Colour Library Books

THE ART OF
GOOD COOKING

Contents

Introduction

The art of good cooking begins with the selection of fresh ingredients in the best possible condition and ends with a delicious meal that is elegantly presented and perfectly complemented by a carefully chosen bottle of good wine. All you need is a sound knowledge of food and basic cooking techniques, imaginative ideas for attractive food presentation and some advice on choosing and serving wine. All this, and more, you will find in this book.

The Art of Good Cooking combines an indispensable guide to food and cookery with a very useful introduction to the wines of the world. 'The Cook's Guide' tells you all you need to know about food. You will find detailed, easy-to-follow information on how to select, store, prepare, cook and serve every type of food, from basic everyday ingredients to unusual fish, shellfish and exotic fruits and vegetables. The clear instructions given here, often with step-by-step colour photographs, will inspire you to use ingredients you lacked the confidence to try

Colour Library Books

THE ART OF
GOOD
COOKING

COLOUR LIBRARY BOOKS

CLB 1951

This edition published 1987 by Colour Library Books Ltd,
86 Epsom Road, Guildford, Surrey.

© Marshall Cavendish Limited 1987
Prepared by Marshall Cavendish Books Ltd,
58 Old Compton St, London W1V 5PA

Printed in Spain

ISBN 0 86283 532 1

Some of this material has previously appeared in the Marshall
Cavendish partwork *Carrier's Kitchen*.

Weights and measures
Both metric and imperial measurements are
given. As these are not exact equivalents,
please work from one set of figures or the
other. Use standard measuring spoons.

Time symbols
The time needed to prepare the dish is given
on each recipe. The time symbols are as
follows:

quick to prepare

takes up to 1 hour to prepare

time-consuming to prepare

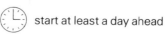 start at least a day ahead

before, and the wide choice of tempting recipes will give you plenty of scope. The guide is illustrated in full colour throughout, helping you identify particular cuts of meat or more unusual fruits and vegetables, and making the recipes, seen in their finished state, impossible to resist.

If you take the trouble to get the food just right you will want to be sure that the wine you serve with it will make the perfect accompaniment. 'The Wine Guide' is all about wine – where it comes from, how it is made, what is to be understood from its labels, and what wines to serve with what food. It is a journey through the wine-growing parts of the world, stopping off en route to sample the local wines. When you have completed your journey through its pages you will know exactly which wine you want to serve with the meal you have created.

'The Wine Guide' ends with a selection of recipes, each to be served with a recommended wine. There are starters, main dishes and desserts, all illustrated in colour, making it the ideal recipe source when you are planning to entertain. Use these recipes with their wine suggestions, or select recipes from other parts of the book and 'mix and match' with various wines in deliciously enjoyable experiments. Combine your skill at selecting wine with the knowledge you have gleaned from 'The Cook's Guide' to create memorable meals that are each a work of art.

The Cook's Guide

I can honestly say – and I speak as someone who has written around twenty cookery books myself – that 'The Cook's Guide' caters for everyone who is interested in cooking, at whatever level. It is for those who find cooking an increasingly creative and absorbing hobby and for those who want to produce the most tasty and appetizing food from good basic ingredients.

Clearly and sensibly planned, 'The Cook's Guide' is divided into sections covering poultry, meat and game; fish and shellfish; vegetables; fruit; herbs and spices. In each section, whether it is dealing with a main ingredient or the 'personality' flavourings like herbs and spices, there is a brief pen portrait of the food in question. Once you have delved into the earliest known methods of cultivation, how it is processed and the forms in which it is available, you are ready to handle it with confidence.

Whether you are planning a small family meal or a large party, you will find all the help you need here, starting with exactly how much of each ingredient to buy. Thoroughly practical and down-to-earth shopping advice is offered for each ingredient in turn. You will learn how to tell when brassicas and leafy greens are 'over the top' and likely to taste bitter; how to get the timing of melons and avocados absolutely right, and since it isn't every day that you buy one, when a lobster is cooked to perfection. And if you want to know about freezing, there's plenty of helpful advice on methods, storage and thawing times.

As you become ever more enthusiastic and confident, you will certainly want to know how to tackle the basic tasks of food preparation. Many of these, like jointing a chicken, filleting fish, cleaning a crab and preparing globe artichokes, are shown in a series of instructive step-by-step photographs.

The many basic techniques of cooking are explained at length, simply and in general terms. Once you master these, you can easily create your own recipes. But there are plenty of recipes here to fire your imagination, many of which combine familiar ingredients with new and interesting flavours. I challenge anyone to resist reaching for their apron when they read through the recipes for herb pâté, veal with ginger cream sauce or seakale and cheese pancakes.

There's no arguing that the success of a dish lies in the care and attention you give to the cooking, but often it's the presentation that wins you more compliments. Throughout the book you will find witty ideas and decorative ways to ensure your dishes look as appetizing as they undoubtedly taste.

With 'The Cook's Guide' beside you and the combined experience, imagination and skill of the authors behind you, you will find it rewardingly easy to make your culinary dreams come true.

Pamela Westland

Poultry, Meat and Game

For centuries, the quality of our meat has influenced much that is best in our cookery traditions. Today, while there is a trend towards eating less meat, most of us still rely on meat as the basic ingredient for our main meals. Good quality meat has never been cheap, and nowadays it is ever more vital to make sure that we really are getting value for money.

Cultivate a good butcher, or shop at a reliable supermarket where the meat is fresh looking and where you are able to purchase exactly the cuts and weights you require for your recipe.

Choose an appropriate cooking technique for the cut of meat that you have bought – cheaper, coarser cuts that need long slow cooking will be ruined by high-temperature roasting – and follow the detailed instructions given in this chapter to be sure that you carry out the basic cooking techniques correctly.

Expand your repertoire of traditional recipes and be aware of new combinations of meat and pasta, vegetables or pulses. Everyday meals that make economic sense may

well have to contain less meat than before – in this section there are many recipes from all over the world which make a virtue of stretching a small quantity of meat so that it goes further.

Be open, too, to the choice that is available – different cuts and varieties of meat. For example, venison and poultry, other than chicken and turkey, are increasingly available. In this chapter you will find all the information and recipes you need to enable you to include these more unusual types of meat in your cooking.

Chicken

Cooks of all nationalities have found the delicate meat of chicken an ideal base for creative dishes. Thanks to modern rearing methods chicken can now be a once-a-week meal instead of an occasional treat and you can afford to try out some of the more unusual and exotic ways with chicken in your own kitchen.

You can buy chicken in a variety of sizes and forms to suit your requirements: from a tiny poussin which will feed only one to a large capon which will make a meal for 8. You can buy them fresh, chilled or frozen; whole, in quarters or in smaller cut portions; cooked or even smoked; the giblets and livers are sold separately by weight.

Most chickens nowadays are reared under controlled conditions designed to put on maximum flesh in minimum time. The result is uniformly young and tender birds, and choosing one in preference to another is largely a matter of the weight and number of servings required (see Buying guide).

Buying chicken

Fresh chicken: whole birds can be bought fresh from farms, poulterers and butchers, sold by weight and usually oven-ready (i.e. plucked, drawn and trussed). Look for a plump breast, smooth, unbroken skin and pliable breastbone tip. If the chicken is wrapped, check that the film covering looks fresh and is unbroken. Never buy bruised or discoloured birds. The giblets (neck, gizzard, heart and liver) are often, but not always, tucked inside the bird in a polythene bag. If you particularly want giblets, remember to ask for them. Use giblets for making a well-flavoured stock.

● **Giblet stock:** Put giblets in a saucepan with a small onion, carrot and perhaps a chopped celery stick or some parsley stalks. Add 1 L/2 pt water, salt and a few peppercorns. Bring to boil, cover and simmer for 2 hours. Strain and use in gravy.

New York dressed birds, i.e. those with the head and feet left on and hung for several days to bring out the flavour, should be ordered in advance. You pay for pre-dressed weight. The marks of a young bird are pale yellow legs and a pliable beak.

Chilled chicken: whole birds and portions are sold from refrigerated (as distinct from frozen food) cabinets in large supermarkets. Before it is packed in film bags and refrigerated, the chicken is air-chilled, which keeps the flesh dry, unlike the iced water chilling method often used for frozen birds. Check for freshness against the 'sell by' date.

Frozen chicken: whole birds and portions are sold from frozen food cabinets (operating at −18C /0F or below) in supermarkets and freezer centres. The birds are sealed in moisture/vapour-proof bags and frozen immediately. As frozen chicken stays frozen without deteriorating during transport, distribution costs are lower and frozen birds are usually slightly cheaper than fresh or chilled. Check that the wrapper is undamaged and that there are no obvious signs of excess frozen liquid inside.

Chicken portions are convenient for single servings or for a recipe requiring a particular cut, and are available fresh or chilled as well as frozen. They are sold singly, by the kilo or in multiple packs of quarters or legs, thighs, breasts or wings.

Storing chicken

Both raw and cooked chicken is very perishable and unless it is handled with care can be a health hazard, especially under warm and humid conditions. But this can be avoided by taking a few simple precautions.

Fresh and chilled chicken: immediately after buying, discard the wrapping and remove the giblets, if any, from inside the bird. Refrigerate the chicken right away, loosely covered with film or foil so that air can circulate freely. Use within 2 days.

Chicken giblets: raw or cooked, these are very perishable, so if you cannot use them immediately, freeze them in polythene bags.

Cooked chicken: cool as rapidly as possible in a cold, airy place, or by standing casseroles in ice-cold water. When cold, keep in the refrigerator. When reheating, bring to simmering point and maintain for several minutes at this temperature before serving.

Using frozen chicken

Transfer whole frozen birds or portions while still solidly frozen to your home freezer and use within 3 months.

Thawing: it is essential to thaw frozen chicken completely, otherwise it cannot cook through evenly, and undercooked poultry can cause food poisoning. Remove the chicken from its wrapping, stand on a plate and cover loosely with foil. Slow thawing in the refrigerator is ideal, because it maintains the texture of the chicken better, but this takes about twice as long as thawing at room temperature. If the bird

Portioning a chicken

1 Cut along and through the length of the breastbone, close to the centre where the bone rises up.

2 Open out the bird and cut along the length of the backbone. (For a less bony portion, cut away the backbone entirely.)

3 Lay the chicken halves skin side up, and cut diagonally behind the thigh, through the ball and socket joint, to separate the leg from the wing and breast.

4 If you need to divide the chicken into 8, cut each portion again. Cut the drumstick free from the thigh through the 'knee' joint. Then hold the wing joint steady with your spare hand. Cut diagonally towards the wing, allowing a good piece of breast with the portion. Slide the knife along the rib cage bone then cut the wing free.

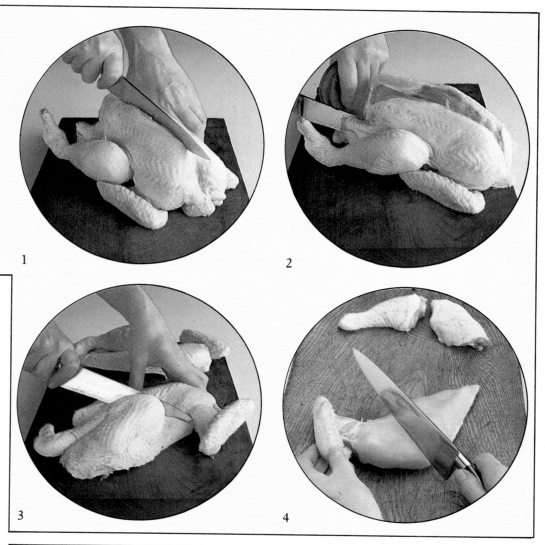

contains a bag of giblets, remove this as soon as it is sufficiently thawed.

Allow a 1.5–1.8 kg /3–4 lb bird at least 24 hours to thaw in the refrigerator, or 12 hours at room temperature. Portions need about 12 hours to thaw in the refrigerator, or 6–8 hours at room temperature.

Jointing a chicken

It is not always possible to find raw joints of the exact size or shape for a particular dish. But a sharp cook's knife and chopping board are all you need to cut up a young bird just the way you want: the portions cost less this way, too. Follow the very simple method (shown in the pictures) of dividing a bird into 4 equal-sized joints (2 breast and wing, 2 leg and thigh), and you will retain most of the carcass; this is efficient for stewing too, as the bones flavour the dish. For sautéing or stir-frying the portions can be divided further as shown in the pictures.

If you need 6 or 8 good-sized portions for frying, cut up 2 small birds into 4 pieces each, and freeze any unwanted portions. If necessary give the knife a sharp tap with a weight to cut through bony bits. Remove the giblets and wash and dry the chicken before you start jointing. Remove the leg shanks (below the 'knee' of the chicken), the wing tips (the triangular 3rd joint of the wing), the parson's nose (the fatty triangular lump at the vent) and the surplus neck skin. Afterwards trim away any remaining scraps of untidy skin from the portions with kitchen scissors and keep for stock.

Cooking chicken

Oven-ready chicken needs very little preparation. If necessary, trim off any stubby feathers, then wash the bird thoroughly under running cold water. Pat dry inside and out with absorbent paper.

Skinning: cook young chicken with its skin on whenever possible, as the skin contains flavour and helps to keep the flesh beneath moist and succulent. When the recipe directs you to remove the skin (for example with chicken breasts) simply loosen the skin with your fingers and then pull it off. The coarse skin of boiling fowls can be removed after cooking and before serving.

Buying guide

Type (alternative names in brackets)	General description	Weight range	Average servings	Best ways to cook
Poussin (Double poussin)	bird up to 6 weeks old	small: about 500 g /1 lb large: about 1 kg /2 lb	1 2	fry, spit roast, casserole whole or halve and grill
Small oven-ready chicken (roaster) (spring chicken) (broiler/fryer, U.S.)	young, tender bird, ideally sized for quartering	1–1.5 kg /2–3 lb	3–4	joint into portions and grill, fry, casserole or bake
Large oven-ready chicken (roaster)	young, tender bird for cooking whole	1.5–2.25 kg /3½–5 lb	4–8	oven or spit roast, pot roast or casserole, poach
Capon (poularde = hen reared like capon)	cock bird castrated and reared to produce more white meat	2–3.5 kg /4½–8 lb	6–12	oven roast, pot roast or poach
Boiling fowl	retired breeding bird aged over 1 year	1.8–3.6 kg /4–8 lb	6–10	poach
Boiling hen	retired egg-producing bird	1.5–2.25 kg /3½–5 lb	4–8	poach

Roasting

This is probably the most popular way of cooking a whole chicken. There are 2 basic methods: English and French. In English roasting the chicken is roasted breast upwards and the flesh kept moist by basting frequently or by covering the breast with pork fat or streaky bacon rashers. Roast the bird at 180C/350F/gas 4, for 40 minutes per kg/20 minutes per lb, plus 20 minutes.

In French roasting, you turn the bird as well as basting it. Insert some seasoned herb butter into the cavity and brush the skin all over with melted butter. Roast the bird on its side for 20 minutes at 220C/425F/gas 7; turn and cook on the other side for 20 minutes, then lower the heat to 180C/350F/ gas 4 and cook breast upwards for remaining cooking time calculated as above.

To test that the chicken is cooked, push a skewer through the thickest part of the leg; the juices should run clear and golden.

Pot roasting

The bird is browned in butter and oil, then cooked whole in the steam that collects in the casserole. Use a flameproof casserole with a level base and a tight-fitting lid into which the bird fits snugly.

1 Season the body cavity of a washed and dried chicken with salt and pepper, insert 15 g /½ oz butter and 15 ml /1 tbls fresh herbs (tarragon is a good choice) or 5 ml /1 tsp dried. Retruss if necessary.

2 Heat 25 g /1 oz butter and 15 ml /1 tbls oil in the casserole. When moderately hot put in the chicken on its side and brown the skin slowly. Continue turning the bird now and then for about 15–20 minutes until it is golden all over. Lift out the chicken. Heat the oven to 180C /350F /gas 4.

3 Add a sliced onion, carrot and 2 stalks of celery, a bay leaf and sprig of thyme or rosemary to the remaining fat in the casserole and fry gently for 5 minutes.

4 Season the skin and replace the bird, breast upwards, on top of the vegetables. Cover with well-buttered foil or greaseproof paper, then put the lid on tightly.

5 Transfer the casserole to the centre of the oven and cook for 42 minutes per kg /20 minutes per lb plus 20 minutes. Check that the bird is cooked by piercing the thigh with a skewer: the juices should run colourless.

6 Place the chicken on a serving dish and keep hot. Add 275 ml /10 fl oz chicken stock to the juices in the casserole, bring to the boil and skim off the surface fat. Stir in 15 g /½ oz cornflour blended with 30 ml /2 tbls medium dry sherry and simmer for several minutes. Season to taste, strain, add some chopped fresh herbs if available and hand round when serving the chicken.

Grilling

This is a simple, speedy way of cooking poussin halves or chicken quarters. The secret of success depends on keeping the surfaces of the meat well basted with melted butter, oil or a marinade during cooking, and maintaining a moderate heat throughout. The surfaces do not need sealing under fierce heat as those of a steak do.

1 If you have time, marinate the portions for at least 3 hours before cooking, in a mixture of olive oil and lemon juice flavoured with garlic and herbs. Turn frequently and keep refrigerated. Otherwise simply wash and dry the portions and run a metal skewer horizontally through each to keep them flat. Brush liberally with melted butter or oil and season well with salt and freshly ground black pepper.

2 Heat the grill to moderate heat. Lay the chicken portions skin side down on the grilling rack and position the pan 13–15 cm /5–6 in below the heat. Cook for 10–15 minutes depending on thickness, brushing with butter and basting frequently.

3 Turn skin side up, baste and continue grilling for another 8–12 minutes, until the juices run colourless when the chicken is pierced in the thickest part.

4 Serve the chicken with the pan juices poured over, accompanied by a green salad and chips or sauté potatoes.

Braising and casseroling

Cook portions rather than whole birds by this method. First the chicken and cut-up vegetables are browned in fat, and then a small amount of liquid and seasonings are added. By varying the vegetables, liquid and seasonings you can make a vast range of chicken dishes, from everyday casseroles to classic dishes.

In casseroled chicken dishes the liquid can be thickened in the early stages of preparation or at the end of cooking. Use a low heat on top of the stove or, if more convenient, a moderate oven (180C/350F /gas 4). The dish can be cooked and served in a heavy-based flameproof casserole.

1 Wash and dry the chicken joints and season them well with salt and freshly ground black pepper.

2 For 4 chicken quarters heat 25 g /1 oz butter and 15 ml /1 tbls oil in a casserole and fry the portions on both sides until golden-brown. Lift out and reserve.

3 Add to the fat in the pan chopped or sliced onions, shallots or leeks, celery and strips of unsmoked streaky bacon. Fry gently for 5 minutes, stirring occasionally.

4 Sprinkle 15 ml /1 tbls flour over the vegetables, stir well and fry for 12 minutes.

5 Stir in about 300 ml /10 fl oz stock, cider or wine and bring to the boil.

6 Return the chicken portions to the pan, add herbs and more vegetables such as skinned and chopped tomatoes, blanched and sliced sweet peppers or whole button mushrooms. Cover the pan tightly and simmer very gently until tender, or cook in a moderate oven, for about 40 minutes.

7 Skim off surface fat, check seasoning and serve.

Frying

Deep-fat frying: a rapid way of cooking small portions of raw chicken such as drumsticks, thighs or breasts, so that they are crisp and golden outside and moist inside. Chicken fried this way is traditionally served in a basket lined with paper napkins. To deep fry safely and successfully you need either a thermostatically controlled electric frier (in which case you will follow the manufacturer's temperature and timing instructions) or a deep pan specially fitted with a wire basket. A thermometer will tell you when the fat has reached the correct temperature for frying. Coating with beaten egg and breadcrumbs prevents the meat from coming into direct contact with the hot fat, and keeps it deliciously moist.

1 Have ready on a large piece of greaseproof paper some sifted flour well-seasoned with salt and freshly ground black pepper; some well-beaten egg in a shallow plate; and a pile of fine, dry white breadcrumbs on another large sheet of paper.

2 Toss the chicken pieces one at a time in the seasoned flour, dip into the egg and drain off excess, and coat the chicken in the breadcrumbs. Press the coating on firmly. Chill the portions for at least 1 hour in the refrigerator to 'set' the coating before frying.

3 When ready to cook, half fill the pan containing the frying basket with vegetable oil and heat slowly. When the thermometer registers 180C /350F the right frying temperature for chicken has been reached.

4 Place 2 chicken quarters or 4 drumsticks

in the frying basket and lower carefully into the hot fat.

5 Fry steadily until crisp and golden, about 12–18 minutes depending on the thickness of the pieces. Check that the chicken is cooked by piercing the thickest part with a skewer. Drain on crumpled kitchen paper and keep hot while you fry the rest of the chicken.

6 Serve very hot with warm granary bread rolls, a crisp green salad and perhaps some sweetcorn fritters.

Shallow pan covered frying: chicken is a very lean meat and this gentle method of frying keeps it beautifully succulent. Use it for portions and especially for chicken breasts. Cooking is relatively quick, depending on the size and thickness of the portions: allow 15–20 minutes for breasts or 25–30 minutes for quarters. The only equipment you need is a heavy-based frying-pan with a tight-fitting lid, wide enough to hold the portions in a single uncrowded layer. It is an ideal way of cooking up to 4 portions at once.

First the portions are browned and then cooked very gently in the aromatic steam that collects in the covered pan. The cooking juices, with a little stock added, provide a small amount of well flavoured sauce for each portion. A wide range of dishes can be created by adding a little fortified wine to the juices after the chicken portions have been removed. Use marsala, Madeira or dry white vermouth, and boil with the pan juices to reduce. Or thick cream and a little finely grated lemon rind, or orange juice, grated zest and honey, can be added to the pan juices.

1 Wash and dry the chicken portions and then toss in flour well seasoned with salt and freshly **ground** black pepper.

2 For 4 portions heat 40 g /1½ oz unsalted butter and 15 ml /1 tbls oil in a frying-pan. When the foam subsides, put in the chicken portions, skin side down, and fry over moderate **heat** for about 5 minutes on each side, until golden brown all over.

Cock-a-leekie

3 Add optional flavourings such as garlic, thinly sliced onion or leek, button onions and/or sprigs of rosemary, thyme or tarragon, and stir into the fat.

4 Cover the pan tightly, lower the heat and cook very gently until the chicken is tender and the juices run colourless when the chicken is pierced with a skewer.

5 Lift out the chicken and keep hot. Discard the herb sprigs if using, add 60 ml /4 tbls good chicken stock and a squeeze of lemon juice to the pan, or any other flavourings you may be using, and stir to loosen the coagulated juices from the base. Boil up briefly, season to taste and spoon over the chicken.

Poaching

Cooking chicken in water well flavoured with vegetables and herbs, sometimes in the same pot with a piece of beef or pickled pork, was originally to tenderize old, tough farmyard fowls. It produced both soup and a main-course dish. It is economical on fuel as the cooking is done over very low heat, and can be used to cook young birds too. It is by far the best way of cooking chicken that is to be eaten cold, as it keeps the meat so moist.

The breast of a young bird is tender enough to cook in the steam, and you need to use only a little liquid. Choose a pot into which the bird will fit snugly and pour round liquid to come halfway up the bird. This results in a concentrated broth which will make a well-flavoured sauce.

If more broth is required for a soup, simply increase the amount of liquid, and if you want to strengthen the flavour, add a chicken stock cube before you start to cook. When cooking an older and tougher boiling fowl, add enough water just to cover the bird and extend the simmering time until it is tender. The success of the method lies in simmering as gently as possible throughout the cooking time. Allow 40 minutes per kg /20 minutes per lb for chicken and 75–85 minutes per kg /35–40 minutes per lb for boiling fowl.

1 Season the body cavity of the washed bird with salt and freshly ground black pepper, and insert a slice or two of lemon and several sprigs of parsley.

2 Choose a deep saucepan into which the bird will fit snugly. Put in the washed giblets (except the liver), a bay leaf, some peppercorns, a few small onions and carrots, 2 sticks of celery cut into chunks and 5 ml /1 tsp salt. Put the bird, breast uppermost, on top. (More vegetables can be added when the amount of water is increased with a boiling fowl, but they will be overcooked and only fit for soup.)

3 For a chicken add enough cold water (about 600 ml /1 pt) to give a depth of 2.5 cm /1 in in the pan, but for a boiling fowl add enough water just to cover the bird. Bring slowly to simmering point, skimming off any grey scum as it rises.

4 Cover the pan tightly and simmer gently until the juices run colourless when the flesh is pierced.

5 Serve with a sauce made from some of the strained, thickened broth, accompanied by the vegetables from the pan.

Cock-a-leekie

This dish from Scotland makes both a substantial soup and a main course. The chicken can be served hot with a sauce made from some of the strained broth, or cold next day as a salad.

soaking prunes overnight, then 1 hour 35 minutes

Serves 4–6
1.8 kg /4 lb oven-ready chicken
salt and freshly ground black pepper
1 large onion, chopped
1 chicken stock cube
500 g /1 lb leeks, trimmed and washed
100 g /4 oz prunes (optional), soaked overnight
  and stoned
30 ml /2 tbls long-grain rice (optional)
30 ml /2 tbls finely chopped parsley

1 Wash the chiken and season generously inside and out. Put into a deep saucepan with the giblets (except the liver) and 1.1 L /2 pt cold water. Bring slowly to the boil and skim off any grey scum as it rises.
2 Add the onion and crumbled stock cube, cover tightly, reduce heat and simmer very gently for 1 hour.
3 Meanwhile cut the leeks in thin diagonal slices. At the end of the hour, add the leeks and the prunes, and rice if using, to the pot. Continue simmering for 20 minutes. Test the chicken: the juices should run colourless when the chicken is pierced with a skewer.
4 Lift out the chicken and giblets. Taste the broth, correct the seasoning, and serve sprinkled with parsley, and with some shreds of the cooked chicken if you want a more substantial soup.

Chicken salad caprice

1 hour 15 minutes including chilling time

Serves 4
45 ml /3 tbls mayonnaise
45 ml /3 tbls soured cream
15 ml /1 tbls horseradish cream
350 g /12 oz cooked chicken, in bite-size pieces
1 grapefruit or orange, peel and pith removed,
  segmented and roughly chopped
crisp lettuce leaves
1 crisp red-skinned apple
15 ml /1 tbls lemon juice
a few black grapes, halved and seeded

1 Mix the mayonnaise and soured cream together, adding enough horseradish to give a distinct tang. Stir in the chicken and grapefruit or orange, cover and refrigerate for up to 1 hour.
2 Line a shallow salad bowl with lettuce leaves and pile the chicken and grapefruit or orange in the centre.
3 Quarter, core and slice the apple and toss the slices in the lemon juice. Arrange the slices all around the edge of the salad bowl and garnish with the grapes.

Florentine chicken livers

25 minutes

Serves 4
225 g /8 oz chicken livers
75 g /3 oz butter
15 ml /1 tbls finely chopped shallot or spring
  onion
4 fresh sage leaves
30 ml /2 tbls oil
8 oval slices from a French loaf, cut 5 mm /1/4
  in thick
15 ml /1 tbls grated Parmesan cheese
salt and freshly ground black pepper
15 ml /1 tbls chopped parsley

Coq au vin rouge

1 Wash the livers and cut away any tissue or green areas; chop them fairly finely.
2 Melt 40 g /1½ oz of the butter in a small pan and fry the shallot or spring onion and sage leaves gently together for 5 minutes. Discard the sage leaves.
3 Add the livers to the pan and cook gently, stirring frequently, for 5–6 minutes until just cooked.
4 Meanwhile heat the remaining butter with the oil in a shallow frying-pan and when hot and foaming fry the bread slices on both sides until crisp and golden brown. Drain on absorbent paper.
5 Stir the Parmesan cheese into the livers and season to taste. Heat for a moment or two. Spread the livers over the fried bread, sprinkle with parsley and serve hot.

Coq au vin rouge

🍴🍴🍴 1 hour 40 minutes

Serves 4

1.5 kg /3 lb oven-ready chicken, cut into
*   quarters, with backbone removed*
1 medium-sized onion, sliced
1 carrot, sliced
2 garlic cloves, cut in half
1 sprig of thyme
1 bay leaf
425 ml /15 fl oz red wine
15 ml /1 tbls tomato purée
salt and freshly ground black pepper
40 g /1½ oz butter
30 ml /2 tbls oil
16 button onions, peeled
100 g /4 oz thick slices unsmoked streaky
*   bacon, rind removed and cut into strips*
45–60 ml /3–4 tbls brandy
175 g /6 oz button mushroom caps, wiped
For the beurre manié
15 g /½ oz butter, softened
15 g /½ oz flour
For the garnish
fried bread croûtons
sprigs of fresh parsley

1 Put the washed giblets, backbone and trimmings from the chicken into a saucepan. Add the onion, carrot, garlic, thyme, bay leaf, wine, tomato purée, seasoning and 150 ml /5 fl oz water. Bring to the boil, then simmer, uncovered, for 20–30 minutes until the liquid has reduced to about half. Strain into a jug.
2 Heat 15 g /½ oz butter with 15 ml /1 tbls oil in a heavy-based pan and fry the button onions over moderate heat for about 10 minutes, rolling them around the pan to brown evenly. Add 150 ml /5 fl oz water, cover tightly and simmer gently for 20–30 minutes, until tender.
3 Heat the remaining butter and oil in a flameproof casserole and fry the strips of bacon for a few minutes.
4 Wash the chicken portions, pat dry with absorbent paper; season lightly. Place them skin side down in the casserole with the bacon and fry for 5–6 minutes until golden. Turn the portions, cover the casserole and fry gently for another 5 minutes.
5 Heat a ladle, pour the brandy into it and set alight with a match. Pour it flaming over the chicken. Shake the pan gently to distribute the flames evenly.
6 When the flames die down, pour the strained wine liquid into the pan containing the chicken, cover tightly and simmer very gently for 40 minutes. Add the mushrooms for the last 5 minutes of cooking.
7 Lift out the chicken portions and arrange skin side up on a heated serving dish. With a slotted spoon remove the mushrooms and bacon strips and scatter evenly over the chicken.
8 Strain any remaining liquid from the onions into the casserole, arrange the onions round the chicken on the dish and keep hot.
9 Measure the liquid remaining in the casserole; there should be no less than 275 ml /10 fl oz. If there is more, reduce it by boiling rapidly, uncovered. Season to taste.
10 Blend the butter and flour to form the beurre manié paste. Bring the liquid in the casserole to simmering point. Using a wire whisk, whisk in the beurre manié little by little, until the sauce is lightly thickened and shiny.
11 Spoon the sauce over the chicken and garnish with croûtons and parsley.

Chicken Kiev

Chicken Kiev is the most famous of all deep fried chicken dishes. Raw chicken breast portions are usually available chilled in good supermarkets, but if you cut the breasts from 2 plump 1.5 kg /3 lb fresh or chilled chickens at home you will have the wing joint attached. Decorate this with a cutlet frill for a truly professional finish that looks very pretty at a party. Warn guests that liquid butter may spurt from inside the chicken when cut.

 🍴🍴 making butter ahead, then 1¾ hours including chilling

Serves 4

4 raw chicken breasts weighing not less than
*   200 g /7 oz each*
100 g /4 oz fresh butter
2.5 ml /½ tsp finely grated lemon zest
15 ml /1 tbls lemon juice
1 clove garlic, finely crushed
15 ml /1 tbls finely chopped parsley or mixed
*   parsley, tarragon and chervil*
salt and freshly ground black pepper
25 g /1 oz flour
2 medium-sized eggs, beaten
fine dry white breadcrumbs for coating
oil for deep-fat frying

1 Several hours in advance, cream the butter with the lemon zest and juice, the garlic and herbs; season to taste with salt and pepper. Form into a rectangular block roughly 6 cm /2½ in long and chill until very firm.
2 With a knife cut off chicken wings, if any, below the first joint, and free the breasts of all other bones. Peel off the skin and discard.
3 Lay the breasts flat, cut side uppermost and with the thickest side towards you. With a small sharp knife cut a horizontal pocket along the centre of the breast to within 25 mm /1in of either end, taking care not to cut right through the flesh.
4 Cut the butter into 4 fingers and insert 1 piece lengthways in each pocket. Press the open edges of the pocket together to enclose the butter completely.
5 Season the flour liberally with salt and pepper, coat the breasts all over, and shake off any surplus flour.
6 Dip the breasts one at a time in beaten egg, drain for a moment, then turn them over and over in the dry breadcrumbs until thoroughly coated. Press the coating on firmly with a flat knife.
7 Repeat the egg and crumbing process again. Then refrigerate the breasts for at least 1 hour to 'set' the coating.
8 When ready to cook, heat the oil in a deep-fat frier to 180C /350F. Lower the joints carefully, 2 at a time, into the fat and fry for 12–15 minutes, until golden-brown and cooked through. Drain on crumpled absorbent paper and keep hot while frying the remaining breasts.
9 Slip a cutlet frill on each wing joint and serve piping hot.

Chicken Kiev

17

Chicken breasts Leoni

⏱ 35 Minutes

Serves 4
4 chicken breasts, boned and skinned
½ lemon
25 g/1 oz flour
salt and freshly ground black pepper
2 small eggs
50 g/2 oz Parmesan or dry mature cheese
30 ml/2 tbls oil
25 g/1 oz butter
12–16 cooked asparagus spears (fresh, frozen or canned), to garnish
lemon slices and parsley, to garnish

1 Lay the chicken breasts between damp greaseproof paper and flatten gently with a rolling pin until about 10 mm/ ½ in thick. Rub the chicken lightly with the cut side of the lemon, squeezing the lemon gently to extract a little juice.
2 Season the flour liberally with salt and pepper and coat the chicken with the seasoned flour on each side. In a deep plate beat the eggs with 30 ml/2 tbls of the cheese.

3 Heat the oil and butter in a shallow frying-pan. When it is hot dip the chicken breasts one at a time in the beaten egg, coating each side, then lower into the fat.
4 Fry over moderate heat, turning once, 5–6 minutes each side until golden and just cooked through. Meanwhile heat the grill.
5 With a fish slice transfer the cooked chicken breasts to the grill rack, lay 3–4 drained asparagus spears on each and sprinkle with the remaining grated cheese. Grill gently for 2–3 minutes until the cheese melts.
6 Arrange the chicken on a hot serving dish. Garnish with lemon slices and parsley.

Poulet à l'estragon

⏱ 1½ hours

Serves 4–6
1.8 kg/4 lb chicken
50 g/2 oz butter
30 ml/2 tbls chopped fresh tarragon leaves
1 garlic clove, crushed
salt and freshly ground black pepper
15 ml/1 tbls oil
50 ml/2 fl oz brandy
75 ml/3 fl oz thick cream

Chicken breasts Leoni

1 Heat the oven to 190C/375F/gas 5. Mash together the butter, tarragon, garlic, salt and pepper. Divide the mixture into three.
2 Gently push your fingers between the skin and the breast of the chicken and insert one third of the butter mixture on each side of the breast, under the skin. Flatten the butter slightly by patting the skin. Put remaining butter into the cavity of the bird.
3 Rub a little oil on the outside of the bird. Arrange the chicken so it rests on one breast on a rack in a roasting tin and roast for 35 minutes. Turn it onto the other side and roast for a further 35 minutes.
4 Remove the tin from the oven, lift off the bird, take out the rack, return the bird.
5 Put the brandy into a soup ladle and warm it gently. Set a match to it and pour it over the chicken. When the flames subside, carefully remove the chicken, tipping the juices from the cavity into the tin. Place the bird on a serving dish and keep warm.
6 Add the cream to the pan and warm it through gently, stirring well to incorporate all the juices. Pour the sauce over the chicken and serve immediately. If you prefer more sauce, add some chicken stock to the pan before the cream.

Lamb and mutton

The sweet meat of lamb is weekly fare in many parts of the world. It was the earliest animal to be domesticated and is traditionally eaten at Easter feasts. Lamb is simple to cook, as many of the cuts can be either roasted or grilled.

About 12,000 years ago, somewhere in the Middle East, man took a very important step when he rounded up some wild sheep as a flock to keep them under supervision. He wisely selected an animal that provided meat for eating and also wool for clothing and milk for drinking and making cheese. Sheep could also withstand winter and live on rough grazing land that could support no other form of agriculture. During the Middle Ages sheep were bred for their wool more than their meat and the great churches built with the profits of the wool trade are still standing.

The rapidly growing urban population in the 19th century created an increased demand for meat. This was met by a breeding programme which is still continuing to produce leaner meat, that could then be sold at a younger age. A ship, the 'Dunedin', with refrigeration equipment sailed from New Zealand in 1882 with carcasses and this began a trade, still maintained, of lamb being exported from the southern hemisphere to the northern.

For many centuries roasting was only possible on turning spits at outdoor feasts or in the kitchens of great houses. Baking at home had to wait for the development of the domestic oven. Hence the stewpot was the universal way of cooking.

Every sheep rearing country has evolved its own lamb recipes. Persian and Turkish cookery specialize in delicate dishes combining lamb with apricots, quinces, raisins and almonds. The Greeks cook it with olive oil, lemon juice and oregano, the Moroccans with a subtle mixture of spices. Dishes consisting of minced lamb with aubergine, tomatoes, onions and green peppers are popular throughout the Middle East. The French prefer young lamb to be underdone rather than overcooked and often combine mature lamb with potatoes or haricot beans.

Choosing lamb

Lamb from hill farms is often leaner and tastier than the fat meat of lowland-reared sheep. The most highly-prized lamb in Europe comes from Wales and coastal salt marsh areas such as Romney Marsh in England and the salt meadows of Brittany and Normandy.

Look for pink, firm and fine-grained flesh and dry, white fat. Freshly cut meat surfaces will have a slightly moist appearance. Legs and shoulders should look plump and rounded and have a thin covering of fat beneath a pliable outer skin. Avoid both very lean, rangy carcasses and very fat ones. As the lamb ages the flesh colour deepens and the meat acquires a more mature flavour. Once past its first birthday lamb is generally described as mutton.

The flavour of mature lamb or young mutton has many devotees; the joints tend to be a little larger but can be cooked in the same way as lamb, allowing extra time and using a lower temperature, if roasting.

Lamb produced in Europe and North America is available from March through to November, with supplies reaching their peak between August and November. In the southern hemisphere the season is reversed; New Zealand supplies are available from the beginning of the year.

Storing lamb

In the shops lamb is usually kept under refrigeration, so it should be transferred to your own refrigerator as soon as possible. Unwrap the meat, stand it on a plate and cover it loosely with foil or cling film to prevent the surface drying. Place it on the shelf below the frozen food compartment where it should keep for up to three days. In fact keeping lamb for a few days before cooking helps to develop the full flavour and tenderness, especially if the lamb has not been hung in the butcher's cold store for at least four days. This applies to imported frozen lamb, which the butcher has thawed before selling and even more so to imported lamb which is still frozen when you buy it. If no refrigerator is available, store the unwrapped lamb for up to 2 days inside a meat safe in a cool larder where the air can circulate freely.

Store cooked meat for 1–2 days in a cool larder or 2–3 days in a refrigerator.

Fruit-stuffed shoulder of lamb

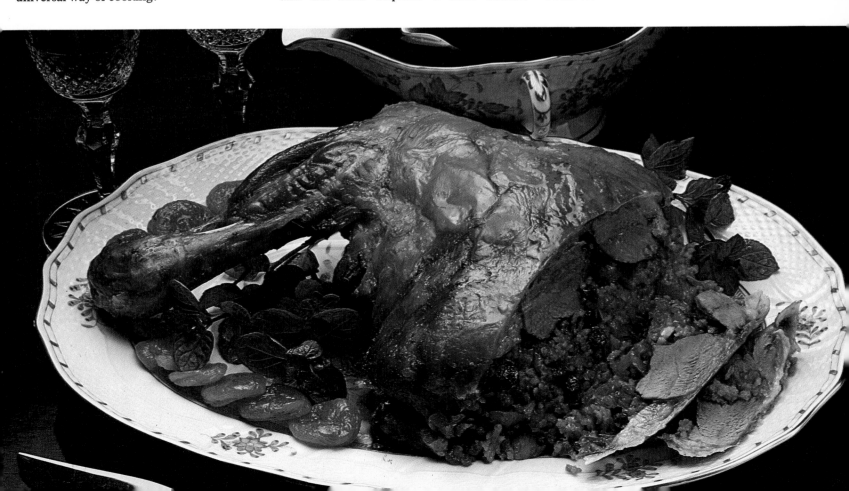

Buying and cooking guide to lamb

Cut and weight	Butchering	Cooking methods	Cut and weight	Butchering	Cooking methods
Leg very lean top quality meat 1.25–2.25 kg /2¾–5 lb	1 whole 2 halved, if large, into fillet and knuckle end 3 from fillet end cut: 5 mm /¼ in or 25 mm /1 in slices; or 10 mm/½ in leg chops; or 4 cm /1 in cubes	1 roast or braise 2 roast fillet; braise or slow roast knuckle end 3 fry or grill slices and chops; grill kebabs, casserole cubes	**Loin** top quality meat with fat cover. Chump end bonier than neck end. 1.5–2.25 kg / 3–5 lb	1 whole (ask butch-er to chop the bone to help carving) 2 halved, if large, into best loin and chump 3 boned out 4 chops either loin or chump	1 roast 2 roast 3 stuff, tie and roast, or braise 4 fry or grill
Shoulder sweet eating meat but fattier than leg 1.25–2.5 kg /2¾–5½ lb	1 whole 2 halved, if large, into blade joint and knuckle joint 3 boned; use whole or cube 4 minced	1 roast 2 roast or braise 3 stuff, tie and roast or braise; cube for casser-oles, or kebabs 4 hamburgers	**Saddle** both loins still joined by the backbone 3.5–5 kg /8–11 lb	whole (including tail which is usually split and curled)	Roast: cook fat side uppermost. Cover for first ⅔ of cooking time, then baste frequently and brown surface
Best end of neck versatile cut of sweet meat with covering of fat; consists of 6–8 cutlets joined by back (chine) bone 700 g–1 kg /1½–2¼ lb	1 whole (ask butch-er to chop joint to facilitate carving) 2 two best ends butchered to form a Guard of Honour or a Crown Roast 3 boned 4 noisettes (large lamb only) 5 cutlets	1 roast 2 roast 3 stuff, tie and roast 4 grill or fry 5 grill or fry; allow 2 each	**Middle neck and scrag** very bony but good flavour if slow cooked with moisture; 1.25–2.25 kg /2¾–5½ lb **Breast** economical thin strip of skinny meat including rib bones and fat 700 g /1 kg /1½–2¼ lb	1 chopped with bones 2 neck fillet tender strips of boneless meat (from large lambs only) 1 whole, if large enough to bone, stuff and roll 2 cut into riblets	1 hot pots and stews 2 cube for kebabs or casseroles, add herbs and spices; the bones make good stock 1 stuff, tie and braise or slow roast 2 simmer to tenderize, then cook in barbecue sauce

Cooking lamb

Lamb sold nowadays is young, usually between three and six months old. Only very occasionally, and then in a country butcher's shop, are you likely to find herb-scented lamb from a hill farm which may be a little older. All joints, other than middle neck, scrag and breast are suitable for roasting, and all chops for frying or grilling. So the choice is entirely up to you.

The roast or grilled meat of early-season lamb is so delicate that it needs no embel-lishment other than a fresh tasting fruit jelly to accompany it. Later, as the season progresses, the flavour of the meat can be enhanced and varied by subtle additions of garlic, herbs (especially rosemary or tarra-gon), marinades, fruit stuffings and sweet-sour glazes.

Roasting

Roasting is suitable for all joints other than middle neck and scrag, or breast. To reduce shrinkage and maximize the flavour, cook lamb in a moderate oven, 180C /350F /gas 4. For boned and stuffed joints weighing 1.5–2.5 kg /3¼–5½ lb, allow 1 hour per kg /30 minutes per lb, plus 30 minutes for both. For joints cooked on the bone reduce this time to 50 minutes per kg /25 minutes per lb, plus 25 minutes, especially if you like the lamb pink and succulent rather than well done.

If you are using a meat thermometer, push it into the thickest part of the meat but without touching any bone. For pink, succulent meat it should register 77C /170F, for well done meat 80C/176F.

After roasting and dishing up meat, allow it to 'rest' in a warm place before carving.

Braising

Braising is suitable for leg, shoulder, chump chops or stuffed joints. A moist and gentle method of cooking, it is ideal for mature lamb. Use a heavy-based pan into which the meat fits snugly.
1 Heat enough oil or dripping to thinly cover the base of the pan and fry the meat, turning, until all surfaces are lightly browned. Remove meat temporarily.
2 Add enough thickly sliced vegetables to make a thick covering for the base of the pan and fry until lightly browned. Pour off excess fat.
3 Add sufficient stock, water, cider or wine to almost cover the vegetables. Season with salt and pepper and tuck in a bay leaf or sprig of thyme.
4 Replace the meat on top of the vege-tables. Cover tightly and simmer very gently on top of the cooker, or in the oven at 170C /325F /gas 3, for a minimum of 1½ hours, allowing 80 minutes per kg /40 minutes per lb for joints. Check from time to time and add more liquid if needed.

5 Serve the meat surrounded by the strained vegetables. Use the liquid for gravy. Pot roasting is almost identical to braising except that no liquid is used or, occasionally, a little wine or cider.

Grilling

Grilling is suitable for all chops and cutlets – these should preferably be 20–25 mm /¾–1 in thick – and for kebabs. It is a speedy method of cooking under the radiant heat. To prevent the meat surface drying, keep the meat well basted with oil, or a suitable sauce, throughout the cooking. For extra flavour marinate mature lamb for 2 hours before cooking, then baste with the mari-nade.
1 Heat the grill until glowing red. Wipe the meat with damp absorbent paper, brush both sides liberally with oil and season with freshly ground black pepper.
2 Lay the meat flat on the grill rack and cook close to the heat for 1–2 minutes each side until the surfaces are sealed.
3 Depending on the type of grill, either reduce the heat or move the grill pan to its lowest position.
4 Continue cooking gently, turning (using a palette knife and spoon to avoid piercing the meat) and basting every few minutes, until cooked to your taste: about 7–10 minutes for thin cutlets; 10–15 minutes for thicker chops or kebabs.

Identifying various cuts of lamb: 1 Leg of lamb and leg fillet 2 Tenderloin 3 Loin and loin chops 4 Shoulder of lamb and shoulder chops 5 Cutlets and a best end of neck (rack of lamb) 6 Breast of lamb 7 Middle neck 8 Butterfly chops

5 Season with salt and serve immediately, garnishing chops and cutlets with pats of herb-flavoured butter and accompanied by a crisp salad.

Shallow frying

Shallow frying is suitable for cutlets, slices and chops up to 25 mm /1 in thick. A quick cooking process, it is especially suitable for thin cuts because frying is less drying than grilling. Always use a heavy-based frying-pan that spreads the heat evenly, and carefully control the heat.

Open frying is used for tender (and fully thawed) cuts of lamb, which can be coated before cooking with seasoned flour or egg and breadcrumbs, or left uncoated.

Covered frying is preferable for mature or still-frozen lamb. After the initial frying and sealing, cover the pan to retain steam and help tenderize the meat.

1 Cover the base of the pan with a thin film of oil for frying uncoated meat, but a little more (about 6 mm /¼ in) for meat coated with egg and crumbs. Heat the oil until sizzling hot.

Carcass cutting

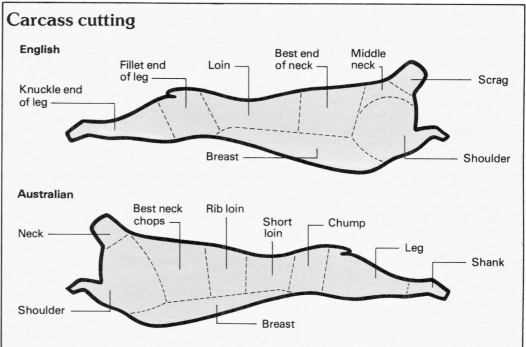

There is no standard way of cutting a lamb carcass, and methods differ from country to country and from district to district. The diagrams show the commonest British and Australian methods, but even the British method varies from place to place in the United Kingdom. In Scotland the shoulder is not usually cut as a separate joint. Instead each side of the forequarter is boned, rolled and tied, then cut into smaller joints.

2 Immediately before frying, pat uncoated meat dry with absorbent paper to aid browning. Cook the meat briskly for 1–2 minutes on each side until the surfaces are lightly browned and sealed.

3 Reduce the heat and continue frying, turning once, until the lamb feels firm but has a little give. The total cooking time for 10 mm /½ in thick chops is 10–12 minutes for open frying and 12–15 minutes for covered frying.

4 Drain, season to taste and serve on very hot plates.

Casseroling and stewing
Best for cubes of boneless shoulder meat or breast, or chopped middle neck and scrag, this is a flavoursome way of simmering small pieces of lamb in a little liquid, with added vegetables and herbs, all in a tightly-covered pot. Stewing and casseroling are virtually identical but the first is cooked on top of the cooker and the second in a slow oven. There are many variations of the method but two main forms. For the cold start method – often used for neck and scrag chops – the lamb is barely covered with cold liquid, brought slowly to simmering point and cooked very gently, covered, for about 2 hours.

For the fry start method – used for cubes of shoulder meat or neck chops – the surfaces of the lamb are first sealed by frying and the liquid and vegetables are then added.

Boiling
Boiling is used for mutton or mature lamb and is also one of the traditional methods of cooking leg of mutton. The meat is gently simmered in water or stock.

1 Wipe the meat and trim if necessary. Put it in a deep pan in which it fits snugly. Add cold water to cover the meat, bring slowly to the boil and remove the scum.

2 Add 15 ml /1 tbls of salt for every 1.5 L /2½ pt of water added. Cover the pan tightly and simmer for 40 minutes per kg /20 minutes per lb, plus 30 minutes.

3 Add small or cut-up root vegetables 1 hour before the end of the cooking time.

4 Serve the drained meat on a hot dish with the vegetables around it. Make a sauce with some of the cooking liquid.

To complement lamb
Certain fruits, herbs and spices have an affinity with lamb and seem to enhance the flavour of the meat.

Fruit jellies: redcurrant jelly is the best known, but quince, medlar, bramble and gooseberry all go well with lamb.

Spices: ginger, cinnamon, coriander or curry powder added to the flour used for coating lamb all emphasize its flavour.

Citrus fruit: add orange or lemon juice to the gravy, or serve wedges with grilled meat.

Herbs: aromatic herbs such as sprigs of rosemary, oregano or lemon thyme, tucked around the joint, lend a subtle distinction to roast lamb. Use either by themselves or with slivers of garlic. In many parts of the world mint is synonymous with lamb – Americans prefer mint jelly, the English mint sauce.

Buying lamb for the freezer
Lamb freezes very successfully and it is a great convenience to have a stock of both joints and individual portions in the freezer. The immediate questions that arise are which cuts, how much, and when and where to buy.

Fresh lamb: lamb can be bought fresh (for freezing down at home or by the butcher) or ready frozen by the supplier. The weight of a carcass is about 12.5–20 kg /28 lb–44 lb. In the northern hemisphere supplies increase and the price drops as the season progresses. For bulk buying prices wait until late summer. Ask your local butcher for advice on this point.

To develop its full flavour and tenderness fresh killed lamb should be aged by hanging in the butcher's cold store for at least four days before it is frozen. Check this point when buying the lamb. When buying ready frozen you are dependent upon the judgment of the supplier as to quality, because there is no way of assessing this once the lamb is frozen. Choose fresh lamb in the normal way.

Frozen lamb: if this is imported, it will be frozen before leaving the country of origin. It is important that you buy only lamb that is still frozen and has not been allowed to thaw out, as handling and re-freezing could involve the risk of contamination. Carcasses tend to be smaller than fresh lamb: 8–16 kg /18–36 lb. Frozen lamb is, of course,

available all year round, but the new season's 'spring lamb' usually starts to arrive in the northern hemisphere from the southern from January onwards.

Once frozen you cannot 'see' the quality, but the New Zealand Meat Producers' Board carefully examines and grades all exported carcasses. Ask your butcher for a 'PL' carcass if you want especially small joints. The larger 'PM' carcass is better for legs and shoulders large enough to divide into two joints each, or if you plan to have it cut into chops and portions.

Ordering frozen lamb
This must depend on your life style, the number in the family and their preferences, as well as the freezer space available. Do you need joints or quickly cooked portions, or a combination of both? If you enjoy cooking and can use all the cuts, including the neck and breast, then a whole carcass is probably the most economical purchase. Consider whether you would be happier buying selected cuts, for example shoulders, legs or chops, which you use most often. Working people find individual cuts invaluable because they do not necessarily have to be thawed before cooking.

Ordering the meat: when buying fresh lamb from a family butcher – as opposed to ready-packed cuts from a store or frozen food centre – you can specify *exactly* how you want the meat cut (see chart on *page 21*). Also specify that you want the lamb aged for at least 4 days before it is cut up. Arrange the time of delivery so that you can set the fast freeze switch in operation 2

Thawing times for frozen lamb

Cut	in a refrigerator
Large joint 1.5 kg /3¼ lb or more	12–14 hours per 4 kg 6–7 hours per lb
Small joints under 1.5 kg /3¼ lb	6–8 hours per kg 3–4 hours per lb
Chops or slices	5–6 hours

Lamb freezer facts
Freezer space needed: allow about 43½ L /1½ cu ft for up to 16 kg /35 lb lamb on the bone.

Storage times: at –18C/0F:
joints and cuts – up to 9 months
offal and mince – up to 3 months

How supplied: jointed and on the bone as:
whole carcasses (2 legs, 2 shoulders etc.)
    sides (1 of each cut)
hindquarters (leg and loin)
forequarters (shoulder, neck, best end and breast)
individual joints or portions (shoulders, legs, loin chops, etc.)

Bandsaw method for frozen lamb

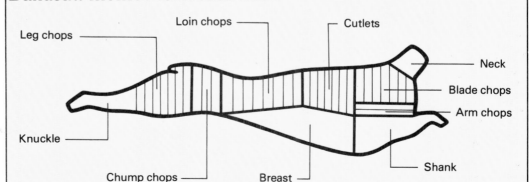

Leg chops — Loin chops — Cutlets — Neck — Blade chops — Arm chops — Shank — Breast — Chump chops — Knuckle

This is a way of cutting up a frozen-solid carcass to obtain the maximum number of individual portions for freezer storage, or for a large-scale barbecue. (It is not suitable for thawed carcasses.) Single chops and cutlet portions are obtained from a side of lamb, double cutlets or chops from a whole carcass.

hours before the meat is delivered. If either freezing space or your own time is very limited, you will find it more convenient to buy ready frozen lamb.

Thawing frozen lamb

Unless you are certain that the lamb was aged before freezing the meat, it will be tenderer and juicier if allowed to thaw out slowly and completely before it is cooked. There is no guesswork involved, because you simply follow your customary times and temperatures. Most cooks agree that moderate temperature roasting, at 180C/350F/gas 4, gives the most satisfactory results. Boned and rolled meat must always be fully thawed before cooking.

Cooking still-frozen lamb

If there is simply not enough time to thaw the meat (and if you are sure that it was aged before freezing) then cook it from frozen. Cook small joints of up to 1.5 kg/3¼ lb for 90 minutes per kg/45 minutes per lb at 180C/350F/gas 4. When cooking joints from frozen you should use a meat thermometer to check that the joint is cooked right through to the centre. Insert the thermometer into the centre of the thickest part of the joint when soft enough without touching a bone. The meat will reach 77–80C/170–180F when cooked.

For stewing the meat can be started from frozen in casseroles and hot pots. Cook it for about 30 minutes longer than usual. Cutlets or chops can be fried or grilled from frozen, but cook these at a lower temperature and allow extra time for thawing as well as cooking.

Hints on freezing cooked lamb

● Time and fuel can be saved by cooking double or treble quantities of casseroles and pies and freezing them.
● Cool the cooked dishes as quickly as possible, refrigerate until chilled and then freeze. Foil containers are useful as they are suitable for both oven and freezer.
● Pie fillings can be covered with raw pastry before freezing, but potato toppings or dumplings should be added when reheating for serving.
● Slices of roast lamb tend to become dry unless they are completely covered with a gravy or sauce before freezing.
● Cooked dishes can be reheated straight from the freezer, but allow enough time in the oven to heat right through to the centre (about 1 hour in a moderate oven for a family size stew or pie).

French spring lamb

Navarin printanier

This is a colourful and fresh-tasting casserole of spring lamb combined with a selection of tender new season's vegetables.

2½ hours

Serves 4
25 g/1 oz butter
15 ml/1 tbls oil
700 g/1½ lb boneless lean shoulder lamb, cut in 25 mm/1 in cubes
10 ml/2 tsp sugar
15 ml/1 tbls flour
salt and freshly ground black pepper
450 ml/15 fl oz chicken stock
15 ml/1 tbls tomato purée
1 clove garlic, crushed
bouquet garni of bay leaf, sprig each of thyme and parsley, tied together
8 button onions, peeled
8 baby carrots, scraped
12 tiny new potatoes, scraped
150 g/5 oz shelled peas or young broad beans

French spring lamb

1   Heat the butter and oil in a flameproof casserole (with a lid) large enough to hold all the ingredients.
2   When hot, fry the meat briskly, in two batches, stirring frequently, until lightly browned. Strain off excess fat and return all the meat to the pan. Sprinkle in the sugar and stir until lightly caramelized.
3   Heat the oven to 150C/300F/gas 2.
4   Add the flour and generous seasonings of salt and pepper to the meat, lower the heat and stir for a minute or two until the flour is lightly coloured. Add the stock, tomato purée, garlic and bouquet of herbs and stir until simmering.
5   Cover the casserole tightly; transfer to the centre of the oven. Cook for 1 hour.
6   Skim excess fat from the surface of the casserole, then add the onions, carrots and potatoes, pushing them under the surface of the sauce. Cover and cook for a further 40 minutes.
7   Stir in the peas or broad beans, cover and cook for another 15 minutes or until all the ingredients are tender.
8   Skim off any surface fat, discard the bouquet of herbs and check the seasoning. Serve from the casserole.

Noisettes of lamb Cumberland

Noisettes are boneless cutlets prepared from meaty best ends of neck of lamb.

🕯 40 minutes

Serves 4
8 small noisettes of lamb, prepared from a
   1 kg/2¼ lb best end (see right)
freshly ground black pepper
15 ml/1 tbls oil
25 g/1 oz butter
salt
For the Cumberland sauce
150 ml/5 fl oz meat stock
60 ml/4 tbls redcurrant jelly
15 ml/1 tbls Worcestershire sauce
30 ml/2 tbls lemon juice
15 ml/1 tbls cornflour
For the garnish
cooked peas
small cooked carrots
watercress sprigs

1　Pat the noisettes dry with absorbent paper and season with pepper. Heat the oil and butter in a large frying-pan, and when hot brown the noisettes quickly on both sides.
2　Reduce the heat and cook gently until tender, about 10–12 minutes, turning once.
3　Season the noisettes with salt, lift out and arrange, overlapping, in a circle around a hot serving dish. Keep hot.
4　Pour off all but 30 ml/2 tbls of fat from the pan. Add the stock, redcurrant jelly, Worcestershire sauce and lemon juice and stir over gentle heat until blended.
5　Mix the cornflour with 30 ml/2 tbls water, stir into the pan and boil for 1 minute, stirring. Spoon over the noisettes.

Noisettes of lamb Cumberland

6　Arrange the peas and carrots around the noisettes and, just before serving, the watercress in the centre.

● To prepare noisettes at home, lay the skinned best end fat side down and cut the meat from the bones with a sharp knife. Season, roll up tightly and tie at 25 mm/1 in intervals with fine string. Cut between the string into noisettes.

Fruit-stuffed shoulder of lamb

As a change from a completely boned shoulder ask the butcher to remove the blade bone only. Then, when served, you have the choice of meat on the bone or stuffed. You can use any stuffing: this apricot flavoured rice stuffing (shown on *page 19*) complements the meat well.

🕯 overnight soaking fruit,
   then 2¾ hours

Serves 8–10
1.5–2 kg/3¼–4½ lb shoulder of lamb, with
   blade bone removed
salt and freshly ground black pepper
For the stuffing
25 g/1 oz butter
1 medium onion, finely chopped
100 g/4 oz long-grain rice, cooked and drained
75 g/3 oz dried apricots, soaked overnight then
   drained and chopped
30 ml/2 tbls seedless raisins, soaked with the
   apricots and drained
30 ml/2 tbls chopped walnuts
finely grated zest of 1 lemon
2.5 ml/½ tsp ground coriander
2.5 ml/½ tsp ground ginger
salt and freshly ground black pepper

1　To make the stuffing melt the butter in a saucepan and fry the onion gently for 6 minutes, stirring frequently. Add the remaining ingredients, with salt and pepper to taste, and mix thoroughly.
2　Wipe the meat with damp absorbent paper and season with salt and pepper.
3　Heat the oven to 180C/350F/gas 4. Fill the blade bone cavity with stuffing and pin the edges of the meat together with a thin skewer. Put any remaining stuffing in a covered casserole and cook on the shelf below the meat for the last ½ hour of cooking time.
4　Lay the meat on a rack in a roasting tin with the loose blade bone below the rack to improve the gravy. Cook for 60 minutes per kg/30 minutes per lb, plus an additional 30 minutes for both.
5　Transfer the cooked meat to a hot serving dish and arrange the extra stuffing beside it. Serve with gravy made in the usual way from the skimmed meat juices.

Leg of lamb Sardinian style

A colourful and flavoursome way of cooking a leg of mutton or lamb, this method is especially convenient when cooking facilities are limited to a single hot plate or a camp fire.

🕯 1¾ hours

Serves 6
leg of lamb weighing about 1.5 kg/3¼ lb
salt and freshly ground black pepper
3–4 cloves garlic, peeled
fresh rosemary
45 ml/3 tbls olive oil
1 onion, finely chopped
800 g/1 lb 12 oz canned peeled tomatoes
15 ml/1 tbls sugar

1　Wipe the lamb with damp absorbent paper, cut away any excess fat and rub the meat all over with salt and pepper. Cut the garlic cloves into thin slivers and divide the rosemary into sprigs.
2　With a pointed knife make nicks over the surface of the lamb and insert a piece of garlic and a sprig of rosemary into each.
3　Heat the oil in a flameproof casserole and fry the lamb, turning frequently, until lightly browned.
4　Add the onion and fry for a minute, then press the tomatoes and their liquid through a coarse sieve into a pan.
5　Add the sugar, bring to the boil and season to taste. Cover the pan tightly and simmer very gently until the lamb is tender, allowing about 40 minutes per kg/20 minutes per lb, plus 20 minutes, turning once. Check the cooking from time to time, adding a little more liquid if it evaporates too rapidly.
6　Transfer the lamb to a hot serving dish. Skim any surface fat from the liquid and boil rapidly, uncovered, until reduced to a rough textured sauce. Season and serve with the meat.

Pork

Succulent roasts with crispy golden crackling, steaks in a piquant tomato and olive sauce, spare ribs and beans in a rich, fruity sauce . . . pork is one of the most delicious of meats, is good value for money and is very versatile.

Apart from countries where pork is taboo on religious grounds, the pig has probably been man's most common source of meat.

Nowadays pig production is a highly organized and scientifically controlled industry. And because porkers are only four to five months old when slaughtered, pork is a much leaner meat than it used to be. Its price compares favourably with other meats, particularly for those with time to spend on cooking the economical fore-end pork cuts.

Cured pork is used for bacon and ham (*pages 47–53*) and is also much used for sausages (*pages 71–75*).

Buying and storing pork

Unlike beef, pork is not improved by ageing but is eaten fresh. When buying pork, look for fine-grained, firm and pale pink flesh, covered by not more than 15 mm /½ in of creamy white fat and a thin, supple outer rind. Avoid over-fat pork which is wasteful (or at least ensure that the butcher trims it before weighing).

Modern refrigeration has made pork an all-year-round meat, but prices fluctuate a little according to supply and demand. There is also a considerable price difference between the prime cuts in high demand and those that need more time to prepare.

When buying, allow 100–175 g /4–6 oz boneless pork per person or, depending on the amount of bone it contains, 175–275 g /6–10 oz of pork on the bone.

Buying pork for the freezer

From time to time special offers of pork legs or fore-ends are too good to miss, especially when you can freeze the surplus. For large families which can make use of the various cuts, a whole or half side can be a good investment. Before buying check the quality carefully and be prepared to freeze the pork as soon as it is delivered.

Individual portions cook successfully from frozen, especially when pan-braised, for roughly half as long again as normal.

Loin of pork with orange

Cooking pork

Pork can be cooked by many different methods, and its subtle flavour combines readily with such a variety of ingredients that there is virtually no end to possible recipes. But remember that whatever method you use the full flavour of pork develops only with slow and thorough cooking, and that undercooked pork is unpleasant to eat and can be a potential health hazard. To check that pork is thoroughly cooked, pierce the thickest part of the meat with a fine skewer. If the juices are clear, the meat is done; if the juices are pink, the meat is not yet done, so continue cooking until they run clear.

25

Hand   Loin   Leg

From the shoulder: 1 blade end joint, 2 spare rib chops. Belly: 3 whole belly including spare ribs, 4 streaky end belly. From the loin: 5 tenderloin, 6 chump end of loin, 7 loin chops. From the leg: 8 chump chops, 9 leg escalopes, 10 leg steaks.

The prime joints make superlative roasts, while the medium-quality cuts produce succulent pot roasts, braises and casseroles – in fact, these moist methods of cooking are particularly well suited to today's leaner pork. Even the skeletal rib bones make delicious Chinese-style spare ribs.

The Chinese, in fact, use pork often, in quick dishes using stir-fried pork and savoury noodles and also in more time-consuming ones such as the delicious long-steamed pork pudding.

The fatter cuts of pork supply the succulence lacking in lean meats such as veal, poultry and liver, hence the use of belly pork combined with these meats in pâtés, stuffings and casseroles.

Our forebears were very aware of the advantages of combining fat pork with pulse vegetables like haricot beans – the result is a heritage of classic economy recipes such as Boston baked beans.

Compared with other meats pork is rather rich and some people find it a little indigestible. This effect is lessened by combining pork with ingredients that provide sharply contrasting textures and flavours. Many fruits do the job admirably, especially apples in various forms – baked, fried in rings, as a sauce, or raw in salads. Other sharp fruit sauces such as gooseberry, plum, rhubarb and cranberry make a welcome change. Prunes with pork is a French classic and apricots are delicious in a stuffing (see recipe). Citrus fruits make a perfect contrast (see recipe).

A little dry white vermouth or reduced white wine or dry cider cuts the richness and improves the flavour of a gravy. A dash of wine or cider vinegar will often do.

Many herbs and spices enhance the flavour of pork, and it is never a mistake to rub a joint with salt, freshly ground black pepper and herbs an hour or two before cooking, and, if you like, spike it with slivers of garlic too. Flavourings that marry well with pork include mustard, juniper berries, coriander, cumin, ginger, soy sauce, rosemary, horseradish, sage, thyme and caraway.

Roasting

Any joint of young pork with a covering of fat can be roasted either on the bone or boned and rolled. But the less prime cuts are more succulent if either pot roasted or stuffed with a moist filling.

When timing the roast remember that boned and rolled joints take longer to cook than cuts on the bone, and thick cuts longer than thin ones. Take the joint from the refrigerator in time for it to come to room temperature or allow an extra 15 minutes in the oven. If using a meat thermometer cook to a temperature of 82C/180F. For a tasty roast, cook at high temperature, 230C/450F/gas 8, for 15 minutes, then reduce the heat to 160C/325F/gas 3 and roast for a further 35–39 minutes per kg/16–18 minutes per lb until cooked through and tender.

Thawing times for frozen pork

Cut	In a refrigerator	At room temperature
Large joint	8–14 hours per kg	4–8 hours per kg
1.5 kg /3¼ lb or more	4–7 hours per lb	2–4 hours per lb
Small joint	6–8 hours per kg	4–6 hours per kg
under 1.5 kg /3¼ lb	3–4 hours per lb	2–3 hours per lb
Chops or steaks	5–6 hours	2–4 hours
25 mm /1 in thick		

Crackling is an English speciality. (In French cooking the rind is always removed.) The rind of all cuts, except perhaps the belly, can make crisp crackling, but that of the loin and leg are best quality. When buying the joint, ask the butcher to score the rind closely, not more than 5 mm /¼ in apart, in the same direction that you will carve, and deeply, right through to the fat beneath – he has a special knife for this.

Before cooking, brush the rind lightly with oil and rub in salt and pepper. The rind will keep the meat moist; for crisp crackling don't cover or baste the joint. If necessary, increase the oven heat for the last 15 minutes to crisp it.

If the rind has been removed but you still want some crackling, prepare it as above. Cook on a rack, uncovered, in a separate tin.
Crisp crust for rindless joints: baste the joint gently while roasting, then increase the heat for the last 20 minutes of cooking and spread the fat side of the joint thinly with made mustard and thickly with dried breadcrumbs mixed with a little brown sugar.

Pot roasting

Oven pot roasting is an excellent way of cooking all joints of pork (though it will not produce crackling). The meat becomes beautifully tender and succulent in the steamy atmosphere of a covered casserole, and is particularly good eaten cold. The joint can be left on the bone, or boned and rolled or stuffed. Use a flameproof casserole in which the meat fits fairly closely.
1   Heat the oven to 170C /325F /gas 3. If necessary, tie the meat into a neat shape and pat dry with kitchen paper.
2   Heat 30 ml /2 tbls oil or lard in the casserole and, when it sizzles, brown the pork on all sides. Lift out and reserve.
3   Add a sliced onion and a sliced carrot, a bouquet garni and, if liked, a clove of garlic. Stir, cover and cook gently for 5 minutes.
4   Season the meat and replace, fat side uppermost, on the vegetables. Add the bones and/or skin, if available. Cover tightly and cook in the centre of the oven, allowing 1 hour 15 minutes per kg /35 minutes per lb, plus 35 minutes, or until a meat thermometer in the thickest part registers 82C /180F. Baste once or twice with the pan juices.
5   When cooked, remove the meat to a hot platter and discard any trussing strings. Skim off most of the fat from the pan juices. Add about 150 ml /5 fl oz liquid (dry cider, white wine, stock or water) and stir to loosen any residue from the base of the pan. Boil briskly for a minute or two, check the seasoning and strain into a hot sauce-boat.

Carcass cutting

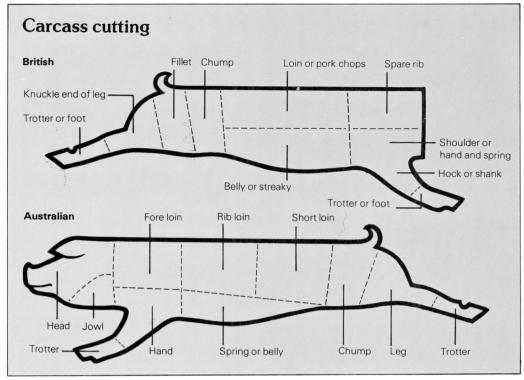

Buying and cooking guide to pork

Cut and weight	Butchering	Cooking methods
Leg Very lean; thin covering of fat and rind Makes good crackling 4-6 kg /8-12 lb	Whole Joints: lean fillet end; bonier knuckle end; Leg steaks Escalopes	Roast–can be boned and rolled or stuffed Roast or braise; knuckle end can be boned and stuffed Grill or braise Sauté
Shoulder Fat and lean meat but good flavour 2.3-3.6 kg /5-8 lb	Joint cut from boned and rolled shoulder Blade joint Spare rib joint or chops	Pot roast or braise Roast–can be boned and stuffed Grill or bake in sauce; cube for stew or kebabs; mince
Belly An economical cut with high proportion of fat 2-4 kg /4½-8½ lb	Streaky end Thick end Thin slices Thick slices Chinese spare ribs	Good pickled or boned and stuffed Roast Grill, bake or fry Cube for casseroles, mince for pâtés Barbecue or bake

Cut and weight	Butchering	Cooking methods
Chump end Prime meat with good crackling; fairly high proportion of bone 1.4-1.6 kg /3-3½ lb	Whole Chops	Roast–can be boned and rolled Braise
Loin Finest roasting pork; makes excellent crackling 2.5-4.5 kg /5½-10 lb	Whole – ask the butcher to chine the joint French-style joint – without rind, fat or bones; meat tied Tenderloin Loin chops – large and meaty Rib chops with long bone	Roast Roast or braise, plain or stuffed Split, stuff and braise, bake en croûte, make into escalopes or cube for kebabs Grill, fry or bake Grill, fry or bake
Hand and spring Good value cut; ideal for pickling 2.3-3.6 kg /5-8 lb	Whole; hand can be boned and tied	Long slow cooking– pot roast, braise or simmer

Frying and grilling

Pork chops and fillet can be shallow-fat fried. Trim some of the fat, season with pepper and leave meat to come to room temperature. Add salt just before cooking. Heat a mixture of butter and oil in a heavy frying-pan and sear the meat quickly for 2 minutes on each side. Lower heat and cook for 6–10 minutes on each side.

Prepare chops similarly for grilling. Heat grill to maximum, brush grid with oil and grill 7.5 cm/3 in away from heat for about the same time until chops are well done.

Pan braising for chops or steaks

For lean pork cuts, slow cooking in a covered pan is the most reliable of all methods. A wide, heavy-based pan with a lid is ideal for cooking several portions at once.

1 Cover the base of the pan with a minimal film of oil or lard and heat until sizzling.

2 Pat the pork portions dry with absorbent paper, season to taste and fry briskly for 2 minutes each side, to seal and brown.

3 Reduce the heat to low, cover the pan tightly and cook very gently for 7–9 minutes each side, until juices run clear. Lift out the meat and keep hot.

4 Skim off surface fat from the pan juices. Add about 150 ml/5 fl oz liquid (dry cider, white wine, or stock) for 3–4 chops or steaks and boil rapidly until well reduced. Check the seasoning and 'lift' the sauce with a dash of horseradish cream or your favourite mustard or mellow it with a little cream. Spoon over the pork and sprinkle with freshly chopped herbs.

Pork specials

Rind: that tough but pliable skin, known as *couenne* in the French kitchen, adds a gelatinous, enriching quality to stocks and gravies, stews and braises. For instance, you'll often find it specified in recipes for French *daubes*. It is rich so use it sparingly, cut in small pieces.

Back fat is the firm fat covering the back of the pig immediately under the rind. Cut in thin slices, it is used for tying over (barding) lean joints or poultry breasts. Cut in matchsticks it becomes the 'sewing thread' for larding lean joints.

Caul is the lacy veil of fat lining the stomach, and is sometimes obtainable from country butchers. After soaking and softening in tepid water it is ready for topping pâtés or wrapping around faggots or other minced meat mixtures.

Apricot-stuffed blade of pork

🕐 🍴 soaking apricots overnight, then 2½ hours

Serves 5
1.1 kg /2½ lb lean blade of pork, weighed after boning (keep bones)
salt and freshly ground black pepper
oil for rubbing
15 ml /1 tbls flour
125 ml /5 fl oz chicken stock
125 ml /5 fl oz dry white wine or cider

For the stuffing
50 g /2 oz dried apricots, soaked overnight, drained and chopped
1 large cooking apple, peeled and chopped
40 g /1½ oz fresh white breadcrumbs
juice and finely grated zest of ½ lemon
salt and freshly ground black pepper
1 small egg, beaten

1 Heat the oven to 170C /325F /gas 3. Make the stuffing by mixing all the ingredients thoroughly. With a sharp knife, cut a deep pocket horizontally through the centre of the joint. Fill with the stuffing and reshape the joint, if necessary securing with skewers.

2 Season the joint generously with salt and pepper and rub the rind with oil. Place the bones in the bottom of a roasting tin and stand the joint, rind uppermost, on a rack over them. Cook for 2 hours, or until the juices run clear.

3 When it is cooked, lift the joint onto a hot serving platter and keep warm while you make the gravy.

4 Pour off all surplus fat from the roasting tin, add the flour to the tin and cook for 1 minute, stirring with a wooden spoon. Stir in the stock and wine or cider, bring to the boil and simmer for 5 minutes. Season with salt and pepper, strain into a hot sauce-boat and serve the joint and the gravy at once.

Pork escalopes mimosa

These escalopes look summery with their yellow, white and green garnish.

🍴🍴 30 minutes, plus 30 minutes chilling (optional)

Serves 4
500 g /18 oz pork tenderloin, trimmed
well-seasoned flour for dusting
1 large egg
75 g /3 oz dry white breadcrumbs
15 ml /1 tbls oil
25 g /1 oz butter
1 large lemon in 8 wedges
chives
flat-leaved parsley
For the mimosa garnish
1 large egg, hard boiled, with the yolk sieved and the white finely chopped
5 ml /1 tsp finely grated lemon zest
15 ml /1 tbls snipped chives, spring onion tops or parsley

1 Using a sharp knife, cut the pork across into 10 mm /⅓ in slices. Lay each slice flat between 2 pieces of dampened greaseproof paper and beat gently with a rolling pin.

Pork escalopes mimosa and Quarterdeck pork and bean casserole

---

Quarterdeck pork and bean casserole

soaking and cooking beans if necessary, then 2½ hours

Serves 6

1 kg /2 lb lean boneless shoulder of pork
40 g /1½ oz flour
5 ml /1 tsp curry powder
salt and freshly ground black pepper
30 ml /2 tbls oil
1 large onion, thinly sliced
30 ml /2 tbls black treacle
150 ml /5 fl oz boiling water
425 g /15 oz canned peeled tomatoes
1 bay leaf
275–350 g /10–12 oz drained haricot or butter beans, cooked or canned
celery leaves, to garnish (optional)

1 Heat the oven to 170C /325F /gas 3. Trim the pork of excess fat and cut it into neat 25 mm /1 in cubes.
2 Mix together in a bowl the flour, curry powder and generous seasonings of salt and pepper. Add the pork cubes and toss until all the coating adheres to the meat.
3 Heat the oil in a deep flameproof casserole and fry the onion over gentle heat for 5 minutes, stirring occasionally. Raise the heat, add the pork and stir for 1–2 minutes, until the oil has been absorbed
4 Dissolve the treacle in the boiling water and add to the casserole with the tomatoes and their juice and the bay leaf. Bring to simmering point, cover tightly and cook in the centre of the oven for 1–1½ hours.
5 Stir in the beans, cover and continue cooking for another 30 minutes. Check the seasoning and serve from the casserole, garnished with celery leaves if wished.

Pork steaks siciliana

1 hour 15 minutes

Serves 4

4 pork steaks, 15 mm /½ in thick, trimmed
about 15 ml /1 tbls well-seasoned flour
30 ml /2 tbls oil
1 large onion, thinly sliced
1–2 garlic cloves, finely chopped
90 ml /6 tbls Marsala
425 g /15 oz canned peeled tomatoes
1.5 ml /¼ tsp oregano
50 g /2 oz small black or green olives, or a mixture
salt and freshly ground black pepper (optional)

1 Sprinkle the steaks generously with the seasoned flour and rub in lightly.
2 Heat the oil in a wide frying-pan with a lid. When it sizzles, fry the steaks quickly 1–2 minutes each side, until pale gold. Remove them from the pan, lower the heat, add the onion and fry for 5–6 minutes, then add the garlic and cook for 1 minute.
3 Return the steaks to the pan and pour in the Marsala. Raise the heat and boil quickly until the liquid is reduced by half.
4 Press the tomatoes with their juice into the pan through a coarse strainer, add the oregano and bring to the boil. Cover tightly and simmer very gently for 40 minutes.
5 Add the olives and simmer for 5 minutes or until the meat is very tender. Arrange the pork steaks overlapping on a hot serving platter and keep warm.
6 Stir the sauce vigorously with a wooden spoon to loosen any juices from the base of the pan and, if necessary, boil rapidly for a few minutes to reduce to a purée consistency. Add salt and pepper if needed, pour over the steaks and serve at once.

Loin of pork with orange

This joint, which is equally good served hot or cold, has a crisp, spicy crust.

2 hours 25 minutes

Serves 8

1.4 kg /3 lb loin of pork, weighed after skinning and boning (keep skin and bones if possible)
salt and freshly ground black pepper
1–2 garlic cloves, finely chopped
30 ml /2 tbls freshly chopped parsley
5 ml /1 tsp freshly chopped marjoram or 2.5 ml /½ tsp dried marjoram
30 ml /2 tbls oil
200 ml /7 fl oz chicken stock
juice of 1 large orange
45–60 ml /3–4 tbls orange liqueur
15 ml /1 tbls French mustard
45 ml /3 tbls dry white breadcrumbs
15 ml /1 tbls soft light brown sugar
2–3 seedless oranges separated into segments, to garnish
sprigs of watercress, to garnish

1 Heat the oven to 170C /325F /gas 3. Sprinkle the inside of the loin of pork with salt, pepper, garlic, parsley and marjoram. Form it into a neat roll, fat side outwards, and tie at intervals with string.
2 Heat the oil in a flameproof casserole into which the meat fits closely. When it sizzles, brown the meat lightly on all sides.
3 Gently heat the chicken stock then add it to the casserole. Tuck the bones and pieces of skin, if available, around the meat, cover the casserole and cook for 1¾ hours.
4 Discard the bones and skin. Pour the orange juice and liqueur over the meat, spread the meat thinly with mustard and sprinkle with the breadcrumbs and sugar. Return to the oven and cook, uncovered, for 15 minutes or until the juices run clear and the topping is crisp and golden.
5 Lift the meat onto a hot serving platter, remove the string and keep warm. Degrease the pan juices, add the orange sections and heat for 2 minutes. Using a slotted spoon, arrange the orange sections in groups around the meat and tuck sprigs of watercress between the groups of orange. Check the gravy for seasoning, pour into a sauceboat and serve at once.

---

2 Dust each escalope lightly on both sides with seasoned flour. Beat the egg with 10 ml /2 tsp water, dip each escalope in the egg and then toss in the breadcrumbs until well coated. Lay flat on greaseproof paper and press on the coating with a palette knife. If possible, leave the meat in a cold place, lightly covered, for at least 30 minutes for the coating to firm up.
3 When ready to cook, heat the oil and butter in a large frying-pan. When sizzling, fry as many of the escalopes as the pan will hold for 3–4 minutes on each side, until golden and cooked through. Lift out, drain on crumpled absorbent paper and keep warm while you cook the remainder.
4 Meanwhile, combine the hard-boiled egg, lemon zest and chives, spring onion or parsley to make the mimosa garnish. When all the escalopes are cooked, pile them on a warmed serving platter, sprinkle with the garnish and arrange the lemon wedges in the centre with the chives and parsley.

✱✱✱ The egg and breadcrumbed escalopes can be layered flat between cling film, overwrapped with foil and frozen. They can then be cooked from frozen, allowing an extra few minutes cooking time.

Beef

Though the roast beef of Old England brings to mind visions of enormous joints spit-roasting over an open fire, the beef we now enjoy is infinitely more tender and succulent, even though it comes from a very much smaller joint.

Cattle were first domesticated about 10,000 BC from the wild ox, and selective breeding has gone on ever since. Today, there are 277 breeds, of which 33 are the best beef-producing strains, lean and tender. The farmer aims at an optimum time to keep his beasts – usually 1½–2 years; one year is too short, resulting in steers (young males) with little flavour, and more than 2 years can become uneconomic.

Choosing beef

More than other meats, the quality of beef is dependent on how the butcher handles it, from hanging the carcasses in his cold store to cutting up and preparing the joints – so find a reliable butcher and make use of his knowledge.

Beef should be hung for at least 8–10 days before it is sold. Without hanging the meat will lack flavour and can never be very tender no matter how carefully it is cooked.

Buy the prime joints for quick cooking methods, such as roasting or grilling, and cook the economical cuts which require longer, slower cooking with added liquid by methods such as braising or casseroling. It is a waste of time and money to cook any cut of beef by an unsuitable method (see chart).

When choosing beef, remember that colour is not a reliable indicator of quality, as the flesh darkens upon exposure to air, the appearance can also be affected by the shop lighting. The meat should look fresh and moist but not watery. There should be very little gristle between the fat and the lean if the meat is from a young animal, and the fat should be firm, dry and cream or white in colour. The lean or prime cuts should look smooth and velvety while more economical cuts will have a coarser texture.

Storing beef

Remove the shop wrapping, put the beef on a clean plate, loosely covered with foil or cling film, and store in the refrigerator. Joints and steaks can be kept for up to 4 days, stewing meat for up to 2 days and mince for one day. Without a refrigerator, the storage times are halved. The more cut surfaces the meat has, the shorter time it should be kept, so if you are chopping or mincing at home, do it just before cooking. Cooked meat can be kept for 1–2 days in a cool place (maximum 13C /55F), 2–3 days in the refrigerator and 3–6 months in the freezer (provided there is no bacon in the cooked dish).

Preparing and cooking beef

To prepare a joint of beef for cooking, remove it from the refrigerator and wipe with a clean, damp cloth. Rub with dry mustard, if wished, and freshly ground black pepper – no salt at this stage as it tends to draw out the meat juices. Allow it to stand at room temperature for 2–3 hours before cooking.

Quantities: for meat with a large amount of bone, allow 275–350 g /10–12 oz per person. Meat with a small amount of bone should be calculated at 225–275 g /8–10 oz per person. Steaks for grilling or frying should be 175–225 g /6–8 oz per portion, while for stewing beef, boned and rolled roasts, or minced beef you will need 125–175 g /4–6 oz per person.

Roasting

Roasting is only suitable for the prime joints: sirloin or rib roast (on the bone or boned and rolled), fillet and topside.

Choose a joint on the bone for the finest flavour, or boned and rolled for easier carving. It should weigh at least 1 kg /2 lb for a boned joint – more if it is unboned. Anything smaller will shrink too much during roasting and would be better pot roasted.

To retain its full succulence and flavour, brown the meat initially on all sides at a high temperature to seal in the juices. The temperature is then lowered and the meat cooked slowly for every joint except fillet. This slower cooking also keeps shrinkage to a minimum – a most important factor when using high-priced cuts. (See *page 32* for roasting times.)

Once cooked, season the joint with salt and more pepper to taste, transfer it to a hot plate and leave to stand in a warm place for 10–15 minutes to let the joint juices 'settle', making carving easier and giving you time to make the gravy. Fillet is again the exception to this – it should be served immediately. Heat the plates well and see that all accompaniments are steaming hot.

Using a meat thermometer: insert the thermometer into the centre of the meat before cooking, taking care not to touch the bone. Centre temperatures of the meat should read 60C /140F for rare, 70C /160F for medium, and 80C /180F for well done.

Sirloin and rib roast: spread the joint with 50 g /2 oz good meat dripping and place it, fat side up, in a roasting tin. Unless the joint has a bone to stand on, stand the joint on a

On the slab, left: sirloin on the bone and fore-rib. In trays, top row: cubed shin, silverside and topside. Middle row: entrecôte steaks, cubed top rump, Fillet and rolled brisket. Bottom row: blade both sliced and cubed, rump steak, sliced leg and cubed clod

Buying and cooking beef: the first five listed are the quality cuts

Cut and weight	Butchering
Sirloin sold with or without the fillet; tender, prime beef with a thin covering of fat; 6.5–9 kg /15–20 lb	Joint on the bone 2.7–3.6 kg /6–8 lb Joint boned and rolled 2–2.5 kg / 4½–5½ lb Sliced into steaks 20 mm /¾ in up
Fillet undercut from the sirloin; very tender, lean, prime beef; often sold barded; 1–1.8 kg /2–4 lb	Whole Sliced into steaks 25 mm /1 in up Minced
Rump lean, prime cut with a narrow border of fat; less tender than sirloin or fillet but good flavour; 5 kg /11 lb	Sliced into steaks 15 mm /½ in up
Topside very lean cut; about 7.3 kg/ 16 lb	Joint, often sold rolled and barded average joint 1.4–1.8 kg /3–4 lb
Rib roast or Fore rib traditional roast beef joint; about 4 kg /9 lb	Joint on the bone 1.8 kg /4–5 lb up (sometimes sold with bone cut short) Joint boned and rolled 1.4–1.8 kg / 3–4 lb up
Leg (hind leg) lean meat, high proportion of connective tissue; 2.7 kg /6 lb	Cubed or thickly sliced for cutting up
Shin (fore leg) lean meat, high proportion of connective tissue; 1.4 kg /3 lb	Cubed or thickly sliced for cutting up

Cooking methods	Cut and weight	Butchering	Cooking methods
	Silverside		
Roast	streaky, coarse-grained meat;	Joint, fresh	Pot roast or braise
Roast	about 6.5 kg /15 lb	Joint, salted 1.8 kg /3–4 lb	Boil with dumplings
Grill or fry	**Top rump (thick flank)**	Boneless joint	Pot roast
	lean meat; similar to topside but	Sliced	Braise
	not as tender; 5.9 kg /13 lb	Cubed	Casserole, stew, use
Roast			in pies or puddings
Grill or fry			
Steak tartare			
	Thin flank		
	coarse-grained meat layered with	Joint on the bone, fresh	Pot roast
Grill or fry	fat; about 4.5 kg /10 lb	Joint boned and rolled, fresh	Pot roast or braise
		Joint boned and rolled,	Boil and press to
		salted	serve cold
	Brisket		
	coarse-grained meat layered with	Joint boned and rolled, fresh	Braise
Roast (best rare)	fat; about 5.4 kg /12 lb	Joint boned and rolled,	Boil and press to
or pot roast		salted	serve cold
	Top rib		
Roast	lean, medium-quality meat; about	Joint boned and rolled	Pot roast or braise
	6.5 kg /15 lb	Thickly sliced	Braise
Roast	**Chuck and blade (braising steak)**		
	lean, medium-quality meat with	Cubed	Casserole, stew, use
	good flavour; about 12 kg /27 lb		in pies or puddings
Long, slow cooking in		Sliced	Braise
casserole or stew			
	Neck and clod		
	good flavour; produces rich	Cubed	Casserole or stew
Long, slow cooking in	gravy during long, slow cooking	Minced (2nd quality)	Pâtés, stuffings, etc.
casserole or stew			

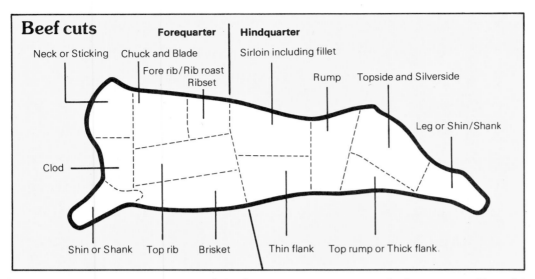

Beef cuts

Forequarter
- Neck or Sticking
- Chuck and Blade
- Fore rib/Rib roast Ribset
- Clod
- Shin or Shank
- Top rib
- Brisket

Hindquarter
- Sirloin including fillet
- Rump
- Topside and Silverside
- Leg or Shin/Shank
- Thin flank
- Top rump or Thick flank

wire rack, keeping the meat clear of the fat in the bottom of the pan. When you reduce the oven temperature (see below), add 60 ml /4 tbls warm water or red wine to the pan and baste the joint from time to time with the pan juices.

Joints on the bone weighing up to 3 kg /6 lb need an initial 15 minutes at 220C /425F /gas 7, then turn the heat down to 170C /325F /gas 3 and cook for 35 minutes per kg /16 minutes per lb for rare; 45 minutes per kg /20 minutes per lb for medium; and 65 minutes per kg /30 minutes per lb for well done.

Boned and rolled joints up to 3 kg /6 lb need, after the initial 15 minutes, 33 minutes per kg /15 minutes per lb for rare, 55 minutes per kg /25 minutes per lb for medium and 1 hour 15 minutes per kg /35 minutes per lb for well done.

Topside: as this is a very lean joint, it must be barded with pork fat before roasting as sirloin or rib roast. Topside is best served rare as it can become dry and tough if the cooking time is extended. If you dislike rare meat, pot roasting gives an excellent result.

Fillet: unlike the other roasts, fillet should be cooked at a higher temperature throughout. As the size of a large fillet will vary greatly from one end to the other, turn in the thinner end and tie it neatly into an even shape. Then, either bard the fillet with pork fat, or turn it in a pan of hot dripping to seal the juices and provide a coating of fat. Place the joint on a rack in a roasting tin, add 45–60 ml/3–4 tbls warm water or red wine and roast at 220C/425F/gas 7 for 22 minutes per kg/10 minutes per lb for rare, or 33 minutes per kg/15 minutes per lb for medium. Serve immediately with a wine gravy and horseradish cream.

Roast meat to eat cold is always roast only until rare. Do not carve off any slices or pierce the joint with a fork, but allow it to become cold before cutting. This way it retains all the juices. Carve into very thin slices.

Grilling

A quick-cooking method, this is suitable only for tender, top-quality cuts such as fillet, sirloin or rump steak. Make sure the steaks are all the same thickness to ensure even cooking. For successful grilling, they should be 20 mm /¾ in or more. Heat the grill 10 minutes before you start to get it really hot. Trim away any excess fat if necessary, then cut the remaining fat at intervals to prevent it curling.

Just before grilling, brush the steaks with a mixture of melted butter and oil and season with a little salt. Place them on a rack below the grill about 7.5 cm /3 in from the heat and cook them for 2 minutes on each side at high heat to seal in the juices. Then lower the heat and cook, turning once, until done. Careful timing is important. Grill for 2–5 minutes each side, according to cut and how you like your steak.

If you are doubtful about whether the steak is cooked, press it with your finger. If rare, it is spongy and springs back, if medium, it still has a certain amount of give, but if well cooked it will feel quite firm. If you are still unsure, cut a small slit in the steak and take a look – it can then easily be returned for extra cooking if necessary. Serve the steaks with pats of flavoured butter.

Pan frying

Another quick-cooking method for tender cuts: prepare the steaks as for grilling. Heat 30 ml /2 tbls oil and 25 g /1 oz butter in a really heavy, well-seasoned frying-pan. When the fat is really hot, and the foaming has subsided, fry the steaks over high heat for 2 minutes until well browned on one side. Turn them and sear the other side. Reduce the heat and cook for 2½–6 minutes each side for sirloin and rump, 4–10 minutes each side for fillet. Season with salt before serving.

Minute steak (a thin slice from the top part of the sirloin) and flash-fry steak (pre-tenderized thin steak) may also be cooked in the same way but they only require one minute each side.

Braising

This method produces tender, succulent joints from the less tender cuts of beef, such as topside, top ribs, brisket, flank and fresh silverside. It is also suitable for thick slices of buttock or braising steak.

Tie the meat into a neat joint, then weigh it and pat dry. Choose a deep, heavy pan with a close-fitting lid to hold the joint or slices of meat snugly.

Melt 30–45 ml /2–3 tbls dripping in the pan and fry the meat until it is lightly browned all over. Fry a mixture of sliced vegetables – carrots, onions, celery and swedes – in the remaining fat. Pour in stock, wine or cider to almost cover the vegetables. Add a bay leaf and season.

Replace the meat on top of the vegetables, and put a piece of buttered paper over the meat. Cover and cook very gently on top of the cooker or in the oven at 170C /325F /gas 3, allowing 1 hour 40 minutes per kg /45 minutes per lb (approximately 3 hours for a joint, 1½–2 hours for steak). Serve the vegetables and juices from the pan with the meat, or purée the vegetables and stock in a blender to make a smooth sauce and serve this with the meat.

Pot roasting

A combination of frying and steaming, this is a very suitable method of cooking very lean meats which may dry out during cooking, or for less tender joints. It is also a good way to produce a 'roast' without an oven.

Topside, brisket, flank and top ribs are all suitable. The method of cooking is the same as braising but without any added liquid or vegetables. After frying the meat, cover the pan tightly with a lid and cook very gently on top of the cooker, following the times given for braising, but turning the meat every half hour.

Stewing and casseroling

Long, slow cooking with added liquid produces delicious, tender meat, even when using the tougher, inexpensive cuts.

A cold-start casserole is the only method that will tenderize really tough meat (any initial frying would only make the muscles contract). If you have economically bought the cheapest stewing beef, usually the muscular shin or the coarse-grained leg, or clod and sticking (from the neck and chest), or have partially defrosted beef which is to cold and wet for frying at the point when cooking must commence, this is the method that will give best results. It will also give a casserole which is largely free from fat (which may be an advantage for some people) and one with a rich succulent gravy.

Cut the beef into small pieces, not more than 25 mm /1 in square, and remove all visible fat and really thick tendons as you go. Add vegetables, usually roots, chopped to equally small shapes, cereals such as barley, herbs and seasonings. Pack the casserole as tightly as you can, because the amount of liquid (stock, cider or wine) used should always be small or a rich gravy will not result. Just cover the ingredients with liquid, bring very slowly to the boil, then reduce the heat to the barest simmer. In an oven this can be achieved by starting at 150C /300F /gas 2 for about 30 minutes and then turning the oven down to 140C /275F /gas 1. Cooking will take 4 hours or more.

Fresh vegetables with a shorter cooking time may be added 30 minutes before the end of cooking. When the meat is tender the surface may be blotted of any fat, if you wish, or this may be stirred in. Cold-start casseroles are usually served with unthickened gravy, although potatoes may be cooked in the casserole which are then mashed and blended thoroughly into the liquid to make gravy.

For a fry-start casserole use best-grade stewing steak, flank, chuck and blade or skirt. Trim any excess fat from the meat, then cut it into large cubes and coat in seasoned flour. For best flavour render the beef fat first, strain it and then use this fat to fry the meat.

It is essential to keep batches small when frying meat for a casserole, otherwise the sides will not be seared, but will give off liquid which will improve the gravy but detract from the flavour of the meat. Fry the meat quickly to brown all over. Put it in a pan or casserole with fried vegetables and cover with stock or a mixture of stock and wine, beer or cider (no more than 750 ml per kg /10 fl oz per lb). Add herbs and seasonings to taste. Traditionally a stew is cooked on top of the cooker in a heavy pan with a tightly fitting lid very, very gently – the liquid should barely be simmering – for 2–3 hours or until the meat is really tender.

To casserole the meat (done in the oven), cook in an ovenproof casserole with a tightly fitting lid in an oven heated to 150C /300F /gas 2, for 2–3 hours or until tender. Serve with potatoes, pasta or plain boiled rice to soak up the gravy.

Thawing times for frozen beef

Cut	In a refrigerator	At room temperature
Large joints – 1.5 kg /3¼ lb or more	12–14 hours per kg /6–7 hours per lb	4–5 hours per kg /2–3 hours per lb
Small joints – under 1.5 kg /3¼ lb	6–8 hours per kg /3–4 hours per lb	2–4 hours per kg /1–2 hours per lb
Steaks or stewing steaks 25 mm /1 in thick (not diced)	5–6 hours	2–4 hours

Boiling

This is a confusing term as the cooking liquid must never boil, only simmer gently. It is good for tenderizing tougher, whole joints of boned and rolled silverside and fresh or salted brisket.

The joint must be neatly tied to keep it in shape during the cooking. Soak the salted joint in fresh, cold water for 2 hours before cooking it. Remove it from the water and weigh it.

Choose a deep, heavy pan with a close-fitting lid, and sit the meat on a pad of folded foil or over 2 metal skewers crossed in the bottom of the pan to prevent the meat sticking. Add cold water to just cover the joint.

Bring the water very slowly to boiling point and skim off any scum. Add an onion, 2 cloves, 6 black peppercorns, a bouquet garni, and salt if using fresh meat, then simmer, covered, allowing 1 hour 45 minutes per kg /45 minutes per lb.

Add sliced, fresh root vegetables for the last hour of cooking if wished. Serve the joint hot with boiled carrots and onions, dumplings (added to the beef for the last 20 minutes of cooking time), boiled potatoes and parsley sauce. To serve cold, allow the meat to cool slightly in the liquid, then weight down until cold and serve with assorted pickles and salads.

Minced beef

Many butchers sell two qualities of beef mince. The higher quality is generally leaner with less fat and connective tissue and is suitable for lasagne, spaghetti bolognese, chilli con carne, meat loaves etc. These dishes rely mainly on the meat content and too much fat would spoil the dish. The second quality is suitable for use in stuffings or with other ingredients which will counteract the richness of the fat.

To complement beef

Plain roast or grilled steaks usually need no more than a little mustard, horseradish sauce, or pats of savoury butter, flavoured with parsley and lemon, or anchovy. Any of the following ingredients added sparingly in the preparation of beef casseroles or made-up dishes can greatly enhance the flavour.

Spices and herbs: whole juniper berries, cloves, cinnamon, ginger, curry powder, bay leaves, thyme, parsley and chives.

Vegetables and fruits: onion, garlic, mushrooms, tomatoes, finely grated orange and lemon zest, green or red peppers, carrots, swedes and parsnips.

Wines and spirits: red wine, sherry, brandy, orange-based liqueurs or beer.

Sauces: tomato purée, Worcestershire sauce, mushroom ketchup, anchovy essence, soy sauce, English or Dijon mustard, horseradish sauce.

Buying beef for the freezer

Buy beef from a well-tried, reliable source and check that the beef has been well hung. With a large quantity get the butcher to freeze it for you, packaged into cuts suited to your particular needs and labelled. Always check what is included in the deal – is it sold by weight to include bones and trimmed fat or by weight for prepared joints, in which case the price will be higher?

The best time to buy a side or quarter of beef is in the autumn when prices are generally lowest, as grass-fed cattle are often slaughtered rather than kept on through the

Roast beef

winter. If, however, you are buying on a smaller scale, look for bargain packs of stewing or casserole steaks in the summer when demand is low.

Bulk buying can be a considerable saving but there are three things to consider: the financial outlay will be large, a minimum of 100 L /3½ cu ft of freezer space will be needed (for a quarter carcass), and will the family happily eat all the various cuts supplied? For large families accustomed to eat a lot of meat it can be a sound investment, but for many homes smaller packs of favoured cuts are more practical.

Ordering frozen beef

Most beef for the freezer is sold boned and trimmed. If any cuts are required on the bone, this should be made clear when ordering.

Hindquarter: includes a good proportion of prime roasting, grilling and frying cuts, with approximately 20% braising and stewing beef.

Forequarter: produces approximately 15% roasting cuts, 55% pot roasting or braising meat with 30% for casseroles, stews and mincing.

Smaller bulk buys: the possibilities are rump, usually sold on the bone with fat and trimmings, approximately 9–13.5 kg /20–30 lb in weight; rump and loin, which is the rump plus sirloin and flank; and top piece which consists of the topside, silverside, thick flank and leg. Alternatively make your own choice of sirloin, topside, rump steaks, casserole or stewing packs, etc.

Cooking frozen beef

Defrost joints in the refrigerator (see chart on *page 33*). Bring them up to room temperature for 2 hours prior to cooking. Cook in the normal way. Boned and rolled meat, and larger joints, should always be fully thawed before cooking, as should pot roast and boiling joints.

Cooking still-frozen beef: to roast a joint on the bone under 1.8 kg /4 lb, heat the oven to 180C /350F /gas 4 and allow 1 hour 5 minutes per kg /30 minutes per lb plus 30 minutes for medium-rare, 1 hour 12 minutes per kg /35 minutes per lb plus 35 minutes for well done. It is advisable to use a meat thermometer – press it into the meat once sufficiently thawed–so that cooking time can be extended if necessary.

Thawing and refreezing: meat taken from the freezer and thawed may then be cooked and refrozen, provided it is cooled quickly before freezing.

Steak with green peppercorn sauce

Steak with green peppercorn sauce

Use whole green peppercorns to give a hot but more subtle peppery flavour than the traditional black peppercorns.

bringing the steaks to room temperature, then 15 minutes

Serves 4
4 × 175–225 g /6–8 oz sirloin or rump steaks, 25 mm /1 in thick, at room temperature
25 g /1 oz flour
salt and freshly ground black pepper
pinch of ground thyme
25 g /1 oz butter
125 ml /4 fl oz dry white wine
150 ml /5 fl oz chicken stock
60 ml /4 tbls thick cream
10 ml /2 tsp green peppercorns, well rinsed
watercress, to garnish

1 Put the flour on a flat dish and season with salt, pepper and thyme.
2 Wipe the steaks dry with absorbent paper and then coat on both sides with the flour.
3 Heat the butter in a large frying-pan over medium-high heat until foaming subsides.
4 Fry the steaks quickly 2 minutes on each side. Reduce the heat to medium and cook for a further minute on each side. Transfer them to a hot serving dish and keep warm.
5 Add the wine to the juices remaining in the pan and scrape the sides well to loosen all the sediment. Boil very rapidly until reduced to 15–30 ml /1–2 tbls. Add the stock and boil rapidly again until it is reduced by half. Remove from the heat, pour in the cream and stir well. Return briefly to the heat, taking care that the sauce does not boil. Stir in the peppercorns.
6 Drain any juices from the steaks into the sauce, stir to blend, then pour it over the steaks. Garnish the dish with watercress and serve the steaks immediately.

Beef rolls Bellagio

2¼ hours

Serves 4
700 g /1½ lb topside cut into 4 slices
salt and freshly ground black pepper
30 ml /2 tbls dripping
1 large onion, finely chopped
1 large garlic clove, crushed
4 stalks celery, finely chopped
100 g /4 oz fresh white breadcrumbs
25 g /1 oz butter
15 ml /1 tbls olive oil
400 g /14 oz canned tomatoes, chopped
30 ml /2 tbls tomato purée
5 ml /1 tsp dried basil
1 green pepper, seeded and chopped
5 ml /1 tsp sugar
15 ml /1 tbls wine vinegar
pasta shells, to serve

1 Beat each slice of beef between sheets of greaseproof paper with a meat bat to flatten. Cut each piece in half to make 8 slices. Season them well with salt and pepper.
2 To prepare the stuffing, heat the dripping in a saucepan and gently fry half the onion with the garlic and celery for 5–8 minutes until softened. Stir in the breadcrumbs and season to taste with salt and pepper.

3 Spread each slice of beef with some stuffing, tuck the edges in to neaten and roll up firmly from the shorter edge. Tie securely with fine string.
4 Heat the butter and olive oil in a flameproof casserole and sauté the beef rolls, turning them until browned all over.
5 Mix together the chopped tomatoes and their juices, tomato purée, dried basil, green pepper and remaining chopped onion. Add the sugar and vinegar. Season well and pour over the prepared meat.
6 Cover with a lid and simmer gently for 1½ hours or until the meat is tender.
7 Remove the beef rolls from the casserole with a slotted spoon and cut off the string. Arrange the rolls on a hot serving dish and coat with the sauce. Serve with freshly cooked pasta shells.

Glazed boiled beef

overnight soaking, 3–4 hours, then cooling plus 45 minutes

Serves 6–8
1.6–1.8 kg /3½–4 lb boned and rolled
  salted silverside or brisket
1 large onion, sliced
2 large carrots, sliced
2 sticks celery, sliced
8 whole black peppercorns
1 bay leaf

Beef rolls Bellagio

For the glaze
12 cloves
75 g /3 oz soft brown sugar
2.5 ml /½ tsp dry mustard
5 ml /1 tsp powdered cinnamon
30 ml /2 tbls thin honey
10 ml /2 tsp lemon juice

1 Put the joint in a large bowl, cover with cold water and soak for several hours or overnight.
2 Rinse the meat well in cold water and place in a large saucepan. Add the vegetables, peppercorns and bay leaf. Pour in cold water to cover.
3 Bring the water slowly to the boil, remove any scum from the surface, then reduce the heat to really low, cover the pan with a lid and simmer until tender, about 3–4 hours. Allow the meat to cool in the cooking liquid.
4 Heat the oven to 180C /350F /gas 4.
5 Drain the beef well and place in a small roasting pan.
6 Press the cloves into the fat. Mix together the sugar, mustard, cinnamon, honey and lemon juice and spoon over the top of the meat.
7 Bake in the centre of the oven for about 45 minutes, basting occasionally during cooking, then serve hot with mustard sauce or cold with pickles and salad.

Braised beef in aspic

Boeuf à la mode d'été

⏱ 🔪🔪🔪 18–24 hours marinating, then 10–11 hours plus setting

Serves 6–8

1.8–2 kg /4–4½ lb rolled topside of beef, larded and barded
1 calf's foot or pig's trotter, blanched and split
50 g /2 oz piece of lean bacon, blanched and diced
15–30 ml /1–2 tbls oil (optional)
600 ml /1 pt beef stock
7.5 ml /1½ tsp powdered gelatine (optional)
For the marinade
2 medium-sized onions, chopped
3 carrots, chopped
2 celery stalks, chopped
1 garlic clove, crushed
600 ml /1 pt red wine
bouquet garni
8 black peppercorns
15 ml /1 tbls oil
For the garnish
500 g /1 lb young carrots, cut into 5 cm /2 in lengths and cooked
500 g /1 lb French beans, trimmed and cut into 5 cm /2 in lengths and cooked
salt

1 Combine all the ingredients for the marinade, except the oil, in a large, deep bowl. Add the beef and pour over the 15 ml /1 tbls oil. Cover and leave to marinate in the refrigerator for 18–24 hours, turning the meats occasionally.
2 Remove the meat from the marinade and pat dry. Strain the marinade and reserve the liquid and the vegetables and bouquet garni separately. Heat the oven to 150C /300F /gas 2. Scrub the calf's foot in cold water, then drain and cut it into pieces.
3 In a large flameproof casserole, fry the diced bacon until browned, adding a little oil if necessary. Remove the bacon with a slotted spoon and reserve. Place the beef in the casserole and brown well on all sides over a high heat. Remove the meat and reduce the heat. Add the reserved marinade vegetables to the casserole and cook gently until lightly coloured.
4 Return the beef to the casserole, placing it on top of the vegetables. Tuck the pieces of calf's foot around the meat. Add the diced bacon, reserved bouquet garni, strained marinade and beef stock.
5 Bring to the boil, cover the casserole and transfer to the oven. Braise the beef for 3½–4 hours or until very tender, regulating the heat so the liquid barely simmers.
6 Allow the beef to cool until tepid, then remove it from the casserole and cool

completely, wrap in foil and chill for 5–6 hours. Strain the liquid, cool and chill.
7 For the garnish, cook the carrots and beans separately in boiling salted water until tender; refresh in cold water, drain and pat dry. Cover and chill until required.
8 Prepare the aspic. Remove the layer of fat from the surface of the chilled stock. If the stock has not gelled to a firm consistency, sprinkle the gelatine over 60 ml /4 tbls water and leave to soak.
9 Warm the stock gently in a heavy-based saucepan until liquid (do not overheat or it will sour). Strain the stock through a muslin-lined sieve and blot any remaining fat from the surface with absorbent paper. Dissolve the soaked gelatine, if using, over a low heat, and stir into the stock.
10 Remove the outer fat and the string from the beef and carve the meat into thin slices.
11 Arrange the slices of meat, overlapping on a large serving plate with the cooked carrots and beans on either side. Spoon syrupy aspic over the meat and carrots to glaze. Chill till set, then cover the dish with clingfilm and refrigerate.
12 Meanwhile pour the remaining aspic into a small dish to a depth of 5 mm /¼ in and chill till set. When ready to serve, turn out the aspic, chop it and use to garnish the braised beef and vegetables.

Veal

Veal, fine-grained and delicately flavoured, is the gourmet's choice for classically elegant dishes, from fragile escalopes to decorative galantines, yet the luxury cuts are matched in goodness by modest ones, made into stews and simple patties. Another young animal – kid – is also included here.

Veal is calf's meat, the best coming from beef 2½ to 3 months old. There are 3 types of veal: unweaned 'bobby' calves, marketed within 2 to 4 weeks from birth, have almost white flesh and a very mild flavour, but the carcasses yield little meat. This veal, almost invariably, is cubed and sold as 'pie veal'. Grass-fed meat from weaned calves is darker in colour than any other, as well as being tougher and more strongly flavoured. The third type, until recently mainly exported by Holland but now a standard European way of raising veal, comes from relatively large calves which are kept indoors and fed on a diet of milk replacer. The veal they yield is as fine-grained and almost as pale and gently flavoured as bobby veal.

Buying and storing veal

Veal is becoming more popular than it was, and frozen, Dutch-style veal in particular is easier to get than a few years ago; escalopes, for instance, are sometimes available in supermarkets, although if you want a large joint or a particular European cut you will have to order it in advance from one of the larger supermarkets or a specialist butcher.

Veal tends to be expensive, so make sure you buy the best quality: look for finely grained flesh which is white or only just very pale pink. Never buy wet or flabby veal, or meat which is brownish or mottled. Avoid, too, large pale joints which look 'blown up' – this may be the result of bleeding old veal to lighten its colour, and when cooked the meat will deflate and be tough. However, do not worry if there are air bubbles around the bones of small animals at the joints and along the flank; small carcasses, especially, are often inflated to make skinning easier, and these bubbles can be punched out with your fist before you cut up or cook the meat.

You will need 225–275 g /8–10 oz per serving of veal on the bone; 100–175 g /4–6 oz of boneless veal.

Refrigerate veal, loosely covered, as soon as you get it home, and use it within 2 days. ✳✳✳✳ Veal tends to lose flavour when frozen so it is not, as a rule, a good meat to freeze except for some special reason. If you do freeze it, double wrap it and freeze for up to 6 months. You can, however, successfully freeze uncooked veal in a mild marinade and cooked veal, without garlic.

Cooking veal

Veal's delicate flesh and flavour demand close attention because the meat can become rubbery and tasteless if it is overcooked, yet it must be well cooked through. Since young veal, especially, has much less natural fat than other meats, it needs handling in ways which keep it moist or which provide extra fat to supplement its own supply.

Marinating the meat is one way of giving some cuts extra moisture, while larding (threading long strips of fat salt pork through the meat with a larding needle) and barding (covering the meat with a thin sheet of pork fat or several slices of bacon) are good ways to moisturize large cuts, and a moist or fatty stuffing is also helpful. Thin veal pieces such as escalopes are usually coated with egg and breadcrumbs or flour to hold in any natural moisture.

A skewer can be used to test large joints for readiness; pierce them to see if the meat juices run clear. But a meat thermometer is a better guide for oven-cooked joints: it should give an interior reading of 80–82C /176–179F.

Some people find the natural flavour of veal rather bland, and certainly it welcomes herbal flavourings and rich, flavoursome sauces. Rosemary, basil and marjoram go particularly well with veal, and so do paprika, sweet peppers and tomatoes. Wine, cheese and cream all marry well with it, making it the ideal meat for a rich, 'special-occasion' dish.

Surprise escalopes

Carcass cutting

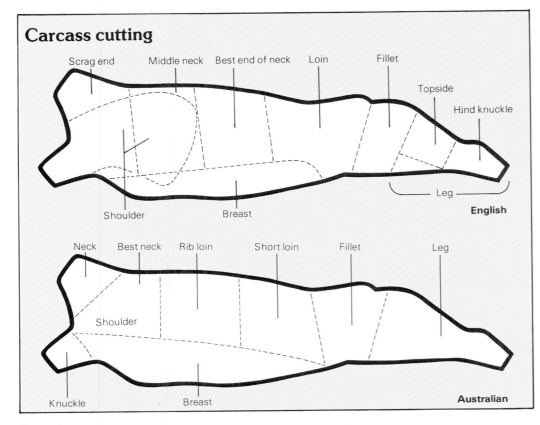

Scrag end · Middle neck · Best end of neck · Loin · Fillet · Topside · Hind knuckle · Shoulder · Breast · Leg · **English**

Neck · Best neck · Rib loin · Short loin · Fillet · Leg · Shoulder · Knuckle · Breast · **Australian**

Roasting

A large joint stays moister than a small one, and any left over can be set in jellied stock to eat cold. Choose young meat to roast.

Open roasting: although any prime cut of veal can be open roasted on a rack in a baking tin, it must be cooked slowly so the flesh is tender, and its scanty natural fat and moisture must be supplemented. Bring the meat up to room temperature well before putting it in the oven. Stuff the meat if wished; otherwise, lard or bard the joint as described on the previous page, or simply spread it with fat. For extra succulence, add a little water, marinade, stock or wine to the tin.

Another, almost foolproof, way to make sure the meat stays moist is to roast it in a loose foil package well smeared with fat inside and with a little liquid in the package.

Open or foil-wrapped, roast a veal joint at 200C /400F /gas 6 or slightly higher for 15–30 minutes, then at 170C /325F /gas 3, allowing 55–66 minutes per kg /25–30 minutes per lb in all; open up the foil package, if used, to let the meat brown for the last 15 minutes.

Pot or casserole roasting: there is not really much difference between roasting the meat in a foil package and roasting it in a container with a lid. The meat is either seared at a high oven temperature like open-roasted meat before the casserole is closed, or turned in a little fat to seal the outside surfaces. If the meat is being larded, the larding can be done first, but barding should be done after searing.

French cooks usually sear some veal bones with the meat and add them to the pan to make the beautiful, condensed, almost sticky pan-juice gravy which should accompany all roasted veal. A little wine or stock in the bottom of the pan helps to make the gravy, and also keeps the veal moist. Diced root vegetables added to the pan give extra flavour.

Braising

Braising is a good method of cooking both large pieces of veal and smaller, cheaper cuts which benefit from really slow cooking. Because they are oven-stewed on a bed of vegetables and, sometimes, chopped bacon, the veal keeps really moist. The vegetables and bacon, and meat if you wish, are sealed in hot fat. Then enough liquid is added to moisten them well. Stock or a mixture of stock and wine with a bouquet garni for extra flavour, can be used. Then they are cooked slowly in a covered casserole.

Ossobuco is a famous Italian dish which uses braised shin of veal, served with a

Buying and cooking guide to veal

Cut and weight (Dutch-style veal)	Butchering	Cooking methods
Leg Prime cut; lean with a thin layer of outside fat; 18 kg /40 lb	Hind knuckle and shin Hock or knuckle end Topside (*noix*) Fillet end (boneless) Escalopes and scaloppine	Braise, make into pies and patties Braise Braise Roast – can be rolled or stuffed Fry
Fillet Tenderest and most expensive cut; 1.1 kg /2½ lb	Whole Steaks or medallions	Lard and roast or pot roast Fry or grill
Loin Succulent; lean with an outside layer of fat; 5.4 kg /12 lb	Whole – on bone or boned and rolled Chump (rear end of loin) Chops	Roast or pot roast Braise if whole; fry, grill or bake chops Fry or bake
Best end of neck Medium-quality cut; 4 kg /9 lb	Whole Cutlets	Roast, pot roast or braise Fry, grill or braise
Breast Lean but coarse textured; needs slow, moist cooking; 6 kg /13¼ lb	Whole, boned	Stuff and roast, braise, stew or make into a galantine
Shoulder Tender, lean meat slightly marbled with fat. Difficult to carve so usually boned and rolled; 10 kg /22 lb	Oyster (shoulder with fore-knuckle removed) Joints	Roast or pot roast Roast; or cube for brochettes, pies, stews
Neck Coarse textured, very bony meat with a good flavour; 10 kg /22 lb	Middle neck Scrag	Fry, grill, braise or stew cutlets; make boned meat into pies and patties Stew; make into pies, patties, soups

topping of garlic, lemon zest and parsley, while in traditional Hungarian goulash shoulder or leg is braised with caraway seeds, paprika and tomatoes.

Frying

Prime small cuts of young or Dutch veal are ideal for frying because the tender meat does not toughen. Bring the meat to room temperature before frying. Use a mixture of oil and butter, and take care not to overcook the meat. Do not dry-fry veal: the already dryish meat will char.

Chops: you can use loin or chump chops, or the thinner best end chops sometimes called cutlets. Ask the butcher to trim off any protruding bits of bone so that the chops will lie flat in the pan, but do not let him cut off the thin layer of creamy white fat around one side. Slash this fat at intervals before frying to prevent the chops curling.

Sear veal chops in very hot fat for 2–3 minutes each side (4 minutes if very thick), then cover and cook gently for 6–8 minutes, or until the juices run clear.

Fillet steaks or medallions: these are 25 mm /1 in thick slices cut across the long fillet muscle, and are the most luxurious of all veal cuts. Treat them like the gold dust their cost represents: fry them for only 1–2 minutes each side.

Escalopes and scaloppine: escalopes can be cut on the bias from the topside or across the grain of a boned leg muscle in European style. They should be very thin, and weigh 75–100 g /3–4 oz each. Thin, small slices from the ends of the muscle can be used for the tiny escalopes weighing about 25 g /1 oz each, which the Italians call *scaloppine* or *piccate*. English-cut escalopes from the fillet end of the leg need to be placed between sheets of greaseproof paper and beaten with a cutlet bat, or, alternatively, a rolling pin, until they are very thin.

Escalopes and scaloppine should be coated with flour or with egg and fresh breadcrumbs before being fried or sautéed. Handle the pieces with tongs rather than spearing to prevent 'bleeding'.

Wiener Schnitzel is a Viennese classic, but Surprise escalopes (see recipe) are just as good.

Grilling

Except for medallions, veal tends to dry out and become chewy when plainly grilled. If you want to grill chops, marinate them first. Escalopes can be protected from drying out by stuffing them: either spread the stuffing on the escalope and roll it up, or sandwich the chosen stuffing between 2 escalopes, then coat the sandwich and grill. Alterna-

tively, sandwich with minced veal with some fat added. Small cubes of veal can be grilled on kebab skewers after marinating in an oil and lemon juice mixture. Fried or roasted veal dressed with a topping, for instance of grated cheese, is excellent if popped under the grill just long enough to melt and glaze the topping.

1 boneless fillet end, 2 boned breast, 3 boned oyster, 4 hind shin, 5 best end of neck, 6 loin, 7 fillet with one medallion cut off, 8 hock, 9 boned and rolled loin, 10 escalope from topside, 11 chump chop, 12 chop, best end of neck, 13 boned scrag, 14 boned and rolled scrag

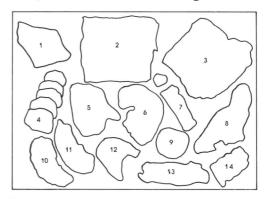

Stewing and steaming

The cheaper cuts of veal can be stewed or boiled. The boned breast is stuffed and boiled to make a classic galantine, or it can be covered with a tunafish mayonnaise for the Italian vitello tonnato. Blanquettes and fricassees are French stews enriched with cream and egg yolks.

Small, tender pieces of young veal can be steamed to make a nourishing dish suitable for invalids.

Kid

Kid is the young male goat, and is best eaten when it is between 4 weeks and 3 months old. It is considered a great delicacy in all the Mediterranean countries.

Allow 175 g /6 oz kid off the bone or 225 g /8 oz on the bone per portion.

**** Freeze kid in the same way as venison (page 67), but do not hang it.

Cooking kid: very young kid is delicious roasted (33 minutes per kg /15 minutes per lb), the rest better for stews (65–80 minutes per kg /30–40 minutes per lb).

Young kid roasted with garlic, rosemary and white wine is a traditional Italian Easter dish. In Corsica a whole kid is stuffed with chopped veal, pork and spinach and spit-roasted, while the Greeks rub kid with lemon and herbs before roasting or grilling.

In Spain kid is stewed, with its liver, in white wine with sweet peppers and garlic and in Ireland kid is made into a stew with white wine and vegetables.

Farmer's veal hock

🔪🔪 2 hours 45 minutes

Serves 4

1 kg /2 lb 3 oz meaty veal hock (or knuckle end of leg), cut into 4 thick slices
100 g /4 oz oz streaky bacon with rind, in 15 mm /1½ in squares
30 ml /2 tbls oil
1 medium-sized carrot, coarsely chopped
1 medium-sized onion, coarsely chopped
25 g /1 oz butter, plus extra for greasing
150 ml /5 fl oz medium-dry still cider
salt and freshly ground black pepper
150 ml /5 fl oz condensed cream of chicken soup
flat-leaved parsley, to garnish

1 Heat the oven to 150C /300F /gas 2. Drop the bacon pieces in boiling water and simmer for 2 minutes, then drain and dry on absorbent paper.
2 Pour the oil into a flameproof casserole which will just hold all the ingredients. Place over a moderate heat and, when it is hot, add the bacon, carrot and onion. Cook, stirring, for 2 minutes, without letting them colour.
3 Add the butter and, as soon as it melts, put in the veal. Cook for 5 minutes, turning

Farmer's veal hock

to colour the slices on both sides. Pour in the cider and cook, uncovered, for 5 minutes. Season with salt and pepper, then pour the soup over the veal. Cover with a piece of buttered paper, then with a lid.
4 Cook in the oven for 2 hours, basting the meat with the cooking juices twice while cooking. Remove the lid after 1 hour, leaving the paper on top.
5 Remove the paper, raise the oven temperature to 220C /425F /gas 7, and cook the veal for a further 10–15 minutes, until the surface of the dish is lightly glazed. Skim any excess fat from the top, garnish with a sprig of flat-leaved parsley and serve at once, from the casserole.

Veal scaloppini with Gorgonzola

🔪 25 minutes

Serves 4–6

12 small, thin veal slices, 40 g /1½ oz each
7.5 ml /1½ tsp flour, plus extra for dredging
45 ml /3 tbls olive oil
125 ml /4 fl oz brandy
75 g /3 oz chilled unsalted butter, cut into small pieces
100 g /4 oz Gorgonzola cheese, without rind, chopped
125 ml /4 fl oz thick cream

1 If the veal slices are English cut, beat them out with a bat until very thin. Dredge them well with flour.
2 Heat 15 ml /1 tbls oil in frying-pan which will hold 4 slices side by side. Over fairly high heat, fry the scaloppini for 30 seconds on each side, until just cooked through. Remove with tongs to a warmed serving platter and keep warm while you cook the remaining scaloppini in 2 batches. Remove from the pan.
3 Reduce the heat to low, add the brandy to the pan and sprinkle with 7.5 ml /1½ tsp flour. Stir with a wooden spoon to scrape up any crusty bits, and boil rapidly until the sauce is reduced by half.
4 Add the butter and cook, stirring, until it melts, then immediately stir in the cheese and cream. Cook, stirring, until the cheese is fully melted. Coat the scaloppini with the sauce and serve at once.

Surprise escalopes

🔪🔪 35 minutes

Serves 4

8 × 50 g /2 oz veal escalopes
225 g /8 oz onion, chopped
75 g /3 oz butter
1 medium-sized ripe avocado
salt and freshly ground black pepper
2 small eggs
flour for coating
sprigs of parsley, to garnish
mashed potatoes, to serve
buttered carrots, to serve

1 If the escalopes are English cut, beat them out with a bat until very thin.
2 In a large, heavy frying-pan, simmer the onion gently in the butter until it is soft and transparent. Remove the pan from the heat and transfer the onion to a bowl with a slotted spoon.
3 Halve and stone the avocado. Scoop the flesh into the onion and mash thoroughly with a fork, mixing well. Spread the mixture over 4 of the escalopes and place the remaining 4 on top. Trim any ragged edges and season on both sides with salt and pepper.
4 Beat the eggs lightly in a shallow dish. Dredge the escalope sandwiches on both sides with flour, then dip in the egg, coating thoroughly. Dredge again with flour.
5 Reheat the butter in the pan until it sizzles. Add the escalope sandwiches (in 2 batches if necessary) and fry for 5 minutes each side.
6 Place on a warmed serving platter, garnish with parsley and serve at once, with mashed potatoes and buttered carrots.

Veal chops baked in foil

 45 minutes

Serves 2
2 × 225 g /8 oz Dutch-style veal chops, 20 mm /³/4 in thick
45 ml /3 tbls seasoned flour
45 ml /3 tbls olive oil
100 g /4 oz prosciutto, chopped
3 cooked or canned artichoke bottoms, drained and chopped
4 button mushrooms, chopped
30 ml /2 tbls dry gin
30 ml /2 tbls dry white vermouth
75 ml /5 tbls thick cream
10 ml /2 tsp Dijon or Meaux mustard
salt and freshly ground black pepper

1 Flatten the veal chops slightly and slash the fat at intervals. Place the seasoned flour in a plastic bag and toss the chops in it.
2 Heat the oil in a heavy frying-pan over a fairly high heat. Add the chops and sauté them for 3–4 minutes on each side, or until they are golden brown, then transfer to a plate. Heat the oven to 200C /400F /gas 6.
3 Add the ham, artichoke bottoms and mushrooms to the pan. Return it to moderate heat and cook, stirring, for 3 minutes. Add the gin and vermouth and cook for 1 minute, then stir in the cream and simmer for 3–4 minutes, until the sauce is well blended and thickened – do not let it separate. Stir in the mustard and season to taste. Remove the pan from the heat.
4 Cut two 30 cm /12 in squares of foil. Place a chop in the centre of each square and divide the ham mixture between them. Fold up the foil to make 2 parcels with air space inside, place them on a baking sheet and cook in the oven for 20 minutes.
5 To serve, place each parcel of veal on a warmed dinner plate. Each diner opens his or her own parcel.

Veal and ratatouille patties

1 hour 10 minutes, including chilling

Serves 4
450 g /1 lb lean raw veal, without gristle or tendons, cubed (grass-fed veal may be used)
150 ml/5 fl oz canned ratatouille
1 garlic clove, finely chopped or crushed
2.5 ml /¹/2 tsp dried basil
salt and freshly ground black pepper
50 g /2 oz boiled ham, cubed
50g /2 oz cooked white or browned rice (25 g /1 oz raw rice)
30 ml /2 tbls freshly chopped parsley
15 ml /1 tbls beaten egg
flour for coating
30 ml /2 tbls oil
40 g /1¹/2 oz butter
150 ml /5 fl oz strong veal or chicken stock
10 ml /2 tsp tomato purée
creamed chopped spinach, to serve

1 Put the ratatouille in a saucepan and sprinkle with the garlic. Add the basil and season lightly with salt. Simmer gently for 5 minutes, or until most of the liquid has disappeared, stirring often. Remove from the heat and let cool.
2 Combine the veal, ham and rice and put them through a mincer. Mix in the ratatouille and parsley. Season to taste and work in the egg.
3 With floured hands, shape the mixture into 8 patties, about 15 mm /¹/2 in thick. Chill in the refrigerator for 30 minutes to firm up.
4 Heat the oil and 30 ml /2 tbls butter in a heavy frying-pan large enough to hold the patties in 1 layer. Dredge the patties with flour and fry them for 2 minutes on each side over a high heat, then reduce the heat and cook turning once, for 10 minutes.
5 Remove the patties from the pan with a

Veal and ratatouille patties
___

fish slice and keep warm. Add the stock and tomato purée to the pan. Raise the heat and boil, stirring constantly, until the sauce is reduced to about 75 ml /3 fl oz. Whisk in the remaining butter.
6 Serve the patties on a bed of creamed spinach with a little sauce poured over each.

Veal cutlets with apples and port

30 minutes

Serves 6
6 best-end veal cutlets or small leg steaks about 20 mm /³/4 in thick
125 ml /4 fl oz clear honey
125 ml /4 fl oz tawny port
pinch of dried mixed herbs
pinch of freshly grated nutmeg
50 g /2 oz unsalted butter
salt and white pepper
450 g /1 lb crisp eating apples, peeled, cored and sliced
45 ml /3 tbls lemon juice

1 Warm the honey just until it is liquid. In a jug, mix it with the port, mixed herbs and nutmeg.
2 Heat the butter in a large, deep frying-pan with a lid over moderately high heat. Add the chops and brown them quickly on each side. Sprinkle them with salt and pepper and reduce the heat to low.
3 Pour in the port mixture, cover and simmer for 4 minutes. Add the apples and sprinkle them with salt and pepper. Spoon some of the sauce over the apples. Cover the pan and simmer for 5 minutes.
4 Stir the lemon juice into the sauce and simmer, uncovered, for 3 minutes. Turn the contents of the pan into a warmed, shallow serving dish and serve at once.

Liver and kidneys

One of the most delicious of all breakfasts is kidneys grilled with bacon. Fried liver served with masses of soft golden onion rings, Lyon-style, is an attractive supper dish. Learn how to make the most of these tasty, economical, and nutritious meats.

It is not surprising that liver and kidneys are the most popular of the internal meats variously known as offal, variety meats and fancy meats. They both provide quickly cooked and deliciously tasty meals, on their own or combined with other meat, and many dishes from these less fashionable parts of the animal can be found among the world's classic recipes.

They are also very nutritious, supplying substantial amounts of protein, iron and vitamins. Liver has the advantage of being a very lean meat, rich in iron, vitamin A and several of the important B group vitamins; it is especially valuable in preventing and treating various forms of anaemia. Kidney supplies a wide variety of nutrients, including iron and vitamins.

Buying and storing liver

Liver should be eaten when very fresh (it is never hung like other meat), so avoid any that looks dull or dry, especially if it has a bluish tinge or smells unpleasant. It is normally sold by weight, sliced along the length of the lobe into 5–10 mm /¼–½ in slices. If you buy it from a traditional butcher you can specify the thickness of slice required, or, better still, buy the liver in one piece and slice it freshly at home just before cooking. This is easy to do and is advisable when you need it cut in a special way for a particular recipe.

Liver is also very economical, there is virtually no waste and it is very rich, so you need allow only 100–125 g /3½–4 oz per portion, whatever the cooking method.

Liver should be eaten on the day of purchase or within 24 hours if it is kept refrigerated. Unwrap the liver, put it on a plate, and cover lightly with transparent film or foil.

✳✳✳ Prepare the liver as for cooking, then wrap closely in freezer film or kitchen foil. Freeze the slices flat, interleaved with transparent film to aid separation. To use frozen liver, thaw in the refrigerator for about 2 hours, then cook from partially frozen, allowing a little longer cooking time. Frozen liver is easy to cut into very thin slices if a recipe requires it.

Types of liver

The livers of various animals differ from each other in flavour, texture and cost but they are similar in shape and structure, so minimal preparation is common to them all.

Calf's liver: the finest and the most expensive kind of liver, it is often difficult to obtain. It has an excellent flavour and a smooth texture and is exceptionally tender. It is best fried or grilled and it should be moist and slightly pink in the centre, never overcooked, which will make it unpleasantly hard and tough.

Lamb's liver is the next best to calf's liver. Its flavour is a little more pronounced and variable but it is still very tender. Fry, grill or casserole it.

Pig's liver is cheaper than calf's or lamb's liver, and darker in colour, with a slightly stronger flavour. This can be modified, if wished, by soaking the liver in milk for an hour or so before cooking. It is the best liver to use for pâtés, faggots and stuffings. It is also good fried or casseroled.

Ox liver is larger, coarser and much stronger in flavour than the other livers, but it is considerably cheaper. It is not recommended for frying or grilling. Soak it in milk or slightly salted water for 2 hours then cook very gently by casseroling or braising.

Chicken livers: although these are technically giblets they are prepared and used in a similar way to other livers. Each chicken yields one small liver weighing 25–50 g /1–2 oz. Chicken livers can also be bought by weight, either loose or frozen in cartons. They are very rich in flavour and therefore often used in small quantities. After freezing their texture is inclined to be very soft, but this is no problem when they are used in pâtés or sauces. You can use up a single liver in liver and bacon rolls to serve with the chicken, or add it to the stuffing. Alternatively collect the livers in the freezer until you have enough for a recipe.

Preparing and cooking liver

Wash the liver briefly under cold running water and pat dry with absorbent paper. If the liver is in one piece, remove any outer skin then slice along the length of the lobe into even slices of the required thickness. Cut out any large veins.

To prepare chicken livers wash them under running cold water and drain thoroughly on absorbent paper. Cut away any white veins, discoloured areas, or gall sacs. The green stain left by the gall gives a very bitter taste and must be removed.

Liver contains very little natural fat and will easily become solid and unpalatable if it is overcooked. The most successful ways of cooking are by lightly grilling, frying or gently casseroling. Also the flavour of liver is rather rich and benefits from the addition of salty or piquant ingredients. Crisply grilled streaky bacon is an ideal partner, fried onions another. Quick sauces made in the pan with the juices left after frying the liver are good accompaniments, flavoured with wine, lemon or orange juice, wine vinegar, mustard, soy sauce or herbs.

Frying: cut the liver into even slices 5–10 mm /¼–½ in thick and coat with well-seasoned flour. This helps to seal the liver and keep it moist when it is fried. Heat a little bacon fat, dripping, oil and butter, or olive oil in a shallow frying-pan. When sizzling, fry the liver over moderate heat for 2–3 minutes, depending on thickness, just until beads of blood appear on the surface. Turn the slices and cook another 2–3 minutes. Serve immediately with thin bacon slices fried in the pan before the liver was cooked, or a sauce made with pan juices.

Grilling: cut the liver into even 10 mm /½ in thick slices. Heat the grill to moderate and heat a little oil in the base of a shallow flameproof dish large enough to hold the liver slices in a single layer. Grease each slice of liver by turning it in the hot fat, using tongs, then grill under moderate heat for 1–2 minutes. Season the liver lightly then turn the slices over and completely cover with thin slices of rindless streaky bacon. Grill for another 2–3 minutes, or until the liver is just cooked and the bacon crisp. Serve with the pan juices poured over.

Types of kidney

According to the animal of origin, kidneys differ considerably in flavour and texture and dramatically in size and shape. For this reason the methods of preparation vary as well as the ways of cooking.

Lamb's and sheep's kidneys are small, weighing 25–50 g /1–2 oz each. Imported kidneys are sold by weight, either frozen or thawed, and are usually skinned. Fresh

Kidneys Dijonnaise

kidneys are firmer in texture and are sometimes available still encased in their surrounding suet.

To prepare the kidneys cut through the suet and pull it away. Then with a sharp knife nick the membrane that covers the kidney on the rounded side. Draw the skin back until it is only attached at the core. Cut a deep V-shape with scissors on either side of the core so that you can remove the core and the skin together. Rinse the kidneys under cold running water and pat dry with absorbent paper. Halve them for grilling, frying or braising.

Pig's kidneys are similar in shape to lamb's, but larger, averaging 100–150 g /4–5 oz each. The flavour can be a little strong, but this can be modified by soaking the kidneys in slightly salted water for 2 hours before cooking, or by blanching them. Fresh kidneys have a firmer texture than frozen or defrosted kidneys. They are prepared like lamb's kidney and are also ideal grilled, fried or casseroled; allow 1 per portion.

Veal kidneys are larger and more expensive than lamb's or pig's kidneys and different in shape and structure, consisting of numerous segments joined to a central core. Their size varies according to the age of the calf. They are considered the choicest kidney of all, as they are very tender and mild, but are often scarce and difficult to obtain.

If the kidneys are to be baked whole leave a little of the surrounding fat in place to keep them moist in the oven. Otherwise remove any fat and the thin covering of membrane. Then cut across into 5 mm /¼ in slices. It is important not to overcook veal kidneys, otherwise they harden and their delicate flavour is lost. Slice then fry them briefly and serve them in a sauce, or bake them whole in their suet covering. Allow 100 g /4 oz per portion.

Ox kidneys are similar in structure to veal kidneys but are larger and darker in colour and much stronger in flavour. They are usually bought by weight, sometimes ready prepared and diced. If the kidney is in a piece, soak it in lightly salted water for 2 hours before using. Then slice vertically in half, cut out the central core and cut the flesh into dice. Long, slow, moist cooking is necessary to tenderize ox kidneys, and they are used for flavouring steak pies and puddings, casseroles and soups. Allow 125–175 g /4–6 oz per 450 g /1 lb beef.

Suet is the hard fat from around the kidneys, beef suet being the best flavoured and most often used in cooking. Lamb suet does not keep so well as it has a higher water content; it can develop a slightly tallow flavour. Fresh suet is now difficult to obtain, but commercially prepared shredded suet is available in packets. This is used for making suet pastry crust for pies and puddings and dumplings for stews.

Buying and storing kidneys

Kidneys must always be eaten very fresh. Look for plump, firm kidneys of a good brown colour, avoiding any that look dull or mottled or that smell unpleasant. Lamb's and ox kidneys are sometimes sold in suet, which should be firm and white.

Kidneys, like liver, should be eaten on the day they are bought. If they are to be kept in the refrigerator store in the same way as liver. Frozen kidneys should be thawed before preparing and cooking. Leave for 5 hours in the refrigerator or 2½ hours at room temperature.

Cooking kidneys

With the exception of ox kidney which requires long, slow, moist cooking to tenderize it, other kidneys can be cooked fairly briefly. This seals the outside while the inside remains juicy and slightly pink. Careful timing is essential, as overcooking hardens and toughens all kidneys. Firm-textured, fresh lamb's or pig's kidneys are excellent grilled. Frozen kidneys, which tend to be softer, are better fried and served in a pan sauce incorporating their juices.

Kidneys are very lean and have a rich flavour which, like liver, is emphasized by the addition of piquant flavours such as mustard, spices, wine and herbs, and softened by cream, yoghurt or butter. A pat of chilled chive or garlic butter, for instance, is the perfect finish for plain grilled kidneys. Small quantities of kidney make delicious pancake or omelette fillings and stuffings for baked potatoes and baked onions.

Grilling: use fine-textured fresh lamb's or pig's kidneys. To prepare the kidneys for grilling spatchcock them. Lay the kidney on a board and hold it flat with one hand, slice through horizontally from the curved side towards the core, without cutting through completely. Then open the kidneys out flat. Because they curl when grilled, use 1–2 metal skewers or cocktail sticks to hold them flat, taking a large 'stitch' through the middle. Heat the grill and prepare a slice of toast for each serving. Lay the kidneys, cut side uppermost, in a flameproof dish and smear with softened butter. Grill the kidneys for 3–4 minutes, depending on size. Season lightly, turn, spread with butter and grill for another 3–4 minutes until pink inside but not bloody. Remove the skewers or cocktail sticks, arrange the kidneys on the buttered toast, pour the pan juices over them and top with a knob of butter.

Pan frying: lamb's, sheep's, pig's or veal kidneys are all suitable for pan frying. To prepare the kidneys, halve them if they are small or slice them if they are large. In a large frying-pan melt 25 g /1 oz butter and 15 ml /1 tbls oil per 450 g /1 lb kidneys. When sizzling, fry the kidneys briskly, tossing frequently, for 2 minutes, until they change from pink to grey. Add a crushed clove of garlic, some chopped parsley and chives, and simmer for 2 minutes. Finally stir in 30 ml /2 tbls of lemon juice or wine and a large knob of butter and simmer for another 2 minutes until the kidneys are tender but slightly pink inside, and the sauce is syrupy. Season to taste and serve with crisp croûtons of fried bread.

1 Wash the kidneys in cold water, pat dry and remove any skin or core. Cut each kidney in half lengthways. Dust lightly with the flour.
2 Melt the butter in a large, shallow frying-pan. When sizzling put in the kidneys and fry fairly briskly for 2–3 minutes, turning them so that they seal and change colour on each side. Remove the kidneys with a slotted spoon and reserve.
3 Add the shallots or onion and fry very gently, 2 minutes if using the shallots or 5 minutes for the onion.
4 Add the wine and lemon juice and boil rapidly until they are reduced to one quarter of their original quantity.
5 Off the heat stir in the cream and mustard. Return the kidneys and their juices to the pan and season lightly with salt and pepper. Reheat gently without boiling, stirring frequently, for 5 minutes. Serve immediately, sprinkled with the parsley, on a bed of plain boiled rice.

Chicken liver sauce with tagliatelle

1 hour

Serves 4
65 g /2½ oz butter
50 g /2 oz onion, finely chopped
50 g /2 oz smoked streaky bacon, rind removed and finely chopped
225 g /8 oz chicken livers
50 g /2 oz mushrooms, finely chopped
15 ml /1 tbls flour
30 ml /2 tbls Marsala or medium sherry
275 ml /10 fl oz chicken stock
15 ml /1 tbls tomato purée
salt and freshly ground black pepper
175–225 g /6–8 oz green tagliatelle
50 g /2 oz freshly grated Parmesan cheese

1 Melt 40 g /1½ oz of the butter in a saucepan and sauté the onion and bacon over low heat for 6–8 minutes, stirring occasionally.
2 Meanwhile, wash the chicken livers, drain well and remove any white veins or discoloured areas. Chop them fairly finely.
3 Increase the heat under the pan, add the chicken livers and mushrooms and cook, stirring constantly, for 1–2 minutes. Stir in the flour and cook for another minute.
4 Add the Marsala or sherry and allow to bubble until it is almost evaporated. Then stir in the stock, tomato purée and salt and pepper to taste. Bring to the boil, cover and simmer very gently for 30–40 minutes.
5 About 10 minutes before the sauce is ready, drop the pasta into a large pan of fast boiling salted water and cook, uncovered, until just tender.
6 Drain thoroughly, return to the pan with the remaining butter and toss lightly.
7 Check the seasoning of the sauce and serve the pasta on very hot plates with the sauce spooned over it. Hand the Parmesan cheese separately.

Stir-fried liver

30 minutes

Serves 4
450 g /1 lb pig's liver, in one piece
15 ml /1 tbls cornflour
5 ml /1 tsp salt
5 ml /1 tsp ground ginger
15 ml /1 tbls medium-dry sherry
5 ml /1 tsp oil
50 g /2 oz lard or dripping
1 large garlic clove, crushed
25 ml /1½ tbls coarsely chopped spring onion tops
For the sauce
25 ml /1½ tbls soy sauce
15 ml /1 tbls medium sherry
15 ml /1 tbls tomato purée
25 ml /1½ tbls wine vinegar
25 ml /1½ tbls chicken stock
5 ml /1 tsp sugar

1 Wash the liver under cold running water and pat dry with absorbent paper. Trim away all traces of thin outer skin or veins. With a sharp knife cut down into 3 mm /⅛ in thick slices and then into 25 mm /1 in strips.
2 In a bowl combine the cornflour, salt and ginger. Blend in 30 ml /2 tbls water, the sherry and oil and mix until smooth.
3 Add the liver slices and gently turn to coat with the cornflour mixture. Leave to stand for 15 minutes.
4 In a mixing bowl combine all the sauce ingredients until well blended.
5 Heat the lard or dripping in a frying-pan over moderate heat. When sizzling add the liver, spreading the pieces evenly over the pan. Increase the heat and cook briskly, stirring, for 30 seconds.
6 Sprinkle in the garlic and spring onions and continue stir-frying for another 30 seconds. Pour the sauce mixture into the pan, bring to the boil and cook, stirring constantly, for a further 30 seconds. Serve immediately with boiled rice.

Kidneys Dijonnaise

Tender kidneys in a creamy, mustard-flavoured sauce is a quickly prepared dish.

30 minutes

Serves 4
550 g /1¼ lb lambs' kidneys
10 ml /2 tsp flour
50 g /2 oz butter
50 g /2 oz shallots, or onion, finely chopped
150 ml /5 fl oz dry white wine or dry vermouth and water mixed
15 ml /1 tbls lemon juice
150 ml /5 fl oz thick cream
25 ml /1½ tbls Dijon yellow mustard
salt and freshly ground black pepper
chopped parsley, to garnish

Kidney stroganoff

This dish, which is best made with firm-textured fresh kidneys, is a sophisticated way of serving offal.

♦ 40 minutes

Serves 4
450 g /1 lb fresh lambs' or pigs' kidneys
50 g /2 oz butter
30 ml /2 tbls oil
225 g /8 oz onion, thinly sliced
225 g /8 oz mushrooms, thinly sliced
60 ml /4 tbls dry vermouth
150 ml /5 fl oz soured cream
salt and freshly ground black pepper
boiled rice, to serve
chopped fresh parsley, to garnish
4 lemon wedges, to garnish

1 Wash the kidneys under cold running water, drain and pat dry with absorbent paper. Peel off the thin membrane, if any, and snip out the central core with scissors. Cut the kidneys into thin slices.
2 Heat half the butter and half the oil in a large frying-pan. When sizzling fry the kidneys briskly for 2–3 minutes, stirring frequently. Remove from the pan with a slotted spoon and reserve.
3 Add the remaining butter and oil to the pan and when melted add the onion and sauté very gently for 10 minutes until it begins to soften.
4 Increase the heat a little, add the mushrooms and fry for another minute or so, stirring constantly.
5 Return the reserved kidneys to the pan, add the vermouth, cover and simmer for 2–3 minutes.
6 Finally stir in the soured cream and generous seasonings of salt and pepper and heat very gently, without boiling, for another minute.
7 Serve the kidneys in the centre of a bed of rice, sprinkled with parsley and garnished with lemon wedges.

Steak and kidney pudding

♦♦ 4–5 hours

Serves 4
For the suet crust pastry
butter for greasing
175 g /6 oz self-raising flour
75 g /3 oz shredded suet
1.5 ml /¼ tsp salt
For the filling
450 g /1 lb chuck steak
175 g /6 oz ox kidney
25 ml /1½ tbls flour
salt and freshly ground black pepper
1 medium-sized onion, finely chopped
150 ml /5 fl oz well-flavoured beef stock
sprig of parsley, to garnish (optional)

1 Thoroughly butter the inside of an 850 ml /1½ pt pudding bowl and a piece of double thickness greaseproof paper large enough to cover the top generously.
2 To make the suet crust mix the flour, suet and salt together in a basin, then mix to a soft, elastic dough with about 90 ml /6 tbls cold water.
3 Turn on to a lightly floured surface, knead briefly, then roll into a circle about 5 cm /2 in larger all round than the bowl top.
4 Cut out one quarter of the dough and reserve for the lid. Line the bowl with the rest of the pastry, damping and joining the cut edges in the bowl. The pastry should extend just above the bowl rim.
5 Cut the steak into 5 mm /¼ in thick slices, then into strips about 2.5×7.5 cm / 1×3 in. Wash the kidney, remove the white central core and cut the kidney into small pieces.
6 Season the flour and toss the steak and kidney pieces in it. Roll a piece of kidney inside each strip of meat and pack into the lined bowl, sprinkling each layer with chopped onion. Add enough stock to come halfway up the bowl.
7 Turn the pastry edges down over the meat and brush with water. Roll the remaining pastry into a circle to fit exactly inside the top of the basin, and press the edges to seal.
8 Pleat the buttered greaseproof paper down the centre to allow the pudding to expand while cooking, and cover the bowl with it. Then cover the paper with a piece of foil. Twist the edges to form a tight cap, or tie in place with string.
9 Lower the bowl into a large saucepan containing fast boiling water to reach halfway up the bowl. Cover tightly with the lid.
10 Steam steadily for 3½–4½ hours, the longer the better, topping up the pan with boiling water as necessary.
11 To serve remove the bowl from the pan and stand it on a plate. Take off the foil and paper, make a hole in the centre of the crust and add the rest of the beef stock. Knot a clean table napkin around the bowl and serve garnished with parsley, if wished.

Steak and kidney pudding

Pork butcher's pâté

Pâté de foie du porc is typical of the rough textured pâtés found in family-owned French charcuteries. The pig's liver and fat belly pork balance each other to provide a rich, moist texture enlivened by the characteristic flavourings of garlic, brandy and spices. This makes an ideal starter or lunch dish.

🕐 ♪♪♪ 3¾ hours, including standing, then overnight chilling

Serves 4–6

225 g /8 oz pig's liver, washed and dried
225 g /8 oz fat belly pork, rind removed
50 g /2 oz cooked gammon fat
1 garlic clove, crushed
4 juniper berries, crushed
large pinch of powdered mace
salt and freshly ground black pepper
15 ml / 1 tbls dry white wine
30 ml /2 tbls brandy
2 thin slices unsmoked streaky bacon
2 bay leaves

Pork butcher's pâté

1 Mince the liver and the pork together fairly coarsely, and put in a mixing bowl.
2 Add the gammon fat, cut in 5 mm /¼ in dice, the garlic, juniper berries, mace, a little salt and plenty of freshly ground black pepper, and the wine and brandy. Mix well.
3 Turn the mixture into a deep 600 ml / 1 pt ovenproof terrine and smooth the surface with a palette knife.
4 Cut the bacon slices across the grain into 5 mm /¼ in strips. Scatter these over the pâté surface; lay the bay leaves on top.
5 Cover and leave to stand for about 2 hours so that the flavours can blend.
6 Heat the oven to 170C /325F /gas 3. Stand the terrine in a baking tin and pour in hot water to come halfway up the sides of the terrine.
7 Cook in the centre of the oven for 1 hour, then uncover and continue cooking for 15–20 minutes to dry the bacon.
8 Remove the terrine from the baking tin and when quite cold cover and refrigerate for 12 hours before serving.
9 Remove the bay leaf and serve the pâté from the terrine with crusty French bread or hot toast.

Crispy topped liver

♪♪ 1 hour

Serves 4

450 g /1 lb pig's or lamb's liver, cut in 10 mm /½ in thick slices
25 g /1 oz bacon fat or dripping
25 g /1 oz flour
salt and freshly ground black pepper
8–10 thin slices smoked streaky bacon, rinds removed
For the topping
40 g /1½ oz butter
1 medium-sized onion, finely chopped
1 celery stalk, finely chopped
65 g /2½ oz fresh white breadcrumbs
5 ml /1 tsp finely grated lemon zest
2.5 ml /½ tsp dried oregano or sage
15 ml /1 tbls chopped fresh parsley
1 medium-sized egg, beaten
salt and freshly ground black pepper

1 Wash the liver under cold running water and pat dry with absorbent paper. Trim away any skin or large veins.
2 To prepare the topping, melt the butter in a saucepan and gently fry the onion and celery for 5 minutes. Off the heat stir in the breadcrumbs, lemon zest, dried herb, parsley, beaten egg and seasonings.
3 Heat the oven to 180C /350F /gas 4. Choose a shallow baking tin (which is large enough for the liver slices to lie flat in a single layer) and use the bacon fat or dripping to grease it thickly. Put it in the oven to heat.
4 Meanwhile, season the flour and toss the liver in it until it is well coated.
5 Remove the baking dish from the oven and arrange the liver slices on the base. Spoon the topping evenly over the liver, press lightly, then cover completely with the bacon slices. Bake in the centre of the oven for 30–35 minutes until the liver is cooked.

Bacon, gammon and ham

Everybody knows how perfectly bacon slices go with fried eggs or liver, but there are many ways to use the wide range of other bacon cuts. A beautiful cold ham is a universal favourite for a buffet party; a gammon is considerably cheaper and can be glazed in all the traditional ways.

There is sometimes confusion over the use of the terms bacon, gammon and ham, so bear in mind the following simple guidelines. Bacon is the term used to describe a cured side of pork. Gammon (the best joint of meat) is the hind leg cut from the cured bacon side.

Ham was traditionally the hind leg cut from a fresh pig carcass and then cured separately – the kind one used to see hanging from a hook up the chimney in a farmhouse kitchen. Nowadays cooked gammon is quite often described as ham.

Curing meat is an ancient and traditional rural craft. Over the years farmers' wives added ingredients such as treacle, herbs or cider to the basic dry salt or brine, and bacon cures developed regional characteristics, throughout Europe and the U.S. Although the brine tanks and salting vats have long since left the farms for centralized factories, some of the regional names such as Wiltshire for bacon or Virginia for ham are still used, but they refer now to the method of cure rather than the place of origin. Modern terms such as Sweet Cure, Mild Cure or Honey Roast indicate the ham or bacon is milder than traditional cures.

After salting or brining, bacon or ham may or may not be smoked for additional flavour. These processes are preservative, meaning that the meat can be kept longer than freshly-killed pork, but the meat is still raw. Curing and maturing ham takes much longer than curing bacon, which accounts for the higher cost of real, traditional ham.

Ham

For ham, the leg is taken from a side of pork and cured separately. It may be cut on the curve round the bone or straight across, when it is called a short cut ham. Different kinds of traditional ham have acquired their individuality from variations in their preparation. The cure, which is basically a dry-salting, brining or sweet pickling process, is followed by an extended drying and maturing period. The hams may be heavily or lightly smoked over different types of aromatic wood.

York ham and prosciutto

47

Some celebrated hams

Many varieties of ham have to be cooked before they are palatable, either by the supplier or at home. Other hams are specially cured to be eaten raw, though some of them may be used in cooking in various ways.

Hams eaten cooked: York ham, originally from the North of England, is a cure known all over the world. The ham is mild and pale pink, darker near the bone. It is considered the best ham for eating cold, though it is also delicious served hot. It is always made with a dry-salt cure, but may be lightly or heavily smoked.

Another famous British ham is Suffolk ham which is sweet-treacle-cured and then smoked. Bradenham ham is cured in molasses and spices according to an 18th century recipe and is easily recognizable by its black rind. Irish hams are usually dry-salted and then boned, before being smoked over peat: Limerick and Belfast hams are well known.

American hams are dry-salted with a secret cure and then smoked over apple and hickory wood. Virginia hams, and in particular Smithfield hams, are known all over the world. The true Virginian ham comes from pigs fed on peanuts and peaches and it is matured for up to 18 months. Pigs for Kentucky hams, on the other hand, are grain-fattened after a diet of acorns, beans and clover.

Paris ham, which is also called *jambon blanc* (white ham), is actually very pale, delicate pink. It is only very lightly cured in brine and is either very lightly smoked or not smoked at all. Paris ham is always boiled – usually to eat cold.

The finest ham for serving hot is the Prague ham, *Pragerschinken*, from Czechoslovakia. This is brined for several months and then smoked over beech sawdust. Serve it baked or boiled (though it can be eaten without cooking).

Hams eaten raw: *prosciutto*, Italian for ham (pronounced proshooto), is used almost synonymously with 'raw ham', and the most famous raw ham comes from Parma in Italy. It is dark salmon in colour, and semi-opaque, not unlike smoked salmon in appearance. Strictly, it should be called *prosciutto crudo* (*crudo* means raw), as Italy also produces less famous hams for cooking, called *prosciutto cotto*. Traditionally it is obtained from 8-week-old pigs, which are cured by dry-salting, but not smoked. In Italy, San Daniele prosciutto is almost as well known as Parma ham.

Spanish *serrano* (mountain ham) is perhaps the nearest ham to prosciutto. It comes from the black-coated Iberian pig which runs free in the forests, and as a result the meat is rather tougher. The best hams come from the Huelva region where they are traditionally matured in the mountains – hence the name.

Bayonne is the best-known French raw ham. It is wine-cured and, unlike the raw hams of Spain and Italy, it is smoked, wrapped up in straw. *Jambon de Bayonne* is usually eaten raw as a first course, but may also be used in cooking in a variety of ways, for example in egg dishes and in ragoûts. *Jambon de Toulouse* is another famous

French ham that is eaten raw and may also be included in cooked dishes: it is merely salted and dried, not smoked. The delicately smoked Ardennes ham, from Belgium, also has an international reputation.

Germany is renowned for strongly smoked hams. Best-known is Westphalian ham, which is cured with juniper berries and smoked at a low temperature over ash or beech. It is much darker in colour than other raw ham. Mainz ham, which is also sometimes cooked, is another popular German ham. There is also Lachsschinken; *schinken* means ham in German, but this pink raw meat is actually lightly cured and smoked pork loin.

Buying and storing ham

Ham for eating raw: this can be bought freshly sliced from delicatessens or in vacuum packs from supermarkets. It should be sliced paper thin and there should be no sign of the meat drying out. Allow 40–50 g /1½–2 oz per person.

Raw ham for cooking: whole raw hams are ideal for buffet parties but may be difficult to buy, even from specialist suppliers.

A whole raw ham weighs 7–8 kg /15–18 lb (half hams are sometimes available). About one-fifth of raw ham will be the weight of the bone. Remember that the cooking will also shrink the final weight of the meat by another fifth. If raw ham has a slight bluish bloom on it from the cure, scrape this off after soaking and before cooking. A whole ham is a large object and you will need a large pan for boiling it. So consider whether you would not do better to buy a ready-cooked ham.

Ready-cooked ham: whole hams, or half a ham, may be obtained from a specialist delicatessen or supplier. Sometimes they are available with the knuckle bone in, but the shank bone removed. Like this they retain their elegant appearance, but are much easier to carve, being meat all the way through except at the end.

In some delicatessens ham may be carved or sliced to order, but cooked ham is widely available, vacuum-packed, from supermarket chilled cabinets. With the ham you will also find a cooked meat which may be described as 'picnic ham' or 'ham shoulder'. This may be cured in the same way as ham,

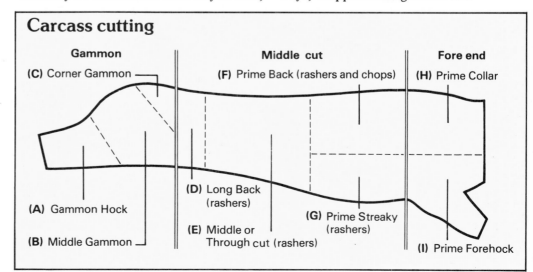
Fore end

but it is from the shoulder of the pig, rather than being the finer meat from the hind leg and, therefore, is not legally ham. Its texture and quality are inferior to real ham but it, nevertheless, supplies a cheaper substitute. Allow about 50 g /2 oz ham per person when serving for a salad.

Canned hams are ready-cooked and are widely sold and exported. Danish, Polish and Dutch are the best-known. However, if you intend to keep one as a store-cupboard standby, you must be sure to buy a small one. A sterilized or pasteurized ham of 1 kg /2¼ lb can be safely kept in a cool place for up to 6 months.

Storing: in theory a whole, uncooked ham can be hung until ready for use. In practice it is difficult to find a dry, airy place between 1–15C /34–60F. Refrigerate bought slices of cooked ham in cling film or foil for 1–2 days. Store joints for up to 5 days, wrapped in cling film or foil.

Carcass cutting

Gammon

(C) Corner Gammon

(A) Gammon Hock

(B) Middle Gammon

Middle cut

(F) Prime Back (rashers and chops)

(D) Long Back (rashers)

(E) Middle or Through cut (rashers)

(G) Prime Streaky (rashers)

Fore end

(H) Prime Collar

(I) Prime Forehock

Gammon

Fore end is the neck and shoulder and contains a mixture of lean and fat. The meat is coarser and cheaper than gammon. It absorbs a lot of salt during curing and needs more soaking than other cuts before cooking (for details on soaking, see *page 50*). Fore end is usually cut into economically priced joints, as follows.

Collar (**H**) is the better part of the fore end and weighs up to 4 kg /9 lb. It is usually boned and tied and divided into smaller joints suitable for boiling or braising. Collar is sometimes sliced.

Forehock (**I**) contains the knuckle bone, but is often sold boned and rolled into small joints suitable for boiling or braising.

Buying bacon and gammon

Bacon will keep longer than uncured meat, but is nevertheless perishable, with a very limited shelf life, so when choosing it is important to look for signs of freshness. Fresh bacon has very firm, white fat and moist, pink (but not 'wet'-looking) meat. It should smell mild and pleasant, never stale or strong, and bacon rashers should not be curling at the edges.

Cut to order: this traditional service is now rare, but still available in some first-class grocers or delicatessens where sides of bacon or whole gammons are on display. These shops will cut joints, and slices (rashers) of specified thickness, as required. Bacon scraps are sometimes available at a lower cost, these are excellent for use in quiches and stews.

Film wrapped: ready-cut joints or slices (rashers) wrapped in transparent film are normally marked with the cut, weight and price. Vacuum-packed joints and rashers are pre-packed in thick polythene. The vacuum packing extends the shelf life of the bacon considerably: note the 'sell-by' or 'open by' date and any cooking instructions.

Boil-in-the-bag: small joints are packed in a special transparent film able to withstand boiling water. Follow the label instructions and do not attempt to boil-in-the-bag any joint not so labelled.

Storing bacon and gammon

Treat vacuum-packed bacon as fresh once opened. Wrap joints or rashers closely in cling film or foil and store in the refrigerator for up to 5 days or as directed. Refrigerate home-cooked bacon joints for 3–4 days, and bought, sliced cooked gammon for 24 hours.

❄❄❄❄ Closely wrap fresh bacon in foil, heavy-duty cling film or polythene, excluding as much air as possible. Layering slices or chops with film makes them easier to separate for cooking. Seal and label.

Because of its salt content, bacon has a shorter storage life in the freezer than other meat, for the salt acts as a pro-oxidant in freezing conditions, making the bacon taste rancid if kept too long. Smoke is an anti-oxidant, so smoked bacon keeps longer than unsmoked. Raw smoked joints will keep for up to 8 weeks, slices and chops for up to 4 weeks. Unsmoked joints will keep for up to 5 weeks, slices and chops for up to 2 weeks. Vacuum-packed joints, smoked and unsmoked, will keep up to 4 months in

❄❄❄❄ Heavily smoked ham will keep longer in the freezer than unsmoked or lightly smoked ham. A portion of a home-cooked ham will freeze only for 3–4 weeks. A vacuum-packed ham, however, can be frozen for 4 months. Dishes with cooked ham in them should not be kept frozen for longer than a few weeks.

Bacon

Bacon is the cured but raw side of a specially bred pig. The meat is immersed in brine for a specified period and then 'matured' by hanging in a cool, air-controlled atmosphere.

Unsmoked bacon (also known as green, plain, pale or white bacon) is matured for only about 1 week. It has a light-coloured rind, pale pink meat and mild flavour.

Smoked bacon is matured bacon which has been smoked for up to 8 hours. It is slightly drier, with a richer flavour and deeper colour than unsmoked bacon. It is also tastier and enjoys a slightly longer storage life, but is marginally more expensive.

Cuts of bacon and gammon

Sides of both smoked and unsmoked bacon are cut into joints, slices and thin slices known as 'rashers' in Britain. The diagram illustrates the main divisions and shows where the different cuts come from.

Gammon: this is the most expensive part of the bacon side and consists of prime quality solid meat with a thin covering of fat. It weighs up to 8 kg /17 lb and can be bought whole, on the bone or boned out, and is often cooked and sold sliced by specialist grocers. For home use it is usually cut into smaller joints, as follows.

Middle gammon (**B**): the prime cut from the centre of the gammon, with a high ratio of lean to fat. It weighs up to 3.5 kg /8 lb

whole and is usually sold boned and tied and cut into smaller joints. Bake in foil, boil, parboil and bake, or braise.

Gammon steaks and slices: steaks, which are 5–10 mm /¼–½ in thick, and 5 mm /¼ in thick slices (rashers) are sliced from the middle gammon. They are prime lean cuts for grilling or frying.

Corner gammon (**C**) is a small, triangular, boneless cut weighing up to 1.5 kg /3 lb. Cook as for middle gammon.

Gammon hock (**A**): this cut from the shank (or knuckle) end can vary in size from half the gammon to a small, bony, shank end. The meat at the shank end is rather sinewy, so short cut joints are best boiled and used for stock or soup. However, a half-leg gammon hock is a meaty joint of handsome shape with plenty of surface area for glazing. Boil, parboil and bake, or braise.

Middle cut: the whole of this central area is usually sliced into bacon rashers. Middle cut joints, which may need to be ordered specially, have a fairly high ratio of fat to lean meat, and are often rolled and tied.

Back bacon (**F**) is prime lean meat with a fine flavour and a thin covering of fat, which provides thin slices (rashers), chops or a joint suitable for baking or braising.

Streaky bacon (**G**) is an economical cut consisting of alternate layers of fat and lean meat. It may be sold thinly sliced to grill or fry or as a joint, best boiled or braised.

Middle cut or Through cut (**E**) provides very long thin slices (rashers) with lean meat from the back at one end and streaky bacon at the other. The joint is a similar mixture of lean meat and streaky; it is very suitable for stuffing as it can be rolled so easily.

Long back (**D**) provides large, substantial slices (rashers) to grill or fry; when thickly cut they can be cubed and used for either casseroles or pies.

the freezer; vacuum-packed slices and chops up to 3 months. Home-cooked joints will keep for not more than 3–4 weeks.

A little chopped bacon is often fried with the onions when a base is being prepared for a casserole. If, however, you are preparing a casserole to freeze, it is wiser to leave the bacon out, as cooked dishes containing bacon are liable to develop an 'off' flavour if kept frozen longer than a few weeks.

Soaking ham and bacon joints

Today's refrigerated bacon is less heavily brined than formerly, and in fact a joint may not need soaking at all to rid it of excess salt. Generally speaking, sweet or mild cure bacon does not need soaking and unsmoked needs less soaking than smoked. For small unsmoked or smoked joints, 2–3 hours soaking in cold water is usually sufficient. Allow the longer time for fore-end cuts and for joints to be baked in foil. Soak a whole gammon or fore end for about 8 hours or overnight. Soak a whole or half ham for about 24 hours.

For small bacon joints, a quick alternative to soaking is blanching. Simply cover the joint with cold water, bring very slowly to the boil then drain and cook by your chosen method.

Cooking a whole ham

Whole hams present a special problem because of their size; you will need a large, preserving pan or stock pot to boil a ham in. Alternatively, consider cooking it in the oven. It may be baked in foil (see right) or in a plain paste of flour and water, which is discarded after cooking (follow the times given in the chart on *page 51*).

The method for boiling is identical to that for smaller gammon joints (follow the instructions below).

Cooking ham and bacon joints

Bacon is an easy meat to cook and there is a wide choice of joints. In assessing value for money, notice whether the joint is on the bone or boneless, and look for the proportion of fat and rind to lean meat. Many pre-formed and pre-packed bacon rolls are rindless with a very mild taste; cook smoked bacon if you like a more distinctive flavour. Follow any special directions given on the pack or, if none, cook by any of the following methods.

Boiling: this is one of the simplest ways of cooking ham or bacon.

1 Wash and weigh the joint and calculate the cooking time allowing 44 minutes per kg /20 minutes per lb, plus 20 minutes up to 4.5 kg /10 lb. A whole gammon or ham will need 33 minutes per kg/15 minutes per lb cooking time.

2 Put the joint in a large saucepan, cover completely with cold water and bring slowly to simmering point.

3 Remove the pan from the heat. Skim the scum from the surface of the water. If liked, add 15 ml /1 tbls Demerara sugar or black treacle, a few peppercorns and 2 bay leaves for extra flavour. Root vegetables such as carrots, parsnips or turnips for serving with the joint may be added. Return the pan to the heat, cover tightly and simmer gently,

calculating the cooking time from this point. Ham or gammon joints should never boil, as this toughens the meat, just simmer very gently.

4 When a small joint is cooked, lift it out and carefully peel off the rind, if any. Reserve the cooking liquid for use as stock for a soup. Leave a large gammon or ham in the cooking liquid to cool to a temperature when it can be easily handled. Then remove it and strip off the rind.

5 Serve plain, coated with browned breadcrumbs or glazed.

6 If a large gammon or ham is to be served cold allow it 12 hours for cooling and setting before carving.

Baking in foil: this method preserves all the natural flavour in the joint, so pre-soaking or blanching is advisable (see left).

1 Weigh the prepared ham or bacon, then calculate the cooking time and heat the oven according to the chart on *page 51*.

2 Wrap the joint loosely in a large piece of foil, sealing the edges over top of joint.

3 Place the joint on a rack in a baking tin and pour a cupful of water into the tin.

4 When the calculated cooking time is up, remove the joint from the oven, open the foil and peel off any rind. Carefully reserve the juices that will have collected in the foil, and use them to make a sauce to serve with the bacon. Serve plain or glazed.

Parboiling and baking: this combination of boiling and baking requires a little more attention than plain boiling or baking, but the cooked bacon has a particularly good

flavour and texture. Parboiling and baking is especially suitable for joints to be stuffed and for shoulder cuts. Soaking is not normally necessary.

1 Weigh the joint and calculate the cooking time as for baking in foil.

2 Boil the joint as above for half the total calculated cooking time if the joint is small, then drain, stuff if wished, wrap in foil and complete the cooking as for baking in foil. For a large gammon or ham bake for the last hour of the calculated cooking time.

Braising is a flavourful method of cooking a small bacon joint in a casserole in the oven.

1 Soak or blanch the joint (see left).

2 Weigh the prepared joint and calculate the cooking time, allowing 77 minutes per kg /35 minutes per lb, plus 35 minutes.

3 Heat the oven to 180C /350F /gas 4. Choose a deep, flameproof casserole into which the joint will fit comfortably.

4 Melt about 25 g /1 oz butter in the casserole and fry a mixture of diced carrot, celery and onion or leek (enough to cover the base to a depth of 4 cm /1½ in), until lightly browned.

5 Add a bay leaf, a sprig of thyme, some freshly ground black pepper and enough stock, cider or water mixed with wine to barely cover the vegetables. Set the drained joint on top.

6 Bring to simmering point, cover tightly and cook in the centre of oven.

7 When the joint is cooked, remove it from the casserole and strip off the rind. Discard the herbs.

8 Serve the joint sliced, with the vegetables, using the stock to make a sauce.

Stuffed bacon roll

Serving ham and bacon joints

Complement the slight saltiness of a hot bacon joint or ham with either a sweet, tangy sauce such as Madeira (see recipe), Cumberland, apple and raisin or cranberry, or with a creamy white sauce well flavoured with chopped parsley or chopped boiled onions.

All root vegetables are excellent served with bacon joints, especially glazed carrots; cauliflower, broad beans, celery and spinach are other favourites. Many people also find that the succulence of a fruit garnish, especially peaches, apricots or pineapple, adds to their enjoyment of bacon. For special occasions, choose one of the rich golden glazes described below to enhance the appearance of a joint served hot or cold, especially one with a large surface area of fat.

Glazing ham and bacon joints

Glazing is a classic way of treating a ham. Nowadays it is a glamorous way of treating a smaller gammon or bacon joint.
1 Cook the joint to within 30 minutes of the calculated cooking time by any of the 4 basic methods described.
2 Increase the oven heat (or heat from cold) to 200C /400F /gas 6.
3 Peel the rind, if any, off the joint, leaving the fat surface exposed. If foil wrapped, leave the foil around the lean meat to keep it moist.
4 Spread the fat with your chosen glaze and bake for the remaining calculated cooking time, basting from time to time, until the fat is crisp and golden.

Baking ham, gammon and bacon joints

Cut and weight	Oven temperature	Minutes per kg /1 lb		
Whole ham or gammon on the bone				
7.5–7.7 kg /16–17 lb	180C /350F /gas 4	44	20	plus 20
Gammon joints				
up to 1.5 kg /3 lb	190C /375F /gas 5	66	30	
up to 2.7 kg /6 lb		55	25	
over 2.7 kg /6 lb		42	20	
All other bacon and gammon joints				
up to 1.5 kg /3 lb	190C /375F /gas 5	77	35	
up to 2.7 kg /6 lb		66	30	
over 2.7 kg /6 lb		55	25	

★ Meat thermometer check: when cooked the centre of the bacon joint should never be below 70C /160F.

The following quantities are suitable for a 1.5–1.8 kg /3–5 lb joint; double or treble for a whole ham.

Sugar and clove glaze: with a sharp knife score the exposed fat in a diamond pattern. Press 30–45 ml /2–3 tbls Demerara sugar evenly over the fat surface, stud each diamond (or intersection) with a whole clove, and bake.

Honey glaze: blend 30 ml /2 tbls clear honey with 30 ml /2 tbls soft brown sugar and 5 ml /1 tsp made mustard. Spread over the fat surface, and bake.

Apricot glaze: mix 30–45 ml /2–3 tbls sieved apricot jam with 5 ml /1 tsp ground cloves or dry mustard, 15 ml /1 tbls soft brown sugar and 10 ml /2 tsp lemon juice. Spread the glaze over the fat surface, and bake.

Orange glaze: mix 30 ml /2 tbls soft brown sugar with 15 ml /1 tbls clear honey and 15 ml /1 tbls orange juice. Spoon half over the fat surface, and bake for 15 minutes. Then arrange thin slices cut from a seedless orange over the surface, fixing each to the fat with a clove. Spoon over the remaining glaze and finish baking.

Crispy topping: mix 15 ml /1 tbls clear honey with 15 ml /1 tbls wine vinegar and spoon over the fat. Sprinkle with equal parts of mixed brown sugar and dry breadcrumbs, and bake till crisp.

Brown crumb finish: cook the joint completely before removing the rind. Sprinkle dried brown breadcrumbs thickly and evenly over the warm fat, pressing them in firmly with a palette knife.

Cooking bacon rashers and steaks

Best back or long back slices (rashers) should be used whenever lean bacon is required, for example bacon and egg or a mixed grill. Remove any rind and bones. Streaky bacon is ideal for adding extra flavour and succulence, for barding meat and poultry, for grilling in kebabs, frying with liver, lining a terrine or 'thatching' a savoury pie on top. Angels on horseback – oysters wrapped in streaky bacon rashers – are delicious as a savoury in place of a sweet course or as a cocktail titbit, and streaky bacon makes decorative rolls for garnishing. Grilled till crisp, then crumbled, streaky bacon adds texture and an attractive garnish to soups, casseroles and vegetable dishes such as cauliflower cheese.

Steaks and chops make quick and substantial main course dishes. Grill or fry them. Remove any rind or bones and snip the fat around the edges at 25 mm /1 in intervals to prevent them curling. Serve them with a vegetable in sauce or with juicy vegetables such as tomatoes, mushrooms or courgettes.

Grilling: heat the grill to medium. Brush lean steaks or chops with fat on both sides to prevent sticking and drying, and arrange flat on the grill rack. Arrange thin slices (rashers) overlapping, so that the lean of one rasher is covered and protected by the fat of the next. Grill 5 mm /¼ in thick steaks or chops for 8–10 minutes, turning once. Grill rashers for 2–3 minutes, turning once.

Frying: use a lightly greased frying-pan over a medium heat. Lay steaks or chops flat in the pan. Fry 5 mm /¼ in steaks or chops for about 10 minutes, turning once. Overlap thin rashers and fry for 3–4 minutes, turning once, until the fat is transparent. Use the bacon fat left in the pan to add extra flavour to fried bread or mushrooms, or apple rings.

Serving raw ham

Top quality raw ham is best served in wafer thin slices as a first course. In Italy it is often served with slices of sweet, juicy melon or with ripe figs. Accompany it with very thin, generously buttered, brown bread. Raw ham also makes excellent open sandwiches and cocktail canapés.

Using cooked ham or cold bacon

Cooked ham is very useful and versatile in the kitchen. Cooked bacon, however, is cheaper and will serve many of the same purposes. So it is worth buying a good size bacon joint to have some left over.

Use ham or boiled bacon slices for salads and sandwiches. Add chopped ham or bacon to risottos, or use as a filling for omelettes and pancakes, or in vol-au-vents, or add to a cream sauce to serve with pasta such as maccaroni or tagliatelle.

Minced ham or bacon will improve the stuffings of poultry, white fish and vegetables such as mushrooms, courgettes, tomatoes and peppers. Ham or bacon rind and bones will give flavour to lentil, pea or mixed vegetable soup.

Glazed pineapple gammon steaks

⏱ 20 minutes

Serves 4

*4 smoked gammon steaks, weighing 100–150 g
/4–5 oz each*
40 g /1½ oz butter, melted
22.5 ml /1½ tbls Dijon mustard
4 or 8 pineapple rings, fresh or canned, drained
22.5 ml /1½ tbls Demerara sugar
watercress sprigs, to garnish

1   With scissors, cut off the gammon rind if any, and snip around the edges of the steaks at 25 mm /1 in intervals, to prevent them from curling under the heat. Heat the grill to medium.
2   Brush both sides of each steak with melted butter, lay the steaks on the grill rack, and cook for 4 minutes. Turn the steaks over, spread with mustard and grill for a further 3 minutes.
3   Arrange one or two pineapple rings on each steak and brush with the remaining melted butter. Sprinkle the sugar evenly over the fruit and gammon, and grill for another 2–3 minutes, increasing the heat if necessary, until lightly browned and glazed.
4   Serve immediately, garnished with watercress.

Stuffed bacon roll

⏱ 3 hours soaking,
then 2½ hours

Serves 8–12
*1.5–1.8 kg /3–4 lb rolled middle cut bacon
    joint (back and streaky)*
15 ml /1 tbls Demerara sugar
butter for greasing
For the stuffing
50 g /2 oz butter
1 celery stalk, finely chopped
175 g /6 oz mushrooms, coarsely chopped
30 ml /2 tbls chopped parsley
finely grated zest of 1 lemon
5 ml /1 tsp dried mixed herbs
75 g /3 oz soft white breadcrumbs
1 medium-sized egg, beaten
salt and freshly ground black pepper

1   Cover the bacon joint with cold water and soak for 3 hours. Then drain, weigh and calculate cooking time as for baking in foil *(page 51)*.
2   Put the joint in a large saucepan, cover with cold water, bring to the boil, cover and simmer gently for half the calculated time.
3   Meanwhile, make the stuffing. Melt 25 g /1 oz of the butter in a frying-pan and fry the celery gently for 5 minutes. Add the mushrooms and fry for another 3 minutes. Off the heat, stir in the parsley, lemon zest, herbs, breadcrumbs, egg and salt and pepper to taste.
4   Heat the oven to 190C /375F /gas 5. Drain the joint, remove the string and peel off the rind.

5   Unroll the joint and lay it flat, spread the stuffing on the inside, then re-roll and tie with string.
6   Place the joint in a deep, lightly greased casserole and dot with the remaining butter. Cover, transfer to centre of oven and bake.
7   About 30 minutes before the end of the cooking time, uncover the casserole, sprinkle the top surface of the joint with sugar, and allow it to brown a little.
8   Remove the string and serve hot, or leave the string on while the joint cools and serve cold, carved in slices.

Ham and chicory gratin

When chicory is not available, or you are in a hurry, a large can of drained celery hearts or asparagus spears makes an equally delicious filling.

⏱ 1 hour

Serves 4–6
6 heads of chicory
15 ml /1 tbls lemon juice
salt
6 thin slices of cooked ham
butter for greasing
50 g /2 oz butter
25 g /1 oz flour
300 ml /10 fl oz milk, heated
2 shakes of cayenne pepper
1.5 ml /¼ tsp grated nutmeg
*100 g /4 oz mature Cheddar cheese, finely
    grated*
30 ml /2 tbls dry white breadcrumbs
parsley sprigs, to garnish

1   Remove any discoloured outer leaves from the chicory, and with a small pointed knife remove the hard core from the base of each head.
2   Add the lemon juice to a large saucepan of boiling, salted water, drop in the chicory, cover and cook gently for 15–20 minutes, until just tender. Drain thoroughly, reserving a little of the cooking water, then press the chicory in a clean tea-towel to remove surplus water.
3   Wrap each head of chicory in a slice of ham and lay the rolls side by side in a well buttered, shallow baking dish. Heat the oven to 190C /375F /gas 5.
4   Melt 25 g /1 oz of the butter in a saucepan, add the flour, stir and cook gently for 1 minute. Gradually beat in the milk and bring to the boil, beating continuously, until the sauce is thick and smooth. Add the cayenne, nutmeg and two-thirds of the cheese, and stir until melted. Then beat in 15–30 ml /1–2 tbls of the reserved cooking liquid to dilute the sauce to a pouring consistency. Check the seasoning.
5   Pour the sauce evenly over the ham and chicory rolls and sprinkle with the remaining cheese mixed with the breadcrumbs. Dot with the rest of the butter.
6   Bake in the hottest part of the oven for 20–30 minutes until bubbling and golden brown. Serve garnished with parsley sprigs.

Gala gammon with spiced peaches

Gala gammon with spiced peaches

For a dinner party or celebration meal, choose a middle gammon joint with a large surface for glazing. Spiced peaches complement its flavour and texture.

⏱ overnight marinating peaches, soaking gammon then 1½ hours

Serves 8–12
1.5–1.8 kg /3–4 lb middle gammon joint
15 ml /1 tbls brown sugar
6 peppercorns
2 bay leaves
For the spiced peaches
425 g /15 oz canned peach halves in syrup
45 ml /3 tbls wine vinegar
30 ml /2 tbls brown sugar
small piece of root ginger
6 cloves
2 allspice berries
25 mm /1 in piece of cinnamon stick
For the glaze and garnish
60 ml /4 tbls of the spiced peach syrup
30–45 ml /2–3 tbls Demerara sugar
whole cloves
30 ml /2 tbls redcurrant jelly
watercress sprigs

discoloured outer skin from the fennel, then slice the bulb very thinly, reserving the fennel foliage for garnishing.

4 Stir the fennel into the cold potato salad and spoon into a shallow salad bowl. Cut the ham into 25 mm /1 in matchstick strips and scatter evenly over the surface.

5 Arrange the egg quarters on the top of the salad, radiating from the centre, and garnish with tufts of fennel foliage.

Braised gammon with Marsala sauce

2½–3 hours

Serves 6–9
1.1–1.5 kg /2½–3 lb smoked corner gammon
25 g /1 oz butter
15 ml /1 tbls oil
1 large onion, sliced
2 large carrots, sliced
3 celery stalks, sliced
1 bay leaf
1 sprig of thyme
freshly ground black pepper
some mushroom stalks if available
10 ml /2 tsp tomato purée
300 ml /10 fl oz beef stock
300 ml/10 fl oz Marsala
25 g /1 oz butter blended with 20 g /¾ oz flour
creamed spinach and buttered small carrots, to serve

1 Weigh the joint and calculate the cooking time, allowing 77 minutes per kg /35 minutes per lb, plus 35 minutes.

2 Put the joint in a large saucepan, cover with cold water, bring slowly to the boil, then drain. Meanwhile, heat the oven to 180C /350F /gas 4.

3 Heat the butter and oil in a deep flameproof casserole, into which the joint will fit fairly snugly, and gently fry the onion, carrot, celery, bay leaf and thyme for 10 minutes, stirring occasionally, until lightly browned.

4 Season the fried vegetables with pepper, and add the mushroom stalks, the tomato purée dissolved in the stock, and two-thirds of the Marsala. Set the gammon joint, rind uppermost, on top, and bring to simmering point.

5 Cover the casserole tightly, transfer to the centre of the oven and cook for the calculated time.

6 Lift out the gammon and peel off the rind. Carve and arrange the slices overlapping on a heated serving dish. Keep warm.

7 Strain the cooking liquid into a saucepan, pressing the vegetables to extract their juices. Add enough of the remaining Marsala to give the sauce a fine flavour, and bring to simmering point.

8 Over a low heat, whisk in the blended butter and flour (beurre manié), a tiny piece at a time, and stir until the sauce is lightly thickened and glossy. Check the seasoning.

9 Spoon some of the sauce over the joint, and serve the rest in a sauceboat. Garnish the serving dish with alternating heaps of creamed spinach and buttered carrots.

---

1 Prepare the spiced peaches. Drain the peach syrup into a small saucepan, add the vinegar, sugar and spices, cover and simmer very gently for 15–20 minutes, until well spiced. Put the peaches in a bowl, strain the syrup over, cover and leave overnight.

2 Next day, soak the gammon joint in cold water for 3 hours. Then drain, weigh the joint and calculate the cooking time, allowing 44 minutes per kg /20 minutes per lb, plus 20 minutes.

3 Put the joint in a deep saucepan, cover with cold water, and add the brown sugar, peppercorns and bay leaves. Bring slowly to the boil, cover and simmer for 30 minutes less than the calculated cooking time.

4 Heat the oven to 200C /400F /gas 6. Drain the joint and carefully peel off the rind. Score the fat into diamond shapes.

5 Place the joint in a deep ovenproof casserole, fat side up, and spoon over 60 ml /4 tbls of the spiced peach syrup. Press the Demerara sugar evenly over the surface and stud each diamond with a clove.

6 Bake the joint uncovered in the oven for the rest of the cooking time until the surface is richly golden, basting now and then. While the joint is baking, heat the spiced peaches in the remaining syrup in a covered flameproof dish, in the oven.

7 Place the gammon on a heated serving dish. Surround with watercress and peach halves, cut side up, and spoon 5 ml /1 tsp redcurrant jelly into each peach.

Potato, fennel and ham salad

45 minutes

Serves 4
500 g /1 lb new or waxy old potatoes, scrubbed
salt
1 large bulb of fennel, with foliage attached
225 g /8 oz cooked ham, cut in thick slices
1 hard-boiled egg, quartered lengthways, to garnish

For the dressing
15 ml /1 tbls wine vinegar
1.5 ml /¼ tsp dry mustard
large pinch of salt
90 ml /6 tbls olive oil
15 ml /1 tbls snipped chives or finely chopped spring onion tops
15 ml /tbls chopped parsley

1 Cook the potatoes in their skins in boiling salted water until just tender. Meanwhile prepare the dressing by putting all the ingredients into a screwtop jar and shaking until blended.

2 Drain and peel the cooked potatoes and cut into 8 mm /⅓ in dice. While still hot, add the dressing, stir lightly, cover and leave until cold.

3 With a potato peeler pare away any

Game birds

Wild birds, called 'feathered game', are much prized by gourmets. Grouse, partridge, pheasant, wood pigeon, wild duck, snipe and woodcock all feed on food not available to farm-raised birds and this gives their flesh a distinctive gamey flavour. Correctly hung, prepared and cooked they make an absolutely delicious meal.

Game birds are distinct from domestic poultry because they spend a great deal of time on the wing and this develops strong muscles. Quail and guinea fowl are in origin wild fowl, although nowadays they are farm-reared for the table. They are dealt with in detail on *pages 58–61*.

Types of game bird
Pheasants, the most handsome of the large game birds, have a strong flavour. They are often sold as a 'brace' – a pair. The cock is the larger of the two, with russet feathers, a long, sweeping tail and a bright green top to his head. The hen has muted brown plumage.

A partridge is slightly smaller in size than a pheasant and the flavour is more delicate – nearer to that of a chicken. Both sexes have greyish breasts, barred wings and a chestnut-coloured head.

The red grouse is Britain's best-known game bird, with a strong gamey flavour. The male has a red mark round the eyes, a dark back and white breast going down to give a trouser effect over the legs. The female has brownish plumage with dark bars. There is also a black grouse, tiny ptarmigan and the large capercaillie – all rarely seen.

Of the wild ducks, mallard is perhaps the most familiar. The male has brilliant green head feathers, the female is less conspicuous with brownish feathers. Teal is much smaller and is also beautifully coloured, while widgeon is between the mallard and the teal in size.

Wood pigeons are small, grey-brown birds, much shot as farm pests. On the other hand conservationists are trying to protect snipe, woodcock and plovers. These are all similar small birds with long bills, served whole.

Game seasons
To conserve game stocks there are closed seasons while the birds are breeding and shooting is not permitted. These vary from one country to another. The seasons for the United Kingdom are given in the chart. However frozen game birds may be available out of season.

Buying a game bird
A bird for the table should have been shot in the head (the aim of all good huntsmen). Pellets in the body could shatter the rib cage, resulting in splinters of bones in the flesh, or enter the stomach, spoiling the bird's appearance.

A good retailer will classify birds as 'young' and suitable for roasting, or as 'casserole' birds. Generally speaking you can identify a young bird by its relatively smooth legs, moist, supple feet and tender pinions (the long wing-tip feathers). If your retailer specializes in game he should be able to stock quail (which are farmed) and pigeon throughout the year. He may also have frozen birds out of season. Grouse, partridge, pheasant and wild duck may be in stock in season in the U.K.; snipe and woodcock, on the other hand, will always need to be ordered specially.

Preparing game birds
If you are given game birds still in feather, your best plan is to take them to a poulterer who, for a fee, will hang, pluck, draw and truss them for you. It is important to know how long birds need to be hung. In some cases it may be more than a week before they are ready for eating. If you are buying ready-prepared birds, say when you want to eat them and ask the retailer for birds that have been hung the correct length of time.

Hanging tenderizes the flesh and intensifies the flavour. The length of time to achieve the right condition differs from one game bird to another. Pigeon (and quail) are never hung and young game birds, shot early in the season, require the minimum length of hanging time. Young grouse shot on the opening day of the season, 'the glorious twelfth', as it is called in Scotland, are traditionally cooked on the same day.

If hanging birds yourself, hang them securely by the beak, unplucked and un-

Buying and roasting game birds

Birds and servings	Shooting season in United Kingdom	Approximate hanging time	Temperature and roasting time
Grouse 2	12 August–10 December (best August–October)	2–4 days	190C /375F /gas 5 35 minutes
Partridge 1–2	1 September–1 February (best October–November)	3–5 days young birds 10 days older birds	220C /425F /gas 7 30 minutes
Pheasant hen 3; cock 4	1 October–1 February (best November–December)	3 days young bird 10 days older birds	190C /375F /gas 5 45–60 minutes
Pigeon 1	No closed season (best August–October)	Not hung (empty crop quickly)	220C /425F /gas 7 20 minutes
Snipe 2 birds each	12 August–31 January (best November)	3–4 days	220C /425F /gas 7, 6– 15 minutes undrawn
Wild Duck Mallard 2–3	1 September–20 February (best November–December)	2–3 days (drawn)	220C /425F /gas 7 25–30 minutes
Teal 1	1 September–31 January (best December)	2–3 days (drawn)	220C /425F /gas 7 10–15 minutes
Widgeon 1	1 September–31 January (best December)	2–3 days (drawn)	220C /425F /gas 7 15–25 minutes
Woodcock 1	1 October–31 January (best November–December)	3 days	220C /425F /gas 7, 10– 15 minutes undrawn

A good way to freeze birds for braising or casseroling is in a marinade; this adds flavour and saves time. Combine 300 ml /11 fl oz red wine, 30 ml /2 tbls olive oil, 6 crushed peppercorns, a crumbled bay leaf and a pinch of dried thyme in a large freezer bag. Add the birds, expel all air, seal, label and freeze. Defrost them in the bag for 24–36 hours in the refrigerator, turning the bag regularly.

Buying frozen game birds is a convenience – and often your only option if supplies are uncertain. Remember that frozen birds are more likely to be tough (there is no way to check quality). Unless you have great confidence in your supplier, you would do better to braise or casserole them rather than roast or grill.

Defrost game birds slowly in the refrigerator for 24 hours. Cook them within 24 hours or they are likely to become higher. Dishes of cooked game can be frozen for 1 month, though it is not good practice to defrost game, cook the dish and then freeze it.

Cooking game birds

Young birds are delicious served plainly roasted with the traditional accompaniments of game chips (wafer-thin fried potatoes) or fried breadcrumbs (see recipes) and gravy or bread sauce. Since the meat is firm and dry, good barding with bacon or pork fat is essential. Small birds to serve one person may be served on a croûte, which can be spread with pâté mixture if you wish. Red cabbage, braised celery and puréed swedes or parsnips are perfect vegetable accompaniments for game birds.

Very small birds like quail and snipe can be grilled, and for this they are usually spatchcocked. To do this cut the bird along the backbone and then turn it over and open it out. Press hard on the middle of the backbone so that the bird lies completely flat.

Older birds are best braised or casseroled and are delicious well marinated before casseroling. Partridge is traditionally cooked in a casserole with cabbage. Rich sauces containing port or redcurrant jelly are popular with game birds.

Pigeon pie is a classic English recipe, and a raised game pie is delicious eaten cold, and perfect for a picnic as it cuts so easily. Any left-over meat from a roasted game bird can be used for a tasty pâté or terrine (potted pheasant is a traditional recipe).

Game stock: a delicious stock can be made very easily by simmering the giblets in lightly salted water until the liquid is strongly flavoured. Make a richer stock by adding the crushed carcass, a bouquet garni and a few juniper berries to the giblets. Strain before using. You can make a wonderful soup from this stock by simmering a little sliced onion, leek, carrot and celery in it, then liquidizing and thickening the mixture with a beurre manié. Season it to taste with freshly ground black pepper, a little port or lemon juice if you wish, and redcurrant jelly.

drawn in a cool, airy place. Take care that they do not touch each other and make sure they are safe from pets. As a general rule game birds are ready for cooking when the tail feathers can be plucked out easily, but check at regular intervals because a warm, humid atmosphere hastens the maturing process. It is a wise precaution to remove some feathers round the vent at the back end of the bird and to test occasionally if you get a gamey whiff as you approach.

The longer older birds are hung the more tender they will be when cooked, particularly if the recipe requires a short cooking time and if you want the flesh to have a slight pinkness. Hanging may take up to 10 or even 14 days if the birds are to be 'high', though very strong flavour is less popular now than it used to be.

Plucking and drawing: after hanging, the birds are plucked, drawn (that is, gutted) and trussed, although woodcock and snipe are traditionally cooked undrawn. Your poulterer will also truss for you, although if you wish to stuff the bird, you will have to retruss it yourself.

Trussing keeps the body compact for cooking and carving. The method is the same as for domestic poultry (*page 63*). Place the ends of the legs into the vent of the bird or into the slit made for drawing.

Barding is necessary to keep the flesh moist during cooking. Lay slices of fat streaky bacon over the breast and thighs and tie at regular intervals with fine string.

Storing and freezing game

Once plucked, keep game birds loosely wrapped in the refrigerator for up to 2 days.

✱✱✱✱ Game birds should be fully hung, then plucked and drawn as near freezing time as possible. If the bird already smells high, overwrap in foil (first overwrapping the legs in foil if they protrude), then seal the bird in a freezer bag and label. Freeze for up to 6 months.

Wild duck terrine

 1 hour marinating, 2¾ hours, then 24 hours chilling

Serves 6

1 large wild duck (mallard), or 2 smaller
   game birds
30 ml /2 tbls brandy
juice of 1 large orange
250 g /8 oz chicken livers
1 large onion, coarsely chopped
50 g /2 oz fresh white breadcrumbs
1 clove garlic, finely chopped
8 slices streaky bacon, de-rinded
3 bay leaves plus extra, to garnish
6 juniper berries plus extra, to garnish
lettuce leaves and orange slices, to garnish

1 Slice the breast of the duck as thinly as possible and marinate the slices in the brandy and orange juice for 1 hour.
2 Heat the oven to 180C /350F /gas 4. Remove all the remaining flesh from the duck and mince with the chicken livers and onion. Mix the breadcrumbs, garlic and the marinade from the breast slices.
3 Stretch the bacon rashers with a palette knife and use to line a 1 L /1¾ pt terrine. Put in half the minced duck mixture, cover with the slices of breast and add the rest of the minced mixture. Press bay leaves into the surface, scatter over the juniper berries and cover with a lid or foil.
4 Stand the dish in a roasting tin and pour in hot water to come half-way up the sides of the dish. Cook in the oven for 2 hours.
5 Drain the liquid from the terrine, remove the bay leaves and juniper berries, then press under a weight, cool and chill for 24 hours. Turn out on to a serving platter. Garnish with bay leaves, juniper berries, lettuce leaves and orange slices.

English pigeon pie

The breasts on a pigeon make up 90% of the meat on the bird so it is really not extravagant to make the pie with the breast only. If you wish, the birds do not even have to be plucked; part the feathers and split the skin along the breastbone with a pointed knife. Pull it back and ease the breasts away from the bone

1¼ hours

Serves 4

300 g /11 oz beef skirt or rump steak, cut into
   small cubes
30 ml /2 tbls seasoned flour
butter for greasing
2 medium-sized eggs, hard-boiled
4 pigeons, breasts only
150 ml /5 fl oz chicken stock
5 ml /1 tsp Worcestershire sauce
30 ml /2 tbls port
salt and freshly ground black pepper
15 ml /1 tbls chopped parsley
400 g /14 oz made weight frozen puff pastry,
   defrosted
1 medium-sized egg, beaten

1 Coat the cubed meat in the seasoned flour and place in the bottom of a 1 L /1¾ pt greased pie dish. Halve the hard-boiled eggs and arrange them over the meat, alternately with the pigeon breasts. Mix the stock with the Worcestershire sauce and port and season to taste with salt and pepper. Pour into the pie dish and sprinkle over the parsley.
2 Heat the oven to 220C /425F /gas 7. Roll out the pastry 4 cm /1½ in larger than the pie dish all round and cut the lid from this, leaving it slightly larger than the rim. Cut a strip to fit around the rim of the pie dish. Brush the edge of the dish with beaten egg, press on the strip and brush it with egg. Place the lid on the pie and press the edges to seal. Knock up the edges with a sharp knife and flute them.
3 Brush the pie all over with egg. Decorate with leaves cut from the pastry trimmings if wished, brushing them over with egg. Cut a steam vent in the pastry and then rest the pie in the refrigerator for about 15 minutes.
4 Bake in the oven for 20 minutes, then reduce the heat to 190C /375F /gas 5 and continue cooking for a further 40 minutes, covering the top with a sheet of aluminium foil, if necessary, to prevent the pastry over-browning.

---

*Wild duck terrine and Partridge
with red cabbage and chestnuts*

Pheasant with apples and cream

1 hour

Serves 4

1 large, young cock pheasant, trussed
75 g /3 oz unsalted butter
2 large slices of streaky bacon
salt and freshly ground black pepper
2 large, sweet dessert apples, peeled, cored
   and sliced
75 ml /3 fl oz calvados or brandy, warmed
5 ml /1 tsp flour
200 ml /7 fl oz thick cream, whipped

1 Put 25 g /1 oz butter and the bacon slices in a deep, heavy-based saucepan, into which the pheasant will fit snugly. Heat gently until the fat runs from the bacon. Add the pheasant and brown lightly on all sides. Turn breast upwards and season well with salt and pepper. Cover the pan and cook over a moderate heat for 15 minutes.
2 Turn the pheasant on to one side, baste well and cook, covered, for a further 15 minutes. Then turn on to the other side, baste again, cover and continue cooking for a further 15 minutes. Test with a skewer: if pink juices still run and you like your game birds well cooked, cook for 5 minutes more.

3   Meanwhile, melt the remaining butter in a small saucepan and cook the apple slices until soft and golden. Keep hot.
4   Put the pheasant on to a heated serving dish, divide it into 4 portions and keep hot.
5   Strain the pheasant cooking juices from the pan into a small saucepan, reheat until they begin to bubble, then pour in the calvados or brandy. Set alight and shake the pan gently over heat until flames die down.
6   In a cup, mix the flour with 15 ml /1 tbls cream and stir the mixture into the contents of the pan. Gradually whisk in the rest of the cream and continue cooking over a moderate heat, stirring all the time, until the sauce thickens. Season to taste with salt and pepper and cook very gently without boiling for a further 2 minutes, then pour over the pheasant. Serve the apples separately or arrange them round the bird.

Partridge with red cabbage and chestnuts

This recipe serves 2 but it is easy to multiply the ingredients for 4 people if you have a large enough casserole. For older birds, extend the cooking time by about 30 minutes until the legs feel tender when tested with a fine skewer.

♏♏ 2–2½ hours

Serves 2
150 g /5 oz chestnuts in their skins
salt
25 g /1 oz bacon or pork dripping
50 g /2 oz streaky bacon, de-rinded and chopped
2 young partridges, trussed
500 g /1 lb red cabbage, shredded
freshly ground black pepper
250 ml /9 fl oz dry cider

1   Heat the oven to 170C /325F /gas 3. Make slits in the rounded sides of the chestnuts. Boil them in salted water for about 15 minutes then drain and remove both outer and inner skins.
2   Melt the dripping in a flameproof casserole over a medium heat and fry the bacon pieces until golden. Remove the bacon from the pan with a slotted spoon. Add the partridges to the fat, brown them on all sides, then remove.
3   Place half the cabbage in the pan, then the bacon and partridges, breasts uppermost. Season the birds generously with salt and pepper, and add the chestnuts and the remaining cabbage. Pour over the cider and lay a piece of foil over the cabbage to keep it moist. Put the lid on the casserole and place in the oven for 1½–2 hours. Serve with plain boiled potatoes.

Roast pheasant

♏ 1 hour

Serves 3 with a hen; 4 with a cock pheasant
1 young pheasant, trussed and tail feathers reserved for the garnish
salt and freshly ground black pepper
20 g /¾ oz butter
1 large slice of streaky bacon
5 ml /1 tsp flour
sprigs of watercress
fried crumbs (optional – see below)
For the gravy
25 g /1 oz butter
25 g /1 oz flour
250 ml /9 fl oz giblet stock, strained and well seasoned
5 ml /1 tsp lemon juice
30 ml /2 tbls sherry or Madeira
For the game chips
2 medium-sized potatoes
iced water
oil for deep-frying
salt

1   Heat the oven to 190C /375F /gas 5. Season the bird well, inside and out, with salt and pepper. Place a small piece of the butter in the cavity and smear the rest over the outside of the bird. Lay the slice of bacon on the breast and secure with string.
2   Place the bird on a trivet in a roasting tin. (If liked, place the breast downwards so juices flow into meat for first half of roasting time.) Roast in the oven for 40 minutes.
3   Make the game chips. Heat the oil in a deep-fat frier to 180C /350F (a bread cube will brown in 60 seconds). Peel and slice the potatoes very thinly with a mandolin cutter. Soak in the iced water for 5 minutes. Drain and pat dry. Put in the frier basket and immerse in the hot oil for 1 minute, turning with a slotted spoon. Drain and keep warm.
4   Increase the heat of the oil to 190C /375F (a bread cube will brown in 50 seconds). Plunge the chips in again and cook until brown, 30–60 seconds. Drain well, salt them and keep warm. Make the fried crumbs, if serving, see below.
5   After 40 minutes cooking remove the bacon from the bird, sprinkle the flour over the breast and return it to the oven, breast uppermost, for a further 5 minutes, to brown; transfer to a warmed serving dish.
6   Meanwhile start making the gravy. Melt the butter in a small, heavy-based saucepan, stir in the flour and cook over a low heat, stirring, for 2–3 minutes. Add 15–30 ml /1–2 tbls drippings from the roasting tin and the giblet stock. Stir in the lemon juice and sherry or Madeira, and bring to the boil, stirring constantly. Simmer for 3 minutes, adjust seasonings. Transfer to a sauce-boat.
7   Garnish the pheasant with watercress, game chips and fried crumbs. Arrange tail feathers. Pass gravy separately.

● Fried crumbs: melt 25 g /1 oz butter and add 5 ml /1 tsp oil. Add 75 g /3 oz fresh white breadcrumbs and stir over a low heat until the butter is absorbed. Increase heat slightly; fry until evenly brown. Keep hot.

Ducks, geese, guinea fowl and quail

These birds are sometimes neglected, since chicken and turkey are cheaper and more widely available. However, guinea fowl is a pleasant change from chicken, while a duck or goose makes an ideal dish for a special occasion and quail, the smallest of the game birds, is the most easily prepared.

Ducks bred domestically are larger than wild ducks, which are covered in the section on game birds (*page 54*). The terms duck and duckling are used fairly loosely, although strictly speaking a duckling should be between six and twelve weeks old. Ducks have a high fat content and do not have all that much meat in proportion to their frame, but their dark-coloured flesh is deliciously rich and succulent, with a distinctive flavour. They are available all the year, being at their best in early to late spring.

Geese are larger than ducks, but the proportion of bone to meat is even higher. Geese are also very fatty, with creamy white flesh which becomes light brown when cooked and has a faintly gamey flavour. A gosling is a young goose not more than six months old. Geese are not seasonal, but are at their best from winter to late spring. In fact it can be difficult to obtain a fresh goose during the summer months.

Guinea fowl are cooked like game but are now bred domestically. They are about the same size as pheasants or small chickens. They are hung for several days, so that their flesh has a slight gaminess reminiscent of pheasant. They are not seasonal, but are at their best from spring to early summer.

Quail are the smallest of the game birds, reared on special game farms, and are available all through the year. They should be eaten as soon as possible after being killed: flavour and tenderness are not improved by hanging. In the Northern hemisphere, they are at their best from June to September.

Buying and storing

All these farm-bred birds are available fresh from poulterers.

New York dressed birds are plucked but not drawn and have the head and feet still attached. You pay less per kg /lb for birds dressed this way but you pay for the head, feet and innards, which can amount to one-third or even more of the total weight. If you do buy birds prepared this way, look for flexible bills (or soft beaks) and feet: webbing of ducks' feet should be soft enough to be easily torn. Ducks should be plump but not over-fattened, or there will be a layer of fat beneath the skin which makes it difficult to get the skin crisp when it is roasted. Geese should have a plump breast, and the flesh should be light pink rather than brownish in colour. With guinea fowl, judge the appearance as you would for chicken: look for a plump breast, white flesh and smooth-skinned feet. The flesh will be much drier than that of chicken. The poulterer will normally clean the bird and remove the head and feet for you after weighing it.

Oven-ready birds are cleaned, plucked and trussed, ready for the oven. Many poulterers sell the birds this way: giblets may or may not be sold with the birds. Prepackaged oven-ready birds are also available from chilled cabinets in supermarkets. Quail, which are cooked undrawn, are sold oven-ready. Look for a well filled out breast and make sure you are buying a young bird with no traces of feathers; feathers in older birds do not pluck so easily.

✱✱✱ Deep-frozen ducks, geese and guinea fowl are available all the year round in supermarkets and freezer centres. This is the cheapest way of buying: a frozen goose will cost only about half the price of a fresh one, though the quality may not be as high. Frozen birds must be totally thawed before cooking, but great care is needed when defrosting since spoilage is likely to be more rapid than is to be expected with chicken or turkey because of the fatty flesh. Quail are not available frozen.

How much to buy: allow at least 500 g /1 lb duck and 700 g /1½ lb goose per serving. A good-sized guinea fowl will usually serve 4 people; smaller birds serve 2. With quail, always allow at least 1 bird per person.

Steam-roasted quails

Cooking the birds

Roasting duck: this is a favourite cooking method, as it gets rid of much of the fat. Ducks for roasting should always be young and tender. Before roasting, season inside and out with salt and freshly ground black pepper, and prick the skin all over with a skewer or roasting fork. Place on a rack in a roasting tin and roast at 180C/350F/gas 4 for 55 minutes per kg/25 minutes per lb. Roast duck is traditionally served with tangy fruit, which complements the rich meat. You can also ring the changes with stuffings for roast duck: sage and onion, apple and potato, or apple and prune. Vegetable accompaniments to roast duck should be kept very simple: boiled new potatoes and peas are traditional.

Casseroling duck: older ducks can be braised very successfully or cooked till tender in a cassoulet with dried haricot beans. Dry-salted, baked duck is a speciality of Wales.

Cold duck: a boned bird set in its own jellied stock makes a wonderful galantine, perfect for a buffet supper party. A terrine of duck has a superb flavour and texture.

Duck stock: the giblets and duck carcass can be used to make a rich soup stock.

Roast goose is traditionally served with a variety of stuffings and sauces. Potato and onion, or chestnut and apple stuffing absorbs the fat effectively, and the sharpness of apple sauce also sets off the richness. Before roasting, remove any pieces of fat from around the vent, prick the fatty parts of the goose with a fork, place on a rack in a roasting tin and cook at 200C/400F/gas 6 for 15 minutes or until the fat begins to run. Remove goose from oven and tip the fat from the body cavity into a dish. Return goose to oven and repeat this cooking and draining process 2 or 3 more times. Season goose inside and out, stuff, and continue roasting at 170C/325F/gas 3 for 1¼–2 hours, depending on size. Prick bird occasionally and turn over half-way through, turning the bird breast side up 10–15 minutes before the end of cooking time.

Smoked goose breast, served raw and thinly sliced, is considered a great delicacy in Germany and Poland.

Goose giblets: these are the neck, gizzard, heart, liver, wing tips and feet. For a delicious gravy to serve with roast goose, make a stock from the giblets, then blend 50 ml /2 fl oz soured cream with 10 ml /2 tsp flour and 20 ml /4 tsp water and add this to 400 ml /14 fl oz stock; bring to the boil, stirring, and simmer until thick.

The goose liver is much prized, and may be specially fattened by forcible feeding (sometimes up to 1.8 kg /4 lb) to make *pâté de foie gras*. This luxury pâté is made in Strasbourg and the Périgord region of France, where chopped black truffles are added to it.

Guinea fowl can be roasted or braised like chicken or pheasant. When roasting guinea fowl, be sure to add plenty of extra fat to prevent the flesh from drying out. Thin giblet gravy and game chips or fried breadcrumbs are traditional accompaniments.

Quail can be roasted, sautéed, casseroled or grilled. Because quail are so small they are usually eaten undrawn, and look attractive served neatly on a croûte of toasted or fried bread.

Goose giblets in parsley sauce

2¼ hours

Serves 2

goose giblets (neck, gizzard, heart, feet and wing tips)
salt and freshly ground black pepper
3 black peppercorns
pinch of dried oregano
1 bay leaf
25 g /1 oz butter
25 g /1 oz flour
25 g /1 oz chopped parsley
1 medium-sized egg yolk, beaten

1 Split the gizzard, peel off the inner lining and discard. Cut the claws from the goose feet and discard. Blanch the feet in boiling water for 2–3 minutes, then remove the scaly skin. Cut the neck into 5 cm /2 in pieces. Thoroughly wash all the giblets.

2 Place the prepared giblets in a saucepan, add water to cover, a little salt, the peppercorns, oregano and bay leaf. Bring to the boil, cover and simmer for 1½–2 hours, or until soft. Remove the giblets from the stock and keep warm in a serving dish.

3 Boil the stock until reduced to about 300 ml /10 fl oz and strain.

4 Melt the butter in a saucepan, stir in the flour and cook, stirring, for 2 minutes. Gradually add the measured giblet stock and bring to the boil, stirring constantly. Add the parsley, season to taste and simmer for 5 minutes. Remove from the heat, spoon a little of the hot sauce into the egg yolk, beat well then beat the yolk mixture into the bulk of the sauce. Pour the sauce over the giblets. Serve with boiled potatoes and a green or mixed salad.

Steam-roasted quails with chicken liver stuffing

40 minutes

Serves 2

4 quails, drawn
salt and freshly ground black pepper
4 chicken livers
40 g /1½ oz butter
1 large carrot, finely chopped
1 medium-sized onion, finely chopped
30 ml /2 tbls brandy
100 ml /4 fl oz strong chicken stock
boiled rice, to serve
sprigs of watercress, to garnish

1 Heat the oven to 220C /425F /gas 7. Season the quails inside and out with salt and pepper and put 1 chicken liver inside each bird.

2 Melt the butter in a shallow flameproof casserole and in it brown the quails on all sides, then remove them.

3 Add the carrot and onion to the fat remaining in the casserole and stir well. Place the quails on top, cover, and cook in the oven for 15 minutes. Uncover and cook for a further 10 minutes, then remove from the oven.

4 Heat the brandy, pour it over the quails and set alight. When the flames subside, remove the quails and keep hot while you finish preparing the vegetables.

5 Add the stock to the carrot and onion in the casserole and boil, stirring occasionally, for 3–4 minutes, or until the liquid has almost completely evaporated. Check the seasoning.

6 Spread the rice over a heated oval serving dish, spoon the carrot and onion mixture into the centre, and place the quails on this. Garnish the dish with sprigs of watercress.

Goose liver with grapes

🍶 30 minutes

Serves 2–3
1 goose liver (about 500 g /1 lb)
15 ml /1 tbls goose fat
150 ml /5 fl oz port or medium sherry
5 ml /1 tsp salt
about 20 grapes, seeded (mixed black and white, if possible)
freshly ground black pepper
boiled rice, to serve

1 Carefully cut the gall bladder from the goose liver, taking care not to damage it, as otherwise the liver may taste bitter.
2 Melt the fat in a small saucepan, add the liver and cook gently for 20 minutes, turning once.
3 Pour off the fat and add the port or sherry and the salt to the pan. Simmer for 5 minutes, then add the grapes. Continue cooking gently for a further 3 minutes, or until the grapes swell; do not allow them to disintegrate.
4 Season the cooking liquid with pepper, cut the liver into neat pieces and serve on a bed of fluffy boiled rice, with the sauce.

Duck in vinegar jelly

🍶🍶 3 hours plus chilling time

Serves 4
2.3–2.8 kg /5–6 lb duck (dressed weight)
45 ml /3 tbls dry white wine
45 ml /3 tbls white wine vinegar
1 chicken stock cube, crumbled
2 bay leaves
4 black peppercorns
1 medium-sized egg white, lightly beaten
1 egg shell, crushed
salt and freshly ground black pepper
15 ml /1 tbls gelatine
8 thin orange slices, halved

1 Place the duck in a large saucepan into which it will fit comfortably. Add the wine, vinegar, stock cube, bay leaves and peppercorns and pour in enough water to cover. Bring to the boil, cover and simmer for 2–3 hours, or until the duck is tender.
2 Lift out the duck and reserve.
3 Strain the stock into a clean saucepan, add the egg white and shell and boil the stock until it clears and is reduced to about 600 ml /1 pt.
4 Strain the stock into a bowl, skim away any fat from the surface and season to taste with salt and pepper. Stir the gelatine into the hot stock until completely dissolved. Allow to cool.
5 Meanwhile, remove the skin and bones from the duck and cut the flesh into large, neat pieces. Arrange them in a lightly oiled 1 L /1¾ pt mould. Carefully pour over the cooled stock and chill until set. Turn out to serve. Garnish with orange slices.

Roast goose with potato stuffing

Roast goose with potato stuffing

🍶🍶 2¼–3 hours

Serves 4–6
2.8–4 kg /6–9 lb goose, dressed weight
For the stuffing
1 kg /2 lb potatoes, cut into 20 mm /¾ in cubes
50 g /2 oz butter
1 medium-sized onion, chopped
15 ml /1 tbls chopped parsley
goose heart and liver, finely chopped
300 ml /10 fl oz goose or chicken stock
5 ml /1 tsp salt
freshly ground black pepper

1 Prepare the goose for roasting (*page 59*). Heat the oven to 200C/400F/gas 6 and cook the goose for 15 minutes, or until the fat begins to run. Remove the goose from the oven and drain off the fat from the cavity into a dish. Return the goose to the oven and repeat the cooking and draining process 2 or 3 times.
2 Meanwhile, make the stuffing. Cook the potatoes in salted water for 10 minutes. Drain. Melt the butter in a saucepan and in it cook the onion until golden. Add the parsley and the chopped goose heart and liver, and cook gently for 5 minutes. Stir in the cooked potato and the stock, mix well and season to taste with salt and pepper.
3 Use the potato mixture to stuff the goose at the vent end. Sew up the vent and tie the legs together.
4 Reduce the oven heat to 170C /325F /gas 3. Place the stuffed goose, breast side up, on a rack in a roasting tin and roast for 1¼–2 hours, depending on the size of the bird. Prick the skin occasionally during the cooking time to release the excess fat, and turn the bird over half-way through the cooking time. Turn the goose breast side up on the rack 10–15 minutes before the end of the cooking time.
5 When the goose is cooked (the thigh joint will move easily in its socket) remove to a warm serving dish and keep hot.
6 Serve with red cabbage and gravy made from goose giblets.

● Redcurrant stuffed apples are a delicious garnish for roast goose, served as an alternative to stuffing. Poach 4 apples, peeled, halved and cored, in 250 ml /9 fl oz dry white wine with 100 g /4 oz sugar, until tender but not disintegrating. Arrange the apple halves round the goose on the serving dish, and fill the cavity of each apple half with 5 ml/tsp redcurrant jelly.

Roast duck with olives

🍴🍴 3 hours

Serves 4
1.8–2.3 kg /4–5 lb duck (dressed weight)
salt and freshly ground black pepper
For the sauce
30 ml /2 tbls duck dripping or butter
*50 g /2 oz streaky bacon, de-rinded and
   chopped*
1 small carrot, diced
1 small onion, chopped
*25 g /1 oz mushrooms or mushroom stalks,
   chopped*
1 stick celery, chopped
25 g /1 oz flour
300 ml /10 fl oz duck giblet stock
30 ml /2 tbls tomato purée
1 bouquet garni
salt and freshly ground black pepper
2.5 ml /¹/₂ tsp French mustard
150 ml /5 fl oz dry white wine
24–30 stuffed green olives, rinsed and drained
For the garnish
sprigs of watercress
julienne strips of carrot, cooked

1 Heat the oven to 180C /350F /gas 4.
Weigh the duck and calculate the cooking
time, allowing 55 minutes per kg /25 minutes per lb. Wash the duck quickly with
warm water, inside and out, and dry it with
a clean cloth. Rub the bird all over with salt.
2 Prick the duck skin all over, then place
the bird, breast side up, on a rack in a
roasting tin and roast in the centre of the
oven for the calculated time.
3 Meanwhile, prepare the sauce. Melt the
dripping or butter in a saucepan, add the
bacon and fry for 2 minutes, until lightly
coloured. Add the carrot, onion, mushroom
and celery, and fry for a further 5 minutes,
until lightly browned. Stir in the flour, mix
well and continue cooking until the mixture
turns golden brown. Remove from the heat
and gradually blend in the stock and tomato
purée. Add the bouquet garni and bring to
the boil, stirring constantly, until the sauce
thickens. Season well to taste with salt and
pepper, reduce the heat and simmer for 1
hour, stirring occasionally to prevent
sticking.
4 Remove the bouquet garni, then pass
the sauce through a sieve, or leave it to cool
slightly then purée it in a food processor or
blender. Transfer to a shallow, ovenproof
dish. Stir in the mustard, wine and olives.
Check the seasoning.
5 Divide the cooked duck into 4 portions,
arrange them in the dish and spoon a little
sauce over each.
6 Raise the oven heat to 200C /400F /gas 6
and cook the duck in the sauce for 20
minutes, or until well heated through.
7 Serve garnished with sprigs of watercress and strips of carrot. Creamed potatoes
and green beans or Brussels sprouts would
be good vegetable accompaniments.

Roast duck with olives

Braised guinea fowl with brandy and soured cream

🍴🍴 1 hour

Serves 4
75 g /3 oz butter
*75 g /3 oz thickly sliced streaky bacon,
   de-rinded and cubed*
*1.4 kg /3 lb guinea fowl (dressed weight),
   jointed*
salt and freshly ground black pepper
500 g /1 lb button onions
60 ml /4 tbls brandy
2 cloves garlic, crushed
600 ml /1 pt chicken stock
15 ml /1 tbls tomato purée
5 ml /1 tsp sugar
*15 ml /1 tbls chopped fresh basil or 5 ml /1 tsp
   dried basil*
100 g /4 oz button mushrooms
15 ml /1 tbls flour
1.5 ml /¹/₄ tsp ground nutmeg
75 ml /3 fl oz soured cream
For the garnish
50 g /2 oz fried bread croûtons
chopped parsley

1 Melt 25 g /1 oz of the butter in a
flameproof casserole and in it fry the bacon
cubes until golden. Remove the bacon from
the casserole with a slotted spoon.
2 Season the guinea fowl joints with salt
and pepper. Add to the casserole and fry
gently until browned all over. Return the
bacon to the casserole; add the onions.
Continue frying until the onions begin to
colour. Heat the brandy, pour it into the
casserole and set alight.
3 When the flames subside, add the garlic,
stock, tomato purée, sugar and basil, and
stir well. Bring to the boil, cover and
simmer over a low heat for about 40
minutes, or until the guinea fowl is tender.
4 Transfer the guinea fowl and onions to a
warm serving dish and keep hot. Boil the
liquid in the pan until reduced to about 500
ml /18 fl oz, and remove from the heat.
5 Meanwhile, melt the remaining butter
in a frying-pan and sauté the mushrooms for
about 2 minutes. In a bowl, blend together
the flour, nutmeg, 30 ml /2 tbls water and
the soured cream. Add the mushrooms and
soured cream mixture to the liquid in the
casserole, and stir well. Bring to the boil,
stirring constantly, and simmer for 3 minutes.
6 Adjust the seasoning if necessary and
pour over the guinea fowl in the dish. Serve
garnished with croûtons and parsley.

Turkey

Turkey, once a prized delicacy, is now widely available—and not just in the form of an enormous monster too big for your roasting tin. Casseroled, sautéed or made into a mousse, it can fit any occasion from the simplest of summer picnics to the grandest of dinner parties.

Turkeys at one time were quite rare and eaten only on special occasions, hence their association with Christmas and Thanksgiving. Nowadays, though, modern production techniques mean that turkeys of all sizes can be bought all year round.

The turkey is native to North and Central America and was domesticated by the Mexicans before the Spanish arrived. Wild turkeys can still be found in some parts of the U.S. and Mexico; they are smaller and gamier than domesticated ones.

Buying turkey

Turkeys are available either fresh, chilled or frozen. Whichever you buy, the breast should be plump and white, the drumsticks firm and rounded.

New York dressed turkeys: on a fresh or New York dressed turkey, which is the one seen hanging in the butcher's window at Christmas—plucked but with head and feet still attached – look for smooth black legs; these indicate a young and therefore tender bird.

Hens are usually reckoned to be more tender than cocks, though modern breeders say there is little difference. Both are hung for five to seven days after killing to tenderize them. These are the turkeys favoured by traditionalists, but they do work out more expensive as you pay for the weight of the head, innards and feet as well as the edible part of the bird.

Chilled turkeys have had their innards removed; they are then dressed for the oven on the farm before they are air-chilled. This process involves no intake of water (unlike deep freezing), so there is no weight loss later on. They are usually available from butchers and supermarkets, prewrapped and with the giblets wrapped separately inside them. Chilled turkeys range in weight from 2.5-11 kg /5-25 lb.

Frozen turkeys are sold oven-ready in the same sizes as chilled turkey. This is the cheapest way to buy turkey, though the weight includes extra water. Lengthy, slow thawing is a necessity to make the bird tender and safe to eat (see chart opposite).

There is a variety of frozen turkey called the self-basting turkey. This has had butter or vegetable oil injected under its skin before freezing and thus needs no basting during roasting.

Turkey joints and breasts, as well as escalopes cut from the breast, are available, either frozen or chilled, from many shops.

These are ideal when you want to eat turkey at one meal only, or when a particular cut is required for a recipe.

Turkey rolls, cooked or uncooked, consist of boned and rolled turkey meat. They may be made of white or dark meat only, or a combination. Sometimes they are sold barded with pork back fat. Uncooked turkey rolls may be plainly roasted or braised in a sauce (see recipe).

Smoked turkey is much loved in central Europe and is becoming more popular elsewhere. It is usually sold precooked; it has a delicate, smoky flavour.

Quantities to buy: if buying a whole turkey, allow 350-450 g /12 oz-1 lb per person for a bird weighing up to 7.5 kg /16 lb; 450-550 g /1-1¼ lb per person for a bird weighing between 7.5-10.5 kg /16-23 lb. A really big bird, between 10.5-11.5 kg /23-25 lb, will give 16-20 servings. If you buy a fresh turkey, allow 1.4 kg /3 lb for the weight of the head, feet and innards. Remember about 5% of the weight of a frozen bird is water.

If you are buying turkey joints, one drumstick or wing will usually be sufficient for one person, while for breast meat you should allow 175 g /6 oz, since there is no bone or fat to consider. For a cold buffet a turkey roll is ideal, as it is quick to carve and there is no wastage. Allow 125-175 g /4-6 oz per person.

Storing turkey

A fresh turkey or turkey roll, loosely covered on a plate, will keep for up to two days in the coldest part of the refrigerator. Giblets should be kept separately and cooked on the day of purchase. Simmer

---

Roast turkey with smoked oyster stuffing

Trussing a turkey

With the breast uppermost, pass a needle and string through the left thigh, just above the joint of drumstick and thigh. Push the needle through the bird and out the other leg, through the same place.

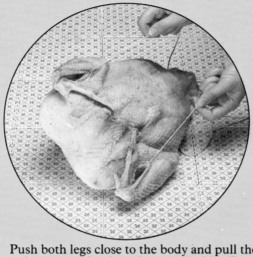

Push both legs close to the body and pull the string out with a length on each side. Turn the bird onto its breast. Carry the string down to the wing on the same side and loop it round the elbow joint.

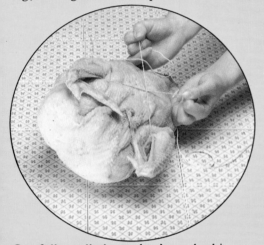

Carefully pull the turkey's neck skin over the back of the bird, then tuck the wing tips over to hold them. Holding the strings taut, pull them round and cross them in the middle of the turkey's back.

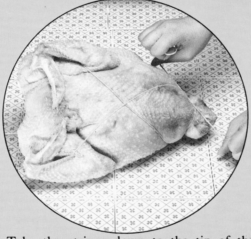

Take the strings down to the tip of the drumsticks. Wind the string twice around the parson's nose and the leg tips, pulling it tightly, then tie securely and cut off any excess string.

with flavourings to make stock for the turkey gravy. Follow the manufacturers' instructions for storing chilled turkeys.

✳✳✳ Freeze fresh or frozen whole (unstuffed) turkeys or turkey joints, wrapped first in aluminium foil, then in freezer bags, for up to one year. Cooked turkey can be frozen for up to three months. Freeze giblets raw (with the liver packed separately) or cooked, wrapped in freezer bags, for up to three months.

Thawing frozen turkey should be done with the bird on a rack over a tray at the bottom of the refrigerator. Remove the wrapping and extract the bag of giblets from inside as soon as possible. Never try to speed up the thawing process—a partially defrosted bird may never reach a sufficiently high oven temperature to kill any bacteria present, and so is dangerous to eat.

Joints and breasts obviously need less time than a whole bird, but should still be thawed for at least 12 hours.

Thawing in the refrigerator

Weight	Time
2.3-3.6 kg /5-8 lb	20-36 hours
3.6-5 kg /8-11 lb	36-42 hours
5-5.9 kg /11-13 lb	42-48 hours
5.9-9 kg /13-20 lb	48-60 hours
9-11.3 kg /20-25 lb	60-72 hours

Preparing turkey for roasting

If you have bought a fresh bird there may be a few quills left on—a sharp tug will quickly remove these. Use pliers if they are deeply buried. Frozen and chilled birds are always fully plucked.

Rinse the bird in cold water and pat dry inside and out. Season inside with salt and pepper before stuffing. If you are not stuffing the bird, put a lemon cut in half, 2-3 sprigs of fresh herbs and some garlic, if you like it, as well as salt and pepper, inside the cavity to give a delicate flavour to the meat and juices.

Stuffing: traditionally two stuffings are used, one in the body cavity and one at the neck end. Never fill the body cavity more than half full to ensure the inside of the bird cooks fully. If you are using one stuffing only, stuff the neck. Secure the neck skin by pulling it over the back of the bird, then take a 'stitch' through it with a small skewer.

Stuffings can be sausage-meat – with chestnuts or without – or sage and onion, a veal forcemeat or a herb and celery stuffing. Smoked oysters give an unusual flavour (see recipe). Allow 60–100 g stuffing per kg turkey or 1-1½ oz per lb.

Trussing makes a large roast look more attractive. Use a trussing needle and fine string (never plastic or nylon which would melt).

Place the bird breast uppermost and thread the needle through the left leg just above the thigh bone near the thigh and drumstick joint. Pass the needle through the body of the turkey and then through the opposite leg; then push both legs tight against the body. Leaving a sufficient length of string on either side of each leg, turn the bird breast side down, carry the string through the elbow joint of each wing, then twist the wing tips under the neck of the bird to hold the neck flap in place. Cross the strings over in the middle of the back and tie down the legs by winding the string round the ends of the drumsticks and round the parson's nose, then tie firmly.

Roasting turkey

Never put a turkey into the oven straight from the refrigerator–bring it to room temperature first. Allow at least 2 hours for a big turkey, plus stuffing and trussing time.

When the turkey is stuffed and trussed, place it on a rack in a roasting tin and either bard it with strips of streaky bacon or cover it with a piece of buttered muslin which can be saturated with fat. Alternatively, the turkey can be spread all over with a paste of softened butter and salt and covered with a dome of aluminium foil. Remove this 20 minutes before the end of cooking to brown the skin. Unless you have bought a self-basting turkey, regular basting will be necessary to prevent the meat becoming dry.

Roast turkeys for 15 minutes at 220C /425F /gas 7 to brown, then turn down the heat to 170C /325F /gas 3 to complete cooking. Weigh the bird after stuffing. As a general guide, allow 43 minutes per kg /20 minutes per lb for well cooked meat. The chart times allow for opening the oven doors several times for basting. Rare meat and smaller birds will need a little less time. If the breast appears to be getting over-

Roasting times for large turkeys

Weight	Hours
4-4.5 kg /9-10 lb	3½-4
4.5-5.4 kg /10-12 lb	4-4½
5.4-6.8 kg /12-15 lb	4½-5
6.8-7.7 kg /15-17 lb	5-5½
7.7-9 kg /17-20 lb	5½-6
9-11.3 kg /20-25 lb	6-7

cooked, cover it with foil until the leg meat is done. A skewer inserted in the thickest part of the leg should produce clear juices when cooked; the leg should wiggle easily in its socket.

Carving and serving roast turkey

Plan your cooking to allow at least 10 minutes setting time at the end of cooking; during this make the gravy and dish up.

A small turkey can be carved and jointed like a chicken. Serve a leg or wing plus some breast meat and stuffing to each person. A large bird is best carved before the meal begins and kept warm until needed.

Traditional accompaniments include chipolata sausages and forcemeat balls wrapped in bacon, and cranberry and bread sauces. Try chopping up the turkey liver, sautéing it in a little butter, and then adding it to bread sauce.

Other ways of cooking turkey

There are many other ways of cooking a turkey beside roasting it. Braised or casseroled joints are delicious cooked in wine or a spicy gravy (see recipe). The breasts can be sautéed or deep fried, or wrapped in bacon and grilled. Try marinating them first (see recipe) to make them extra tender and flavourful.

Drumsticks are the classic ingredient for devilled turkey and are ideal for a picnic. But they can also be casseroled, or you can remove the bone and stuff the cavity with finely chopped chestnuts and mushrooms before roasting.

Left-over turkey

Left-over turkey need not be dull. Properly cooked in the first place, it should be as tender and succulent cold as it was hot, and is delicious in a salad with mayonnaise, celery and apple.

Turkey mousse (see recipe) is an elegant way of presenting leftovers. Or use cooked turkey as a filling for pancakes, topped with a white or cheese sauce and served with pasta, or make it into a pie.

Turkey and water chestnut soup

making and cooling stock, then 15 minutes

Serves 4

1 turkey carcass, with any left-over stuffing and
* gravy*
1 large onion
3 cloves
2 bay leaves
1 blade of mace
1 sprig of thyme
2-3 sprigs of parsley
juice and grated zest of 2 oranges
salt and freshly ground black pepper
pinch of freshly grated nutmeg
200 g /7 oz canned water chestnuts, drained
* and finely chopped*
15 ml /1 tbls finely snipped fresh chives, to
* garnish*

1 Put the turkey and any stuffing into a large saucepan and cover with cold water. Add the onion stuck with the cloves, the bay leaves, mace, thyme, parsley and orange zest. Bring to the boil over a high heat, then reduce the heat and simmer very gently for 3-4 hours.
2 Strain the stock into a large shallow bowl (this will speed up the cooling process) and leave to cool.
3 When the stock is cold, skim off any fat from the top and return to the rinsed-out pan. Boil over a high heat until the stock has reduced to about 1 L /2 pt.
4 If you have any left-over gravy, skim the fat off and add the gravy to the stock. Lower the heat and stir in the orange juice, salt, pepper and nutmeg. Add the water chestnuts and simmer for 5-10 minutes, pour into a warmed soup tureen, garnish with the chives and serve at once.

Turkey fricassee in coconut gravy

Coconut milk is often used in Oriental cookery. It makes a lovely, thick sauce and gives an Eastern touch to this unusual fricassee.

making coconut milk, then 1 hour 40 minutes

Turkey fricassee in coconut gravy

Serves 6

6 turkey joints, wings or drumsticks
salt and freshly ground black pepper
60 ml /4 tbls sesame oil
2 large onions, thinly sliced
2 garlic cloves, crushed
2 red chillies, seeded and chopped
20 ml /4 tsp coriander seeds, crushed
10 ml /2 tsp cumin seeds, crushed
grated zest of 1 lemon
5 ml /1 tsp ground ginger
575 ml /1 pt coconut milk (see below)
50-275 ml /2-10 fl oz turkey or chicken stock
15 ml /1 tbls finely chopped fennel fronds

1 Rub the turkey joints with salt and pepper. Heat the oil in a large saucepan over a moderate heat, add the sliced onions and sauté for 5-10 minutes, or until soft.
2 Add the turkey, garlic, chillies, coriander and cumin seeds, lemon zest and ginger. Cook for 4-5 minutes, stirring.
3 Pour in the coconut milk and 50 ml /2 fl oz stock. Bring to the boil, then reduce the heat and simmer, covered, for 40-50 minutes.
4 Uncover the pan and simmer for a further 20-30 minutes, adding more stock if needed. Check the seasoning and adjust if necessary. Put in a warmed serving dish, garnish with the fennel and serve.

● Coconut milk: soak 75 g/3 oz desiccated coconut in 600 ml/1 pt boiling water for 1 hour, then drain through muslin, discard coconut and use liquid.

and cook until it stops bubbling, about 2 minutes. Push the onions to the sides of the pan, add the remaining oil, then the turkey.

3 Turn it to brown on all sides, then add 60 ml /4 tbls stock. Stir well, bring to just under boiling point and then simmer gently, covered, for 30-40 minutes, until the turkey is tender and cooked through. Turn the roll frequently during cooking, adding more stock if the sauce seems to be drying up.

4 Lift the roll onto a warmed serving platter, slice thinly and keep warm. Add the yoghurt to the saucepan over a very low heat, stirring thoroughly to remove any lumps. Check the seasoning, pour the sauce over the turkey and serve at once.

Turkey patties in spicy basil sauce

 1 hour 20 minutes

Serves 4
350 g /12 oz cooked turkey meat, minced
3 medium-sized eggs
5 ml /1 tsp coriander seeds, crushed
2.5 ml /½ tsp blades of mace, crushed
salt and freshly ground black pepper
15 ml /1 tbls olive oil (optional)
fresh white breadcrumbs for coating
50 g /2 oz butter
For the sauce
30 ml /2 tbls olive oil
1 large onion, very finely chopped
1 garlic clove, finely chopped
1 small green chilli, seeded and chopped
400 g /14 oz canned tomatoes
45 ml /3 tbls freshly chopped basil
salt and freshly ground black pepper

1 In a large bowl, beat 2 of the eggs. Add the minced turkey and beat well. Add coriander seeds, mace and salt and pepper to taste and mix well. If the mixture seems too dry, add the olive oil.

2 Beat the remaining egg in a shallow bowl and place the breadcrumbs on a plate.

3 Form the turkey mixture into 8 patties about 5 cm /2 in in diameter and 6-12 mm /¼-½ in thick. Dip each patty in the egg and then into the breadcrumbs, making sure each is well coated. Place on a plate in the refrigerator to firm up while you make the sauce.

4 To make the sauce, heat the oil in a large saucepan over a low heat. Add the onion, garlic and chilli and cook gently for about 25 minutes, until the onions are very soft.

5 Purée the tomatoes and basil in a blender. Add to the saucepan and season with salt and pepper. Simmer gently for 10 minutes or until the sauce is thick.

6 Shortly before the sauce is done, melt the butter in a large frying-pan and add the patties, 4 at a time, so that they sit comfortably in one layer. Fry for 3-4 minutes each side, until crispy and golden. Remove with a slotted spoon and keep warm while you fry the remaining patties.

7 Place the turkey patties on a large warmed serving platter, pour the sauce over and serve at once.

Turkey mousse

This light and creamy mousse is perfect for lunch served with French bread or, served in individual ramekins with hot buttered toast, as a starter.

20 minutes
plus 4-5 hours setting

Serves 4-8
275 g /10 oz cooked turkey meat, minced
275 ml /10 fl oz thick Bechamel sauce
2 large eggs, separated
30 ml /2 tbls fresh dill, finely chopped
5 ml /1 tsp freshly grated nutmeg
2-3 dashes Tabasco sauce
salt and freshly ground black pepper
25 g /1 oz powdered gelatine
To serve
tomato and onion salad
1 crisp lettuce, finely shredded

1 Mix the minced turkey with the bechamel. Beat in the egg yolks, dill, nutmeg, Tabasco and salt and pepper to taste, remembering that once chilled the mousse will not seem so highly flavoured.

2 Sprinkle the gelatine over 45 ml /3 tbls cold water in a small bowl and set the bowl in a pan of barely simmering water until the gelatine dissolves.

3 Pour a little of the melted gelatine into an 850 ml /1½ pt ring mould and swirl round so that the mould is evenly coated. Put the mould into the refrigerator to chill while finishing the mixture.

4 Add the remaining gelatine to the turkey mixture, beating well. Whisk the egg whites until stiff, then fold gently but thoroughly

Turkey mousse

into the turkey mixture. Pour into the chilled mould and leave in the refrigerator for 4-5 hours to set.

5 When ready to serve, dip a tea-towel into very hot water, wring out and place over the mould for a few seconds. Place a plate over the mould and invert quickly, tapping the top of the mould if necessary to dislodge the mousse.

6 Pile the tomato and onion salad into the centre of the mousse, surround with the finely shredded lettuce and serve.

Turkey roll with paprika sauce

1 hour 15 minutes

Serves 4-6
1 rolled turkey breast, about 1 kg /2 lb 3 oz
120 ml /8 tbls olive oil
2 large onions, finely chopped
10 ml /2 tsp sugar
30 ml /2 tbls paprika
10 ml /2 tsp ground allspice
60 ml /4 tbls dry white wine
60-120 ml /4-8 tbls light stock
275 ml /10 fl oz yoghurt
salt and freshly ground black pepper

1 Heat 60 ml /4 tbls oil in a large saucepan over a low heat and add the onions and sugar. Sauté for 10 minutes or until the onions are soft and golden.

2 Add the paprika and allspice and cook for a further 2-3 minutes. Pour in the wine

Turkey escalopes marinated in sherry

 24 hours marinating, then 30 minutes

Serves 4
4 × 150-175 g /5-6 oz turkey escalopes
30 ml /2 tbls olive oil
15 ml /1 tbls thick cream
chopped fresh coriander leaves, to garnish

For the marinade
65 ml /2½ fl oz dry sherry
50 ml /2 fl oz olive oil
4 ml /¾ tsp fresh lime juice
2.5 ml /½ tsp cumin seeds, crushed
2.5 ml /½ tsp fenugreek seeds, crushed
1.5 ml /¼ tsp coriander seeds, crushed
2.5 ml /½ tsp clear honey
1 garlic clove, crushed
salt and freshly ground black pepper

1 Combine the marinade ingredients in a large bowl and add the escalopes. Leave in a cool place for 24 hours, turning several times.
2 Heat the olive oil in a large frying-pan over a low heat. When it is nearly smoking, remove the escalopes from the marinade (do not dry) and place in the pan in one layer.
3 Raise the heat to seal the escalopes on both sides. Then lower the heat to low and sauté gently for 10-12 minutes each side, until crisp on the outside and tender inside. Remove with a slotted spoon to a warmed serving platter and keep warm.
4 Add the remaining marinade to the pan and bring to the boil. Let it bubble for 1-2 minutes, stirring constantly, then lower the heat and add the cream. Stir well but do not allow the sauce to boil. Pour over the escalopes, garnish and serve at once.

● New potatoes garnished with fresh coriander leaves go well with this.

Roast turkey with smoked oyster stuffing

3½ hours

Serves 10-12
3.6 kg /8 lb turkey, dressed weight
1 lemon, cut in half
salt and freshly ground black pepper
8 thin slices of streaky bacon
125-175 g /4-6 oz butter
15 ml /1 tbls whisky
sprigs of watercress, to garnish
thin slices of lemon, to garnish

For the stuffing
75 g /3 oz butter
2 medium-sized onions, finely chopped
4 sticks celery, chopped
1 small green pepper, finely chopped
125 g /4 oz button mushrooms, thinly sliced
30 ml /2 tbls finely chopped parsley
125 g /4 oz fresh white breadcrumbs
2.5 ml /½ tsp dried marjoram
2.5 ml /½ tsp dried thyme
2.5 ml /½ tsp freshly grated nutmeg
salt and freshly ground black pepper
125 g /4 oz canned smoked oysters, chopped
15 ml /1 tbls whisky

1 First make the stuffing: melt the butter in a large frying-pan and cook the onions, celery, green pepper, mushrooms and parsley until soft, about 15 minutes.
2 Place the mixture in a large bowl and stir in the breadcrumbs. Add the marjoram, thyme, nutmeg and salt and pepper. Add the oysters, together with any liquid from the can, and the whisky and stir well.
3 Heat the oven to 220C /425F /gas 7.
4 Wipe the turkey inside and out with a damp cloth, dry, then pack the stuffing into the cavity. Truss the bird, then rub the skin all over with the lemon and season with salt and pepper. Lay the bacon slices over the breast and place in a roasting tin.
5 Melt 125 g /4 oz butter in a small saucepan. When it is bubbling, pour over the turkey. Cover the turkey loosely with foil and place in the oven. After 15 minutes turn the heat down to 170C /325F /gas 3 and cook for a further 2-2½ hours, basting every 15 minutes with the melted butter. Melt more butter for basting if necessary. Remove the bacon slices when the bird is almost cooked, to allow the breast to brown. When the juices run clear if the thickest part of the turkey is pierced with skewer, the turkey is done.
6 Place the turkey on a warmed serving platter, remove any strings, garnish with watercress and lemon slices and keep warm in the turned-off oven while you make the gravy.
7 Skim the fat from the cooking juices and add 30-45 ml /2-3 tbls water to the roasting tin. Bring to the boil, add the whisky and boil for 2 minutes. Pour into a warmed sauce-boat and serve with the turkey.

Turkey escalopes marinated in sherry

Venison, hare and rabbit

Venison, hare and rabbit are the prize game animals. With their sweet, gamey flavours, they can be cooked in many ways to provide a variety of delicious dishes, from succulent roasts and rich casseroles to hearty pies.

Venison, hare and rabbit, collectively called 'furred game', were once a common sight on medieval dining tables. Now, with most of the royal forests gone, and land-hungry farmers and urban planners at their heels, these animals are much rarer. Rabbit suffered the additional hazard in the 1950s of the fatal disease myxomatosis. But venison is increasingly being raised commercially and wild rabbit is again safe to eat, so we can once more enjoy the dishes that were such a feature of banquets in olden days.

Rabbits are now widely bred for the table and these animals are less gamey in taste.

Venison
The term venison used to cover any wild animal hunted for food but now applies only to deer: antelope, elk, reindeer, roe, fallow and red deer. The male, or buck, is better for eating than the female, but neither should be more than three years old, the prime animals being between 18 months and two years old.

The meat should be dark and firm, the fat a clear, creamy white. Even when very high it should have only a gamey, meaty smell with no trace of ammonia. Venison is by nature dry and tough, but these problems are easily overcome – the first by larding or barding the meat, the second by hanging and marinating it.

Venison should be well hung. The exact length of time depends on how high you like it, but 12–21 days is average. As it is very rich, a portion of 175 g /6 oz boneless meat (225 g /8 oz on the bone) should be adequate.

The seasons for shooting male and female venison, as well as the different species, vary, but some venison, either fresh or frozen, is available all year round.

Buying and storing: unless your local retailer specializes in game, you will probably have to order venison. Specify whether you like it well hung or not. Some retailers, however, stock stewing venison which is already chopped.

Store venison in the refrigerator in a marinade. It can be kept for up to three days, provided it is completely submerged in the liquid.

❋❋❋❋   When you order venison you may have to take a whole haunch or shoulder. It should be fully hung before freezing. If the meat is already frozen, ask the butcher to cut the part you want for immediate use and keep the remainder frozen. You can then store this in your own freezer for up to six months (depending on its initial date of freezing). Fresh venison should be cut into small joints, steaks or chops, wrapped individually in cling film, then put into

---

Baked rabbit in lemon sauce

polythene bags and frozen. Stewing venison can be chopped and frozen in a marinade – just put the meat and marinade in a large freezer bag, expel all air and seal. Defrost in the bag for 36 hours, turning regularly.

Hare
Hare and rabbit look similar but they are different species, the hare being bigger, with longer ears and hind legs. Young hares can be recognized by their short necks, long joints and thin saddle. The ears are soft and tear easily, while an older hare has a clearly defined cleft in the lip. The meat is a dark reddish brown – the darker it is, the longer the hare has hung.

A leveret is a hare less than one year old. It has a small, bony knob near the foot which disappears as the animal grows older. The dressed weight of a leveret is 450–700 g /1–1½ lb, that of a young hare 1.1–1.4 kg /2½–3 lb, and that of an older hare up to 2 kg /4½ lb. An older hare will feed six people, a young hare four, but a leveret only two. Hare is in season from late summer to early spring, but at its best in early winter.

Hare should hang by its hind legs, unskinned and in a cool place, for four or five days. A bowl is placed under the head to collect the blood. Your butcher will skin and paunch the hare (removing the entrails) for you after hanging.

Buying and storing: unless your local retailer specializes in game, you will probably have to order hare. Specify whether you want a young or older animal and whether you want it hung. If you want the blood of the hare, ask for the hare to be hung and the blood collected and kept for you, together with the heart, liver and kidneys.

After hanging the meat may be kept in a marinade for up to three days, provided it is completely submerged. The liver, kidneys and heart must be submerged as well. Add 5 ml /1 tsp vinegar to the blood and refrigerate, covered.

❋❋❋❋   If you are buying a hare for freezing, ask for it to be fully hung and discard blood and entrails. If you are hanging it yourself, collect the blood after the first day, add 2.5 ml /½ tsp vinegar and freeze immediately. After fully hanging, do not freeze the remaining blood or offal.

After skinning, wash the hare joints and pat dry. Wrap well and freeze for up to six months. Frozen hare should be casseroled rather than roasted.

Rabbit
Rabbit is widely available as 'hutch' or tame rabbit. More delicate in taste than wild rabbit, it is easily distinguished by its uniformly pale flesh. The flesh of the wild rabbit is much darker, especially at the joints.

A wild rabbit should always be eaten when young, but a tame rabbit will be tender even when old. If a wild rabbit's kidneys are buried in fat, the animal is sure to be tender; if the fat is a golden yellow, it will be particularly tasty.

Rabbits are not normally hung but drawn immediately on killing and should be eaten within three to four days. Rabbit is available all year round, both fresh and frozen.

The weight of both wild and hutch rabbit, dressed, is 700 g–1.1 kg /1½–2½ lb when young, up to 1.6 kg /3½ lb if older. One rabbit will feed four; one front leg and half a saddle make up one portion.

Buying and storing: you will probably have to order wild rabbit, which should always be young. You can tell if it is young by the ears, which tear easily. The butcher will skin and paunch it for you. Age is not important when buying a tame rabbit, unless you want to sauté it. In that case, look for small, plump legs and a small saddle.

Most butchers now sell frozen tame rabbit, much of which comes from China. Many supermarkets also sell blocks of frozen, boneless rabbit; this is best used for casseroles or pies.

Tame rabbit should be cooked within 24 hours of purchase. Wild rabbit can be kept in a marinade for up to three days, as long as the meat is completely covered by the marinade.

✳✳✳✳ Rabbits should be skinned and paunched immediately for freezing. Joint if wished and wrap. They will keep for six months, but should be casseroled, not roasted.

Preparing and cooking

If you have been given some furred game most butchers will, for a fee, hang, skin and paunch it for you.

Marinating: venison and hare should always be marinated for 24–48 hours to tenderize and flavour it. The marinade should contain wine, some port or brandy, an onion, herbs and spices and a little olive oil. Sometimes wine vinegar mixed with water replaces the oil. Exact quantities vary considerably (see recipes) and other spirits may be substituted for the wine; in Spain sherry is used, in Normandy cider and a little calvados are popular. The meat should be turned regularly to soak it thoroughly in the marinade which can be used later to make the sauce or gravy.

Larding: after marinating you can, if you wish, lard a venison joint or hare before roasting. This entails threading small pieces of fat pork all over the meat about 15 mm /½ in deep. However, provided that you cook the roast with plenty of fat and baste it constantly, larding is not necessary.

Venison: the haunch of venison is the best part to roast, the fillet being used for steaks and the loin for chops or cutlets. These should first be pounded with a mallet, then brushed with melted butter and grilled. All roasts, steaks and chops should be served rare rather than well done. The shoulder is used for stews, game pies or pasties, galantines and pâtés, as well as potted venison.

In Germany, venison is often marinated in buttermilk which is then added during the roasting, with some cranberry jelly put in at the end, and traditionally served with dumplings and red cabbage. Italians like to add cherries and whole coriander seeds to braised venison. Soured cream is often used in Scandinavian and Balkan kitchens and is also delicious with hare (see recipe).

Hare: the most important task in the preparation of hare is the removal of the bluish, thin membrane which holds the joints together. Use a thin-bladed knife for this job.

Only young hares should be roasted and they are best too for jugged hare, but older animals are ideal for brawns, pâtés and pies. The blood, with a few drops of vinegar added to prevent coagulation, is often used to enrich the sauce.

A delicious Italian recipe for hare uses the juice of six lemons as a marinade, in which the hare is then cooked, with the addition of olive oil, some red wine, oregano and 12 garlic cloves – the result is spectacular.

Rabbit: wild rabbit, stronger and gamier than its tame cousin, is best used for casseroles with rich sauces and in gamey pies (see recipe). It is better for having been marinated 2–3 hours or overnight before cooking. Tame rabbit is excellent with delicate sauces: in France it is cooked with prunes, red wine and cognac. Very young tame rabbit can be sautéed in butter with a little cream and brandy added to the pan juices just before serving. Potted rabbit is best made with the wild animal but delicious rillettes can be made from tame rabbit if you wish to preserve it.

Stocks and soups can be made from venison bones or the crushed carcass of a hare or rabbit. Simmer in lightly salted water with onion, celery and a bouquet garni until rich in flavour. For a soup, add any left-over meat and gravy, a drop of port or brandy (lemon juice for rabbit) and season well.

Roast venison with cranberry tartlets

🕐 🍴🍴 24–48 hours marinating, then 2 hours 35 minutes

Serves 6–8

1.5–2 kg /3½–4½ lb well-hung haunch of venison
125 g /4 oz butter, more if necessary
15 ml /1 tbls cranberry jelly
10 ml /2 tsp Dijon mustard
For the marinade
575 ml /1 pt dry red wine
75 ml /3 fl oz brandy
30 ml /2 tbls olive oil
1 large onion, thinly sliced
2 bay leaves
4 large sprigs thyme
4 large sprigs lavender leaves (optional)
large pinch of freshly grated nutmeg
1 garlic clove, crushed
6 black peppercorns, crushed
pinch of salt
For the tartlets
225 g /8 oz flour
pinch of salt
150 g /5 oz butter
flour for dusting
180 ml /12 tbls cranberry jelly

1 Combine all the marinade ingredients and pour over the venison. Leave in a cool place for 24–48 hours, turning the joint frequently.

2 Heat the oven to 220C /425F /gas 7. Make the pastry. Sift the flour with the salt, then rub in 125 g /4 oz butter with your fingertips until the mixture resembles fine breadcrumbs. Add 50–75 ml /2–3 fl oz iced water very gradually, until the dough is fairly soft but not sticky.

3 Flour a board and roll the dough out thinly. Using a 6.5 cm /2½ in diameter cutter, cut out 12 circles. Grease 12 tartlet tins with the remaining butter, insert the pastry circles, line with foil and beans and bake for 4–5 minutes. Remove the foil and beans and continue baking for 4–8 minutes, until cooked and golden. Remove from the oven.

4 Lower the heat to 180C /350F /gas 4. Melt the butter in a roasting tin. Remove the venison from the marinade, reserving the marinade. Place the joint in the tin and baste well with the butter. Cook for 1–1½ hours, depending on the size of the joint and how rare you like your meat. Baste frequently, using more butter if necessary.

5 When cooked, place the venison on a warm serving platter. Lower the oven heat to 150C /300F /gas 2 to keep the venison warm while you make the gravy. Put the tartlet shells into the oven to warm.

6 Strain the reserved marinade into the roasting tin and boil for 2–3 minutes on a high heat. When slightly reduced, lower the heat and add 15 ml /1 tbls cranberry jelly and the mustard. Stir until they dissolve and pour into a warmed sauceboat.

7 Remove the tarts from the oven and put 15 ml /1 tbls cranberry jelly into each one. Arrange around the joint and serve with the gravy handed round separately.

/300F /gas 2, cover the platter with foil and return to the oven to keep warm.

7 Add the strained marinade to the juices in the roasting tin and reduce slightly on a medium heat, stirring constantly. Reduce the heat to low, add the remaining soured cream and stir for another 2 minutes. If using, add the blood and mix in well. Remove from the heat and pour into a warmed sauceboat.

8 Take the hare from the oven, remove the foil, pour a little gravy over each joint, garnish with the flat-leaved parsley and serve at once, with the rest of the gravy and the redcurrant jelly handed separately.

Baked rabbit in lemon sauce

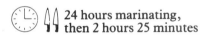 1 hour 10 minutes

Serves 4
900 g /2 lb rabbit, jointed
salt and freshly ground black pepper
15 ml /1 tbls olive oil
15 ml /1 tbls lemon juice
75 g /3 oz softened butter
5 ml /1 tsp dried tarragon
2.5 ml /½ tsp dried oregano
lemon slices and watercress, to garnish
For the sauce
50 g /2 oz butter
15 ml /1 tbls flour
125 ml /4 fl oz chicken or other light stock
25 ml /1 fl oz dry white wine
15 ml /1 tbls lemon juice
150 ml /5 fl oz thick cream

1 Heat the oven to 190C /375F /gas 5. Season rabbit joints. Place them in a roasting tin.
2 Mix the olive oil with the lemon juice and pour over the rabbit. Mix together the softened butter, tarragon and oregano. Spread this paste evenly over the rabbit joints, place 2 lemon slices on each joint and bake for 30–40 minutes or until the rabbit is done, basting from time to time.
3 Meanwhile, make the sauce. Melt the butter in a small saucepan and stir in the flour. Add the stock and wine gradually, stirring constantly. Add the lemon juice and bring to a simmer. Simmer for 4 minutes, stirring, then add the cream and blend.
4 Remove the rabbit from the oven and arrange on a warmed serving platter, garnishing with the lemon slices. Keep warm. Pour any juices from the roasting tin into the sauce and stir thoroughly. Pour over the rabbit and serve immediately.

● You can vary this recipe slightly by coating the rabbit with a tarragon mustard, instead of the herb butter. Use 10–15 ml/2–3 tsp finely chopped fresh tarragon or 5 ml/1 tsp dried tarragon (infused for a few minutes with 1 tbls boiling water). Mix the fresh or infused tarragon with 1 tbls Dijon mustard and spread this on each joint before baking. Omit the lemon juice from this version of the recipe.

Roast hare with soured cream

Roast hare is considered by many to be even finer than venison.

⏰ 🍴🍴 24 hours marinating, then 2 hours 25 minutes

Serves 4
1 young hare, with liver, heart and kidneys, blood optional
few drops of white wine vinegar (optional)
4 large rashers fat bacon
75–100 g /3–4 oz butter, melted
25 g /1 oz flour
150 ml /5 fl oz soured cream
flat-leaved parsley, to garnish
redcurrant jelly, to serve
For the marinade
600 ml /1 pt dry white wine
50 ml /2 fl oz olive oil
25 ml /1 fl oz white wine vinegar
15 ml /1 tbls dried oregano
2 large sprigs thyme
salt and freshly ground black pepper
For the stuffing
225 g /8 oz canned chestnuts, drained and chopped
15 ml /1 tbls freshly chopped parsley
10 ml /2 tsp dried oregano
10 ml /2 tsp dried thyme
100 g /4 oz sausage-meat
50 g /2 oz fresh white breadcrumbs
salt and freshly ground black pepper
1 medium-sized egg

Roast hare with soured cream

1 If you wish to use the blood in the gravy, add a few drops of vinegar to prevent coagulation, and place the liver, heart and kidneys in the blood, cover and refrigerate. If you are not using the blood, keep the liver, heart and kidneys loosely covered in the coolest part of the refrigerator.
2 Place the hare in a large bowl and cover with the marinade ingredients. Leave in a cool place for 24 hours, turning occasionally.
3 Heat the oven to 190C /375F /gas 5. Remove any membranes and greenish-yellow spots from the liver. Wash the liver, heart and kidneys thoroughly, chop them finely and combine with all the stuffing ingredients except the egg. Mix thoroughly, then add the egg and stir well.
4 Remove the hare from the marinade, pat dry and put the stuffing into the 2 cavities under the front and back legs. Lay the bacon rashers over the hare and tie or skewer firmly. Place the hare in a roasting tin, baste well with melted butter and cover with foil. Cook for 1½ hours, basting every 15 minutes.
5 Remove the foil, dredge the hare with the flour, baste with 30 ml /2 tbls soured cream and return to the oven for 15 minutes to brown.
6 Remove the hare from the oven. Take out the stuffing and pile in the centre of a large, warm serving platter. Joint the hare with a stout-bladed knife and arrange around the stuffing with a bacon rasher on each joint. Lower the oven heat to 150C

Wild rabbit pie

This delicious pie is equally good for a picnic or as a supper dish. It can be made with tame rabbit but will not taste as gamey.

 ⏱ 🥄🥄🥄 3 hours 40 minutes, plus cooling and chilling

Serves 4–6
1 wild rabbit, jointed
1 L /2 pt strong beef stock
15 ml /1 tbls gelatine (if using stock cubes rather than home-made stock)
225 g /8 oz button mushrooms, thinly sliced
50 g /2 oz butter
5 ml /1 tsp freshly grated nutmeg
2.5 ml /¹/₂ tsp dried sage
5 ml /1 tsp dried marjoram
salt and freshly ground black pepper
225 g /8 oz smoked ham, in julienne strips
3 medium-sized eggs, hard boiled and sliced
30 ml /2 tbls port or brandy
flat-leaved parsley, to garnish (optional)
raw onion rings, to garnish (optional)

For the pastry
225 g /8 oz flour
pinch of salt
150 g /5 oz butter
flour for dusting
milk
1 medium-sized egg yolk, beaten

1 Put the rabbit and the stock in a large saucepan and bring to boiling point over high heat. Turn the heat to low and simmer gently for about 1 hour, or until the rabbit is tender.

2 Meanwhile, make the pastry. Sift together the flour and salt and rub in 125 g/ 4 oz butter with your fingertips until the mixture resembles fine breadcrumbs. Gradually add 50–75 ml /2–3 fl oz iced water, until the dough is soft but not wet.

3 Flour a board and roll out the pastry fairly thinly. Cut off one-third and reserve for the lid and trimmings. Roll out the remainder large enough to line a 1.7 L /3 pt rectangular dish or small roasting tin. Cut off one-third of the reserved pastry for trimmings and roll out the remainder into an oblong for the lid. Roll out the remaining pastry thinly and cut out 6 leaves, rolling what is left into a long, thin piece between the palms of your hands. Cut in half and twist the 2 pieces together, pinching at the ends to join them.

4 Grease the loaf tin with the remaining butter and line with the large piece of pastry.

5 Remove the rabbit from the stock with a slotted spoon and leave to cool. Meanwhile boil the stock hard until it has reduced to about 275 ml /10 fl oz, and keep warm. If using stock made from cubes rather than home-made, dissolve the gelatine in 30 ml /2 tbls water and add to the stock.

6 Sauté the sliced mushrooms in the butter until they begin to give off their juices, then drain and reserve.

7 When the rabbit is cool, remove all the flesh from the bones and divide into 2

Wild rabbit pie

portions. Finely chop one half and put the other half through the mincer.

8 Heat the oven to 200C /400F /gas 6. In a bowl, mix the minced rabbit with the nutmeg, sage and marjoram. Put half the chopped rabbit in the bottom of the lined loaf tin and season with salt and pepper. Cover with half the mushrooms, then add a layer of half the minced rabbit and season.

9 Add the ham in one layer, then the slices of hard-boiled egg. Cover with the remaining minced rabbit, then the rest of the mushrooms, finishing with a layer of chopped rabbit. Add the port or brandy to the stock and pour enough over the rabbit to just cover the top layer of meat. Reserve the remainder, keeping it in a warm place so it does not set.

10 Brush the outer edges of the pastry lining the tin with milk and put on the lid, pressing firmly. Make 3 slits in the lid. Place the pastry twist around the edge of the lid, and the leaves around the slits, brushing the pastry with milk to fasten. Brush all over with beaten egg yolk and bake for 20 minutes.

11 Lower the heat to 150C /300F /gas 2 and bake for a further 30 minutes, covering the pie with foil if it is browning too much. Remove from the oven and cool.

12 When it is cool, pour in more stock through the slits in the lid until the pie is full. Refrigerate overnight and serve well chilled, garnished with flat-leaved parsley and raw onion rings, if wished.

Cooked and dried sausages

Salami, peperoni, frankfurter, *Bratwurst*, blood pudding – these are just a few of the bewildering variety of cooked and dried sausages available. Learn about all the different kinds, and how to prepare and use them.

Most delicatessens stock a wide variety of sausages, but they are almost all just variations on one basic product – meat – and are easy to use, given a few simple facts.

Although they vary so much in looks and flavour, treated sausages can be divided into two main categories: sausages that have been prepared by cooking, and those prepared by drying.

The meat may be puréed, minced or quite coarsely chopped, and may have solid chunks of lean meat or white fat in it, as well as spices, nuts or vegetables. It may come from any animal, although pork is included in most sausages and is often the only meat used. Most European cooked and dried sausages, apart from their flavourings, contain just meat and fat. Nearly all British sausages, on the other hand, contain preservatives and cereals.

Most sausages have a covering or casing of some sort. Traditionally, this is some membraneous part of an animal's 'innards' – usually sections of intestine. Today, most commercially prepared sausages are put into edible synthetic casings of cellulose.

There are two sorts of cooked sausage. The first is made from fresh or very lightly salted raw meat and is fully cooked, usually by steam heating. The second is generally lightly salted and/or smoked, and is then partly or fully cooked by scalding in boiling liquid. Some sausages of both sorts can be skinned, sliced and served just as they are. However, others are improved by reheating, and some need to be fully recooked.

Certain types of raw sausage may simply be salted and dried in the air, or may be either lightly or heavily smoked to dry and preserve them. They are classified as semi-dried if they have lost less than 20% of their moisture, or fully dried if over 20% of the moisture has been removed.

Steamed fresh meat sausages

Fresh meat sausages are made of very finely minced meat or offal. One distinct group is the various liver sausages, which are usually greyish, soft, smooth pastes. They are ready to use: peel off any coating of white fat first.

Names to look for include *saucisson au foie de porc* and *Leberwurst*.

Even more distinctive are the black puddings, or *boudins noirs*, containing blood, often with cubes of solid fat embedded in the firm smooth paste. Most really are black or very dark, so are easy to identify. They are usually smooth skinned, although some, including *morcilla* from Spain, may be slightly wrinkled. All the blood sausages

A selection of sausages usually cooked before serving. Hanging, from the left: Cotechino, Chorizos, Frankfurters, Zampone, Kabanos, Mettwurst. Below: 1 Lap cheong, 2 Bockwürste, 3 Boudins noirs, 4 Cervelas, 5 Knackwürste, 6 Morcillas, 7 Andouillettes, 8 Lo chou cheong

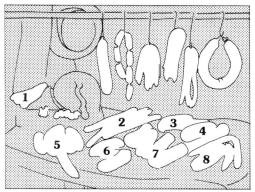

must be recooked before use: place in boiling water and cook pieces for 15 minutes, small boiling rings for 25–30 minutes, large rings for up to 50 minutes.

A third group of steamed sausages consists of the bland Italian *mortadella* and Bologna sausages. They are among the largest of the sausages, traditionally encased in a beef or pig's bladder. The best *mortadella* sausages are made of pure pork; others are made of mixed meats. They are sometimes flavoured with peppercorns or pistachios, and have a spongy, rather rubbery texture. Bologna sausages are a mild mixture of beef and pork. Both are usually served cold.

The stubby little German *Teewurst* is a soft, smooth, spreadable paste of minced pork and beef, usually bright salmon-pink in a tan jacket. It is smoked and often highly spiced.

Most of the various French *andouilles* and *andouillettes*, which consist mainly of tripe or similar offal, are boiled, white, log-shaped sausages. They are best eaten hot: slash their tops, grill and serve with mustard sauce. The odd Italian *zampone* is a pork sausage stuffed into a boned pig's trotter instead of a casing, and boiled and served hot.

Scalded sausages

Some scalded sausages are ready to serve; others need recooking. The first kind are often sold thinly sliced in vacuum packs, and they may contain jelly or large solid pieces of meat, mushrooms or other solid food. German veal sausage with pieces of ham (*Schinken Kalbfleischwurst*) and ham sausage with aspic and pistachio nuts (*Bauernsülze*) are ready-to-serve sausages.

The most famous lightly smoked sausage for reheating is the frankfurter. Like almost all sausages of its type, it is a finely minced, almost spongy paste. You can buy 'franks' from a chilled cabinet or in cans; most are 'hot dog' size but tiny cocktail ones are also available. They come in various colours as well as sizes, because each manufacturer tints his franks to suit the taste of his local purchasers. Wieners, Viennas or *Wienerwürste* are often confused with franks, but they were originally different sausages. Kosher franks are red and made wholly of beef, with garlic sometimes added. Cook medium-sized franks in simmering water, stock or a mixture of water and wine for 15–20 minutes. (Big franks take longer; cocktail franks take less time.) Serve them in buns, in dishes containing sauerkraut, or sliced in salads. They can also be barbecued.

You are likely to see several other kinds of lightly smoked sausage for reheating. *Bratwursts* are pale and vary in texture; they can be boiled, baked or fried. *Extrawurst* is a dull, spongy sausage, occasionally fried in slices, although it is usually served as it is. *Bockwurst* is extra long and, like its cousin the dumpy *Knackwurst*, has a closely knit, slightly spongy pink inside like a frank. Both should be steamed or poached thoroughly to reheat them, whether they are fried or grilled afterwards or not; so should other, similar, light spongy sausages.

Italian *cotechino* is a large, mottled sausage which should be boiled whole for 2 hours. It can then be cooled and fried, if wished. Polish *Kielbasa*, a garlicky, fairly coarse sausage, should be boiled for 1–2 hours, cut up and fried or casseroled.

Some lightly smoked sausages, shaped into boiling rings, are boiled whole, then cut up for serving. Others are straight, but also meant for boiling. One is the Alsatian *saucisse de Strasbourg*, which is very similar to a frankfurter. Another is the lightly smoked *cervelas* or *cervelat*, which the British call a saveloy. Once made of pigs' brains, it is now made of minced pork, beef and bacon fat. In France it is served hot, with hot potato salad, but it can also be cooled after boiling and served thinly sliced. Other finely minced sausages can also be served hot or cold. The red-skinned Hungarian and smoked pork sausages made in Britain in the shape of boiling rings are two.

Dried sausages for cooking

A few sausages are only lightly dried and strongly spiced. They are designed for recooking and include the Spanish and Mexican *chorizo* and Polish *kabanos*. Usually lightly dried sausages are blanched then added in chunks to pulses, pasta, meat or vegetable stews. The French *saucisse de Toulouse*, a very heavily dried sausage, Dutch *Rookwurst* and Spanish *butifara*, as well as some of the French *saucissons secs* (a general term meaning dried sausages) are used in the same way.

Lap cheong and *lo chou cheong* are mottled, red and white Chinese pork sausages, which should be boiled or steamed.

Dried sausages should be blanched before frying or grilling. Put whole small sausages or pieces into boiling water. Reduce the heat so that the water simmers, then cook for 4–5 minutes, depending on size. Drain and pat dry on absorbent paper.

Dried sausages for slicing

There are literally hundreds of types, because not only every sausage-making country but most regions, and even many towns, especially in Italy and France, make their own version of each well-known type. Each manufacturer claims fiercely that his is the original and the best. It would be quite impossible to learn all the individual names, so your wisest course is just to remember the names of the main types, and a few renowned versions, and to experiment by tasting others if you come across them.

By far the best known of all these sausages are the dozens of salamis. Italian ones vary from mild to strongly spiced, and come in a range of sizes. They are air-dried and/or smoked, made of coarsely minced pork, often combined with other meats. The Bolognese and Genovese versions are considered the best ones by many connoisseurs. German salamis also vary. They are

usually made of beef and pork and may have white jackets. Danish salamis are bright red and usually sold in vacuum packs. There is a Corsican salami called *coppa* which is smoked over a chestnut fire. Many other countries make their own versions of salami, including Hungary, Poland, Switzerland and Spain.

Another big group of sausages is the dried *cervelats*; most countries produce a mild, dried, stumpy, long-lasting cervelat as well as the boiling version. It is a good choice for anyone who does not care for the spicier flavour of salami. Poloneys, made all over Europe, contain cereal and often herbs, and are brightly dyed after being smoked.

German sausages which you may come across are the *Braunschweigerwurst* or Brunswick sausage (there is also a boiling version of this), *Bierschinken, Bierwurst, Mettwurst* (which is rather messy to eat raw but is delicious fried or sliced and used to top

Ready-to-eat sausages. Top row, from the left: Schinkensulzwurst; Bierschinken, Mortadella, Leberwurst

pizzas), *Jagdwurst, Kalbsleberwurst, Plockwurst, Katenrauchwurst, Schinkenwurst* and *Schinkenplockwurst* (both of which tend to fall apart when sliced unless they are chilled first) and *Zungenwurst*. Good sausages from other countries include *rosette* (France), *boutefa* (Switzerland), *salchichón* (Spain), *gyulai* and *czaba* (Hungary), but there are dozens of others.

Buying and storing sausages

Sausages for eating cold are widely available, but if you want a sausage for cooking or an unusual one for eating raw, you will have to search harder. You may find what you are looking for in an ethnic grocery. And although they differ markedly in flavour and pungency, sausages meant for cooking are, to a large extent, interchangeable. If you cannot get the one you want, you will almost always be able to find one reasonably like it which will do instead; just make sure that you substitute a garlic sausage only if your recipe specifies a garlicky one.

It is often difficult, when faced with a variety of unlabelled sausages, to know whether they are to be eaten cold or cooked first. Pre-sliced, vacuum-packed sausages and those set in jelly or with large, solid pieces of meat or other solid food embedded in them are ready to eat. So, almost all the time, are those with a coating of fat surrounding them. A sausage with a shape and consistency similar to that of a frankfurter is usually meant to be served hot. The safest thing is to ask!

Assessing quality: the quality of pre-packaged sliced sausage is easy to assess through the plastic: reject any which looks wet or gummy. Whole sausages should fill their casings smoothly and there should be no signs of seepage. Cut surfaces should be slightly glossy and evenly coloured. Never buy 'weeping' or mouldy sausages.

Storing: liver sausages, blood sausages and other fresh meat sausages and boiling rings, as well as lightly smoked scalded sausages, must be refrigerated and used within three days. Semi-dried sausages must also be refrigerated, but they should keep well for three weeks or more. It is best to refrigerate fully dried sausages as well, but they will keep for a month or longer. Cover cut ends of sausage smoothly with cling film, then wrap the sausage closely in plastic wrapping or foil.

✳✳✳ Mild sausages and made dishes containing them can be frozen, closely wrapped, for up to three months. Garlicky and strongly spiced sausages may develop 'off' flavours after three or four weeks.

Serving sausages

Except for soft spreadables such as liver sausage, sausages for eating raw are served thinly sliced. To slice a sausage, first remove any transparent outer covering on a jacketed sausage, but not the jacket itself or any other casing. Cut into slices on the diagonal, then remove the thin ring of casing or fat surrounding each slice.

Serve sliced sausages as part of a cold platter or in sandwiches. Mix chopped or thinly sliced sausage with vegetables, pulses, pasta or hard-boiled eggs and bind with a dressing to make a salad. Combine liver sausage with soft cheese to make a quick pâté.

Sausages can be served hot in even more ways: garlic sausage is used to spice up Dutch lentil soup, Madrid stew has both chorizo and morcilla added, and in Germany Bratwurst is baked in a brioche-type pastry (see recipe). In south-western France, the famous bean and meat stew called cassoulet traditionally gets its character from a saucisse de Toulouse, but chorizo does very well too.

Plainly cooked sausages go well with potatoes or scrambled or fried eggs, and, of course, can be eaten on their own with or without a variety of mustards.

Sausage and leek hot-pot

🍴🍴 1 hour 15 minutes

Serves 4
900 g /2 lb leeks, trimmed and thickly sliced
3 large potatoes, thickly sliced
425 ml/15 fl oz chicken stock
75 ml /5 tbls medium dry white wine
225 g /8 oz saucisson vaudois or Bierwurst,
   in one piece
225 g /8 oz rindless smoked middle bacon slices
15 ml /1 tbls flour
15 ml /1 tbls milk
pinch of freshly grated nutmeg
pinch of dried thyme
pinch of dried basil
salt and freshly ground black pepper

1 Place the leeks and potatoes in a flameproof oven-to-table casserole with 250 ml /9 fl oz of the stock. Add the wine. Place over low heat, cover and cook gently for 40 minutes, or until the potatoes are tender but not broken.

2 Meanwhile, cut the unskinned sausage into 15 mm /½ in slices. Cut any large slices in half across. Put the sausage and the bacon in a second pan with the remaining stock, cover and poach over very gentle heat for 10 minutes.

3 Cream the flour with the milk and stir it into the casserole. Add the nutmeg and herbs and season lightly with salt and pepper. Stir lightly to mix.

4 Drain the bacon and sausage. Skin the sausage. Arrange the bacon in a flat layer on top of the vegetables, then place the sausage slices in a line on top. Cover the casserole, reduce the heat and simmer very gently for 15 minutes. Serve hot from the dish.

Bratwurst in pastry

🍴 1 hour 30 minutes,
plus 1 hour proving

Serves 6
5 ml /1 tsp dried yeast
5 ml /1 tsp sugar
pinch of salt
60 ml /4 tbls warm milk
350 g /12 oz flour
1 medium-sized egg, beaten
50 g /2 oz butter, melted and cooled
*450 g /1 lb Bratwurst (or saveloys or white
pudding)*
flour for rolling out
butter for greasing
*milk for dough (if necessary) and for brushing
pastry*

Sausage and leek hot-pot

1   Put the yeast, sugar, salt and warm milk in a warmed jug and leave for 10–15 minutes, until frothy.
2   Place the yeast mixture, flour, egg and butter in a food processor and process to a smooth dough, adding a little extra milk if needed. Alternatively, work all the ingredients together in a bowl, then knead well for 5 minutes.
3   Put the dough into a bowl and leave it in a warm place for 45–60 minutes, until well risen. Meanwhile, skin the sausages.
4   Heat the oven to 190C /375F /gas 5. Roll out the dough on a floured surface into a rectangle about 35 × 30 cm /14 × 12 in; it should be about 5 mm /¼ in thick. Pile the sausages in the centre. Fold the dough over the sausages to make a parcel. Place it on a well-buttered baking sheet with the cut edges underneath, and brush with milk.
5   Bake for about 50 minutes, until golden brown. Serve sliced, hot or cold.

Salami and bean soup

This satisfying Italian soup, *minestra di fagioli,* is traditionally made with smoked turkey or goose breast, but you can use cooked meat and smoked salami instead.

🍴 55 minutes

Serves 6–8
50 g /2 oz butter
50 ml /2 fl oz oil
1 medium-sized onion, finely chopped
4 garlic cloves, crushed
*75 g /3 oz cooked goose meat (smoked if
available), coarsely chopped*
*75 g /3 oz Italian salame di oca (goose salami)
or mild Danish or German salami, coarsely
chopped*
*400 g /14 oz canned tomatoes, drained and
sieved*
2.5 ml /½ tsp chilli powder
200 g /7 oz elbow macaroni
salt
2.5 ml /½ tsp powdered rosemary
2 chicken stock cubes, crumbled
425 g /15 oz canned cannellini beans, drained
freshly chopped parsley, to serve

1   Heat the butter and oil in a large saucepan. Add the onion, garlic, goose meat and salami, and fry until golden, stirring frequently.
2   Add the tomatoes, chilli powder and 50 ml /2 fl oz water. Stir once, reduce the heat, cover and simmer for 20–25 minutes, stirring occasionally, until it is fairly thick.
3   Meanwhile, cook the macaroni in fast-boiling salted water until it is almost tender. Drain.
4   Add the rosemary, a pinch of salt, the crumbled stock cubes and 1.5 L /2½ pt water to the soup. Stir well, bring to the boil, then boil gently for 10 minutes.
5   Add the drained beans and macaroni, reduce the heat and simmer for 5–6 minutes to heat the beans through. Serve sprinkled with the chopped parsley.

Mexican-style sausage pie

If you make this in a spring-release tin and remove the sides for serving, it will look like a savoury many-layered gateau.

🍴 2 hours

Serves 4–6
3 × 100 g /4 oz chorizos
*175 g /6 oz Philadelphia full-fat soft cheese,
at room temperature*
butter for frying and greasing
75 g /3 oz Cheddar cheese, grated
*3 medium-sized eggs, hard boiled and
chopped*
For the sauce
45 ml /3 tbls corn oil
1 medium-sized onion, finely chopped
*400 g /14 oz canned tomatoes, sieved
with their juice*
3–4 drops Tabasco sauce
5 ml /1 tsp dried basil or oregano
2 bay leaves
salt and freshly ground black pepper
For the pancakes
100 ml /3½ fl oz milk and water mixed
1 medium-sized egg
1.5 ml /¼ tsp salt
40 g /1½ oz flour
15 g /½ oz cornmeal
15 ml /1 tbls butter, melted

1   First make the sauce: heat the oil in a saucepan, add the onion and fry until it is soft but not browned. Add the sieved tomatoes and the remaining ingredients. Stir well, partly cover the pan, reduce the heat and simmer for 30 minutes. Cool to tepid, then remove the bay leaves.
2   Meanwhile, put all the pancake ingredients into a food processor or blender and blend to make a thin batter.
3   Grease a frying-pan with butter then use the batter to make six 15 cm /6 in pancakes, not too thin, brushing with extra butter as necessary. Reserve the pancakes.
4   Heat the oven to 180C /350F /gas 4. Skin the chorizos, crumble them and fry them in their own fat in a frying-pan until lightly browned. Drain well on crumpled absorbent paper. Soften the soft cheese with the back of a spoon.
5   Coat the inside of a round casserole or spring-release tin 15 cm /6 in in diameter with butter. Place one pancake in the bottom. Sprinkle evenly with some of the crumbled chorizo, grated cheese and hard-boiled egg. Dot with soft cheese and spoon a little sauce over.
6   Repeat the layers until all the ingredients are used up, ending with a layer of sauce. Bake for 30 minutes and serve hot, cut in wedges.

● In Mexico, this would be made with soured cream instead of the soft cheese and tortillas instead of the pancakes. It would be known as a *sopa seca* or dry soup and would come between the soup and main course as part of the main meal of the day.

Fish and Shellfish

It is frequently said that for a nation which is completely surrounded by water we are astonishingly ignorant about fish. Many people seem nervous of buying fresh fish or shellfish, or of straying away from the fish and chip shop favourites: coley, cod, haddock and plaice.

Certainly fish must be very fresh to be enjoyed fully. If you have a good fishmonger near you support him by shopping there regularly. Some supermarkets now sell fresh fish and if they are large enough to have a quick turnover, the fish you buy should be good.

Fish is a vital part of a healthy diet, and it is available at a reasonable price. Nutritionists believe we should increase the amount of oily fish we eat – whether it is herring or the more expensive salmon.

Some people are anxious about the preparation that is sometimes involved in cooking fish – cleaning, gutting, filleting – or, in the case of shellfish, getting the shells open and removing the inedible parts. None of these techniques is difficult: follow the detailed information given in this chapter and you will soon master them.

Different types of fish are beginning to appear more often at the fishmonger's. This is partly because of depletion of stocks of the more traditional fish and partly as a result of demand, both from ethnic communities and from people who have holidayed abroad, for varieties such as squid, red mullet and monkfish. Make good use of the information and recipes in this chapter and be as adventurous as you would like to be.

Mackerel and herring

Mackerel, herring, sprat, shad, sardine, pilchard, smelt and anchovy — together they make up one of the largest collections of seafood in the world. They do not belong to the same family, but they share the common features of having a relatively high oil content and being delicious to eat.

It makes sense for a cook to group these highly nutritious fish together because of their similar flesh, but you would not find them all in the same glass case in a natural history museum. The mackerel is closely related to the much larger tuna fish, while the smelt belongs to the same zoological order as the salmon and trout. Other members of this group — sprat, shad and

pilchard – are members of the extensive herring family, to which the anchovy is distantly related. Mackerel and herring are economically the most important members of the group.

Mackerel must be bought very fresh. There used to be a law in Britain which permitted them, alone among fish, to be sold on Sundays, just because they would spoil if kept for an additional day. International competition in mackerel fishery and the trend towards marketing much of the catch as smoked mackerel, have pushed prices up a little, but the mackerel is still outstandingly good value.

Herrings are mysterious fish which swim in large, sometimes vast shoals. They have a history of being unpredictable, glut followed by scarcity. In the Middle Ages, when herring was one of the main articles of commerce in northern and western Europe and one of the principal props on which the wealth and political power of the Hanseatic League, a powerful trade and political association, rested, there was constant talk that herrings were a disappearing commodity. Similar complaints are still voiced today. No one has yet discovered why the large herring shoals have disappeared and reappeared over the centuries, nor why the best grounds for catching them change from time to time. Overfishing may be causing a dwindling of stocks but, on past experience, it is just as likely that the herring will come back again in large numbers. Happily herrings are still fairly easy to buy and not expensive.

Sardine or pilchard: pilchards are not, as is sometimes supposed, a different species of fish, but simply an adult sardine. Traditionally both sardines and pilchards have been marketed in canned form and very good they can be too, especially if you go to some care to choose the better quality canned fish available from France, Spain, Portugal and northern Africa. Canned sardines are the only ones many people know. In Spain and Portugal sardines are eaten freshly grilled over charcoal. Now that sardines are frozen in bulk they can be thawed and used as fresh. It is well worth buying frozen sardines and using them for a main course, rather than as the hors d'oeuvre or snack usually prepared from cans.

Sprats are usually sold in cans, but they can be bought and used fresh. The best canned sprats come from the Baltic republics of the Soviet Union and from the Baltic coast of Germany. The Baltic is less salty than the North Sea and for that reason there are fewer species of fish in it. It suits the sprat population which thrives in large numbers and is consequently one of the most important Baltic fish.

Whitebait are a standard starter on British restaurant menus, and their popularity goes back to the 18th century, when whitebait dinners at Greenwich were popular for all classes alike. Until the end of the 19th century these tiny silver fish were believed to be separate species. In reality they are, in Europe, a mixture of young fish, young herrings and sprats and related species. The fish differ in North America, and in Australia the term is applied to small fish of quite different families.

Shad, a notoriously bony fish, is available in Europe on a limited scale only, although they are highly appreciated in France. In America there are several species available and shad roe is considered a great delicacy.

Smelt is higher valued in the kitchens of Normandy, Canada and New England than it is in the British Isles. Smelt have a very distinctive smell when fresh: some people say it is like the smell of cucumber, while others liken it to the scent of violets. Like the sprat the smelt will live happily in waters which are not very salty including a few land-locked waters.

Buying and storing fish

You will want to be sure that the fish is fresh: look for the classic tell-tale signs. Be sure that the eyes are bright and stand out properly. Dull sunken eyes are a bad sign. Inspect the gills by raising the gill covers at the back of the head; they should be moist and red, not grey. The body of the fish should be firm to the touch; if you touch it, your finger should not leave an impression. The fish should smell fresh and salty, but it should not smell too strongly.

If you are buying herring or mackerel, there is another factor to consider. When they are ready to spawn (the females are with roe and the males with milt), they will be in prime condition. If they are taken just after spawning, they will be lean and flabby. Buy them if they are plump or firm but not if they seem thin or emaciated.

Note the price - cheapness can be both a good and a bad sign. Sometimes if a fish is priced low the fishmonger may be trying to get rid of it before it goes off - it may not be as fresh as it ought to be. On the other hand it could reflect a glut when the fishmonger hopes that a lower price will shift larger quantities than normal.

✶✶✶✶ If you buy frozen fish, they are likely to be frozen whole. If they are not already sealed in a protective wrapping, and you intend to keep them for some time, wrap them tightly. Fish of this oily type can be frozen for 3 months, though it is wise to keep them for less than this to allow for the time spent in commercial freezers. Cooked fish dishes can be kept frozen for 1 month.

Freezing down your own fish is only practical if it is really fresh – it should be done within 12 hours of the fish leaving the water, or within about 2 hours for mackerel. This means that you or a member of your family caught the fish, or you have bought it directly off the boat which netted it. Never freeze fish that have been through the retail trade. They may well have been frozen and thawed once already.

Top centre, sprats; to the right and left, mackerel with anchovies between. Centre, sardines, herrings below. Bottom, sprats.

How to clean a fish

To scale herring etc, hold the fish by the tail and use the blunt side of the knife to scrape off the scales towards the head. Rinse the fish under running cold water.

To gut a fish, make a slit along the belly from below the head, two-thirds of its length. Scrape out the guts and black skin, salt inside the cavity then wash.

Cut off the fin along the backbone and the gill covers, which are little fins behind the head. Cut off the head behind the gill opening and the tail if the recipe requires.

How to fillet and bone a fish

To make two fillets from a gutted, headless, tailless fish, cut along backbone from head end to tail down through the flesh, splitting the fish and exposing the bone. Lift this out.

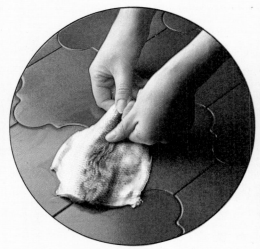

To split open a gutted, headless fish, cut the fish through the belly cavity through to the tail. Turn the fish over and press down on its back to open it out flat.

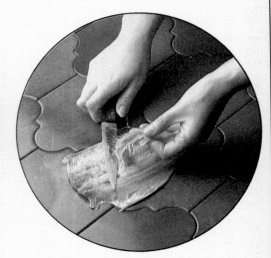

Lift up the backbone from the head end. Cut it free just above the tail, keeping the tail on if the recipe requires. The fish can then be layered flat or rolled from head end.

Preparing the fish

Scaling: not all fish have scales; the mackerel for example is smooth-skinned. But herrings do and these have to be removed as even one or two, unexpectedly encountered by the eater, will spoil the pleasure of the dish. Sardines, pilchards and anchovies have scales that are very loosely attached. You may find that all their scales have come off before you start work. Use a knife, or one of the special scaling implements which you can buy at any good cookery equipment store. Scaling is shown in the step-by-step pictures (*page 79*). If convenient, scale fish under water. Run your hand carefully over the fish from tail to head when you have finished to make sure that no scales are left.

Gutting is shown in the step-by-step pictures (*page 79*). It is straightforward after the first time. Reserve the roe or milt if this is present. You can recognize these as they are both long smooth sacs of milky colour. The stomach contents are best removed on to newspaper, so that they can be wrapped and discarded quickly and there is the minimum of blood. Gutting can also be done under running water. Washing the cavity afterwards is essential to remove all trace of blood and any black skin on the stomach wall.

Splitting the fish is entirely dependent on the requirements of the recipe. Briefly there are three different ways of doing it. If the recipe requires fillets, then the quickest thing is to remove the head and tail and to cut down the backbone through the fish, as shown in the picture, cutting the fish in two lengthways and removing the bone.

If the fish is to be opened flat, for rolling up or for layering, split the headless fish up through the stomach cavity. By pressing down firmly on the back as shown in the picture the fish will open up and the backbone work loose in one rhythmical operation. Cut the bone free and discard it.

If the fish is to be stuffed whole with the head on, cut up through the stomach cavity until the bone is exposed, but without piercing the outside skin. Cut the bone free at head and tail and lift out.

Fillets: you will notice that most of these fish, especially mackerel and herring, have a strip of brown meat running along outside the white meat. This is quite in order: the brown meat is particularly nutritious.

Cooking the fish

Mackerel: as it has a fairly high oil content you will find plain grilling is one of the most satisfactory ways of preparing mackerel. It is also good baked, especially if you add an ingredient with an acid nature to balance the oiliness. Traditionally gooseberries are used for this but rhubarb is also well-suited to mackerel. There are many mackerel recipes in which the mackerel might be described as instant cured, in that vinegar or white wine is used. The fish are ready to eat immediately, hot, or to be served cold the same day. The French mackerel with white wine (*maquereaux au vin blanc*) is a classic of this kind and makes an excellent first course. From Denmark come *gravad makrel,* a sort of 'instant cure' with herbs, which requires no cooking. If you prefer poached fish, mackerel is delicious prepared in this way.

Herring: so many herrings are consumed in a cured state as rollmops or kipper, that people forget how good fresh herring can be. The Dutch eat the first herring of the season, known as green herring (*groene haringen*), raw. Freezing does not make any difference to the flavour of these raw herring, which are usually eaten with a little chopped onion. In Scandinavia herring is used to make a soup. It is also very popular grilled. A delicious breakfast dish from Scotland is made from herring coated in medium-fine oatmeal and fried.

The 'instant cure' recommended for mackerel can also be applied to herring. A Scottish delicacy is soused herring which can be eaten hot, as a high tea dish or allowed to cool, and served cold as a starter.

Another Scottish recipe is for tatties 'n herrin. This was originally a way of dealing with salted herring, but it can also be used for fresh herring. Steam them with potatoes, but be sure to let everything drain before serving so that the potatoes are mealy and the herring not soggy.

Tart apples can be combined successfully with herring. A sauce made from apples is a good accompaniment to grilled herring, but the most usual accompaniment is mustard sauce.

There are many ways of using herring in a salad. Dutch herring salad started off as a way of serving salted herring, but it is very good made with fresh herrings. Lightly grill them then cool, fillet and chop them. Combine the chopped herring with chopped green apple, diced cooked beetroot, chopped hard-boiled eggs, a little chopped veal (if you have some), mashed potato and toss in a dressing of three parts of olive oil to one of vinegar.

Sprats can be grilled, but this fish is at its best when it is cured, smoked or canned.

Whitebait: handle them as little as possible by using a colander, a flouring bag and a large strainer spoon. They are best deep fried (see recipe).

Shad are described as 'planked' in the United States when they are prepared and cooked on a well-seasoned (in terms of age) plank of wood. Take a good sized shad weighing 2 kg /4½ lb, clean it and split it open. Place the skin side down on the hardwood, which has been brushed with melted butter, and cook it in a hot oven for 20 minutes. Although it will taste good, this method of cooking does not soften the numerous small bones for which the shad is notorious. The traditional way of softening the bones to the point at which you can eat them without discomfort is to cook the shad with sorrel. Sorrel contains a compound of oxalic acid, and many people believe this to be responsible for the softening. Another view is that it is a long cooking process which has this softening effect.

If you are grilling a large shad, be sure to score the side first. Serve grilled shad with a delicate sauce bearnaise. Shad is also delicious poached in a court-bouillon. Use the head and tail of the fish for the court-bouillon. Serve poached shad with beurre blanc.

Fresh sardines are best grilled and need no accompaniment, other than a squeeze of lemon.

Fresh pilchards, of course, are larger than sardines and they can be stuffed and baked. There is an old Cornish method for grilling them called 'scrowling'. Split the cleaned fish open, place two together, skins outside and cook them on a gridiron, turning them once.

Star-gazy pie is another traditional Cornish recipe – it has an unusual and attractive appearance. To make this, clean the pilchards and place them in a pie dish, tails in the middle and heads around the outside of the dish. Put a pastry covering over them, leaving their heads poking out. Bake the whole dish for 45 minutes. The theory is that the valuable juices in the head drip back into the dish while it is cooking.

Smelt are usually served fried. Scale and gut them, thread them through the eyes on skewers, dip them in milk, flour them and deep-fry for a short time in hot oil, so that they come out crisp and crunchy. There is a Canadian method of preparing smelts with a coating of ground almonds (see recipe), which can also be used for other fish in this group.

Fresh anchovies, or frozen ones, which have been allowed to thaw, can be grilled like fresh sardines. Anchovies are used very adventurously in many parts of the world. The Turks and Italians use them well; the Turks even make an anchovy bread.

Whitebait

Their preparation is very simple, but make sure you handle them as little as possible. Make full use of colanders, a flouring bag and a slotted spoon.

 40 minutes

Serves 4–6
1 kg /2 lb whitebait
flour, seasoned with salt and pepper
vegetable oil for deep-frying
cayenne pepper (optional)
2 lemons, cut in wedges
thinly sliced buttered bread to serve

1 Wash the whitebait, drain them thoroughly and put them, in two successive batches, in an open plastic bag with enough flour in it to coat them. Shake well until they are all coated, then transfer them to a dry sieve or colander and shake them to get rid of surplus flour.
2 Meanwhile heat the oil in a deep-frier to 190C /375F or until a cube of bread browns in 50 seconds. Using a large slotted spoon dip a few whitebait into the hot fat for just 1 minute. They should be slightly coloured but not browned.
3 Lift out the fish with the spoon, drain for a few seconds, then turn the whitebait on to absorbent paper to drain. Keep them hot in the oven. Repeat with successive batches of whitebait, making sure that the oil had reached the right temperature before adding each new batch.
4 Sprinkle the cooked fish lightly with cayenne pepper if you like. Serve immediately with lemon wedges and thin slices of buttered brown bread.

Fresh anchovies au gratin

Alici ammollicate

Fresh anchovies are baked briefly under a savoury coating of parsley, garlic and breadcrumbs in this Italian dish.

 30 minutes cleaning
 then 15 minutes cooking

Serves 6
1 kg /2 lb fresh anchovies
150 ml /5 fl oz olive oil
3 garlic cloves, finely chopped
2 sprigs of parsley, chopped
60 ml /4 tbls soft breadcrumbs
salt and freshly ground pepper

1 Heat the oven to 220C /425F /gas 7. Wash and gut the fish. Remove their heads, tails and backbones. Arrange them in a shallow, oiled oven dish and pour most of the olive oil over them. Reserve a little olive oil for later use. Sprinkle with finely chopped garlic and the seasoning.
2 Mix the parsley with the breadcrumbs and moisten with the remaining olive oil. Distribute the mixture evenly over the fish and bake for 15 minutes. Serve hot.

● For a different flavour use a popular Neapolitan version called *alici areganate*. Sprinkle the fish with chopped garlic and parsley, salt and pepper and oregano before baking.
● Substitute fresh sardines or small herrings for the anchovies.

Whitebait

Marinated mackerel

Gravad makrel

One of the most famous fish dishes in Scandinavia is *gravlax*, which is fresh salmon marinated with dill. In Denmark less expensive mackerel is used to produce a dish which is not quite such a delicacy, but still very good indeed.

🕐 🍴🍴 15 minutes cleaning,
then 12–18 hours marinating

Serves 4
*2 large or 4 small fresh mackerel, cleaned
  boned and filleted*
45 ml /3 tbls sugar
60 ml /4 tbls salt
15 ml /1 tbls ground white pepper
*120 ml /8 tbls fresh dill, roughly chopped
sprigs of fresh dill*

1   Mix the sugar, salt and pepper well in a bowl. Lay the fillets out flat, skin side down, and sprinkle each fillet with the mixture. Then cover each fillet with a layer of roughly chopped dill.
2   Scatter dill sprigs over a large flat platter. Lay one of the fillets, skin down on top of the dill sprigs. Put another fillet on top head to tail and skin side up. Arrange the remaining fillets in pairs the same way.
3   Sprinkle the arranged fish with the remaining roughly chopped dill, then cover with foil and a wooden board pressed down with a 2 kg /4½ lb weight. Leave in the refrigerator for 12–18 hours, but no longer than this.
4   To serve, scrape the dill and seasonings off the fillets. Using a very sharp knife cut the fillets in thin slices, starting at the tail, as you would with smoked salmon. Lay the cut slices overlapping each other on a serving plate.

Mackerel with rhubarb

Rhubarb makes an unusual combination with mackerel, but in fact the tartness of the rhubarb goes well with the fish.

🍴🍴 45 minutes

Serves 4
*4 fresh mackerel, filleted to give 8 fillets,
  (about 1 kg /2 lb weight)*
50 g /2 oz butter or margarine
1 large onion, finely chopped
*225 g /8 oz young rhubarb, trimmed and
  chopped*
salt and freshly ground pepper
30 ml /2 tbls fresh breadcrumbs, toasted
watercress, to garnish (optional)
For the sauce
*500 g /1 lb young rhubarb, trimmed and
  chopped*
30 ml /2 tbls sugar
a little grated lemon zest

Mackerel with rhubarb

1   Heat the oven to 200C /400F /gas 6 and grease a large ovenproof dish.
2   Melt the margarine in a pan and add the chopped onion. Cook over moderate heat until the onion is transparent. Add the chopped rhubarb and salt and pepper to taste and simmer gently, uncovered, for 5 minutes. Remove the pan from the heat and stir in the breadcrumbs.
3   Lay the mackerel fillets out flat, skin side down, and dividing the stuffing between them spread it out over each fish. Roll up each fillet to enclose the stuffing and put them in the prepared ovenproof dish. Cook them in the oven for 15–20 minutes.
4   Meanwhile make the rhubarb sauce. Place the chopped rhubarb, sugar and lemon zest with 30 ml /2 tbls water in a saucepan and stew over moderate heat for about 10 minutes, or until the rhubarb is quite soft.
5   Then press the rhubarb mixture through a fine sieve or blend to a purée. Reheat sauce and pour over mackerel. Serve garnished with watercress.

Baked herring

Harlinger haringschotel is a baked herring from Harlingen in Holland. It is best made with plump young herring, which are usually available in the spring.

🍴🍴 1 hour soaking fillets,
then 90 minutes

Serves 4
4 fresh herrings, cleaned and filleted
75 g /3 oz butter
4 shallots, chopped
275 ml /10 fl oz yoghurt
4 medium-sized eggs, separated
4 large potatoes, boiled and mashed
2.5 ml /½ tsp sugar
2 pinches of salt

1   Steep the fillets in cold water for 1 hour, then drain and cut them into small chunks.
2   Heat the oven to 180C /350F /gas 4. Melt a quarter of the butter in a frying-pan and sweat the shallots until they are translucent. Remove the shallots and let them cool, then combine them with one third of the

yoghurt and all of the chopped fish.

3 Meanwhile, melt the rest of the butter in the pan and stir in the remaining yoghurt, the egg yolks and the mashed potato. Beat the egg whites until they are stiff, then fold them into the mixture. Add the sugar and salt.

4 Butter an ovenproof dish and place half the egg and potato mixture in the bottom. Cover the potato layer with the herring mixture and finally top with the rest of the egg and potato mixture. Bake in the oven for 45 minutes.

● Another Dutch version uses soured cream instead of the yoghurt.

Smelts with almond coating

◖◖ 50 minutes

Serves 6
1 kg /2 lb fresh smelts
salt
60 ml /4 tbls flour
2 medium-sized eggs, beaten
200 g /7 oz ground almonds
100 g /4 oz butter, melted
lemon wedges, to serve

1 Heat the oven to 450F /230C /gas 8. Remove the fin from the back of each smelt, and the five fins on each underside, by pulling them forward and away from the fish. Remove the heads. Clean each fish and then spread it out in butterfly fashion, skin side up. Hit it with a flat, heavy object along the back, in four or five places. Then turn it over and you will find that the backbone comes away easily, with the tail.

2 Rinse and dry the fish, sprinkle them on both sides with a little salt, then fold them back into their original shape. Roll them in flour, shake off the excess and dip them in the beaten egg. Drain off any excess egg liquid. Roll the smelts in the ground almonds and pat this last coating on so that it adheres well.

3 Line a wide, shallow baking tin with foil, grease it and lay the fish in it side by side. Pour the melted butter evenly over them. Bake in the oven for 10 minutes. Garnish with lemon wedges and serve.

Slow-oven shad

◗ 2½ hours

Serves 4
1 kg /2 lb shad, uncleaned
25−50 g /1−2 oz breadcrumbs, soaked in milk
45 ml /3 tbls parsley and chives, chopped
100 g /4 oz butter
100 g /4 oz sorrel, washed
275 ml /10 fl oz dry cider
salt and freshly ground black pepper
sprigs of parsley and lemon slices, to garnish

Turkish-style anchovies, with rice

1 Heat the oven to 140C /275F /gas 1. Scale, gut and wash the shad. Cut out the gills with scissors and trim off the fins but leave on the head. Mash up the roe or milt with a fork. Squeeze the milk out of the breadcrumbs and then mix this with the herbs into the roe or milt. The result should be fairly thick paste. Use this to stuff the gut and gill cavities of the fish.

2 Butter an ovenproof dish, line it with sorrel leaves and place the fish in it. Season the fish and sprinkle any surplus stuffing around it.

3 Add 30 ml /2 tbls of cider and dot most of the remaining butter over the dish. Cook in the oven for 2 hours, basting regularly and adding the remaining cider and more knobs of butter. Garnish with parsley and lemon slices to serve.

● If you have sorrel growing or can pick it wild, then take advantage of its natural affinity with shad by serving it as a vegetable accompaniment, either whole or as a purée, to this dish.
● If you cannot find sorrel, spinach is a suitable alternative.

Turkish-style anchovies, with rice

Turkish fishermen have a special manual about the fish which they catch in the Black Sea, the Sea of Marmora and the Mediterranean. In the section on fish cookery the anchovy emerges as top fish and this is the best recipe.

◖◖ 30 minutes cleaning then 45 minutes

Serves 6
1 kg /2 lb fresh anchovies
salt and freshly ground pepper
125 g /4 oz butter
2 medium-sized onions, chopped
30 ml /2 tbls pine nuts
400 g /14 oz long-grain rice
30 ml /2 tbls currants
5 ml /1 tsp allspice
5 ml /1 tsp cinnamon
5 ml /1 tsp sugar
a little extra melted butter

1 Clean and debone the anchovies, removing the tails and heads. Sprinkle 5 ml /1 tsp salt over the fish.

2 Heat the butter in a pan, add the onion and the pine nuts, and let the onion brown slightly. Add the long-grain rice and cook over low heat, stirring constantly, for 10 minutes.

3 Add 1 L/1¾ pt water. Add currants, allspice, cinnamon, sugar and seasoning. Raise the heat until the water boils. Reduce to a medium heat for a few minutes and then to low heat as the water begins to be absorbed. Cook until the rice is ready − about 20 minutes.

4 Grease or oil a flameproof dish suitable for serving. Arrange half of the anchovies in a single layer in the dish. Put all of the rice mixture on top of them, then add a second layer of the fish in two even rows. Pour over the extra melted butter, cover the dish and cook on a medium heat for 10−15 minutes. Serve immediately.

Cod and other white fish

Make a soothing, chunky fish chowder, casserole fish fillets in a spicy tomato sauce, or combine cooked fish with mayonnaise and fresh herbs for a creamy salad – learn about round white fish and some different ways to cook them.

'Round' is a convenient term for describing all fish that are roughly cylindrical in shape, and is used chiefly in connection with white fish such as cod, haddock, coley, hake and whiting. The flesh of these fish has a low fat content and is therefore whitish in colour. White fish are high in protein and low in fat.

Round fish with flesh a little darker in colour, such as hake and bass, contain appreciably more oil, but not as much as the oily fish such as herring and mackerel.

Although round white fish have many similarities – they are all ocean fish, for one – it is a mistake to think that they all taste alike – their flavours, though generally bland, differ considerably. Even fish of the same species taste different depending on the season when caught and where they have been feeding, as well as the length of time between catching and eating. The texture of various species varies too.

Types of white fish

Cod is a large fish with a greyish green back mottled with olive, which shades to a white belly. It has a large barbule beneath the jaw – a little 'feeler' that gives the effect of a beard. It is a low-fat fish with white, firm and flaky-textured flesh. Small fish are known as codlings, and have a more delicate flavour and texture. Certain fish in Australia are called cod but are actually perch; however, some true cod is found there, both fresh and frozen.

Salt cod has been gutted, highly salted and then dried. It must be soaked in cold water for 12–48 hours, with the water changed several times. It is then skinned, boned and gently poached. It is especially popular in the Mediterranean. Stockfish is cod, hake or ling which has been wind-dried without salting.

Haddock has a grey back which shades through silver grey to a white belly. It is easily identified by a dark 'thumb mark' on each shoulder. Like cod, its flesh is white, firm and flaky, with a low fat content. It is imported, frozen, into Australia.

Hake is a long, slender fish with a grey back, silvery flanks and a silver-white belly, usually sold in the form of fillets or steaks. Best eaten very fresh, it has a highly esteemed flavour and a soft-textured flesh with a low fat content and very few bones. It is sometimes known as gemfish in Australia.

Coley or saithe has a very dark greenish black back, shading to dull silvery sides and belly. Usually sold as fillets or steaks, it is a low-fat fish whose firm flesh is easily identified as a distinct greyish pink colour when raw. It turns white on cooking. It is not available in Australia.

Ling is a long fish with a greenish brown back with light markings and a grey belly. A low-fat fish with a firm texture and white flesh, it is usually sold as fillets, and is sometimes available in Australia.

Flake, dogfish, huss, and rigg are alternative names which cover a variety of small sharks. They have sandy brown backs and sides and cream-coloured bellies, but are always sold skinned. Flake has very firm, meaty, dense flesh which is pinkish in colour, and contains one central bone, so is very easy to fillet. It should be eaten very fresh. Flake is available in Australia.

Bass or sea bass is a handsome fish, with small steely grey scales covering the back and sides. It has very white flesh with a firm texture, few bones and a fine flavour. It is not available commercially in Australia.

Pollack or lythe has a dark metallic green back which shades to a grey green with lighter spots. Its lower jaw is the longer. It is a low-fat fish with white, fairly firm flesh which is very bland in flavour. It is usually sold as fillets or steaks, but is not available in Australia.

Whiting is a small fish; sandy grey-green in colour, shading to silver flanks and belly. Its white, soft-textured flesh has a very low fat content and a delicate flavour. Its skin is very thin and can be difficult to remove. Whiting is sold whole or as fillets.

Australian whiting is a different species from that found in the North Atlantic, but does have similar characteristics.

Bream: sea bream describes several North Atlantic fish. True sea bream is round rather than cylindrical and is covered in coarse scales. Its firm white flesh has a delicate flavour. Bream is a very popular ocean fish in Australia. It also has firm white

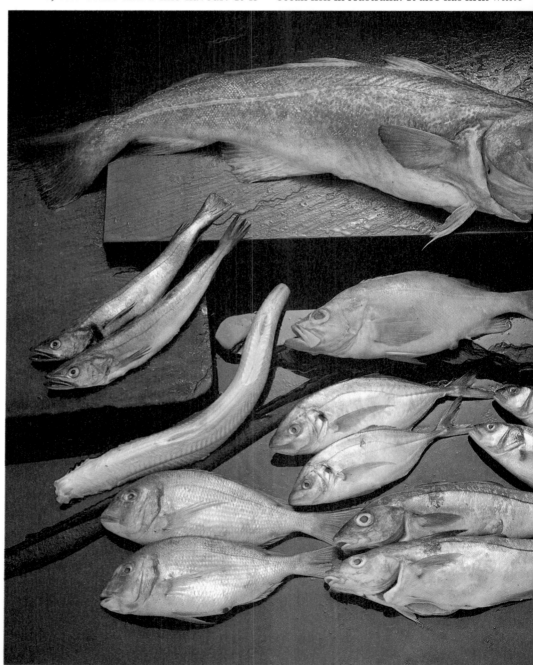

flesh with a delicate flavour.

Snapper, with its pink to deep red scales and pointed snout, is a favourite Australian and American fish. It has firm white flesh with a pleasant flavour but is slightly dry.

Flathead is another popular Australian fish, with a long tail and a flat-topped head. Its firm flesh is meaty with a fine flavour.

Trevally is a small, round, silvery Australian fish with a sweet flavour and firm flesh.

Buying and storing white fish

The best time to buy fish is when the species is in season and therefore plentiful and in prime condition. Ask your fishmonger's advice about this, because seasons vary in different parts of the world.

The sooner fish is eaten after catching the better the taste and texture, so when choosing fish look for clear, bright eyes, shiny skin and bright red gills. The flesh of filleted fish should be firm, regain its shape when pressed with a finger, and have no blood

clots or bruise marks visible. There should be very little smell.

The variety of frozen fish is limited to the more popular species in general, but if quick frozen soon after catching the quality can be excellent, and the fish virtually fresher than 'fresh' fish which has journeyed long distances. Buy from shops which rotate stocks conscientiously and where the turnover is brisk, because quality deteriorates if fish is kept frozen for long periods.

How to buy round white fish: small fish, weighing between 250–350 g /9–12 oz, are usually sold whole. Allow one per person.

Medium-sized fish range in weight from 350 g–2.3 kg /12 oz–5 lb. Allow 225 g /8 oz per person when buying a whole fish for poaching or stuffing; 150–175 g /5–6 oz when buying fillets.

Large fish weighing over 2.3 kg /5 lb are usually sold cut up in portions. The head and shoulders are usually poached and used for fish stock, fish cakes, pies and soups. Cutlets and steaks are slices cut across the fish about 25 mm /1 in thick. Cutlets come from the belly end of the fish and so will be horseshoe-shaped. Steaks are solid meat with the backbone running through the centre. Allow 175 g /6 oz per person.

Cutlets can be stuffed and baked or grilled; steaks can be cooked by any method. The middle cut is a large piece of fish for baking or poaching. Allow 175 g /6 oz per person. The tail piece is poached or baked. Allow 225 g /8 oz per person.

Storing: To enjoy fresh fish at its best, eat it as soon after purchase as possible, preferably on the same day. At any rate, keep it no longer than 24 hours. To store, unwrap the fish, rinse it quickly under the cold tap, pat dry with absorbent paper, place on a dish and sprinkle lightly with salt. Cover loosely and refrigerate until time to cook.

❄ ✳✳✳ Frozen fish should be transferred to your home freezer while still firmly frozen, and stored for up to three months. Do not freeze fish yourself unless you have caught it or bought it, freshly caught, from the fisherman.

Preparing white fish

White fish is usually gutted at sea and then prepared for sale, according to species and size, by the fishmonger. Preparation at home involves, in the case of a whole fish, cutting off fins with kitchen scissors and scraping the body cavity with the back of a knife to remove any black membrane and, if you have bought fillets, skinning them if wished. Some people like to eat fish skin, especially if coated with crumbs or batter and crisply cooked.

Cooking white fish

Although most of the round white fish do not fall naturally into the gourmet class, it is less than fair to dismiss them as dull and uninteresting. Cooked with flair and imagination, these fish will reward you with tasty, satisfying and economical dishes.

Centre top: cod; second row: two coley, sea bream, bass; third row: skinned flake, two trevally, two hake; front: two snapper, two haddock, two whiting

The importance of freshness has already been stressed. After that, the golden rules when cooking round white fish are:
● avoid overcooking – cooked fish will be opaque and part easily from the bone when the thickest part is pierced with a knife tip; a white curd may have formed between the flakes;
● add colour with additional ingredients or garnishes;
● add richness in the form of a creamy sauce, oily marinade, buttery baste or stuffing, or a herb mayonnaise;
● provide texture contrast by means of a crisp coating or topping, chopped vegetables or nuts;
● season generously and add strong flavours such as cheese, bacon, onion, leek, garlic, mustard, horseradish, lemon, lime, spices and herbs.

Generally speaking, one round white fish recipe is interchangeable with another, but you do need to consider the varying textures of different species. Grilling, for instance, requires a firm-textured fish not likely to break when turned or fall off the skewer. Soft-textured fish are best baked or steamed, or coated with egg and crumbs and fried.

Cod can be cooked by any method. Battered and deep-fried cod is a classic.

Haddock can also be cooked in any way. Small haddock are often cooked whole, stuffed and baked.

Hake can be cooked by any method; it is good cold with mayonnaise (see recipe).

Coley is inclined to be dry, so is best cooked with added fat. Try it instead of cod in fish pies and soups.

Ling is good poached and served with a creamy cheese sauce, or try it in pies and soups.

Flake can be used in soups and casseroles. It is good fried and served with a rich, piquant sauce, or cold with a garlic-flavoured mayonnaise.

Bass is usually cooked whole – remove the scales first, unless the fish is to be skinned before serving. Larger fish are usually poached or baked in the same way as salmon; smaller ones grilled or poached like trout. It is excellent cold.

Pollack can be cooked by any method. Add a rich sauce or savoury butter.

Whiting is best cooked when very fresh by poaching, baking or frying.

Sea bream: larger fish can be poached or baked; smaller ones grilled whole.

Bream can be cooked by any method, though is most often baked.

Snapper: small fish or fillets are often baked with a stuffing; steaks or fillets are good poached and served with an oyster or tomato sauce.

Flathead can be cooked by any method. It is usually filleted first.

Trevally must be eaten very fresh. It can be cooked by any method.

Cooking frozen fish fillets: thaw sufficiently to flatten or separate the fillets and then poach, steam, grill, bake or shallow fry, cooking gently and allowing time for thawing as well as cooking, about half as long again as usual. Thaw fillets completely before deep frying.

Gefilte fish

This traditional Jewish dish often contains carp as well as white fish. Some fishmongers sell a minced fish mixture ready for making it, but if you are mincing the fish at home, buy at least two different kinds.

🔪🔪 45 minutes,
plus 1 hour or more chilling

Serves 4–6
700 g /1½ lb mixed white fish fillets (cod, haddock, whiting, hake, etc)
7.5 ml /1½ tsp salt
100 g /4 oz onion, chopped
1 large egg
30 ml /2 tbls oil
large pinch of ground white pepper
30 ml /2 tbls freshly chopped parsley
about 45 ml /3 tbls matzo meal
dry white breadcrumbs for coating
oil for frying

1 Wipe the fish with damp absorbent paper, sprinkle the cut surfaces with the salt and refrigerate for 30 minutes to 1 hour.
2 Skin the fillets and cut into large pieces. Pass the fish and onion through the coarse blades of a mincer or chop coarsely in a food processor.
3 In a bowl, beat together the egg, oil, pepper, parsley and 15 ml /1 tbls water. Beat in the minced fish and 45 ml /3 tbls matzo meal. The mixture should be stiff enough to hold its shape; if necessary, add a little more water or matzo meal.
4 Take a heaped tablespoon of mixture at a time and, with wetted hands, form into balls. Flatten into cakes and coat with breadcrumbs. Leave to firm up in the refrigerator for 30 minutes or until ready to fry.
5 Heat about 10 mm /⅓ in oil in a large frying-pan. When it sizzles, fry the cakes in batches, about 5 minutes each side, until golden brown and cooked through. Serve hot or let cool and serve cold.

North Sea chowder

🔪🔪 defrosting prawns if necessary,
then 50 minutes

Serves 4
25 g /1 oz butter
75 g /3 oz salt pork or unsmoked streaky bacon, rinded and chopped
250 g /9 oz onion, finely chopped
15 ml /1 tbls flour
300 ml /10 fl oz milk
bouquet garni consisting of 2 celery stalks, 1 bay leaf, 1 blade mace
350 g /12 oz potatoes, in 15 mm /½ in cubes
500 g /1 lb cod or haddock fillets, skinned and cut into 25 mm /1 in pieces
100 g /4 oz peeled prawns, defrosted if frozen
60 ml /4 tbls thin cream or evaporated milk
2 ripe tomatoes, blanched, skinned, seeded and chopped (optional)
salt and freshly ground black pepper
30 ml /2 tbls freshly chopped parsley or chives

1 Melt the butter in a large saucepan and gently fry the salt pork or bacon and the onion for 5 minutes, or until it begins to brown.
2 Stir in the flour and cook gently for a minute, then gradually stir in 450 ml /16 fl oz water and the milk. Add the bouquet garni and potatoes. Bring to the boil, cover and simmer gently for 10 minutes.
3 Add the fish and simmer for 5 minutes, then add the prawns, cream or evaporated milk, tomatoes if using, and generous amounts of salt and pepper. Heat gently for 2–3 minutes.
4 Remove the bouquet garni and serve at once in deep soup bowls, sprinkled with the parsley or chives.

● This soup, which is a meal in itself, should be accompanied by plain crackers or hot buttered toast. Use mussels or scallops instead of the prawns, if you wish.

Mustard-grilled cod cutlets and North Sea chowder

Mustard-grilled cod cutlets

🔪 30 minutes

Serves 4
4 cod cutlets, trimmed
salt and freshly ground black pepper
15 ml /1 tbls lemon juice
75 g /3 oz butter, softened
30 ml /2 tbls Dijon or other mustard
30 ml /2 tbls dry white breadcrumbs
50 g /2 oz grated mature Cheddar cheese
30 ml /2 tbls freshly chopped parsley
2 small firm tomatoes, halved
watercress, to garnish

1 Rinse the fish under cold running water, pat dry with absorbent paper and sprinkle with lemon juice, salt and pepper.
2 Cut the onion, carrot, celery and cucumber into 25 mm /1 in lengths and then into julienne shreds. Place the onion, carrot and celery in a small saucepan with 15 g /½ oz butter and 150 ml /5 fl oz water. Bring to the boil, cover and simmer gently for 10 minutes. Add the cucumber and simmer for another 5 minutes.
3 Meanwhile, place the fish steaks side by side in a wide, shallow saucepan and add the cider. Bring to simmering point, cover and poach gently for 10–12 minutes, until just cooked.
4 With a fish slice, lift the steaks onto a hot serving dish, leaving the fish stock in the pan. Remove and discard the skin and central bones.
5 When the vegetables are just tender, strain their cooking liquor into the fish stock. Spoon a few of the vegetables over each piece of fish and pile the rest in the centre of the dish. Cover and keep warm.
6 Beat the remaining butter and the flour to a smooth paste. Add in small pieces to the simmering fish stock and stir vigorously until boiling. Add the cream, check the seasoning, heat through and spoon over the fish. Sprinkle the parsley over the vegetables in the centre of the dish and serve.

Whiting pinwheels

♩♩ 50 minutes

Serves 4
4 whiting fillets, not less than 200 g /7 oz each
salt and freshly ground black pepper
75 g /3 oz butter, softened
100 g /4 oz mushrooms, finely chopped
50 g /2 oz fresh, fine white breadcrumbs
5 ml /1 tsp finely grated lemon zest
30 ml /2 tbls freshly chopped parsley
a little lemon juice
lemon wedges, to garnish
parsley sprigs, to garnish

1 Heat the oven to 190C /375F /gas 5. Wipe the fish fillets with damp absorbent paper and lay, skin side down, on a board. Cut each in half lengthways, making long strips, and sprinkle lightly with salt.
2 Melt 65 g /2½ oz butter in a small saucepan and fry the mushrooms for 2 minutes. Stir in the breadcrumbs, lemon zest, parsley, salt and pepper to taste, and enough lemon juice to give the stuffing a spreading consistency.
3 Using a round-bladed knife, spread each strip of fish with the stuffing. Roll up from tail to head and place the rolls side by side in the dish. If they fit closely, the rolls will be held in shape; otherwise, secure each with a small skewer or cocktail stick.
4 Using 15 g /½ oz butter, grease a shallow oven-to-table dish large enough to hold the pinwheels in a single layer, and a piece of greaseproof paper to cover them.
5 Cover with the buttered paper and bake for 15 minutes, then serve hot, garnished with the lemon wedges and parsley sprigs.

1 Rinse the cutlets under cold running water, pat dry with absorbent paper and sprinkle with salt, pepper and lemon juice.
2 Heat the grill to medium. Mix the butter and mustard to a cream and season with salt. Spread half the butter over one side of the cutlets. Lay the cutlets buttered side down in a shallow flameproof dish large enough to hold them in a single, uncrowded layer. Spread the rest of the butter over the fish.
3 Grill for 5 minutes, then turn carefully and grill for another 3 minutes.
4 Mix together the breadcrumbs, cheese and parsley and sprinkle thickly over the fish, then baste well with the melted butter in the dish. Gently press the halved tomatoes, cut side up, into the spaces between the cutlet flaps and continue grilling gently for another 5 minutes, or until the topping is crisp and golden. Serve hot from the dish, garnished with sprigs of watercress.

Haddock steaks bretonne

♩♩ 55 minutes

Serves 4
4×175–225 g /6–8 oz haddock, cod or hake
  steaks
15 ml /1 tbls lemon juice
salt and white pepper
1 small onion
1 medium-sized carrot
2 celery stalks
¼ medium-sized cucumber
25 g /1 oz butter
150 ml /5 fl oz dry cider
15 ml /1 tbls flour
45 ml /3 tbls thin cream
15 ml /1 tbls freshly chopped parsley

Fish mayonnaise with four herbs

🕐🕐 defrosting prawns if necessary, then 1 hour 30 minutes

Serves 4–6
900 g /2 lb haddock or hake fillets
salt and freshly ground black pepper
juice of 1 large lemon
90 ml /6 tbls olive oil
45 ml /3 tbls freshly chopped mixed herbs –
parsley, chervil, tarragon and chives
300 ml /10 fl oz thick mayonnaise
30–45 ml /2–3 tbls thin cream
For the garnish
2 medium-sized eggs, hard boiled and quartered
2 firm tomatoes, quartered
a few sprigs of watercress
50 g /2 oz peeled cooked prawns, defrosted if
frozen
15 ml /1 tbls freshly chopped parsley

1 Place the fish in a shallow pan with a small amount of cold water, 10 ml /2 tsp salt and 15 ml /1 tbls lemon juice. Bring to simmering point, cover and poach gently for about 10 minutes, or until just cooked. Drain, remove all skin and bones and flake coarsely.
2 Put the fish into a bowl and, while it is still hot, add the oil, the remaining lemon juice, the herbs and salt and pepper to taste. Mix gently but thoroughly, cover and set aside until cold, about 1 hour.
3 When ready to serve, pile the fish in the centre of a serving dish. Thin the mayonnaise to a thick coating consistency with the cream and spoon over the fish.
4 Arrange the eggs, tomatoes and watercress around the base of the salad. Scatter the prawns over the mayonnaise, sprinkle with the parsley and serve.

Fish fillets marinara

🕐 1 hour 10 minutes

Serves 4
700 g /1½ lb flake, skinned and cut into 7.5 cm
/3 in lengths
seasoned flour for coating
25 g /1 oz butter
30 ml /2 tbls oil
chopped parsley, to garnish
For the sauce
25 ml /1½ tbls olive oil
100 g /4 oz onion, finely chopped
100 g /4 oz carrot, finely chopped
1 large garlic clove, crushed
800 g /1¾ lb canned tomatoes
15 ml /1 tbls tomato purée
10 ml /2 tsp sugar
salt and freshly ground black pepper

Fish mayonnaise with four herbs

1 First, make the sauce. Heat the oil in a saucepan and fry the onion and carrot very gently for 5 minutes. Add the garlic, the tomatoes and their juice, tomato purée, sugar and salt and pepper to taste. Bring to the boil, cover and simmer very gently for 40 minutes, or until thick.
2 While the sauce is cooking, rinse the fish under cold running water and pat dry with absorbent paper. Roll the fish in seasoned flour to coat thoroughly, then shake off excess flour.
3 Heat the butter and oil in a shallow frying-pan and when it sizzles, fry the fish, a few pieces at a time, over fairly brisk heat, until golden on each side. As each piece is browned transfer it to a shallow flameproof casserole, arranging the pieces side by side in a single layer.
4 When the sauce is cooked, beat well to break up any large pieces of tomato, adjust the seasoning, bring to the boil and pour over the fish. Cover the casserole and simmer over very low heat for 10 minutes, until the fish is cooked through. Serve very hot from the casserole, sprinkled generously with chopped parsley.

● The sauce can be made in advance if wished; it freezes well.
● Cod or another firm-textured fish can be substituted for flake in this recipe.

Cider cod

⌛ 30 minutes

Serves 4
500 g/1 lb cod fillets
350 g/12 oz tomatoes, halved
100 g/4 oz mushrooms
300 ml/10 fl oz dry cider
salt and freshly ground black pepper
25 g/1 oz butter
25 g/1 oz flour
75 g/3 oz Cheddar cheese, grated

1 Heat the oven to 190C/375F/gas 5. Divide the cod into 4 portions and place them in the bottom of a greased ovenproof dish. Top the cod with the tomatoes and mushrooms, pour over the cider and bake in the oven for 15 minutes.
2 Drain the liquid from the cod into a jug, cover the fish with foil and keep it warm. Melt the butter in a saucepan over low heat, add the flour and stir for 2 minutes. Remove from heat and stir in cider liquor. Season.
3 Place the pan over medium heat and simmer, stirring continuously, for 2 minutes. Pour sauce over fish, sprinkle over the cheese and place under grill for 5 minutes or until golden.

Cod steak in crab sauce

⌛ 1 hour 40 minutes

Serves 4
4 large cod steaks, 25mm/1 in thick
For the court bouillon
600 ml/1 pt dry white wine
15 ml/1 tbls white vine vinegar
2 small onions, finely chopped
1 bouquet garni
1 sprig of fennel
16 black peppercorns
For the crab sauce
100 g/4 oz butter
45 g/1½ oz flour
50 g/2 oz crab pâté
3 medium-sized egg yolks
5–10 ml/1–2 tsp lemon juice
75–125 ml/3–4 fl oz thick cream
salt and freshly ground black pepper
75g/3 oz pimento-stuffed olives

1 Place the ingredients for the court bouillon in a large saucepan with 600 ml/1 pt water and bring to the boil over high heat. Lower the heat and simmer for 30 minutes.

2 Strain the court bouillon and return to the rinsed-out pan. Add the cod steaks and simmer for 15–20 minutes, or until just cooked. Remove with a slotted spoon.
3 Remove the skin and the centre bone, if wished. Arrange the steaks on a serving platter and keep warm.
4 Boil the court bouillon rapidly until it is reduced to 600 ml/1 pt. Strain and reserve.
5 Melt 50 g/2 oz butter in a saucepan over low heat. Stir in the flour, cook for 2 minutes, then beat in the crab pâté. Add the reduced court bouillon a little at a time. Then stir for 5 minutes over gentle heat, or until the sauce is slightly reduced and thickened.
6 In a small bowl, beat the egg yolks with 5 ml/1 tsp lemon juice. Add 50 ml/2 fl oz cream and mix thoroughly. Add to the sauce, stirring, and cook over low heat for 2–3 minutes. Do not allow the sauce to boil. Add the remaining butter in small knobs, mixing well after each addition.
7 Adjust the seasoning, adding the remaining lemon juice, if necessary. Then add a further 25–50 ml/1–2 fl oz cream, to give the sauce a thin pouring consistency. Slice the olives and stir them into the sauce. Pour over the fish and serve at once.

Cod steak in crab sauce

Flat fish

Sole and turbot, with their firm flesh and superb flavour, can be made into classic dishes that will impress all who sample them. Plaice and flounder are, perhaps, less glamorous, but all flat fish are worth knowing about, as they are readily available and simple to prepare.

Flat fish are some of the most delicately flavoured fish; perfect cooking is needed to enhance but not swamp their taste. Jonathan Swift, the author of Gulliver's Travels, summed it up by saying: 'Fish should swim thrice; first it should swim in the sea, then it should swim in butter and, at last, sirrah, it should swim in good wine.' Or it may 'swim' poached in court bouillon before being served with a sauce.

Sole, plaice, halibut, flounder and turbot are all members of the order of flat fish. All fish start life as round, but some of them – the flat fish – have the habit of lying on their sides on the sea bed. When a flat fish is one to two months old, the eye that is underneath works its way around to the top, and, while the skin underneath stays thin and white, the skin on the upper side thickens and darkens, and can change colour to match the sand on which it lies. Some flat fish, such as turbot, brill and megrim or whiff, lie on their left sides and are known as 'left-handed' while plaice, flounder, sole, witch, dab and halibut are 'right-handed'.

John Dory and skate (ray), belong to different orders of fish, but they are usually grouped with the flat fish because of their shape.

Types of small flat fish

Sole is the noblest of the 'noble fish', its texture delicate yet firm. The flesh comes easily away from the bone and is very easily digested. One of the great pleasures of restaurant dining is to see a skilled waiter effortlessly remove a whole side of the flesh in one movement – but the secret of success, of course, belongs to the cook, not the waiter.

There are many species of sole. The choicest is often called Dover sole. It is streamlined in shape compared to other flat fish, almost oval with narrow fins. Its upper side has brownish-grey blotchy skin. A

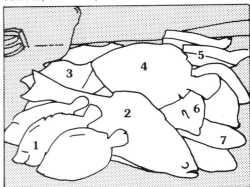

A selection of flat fish: 1 Lemon soles; 2 Halibut; 3 Skate wings; 4 Turbot; 5 Brill cutlets; 6 Plaice; 7 Dover soles

Plaice with oranges

This inexpensive but impressive dish is excellent for a buffet as it can be made well in advance of serving.

1 hour plus cooling

Serves 4–8
2 × 900 g /2 lb plaice, in 8 fillets and all skin removed
juice of ½ lemon
3 oranges
salt and freshly ground black pepper
butter for greasing
40 g /1½ oz butter, in small pieces
150 ml/5 fl oz mayonnaise
paprika, to garnish
50 g /2 oz canned anchovy fillets, drained
30 ml/2 tbls vinaigrette dressing

1   Heat the oven to 180C /350F /gas 4. Wash the fillets of plaice and dry them well with absorbent paper. Sprinkle with the lemon juice and the juice of half an orange. Season with salt and pepper. Finely grate the zest of 1 orange over the fish and roll up the fillets, beginning at the head end. Secure with wooden cocktail sticks and lay them in a buttered ovenproof dish.
2   Squeeze the juice of half an orange over the fish, dot with the butter and cover the dish with buttered greaseproof paper or foil. Bake in the centre of the oven for about 20 minutes, or until the fillets are tender but still firm. Remove the dish from the oven and leave to cool.
3   Lift the cold fillets carefully on to a shallow serving dish and remove the cocktail sticks.
4   Add the juice of half an orange to the mayonnaise, a drop at a time, and stir in the grated zest of half an orange. Coat the fillets with the mayonnaise and sprinkle lightly with the paprika. Halve the anchovy fillets lengthways and arrange 2 halves over each little 'parcel' of fish.
5   Peel the remaining 1½ oranges, removing all the pith, and cut them into thin slices with a sharp, serrated knife. Dip the slices in the vinaigrette and serve separately as an accompaniment.

Sole Colbert

Use a deep-fat frier with a large frying basket. The fish is fried with the bone in it for maximum flavour but the bones are cleverly removed before serving.

45 minutes

Serves 4
4×275–350 g /10–12 oz sole
seasoned flour for coating fish
2 medium-sized eggs, beaten
fine breadcrumbs for coating fish
oil for deep frying
sprigs of parsley, to garnish
For the maitre d'hotel butter
100 g /4 oz butter, softened
15 ml /1 tbls finely chopped parsley
juice of ½ lemon
salt
pinch of cayenne pepper

1   First make the maitre d'hotel butter. Blend the ingredients together well and form into a sausage shape on a piece of foil. Roll up and chill well.
2   Skin one sole on both sides, leaving the head intact. Lay it, top side uppermost, on a chopping board and, with the point of a sharp filleting knife or other knife, make an incision starting about 25 mm /1 in below the head. Cutting through to the bone, cut down in a straight line to within 4 cm /1½ in of the tail. Now loosen the fillets from the bone starting on the top left hand side, and going downwards, sweeping the knife round horizontally in a crescent movement. Repeat on the right hand side so that the fillets are only attached at the head, tail and fins.
3   Roll the fillets back from the centre towards the fins, exposing the bones. Snip the backbone with scissors in 3 places, near the head, in the centre and near the tail, just enough to make it easy to break and lift out when the fish is cooked. Repeat with the other soles.
4   Pat the fish dry, dust all over with seasoned flour. Dip each fish first in the beaten eggs, then in the breadcrumbs, making sure that the crumbs stick to the flesh by patting them on firmly with the side of a broad-bladed knife.
5   When you are ready to cook, heat the oil in a deep-fat frier with the frying-basket in place. Heat to 190C /375F or until a 25 mm /1 in cube of day-old bread turns golden brown in 50 seconds. Lower the fish one at a time into the oil in the frying basket. When it becomes golden brown, lower the heat so that the crumbs do not burn; the sole will take 6–8 minutes to cook. (For a perfect result, place a slightly smaller frying basket on top of the fish to keep it even and flat.) Repeat with the other fish in turn.
6   As each fish is cooked, drain on crumpled absorbent paper. Carefully ease out the backbones and keep warm on a serving dish. Cut the maitre d'hotel butter into rounds, and arrange these in the cavities of the fish. Garnish then serve at once.

Sole Colbert

Sole Dugléré served cold

Fillets of John Dory Pierre Chapelle

In this recipe, golden fillets of John Dory are served on a bed of pilaff rice.

🔪🔪 making fish stock,
then 35 minutes

Serves 4
1 kg /2 lb John Dory, filleted, with the head, skin and trimmings reserved
2 medium-sized eggs, beaten
salt and freshly ground black pepper
fine breadcrumbs for coating
75 g /3 oz butter
For the fish stock
100 ml /3½ fl oz dry white wine
1 slice of carrot
1 slice of onion
1 bay leaf
For the pilaff
25 g /1 oz butter
120 ml /8 tbls chopped onion
1 small clove garlic, finely chopped
4 ml /scant tsp curry powder
4–6 large tomatoes, blanched, skinned, seeded and roughly chopped
150 ml /5 fl oz chicken stock
175 g /6 oz Patna rice
salt and freshly ground black pepper

1 Make a fish stock with the head bones, trimmings and white skin of the John Dory: rinse them thoroughly, chop them roughly and place in a saucepan with 100 ml /3½ fl oz cold water, the wine and a little salt. Place the pan on a low heat and bring to the boil, skimming off any scum that rises to the surface. Add the remaining ingredients and simmer gently, uncovered, for about 25 minutes. Strain the stock through a muslin-lined sieve and reserve 150 ml /5 fl oz.

2 Make the rice pilaff: melt the butter in a saucepan, add the chopped onion and cook it until it is soft but not browned. Stir in the garlic and curry powder and cook for 1 minute, stirring, then add the chopped tomatoes, the chicken stock and the reserved fish stock. Bring to the boil, shower in the rice, season with salt and pepper, cover and simmer gently for about 15 minutes.

3 While the rice is cooking, fry the fish. Season the eggs with salt and pepper. Dip the John Dory fillets in the egg, then in the breadcrumbs. Shake off any surplus crumbs. Melt the butter in a shallow frying-pan and heat it until the foaming subsides. Add the fish fillets and fry them for about 3 minutes on each side, until they are golden brown. Drain them on absorbent paper and keep warm until the rice is cooked, if necessary.

4 With a fork, pile the rice on a warmed serving dish. Arrange the John Dory fillets on top and serve at once.

Sole Dugléré

Sole Dugléré is a classic French dish named after a 19th century Parisian café proprietor. In this recipe the fish is served cold although the hot version of the dish is better known.

🔪🔪 making fish stock,
then 1 hour plus cooling

Serves 4
2×550 g /1¼ lb Dover soles, in 8 fillets, with bones and trimmings reserved
75 g /3 oz unsalted butter
salt and freshly ground white pepper
2–3 shallots, finely chopped
4 large tomatoes, blanched, skinned, seeded and chopped
150 ml /5 fl oz dry white wine
50 g /2 oz flour
150 ml /5 fl oz thick cream
1 medium-sized egg yolk
few drops of lemon juice
chopped parsley, to garnish
For the fish stock
1 slice of carrot
1 slice of onion
1 bay leaf
15 ml /1 tbls dry white wine

1 Skin the soles, and reserve. Use the bones, trimmings and white skin to make fish stock. Rinse them thoroughly, chop them roughly and place in a saucepan with 200 ml /7 fl oz cold water and a little salt. Place the pan on a low heat and bring to the boil, skimming off any scum that rises to the surface. Add the remaining ingredients and simmer gently, uncovered, for about 25 minutes. Strain it through a muslin-lined sieve and reserve 150 ml /5 fl oz.

2 Thoroughly grease a large shallow flameproof dish with 15 g /½ oz butter. Wash the sole fillets and pat them dry with absorbent paper. Arrange them in a single layer in the dish and season with salt and white pepper. Sprinkle with the chopped shallots and cover with the chopped tomatoes. Pour in the strained stock and the wine and cover with buttered greaseproof paper.

3 Bring the contents of the dish to simmering point on a medium heat, then lower the heat and poach the sole gently for about 7 minutes, until the fish is cooked through but still firm.

4 Lift out the cooked fillets carefully, drain them and leave to get cold.

5 Meanwhile, make a beurre manié by mashing together 25 g /1 oz butter and 50 g / 2 oz flour. Bring the fish cooking liquid, with the shallots and tomatoes, to the boil. Boil quickly to reduce it by at least a quarter. Remove the pan from the heat and stir in the cream. Add the beurre manié in small pieces and whisk until absorbed.

6 Melt 40 g /1½ oz butter in a small pan on a low heat. Stir in the egg yolk and blend this mixture into the cream sauce. Correct the seasoning and leave the sauce to cool.

7 Just before serving, arrange the sole fillets on a large dish and sprinkle with a few drops of lemon juice. Coat the fish with the sauce and sprinkle with chopped parsley.

Salmon and trout

The salmon is considered the 'king of the river' by gourmets, and is indeed delicious. But its less expensive relatives, including the trout and the salmon trout, are easy to cook and good to eat.

Salmon and salmon trout (also known as sea trout) are marine fish, but they are spawned and spend their early lives in fresh water. Brown and rainbow trout, grayling and char live entirely in fresh water, although they belong to the salmon family.

Salmon have an interesting life cycle. Eggs remain buried in gravel for several months, then hatch. Newly hatched fish remain attached to their yolk sacs until all the nourishment the sacs can provide has been absorbed. They then emerge from the gravel and, when they are between three and four years old, begin their journey towards the sea, where growth is rapid. A few fish, known as grilse, return to the rivers in the same year, but most remain at sea for several years before returning to their native rivers, finding their way back through some mysterious instinct. However, this journey against the current, often through rapids and up waterfalls, is so exhausting that many die en route. Having arrived at the upper reaches of the fast-flowing river, the chosen spawning ground, the female scoops a shallow trench in the gravel and lays her eggs, which are then fertilized by the male. The great majority of salmon die right after spawning, but a few manage to return to the sea and survive.

Types of fish

The Atlantic salmon lives in the northern waters of the Atlantic Ocean and migrates upstream in North America, Britain and Europe during the breeding season. Its skin is shiny grey on its back, with a white belly. It has a forked tail and plump body. It is at its best from May to July.

Grilse are available fresh during early summer, or frozen. They are young salmon which have spent one year at sea.

The Pacific salmon is found around the west coast of America. It is larger than its Atlantic relative, with a flatter body. It is available frozen all year round.

Other subspecies of salmon are more or less landlocked, migrating in North America to the Great Lakes and in Scandinavia to the Baltic Sea. Both these bodies of water provide less nourishment than the open seas, so the fish remain smaller and are considered by many to be inferior in flavour to the Atlantic and Pacific salmons.

In Australia, the fish known as salmon or bay trout is actually a member of the perch family.

Salmon trout have a life cycle similar to that of the salmon, but they do not travel very far into the sea, and return earlier to fresh water. The males are reddish in colour; the females silvery and, like salmon, the flesh is pink after cooking. They are best from March to July.

Rainbow trout, natives of North America, are the most common trout in Britain, Europe and North America, where they are easily available fresh or frozen because plentiful supplies come from trout farms. They have attractive silvery markings with a shimmering pink band from head to tail and are available all year round. Occasionally these are available with red flesh, when they are known as 'red trout'.

Brown trout: these golden brown fish inhabit many streams and rivers in Britain and Europe. They are at their best from March to September, but are rarely available in shops.

Grayling is another member of the salmon family, a freshwater fish recognized by its long dorsal fin which is 'rayed'. It is at its best in winter, but is difficult to find in shops.

Char, another freshwater relative, is found in Britain and Europe, and is recognized by the black spots on its sides. Like grayling, it is at its best in winter but is difficult to buy.

Buying and storing

When buying, look for bright eyes, scarlet gills and firm flesh which will not remain dented when pressed. A headless fish has probably been frozen and defrosted.

Steaks and cutlets should look firm and bright.

Amounts to buy: if you are buying a small salmon or salmon trout (under 1.5 kg /3½ lb

Salmon steaks poached in red wine

Skinning and boning a whole fish

Place the fish on damp greaseproof paper. With a sharp knife, cut the skin halfway along the bottom of the fish, across the tail, along the top and below the head.

Peel the skin away, using the knife to separate it from the flesh. Discard skin and scrape away the brown flesh from the middle of the fish.

Using the paper, roll the fish onto a serving platter and repeat the skinning process on the other side. Work the knife along the fish between the upper fillet and the bone.

Using two fish slices, lift the upper fillet away from the backbone and place it to one side. Snip through the backbone at head and tail and lift off, then replace upper fillet.

---

including head and tail, you will need 200–225 g /7–8 oz per person. Portions of larger fish need weigh only 150 g /5 oz. One whole trout per person is usually served. For salmon and salmon trout middle-cut steaks, allow 150–175 g /5–6 oz; tail piece steaks: allow 200 g /7 oz per serving.

Storing: always cook fish on the day of purchase, if possible; at any rate never keep it longer than 24 hours. To store in the refrigerator, unwrap, then place the fish on a clean plate and cover loosely with foil.

✳✳✳✳ To freeze a fresh fish, gut it then wash and drain it well. Open freeze it on a tray until firm, then pack and freeze for up to three months.

Preparing salmon and trout

Gutting: using a sharp, pointed knife, make a slit along the belly of the fish. Place your fingers under the gills and pull out all the entrails, working down the belly of the fish. Large salmon require some strength to gut.

Run your finger down the length of the backbone to remove the dark membrane which lies against it. If it is necessary to remove the head, cut it off just below the gills.

Trimming: the salmon family are often served with their heads on. In this case, remove the eyes with a sharp pointed knife. Before cooking trim away the gills and fins and cut a deep 'V' shape into the tail with kitchen scissors. Rinse the fish in cold water and dry well with absorbent paper immediately after trimming.

Cutting large fish into steaks: gut the fish and remove the head below the gills. Cut the fish in even slices about 4 cm /1½ in thick, cutting through the flesh and backbone with a sharp knife.

Skinning salmon and salmon trout: when serving hot, the fish can be served in its skin if it has been scaled (*page 79*) and had its fins trimmed, or it can be served with its upper skin removed.

When cold, the fish should be either half or completely skinned. If it has been cooked unscaled, it must be completely skinned. Place the fish on a sheet of damp greaseproof paper. Using a sharp knife, make a cut in the skin along the top of the back, across the tail, around the head and along the belly of the fish. Lift the skin away from one end, using the knife to separate it from the flesh. Scrape away the brown flesh from the middle of the fish. Lifting with the paper, roll the fish over and repeat on the other side, if wished.

Removing the bone: if the bone is removed from a salmon before it is glazed (see pictures), this makes portioning considerably easier, as each person takes a top-to-bottom slice through the whole fish. It is, however, optional. If you do not do it neatly, removing and replacing the fillets without breaking them, the appearance of the fish may be spoilt. By the alternative method the top fillets are removed during serving. The backbone must then be cut at the head and tail and removed to allow the lower fillets to be served.

Cooking salmon and trout

Fish of the salmon family, with their firm, moist flesh, can be poached, baked, grilled, shallow fried or steamed.

Poaching: whole fish are often poached. Use a fish kettle if you have one – it will have a removable grid for draining. Or enclose the fish in muslin so you can lift it out of the liquid after cooking. Use either lightly salted water or a court bouillon for poaching. The liquid should never rise above simmering point, otherwise the flesh of the fish will break up. Fish may also be poached in a roasting tin in the oven at 180C /350F /gas 4 – but make sure your fish will fit in the tin first!

Cook whole fish weighing over 2.3 kg /5 lb for 18 minutes per kg /8 minutes per lb; fish weighing between 1–2.3 kg /2–5 lb for 22 minutes per kg /10 minutes per lb; fish weighing less than 1 kg /2 lb for 22–33 minutes per kg /10–15 minutes per lb. Steaks and cutlets take between 10 and 20 minutes, according to thickness.

Poaching to serve cold: if you plan to decorate a whole, cold fish, the fish is best cooled in the cooking liquid. To avoid overcooking, cook it by the Scottish method. Lay the fish on a rack in a fish kettle or other large pan. Pour in court bouillon or enough cold water to cover the fish by 25 mm /1 in. Add 45 ml /3 tbls salt to every 4.5 L /8 pt water and bring slowly to the boil. As soon as the water reaches a fast boil, remove the pan from the heat, skim, cover the pan closely and set aside in a cool place (not the refrigerator) until it is almost cold. This method can be used for any size of fish.

Presenting a poached fish: a cold, skinned fish is beautiful when decorated and glazed. Cut vegetable shapes, dip them in aspic and arrange on the fish. Then coat the fish with a layer of aspic. This can be made either from aspic crystals or stock and gelatine (see recipe for Salmon with green mayonnaise). If you are using a good court bouillon to poach the fish, reduce this to make aspic (see recipe for glazed salmon trout). Any remaining aspic can be cubed and arranged around the fish as a garnish.

All the salmon family are excellent poached and served hot or cold with mayonnaise, green mayonnaise (see recipe), rémoulade (mayonnaise flavoured with gherkins, capers, spring onions, herbs and anchovy essence), hollandaise or tartare sauces. Cutlets or steaks may be served and decorated in the same way as whole fish. The classic garnishes for cold salmon include small aspics of shellfish, little tartlets filled with a macédoine of vegetables, caviare, fish mousse or a vegetable purée. Cucumber salad is a usual accompaniment.

In Russia, flaked poached salmon is made into an elaborate pie called koulibiac.

Baking: whole fish or cutlets may be baked in a casserole or wrapped in buttered foil (see recipe). This is a good method to use for stuffed fish.

Grilling is suitable for small whole fish such as trout, as well as steaks and cutlets of salmon and salmon trout. If you are grilling a whole fish which is very thick, make three diagonal slashes in the flesh to allow the heat to penetrate throughout. Brush surfaces with melted butter or a mixture of oil and butter, and baste again during cooking. Grill under a moderately high heat for 5–7 minutes each side for medium-sized trout and other whole fish and 10-15 minutes (total cooking time) for steaks and cutlets. Turn these halfway through cooking, if wished. Plain grilled fish is often served with watercress and a savoury butter flavoured with anchovy or parsley and lemon.

Shallow frying is a delicious way of cooking small whole fish such as trout. They are usually coated in seasoned flour and fried in butter or a mixture of butter and oil for about 6 minutes each side (see recipe).

Steaming: steaks of larger fish or whole trout may be steamed over boiling water and served with a sauce.

Salmon steaks poached in red wine

🔪 25 minutes

Serves 4
4 salmon steaks, about 175 g /6 oz each
1 medium-sized onion, chopped
1 medium-sized carrot, finely diced
275 ml /10 fl oz dry red wine
salt and freshly ground black pepper
6–8 large croûtons fried in butter, to serve

1 Place the salmon steaks in a shallow pan and cover with the onion and carrot. Pour in the wine and season with salt and pepper. Cover and poach very gently for 15 minutes.
2 Carefully lift the steaks with a fish slice, allow to drain briefly, then arrange them in a warmed serving dish and keep hot.
3 Boil the liquid in the pan until it is reduced to about 150 ml /5 fl oz, then check the seasoning and spoon the reduced liquid and the vegetables over the salmon. Garnish with the croûtons and serve at once.

Trout meunière

🔪 15 minutes

Serves 4
4 trout complete with heads and tails, cleaned (about 225 g /8 oz cleaned weight)
60 ml /4 tbls seasoned flour
75 g /3 oz butter
10 ml /2 tsp lemon juice
30 ml /2 tbls chopped parsley
lemon slices, to garnish
flat-leaved parsley, to garnish

Trout meunière served with new potatoes garnished with a sprig of mint

1 Coat the fish with seasoned flour and shake off any excess. Melt 50 g /2 oz of the butter in a large frying-pan, put in the fish and fry on a moderately high heat for about 6 minutes. Turn the trout carefully and fry for a further 6 minutes, or until cooked through and golden brown.
2 Remove the trout to a warm serving platter, sprinkle with the lemon juice and parsley and keep warm.
3 Add the remaining butter to the pan and heat until it becomes nut brown in colour. Pour over the trout, garnish and serve.

● For a more elaborate version of this recipe, add 20 ml /4 tsp lemon juice and 15 ml /1 tbls capers to the pan before pouring the juices over the trout.

Glazed salmon trout

🔪🔪🔪 1 hour 30 minutes

Serves 6
1 salmon trout complete with head and tail,
  cleaned (about 1.4 kg /3 lb cleaned
  weight), trimmed
200 ml /7 fl oz dry white wine
1 small onion, sliced
3 black peppercorns
1 bay leaf
1 slice of lemon
salt and freshly ground black pepper
butter for greasing
7.5 ml /1¹/₂ tsp gelatine
30 ml /2 tbls dry sherry or water
1 medium-sized egg white plus the eggshell
¹/₂ small cucumber, thinly sliced
1 hard-boiled egg, thinly sliced
250 ml /9 fl oz thick mayonnaise
50 g /2 oz jar Danish caviare-style lumpfish roe

1 Heat the oven to 180C /350F /gas 4.
Wrap the fish loosely in muslin and place it
in a roasting tin, curling it slightly if
necessary. Pour in the wine and 200 ml /7 fl
oz water and add the onion, peppercorns,
bay leaf, lemon slice and a pinch of salt.
2 Butter a large piece of foil and form it
into a dome to cover the tin without
touching the fish. Cook in the oven for 30
minutes, basting once with the liquid in the
tin. Leave to cool in the liquid.
3 Lift the fish out carefully and drain it
well. Remove the muslin and place the fish
on a serving platter and chill.
4 Sprinkle the gelatine over the sherry or
water. Strain the fish-cooking liquid into a
pan and boil until it is reduced to about 200
ml /7 fl oz. Season if necessary.
5 To clarify the fish stock, whisk the egg
white and add to the pan with the crumbled
shell and soaked gelatine. Whisk well until
the liquid rises to the top of the pan.
Remove the heat and let settle for 5 minutes. Replace on the heat, boil up again,
then draw aside and leave for 5 minutes.
6 Scald a piece of muslin in boiling water
and wring it out. Place a sieve over a bowl
and line it with a double thickness of
muslin. Push the egg white froth to one side
and, if the liquid looks clear and sparkling,
ladle it into the muslin. If the liquid is not
quite clear, repeat the boiling up process
once more. Let the aspic cool until syrupy.
7 Slit the skin around the tail and behind
the gills on the head of the fish. Carefully
remove the skin from the upper half without
damaging the flesh. If wished the fish may
be rolled over and the second side skinned.
Remove the upper two fillets carefully with
fish slices and cut out and remove the bone
(see pictures *page 96*). Re-form the fish.
8 To decorate the fish, dip cucumber
slices in aspic and arrange a 'ruff' around
the head of the fish, covering the gills.
Arrange a line of alternate slices of cucumber and egg dipped in aspic, overlapping,
down the centre. Coat the fish with a thin
layer of aspic. Allow to set, then chill.
9 Garnish with piped rosettes of mayonnaise and mounds of roe. Serve at once.

Poached stuffed trout

**The flavour of this dish is enhanced by the
use of wine and vermouth, but it is also
excellent made with dry cider.**

🔪🔪 2 hours chilling,
     then 40 minutes

Serves 4
4 trout complete with heads and tails,
  cleaned (about 225 g /8 oz cleaned weight)
butter for greasing
90 ml /6 tbls dry white wine
30 ml /2 tbls dry white vermouth
50 g /2 oz butter
2 small shallots, finely chopped
50 g /2 oz hazelnuts, toasted and chopped
2.5 ml /¹/₂ tsp dillweed
60 ml /4 tbls dry wholemeal breadcrumbs
salt and freshly ground black pepper

1 Place the trout in a buttered ovenproof
dish and pour over the wine and vermouth.
Cover and chill for at least 2 hours.
2 Heat the oven to 180C /350F /gas 4.
Melt half the butter in a frying-pan and fry
the shallots gently until soft. Stir in half the
hazelnuts, the dillweed and the breadcrumbs. Season generously with salt and
pepper. Use to stuff the trout, then reshape
the fish and return to the dish.
3 Pour in 150 ml /5 fl oz water and
sprinkle each fish with a little salt and
pepper. Cover lightly with a sheet of buttered foil. Cook the fish for 20 minutes,
basting once with the juices in the dish.

*Glazed salmon trout and Cold baked
salmon with green mayonnaise*

4 Just before the fish is cooked, melt the
remaining butter in a small frying-pan. Toss
the rest of the hazelnuts in it until they are
hot. Scatter the fried nuts over the trout and
serve hot from the dish.

Salmon trout steaks with cucumber sauce

🔪 30 minutes

Serves 4
4 salmon trout steaks, about 175 g /6 oz each
salt
freshly ground black pepper
butter for greasing
40 g /1¹/₂ oz butter, melted
lemon slices, to garnish
parsley sprigs, to garnish
For the cucumber sauce
1 small cucumber, peeled and diced
salt and freshly ground white pepper
50 g /2 oz butter
150 ml /5 fl oz hot bechamel sauce
30 ml /2 tbls thick cream
15 ml /1 tbls very finely chopped parsley

1 Season the salmon trout steaks on both
sides with salt and pepper. Place them in a
grill pan lined with buttered foil and brush
with melted butter. Cook under a moderately hot grill for about 6 minutes. Turn

carefully and brush again with butter. Continue cooking for a further 5–6 minutes, or until the fish flakes easily.

2   Meanwhile, make the sauce: blanch the diced cucumber in boiling salted water for 1 minute and drain well. Melt the butter in a saucepan, add the cucumber and cook, stirring occasionally, until the cucumber is tender and the liquid has evaporated. Stir in the bechamel sauce and reheat to boiling point. Stir in the cream, season to taste and stir in the chopped parsley. Pour into a sauce-boat.

3   Transfer the fish steaks to a warm serving dish and garnish with the lemon slices and parsley sprigs. Serve the sauce separately.

Grilled trout with fennel

 45 minutes

Serves 4
4 small heads of fennel
75 g /3 oz butter
60 ml /4 tbls dry white breadcrumbs
finely grated zest and juice of 1 large lemon
2.5 ml /1/2 tsp dried marjoram
1.5 ml /1/4 tsp ground bay leaves
salt and freshly ground black pepper
4 trout complete with heads and tails, cleaned (about 225 g /8 oz cleaned weight)
60 ml /4 tbls seasoned flour
about 75 ml /3 fl oz dry white wine
30 ml /2 tbls oil

1   Trim the heads of fennel, remove a little of the stalk from the top of each head and keep for the stuffing. Reserve the green feathery leaves for the garnish. Cut each head in quarters.

2   Finely chop enough of the reserved fennel stalks to give 60 ml /4 tbls chopped fennel. Melt 25 g /1 oz butter in a pan, add the chopped fennel and cook gently until soft. Stir in the breadcrumbs, lemon zest, marjoram and bay leaves and season generously with salt and pepper. Use this to stuff the trout, then reshape the fish and coat them with seasoned flour.

3   Make the lemon juice up to 150 ml /5 fl oz with wine and place in a pan large enough eventually to take the fennel. Add a pinch of salt and 25 g /1 oz butter. Heat gently until the butter melts, then add the fennel quarters and turn them until coated with the wine mixture. Bring to the boil, cover and cook gently for about 10 minutes, or until the fennel is just tender and has absorbed the liquid.

4   Meanwhile, melt the remaining butter with the oil and pour about one-third of this into a foil-lined grill pan. Put in the fish, pour the remaining butter and oil over and cook under moderately high heat for 7 minutes, or until golden brown. Turn the fish carefully and cook for a further 7 minutes, or until golden brown on the other side.

5   Transfer the trout to a warmed serving dish, spoon over any buttery pan juices and arrange the cooked fennel at either end of the dish. Chop the fennel leaves and scatter over the fish, then serve at once.

Cold baked salmon with green mayonnaise

 1 hour 50 minutes plus cooling

Serves 10
1 salmon, complete with head and tail (about 2 kg /4 1/2 lb cleaned weight), cleaned and trimmed
salt
1 medium-sized onion, sliced
1 lemon, sliced
2-3 bay leaves
butter for greasing
1/2 large cucumber, unpeeled and thinly sliced
1 small bunch of radishes, thinly sliced
400 ml /14 fl oz liquid aspic (made from crystals)
flat-leaved parsley, to garnish
For the green mayonnaise
45 ml /3 tbls finely chopped mixed herbs (tarragon, dill, chervil, chives, parsley)
4 large spinach leaves, blanched
500 ml /18 fl oz mayonnaise
salt and freshly ground black pepper (optional)

1   Heat the oven to 180C /350F /gas 4. Sprinkle the salmon with salt, pack the cavity with sliced onion, lemon and bay leaves to keep its shape and wrap it loosely in well-buttered foil, making an airtight parcel. Place on a baking sheet and cook for 50 minutes. Let it cool wrapped in the foil.

2   Make up the aspic using aspic cystals according to the packet directions. Leave this to cool.

3   When the fish is cold, unwrap it and transfer it to a very large platter, being careful not to break it up. Remove and discard the onion, lemon and bay leaves. Slit the skin neatly across the tail and behind the gills at the back of the head. Remove the skin from the upper half of the salmon, being careful not to damage the flesh. If wished remove the two upper fillets carefully with two fish slices. Cut the backbone at the head and tail end and remove it and all small bones, especially round the cavity (see pictures *page 96*). Replace the upper fillets.

4   Use the aspic when it is syrupy, dipping the decorations into the aspic and then applying them to the fish so they stick. To garnish the fish, arrange a line of cucumber slices, overlapping, down the centre of the fish and then a line of radish slices, also overlapping, down each side of the cucumber. Put a 'ruff' of cucumber or radish slices around the head. Chill well.

5   Heat the aspic again to make it syrupy if necessary and coat fish with a thin layer. Let set. Coat again to glaze. Chill until set.

6   Meanwhile, make the green mayonnaise. Pound the herbs and press through a sieve with the spinach leaves. Beat the purée into the mayonnaise and add salt and pepper if wished. Clean up any spills on the serving platter and garnish with parsley and more cucumber slices. Hand the sauce separately.

Smoked fish

Start the day as the Victorians did, with hot, creamy kedgeree, have kipper and kidney bean salad for lunch, or impress your dinner guests with an elegant smoked cod mousse – smoked fish is delicious, nutritious and easy to use.

Succulent pairs of chestnut-coloured kippers; wafer-thin coral slices of smoked salmon; tasty smoked trout – they are all the delicious descendants of a chance prehistoric discovery. For the process of smoking fish is thought to have developed from the age-old method of preserving fish by wind drying. Anxious to hasten a process entirely at the mercy of the elements, prehistoric man must have hung fish on poles over wood or peat smoke, and both dehydrated and preserved the fish. This was a vital breakthrough, extending the safe-keeping period of the summer's catch through the long winter ahead.

Later, fishermen learned to begin the dehydration process by layering the fish in salt or soaking it in brine, thus shortening the smoking time. Salting became the primary method of preserving fish in most of Europe, from the brine-pickled herrings of Scandinavia to the tough-as-leather salt cod of Spain and Portugal. Smoked fish has survived the invention of all present-day methods of preservation and in Britain is a national speciality. For now, with refrigerated storage and freeze-drying, there is no need for brining and smoking. Indeed, fish is now only lightly smoked, enough to impart flavour, but not enough to increase its keeping properties substantially.

The smoking process

There are two alternative ways of smoking fish and each one produces a different result. 'Hot smoking' produces cooked, ready-to-eat fish. 'Cold smoking', however, takes place at a much lower temperature, and it produces a smoky-tasting fish which usually needs to be cooked before it is eaten.

In both methods, the first step is to remove as much moisture as possible from the fish. The fish is either layered with dry salt or soaked in brine. The next step is to process the fish in kilns or chambers in smoke produced from smouldering hardwood chips or sawdust. It is the herbs or spices used in the brine, and the type of wood used, that give the individual flavours.

You can buy home-smoking appliances which make it easy to hot-smoke fish at home or, preferably, on the beach, where you can smoke the fish straight off the boat. Remember that for smoking, as for all consumption, fish must be in absolutely perfect condition.

Hot-smoked fish

These fish tend to be relatively expensive, but are ready to eat and therefore one of the most natural and nutritious forms of 'convenience food'.

Eel: smoked eel is not widely available, but you can sometimes find it, either filleted or on the bone, at delicatessens. The flesh should be firm but pliable.

Serve smoked eel as a first course. Allow about 50 g /2 oz per person, and serve it, sliced, on a bed of shredded lettuce with lemon wedges, cayenne pepper and thin slices of brown bread and butter.

Arbroath smokies: small haddock or whiting are cleaned, salted and hung, without being opened out, to be smoked over oak or silver birch chips until the outside is a pale copper colour and the inside is tender.

Although they are technically hot-smoked and therefore do not need further cooking, Arbroath smokies are usually brushed with butter and lightly grilled or fried before serving. They are one of the most delicious of breakfast luxuries.

Bucklings: these are herrings that have been gutted, beheaded and partially dehydrated in brine, then smoked. The skin should be silvery-gold and the flesh a pale golden colour with a soft, moist texture.

To serve, skin the fish – dipping in boiling water for a few seconds makes it easier to peel the skin away – and serve it whole. Fillet very large fish. Serve simply with lemon wedges, cayenne pepper and brown bread and butter. Bucklings make excellent pâtés and are good in salads, especially combined with hard-boiled eggs.

Mackerel: one of the most readily available of smoked fish, whole or filleted mackerel make a delicious instant lunch or supper.

Allow about 75–100 g /3–4 oz per person and serve with wedges of lemon. Smoked mackerel makes a delicately flavoured pâté (see recipe) and can be pounded and mixed with softened butter, cream cheese, cream or sieved cottage cheese.

Trout are first gutted and then smoked on the bone. Check that the skin is shiny and looks as if it has just been lightly brushed with oil. Dry skin indicates dry flesh.

For a first course or a light lunch or supper dish, allow one small whole fish per person, weighing about 175 g /6 oz. For a more substantial meal, allow about 200–225 g /7–8 oz each. When serving the fish whole leave on the head and tail. The skin may be removed just before serving.

Horseradish and trout are a good combination of flavours – serve horseradish sauce with whole smoked trout, or mix horseradish into mayonnaise for a salad. Or, just as delicious, serve simply with lemon, pepper and brown bread and butter.

Cold-smoked fish

Bloaters and red herrings: both are processed from herrings. Bloaters are dry-salted and very lightly smoked without being gutted first. They are recognizable by the bright silvery sheen of their skins. Red herrings are heavily salted and also smoked ungutted, but they are not easily obtainable – you might find them in Cypriot or West Indian food shops.

To serve, lightly grill or fry bloaters or red herrings in butter, using a low heat.

Cod: sometimes sold as 'smoked fillet', and often coloured a bright golden yellow artificially, smoked cod is at its best from May to October in the Northern hemisphere. It has many uses in cooking but is not considered to have such a fine flavour as smoked haddock.

It can be gently poached in milk or water, fried, grilled or baked. After cooking, you can flake it into scrambled eggs, pancake fillings or omelettes, add it to cheesy fillings for open flans or stir it into horseradish or tomato mayonnaise in salads.

Haddock: large haddocks are filleted before smoking and many are artificially dyed bright yellow or dull orange to simulate the colour that was achieved by long smoking processes. Those sold as 'golden cutlets' are the small fish, filleted and smoked. They may need soaking for 2 hours before cooking if the cure was very salty.

Serve smoked haddock in the same ways as smoked cod (see above).

Kippers: said to be a favourite of the late King George VI, kippers are herrings in yet another guise. They are first split, gutted, slightly dehydrated in brine and then smoked. The best flavour is to be found in the undyed kippers that are smoked to a deep yellowish-brown, but many are now dyed to a deeper red-chestnut shade. They are available all year round, but at their best from August to April in the Northern hemisphere, and can be bought whole, boned, filleted, canned and vacuum-packed as 'boil in the bag' products. The best are said to come from Northumberland, Loch Fyne and the Isle of Man.

Kippers can be served without further cooking if they are very fresh – try them

A selection of smoked fish: 1 golden cutlets (whiting); 2 mackerel fillets; 3 kipper fillets; 4 cod fillets; 5 haddock fillets; 6 kippers; 7 trout; 8 mackerel; 9 Arbroath smokies; 10 eel; 11 cods' roe (see page 131); 12 sprats; 13 salmon

marinated in oil and lemon juice or wine vinegar. In this they are an exception to the rule that all cold-smoked fish must be cooked. They can be lightly grilled or poached, but enthusiasts insist that the best way to cook them is to jug them, that is, dip them, head first, into a jug of boiling water for 5 minutes, then drain, pat them dry and serve on hot plates with little pats of butter. Kippers also make very good pâtés.

Salmon: Scottish and Irish salmon are held to be far superior in flavour, though more expensive, than the Pacific and darker-coloured Canadian salmon. The fish is dry-salted and then smoked over oak chips. The flesh should be dense and slightly glossy. Smoked salmon is available as a whole side, half side (both more suitable for a big buffet party), or thinly shaved into almost translucent slices and sold by weight or in vacuum packs. You often find smoked salmon trimmings at a more reasonable price.

Smoked salmon is the king of smoked fish, to be presented at its simplest – serve it with lemon wedges, cayenne pepper and the thinnest possible slices of brown bread and butter. Trimmings can be made into pâtés, mousses, dips or quiches. The flavour of smoked salmon is so pronounced that a little goes a long way.

Sprats: the smallest of the smoked fish, sprats are members of the herring family. They are relatively inexpensive, though not very readily available.

Serve them grilled, shallow fried or tossed in seasoned flour and deep fried. Sprats are served whole to be filleted on the plate.

Buying and storing smoked fish

Whole smoked fish such as trout and sprats should have crisp, glossy skins without any signs of shrivelling. Filleted fish should be slightly moist but never slimy. Signs to avoid are dryness and lack of lustre.

Since fish is not now smoked as a means of preservation, it should not be kept for very long. Keep smoked herrings for a maximum of 3 days, kippers for up to 5 days, and other smoked fish for up to 4 days. Store it in the refrigerator, well wrapped so that it keeps its flavour to itself. A light wrapping of greaseproof paper inside a lidded plastic box is ideal.

❋❋❋❋ Smoked fish can be stored in the freezer for up to 1 month.

Cooking smoked fish

Ideas for cooking and serving smoked fish have appeared under the individual headings, but here are some more general suggestions:

Smoked fish are delicious flaked into salads, especially with a lemon or orange flavoured vinaigrette dressing, and they are also ideal for pâtés, which you can serve in chilled empty lemon shells or orange halves, for dramatic presentation. Smoked fish pâté is super scooped up with fresh raw vegetables, or spread on cocktail canapés.

Smoked fish give a particularly delicate flavour to soups such as chowders. With the addition of potatoes, sweetcorn and carrots, the chowder becomes a meal in a pot, needing nothing more than fresh, crusty bread and, perhaps, a glass of cider.

All smoked fish combines especially well with eggs and cream, and never better than in a quiche which can be served as a first course, lunch or supper dish, or part of a buffet meal. You can even start your day with smoked fish; try kedgeree, the traditional Victorian breakfast dish of fish, rice and eggs, grilled or fried Arbroath smokies, or smoked haddock stirred into scrambled eggs.

A final word on cooking with smoked fish – you can minimize the smell by wrapping fish for grilling, baking or boiling in foil and sealing the parcel well all round. All the smell and flavour will be trapped inside.

Smoked cod mousse

〰 40 minutes
〰 plus 2 hours setting time

Serves 4–6
225 g /8 oz cooked, smoked cod
10 ml /2 tsp powdered gelatine
6 medium-sized eggs, hard-boiled
90 ml /6 tbls mayonnaise
5 ml /1 tsp anchovy essence (optional)
60 ml /4 tbls thick cream
salt and freshly ground black pepper
pinch of cayenne pepper
1/4 small cucumber, thinly sliced, to garnish

Smoked mackerel pâte

1 Flake the cooked smoked cod and remove any small bones. Set it aside.
2 Pour 30 ml /2 tbls water into a cup, sprinkle on the gelatine and stand the cup in a bowl of hot water. Stir occasionally until the gelatine has dissolved, about 10 minutes.
3 Meanwhile, coarsely chop 5 of the hard-boiled eggs, reserving the remaining one to garnish the mousse.
4 Mix together the mayonnaise, anchovy essence (if using), cream, flaked fish, dissolved gelatine and chopped eggs. Stir until the gelatine is completely distributed throughout the mixture. Season to taste with salt, pepper and cayenne pepper.
5 Rinse an 850 ml /1½ pt soufflé dish with cold water. Pour in the fish mixture and cover. Chill in the refrigerator for 2 hours, or until the mousse is set.
6 If you wish to turn out the mousse, run a knife around the edge, put a serving plate over the top, invert the dish and give a sharp shake so that the mousse is turned out on to the plate. Or you can leave the mousse in the dish.
7 Thinly slice the remaining hard-boiled egg and arrange the slices in a ring round the edge of the mousse alternating with the slices of cucumber.

Smoked mackerel pâté

⅄ 15 minutes

Serves 4
350 g /12 oz smoked mackerel fillets
150 ml /5 fl oz soured cream
100 g /4 oz cream cheese
25 g /1 oz butter, at room temperature
salt (optional)
large pinch of cayenne pepper
5 ml /1 tsp grated orange zest
30 ml /2 tbls orange juice
4 small orange shells
4 small bay leaves, to garnish

1 Strip away the skin fom the mackerel, and finely flake the flesh, discarding any small bones.
2 Put the soured cream, cream cheese, softened butter and flaked mackerel into a blender and blend until the mixture forms a soft paste, scraping the sides of the container once or twice, if necessary.
3 Season to taste with salt, if needed, and cayenne pepper and add the orange zest and a few drops of the orange juice. Blend again, add a little more orange juice and blend. Continue until all the orange juice is incorporated.
4 Cut a thin slice from the base of each orange shell so that the shells can stand without toppling. Spoon in the pâté and shape it into a mound at the top. Loosely cover the filled orange shells and chill.
5 Stick a bay leaf into the top of each mound of pâté before serving.

Smoked trout with mustard sauce

⅄ 10 minutes

Serves 4
4 small smoked trout, 175 g /6 oz each
For the sauce
150 g /5 fl oz thick cream
10 ml /2 tsp made mustard
a few drops of lemon juice
salt and freshly ground black pepper
15 ml /1 tbls chopped chives
To serve
shredded lettuce
shapes cut from hard-boiled egg white
1 tomato, blanched, skinned, seeded and cut into shapes
1 lemon, sliced

1 To make the mustard sauce, whisk the cream until it is just thick but not stiff. Beat in the mustard, lemon juice, salt and pepper and stir in the chives.
2 Cut the skin of each trout across the head and tail, and neatly peel off the skin.
3 Cover a serving plate with the lettuce and arrange the trout on it. Garnish with the egg white shapes, tomato shapes and lemon slices. Serve the sauce separately.

Smoked salmon quiche

⅄⅄ 1¼ hours

Serves 4–6
shortcrust pastry made with 175 g/6 oz flour
4 large eggs
150 ml /5 fl oz thick cream
150 ml /5 fl oz thin cream
30 ml /2 tbls chicken stock or milk
freshly ground black pepper
pinch of cayenne pepper
pinch of grated nutmeg
100 g /4 oz smoked salmon trimmings
10 ml /2 tsp chopped parsley

1 Heat the oven to 200C/400F/gas 6.
2 Line a 20 cm/8 in flan tin with the pastry, then with foil and beans, and bake blind for 10 minutes. Remove the foil and beans and bake for 8 minutes more. Reduce heat to 180C/350F/gas 4.
3 Whisk together the eggs, thick and thin creams and stock or milk, and season with black pepper, cayenne pepper and a pinch of nutmeg.
4 Remove any bits of skin from the smoked salmon trimmings and arrange them in the pastry case, stir the parsley into the egg and cream mixture and pour it over the salmon. Bake in the centre of the oven for 30–40 minutes until filling is just set.
5 Leave the quiche to cool a little in the tin, then transfer it to a serving dish. Serve warm.

Kipper and kidney bean salad

⅄ 15 minutes
plus 30 minutes standing

Serves 4
175 g /6 oz cooked or canned red kidney beans
350 g /12 oz kipper fillets, skinned and flaked
1 small onion, thinly sliced
1 garlic clove, crushed
For the dressing
60 ml /4 tbls olive oil
15 ml /1 tbls orange juice
15 ml /1 tbls red wine vinegar
salt and freshly ground black pepper
5 ml /1 tsp grated orange zest
To serve
lettuce leaves
1 lemon, quartered

1 If you are using canned kidney beans, drain them, then rinse in cold water and drain again. Toss together the flaked kippers, beans, onion and garlic.
2 To make the dressing, shake together the oil, orange juice, wine vinegar, and salt and pepper to taste. Stir in the orange zest and pour the dressing over the salad. Cover and leave at room temperature for about 30 minutes.
3 Just before serving, arrange some lettuce leaves on a serving dish, or in 4 individual salad bowls, spoon on the salad and garnish with the lemon wedges.

Smoked trout with mustard sauce

Lesser known fish

Go Greek tonight with grilled swordfish kebabs, try red mullet cooked Italian-style, or make the classic French pike dumplings called quenelles. Learn about these and other less familiar fish.

The oceans, rivers and lakes of the world are full of fascinating fish, some which are not very well known, and others which do not fit easily into the major categories covered in this chapter.

Some fish, such as the red mullet, are beautiful. Others, like the ferocious-looking monkfish, are beheaded before reaching the fishmonger for fear of frightening the customers . . . yet both are delicious to eat. So whenever you see an unfamiliar species for sale try it, or you may miss out on a rare treat or an interesting bargain.

For information on buying and storing fish, see *page 79*.

Saltwater fish

Conger eel: shape apart, there is little similarity between conger eel and river eels. Congers are very much larger and coarser, and have substantial flesh which needs long cooking to tenderize it. They are usually sold skinned; the centre and head end are preferred to the tail end, which is bony. Stew congers with strongly flavoured ingredients or use them for fish soups.

Garfish: the garfish is a very long fish (its nickname is the sea needle) with bright green bones. Its flesh can be a bit dry but it has a good flavour. Poach or fry it.

Grey mullet: in Australia, where red mullet is rare, this handsome, silvery grey fish with its large scales is known simply as mullet. It can be recognized by a series of dark lines from head to tail on the upper part of the body. It is caught in coastal waters and estuaries throughout the oceans of the world. When caught in clean waters it is a good fish with firm white flesh. Mullet caught in brackish estuaries can taste muddy and needs cleaning in salt water.

Grey mullet are usually sold whole, weigh from 450 g–1.8 kg /1–4 lb, and need scaling and gutting. Small fish can be grilled, larger fish poached or baked, whole or in fillets. A rich sauce complements the delicate flavour. Baked grey mullet served in a pie is a traditional Cornish dish.

Monkfish or angler-fish: a flattened, cone-shaped tail is all you are likely to see of this aggressive, huge-headed fish, yet it is one of the most prized Mediterranean fish, and is also found in the North Sea. The firm, milky white flesh of the tail is lobster-like in texture and taste, and boneless except for the central spine. Tails weigh from 225 g /8 oz to over 2 kg /4½ lb.

Whole tails can be baked with moist vegetables, or poached and served with a sauce. Any leftovers make an excellent salad. Small cubes can be grilled *en brochette*. Egg and breadcrumbed and deep fried, they can pass for scampi! Try strips of monkfish in any scampi recipe.

Pompano, bluefish and amberjack are a group of fish with bluish backs and silver bellies, popular on the Atlantic coast of America as well as in the Mediterranean. Their white, compact flesh makes good eating. The pompano has a very divided tail and sharply raked fins. The scad or horse mackerel is related, but not of such high quality. Cook these fish by any method.

Red gurnard: the best of the gurnard species, red gurnard is recognized by its bright colour – it is called the sea robin – and cone-shaped body tapering from a large, bony head. On either side of it extends a pair of fan-shaped fins that look like wings. This fish has a good flavour and firm flesh, but beware the sharp spines and fine bones.

Red gurnard weigh 225–700 g /8 oz–1½ lb and are sold whole. The head accounts for up to half the weight so allow at least 350 g /12 oz per person. Bake prepared (beheaded and skinned) whole fish with moist vegetables and cheese or cook *en papillote*.

Swordfish kebabs

Making quenelles

Whip the cream stiffly, then fold it into the puréed fish and egg mixture, gently but thoroughly. Chill the mixture 3–4 hours in the refrigerator.

Using two wet dessertspoons, shape the quenelles mixture into plump oval shapes. Keep a bowl of water nearby to dampen the spoons.

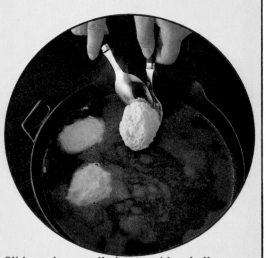

Slide each quenelle into a wide, shallow pan containing barely simmering salted water and poach for 8 minutes, turning them once.

Larger fish can be filleted and skinned, then cooked as white fish fillets. There is also a grey gurnard, which is best baked.

Red gurnard is available in Australia; latchet is an Australian gurnard of lesser quality.

Red mullet: beloved of the ancient Romans, this bright red little fish, distinguished by long twin barbels (feelers) under the jaw, is still a popular fish along the Mediterranean. Some people consider it the finest fish of all. It is sometimes called the 'sea woodcock' because the liver, which should always be replaced after gutting, gives it a slightly gamey taste.

Red mullet are always sold, and usually cooked, whole, but need scaling and cleaning. One 225 g /8 oz fish provides an average portion; larger fish can be cooked whole and then filleted. Numerous recipes exist for both hot and cold red mullet, almost invariably based on grilling or frying in butter.

Red mullet is occasionally available in Australia, where it may be known as goatfish.

Shark: porbeagle and tope are members of the shark family likely to appear on the fishmonger's slab from time to time. These vast fish are usually skinned and sold in steaks or tail pieces. Don't be put off by the slight ammonia smell common to all members of the shark family – this quickly disperses on cooking. Except for the central spine, sharks are bone free, with smooth greyish skins. The flesh is almost veal-like in texture.

Fry or grill shark steaks and serve with a tasty sauce, bake *en papillote*, or cut into chunks for fish steaks or kebabs. In Australia, shark is known as flake.

Swordfish is a long, slender fish distinguished by a sharp, sword-like protrusion which can account for one-third of its length (generally 2–3 m /6½–10 ft).

Swordfish is usually sold as steaks; the flesh is fine-grained, firm and meaty. Swordfish steaks are excellent grilled, either whole or as kebabs (see recipe), or braised

with juicy vegetables. You may also come across it smoked.

Tuna or tunny: various members of the tuna family (which includes the bonito, skipjack and albacore) are found along the Mediterranean, Atlantic and Pacific, as well as in Australia. The flesh of these handsome, silvery, smooth-skinned fish, so familiar in cans, is reddish, firm, oily and almost meat-like.

Tuna is sold in slices or pieces; the belly is the most delicate part. High-quality tuna slices can be grilled or fried, but a safer method for coarser parts is to braise the fish with vegetables.

Weever has sharp, poisonous spines, a greyish-brown back and creamy belly. Found buried on the sandy beaches of the Mediterranean, Britain and Australia, it is a good eating fish with firm flesh. Fillets can be marinated and grilled, or battered and deep fried. Use small weevers in stews or fish soups.

Freshwater fish

Any stubborn scales on freshwater fish are more easily removed if the fish is plunged briefly into boiling water before scaling. The flavour of fish caught in muddy waters benefits from several hours of soaking after preparation in water acidulated with vinegar (use 75 ml/5 tbls vinegar to every 2 L/3½ pt water).

Carp is one of the best freshwater fish, with firm, sweet-tasting flesh. Its roe is considered a delicacy. Carp can grow to a great age and size, but those of 1.1–1.8 kg /2½–4 lb are preferable. Carp can be cooked by any method; stuffing and baking, or braising in a sweet and sour sauce are the most popular, but fried carp steaks are also delicious. Carp is available in Australia.

Eels and elvers: although born at sea, these slender, silvery fish spend most of their lives in rivers and lakes. Buy eel live if possible and let the fishmonger kill, skin, clean and cut it up. The flesh is rich in oil. Marinate eel, then grill or bake on a grid so the fat can

drain away, or make into a pie or a stew. Eel simmered in a well-flavoured court bouillon which sets to a jelly on cooling is the famous speciality of London's East End, jellied eels.

Elvers are thread-like baby eels, about 6.5 cm /2½ in long. They are available in season at the mouths of certain rivers, and are sold by weight. Wash them thoroughly in salted water, toss in seasoned flour and deep fry, or parboil and cool, then shallow fry in butter with garlic and parsley. Both eels and elvers are available in Australia.

Perch is a good eating fish, but one that should be cleaned and scaled immediately after being caught. Fry it in butter, poach and serve with a rich sauce, or stuff and braise it. Murray cod is an Australian perch (see below).

Pike is a large fish with a dark body mottled with cream and with mottled fins and tail. The thrusting bottom jaw is full of teeth. It is highly regarded in France, where it is known as *brochet*. Its white flesh is incredibly bony and inclined to be dry. Pike is best poached and served with a rich sauce, braised on a bed of vegetables or fried in butter. It is much used for mousses and quenelles (see recipe) and can also be stuffed and roasted.

Australian sea pike (snook) is a different fish but makes good eating.

Other freshwater fish: gudgeon are small fish which must be cooked very fresh. Bream and barbel are related to carp and need well-seasoned sauces. Similarly, tench are not very highly regarded for culinary purposes. However, the mottled burbot is highly rated on the European continent. The zander or pike-perch, which has a bulbous head and backward-sloping teeth, is popular in Central Europe, where it is considered to have a flavour not unlike sole, but it is not highly regarded elsewhere.

Some Australian fish

Barracouta is a large fish, usually purchased as fillets. It has oily white flesh with a good flavour.

Barramundi or a giant perch is considered to be one of Australia's finest food fishes, with firm, white, tender flesh. The average weight is about 4.5 kg /10 lb. Barramundi is good baked, but it can also be grilled or poached.

Catfish, also known as rockfish or wolf-fish, is a fierce-looking North Atlantic and Australian fish with protuberances round the mouth which look like a cat's whiskers. However, it is usually sold beheaded, skinned and cut in pieces. It has a firm texture and good flavour. Fry it and serve with a sauce, or use for fish pie or a stew.

Gemfish is a popular fish with a good texture and flavour. Usually sold in fillets, it can be cooked by any method.

Kingfish is a large fish with good eating qualities. The yellowtail is one of the best varieties. Kingfish is best baked, either whole or as steaks.

Mulloway: sometimes known as butterfish or jewfish, this is an oily fish with a good flavour. Fish weighing over 5 kg /11 lb often have a coarse texture. Mulloway is usually sold as steaks, which can be poached, fried, or marinated and then grilled.

Murray cod is a highly esteemed Australian perch. It is a large fish with a delicate flavour. Cook as perch.

Red emperor is a North Australian reef fish which is excellent for eating. It is best baked or braised.

Pike quenelles with prawn sauce

Pike, which needs painstaking boning, is traditional for these light and creamy dumplings, but other firm-fleshed fish such as monkfish, turbot, sole, John Dory or whiting make delicious quenelles.

35 minutes, 3–4 hours chilling, making sauce, then 20 minutes

Serves 4
225 g /8 oz boned, skinned pike (up to 500 g /1 lb before boning)
2 large eggs
90 ml /6 tbls thick cream
salt and freshly ground white pepper
freshly grated nutmeg
prawn sauce (see below), to serve
peeled prawns, lemon slices and parsley sprigs, to garnish

1 Cut up the fish roughly and reduce it to a purée, with the eggs, in a food processor or strong blender. Press the purée through a fine sieve into a bowl.
2 Whip the cream until it is stiff enough to hold its shape, then fold lightly but thoroughly into the fish. Season to taste with salt, pepper and nutmeg. Cover and re-

frigerate for 3–4 hours to firm the mixture.
3 Prepare the sauce and keep it hot.
4 Fill a wide, shallow pan with salted water and bring to simmering point.
5 Using wet dessertspoons, take a heaped spoonful of the fish mixture and shape it into a plump oval (see pictures, *page 105*).
6 Slide the quenelle into the barely simmering liquid and repeat, cooking the quenelles in 2 batches to avoid overcrowding if necessary. Poach for 4 minutes each side, maintaining the water at a bare quiver throughout – if cooked too quickly the quenelles will disintegrate.
7 Lift out with a slotted spoon, drain on absorbent paper and arrange in each of 4 warmed, individual dishes.
8 Spoon the sauce over the quenelles, garnish with the prawns, lemon slices and parsley sprigs and serve at once.

● Prawn sauce: melt 20 g/¾ oz butter in a heavy-based saucepan and stir in 1½ tbls flour. Cook over low heat for 1–2 minutes, stirring, then add 225 ml/7½ fl oz fish or chicken stock. Stir until creamy, simmer gently for 20 minutes then add 150 ml/5 fl oz thick cream and continue cooking for 25 minutes, stirring occasionally. To finish: sauté 175 g/6 oz chopped prawns in 20 g/¾ oz butter, season to taste and add to sauce.

Poached grey mullet with herb sauce

This method of making a concentrated court bouillon and then diluting it eliminates the usual cooling time and allows the fish to be cooked immediately.

1–2 hours chilling, then 1 hour

Serves 4
1 grey mullet, about 1 kg /2 lb 3 oz, scaled and
*   gutted, with head left on*
salt
lemon slices, to garnish (optional)
fresh fennel leaves, to garnish (optional)
For the court bouillon
175 g /6 oz onion, sliced
1 large carrot, sliced
10 black peppercorns, lightly crushed
15 ml /1 tbls sea salt
large bouquet garni
45 ml /3 tbls white wine vinegar
For the sauce
2 medium-sized egg yolks
5–10 ml /1–2 tsp Dijon mustard
3–4 drops of tarragon vinegar
30 ml /2 tbls freshly chopped herbs – parsley,
*   fennel, chervil, chives, as available*
50 g /2 oz butter
salt and freshly ground black pepper

1 Sprinkle the gut cavity of the fish with salt and refrigerate for 1–2 hours.
2 Prepare the court bouillon. Place the onion, carrot, peppercorns, sea salt, bouquet garni and vinegar in a fish kettle, large casserole or saucepan and add 1.1 L /2 pt cold water. Bring to the boil and simmer for 30 minutes.
3 Add 600 ml /1 pt cold water to reduce the temperature, then lower the fish in gently, curving it to fit the pan if necessary and adding more water as needed to just cover the fish.
4 Bring slowly to simmering point, then cover, lower the heat and simmer gently, with the liquid barely quivering, for 10 minutes. Turn off the heat and leave the fish in the water for a further 10 minutes.
5 Meanwhile, prepare the sauce. Beat the egg yolks, mustard, vinegar and herbs together in a bowl. Barely melt the butter and add, little by little, to the sauce, stirring vigorously all the time. Season to taste with salt and pepper.
6 Lift the fish carefully from the liquid, drain thoroughly and arrange on a hot serving platter. Gently peel off and discard the skin and blot off any liquid from the platter with absorbent paper. Spoon the sauce over the fish, garnish with lemon slices and fennel leaves, if wished, and serve the fish at once.

Poached grey mullet with herb sauce

Swordfish kebabs

Swordfish is particularly good grilled, especially on an open fire.

3–4 hours marinating, then 25 minutes

Serves 4
550 g /1¼ lb swordfish steaks, about 25 mm /1
*   in thick*
30 ml /2 tbls olive oil
30 ml /2 tbls lemon juice
a few slices of raw onion
salt and freshly ground black pepper
100 g /4 oz streaky bacon slices, cut into squares
8 bay leaves, halved
175 g /6 oz button mushrooms
buttered rice, to serve
4 lemon quarters, to garnish

1 Remove all skin and bone from the fish and cut into 25 mm /1 in cubes. Place in a bowl with the oil, lemon juice, onion and salt and pepper. Stir, cover and marinate for 3–4 hours, stirring occasionally.
2 Strain off the marinade and reserve. Discard the onion. Arrange alternately on 4 long skewers the fish, bacon, bay leaves and mushrooms.
3 Heat the grill to moderate or, if you are barbecuing the fish, wait until the flames die down and the embers are red hot. Brush the kebabs with some of the marinade. Grill for 12–15 minutes, turning and brushing with marinade several times, until cooked.
4 Serve the kebabs on a bed of buttered rice, accompanied by lemon quarters.

Calabrian mullet

30 minutes

Serves 4
4 red mullet, about 225 g /8 oz each, scaled,
*   cleaned and gutted, with heads on and*
*   livers replaced*
45 ml /3 tbls well-seasoned flour
45 ml /3 tbls olive oil
15 ml /1 tbls chopped fresh marjoram or
*   5 ml /1 tsp dried marjoram*
40 g /1½ oz butter
30 ml /2 tbls drained capers
12 black olives, stoned and cut into slivers
15 ml /1 tbls lemon juice
5 ml /1 tsp finely grated lemon zest
15 ml /1 tbls freshly chopped parsley
lemon slices, to garnish

1 Coat the fish with seasoned flour, shaking to remove any surplus.
2 Heat the oil and marjoram in a large, heavy frying-pan and fry the mullet over moderate heat for 6–8 minutes each side, until crisp, golden and cooked through. Lift onto a hot serving platter and keep warm.
3 Heat the butter in a small saucepan until it is just beginning to turn brown, then remove the pan from the heat and stir in the capers, olives, lemon juice, zest and parsley.
4 Spoon the sauce over the fish, garnish the dish with lemon slices and serve at once.

Shrimps, prawns and scampi

Potted shrimps, prawn cocktails and deep-fried scampi are among the most popular restaurant dishes. But there are many other ways of cooking these delicious shellfish: try some of them for a real treat and dine out at home.

Shrimps, prawns, scampi and the fresh-water crayfish are crustaceans, as distinct from the other big family of shellfish: the molluscs. The latter includes oysters, clams, scallops, cockles, mussels, winkles and snails. Unlike the molluscs, which have a solid outer shell, crustaceans have hard, horny external skeletons. These are segmented to allow for movement and periodically shed as the shellfish outgrow them.

Shrimps, prawns and scampi inhabit inshore waters throughout the world, but the crayfish is found in fresh water. These shellfish are grey or almost transparent before cooking and acquire their pink, red or brownish colour when cooked. They are very nutritious and their flavour is unbeatable, which makes them universal favourites.

Shrimps

Shrimps inhabit sandy seabeds and in some areas can be harvested at low tide in push nets. In European waters there are two distinct families, which are called after the colour they become when cooked. The pink shrimp is mainly restricted to British waters, but the brown shrimp swims round shores from Norway to the Mediterranean: it is called *crevette grise* in France and *gamberetto grigio* in Italy. Most North Americans describe as 'shrimp' the larger crustaceans which are known as 'prawns' in European countries.

The distinction between prawns and shrimps in Europe is mainly one of size – shrimps are tiny, prawns are larger – and this is now being backed by EEC regulations. Because shrimps are so small, they cannot be shelled mechanically. So if you are serving tiny shrimps, let your guests peel their own, or look for recipes that require only a small weight of peeled bodies.

Prawns

Prawns are fished off rocky coasts in many parts of the world. The small to medium-size northern prawn, caught in the cold waters off Greenland, Canada and Norway, has a fine taste and texture and is widely used for canning and freezing. The common prawn of the northern hemisphere is semi-transparent or grey in colour and turns pinkish red after cooking. It is called *crevette rose* in France and *gamberello* in Italy.

The Mediterranean has several distinct species of prawn and these are exported and sold as 'Mediterranean prawns'. They are often considerably larger than the common prawn, with a firm texture, bright red colour and excellent flavour. The French *crevette rouge*, the Italian *gambero rosa* and the Spanish *gamba* are all in this group.

Prawns caught in very warm waters tend to be tougher and less tasty. Malaysian prawns are fairly small, but king prawns (also called Pacific and jumbo prawns and 'green' prawns in Australia because of their green-greyish colour when raw) are particularly large and can weigh up to 50 g /2 oz each. These are caught in the Indian and Pacific Oceans (especially off the North Australian coast) and also in the Caribbean and off the West African coast.

Scampi

This Italian name is increasingly used for a shellfish which is a miniature member of the lobster family, and is sometimes called a Norway lobster. Over half the shellfish consists of a huge pair of claws, which have hardly any meat inside them. It is the scampi tails that are most often eaten. The body covering is much stronger than that of a prawn, and more difficult to remove.

Scampi are fished in Atlantic waters from Iceland to Morocco. Another name by which they are known is Dublin Bay prawn for it was in Dublin Bay that large catches from northern waters were sold at one time. In France they are called *langoustines*. Scampi caught in the Adriatic are very large.

Fresh-water crayfish

These shellfish are similar in appearance to scampi, but are generally smaller. Unlike shrimps, prawns and scampi, they only live in rivers and lakes, in chalky districts. They are abundant in Norway and France, where they are considered a special delicacy, and in other parts of Central Europe and North America. In Australia fresh-water crayfish are called yabbies and are found in most parts of the continent. These small, dark grey shellfish are distinct from the much larger spiny sea lobster, which is sometimes rather confusingly also called crayfish or crawfish. (Spiny lobsters are covered on *page 121*).

Peeling cooked shrimps and prawns

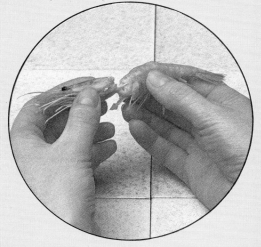

Straighten the prawns out and pull off the whole head with a twisting movement. (Reserve the heads if needed for stock.)

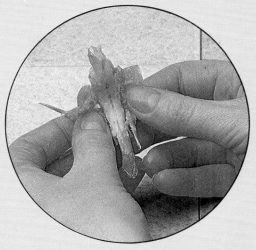

Insert your fingers under the legs and pull upward over the saddle of the prawn, exposing the pink body.

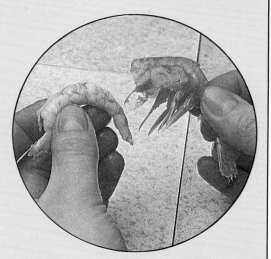

Hold firmly onto the body and pinch the tail to release pressure. Pull the body out of the remaining shell in one piece.

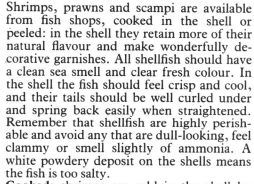

Scampi with their heads on and prawns

Buying shellfish

Shrimps, prawns and scampi are available from fish shops, cooked in the shell or peeled: in the shell they retain more of their natural flavour and make wonderfully decorative garnishes. All shellfish should have a clean sea smell and clear fresh colour. In the shell the fish should feel crisp and cool, and their tails should be well curled under and spring back easily when straightened. Remember that shellfish are highly perishable and avoid any that are dull-looking, feel clammy or smell slightly of ammonia. A white powdery deposit on the shells means the fish is too salty.

Cooked: shrimps are sold in the shell by weight or volume. A mug of 1 pt measure is equal to about 250 g /8 oz; this will yield 100–150 g /3½–5 oz peeled shellfish, depending on size and condition. If you are buying them for garnishing, this weight should yield 12–20 prawns, depending on their size.

In summer the prawns may be with roe: hundreds of little coral-coloured eggs packed between the legs. The roe is eatable, but will detract from the tail weight. Allow a minimum of 50 g /2 oz peeled shellfish per person, if serving as a starter. If you are buying larger prawns, such as king prawns, allow 2–6 per person, according to the dish.

Scampi is always sold cooked (unless frozen) and is hard to find with the head. A scampi tail in the shell weighs from 50–100 g /2–4 oz. Allow 2–5 tails per person, according to size and the recipe. As crayfish are rather smaller, allow 4–8 per person.

Frozen is a safe way of buying these shellfish; it also enables people far from the sea to enjoy their delicate flavour. Fish shops sell cooked shellfish frozen solid or loose and semi-thawed, peeled or in the shell. Deep-frozen prawns are available cooked and peeled and in the shell from the frozen food cabinets in supermarkets. Scampi and king prawns are frozen raw. You can also buy quick-frozen potted shrimps, and ready-breaded frozen scampi.

Thawing: shellfish need to be fully thawed before being used. Follow any label directions carefully. Defrost overnight in a refrigerator, or at room temperature for 2–3 hours, leaving them in the bag in which they were bought if possible. Once thawed, shellfish should be kept refrigerated and eaten within 24 hours. Drain thoroughly before using; use juice in soups or stocks.

❉❉❉❉ If you have sufficient freshly caught shellfish it is worth freezing them at home. They will keep for up to 1 month. Wash shrimps and prawns thoroughly in fresh cold water. Boil in lightly salted water until they just turn pink, 2–4 minutes. Cool in the cooking liquid, then drain thoroughly and dry. Open freeze, then bag. Freeze scampi tails raw and unpeeled. Wash the tails, dry and pack tightly into polythene bags. Cook from frozen in boiling salted water; simmer for 4–6 minutes.

Do not freeze store-bought shellfish: they are likely to have already been frozen and thawed once, and refreezing can be a serious health hazard.

Preserved shellfish

Canned shrimps and prawns have a less fine flavour and texture than fresh or thawed frozen fish, but have their uses as a store-cupboard standby. Dried shrimps are used in some national cuisines, such as that of Brazil, but are not easy to get hold of except in specialist shops.

Boiling live shellfish

If you are lucky enough to catch or be given a quantity of live shellfish, or been able to buy it fresh, it must be cooked as soon as possible. Boiling is the best way of preserving the delicious sea-fresh flavour. Keep them in a bucket of sea or salted water until you are ready to cook. Time the cooking carefully as shellfish cook quickly and the texture will be spoiled if they are overdone.

1 Bring a large pan of fresh water to the boil and add 25 g /1 oz sea or rock salt to

each 600 ml /1 pt water in the pan.

2 Plunge the well-drained shellfish into boiling water, then bring to the boil again. Boil shrimps just until they lose their transparency and change colour, about 1–2 minutes. Boil prawns until they change colour, 2–6 minutes, depending on size. Boil whole scampi or scampi tails in the shell for 5–6 minutes, depending on size.

3 Drain them immediately, and if serving cold, rinse in cold water to prevent further cooking. If serving hot, eat at once.

Serving freshly-boiled shellfish

Freshly boiled shellfish is at its best served very simply so that its delicate taste can be enjoyed to the full. When possible, serve prawns or scampi in their shells so that their beautiful appearance can be appreciated.

Arrange cold prawns or whole scampi if you can get them on a bed of crushed ice and garnish with lemon wedges and fronds of feathery herbs or even seaweed. Serve scampi piled in a circle with their tails to the centre of the platter and their decorative claws facing the edge of the dish. Put a bowl of thick, lemon-flavoured mayonnaise in the centre of the dish, or serve a vinaigrette dressing made with olive oil, a little lemon juice, seasonings and chopped herbs to taste. Provide a salt and a pepper mill, large cloth napkins, and finger bowls.

Large, freshly caught scampi or crayfish served hot from the boiling pot with a simple sauce of melted butter, lightly sharpened with lemon juice, is a popular Scandinavian dish. Make it easy for diners to get at the meat by splitting the back of the tail shell with a sharp knife. Everyone then shells his own fish and dips them in the butter before eating.

Using shellfish

The concentrated flavour of shrimps makes them excellent starters. Make your own shrimp paste, shrimp butter or potted shrimps, and serve at room temperature with thin slices of wholemeal bread. Add peeled shrimps or small prawns to sauces for white fish or use them in fillings for seafood quiches or pancakes. Stuff hard-boiled eggs, hollowed-out tomatoes or cucumber cases with prawns mixed with mayonnaise. Shrimps and prawns also go well with rice.

Small, peeled, frozen or canned prawns are good in soups, or in cooked spicy dishes like curries, where the original fish flavour is not quite so important.

Use large, peeled, fresh prawns in salads and starter cocktails or for Chinese-style stir-fried dishes. King prawns can be marinated, then grilled or barbecued. Or sauté whole prawns in the shell in oil with garlic and herbs, and serve piping hot. Scampi tails can be deep-fried in a light batter and served with tartare sauce, or shallow-fried in butter.

Serve crayfish freshly boiled, or add the tails to a velouté sauce to make sauce Nantua. Scampi are the correct garnish for chicken Marengo. You can use crayfish in any scampi recipe – or use prawns or scampi where crayfish are specified.

Prawn bisque

Prawn appetizers

⌛ 15 minutes
plus 30 minutes chilling

Serves 4
1 × 250 g /8 oz bulb of fennel, shredded
300 ml /10 fl oz natural yoghurt
1 small garlic clove, crushed
10 ml /2 tsp lemon juice
½ cucumber, unpeeled and cut into 5 mm /¼ in dice
250 g /8 oz frozen peeled prawns, thawed and drained
salt and freshly ground black pepper
4 large crisp lettuce leaves, to serve
parsley, to garnish

1 Trim coarse or discoloured skin from the fennel bulb and reserve any green fronds. Slice the bulb thinly, then cut into shreds.
2 Mix the yoghurt, garlic and lemon juice together in a bowl and stir in the shredded fennel and diced cucumber.
3 Reserve a few prawns for garnishing and stir the rest into the yoghurt mixture. Season to taste with salt and pepper and chill for 30 minutes to allow the flavours to blend.
4 Place the lettuce leaves on 4 small plates and divide the prawn mixture between them. Snip the fennel fronds and a little fresh parsley over the surface of each, and garnish with the reserved prawns.

Prawn bisque

The basis of this attractive soup is the stock which is made with the heads and shells of prawns.

⌛ 50 minutes

Serves 4–6
350 g /12 oz cooked unshelled prawns
250 g /8 oz raw fish trimmings
1 medium-sized onion, sliced
15 ml /1 tbls tomato purée
1 bay leaf
3 thin strips lemon zest
25 g /1 oz butter
25 g /1 oz flour
salt and freshly ground black pepper
pinch of grated nutmeg
10 ml /2 tsp lemon juice
60 ml /4 tbls thick cream to serve

1 Peel the prawns. Put the heads and shells into a large saucepan.
2 Add the fish trimmings, onion, tomato purée, bay leaf and lemon zest to the pan, cover with 900 ml /1½ pt cold water, bring to the boil. Simmer gently for 20 minutes.
3 Strain the contents of the pan into a bowl through a nylon sieve and discard the debris left in the sieve.
4 Melt the butter in the rinsed-out pan. Add the flour and cook, stirring gently, for 2 minutes. Gradually blend in the fish stock,

stirring all the time. Reserve 60 ml /4 tbls of the soup, then bring the rest to the boil and simmer for several minutes.

5 Reserve a few small peeled prawns for garnishing, if you wish, and purée the rest in a blender with the reserved 60 ml /4 tbls of the soup. Stir the puréed prawns into the soup and season to taste with salt (if needed), pepper, nutmeg and lemon juice.

6 Serve in heated soup bowls topped with a swirl of cream and reserved prawns.

Coral reef prawns

🍴 30 minutes

Serves 4
250 g /8 oz long-grain rice
125 g /4 oz butter
15 ml /1 tbls olive oil
30 ml /2 tbls finely chopped shallots or spring onion bulbs
16 king or Mediterranean prawns, lightly boiled and peeled, or 500 g /1 lb large frozen prawns, defrosted and drained
60 ml /4 tbls brandy
5 ml /1 tsp lemon juice
salt and freshly ground black pepper
300 ml /10 fl oz thick cream
30 ml /2 tbls chopped parsley
30 ml /2 tbls shredded fennel or green pepper
30 ml /2 tbls chopped chives or spring onions
paprika pepper
lemon wedges, to garnish

Coral reef prawns

1 Bring a large saucepan of salted water to the boil and cook the rice for 15–20 minutes until tender. Drain well, and keep the rice warm in a covered bowl set over a pan of simmering water or in a covered flameproof dish in the oven, while you cook the prawns.

2 Heat 50 g /2 oz of the butter and the oil in a large, heavy-based frying-pan, and cook the shallots or spring onions over a gentle heat for 2 minutes. Add the prawns, stir and cook very gently for a further minute.

3 Add the brandy to the pan and heat through for 1 minute. Then set the contents of the pan alight and shake the pan gently to distribute the flames evenly.

4 When the flames die down, add the lemon juice and season the mixture lightly with salt and generously with freshly ground black pepper. Stir and heat through gently for 1 minute.

5 Add the cream and heat gently without boiling for a few minutes until the cream thickens. Check the seasoning.

6 Fork the remaining butter into the rice, until it is melted, then stir in the parsley, fennel or green pepper and chives or spring onion tops. Spread the rice in a layer on a hot serving dish. Spoon the creamed prawns into the centre and sprinkle generously with paprika. Serve at once, garnished with lemon wedges.

● This is a perfect dinner party dish.

Rich shrimp paste

🍴🍴 shelling the shrimps
then 30 minutes plus chilling

Serves 6
600 ml /1 pt cooked brown shrimps, peeled, with heads and shells reserved
250 g /8 oz whiting or plaice fillet
2 pinches of cayenne pepper
1.5 ml /1/4 tsp powdered mace
2 drops anchovy essence
150 g /5 oz butter
lemon wedges for serving

1 Put the heads and shells in a saucepan, cover with cold water, bring to the boil, then simmer for 5 minutes.

2 Strain through a nylon sieve and reserve the amber-coloured liquid, discarding the debris. Poach the white fish fillet in the shrimp liquid over low heat for 10 minutes.

3 Cool slightly, then drain. Discard any skin or bones and pound the fish to a very smooth paste in the saucepan with a spoon.

4 Beat in the cayenne, mace, anchovy essence and 75 g /3 oz butter. When the mixture is smooth, stir in the shrimps and heat through over low heat, stirring gently.

5 Press into 6 small ramekins of about 6 cm /2½ in diameter; smooth the surface.

6 Slowly melt the remaining butter and spoon it over the surface of each ramekin. Eat the paste within 2 days of making. Serve with lemon wedges.

Crab

Fortunately for its many devotees, crab is an easily obtainable and still affordable luxury, particularly if you prepare it yourself. It can be made into a great variety of delicious dishes, both hot and cold.

There are many different species of crab, all of which are encased in hard shells. These shells are cast off – or moulted – each summer, to allow the crab to grow.

Types of crab
Edible or common crab: this is the most familiar crab in Northern Europe. It is found on the European side of the Atlantic and in the Mediterranean, and is caught in baited crab pots laid in rocky coastal waters. The common crab is large (up to 30 cm /12 in wide), with a brownish red upper shell which becomes lighter red when boiled. It has eight legs and two large, powerful front claws.

Spider or spiny crab: this crab is most popular in the Mediterranean, although it is also found along the European Atlantic coast, off the coast of Japan, where they grow to huge size, and around Australia. Its round body and long legs (which are both horny) give it a distinctly spidery shape. Its meat is very good to eat – some people say it is even sweeter than the common crab, and the shells make particularly attractive containers for single-portion crab dishes.

Blue crab: the blue crab is exceedingly popular along the eastern coast of North America – it is said that about 200 million blue crabs are caught in Chesapeake Bay each year – but it is also found in the eastern Mediterranean. It is small, with a bluish shell which turns red when cooked; its meat is of a high quality. The blue swimming crab of Australia, one of Australia's best eating crabs, is related.

Shore crabs: the green crab is a small, greenish-coloured crab familiar along sea shores on both sides of the Atlantic and in the Mediterranean. It is usually made into soups. The Australian mud crab, which is dark olive green to brown, has delicious claw meat, but the body meat is less good.

Soft-shell crab is not a separate species, but a crab caught immediately after moulting, before its new, larger shell hardens. In Venice, tiny shore crabs (*molecchie*) are commercially cultivated and sold as soft-shell crabs, and in America small blue crabs are caught for this purpose.

Soft-shell crabs are available frozen. They can be sautéed in butter, grilled or deep fried and eaten whole, claws and all.

Queen or snow crab is found in the cold northerly waters off Canada and Japan. It has a large yield of white leg meat, and is exported frozen and canned.

King crab: the Japanese or Alaskan King crab is found in the cold waters of the north Pacific and averages 4.5 kg /10 lb in weight. Harvested in mid-winter, the flesh is often exported frozen. Tasmanian crabs can be even larger; they make excellent eating but are difficult to find, even in southern Australia.

Buying and storing crab
Buying: fresh crab is available most of the year, but is at its best and most plentiful in the summer.

If you are buying a live crab, choose one that feels heavy for its size and which responds with a vigorous action when touched. A medium-sized crab, according to species, is better value for money than a large or small one, as it will have the highest proportion of flesh to shell. A good fishmonger will advise you. Handle the crab from the back, keeping your hands out of reach of its claws.

If you want a cooked crab, buy it from a reputable fishmonger to be sure it is fresh. Choose one with claws and legs intact; it should feel heavy for its size and shouldn't sound watery when shaken. A good fishmonger will always open the crab and show you its contents, and if asked he will

Crabmeat and grapefruit salad

Cleaning a cooked crab

Place the crab on its back with the tail end facing you. Remove the claws as close to the body as possible by twisting them very sharply inwards.

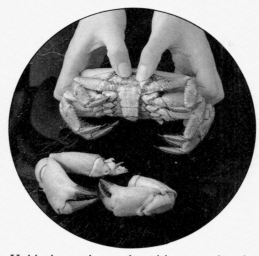

Hold the crab steady with your thumbs under the tail flap. Push downwards with your thumbs until the body breaks away from the shell.

Turn the shell so that the mouth faces you. With your thumbs, press down on the mouth of the crab until it breaks cleanly away with a click.

Remove and discard the mouth and the stomach sac immediately below it. Scoop out all the soft yellowish-brown meat, together with any coral.

Pull off and discard the grey lungs or 'dead men's fingers', then scrape any brown meat clinging to the body into the bowl containing the brown meat.

Twist off the legs. Dig out the meat from the leg sockets and central sections with the skewer, taking care to free the meat of every bit of splintered shell.

To remove the delicate meat from the claws, twist the smaller part of each claw back on itself so it breaks off from the larger section. Scoop out the white meat.

Crack the first leg joints (those closest to the body) with the back of the blade of the knife or cleaver, then remove all the white meat with a teaspoon.

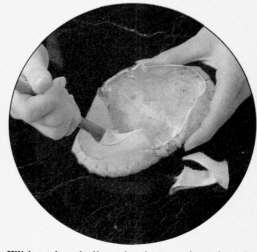

Widen the shell cavity by tapping sharply along the inside of the natural line marking with the handle of the wooden spoon, then break away the surplus shell.

quickly remove the inedible parts for you. You can also buy 'dressed' crab in its shell. This is not the famous dish of the same name, but simply ready-prepared crabmeat; the brown meat usually contains some breadcrumbs or rusk.

The contents of the common crab vary considerably depending on the season, fishing ground and skill of the person preparing the crab; therefore the average meat yield can range from about one-third to one-half of the total cooked weight. A good 1.1 kg /2½ lb crab should give four main course or eight starter servings.

The claws, legs and inner body contain white meat, while there is brown meat just inside the body shell. The female (hen) crab yields more brown than white meat, and prior to spawning a considerable amount of this will be the red coral or roe. A male (cock) crab, with its larger claws, can provide almost as much white as brown meat. To tell the difference between the sexes, look at the shape of the tail flap: the hen has a broad, apron-shaped flap, the cock a narrow one.

Crabmeat is also available canned and frozen. The white and brown meat may be sold separately or in combination; anything labelled queen or snow crab is likely to be mostly white meat.

Storing: a live crab is best cooked as soon as possible, though it can be kept in a bucket of water up to 24 hours, with its claws bound in an elastic band. Cooked crab should be eaten the same day, although it can be stored, loosely covered, in the refrigerator for up to 24 hours.

✱✱✱✱ A freshly home-cooked whole crab or separate packs of brown and white meat can be wrapped in polythene bags and frozen for up to one month. Make sure purchased frozen crab meat does not partially defrost in transit to your freezer. Store for up to 1 month. Defrost, wrapped, in the refrigerator for several hours and use immediately after thawing.

Killing and cooking a live crab

The best-tasting crabmeat comes from a crab you have cooked yourself, but this means that you will have to kill it. This should be done just before you cook it. The most humane method is to spike it through its nerve centre: if you insert a sharp, pointed rod at several different angles just above the mouth, the crab should die almost immediately.

The most usual method of cooking a crab is to boil it, though it can also be sautéed, fried, steamed or baked. To boil, lower the crab into well-salted, fast-boiling water, lower the heat and simmer for 15 minutes for the first 500 g /1 lb plus 10 minutes for each additional 500 g /1 lb. Then drain in a colander, hold under cold running water for a few minutes and cool at room temperature until cold – three or four hours.

Removing the crabmeat

Make sure your crab is completely cold before you start, and allow yourself about half an hour for the job. First assemble a large chopping board, a heavy knife or cleaver, a large wooden spoon, a small teaspoon, a skewer, three bowls – one for white meat, one for brown meat and one for debris – and newspaper to wrap the debris when finished.

Remove the body meat by following the first five step-by-step pictures (*page 113*). The most fiddly job is easing the white meat from the centre maze of thin-shelled sections. With the knife or cleaver, split the body downwards into halves or quarters, depending on the size of the crab. Patiently dig out the meat (step 6). When all visible meat has been removed, crack the pieces open with the wooden spoon handle and remove the remainder of the meat. Make sure you remove all shell splinters.

Break the claws apart (step 7). With the back of the blade of the knife or cleaver, tap sharply around the broadest part of the remaining sections until the shell cracks and can be parted. Extricate the meat with fingers and skewer, keeping the pieces of meat as large as possible.

Remove the meat from the first leg joints (step 8). Larger crabs have edible meat in the second joints as well, though you may prefer to keep the legs (minus the first joints) for a garnish: in this case, rub each leg with absorbent paper moistened with a few drops of vegetable oil to give it a sheen, and use the legs individually or join several into a bracelet to serve as a platform for holding the filled shell steady.

If you want to keep the shell to use it for serving the crabmeat, widen the cavity (step 9), then scrub the shell under hot water, dry it and rub it with oiled absorbent paper. The prepared shell can be kept and used over and over again, like a scallop shell.

Using crabmeat

The white and brown meats are very different in character. The richly flavoured creamy brown meat varies from soft to firm, according to the season. Coral from the hen crab is rich in colour as well as flavour, and can be sieved for garnishing or used for a savoury butter. Dressed crab is a classic, and very delicious. The white and brown meats are seasoned and arranged decoratively in the shell, then garnished with sieved hard-boiled egg and parsley.

Cooked crab dishes have a richer flavour when they include a good portion of brown meat, especially crab soups, quiches and tartlets and scalloped dishes (see recipe). Cold crab dishes such as mousses and salads are also tastier if they contain brown meat, but some people prefer the white meat and find it more digestible. Although the white meat is more delicate in flavour it is inclined to be dry, and is enhanced by being combined with mayonnaise, cream or avocado-based sauces (see recipe for crab salad with guacamole).

Even a small amount of crabmeat can make a deliciously different starter. Combine it with mayonnaise and use it to stuff avocadoes or hard-boiled eggs, or with finely diced cucumber to stuff hollowed-out tomatoes. Or combine crabmeat with a thick cream sauce, form the mixture into balls and deep fry for *délices de crabe*.

Crabmeat can be successfully combined with other seafoods in salads or fish stews.

Crabmeat and grapefruit salad

⚐⚐ extracting crabmeat if necessary, then 15 minutes

Serves 4
2 large pink grapefruit
crisp leaves of red radicchio or Webb's lettuce
225 g /8 oz fresh, frozen or canned crabmeat, white, brown or mixed
60 ml /4 tbls thick mayonnaise
1.5 /1¼ tsp Dijon mustard
15 ml /1 tbls thick cream
salt and ground white pepper
10–15 ml /2–3 tsp tomato ketchup
sprigs of fresh chervil or finely snipped chives, to garnish

1 Using a serrated knife, peel the rind and pith from the grapefruit, then cut out the segments, discarding the pips.
2 Arrange the radicchio or lettuce leaves and grapefruit segments neatly on each of 4 serving dishes. Pile the crabmeat in the centre.
3 Mix together the mayonnaise, mustard and cream. Add salt and pepper to taste, and enough ketchup to colour the mixture a delicate pink.
4 Spoon a little of the dressing over each portion of crab, garnish with chervil or chives, and serve.

● Ordinary grapefruit can be used instead of pink grapefruit. Sprinkle it with 5 ml /1 tsp sugar first.

Crab and melon appetizer and Crab salad with guacamole

1   Mash or beat the crabmeat to a rough purée. Include the coral if you are using a female crab.
2   Melt 25 g /1 oz butter in a saucepan, add the flour and stir over a low heat for a minute. Blend in the milk, stirring, bring to the boil and simmer gently for 3–4 minutes.
3   Stir in the cream, mustard, Worcestershire sauce, sherry and half the cheese. Season highly with salt, black pepper and cayenne pepper. Add the crabmeat, mix thoroughly and turn into the baking dishes.
4   Combine the breadcrumbs and the remaining cheese and sprinkle over the crab mixture. Dot with the remaining butter, cut into flakes, and refrigerate if not cooking immediately.
5   When ready to serve, heat the oven to 200C /400F /gas 6. Cook until the crab is heated through and the top is lightly browned, 20–25 minutes. Garnish with slices of hard-boiled egg, watercress or parsley sprigs and the shortened crab legs, if you are using a fresh crab. Serve at once.

Crab and melon appetizer

This unusual starter salad has a fresh and summery combination of flavours and textures.

🍴🍴 40 minutes

Serves 4
1 freshly boiled crab, about 800 g /1¾ lb
oil for rubbing
lettuce leaves
1 medium-size ripe honeydew melon
juice of 1 lime or ½ lemon
60 ml /4 tbls thick mayonnaise
salt and freshly ground black pepper
pinch of cayenne pepper
paprika, to garnish

1   Remove the meat from the body and claws of the crab, keeping the white and brown meat separate.
2   Break off the section nearest the body of each leg, and add the meat to the other white meat. Trim the remaining section of each leg, rub with oiled absorbent paper and reserve. Line each of 4 serving plates with lettuce leaves.
3   Cut the melon lengthways into quarters and remove the rind and seeds. Divide each quarter in half again lengthways and arrange 2 sections, with ends touching, on each of the serving plates. Squeeze a little lime or lemon juice over the melon sections.
4   Mash the brown meat with the mayonnaise and season to taste with salt, black pepper and cayenne pepper. Spoon this mixture into the spaces between the melon sections.
5   Arrange the white meat along the centre of each salad, on top of the brown meat. Sprinkle with paprika, arrange the crab legs at one end and serve.

Crab salad with guacamole

Choose frozen queen crabmeat, which is all white meat, for this recipe.

🍴🍴 thawing crabmeat, then 20 minutes plus chilling

Serves 6
500 g /1 lb frozen white crabmeat, just thawed
350 g /12 oz carrot, coarsely grated
45 ml /3 tbls vinaigrette dressing
30 ml /2 tbls freshly chopped parsley
1 cucumber, very thinly sliced
For the guacamole
1 large, ripe avocado
15 ml /1 tbls lemon juice
15 ml /1 tbls finely grated onion or 1 small garlic clove, crushed
30 ml /2 tbls olive oil
salt and freshly ground black pepper
pinch of sugar
pinch of cayenne pepper or chilli powder (optional)
1 medium-sized tomato, blanched, skinned, seeded and chopped

1   First prepare the guacamole. Halve the avocado, remove the stone and scoop the flesh into a bowl. Add the lemon juice, onion or garlic and oil and beat with an electric or rotary whisk until smooth.
2   Season to taste with salt, pepper and sugar, adding cayenne pepper or chilli powder if wished. Stir in the tomato, cover and refrigerate until ready to serve.

3   Combine the carrot, vinaigrette and parsley. Set aside to let the flavours blend.
4   To serve, stir the guacamole and place it in a small bowl in the centre of a flat serving dish. Edge the dish with overlapping cucumber slices and fill the space between with the carrot salad. Arrange the flaked crabmeat over the carrot and top with the larger pieces of crab.

Gently devilled crab

Make this in 6 cocotte dishes for a starter, or in 4 small crab shells or gratin dishes for a main course. It can be prepared ahead of time.

🍴 defrosting crabmeat if frozen, then 45 minutes

Serves 4–6
350 g /12 oz fresh or frozen crabmeat, brown and white mixed
65 g /2½ oz butter
25 g /1 oz flour
275 ml /10 fl oz milk
30 ml /2 tbls thin cream
5 ml /1 tsp Dijon mustard
10 ml /2 tsp Worcestershire sauce
30 ml /2 tbls medium sherry
25 g /1 oz finely grated Parmesan cheese
salt and freshly ground black pepper
pinch of cayenne pepper
90 ml /6 tbls dry white breadcrumbs
For the garnish
1–2 medium-sized eggs, hard boiled and sliced
watercress or parsley sprigs
shortened crab legs (optional)

Mussels and other shellfish

Few foods bring so much savour to our meals as molluscs, the small marine creatures that live in shells. They range from prestigious oysters to humble cockles, and include mussels, scallops, clams, winkles and whelks.

Sea creatures that live inside a 'seashell', of the kind that you would pick up on a beach, are called molluscs. Best to eat are the bivalves, which have a pair of shells. These include oysters, mussels, scallops, clams and cockles. Edible molluscs in single shells include abalone, whelks and winkles, and limpets.

Buying and storing molluscs

Alas, in these days of polluted waters, some molluscs can be a source of food poisoning, so it is essential that you do not gather your own shellfish, and that you buy from a reputable fishmonger. He will sell only molluscs known to be safe to eat, either because they have been through a purification process or have been cultivated in, or gathered from, approved grounds.

With the exception of scallops, molluscs decompose rapidly and should always be kept very cool and eaten or cooked on the day of purchase. If you buy cooked molluscs, it is always best to eat them the day you buy them.

✳✳✳✳ Do not freeze molluscs unless you are sure they have been gathered or taken from their purifying water the same day. Use within one month.

Clams and oysters are usually frozen raw. To freeze your own, open them over a muslin-lined strainer with a bowl beneath to catch the juices. Wash in cold water with 30 ml /2 tbls salt added to each 600 ml /1 pt water. Drain and pack in rigid containers with the strained juices. To serve raw, thaw unopened in the refrigerator for 6–8 hours. To cook, add frozen to a hot soup or sauce and heat gently for 4–6 minutes.

Scallops should be removed from their shells, cleaned, washed thoroughly in salted water, rinsed, drained then packed for freezing. Thaw overnight in the refrigerator, then cook as fresh scallops.

Mussels, cockles, whelks, winkles, limpets and pipis should be cooked, shelled, washed thoroughly in salted water, rinsed and drained. Pack in their juices in rigid containers. Freeze mussels in their shells. Thaw in the refrigerator for 6–8 hours.

Bivalves

Oysters: it is difficult to imagine that only 100 years ago oysters were cheap and plentiful. Nowadays their rarity puts them into the luxury class; some people eat them as an aphrodisiac. Flavours and colours vary according to species and the area of cultivation. The best in the Northern hemisphere are the flattish, round-shelled oysters such as the British natives (Royal Whitstables, Helfords and Colchesters), the French Belons and Marénnes and the American Blue Points. Usually cheaper are the elongated, rough-shelled Portuguese-type oysters and the large Pacific oysters with triangular shells and frilly edges. The Pacific oyster is the largest available in Australia, but the Sydney rock oyster has the best flavour.

Some species are available all year round, others are not on sale during the summer months. For serving raw, buy the best available, but ask your fishmonger's advice because the grades refer to the size of the shell, not the quality of the oyster (largest are grade 1, smallest are 'buttons'). Cheaper oysters are best cooked.

Oysters are sold in tens or dozens in their shells; they are also sold shucked (removed from their shells). Shucked oysters are also sold frozen, canned and dried (dried ones can be found in Chinese shops), and you can buy smoked oysters in cans.

Your fishmonger will open oysters for you if asked, but the precious liquid will be lost.

So open oysters yourself just before serving, thereby retaining all their exquisite sea-fresh flavour and juices.

Wrap a clean, thin cloth around your left hand (assuming you are right-handed) and place the oyster in the left palm, flat side uppermost and hinge towards you. Slip the point of a short, blunt knife under the hinge and into the oyster. Holding the oyster firmly with your left hand, twist the knife until the shells are forced apart. Lift off and discard the flat shell. Still holding it firmly so that the juices don't spill, slip the knife under the oyster to free it from the curved shell, then flick away any chips of shell on the oyster with the point of the knife.

Your oysters are now ready to serve *au naturel*. Serve six or more per person, arranging the oysters in the curved shells on dinner plates strewn with finely crushed ice. (If you own specially indented oyster dishes, use those.) Embed the oysters firmly in the ice with the shell hinges pointed towards the centre. Serve with lemon wedges and very thinly sliced brown bread and butter, and have cayenne pepper or Tabasco sauce ready for those who like them.

When cooking oysters, the vital point to remember is to cook them only until they curl. If you overcook them they will toughen and spoil. Perhaps the most famous oyster dish is oysters Rockefeller, in which oysters on the half shell are baked with a Pernod-flavoured spinach and butter topping. But they are also delicious made into fritters and soups.

Mussels are one of the most popular molluscs. Their smooth, blue-black shells generally range in size from 4–6.5 cm /1½–2½ in. The small mussels cultivated off the Atlantic coast of France are especially sweet and delicious.

Mussels are available from autumn to spring, but are best in winter. Fresh mussels in their shells are sold by volume or weight; allow 300 ml /½ pt or 250 g /8 oz per person for a first course, two or three times that amount if they are to be served as a main course. You can also buy frozen shelled mussels, and mussels in cans or jars.

Before cooking, mussels must be thoroughly scrubbed with a hard scrubbing brush under cold running water. Discard any that are open or cracked. Pull away the hair-like strands attached to the hinge (known as the beard) and scrape off any encrustations with a sharp knife, then drop

1 Colchester clams, 2 mussels, 3 whelks, 4 abalone, 5 Portuguese oysters, 6 Pacific oysters, 7 Colchester oysters, 8 Great scallops, 9 cockles, 10 winkles

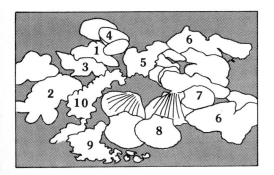

Opening an oyster

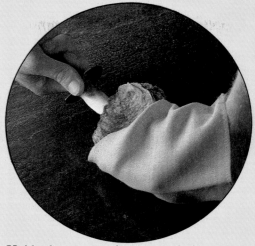

Hold the oyster in your cloth-wrapped palm, hinge towards you. Insert the point of a short knife under the hinge.

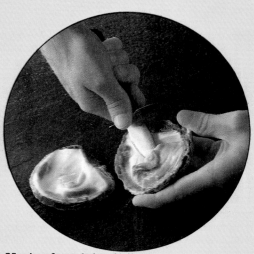

Having forced the shells apart, slip the point of the knife under the oyster to free it from the curved shell.

the mussels in a bowl of clean, cold water. To open mussels, put them in a wide, heavy-based pan with a little dry white wine and some flavourings – chopped onion or shallot, herbs, salt and pepper. (They can also be placed in the pan with no additional ingredients, just the water clinging to them.) Cover tightly and cook over a high heat, shaking occasionally, for 5–7 minutes. Strain the liquor through a muslin-lined strainer into a bowl to collect the juices, and discard any mussels still tightly shut.

Once cooked, mussels should be eaten right away, before they have a chance to toughen or lose flavour. Try them in a cream sauce, flavoured with saffron or in a mild curry. The marvellous aroma arising from a steaming hot dish of *moules marinière* – the classic French recipe for mussels, mussel soup or garlic stuffed mussels is an essential part of their enjoyment.

When serving cold, cool rapidly and eat as soon as possible. Lacking any natural fat, mussels combine particularly well with creamy sauces, mayonnaise or vinaigrette. Small quantities of mussels can make a memorable omelette filling, a stuffing for fish fillets, or a colourful sauce or garnish.

Scallops, with their firm white flesh and orange coral, are delectable, if rarer than they were. In medieval Europe the scallop shell was the sign of the pilgrim. *Coquilles St. Jacques* are still named in France after the patron saint of Santiago de Compostela in northern Spain. The most common specie in Northern Europe is the Great scallop. Queens are much smaller and Bay scallops (popular along the Atlantic coast of the U.S.) smaller still. Scallops are also abundant in Australia.

Theoretically they are available all year round, but in practice supplies are erratic. Scallops are most often sold opened and cleaned, but still attached to the flat shell. Frozen, shelled scallops are sold by weight. Allow 75–100 g /3–4 oz per person for a main course. If you are buying them in their shells, two large scallops per person are

usually sufficient, but you will need three to six if they are smaller.

Scallops can be opened in the same way as oysters, but an easier way is to arrange them in a single layer on a baking sheet and place them into an oven heated to 200C /400F /gas 6 or under a hot grill; as soon as the shells open (two to three minutes) remove the scallops from the heat and clean them.

To clean, slip a knife between the scallop and the half shell to which it is attached in order to separate them. Remove all the fringe area and the black intestinal thread, retaining only the white cushion and orange roe, and wash thoroughly.

Scallops can be poached, sautéed, grilled or deep or shallow fried (see recipe). As with other molluscs, the important thing to remember is not to overcook them. If they are poached, the roe can be separated from the white before cooking, and then be cooked for a shorter time.

Clams: there are various species and sizes, their shells ranging from 7–16 cm /3–6 in across. Among the tastiest are the European Palourde and Praire, the American Quahog and the Toheroa from New Zealand. Clams are very popular in the U.S. and are cultivated along both the Atlantic and Pacific coasts. They are at their best during the summer, though they are usually available all year round.

Fresh live clams in their shells are sold in tens or dozens. Allow 8–12 or more per person, depending on size, and check that their shells shut tightly when tapped – this is a sign that the clam is alive and well.

You can buy frozen shelled clams, canned clams, whole or minced, and clam juice.

Clams are eaten either cooked or raw, though large or frozen clams are best cooked. Clams can be opened by the oyster method. You can also use the mussel method for small ones, and the dry-heat scallop method for large ones. Take care to conserve the liquor, which is full of flavour. After opening, remove the black-tipped tube and wash thoroughly.

When clams are opened by the mussel method they simply need reheating, with their liquor, in a soup, sauce or chowder. Clams are a very popular ingredient in Italian pasta sauces (see recipe), and can be made into tasty fritters. Chopped clams combined with bacon and a creamy egg custard make a good filling for tartlets, which could be served as an unusual starter.

Cockles are small heart-shaped molluscs, heavily ridged, found buried in sand banks, usually 25 mm–5 cm /1–2 in across, although they can be larger. They are found throughout Europe and in Australia, and are especially popular in Britain.

They are available all year round, but best during the summer. They are sold cooked and shelled, fresh, frozen or bottled.

In Britain cockles are popularly eaten from a shallow dish, sprinkled with pepper and vinegar, but they can be included in shellfish salads, reheated briefly in a velouté sauce to enliven poached white fish or in a mornay sauce to add flavour to hard-boiled eggs, or added to a fish pie.

Pipis are small bivalves found in Australia with triangular or wedge-shaped shells. They can be eaten in the same way as cockles.

Single-shelled molluscs

Abalone is held in great esteem in the Channel Islands, where it is known as ormer, and in the Orient. The beautiful lining of its large shell – pearly purple, green and silver – is more familiar to many people than the creature inside.

Abalone is imported from Asia, mostly in cans but also dried. If you can find it fresh (say, in the Mediterranean or Australia), it will be either live in the shell or shucked. Frozen, shucked abalone is sold by some fishmongers. Remove the dark gut section and the black frill, then wash the meaty foot and beat it with a wooden mallet, whole or in thin horizontal slices.

It can be eaten raw (if fresh) or cooked. Be sure it is cooked briefly, otherwise it will toughen. It can be marinated or egg-and-breadcrumbed, then sautéed in butter, poached in white wine with onion and herbs, or chopped and added to soups and stews.

Winkles or periwinkles: these tiny creatures in their dark spherical shells are the smallest molluscs marketed (maximum length is 25 mm /1 in).

They are sold, ready cooked, all year round, and are considered tasty morsels by their devotees, who mostly eat them cold with malt vinegar and brown bread and butter. The diner requires a pin to 'winkle' the flesh out of the shell. Stick the pin into the flesh at an angle, then turn the shell with your other hand. The flesh will unwind like a corkscrew. As with other pre-cooked molluscs, the surest guarantee of freshness is to buy from a reliable fishmonger.

Whelks are much larger than winkles (10–15 cm /4–6 in) and live in handsome whorled shells, but are not as tasty. They are usually bought ready cooked in their shells, which are smashed for easy extraction; or they may be shucked. They are at their best during the summer months. Whelks are also sold bottled in vinegar. Whelks are usually eaten cold, cut lengthways into slices, with salt, pepper and vinegar, but can also be crumbed and fried.

Limpets have cap-shaped shells 25 mm–5 cm /1–2 in in diameter. They can be eaten raw or cooked, in soups, boiled or fried. They are rather tough and, many people say, not particularly tasty.

Scallops with bacon

〠 55 minutes

Serves 4
24 small scallops (Queens), or 12 larger ones
  shelled and cleaned
45 ml /3 tbls flour
salt and freshly ground black pepper
2 small eggs
75 g /3 oz dried white breadcrumbs
6 slices unsmoked streaky bacon, diced
oil for frying
30 ml /2 tbls freshly chopped parsley
lemon wedges, to garnish

New England oyster stew and Scallops with bacon

New England oyster stew

opening oysters if necessary, then 10 minutes

Serves 4
36 small oysters in their shells, opened
425 ml /15 fl oz milk
200 ml /7 fl oz thick cream
25 g /1 oz butter
salt and freshly ground black pepper
a dash of Tabasco sauce or a pinch of cayenne
pepper
paprika, to garnish
crackers or rusks, to serve

1 Strain the liquor from each oyster through a muslin-lined strainer into a small saucepan. Rinse the oysters in cold water to remove any flakes of shell and add the oysters to the liquor.
2 In another saucepan bring the milk, cream and butter just to simmering point.
3 Bring the oyster liquor to simmering point and cook very gently for 2 minutes. Add the oysters and their liquor to the hot milk and season to taste with salt, pepper and Tabasco or cayenne.
4 Serve at once in heated soup cups, garnished with a sprinkling of paprika and accompanied by crackers or rusks.

Oyster florentine gratin

40 minutes

Serves 4
24 small oysters, shelled
65 g /2½ oz butter plus extra for greasing
20 g /¾ oz flour
150 ml /5 fl oz hot milk plus extra if necessary
60 ml /4 tbls thick cream
40 g /1½ oz freshly grated Parmesan cheese
salt and ground white pepper
a pinch of cayenne pepper
700 g /1½ lb spinach, prepared
paprika, to garnish

1 Melt 25 g /1 oz butter in a small pan, add the flour and cook gently for a minute, stirring. Add the hot milk and beat with a small wire whisk until smoothly blended. Stir constantly until it boils, then stir in the cream, three-quarters of the cheese and salt, pepper and cayenne to taste.
2 Leave the sauce to simmer and reduce, stirring now and then, while you cook the spinach and oysters.
3 Put the washed (but not dried) spinach leaves into a large saucepan, cover and cook over a moderate heat, stirring occasionally, for 10–15 minutes, until tender. Turn into a strainer and drain well, pressing to extract as much moisture as possible. Chop finely, return to the saucepan, season to taste and stir in 25 g /1 oz butter.
4 Spread the spinach over the base of 4 heated and buttered deep scallop shells or

cocotte dishes and make a depression in the centre. Keep hot. Heat the grill to moderate.
5 Tip the oysters and their juices into a small pan and poach over gentle heat for 2 minutes. Immediately strain the juices through a muslin-lined strainer into the cheese sauce. Divide the oysters between the spinach-lined dishes.
6 Stir the sauce briskly. It should be of a creamy coating consistency. If it is too thin, boil it quickly to reduce; if too thick, add a little hot milk. Check the seasoning and spoon over the oysters.
7 Sprinkle with the remaining cheese, dot with the remaining butter and slip under the hot grill for a minute or so until golden. Garnish each with a sprinkling of paprika and serve at once.

Vermicelli marinara

cleaning and preparing shellfish, then 1 hour 15 minutes

Serves 4
1 L /2 pt fresh mussels in their shells, cleaned
and prepared
about 20 small clams, cleaned and prepared
75 ml /5 tbls olive oil
1 medium-sized onion, finely chopped
2–3 garlic cloves, crushed
550 g /20 oz ripe tomatoes, blanched, skinned,
seeded and chopped, or 400 g /14 oz canned
peeled tomatoes
15 ml /1 tbl tomato purée
salt and freshly ground black pepper
350 g /12 oz vermicelli
30 ml /2 tbls freshly chopped parsley
15–30 ml /1–2 tbls freshly chopped basil

1 Heat 45 ml /3 tbls olive oil in a saucepan and fry the onion gently for 5 minutes, until it is beginning to soften.
2 Stir in the garlic, then add the tomatoes, tomato purée and salt and pepper. Bring to the boil and simmer, uncovered, for about 20 minutes, or until most of the liquid has evaporated and the tomatoes are reduced to a rough purée.
3 Lower the vermicelli into a large pan of fast-boiling, well-salted water and boil uncovered for a few minutes, until the pasta is just tender. Drain thoroughly.
4 Meanwhile place the wet mussels in a wide pan. Cover and shake over a high heat just until the shells open. With a slotted spoon, transfer the mussels to a bowl, discarding any that do not open. Strain the mussel liquor through several thicknesses of muslin into the tomato sauce.
5 Repeat this process with the clams. Simmer the sauce until it is thick, then season to taste.
6 Remove the shellfish from their shells, leaving a few of each in their shells for garnishing. Add the shellfish to the sauce and heat through.
7 Heat the remaining oil in a shallow flameproof serving dish. Off the heat add the drained vermicelli and toss with 2 forks until it glistens. Pour the sauce over, garnish with the reserved shellfish, sprinkle with the herbs and serve at once.

1 Pat the scallops dry with absorbent paper. Season the flour generously with salt and pepper and put in a polythene bag. Break the eggs into a deep soup plate, add 10 ml /2 tsp cold water and beat lightly. Pile the breadcrumbs in the centre of a large piece of greaseproof paper.
2 Drop the scallops, several at a time, into the flour and shake thoroughly. Remove, dip in the egg, then toss in the breadcrumbs.
3 Arrange the coated scallops on a plate in a single layer and leave in the refrigerator for about 30 minutes for the coating to set.
4 When ready to cook, fry the bacon gently in a heavy frying-pan, without additional fat, for about 5 minutes, until crisp. Stir frequently. Remove the bacon with a slotted spoon and keep hot.
5 Add enough oil to the bacon fat in the pan to give a depth of about 15 mm /½ in. Heat until sizzling, then fry half the scallops until crisply golden and just cooked through, about 5–6 minutes in all, turning once. Remove with a slotted spoon, drain on crumpled absorbent paper and keep hot while you fry the rest.
6 Divide the scallops between 4 deep scallop shells or individual gratin dishes and sprinkle with the diced bacon mixed with the chopped parsley. Garnish with the lemon wedges and serve very hot.

Mussel and potato salad

Serve this colourful salad for lunch on a warm day, accompanied by crusty bread and some dry white wine.

⏳⏳ preparing mussels,
then 1 hour plus cooling

Serves 4

1½ L or 1 kg /2 pt or 2 lb mussels in their
    shells, cleaned and prepared
450 g /1 lb small new potatoes
60 ml /4 tbls dry white wine
2 shallots, chopped
a sprig of thyme
a few parsley stalks
salt and freshly ground black pepper
1 tender stalk of celery, thinly sliced
60 ml/4 tbls vinaigrette dressing
30 ml /2 tbls cooked peas

1 Place the mussels in a wide saucepan with the wine, shallots, thyme, parsley and several grinds of pepper. Cover and cook over high heat for 5–6 minutes, shaking the pan frequently.
2 Remove the mussels as they open. Reserve a few in their shells for garnishing and discard the remaining shells, plus any mussels that fail to open.
3 Set the mussels aside to cool, then strain the cooking liquid through a muslin-lined strainer into a small pan.
4 Boil the potatoes in lightly salted water until just tender, then drain, skin and cut into 5 mm /¼ in slices. As soon as the potatoes are sliced, boil the mussel liquor briskly until well reduced, then pour over the potatoes and set aside until cold.
5 To serve, drain any surplus liquid from the potatoes and spread the potatoes and celery in a shallow serving dish. Arrange the mussels on top and spoon the vinaigrette over.
6 Sprinkle the peas over the top and surround the salad with the reserved mussels.

Cod, cockle and shrimp pie

⏳⏳ defrosting shrimps and pastry,
then 1 hour 30 minutes

Serves 4–6

700 g /1½ lb thick fillets of cod
125 g /4 oz shelled, cooked cockles
125 g /4 oz peeled shrimps or small prawns,
    defrosted if frozen
275 ml /10 fl oz milk
1 small onion, sliced
1 bay leaf
6 black peppercorns, lightly crushed
salt and freshly ground black pepper
40 g /1½ oz butter
25 g /1 oz flour
2 medium-sized eggs, hard boiled and quartered
30 ml /2 tbls freshly chopped parsley
225 g /8 oz made weight puff pastry, defrosted
    if frozen
beaten egg, to glaze
a sprig of parsley, to garnish

Mussel and potato salad

1 Cut the cod into several pieces and place in a saucepan with the milk, onion, bay leaf, peppercorns and a little salt. Bring slowly to simmering point, then cover and cook gently for 12–15 minutes, until the fish is done. Strain off and reserve the liquid, discarding the onion, bay leaf and peppercorns.
2 Heat the oven to 220C /425F /gas 7. Melt 30 g /1¼ oz butter in a small saucepan, stir in the flour and cook gently for 1–2 minutes. Add the strained milk and whisk briskly until boiling and thickened. Simmer for several minutes.
3 Meanwhile remove any skin or bones and flake the fish coarsely. Stir into the sauce and add the cockles and shrimps or prawns (reserving a few for garnishing), the hard-boiled eggs, parsley and salt and pepper to taste.
4 Use the remaining butter to grease a 1.1 L /2 pt pie dish and turn the fish mixture into it.
5 Roll out the pastry thinly and cut out a lid to cover the pie. Cut strips from the trimmings and fit round the moistened edge of the pie dish. Moisten the strip and cover with the lid. Knock up and flute the edges.
6 Make a steam vent in the centre of the lid and surround with small pastry circles cut from the trimmings. Brush the pastry with the beaten egg.
7 Bake in the hottest part of the oven for 25 minutes or until the crust is golden. Pile the reserved cockles and shrimps or prawns in the centre and top them with a sprig of parsley. Serve the pie at once.

Lobster

Lobster, gleaming in its bright red shell, looks, and is, one of the world's greatest luxuries. Buy only the best and, however you cook it – as a stuffing for crêpes, in a creamy soup with spinach, or simply grilled with brandy and butter – it will live up to its reputation as 'king of the crustaceans'.

The true lobster is a ten-legged salt-water crustacean found only in northern waters: the common European lobster *(Homarus gammarus)* is found from the Mediterranean to Norway while the common North American lobster *(Homarus americanus)*, which is slightly larger, inhabits the waters from Labrador down to South Carolina.

In warmer waters the spiny lobster *(Palinurus elephas* and *Palinurus vulgaris)*, also known as *langouste* (in France), rock lobster (in the U.S.), crawfish (in Britain) or crayfish (in South Africa), takes over. Reddish brown with yellow and white markings, as opposed to the blue-black of the true lobster, its great differences are the long feelers which can give you a nasty whiplash and the lack of the huge claws which provide the most delicate meat in the true lobster.

In Australia, besides the spiny lobster, bugs or bay lobsters *(Thenus orientalis* and *Ibacus peronii)* are found. They are much smaller – about 15 cm /6 in long – and have no claws. The tail meat can be used in lobster recipes but you will need about six bugs per person.

Grilled brandied lobster

Buying and storing lobster

The ideal weight for a lobster is 450-700 g /1-1½ lb, and a lobster in this size range will serve one person or more, depending on the recipe and whether it is being served as a starter or main course. Spiny and European lobsters can be used interchangeably in recipes as roughly the same weight of flesh is found in relation to shell, despite their different shape.

The female lobster, or hen, is slightly smaller than the male, or cock, and is thought by some to be superior in flavour. In season you will find the roe or coral, a collection of round orange eggs snuggling inside the tail fins and the hindmost legs. The coral makes a delicious addition to sauces. Both sexes are in season, in the northern hemisphere, from April to November, and are at their best – and cheapest – during the summer.

Lobster should always be bought absolutely fresh and used as soon after purchase as possible. A cooked lobster is best eaten the same day, though it can be kept, loosely wrapped, in the refrigerator for 24 hours. A live lobster can be kept in a sink or bucket of water and cooked the next day but make sure its pincers are tightly bound with thick elastic bands; they are very strong and can deliver a painful nip!

If a live lobster is in good condition it will be active: a languid creature will have spent too long a time out of water, gradually wasting away. So always pick up a lobster to test for weight – it should feel heavy in proportion to its size. It's safest to pick it up by its head, with its body away from you, and making sure its claws are well tied. Avoid lobsters covered in barnacles as this is usually a sign of old age.

If you are buying a cooked lobster, the tail should be coiled tightly against the body and should spring back quickly if you pull it out; if you squeeze the body it should feel firm and hard. Lobsters with tail flesh coloured dark green to black should never be bought: they have either not been properly cooked or have been dead some time before cooking.

You can buy frozen lobster and spiny lobster tails, but the flavour will not be as good: use them in soups, pancakes or curries.

✳✳✳✳ You can freeze lobsters that you have boiled yourself. Freeze them in or out of their shells for up to one month.

Killing and boiling a lobster

There has been some controversy as to the most humane way to kill a lobster but it is now generally agreed that to plunge it, head first, into boiling water is the quickest method. The noise that sounds like a scream in fact is not, but is merely air being expelled.

The water should be heavily salted: 175-200 g/6-7 oz salt to 1.7 L /3 pt water, or use

Preparing a boiled lobster

Split the lobster, then cut off the claws and crack them with a sharp diagonal blow.

Pull out and discard the greyish, feathery gills, from both sides of the body.

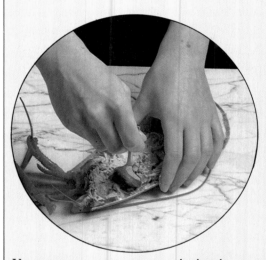

Use a teaspoon to scrape out the head meat, the liver and the coral, if there is any.

Extract the tail and claw meat, keeping the pieces as large as possible.

seawater with enough salt added so that an egg will float. Boil the lobster 10 minutes per 450 g / 1 lb; a small lobster weighing just that may need a little extra time. The shell will turn bright red as it cooks. You can tell if the lobster is cooked by the opaque colour of the tail flesh and by its springiness to the touch. Remove it from the water and let it cool at room temperature if you are not eating it at once.

If you want raw lobster for a recipe, you can kill it with a knife or cleaver, either down the middle line of its body or between the body chell and tail. But boiling for 1-2 minutes will kill it with less aggravation, and the results will be just as good.

Removing the meat from a lobster
Place the lobster on a work surface with its head away from you and, using a cleaver or heavy-bladed long knife, make a split down the middle of its back (unless you have already done so in order to kill it). Cut off the claws (if you have the large-clawed European variety) and crack them, diagon-

ally across, with a sharp blow.

In the head of the lobster is its stomach or grit sac. It is like a little bag; it comes out easily and must be discarded. Running from this along to the tail is the gut, which resembles a thin black cord. Pull it out and discard it. The only other parts of the lobster not used are the feathery gills, situated in cavities on either side of the body, between the creamy white head meat and the small legs. They should be removed after scraping out, with a teaspoon, all the head meat and the greenish liver, or to-mally, which is one of the most delicious parts of the lobster. Reserve it, with the head meat, for adding to sauces. If you are dealing with a hen lobster remove the coral or roe from beneath the tail; it will be bright red in a cooked lobster, greyish in an uncooked one. Reserve separately. Any soft pinkish meat underneath the gills should be scraped out and added to the head meat.

The tail flesh is next to come out and should pull away easily in one piece, with its red coating of skin intact.

If you are dealing with a large-clawed variety, next extract the meat from the claws by pulling. Cut vertically through the meat and remove and discard the blade of cartilage in the centre. Pull the pink flesh from the little claws out in one piece and keep whole. The legs can now be broken off. Cut them at each joint and squeeze out the flesh by pressing the shell between thumb and forefinger from the bottom upwards. This can be added to the liver and head meat for use in the sauce or can be kept with the tail and claw meat if you want a smoother sauce.

Cooking lobster
In restaurants one usually encounters lobster cooked in one of the rich classic sauces – lobster à l'américaine, lobster thermidor and lobster Newburg are famous examples. While these are undoubtedly delicious, it sometimes seems a pity not to let the lobster's own delicate flavour come out to the full; a freshly killed lobster, topped with lots of melted butter and simply grilled for 10-15 minutes if raw, or blanched for only a few minutes to heat through if boiled, and served with freshly ground black pepper and lemon wedges, is equally good. For a slightly grander version, add brandy and just a little cream (see recipe).

Serving the lobster in its half shell is traditional, but if you want to make the lobster go further than one between two people, it is better to take it out of the shell and serve it with a sauce, either on a bed of rice or, more unusually, in parcels of filo pastry (see recipe). A combination of cooked lobster with chive sauce is very elegant and easy to adapt to the spiny lobster. If you have only one small lobster and want to 'stretch' it between four use it to make a lobster sauce, which could accompany poached white fish.

If you want to serve the lobster cold, blanch it for five minutes in some heavily salted water, then drain and complete the cooking in a court bouillon (with a little salt, pepper, thyme and a bay leaf added to the water). Cool it on its back so that some of the liquid is retained in the shell, to be absorbed by the flesh, keeping it moist and succulent. The liver and head meat is usually folded into the accompanying mayonnaise, which can be varied with different herbs (fresh dill and tarragon go well, while a few crushed lemon balm leaves add a deliciously tangy flavour). Or add 15 ml /1 tbls cognac or gin to the mayonnaise for an added kick. Dressing the lobster with yoghurt (see recipe) makes a piquant and less rich dish.

Lobster can also be made into soups. For sheer luxury use the whole lobster but make it go further by adding some chopped spinach as in lobster pottinger (see recipe). In the classic *bisque d'homard* the shell is used to make the stock, which is thickened by puréed flesh and cream beaten with egg yolks. A very tasty soup can be made, though, using just the meat from the small claws or from a small lobster. If you have just the shell left over, it can be used to make a lobster glaze which can be added to enrich a soup or sauce.

Lobster crêpes

🔪🔪🔪 making the crêpes,
then 1 hour 50 minutes

Serves 4-8
700 g /1½ lb freshly boiled lobster
50 g /2 oz butter, plus extra for greasing
1 medium-sized onion, finely chopped
30 ml /2 tbls flour
2.5 ml /½ tsp soy sauce
2.5 ml /½ tsp Dijon mustard
2.5 ml /½ tsp dried tarragon
15 ml /1 tbls lemon juice
5 ml /1 tsp Pernod
salt and freshly ground black pepper
8×18 cm/7 in crêpes (see below)
15 ml /1 tbls freshly grated Parmesan cheese
For the bouillon
150 ml /5 fl oz white wine
1 bouquet garni
2 bay leaves
6 white peppercorns
2 sprigs of fresh dill

1 Extract the meat from the lobster. Dice tail and claw flesh (if present) and reserve in a bowl; place liver and coral in another.
2 Squeeze the flesh from the legs and add to the tail and claw meat. Put the leg shells into a large saucepan with the bouillon ingredients. Remove and discard the feathery gills, chop lobster shell and add to pan.
3 Add 850 ml /1½ pt cold water and bring to boiling point over a brisk heat. Lower the heat and simmer gently for about 30 minutes, until reduced to about 425 ml /15 fl oz.
4 Strain the bouillon through a fine sieve, cool and reserve.
5 Melt 25 g /1 oz butter in a heavy-based frying-pan over medium heat, add the onion and sauté for 8-10 minutes, until soft and golden. Remove with a slotted spoon and keep warm. Add the diced tail and any claw flesh and sauté for 3 minutes, then remove and keep warm.
6 Add the remaining butter to the pan and melt it, then stir in the flour to form a roux. Gradually pour in the reserved bouillon, stirring constantly. Add the soy sauce, mustard, tarragon, lemon juice and Pernod and cook for 7-8 minutes, stirring, until the sauce thickens slightly.
7 Add the liver and coral and salt and pepper to taste, stir well and remove from the heat. Heat the grill to high.
8 Divide the reserved lobster meat and onion between the crêpes, topping each with 15 ml /1 tbls sauce. Roll up the crêpes and arrange in a greased flameproof dish.
9 Pour over the remaining sauce, sprinkle with the Parmesan cheese and grill for 4-5 minutes, until the cheese is melted and the sauce golden and bubbling. Serve at once.

● Crêpes: prepare a batter using 75 g/3 oz flour, 2.5 ml/½ tsp salt and 2 medium eggs. Stir in 30 ml/2 tbls melted butter, then 150 ml/5 fl oz milk. Strain through a sieve and leave to stand for 2 hours. To fry, heat and grease pan, then use 45 ml/3 tbls batter for each crêpe. Cook for 1 minute each side, greasing pan between crêpes. Keep warm.

Dressed lobster

🔪🔪 45 minutes

Serves 6
2 × 700 g /1½ lb freshly boiled hen lobsters
125 ml/4 fl oz vinaigrette dressing
1 head of curly endive, shredded
6 hard-boiled eggs, quartered lengthways
30 ml /2 tbls finely chopped fresh parsley, to garnish
boiled new potatoes or thin slices of buttered brown bread, to serve
For the yoghurt dressing
150 ml /5 fl oz yoghurt
2.5 ml /½ tsp tomato ketchup
1.5 ml /¼ tsp Worcestershire sauce
2-3 drops Tabasco sauce
1.5 ml /¼ tsp Dijon mustard
5 ml /1 tsp olive oil
5 ml /1 tsp clear honey
1.5 ml /¼ tsp tomato purée
juice of ¼ lemon
salt and freshly ground black pepper

1 Remove the tail and claw flesh (if present) from the lobster, chop coarsely and put into a bowl with the vinaigrette. Let stand for 20 minutes.
2 Remove the coral from the lobster and reserve. Remove the liver and place in a bowl. Add the ingredients for the yoghurt dressing to the liver and whisk well.
3 Arrange the shredded endive around the edge of a serving platter and place the egg quarters on this.
4 Remove the lobster flesh from the vinaigrette with a slotted spoon and add to the dressing. Toss to coat thoroughly.
5 Pour the vinaigrette over the endive and eggs and sprinkle with the chopped parsley. Pile the lobster into the centre of the dish, garnish with the reserved coral and serve at once, with boiled new potatoes or thin slices of buttered brown bread.

● Instead of yoghurt, you can use soured cream or a walnut oil mayonnaise. If using the mayonnaise, top the dressed lobster with finely chopped walnuts.

Lobster crêpes

Potted lobster

If you are given a lobster that you cannot eat immediately, this is ideal as it will keep well in the refrigerator for several days.

🔪🔪 1 hour, plus cooling and 4 hours or more chilling

Serves 4-6
700 g /1½ lb freshly boiled hen lobster
65 g/2½ oz butter
salt and freshly ground black pepper
pinch of cayenne pepper
15 ml /1 tbls gin
75 ml /3 fl oz thick cream
sprigs of watercress, to garnish (optional)
toast, to serve

1 Extract all the flesh, the liver and the coral from the lobster. Chop finely and place in a saucepan with 25 g/1 oz butter, salt, black and cayenne peppers and gin.
2 Cook over a low heat for 20 minutes, stirring occasionally. Add the cream and mix well, then cook for a further 10 minutes until mixture is smooth and very thick.
3 Blend the mixture in a food processor or press it through a fine sieve, so it is very smooth, then press into 4-6 ramekins and leave to cool.
4 Heat 40 g/1½ oz butter in a pan until foaming. Remove from heat and let stand for 1 minute, then strain through a fine sieve over the cold lobster mixture. Cool, then put into the refrigerator for at least 4 hours to chill thoroughly.
5 Garnish with sprigs of watercress, if wished, and serve with toast.

Grilled brandied lobster

🔪🔪 55 minutes

Serves 4
2 × 700 g /1½ lb freshly boiled lobsters
50 g /2 oz butter
30 ml /2 tbls brandy
45 ml /3 tbls thick cream
salt and freshly ground black pepper
halved lemon slices, to garnish
crisp salad, to serve
For the topping
75 g /3 oz butter
60 ml /4 tbls fresh white breadcrumbs
pinch of cayenne pepper

1 Remove the tail flesh from the lobsters and cut into large chunks. Crack the claws (if present) and extract the meat from them, cut it into chunks and add to the tail flesh.
2 Remove the coral and reserve. Remove the liver and soft pink flesh and reserve separately. Squeeze the flesh from the legs and add to the liver.
3 Wash the shells thoroughly, discarding the feathery gills. Pat the shells dry with absorbent paper.
4 Melt the butter in a large, heavy-based

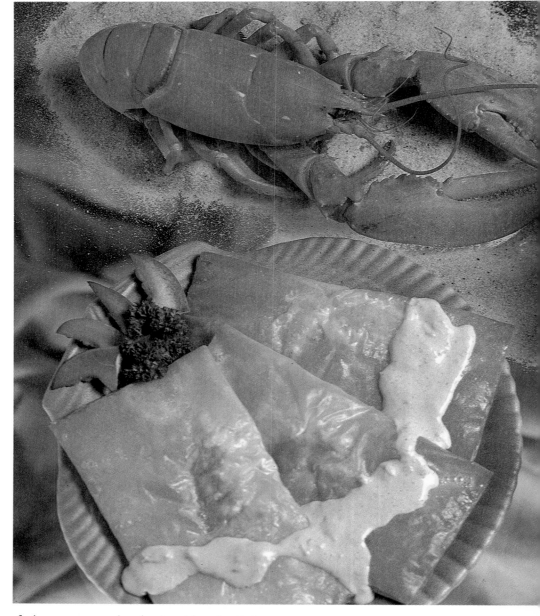

frying-pan over a low heat and brush a little of it inside the shells. Add the tail and claw flesh to the pan and sauté gently, stirring, for 3-4 minutes.
5 Pour the brandy into a ladle, warm it, then ignite and pour over the lobster. Stir until the flames die down, then remove the lobster with a slotted spoon and pile into the 4 half shells.
6 Pound the liver mixture, then add to the pan, stirring well. Add the cream, a little salt, and lots of black pepper and stir for 2-3 minutes over a low heat. Pour a quarter of the sauce over the lobster in the shells.
7 Heat the grill to high and make the topping: melt 50 g /2 oz butter in a heavy-based frying-pan, add the bread-crumbs and reserved coral. Stir well and cook gently for 2 minutes. Divide the mixture between the shells, dot with the remaining butter and sprinkle with cayenne pepper.
8 Put the shells under the grill for 2-3 minutes, until the butter has melted and the topping is bubbling. Serve at once, gar-nished with halved lemon slices and accom-panied by a crisp salad.

Lobster pottinger

Pamper your dinner party guests with this deliciously extravagant soup. The green of the spinach purée contrasts prettily with the creamy coral of the lobster soup. A pottinger is a bowl with handles on either side, and was used to serve soup in medieval England.

🔪🔪🔪 1 hour 30 minutes

Serves 4
450-700 g /1-1½ lb freshly boiled hen lobster
65 g /2½ oz butter
1 small mild onion, finely chopped
1 celery stalk, finely chopped
150 ml /5 fl oz Madeira
1 bouquet garni
salt and freshly ground black pepper
75 g /3 oz fresh cooked spinach, chopped, or frozen chopped spinach, defrosted
freshly grated nutmeg
150 ml /5 fl oz thick cream

Lobster in filo parcels

Lobster encased in thin, crispy filo pastry and served with a creamy sauce makes a dish fit for a king! When a large-clawed lobster is used, garnish with claw tips.

♀♀♀ 1 hour 10 minutes

Serves 6

2 × 700 g /1½ lb freshly boiled lobsters
90 ml /6 tbls melted butter
140 g /4½ oz butter
45 ml /3 tbls whisky
18 sheets filo pastry, about 23 cm /9 in square
5 ml /1 tsp paprika
salt and freshly ground black pepper
7.5 ml /1½ tsp lemon juice
275 ml /10 fl oz thick cream
fresh parsley sprigs, to garnish

1 Remove the flesh from the lobster tails and claws (if present). Chop off the red tips of the claws and reserve separately. Cut the remaining flesh in large chunks.
2 Squeeze out the leg flesh and put into a mortar. Remove the liver and coral and pound with the leg meat in the mortar.
3 Heat the oven to 230C /450F /gas 8. Grease a baking sheet with melted butter.
4 Melt 65 g /2½ oz butter in a heavy-based frying-pan and add the tail and claw flesh, keeping it on one side of the pan. Put the claw tips on the other side. Sauté for 3 minutes, turning the lobster flesh over gently to heat through, then flambé with the whisky.
5 Remove the claw tips with a slotted spoon and keep warm. Use the remaining melted butter to brush the sheets of filo pastry on one side.
6 Divide the tail and claw flesh evenly between 6 sheets of pastry. Fold both sides over to encase the lobster completely, then fold the tops and bottoms under. Wrap each parcel in 2 more sheets of buttery filo in the same way. Brush the outsides of the parcels with any butter remaining.
7 Put the parcels on the baking sheet and bake for about 6 minutes, or until the pastry is puffed and golden.
8 Meanwhile, make the sauce by melting the remaining butter in the frying-pan over medium heat. Add the pounded mixture together with the paprika, salt and pepper and lemon juice and stir for 2 minutes.
9 Gradually stir in the cream, being careful not to let the sauce boil. Continue stirring over a very low heat for 3-4 minutes.
10 Remove the parcels from the oven and place on a warmed serving platter. Pour a little of the sauce over each parcel. Garnish with the reserved claw tips and parsley sprigs and serve at once, with the remaining sauce in a warmed sauce-boat.

● Instead of filo pastry, you can use good-quality puff pastry, very thinly rolled out. In this case, of course, the pastry does not have to be brushed with melted butter.

1 Remove the tail flesh from the lobster, finely chop and put into a bowl. Add the liver, coral and leg flesh. Extract the flesh from the claws and reserve separately (keep back one-quarter of the flesh as a garnish if using spiny lobster).
2 Remove and discard the gills. Chop the shell with a stout-bladed knife and reserve.
3 Melt 25 g /1 oz butter in a heavy-based saucepan over a moderate heat, add the onion and celery and sauté for 5 minutes until soft. Add the chopped lobster shell and stir for 2-3 minutes. Pour in the Madeira and let it bubble for 2 minutes, then add the bouquet garni and cover with 850 ml /1½ pt cold water.
4 Bring quickly to the boil, then lower the heat and simmer gently for about 30 minutes, until it is reduced to just over 600 ml /1 pt. Turn off the heat and let it cool slightly.
5 Remove the bouquet garni and pour the contents of the pan, including the finer pieces of shell, into a blender and blend for 2-3 minutes.
6 Pour through a muslin-lined sieve to remove any pieces of shell remaining (of which there will probably be a fair amount).

From the left, Lobster in filo parcels, Potted lobster and Lobster pottinger

Discard these and return the liquid to the blender, together with the chopped tail meat, liver and coral. Blend until smooth, then return the liquid to the rinsed-out saucepan, reserving 90 ml /6 tbls soup in the blender.
7 Chop the reserved (claw) flesh into small pieces and add to the soup. Season with salt and freshly ground black pepper, then whisk in 25 g /1 oz diced butter over a low heat. Let the soup simmer very gently while you prepare the spinach.
8 Add the chopped spinach to the reserved soup in the blender and blend together. Melt the remaining butter in a small saucepan over a low heat. Add the spinach and season with salt, pepper and nutmeg. Reserve.
9 Stir the cream into the lobster soup and heat through gently; do not allow it to boil. Pour into a warmed soup tureen, then pour the spinach purée into the middle of the lobster soup. Stir to give a marbled effect, then serve at once.

125

Squid, octopus and cuttlefish

Some of the most delicious seafood dishes are made from squid, octopus or cuttlefish. It is well worth taking the time to prepare them, as they are inexpensive and can be cooked in many different ways to provide an authentic Mediterranean meal.

Squid, octopus and cuttlefish are all molluscs (creatures without a backbone) belonging to the *cephalopod* group. Cephalopod means 'head-footed' and refers to the way the tentacles of the creature are attached to the head, which often travels at the rear.

The three have certain characteristics in common: they all have ink sacs – the ink is squirted at a predator while they make their getaway behind the black cloud. They all have tentacles with suckers surrounding their mouths and a hollow muscular sac, containing the gills and internal organs. This sac is filled with water and then contracted, expelling the water, so the creature can propel itself along.

Since ancient times Mediterranean peoples have highly prized these creatures for food, although elsewhere in the world only the Japanese hold them in the same regard.

From the left: cuttlefish, octopus, two squid

There are over 350 varieties of squid, ranging in size from tiny to giant. They are torpedo-shaped, with an arrow-shaped fin which extends on either side of the body and tapers to the tail, and have eight short tentacles and two long ones, all with suckers. The long ones are normally kept retracted, ready to shoot out at their prey.

Cuttlefish have bigger, flatter bodies than most squid with a rounded swimming fin right round the body, or sometimes in lobes at the tail. They have eight short tentacles with suckers and two long ones with 'spoons' on.

Not all of the hundreds of varieties of octopus are good for eating, but the best have been compared to lobster. The small Mediterranean octopus is excellent, 20-25 cm /8-10 in long with the tentacles stretched out. Mediterranean fishermen say it should be bashed against the rocks 99 times but, in any case, all octopus, fresh or frozen, should be beaten well with a rolling pin or bottle to tenderize the flesh.

Buying and storing cephalopods

Squid and octopus are not easy to find: cuttlefish are even more difficult. They are all most likely to be found in areas with large Mediterranean populations, and are more likely to be found frozen than fresh. You may be able to order them frozen from your fishmonger. California now exports large quantities of frozen squid and freezing tenderizes these creatures. Frozen squid and cuttlefish have the ink sacs removed.

The length of these sea creatures is measured from the tip of the bunched tentacles to the rear of the body. If the squid are very tiny (5 cm /2 in long) allow 6-8 per person; for larger ones (20 cm /8 in) allow 2-3 per person. Cuttlefish make the tenderest eating when they are 25 cm /10 in long and weigh about 450 g /1 lb. If stuffing, choose a small one and allow one per person; if stewing, a larger one will feed two people. Octopus lose a lot of liquid and shrink in cooking, so allow one per person if they are 25-30 cm /10-12 in in length.

Buy cephalopods on the day you intend to eat them if they are fresh, and store, loosely covered, in the refrigerator.

Squid, octopus and cuttlefish are available canned in various sauces. They make delicious appetizers and can be bought in specialist shops. These shops may also have them dried.

**** Never attempt to refreeze partially defrosted squid, octopus or cuttlefish.

Solidly frozen squid, octopus and cuttlefish can be frozen for up to 6 months; defrost in the refrigerator for 24 hours. A dish of any of the three stewed or casseroled may be frozen for up to 4 weeks.

Preparing cephalopods

Preparing squid: the preparation and cleaning process sounds complicated but once mastered is quickly done. Hold on to the tentacles and pull. The head and internal organs will slip out of the body. Cut off the tentacles just beyond the head and reserve. If you want the ink, remove the ink sac; this is attached to the head and is long and narrow, the black ink showing clearly through the white enclosing membrane. Cut it away, being careful not to break it, and put it into a bowl. The head and internal organs can now be discarded.

Slip out the bone from inside the pouch of the body. It looks like a transparent plastic pen nib and is held in place by a flap which is easily retracted.

Thoroughly rinse out the inside of the body with cold water and then rub off the pinkish outer membrane. Rinse the tentacles in the same way. You will be left with a milky white body with two flaplike fins (quite edible) and tentacles ready for cooking.

Preparing octopus: stretch the octopus out and cut off the tentacles just above the eyes, then pull the head out gently: some of the internal organs will come away with it. Turn the body inside out, clean thoroughly under running water, removing the remaining internal organs and cutting away the beak-like protuberance at the base of the tentacles. Rinse the tentacles. Turn the octopus right way out and put it and the tentacles between two sheets of greaseproof paper. Beat well. The ink is rather musky in taste and is not normally used. The octopus is now ready for the preliminary cooking.

Preparing cuttlefish: lay the cuttlefish out flat, cut off the tentacles and reserve. Make a slit at one end of the body and pull out the flat porous bone. Continue the slit down the body, remove the head and insides and cut off the parrot-like beak. Wash very thoroughly in running water and, using a sharp pointed knife, slip off the outer membrane. Prepare the tentacles in the same way and rinse well.

Cooking cephalopods

Cooking squid: there are dozens of recipes in Mediterranean cookery for squid—fried, stewed, grilled, stuffed. Small squid, dipped in batter and deep fried, are particularly delicious. Indonesian fried squid with tamarind is a very good variant or try squid with fresh tomato sauce. Squid cooked in its ink (*calamares en su tinta*) is a famous Spanish dish; squid are also delicious cold (see recipe) and are excellent stuffed with herb-flavoured rice.

The stuffing for cuttlefish (see recipe) can also be used for larger squid—they will need less cooking, about one hour. Both squid and cuttlefish can be stuffed with mixtures of onions, garlic, anchovy fillets and parsley, or tomatoes, onions, garlic and breadcrumbs.

Preparing squid, octopus and cuttlefish

Pull on the squid tentacles to remove the internal organs, then separate the ink sac from the body. Cut off the tentacles beyond head.

Slip out the transparent 'spine' from inside the pocket, which is the squid's body. It is held by a tiny flap, which retracts easily.

Slit the cuttlefish the length of the body and remove the bone. Reserve the ink sac if needed. Cut off tentacles beyond the head and reserve.

Stretch out the octopus tentacles, then make a cut round the head above the eyes. Pull gently to remove the organs. Cut off tentacles and beak.

Cooking cuttlefish: simmering stuffed cuttlefish is one of the best ways of cooking it: the long, slow simmering ensures great tenderness. Spinach and herbs stuffings are particularly good, or minced pork, fennel and parsley (see recipe). Or try a raisins, pine nuts and rice stuffing. Cuttlefish make a delicious stew (see recipe) but, unlike squid and octopus, it is rarely served cold.

Cooking octopus: there are two methods of cooking octopus. Both give good results, although the second is probably better for large octopus.

The traditional Spanish method is to drop the body and tentacles into a large pan of unsalted boiling water with a cork (this tenderizes the flesh, though no one knows why) and a potato (a small one for a small octopus; a larger one for a medium-sized octopus). Barely simmer until the potato is soft, about 45 minutes to one hour, when the octopus will be ready. Remove from the pan, cool and then peel away the skin and rub off the horny suckers.

For the second method, put the octopus into a glass ovenproof dish with plenty of room to spare, and cover. Do not add water or seasoning. Cook in an oven heated to 150C /300F /gas 2 for one to two hours. The octopus will give out a lot of dark red liquid and when it can be pierced easily with a knife tip it is done. Discard the liquid and rinse the octopus. Peel off the skin and rub off the suckers. Now plunge the octopus into a pan of boiling water with a bay leaf, a peeled onion and a large pinch of salt. Cook for 10 minutes or until a fork slips easily into the flesh. Remove from the heat and cool.

Whichever method you use, once the preliminary cooking is completed the octopus is ready to be served cold with olive oil and lemon juice, garnished with parsley, or with either a garlic or an avocado mayonnaise. Or the octopus can be reheated in a sauce. Any sauce suitable for lobster can be used, or mix the octopus with squid and cuttlefish and cook in red wine with tomatoes, garlic and onions for an authentic provençal seafood stew.

Squid and prawn salad

Grilled baby squid

♦♦♦ cleaning the squid,
then 30 minutes

Serves 4
*900 g /2 lb baby squid, cleaned weight (about
   1.4 kg /3 lb uncleaned)*
90 ml /6 tbls olive oil
45 ml /3 tbls tomato purée
2 large garlic cloves, crushed
juice of 1 lemon
salt and freshly ground black pepper
saffron rice, to serve

1 Slice the squid into fine rings. Chop the
tentacles finely and keep separate. Place the
rings at one end of the grill pan (with the
grid removed) and the tentacles at the other.
2 Heat the grill to high. Mix the oil with
the tomato purée and garlic and pour over
the squid. Grill for 18-20 minutes, turning
often.
3 Place the squid rings on a warmed
serving platter and pile the tentacles on top.
Pour over any juices remaining in the
grill pan, sprinkle with the lemon juice,
season with salt and pepper and serve at
once, with a bowl of saffron rice.

Cold octopus with paprika

This is a speciality of the octopus bars of
**Madrid, where it is served as a *tapa* or
hors d'oeuvre. Served with crusty French
bread, it makes a good appetizer.**

🕐 ♦♦ cleaning and cooking,
then 24 hours marinating

Serves 4
*1 medium-sized octopus, 450 g /1 lb cleaned
   weight (900 g /2 lb uncleaned)*
150 ml /5 fl oz olive oil
1 garlic clove, crushed
15 ml /1 tbls paprika
½ Spanish onion, finely chopped
juice of 1 lemon
salt and freshly ground black pepper
30 ml /2 tbls finely chopped parsley

1 Cook the octopus according to either of
the methods on *page 127*. Skin and chop
finely. Place in a bowl and add the oil,
garlic, paprika and onion. Leave in a cool
place (not the refrigerator) for 24 hours.
2 Turn out onto a serving platter, sprinkle
with the lemon juice, season with salt and
pepper, sprinkle with the parsley and serve.

Squid and prawn salad

Serve this fresh-tasting salad as a starter
for eight people or as a lunch dish for
four.

♦♦♦ cleaning the squid,
then 1 hour 15 minutes

Serves 4-8
*900 g /2 lb squid, cleaned weight (1.4 kg /3 lb
   uncleaned)*
225 g /8 oz boiled, shelled prawns or shrimps
3 small onions, finely chopped
15 ml /1 tbls sugar
60 ml /4 tbls olive oil
juice of 1 lemon
1 medium-sized crisp lettuce, finely shredded
1 medium-sized avocado, sliced
45 ml /3 tbls vinaigrette dressing
salt and freshly ground black pepper
15 ml /1 tbls finely chopped parsley

1 Combine the onions and sugar in a bowl
and leave to stand for 1 hour.
2 Meanwhile, cook the squid. Heat the
grill to high. Slice the body of the squid into
fine rings and the tentacles into short strips.
Place in the grill pan (with the grid re-

moved), pour over the oil and lemon juice and grill for 20 minutes, turning often. Leave to cool.

3 Arrange the shredded lettuce on a serving platter and top with the avocado slices. Pour over the vinaigrette dressing.

4 Mix the squid with the chopped onions and salt and pepper to taste. Pile on top of the avocado, garnish with the prawns or shrimps and parsley and serve.

Stuffed cuttlefish with parsley sauce

cleaning,
then 3 hours 45 minutes

Serves 4
*4 medium-sized cuttlefish, together 900 g /2 lb
   cleaned weight (1.8 kg /4 lb uncleaned)*
60 ml /4 tbls olive oil
1 Spanish onion, finely chopped
275 ml /10 fl oz dry white wine
30 ml /2 tbls tomato purée
flat-leaved parsley, to garnish
For the stuffing
275 g /10 oz lean pork, finely minced
1 large onion, finely chopped
90 ml /6 tbls parsley, finely chopped
1 small head fennel, finely chopped
2 medium-sized egg yolks, beaten
large pinch of cayenne pepper
salt and freshly ground black pepper
For the parsley sauce
100 g /4 oz parsley, chopped
2 garlic cloves, chopped
45 ml /3 tbls olive oil
salt and freshly ground black pepper

1 To make the stuffing, chop the tentacles of the cuttlefish finely and combine with the pork, onion, parsley and fennel. Add the egg yolks to bind the mixture, add the cayenne pepper and salt and black pepper to taste and mix well.

2 Divide the stuffing into 4 and put a portion into each cuttlefish body, rolling the body around the stuffing and fixing firmly with cocktail sticks.

3 In a large saucepan, heat the oil and sauté the onion for 5 minutes. Add the wine and tomato purée, put in the cuttlefish and cover with water. Bring quickly to the boil, then turn down the heat and barely simmer for 3 hours.

4 Meanwhile, make the parsley sauce. Combine the parsley, garlic and olive oil in a blender and purée. Pour the mixture into a large frying-pan, add salt and pepper to taste and simmer gently for 30 minutes, stirring occasionally.

5 Test the cuttlefish with a fork – if it slips in easily they are done. Remove them from the pan with a slotted spoon and keep warm on a warmed serving platter.

6 Bring the cuttlefish cooking liquid to a fast boil and reduce to 275 ml /10 fl oz. Add this to the parsley sauce and simmer for 10 minutes or until it is slightly reduced. Pour over the cuttlefish, garnish with the flat-leaved parsley and serve at once.

Stuffed cuttlefish with parsley sauce

Spicy cuttlefish stew

cleaning,
then 1 hour 45 minutes

Serves 4
*2 medium-sized cuttlefish, together 450 g /1 lb
   cleaned weight (900 g /2 lb uncleaned)*
30 ml /2 tbls olive oil
1 large onion, finely chopped
1 garlic clove, crushed
400 g /14 oz canned tomatoes
1 red chilli, seeded and finely chopped
1 bay leaf
30 ml /2 tbls finely chopped parsley
2.5 ml /1/2 tsp ground allspice
150 ml /5 fl oz dry red wine
salt and freshly ground black pepper

1 Chop the cuttlefish into 25 mm /1 in squares and the tentacles into 25 mm /1 in lengths. Put into a large saucepan with 275 ml /10 fl oz water and bring to the boil, then reduce the heat and simmer for 30-40 minutes, until the cuttlefish can be cut with the edge of a spoon. Strain and reserve the cooking liquid.

2 Heat the oil in the rinsed-out saucepan and sauté the onion and garlic for 5 minutes. Add the cuttlefish, tomatoes, chilli, bay leaf, parsley, allspice, wine and the reserved cooking liquid. Simmer gently for 45 minutes.

3 Add salt and pepper to taste, pour into a warmed serving bowl and serve.

● Rice with raisins and pine nuts makes a delicious accompaniment to this stew.

Caviar and other fish roes

Melt-in-the-mouth herring roes on hot buttered toast; sparkling red or black lumpfish roe dramatically topping a mousse; thick golden slices of crumbly cod's roe – roe comes in many forms and offers a wide choice of dishes.

Hard or soft, roes are a delicacy that can be served as a main ingredient or garnish in dishes from breakfast through to supper. Endlessly versatile, whether bought fresh, frozen or canned, roe spans the entire price scale, too, from awesomely expensive caviar to cheap and cheerful herring roe.

Hard roes come from female fish; soft roes from males. In many species, the roe is so small that it passes almost unnoticed and is cooked with the fish, though it can always be taken out and used as a garnish or stirred into an accompanying sauce. In others, the roe is large enough to be considered as a separate ingredient and is sold separately.

Sevruga caviar, centre; on the left from the top, baked potato and brioche, both with cod's roe and soured cream, fried hard herring roe; front, soft herring roe; on the right, red and black lumpfish roe

Caviar

The king of the roes, caviar is far and away the most rare and therefore the most expensive. It is the salted hard roe of sturgeon, now mainly fished in the Caspian Sea.

There are three main types of caviar. Beluga has large grains varying from pale grey to black and comes from the largest fish (16-20 years old). This is the most expensive. Then there is the rarest type, osetr, which can be golden brown, grey, green or black and comes from slightly younger and smaller fish. And last, sevruga, the cheapest of the three, which has smaller grains and comes from seven to ten year old fish.

Buying and storing caviar: when caviar is available fresh, it should be eaten within one day. However, most is pasteurized and sold in jars or cans. This process does diminish the flavour somewhat, but without it the delicate roe would not travel. Pressed caviar is also available, canned or frozen. In block form like this, it is relatively less expensive and has a slightly saltier flavour than the pasteurized.

Store caviar in the coldest part of the refrigerator, and eat as quickly as possible. It should not be frozen (except in the case of already frozen pressed caviar).

Allow 25–40 g /1–1½ oz caviar per person when it is to be served on its own.

Serving caviar: caviar is always served well chilled, often dramatically sent to the table in its jar, surrounded by crushed ice. As an appetizer it is eaten with hot toast served with butter and lemon wedges – a squeeze of lemon brings out the flavour – and as a cocktail nibble, on small, dry, unsalted biscuits. A traditional Russian dish is blinis, buckwheat yeast cakes filled with soured cream and caviar (this is often prepared, and is still delicious, with mock caviar).

Mock caviar

Almost inevitably, when there is a product that is priced out of reach of enthusiastic family cooks, there will be imitations and substitutes, and caviar certainly has its look-alikes. But this is not to say that they are not enjoyable or without merit in their own right – and at least they are affordable!

Lumpfish roe is a popular alternative to caviar. Lumpfish are caught off Iceland and Greenland. The roe of the female has large, shiny eggs which are sandy-coloured when fresh. They are rinsed to separate the grains, salted and then coloured either black or deep red. Lumpfish roe, in small jars, is widely available in shops and supermarkets and can be stored, unopened, in the larder but once opened should be used within two days and kept refrigerated.

Salmon roe: the golden-red roe of Canadian red salmon is sometimes available in jars. While it does not have the true taste of caviar, it does have a very pleasant and characteristic flavour all its own.

Shellfish roe: not exactly a caviar substitute, but with a similar appearance, the roe of shellfish is a delicacy too good to discard unknowingly with the shells. If you are dressing a crab, scrape out any brownish-orange eggs you find under the tail. These have a very delicate and absolutely delicious flavour and can be used to garnish the crab.

Prawns have bright orange eggs held firmly between the legs. When shelling prawns at the table, it is quite permissible to suck them from the shell. If you are preparing fresh prawns in the kitchen, it is worth making a special feature of the roe, perhaps sprinkling it on top of mayonnaise.

Serving mock caviar: mock caviars, as well as the real thing, are most often used as toppings and garnishes or served as they are, so none of their beauty is lost. As an appetizer or part of a salad plate, stuffed hard-boiled eggs topped with mock caviar taste luxurious; cold haddock or salmon mousse goes up in the world with a mock caviar garnish – possibilities are endless.

A typically Scandinavian way to serve lumpfish roe is on hot buttered toast, topped with a thick onion ring with a raw egg yolk in its centre. Grind some black pepper on top and serve at once.

Any mock caviar, but particularly lumpfish roe, makes a tasty butter to serve with grilled, steamed or poached fish.
● Cream 100 g /4 oz unsalted butter until it is soft, then stir in 20 ml /4 tsp red lumpfish roe. Season with freshly ground black pepper and a few drops of lemon juice, shape into a roll and wrap in foil or greaseproof paper. Chill then slice to serve.

Grey mullet roe

Botargo or taramà, the salted and dried female roe of grey mullet, is native to the Mediterranean. It has a black skin and is orangey-brown in the centre. Refrigerate in a polythene bag for up to a week.

It is the roe used to create taramasalata. As an appetizer, it is delicious boiled (simply drain if canned), thinly sliced and served lightly sprinkled with good olive oil, lemon juice and freshly ground black pepper. Accompany with brown bread.

Cod's roe

The hard roe of large female codfish can be quite large – it is nothing for a single piece to weigh well over 450 g /1 lb.

Buying and storing cod's roe: cod's roe is sold 'fresh' in three forms: uncooked, simply boiled (in both these cases it is a deep

parchment colour) and smoked. Smoked cod's roe varies in colour from bright red to pale browny-orange, and is available and ready to use in jars as well as by the piece.

Roe should feel soft to the touch – never dry or hard. You can also buy pressed cod's roe which is cooked in its can.

Cooking and serving cod's roe: to cook fresh cod's roe, tie it in a piece of scalded muslin and cook in boiling, salted water for ½–1 hour, depending on size. Drain, unwrap and cool, then gently peel off the skin and pat the roe dry.

Boiled cod's roe is usually given a crispy coating and fried to a tempting golden brown. Slice thickly (about 15 mm /½ in thick), toss in flour, then in beaten egg and finally in dried breadcrumbs or fine oatmeal. Fry on both sides in butter until the slices are coloured and the coating is crisp. A salad of chopped gherkins stirred into yoghurt or soured cream goes well.

In Norway, boiled cod's roe is sliced and fried in butter until it is only just turning yellow, then used to garnish grilled or poached fish.

Pressed cod's roe can be sliced and served as it is, or egg-and-breadcrumbed and fried.

Before using smoked roe, it is advisable to taste a little. If it is too salty, skin the roe and soak in cold water for at least one hour, changing the water once or twice. Smoked cod's roe is most often made into taramasalata, but it can also be combined with cream or cottage cheese to make a dip, or with soured cream to top jacket potatoes. You can also use it to fill pancakes or to top open sandwiches with a bland cream cheese or egg base.

Deep-fried soft roes

Herring roe

Hard and soft herring roes are sold fresh or canned. Hard roes are a golden brown; soft ones are paler in colour and much creamier in texture.

Cooking: blanch soft roes in boiling, salted water for 2 minutes, then drain, pat dry and toss in lightly seasoned flour. Either brush with melted butter and cook under the grill or fry them in butter, then serve on hot buttered toast with wedges of lemon.

Soft roe butter can be used as a topping for grilled fish or as a spread for canapés:
● Fry roes in butter with a sprinkling of lemon juice, allow to cool, then mash them to a paste and beat them with twice their weight of softened butter. Season with salt, pepper and made mustard, form into a roll and wrap in foil or greaseproof paper. Refrigerate for up to 24 hours.

Hard herring roes are delicious lightly floured or tossed in flour, egg and breadcrumbs and fried in butter. Serve them with fried eggs, on toast, or as a fish garnish.

Storing cod's and herring roes

Store fresh roes, lightly wrapped, in the coldest part of the refrigerator for up to 24 hours. Smoked cod's roe will keep for up to a week, closely wrapped in greaseproof paper in a sealed container.

✳✳✳✳ Only freeze very fresh roes that you are sure have not been frozen and thawed – most roes that you buy have been. Wash, pack in small rigid containers and freeze for up to two months. Smoked cod's roe can be frozen for up to one year.

Smoked cod's roe dip

⚐ 20 minutes
plus chilling

Serves 6
150 g /5 oz smoked cod's roe
1 garlic clove, crushed
75 ml /5 tbls olive oil
150 ml /5 fl oz yoghurt
100 g /4 oz cottage or cream cheese
15 ml /1 tbls lemon juice
30 ml /2 tbls freshly chopped parsley
freshly ground black pepper
pink or red food colouring (optional)
raw vegetables and cocktail biscuits, to serve

1 Pour boiling water over the smoked cod's roe, let soak for 5 minutes, then drain. Peel away the skin.
2 If you have a blender you can make the dip in a matter of seconds. Alternatively beat the mixture in a bowl with a fork: break up the roe, add the garlic and beat well. Gradually pour on the olive oil, beating all the time. Beat in the yoghurt and cheese and, when the mixture is smooth, stir in the lemon juice and parsley and season to taste with pepper. If the mixture is very pale, add a drop of food colouring.
3 Turn the dip into a serving bowl, cover and chill. Serve with 'dip sticks' of crisp raw carrots, green pepper strips and cauliflowerets, and with cocktail biscuits.

Cod's roe paste with scrambled eggs

This makes a tasty snack, but the paste could also be served with hot buttered toast as a first course.

⚐ 20 minutes

Serves 4
150 g /5 oz boiled cod's roe, skinned
100 g /4 oz plus 15 ml /1 tbls softened unsalted butter
5 ml /1 tsp anchovy essence
few drops of lemon juice
salt and freshly ground black pepper
pinch of cayenne pepper
8 medium-sized eggs
30 ml /2 tbls thin cream or milk
4 slices toast, to serve
parsley sprigs, to garnish

1 Mash the cod's roe and beat it with 100 g /4 oz butter, the anchovy essence, lemon juice, salt, black and cayenne peppers. For a really smooth paste, you can reduce it to a purée in a blender.
2 Melt the remaining butter in a small pan. Beat together the eggs, cream or milk and salt and pepper to taste. Cook the eggs over gentle heat until lightly scrambled.
3 Spread the cod's roe paste thickly on the slices of toast, spoon on the scrambled eggs and garnish with the parsley. Serve hot.

Soft roe omelette with lumpfish roe butter

This luxurious-looking omelette can serve as a starter or a light main course.

⚐⚐ making lumpfish roe butter, then 25 minutes

Serves 4
225 g /8 oz soft herring roes
salt and freshly ground black pepper
75 g /3 oz butter
1 small onion, finely chopped
100 g /4 oz button mushrooms, sliced
8 medium-sized eggs
lumpfish roe butter (page 131), to serve

1 Blanch the roes in a large pan of boiling, salted water for 2 minutes, drain and dry.
2 Melt 50 g /2 oz butter in a pan and fry the roes, turning them often and breaking them up with a wooden spoon, for 5 minutes. Lift out and keep warm. Fry the onion over moderate heat for 3 minutes, then add the mushrooms and cook for 2 minutes. Return the roes to the pan.
3 Melt the remaining butter in a large frying-pan. Beat the eggs and season with salt and pepper. Pour the eggs into the hot butter, tilt the pan and cook the omelette until it is set on the outside but still runny inside. Slide in the roe mixture, fold over the omelette and slide it onto a heated serving plate. Top with pats of lumpfish roe butter and serve at once.

Smoked cod's roe dip

Caviar eggs en cocotte

Here is an easy appetizer that looks dramatically different. Thinly sliced brown bread and butter go well.

⚐ 20 minutes
plus 1 hour setting time

Serves 6
6 large eggs
400 g /14 oz canned clear consommé
5 ml /1 tsp gelatine
15 ml /1 tbls medium-dry sherry
100 g /4 oz red caviar or lumpfish roe
parsley or watercress, to garnish
1 lemon cut into 6 wedges, to serve

1 Poach the eggs for 3–4 minutes, until the whites are set and the yolks still slightly runny. Transfer them at once to a bowl of cold water to prevent further cooking.
2 Pour 15 ml /1 tbls consommé into a small bowl, sprinkle on the gelatine and stand it in a pan of hot water. Stir until the gelatine has dissolved.
3 Gently heat the remaining consommé and the sherry in a small pan, then stir in the gelatine mixture. Remove the pan from the heat and pour a 10 mm /⅓ in deep layer of the consommé into six 150 ml /5 fl oz ramekins. Put them into the refrigerator for about 30 minutes to set. Meanwhile, stand the pan of consommé in hot water to prevent it from setting.

4 Trim the eggs if necessary and pat them dry on crumpled absorbent paper. Place them on the consommé layer in the dishes. Spoon the lumpfish roe on top of the eggs, shaping it into the form of heavy bunches of grapes. Use a parsley or watercress stem to make each stalk.

5 Spoon the remaining consommé gently around the eggs, without disturbing the roe and refrigerate for about 30 minutes, until the consommé is firm. Garnish each dish with a parsley or watercress sprig and serve with a wedge of lemon.

Deep-fried soft roes

Crisp on the outside, smooth and soft inside, these roes make a delicious first course. For a more substantial dish, serve with grilled bacon slices.

20 minutes
plus 1 hour standing time

Serves 4
12 large soft herring roes
salt
oil for deep frying
watercress sprigs, to garnish
1 lemon, quartered, to serve
For the batter
100 g /4 oz flour
pinch of salt
15 ml /1 tbls olive oil
1 large egg white

1 Blanch the roes in a large pan of boiling, salted water for 2 minutes, drain and pat dry on crumpled absorbent paper.

2 To make the batter, sieve together the flour and salt into a bowl, stir in the oil and beat in 175 ml /6 fl oz lukewarm water. Cover and set aside for about 1 hour.

3 Heat the oil in a deep-fat frier to 200C /400F or until a small cube of stale bread will brown in 40 seconds. Whisk the egg white until stiff and lightly fold it into the batter.

4 Dip the roes into the batter, shake off any excess and fry them, a few at a time, in the hot oil. Remove the roes, drain on absorbent paper and keep warm while you fry the remainder. Arrange on a heated serving dish, garnish with the watercress and serve at once, with the lemon quarters.

Herring roe mousse

Mild and with a subtle flavour, soft herring roes make an unusual mousse for a first course or light summer meal.

35 minutes
plus 1 hour 50 minutes chilling time

Serves 6
75 g /3 oz butter
450 g /1 lb soft herring roes
400 g /14 oz canned clear consommé
15 g /1/2 oz powdered gelatine
40 g /11/2 oz flour
2 medium-sized eggs, separated
salt and freshly ground black pepper
juice and grated zest of 1/2 lemon
150 ml /5 fl oz thick cream
1 red pepper, cut into decorative shapes, to garnish
a few parsley stalks, to garnish

1 Melt half the butter in a frying-pan and fry the roes, turning them often, for 5 minutes, until they are firm but not brown. Remove with a slotted spoon and set aside.

2 Pour 30 ml /2 tbls consommé into a small bowl, sprinkle on the gelatine and set in a pan of hot water. Stir to dissolve the gelatine, then stir into the remaining consommé.

3 Pour the juices from the pan into a measuring jug and make up to 300 ml /10 fl oz with consommé. Stand the remaining consommé in hot water to prevent it from setting.

4 Melt the remaining butter in a small saucepan, stir in the flour and stir over low heat for about 2 minutes. Pour on the measured consommé mixture and stir until smooth. Remove the pan from the heat and allow to cool for a few minutes. Tip the mixture into a blender, add the egg yolks and herring roes, salt, pepper, lemon juice and zest. Blend until smooth. (Alternatively, sieve the roes and beat the mixture by hand.)

5 Turn the mixture into a bowl and set aside for 15-20 minutes, until it begins to set. Whisk the cream lightly, then whisk the egg whites until stiff. Stir the cream into the fish mixture, then gently fold in the egg whites. Check the seasoning, turn into a serving dish and refrigerate for about 1 hour or until set.

6 Decorate the mousse with pieces of red pepper cut into flower shapes, with parsley to represent stalks. Spoon on a thin layer of the remaining consommé and chill for about 30 minutes, or until this has set.

Caviar eggs en cocotte

133

Vegetables

The number of sections within this chapter is an indication of the incredible range of vegetables which is now available to us – from the homely potato and leek to the most exotic imports. Interest in this exciting range, in growing for the table and in the health-giving properties of vegetables has led to a great change in our attitude towards cooking and serving them.

Soggy, over-boiled 'veg' is steadily becoming a relic of the past – the cooking method for any vegetable should aim to retain as much of the natural goodness and flavour as possible. This usually means cooking for a short length of time and in a minimum amount of water or steaming the vegetables, which keeps the colour and flavour intact.

Vegetables are once again valued as an important part of the meal. There is no need to stick to the same cooking method day in, day out for any one particular vegetable – and certainly if you are a gardener, and have, say, a glut of courgettes or runner beans, the variety is enormous. Similarly, salads are now served more frequently and can be made up of a wide selection of raw vegetables.

While the range of frozen vegetables and the constant supply of imported vegetables is useful, do not ignore the value of vegetables in season. The appearance of different vegetables month by month provides the culinary imagination with the stimulation it needs to create a variety of dishes according to the season. It makes sense economically to stick with what is in season, and what could taste more luxurious than the first crop of peas or beans, new baby carrots, or roast parsnips after the first hint of frost?

Cauliflower, broccoli and calabrese

Enjoy cauliflower cheese in a new and different form, broccoli tossed in soured cream mayonnaise with brandied raisins, and tender green calabrese spears with a rich buttery sauce. Learn how to cook these nutritious vegetables to retain their shape, texture and taste.

The tightly closed flower bud is the portion we eat of cauliflower, broccoli and calabrese. Members of the Brassica family and therefore close relations of the cabbage, they are native to the Mediterranean region and Asia Minor.

Cauliflower produces heavy, tightly packed clusters of white flower buds on a single stout stalk. Because of its appearance, it used to be known as 'curds'. There are both summer- and winter-harvesting varieties of cauliflower; in winter the leaves are wrapped around the heads as protection from frost.

The most widely known variety of broccoli in Northern Europe is the purple sprouting type, which has small clusters of deep purple flower buds sprouting at intervals up the stem. More recent is the 'hearting' broccoli, which has a central cluster of buds as well as side sprouts, and can be purple (from South Africa), white or green, according to variety.

And then there is 'Italian broccoli', more commonly known as calabrese. A green sprouting broccoli, the heads are usually more substantial than the purple sprouts but they are completely interchangeable.

Buying and storing

When buying cauliflowers, choose ones with compact, milky white heads. Avoid yellowing ones with clusters beginning to open out. Broccoli and calabrese clusters, too, should be tight, firm and compact. Do not buy the very thin, spindly shoots – the second growth of the plants – which can be bitter.

Cauliflowers are usually available all year round. Purple sprouting broccoli is sold in winter and early spring, and calabrese arrives in the autumn. Both cauliflower and broccoli are available frozen.

Store cauliflower, broccoli and calabrese loosely wrapped in a polythene bag at the bottom of the refrigerator for up to three days. Once cooked, store in covered containers in the refrigerator for up to two days.

**** Blanch cauliflower florets, broccoli and calabrese spears in boiling, salted water for 3–4 minutes, according to size. (Adding 10 ml /2 tsp lemon juice to each 1 L /2 pt water when blanching cauliflower helps to preserve the colour.) Drain, cool quickly in iced water, then drain again. Pack in rigid containers or heavy polythene bags and freeze for up to a year.

Cook from frozen; either boil for 5–8 minutes or steam for 8–10 minutes, until the vegetables are only just tender.

Preparing

Cauliflower may be cooked whole, halved, quartered, in large or small groups of florets. If it is to be cooked whole, cut off all but the smallest inner leaves and wash thoroughly under cold running water. If there are many insects, soak the cauliflower in salted water for up to 10 minutes, but soaking does destroy much vitamin C. Cut a deep cross in the stalk to ensure even cooking.

To serve in florets, first cut into evenly sized pieces, then wash thoroughly and drain. There is no need to waste the stalk – either chop it and cook it with the florets, or shred it and serve it raw in a salad.

To prepare broccoli and calabrese, trim off the tough lower part of the stems and cut a cross in the bottom of thick ones. It might also be necessary to pare the lower parts of thick stems. Large heads of 'hearting' broccoli may be cooked whole, halved or quartered. To stir-fry the vegetables, slice thinly on the diagonal.

Cooking

All three vegetables take well to simple methods of cooking and benefit from a delicate sauce or a crisp and crunchy garnish.

Cook cauliflower in the minimum of water – whole heads are best 'steam-boiled' in a covered pan in about 5 cm /2 in of salted water with a little lemon juice and, if you like, a bay leaf, a few parsley stalks or a bouquet garni. Cook for 12–15 minutes; test for doneness with a fine skewer or the point of a sharp knife – it should be just tender. Large florets can be stood upright in very little water and cooked in the same way, for 5–8 minutes.

Large or small florets cook well by steaming, too. Sprinkle with salt, pepper and lemon juice and steam for 5–10 minutes. Or braise large florets in very little chicken stock and butter, well seasoned and, if you like, lightly spiced with mace or nutmeg. A dish described as 'du Barry' will contain cauliflower, as it was much liked by Louis XV's mistress.

All these methods can be used to cook broccoli and calabrese. Never add bicarbonate of soda to the cooking water to preserve the colour – it's a sure way of destroying the vitamin C. And never nurture fond hopes of serving bright purple broccoli, as colourful as the moment it was harvested. However you cook it, it will still turn bright green. Tie long spears in bundles, as for aspar-agus, or stand them in a pan small enough to hold them upright. Cook them in the minimum of water or stock for 7–10 minutes. For steaming, allow 10–12 minutes.

Cauliflower and the tender spears of broccoli and calabrese may be served raw as part of a salad; or use cauliflower florets as 'dip-sticks' for creamy pâtés and dips.

Serve the vegetables, lightly cooked, in salads – toss them in vinaigrette while they are still hot, let cool and then combine them with mixtures such as cooked, dried beans, raisins and walnuts, or onion rings and grated raw carrot, or orange segments and tender lettuce hearts. Try cauliflower florets tossed with black olives, anchovies and garlic croûtons in a lemony vinaigrette. Indeed, croûtons, fried breadcrumbs, nuts, sunflower or sesame seeds all make contrasting toppings for cauliflower.

All these vegetables have a special affinity with cheese, cream and butter. Cauliflower cheese, perhaps the best-known example, is a popular family meal, but for a change, try broccoli cheese with browned almonds on top. Serve steamed cauliflower with browned butter poured over, or sprinkled with grated cheese and browned under the grill, or make a purée of broccoli mellowed with thick cream.

Make a cream of cauliflower or broccoli soup and serve it hot or cold, with a garnish of crisp croûtons or soured cream and paprika.

One of the classic ways to serve broccoli or calabrese is with hollandaise sauce, but it is just as delicious with a mousseline sauce (see recipe).

Stir-fry broccoli with prawns and almonds or combine it with eggs, either tossed in cheese in a creamy omelette, or baked in a slightly spiced quiche.

Broccoli and raisin salad and Cauliflower and cream tarts

Broccoli and raisin salad

Begin the day before by marinating the raisins in brandy, for a very special blend of flavours.

 overnight marinating, then 30 minutes

Serves 4
100 g /4 oz seedless raisins
45 ml /3 tbls brandy
450 g /1 lb broccoli, cut into florets
salt
2 large carrots, cut into matchstick strips
lettuce leaves, to serve
30 ml /2 tbls walnut halves, to garnish
For the dressing
60 ml /4 tbls mayonnaise
30 ml /2 tbls soured cream
15 ml /1 tbls cider vinegar
5 ml /1 tsp clear honey
salt and freshly ground black pepper

1 Put the raisins and brandy in a lidded jar, cover, shake well and leave to marinate overnight (or longer). Shake the jar occasionally, if convenient.
2 Steam the broccoli florets over boiling, salted water for 6–7 minutes or until they are barely tender, cool quickly and dry on absorbent paper.
3 To make the dressing, combine the mayonnaise, soured cream, vinegar, honey and salt and pepper to taste.
4 Just before serving, drain the raisins and toss them with the broccoli and carrots. Stir in the dressing. Cover a serving dish with lettuce leaves, pile the salad onto the lettuce and garnish with the walnut halves.

● If there is any brandy remaining in the jar, you can top it up, and add more raisins, to make a delicious topping for ice cream.

Cauliflower and cream tarts

Serve these tarts as an unusual and substantial first course, or as a light lunch or supper dish with salad.

making and chilling pastry, then 1 hour 10 minutes

Serves 6
40 g /1½ oz butter plus extra for greasing
shortcrust pastry made with 225 g /8 oz flour
2 medium-sized carrots, finely diced
½ small cauliflower, divided into small florets
salt and freshly ground black pepper
1 small onion, finely chopped
1 garlic clove, finely chopped
50 g /2 oz button mushrooms, thinly sliced
15 ml /1 tbls flour
225 ml /8 fl oz thin cream
pinch of freshly grated nutmeg
2 bay leaves
15 ml /1 tbls chopped fresh marjoram, or 5 ml /1 tsp dried
flat-leaved parsley, to garnish

1 Heat the oven to 220C /425F /gas 7. Grease the holes of a 12-hole deep bun or muffin tin well.
2 Roll out the pastry 3 mm /⅛ in thick and line the tins. Prick the bases with a fork, line with foil and beans and bake blind for 10 minutes. Remove from the oven and remove the foil and beans. Reduce the heat to 190C /375F /gas 5.
3 Steam the carrots and cauliflower separately over boiling, salted water until they are just tender.
4 Melt 25 g /1 oz butter in a small pan and sauté the onion and garlic over moderate heat for 4 minutes, stirring once or twice. Add the mushrooms, stir and sauté for a further 2 minutes. Stir in the carrots and cauliflower and remove from the heat. Spoon the vegetables into the pastry cases.
5 Melt 15 g /½ oz butter in a saucepan, stir in the flour and gradually pour on the cream, stirring. Add the nutmeg and bay leaves and bring to the boil, stirring. Simmer for 5 minutes. Remove the bay leaves, season with salt and pepper and stir in the marjoram.
6 Pour the sauce over the vegetables and return to the oven. Bake for 15 minutes, arrange on a serving plate, garnish with flat-leaved parsley and serve at once.

Calabrese with mousseline sauce

Calabrese with mousseline sauce

⧘ 20 minutes

Serves 4–6
900 g /2 lb calabrese spears
salt
10 ml /2 tsp lemon juice
For the mousseline sauce
1 medium-sized egg
3 medium-sized egg yolks
15 ml /1 tbls lemon juice
salt and white pepper
175 g /6 oz unsalted butter, melted
45 ml /3 tbls thick cream, whipped

1　Tie the calabrese spears into a bundle. Boil 5 cm /2 in water in a large saucepan and add salt and the lemon juice.
2　Stand the bundle of calabrese spears in the boiling water with flower ends upwards. Cover the pan, return to boil and boil for 7–10 minutes, until just tender. Drain and keep warm.
3　Put the egg, egg yolks and lemon juice in the top of a double boiler or in a bowl placed over a pan of simmering water. Season with salt and pepper. Beat with a wire whisk until the mixture thickens, then slowly pour in the melted butter, still beating. When the sauce is on the point of setting, remove the pan from the heat and stir in the whipped cream.
4　Arrange the calabrese spears on a heated serving dish, spoon over a little of the sauce and pour the rest into a heated sauce-boat. Serve the calabrese and sauce at once.

Cauliflower curry

⧘⧘ 45 minutes

Serves 4
45 ml /3 tbls oil
2 large onions, sliced
10 ml /2 tsp garam masala
5 ml /1 tsp ground cumin
2.5 ml /½ tsp paprika
2.5 ml /½ tsp turmeric
2.5 ml /½ tsp salt, more if needed
1 large cauliflower, cut into florets
2 green peppers, sliced
300 ml /10 fl oz hot chicken stock
15 ml /1 tbls tomato purée
2 large tomatoes, blanched, skinned, seeded and quartered
15 ml /1 tbls chopped coriander leaves or mint, to garnish

1　Heat the oil in a large saucepan and sauté the onions over moderate heat for 4 minutes, stirring occasionally. Stir in the spices and salt and cook, stirring, for 1 minute. Stir in the cauliflower and peppers and cook for 3 minutes, stirring once or twice.
2　Mix together the stock and tomato purée, pour onto the vegetables and bring to the boil. Cover, lower the heat and simmer for 20 minutes.
3　Add the tomatoes and simmer for 2 minutes. Taste the sauce and add more salt if needed, then pour into a warmed serving dish and serve, garnished with the coriander or mint.

● Side dishes of chopped banana rolled in desiccated coconut, onion rings, yoghurt and chutneys make good accompaniments.

Cauliflower cheese fritters

⧘ 25 minutes

Serves 4
1 large cauliflower, cut into florets
salt and freshly ground black pepper
30 ml /2 tbls flour
5 ml /1 tsp freshly chopped parsley
1 medium-sized egg, beaten
10 ml /2 tsp thin cream
oil for deep frying
50 g /2 oz freshly grated Parmesan cheese
shredded lettuce and watercress sprigs, to garnish
1 lemon, quartered, to serve

1　Steam the cauliflower florets over boiling, salted water for about 6 minutes, until they are barely tender. Cool quickly and dry on absorbent paper.
2　Season the florets with salt and plenty of pepper. Combine the flour and parsley on a plate, and mix together the egg and cream in a small bowl. One at a time, toss the florets first in the flour to coat thoroughly, then in the egg and cream mixture.
3　Heat the oil in a deep-fat frier to 200C /400F. At this temperature a cube of bread will brown in 40 seconds.
4　Drain off any excess egg and roll the florets in the cheese, lift out, then roll in the cheese again.
5　Deep fry the fritters for about 4–5 minutes, until they are crisp and golden brown. Drain on absorbent paper and serve the cauliflower cheese fritters at once, garnished with the lettuce and watercress and accompanied by the lemon wedges.

Cabbage, kale and Brussels sprouts

Cabbage, kale and Brussels sprouts too often suffer from over-boiling, but are delicious if cooked till just tender. They are also tasty cooked in soup or a hot-pot, and served raw in salads.

Cabbage, kale and Brussels sprouts belong to the *Brassica* family, which probably originated in the countries around the eastern Mediterranean and in Asia Minor: cabbages of all kinds still feature prominently in the cuisine of these regions. The labourers building the Great Wall of China were fortified with nutritious cabbage, and the Greeks ate it before and after heavy drinking sessions. The Romans carried cabbage to northern Europe.

Cabbage has changed a great deal through the centuries: it was not until the 16th century that firm, round-headed cabbages appeared. Since the 1960s varieties of cabbage and Brussels sprouts have been bred which have done much to eliminate the sulphurous taste and lingering cooking smell that at one time made them unpopular vegetables.

There is plenty of truth in the saying 'cabbage is good for you' — indeed, all brassicas are. They contain calcium, iron and other minerals, and vitamins A and C.

Types of brassica
Many different varieties of cabbage are cultivated; they can be dark or light green, nearly white or red, with either smooth or curly, almost frilled leaves. They may also be tightly packed or loose round a central heart.
Green cabbages are the most widely grown. They are planted right through the year, so are always available.
Spring cabbage does not mean a cabbage planted or harvested in the spring, but refers to one that is cut young, when the heart is only partially developed.

Savoy cabbage is a highly regarded variety: it is pale green and has darker green outer leaves ribbed with thick, fleshy veins, which give the vegetable its wrinkled appearance. It is milder in flavour than some other green cabbages.
White and red cabbages both have very firm, tight heads, and are smooth-leaved.
Kale is also known as curly kale, borecole and, in the U.S., as collards or collard greens. It is an 'open' form of cabbage, with heavily frilled, bluish-green leaves. It is the hardiest brassica and will thrive even in a harsh winter climate. The leaves are coarse and strong-flavoured and are regarded by many as an acquired taste.
Brussels sprouts are like miniature, tight-headed cabbages growing at the base of leaf nodes all the way up tall stalks. They are a comparatively new addition to our diet. It is sometimes said that they should be eaten only after they have been nipped by the frost, to get the best flavour, but this is a matter of taste.

Buying and storing
Look for cabbages with compact heads and firm, crisp leaves, avoiding any that are discoloured. A good cabbage should weigh heavily when held in the hand: this means it will have a firm, undamaged centre.

At the back, on left and right, green cabbages; in the centre, red cabbage and front left, white cabbage shredded

Hard cabbages will keep a week or more, soft-headed ones a few days. Cooked cabbage will keep covered in the refrigerator for a couple of days, but should really be used as soon as possible. Brussels sprouts are at their best when young and small and really firm: once they open out, they lose their sweetness. Avoid any with soft, wilted heads and yellowish leaves. Sprouts will keep for up to 2 days in a plastic bag in the refrigerator, and cooked and covered for the same time.

**** It is not generally considered worth freezing cabbage, since it is available all year round. Blanch Brussels sprouts in boiling, salted water for 3–5 minutes, kale for 4 minutes. Drain, cool at once in iced water for the same time as for blanching, then drain again thoroughly. Bag, seal, label and freeze for up to a year. Commercially frozen Brussels sprouts are a good buy when fresh ones are not available.

Preparing brassicas
Strip off the outer leaves of 'loose' cabbages, discarding any that are tough or discoloured, and strip or cut off the hard stalks. Cut firm cabbages in half, remove the core by cutting out a deep V, then cut each half into 2 or 3 pieces, or shred finely in a food processor or with a very sharp knife.

Strip kale leaves from the stalks and tear large leaves into 2 or 3 pieces. Remove any wilting outer leaves of Brussels sprouts, trim the stalk ends close to the leaves and, with a small, sharp knife, cut a deep cross in the stalk to allow the heat to penetrate. Wash all vegetables thoroughly in cold water and drain well. If you have to prepare them in advance, dry them and keep them in a polythene bag in the refrigerator, until you are ready to cook.

Cooking brassicas

Cabbage to be served as a vegetable accompaniment can be cooked in a number of ways. Chunks can be boiled in salted water or chicken stock, perhaps with an onion studded with cloves, in a covered pan for not longer than 8–10 minutes – take care not to overcook them! Chop the cabbage and toss it in butter and flavour with caraway seeds if liked. Shredded cabbage is better steamed, and can also be braised in melted butter, then cooked in a little well-seasoned chicken stock for 5–10 minutes until all the liquid is absorbed. Cabbage stir-fried in the Chinese manner is deliciously crisp.

Cabbage makes hearty soups, much favoured in French country cooking. Cabbage leaves can be used instead of vine leaves to make steamed *dolmades*-style parcels with a savoury minced meat and rice filling. White cabbage is ideally suited to casserole cooking, since the firm leaves do not disintegrate, and is also the variety used for Sauerkraut (see recipe), the pickled cabbage which features prominently in central European cuisine: sauerkraut is the traditional accompaniment to frankfurters and can be bought in cans. Left-over cabbage is delicious combined with potato in bubble and squeak or colcannon, as the Irish version is called. Either white or red cabbage is excellent shredded in crunchy salads such as coleslaw.

Pickled red cabbage can be bought in cans; fresh red cabbage is delicious cooked slowly with onions, apples and spices, and is traditionally served with roast goose, partridge and pheasant, but is equally enjoyable with pork, boiled bacon or sausages.

Kale is best cooked simply – boiled or steamed – and served as an accompaniment rather than in a dish with other ingredients; as its flavour is very pronounced.

Brussels sprouts are excellent boiled, steamed or braised, and are traditionally served with chestnuts (see recipe); try them too with butter-fried croûtons, diced fried bacon or a crisp topping of fried breadcrumbs and chopped nuts, or purée them with cream and flavour with nutmeg. Brussels sprouts can also be successfully used in dishes on their own – like a soup or soufflé (see recipes). Shredded young sprouts make an unusual addition to a mixed green salad, and with sliced chicory, orange segments and walnuts make an interesting side salad.

Stuffed cabbage

🕔 2 hours

Serves 4
1 small white or green smooth-leaved cabbage
50 g /2 oz butter
1 medium-sized onion, sliced
1 clove garlic, crushed
350 g /12 oz sausage-meat
5 ml /1 tsp dried mixed herbs
100 g /4 oz 1-day-old white breadcrumbs
salt and freshly ground black pepper
50 g /2 oz walnuts, chopped
1 hard-boiled egg, finely chopped

Stuffed cabbage

1 Remove any discoloured or loose outer leaves from the cabbage until it is a neat, round shape. Blanch it whole in a saucepan of boiling, salted water for about 4 minutes, then drain it thoroughly.
2 Transfer the cabbage to a board and, using 2 spoons, gently pull the leaves outwards to make a hollow in the centre. With a curved grapefruit knife, carefully cut out the centre of the cabbage, without cutting through to the base. Chop the removed cabbage centre finely.
3 Melt half of the butter in a large frying-pan and fry the onion over a moderate heat for 3 minutes. Add the garlic and fry for 1 minute, stirring. Add the sausage-meat and stir until it is evenly browned. Stir in the herbs and half of the breadcrumbs and season with salt and pepper. Add the chopped cabbage and mix well.
4 Spoon the filling into the cabbage shell and wrap the whole cabbage tightly in foil. Put a trivet in the bottom of a large saucepan, half fill it with boiling water, add the cabbage parcel and cover the pan. Boil, topping up with boiling water when necessary, for 1½ hours or until the cabbage is tender when pierced with a fine skewer.
5 To make the topping, melt the remaining butter in a small frying-pan, add the walnuts and remaining breadcrumbs and fry over a moderate heat until the mixture is dry. Stir in the chopped egg.
6 Unwrap the cabbage, transfer it to a heated serving dish and top it with the golden crumb mixture. Serve very hot.

Brussels sprouts purée

Try this different way of cooking sprouts: the purée is delightfully creamy.

🕔 25 minutes

Serves 4
700 g /1½ lb Brussels sprouts, prepared
150 ml /5 fl oz thin cream
225 g /8 oz cold mashed potato
50 g /2 oz butter, melted
salt and freshly ground black pepper
grated nutmeg

1 Boil or steam the Brussels sprouts until just tender. Drain them thoroughly and purée them with the cream in a blender or through a food mill, stirring in the cream.
2 Put the mashed potato in a large bowl, pour on the melted butter and beat in the Brussels sprouts purée until completely smooth. Season to taste with salt, pepper and nutmeg and turn into a heated serving dish.

● This purée can be used as the basis of a deliciously light soufflé. Beat 3 large egg yolks, beat them into the cooled purée, then fold in 4 stiffly beaten egg whites. Turn into a greased 850 ml /1½ pt soufflé dish and bake in an oven pre-heated to 190C /375F /gas 5 for 45 minutes, until the soufflé is well risen and golden. Serve at once.

Brussels sprouts soup

⏱ 30 minutes

Serves 4
25 g /1 oz butter
1 medium-sized onion, sliced
700 g /1½ lb Brussels sprouts, prepared
850 ml /1½ pt chicken stock
salt and freshly ground black pepper
grated nutmeg
150 ml /5 fl oz thick cream
To garnish
2 slices of lean bacon, rind removed

1 Melt the butter in a large saucepan, add the onion and cook over a moderate heat for 3-4 minutes until the onion is soft but not brown.
2 Cut any very large Brussels sprouts in half. Add the sprouts to the pan with the stock, bring to the boil, cover the pan and simmer for 20 minutes. Remove the pan from the heat and purée the contents in a blender or through a food mill.
3 Return the purée to the rinsed pan, season to taste with salt, pepper and nutmeg, and stir in the cream. Heat gently without boiling.
4 To prepare the garnish, dice the bacon and fry it in a non-stick pan over a moderate heat until it is crisp and dry. Remove the bacon from the pan with a slotted spoon and set aside.
5 Pour the soup into a heated tureen or individual soup bowls and sprinkle with the bacon. Serve immediately.

Beef and red cabbage casserole

Rich and lightly spiced, this is an ideal dish for an informal supper party. The casserole can be prepared in advance, then reheated just before serving. The beer gives the sauce a rich colour.

⏱ 1½ hours

Serves 4-6
25 g /1 oz butter
1 kg /2¼ lb topside of beef in one piece
1 large onion, thinly sliced
700 g /1½ lb red cabbage, shredded
15 ml /1 tbls red wine vinegar
150 ml /5 fl oz brown ale or Guinness
30 ml /2 tbls redcurrant jelly
6 juniper berries, crushed
2 bay leaves
salt and freshly ground black pepper
5 ml /1 tsp soft brown sugar (optional)

1 Heat the oven to 180C /350F /gas 4. Melt the butter in a large, flameproof casserole, and brown the meat on all sides. Remove from pan and keep warm.

Beef and red cabbage casserole

2 Over a moderate heat, fry the onion in the casserole for about 3 minutes, stirring occasionally, then add the shredded cabbage. Stir well, then add the vinegar, beer, redcurrant jelly, juniper berries and bay leaves. Stir until the jelly has melted. Season with salt and pepper and return the meat to the casserole.
3 Cover the casserole and cook in the oven for 1¼ hours, or until the meat is tender when pierced with a fine skewer. Remove and discard the bay leaves, taste the juices and adjust the seasoning if necessary. Add the brown sugar, if you like, to make the sauce even richer.
4 Transfer the meat to a heated serving dish and spoon the red cabbage and the meat juices round it. Serve with mashed potatoes and runner beans.

Pork and cabbage hot-pot

The cabbage absorbs the flavours of the meat and sage, yet remains crisp.

⏱ 55 minutes

Serves 4
25 g /1 oz butter
1 large onion, sliced
1 clove garlic, crushed
4 large pork chops, trimmed of excess fat
500 g /1 lb white cabbage
salt and freshly ground black pepper
150 ml /5 fl oz hot chicken stock
45 ml /3 tbls tomato purée
5 ml /1 tsp dried sage
pinch of ground nutmeg
fresh sage leaves, to garnish, if available

1 Heat the oven to 190C /375F /gas 5. Melt the butter in a frying-pan. Add the onion and cook, stirring occasionally, for 3 minutes. Add the garlic and cook for 1 minute more. Add the chops and cook for about 8 minutes, turning them once to brown them well on both sides.
2 Meanwhile, discard any discoloured leaves from the cabbage and separate the remaining leaves, discarding the tough core at the centre. Tear the large leaves in half.
3 Remove the onion and chops from the pan with a slotted spoon, and layer them with the cabbage in a casserole. Season well with salt and pepper.
4 Mix together the stock, tomato purée, dried sage and nutmeg, and pour over the chops and vegetables in the casserole. Cover and cook in the oven for 45 minutes, or until the chops are tender. Serve very hot, garnished with sage leaves if available.

Sauerkraut

The name means 'pickled cabbage' and this is a centuries-old way of preserving white cabbage.

🕐 ∮∮∮ 1 hour,
then 4–4½ weeks fermenting

Makes about 1.5 kg /3¼ lb
2 kg /4½ lb white cabbage, finely shredded
75 g /3 oz coarse salt
4 bay leaves, crumbled
5 ml /1 tsp caraway seeds (optional)

1 Use a large, deep earthenware or porcelain container (a casserole is suitable). Sprinkle a layer of salt in the base, add a layer of cabbage, sprinkle with pieces of bay leaf and a few caraway seeds if using, then with another layer of salt. Continue adding the layers to the dish, finishing with a sprinkling of salt.
2 Scald a piece of muslin or cheesecloth in boiling water and use it to cover the container. Put a plate on top of the cloth and then a heavy weight to keep the cabbage compressed and immersed in the brine that will form from the juices and salt.
3 Leave the container in a warm place with a steady temperature (about 20C /68F) for a few days until fermentation starts (when bubbles rise). Once fermentation has started, transfer the container to a cooler place (about 10C /50F) for 3–4 weeks until the fermentation has stopped (when the bubbles have stopped rising).
4 Throughout the fermenting time, skim off the scum every 1–2 days. Replace the cloth each time with a freshly sterilized one and wash the plate.
5 Keep the sauerkraut for short-term use (3-4 days) in a covered container in the refrigerator.
6 For longer-term storage, drain off the brine into a large saucepan, bring it to the boil, add the sauerkraut and bring back to the boil. Warm sterilized preserving jars in a very low oven, then pack in the sauerkraut and hot brine. Cover tightly and place the jars on a trivet in a large pan of water. Bring the water to the boil and boil for 25 minutes.
7 Remove the jars and test them for seal: remove the closures and carefully try lifting up the jars by their lids. If any lids are not properly sealed, use the contents within a 3–4 day period. Otherwise, label them, cool and store in a cool, dry, airy place for up to 1 year.

● Sauerkraut must always be well drained before serving; it can also be rinsed in cold water if you prefer a less salty taste.

Brussels sprouts with chestnuts

Bubble and squeak

In Victorian times, this was a popular dish in pubs. The name refers to the noise it makes when frying.

∮ 10 minutes

Serves 4
500 g /1 lb cold cooked potatoes, mashed
500 g /1 lb cold cooked cabbage or Brussels sprouts, or a mixture of both
salt and freshly ground black pepper
50 g /2 oz beef dripping or butter
5 ml /1 tsp vinegar

1 Put the potatoes and greens in a bowl and stir with a fork to break them up. Mix together thoroughly and season well with salt and pepper.
2 Heat the dripping or butter in a frying-pan and add the vegetables. Press the mixture down with a wooden spoon. Fry over a moderate heat for 6–7 minutes, turning occasionally, until the mixture is lightly browned, crisp and dry.
3 Sprinkle the bubble and squeak with the vinegar and turn it on to a heated serving dish. Serve with cold roast meat or poultry or with boiled beef.

Brussels sprouts with chestnuts

This combination is a favourite with Christmas turkey, and delicious with all roast meat, poultry and game.

∮∮ 1¼ hours

Serves 4
350 g /12 oz chestnuts in their skins
40 g /1½ oz butter
275 ml /10 fl oz chicken stock
700 g /1½ lb Brussels sprouts
salt and freshly ground black pepper

1 Prick the skins of the chestnuts, put them in a saucepan, cover with cold water and bring to the boil. Turn off the heat, remove the chestnuts one at a time with a slotted spoon. Peel off the tough outer and papery inner skins. Cut the chestnuts in half.
2 Heat half the butter in a saucepan and add the chestnuts. Stir over a moderate heat for 1 minute to coat them in butter. Pour on the stock, cover the pan and bring to the boil. Simmer for 1 hour, or until the chestnuts are tender and the stock has been absorbed. Check from time to time that the pan has not dried out.
3 Meanwhile prepare the Brussels sprouts and boil or steam them until they are just tender. Drain them thoroughly.
4 Melt the remaining butter in a saucepan, add the cooked chestnuts and Brussels sprouts, season well with salt and pepper and stir to mix thoroughly. Turn into a heated serving dish; make sure there are plenty of chestnuts on top.

Spinach and leafy greens

Greens are much more than good for you. Cooked in soups, flans and pancake fillings, served with herb butter, a creamy sauce or a dash of spice, they are versatile and delicious. Careful preparation and accurate timing can turn them into the memorable dish of a meal.

For centuries leafy greens which grew wild and could be gathered freely formed an important part of the peasant diet throughout Europe and the Middle East, for country people knew well what modern children are reluctant to accept: that greens are, indeed, good for you.

Spinach is much richer in protein than other leaf vegetables; it also has a high vitamin A content. However, despite the advocacy of the Popeye cartoons, the iron it contains is indissoluble and so effectively unobtainable. Spinach is thought to have originated in Persia, and was eventually brought to Northern Europe in the 16th century, where it has been grown ever since.

Spinach beet: a number of members of the beetroot family are cultivated for their leaves, rather than the root. Although beets have no relation to spinach their flavour is mild and spinach-like and so the plant is sometimes called perpetual spinach.

Chard, also called Swiss chard or seakale beet, is another vegetable of the beetroot family with an almost perpetual cropping season. The leaves are shiny dark green, large as a plate with a conspicuous stalk, fleshy and white. There is a variety with red stems called rhubarb chard or ruby chard in the U.S. To eat, the green leaf and the tasty stalk are cooked separately.

Good King Henry, called mercury or wild spinach, also has spinach-tasting leaves which are arrow-shaped. Its shoots, when very young and tender, can be tied in bundles, cooked and eaten like asparagus.

New Zealand spinach: discovered by members of Captain Cook's expedition to Australasia in 1770, this fleshy-leaved plant is not a spinach at all, but it flourishes in warmer climates and has a sweet, mild and very pleasant flavour.

Chinese cabbage: called *bok choy* in China, to distinguish it from the all-white Chinese cabbage which is sold under the name of 'Chinese leaves', this cabbage has broad dark leaves, tapering to a narrow-margined stalk. It belongs to the Brassica family and is usually stir-fried.

Turnip tops may be eaten as a green vegetable. The leaves are frilly and they are sold in bunches including the buds of a yellow flower. The flavour is mild and turnip-like. Cook them as for spring and winter greens.

Spring and winter greens are members of the Brassica family, with a more familiar cabbage taste. In the United States they are known as collards and they form the basis of many soul food dishes of the black communities in the South. These greens can be a welcome stand-by when fresh green vegetables are wanted throughout the winter. They become more succulent and less bitter as spring progresses.

Nettles are good to eat when young. Cut them with gloves on and do not use ones from roadsides, which may have been sprayed with chemicals. They can be used to make a tasty soup.

Leafy greens, clockwise from the top: chard, spinach, spring greens, bok choy

Buying and storing

Spinach is available almost all the year round, since there are both summer and winter types. Summer spinach, with its lighter, brighter leaves and more delicate flavour, is perhaps a better introduction to the vegetable for those who might harbour some prejudice. Winter spinach has very dark green leaves which are coarser and have a slightly bitter, acidy flavour, and coarser, thicker stems which are usually discarded.

When buying greens, avoid any with wilting or yellowing leaves, or (except for turnip tops) seedheads which have already formed on the plant. When buying chard or seakale beet, examine not only the leaves but also the stems—these should be thick, fleshy (but not stringy) and stiff. Floppy stems indicate loss of freshness and quality. According to variety, stems may be milky white or tinged with purplish red.

Spring greens, if they are to be enjoyed at their best, must be crisp and sound almost crackly when handled. Again, avoid any that are limp, wilting or turning yellow or, worse, brown at the edges.

To store, pack leafy greens loosely in a large polythene bag and keep them in the salad drawer of the refrigerator for no more than two days. Once cooked, leafy greens can be stored in the refrigerator in a covered container for up to three days, but after that they acquire an unpleasant bitterness.

✱✱✱✱ All the leafy greens can be frozen successfully. Wash leafy greens, blanch for 2 minutes in boiling, salted water, cool in cold water, drain and press out excess moisture. Chop the leaves if you wish, then pack into boxes or polythene bags. Freeze spinach and chard leaves up to one year, greens for 6 months.

Select tender young stalks of Swiss chard, trim and wash well, then grade into bundles of even size. Blanch for 2–4 minutes, according to thickness, cool and drain. Pack into rigid boxes or cartons and freeze for up to 6 months.

Preparing leafy greens

Spinach and other greens need very thorough washing to rid them of all the grit and sand they contain. If the leaves are to be eaten raw in a salad, they must be completely dried first.

The fine ribs or stalks through the centres of summer spinach and very young winter spinach leaves need not be removed, but the tough stalks of spinach and spring and winter greens should be discarded—run a sharp knife down each side, cutting away the leaf in two parts. Strip off edible chard stalks in the same way, and trim them neatly at each end. These are then used for a separate recipe.

Cooking leafy greens

Care and accuracy in cooking is the make-or-break factor for leafy greens. Overcooking toughens them and robs them of both flavour and nutrients, and failure to press out or evaporate away the last drop of moisture can send them to the table surrounded by a moat of green liquid—not a very pleasant sight!

Spinach: since spinach has a very high water content, and collapses dramatically on contact with heat, a lot of the fresh vegetable goes only a little way—allow at least 225 g /8 oz of fresh leaves per serving.

There are four distinctly different ways to cook spinach; all are effective. The first is to put the washed and drained leaves into a very large, well-buttered pan, with only the water still clinging to the leaves. Sprinkle lightly with salt, cover and cook over a moderate heat, stirring occasionally, for 10-15 minutes, then turn the leaves into a colander or sieve and press gently to force out the moisture.

Return the leaves to the pan with a little butter, season with salt, pepper and nutmeg, add a dash of lemon juice and stir over gentle heat to evaporate any lingering moisture and to reheat. Turn into a heated dish and serve very hot.

The second method involves cooking the leaves uncovered in a large pan of boiling, salted water with a large pinch of sugar for 10-15 minutes, then draining, refreshing in cold water and draining again. The leaves are then pressed dry and reheated. Supporters of this method maintain that the spinach is more digestible and less likely to have an acidy or metallic taste.

A nouvelle cuisine way of cooking spinach is to put the leaves into a hot, buttered pan only until they wilt. The leaves are then removed before they darken and

Spinach pâté

may be used as a bed for fish or meat.

You can also cook the washed and well-drained leaves by stir-frying, in the Chinese style, with chopped garlic and spring onions.

To give cooked spinach a softer flavour, add thick or thin cream, soured cream, thickened yoghurt or bechamel sauce.

Other last-minute flavourings give the vegetable a different personality—try very finely chopped onion, spring onion or shallot, or crushed garlic added when the spinach is returned to the pan to reheat, or chopped fresh herbs such as rosemary, parsley or thyme stirred in just before serving.

Cooked spinach is the basis of the well-known eggs florentine, where poached or boiled eggs are served on a bed of cooked spinach and topped with cheese sauce. Combined with cream and cheese, spinach makes a tasty flan or pancake filling; or combine spinach with cream and chicken stock to make a quick spinach soup.

Cooked spinach can be pressed through a sieve or whizzed in a blender to make a purée. Mixed with a little cream and well seasoned, this can be used to fill tiny tartlet cases, tomato shells or artichoke bottoms.

Spinach beet or chard: the leaves of these varieties can be cooked in the ways described above. Very young stalks can be washed, dried and finely sliced to serve in a salad—with orange segments and walnuts, for example—or cooked stalks can be served as a separate course or unusual salad in their own right: mix them, while still hot, with vinaigrette or lemon dressing, allow them to cool, then sprinkle with chopped herbs or sunflower seeds.

To cook the stalks, put them in a pan with just enough boiling, salted water to cover, cover the pan and simmer for 5 minutes, or until the stalks are tender. Drain well, return to the pan with a knob of butter and season with salt, pepper and lemon juice. Serve with cheese or hollandaise sauce, if wished.

Another way to cook them is to simmer them, covered, with 25 g/1 oz butter and 60 ml/4 tbls chicken stock to 450 g/1 lb stalks (enough for six people). Cook for 5-10 minutes and season with salt, pepper and lemon juice.

Spring and winter greens: after washing, cut off the tough stalks (these can be finely sliced and used as a crunchy salad ingredient), then cook the leaves in the very minimum of boiling, salted water—use just enough to cover. Add a knob of butter, cover and cook for 10-15 minutes, stirring occasionally. Test the greens with the point of a sharp knife and drain them as soon as they are tender. Toss them in melted butter, season well with salt and pepper and add some chopped fresh parsley or chives. Garnish with thinly sliced onion rings, finely chopped spring onion or chopped hard-boiled egg and serve very hot.

Spinach pâté

This is a quick-to-prepare first course that, with the addition of a salad, would make a delightful summer lunch.

🍴 30 minutes
plus 1 hour chilling

Serves 4
225 g/8 oz young spinach leaves, cooked, drained and finely chopped
25 g/1 oz butter
6 spring onions, finely chopped
30 ml/2 tbls chopped fresh mint leaves
15 ml/1 tbls thin cream
150 g/5 oz full-fat cream cheese
salt and freshly ground black pepper
pinch of cayenne pepper
15 ml/1 tbls lemon juice
4 thin slices of lemon, to garnish
hot granary rolls or toast fingers, to serve

1 Melt the butter in a pan and sauté the spring onions over moderate heat for 2-3 minutes, stirring occasionally. Add the chopped mint and spinach and mix well. Remove from the heat and leave to cool.
2 When the spinach mixture is cool, stir in the cream, cream cheese, salt, pepper, cayenne pepper and lemon juice. Reduce to a purée by blending in 2 batches.
3 Divide the pâté between 4 individual ramekin dishes and smooth the tops. Cover and chill in the refrigerator for at least 1 hour. Garnish each with a slice of lemon and serve with hot granary rolls or toast fingers.

Meat loaf with spinach filling

Spinach makes a flavourful filling for a standard meat loaf recipe. For added colour, serve it with a lightly seasoned tomato sauce. Any leftovers are delicious cold, with a salad.

🍴 2 hours 20 minutes

Serves 6
350 g/12 oz pork sausage-meat
350 g/12 oz minced beef
1 medium-sized onion, finely chopped
45 ml/3 tbls fresh white breadcrumbs
15 ml/1 tbls freshly chopped mint leaves, or 5 ml/1 tsp dried mint
5 ml/1 tsp freshly chopped thyme, or 2.5 ml/1/2 tsp dried thyme
salt and freshly ground black pepper
2.5 ml/1/2 tsp ground coriander
45 ml/3 tbls strong beef stock, or water and stock cube
1 medium-sized egg, beaten
butter for greasing
buttered new potatoes, to serve

Meat loaf with spinach filling

For the filling
15 ml/1 tbls olive oil
1 small onion, finely chopped
450 g/1 lb fresh spinach, cooked, drained and finely chopped
50 g/2 oz low-fat cream cheese or other cream cheese
salt and freshly ground black pepper

1 In a large bowl, mix together the sausage-meat, minced beef, onion, breadcrumbs and herbs and season with salt, pepper and coriander. Stir in the stock and beaten egg, beat well, cover and chill in the refrigerator while you make the filling.
2 To make the filling, heat the oil in a pan, sauté the onion, stirring occasionally, for 3 minutes, then add the spinach. Remove the pan from the heat and allow to cool. Stir in the cream cheese and season well.
3 Heat the oven to 180C/350F/gas 4. Grease a 1 L/1½ pt loaf tin. Spread half of the meat mixture in the tin and smooth the top. Cover with the spinach mixture, then top with the remaining meat. Cover the tin with a double layer of foil.
4 Stand the tin in a roasting tin filled with boiling water to come half-way up the sides of the loaf tin. Cook in the centre of the oven for 1½ hours. Allow to cool in the tin for 5 minutes, then turn out onto a heated dish and serve with buttered new potatoes.

Spinach and bacon salad

♦ 25 minutes

Serves 4
225 g /8 oz young summer spinach leaves
100 g /4 oz bacon slices, in 15 mm /¹/₂ in
squares
100 g /4 oz button mushrooms, thinly sliced
30 ml /2 tbls freshly snipped chives
For the croûtons
25 g /1 oz butter
15 ml /1 tbls oil
1 garlic clove, crushed
2 × 15 mm /¹/₂ in thick slices of white bread cut
from a large loaf, cubed
For the dressing
45 ml /3 tbls olive oil
15 ml /1 tbls cider vinegar
salt and freshly ground black pepper
1 garlic clove, crushed

1 Chop or tear the spinach leaves and place them in a salad bowl.
2 Fry the bacon squares in a non-stick frying-pan over moderate heat, stirring frequently, until they are crisp. Remove them from the pan with a slotted spoon, toss them on absorbent paper and allow them to cool.
3 To make the croûtons, heat the butter and oil in a frying-pan, add the garlic and fry over moderate heat for 1 minute. Add the bread cubes and fry, stirring frequently, until they are crisp and golden. Toss them on absorbent paper and allow to cool.
4 Toss the mushrooms and chives with the spinach and add the bacon. Make the dressing: beat together the oil and vinegar, season with salt and pepper and stir in the crushed garlic. Add the croûtons to the salad, pour over the dressing, toss to coat the leaves, and serve at once.

● Chopped or sliced hard-boiled eggs make a good addition to this salad.

Spinach and bacon salad

Chard stalks in cream sauce

♦ 35 minutes

Serves 4
24-28 large chard stalks, in 5 cm /2 in lengths
1 small onion, thinly sliced
60 ml /4 tbls chicken stock
5 ml /1 tsp lemon juice
40 g /1¹/₂ oz butter
salt and freshly ground black pepper
15 ml /1 tbls flour
275 ml /10 fl oz thin cream
100 g /4 oz flaked almonds, toasted
15 ml /1 tbls freshly chopped parsley, to garnish

1 Place the chard stalks in a saucepan with the onion, chicken stock, lemon juice, butter, salt and pepper. Cover the pan, bring to the boil and simmer for about 10 minutes, or until the stalks are tender. Remove the lid and increase the heat if necessary to evaporate the liquid.
2 Stir in the flour and gradually pour on the cream, stirring all the time over a low heat. Do not allow the sauce to boil. Adjust seasoning and stir in the almonds, reserving a few for the garnish.
3 Turn into a heated serving dish and garnish with the parsley and the reserved almonds. Serve at once.

Spring greens and hazelnut soup

♦♦ 45 minutes

Serves 4
450 g /1 lb tender young spring greens
salt and freshly ground black pepper
50 g /2 oz butter
1 medium-sized onion, sliced
850 ml/1¹/₂ pt chicken stock
60 ml /4 tbls thin cream
50 g /2 oz shelled hazelnuts, chopped
pinch of sugar

1 Strip off and discard the tough stalks from the greens. Blanch the leaves in a large pan of boiling salted water for 5 minutes, then drain well. Cut one large leaf into very thin strips and reserve for the garnish; chop the remainder and set aside.
2 Melt the butter in a large saucepan and sauté the onion over moderate heat for 3 minutes, stirring occasionally. Add the chopped greens, stir well and simmer for 3-4 minutes. Pour on the chicken stock and bring to the boil. Cover the pan and simmer for 20 minutes, then purée in a blender.
3 Return the purée to the rinsed-out pan, stir in the cream and hazelnuts, taste and season with salt, pepper and a pinch of sugar. Heat gently, stirring. Serve hot, garnished with the reserved leaf strips.

● To enhance the colour of this soup, add 1-2 drops of green food colouring.

Leeks

Leeks are often served as a cooked vegetable, but they make first-class soups and are delicious baked, farmhouse-style, in a pie. When raw, their slightly sweet, spicy taste gives a lift to salads.

Wild leeks are thought to have originated in the eastern Mediterranean, and their cultivation dates back to at least 3500 BC, when they were grown by the Sumerians as a flavouring for their staple diet of beans and barley. In Britain, few vegetables except leeks survived the withdrawal of the Romans and the following Dark Ages. Under the Saxons they grew so freely that their name, 'leac tun', came to mean 'kitchen garden'. Indeed, in Wales they became a national emblem.

Leeks are a member of the numerous onion family, and one of its mildest, sweetest forms. Rather like larger cousins of spring onions, they are long and thin, blanched white at the base and with green tops. Their average length is 20-30 cm /8-12 in and they can be as much as 5 cm /2 in across, but when very large, they are suited more for the prize table at the horticultural show than for cooking, although large leeks can be used in hearty soups and stews.

Leeks are remarkably versatile. They can be eaten raw or cooked, hot or cold, as a flavouring or as a vegetable, and are in season from winter through early spring.

Vegetable hotpot

Buying and storing leeks

Look for well-blanched specimens with tightly rolled leaves. Once the leaves splay out at the top they become tough and are useful only to flavour stocks and soups. Avoid any that are bruised, discoloured or flabby; small and medium-sized leeks are tastier and more tender than large ones.

If you have a garden, one of the best ways to store large quantities of leeks is to dig a trench and 'heel them in' so that the white parts are well covered with soil. This way they will keep fresh for a month or more.

To store leeks in the refrigerator, cut off the rootlets and the tough tops of the leaves, and put the leeks in a plastic bag or in the salad drawer, where they will stay fresh for up to five days. Do not leave unwrapped leeks in the main part of the refrigerator or they will impart their flavour to other foods. Cooked leeks can be stored in a covered container in the refrigerator for two days.

✳✳✳ Freeze only the freshest small or medium-sized leeks. Wash them thoroughly and blanch, sliced, for 1 minute, or whole for 2 minutes. Cool rapidly, drain very thoroughly, pack in boxes or polythene bags and freeze. Cooked leeks and dishes containing them can be frozen.

Preparing leeks

Leeks are made up of many layers of leaves like concentric tubes, one inside the other, and they need very thorough washing to remove every trace of dirt and grit.

Cut off the rootlets and the toughest part of the green tops and discard. Using the point of a sharp knife, slit from root to top through the outer one or two discoloured layers and discard these also.

If you need whole leeks for a recipe, slit each leek from root to top, from the outside through to the centre. Gently open out the leek and hold it, root end upwards, under cold running water until all the grit has been washed away. Close the leek again and stand it, head down, in a jug of cold water for 2 minutes, then drain well.

If sliced leeks are needed, it is easier to slice the leeks first, then put them in a colander and wash thoroughly under cold running water.

Using leeks

As a flavouring: leeks were one of the original pot-herbs of country stews, and are used to flavour the court bouillon in which fish is cooked, or the stock in which ham, bacon or mutton is boiled. They are also used in a bouquet garni; use a leek as a container for the mixed herbs – slit it in half lengthways, push in stalks of parsley and thyme and a bay leaf, and tie with string.

The white of the leek is the 'delicacy' but all except the toughest and most fibrous green part can be used for flavouring. This makes leeks a dual-purpose – and highly economical – vegetable.

Using leeks raw: tender young leeks can be eaten raw in salads. Like this, they have a much more pronounced onion flavour than when they are cooked.

● Slice thinly and push out the centres to form rings. Toss with torn lettuce leaves and watercress sprigs, or with endive and chicory, or combine them with tomato and apple slices and chopped fresh mint.

● A slice of raw leek can be steeped in salad oil or white vinegar for up to 10 days (and then discarded): the resulting flavoured oil or vinegar used in a vinaigrette dressing will give a subtle, tart-sweet flavour that is refreshing with green salads and ones containing oranges.

Cooked leeks: leeks can be simmered in salted water, braised in butter and a very little stock or water, poached in stock with parsley and a bay leaf, or steamed. It is important not to overcook them as they can easily become mushy.

Whole young leeks take about 10-12 minutes to cook by the first three methods, 15 minutes by steaming. But the actual time depends on the age and size of the vegetables: older, larger specimens naturally take a little longer, and sliced leeks cook more quickly. Test them by piercing with a fine skewer or sharp knife and be ready to remove them from the heat the moment they begin to feel tender.

Unless they are to be served in the sauce in which they have been cooked, drain the leeks very thoroughly on crumpled absorbent paper. Then toss in a pan with seasoned melted butter until they are just heated through.

Serving cooked leeks: partly cooked leeks (boiled for 5-6 minutes and well drained) make a delicious first course tossed while still warm in vinaigrette dressing and combined with fresh herbs and other vegetables such as carrots (see recipe), tomatoes or thinly sliced raw celery. They can be garnished with finely chopped hard-boiled eggs, black olives, breadcrumbs crisply fried in butter, chopped walnuts, or sunflower seeds.

● Sliced steamed leeks are good cooled and tossed in a dressing of soured cream sharpened with a little horseradish sauce, or in a tomato mayonnaise.

● For leeks à la grecque, bring whole leeks just to the boil in a well-seasoned dressing of white wine, water and olive oil flavoured with coriander seeds. Simmer until just tender, then serve them in the dressing, either hot or cold.

● Top partly cooked and well-drained leeks with a cream sauce, cover with a layer of mashed potatoes, and bake until the potatoes are golden, or mix with tomatoes, cover with a cheese sauce, and bake.

Leeks, cream and cheese have many successful combinations – try filling savoury pancakes with chopped cooked leeks folded into a creamy cheese sauce, or covering cooked leeks with a Welsh rarebit mixture and browning under the grill.

Vichyssoise (see recipe) is a classic cold soup made from the last leeks of spring, and for winter there are many hearty, robust soups, casseroles and stews which combine leeks with vegetables, meat or fish.

Vichyssoise

🕯 1 hour

Serves 6-8
50 g /2 oz butter
*1 kg /2 lb leeks, trimmed of green tops,
    cleaned and sliced*
100 g /4 oz potatoes, peeled and sliced
1 L /1¾ pt chicken stock
salt and freshly ground black pepper
large pinch of freshly grated nutmeg
425 ml /15 fl oz thin cream
30 ml /2 tbls snipped chives

1 Melt the butter in a saucepan over a low heat. Add the sliced leeks, cover and cook very gently for 15 minutes, stirring occasionally. Do not allow the leeks to brown.
2 Add the potatoes and chicken stock to the pan, cover and simmer for 20 minutes.
3 Purée the soup through a sieve or in a blender. Season with salt, pepper and nutmeg.
4 Leave the purée to cool, then stir in most of the cream and chill. When ready to serve, turn the soup into a chilled tureen, swirl the remaining cream over the surface and garnish with snipped chives.

● Vichyssoise proper is always served chilled. The hot version, leek and potato soup, is also good. To serve hot, return the purée to the rinsed-out pan, stir in most of the cream and reheat gently without boiling.

Vichyssoise

Leek and carrot salad

🕯 15 minutes

Serves 4
8 small, tender leeks, trimmed and cleaned
1 large carrot, cut into matchstick lengths
For the dressing
45 ml /3 tbls vegetable oil
15 ml /1 tbls red wine vinegar
salt and freshly ground black pepper
pinch of mustard
pinch of sugar
15 ml /1 tbls chopped fresh parsley
5 ml /1 tsp chopped fresh mint
1 hard-boiled egg, finely chopped, to garnish

1 Partly cook the leeks in a large saucepan of boiling salted water for 5 minutes. Drain thoroughly and pat dry with crumpled absorbent paper. Arrange the leeks on a serving dish and place the carrots in a strip down the centre.
2 Shake together the dressing ingredients and pour over the leeks and carrots.
3 Just before serving, arrange the chopped hard-boiled egg in strips on each side of the carrots.

● This can be prepared 2 hours in advance, covered, and left at room temperature.

Creamy leek pie

This double-crusted pie with its rich filling needs only a green salad to make a nourishing family meal.

making and resting pastry then 1¼ hours

Serves 4

shortcrust pastry made with 350 g /12 oz flour
butter for greasing
50 g /2 oz butter
750 g /1½ lb small leeks, trimmed of green tops, cleaned and sliced
100 g /4 oz lean ham, trimmed of fat and diced
1 medium-sized egg
1 medium-sized egg yolk
275 ml /10 fl oz thick cream
salt and freshly ground black pepper
pinch of freshly grated nutmeg
milk, to glaze

1 Heat the oven to 190C /375F /gas 5.
2 Roll out half the pastry and use it to line a lightly greased 20 cm /8 in diameter pie plate. Roll out the remaining pastry to make a lid and set it aside in a cool place.
3 Melt the butter in a saucepan and fry the sliced leeks gently for about 10 minutes, until they are tender but not brown. Remove from the heat and stir in the diced ham. Using a slotted spoon, scatter the leek and ham mixture over the pastry base.

4 Using a wooden spoon, beat together the egg, egg yolk and cream. Season lightly with salt, pepper and nutmeg. Pour the cream mixture over the leeks and ham.
5 Brush the rim of the pastry base with milk. Lay the pastry lid on top; trim, knock up, and flute the edges. Brush the pastry lid with milk. Use the pastry trimmings to make leaf or other decorative shapes and press gently on the pastry lid. Brush the decorations with milk.
6 Bake the pie for 30-35 minutes, until the pastry is cooked and golden brown. Serve the leek pie hot or cold.

Vegetable hotpot

2 hours 10 minutes

Serves 4

50 g /2 oz butter
2 large carrots, sliced
1 small turnip, diced
2 stalks celery, thinly sliced
12 small leeks, including green tops, cleaned and thickly sliced
25 g /1 oz flour
425 ml /15 fl oz chicken stock, or water and stock cube
salt and freshly ground black pepper
5 ml /1 tsp Worcestershire sauce
30 ml /2 tbls chopped fresh parsley
500 g /1 lb potatoes, peeled and sliced
50 g /2 oz grated Cheddar cheese
finely chopped parsley, to garnish

1 Heat the oven to 180C /350F /gas 4.
2 Melt the butter in a frying-pan and fry the carrots, turnip and celery over a low to medium heat for 7-8 minutes, stirring often to prevent them from browning. Remove the vegetables with a slotted spoon and put them into a 1 L /2 pt ovenproof casserole.
3 Add the leeks to the fat in the pan and fry them for 2-3 minutes, turning often so they do not brown. Add to the casserole.
4 Stir the flour into the butter remaining in the pan, then gradually pour on the stock, stirring. Bring to the boil, stirring, then season with salt, pepper and Worcestershire sauce. Simmer for 3 minutes, then mix in the parsley. Pour the sauce over the vegetables and toss carefully to mix.
5 Arrange the sliced potatoes in overlapping circles on top of the vegetables. Cover the casserole with a lid or with foil, stand it on a baking sheet and cook for 1½ hours, or until the potatoes are tender.
6 Heat the grill to high. Sprinkle the cheese over the potatoes and grill until well browned. Garnish with parsley and serve.

Baked leeks

1 hour

Serves 4

300 ml /10 fl oz chicken stock
8 medium-sized leeks, trimmed of green tops and cleaned
50 g /2 oz butter
4 slices bacon, rinded and diced
30 ml /2 tbls flour
150 ml /5 fl oz thick cream
50 g /2 oz Cheddar cheese, grated
salt and freshly ground black pepper
8 thin slices of ham, 25 g /1 oz each
butter for greasing
60 ml /4 tbls fresh white breadcrumbs

1 Heat the oven to 190C /375F /gas 5.
2 Bring the chicken stock to the boil in a medium-sized, heavy-based saucepan. Add the leeks and cook for 7-8 minutes, until they are barely tender. Drain the leeks, reserving the stock, and leave to cool.
3 Add half the butter to the rinsed-out pan and place over a medium heat. When the butter is melted, add the diced bacon and fry for 5 minutes. Away from the heat, stir in the flour. Return the pan to a low heat, stir for 2 minutes and remove from the heat.
4 Measure out 125 ml /4 fl oz of the stock and slowly pour into the pan, stirring constantly. Return the pan to the heat and bring the sauce to the boil. Add the cream and bring the sauce back to the boil. Beat in half the cheese and season to taste with salt and pepper. Set the cheese sauce aside.
5 Wrap 1 slice of ham around each leek. Arrange the leek rolls in a buttered, shallow ovenproof dish and pour over the sauce.
6 Melt the remaining butter in a small heavy-based saucepan. Stir in the breadcrumbs and remaining cheese. Sprinkle the mixture over the cheese sauce. Bake for 30 minutes, or until the topping is golden.

Leek and carrot salad

Unusual shoots and leaves

If you are bored with familiar vegetables, why not try something more unusual? Wrap quails in vine leaves to keep them moist and flavourful, fill pancakes with seakale and a cheesy sauce, or add sorrel to haricot beans to make an ordinary soup extra special.

Fennel is a bulbous-shaped vegetable with a swollen leaf base, and is related to celery. Seakale and cardoons produce leaf stalks which must be blanched, or forced, for eating. They can be eaten either cooked or raw. Vine leaves and sorrel are delicious, tender leaves which are used to complement and flavour other ingredients, though they are not usually eaten on their own.

Fennel

The fennel we are referring to here is often called Florence, Florentine or sweet fennel in order to distinguish it from the herb to which it is closely related. Its flavour is nutty and fresh, with a hint of liquorice.

Buying and storing fennel: when buying fennel, avoid any bulbs which look slightly shrivelled or brown around the base. Fennel from southern Europe is most often available in the winter, although it will grow as far north as Britain in summer. It will keep for up to a week in a polythene bag at the bottom of the refrigerator.

✳✳✳ Freeze for use in cooked dishes; quarter, blanch in boiling water for 3–5 minutes, drain, cool in cold water and drain again. Then dry, pack in freezer bags and freeze for up to 6 months.

Preparing fennel: after rinsing, cut off the thin ends of the stalks; these can be used to flavour soups or stews. The bulbs are usually cut into quarters lengthways, then sliced or chopped if wished. The leaves may be chopped and added to the finished dish.

Cooking and using fennel: in salads, raw fennel goes well with oranges, grapes, celery, radishes, Chinese cabbage and red and green peppers. A little grated cheese added to the dressing will enhance the flavour. An unusual first course would be a salad of fennel and walnuts or diced Gruyère cheese.

Quartered fennel bulbs can be simmered in lightly salted boiling water for 10 minutes, drained and served with melted butter and the chopped leaves, or with a cheese sauce. Fennel halves are delicious braised in chicken stock and served with roast chicken. To sauté fennel, cut the quartered bulbs into 5 mm/¼ in slices and cook gently in butter or oil with chopped garlic. Herbs or orange segments can be added just before serving. Fennel can also be stir-fried, and boiled fennel can be puréed and added to a white sauce to coat hard-boiled eggs, grilled or poached white fish or baked ham.

Seakale

Seakale, also known as silver-beet, was popular in Britain and northern Europe in the 19th century but it has since been almost forgotten. It is blanched by having sand or shingle piled round it to keep it white and looks a bit like a head of white celery, with pale green, tightly curled leaves on the ends of the shoots. Its flavour is nutty and delicate and is often compared to that of asparagus.

Buying and storing seakale: if you are lucky enough to find seakale in the shops in the spring, it should be very white. Keep it in the dark until you cook it or it will turn green and become bitter. It is best used on the day you buy it and should not be frozen.

Preparing seakale: separate the stalks and wash them well. Trim away the leaves, which can be chopped and added to salads. Cut away and discard any parts of the stalks that are discoloured.

Cooking and using seakale: to cook seakale, tie the stalks in bundles. If the stalks are very wide, they can be cut in half lengthways. Cook the bundles in a large pan of boiling, salted water for 20–30 minutes if the shoots are young and tender, up to 50 minutes if they are older. (In this case it is best to change the water halfway through.)

As seakale is such a rare vegetable, it is probably best served as a first course so that you can really appreciate it. Melted butter and a sprinkling of freshly grated Parmesan cheese make a good accompaniment, or serve it with hollandaise sauce. Seakale can also be served au gratin or, if you have enough, in pancakes (see recipe).

Cardoons

The cardoon was a popular vegetable in Britain and Europe in the 17th and 18th centuries, but is now rarely grown.

When blanched, cardoons have white stalks, thick, prickly leaves and a thick, fleshy root, all of which are edible. Their flavour resembles that of globe artichokes, to which they are related. Indeed, the leaves of globe artichokes can be blanched and eaten in the same way as cardoons. You are unlikely to find these leaves in the shops, though, and would have to grow them in your own garden for blanching.

Buying and storing cardoons: most European cardoons now come from Cyprus and are available from late March until June. They are not available in Australia. When buying, look out for fresh, translucent and firm-textured stalks.

Washed and trimmed, cardoons can be kept for 5 days in a polythene bag in the refrigerator.

✳✳✳ Cardoons can be frozen and used as a hot vegetable or in soups. Prepare the stalks, blanch them in boiling water for 3 minutes, drain, cool under cold running water and drain again, then dry, pack and freeze for up to a year.

Preparing cardoons: discard the tough outer stalks, as well as any wilted ones. Cut away the prickles from the inner stalks, remove any stringy pieces and cut the stalks into 7.5 cm /3 in lengths. If you intend to serve them raw, remove the thin skin from the inside of the stalks.

Cut away the prickles from the heart and root and rub them with a cut lemon to prevent discoloration. Cut the leaves into 10 cm /4 in pieces and rub these with a cut lemon.

Cooking and using cardoons: the best stalks can be eaten raw. In Italy they are served with anchovy and garlic sauce (see recipe). To cook the stalks and heart, simmer them in water or stock for 1½ hours, or braise them for the same length of time in an oven heated to 180C /350F /gas 4. Serve them simply with some melted butter or with a velouté sauce made from the cooking liquid.

The leaves should first be blanched in boiling water for 15 minutes, drained, then cooked for a further 1½ hours in stock and served with melted butter or lemon juice and chopped fresh herbs, or a sauce made from the stock.

Vine leaves

Vine leaves can be picked from any grape vine, as long as the vines have not recently been sprayed. The tenderest leaves are the three or four nearest the tip.

Buying and storing vine leaves: fresh vine leaves can be bought in ethnic shops and markets throughout the summer, or you can buy them preserved in brine in tins or vacuum-sealed packs. A 500 g /1 lb tin contains 50–60 leaves.

If you have a lot of fresh leaves and wish to preserve them, blanch them for one minute in boiling, salted water, drain and dry them, then pack into wide, shallow jars and pour in enough olive oil to come 15 mm /½ in above the top of the leaves. Seal tightly and use as you would those preserved in brine.

✳✳✳ Vine leaves should not be frozen on their own, but you can freeze stuffed ones for up to 6 months.

Preparing vine leaves: to prepare fresh vine leaves for cooking, trim off the stems and blanch the leaves in boiling, salted water for one minute, drain and refresh in cold water. Preserved leaves need simply to be rinsed under cold water.

Using vine leaves: vine leaves can be chopped raw into salads; or they can be dipped in batter and deep fried. Their most popular use, however, is as a wrapping for other ingredients. Small vine leaf parcels (called *dolmades* in Greece, *dolmas* in Turkey) are served hot or cold. The most popular hot filling is a mixture of lamb and rice, with spices, fresh herbs and often currants added. Fillings for cold vine leaves include tomatoes and rice, or a purée of cooked chick-peas. Stuffed vine leaves are very easy to prepare for yourself (see recipe) but tinned ones are also available.

In France, vine leaves are wrapped around small birds such as quail or ortolans to preserve and enhance the flavour and keep the birds moist. In Italy, wild mushrooms are baked in a vine leaf-lined dish, covered with more leaves.

Sorrel

There are two types of sorrel, French sorrel and common or garden sorrel. The common sorrel grows wild in most parts of Europe and can be used for cooking; it is the French sorrel, however, which has the most delicate flavour. Its leaves are dark green, glossy, slightly arrow shaped and often wrinkled, with a light, lemony flavour and a slightly acid quality. If a recipe specifies sorrel and none is available, use spinach.

Buying and storing sorrel: French sorrel is mostly grown in gardens, but some is available from specialist shops during the summer. It can be stored in a polythene bag in the refrigerator for 2 days.

✳✳✳✳ Bunches of sorrel or the coarsely chopped leaves can be stored in freezer bags (first wash and dry them) for up to 2 months. Freshly picked leaves can be cooked and puréed, then frozen for up to 8 months.

Preparing sorrel: to prepare sorrel for cooking, cut off the stem level with the leaf. If the leaves are large and the stems tough, the whole mid-rib should be torn away. Wash the leaves and dry them well.

Cooking and using sorrel: the basic method of cooking sorrel is to cook it in melted butter over a low heat until it wilts and becomes dull green in colour. This 'melted' sorrel can be used as a base for fish or added to a bechamel sauce which is then sieved to make a pale green purée. This purée can be used as the basis of a soufflé or it can be thinned with stock and more milk to make a soup. Or add some scalded thick cream to the melted sorrel. Both this and the bechamel-based sauce can be served with poultry, white fish or eggs.

● To make a sorrel omelette, soften 4 chopped sorrel leaves in butter and add 60 ml /4 tbls scalded thick cream. Off the heat, thicken the mixture with an egg yolk. Make a 2-egg omelette in the usual way, spread it with the sorrel purée, fold it over and serve.

A little finely chopped raw sorrel makes a refreshing addition to green summer salads, and some can be added to cream cheese to make a piquant sandwich filling.

Parcels of quail

 1 hour

Serves 4-8
16 vine leaves
8 small sprigs of thyme
8 sage leaves
8 quail
50 g /2 oz butter, softened, plus butter for
* greasing*
4 black olives, halved and stoned
2 slices streaky bacon, trimmed of rind
sage leaves and thyme sprigs, to garnish

1 If the vine leaves are fresh, blanch them in boiling water for 1 minute, drain and refresh with cold water, then drain again. If they are preserved in brine, rinse them thoroughly in cold water.

2 Heat the oven to 200C /400F /gas 6. Put a sprig of thyme and a sage leaf inside each quail. Spread each quail with a little softened butter.

3 Put an olive half on top of each quail. Cut each bacon slice into 4 evenly-sized pieces and place a piece of bacon on top of each olive half. Wrap each quail in 2 vine leaves and then in a piece of buttered foil approximately 25 cm /10 in square. Seal the foil tightly to keep the vine leaves in place.

4 Lay the parcels in a large, flat, oven-proof dish and cook in the oven for 35 minutes. Lift the parcels out onto a hot serving platter, remove the foil, garnish with sage and thyme and serve.

Parcels of quail

Cardoons with garlic and anchovy sauce

This Italian dish, known as *bagna cauda*, can be served as a first course or as a snack. Fennel, celery or carrots can be used as well as or instead of the cardoons.

25 minutes

Serves 4
stalks of 1 cardoon
6 anchovies in brine, filleted and rinsed, or 12
  canned anchovy fillets, drained
175 ml /6 fl oz olive oil
4 garlic cloves, crushed
75 g /3 oz butter, in small pieces

1 Use only the soft inner stalks of the cardoon. Trim away the leaves and any stringy pieces of stalk, as well as the thin skin from the insides of the stalks. Cut the stalks into 7.5 cm /3 in lengths and divide them between 4 plates.
2 Finely chop the anchovies. Heat the oil in a saucepan over a medium heat. Add the garlic and cook until it begins to sizzle. Stir in the anchovies and cook for 2 minutes, stirring, then remove the pan from the heat.
3 Beat in the butter, then continue beating until the sauce thickens slightly. Pour the sauce into 4 small, very hot dishes and place the dishes on the plates. Serve at once.
4 To eat, dip the pieces of cardoon into the sauce with a fork or your fingers.

Sorrel and haricot bean soup

15 minutes, then 2 hours soaking, then 2 hours

Serves 4
250 g /8 oz dried haricot beans
15 ml /1 tbls oil
1 bay leaf
1 small onion, thinly sliced
750 ml /1 pt 7 fl oz chicken stock
40 g /1½ oz butter
150 g /5 oz sorrel leaves, finely chopped
150 ml /5 fl oz thin cream
salt and freshly ground black pepper
30 ml /2 tbls freshly chopped parsley, to serve

1 Put the haricot beans into a saucepan, cover with cold water, bring to the boil and boil for 15 minutes. Remove the pan from the heat and soak the beans for 2 hours.
2 Drain the beans and return them to the saucepan. Cover with fresh cold water, add the oil, bay leaf and onion and bring to the boil. Cover and simmer for 1½ hours or until the beans are tender.
3 Drain the beans, discarding the bay leaf. Rub the beans and onion through the medium blade of a vegetable mill. Gradually mix in the chicken stock.
4 Melt the butter in a saucepan over a medium heat. Stir in the sorrel leaves and cook until they are wilted and dark green in colour. Rub them through a sieve into the soup, add the cream and salt and pepper to taste. Reheat gently, then serve, sprinkled with the chopped parsley.

Haddock with sorrel

55 minutes

Serves 4
750 g /1 lb 10 oz fresh haddock fillets
100 ml /3½ fl oz dry white wine
1 medium-sized onion, thinly sliced
1 medium-sized carrot, thinly sliced
1 celery stalk, chopped
1 bouquet garni
5 ml /1 tsp black peppercorns
50 g /2 oz sorrel leaves, chopped
125 g /4 oz fromage blanc or curd cheese
celery leaves, to garnish

1 Skin the haddock fillets, reserving the skin. Cut the fish into small serving pieces.
2 Put the skin into a saucepan with 300 ml /10 fl oz water, the wine, onion, carrot and celery, bouquet garni and peppercorns. Bring to the boil, then boil gently, uncovered, for about 20 minutes or until the liquid is reduced by half.
3 Strain the liquid into a wide-based saucepan and bring it just to boiling point. Add the haddock pieces and poach for about 3 minutes, or until cooked through but still firm. Lift them onto a warmed serving dish with a slotted spoon and keep warm.
4 Add the sorrel to the simmering liquid and cook for 1 minute, then transfer the sorrel and the liquid to a blender or food processor. Add the fromage blanc or curd cheese and work until smooth.
5 Reheat the sauce very gently, then spoon over the haddock, garnish with the celery leaves and serve.

Vine leaves stuffed with rice and aubergines

🍴🍴 1 hour 40 minutes

Serves 4
20 vine leaves
300 g /11 oz aubergines, finely chopped
15 ml /1 tbls salt
175 g /6 oz long-grain rice
250 g /8 oz tomatoes, blanched, skinned,
*   seeded and finely chopped*
5 ml /1 tsp paprika
2.5 ml /1/2 tsp cinnamon
1.5 ml /1/4 tsp cayenne pepper
150 ml /5 fl oz chicken stock
150 ml /5 fl oz tomato juice

1 If the vine leaves are fresh, blanch them in boiling water for 1 minute, drain, refresh with cold water and drain again. If they are preserved in brine, rinse them thoroughly in cold water.
2 Put the chopped aubergines in a colander and sprinkle with the salt. Let them drain for 20 minutes, then rinse in cold water and pat dry with absorbent paper.
3 Heat the oven to 200C /400F /gas 6. Mix together the aubergines, rice, tomatoes, paprika, cinnamon and cayenne pepper.
4 Lay a vine leaf on the table, veined side uppermost. Place 1 heaped tablespoonful of the stuffing mixture on the stalk end. Fold over the stalk end, then the 2 sides, then roll up the leaf.
5 Continue stuffing the vine leaves until the stuffing and leaves are all used up. Place the stuffed leaves in a large, flat ovenproof dish with the folded-over tips of the leaves underneath.
6 Mix together the stock and the tomato juice, pour over the vine leaves and cook, uncovered, for 45 minutes, then place on a hot serving platter and serve at once.

Fennel with tomatoes

🍴 45 minutes

Serves 4
350 g /12 oz fennel
60 ml /4 tbls olive oil
1 large onion, thinly sliced
1 garlic clove, finely chopped
1.5 ml /1/4 tsp cayenne pepper
350 g /12 oz tomatoes, blanched, skinned,
*   seeded and chopped*
25 g /1 oz freshly grated Parmesan cheese
flat-leaved parsley, to garnish

1 Trim the fennel, cut it into quarters lengthways and thinly slice it.
2 Heat the oil in a large frying-pan on a low heat. Add the onion and garlic and cook for 2 minutes, stirring. Add the fennel and cayenne, stir, cover the pan and cook gently for 10 minutes.
3 Mix in the tomatoes and cook them,

uncovered, for a further 10 minutes, or until they are very soft.
4 Turn the vegetables into a warmed serving dish, scatter the cheese over the top, garnish with parsley and serve at once.

Seakale and cheese pancakes

🍴🍴 1 hour 10 minutes

Serves 4
500 g /1 lb seakale
salt
25 g /1 oz Gruyère cheese, grated
For the pancakes
125 g /4 oz flour
1/4 nutmeg, grated
pinch of salt
15 ml /1 tbls freshly grated Parmesan cheese
1 medium-sized egg
1 medium-sized egg yolk
150 ml /5 fl oz milk
75 ml /5 tbls olive oil
For the cheese sauce
25 g /1 oz butter
25 g /1 oz flour
300 ml /10 fl oz milk
50 g /2 oz Gruyère cheese, grated

Fennel with tomatoes

1 First make the pancake batter: put the flour, nutmeg, salt and Parmesan cheese in a bowl and make a well in the centre. Place the egg and egg yolk in the well and beat in the flour from the sides of the well, a little at a time. Mix together the milk and 150 ml /5 fl oz water and beat half this mixture gradually into the flour. Beat in 15 ml /1 tbls of the oil and finally the remaining milk and water. Leave the batter in a cool place for 30 minutes.
2 Meanwhile, make the sauce. Melt the butter in a saucepan over a medium heat. Stir in the flour and cook for 1 minute. Stir in the milk, bring to the boil and stir until the sauce thickens. Remove the pan from the heat and beat in the cheese. Cover and keep warm while you cook the seakale and make the pancakes.
3 Tie the seakale shoots into 4 bundles and cook them in a large pan of boiling, salted water for 20-30 minutes, or until tender.
4 While the seakale is cooking, make 8 pancakes from the batter, using 45 ml /3 tbls batter for each and frying each one in 7.5 ml /1/2 tbls oil. Keep warm.
5 Drain the seakale well and split each bundle in 2. Lay half a bundle of seakale on one half of each of the pancakes. Spoon the sauce over the seakale and fold over.
6 Transfer the pancakes to a warm, flat serving dish, scatter 25 g /1 oz Gruyère cheese over the top and serve at once.

Olives

Olives, green, and black, large and small, are an important and historic ingredient in the kitchen. With their distinctive, slightly astringent taste, they can be served as a dish on their own, used as a garnish or as an important flavouring in a sauce or casserole.

The first man to taste a wild olive must have had great culinary imagination, for the fresh olive is quite inedible owing to the presence of an extremely bitter alkaloid. This is removed by soaking the olives in an alkaline solution or lye, which is allowed to penetrate two-thirds of the fruit but not as far as the stone, leaving a slight bitterness giving the characteristic taste. The olives are then washed to remove the soaking solution. Salt can also remove the bitterness, and olives are often stored in brine where they will keep many months.

Olives have been cultivated from time immemorial. The olive tree is an evergreen, native to all the countries of the Mediterranean except Egypt. It was introduced to the United States, South America, Australia and China, but it is Europe that accounts for more than three-quarters of the world's cultivated olives. And just three countries account for most of that production: Spain, Italy and Greece. Nearly all of these olives, though, go into the making of olive oil.

Types of olive
There are hundreds of varieties of olive grown for table use and oil extraction. In California the Mission variety is grown almost exclusively for eating, while they tend to grow the Sevillana and Manzanilla in Spain and the Ascolane and Corate in Italy.

Black olives for eating are mature, while green olives for the table are picked or shaken off the tree when fully grown but still unripe. The soft red olives that come from Italy are picked when they are just beginning to ripen—these are hard to find but worth looking for.

Jars of olives neatly packed on supermarket shelves give no clue to the enormous variety found in the market-places of Spain, Italy and Greece. From Greece come tiny, crinkled black olives with a pungent, salty taste; enormous succulent purple-black olives; large green olives which are cracked and flavoured with coriander seeds, and 'sour' olives—small green ones cracked and stuffed with cumin seeds.

In Spain, green olives are stoned and stuffed with slivers of pimento, almond or anchovy, or marinated for many months in olive oil flavoured with garlic, thyme, fennel and other herbs.

In Italy, small black olives are often stoned and marinated in oil flavoured with garlic and oregano or rosemary.

Buying and storing olives
It is not always easy to tell a good olive just by looking at it. Very often the small, shrivelled-looking ones can be the most delicious, although on the whole a plump and shiny olive will probably be a tasty one. Whenever possible, buy olives loose and store them in glass jars, covered with olive oil. If you can only buy them in bottles or packets in brine, rinse off the brine and then store in oil. Do not store in the refrigerator; a cool larder is perfect and they should last many months. Check periodically, though, and if any mould should appear, rinse the olives quickly in warm water, discarding the oil and any really mouldy olives, and then store in a clean jar with new oil.

**** Fresh olives do not freeze well. There is no need to freeze them in any case as they keep so successfully in oil, but they can be frozen when used in a cooked dish.

Spicy lamb with black olives

Flavouring olives
If you cannot find stuffed or marinated olives where you shop, then buy plain green or black ones, stone them and stuff them yourself. There are gadgets available for stoning olives which make it an easy process. You can then either put the flavouring into the cavity or scatter it between each layer of olives in the jar before covering with oil. Almost any herb (except mint) can be used, and coriander and cumin are the best spices; or use garlic.

Olives can also be stuffed just before serving with a flavoured butter or smooth pâté – this is particularly nice when they are to be served as a snack with drinks.

Using olives
Olives can be used in so many different ways–the only dish you cannot add them to is the dessert!

Olives cleanse and stimulate the palate and are thus marvellous with drinks before dinner or as an appetizer. Olive and cheese pâté (see recipe) is a delicious and delicate start to a meal, as are anchovy-stuffed olives

encased in cream cheese, then rolled in black caviar or lumpfish roe, chilled and served on a bed of finely shredded lettuce.

An appetizer much loved in Victorian times consists of large green olives stuffed with watercress butter, set in chicken aspic in small moulds. These are turned out onto croûtons spread with watercress butter and then daintily garnished with sprigs of fresh watercress.

Greek Cypriots make a delicious coarse bread with black olives worked into the dough.

Olives go beautifully with fish–green olives with a firm white fish such as cod or haddock, black with stronger-flavoured fish such as sardines and red mullet. Both black and green olives go with chicken (see recipe). Breast of veal stuffed with force-meat and chopped black olives, casseroled in white wine and tomatoes is a very popular dish in France, as are beef stews and duck roasted or casseroled with olives.

Olives give an added zing to a quiche or even to scrambled eggs. In Italy olives are much used in pasta dishes and pizzas and are also used to stuff small birds such as pigeons and plovers. Lamb and olives is a popular flavour combination in the Middle East.

Ordinary salads can be pepped up with the addition of a few olives: black ones with a potato and onion salad dressed with a mustardy vinaigrette, or with a tomato salad sprinkled with a little olive oil. A delicious salad can be made with cold roast beef (preferably rare), cut into strips, mixed with small stoned black olives and dressed with soured cream and lemon juice. Lettuce hearts, avocado chunks and a few Italian red olives dressed with a ravigote sauce (vinaigrette with capers, onions, parsley, chives, tarragon and chervil) make an elegant and spectacular salad to go with cold lobster or prawns.

And don't forget the simple ways of serving olives. Nothing is more perfect on a hot summer day than a picnic lunch with bowls of shiny black olives, large green olives flavoured with coriander, garlicky salami and crusty bread washed down with a bottle of chilled Beaujolais.

Olive and cheese pâté

🕛 15 minutes,
plus 30 minutes or more chilling

Serves 6
225 g /8 oz Ricotta cheese
100 g /4 oz San Gaudenzio or mild Gorgonzola
100 g /4 oz butter, softened
1 garlic clove, crushed
10 ml /2 tsp freshly chopped parsley
100 g /4 oz large green olives, stoned
hot buttered toast, to serve

1 Mash the cheeses together with the butter to form a smooth paste. Add the garlic and parsley and mix well.
2 Reserve a few olives for decoration and finely chop the rest. Stir into the cheese mixture, put into an earthenware terrine, pressing down well, and chill in the refrigerator for at least 30 minutes.
3 Garnish with the reserved olives, cut in half, and serve with hot buttered toast.

Spicy lamb with black olives

🔪🔪 2 hours 25 minutes

Serves 6
900 g /2 lb boned shoulder of lamb
60 ml /4 tbls olive oil
1 large aubergine, cut into chunks (unpeeled)
1 large Spanish onion, finely chopped
5 ml /1 tsp coriander seeds, crushed
5 ml /1 tsp mustard seeds, crushed
5 ml /1 tsp fenugreek seeds, crushed
5 ml /1 tsp turmeric
5 ml /1 tsp ground ginger
2.5-5 ml /1/2-1 tsp chilli powder
3 garlic cloves, crushed
60 ml /4 tbls finely chopped fresh mint
400 g /14 oz canned tomatoes
225 g /8 oz large black olives, stoned
salt and freshly ground black pepper
150 ml /5 fl oz yoghurt
cooked rice, to serve
sprig of mint, to garnish

1 Cut the lamb into 25 mm /1 in cubes, trimming off excess fat.
2 Heat the oil in a large saucepan and brown the meat on all sides over a high heat. Remove with a slotted spoon. Add the aubergine and onion to the pan and sauté for 5 minutes over a medium heat. Add the coriander, mustard, fenugreek, turmeric, ginger and chilli and stir for 2 minutes.
3 Add the garlic, mint and tomatoes and return the meat to the pan with 575 ml /1 pt water. Bring to simmering point, cover and cook gently for 1/2 hour, then uncover and cook for a further 3/4-1 hour. The meat should be tender and the sauce very thick.
4 Add the olives and cook for a further 5 minutes. Add salt and pepper to taste, pile onto a bed of cooked rice and spoon the yoghurt on top. Garnish, then serve at once.

Tomato and olive sauce for pasta

This is a simple and delicious sauce which is ideal for pasta.

⏲ 40 minutes

Makes about 600 ml /1 pt
30 ml /2 tbls olive oil
1 large Spanish onion, finely chopped
2 garlic cloves, crushed
15 ml /1 tbls dried oregano
400 g /14 oz canned tomatoes
2 anchovy fillets, pounded
15 ml /1 tbls dry white wine
100 g /4 oz small black olives, stoned
salt and freshly ground black pepper
boiled pasta, to serve

1 Heat the oil in the saucepan and add the onion and garlic. Sauté over moderate heat for 5 minutes, then add the oregano and sauté for a further 2 minutes.
2 Add the tomatoes, mashing with a wooden spoon. Bring to boiling point over a high heat, then reduce the heat and simmer for 10 minutes.
3 Add the anchovies, wine and olives. Season to taste with salt and pepper and simmer for a further 5-15 minutes, depending on how thick a sauce you want. Serve immediately over boiled pasta.

● This will keep for 2 days in the refrigerator, covered with 15 ml /1 tbls olive oil.

Olive chicken with pine nut rice

🍴🍴 1 hour 40 minutes

Serves 6
1.8 kg /4 lb chicken
1 lemon, cut in half
450 g /1 lb olives flavoured with coriander
juice of 1 lemon
5 ml /1 tsp coriander seeds, crushed
For the rice
30 ml /2 tbls olive oil
50 g /2 oz pine nuts
275 g /10 oz long-grain rice
575 ml /1 pt chicken stock

1 Heat the oven to 190C /375F /gas 5. Wash the chicken inside and out and pat dry. Place one half of the lemon inside the cavity, cut side facing out. Stuff with the olives, pushing well in, then put the other lemon half in, zest side out, to seal the neck.
2 Place the chicken in a chicken brick, pour over the lemon juice and scatter the coriander seeds over the breast and legs. Cook for 1½ hours, or until done.
3 Thirty minutes before serving make the rice. Heat the oil in a large saucepan, add the pine nuts and sauté gently until golden but not brown, about 5 minutes.
4 Add the rice and stir over a medium heat for 2-3 minutes, until the grains are transparent. Pour in the chicken stock, bring to the boil, then simmer gently, covered, for 15-20 minutes, until all the stock is absorbed and

Olive and cabbage salad

the rice is tender but not mushy. Pile onto a warmed serving plate.
5 Remove the chicken from the oven, place on top of the rice, pour the juices from the brick into a sauce-boat and serve at once.

● You can roast the chicken in an uncovered roasting tin, if you baste it with 30 ml /2 tbls olive oil. But the flavour and succulence of a chicken cooked in a brick is far superior.

Olive and cabbage salad

⏲ 20 minutes
plus 30 minutes standing

Serves 4
1 small white cabbage, finely shredded
125 ml /4 fl oz olive oil
100 g /4 oz Feta cheese, crumbled
100 g /4 oz large Greek black olives, stoned
100 g /4 oz anchovy-stuffed green olives
freshly ground black pepper

1 Place the cabbage into a large salad bowl and dress with the oil. Crumble the cheese over the cabbage and add the olives.
2 Season with freshly ground black pepper—you will not need any salt as the cheese is quite salty – and toss everything 2 or 3 times. Let the salad stand for 30 minutes so the flavours blend.

Onions, shallots and garlic

Onions have been an invaluable flavouring in cooking for at least 5000 years. Garlic or some form of onion is essential for many meat, fish, poultry, game and vegetable dishes and numerous soups and sauces. Onions are a delicious vegetable in their own right too, whether they are braised, boiled, fried, stuffed and roasted, or simply baked in their skins.

At first sight the small round pickled onions we enjoy with cheese and cold meat seem to have little in common with the tightly packed bulbs of garlic that give a Mediterranean flavour to food, or with the huge mild Spanish onions. Yet they are all members of the *Allium* family, which also includes shallots, spring onions and Welsh onions.

Ordinary onions, revered by the ancient Egyptians as too sacred to eat, are now the most widely used vegetable as flavouring. Although not particularly nutritious, they aid our enjoyment of other food. Ordinary onions range in size from small to very large; they have a pungent white flesh encased in layers of papery brown skin. They are suitable for baking, roasting, braising, boiling and frying and can be used raw in salads or as a garnish.

Pickling or pearl onions (also called button onions) are ordinary onions picked while the bulbs are immature – the size of a large walnut. Cook them whole in dishes where their neat, compact shape is shown to advantage – coq au vin for example, or a salad prepared à la grecque. If you enjoy a pickle with a real 'bite', button onions are the best choice for preserving. They can also be braised or included in composite vegetable dishes.

Spanish or Bermuda onions and the Italian red and the Breton onions have a milder, sweeter flavour than ordinary onions, which they can replace in almost any dish. In some countries they are eaten raw, almost like a fruit. They are ideal for salads and baking (but too sweet for puréed soups or sauces).

Shallots grow in clusters of 6–12 bulbs around the stem. Shallots resemble pickling onions in that the bulbs are small and have a papery brown skin and sometimes a purple inside skin; their flavour is much finer. Use shallots instead of pickling onions if you want a more delicate result. Shallots are favoured in the regional cooking of northern France and are the classic choice for marinades and for fine-flavoured sauces such as bearnaise and bordelaise.

Garlic also grows in clusters; a complete cluster is sometimes called a head, an individual bulb is called a clove. A native of Mediterranean countries, garlic is also grown in cooler climates. There are many varieties, some deep purple, others white in colour. Garlic is used both raw and cooked (which considerably tames its pungent flavour).

Spring or salad onions are called scallions in the U.S. Very slender and mildly flavoured, these are the perfect salad onions.

Back (left to right): spring onions, ordinary onions, Spanish onions; front: pickling onions, shallots, red onions, garlic; strung dried garlic hanging on wall

Chopping onions the French way

Place the peeled, halved onion, cut side down on a board. Make several horizontal cuts toward the root end with a sharp knife, without cutting through at the root end.

Place your fingers across the onion. Now cut the onion lengthways, not quite through at the root end. Steady it with your fingers, and retract your fingertips as you cut.

Now hold the onion with your fingers toward the tip. Cut across the onion, just clear of your fingertips, retracting as you cut. The onion will fall into tiny dice.

You can snip their hollow leafy tops in winter to use as a herb instead of chives.

Welsh onions are (despite the name) grown mainly in China and Japan and are not often commercially available elsewhere. They are similar to spring onions but grow in bunches and each narrow bulb is encased in a brown skin. They are also called Japanese bunching onions. Use them raw like spring onions, or in stews.

Tree (or Egyptian) onions – also rarely seen fresh – have tiny, extremely pungent buds growing at the top of the stem. These can be pickled in vinegar or brine; they are processed commercially and sold as cocktail onions. They can also be used in cooked dishes and, sparingly, in salads.

Prepared onions: pickled onions and baby pickled cocktail onions are a popular supermarket buy. You can also buy small pearl onions frozen, and accelerated freeze-dried onions, which are reconstituted in water.

Onion products: onion powder and dried onion flakes are a useful emergency standby; in oriental countries onion seed is used as a spice. Garlic salt and garlic pepper impart a subtle flavour to cooked dishes; minced garlic 'crystals' and dried garlic flakes are more pungent.

Buying and storing onions

Ordinary onions are available all year round. Choose firm, unbruised bulbs and store, tied in ropes or hanging in nets, in a cool, airy place. Check for dampness and discoloration. Once peeled, onions stale quickly; wrap cut pieces tightly in cling film, refrigerate and use within 1–2 days.

Spring onions are available most of the year. They do not keep well, so buy in small quantities. Shallots are only available in late summer and they do not store as well as onions.

You can buy garlic loose, in small nets or on ropes. The bulbs should be full and unblemished. Stored in a dry, warm, airy place, garlic will keep for up to 6 months.

Stringing onions: just rub any loose outer skins off dry bulbs and pull off all but 10 cm /4 in of the leaf ends. Cut a long piece of stout string or twine into three lengths; knot together at the top and hang at a convenient working height. Plait the strings, trapping the leaf end of an onion on either side as you work and pulling the string tightly to secure it. (You can string garlic bulbs in the same way as onions.)

Store in a cool, airy place and pull the onions out as you need them. Check regularly for dampness, using any that start to discolour first.

✱✱✱✱ Onions usually freeze well, but they are not a good use of scarce freezer space, as they are readily available throughout the year. Chopped raw onion will freeze happily for 1 month, if it is not convenient to use it up. You may also like to store a small quantity of slices, lightly fried in butter. These can then be added, frozen, to quick-cooking dishes.

Pickling onions are time consuming to prepare so you may find it more convenient to prepare and freeze them ahead. Top and tail them, then blanch them, unpeeled, for 2 minutes in boiling water, then remove the skins. Open freeze, then put in bags. Label them with name and date and store for 3 months.

To avoid changes in flavour it is advisable not to freeze any dishes containing garlic for a longer period than 1 month.

Preparing onions

Ordinary and Spanish onions: peel large onions under cold running water to reduce irritation to your eyes. Or blanch the onions first in boiling water for 3 minutes, then drain and pat dry. (Sliced and chopped onions can also be blanched before further cooking to reduce some of their pungency and make them more digestible.)

Trim the top and root end, peel away the skin and first fleshy layer if it is discoloured. Cut onion in half lengthways, place cut side down and cut across into slices or chop the onion (see pictures). Peeled, whole onions can be sliced straight across into complete rings of varying thickness.

● To cut onions into 4 for kebabs, so that they do not disintegrate, just cut 2 good slices off opposite sides. Then halve the remaining core through the middle. Thread the pieces of onion on to the skewer through the inner skin.

● For onion juice, grate the onion and spoon up juice from base of grater; or, chop, put in a garlic press and squeeze.

Pickling onions: top and tail, then pour over boiling water to cover; leave 5 minutes. Drain and cool, rub off skins and membrane. Cut a cross at root ends to help salt penetrate and ensure onions stay whole.

Spring onions: trim the green tops and slip off the outer layer covering the bulb; chop or leave whole.

● To make an attractive tassel for a garnish, cut off most of the green tops. Make several slits close together down from the top. Put the onions in iced water for 1 hour. The tops will curl back (see picture). Use to garnish salads or a cheese board.

Shallots and Welsh onions: separate the bulbs, top and tail; pull off skin and the first layer of flesh too.

Garlic: peel papery skin from bulb and pull off as many cloves as you need. Trim away root end and peel off skin. Cut away any discoloured parts (they impart a rancid taste). Peeled garlic cloves may be lightly crushed with the flat of a knife and included in dishes such as casseroles. Large quantities of garlic may be minced with a fine blade.

● To crush garlic, put the peeled, chopped clove on a flat surface with a little salt and mash to a paste with the flat of a knife. This is extremely useful for dishes such as salads which are eaten raw, as it eliminates the possibility of anyone being served pieces of raw garlic which would overwhelm the flavour.

Using onions

Ordinary onions are used to flavour soups, stocks, sauces, stews, casseroles, stuffings, braised vegetable dishes and savoury breads as well as chutneys, pickles and relishes. They can be baked, with or without stuffing, braised, boiled or fried as a vegetable. As a main ingredient they are supreme in French onion tart (see recipe) and that melt-in-the-mouth potful, French onion soup.

The flavour of onions is affected by the way they are cooked. The longer the cooking and the higher the temperature, the more 'acrid' they become. Well-browned onion rings are just right with a homely dish

of sausages, but browning would ruin a light sauce or a very delicate dish. Onions give off a great deal of moisture during cooking, so it is best to seal meat for stews and casseroles before frying the onions.

Using garlic

Raw garlic has a strong, almost fierce flavour. (It is most pungent minced or crushed.) It is used in sauces like *skordhalia* (see recipe) and the Italian *pesto*. Cooked slowly, garlic mellows and becomes almost sweet; finely chopped garlic loses its piquancy quite quickly and whole heads of garlic (often called for in fish soups and stews) taste sweeter still. A single clove added to a casserole brings out the flavour of the other ingredients; slivers of garlic pressed into slits made in a joint of lamb or pork before roasting enhance the meat. To give a scent of garlic to green salads, rub half a clove around the salad bowl or steep a cut clove in the dressing.

Fried onion rings

These golden onion rings are delicious with grilled or roast meat, especially steak and chicken. Since they are crisp they can also be served with drinks.

▽ 25 minutes

Steak with Fried onion rings

Serves 4
2 large onions, peeled, trimmed and thinly sliced into rings
vegetable oil for deep frying
For the batter
50 g /2 oz flour
1.5 ml /1/4 tsp bicarbonate of soda
large pinch of cream of tartar
large pinch of salt
1 medium-sized egg
45 ml /3 tbls milk
5 ml /1 tsp melted butter

1 Make the batter. Sift the flour with the bicarbonate of soda, cream of tartar and salt into a bowl. Combine the egg and milk in a large bowl and beat together with a wooden spoon; stir in the melted butter. Add the sifted flour mixture to the egg mixture and beat well until the batter is smooth and glossy.

2 Heat the oil in a deep-fat frier to 190C /375F; at this temperature a cube of stale bread should brown in 50 seconds.

3 Using tongs or a fork, dip the onion rings, a few at a time, into the batter. Fry the coated onion rings in batches for 3–4 minutes until they are puffed up and golden. Remove the cooked onion rings with a slotted spoon, drain them on absorbent paper and keep them warm while you fry the remainder.

Soubise sauce

Serve this creamy onion sauce with roast lamb or veal, grilled chops, or ham.

55 minutes

Serves 4
450 g /1 lb onions, peeled and thinly sliced
75 g /3 oz butter
large pinch of salt
40 g /1½ oz flour
425 ml /15 fl oz milk
150 ml /5 fl oz thin cream
freshly ground black pepper
pinch of freshly grated nutmeg

1   Melt the butter in a large, heavy-based saucepan over a very low heat. Add the onions and salt, stir well. Cover and sweat very gently, till the onions are soft but not brown.
2   Off the heat, stir in the flour; return the pan to a low heat and stir for 3 minutes. Meanwhile bring the milk to the boil in a small pan and remove from the heat.
3   Off the heat, gradually pour the boiling hot milk on to the onions, stirring constant-ly. Simmer the onion sauce gently for 15 minutes, stirring occasionally.
4   Pureé the sauce through a fine nylon sieve or an electric blender. Return the pureé to the rinsed out pan and reheat gently to simmering point. Stir in the cream and season with salt, pepper and nutmeg.
5   Serve the sauce immediately; or, turn it into a heatproof bowl, cover with dampened greaseproof paper and stand in a pan of very hot water until ready to serve.

Pickled onions

2 days soaking plus 1 hour, then 3 weeks maturing

Makes 1.5–1.7 kg /3–4 lb
1 kg /2¼ lb pickling onions, trimmed
225 g /8 oz coarse salt
50 g /2 oz sugar
600 ml /1 pt white wine vinegar
5 ml /1 tsp whole cloves
5 ml /1 tsp mustard seed
4 dried red chillies
2.5 ml /½ tsp black peppercorns
1 bay leaf, crumbled

1   Place the onions in a bowl, cover with boiling water and leave for 5 minutes. Drain the onions and, while they are still warm, rub off the skins. Cut a cross at the root end of each onion both to help them stay whole and for the salt to penetrate.
2   Combine half the salt with 1.2 L /2 ¼ pt water in a large bowl and stir until the salt has dissolved. Add the onions and cover them with a large plate so they are complete-ly immersed in the brine. Place a weight on the plate and leave onions to soak 12 hours.
3   Drain the onions and wash the bowl. Make fresh brine with the remaining salt and 1.2 L /2¼ pt water; add the onions, cover with a weighted plate and leave to soak for 36 hours.
4   Drain the onions and pack them into cleaned, warmed preserving jars.
5   Combine the sugar and vinegar in a stainless steel, enamelled or aluminium pan. Stir over a low heat until the sugar has dissolved. Add the spices and crumbled bay leaf. Bring the vinegar syrup to the boil and boil for 5 minutes. Remove the pan from the heat and leave the spiced vinegar to cool.
6   Pour the spiced vinegar over the onions so that they are completely covered. (If you prefer, strain the vinegar first to remove the spices.) Seal the jars with vinegar-proof covers, label and store in a cool, dry place. They will be ready to eat within 3 weeks and are best eaten within 6 months.

Jars of pickled onions

Garlic sauce

In Greece, this creamy garlic sauce is called *skordhalia* and served with deep-fried vegetables or fish – battered covered aubergine slices are particularly deli-cious. It will keep for up to 1 week in an airtight container in the refrigerator.

20 minutes plus chilling

Serves 4
100 g /4 oz stale white bread, crusts removed
6 garlic cloves, peeled
salt
250 ml /8 fl oz olive oil
15 ml /1 tbls lemon juice
15 ml /1 tbls white wine vinegar
freshly ground black pepper

1   Cut the bread into pieces and place in a bowl; pour on just enough water to cover and soak for 5 minutes.
2   Turn the soaked bread into a fine sieve and drain off the water. Using a wooden spoon, gently press the bread against the sieve to extract any remaining liquid.
3   Mince or crush the garlic with 2.5 ml /½ tsp salt. Purée the garlic and bread in a blender, or use a pestle and mortar to pound the garlic to a smooth paste and gradually beat in the bread.
4   Add the olive oil, a little at a time, and pound or blend until it is completely absorbed by the bread. When all the olive oil has been incorporated, blend in the lemon juice and wine vinegar. Season to taste with salt and black pepper and con-tinue blending the sauce again until it is smooth and creamy. Turn into a bowl if necessary. Cover the sauce with cling film, chill for 30 minutes, or until needed.

French onion tart

A classic French country dish, onion tart is popular as a first course, or as a light but rich lunch or supper dish.

🕐🕐 1½ hours including 30 minutes chilling pastry

Serves 6
175 g /6 oz flour
2.5 ml /½ tsp mustard powder
2.5 ml /½ tsp salt
pinch of cayenne pepper
100 g /4 oz butter
75 g /3 oz Cheddar cheese, grated
1 large egg yolk, lightly beaten
butter for greasing
For the filling
100 g /4 oz butter
2 large onions, finely chopped
15 ml /1 tbls flour
3 medium-sized eggs
150 ml /5 fl oz thin cream
150 ml /5 fl oz thick cream
salt and freshly ground black pepper
pinch of ground nutmeg

1 To make the pastry, sift the flour, dried mustard, salt and cayenne pepper into a bowl. Cut the butter into small pieces and rub it into the dried ingredients, using your fingertips, until the mixture resembles fine breadcrumbs. Stir in the cheese. Mix to a stiff paste with the egg yolk and 20–25 ml /4–5 tsp water.
2 Turn the dough onto a lightly floured surface and knead gently until smooth. Wrap the dough in cling film and chill for at least 30 minutes.
3 Heat the oven to 200C /400F /gas 6. Roll out the dough on a lightly floured surface. Carefully wrap it loosely round the rolling pin and unroll it gently over a greased 23 cm /9 in flan case. Press the pastry gently into the case and trim neatly. Prick the base of the dough all over with a fork.
4 Line the pastry case with foil and fill it with baking beans. Bake blind for 10 minutes, then remove from the oven. Turn down the oven to 180C /350F /gas 4. Discard the foil and beans, then bake the pastry case for a further 8 minutes. Allow the pastry case to cool slightly before adding the onion filling.
5 Meanwhile make the filling. Melt the butter in a small pan. Fry the onions over a low heat for 12–15 minutes, stirring frequently, until they are transparent. Remove the pan from the heat and allow the onions to cool.
6 Stir in the flour. Beat together the eggs, thin and thick cream and beat into the onion mixture. Season with salt, pepper and nutmeg.
7 Turn down the oven to 170C /325F /gas 3. Pour the filling into the pastry case and bake for 35–40 minutes, until set and golden brown. Serve the tart very hot, as a first course, or, with a crisp green salad, it can provide a really appetizing dish for either lunch or supper.

Roast stuffed onions

🕐 1 hour

Serves 4
4 large Spanish onions
salt
50 g /2 oz butter
1 medium-sized onion, peeled and finely chopped
1 garlic clove, peeled and crushed
250 g /8 oz sausage-meat
60 ml /4 tbls fresh white breadcrumbs
10 ml /2 tsp chopped fresh oregano or 5 ml /1 tsp dried oregano
freshly ground black pepper
30 ml /2 tbls thick cream
25 g /1 oz Cheddar cheese, grated
tomato sauce, to serve (optional)

1 Peel the Spanish onions and trim away the root ends and brown parts at the top. Parboil the onions in boiling salted water for 10 minutes; drain them well and leave until they are cool.

2 Melt half the butter in a heavy-based frying-pan. Add the finely chopped onion and fry over a moderate heat for 3 minutes. Stir in the crushed garlic, the sausage-meat, 45 ml /3 tbls of the breadcrumbs and the oregano and season to taste with salt and black pepper. Cook, stirring occasionally, for 10 minutes. Stir in the cream and remove the pan from the heat.
3 Heat the oven to 190C /375F /gas 5.
4 Gently open out the cooled onions; using a small spoon, scrape out and reserve the centre of the bulbs. Chop half the reserved onion flesh and stir it into the filling. Divide the filling between the onions and arrange them in a buttered, shallow ovenproof dish.
5 Melt the remaining butter in a small, heavy-based saucepan. Remove from the heat and stir in the remaining breadcrumbs and the grated cheese. Sprinkle the breadcrumb mixture over the stuffed onions in the ovenproof dish.
6 Bake the onions for about 30 minutes, until they are tender and the filling is crispy-brown on top. Serve with a well-flavoured tomato sauce, if liked.

Asparagus

Fresh asparagus is the most delicious of the tender early summer vegetables. Its delicacy, brief season and high cost mean that it needs special care in cooking and serving, to do full justice to both flavour and texture.

Asparagus belongs to the lily family, and it is the common variety that is cultivated as a vegetable. Highly prized by the ancient Greeks and Romans, asparagus is now widely grown in most temperate and subtropical parts of the world. Unfortunately the asparagus season is very short – from early May to late June in the northern hemisphere – but imported asparagus is available from early February to September, and the jumbo spears grown in California are exported throughout the year.

Grades of asparagus

The part that is eaten is the young spear (stalk and tip), which is either green or white (blanched). Asparagus is graded according to the thickness of the stalk and the plumpness of the buds. The top grade has fat, tender stalks; medium stalks may rate a slightly lower grade, while the thin stalks, sold as 'sprue' or 'grass', cost less but still have a fine flavour. 'Grass', incidentally, is the trade name applied to asparagus in general.

Using asparagus

As a first course: top-quality fresh spears are traditionally served as a separate course, so that the delicate flavour and succulence of each stalk can be relished and savoured. Asparagus makes an ideal starter served simply with melted butter or an appropriate sauce to preserve the distinctive taste. Allow 8–10 fat stalks per serving, or 4–5 oz /100–150 g of thin stalks. The rich smoothness of butter, cream and eggs goes perfectly with asparagus, but too strong or assertive seasonings and flavourings should be avoided: use cheese with caution. Lower grades of asparagus make marvellously delicate soups, mousses, soufflés, custards and flans. Cold asparagus, combined with other lightly cooked mixed vegetables, and dressed with vinaigrette makes an original salad.

As a garnish: even a small amount of asparagus adds distinction when used to garnish bland meat such as chicken breasts, escalopes of veal or braised tongue. The slender spears of green asparagus are very decorative, and even one or two can make a dish attractive. Asparagus tips, sautéed lightly in butter, can transform a simple omelette or dish of scrambled eggs into something that is really special.

Using up asparagus: no part of the vegetable need be wasted. Cook the trimmings and discoloured cut ends with the spears to add extra flavour to the cooking liquor, which will provide an excellent basis for deliciously flavoured soup.

Buying asparagus

Freshness is all-important to the flavour and eating quality of asparagus, and the shorter the time between picking and cooking the better. The season seldom lasts longer than 6–8 weeks, so unless you grow your own, keep a close watch on the shops in your neighbourhood to catch new deliveries on arrival, especially those from local nurseries, if you live in the country.

You will find that asparagus is most often sold in bundles, sometimes loose. Look for crisp stalks with compact tips, and particularly for moist ends, which indicate that the spears have been cut recently. Be wary of tired-looking, 'woody' stalks with discoloured ends – this may mean that they have travelled too far.

Preserved asparagus

Both whole spears and tips of green and blanched asparagus are canned commercially, and frozen green asparagus is available in packets. Although they lack the fine quality of the fresh vegetable, these products are invaluable, if expensive, standbys for unexpected social occasions. It is certainly worth keeping a tin in your store cupboard.

Preparing asparagus

Young green spears may need no preparation other than trimming any discoloured parts from the cut end. In other cases examine the stalks, and where they begin to feel thick and tough, shave off the skin from this point downwards, using a vegetable peeler or sharp knife. Rinse the stalks in cold water to dislodge dirt or sand, drain well and sort into spears of equal thickness.

Tie in bundles of 8–12 spears with the tips level. Use soft string and tie in two places, just below the tips and towards the bottom. Finally, trim the cut ends so that the stalks are of similar length and the bundles stand firmly in the cooking pan.

If you cannot cook the asparagus immediately you have bought it, stand the bundles upright in 10 mm /½ in cold water, cover with a polythene bag and refrigerate. They will keep for 2–3 days if necessary.

Cooking asparagus

Asparagus stalks need longer cooking than the tips, and the easiest way of solving this problem is to cook them standing upright in simmering salted water to reach two-thirds up the stalks. By this method the tips are steamed and do not overcook, while the tougher stalks are boiled. If you do not have a saucepan that is deep enough, improvise with a domed 'lid' of foil, making it high enough to stand above the tips. Crimp it well at the pan edge to hold in the steam.

Tying the asparagus in bundles helps to hold the tips above the water, but in a wide pan there is a tendency for the bundles to keel over. One way to prevent this is to cook new potatoes (which are in season at the

Make a dome of foil

Use a tall jar for boiling asparagus

Sauces for hot asparagus

Hollandaise: combine 5 ml/1 tsp lemon juice, 15 ml/1 tbls water, salt and white pepper in the top of a double boiler. Put hot, but not boiling water into bottom pan. Add 4 egg yolks and 25 g/1 oz softened butter, diced, to liquid. Stir rapidly until butter is melted and mixture begins to thicken. Gradually add a further 75 g/3 oz butter, diced, beating all the time and never allowing water in bottom pan to boil. Remove from heat and beat for 2–3 minutes, until rich and creamy. Stir in a little lemon juice to taste.

Melted butter: bring 30 ml /2 tbls water to the boil in a small saucepan. Remove from heat, add 100 g /4 oz fresh butter cut into dice and swirl around until the butter melts but remains creamy. Avoid overheating or the butter will become oily and the mixture will separate. Season lightly with lemon juice and white pepper.

Cream sauces: thin a bechamel sauce to a pouring consistency by beating in fresh thin cream. Sharpen lightly with finely grated horseradish, tarragon vinegar or lemon juice, adding finely chopped fresh herbs to taste.

Sauces for cold asparagus

Mayonnaise chantilly: flavour 300 ml/10 fl oz of basic mayonnaise with lemon juice to taste. Just before serving fold in 90 ml/6 tbls lightly whipped cream.

Vinaigrette: use a mild olive oil and make with 4 or 5 parts of oil to 1 part of lemon juice and tarragon vinegar mixed. Add chopped fresh herbs and season well.

Other ways to serve asparagus

Asparagus and cauliflower salad: for a summer lunch dish, arrange cooked asparagus spears radiating from the centre of a round, flat dish. Pile firm florets of cooked cauliflower dressed with vinaigrette in the centre. Top the cauliflower with creamy mayonnaise and sprinkle with chopped mixed herbs. Garnish with sliced or quartered hard-boiled eggs.

Asparagus Flemish-style: for a light supper, serve hot asparagus spears with a soft-boiled egg, salt and pepper, butter and thinly sliced brown bread and butter. Cut off the top of the egg, stir a pat of butter and seasoning into the yolk, and dip each spear in before eating.

Asparagus milanese: this hot dish makes a delicious accompaniment to veal or chicken. Arrange the cooked spears on a buttered flameproof dish and sprinkle the tips lightly with grated Parmesan cheese. Over the cheese pour butter melted to the *noisette* stage: this is when it is just beginning to turn brown and smell nutty. Slip under a hot grill for a minute or so until the cheese begins to melt, then serve immediately.

Asparagus polonaise: this goes particularly well with fish. Arrange well-drained hot spears side by side on individual hot dishes. About 5 cm /2 in below the tips sprinkle a wide band of hard-boiled egg and parsley mixed. Heat some butter to the *noisette* stage (see above), remove from heat and immediately stir in some fine white breadcrumbs (about 25 g /1 oz to 100 g /4 oz butter) and pour over the asparagus.

Asparagus spears with vinaigrette sauce

same time) in the water around the asparagus, or you can place a water-filled jam jar in the centre of the pan, with the bundles standing round it. Another solution is to stand the loose stalks in tall, straight-sided jars – instant coffee jars are very suitable – and fill to just below the tips with boiling salted water. Set the jars in a covered pan of simmering water; cook till tender.

Asparagus boiler: if you cook asparagus frequently, it is well worth buying this specially designed, tall, narrow pan with a perforated inner container, or basket.

Cooking time: this depends on the thickness and quality of the spears; allow from 12–20 minutes for green asparagus and up to 30–45 minutes for large blanched spears. The asparagus is cooked when the thick part of the stalk feels tender when pierced with a sharp knife.

Draining asparagus

Asparagus needs to be drained very thoroughly so that no liquid remains to seep out and dilute the sauce with which it is served. Lift the bundles from the pan, cut the string, and if you do not have a serving dish with a removable perforated drainer, lay the asparagus on a clean, folded tea towel to absorb the liquid before serving. Do not worry if this cools the asparagus a little, as warm rather than very hot spears are much easier to hold in the fingers and dip in the sauce. If serving cold, dip the cooked asparagus spears in cold water and leave them on the tea towel until they have drained and cooled completely.

Serving asparagus

Arrange the spears neatly on individual large plates, warm or cold as appropriate, and hand the sauce round separately. Or if you own a pair of special asparagus tongs, the asparagus will look very attractive served on one large dish from which your guests can help themselves. Beside each place setting put a finger bowl half-filled with warm water with a thin slice of lemon or a decorative flower head floating on it; although pottery soup bowls lack the elegance of glass or silver, they can be very suitable for this purpose. Remember to provide large cloth napkins rather than paper ones, as fingers will frequently need to be dried.

If you find it difficult to mop up a thin sauce when eating asparagus, a trick worth trying is to slip a fork, prongs downward, under your plate to tilt it slightly and concentrate the sauce to one side.

✱✱✱✱ Freshly picked asparagus, either thick stalks or sprue, should be packed in rigid, shallow containers to protect the tips from damage in the freezer. Prepare the stalks as for cooking, and cut to fit the containers. Do not tie into bundles but blanch the stalks loose, allowing 4 minutes boiling time for thick stalks, 3 minutes for medium stalks, and 2 minutes for thin stalks. Plunge at once into iced water for as long as the boiling time. Drain well, chill and then pack into containers. Trimmings can be packaged separately for soups and purées. Storage life is 9–12 months. Cook from frozen in a small quantity of boiling salted water for 5–6 minutes, or longer if necessary, until just tender.

Asparagus rolls

These rolls are very popular at drinks parties and wedding receptions. It is essential to cut the bread paper-thin.

🍴🍴 45 minutes
then 2 hours chilling

Makes about 50 rolls
2 small brown loaves, chilled for 2 hours
350 g /12 oz butter, softened
salt and freshly ground black pepper
2 × 350 g /12 oz cans asparagus tips, drained
150 ml /5 fl oz mayonnaise

1   Remove all the crusts from the loaves and slice the bread very thinly. Butter each slice and sprinkle with a little salt and pepper.
2   Place an asparagus tip on each slice and spread a little mayonnaise on top. Roll tightly and pack the rolls closely together on a serving dish. Cover with a damp tea towel. Serve within 5 hours.

Asparagus soup

Make this delicately flavoured dinner party soup with fresh thin spears or trimmings, or with frozen asparagus. Serve with melba toast or slender bread sticks. When leeks are not available use 2 finely chopped shallots instead.

🍴🍴 45 minutes

Asparagus rolls

Serves 4–6
350 g /12 oz green asparagus
25 g /1 oz butter
1 small leek, white and green parts, washed and finely sliced
8 lettuce leaves, roughly torn
15 ml /1 tbls flour
850 ml /1½ pt mild chicken stock
salt and freshly ground black pepper
2 medium-sized egg yolks
150 ml /5 fl oz thin cream

1   Cut off and reserve about 12 tips for garnishing and chop the rest of the asparagus into 25 mm /1 in lengths.
2   Melt the butter in a saucepan and cook the leek very gently, without colouring, for about 5 minutes. Add the lettuce for the last minute or so, stirring until softened.
3   Sprinkle in the flour and stir well. Stir in the stock and when boiling tip in the asparagus. Cover, reduce heat and simmer for 25–30 minutes, or until very tender.
4   Meanwhile, simmer the reserved tips in a very little salted water for 5–10 minutes, until just tender.
5   Purée the soup in a blender and, if necessary, pass through a sieve to remove any fibrous pieces. Return to the rinsed pan and season to taste.
6   To serve, bring the soup to the boil. Remove from heat, stir in the egg yolks beaten with the cream and reheat gently, stirring, but without boiling again.
7   Strain the cooking liquid from the tips into the soup and stir well. Pour the soup into individual bowls and garnish.

Sprue à la crème

🍴 25 minutes

Serves 4
500 g /1 lb fresh green asparagus sprue or frozen green asparagus
salt and freshly ground black pepper
50 g /2 oz butter
45–60 ml /3–4 tbls thick cream

1   Prepare the asparagus, removing any fibrous or discoloured cut ends. Cut the asparagus 7.5 cm /3 in below the tips and tie the top parts into 4 small bundles with string. Chop the rest of the spears into 10 mm /½ in pieces.
2   Drop the chopped pieces into a small amount of boiling salted water in a wide saucepan, and after the water regains boiling point lay the asparagus bundles on top. Cover and cook gently for 12–18 minutes, or until tender (about 5–6 minutes if you are using frozen asparagus).
3   Lift out the bundles, remove the string and keep warm. Drain the chopped pieces thoroughly, return to the pan and toss over heat to evaporate excess moisture.
4   Add the butter to the pan, and when mixed with the asparagus pieces add the cream and seasonings to taste. Stir and heat gently for a minute or two until the cream thickens.
5   Divide the creamed asparagus between 4 individual warmed gratin dishes. Place a little clump of tips on top of each portion and serve as a first course or side dish.

Asparagus mousses

🕐 25 minutes

Serves 6
350 g /12 oz canned green asparagus
45 ml /3 tbls concentrated chicken stock
15 g /1/2 oz powdered gelatine
150 ml /5 fl oz milk
15 g /1/2 oz butter
15 g /1/2 oz flour
salt and freshly ground black pepper
1 large egg white
125 ml /4 fl oz whipping cream

1 Cut off and reserve 6 of the best asparagus tips for garnishing. Purée the rest of the can contents (spears and liquid) in a blender or through a vegetable mill.
2 Put the stock and gelatine in a small basin, stand it in a pan of boiling water and heat gently, stirring now and then, until dissolved.
3 Heat the milk, butter and flour together in a saucepan, whisking continuously, until a smooth, thick sauce forms. Simmer very gently for 5 minutes.
4 Remove from heat and stir in the dissolved gelatine followed by the asparagus purée. Mix thoroughly, season to taste and set aside until cold.
5 Whisk the egg white until stiff and the cream until softly peaked. Fold first the cream and then the egg white into the cold asparagus mixture, blending lightly but thoroughly.
6 Spoon into 6 individual soufflé dishes of about 8.5 cm /3½ in diameter and refrigerate until set.
7 Before serving, top with the reserved tips. Hand round slices of wafer-thin brown bread and butter separately.

Maltese asparagus

🕐 10 minutes for sauce plus 15–45 minutes for asparagus

Serves 4–6
700 g /1½ lb fresh asparagus spears, prepared
For the Maltese sauce
3 medium-sized egg yolks
juice of ½ large lemon
salt and ground white pepper
175 g /6 oz unsalted butter, at room temperature
finely grated zest of ½ orange
juice of 1 small orange

1 Put the egg yolks, 15 ml /1 tbls of the lemon juice, 15 ml /1 tbls water and a good pinch each of salt and pepper into a small bowl. Beat well with a small wire whisk.
2 Divide the butter into 15 g /½ oz pieces and add one piece to the egg yolks.
3 Rest the bowl containing the eggs over a pan of barely simmering water, checking that the base does not touch the water. Beat steadily until the egg mixture slowly thickens to a creamy consistency. This will take

Turkey and asparagus Apollo

1–2 minutes and it is very important that the mixture does not overheat and curdle. If the sauce shows signs of separating, add 15 ml /1 tbls cold water and beat briskly.
4 Immediately remove the pan from heat and, stirring continuously, beat in the rest of the butter, one piece at a time, making sure that each portion has been absorbed by the egg mixture before adding the next.
5 Finally beat in the orange zest and enough of the orange juice to flavour the sauce and thin it to a coating consistency. Check the seasoning and add extra lemon juice to taste.
6 Keep the sauce warm until the asparagus is ready, by leaving the bowl containing the sauce standing over hot (but not boiling) water and stirring frequently.
7 Prepare a pan of boiling salted water which will cover two-thirds of the asparagus stalks. Stand the bundle of asparagus upright, cover tightly and cook for 15–45 minutes according to the thickness of the stalks. Drain thoroughly and serve accompanied by the sauce in a warm sauceboat.

Turkey and asparagus Apollo

For an elegant lunch or supper, this dish can be made quickly from freezer and store-cupboard standbys. Cooked chicken and ham can be substituted for turkey.

🕐 20 minutes

Serves 4
350 g /12 oz canned asparagus spears
about 350 ml /12 fl oz chicken stock
40 g /1½ oz butter
40 g /1½ oz flour
150 ml /5 fl oz thin cream
10 ml /2 tsp lemon juice
salt and freshly ground black pepper
350 g /12 oz cooked turkey meat
2 hard-boiled eggs

1 Drain the liquid from the asparagus and make up to 425 ml /15 fl oz with chicken stock. Reserve some of the best spears for garnishing and chop the rest into 25 mm /1 in lengths.
2 Melt the butter in a saucepan, stir in the flour and cook gently for a minute. Add the measured liquid and beat briskly until smooth and boiling. Stir in the cream and lemon juice, season, and simmer gently for 5 minutes.
3 Cut the turkey into bite-size cubes and reheat thoroughly in the sauce.
4 Slice one of the eggs thinly and reserve for garnishing. Coarsely chop the other egg and stir into the sauce with the asparagus pieces. Heat through and check seasoning.
5 Turn the mixture into a heated shallow serving dish. Arrange egg slices in the centre with the reserved asparagus spears radiating outwards. Serve hot.

165

Green peas

We can enjoy peas in one form or another all the year round, and frozen and canned peas are very useful standbys. But fresh peas are still an eagerly anticipated treat, unrivalled for their natural sweetness and crispness.

For centuries field peas were dried for use as a staple winter food, but in the 16th century Italian gardeners developed a small, sweet garden pea, the equivalent of what we now call *petits pois* (little peas). Over the next 100 years fresh peas became immensely popular, especially in France, where King Louis XIV would retire behind locked doors in his palace at Versailles to feast on the first peas of the season. The regions of Clamart and St Germain around Paris became famous for the quality of their peas; either name in a recipe indicates that peas are a main ingredient in the dish.

Peas are one of the most nutritious vegetables, providing protein, calcium and vitamins A, B and C. Young peas are rich in natural sugars and are delicious eaten raw, straight out of the pod.

Types of pea
The many types of pea can be loosely classified by whether they are shelled and only the peas eaten, or whether the whole pod is eaten.

Shelling peas are grown for their sweet, nutty-tasting seeds which are removed from the pod for eating.

Garden peas are grown in most parts of the world, except the tropics. The pods, picked when 7.5–10 cm /3–4 in long, each contain a single row of yellow-green or blue-green seeds. The ordinary round garden pea and the larger marrowfat pea are the two basic types of garden pea. Marrowfats are distinguished from other peas by their wrinkled seeds at planting time. They tend to be relatively sweet and are often used for freezing and canning. The smallest and sweetest shelling peas are called petit pois; these are picked when still very young and tender.

Edible-podded peas are cultivated specially for their succulent pods which are tender enough to be eaten whole. They contain tiny seeds, but unlike shelling peas, the pods have no papery lining.

The name of mange-tout peas means 'eat-all' in French. They have long been used for cooking in China, where they are known as snow peas. They are also called sugar peas or Chinese peas and they have only recently become popular in Northern Europe and the U.S.

Asparagus peas were once cultivated as an ornamental plant. They are now grown for their edible pods which have frills right down the length of the pod. They are sometimes called winged peas. The pods must be picked when no longer than 25 mm /1 in or they will be fibrous. They have a mild, slightly aromatic flavour.

Processed peas: commercially frozen peas are one of our most successful freezer vegetables. Cooked from frozen, they need less than half the cooking time of fresh peas and far less cooking liquid than fresh peas.

Canned peas are less like the fresh vegetable than frozen, but are useful in braised and casseroled dishes. When using them remember they usually contain a little added sugar. French canned petits pois are specially good; you can also buy canned pea purée.

Quick-dried (air-frozen) peas in packets, reconstituted by cooking in liquid, take up minimum space in the store cupboard. The section on pulses, *page 194*, covers dried peas.

Buying and storing peas
For maximum flavour and food value, buy only enough for your immediate needs and use on day of purchase. If you do buy peas in advance, keep them in a cool, airy place and use within 24 hours. Wrap mange-tout peas in cling film to keep them fresh.

Shelling peas come into season in spring and last to mid- or late summer. Look for firm, plump, bright green pods; avoid any that are bulging or wizened as the peas inside are likely to be hard and tough. As a guide, 500 g /1 lb pods yields about 175 g /6 oz shelled peas. You should allow 75–100 g /3–4 oz shelled peas per person as a vegetable accompaniment, so buy about 1.5 kg /3 lb peas in the pod to serve 4.

Mange-tout peas are available from February in North America and Northern Europe. The pods should look fresh and crisp, with the row of tiny seeds inside just apparent. Allow 100 g /4 oz per person, less if they are mixed with other vegetables.

✳✳✳ Freeze only very young and tender peas. Blanch for 1½ minutes then cool them in iced water for the same time and drain. Open freeze on trays and bag when firm. They will keep frozen for 9–12 months. Top and tail mange-tout peas, blanch for 2 minutes, cool in iced water for the same time, then drain and pack in containers.

Preparing peas
Shelling peas: pinch the end of the pod to make it open and remove the peas with your thumb. Save the best pods to use in soup.

Mange-tout peas: rinse and drain, then top and tail, and string if necessary. Leave whole or slice into 25 mm /1 in pieces.

Cooking peas
Steamed and boiled: petits pois and other very young garden peas need only simple, brief cooking. Steam the shelled peas over boiling water for about 15 minutes. Or cook them in plenty of simmering water, with a sprig or two of mint if you like, for 5–10 minutes. Test frequently by tasting – when cooked the peas should be tender but crisp.

Drain the peas immediately they are cooked, refresh them in cold water and drain again. To eat immediately, tip them into a dry pan and shake gently over a moderate heat to allow any remaining moisture to evaporate. Season with salt and a little sugar, if needed, to bring out the sweetness; turn them into a heated dish and top with knobs of fresh butter. If you wish they can be reheated in butter or cream before serving. If you do not have enough peas to go round, add some freshly cooked young carrots or sweetcorn.

Braised peas: gentle braising will tenderize larger, more mature peas, though petits pois are often cooked this way too. They can be simmered with some chopped onion for 5–10 minutes, then drained, dried off and tossed in enough cream to coat them lightly. Or try them with button onions and lettuce in the French style.

Pea soups and purées: mature, end-of-season peas have a pasty, floury texture, as their natural sugar has converted to starch. Use them in soups or purée them after cooking, in a blender or food mill, or by passing them through a nylon sieve. If pods have been cooked in the soup, sieving is

Risotto with peas

essential to remove the fibres. For extra body, thicken the purée with sieved cooked rice or puréed potato. Gently reheat the purée, stirring in enough butter or cream to give a fluffy consistency.

A purée of peas is exceptionally versatile: serve it piping hot with any ham or bacon dish, or topped with soft-boiled eggs and garnished with croûtons for a light supper; thin the purée with stock or cream for a nourishing soup. For omelette Clamart, fill an omelette with 30 ml /2 tbls of pea purée.

Cooking mange-tout peas: these are excellent stir-fried in the Chinese fashion. Mange-tout peas can also be steamed for about 10 minutes until tender and served either as a vegetable accompaniment or with melted butter or hollandaise sauce as a first course. Or place the pods in a wide, shallow saucepan with just enough water to cover the base, add a large knob of butter and a pinch each of salt and sugar and bring to the boil; simmer, covered, for a few minutes until the pods are tender. Drain immediately and serve with fresh butter. Cooked mange-tout peas can also be used in salads, or puréed and sieved, and served hot.

Using cooked peas: cooked peas are delicious cold in rice, pasta and potato salads, and can be used in flat omelettes and quiches. Coated with mayonnaise, they make an excellent filling for hollowed-out tomatoes, served as a starter.

Raw peas or very young uncooked mange-tout peas make a colourful and crunchy addition to mixed vegetable salads.

Summer pea soup

1 hour plus chilling time

Serves 4

1.5 kg /3 lb fresh peas in the pod
25 g /1 oz butter
½ Spanish onion, finely chopped
4 outer leaves cos lettuce, shredded
600 ml /1 pt hot chicken or vegetable stock
salt and freshly ground black pepper
150 ml /5 fl oz natural yoghurt
2.5 ml /½ tsp lemon juice (optional)

1 Shell the peas and weigh out 500 g /18 oz. Reserve 3–4 of the best empty pods.
2 Melt the butter in a large, heavy-based saucepan over low heat. Add the onion, lettuce and pea pods. Cover the pan and sweat the vegetables gently for 10 minutes, stirring occasionally.
3 Add the peas to the pan, pour in the hot stock and season with salt and pepper. Bring slowly to the boil, cover, reduce heat and simmer until the peas are very tender.
4 Remove the pan from the heat, discard the pods, and allow the soup to cool slightly. Then reduce it to a smooth purée in a blender, a batch at a time. Add all but 20 ml /4 tsp yoghurt to the final batch of purée and blend this batch again.
5 Pour all the puréed soup into a bowl and chill, stirring occasionally. Just before serving, check the seasoning and sharpen with a few drops of lemon juice if liked. Pour the soup into 4 individual bowls and swirl 5 ml /1 tsp yoghurt into each.

• If you like the flavour of mint, add a sprig when cooking the peas, and float a few mint leaves on top of each bowl just before serving. Omit the lemon juice.

Risotto with peas

This dish, which comes from Venice, is called *risi e bisi* in Italy. It has a creamier, slightly more liquid consistency than the usual risotto, and is served in bowls.

50 minutes

Serves 4

1 kg /2 lb fresh peas in the pod
175 g /6 oz Italian medium-grain rice
50 g /2 oz butter
1 small onion, chopped
50 g /2 oz Italian prosciutto ham, chopped
850 ml–1 L /1½–1¾ pt hot chicken stock
50 g /2 oz freshly grated Parmesan cheese
extra Parmesan cheese for serving

1 Shell the peas and weigh out 350 g /12 oz. Pick over, but do not wash the rice.
2 In a shallow, flameproof casserole, melt half the butter over low heat. Add the onion and cook gently until softened and beginning to colour.
3 Add the chopped prosciutto and cook, stirring, for 1 minute. Add the peas and stir gently with a wooden spoon until they are well coated with butter.
4 Pour in 150 ml /5 fl oz of the hot chicken stock and bring to the boil. Add the rice, then pour in 600 ml /1 pt of the stock. Simmer gently, uncovered and without stirring, for 15–20 minutes, until the stock is almost all absorbed. Slowly stir in 75 ml /3 fl oz of the remaining stock. Cook for a few minutes more until the rice is very tender, adding a little more stock if necessary.
5 Stir in the remaining butter and the 50 g /2 oz freshly grated Parmesan cheese, then add enough of the remaining stock for a creamy, slightly soupy consistency. Ladle into heated soup bowls and serve with extra freshly grated Parmesan handed separately.

Pea tarts

These elegant little tarts are made with a crisp cheese pastry and filled with a creamy pea purée. Provide small plates when serving, as the tarts are fragile.

   1 hour for pastry including chilling time, then 25 minutes

Makes about 12
For the pastry
175 g /6 oz flour
salt and freshly ground black pepper
pinch of cayenne pepper
50 g /2 oz finely grated Gruyère or Parmesan cheese or a mixture of both
100 g /4 oz butter, diced
1 medium-sized egg, separated
For the filling
700 g /1½ lb fresh peas in the pod
pinch of caster sugar
30 ml /2 tbls thick cream or mayonnaise
salt and freshly ground black pepper

1 Make the pastry. Sift the flour with a pinch of salt, black pepper and a pinch of cayenne pepper into a chilled mixing bowl. Stir in the cheese. Rub the butter into the flour and cheese with your fingertips until the mixture resembles breadcrumbs.
2 Beat the egg yolk with 5 ml /1 tsp water and mix it into the rubbed-in mixture with a fork. Continue mixing until the ingredients

Pea tarts

begin to cling together, then gather the pastry into a ball with your fingers.
3 Tip the pastry on to a lightly floured surface and knead briefly until smooth. Wrap in cling film and chill for 30 minutes.
4 On a lightly floured surface, thinly roll out the pastry and use to line 12 or so tartlet tins or small barquette (boat-shaped) moulds. Chill for 10–15 minutes. Meanwhile, heat the oven to 200C /400F /gas 6.
5 Place the moulds on a baking sheet and line with foil and beans. Bake blind for 10 minutes. Remove foil and beans and lightly brush the insides of the pastry cases with the beaten egg white. Bake for a further 5 minutes. Cool the pastry cases slightly, then carefully unmould and leave to cool completely on a wire rack.
6 Shell the peas and weigh out 250 g /8 oz. Cook the peas in a saucepan of simmering, lightly salted water, with a pinch of sugar added, until tender. Drain the peas and refresh them in cold water for 3–4 minutes, then drain thoroughly again.
7 Combine 100 g /4 oz of the drained peas with the cream or mayonnaise and reduce to a smooth, thick purée in a blender. Season with salt and pepper to taste.
8 Spread the purée evenly in the cold pastry cases. Divide the remaining whole peas between the tarts, arranging them neatly over the purée. Serve within 2 hours of filling as an appetizer or garnish.

Chicken with green peas

   1½ hours

Serves 4
4 chicken quarters
salt and freshly ground black pepper
4 slices streaky bacon, rinded and cut into strips
25 g /1 oz butter
1 medium-sized onion, chopped
50 g /2 oz button mushrooms, sliced
15 ml /1 tbls flour
400 ml /14 fl oz hot chicken stock
5 ml /1 tsp dried mixed herbs
1 kg /2 lb fresh peas in the pod
parsley sprigs to garnish

1 Rinse the chicken quarters in cold water and dry thoroughly on absorbent paper. Rub salt and pepper into the chicken all over with your fingers.
2 Sauté the bacon strips in a large, shallow, flameproof casserole over low heat until the fat runs and the bacon is cooked. Remove the bacon with a slotted spoon and reserve.
3 Add the butter to the casserole. When foaming subsides, put in the chicken quarters skin side down. Cook gently, turning frequently, for 10–15 minutes until browned on all sides. Remove the chicken and reserve.
4 Reduce heat to low. Add the onion and mushrooms to the casserole and cook, stirring, until softened. Sprinkle in the flour, stirring vigorously to blend; cook, stirring constantly, for 1 minute.
5 Gradually stir in the hot stock and the herbs, and bring to the boil, stirring constantly. Return the chicken quarters and bacon strips to the casserole. Cover and simmer for 50 minutes.
6 Shell the peas, weigh out 350 g /12 oz and add these to the casserole. Cover and simmer for a further 10 minutes or until the peas are cooked and the chicken is tender. Skim off any fat from the surface of the dish and correct the seasoning. Serve garnished with parsley sprigs. Creamy mashed potato with nutmeg is a good accompaniment.

Eggs and peas, Jewish-style

Serve with plain grilled tomatoes for a light lunch or supper for children.

   20 minutes

Serves 2–4
1.5 kg /3 lb fresh peas in the pod
freshly grated nutmeg
pinch each of ground cloves and ground mace
salt and freshly ground black pepper
5 large eggs
90 ml /6 tbls thick cream
60 ml /4 tbls butter-fried croûtons

1 Shell the peas and weigh out 500 g /18 oz. Pour 275 ml /10 fl oz water into a large, heavy-based frying-pan and bring to the boil over medium heat. Add the peas, a good pinch of nutmeg and the ground spices and season lightly with salt and pepper.
2 Reduce the heat slightly, cover the pan and simmer gently until the peas are almost tender.
3 Reduce the heat to low. With the back of a metal spoon, make 4 shallow depressions in the peas. Carefully break 1 egg into each hollow. Cover the pan and cook for 3–4 minutes until the eggs are set.
4 Meanwhile, heat the grill to high. In a small bowl, beat together the remaining egg and the cream and season lightly with salt and pepper.
5 When the eggs in the pan are set, pour over the beaten egg and cream mixture. Place the pan under the grill for about 30 seconds until the cream topping is set. Using a slotted spoon, transfer them on to heated plates. Garnish each portion with 15 ml/1 tbls croûtons and serve.

Stir-fried mushrooms with mange-tout peas and cashews

Serve this crunchy, sweet-sour vegetable dish with grilled pork chops or chicken.

20 minutes

Serves 4
250 g /8 oz mange-tout peas
salt
250 g /8 oz button mushrooms
1 small red pepper
15 ml /1 tbls soy sauce
15 ml /1 tbls dry sherry
5 ml /1 tsp clear honey
60 ml /4 tbls sunflower oil
1 garlic clove, chopped
50 g /2 oz cashews

1 Top and tail the mange-tout peas, string if necessary and cut into 25 mm /1 in pieces. Blanch them in a large pan of boiling, lightly salted water for 1½ minutes; drain and refresh them in cold water and drain thoroughly again.
2 Trim, wipe and slice the mushrooms. Core and seed the red pepper and cut the flesh into matchstick strips. In a small bowl, combine the soy sauce, sherry and honey.
3 Heat the oil and garlic in a Chinese wok or large frying-pan over a moderate heat. When the garlic begins to sizzle, add the sliced mushrooms and strips of pepper and stir-fry for 2 minutes. Add the cashews and stir-fry for 1 minute more.
4 Add a good pinch of salt and 60 ml /4 tbls water and boil over high heat until the liquid has almost entirely evaporated. Give the soy sauce mixture a good stir and pour into the pan. Toss the vegetables and nuts in the sauce, then add the mange-tout peas and stir-fry for 1 minute. Serve immediately.

Stir-fried mushrooms with mange-tout peas and cashews

Peas with cream and nutmeg

35 minutes

Serves 4
1.5 kg /3 lb fresh peas in the pod
175 ml /6 fl oz thick cream
salt and freshly ground black pepper
1.5 ml /¼ tsp sugar
freshly grated nutmeg

1 Shell the peas and weigh out 500 g /18 oz. Put them in a large pan of boiling, lightly salted water and cook for about 4–8 minutes until just tender. Drain the peas, then refresh them in cold water and drain again.
2 In a small bowl, whip 30 ml /2 tbls of the cream until stiff and reserve. In a small, heavy-based saucepan, heat the remaining cream over low heat to just below boiling point and keep hot.
3 Tip the drained peas into a large, heavy-based saucepan and shake briefly over moderate heat until any remaining moisture has evaporated. Pour in the hot cream and season to taste with salt, pepper and a pinch of nutmeg. Simmer very gently, uncovered, for about 5 minutes until the cream is reduced and thickly coats the peas.
4 Gently stir in the reserved whipped cream. Turn the peas and cream out into a heated vegetable dish and dust lightly with nutmeg. Serve immediately.

Sweet peppers and chillies

Although they both belong to the Capsicum family, there is a world of difference between the fierce heat of the small chilli and the mild spiciness of the sweet pepper.

Brightly-coloured and exotic, chillies and sweet peppers have come to be associated with the cooking traditions of Mediterranean, Asian and Middle Eastern countries. Yet they are native to the American tropics and comparatively new to Europe and Asia.

It was Columbus who brought them to Europe and he called them 'pepper' because the heat of the chillies so closely resembled the spice he sought. The new flavourings were enthusiastically used in Europe, and within a century or so had spread to Asia and Africa. It took longer for them to be commonplace in Britain–it is only in the last decades they have become easily available.

The sweet or bell pepper is a crisp vegetable, mildly sweet and spicy and eaten raw or cooked. The chilli is only used as a flavouring and it is unwise to eat it raw – although in Latin-American villages there are chilli-eating competitions!

Sweet ripe peppers are dried and ground to make the spice paprika, which is slightly peppery but not hot. Dried chillies are ground to make cayenne pepper and are combined with other spices to make chilli and curry powders and chilli seasoning.

Buying peppers and chillies

The crisp green pepper is an unripe vegetable; as it matures it turns red or, less often, shades of yellow varying from chrome to lemon. Red peppers have the sweetest flavour and the softest texture; yellow ones are both sweet and crisp, and all of them are high in vitamin C. Peppers are more plentiful and cheaper in the summer; choose firm, glossy pods without blemishes.

Chillies are also red or green depending on ripeness. Although in Mexico there are an amazing number of chillies, all differing in flavour and pungency, elsewhere the choice may be limited – but they are always hot! Inside are tiny, cream-coloured seeds; they may look harmless but they are the hottest part of the chilli and should be discarded unless you are prepared for a fiery flavour.

Canned peppers are called pimentos, from the Spanish *pimiento*. They are preserved in brine or spiced vinegar. This softens them, giving them the texture of grilled fresh peppers (see below). Chillies, usually green, can also be bought canned in brine.

Dried red chillies are sold whole or crushed. Dried pepper flakes, which are also sold, can be used direct from the packet if they are to be stewed, otherwise soak them before use. Store like other spices.

Storing peppers and chillies

Whole peppers will keep for a few days in the salad-crisper drawer of the refrigerator. Wrap cut portions in plastic film as exposed edges quickly become mushy.

If you are preparing chillies ahead, or storing left-over canned chillies in the refrigerator, cover them tightly, as their pungency will taint other foods. The traditional methods of keeping chillies include pickling in vinegar or drying out and stringing up like onions.

❋❋❋ Freeze seeded whole peppers for stuffing; blanch them for 3 minutes, refresh, dry, chill and freeze in rigid containers. Store for up to 6 months. Defrost in boiling water and finish parboiling. Strips can be frozen raw; separate the colours, as red peppers soften more quickly than green. Store for up to 6 months. Raw strips may be defrosted and used in salads or added, frozen, to dishes for cooking. Chopped peppers can also be bought ready-frozen.

Using peppers and chillies

Peppers, although distinctively flavoured, are not nearly as pungent as chillies and can be used much more lavishly. They go especially well with tomato-based dishes and those requiring olive oil.

Try including quarters of crisp, raw, sweet peppers in a selection of crudités– yellow segments look especially attractive with sprigs of cauliflower and wedges of Florentine fennel.

Preparing peppers and chillies

Cut a slice from the top of a whole pepper; take out the pith and seeds with a knife. Use the top as a 'lid' for stuffed peppers.

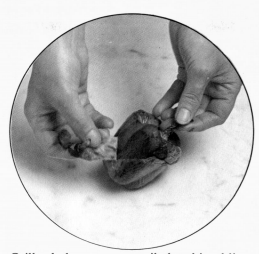

Grill whole peppers until the skins blister and blacken. When they are cool, rub off the skins under running water.

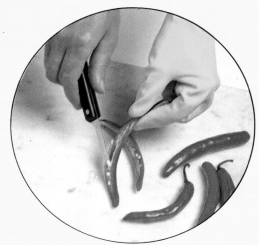

Scrape out chilli seeds with a pointed knife, taking care not to handle the seeds. Then rinse the pods to remove any remaining seeds.

A succulent salad of skinned, grilled peppers make an elegant accompaniment to grilled meat, especially good with lamb. Slices of pepper sautéed in butter would be a delicious alternative. If you want to give a lift to humdrum macaroni or egg dishes, simply add some cooked diced peppers.

Use whole green peppers stuffed for a main course. Fillings can be based on tuna, sausage or left-over meat combined with rice and onions, cheese or nuts for additional flavouring.

Their hot pepperiness makes chillies an ideal condiment for bland foods, such as pulses or rice. They are frequently used in Indian sambals and other fiery relishes, and in sauces.

Latin American cookery, in particular, makes extensive use of the pungent little pods to pep up meat and poultry stews, corn and other vegetable dishes. They are essential in the famous Mexican *mole* (or chilli) sauces, and are traditionally included in creamed avocado sauces such as guacamole. If you are unfamiliar with them, remember a little chilli goes a long way.

Preparing peppers

Seeding: slice off the stem end (keep this for a lid if stuffing). Scrape out the seeds and any pith from the pod and rinse clean.
Blanching softens the texture of raw peppers. Put the seeded pods in cold water, bring to the boil, drain and refresh in cold water.
Parboiling peppers for stuffing makes them easier to fill and shortens the baking time. Simmer for 10 minutes.
Grilling and skinning peppers makes them meltingly soft, and intensifies their sweet rich flavour. Grill them whole (before seeding) so that the juices are sealed in and the flavour concentrated in the flesh. Grilling over charcoal gives the deliciously smoky flavour which characterizes many Mediterranean dishes.

Spear each pepper on a wooden-handled fork and turn it over a gas flame, or under a hot grill, until the skin blisters and blackens. Cover the pepper with a cloth and leave it until it is cool enough to handle. Rub off the skin under cold running water. Better still, although messy, scrape off the skin over a plate and catch the juices to use.

Preparing chillies

Handle chillies with care – they contain a pungent oil which can cause burning in the eyes, nose and throat. Wear a rubber glove, do not touch your face while preparing them and always wash your hands afterwards.

Snap off the stem, split open the pod and scrape out the seeds, then rinse inside the pod thoroughly. Cover dried chillies with hot water and leave them to soak for 1 hour, then drain well and seed in the same way as fresh pods. Use the soaking liquid for flavouring.

Sweet pepper butter

Serve this attractive apricot-coloured butter with grilled fish or steak, or try it with baked potatoes or steamed carrots.

🕯 10 minutes

Makes 150 g/5 oz butter
1 pimento, drained and chopped
15 ml/1 tbls thick cream
1 large pinch of chilli powder
50 g/2 oz butter softened
a squeeze of orange juice
salt and freshly ground black pepper

1 Combine the pimento, cream and chilli powder and reduce to a purée in a blender.
2 Place the softened butter in a mixing bowl. With a spatula or wooden spoon work in the pepper purée, a little at a time. Blend in the orange juice and season to taste.
3 Pack the flavoured butter into a small china dish, cover tightly with cling film or foil and refrigerate until required.

Rouille

Red pepper sauce

Rouille is a Provençal sauce for fish: the name means 'rust'. It also goes well with pasta and it makes a good dip to serve with raw vegetables.

🕯 30 minutes

Makes 175 ml/6 fl oz sauce
1 large sweet red pepper, grilled, skinned, seeded and chopped
1 small red chilli, seeded, blanched and chopped
1 large garlic clove, peeled and chopped
25 g/1 oz fresh breadcrumbs
60 ml/4 tbls olive oil
30-45 ml/2-3 tbls warm fish stock or water
salt and freshly ground black pepper

1 Combine the sweet pepper, chilli and garlic in a blender or mortar. Reduce to a purée or pound to a smooth paste.
2 If using a blender turn the purée into a mixing bowl. Work in the breadcrumbs then gradually stir in the olive oil. Slowly beat in the stock or water and season.

Chilli con carne

🕯 1 hour soaking time,
then 45 minutes

Serves 4
450 g/1 lb chuck steak, trimmed and cubed
4 dried red chillies, soaked in hot water for 1 hour
2 medium-sized onions, peeled and chopped
2 large garlic cloves, peeled and chopped
30-45 ml/ 2-3 tbls vegetable oil
7.5 ml/½ tbls dried oregano
salt and freshly ground black pepper
175-225 g/6-8 oz cooked or canned red kidney beans

171

1 Drain the chillies, reserving the liquid, then seed and coarsely chop them. Combine the chopped chillies, onion and garlic and reduce to a coarse purée in an electric blender or with a pestle and mortar.
2 Heat the oil in a large, heavy-based pan. Add the meat and brown it on all sides. Remove from the pan with a slotted spoon and reserve.
3 Add the chilli purée to the pan and cook for 5 minutes, stirring constantly. Stir in the oregano and salt and pepper to taste. Return the meat to the pan and moisten with a little of the reserved chilli liquid. Cover and cook gently for 10 minutes.
4 Drain the beans, reserving the cooking or canning liquor. Add the beans to the pan, together with some of their liquor, if the mixture is dry. Check and adjust seasoning, adding more of the chilli liquid to taste. Simmer for 15 minutes and serve hot.

Cheese-stuffed peppers

⌇ 1 hour

Serves 4-5
4-5 plump peppers
25 g /1 oz butter
30 ml /2 tbls olive oil
175-225 g /6-8 oz onions, chopped
1 garlic clove, chopped
175-225 g /6-8 oz easy-cook Italian rice
about 300 ml /11 fl oz stock
2 hard-boiled eggs
125 g /4 oz Cheshire or Lancashire cheese, chopped
100 g /4 oz walnuts, chopped
45 ml /3 tbls grated Parmesan cheese
30 ml /2 tbls chopped parsley
5 ml /1 tsp oregano
salt and freshly ground black pepper
100 g /4 oz Mozzarella cheese, sliced in 4

1 Heat the oven to 180C /350F /gas 4. Heat the butter and oil in a large pan over medium heat and fry the onions and garlic until soft. Add the rice and cook, stirring, for about 2 minutes.
2 Slice the lids from each of the peppers and seed them. Parboil the peppers for 10 minutes. Then drain them and turn them upside down until needed.
3 Meanwhile, chop the uncooked trimmings from the lids and add these to the rice. Add the stock to the rice, stir once, cover and cook for 12 minutes, adding more stock as necessary for the larger quantity of rice.
4 Peel and chop the eggs and add these, plus the chopped Cheshire cheese, walnuts, Parmesan, parsley and oregano to the rice and season to taste.
5 Arrange the peppers in a greased baking dish in which they fit snugly. Fill with the stuffing and top with the slices of Mozzarella. Bake for 30 minutes. Serve with ratatouille.

● Do not try to economize by omitting the Parmesan, which is needed to flavour the rice; but you can use Cheddar instead of Mozzarella for the topping for this three-cheese dish.

Cheese-stuffed peppers

Pipérade

This is equally delicious hot or cold. Sprinkle with parsley and garnish with crisp croûtons if serving it hot. If you are serving it cold, turn it into a bowl to cool. Use it to fill a hollowed-out French loaf which has been spread with garlic butter and crisped in the oven. Pipérade is also good in baked tartlet cases.

⌇ 40–50 minutes

Serves 4
50 g /2 oz butter or bacon fat
1 large Spanish onion, peeled and chopped
2 garlic cloves, peeled and chopped
2 medium-sized peppers, seeded, blanched and chopped
3 large tomatoes, skinned and chopped
salt and freshly ground black pepper
8 large eggs, lightly beaten

1 Heat the fat in a large, heavy-based saucepan. Add the onion and garlic and cook for 5-7 minutes until the onion is soft.
2 Stir in the peppers and cook gently for 10 minutes. Increase the heat, add the tomatoes and season lightly. Cook briskly, stirring frequently, for 5-10 minutes until the mixture is soft but not watery.
3 Reduce the heat to low and pour in the eggs. Cook gently, stirring constantly, until the eggs are just set and the mixture is thick and creamy.

● For a spicy Latin American version, add 5 ml /1 tsp each of chilli powder, dried oregano and powdered cumin with the tomatoes.

Pork with peppers

⌇ 40 minutes, then 1¼ hours cooking

Serves 4
4 pork loin chops
salt and freshly ground black pepper
15 ml /1 tbls vegetable oil (optional)
100 g /4 oz button mushrooms
2 medium-sized onions, peeled and chopped
15 ml /1 tbls paprika
200 ml /7 fl oz chicken stock
2 medium-sized peppers, seeded and sliced
15 ml /1 tbls flour
200 ml /7 fl oz soured cream

1 Trim the pork loin chops, reserving any excess fat. Heat a large, flameproof casserole and put in the trimmings. Fry them until they give off their fat, or heat the vegetable oil. Add the chops and sauté until nicely brown, about 5 minutes on each side. Remove the chops with a slotted spoon.
2 Sauté the mushrooms in the hot fat, stirring occasionally, then remove them and reserve with the chops. Add the onions to the pan and cook for about 5 minutes, until golden brown. Sprinkle with the paprika and a pinch of salt. Cook for 2-3 minutes, stirring constantly.
3 Gradually blend in the stock and bring to simmering point. Add the chops, mushrooms and peppers. Season to taste. Cover the casserole with a tight-fitting lid and cook very gently for about 1 hour, turning the chops occasionally.
4 Remove any trimmings. Blend the flour with the soured cream and pour it into the casserole. Cook for a further 5-10 minutes turning the chops occasionally. Check the seasoning and serve.

Greek pepper salad

Mix red, green and, if they are available, yellow peppers to make a crisp and attractive salad. Serve it with kebabs or a rich meat like lamb.

🔪 45 minutes including salting

Serves 4
1 cucumber, sliced
3 large peppers, seeded and cut into rounds
500 g /1 lb firm tomatoes, cut into quarters
bunch of spring onions, trimmed
75 g /3 oz Feta cheese, cubed
50 g /2 oz black olives
For the dressing
2 sprigs of fresh mint
2 garlic cloves, crushed
105 ml /7 tbls olive oil
juice of 1 large lemon
salt and freshly ground black pepper

1 Put the sliced cucumber in a colander. Salt between layers and leave the colander in the sink to drip. Rinse off the salt and dry the cucumber slices on absorbent paper.
2 Arrange the prepared peppers, cucumber and tomatoes in layers in a bowl.
3 Chop the spring onions in half lengthways and add to the salad. Top the salad with the olives and the cubes of Feta cheese.
4 Mix the chopped mint, garlic, olive oil and lemon juice. Add salt and pepper to taste and pour over the salad.

Duck with mole verde

Duck with mole verde

Mole verde is a subtle chilli sauce from Mexico. The name means 'green purée' and the sauce is served with poultry or fish.

🔪🔪 2¼ hours

Serves 4
2.4 kg /5½ lb duck with giblets
pinch of ground cumin
1.5 ml /¼ tsp ground black pepper

Greek pepper salad

For the stock
the duck giblets
1 small carrot, finely chopped
1 small onion, finely chopped
1 garlic clove, finely chopped
7.5 ml /1½ tsp salt
5 peppercorns
For the green purée
350 g /12 oz green (or red) tomatoes
2 × 7.5 cm /3 in green chillies, seeded and chopped
1 small onion, chopped
2 garlic cloves, peeled and chopped
2 large lettuce leaves, chopped
1 small bunch radish leaves
4 sprigs coriander leaves

1 Place stock ingredients in a saucepan, cover with water and simmer for 1½ hours.
2 Meanwhile, prick the duck's skin all over, pulling up the skin with the fork prongs, and being careful not to puncture the flesh. Place a casserole over medium heat and, when hot, brown the duck on all sides. Drain off the excess duck fat periodically and reserve it. Cover the casserole tightly and cook the duck over a low heat for 1 hour or until tender.
3 Prepare the green purée. Cover the tomatoes with boiling water for 1 minute, drain, skin and chop roughly. Put them in an electric blender, add the other purée ingredients and blend until smooth.
4 Strain the giblet stock. Return the liquid to the rinsed-out pan and boil until reduced to 300 ml /10 fl oz.
5 Heat 30 ml /2 tbls of the reserved fat in a saucepan over medium heat and stir in the ground cumin and pepper. Add the vegetable purée and simmer for 5 minutes, stirring occasionally. Reduce heat to low, stir in stock and cook for 15 minutes.
6 When the duck is cooked, allow it to cool a little then cut into serving pieces. Add the purée to the juices in the casserole.
7 Add the duck pieces to the sauce, heat through and serve.

Sweetcorn

Warm, golden spoon bread dripping with butter, creamy fish chowder thick with chewy corn kernels, pancakes tightly rolled around spicy fillings – cooks the world over use their ingenuity when they prepare this vital cereal crop.

Sweetcorn, Indian corn or maize is available in many forms: as corn on the cob, as kernels off the cob, as hominy, which is ground hulled corn. Various kinds of meal are made from corn, as is cornflour (also known as cornstarch). It is used to make an oil, which is popular for frying. It is also turned into a syrup.

Sweetcorn is native to Central America, but has spread to Europe and Africa. In much of Continental Europe, however, it is considered primarily as an animal food, rather than food for the table. Corn has one overwhelming disadvantage: its protein is lower and therefore its nutritional value is less than other cereals. Nor can it be used with yeast to make a dough that rises; all corn breads are dense and flattish.

Buying and storing sweetcorn

Fresh corn: an American saying that corn cobs should not be cut until the kettle is singing on the hob emphasizes the importance of choosing corn that is really fresh. Corn cobs still contained in the green husks with brown silky tops are more likely to be local than trimmed ones. Select cobs with thick, smooth grains which are uniform in colour – layers of pale-coloured kernels at the top are a sign of under-ripeness. Cook fresh corn on the day you buy it. A cob will yield 100 g /4 oz kernels.

✳✳✳✳ Corn can be frozen on or off the cob, but only when it is very fresh and tender. Blanch small cobs in boiling, unsalted water for 4 minutes, large ones for 8. Kernels should be blanched for 2–4 minutes. Drain them, cool quickly, then wrap, label and freeze for up to one year. Cook from frozen.

Canned, frozen and dried corn: packs of frozen corn, on or off the cob, canned corn kernels known as 'niblets', sometimes combined with chopped peppers, and creamed corn are all widely available. Miniature corn

cobs, less than 5 cm /2 in long, are sold in cans or jars in Oriental food shops. Small, hard, dark yellow dried corn seed is sold to make popcorn.

● To make popcorn, heat 15 ml /1 tbls oil in a large pan and add 100 g /4 oz dried corn. Cover tightly and cook over high heat, shaking the pan constantly. The corn will fluff up to 4–5 times its original size. Serve with melted butter and salt or sugar, or press into balls.

Hominy is the large, cooked, starchy endosperm of a hulled maize kernel. Nowadays it is bought in cans, ready to reheat and serve, topped with butter, as an accompaniment to meat. Hominy can be coarsely ground to make hominy grits, sold in packets. Grits

---

Clockwise from top left: whole fresh corn, dried corn, hominy, corn cobs, popcorn. In centre: cornmeal, taco shells

are used to make a breakfast 'porridge' in the American South.

Cornmeals are coarsely ground maize kernels, either yellow or white. The two colours are interchangeable in recipes. They are sold in central Europe under various names. *Polenta* is a yellow Italian cornmeal, and comes either finely or coarsely ground. Look for cornmeals in speciality food shops, though some supermarkets stock yellow cornmeal and polenta. Store cornmeals for up to 2 months, tightly covered, in a cool, dry place.

Masa harina is the cornmeal used to make the flat Mexican pancakes called *tortillas*. The corn is treated with lime before being finely ground. Masa harina is exported. Half and half yellow cornmeal and plain white (wheat) flour can be used as a less good substitute in many recipes. Tortillas themselves are exported canned from Mexico and the US; they can sometimes be found in speciality food shops.

Cornflour, a fine white powdery flour, can be found in every supermarket. Store it for up to 6 months in a cool, dry place.

Cooking sweetcorn

Fresh corn: to prepare whole ears of corn, strip away the dry, papery husks and all the silky threads inside and wash under cold running water. Corn on the cob can be boiled, grilled or baked.

● To boil, put the ears in a pan of boiling, unsalted water and cook for 5–8 minutes if they have just been picked, up to about 20 minutes for older corn. Both the addition of salt and overcooking toughens corn, but 15 ml /1 tbls sugar adds pleasantly to the already sweet natural flavour.

Just-picked cobs can be brushed with melted butter and grilled, turning often, for about 10 minutes. They are especially delicious cooked outdoors on a barbecue. Older cobs should first be partly cooked in boiling, unsalted water for 10 minutes, then thoroughly drained before grilling for another 10 minutes.

Well buttered, seasoned with freshly ground black pepper and closely wrapped in their husks or in foil, corn on the cob can be baked, grilled or boiled. Bake for 30 minutes at 180C /350F /gas 4; grill or boil for 20 minutes.

To eat corn on the cob, spear each end with little sticks specially made for the purpose – or use forks – and rotate as you bite away one strip of kernels at a time.

To serve corn as a vegetable accompaniment rather than as a course in its own right, it is usually more convenient to strip the grains from the cob, and this is almost invariably done when the corn is to be cooked in casseroles and soups. Hold the cob firmly in one hand, stalk end on the work surface, and, using a very sharp knife, slice downward between the core and the grains. Wash and drain the grains well.

When young, tender and very fresh, the kernels can be eaten raw and are good tossed in a salad with cabbage and raisins.

Cook fresh corn kernels in boiling water for 5–8 minutes, or steam them over rapidly boiling water for about half as long again. Corn kernels blend particularly well with

other vegetables: succotash is an American classic made with beans, but corn also goes well with peas and carrots.

For creamed corn, a delicious partner for roast and grilled meat and poultry, simmer the kernels for about 5 minutes in thin cream, then season well.

Both plain or creamed corn kernels can be stirred into batter to make crispy fritters, which with fried bananas make a delicious traditional accompaniment to fried or grilled chicken in chicken Maryland.

Main course dishes can be made with corn kernels: combine them with chicken in a pie. Burgoo is a Kentucky meat stew which uses corn kernels.

Canned and frozen corn should be cooked according to package directions. Canned corn kernels can be drained and added to salads as they are, and you can substitute canned or frozen kernels in most recipes calling for fresh corn, reducing cooking times as necessary.

Hominy grits: it is best to follow package directions when cooking grits, as cooking times vary, but as a general guide, place grits in a saucepan with four times their volume of cold water, bring to the boil, then simmer gently, covered, for about an hour, and serve hot with sugar, honey or treacle and cream, or butter, salt and pepper. Cold grits, set solid, can be sliced and fried, then served hot with sugar or a savoury sauce.

Cornmeals: the ways that cornmeal was – and still is – used regionally in America makes evocative reading: ash bread was baked in the ashes of an open fire, johnnycake (journey cake) was for travellers, cracklin' bread was enriched with crisp little pieces of pork rind, Hush puppies – fritters made with cornmeal, onion, egg and buttermilk – are liked by man and beast.

In Northern Italy, *polenta* is made into a thick porridge and served as an accompaniment to meat. When cold this can be sliced and fried. It can also be made into a main course casserole or layered like lasagne. *Mamaliga* is a similar Romanian porridge, served hot or cold with eggs, cheese, soured cream, onions or cabbage.

Tortillas are the staple flat bread of Mexico and they are eaten with every meal. Hot, they are used to scoop up food, or buttered and eaten as bread. Dipped in a thin spicy sauce and quickly fried, then rolled around a savoury filling, these versatile pancakes are called *enchiladas*, and when they are fried, then shaped into a shell and filled with meat, cheese or vegetables, they become *tacos*. Wrapped in the corn husks, the dough is used to make *tamales* (see recipe).

Once cold, tortillas quickly become stale. They are then broken into soups or stews, rather like croûtons, or made into a casserole with cream and cheese.

Cornflour is most often used as a thickening agent and has little, if any, flavour. It is also colourless; unlike flour it turns transparent when cooked. It is widely used in Chinese cookery to thicken sauces in stir-fried dishes. Much lighter than wheat flour, it can be used to make cake flour in the proportion 3 parts plain flour to 1 part cornflour, when a special flour is not available.

Sweetcorn mornay

🍴 35 minutes

Serves 4
50 g /2 oz butter plus 15 ml /1 tbls melted
  butter
1 medium-sized onion, chopped
40 g /1½ oz flour
425 ml /15 fl oz milk
150 ml /5 fl oz sweet cider
75 g /3 oz grated Cheddar cheese
salt and freshly ground black pepper
800 g /1¾ lb canned sweetcorn kernels,
  drained
30 ml /2 tbls freshly chopped parsley
1 canned pimento, drained and cut into
  strips (optional)
50 g /2 oz fresh wholemeal breadcrumbs
25 g /1 oz walnuts, chopped

1 Heat 50 g /2 oz butter in a saucepan and
fry the onion over moderate heat for 5
minutes. Stir in the flour and gradually pour
on the milk, stirring until the sauce thickens. Pour on the cider and stir until well
blended. Simmer for 3 minutes.
2 Heat the grill to moderate. Remove the
pan from the heat, stir in 50 g /2 oz of the
cheese and season with salt and pepper. Stir
the sweetcorn, parsley and pimento, if
using, into the sauce and mix well.
3 Pour into a shallow ovenproof dish. Mix
together the remaining cheese, the breadcrumbs and walnuts and scatter over the
top. Pour over the melted butter.
4 Grill for 10–12 minutes, or until the top
is crisp and brown, then serve at once.

● This can be cooked in the oven at 190C
/375F /gas 5 instead of under the grill.

Fish and corn chowder

🍴 45 minutes

Serves 6
900 g /2 lb white fish fillets, such as cod, coley
  or haddock
100 g /4 oz fat salt pork, rind removed, cut in
  15 mm /½ in cubes
1 large onion, sliced
25 g /1 oz flour
1.1 L /2 pt milk
450 g /1 lb potatoes, thickly sliced
175 g /6 oz fresh corn kernels
salt and freshly ground black pepper
50 g /2 oz butter, in small pieces
15 ml /1 tbls freshly chopped parsley, to
  garnish

1 Skin the fish and cut into pieces about
7.5 × 4 cm /3 × 1½ in.
2 Place the pork cubes in a large pan over
a medium heat and cook until the fat runs
and the meat browns. Remove the cubes of
pork with a slotted spoon and set aside.
3 Add the onion to the pan and cook until
it is soft, then stir in the flour. Gradually

pour on the milk, stirring. Bring to the boil,
add the potatoes, corn kernels, fish and
pork and season well with salt and freshly
ground black pepper.
4 Cover and simmer for 20 minutes, or
until the fish and vegetables are tender.
Check the seasoning and adjust if necessary.
5 Pour the chowder into a heated soup
tureen, dot with the butter, sprinkle on the
parsley and serve at once.

Spicy pork tamales

🍴🍴 1 hour 30 minutes

Serves 4 as a main course
12 corn husks (optional)
For the pancakes
50 g /2 oz hydrogenated vegetable fat or lard
175 g /6 oz masa harina or polenta
5 ml /1 tsp baking powder
5 ml /1 tsp salt
For the filling
175 g /6 oz lean, minced pork
1 small onion, very finely chopped
1 dried red chilli, seeded and finely chopped
1 tomato, blanched, skinned, seeded and
  chopped
10 ml /2 tsp freshly chopped coriander leaves
  or mint
pinch of salt

1 Soak the corn husks in very hot water
for about 10 minutes, to make them supple,
then drain and pat dry with absorbent
paper. Alternatively, use rectangles of foil,
23 × 10 cm /9 × 4 in.
2 To make the pancakes, cream the fat
until it is light and fluffy. Sift together the
masa harina or polenta, baking powder and
salt. Alternately beat small amounts of the
corn mixture and about 300 ml /10 fl oz
water into the fat, until the dough is smooth
but moist.
3 Arrange corn husks or foil on a working
surface and divide the dough between them,
spreading it out in the centre of each to
make a 9 cm /3½ in square.
4 Mix together the filling ingredients to
form a moist but not runny paste. Divide
the filling between the pancakes, spooning it
into the centre. Fold the sides of the husk or
foil into the centre so that the pancake forms
a 'tube' with a centre join. Fold over the top
and bottom of the wrapping, to enclose the
pancakes completely. Tie the parcels with
fine string.
5 Place the parcels on a steaming rack or
in a colander that fits inside a saucepan.
Cover with foil and then with the lid, and
steam over boiling water for 50 minutes.
6 Untie the strings, wrap the tamales in a
cloth to keep them warm and serve at once.

Fish and corn chowder

Tomatoes

The tomato is actually a fruit, but is used as one of our most versatile and popular vegetables. Cooked in soups, stews, sauces or savoury flans, grilled, baked or fried as a vegetable accompaniment, or eaten raw in salads and sandwiches, tomatoes contribute flavour and goodness to every meal.

Discovered in South America by the Spaniards in the 16th century, the tomato was soon taken back to Spain where it flourished in the hot, sunny climate. From there it reached North Africa and Italy, where it was known as *pomo di Mori* (apple of the Moors), and southern France, where the name was adapted to *pomme d'amour* (apple of love). Tomatoes were first grown in Britain in the mid-16th century, when the red and yellow varieties were equally common.

Tomatoes now grow all over the world in both tropical and temperate climates and are available throughout the year. They thrive in the countries around the Mediterranean – France, Italy, Morocco and Israel. They are also grown on a large scale in the Canary Islands, the Caribbean, South Africa and South America, their original home. In the hotter parts of the world tomatoes are grown in the open, but further north, in Britain, Holland, Germany, northern France and parts of the U.S., they are more successfully grown under glass.

Kinds of tomato

Commercially grown tomatoes usually have small to medium-sized round, uniformly red fruit. The really large, irregularly shaped Mediterranean tomatoes – often ridged and streaked with green and pale orange – are well worth buying when they are available. They are very sweet and delicious eaten raw, although their size also makes them ideal for cooking stuffed. Plum tomatoes, so-called because they are oval in shape, like plums, are usually peeled, processed and sold in cans for export. They are particularly useful for making a good thick purée or for winter cooking, when fresh tomatoes are expensive.

Home-grown tomatoes: if you can grow your own tomatoes, either outdoors or under glass, you will have a much more extensive range from which to choose. Dwarf 'cherry tomatoes' are excellent for home-growing; they are especially nice in salads, either left whole or cut into halves. Yellow tomatoes have a sweet flavour and are particularly decorative because of their

bright colour. They should not be confused with unripened green tomatoes. Some seed firms offer packets of mixed, ornamental tomato seeds. These include pear-shaped tomatoes, cherry tomatoes, some of which grow in decorative clusters, rather like grapes, and unusually coloured tomatoes. A packet of these is well worth trying, to add variety to your garden and cooking.

Buying and storing tomatoes

Make sure that the tomatoes are firm and there is no trace of blackness round the stalk. If you want to eat them on the day of purchase, choose really red ones, but if they are to be kept for a few days, it is best to buy them a little under-ripe. Tomatoes tend to lose their flavour if they are kept in the refrigerator, so keep them uncovered in a bowl in a cool, dark place. This way they should stay fresh for up to 4 days.

Tomatoes can be really cheap in late summer. This is the time to make chutneys and sauces, and tomato purée for freezing. The purée can then be added to soups and casseroles when fresh tomatoes are expensive. To make the purée, chop the tomatoes, put them in a large saucepan and simmer very gently, uncovered, until they are reduced to a thick pulp. This will take about 1½ hours. Cool, then rub through a sieve, or work through the fine blade of a vegetable mill, to remove the seeds.

Jellied tomato and prawn ring

**** Pour the purée into cartons and freeze. It will keep for up to 9 months. Small, firm tomatoes can be frozen whole on trays, then packed into containers and kept frozen for up to 6 months. When thawed they are only suitable for sauces and casseroles and other cooked dishes.

Tomato products

Canned tomatoes are endlessly useful in cooking, and very good value. Italian plum tomatoes, which have a rich red colour and thick juice, are popular.

Tomato purée, paste or concentrate are sold in small cans or tubes. They are good standbys to keep in your store cupboard, but use with caution as they are very strong. Mix sparingly with stock to add to soups and casseroles; add to sauces and salad dressings; beat into eggs for an omelette, or add to a savoury scone mixture.

Tomato ketchup, which is rather like a puréed spicy chutney, is very useful for making sweet and sour barbecue sauces, and it will add piquancy to cold meats as well as to fried food and mixed grills.

Tomato juice is a refreshing, low-calorie drink which is available either bottled or canned. Drink it plain or with a pinch of salt, a dash of Worcestershire or Tabasco sauce and a twist of lemon peel. Add a 25 ml /1 fl oz measure of vodka to 75 ml /3 fl oz tomato juice for a Bloody Mary. Tomato juice can also be used in cooking savoury dishes, mixed with stock or added to stews.

Preparing fresh tomatoes

Some recipes require tomatoes to be skinned and seeded: for skinning tomatoes, see picture. If the tomatoes are very ripe, leave them for only half a minute; if firm and slightly under-ripe, for 1 minute. Do not leave the tomatoes in the water too long or they will start to cook and become very soft and pulpy. To remove the seeds, cut the tomatoes in half and carefully scoop out the seeds with a teaspoon. The tomato flesh is then used alone, for a more concentrated flavour, without the juice, which dilutes salad dressings in particular. To recover the juice that surrounds the seeds, put the seeds in a fine sieve and rub them over a bowl. Use this juice to enrich soups and casseroles.

When you need to slice unpeeled tomatoes thinly for a salad, you may find it helpful to use a knife with a serrated edge.

Using tomatoes

Tomatoes are not only delicious but are also very good for you. They contain significant amounts of vitamins A and C, so they make a healthy contribution to your family's diet.

Cooked tomatoes are a very popular vegetable accompaniment to many dishes – fried breakfast bacon, grilled meat, poached or baked fish. Skinned tomatoes can be sautéed whole in butter with chopped fresh herbs in a covered saucepan. They can also be fried, baked whole or halved in a buttered dish, or halved and grilled. When baking or grilling halved tomatoes, dot each half with butter and sprinkle with herbs, or put half an olive or a cross of anchovy fillets on top. They can also be grilled on a skewer as part of a kebab. Large tomatoes can be baked with a savoury meat or rice stuffing and a crispy breadcrumb topping. Cooked tomatoes make creamy or chunky soups; added to casseroled dishes, they will form a thick, rich sauce that can be simply flavoured with herbs and onions or highly spiced with paprika and cayenne pepper. Tomatoes are delicious cooked with eggs and cheese in savoury quiches, and mixed with mushrooms make an excellent filling for omelettes. Use tomatoes to add colour and flavour to pizzas and cheese dishes, and to make a variety of sauces to eat with pasta and baked dishes; green tomatoes make wonderful chutney. You will also find that tomatoes combine well with other cooked vegetables, particularly with courgettes and aubergines in ratatouille and with peppers in pipérade.

Raw tomatoes: by themselves, mixed with other vegetables or combined with ingredients such as eggs, cheese or chicken, tomatoes make delicious and refreshing

Preparing tomatoes

To remove the skins, place the tomatoes in a bowl and cover with boiling water. Leave ½–1 minute. Drain and peel off the skins.

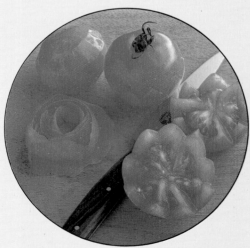

For tomato water lilies, cut round the middle of the fruit in a zig-zag pattern with a small, sharp knife. For tomato roses, thinly pare away the peel in a spiral, and coil it round your finger.

salads. In France they are sliced thinly and served very simply with a herb-flavoured vinaigrette dressing, often as a first course. The Italians combine sliced tomatoes with Mozzarella cheese and chopped fresh basil, sprinkled with olive oil and plenty of freshly ground black pepper. As with all salads, tomatoes should be dressed only just before serving so that they stay sweet and firm. Tomatoes are blended with cucumbers, sweet peppers, herbs and spices in gazpacho, the uncooked Spanish soup that is served ice-cold. Raw tomatoes can be stuffed with a cream cheese mixture and served as a first course. The Spaniards like to rub a cut tomato over a slice of fresh bread, so that it absorbs the juice; then the bread is rubbed with garlic and sprinkled with olive oil and eaten as a snack.

Tomatoes as a garnish: use tomato slices, quarters or wedges for quick and easy garnishes; halve them by cutting round their middles in a zig-zag pattern with a small, sharp knife, or make roses with tomato peel (see picture).

Unblended tomato soup

This is a tasty and inexpensive soup. The canned tomatoes lose any slightly 'tinny' flavour during the cooking.

 35 minutes

Serves 4
800 g /1lb 12 oz canned tomatoes
425 ml /15 fl oz stock
25 g /1 oz butter
1 large onion, finely chopped
60 ml /4 tbls chopped mixed fresh herbs
salt and freshly ground black pepper
60 ml /4 tbls soured cream or natural yoghurt

1 Drain the tomatoes and add the juice to the stock, to make 600 ml /1 pt liquid.
2 Melt the butter in a saucepan over a low heat, stir in the onion and cook until it is soft. Add the tomatoes and herbs, cover and cook for 10 minutes.
3 Mash the tomatoes to a purée, using a potato masher, then pour in the stock. Season well with salt and freshly ground black pepper.
4 Bring the contents of the pan to the boil, cover and simmer for 15 minutes. Remove the pan from the heat.
5 Pour the soup into 4 individual soup bowls and swirl 15 ml /1 tbls soured cream or yoghurt on top of each serving.

● For a special touch, stir in 75 ml /3 fl oz dry sherry or Marsala after the pan is removed from the heat.
● For tomato and leek soup, use 2 medium-sized leeks instead of the onion.
● For tomato and lentil soup, stir in 100 g /4 oz split red lentils (no need to soak them first) when you add the tomatoes to the pan. Pour in the stock immediately, add a bay leaf and simmer for 45 minutes or until the lentils have softened and disintegrated.

Tomato, celery and red pepper relish

This is a tasty and colourful accompaniment to egg and cheese dishes, savoury quiches and hamburgers.

🕒 30 minutes

Makes 350 g /12 oz
250 g /9 oz tomatoes
2 stalks celery, finely chopped
1 medium-sized onion, finely chopped
30 ml /2 tbls olive oil
1 garlic clove, finely chopped
5 ml /1 tsp celery seed
1 sweet red pepper, cored, seeded and finely chopped
45 ml /3 tbls white wine vinegar

1 Scald, skin, seed and finely chop the tomatoes.
2 Heat the oil in a saucepan over a low heat. Stir in the celery, onion, garlic and celery seed, reduce the heat to very low and cook until the onion is transparent.
3 Mix in the tomatoes and red pepper. Add the vinegar and bring the mixture to the boil.
4 Remove the pan from the heat and transfer the relish to a bowl. Allow to become completely cold before serving.

● This relish is not a preserve, but will keep for 3–4 days covered in the refrigerator.

Cheese and tomato tart

🕒🕒 1¼ hours

Serves 6
shortcrust pastry made with 175 g /6 oz flour
350 g /12 oz firm tomatoes
30 ml /2 tbls chopped fresh herbs, including basil if available
6 spring onions, finely chopped
250 g /9 oz curd cheese
4 medium-sized eggs, beaten
125 g /4 oz Cheddar cheese, grated

1 Heat the oven to 200C /400F /gas 6.
2 Line a 20 cm /8 in flan tin with the pastry, then with foil and beans, and bake blind for 10 minutes. Remove the foil and beans and bake for 8 minutes more.
3 Slice the tomatoes thinly and lay the slices in the bottom of the flan case. Scatter over the herbs and spring onions.
4 Put the curd cheese into a bowl and gradually beat in the eggs. Continue to beat until the mixture is smooth. Spoon the curd mixture in an even layer over the tomatoes and cover the top with the grated Cheddar cheese.
5 Bake the tart for 40 minutes, until the filling is set and the top is golden brown. Serve either hot or cold.

Tomato butter

Savoury tomato butters are good for sandwich fillings and as a base for open sandwiches. They melt deliciously into plainly grilled meat or fish. It is best to use unsalted butter and add a variety of extra flavourings to suit particular dishes.

🕒 20 minutes plus 45 minutes chilling

Makes 60 g /2½ oz
50 g /2 oz unsalted butter
pinch of cayenne pepper
10 ml /2 tsp tomato purée
15 ml /1 tbls chopped fresh parsley, basil, thyme or marjoram

1 Put the butter into a bowl and beat until soft, using a wooden spoon.
2 Beat in the cayenne pepper and the tomato purée, 5 ml /1 tsp at a time. Then beat in the chopped herbs.
3 Put the butter on a piece of greaseproof paper and form it into a roll. Roll it in the paper, then chill it for 45 minutes.
4 Cut the chilled butter into pats. The edges of the pats can be trimmed with a small fluted biscuit cutter to give a decorative effect.

● For tomato and lemon butter, which is especially good with veal, add to the tomato butter the finely grated rind of ½ lemon, then beat in 10 ml /2 tsp lemon juice, a few drops at a time.
● For a spicy butter that goes well with lamb, beat into the tomato butter 10 ml /2 tsp Worcestershire sauce drop by drop.
● For tomato and olive butter to top grilled steak, chop 2 stoned black olives very finely and add them to the tomato butter. Use thyme as the herb in the butter.
● For tomato and anchovy butter to serve with fish, use black pepper instead of cayenne and work into the tomato butter 4 anchovy fillets that have been soaked in milk for 15 minutes and then pounded to a paste. Use thyme as the herb in the butter.

Cheese and tomato tart with a bowl of Tomato, celery and red pepper relish

Jellied tomato and prawn ring

This rich red tomato jelly mould (shown on *page 177*) makes a refreshing and attractive starter or light summer lunch dish.

🔪🔪 1 hour plus 1 hour chilling

Serves 8 as a first course, 4 as a main course
750 g /1½ lb ripe tomatoes
juice of ½ lemon
1 medium-sized onion, finely chopped
1 garlic clove, finely chopped
10 ml /2 tsp paprika pepper
pinch of cayenne pepper
4 basil leaves or 5 ml /1 tsp dried basil
200 ml /7 fl oz dry white wine
25 g /1 oz powdered gelatine
oil for greasing
350 g /12 oz peeled cooked prawns
45 ml /3 tbls chopped parsley
For the tomato salad
3 large, firm tomatoes
30 ml /2 tbls olive oil
15 ml /1 tbls lemon juice
10 ml /2 tsp tomato purée
2.5 ml /½ tsp paprika pepper
2 drops Tabasco
sprigs of watercress, to garnish

1   Chop the tomatoes and put them into a saucepan with the lemon juice, onion, garlic, paprika and cayenne pepper, basil and all but 60 ml /4 tbls of the wine. Cover and cook very gently on a low heat for 20 minutes, until the tomatoes are reduced to a purée. Meanwhile soak the gelatine in the rest of the wine.
2   Rub the tomato mixture through a sieve. Return the purée to the rinsed pan, set it on a low heat and stir in the soaked gelatine; continue to stir until it has dissolved.
3   Remove the pan from the heat. Lightly oil a 22 cm /9 in ring mould, then pour in enough of the tomato mixture to come ·15 mm /½ in deep. Put it into the refrigerator for about 15 minutes to set firm.
4   Scatter half the parsley over the set tomato jelly. Cover with the prawns in an even layer and scatter over the rest of the parsley. Pour in the remaining tomato jelly and put the ring into the refrigerator for at least 1 hour, to set.
5   To make the salad, chop the tomatoes fairly coarsely and put them in a bowl. Beat together the oil, lemon juice, tomato purée, paprika pepper and Tabasco, and fold them into the tomatoes.
6   Wring out a tea towel in hot water and hold it around the mould for a few seconds. Place a large flat serving plate upside down on top of the mould and invert the mould and plate. Holding the mould and plate firmly with both hands, give one or two firm shakes to release the jelly from the mould. Fill the centre with the tomato salad and garnish with sprigs of watercress. Serve immediately.

Tomato and tequila cocktail

Cod and tomatoes with aïoli

🔪🔪 1 hour marinating, then 45 minutes cooking

Serves 4
750 g–1 kg /1½–2 lb cod fillets
freshly ground black pepper
juice of 1 lemon
40 g /1½ oz seasoned flour
600 g /1¼ lb firm tomatoes
60 ml /4 tbls oil
1 large onion, quartered and thinly sliced
15 ml /1 tbls chopped fresh basil or chervil, or 30 ml /2 tbls chopped parsley
For the aïoli (garlic mayonnaise)
2 garlic cloves, crushed with 2.5 ml /½ tsp salt
2 medium-sized egg yolks
200 ml /7 fl oz olive oil
juice of ½ lemon

1   Skin the cod and cut it into 2.5 × 5 cm /1 × 2 in pieces. Put them on a flat plate and sprinkle with pepper and lemon juice. Leave them for 1 hour at room temperature.
2   To make the aïoli, put the crushed garlic in a bowl and work in the egg yolks with a wooden spoon, beating very thoroughly. Add 30 ml /2 tbls of the oil, drop by drop, beating all the time.
3   Beat in 10 ml /2 tsp of the lemon juice, then beat in the rest of the oil, adding it in a steady stream. When all the oil has been added, season to taste with any remaining lemon juice, if necessary.

4   Coat the pieces of cod in the seasoned flour. Skin and coarsely chop the tomatoes.
5   Heat the oil in a large frying-pan over a moderate heat. Put in the pieces of cod and brown them for about 1½ minutes on each side. Remove them from the pan with a slotted spoon and reduce the heat.
6   Cook the onion in the remaining oil in the pan until it is soft. Mix in the tomatoes and basil and cook for 1 minute.
7   Put the pieces of cod on top and cook very gently, uncovered, for 4 minutes.
8   Serve the cod with the tomatoes and onions spooned over it. The aïoli may be spread over the top or served separately.

Tomato and tequila cocktail

🔪 10 minutes

Serves 4
600 ml /22 fl oz canned tomato juice
juice of 2 large oranges
100 ml /3½ fl oz tequila
2.5 ml /½ tsp Tabasco
crushed ice
orange rings, to garnish

1   Pour the tomato juice into a large jug and stir in the orange juice, tequila and Tabasco. Stir very well to blend thoroughly.
2   Put enough crushed ice in 4 tall glasses to come quarter way up each glass. Pour in the cocktail, garnish and serve immediately.

Fresh beans

Fresh beans are among the most delicately flavoured and delicious of vegetables. In France and Italy they are considered a great delicacy and are often served as a separate course – either before or after the main course. Cooked until just tender and tossed in melted butter they make a superb accompaniment to meat or fish; cold they are excellent in salads.

Types of beans

French beans are also known as green beans, haricots verts and string beans – even though most are stringless. The most common varieties have slender green pods, round in section, which taper to a small tail. Dwarf beans and Bobbi beans are similar but are thicker.

Fresh white haricot beans are a variety of French bean cultivated mainly for the beans inside the pod which are dried. But they can also be cooked and eaten fresh.

Runner beans have large, flat bottle-green pods and are more popular in England than elsewhere, as they are undeniably coarse.

Lima beans also called Madagascar or butter beans are normally only found fresh in the tropical areas where they grow, but they may be sold frozen. They are also available dried or canned. Fresh lima beans are shelled and simmered like broad beans.

Broad beans have formed part of man's diet since very early times. Fortunately, modern varieties are a vast improvement on the tough earlier bean. With their slightly sharp flavour they are very nutritious, being rich in protein, vitamins and carbohydrates.

Salade niçoise

Buying and storing beans

Look for unblemished pods – French or runner beans that are withered, blackening or bulging are past their best. French beans should be pencil slim: big old beans are really only good for purée. When really fresh, both French beans and runner bean pods should be springy and break crisply in two. Try to buy French beans of the same size and thickness as these will cook evenly. Allow 500 g /1 lb of French or runner beans to serve 3–4 people as a vegetable accompaniment.

There is no way of telling the exact yield after shelling, but as a rough guide buy 1 kg /2 lb (unshelled weight) broad beans to serve 4 people as a vegetable accompaniment.

Store beans in the crisper drawer of the refrigerator: they are best used when fresh, so do not keep them more than 2–3 days.

✳✳✳ Freeze young beans only. Top and tail French beans and string and slice runner beans. Blanch for 1–2 minutes (depending on size) and refresh. Cool, dry and open freeze them, then bag when solid. Pod broad beans, blanch and freeze.

Preparing beans

French beans: rinse them in cold water and drain well. Most varieties are stringless, but if not, string them using the method de-

scribed under runner beans. Top and tail young beans and cook them whole. Larger, older beans need more severe pruning to remove the tough ends. Slice them in half or into thirds for cooking.

Runner beans: rinse, drain and string. When the beans are young the strings can be easily pulled away as you trim the ends; mature beans are best thinly pared all round. Slice them into 25 mm /1 in lengths.

Broad beans: to shell the beans split open the pod by pressing down on the curved edge with your thumb, then run your thumbnail down the edge to open the pod and gently pull out the beans. (Save the best pods for flavouring; include two or three with the beans or use for stocks.)

Once the beans are larger than a big pea, their papery skins are too coarse for eating and must be removed. Skin the beans raw or when cool enough to handle after cooking, depending on the recipe. Slit the skin along the bean's indented edge with your thumbnail, then squeeze out the green kernel.

Cooking French beans

Drop the beans into plenty of boiling lightly salted water and simmer, uncovered (to preserve their colour) for 5 minutes until tender but crisp. Really tiny beans will be cooked by little more than bringing them to the boil. Alternatively steam the beans for 10–12 minutes. Do not overcook as this spoils their fresh flavour and colour. Drain the beans the minute they are done, (save the cooking liquid for stock). If you are serving the beans immediately, toss them briefly over a low heat to dry them off.

Toss the cooked beans with small lumps of butter or parsley butter over moderate heat until heated through, and serve. Or sauté chopped onion and garlic first in the

butter and add a dash of vinegar and the beans; serve with sautéed liver or kidneys.

For a richer dish to accompany plain grills or roasts, stir thick cream with hot beans and season with freshly grated nutmeg. Or soften wedges of skinned and seeded tomato in olive oil or butter, add the beans and stew gently for a minute or two; season and serve with steaks, chops, meat balls and omelettes.

Large mature beans make a fresh-tasting, emerald green purée. Stew the cooked beans briefly in a little butter then, if the purée is very watery, stir it over a moderately high heat, until reduced and slightly thickened. To give it body, blend it with half its volume of puréed rice or potato. Enrich with thick cream or butter and serve piping hot with boiled bacon or gammon.

Frozen beans are an excellent standby; ready-prepared they are quicker to cook than fresh beans, so adjust cooking times.

If you are cooking French beans to serve cold (or cooking them ahead), refresh the beans in cold water immediately after draining. If you leave them to cool slowly, they turn an unappetizing grey and lose their crispness. Reheat just before serving in any of the ways given. For salads, pat the beans dry, toss in dressing and leave to absorb the flavour for 1–2 hours. Alternately, fold in some thick mayonnaise and serve with crudités or a flat omelette.

Cooking runner beans

Cook in plenty of boiling slightly salted water for 5–15 minutes, depending on size and age, until just tender. Drain and dry off as for French beans, and toss in butter. Because they are fairly robust, runner beans can also be stewed or braised. For a change, you could mix them with an equal quantity of cooked, buttered carrots, or finish in any of the ways suggested for French beans.

Cooking haricot beans

In Italy and France the very young, tender pods are treated in much the same way as French beans. Once the small white seeds have formed – but before they have matured – the pods are discarded and the beans are simmered in well-flavoured stock for 30–40 minutes until tender. After cooking, fresh haricots may be finished in cream sauce or generously topped with sautéed onion rings and freshly chopped parsley. Include haricots in soups or puréed and enriched with olive oil, pork or bacon fat. Dress cold beans in a well seasoned olive oil vinaigrette, and garnish lavishly with fresh herbs for a first course or salad.

Cooking broad beans

Broad beans can be eaten during three stages of growth. When very young and tiny – no more than 5–7.5 cm /2–3 in long – the baby beans are tender enough to be eaten raw. In France they are served as a first course, either with other crudités and a garlic-flavoured mayonnaise or shelled at table and seasoned with sea salt. When not so young, they may be cooked and eaten whole with butter. Older beans must be skinned (see preparation) but the cooking methods will be the same.

Yoghurt broad beans

To cook, simmer the beans uncovered in boiling, salted water for 8–10 minutes: do not overcook. Alternatively pour in just enough water to cover the beans, adding salt and a lump of butter. Simmer, covered, until just tender and most of the liquid has been absorbed. Season and add a few drops of lemon juice. Serve with pork, ham or gammon. Simmered beans can be reheated in butter, thick cream or white sauce.

For salad, cook the beans and turn the cooked warm beans in a lemon, garlic or mustard flavoured dressing or in soured cream or well-seasoned yoghurt sharpened with lemon juice. For a richer result mix the yoghurt with an equal quantity of thick mayonnaise.

When the pods are fully grown and mottled with black, the beans inside tend to be mealy and are best puréed through a mouli legumes, or blended and then sieved. Enriched with butter or a few spoonfuls of thick cream, it makes one of the best accompaniments to boiled bacon. Use it to fill baked tartlet cases, crispy croustades, omelettes or pancakes. For a light supper dish serve it piping hot and topped with a poached egg and garnished with crisply fried bacon or onion rings. Thinned down with stock or cream it becomes a delicious, nourishing soup. Serve sprinkled with freshly chopped herbs.

Savory is the classic flavouring for broad beans; add a few fresh sprigs or a pinch of the dried herb to the cooking liquid, but remember it is very pungent and should be used sparingly. Parsley, chervil and sage are all good alternatives. It is always worth adding a few drops of fresh lemon juice to bring out the tangy flavour of the beans.

Yoghurt broad beans

20 minutes, plus 20–30 minutes chilling time

Serves 4
10 cm /4 in piece of cucumber, quartered and seeded
salt and freshly ground black pepper
500 g /1 lb shelled broad beans
30 ml /2 tbls sunflower oil
10 ml /2 tsp lemon juice
50 g /2 oz curd cheese
150 ml /5 fl oz natural yoghurt
30 ml /2 tbls mayonnaise
15–30 /1–2 tbls freshly chopped chives
paper thin onion rings, to garnish (optional)

1 Chop the cucumber into small dice; place in a sieve, sprinkling salt between each layer. Set aside to drain.
2 Skin the beans as necessary, then cook briefly in boiling, lightly salted water until just tender. Meanwhile, combine the oil and lemon juice in a mixing bowl with salt and pepper to taste and whisk well with a fork.
3 Drain the cooked beans, add to the bowl and turn well in the dressing. Set aside.
4 With a wooden spoon beat together the curd cheese and 15 ml /1 tbls of yoghurt until smoothly blended. Beat in the remaining yoghurt, followed by the mayonnaise. Stir in the chives.
5 Rinse the cucumber in cold water, drain and pat dry with absorbent paper. Stir the cucumber into the yoghurt dressing, then pour the dressing over the beans. Stir gently, but thoroughly, and season.
6 Turn the salad into a serving dish, cover and chill in the refrigerator for 20–30 minutes. Garnish with onion rings.

Salade niçoise

A flavoursome main course salad which makes the most of summer vegetables, the ingredients of salade niçoise can be varied to taste: broad beans or peas may replace the potatoes and a little thinly sliced red sweet pepper is sometimes included. Serve it with hot garlic bread.

🍴🍴 1–1½ hours preparation

Serves 4
For the dressing
105 ml /7 tbls olive oil
23 ml /1½ tbls tarragon vinegar
1.5 ml /¼ tsp Dijon mustard
1 large garlic clove, peeled and sliced lengthways in half
salt and freshly ground black pepper
For the salad
225 g /8 oz baby new potatoes, scrubbed
225 g /8 oz French beans, trimmed
200 g /7 oz canned tuna fish, drained and flaked
1 large, crisp lettuce heart, washed and dried
3 medium-sized hard-boiled eggs, shelled
3 medium-sized tomatoes
8 canned anchovy fillets, drained
50–100 g /2–4 oz black olives, stoned
30 ml /2 tbls freshly chopped mixed herbs

1 Put the oil, vinegar, mustard and garlic in a jar with a screw-top lid. Add salt and pepper to taste. Replace the lid tightly and shake vigorously to emulsify the ingredients.
2 Cook the potatoes in boiling, lightly salted water until tender, drain and leave until cool enough to handle. At the same time cook the beans in plenty of boiling, lightly salted water until just tender; drain and refresh in cold water to stop the cooking process, then pat dry.
3 Slice the beans into 5–7.5 cm /2–3 in lengths and place in a medium-sized mixing bowl. Slip the potatoes out of their skins and cut into chunks. Add the potatoes and tuna to the beans and stir lightly to mix.
4 Shake the dressing vigorously once more, then remove and discard the garlic. Pour a generous third of the dressing over the bean and potato mixture and stir gently but thoroughly. Set the bowl aside until the vegetables are quite cold.
5 Tear the larger lettuce leaves into two or three pieces and place the lettuce in a large, fairly shallow salad bowl. Pour over half the remaining dressing and toss the leaves until evenly coated.
6 Spread the tossed lettuce over the base and sides of the bowl, then pile the bean and potato mixture in the centre. Split the anchovy fillets lengthways in half and arrange lattice fashion over the beans and potato mixture.
7 Slice the eggs and tomatoes into quarters and arrange in a ring around the bean and potato mixture. Scatter over the olives. Sprinkle enough of the remaining dressing over the eggs and tomatoes to moisten them; drizzle the rest over the surface of the salad. Scatter over the herbs and serve.

Provençal vegetable soup

🍴🍴 1 hour

Serves 4–6
salt
bouquet garni
1 large potato, peeled and diced
1 large onion, peeled and chopped
1 celery stalk, scrubbed and finely sliced
2 carrots, scraped and sliced
225 g /8 oz French beans
225 g /8 oz runner beans
2 courgettes, topped and tailed but unpeeled
100 g /4 oz pasta shells or macaroni
For the pistou sauce
3–4 large garlic cloves, peeled
60 ml /4 tbls freshly chopped sweet basil leaves
50 g /2 oz freshly grated Parmesan cheese
2 medium-sized tomatoes, skinned, seeded and coarsely chopped
60 ml /4 tbls olive oil

1 Bring 1.7 L /3 pt water with 5 ml /1 tsp salt to the boil in a large flameproof casserole. Add the bouquet garni, potato, onion, celery and carrots. Bring back to the boil, then cover the pan, and simmer for about 10 minutes or until the vegetables are tender.
2 Top and tail the beans and remove any fibrous strings. Slice the French beans in half, slice the runner beans into 15 mm /½ in lengths, and slice the courgettes fairly thickly. Add the beans, courgettes and pasta to the casserole and simmer, uncovered, for 10–15 minutes until tender.
3 While the soup is cooking, prepare the pistou. Pound the garlic and basil, with salt and pepper to taste, to a paste using a mortar and pestle. Gradually work in the cheese, alternating with the tomatoes. Then slowly work in the olive oil, a few drops at a time to start with, to make a thick sauce.
4 Remove and discard the bouquet garni from the soup. Blend 60 ml /4 tbls of the hot soup into the sauce, then stir the mixture into the soup. Check the seasoning.

Provençal vegetable soup

Broad beans with bacon and cream

♦ 30 minutes

Serves 4
500 g /1 lb shelled broad beans, skinned if
* necessary*
100 g /4 oz unsmoked lean bacon slices,
* with rind*
15 g /1½ oz butter
salt and freshly ground black pepper
3 medium-sized egg yolks, lightly beaten
175 ml /6 fl oz thick cream
a good squeeze of lemon juice
freshly chopped savory or failing that, parsley
* or chervil, to garnish*

1 Slice the bacon into thin strips. In a
flameproof casserole over a low heat cook
the bacon strips in the butter for 2–3
minutes without allowing them to become
crisp.
2 Stir in the beans, then pour in about 100
ml /3½ fl oz water to barely cover them.
Season carefully, bearing in mind the saltiness of the bacon.
3 Bring the water to the boil, cover pan
tightly and simmer until the beans are just

tender and most of the liquid has been
absorbed. Shake the pan occasionally during cooking to prevent the beans sticking. If
more than a few spoonfuls of liquid remains
by the time the beans are cooked, reduce it
by boiling rapidly, uncovered.
4 Remove the casserole from the heat and
set aside to cool slightly. Meanwhile, blend
together the egg yolks, cream and 2–3
grindings of black pepper.
5 Pour the egg and cream liaison on to the
beans, stirring constantly with a wooden
spoon. Return the casserole to a very low
heat and cook, stirring constantly, for 5–7
minutes until the sauce has thickened slightly. Do not allow it to come near the boil or
the eggs will scramble.
6 Remove the casserole from the heat, stir
in the lemon juice and correct the seasoning.
Sprinkle over the herbs and serve immediately, straight from the dish.

Runner beans
à la grecque

**This is an excellent way of cooking runner
beans, rendering them crisp yet succulent. The dish can be prepared up to 2
days ahead.**

♦♦ 1 hour plus 40 minutes cooling
   and 10–15 minutes chilling

Serves 4
1 small onion, peeled and finely chopped
60 ml /4 tbls olive oil
60 ml /4 tbls dry white wine or lemon juice
6 parsley sprigs
1 celery stalk
1 bay leaf
1.5 ml /¼ tsp dried thyme
6 black peppers, lightly crushed
6 coriander seeds, lightly crushed
1.5 ml /¼ tsp salt
450 g/1 lb runner beans topped, tailed and
* strings removed*
30 ml /2 tbls freshly chopped mixed herbs

1 Place all the ingredients except the
beans and fresh herbs in a medium-sized
saucepan with 400 ml /14 fl oz water. Bring
to the boil, then cover and simmer for 15
minutes. Slice the beans into 25 mm /1 in
lengths.
2 Add the beans to the pan and stir well.
Bring back to the boil, then cover and
simmer for 5–10 minutes, until tender. Do
not overcook.
3 Using a slotted spoon, transfer the beans
and onions to a dish and cover them.
4 Boil the cooking liquid very briskly for
about 15 minutes or until reduced to about
150 ml /5 fl oz, then strain over the beans.
Leave to cool. Serve the dish tepid or
slightly chilled, garnished with the freshly
chopped herbs, accompanied by wholemeal
rolls as an hors d'oeuvre.

Runner beans à la grecque

Mushrooms

Mushrooms have always been considered a delicacy and a classic garnish to many dishes. Besides making soups and hors d'oeuvres, grills and fritters, mushrooms lend flavour to any dish, classic or homely, to which they are added. Other fungi are also highly prized, including the most rare and expensive of all flavourings – truffles, best known in French cuisine.

Mushrooms are the edible fruiting bodies of a group of leafless, flowerless plants called fungi. According to most folklore, mushrooms were thought to be the results of thunder or lightning bolts striking the ground. The Romans, however, called them the 'food of the gods' for their delicious flavour, which enhances any dish to which they are added.

Wild mushrooms are collected and eaten in Europe, and in Eastern Europe they are preferred to the cultivated variety. In English-speaking countries there is a tendency – unfounded – to regard all except the field mushroom (*Agaricus campestris*) as inedible.

Cultivated mushrooms

The main mushroom cultivated in the West (*A. bisporus*) is closely related to the field mushroom and also to the horse mushroom (*A. arvensis*). A white-capped cultivated mushroom (*A. hortensis*) is popular throughout English-speaking countries; a brown-capped variety is sold in France and on the West coast of the USA.

Mushrooms are graded commercially according to their stage of development. Button mushrooms are small with the thick membrane still covering the gills. These are used for salads, pickling, garnishing and for soups and sauces that need to remain white. At the cup stage the membrane has broken to reveal the gills. Mushrooms at this stage are useful for fritters and vegetable garnishes and for general flavouring in pies, casseroles and soups. You can also stuff them or serve them whole as an hors d'oeuvre or vegetable accompaniment. Flat mushrooms with the gills fully revealed tend to be large. Excellent for grilling, for example for breakfast, they will add dark juice to any dish to which they are added. Mushroom stalks, useful for flavouring, are also sold separately.

Other commercially available mushrooms

Boletus: dried mushrooms are available from several countries. From France they are called ceps (see Wild mushrooms), from Italy *funghi porcini* (little pigs).

Shiitake (*Lentinus edodes*), cultivated in China and Japan, is a brown mushroom with blackish square scales. It is exported and is sold in Chinese supermarkets as 'dried mushrooms'. It can also be grown at home in temperate climates: a few seedsmen and garden centres supply a small ornamental log impregnated with the spawn which will produce a good crop.

Paddy straw mushrooms (*Volvariella volvacea*) are grown on rice straw in the East and are exported canned.

Wood ears ((*Auricularia polytricha*), a gelatinous black tree fungus from China, are exported dried.

Truffles (*Tuber aestivum*), grow underground on tree roots, oak or beech, and are only discovered through their scent. Truffle-hunters use dogs and pigs to sniff them out. Although there are truffles in Britain, the best are found in France and Italy. Best known is the black Périgord truffle (*Tuber melanosporum*) which looks like a small brown potato and the Piedmont white truffle (*Tuber magnatum*). The truffle is the most expensive food in the Western world: a single specimen can cost more than dinner for two in a smart restaurant. Truffles are sold fresh in midwinter in the producing areas, but elsewhere can be bought in minute cans. The black truffle is cooked, the white one usually eaten raw.

The smell of truffle is very pervasive and a few truffle parings will flavour a large quantity of food. Always use the can juices and keep any unused truffle, covered in sherry or its own juice and tightly covered with cling film.

The black specks of truffle can be seen in truffle pâté or the shapes (usually cut into diamonds) decorating expensive restaurant dishes. Use slivers of black olive or minaret mushrooms (see picture) at home as a substitute for truffles when these are specified in the recipe for decoration.

Steak chasseur

Recognizing and using wild mushrooms

Mushroom picking is a much stronger tradition in Europe, for example Poland and Russia in the north and Italy in the south, than it is in English-speaking countries. Sadly the most famous wild mushrooms like ceps, morels, and chanterelles are usually now only on the menu in France unless you pick them yourself. In temperate climates they are more widely available than you might imagine, but their delicate structures and fresh scent deteriorate so quickly that the retail trade no longer handle them.

If you want to pick wild mushrooms always take with you a reliable field guide, full of clear photographs or drawings. Do not eat any wild mushrooms which are rotten, dried-up or wormy. For this reason avoid going mushrooming during or after rain, as a rotten specimen might become waterlogged, swell and look healthy. Also, mushrooms picked in the rain will not dry well. Wild mushrooms may have to be washed to remove insects, and also peeled.

Cep (*Boletus edulis*) is widely eaten in the whole of Europe. It is bun-like with a brown cap from 2.5–25 cm /1–10 in across and yellow flesh; instead of gills it has narrow tubes on the underside of the cap, which looks like a sponge. They grow in clearings in woods (especially beech) in summer and early autumn. These are the favourite mushroom of fine cooking. Fry them in olive oil or use them in any mushroom recipe. They are also sold dried and make an excellent addition to a variety of casseroles and soups.

Fairy ring champignon (*Marasmius oreades*) is one of the most common British wild mushrooms. Lighter brown on top, darker underneath on a slender stem, the centre of the cap rises to a peak. While it is well known for the ruin of many a lawn, its culinary advantages have largely been overlooked. It is very easy to preserve in dried form and is excellent for soups and as an omelette filling.

Puffball (*Lycoperdon* spp) grows in light woodlands and pastures, and can grow so big you cannot put your arms around it. Pick pure white young puffballs, with a smooth white skin, or with a soft mosaic pattern. Slice and coat them in egg and breadcrumbs, then sauté in butter or deep fry in oil.

Blewitts (*Lepiota* spp) have distinctive pale or deep violet-coloured gills and stems. They mainly grow in autumn, under trees or in open grassland and have a pleasant smell. They are particularly good for frying.

Parasol mushroom (*Lepiota procera*) and its close relative shaggy parasol (*Lepiota rhacodes*) are easily recognizable. Both are very large, about 12 cm /5 in across when mature, with a scaly umbrella-like cap, rising to a peak in the middle, and a scaly stem. They grow on grassy banks or in sandy soil near the sea. Good for stuffing and frying.

Chanterelle (*Cantharellus cibarius*), *girolle* in France, is a brilliant yellow-orange colour, which shows up against moss in damp woods (chiefly deciduous) where it grows. It has a firm flesh, shaped like a trumpet with delicate ribs running underneath and smells fruity. It needs to be cooked a little longer than most mushrooms, and has a strong flavour. It is splendid in egg dishes.

Morel (*Morchella esculenta*), *morille* in French, these are also called sponge mushrooms because they are brown and pitted all over like a honeycomb with regular ridges between. Morels are usually split and washed well, in case the cavities contain insects. Morels grow in the spring, unlike the majority of fungi which appear from mid-summer onwards, and can be found on the ground until the first frosts come. You will make best use of them by mixing them into rich cream sauces or serving them in poultry dishes.

Cep

Fairy ring champignon

Puffballs

Shaggy parasol mushroom

Chanterelles

Morels

Oyster mushroom (*Pleurotus ostreatus*), popular in Europe and the East, is a fungus which grows on rotting beech or ash trees. Its shape is like the shellfish, its colour varies with age, blue-grey when young, changing to light or dark brown as it matures. It has white gills underneath.

Drying wild mushrooms

Many wild mushrooms dry well if in good condition, though do not try to dry cultivated mushrooms, oyster or parasol mushrooms. Select really good specimens and trim off any damaged parts. Ceps and related species should be sliced before drying. Chanterelles, fairy ring champignons and morels can be dried whole.

Lay the mushrooms out on a tray or on absorbent paper in a warm dry place – on a rack above an oil-fired stove is ideal – for about 12 hours to remove excess moisture. Thread them on to strings, separate them and hang them horizontally in a warm room, over a radiator or night storage heater, or leave them for several days in an airing cupboard, or an unlit gas oven, with a pilot light. Aim to dry the mushrooms as quickly as possible, so that the maximum flavour is retained. Make sure they are thoroughly dry before storing them in airtight boxes, wrapped in plastic film.

Wood blewitts

Oyster mushrooms

Buying and storing cultivated mushrooms

It is important to use fresh firm mushrooms. Mushrooms should be bought as soon after picking as possible. Avoid those that are wrinkled or brownish, or with blackened or damaged gills. Choose the grade to suit the recipe you are using.

If they are bought fresh, mushrooms can be kept for at least a week before using, although they should, ideally, be used within 3 days of purchase. Leave them in the punnet or paper bag in which they were bought, and store on the lower shelf of the refrigerator or in a cool place.

There are many ways of preserving mushrooms: chutney, ketchup (see recipe), pickle or as a flavouring paste (see recipe).

✱✱✱ Freeze mushrooms whole. Open freeze on a tray, then transfer to a rigid container. These are not suitable for salads, but can be tossed in butter or grilled from frozen as a garnish. Mushrooms will take up less space if they are sautéed first and then packed in small bags. The mushrooms can then be added, unthawed, to soups, stews, etc.

Preparing mushrooms

It is usually unnecessary to peel cultivated mushrooms or to discard the stalks. Wipe dark spore dust from the caps with a damp cloth or a paper. Trim earthy stalk ends or remove them, according to the recipe.

Preparation: button mushrooms are left whole or quartered, according to size. Caps are usually sliced across; the T-shape of the stalk in the cap makes an attractive decorative garnish. Alternatively the stalks may be gently detached and used for another dish and the caps sliced neatly. Mushrooms may also be coarsely chopped, according to the recipe. Use a stainless steel knife to prevent discoloration. The stalks are removed from large flat mushrooms for grilling or stuffing.

Minaret mushrooms: for a decorative garnish, for the top of a fish fillet, etc, hold the mushroom stalk downward and make a series of skin-deep cuts from top to bottom of the caps, not meeting on top and slightly curving. Now reverse the knife and make a second series of cuts only a fraction away, remove the strips in between the cuts.

Preparing minaret mushrooms for use as a garnish for individual fish or steaks

To keep mushrooms white, for a white sauce or soup, they can be cooked in a little water or stock from the recipe with added lemon juice.

Canned mushrooms: though neat in appearance their flavour tends to be diminished. Try tossing the drained mushrooms in a little butter with a spoonful of chopped spring onion. Boil down the can juice and add this to the dish.

Dried mushrooms are expensive but very light: use 50 g /2 oz dried mushrooms as the equivalent of 200 g /7 oz fresh ones. Conversely, if a recipe specifies dried mushrooms and you only have fresh ones, treble the weight given. To reconstitute dried mushrooms, soak them in cold water overnight or in warm water for 30–60 minutes. The stem tips may need discarding. The soaked mushroom is then usually sliced. Use the soaking liquid as a stock to flavour soups and stews; it may need straining first.

Using mushrooms

Mushrooms taste best when sautéed or sweated in butter before being cooked in other ways. Cultivated mushrooms have a softer texture than wild mushrooms, which stand up better to long stewing. Button mushrooms and young ceps can, however, be served raw if they are marinated in oil and lemon juice for 20 minutes first. Tossed with spinach, beans, bacon, prawns and many other salad ingredients they make excellent starters; they are also a classic salad served à la grecque .

Mushrooms combine well with eggs, such as scrambled eggs or omelettes, and are delicious in quiches and tartlets. In cream sauce or on their own they are wonderful on toast. Stuffed with cheese, herbs and breadcrumbs or ham, and grilled or baked, they make excellent hot starters. Sautéed, braised with lemon juice, grilled or fried, they are one of the most popular side dishes.

Mushrooms are used as the base of one of the classic French kitchen flavourings. *Fines herbes* formerly always included mushroom parings, as well as chopped herbs, in the days when mushrooms were always peeled and their skin was a frequent kitchen by-product. Include 1–2 chopped mushrooms or some stalks in with your herbs for flavouring. Duxelles (see recipe) is a dry home-made mushroom paste, also used for flavouring. It is often more convenient to make and store it than stopping frequently to fry small quantities of mushrooms.

Sautéed mushrooms are one of the most popular garnishes and a classic accompaniment to bland white meat, such as veal or poultry, or to fish. The meaty quality of mushrooms means that they can be used to extend meat, for example, in a risotto when the quantity of meat is inadequate for the number of people at table. Dishes garnished with mushrooms are often described as *chasseur* which means 'hunter'. Any dish with Périgord (or related words) in the title contains truffles and this is usually true if they are described as 'Rossini', as this composer was very fond of truffles.

187

Mushroom soufflé

🍴🍴 50 minutes

Serves 4
40 g /1½ oz butter
250 g /9 oz mushrooms, chopped
1 small onion, chopped
100 ml /3½ fl oz milk or thin cream
100 g /4 oz fresh breadcrumbs
3 medium-sized eggs, separated
salt and freshly ground black pepper
pinch of grated nutmeg

1 Heat the oven to 200C /400F / gas 6. Butter a 600 ml /1 pt soufflé dish, line with greaseproof paper and grease again.
2 Melt the butter in a saucepan and add the mushrooms and onion. Cover the pan and sweat the chopped vegetables for 10 minutes until the onions are soft and the mushrooms have given up their liquid.
3 Off the heat add the milk and fresh breadcrumbs, stir in the egg yolks and season to taste.
4 Beat the egg whites until they form stiff peaks. Then carefully fold the mushroom mixture into the whites. Transfer to the prepared dish and sprinkle the top of the soufflé with grated nutmeg. Bake the soufflé for about 30 minutes or until it is well-risen and browned.

Duxelles flavouring

🍴 30 minutes

Makes 175 g /6 oz
25 g /1 oz butter
1 medium-sized onion or 2 shallots, chopped
350 g /12 oz dry young mushrooms or stalks and trimmings, finely chopped
45 ml /3 tbls finely chopped parsley

1 Melt the butter in a saucepan and cook the onions or shallots over low heat for about 10 minutes, until they are soft but not coloured. Add the mushrooms and cook, stirring constantly, until all the liquid has evaporated, about 15 minutes.
2 Add the parsley and cook for 2 minutes or until the mixture is very dry.
3 Turn the duxelles mixture into a small jar, pressing it down well. Cover and keep in the refrigerator, re-covering the jar after each use. Use within 1 week or store in the freezer for up to 3 months.

● To use, add a spoonful to soups, stews and sauces, or add some to stuffings for meat or poultry.
● Add a spoonful of duxelles to hamburger mixtures, or to patties of minced white meat such as pork or veal.
● For hot stuffed eggs, halve 4 hard-boiled eggs. Remove and mash the yolks, and mix in 15 ml /1 tbls duxelles, 15 ml /1 tbls finely chopped parsley, 50 ml /2 fl oz thick bechamel sauce and seasoning to taste. Pile back into the whites and sprinkle with breadcrumbs. Brown under the grill.

King Richard's leek and mushroom soup

This recipe is based on one which appears in the oldest English-language cookery book, the *Forme of Cury* compiled by the 'chef maistes cokes of kyng Richard the Secunde' in the late 14th century.

🍴 40 minutes

Serves 2
2 leeks, finely shredded and chopped
200 g /7 oz mushrooms, chopped
2.5 ml /½ tsp saffron powder
300 ml /10 fl oz chicken stock
25 g /1 oz butter
salt and freshly ground black pepper
pinch of grated nutmeg

1 Dissolve the saffron by heating gently in the stock.
2 In a saucepan, melt the butter and add the leeks and mushrooms. Cover and sweat the chopped vegetables gently over a low heat for 10 minutes or until the leeks are softened and the mushrooms cooked.
3 Add the stock, salt, plenty of pepper and a large pinch of nutmeg. Simmer for 20 minutes, or until the flavours have mingled. Serve hot.

Japanese mushroom fritters

These fritters, made with a light-as-air tempura batter, are delicious as appetizers or as a side dish to grilled meat. In Japan sweet cooking wine, *mirin*, and *daishi* which is a golden, delicate fish-based stock are used for the sauce. Japanese radish, *daikon*, sold as mooli in Europe, is used for the garnish; this is milder than the red radish, with a less peppery taste, and so you will find that turnip is the best substitute for it.

🍴 15 minutes (plus 30 minutes soaking time if using dried mushrooms)

Serves 8
450 g /1 lb mushrooms, ceps, or 150 g /5 oz dried shiitake mushrooms, soaked for 30 minutes in boiling water and patted dry
250 g /8 oz mooli or turnip, coarsely grated
oil for deep frying
For the tempura sauce
250 ml /8 fl oz good chicken consommé or Japanese daishi
30 ml /2 tbls sweet sherry
30 ml /2 tbls soy sauce

King Richard's leek and mushroom soup, Japanese mushroom fritters

For the tempura batter
1 small egg
50 g /2 oz flour
50 g /2 oz cornflour
1.5 ml /¼ tsp salt
1.5 ml /¼ tsp monosodium glutamate
2.5 ml /½ tsp baking powder
1 small ice cube

1 First make the tempura sauce: heat the ingredients together in a small saucepan until the liquid boils. Then remove the pan from the heat and leave the sauce to cool while you make the tempura batter.
2 To make the tempura batter: beat the egg and 75 ml /3 fl oz water lightly together. Using a fork or chopsticks mix the dry ingredients. Lightly beat the egg mixture into them and add the ice cube. The ingredients should just be blended and the batter should be thin and lumpy. Do not beat out the lumps.
3 In a wok or deep-fat frier, heat the oil until it smokes. Use chopsticks to dip one mushroom at a time in the batter, shaking off any excess, then in the oil. Cook the mushrooms for 1–2 minutes, for only as long as it takes for the batter to set and turn pale golden. Remove and drain them on absorbent paper.
4 Serve the mushroom fritters accompanied by the sauce in a small bowl or sauceboat and the grated mooli or turnip in a separate dish.

Steak chasseur

 1 hour 20 minutes

Serves 4
4 × 175-200 g /6-7 oz sirloin steaks
60 ml /4 tbls olive oil
½ garlic clove, cut
salt and freshly ground black pepper
50 g /2 oz butter
350 g /12 oz mushrooms, sliced
1 medium-sized onion, finely chopped
30 ml /2 tbls finely chopped parsley
150 ml /5 fl oz good consommé
65 ml /2½ fl oz madeira or dry red wine mixed
    with 15 ml /1 tbls tomato purée and
    10 ml /1 tsp cornflour
30 ml /2 tbls finely chopped parsley

1 Rub the steaks with 30 ml /2 tbls oil and garlic. Season with pepper, leave 1 hour.
2 Melt half the butter with 15 ml /1 tbls oil in a frying-pan over medium heat. Fry the steaks for about 4 minutes on each side.
3 Melt the remaining butter and oil in a separate pan. Sauté the mushrooms for 5 minutes. Add the onion, cook 1 minute.
4 Remove steaks from pan, season, keep warm. Add the consommé to the pan, boil to reduce by half. Add the wine, boil 1 minute. Stir in mushrooms and parsley. Heat through. Return steaks to pan and serve.

Mushroom ketchup

This seasoning, very popular in Victorian times, is sold commercially but is more difficult to get hold of than the well-known tomato ketchup. A spoonful or so of it will pep up the flavour of a brown sauce or soup. The ketchup needs a lot of mushrooms, but they need not be in top condition, so it is the answer when you can acquire a large quantity cheaply. The sauce can also be made from wild mushrooms. Do not let the mushroom liquid boil, as this will destroy the flavour.

 3–9 days in salt
   then 4 hours

Makes 850 ml /1½ pt
1.5 kg /3 lb mushrooms
150 g /5 oz coarse or sea salt
30 ml /2 tbls allspice
2 blades of mace
15 ml /1 tbls cayenne pepper or
    20 peppercorns
5 whole cloves
2.5 cm /1 in piece ginger root, chopped
15 ml /1 tbls sugar
125 ml /4 fl oz brandy
125 ml /4 fl oz wine vinegar

1 Trim and clean the mushrooms as necessary, then chop them coarsely. Spread them out in an earthenware or enamel-lined pan and cover with the salt. Mix this into the mushrooms with your hands.
2 Leave in a cool place or refrigerator for 3 days, stirring and squashing with a spoon at least once. If you do not have time to cook and finish the pickle immediately, this salting stage may be continued for a maximum of 9 days.
3 When you are ready to make the ketchup, turn the mushrooms and their liquor into a jellybag, or a buttermuslin spread out inside a large colander over a bowl. Squash the mushrooms well with a spoon and then twist and squeeze the bag or cloth to obtain the maximum amount of liquor.
4 Crush the allspice, mace and peppercorns in a mortar with a pestle and add the ginger root and crush again. Add these flavourings plus the cloves to the mushroom liquor with the cayenne pepper, if using, 15 ml /1 tbls coarse salt and the sugar.
5 Pour the liquor into the top pan of a double boiler, bring almost to the boil, then put the pan on to the boiler containing simmering water. Simmer, uncovered, so that the liquid reduces, at the back of the stove, remembering to add more hot water regularly to the bottom pan so that it does not boil dry. Reduce the liquor to 750 ml /1 pt 6 fl oz – about 2½–3 hours.
6 Sterilize 3 small jars or bottles, for example 3 × 300 ml /10 fl oz old soy sauce bottles.
7 Strain the liquor to remove the spices and stir in the brandy and vinegar. Pour into the prepared container(s), using a funnel for bottles. Seal tightly; the ketchup should keep indefinitely until opened, then use fairly quickly. Add a spoonful or so to taste, to sauces, casseroles and soups.

Globe artichokes

Globe artichokes are decorative served whole as an hors d'oeuvre and versatile when used in soups, sauces, salads and casseroles. The bottoms make a luxurious garnish or starter piled high with a savoury filling.

Globe artichokes are large, unopened thistle heads, and at first sight do not seem edible at all. But don't be put off by their formidable appearance, for beneath that prickly exterior there is some delicious nutty flesh.

When very small the immature flower bud of some varieties is tender enough to be eaten whole – cooked and sometimes raw. But the ones that end up in our shops tend to be large, each head weighing about 250–350 g /8–12 oz, and they must be cooked before they are eaten.

At the top of the stalk is a disc of delicious flesh, called the artichoke bottom, from which the leaves grow and each leaf has a pad of this flesh inside at the base – the rest of the leaf is stringy and inedible. Above the base is the bristly choke. This is inedible except when very immature, and so is usually scaped away. Above this is a cone of very soft, purplish leaves inside the stiffer rings of outer leaves.

The thick pad below the leaves, the *fond d'artichaut* in French, is the luxurious portion. It is often called the 'heart' but is more correctly called the bottom, because it is also possible to prepare (or buy canned) from very young artichokes an artichoke 'heart' which is indeed heart-shaped. This is the base of the artichoke cut before the choke has formed and it retains two or three layers of soft inner leaves.

Buying and storing artichokes

Globe artichokes are most plentiful in spring and summer, though imported ones may be bought over a longer season. There are several different varieties, some with flat round heads and smooth-edged leaves, some with large pointed heads and spiny leaves; some so small and soft they can be eaten whole, though these are hard to come by.

Once cut, globe artichokes soon lose their succulence and the leaves toughen and dry. Choose fresh, heavy young heads that are thick and solid with tightly packed leaves. Avoid any with spread-out leaves or with heavily speckled or spotted leaves.

Choose large heads if they are to be served with a filling or if you want to prepare artichoke bottoms. The larger they are the larger the fleshy base will be – and the less fiddly the job of preparing them. Medium-sized heads are perfect to serve whole as a first course. You need the small, special varieties – if you can find them – to serve in recipes where the entire artichokes, leaves and all, are eaten.

Artichokes should be served as fresh as possible, but if necessary keep them for up to 4 days in a strong plastic bag at the bottom of the refrigerator. Artichoke bottoms, large and small for different types of recipes, can be bought canned in brine. You can also buy canned hearts complete with the immature choke and leaves. Canned artichokes should be drained, rinsed and drained again before using.

Ways of preparing artichokes

Scraping the choke from a cooked artichoke before adding a sauce or stuffing.

Preparing an artichoke bottom: cutting off the choke with a sharp knife.

Preparing an artichoke heart: the prepared heart is kept in a bowl of acidulated water.

**** It is possible to blanch trimmed artichokes for 7–10 minutes then refresh and freeze them for up to 6 months. Thaw for 4 hours then complete cooking. Artichoke bottoms and the prepared centres of young, tiny ones can be cooked until almost tender then chilled and frozen for 3 months. Scrapings from the cooked leaves can be frozen (for use in sauces) if lemon juice is added before freezing. Use within 1 month.

Preparing and serving a head

Globe artichoke bottoms, the 'meat' of the vegetable, discolour rapidly on exposure to air, and so it is essential to have ready a bowl of water with lemon juice added in the proportion of 15 ml /1 tbls to each 500 ml /1 pt. Drop the artichokes into this acidulated water each time a cut is made across or into the bottom; otherwise, it will turn an unattractive brownish-black.

To prepare an artichoke to cook and serve whole, cut off and discard the stalk and trim the base so that the vegetable will stand level and steady on a plate. Using a very sharp knife (preferably stainless steel), trim off the outer two layers of leaves, working all around the head with a gentle sawing motion. Lay the artichoke on its side and cut off the top third of the leaves with sharp scissors if wished. Wash thoroughly under cold, running water and leave to soak upside down in a bowl of water for 15 minutes. Drain by standing the heads upside down.

Boiling: artichokes are boiled to serve whole as a first course. Prepare a large pan of boiling, salted water and add 15 ml /1 tbls olive oil, which gives the leaves an attractive sheen, and 30 ml /2 tbls lemon juice, which helps to preserve the colour. (If you wish, you can add flavourings such as small sprigs of herbs – marjoram, oregano, thyme, parsley or bay leaves – or chopped onions, shallots or garlic.) Put in the artichokes, bring the water back to the boil, cover the pan and boil for 30–45 minutes, depending on size. To test, lift one out on a draining spoon and pull off one of the outer leaves. It

should come away easily. Do not overcook, or the characteristic flavour will be lost. To drain, stand them upside down on a draining board.

When the artichokes are to be served cold, it is best to cook them about one hour before the meal, so that they are just cool. A slight miscalculation will do no harm, however – they taste just as good when served warm.

Removing the choke: the head may be served with the choke in place or it may be removed before serving. If it is to be stuffed, the choke and inner leaves are removed to turn the base and outer leaves into a container.

Gently pull the outer leaves open until you can see the soft cap of inner leaves. Hold the top of this and pull it out whole. Underneath is the bristly choke which can be scraped out with a teaspoon. Make sure every bit of choke is removed before you add a sauce or stuffing, then re-form the flower head.

Sauces: hot butter sauce goes well with warm artichokes; vinaigrette, lemon sauce or mayonnaise as well as many sharp white and tomato sauces go well with cold ones. A thicker sauce may be piled into the centre – ravigote, cold fish and prawn sauce go well – for dipping the leaves.

Serving: to serve hot arrange them on a heated serving platter or wrap each one in a cotton napkin. Serve the sauce separately and provide a big plate for discarded leaves.

To eat: the artichokes are dismantled at table leaf by leaf. Spoon vinaigrette onto the plate, round the base of the artichoke. Then pull off a leaf with your fingers and thumb, dip the leaf base into the sauce and put it between your teeth. The soft leaf covering is scraped off as you pull the leaf away. It takes a little practice to perfect the movement of plucking, biting and discarding and it is certainly a conversation stopper! Pull off the inner leaves in a cone and cut off the choke (if present) with a knife and fork. Then cut and eat the artichoke base, together with any filling.

Braised whole artichokes

For a substantial first course or lunch dish, stuff whole raw artichokes, prepared as shown above. Make a filling, choosing from chopped pork, chicken, ham, bacon, mushrooms or nuts, mixed with breadcrumbs or rice. Then braise them in stock for about 1–1½ hours. Or braise whole artichokes in the Greek way. Sauté carrots, potatoes and whole baby onions in olive oil, add the artichokes, stock and herbs and braise. Serve with rice. These dishes are messy to eat, however, as you will have to pull off the hot leaves with your fingers.

Very small, young globe artichokes, cooked in the Provençal manner and eaten with a knife and fork, avoid this problem. Prepare them as usual and rub the outside all over with lemon juice. Pack them upright into a small pan and pour in olive oil to come half way up the vegetables. Cover with water and boil rapidly, uncovered, for 20 minutes or until tender. The water will evaporate and the artichokes cook in oil. Drain, arrange them upside down on a plate and serve with a lightly spiced tomato sauce.

Artichoke bottoms and hearts

To prepare an artichoke bottom, cut off the stalk and then the leaves, cutting round one layer at a time. Gradually work to the centre until the rim of the base is exposed. Dip this at once into acidulated water, then cut out the choke. Dip again into the water and trim and smooth the base. Brush the bottoms with lemon juice and leave in acidulated water until ready to cook.

To prepare an artichoke heart, work on a small artichoke in the same way until you reach the palest green, tender inner leaves. Cut off the tips to neaten them, trim the bottom. Brush with lemon juice and drop into acidulated water until ready to cook. Left-over leaves should not be discarded. Blanch for 3 minutes, then scrape off the fleshy layer from the leaves. Sprinkle it with lemon juice and store in a small covered container. It makes a delicious addition to mayonnaise or a cream sauce for poultry.

Cooking and serving: artichoke bottoms and hearts are blanched in boiling, salted, acidulated water for three minutes, drained and dropped into cold acidulated water. Dry thoroughly before lightly sautéing in butter or a mixture of oil and butter, or tossing in dry breadcrumbs or batter and deep frying, or puréeing to make into a creamy sauce or soup.

They make a tasty addition to casseroles and stews and are especially good with lamb (see recipe), chicken dishes, fillet steak and a medley of other summer vegetables. They are also perfect partners for eggs and are delicious chopped into a dish of scrambled eggs for an elegant brunch dish, or topped with baked eggs and served with hollandaise sauce.

For a really refreshing change in salads, artichoke bottoms or hearts can be boiled, drained, acidulated and dried, and served alone with vinaigrette or mayonnaise. Use them in a fish or crab salad, mix them with cooked haricot beans and onion rings; orange segments and finely chopped fennel bulb; chicory and watercress garnished with walnuts – or what you will.

Artichoke bottoms are perfectly suited, by nature of their shape, to be containers for spoonfuls of a vegetable purée, a mousse, or decorative shapes of salad vegetables set in clear aspic. They make stunning first courses or garnishes.

Deep-fried baby artichokes

30 minutes
plus 2 hours for batter to rest

Serves 4
8 small young artichokes
lemon juice for brushing
oil for deep frying
1 lemon, quartered, to serve
For the batter
100 g /4 oz flour
pinch of salt
45 ml /3 tbls olive oil
1 medium-sized egg white

1 Begin by making the batter. Sift the flour and salt into a bowl, make a well in the centre and pour on the olive oil. Beat to a smooth paste. Gradually pour on 200 ml /7 fl oz water, beating all the time. Cover the bowl and let stand for at least 2 hours.
2 Trim the bases of the artichokes and brush the cut surfaces with lemon juice. Cut off the top one-third of the leaves; also remove the 3 outer layers of leaves.
3 When you are ready to start cooking, whisk the egg white until it is stiff and fold it gently into the batter.
4 Pour the oil into a deep pan and heat it for deep frying.
5 Dip each artichoke into the batter, allowing the excess batter to drain back into the bowl. Fry the artichokes in the hot oil for 6–8 minutes, until the batter is fluffy and golden brown and the artichokes are tender. Remove the pan from the heat, lift out the artichokes with a slotted spoon and drain

them on crumpled absorbent paper. Arrange them on a heated serving dish and serve at once with the lemon wedges.

● Alternatively, you can slice the prepared artichokes lengthways into 4 slices, brushing each slice with lemon juice as you cut it. Dip each slice in batter and deep fry them for 4–5 minutes, until they are tender and golden brown.
● Cooked in this way, globe artichokes are delicious served with hollandaise sauce in which the artichokes can be dipped.

Artichokes with prawn mayonnaise

1 hour, plus 1 hour cooling

Serves 4
4 large globe artichokes, trimmed, washed, soaked and drained
salt
30 ml /2 tbls lemon juice plus extra for brushing
15 ml /1 tbls olive oil
For the mayonnaise
1 small egg yolk
5 ml /1 tsp lemon juice
large pinch of mustard powder
5 ml /1 tsp tomato purée
salt and freshly ground black pepper
pinch of cayenne pepper
225 ml /8 fl oz olive oil
1 bunch watercress, trimmed and separated into sprigs
100 g /4 oz peeled prawns, defrosted if frozen

1 Bring a large pan of water to the boil, add salt, lemon juice and olive oil, then the artichokes. Cook for 35–45 minutes, or until they are done. Drain thoroughly and stand upside down to cool for about 1 hour.
2 Meanwhile, make the mayonnaise. Put the egg yolk into a small bowl, stir in the lemon juice, mustard powder, tomato purée, salt, black and cayenne peppers.
3 Pour the oil into a small jug and gradually pour it onto the egg mixture, a few drops at a time, beating vigorously. When the mayonnaise begins to thicken, pour on the oil in a thin, steady stream, still beating continuously. Taste and adjust seasoning if necessary. If it is too thick, beat in a few drops of cold water.
4 Reserve 4 of the best watercress sprigs for the garnish, finely chop the rest and stir into the mayonnaise. Stir in the prawns.
5 When the artichokes have cooled, gently open out each one, using the base of a small tumbler or the handle of a wooden spoon. Carefully ease out the leaves, leaving the choke exposed. Using a sharp knife, cut away the choke, making sure that there are no prickly remnants. Immediately brush the artichoke bottoms with lemon juice to preserve their colour. Spoon the mayonnaise into the cavities, garnish each artichoke with watercress and serve.

● For a milder filling, omit the chopped watercress from the mayonnaise; use watercress and unpeeled prawns to garnish.

Artichokes with ham and mushroom stuffing

1 hour 20 minutes

Serves 4
4 large globe artichokes, trimmed, washed, soaked and drained
salt
30 ml /2 tbls lemon juice plus lemon juice for brushing artichoke bottoms
15 ml /1 tbls olive oil
425 ml /15 fl oz hot chicken stock
For the stuffing
50 g /2 oz fresh white breadcrumbs
1 small onion, finely chopped
50 g /2 oz lean ham, finely chopped
50 g /2 oz button mushrooms, finely chopped
15 ml /1 tbls chopped parsley
salt and freshly ground black pepper
30 ml /2 tbls olive oil

1 Heat the oven to 190C /375F /gas 5. Cook the artichokes in a large pan of boiling, salted water with the lemon juice and olive oil for 10 minutes, then drain thoroughly.

2 Make the stuffing by mixing together all the ingredients. When the artichokes are cool enough to handle, open them out and scoop out the chokes with a teaspoon. Brush the exposed bottoms at once with lemon juice.

3 Divide the stuffing between the artichokes and gently press the leaves tight around it. Arrange the vegetables in a deep ovenproof dish, in which they fit tightly in a single layer. Pour on the hot stock.

4 Bake the artichokes, uncovered, basting frequently with the stock, for 1 hour or until an outer leaf comes away easily.

5 Serve hot with the remaining stock as a sauce; provide fingerbowls and napkins.

● To eat, pull away the larger leaves one by one, scraping off the fleshy layer with your teeth. Then eat the filling and artichoke bottom using a knife and fork.

Lamb with artichoke hearts

Tender artichoke hearts make a succulent addition to this easy dish.

cooking artichoke hearts, then 40 minutes

Serves 6
75 g /3 oz butter
1 kg /2¼ lb lean leg of lamb, in 15 mm × 5 cm /½ × 2 in strips
6 artichoke hearts, cooked for 30 minutes
10 ml /2 tsp flour
225 ml /8 fl oz dry white wine or dry cider
125 ml /4 fl oz chicken stock
salt and freshly ground black pepper
60 ml /4 tbls thick cream
15 ml /1 tbls chopped parsley, to garnish

1 Melt 50 g /2 oz of the butter in a frying-pan and fry the strips of lamb on a moderately high heat, a few at a time, turning frequently, until they are browned on the outside but still moist and tender inside – about 5 minutes. Transfer the cooked lamb to a warm dish with a slotted spoon, and keep it warm while you cook the rest of the meat.

2 Melt the remaining butter in the pan, lower the heat to moderate and fry the artichoke hearts for 4–5 minutes, turning them once. Transfer them to the dish with the cooked lamb.

3 Stir the flour into the fat remaining in the pan, then gradually pour on the wine or cider and the stock, stirring. Season with salt and pepper, bring the sauce to the boil and simmer for 5–10 minutes, until it is thickened and slightly reduced. Stir in the cream.

4 Return the lamb, artichoke hearts, and any juices that have accumulated, to the pan and heat gently without boiling. Turn out onto a warmed serving dish, garnish with the chopped parsley and serve at once.

Artichokes with prawn mayonnaise and Lamb with artichoke hearts

Dried pulses

The popularity of wholefood and vegetarian cookery in recent years means a colourful range of nutritious dried pulses is now available. Learn all about the different varieties of bean, pea and lentil and how to cook them whole to use as main courses, salads and side dishes.

Pulses are the seeds of pod-bearing or leguminous plants. These peas, beans and lentils were among the earliest vegetable crops to be cultivated and, in their dried form, have been used in cooking for thousands of years.

Pulses mean healthy eating, for they have a low fat content, contain iron and B group vitamins, and are high in protein and dietary fibre or 'roughage'. Unfortunately most do not contain all the essential amino acids the body needs (soya beans are exceptional).

So for a well-balanced vegetarian diet, pulses should be combined with cereals, dairy products, seeds and nuts. Each of these contains some amino acid not found in pulses and together they achieve the perfect protein balance, the equivalent to protein contained in meat or fish.

In fact, most of the traditional ways of serving pulses combine the cooked dried vegetables with food from one of these categories – bread or pasta, rice, eggs, cheese or yoghurt, with other seeds for flavour and nuts for texture. In India spiced lentils, *dal*, are served with rice. In the Middle East dried bean salads dressed with seed or nut oil are served with bread. The Greek salad-dip, *hummus*, is ground chick-peas combined with *tahini* paste made from sesame seeds, and is scooped up on pitta bread. In North Africa bowls of succulent *couscous*, made from semolina, are garnished with chick-peas, which contrast in texture and combine in food value with the soft, steamed grains. In America Boston baked beans, slow-cooked with molasses and fat pork, are traditionally served with steamed, malted brown bread.

Buying and storing pulses

Most supermarkets stock a good range of the most popular dried pulses such as peas, butter beans, haricot beans and lentils, sold in packets under brand names. Others are often displayed in a specialist food section.

A choice of more unusual beans and different varieties of lentil are available in Asian or West Indian shops, in health food shops and buy-in-bulk wholefood shops.

Dried pulses can, in theory, be stored almost indefinitely in covered containers in dry, cool conditions. But the older they are, the tougher they get, and the longer they take to cook (which is why suggested cooking times can be only approximate). Ideally, it is best to buy pulses from a store with a quick turnover, and in quantities you can expect to use within six months. Remember, though, that prices tumble as you buy in greater bulk, so it is a good idea to get together with friends and neighbours, buy your beans by the sackful, and have a weighing-out party.

Canned cooked butter beans, flageolets, red kidney beans and other pulses are less economical than those bought dry, but are a useful store-cupboard standby, to be served in salads, as a vegetable accompaniment, or in composite dishes, when time is short.

Preparing pulses

Washing: even attractively packaged dried pulses should be washed well. Put them in a colander in a bowl of cold water. Discard any that are discoloured along with any gritty substances.

Soaking: most dried pulses need to be soaked before cooking, to replace some of the moisture that has been processed out of them. Use either of the following methods, whichever suits your timetable best. (Lentils are the chief exception, and can be cooked without soaking.)

For long soaking: put the pulses in a large bowl, cover them with about three times their volume of water and leave to soak for 4–6 hours or overnight, if more convenient. This is generally considered to be the best method, with the most tender results.

For short soaking: if time is limited, bring the pulses to the boil in a large saucepan of unsalted water and boil them for 3–5 minutes. Remove the pan from the heat, cover and leave the pulses to soak for 40–60 minutes.

Cooking pulses whole

Pulses may be cooked in the soaking liquid, which will contain the vitamins given off during soaking, but also some gases which can cause indigestion. So, if you prefer, drain the pulses after soaking, rinse them thoroughly in cold running water, and cook in fresh water or stock.

Cooking on top of the stove: put the soaked pulses in a large saucepan and cover them with cold water, vegetable or meat stock. Do not add salt at this stage, as it toughens the pulses, but add other flavourings such as celery, herbs, bay leaf, onion or garlic, and a few grindings of black pepper. Bring the liquid to the boil, reduce the heat and simmer the pulses gently. Add salt to taste at the end of the cooking time.

Pressure cooking with the same additions reduces cooking times by well over half.

Casseroling: all pulses can be cooked successfully with meat and other vegetables in casseroles, but remember to add extra liquid as the pulses soak up a great deal. Check from time to time during cooking in case more is needed.

Electric slow-cooking: boil all pulses except split lentils for 2–10 minutes before adding to the pot.

Dried peas

Chick-peas are native to Asia and play an important part in the national cuisines of Arab and Mediterranean countries. They are light golden brown, like small, round nuts, and very tough. They need long soaking and cooking and can be served in stews, soups or salads, or ground as the base of Greek *hummus*.
Cooking time: after soaking, 3–4 hours.

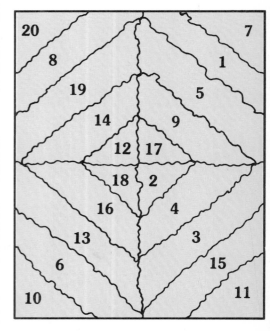

1 Adzuki; 2 Black beans; 3 Black-eyed beans; 4 Borlotti beans; 5 Broad beans; 6 Butter beans; 7 Cannellini; 8 Chick-peas; 9 Flageolets; 10 Ful mesdames; 11 Gungo beans; 12 Haricot beans; 13 Mung beans; 14 Pinto beans; 15 Red kidney beans; 16 Soya beans; 17 Split lentils; 18 Split peas; 19 Whole green peas; 20 Whole lentils

---

Soaking and cooking times

Soaking

in cold water	4–6 hours
in boiling water	40–60 minutes

Pulse	Cooking time*
Adzuki	30–45 minutes
Black beans	1–1¼ hours
Black-eyed beans	1–1¼ hours
Borlotti beans	1–1¼ hours
Broad beans	1½–2 hours
Butter beans	1¼–1½ hours
Cannellini	1–1¼ hours
Chick-peas	3–4 hours or more
Flageolet	1–1¼ hours
Ful mesdames	1–1¼ hours
Gungo beans	2–3 hours
Haricot beans	1¼–1½ hours
Mung beans	30–45 minutes
Pinto beans	1¼–1½ hours
Red kidney beans**	1–1¼ hours
Soya beans	3–4 hours or more
Split lentils	20–35 minutes
Split peas	30–45 minutes
Whole green peas	1½–2 hours
Whole lentils	30–45 minutes

* Average cooking time
** Boil hard for 10 minutes first

Whole green peas are sometimes also called blue peas. After soaking and boiling they can be served in the same way as fresh peas, flavoured with mint and sugar, or stirred to a pulp and served as 'mushy peas', the traditional accompaniment to fish and chips. They make good soups, especially with ham stock.
Cooking time: after soaking, 1½–2 hours.
Split peas are yellow or green peas split in half; yellow ones are more common.
Cooking time: after soaking, 30–45 minutes; unsoaked, 1–1¼ hours.

Dried beans

Adzuki or Aduki are tiny, round, dark red beans with a strong, sweet, slightly nutty flavour, making them ideal to serve with game and rich meat dishes. They also make good vegetarian burgers and loaves. In Eastern countries they are cooked with rice, and used for sweet cakes.
Cooking time: after soaking, 30–45 minutes.
Black beans are kidney beans which are white inside and have black, shiny skins. Also called turtle beans, they figure prominently in the cooking of African and West Indian countries.
Cooking time: after soaking, 1–1¼ hours.
Black-eyed beans: these small, cream-coloured kidney beans with black spots come mainly from California. They are more easily digested than most other pulses, and are the traditional ingredient of Hopping John, the spiced rice and tomato dish of America's Deep South.
Cooking time: after soaking, 1–1¼ hours.
Borlotti beans, also known as rose-cocoa beans, are longish in shape, and an attractive speckled pink in colour. When cooked they are pleasantly moist and slightly sweet.
Cooking time: after soaking, 1–1¼ hours.
Broad beans when dried need long cooking. In Greece they are served cold with fish, onion and olive oil, or with tomatoes.
Cooking time: after soaking, 1–2 hours.
Butter beans are also known as Madagascar or Calico beans. Lima beans are very similar to butter beans. Large, flat and white, they are popular in soups, stews and casseroles and as a vegetable accompaniment, particularly with pork. They are available cooked in cans.
Cooking time: after soaking 1¼–1½ hours.
Cannellini are small, white kidney beans which come from Italy. They can be successfully substituted for haricots.
Cooking time: after soaking, 1–1¼ hours.
Flageolet beans come mainly from Argentina and are considered by many to be the finest of all pulses, since they are harvested when very young and small. They are white or pale green, and are delicious cooked with lamb, or in salads. They are also available cooked in cans.
Cooking time: after soaking, 1–1¼ hours.
Ful mesdames are small round brown beans that come from Egypt. They have an earthy flavour and are good in salads with onion and garlic or herb dressing.
Cooking time: after soaking, 1–1¼ hours.
Gungo beans, also known as pigeon peas, are small and dullish brown. They are used in African and West Indian cooking.
Cooking time: after soaking, 2–3 hours.

Haricot beans, which are small, oval and cream in colour, are the dried seeds of French beans. They come mainly from America, where they are known as navy beans, or Boston beans because they are the main ingredient in the New England baked bean dish. They feature, too, in French Cassoulet (see recipe), and in mixed salads also containing cooked fresh French beans.
Cooking time: after soaking, 1¼–1½ hours.
Mung beans, which are small, round and an attractive bright green, are the seeds of Chinese bean sprouts. They cook quickly and do not need pre-soaking. They have a sweetish flavour and hold their shape well.
Cooking time: after soaking, 30–45 minutes; unsoaked, 45 minutes – 1 hour.
Pinto beans are pink, speckled kidney beans which make eye-catching side dishes or salads. In the American South-West they are served highly spiced with red peppers.
Cooking time: after soaking, 1¼–1½ hours.
Red kidney beans come mainly from the U.S. and Canada, and are traditionally served in chilli con carne and other hot, spicy dishes, as well as in soups and salads. After soaking in cold water, they should be boiled fast for 10 minutes before they are simmered on top of the stove or in an electric slow cooker. This is particularly important, to destroy a poisonous enzyme present in the bean. Red kidney beans are also available cooked in cans.
Cooking time: after soaking, 1–1¼ hours.
Soya beans are the most important of all the pulses, because they contain first-class protein, and in greater quantity, weight for weight, than fish, meat or dairy products. This makes them invaluable in vegetarian diets. They also have many high-protein derivatives – soya flour, miso paste, bean curd, a meat substitute called textured vegetable protein (TVP), and soy sauce.
Soya beans are the toughest of the pulses, and need long soaking and cooking, though a variety called 'soya splits' has been developed, which is partly pre-cooked and can be fully cooked, without soaking, in 30 minutes. Soya beans have virtually no taste, and need plenty of added flavourings.
Cooking time: after soaking, 3–4 hours.

Dried lentils

Lentils are available both whole and split. Soaking is not essential for either type, but does cut down on cooking time.
Whole lentils come mainly from Spain and South America and may be white, green, brown, pink, yellow or grey. They do not disintegrate in cooking and are served as an accompanying vegetable with butter and herbs, and are good in soups and casseroles. The Puy, or French, lentils do not have the earthy taste of other types, and are popular in Italian salads with onion, mint, garlic, olive oil and hard-boiled eggs.
Cooking time: after soaking, 30–45 minutes; unsoaked, 1¼–1½ hours.
Split lentils, or Egyptian lentils, are yellow, orange, pink or red. They do not have any flavour of their own, and disintegrate in cooking, so are usually served as a purée flavoured with herbs and spices.
Cooking time: unsoaked, 30–45 minutes; if soaked, reduce cooking time by 10 minutes.

Cassoulet

This filling dish from the Périgord region of France should always contain one fatty meat, one lean one and one spicy one. It needs no vegetable accompaniment.

⧖ 5 hours

Serves 6
350 g /12 oz haricot beans, soaked and drained
1 large onion, sliced
2 garlic cloves, crushed
1 bay leaf
1 L /1¾ pt unsalted white stock, or water and stock cubes
freshly ground black pepper
3 medium-sized tomatoes, skinned, seeded and finely chopped
500 g /1 lb belly of pork, skinned and cut into thin strips
2 quarters of chicken, skinned, boned and sliced
150 g /5 oz chorizo (spiced Spanish garlic) sausage, or similar, skinned and diced
15 ml /1 tbls chopped parsley
15 ml /1 tbls tomato purée
15 ml /1 tbls whole-grain mustard
75 g /3 oz fresh white breadcrumbs

1 Put the beans, onion, garlic, bay leaf and stock in a large saucepan and bring to the boil. Add freshly ground pepper, cover and simmer for 1 hour.

2 Heat the oven to 150C /300F /gas 2. Drain the beans and reserve the stock. Discard the bay leaf and stir the chopped tomatoes into the beans.

3 Make a layer of the bean and tomato mixture in a 2 L /3½ pt ovenproof casserole, cover with a layer of pork, then layers of more beans, chicken, beans, sausage and beans, seasoning each bean layer with pepper.

4 Stir the parsley, tomato purée and the mustard into the reserved stock and pour over the casserole. Make up with more stock if necessary, just to cover the top layer.

5 Sprinkle on half the breadcrumbs, cover and cook the casserole for 3 hours. Then stir the cooked breadcrumbs carefully into the top layer. Sprinkle on the remaining bread-crumbs and continue cooking, uncovered, for 45 minutes. Serve with a green salad and crusty French bread.

Moors and Christians

This Cuban dish combines pulse and grain. It gets its name from the contrasting black beans and white rice. Topped with a fried egg for each person, it makes a substantial lunch or supper dish. Serve it without the eggs (see picture) as a main dish accompaniment.

2 hours

Serves 4–6
225 g /8 oz black beans, soaked and drained
30 ml /2 tbls vegetable oil
1 medium-sized onion, chopped
1 garlic clove, crushed
1 green pepper, seeded and thinly sliced
1 red pepper, seeded and thinly sliced
2 large tomatoes, skinned, seeded and chopped
salt and freshly ground black pepper
large pinch of cayenne pepper
225 g /8 oz long-grain rice
25 g /1 oz butter
4–6 large eggs
15 ml /1 tbls chopped parsley

1 Cook the beans in boiling, unsalted water for about 1 hour, until barely tender.

2 Heat the oil in a saucepan and fry the onion and garlic over a medium heat for 2 minutes. Add the sliced peppers, stir well and fry for a further 3 minutes, stirring occasionally. Do not allow the vegetables to brown.

3 Add the tomatoes, salt, pepper, cayenne, rice, drained beans and 600 ml /1 pt water. Stir well, cover the pan and simmer very gently for about 45 minutes, until the rice is tender and the liquid has been absorbed. Taste and adjust the seasoning if necessary.

4 Turn on to a heated serving dish and keep warm. Heat the butter in a frying-pan and quickly fry the eggs. Arrange the fried eggs on top of the beans and rice and sprinkle with the parsley.

Moors and Christians

Chick-pea and leek salad

When you are cooking chick-peas for another dish, cook enough for this salad, too – it saves time and fuel.

10 minutes

Serves 4
4 small, young leeks
225 g /8 oz cooked chick-peas (cooked weight)
15 ml /1 tbls lemon juice
45 ml /3 tbls sunflower oil
large pinch of dried mustard
salt and freshly ground black pepper
8–12 black olives, stoned
15 ml /1 tbls chopped parsley
2 tomatoes, quartered, to garnish

1 Trim the leeks, discarding most of the green part (reserve for making soup). Wash the leeks thoroughly and slice thinly into rings.

2 Toss together the leeks and chick-peas.

3 Shake or beat together the lemon juice, oil, mustard and salt and pepper, and pour the dressing over the vegetables. Stir in the black olives.

4 Turn the salad into a serving dish, sprinkle with the parsley and garnish with the tomato wedges. Serve with fresh wholemeal bread.

Brown lentils with mint

This simple Italian dish of whole lentils is delicious with lamb or veal.

1¾ hours

Serves 4–6
45 ml /3 tbls sunflower oil
1 large onion, thinly sliced
2 garlic cloves, crushed
350 g /12 oz whole brown lentils, washed and drained
2 sprigs of mint
salt and freshly ground black pepper
15 ml /1 tbls chopped mint

1 Heat the oil in a saucepan and fry the onion over a medium heat, stirring occasionally, for 3 minutes. Add the garlic and fry for a further minute.

2 Add the lentils and stir for about 3 minutes, until they have absorbed the oil.

3 Pour over 1 L /1¾ pt hot water, add the mint sprigs and bring to the boil. Cover the pan and simmer for 1¼–1½ hours. Remove the mint and season well.

4 Turn into a heated serving dish, sprinkle with the chopped mint and serve hot.

● For a cold hors d'oeuvre for 4, garnish with 2 quartered hard-boiled eggs.
● To reduce cooking time to 30–45 minutes, pre-soak the lentils for 4–6 hours.

Parsnips, turnips, swedes

The glowing colours of a dish of mixed root vegetables heralds the arrival of autumn. Too often parsnips, turnips and swedes are relegated to supplying bulk to stews and casseroles – try them on their own, as purées, or use them in starters, soups or in one of the many traditional recipes.

Parsnips, turnips and swedes each have their own distinctive flavour, colour and texture but they are all cooked in similar ways. They are all swollen roots which act as underground storehouses for the water and nutrients needed by the plant for the winter. They are economical to buy and provide natural fibre and bulk without adding fat to the diet.

Buying and storing
Roots are usually sold washed and this, though convenient, reduces their storage life. It is best therefore to buy them in small quantities. Choose firm, medium-sized roots, free from discoloration and avoid any with wrinkled skins or that feel soft. Allow about 175 g /6 oz of roots weight, per portion.

Storage times vary considerably according to the facilities you have, but on average they will keep for 4–5 days in the salad compartment of a refrigerator or for 3–4 days in a cool, airy larder.

✱✱✱ Parsnips, turnips and swedes can each be frozen separately, or as mixed diced roots, ready to add to a stew. Choose young, firm and freshly dug roots and slice or dice them. Blanch them in batches in boiling water and then refresh for 3 minutes each. Open freeze on trays and then bag the pieces when solid. They can be stored for at least 1 year. Cook them from frozen.

Preparing the roots
Barely peel young roots so that you keep the nutrients that are immediately beneath the skin, or cook young roots in their skins and peel them afterwards. Peel mature roots to remove coarse skins. Always try to prepare the vegetables just before cooking them, but if they have to be prepared ahead, cover them with cold water.

Cooking
Cooking times vary, increasing with age and maturity. Swedes take longer to cook than turnips or parsnips. If diced or sliced, even mature roots will cook in water in 15 minutes, compared with 25–45 minutes if left whole. Pierce them to see if they are done and try not to overcook them. Season generously with salt and freshly ground black pepper and dress with butter, cream, dripping or bacon fat – parsnips need a particularly generous dressing of butter.

Roasting: to serve 4 people cut 700 g/1½ lb roots into evenly-sized pieces and parboil for 5 minutes. Drain, then shake them over the heat for a minute to dry. Roast in about 25 g /1 oz hot dripping or butter and oil in a moderate to hot oven for 45–60 minutes, until tender and golden. Turn them once. Check that they are cooked by piercing them right through to the central core, as this is firmer and more fibrous than the outside, so takes longer to cook.

Braising: quarter young and small roots or dice or slice mature roots. Turn the vegetables in hot fat, using 25 g /1 oz butter for every 500 g /1 lb vegetables. Cover tightly and leave to 'sweat' over gentle heat for 5–10 minutes, shaking the pan now and then. Add 150 ml /5 fl oz stock, season and simmer, covered, on top of the stove for

10–15 minutes or add 60 ml /4 tbls liquid and cook in a slow to moderate oven for 25–40 minutes. Drain off any liquid and sprinkle with chopped fresh herbs.

Cooking in a foil parcel: cut the peeled roots into fine julienne strips, season lightly and wrap in a loose parcel of buttered foil. Bake in a moderate oven for about 45 minutes.

Puréeing: Boil and mash the roots thoroughly or pass through a vegetable mill. To serve the purée as a vegetable add a little butter or thick cream, season to taste with salt, pepper and grated nutmeg, and beat with an electric or rotary whisk until light and fluffy. Alternatively use the purée as a base for a soufflé.

Steaming: cut into 10 mm /½ in dice, season and steam for 20–30 minutes, until just tender. Dress with a generous knob of

butter and chopped herbs before serving.
Simmering: Simmer evenly-sized pieces, in boiling water to almost cover them with 5 ml/1 tsp salt per 500 g/1 lb vegetables until tender – about 15 minutes if diced, 25 minutes if cubed and 30–45 minutes if left whole. Season and dress with butter and chopped herbs.

Using parsnips

Their sweet nutty flavour makes parsnips a good accompaniment to pickled meat such as salt beef, ham and tongue, but their special affinity is with beef. Roast the beef on a trivet, with some quartered parboiled parsnips beneath the meat so that they absorb the meat juices while the beef cooks.

Make fritters from parsnip slices, parboiled for 5 minutes. Drain, then batter and fry in deep fat. These fritters make an

excellent vegetable accompaniment to grilled fish.

As a side dish serve cooked parsnips with plenty of butter – 25 g/1 oz per 500 g/1 lb parsnips – heated until nut brown, with a good squeeze of lemon juice. To reheat cooked parsnips simply slice them thickly, dip in seasoned flour and fry generously in hot butter and oil.

For an old-fashioned parsnip roast, prepare puréed parsnips (see method) with butter or cream, seasoning and plenty of grated cheese. Sprinkle thickly with dried white breadcrumbs, mixed with more grated cheese, dot with butter and brown under the grill. Parsnip cakes were another traditional favourite. Make a parsnip purée with butter, salt, pepper, ground mace and ginger or curry powder and stir in enough mashed potato to slightly stiffen the mixture. Make round cakes, egg and crumb them and fry in hot fat.

Using turnips

Cook young tender turnips whole or cut into quarters. Their slightly peppery flavour and refreshingly succulent texture contrast perfectly with rich meat such as duck, game, pork, ham or lamb.

Fresh young turnips make an excellent raw salad, coarsely grated and dressed with a little vinaigrette plus chopped herbs or drained capers. The particularly light and delicate purée of mashed turnips and potatoes, known as skirlie-mirlie or punch-nep (see recipe) makes an original topping for shepherd's pie or a base for bangers and mash. Enhance the peppery flavour and pale colour of puréed turnips by cooking a bunch of watercress with them.

Add mature turnips to winter casseroles and pies. Cornish pasties are both lighter and juicier if diced turnip replaces half of the potato content. For a supper dish sauté quartered small turnips in butter until tender, adding chopped ham. Serve sprinkled with chopped green fennel foliage or parsley.

Using swedes

These golden fleshed roots are much undervalued. They are harder and denser than turnips and need a rather longer cooking time. When cooked they have a slightly sweetish flavour. Use swedes in any recipe in place of turnips. They are particularly good served as a buttery, well peppered purée (see recipe). They also make a delicate soufflé.

Sausage and swede soufflette

Light and nourishing, this dish of spiced swedes and eggs is a welcome low calorie alternative to sausage and mash. The swedes make a light, soufflé layer on top of the sausages.

⏲⏲ 65 minutes

Sausage and swede soufflette

Serves 2–4
1 kg/2 lb swedes, peeled and cut into
*   25 mm/1 in dice*
salt and freshly ground black pepper
1.5 ml/¼ tsp grated nutmeg
4 large pork sausages or 8 pork chipolatas
25 g/1 oz butter
25 g/1 oz flour
75 ml/5 tbls milk
2 large eggs, separated
2 slices of streaky bacon, chopped
30 ml/2 tbls coarsely grated cheese

1 Cook the swedes in boiling salted water to cover for 15–25 minutes until tender. Drain, mash thoroughly and leave in the pan to dry over low heat for 1–2 minutes. Season well with salt, pepper and nutmeg.
2 Heat the oven to 200C/400F/gas 6.
3 Brown the sausages in a hot greased frying-pan, but do not allow them to cook. Set aside.
4 Melt the butter in a saucepan, stir in the flour and cook gently for a minute, stirring. Remove the pan from the heat and gradually stir in the milk, then bring slowly to the boil, stirring continuously for 2 minutes, until the mixture is thick and smooth.
5 Remove the pan from the heat and beat in the egg yolks, and then the mashed swede.
6 Whisk the egg whites until stiff but not dry and fold lightly into the mixture.
7 Arrange the browned sausages in the bottom of a greased 1.2 L/2 pt casserole or gratin dish and spoon the soufflé mixture over them. Sprinkle the bacon and cheese over the surface.
8 Bake in the hottest part of the oven for 30–35 minutes, until firm and golden. Serve immediately.

Bashed neeps

A traditional accompaniment to haggis, bashed neeps is undoubtedly the most famous way of serving swedes. Check for tenderness while cooking; the time needed for cooking swedes can vary.

⏲ 50 minutes

Serves 4
675 g/1½ lb swede, peeled and cut into
*   25 mm/1 in dice*
salt and freshly ground black pepper
a little grated nutmeg
15 ml/1 tbls thick cream or 25 g/1 oz butter
chopped parsley, chives or chervil, to garnish

1 Put the swede into a saucepan and add boiling water to cover and 5 ml/1 tsp salt. When the water boils again cover the pan and simmer until the swede is tender when pierced, 15–25 minutes.
2 Drain well then mash until smooth using an electric whisk or a potato masher.
3 Season to taste with salt, nutmeg and plenty of freshly ground black pepper. Stir in the cream or butter. Pile the swede in a hot dish and sprinkle with the chopped herbs. Serve very hot.

Skirlie mirlie

You can almost hear the bagpipes playing and see kilts swirling as you mash turnips and potatoes together for this traditional Scottish dish. The Welsh version, called punch-nep, has holes punched in the smoothed surface of the purée into which a little melted butter or bacon fat is poured.

⏱ 45 minutes

Serves 5–6
450 g/1 lb turnips, peeled and thickly sliced
450 g/1 lb floury potatoes, peeled and
*   thickly sliced*
salt
45–60 ml/3–4 tbls creamy milk
25 g/1 oz butter
freshly ground black pepper
For the garnish
chopped fresh parsley or chives
small triangles of crisply fried bread

1   Put the turnips into a pan of boiling salted water, cover and simmer for 15 minutes.
2   Add the potatoes, cover and continue cooking gently for another 15 minutes, or until both the turnips and potatoes are tender. Drain well then mash thoroughly with a potato masher.
3   Add the milk and butter, heat for 1–2 minutes, then whisk with an electric or wire whisk until light and fluffy. Season well with pepper.
4   Pile into a hot dish and serve sprinkled with herbs and garnished with the triangles of fried bread.

White turnip soup

A smooth and delicate white soup, *potage Freneuse* is made special by serving with crisp blue cheese croûtes. *Freneuse* is a district outside Paris which is famous for its turnips.

⏱⏱ 60 minutes

Serves 4–6
40 g/1½ oz butter
675 g/1½ lb turnips, peeled and sliced
1 large onion, peeled and sliced
1 large potato, peeled and sliced
900 ml/1½ pt chicken stock
salt and freshly ground black pepper
300 ml/10 fl oz milk
a little grated nutmeg
chopped fresh parsley, to garnish
For the blue cheese croûtes
40–65 g/1½–2½ oz blue Stilton cheese
15–20 g/½–¾ oz soft butter
4–6 thick, diagonally cut slices French bread

1   Melt the butter in a large saucepan. Add all the vegetables, stir well to coat with the butter, then cover and leave to sweat over low heat for 10 minutes, shaking the pan from time to time.

2   Add the stock and a little salt and pepper, bring to the boil, cover and simmer for 25–30 minutes, until all the vegetables are soft.
3   Purée the soup in a blender or pass through a sieve or food mill. Return the purée to the pan and set on one side.
4   Make the blue cheese croûtes: blend the cheese to a paste with the butter. Toast the bread slices on one side only. Spread the cheese mixture on the untoasted side of the bread, then grill until the cheese melts.
5   Add the milk to the soup, bring to the boil and check the seasoning. Serve sprinkled with parsley.

Caramelized turnips

Syrup-glazed turnips are delicious with duck, roast pork, ham and grilled meats. Of the various methods of preparing caramelized turnips this is the simplest, as the pan needs to be watched only for the last few minutes of cooking, just while the glaze is forming.

Skirlie mirlie

⏱ 35 minutes

Serves 4
600 g/1¼ lb small young turnips, pared and
*   quartered*
salt
25 g/1 oz butter
25 g/1 oz soft brown sugar
30 ml/2 tbls stock

1   Put the turnips into a saucepan, almost cover with boiling water and add 5 ml/1 tsp salt. When the water boils again cover the pan and simmer until the turnips are just tender, 15–20 minutes. Drain off the water leaving the turnips in the pan.
2   Add the butter, sugar and stock and heat fairly briskly for a few minutes, turning the turnips gently now and then, just until they are coated with a shiny, syrupy glaze. Remove from the heat and serve hot.

●   Parsnips can be cooked in the same way.

Cheese and parsnip galette

♩♩ 70 minutes

Serves 4-6
900 g/2 lb parsnips, peeled
salt and freshly ground black pepper
50 g/2 oz butter
15 ml/1 tbls Demerara sugar
30 ml/2 tbls very finely chopped shallot or
*   onion*
10 ml/2 tsp lemon juice
100 g/4 oz Cheddar cheese, coarsely grated
For the garnish
a sprig of parsley
300 ml/10 fl oz tomato sauce (optional)

1   Cook the parsnips whole in boiling salt water until almost tender, from 15–25 minutes. Drain, and when cool enough to handle cut into thin slices.
2   Heat the oven to 220C/425F/gas 7. Use some of the butter to generously grease a 15 cm/6 in deep sandwich tin. Dust with the sugar.
3   Melt the remaining butter and fry the onion gently for about 5 minutes until soft but not coloured.
4   Line the bottom and sides of the prepared tin with overlapping slices of parsnip. Sprinkle with salt, pepper, lemon juice and grated cheese. Fill the tin with the remaining parsnip slices, sprinkling each layer as before.
5   Press a piece of buttered greaseproof paper over the top and bake in the hottest part of the oven for 30–40 minutes, until well browned.
6   Loosen the edges, turn out on to a hot dish and garnish with parsley. Hand round tomato sauce separately, if liked.

Honeyed parsnips

♩ 30 minutes

Serves 4
675 g/1½ lb parsnips, peeled and quartered
salt
25 g/1 oz butter
30 ml/2 tbls orange juice
15 ml/1 tbls lemon juice
30 ml/2 tbls clear honey

1   Cook the parsnips in boiling salted water for 10–15 minutes, until barely tender. Drain thoroughly.
2   In a heavy-based saucepan heat together the butter, orange and lemon juice and honey; when blended add the parsnips.
3   Cook over low heat for 5–10 minutes, turning the parsnips gently now and then, until they are coated with a thick brown syrupy glaze. Serve hot.

Parsnip velour soup

♩ 1 hour

Serves 4–6
50 g/2 oz butter
450 g/1 lb parsnips, peeled and sliced
1 large onion, peeled and sliced
1 stalk celery, washed and sliced
5 ml/1 tsp flour
7.5 ml/1½ tsp curry powder
salt and freshly ground black pepper
900 ml/1½ pt chicken stock
300 ml/10 fl oz milk
45–60 ml/3–4 tbls cream (optional)
For the garnish
25 g/1 oz toasted flaked almonds or 10–15 ml/
*   2–3 tsp chopped fresh chives*

1   Melt the butter in a saucepan, add the vegetables and stir well. Cover the pan and sweat the vegetables over low heat for 10 minutes, shaking the pan now and then.
2   Add the flour, curry powder, a little salt and pepper and cook gently for 1 minute.
3   Add the stock, bring to the boil, cover and simmer for 30 minutes or until all the vegetables are soft.
4   Purée the soup in a blender and return to the pan. Add the milk and bring to the boil.
5   Taste the soup and season with more salt and pepper, if necessary. Stir in the cream if using. Serve hot, sprinkled with toasted flaked almonds or chopped fresh chives.

Parsnip fritters

♩ 30 minutes

Serves 4
550 g/1¼ lb parsnips, peeled and sliced
salt
1 medium-sized egg
25 g/1 oz butter, softened
15 ml/1 tbls flour
50 g/2 oz walnuts, roughly chopped (optional)
oil for frying
maple syrup, or golden syrup heated with a
*   few drops of lemon juice, to serve*

1   Put the parsnips in a pan, cover with boiling water, add 5 ml/1 tsp salt and when the water boils again cover the pan and simmer for 10–15 minutes, until the parsnips are tender when pierced.
2   Drain well, shake over heat for a minute and then mash thoroughly.
3   Beat in the egg, butter, flour and salt to taste. Stir in the walnuts, if using. Leave in a cold place for an hour or so to firm up.
4   To cook, heat enough oil to give a depth of 25 mm/1 in in a shallow pan, and when hot slip in spoonfuls of the parsnip mixture and fry until golden, 2–3 minutes. Turn carefully and fry until golden.
5   Lift out with a slotted spoon, drain on crumpled kitchen paper and keep hot until all are fried. Serve very hot, with syrup.

Parsnip fritters

Beetroot and radishes

Beetroot and radishes are the most colourful of the root vegetables, and are usually used in salads, although they can also be made into delicious hot dishes. Other lesser known radishes are mooli, an Eastern vegetable which has recently become popular in the West, and horseradish, which has long been popular as an ingredient in pungent relishes and sauces.

Beetroot

Beetroot was first cultivated about 2,000 years ago in the Middle East. It was developed from the wild plant called sea beet (*Beta vulgaris*), as also were spinach, mangolds and sugar beet. Beetroot is called beet in the U.S.

Beetroot is grown in most of the temperate regions of the world; Cyprus and Italy are among the leading exporting countries. During the summer and autumn months beetroots are small and round, with a sweeter flavour than during the rest of the year: during the winter, they are larger and a little tougher. Elongated roots, as well as round ones, are grown, but the round shape is the most popular. Both types are purplish-red in colour and taste the same.

Buying and storing beetroot

Raw beetroots are sold trimmed, by weight, or in bunches with either all the foliage or just the lower stems attached. The larger, winter beetroots are always sold trimmed. When buying raw beetroots make sure that the skins look unwithered and that the roots are hard. Store them in a cool, dry, dark place and use them within a week.

Beetroots are often available cooked but unskinned – a time-saver in the kitchen. Always make sure that they are freshly cooked and that the skins look smooth. If the beetroots are dry and wrinkled, they are not freshly cooked. Keep cooked beetroots, unpeeled, in the refrigerator for up to 4 days.

✳✳✳✳ Since beetroots are available all through the year, it will probably only be necessary to freeze them if you grow your own and have a glut. Choose small, young beetroots for freezing. Cook and peel them and freeze them separately on trays, then pack into bags. They will keep for up to 2 months.

Prepared beetroot: throughout the year you can buy packets of small round beetroots that have been cooked, peeled and soaked in vinegar. You can also buy beetroot bottled in vinegar, either whole or sliced, sometimes with sliced onions added.

Using beetroot in cooking

Preparing beetroot: rinse raw beetroots thoroughly under cold running water; do not scrub them as this may break the skin and cause the beetroot to 'bleed' while cooking.

Boiling beetroot: to preserve the colour, never peel beetroots before boiling. Leave on the root and stem ends; just trim the ends, leaving about 25 mm /1 in. Drop the beetroots into lightly salted, boiling water (the addition of a little vinegar helps preserve the colour), cover and simmer until tender.

Small, new beetroots may take as little as 20 minutes to cook, the larger ones up to 1½ hours. To test whether they are done, do not pierce with a skewer, as this will release the purple juice, but see if the skin can be rubbed away easily round the stem end. Once cooked, peel the beetroots while they are still warm.

Beetroot salads: diced or sliced, deep red beetroot flesh contrasts effectively with salad greens. Beetroot also combines well in salads with certain fruits, such as apple and orange; but always mix beetroot into a salad only at the last minute before serving, as the red juice will stain the other ingredients.

Beetroot salads are popular in Eastern Europe and the U.S.S.R. where diced beetroot is traditionally combined with cooked salt or fresh herrings, diced ham or beef, hard-boiled eggs, boiled potatoes and dill pickles.

Beetroot can also make a salad by itself, perhaps with a few thinly sliced onion rings; served this way, it is usually dressed with vinegar, though this should be used sparingly so as not to impair the sweet flavour of the vegetable.

Hot beetroot: boiled beetroot can be served as a hot vegetable accompaniment and is particularly good if it is coated in a cheese or velouté sauce or with soured cream. When serving them this way, keep small beetroots whole, but cut larger ones into 25 mm /1 in chunks. Beetroots can also be braised (see recipe), or roasted, rather like potatoes. For both these methods, peel the beetroots first, keeping small ones whole and cutting the larger ones into chunks. To roast, put the beetroots in a shallow pan of hot butter and cook in the oven (200C /400F /gas 6) for 45 minutes.

Beetroot soup: as beetroot gives a deep red colour to anything it is cooked with, it makes soups (see recipe) and consommés very attractive. In the U.S.S.R. and Poland beetroot is traditionally used to make a famous and delicious soup called *borshch* (also spelt bortsch or borsch), the word being an old Slav one meaning beet. Strained borshch is served as part of the traditional Jewish Passover meal. Apart from the beetroot, which is essential, the other ingredients may vary according to what is available. Other vegetables, particularly cabbage, may be included, and the soup can also be a meal in itself, containing sausage, beef, bacon, game or poultry.

Back row: Scarlet and white radishes; centre: beetroot, elongated radishes and black radishes and, front: horseradish

Soured cream, diced boiled potato or hard-boiled egg are traditional garnishes.

Raw beetroot: of course, you do not always have to cook beetroot. If you like crunchy salads, blanch the beetroot, grate it finely and mix it into a dressing with grated apple or other raw vegetables such as shredded red cabbage or grated carrot.

Pickling beetroot: beetroot has always been a popular vegetable for pickling, as it keeps its flavour and freshness for a long time. A favourite recipe in Jewish households is *chrane*, a relish of beetroot mixed with horseradish (see recipe) served with salt beef.

Beetroot leaves, if they are in good condition, can be added to soups and casseroles, to which they add a spinach-like flavour.

Radishes

Radishes (*Raphanus sativus*) originated in southern Asia. They were cultivated in ancient China and Japan, Egypt and Greece, and have also been known in western Europe for centuries. They grow in most temperate climates and are available all the year round; the main exporting countries are Cyprus, Italy, Holland, Israel and the U.S.

There are many different types of radish, varying in flavour, shape and colour: some taste hotter and more pungent than others; some are round and completely scarlet;

Hot radish and cucumber salad; tongue

some are elongated and white round the tips, or a lighter pink colour; some are white all over. Most are quite small, about 15 mm–3 cm /½ –1¼ in; white radishes are larger, usually about 15–18 cm /6–7 in.

During the winter months, small quantities of black radishes may reach the market. Also known as winter or Spanish radishes, these have a large, bulbous root about 15–20 cm / 6–8 in long; their skin is dark, hence their name, but they are white inside. They have a stronger flavour and coarser texture than summer radishes.

Buying and storing radishes

Locally grown summer radishes can often be bought tied in bunches with the leaves still attached. Make sure that the leaves are a fresh green and not yellowing, and that the radish roots are crisp and firm. Cut off the leaves as they wilt quickly. Wash the radishes and store in the bottom of the refrigerator in a polythene bag for up to four days. To ensure crispness, leave radishes in a bowl of iced water for 2–3 hours before using. Radishes do not freeze well.

Using radishes in cooking

With their peppery taste, radishes are excellent appetizers: the French often eat them with salt, crusty bread and butter.

203

Radishes also make a tasty accompaniment to bread and cheese. Thinly sliced, radishes are a popular salad vegetable: they go very well with watercress, with celery, cabbage and cucumber, and in a salad of lettuce and spring onions. Black radishes need to be grated for salads. All kinds of radish, sliced, may be successfully stir-fried with other vegetables, Chinese style, and then served as a hot vegetable side dish.

Garnishing with radishes

For radish roses, choose very fresh even-sized, unblemished radishes and slice off the stalk. With this end downwards, make three rows of slits round the radish, which will open out into petals. Start at the bottom, holding a small sharp knife almost horizontally, with the point turned downwards, cut a series of round petals. Raise the knife and make a new row of petals which bridge the gaps in the line below. Make a third row if the radish is large enough. Soak the cut radishes in iced water overnight until they open. Trim the tip if wished.

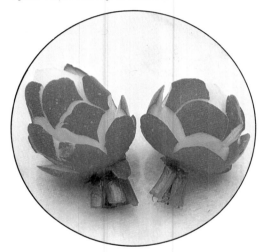

Cut radishes to open up like roses

Mooli

Mooli is closely related to the radish and has a long, white, pointed root which can weigh from 175 g /6 oz to over 1 kg /2¼ lb. It has a crunchy texture and tastes slightly more bitter than radish, but not as hot. Mooli is a popular vegetable in Asia; it has been grown for centuries in China and Japan, where it is known as *daikon*. In Japan it is grated very finely and used as a garnish. It is also pickled in a mixture of soy sauce and sugar and eaten with fish dishes. Because of its association with the Orient it is sometimes called the Japanese radish in Western markets. Kenya is one of the leading exporting countries of mooli.

When buying mooli, be sure the skin is a fresh, pearly white. Store it either in a cool, dry place or in a polythene bag in the bottom of the refrigerator. It will keep for up to a week.

Thinly sliced mooli makes fresh, crunchy salads, either alone or with other vegetables such as cucumber and cabbage. It goes well with gently spiced dressings. Thinly sliced mooli can also be stir-fried; diced, it can be boiled or braised like turnips, and served with plenty of melted butter.

Horseradish

Horseradish (*Armoracia rusticana*) probably originated in south-east Europe and western Asia, and is now cultivated in many temperate areas – it can be found growing in the wild. Its long, thin, slightly twisted roots are coloured rather like a parsnip. If you are lucky enough to find horseradish in a greengrocer's, you must use it immediately as it goes soft quickly.

Horseradish has a hot and fiery taste, so must be treated with caution. It is never served as a separate vegetable, but used as an ingredient in sauces and relishes. The outer part of the root has the strongest taste but the whole root can be used in cooking. Since the fumes are so strong it is wise to use a face mask if you are hand-grating any quantity – an automatic grater is better for horseradish.

● To preserve fresh horseradish, grate it finely, put it into a jar, cover with white wine vinegar and seal. It will keep for about nine months.

● To make your own horseradish cream, mix 75 g /3 oz grated horseradish with 5 ml /1 tsp each mustard powder and sugar, 15 ml /1 tbls white wine vinegar and 150 ml /5 fl oz lightly whipped thick cream. Leave for 15 minutes before serving with roast beef, smoked mackerel or smoked trout.

You can also buy ready-grated preserved horseradish, and jars of horseradish cream or horseradish sauce, though these are rarely as piquant as the home-made kinds.

Stuffed beetroots

Small beetroots, hollowed out and filled with a mixture of curd cheese and orange, make an unusual and attractive starter.

◖◖ 1½ hours

Serves 4
4 round beetroots, each weighing 100–150 g /4–5 oz
175 g /6 oz curd cheese
1 garlic clove, crushed with a pinch of salt
2 large oranges

1 Boil the beetroots until they are tender. Peel them while they are still warm, then allow to cool completely.
2 Cut a slice off the top of each beetroot and reserve. With a teaspoon, hollow out and reserve the centres, leaving shells about 5 mm /¼ in thick. Finely chop half the scooped out beetroot and keep the rest for a salad.
3 Put the curd cheese in a bowl and beat in the garlic. Grate the zest of one of the oranges into the cheese and mix well.
4 Remove all the pith and seeds from the grated orange and finely chop the flesh. Mix the orange flesh into the cheese together with the chopped beetroot.
5 Fill the beetroot shells with the cheese mixture and set the caps on the beetroot.
6 Remove the zest and pith from the second orange. Cut the flesh crossways into 4 thick slices. Serve each beetroot standing on an orange slice.

Mixed vegetable borshch

This is a substantial soup, full of chunky vegetables.

◖ 45 minutes

Serves 6
400 g /14 oz beetroots
1 large onion
200 g /7 oz carrots
200 g /7 oz celery
1.2 L /2¼ pt ham stock
15 ml /1 tbls soft brown sugar
30 ml /2 tbls red wine vinegar
1 garlic clove, crushed with a pinch of salt
freshly ground black pepper
For the garnish
150 ml /5 fl oz soured cream
250 g /9 oz potatoes, boiled and cut into 5 mm /¼ in dice
30 ml /2 tbls chopped parsley

1 Cut all the vegetables into small julienne strips.
2 Bring the stock to the boil, put in the vegetables, sugar, vinegar and garlic and season with the pepper. Cover and simmer for 20 minutes.
3 To serve, ladle the soup into heated individual bowls. Top each one with a portion of soured cream. Scatter the diced potatoes on top and sprinkle over a little chopped parsley.

Braised beetroot dijonnaise

Hot braised beetroot in a mustardy sauce makes a tasty accompaniment particularly for beef dishes.

◖ 1 hour 20 minutes

Serves 4
500 g /1 lb small round beetroots
15 g /½ oz butter
1 medium-sized onion, thinly sliced
200 ml /7 fl oz beef stock
15 ml /1 tbls red wine vinegar
10 ml /2 tsp Dijon mustard
30 ml /2 tbls thick cream
30 ml /2 tbls chopped parsley

1 Heat the oven to 180C /350F /gas 4. Peel the beetroots and keep them whole.
2 Melt the butter in a small, flameproof casserole over a low heat. Fry the onion until soft but not coloured. Add the whole beetroots to the pan and turn them in the butter.
3 Pour in the stock, add the vinegar and stir in the mustard. Bring to the boil. Cover the casserole and cook in the oven for 1 hour.
4 Stir the cream into the hot liquid, transfer to a heated serving dish and scatter with chopped parsley.

Mixed vegetable borshch

Chrane with raisins

This is a sweet variation of the Jewish relish called *chrane*. Serve it with cold beef or cheese.

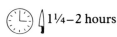 1¼–2 hours

Makes 700 g /1½ lb
350 g /12 oz small beetroots
75 g /3 oz grated horseradish
125 g /4 oz raisins
15 ml /5 fl oz red wine vinegar
salt and freshly ground black pepper

1 Boil the beetroots until tender. Cool, peel and finely grate them. Mix the grated horseradish with the beetroot.
2 Finely chop or mince the raisins and mix them into the beetroot and horseradish. Stir in the vinegar and season well.
3 Put the mixture into sterilized preserving jars and seal tightly. Leave for a minimum of 1 week before opening, then use within a week. This relish will keep for up to 3 months unopened.

Hot radish and cucumber salad

This unusual, hot salad goes particularly well with cold tongue or ham, or smoked mackerel.

 15 minutes

Serves 4
175 g /6 oz radishes
1 large cucumber, unpeeled
30 ml /2 tbls malt vinegar
15 ml /1 tbls grated horseradish
15 ml /1 tbls chopped capers
60 ml /4 tbls olive oil
1 garlic clove, chopped

1 Thinly slice the radishes and cucumber.
2 Mix together the vinegar, horseradish and capers.
3 Heat the oil in a frying-pan over a high heat. Stir-fry the radishes, cucumber and garlic for about 2 minutes until they are beginning to brown.
4 Pour in the vinegar mixture, let it bubble and serve the salad immediately.

Mackerel baked with horseradish

2 hours marinading, then 50 minutes

Serves 4
30 ml /2 tbls grated horseradish
grated zest and juice of 1 lemon
10 ml /2 tsp mustard powder
125 ml /4 fl oz dry white wine
4 small mackerel, filleted
To garnish
30 ml /2 tbls chopped parsley
1 bunch of watercress

1 In a large, flat, ovenproof dish, mix together the horseradish, lemon zest and juice, mustard powder and wine.
2 Turn the mackerel fillets in the mixture and leave them, cut side down, for 2 hours at room temperature.
3 Heat the oven to 180C /350F /gas 4. Turn the mackerel fillets over and then bake them for 25 minutes until they are tender and lightly browned.
4 Serve them, either straight from the dish or on a heated serving platter, garnished with parsley and watercress.

Carrots

Carrots are among the most versatile and popular of the root vegetables. They can be cooked in numerous ways as a side dish, or incorporated into main dishes. They can be served raw in salads, and make colourful garnishes. Grated carrot also adds moist sweetness to cakes and puddings.

Carrots are thought to have been first cultivated in Afghanistan about 2,000 years ago. In their original form they were small, tough and purple-fleshed, quite unlike the vegetable we know today.

Carrots now grow all over the world, particularly in temperate climates, and are available all the year round. The U.S. and Cyprus are two major exporting countries. Carrots are a very healthy addition to the diet, being rich in vitamin A and calcium. They have a high sugar content and were used as a sweetener at a time when sugar was very expensive.

Types of carrot
Most carrots are bright orange-red, although a few varieties are more on the yellow side. Most commercially available carrots are tapering or sausage-shaped, but there are some short, rounded, stump-rooted types available to the home gardener. Carrots have finely divided, fern-like leaves, and can be fun to grow as pot plants.

Early carrots, also called 'young' or 'new' carrots, are available through the summer months. Several are specially cultivated early-maturing varieties, others are main-crop varieties pulled when young. They are smaller, with a more delicate flavour than mature maincrop carrots: these are sown later in the year, are longer-growing, and pulled for winter storage.

Buying and storing
Early carrots are often sold in bunches with the feathery foliage still attached. The foliage should be bright green and the carrots should look crisp and bright. Avoid any that look shrivelled, with yellowing leaves. Young carrots should be eaten as soon as possible after purchase. They will keep at their best for only up to 2 days. Store them, if necessary, in a cool, dry place, with the foliage still attached.

Maincrop carrots are always sold trimmed. They should be firm, with a strong, fresh colour. Avoid any with a light coloured bloom on them, or that are cracked or look soft and withered. Maincrop carrots will keep for up to a week in a cool, dry and preferably dark place. If you have a plastic vegetable rack, line it with newspaper and store the carrots on this, never in a polythene bag.

**** Young carrots freeze better than older ones. Scrub them and either leave them whole or cut them into short lengths. Blanch them in boiling water for 5 minutes, drain and immediately plunge them into iced water for 5 minutes. Drain and freeze in rigid containers, or freeze them separately on trays, then bag. Frozen carrots can be bought whole, sliced or diced, and are also included in frozen mixed vegetables.

Canned whole or sliced carrots are available, as is canned or bottled carrot juice.

Preparing carrots
There is no need to peel young carrots, just scrub them well. Top and tail them by cutting a very small slice off the top of the carrot with the foliage, and removing the tapering root. Cook young carrots whole, but if they are mixed sizes, cut the longer ones so they will cook evenly.

If the outsides of maincrop carrots are blemish-free, they do not need to be peeled, just scrubbed well. If the outsides are marked, scrape or peel the carrots as thinly as possible with a vegetable parer. Cut off a small section at both stalk and root ends. Maincrop carrots are generally sliced or diced for cooking, but can be left whole if they are small. It is important to remove the hard, woody centre from old carrots.

Carrot soup with yoghurt

Cooking carrots

Boiling and steaming: both early and maincrop types can be boiled or steamed. Young carrots take a shorter time to cook: both types, when cooked properly, should be tender but still firm. Plainly cooked carrots are delicious tossed in butter with plenty of chopped fresh herbs: chervil, mint and summer savory complement the delicate flavour of young carrots, and parsley, thyme and marjoram go well with the more robust flavour of older ones. Carrots can also be served mixed into a bechamel or velouté sauce, or coated with seasoned cream, and combine well with broad beans in this way.

Carrot purée: boiled maincrop carrots can be mashed or rubbed through a vegetable mill, and enriched with butter or cream. This can be served scattered with chopped parsley as an accompanying vegetable, or piped to decorate savoury dishes. Carrot purée can also be mixed with other puréed root vegetables such as potato, parsnip or turnip, or used as the basis of a tasty cream soup such as the classic French *potage Crécy*. The flavour of orange also goes well with carrot in a soup.

Glazed carrots: glazing is an excellent way of bringing out all the sweetness and flavour of both early and maincrop carrots. Simmer them in stock to cover with a knob of butter and 5 ml /1 tsp sugar or honey until all the liquid is absorbed and the carrots are thoroughly coated with a syrupy glaze.

Braising carrots: to make a rich winter vegetable dish, braise carrots in stock or a mixture of stock and beer, either by themselves or with other root vegetables. Both new and maincrop carrots can be stir-fried and stir-braised in the Chinese way, either alone or in mixtures of vegetables. If cooked in this way, they need to be very thinly sliced.

Carrot salad: boiled new carrots mixed while still warm into a vinaigrette or mayonnaise dressing and left until they are quite cold are delicious as a salad; served this way they are also very good mixed with lightly cooked peas or broad beans. For a shredded carrot salad, grate or shred maincrop carrots very finely in a food processor: mix with crunchy, diced green peppers, celery or fennel or, for a sweet taste, with apples or raisins.

Carrot juice: use young carrots to make your own juice in a juicer: 500 g /1 lb will yield approximately 200 ml /7 fl oz juice. Serve it either on its own, or mixed with other vegetable juices.

Garnishing with carrots

Grated raw carrot looks attractive floating on the surface of a bowl of pale, creamy soup; add a herb sprig for extra colour.

● To make carrot flowers to garnish a salad, thinly pare strips of carrot lengthways, roll them up and secure with cocktail sticks. Put them into iced water for an hour, then remove the sticks, uncurl the strips and arrange them on top of each other at different angles to form petals. In the centre you can place either a cocktail onion or a stuffed olive, and then anchor from the back with a cocktail stick.

● Cut slices from a large carrot, remove the centres with an apple corer, and use as holders for thin, julienne strips of celery; if these are immersed in iced water for a time, the celery will curl attractively. Use to garnish canapés or hors d'oeuvre or large platters of cold meat.

● Use aspic cutters or tiny biscuit cutters to stamp out a variety of carrot shapes for use in salads and soups.

Carrot flower

Make hollow carrot holders for thin, julienne strips of celery

Carrot shapes can be made with a sharp knife or aspic cutters

Carrot soup with yoghurt

This is a creamy-textured soup with a light flavour of garlic and spice.

🔪🔪 45 minutes

Serves 4
500 g /1 lb carrots, thinly sliced
25 g /1 oz butter
1 large onion, finely chopped
5 ml /1 tsp ground coriander
1 L /1¾ pt chicken or light beef stock
salt and freshly ground black pepper
bouquet garni
10 ml /2 tsp cornflour
150 ml /5 fl oz natural yoghurt
1 garlic clove, crushed with a pinch of salt
1 carrot, coarsely grated, and flat-leaved parsley sprigs, to garnish

1 Melt the butter in a saucepan over a low heat. Stir in the carrots, onion and coriander. Cover and cook gently for 7 minutes.
2 Pour in the stock and bring to the boil. Season and add the bouquet garni. Cover and simmer for 20 minutes until the carrots are soft.
3 Meanwhile, blend the cornflour with the yoghurt in a saucepan. Bring the mixture slowly to the boil, stirring. Simmer for 2 minutes and remove from the heat.
4 Remove the bouquet garni from the cooked carrots. Purée the carrots in a blender with the cooking liquid, or rub through a vegetable mill, until you have a smooth soup. Stir in the garlic.
5 Stir the yoghurt into the soup and reheat, without boiling. Serve the soup in heated individual soup bowls, and garnish each one with grated carrot and parsley.

Stir-braised carrots and celery

🔪 25 minutes

Serves 4
250 g /8 oz carrots
1 small head of celery
60 ml /4 tbls oil
1 garlic clove, finely chopped
150 ml /5 fl oz stock
15 ml /1 tbls soy sauce

1 Thinly slice the carrots and cut the celery into 20 mm /¾ in pieces.
2 Put the oil and garlic in a large frying-pan and set over a high heat. When the garlic begins to sizzle, put in the carrots and celery and stir them for 2 minutes or until the celery is translucent.
3 Pour in the stock and bring to the boil. Stir in the soy sauce.
4 Cover the pan tightly, reduce the heat to moderate, and cook for 10 minutes. The vegetables should be slightly crunchy, with only 30–45 ml /2–3 tbls liquid left in pan.

Shepherd's delight pie

This substantial shepherd's pie has a fluffy, carrot-flavoured topping which differs from the traditional version in colour and taste but is just as delicious.

⅄⅄ 1½ hours

Serves 4-6
For the filling
30 ml /2 tbls oil
25 g /1 oz butter
2 large onions, finely chopped
1 garlic clove, finely chopped
1 medium-sized carrot, finely chopped
1 celery stick, finely chopped
700 g /1½ lb minced beef
250 g /8 oz tomatoes, blanched, skinned and chopped
100 g /4 oz mushrooms, finely chopped
150 ml /5 fl oz dry white wine
30 ml /2 tbls chopped fresh parsley
15 ml /1 tbls chopped fresh marjoram or 5 ml /1 tsp dried marjoram
15 ml /1 tbls chopped fresh thyme or 5 ml /1 tsp dried thyme
salt and freshly ground black pepper
butter for greasing
For the topping
500 g /1 lb carrots, coarsely chopped
100 g /4 oz potatoes, coarsely chopped
1.5 ml /¼ tsp ground nutmeg
salt and freshly ground black pepper
2 medium-sized eggs, separated

1 Heat the oil and butter together in a large frying-pan over a low heat. Stir in the onions, garlic, carrot and celery and cook them gently, stirring occasionally, until they begin to brown.
2 Raise the heat and add the minced beef to the pan with the onions, garlic, carrots, and celery. Cook, stirring, until the meat begins to brown.
3 Reduce the heat and mix in the tomatoes, mushrooms, wine, herbs and seasonings. Cover the pan and simmer gently for 20 minutes, stirring occasionally to ensure that the mixture does not stick.
4 Heat the oven to 200C /400F /gas 6. Boil the carrots and potatoes together for 20 minutes or until soft. Drain, then mash them with a potato masher or fork, or rub them through a vegetable mill until the mixture is smooth. Season with nutmeg, salt and pepper.
5 Beat the egg yolks into the carrot and potato mixture. Whisk the egg whites until stiff but not dry. Fold them gently but thoroughly into the carrot and potato purée with a metal spoon.
6 Put the beef mixture into a large buttered pie dish and pile the carrot and potato purée on top. Spread the purée evenly and then fluff with a fork. Bake the pie for 30 minutes until the top is risen and golden brown. Remove from the oven and serve immediately.

Carrot, fennel and green pepper salad

Boiled beef and carrots

This is a traditional English dish. You can use either new or old carrots.

🕐 ⅄⅄ overnight soaking then 2 hours

Serves 4
1.1 kg /2½ lb salted brisket or silverside of beef
6 cloves
10 black peppercorns
bouquet garni including celery leaves
2 bay leaves
4 medium-sized onions, quartered
700 g /1½ lb carrots
For the dumplings
250 g /9 oz flour
5 ml /1 tsp baking powder
4 allspice berries, crushed
4 juniper berries, crushed
6 black peppercorns, crushed
60 ml /4 tbls chopped parsley
pinch of salt
100 g /4 oz fresh beef suet or chilled beef dripping, grated

Boiled beef and carrots

1 Soak the beef overnight.
2 Put the beef into a large saucepan with fresh water to cover, and add the cloves, peppercorns, bouquet garni, bay leaves and onions.
3 Set the pan over a moderate heat and bring the water to the boil. Skim, then cover and simmer for 1 hour.
4 Meanwhile, make the dumplings. Sift the flour and baking powder into a mixing bowl and add the spices, parsley and salt. Mix in the suet or dripping.
5 Make a well in the centre of the dry ingredients, pour in 125 ml /4 fl oz cold water, and mix to a stiff dough. Divide it into 16 pieces and form into balls.
6 When the beef has cooked for 1 hour, skim the liquid of any fat. Put the dumplings into the saucepan with the beef and cook for a further 10 minutes, then add the carrots. Cook for a further 20 minutes, until the carrots are tender.
7 To serve, take out the beef, carve it into fairly thick slices and arrange them on a large, heated serving dish surrounded by the carrots, onions and dumplings. Pour a little of the cooking liquid over the meat and serve the rest separately in a sauceboat.

Carrot, fennel and green pepper salad

⏱ 35 minutes

Serves 4
250 g /8 oz carrots
250 g /8 oz fennel
2 medium-sized green peppers
1 small cooking apple
30 ml /2 tbls poppy seeds
60 ml /4 tbls olive oil
30 ml /2 tbls sherry or white wine vinegar
1 garlic clove, crushed with a pinch of salt
freshly ground black pepper

1 Grate the carrots, chop the fennel, core, seed and dice the peppers, and core and chop the apple. Mix them together in a bowl with the poppy seeds.
2 To make the dressing, beat the oil, sherry or vinegar, garlic and pepper together until they emulsify, and fold it into the salad. Leave the tossed salad to stand for 15 minutes before serving.

Carrot and pine nut tart

Carrots and pine nuts make a light, spiced filling for this savoury tart. It is the perfect dish for a vegetarian lunch.

⏱ 1 hour 10 minutes

Serves 4–6
500 g /1 lb carrots, thinly sliced
6 medium-sized eggs
5 ml /1 tsp hot Madras curry powder
5 ml /1 tsp cumin seeds
shortcrust pastry made with 225 g /8 oz flour
75 g /3 oz pine nuts

1 Heat the oven to 200C /400F /gas 6. Steam the carrots for 20 minutes or until tender. Cool them slightly.
2 Beat the eggs with the curry powder and cumin seeds. Line a 25 cm /10 in flan tin with the pastry.
3 Arrange the carrot slices in overlapping rings in the base of the flan. Scatter the pine nuts over the top and pour in the beaten egg mixture, making sure the nuts are evenly distributed.
4 Bake the tart for about 25 minutes or until the filling is set and golden brown. Serve warm, with a crisp green salad and potatoes baked in their jackets.

● Chopped walnuts may be substituted for pine nuts.

Carrot cake

⏱ 2¾ hours

Makes a 22 cm /9 in cake
5 large eggs, separated
250 g /8 oz sugar
250 g /8 oz carrots, finely grated
350 g /12 oz almonds, blanched and ground
grated zest of ½ lemon
50 g /2 oz flour
5 ml /1 tsp baking powder
pinch of salt
5 ml /1 tsp ground cinnamon
butter and flour for preparing the tin
For the frosting
125 g /4 oz cream cheese
30 ml /2 tbls thin cream
100 g /4 oz icing sugar, sifted
grated zest of ½ lemon
2.5 ml /½ tsp ground cinnamon
50 g /2 oz almonds, blanched and ground

1 Heat the oven to 180 /350F /gas 4. In a large mixing bowl, whisk the egg yolks until they begin to thicken. Whisk in the sugar and continue whisking until the mixture is thick and frothy.
2 Mix in the grated carrots, ground almonds and lemon zest. Sift the flour with the baking powder, salt and cinnamon and fold into the carrot and almond mixture. Stiffly whip the egg whites and fold them in.
3 Put the mixture in a buttered and floured 23 cm /9 in cake tin and bake the cake for 1 hour 10 minutes or until a fine skewer inserted in the centre comes out clean. Turn the cake on to a wire rack to cool completely.
4 To make the frosting, put the cream cheese in a bowl and beat in the cream until thoroughly blended. Gradually beat in the icing sugar and then add the lemon zest and cinnamon. Beat well.
5 Cut the cake horizontally in half, and sandwich it together with one-third of the frosting. Spread the rest of the frosting over the top and sides.
6 For the decoration, put the ground almonds into a heavy ungreased frying-pan and stir them over a moderate heat until they become light brown. Tip them on to a plate and leave to cool completely. Sprinkle the almonds evenly over the top and sides of the cake.
7 Let the cake stand for 2 hours before serving, to allow the frosting to set.

● It is most important not to use shop-bought ground almonds, but prepare your own at home with a grinder or processor.

Pumpkins, courgettes and other squashes

Small, glossy courgettes, plump, striped marrows, giant, golden pumpkins, vivid, warty crooknecks – all are members of the same family of vegetables. They can be stuffed, steamed or sautéed, made into soups, fritters, soufflés, preserves, pies and even cakes.

Courgettes, marrows and pumpkins, along with other vegetables sometimes collectively grouped under the terms squashes or gourds, are members of the Cucurbitaceae family which probably originated in South America.

Along with beans and sweetcorn, squashes of all kinds – and there are about 700 different species – were one of the staple foods of the American Indians. But these earliest vegetables had no edible flesh and were grown for the large, oily and nutritious seeds which were ground into a meal, the basis of a sauce used to dress tortillas. Marrow and pumpkin seeds were also roasted (called pepitas, they are still eaten today, noisily, like peanuts). Later on the plants were developed to bear fleshy, edible fruits, but were not introduced into Europe until comparatively recently.

Buying and storing squashes

When buying any type of squash, choose ones with firm, unblemished skins and shun any that are soft or discoloured at the stalk or blossom end.

Courgettes (known as zucchini in Italy and the U.S.) are best when small; ideally they are harvested before they are 12.5 cm /5 in long. (Forgotten ones left on the plant can be used in the same way as marrows.) The smooth, glossy skin can be yellow, pale or dark green, and is sometimes striped. You should be able to wrinkle it easily with your fingernail. Courgettes are available all year round.

Marrows or vegetable marrows are green and/or yellow: ridged, speckled or striped. Small is delicious: choose examples no more than 30 cm /12 in long and 12.5 cm /5 in across. Leave the gigantic ones where they belong – at horticultural shows to win prizes for novelty value. Marrows are in season from summer to early autumn.

Pumpkins, with their sweet-tasting flesh, humpy, cushiony shape and brilliant orange skins, are the most eye-catching of vegetables. In Europe they grow up to 45 cm /18 in across and weigh up to 12 kg /25 lb, but American pumpkins have been known to weigh as much as 90 kg /200 lb! You can usually buy a wedge of pumpkin, but make sure it has been wrapped in cling film as exposure to air causes drying. Pumpkin purée, cooked and canned, is available in some speciality shops.

Storing: courgettes, while they are best cooked on the day of purchase, can be stored in the vegetable drawer of the refrigerator for 3–4 days. Whole marrows and pumpkins will keep in a cool, dry place for 3–4 weeks. Cooked squash of all kinds can be stored in a covered container in the refrigerator for 2–3 days.

✳✳✳✳ Courgettes under 8 cm /3 in can be blanched whole for 1 minute, refreshed, cooled, dried, packed in freezer bags and frozen for up to 6 months. Cut larger ones into chunks or slices and blanch for 2 minutes.

Freeze only small, young marrows: peel them, cut into chunks and remove seeds. Then blanch for 2 minutes, refresh, cool, dry, pack in rigid containers and freeze for up to 6 months.

Pumpkins should be peeled, seeded and cut into pieces. Bake, boil or steam until soft, then drain, purée if wished, cool, pack in rigid containers and freeze for up to 1 year.

Preparing squashes

Courgettes: trim off ends, wash and dry. They can be cooked whole, halved lengthways, sliced or diced, and do not need peeling.

Marrows: trim off ends and, if the skin is tough, pare it with a vegetable peeler. If not, wash and dry. To prepare marrow slices for stuffing, cut a slice from one end. Using a small sharp knife carefully make a cut round the centre, then use a vegetable baller or spoon to scrape out seeds and stringy centre fibres. Turn the marrow, cut off a slice from the other end and work towards the middle in the same way.

Whichever way you cook the marrow – halved, sliced or diced – you must remove seed and fibres either before or after cooking.

Pumpkins: cut whole ones in half and then in wedges or slices, remove peel and seeds and slice or dice the flesh.

Degorging: all the squashes contain a lot of water which can dilute delicate sauces, and older ones can be bitter. To remedy this, you can 'degorge' the vegetable. This also prevents it from soaking up too much fat when it is fried. Either sprinkle the cut flesh generously with cooking salt and leave in a colander to drain or (more effectively) tie the salted pieces in a clean tea-towel and hang it up to drain, then force out more moisture by wringing. Either way, thoroughly rinse under cold running water, drain and dry on absorbent paper.

Cooking squashes

Courgettes: halved or sliced, young courgettes can be marinated in vinaigrette and served raw as a salad. Whole, halved or sliced, they take well to steaming over salted water flavoured with a few sprigs of fresh herbs, simmering in a small amount of chicken stock together with plenty of butter or, brushed with oil or melted butter, to grilling. Dipped in flour, egg and breadcrumbs or batter, thickly sliced courgettes may be deep or shallow fried and served, if wished, with a tomato or sweet and sour sauce (see recipe).

Courgettes go well with meat, especially lamb and chicken, and are a good vegetable accompaniment for fish dishes. They make delicious containers for combinations of meat, fish, vegetables, rice, breadcrumbs, cheese, eggs and herbs, which may be served hot or cold.

Courgette flowers (other squash flowers as well) can be made into fritters or chopped into scrambled eggs.

Marrows are perhaps best stuffed: whole, halved or thickly sliced, filled with lentils and cheese (see recipe), or perhaps with sausage-meat, with an Indonesian medley of eggs, minced beef or chicken and prawns, or with a vegetarian mixture of nuts, mushrooms and spices.

Marrows can be steamed, braised, grilled, sautéed or deep fried – the secret is to catch them just before they collapse, while they still have a pleasant crispness. Serve, if you wish, with a cream or tomato sauce.

Because of their capacity to absorb other

flavours, marrows are excellent for preserves such as marrow chutney or marrow and elderberry jam (see recipe).

Pumpkins: the most famous pumpkin dish is probably American pumpkin pie, that classic combination of pumpkin purée, spices and cream which is traditionally served at Thanksgiving dinner. But pumpkin is also successfully used in cakes (see recipe) and pastries and can be fried to accompany roast chicken.

When the flesh is to be sieved or mashed to a purée, boiling is satisfactory, but otherwise steaming assures a better texture. Pumpkin wedges brushed with melted butter can be baked at 180C /350F /gas 4 for 25–30 minutes, and brushed with honey or sprinkled with sugar just before the end of cooking. This way they make a lovely companion to roast poultry or, sprinkled with more sugar and some spice, and topped with thick cream, a trouble-free dessert.

In the West Indies, pumpkin is made into a delicious spicy soup and in Argentina, a whole pumpkin is baked, then filled with a beef stew.

On chair: pumpkin, karelas, kodus. On ledge: courgettes, marrow, kumor, kodus, cymlings

Less familiar squashes

Besides the more familiar vegetables described above, you may come across other sorts of squash. Many of them can be classified as either summer or winter squashes (which can be stored), although, confusingly, some summer squashes can be kept for use over the winter.

Summer squashes, in general, are thin skinned and, if young, do not need peeling (pumpkin is an exception). Besides courgettes and marrows, summer squashes include the bright yellow or orange crookneck with its warty skin and crooked shape, and the custard marrow (pale green), pattypan (white) and cymling (orange), all of which are disc shaped with scalloped edges.

Cook summer squashes in the same way as courgettes; they also make tasty purées with butter, cream and seasoning added.

Winter squashes have hard skins and are always cooked unpeeled. They are usually baked in halves or wedges, then glazed with maple syrup or brown sugar and butter or stuffed with a savoury filling, but they can also be cut into pieces and boiled or steamed. Varieties include the yellow, pear-shaped butternut, the dark green, acorn-shaped acorn squash and the large, thick-skinned, dark green hubbard. The spaghetti marrow or vegetable spaghetti is descriptively named for the tangled mass of fibres in its centre, eaten hot with butter or a tomato sauce or cold with a salad dressing.

Chokos, also called chayotes, are pear shaped and ridged, with creamy white to dark green skins and a delicate flavour.

They range from 7.5–20 cm /3–8 in in length, but are best when small. Boil them and top them with grated cheese, stuff them with a spicy minced beef mixture, serve them cold in an olive oil and lemon juice dressing, or peel, slice thinly, dip in batter and deep fry.

Indian squashes: the *Kodu*, the *Kumor* and the *Karela* (also known as bitter gourd) are among the many varieties of squashes used in Indian and other Eastern cuisines and often found in Oriental food shops. They are usually peeled, chopped and braised with spices.

Marrow rings with lentil stuffing

◢◢ 1 hour 40 minutes

Serves 4

100 g /4 oz split red lentils
45 ml /3 tbls oil, plus extra for greasing
1 small marrow
1 small onion, finely chopped
1 carrot, finely chopped
1 celery stalk, thinly sliced
2 tomatoes, blanched, skinned, seeded and chopped
5 ml /1 tsp dried basil
2.5 ml /1/2 tsp ground coriander
45 ml /3 tbls fresh breadcrumbs
1 medium-sized egg, lightly beaten
30 ml /2 tbls chicken stock or milk
50 g /2 oz Cheddar cheese, grated
salt and freshly ground black pepper
150 ml /5 fl oz chicken stock
15 ml /1 tbls tomato purée

1 Cook the lentils in boiling water until soft, about 35 minutes, then drain.
2 Meanwhile, heat the oven to 180C /350F /gas 4. Grease a shallow baking dish.
3 Cut a slice from each end of the marrow. Cut the marrow into 4 slices about 5 cm /2 in thick and cut away and discard the seeds and tough centre fibres. Arrange the marrow slices in a single layer in the dish.
4 Heat the oil in a frying-pan and sauté the onion, carrot, celery and tomatoes over moderate heat, stirring frequently, for 3 minutes. Remove from the heat and stir in the lentils, basil, coriander, breadcrumbs, egg, 30 ml /2 tbls stock or milk and three-quarters of the cheese. Season and mix well.
5 Divide the filling between the marrow slices, pushing it well down into the cavity of each and piling it into a mound on top.
6 Mix together the chicken stock and tomato purée and add salt and pepper to taste. Pour the sauce round, not over, the marrow slices and sprinkle the remaining cheese over the marrow.
7 Bake for 35–45 minutes, until tender. Serve hot, with the juices as a sauce.

Courgette fritters with sweet and sour sauce

Deep fried in a light but rich batter, these courgettes are served with a sauce that emphasizes their natural sweetness.

2 hours resting, then 50 minutes

Serves 4
600 g /1 lb 6 oz courgettes, thickly sliced
oil for deep frying
boiled rice or noodles, to serve
For the batter
100 g /4 oz flour
2 medium-sized eggs
150 ml /5 fl oz milk
salt and freshly ground black pepper
For the sauce
25 g /1 oz butter
1 medium-sized onion, finely chopped
2 celery stalks, thinly sliced
1 small green pepper, sliced
15 ml /1 tbls tomato purée
30 ml /2 tbls honey
2.5 ml /½ tsp ground ginger
2.5 ml /½ tsp paprika
pinch of freshly grated nutmeg
425 ml /15 fl oz hot chicken stock
50 g /2 oz seedless raisins
50 g /2 oz sultanas
15 ml /1 tbls cornflour
30 ml /2 tbls red wine vinegar
salt and freshly ground black pepper

1 To make the batter, sift the flour into a bowl and beat in the eggs. Gradually pour on the milk and beat until smooth. Season with salt and pepper, cover the bowl and leave to rest at room temperature for about 2 hours.
2 Meanwhile, make the sauce. Melt the butter in a saucepan and fry the onion, celery and green pepper over moderate heat, stirring frequently, for 5 minutes. Stir in the tomato purée, honey, ginger, paprika and nutmeg and immediately pour on the stock, stirring until all the ingredients are well blended. Add the raisins and sultanas, bring to the boil and simmer for 15 minutes.
3 Measure the cornflour into a small bowl, pour on the vinegar and mix to a smooth paste. Stir into the sauce and cook, stirring, until it thickens and clears, about 3 minutes. Season with salt and pepper to taste and keep hot while you fry the courgettes.
4 Heat the oil in a deep-fat frier to 200C /400F or until a 15 mm /½ in cube of day-old white bread browns in 40 seconds.
5 Holding the slices of courgette on a fork, dip them quickly into the batter, hold for a minute over the bowl to allow excess batter to drip off, then deep fry them, a few at a time, until they are puffed up and golden brown. Remove with a slotted spoon, drain on absorbent paper and keep warm while you fry the remainder.
6 Serve the courgettes as soon as possible, in a mound in the centre of a ring of rice or noodles, with the sauce handed separately.

Spaghetti with courgette sauce

35 minutes

Serves 4
30 ml /2 tbls oil
50 g /2 oz butter
2 medium-sized onions, chopped
1 garlic clove, finely chopped
1 green pepper, thinly sliced
450 g /1 lb courgettes, trimmed and cut into 5 mm /¼ in slices
350 g /12 oz tomatoes, blanched, skinned, seeded and sliced
5 ml /1 tsp dried oregano
salt and freshly ground black pepper
350 g /12 oz wholewheat spaghetti
freshly grated Parmesan cheese, to serve

1 To make the sauce, heat the oil and 25 g /1 oz butter in a frying-pan and sauté the onions over moderate heat for 3 minutes, stirring occasionally. Add the garlic, green pepper and courgettes, stir well and sauté for 2 minutes. Cover the pan, lower heat and simmer 10 minutes, stirring occasionally.
2 Add the tomatoes, oregano, salt and pepper and cook, uncovered, over moderate heat for a further 10 minutes. Taste the sauce and add more seasoning if necessary.
3 While the sauce is cooking, cook the spaghetti in a large pan of boiling, salted water 12–13 minutes, or until just tender.
4 Drain the spaghetti and toss it with the remaining butter in a warmed serving dish. Top with the sauce and serve hot, with the cheese handed separately.

Pumpkin cream soup

This soup has a subtle flavour and pretty, pale apricot colour.

1 hour

Serves 4
40 g /1½ oz butter
2 medium-sized onions, chopped
700 g /1½ lb prepared pumpkin, in 25 mm /1 in cubes
600 ml /1 pt chicken stock
pinch of freshly grated nutmeg
1.5 ml /¼ tsp paprika plus extra for garnishing
150 ml /5 fl oz thin cream
salt and freshly ground black pepper
60 ml /4 tbls soured cream

1 Melt the butter in a large saucepan and fry the onions over moderate heat for 3–4 minutes. Do not let them brown. Add the pumpkin, stir well and pour on the stock. Bring to the boil, cover and simmer for 30 minutes.
2 Purée the mixture in a blender or push it through a sieve. Return the mixture to the rinsed-out pan. Stir in the nutmeg, paprika and cream and season with salt and freshly ground black pepper.
3 Reheat gently without boiling, then adjust seasoning if necessary. Pour into warmed soup bowls and top each with a spoonful of soured cream and a pinch of paprika. Serve the soup at once.

Spaghetti with courgette sauce

stirring once or twice if convenient.

3 Wash the elderberries and strip them from the stalks by pushing them off with the tines of a large fork.

4 Turn the marrow and sugar mixture into a large pan, add the elderberries and lemon juice and simmer for about 1 hour, or until the fruit is tender.

5 Bring to the boil and boil rapidly for 10–15 minutes, until setting point is reached; to test, remove the pan from the heat and spoon a little jam onto a cold saucer. When the test sample is cold, push a finger over the surface. If it wrinkles, it is ready. If not, cook for a little longer, then test again.

6 When the jam is ready, pour it into clean, warm jars. Cover them at once with waxed paper circles and then with transparent paper covers. Leave to cool, then label and store in a cool, dry place.

Pumpkin cake

Sweet and spicy with a tangy topping, this moist cake keeps well for 3-4 days.

1 hour 15 minutes,
plus cooling

Serves 8
100 g /4 oz self-raising flour
5 ml /1 tsp ground cinnamon
1.5 ml /¼ tsp freshly grated nutmeg
2.5 ml /½ tsp salt
1 medium-sized egg
40 g /1½ oz soft margarine plus extra to grease
50 g /2 oz caster sugar
50 g /2 oz soft light brown sugar
225 ml /8 fl oz pumpkin purée (fresh or canned)
50 g /2 oz chopped walnuts
50 g /2 oz raisins
For the frosting
15 g /½ oz soft margarine
grated zest of 1 lemon
100 g /4 oz icing sugar, sifted
5 ml /1 tsp lemon juice
15 ml /1 tbls thick cream

1 Heat the oven to 180C /350F /gas 4. Grease a cake tin 18 cm /7 in square.

2 Sift together the flour, cinnamon, nutmeg and salt and beat in the egg. In another bowl, cream together the margarine and sugars and beat until light. Beat the dry ingredients and pumpkin purée alternately into the margarine mixture, then stir in the nuts and raisins.

3 Turn the mixture into the tin and bake in the centre of the oven for 45–50 minutes, or until the cake is done. Leave to cool in the tin, then turn out.

4 To make the frosting, cream together the margarine and lemon zest, add the sugar, lemon juice and cream and beat until smooth.

5 Spread the frosting on top of the cold cake. Draw a fork from side to side, making parallel lines in one direction. Then draw it across 3 or 4 times in the opposite direction to make a wavy pattern. Cut the pumpkin cake into 8 fingers to serve.

Cold pumpkin soufflé

1 hour 30 minutes,
plus 1 hour or more chilling

Serves 6
450 g /1 lb prepared weight pumpkin
1.5 ml /¼ tsp ground cinnamon
1.5 ml /¼ tsp ground ginger
1.5 ml /¼ tsp vanilla essence
45 ml /3 tbls orange juice
15 ml /1 tbls gelatine
3 large eggs, separated
75 g /3 oz soft light brown sugar
150 ml /5 fl oz thick cream, whipped
a few fresh leaves and flowers, to decorate
sponge finger biscuits, to serve

1 Cut the pumpkin flesh from the rind, discard the seeds and tough fibres, and check the weight. Cut into dice and steam or boil until just tender, 10–15 minutes.

2 Drain and then mash, sieve or liquidize to a purée. Stir in the spices and vanilla and leave to cool.

3 Pour the orange juice into a small bowl, sprinkle on the gelatine and stand in a pan of hot water. Stir occasionally until the gelatine has melted.

4 Whisk the egg yolks and sugar until thick and creamy. Stir in the pumpkin purée and then pour in the gelatine mixture in a slow, steady stream, stirring. Fold in the cream and refrigerate until the mixture

begins to set, about 10–15 minutes.

5 Whisk the egg whites until they are stiff, then fold them into the pumpkin mixture using a metal spoon. Turn into a serving bowl and chill for 1 hour or more to set.

6 Decorate the top with a few small leaves and fresh flowers and serve chilled, with sponge finger biscuits.

● In place of the fresh pumpkin you can use 225 g /8 oz canned unsweetened pumpkin purée if you wish.

Marrow and elderberry jam

Rich in colour and delicate in flavour, this jam is perfect with hot scones or toast.

8 hours standing,
then 2 hours plus cooling

Makes about 2.3 kg /5 lb
700 g /1½ lb prepared weight marrow
1.4 kg /3 lb sugar
1.4 kg /3 lb elderberries
juice of 1 lemon

1 Peel the marrow, discard the seeds and tough fibres and check the weight. Cut it into dice of about 15 mm /½ in and place in a large earthenware, china or plastic bowl – do not use a metal one.

2 Sprinkle on the sugar, stir well, cover with a cloth and leave for about 8 hours,

Potatoes

Potatoes tend to be taken for granted as an accompaniment to meat, and indeed there are many ways to serve them as such. But why not try them in a creamy fish soup, buttery gnocchi, or even an almond tart?

Potatoes were originally grown merely for their curiosity value. It is only relatively recently that potatoes have become such an important food crop, once it was discovered that they grew well and could be used in so many ways. Potatoes are also rich in vitamin C, contain some protein, and are not nearly as fattening as their reputation suggests – as long as you don't fry them or smother them in butter, that is!

There are two main potato crops in northern Europe: the new or early crop which comes into the shops in May and lasts until August, and maincrop or old potatoes which are available from September to May.

New potatoes with their waxy texture, are, in general, excellent for boiling or steaming and eating hot or cold in salads. They sauté very well and the larger ones make very good chips. They can also be roasted with meat, and late in the season Maris Peer and Wilja can be jacket baked. Other varieties to look out for include Home Guard, Pentland Javelin and Ulster Sceptre.

Maincrop potatoes: Desirée, King Edward and Maris Piper are good all-round potatoes which can be chipped, sautéed, roasted, jacket baked, boiled and mashed. Pentland Crown, Pentland Dell and Pentland Hawk are not so high in quality, but can also be cooked in any of the ways mentioned above. Maincrop potatoes are not very good for dishes that require firm pieces of potato such as salads or gratins. At the beginning of the season, maincrop potatoes are rather waxy; they become more floury with storage. King Edward and Maris Piper are especially floury.

In Australia, Sebago, Kennebec, Delaware and Pontiac are all-purpose potatoes which are harvested from the different states all year round, so can be both new and maincrop, according to season.

Buying and storing potatoes

When buying potatoes, avoid any with dark-coloured or green patches, cut skins, sprouts or signs of withering. New potatoes should have damp soil sticking to them and their skins should rub away easily. Try to cook them as quickly as possible; in any

case, keep them no longer than two days.

Old potatoes should be evenly shaped and not excessively dirty, although unwashed ones will keep longer than cleaned ones.

If you buy potatoes in a polythene bag, transfer them to a vegetable rack or another container which gives adequate ventilation as soon as you get home. Store them in a cool, dark and dry place far from anything with a strong smell.

Potato products: you can buy frozen chips, duchesse potatoes and potato croquettes, as well as various other frozen potato products. Cook these according to package directions. Instant mashed potato is a useful item to have on hand for making a quick shepherd's pie, for example. Potato flour or starch is used in some dumplings, pastries and cakes.

✱✱✱✱ Since potatoes are available all year round it is not worth freezing them in any quantity. Whole cooked potatoes tend to become leathery and sliced or chopped potatoes in casseroles may break up on thawing. However, it is useful to have a supply of frozen chips and duchesse potatoes on hand.

Fry chips in hot fat for 3 minutes, drain, cool, open freeze, then pack in bags or boxes and store for up to 3 months. Cook from frozen in hot fat until golden.

Pipe out serving portions of duchesse potato mixture (see below), open freeze, then pack and freeze for up to 3 months. To cook, defrost then bake as directed.

Preparing potatoes

Both old and new potatoes are best cooked in their skins – this way they retain more of their vitamins. You can easily slip off the skins after cooking if wished. Simply wash the potatoes well, scrubbing if necessary to get them clean. Cut away any green patches.

If you must peel them before cooking, peel as thinly as possible and immediately place them in a bowl of cold water to avoid discoloration, but do not let them soak too long or they will lose some of their nutrients. Provided they have been scrubbed, the peelings can be used to make vegetable stock, or you can deep fry them in the same way as you fry chips, or bake them and serve with salt, pepper and lots of butter.

Cooking potatoes

Boiling or steaming: choose potatoes which are all the same size. If they are very large, cut them into even-sized pieces. To boil, drop them into lightly salted boiling water and simmer gently until tender – time depends on type and size. A sprig of mint may be added to new potatoes if wished. If the potatoes do start to break up during boiling, pour off the water and finish cooking them by steaming. Remember that steaming takes slightly longer than boiling.

Serve boiled or steamed potatoes hot with butter and a little chopped parsley, warm in a German salad with frankfurters or cold in other salads. It is best to toss the potatoes in the dressing while they are still warm, then add other ingredients later.

Mashing: boil or steam maincrop potatoes, drain if necessary, then dry over a low heat.

New potatoes topped with butter

Mash with a fork or masher, until all the lumps have disappeared. For a very fine texture, rub them through a sieve instead.

● For creamed potatoes, add 25 g /1 oz butter and 15–30 ml /1–2 tbls hot milk to 500 g /1 lb potatoes. Beat the mixture over a low heat until it is light and fluffy and serve as a side dish or use to top a pie.

● For duchesse potatoes, add 50 g /2 oz butter to 500 g /1 lb sieved, mashed potatoes, together with 2 egg yolks and seasoning. Pipe into mounds or use as a decorative border, brush with egg and brown in the oven.

● For croquettes, leave mashed potatoes to cool slightly, then form into small sausage shapes. Dip in beaten egg, then coat thickly with dried breadcrumbs. Deep fry for 2–3 minutes, until golden brown, then drain and fry for another 2–3 minutes.

Sautéing: thickly slice boiled potatoes and sauté in butter and olive oil until crisp and golden. Lyonnaise potatoes are made by cooking the potatoes with sliced onion rings sautéed in butter.

Deep frying is used for such gourmet dishes as game chips and pomme dauphine.

For chips, cut peeled potatoes into sticks, rinse in cold water, drain and dry on absorbent paper. Deep fry in fat heated to 190C /375F until lightly coloured, then drain. Just before serving, return to the hot fat and fry until golden brown, drain again and serve at once, sprinkled with salt.

Jacket baking: choose large, unblemished floury potatoes of about the same size. Scrub well, dry and prick all over with a fork. If you prefer a crisp skin, make a slit all the way around the potato with a knife;

Potato almond tart

do not prick. Place the potatoes on a baking sheet, making sure they do not touch each other. Bake in an oven heated to 220C /425F /gas 7 for about an hour, or until they are soft. Potato bakers cut down on the cooking time as their metal prongs help the heat penetrate to the centres of the potatoes. If you have a potato pot, you can use it to bake potatoes on top of the stove. When the potatoes are cooked, make a slit or cross on top, squeeze gently in a cloth to open and top with butter, soured cream and chives, grated cheese, crisply fried bacon bits, scrambled eggs – use your imagination!

Roasting: peel medium-sized potatoes, coat them in hot fat, then roast in an oven heated to 200C /400F /gas 6 for 50–60 minutes. You can cut down on the cooking time by boiling them for 10 minutes, draining, drying and finishing off in the oven.

Casseroling: peel and slice waxy new potatoes, then let them soak in cold water for a few minutes. Layer them in a greased casserole with butter and milk or stock, seasoning as you go. Add, if you wish, grated cheese, thinly sliced onion, herbs, sliced tomatoes, etc. Cover and bake at 200C /400F /gas 6 for about one hour, or until the potatoes are soft.

Other ways of using potatoes: besides these basic methods, potatoes can be used in cooking in hundreds of ways. They are delicious in soups and are a necessary element in the classic vichyssoise. They can be used in quiches, omelettes, even in scones and sweet tarts (see recipe).

Potatoes and beans in mustard sauce and Potato and prawn salad

Finnish spring soup

This soup is substantial enough to be served as a light main course with a salad and crusty bread.

 35 minutes

Serves 4
500 g /1 lb waxy new potatoes, scraped
1 bay leaf
12 spring onions, cut in half
150 ml /5 fl oz chicken stock
150 ml /5 fl oz milk
1 small cauliflower, separated into florets
600 g /1¼ lb monkfish, cut into chunks
salt and freshly ground black pepper
30 ml /2 tbls freshly chopped parsley

1 Place the potatoes, bay leaf and spring onions in a large saucepan with the stock. Bring to the boil, lower the heat, cover and simmer for 5 minutes.
2 Add the milk and return to the boil. Add the cauliflower and continue simmering for a further 5 minutes.
3 Add the monkfish and salt and pepper to taste, then simmer for 10–15 minutes, until the fish and vegetables are tender. Serve sprinkled with the chopped parsley.

Crécy potatoes

Serve this rich casserole with plainly cooked meat or poultry.

 1 hour 10 minutes

Serves 4
225 g /8 oz carrots, peeled and sliced
salt and freshly ground black pepper
350 g /12 oz waxy new potatoes, peeled and sliced
6 spring onions, sliced
200 ml /7 fl oz milk, more if necessary
150 ml /5 fl oz thick cream
50 g /2 oz Emmental cheese, grated

1 Heat the oven to 190C /375F /gas 5. Drop the carrots into lightly salted boiling water and simmer for 10 minutes, then drain. Meanwhile, boil the potatoes and spring onions in the milk with a little black pepper for 5 minutes. Drain, reserving the milk.
2 Layer the carrots, potatoes and spring onions in a small ovenproof dish, seasoning each layer with salt. Pour in the milk and the cream, and sprinkle the top with grated cheese.
3 Bake, uncovered, for 45 minutes or until tender, checking from time to time to make sure that it is not drying out. If so, add a little hot milk. Serve from the dish.

Meat and potato pie

 1 hour 25 minutes

Serves 4
15 ml /1 tbls oil
1 large onion, finely chopped
350 g /12 oz lean minced beef
15 ml /1 tbls flour
175 ml /6 fl oz strong beef stock
1.5 ml /¼ tsp mixed herbs
salt and freshly ground black pepper
300 g /10 oz new potatoes, peeled and cubed
shortcrust pastry made with 225 g /8 oz flour

1 Heat the oil in a large frying-pan and fry the onion for 2–3 minutes. Add the beef, turn up the heat, and brown well all over.
2 Reduce the heat and add the flour, stock, herbs and salt and pepper to taste. Bring to the boil, stirring all the time. Simmer for 15 minutes, add the potatoes and simmer for a further 10 minutes.
3 Heat the oven to 200C /400F /gas 6. Roll out the pastry and use just over half of it to line a 20 cm /8 in flan tin. Fill with the meat and potato mixture and cover with the remaining pastry. Press the edges together to seal, then trim and flute with your fingers. Prick the top with a fork and bake in the centre of the oven for 30 minutes or until the pastry is golden brown. Serve at once.

Potato oatmeal stew

This dish needs only a green vegetable to make a complete meal.

🔪 45 minutes

Serves 4
30 ml /2 tbls oil
2 medium-sized onions, sliced
350 g /12 oz lean bacon, chopped
45 ml /3 tbls fine oatmeal
15 ml /1 tbls yeast extract
1 kg /2 lb potatoes, peeled and cut into chunks
salt and freshly ground black pepper
75 g /3 oz Cheddar cheese, grated
350 g /12 oz carrots, grated, to serve

1 Heat the oil in a large saucepan. Add the onions and gently fry for 2–3 minutes. Add the bacon and cook for a further 2–3 minutes.
2 Stir in the oatmeal and add 300 ml /11 fl oz water and the yeast extract. Bring the mixture to the boil, stirring all the time, then add the potatoes and salt and pepper to taste. Cover, reduce the heat and simmer for 15–20 minutes, until the potatoes are cooked through. Take care not to overcook or the potatoes will fall apart.
3 Pour into a heated serving bowl, sprinkle the grated cheese on top and serve at once with the grated carrots separately.

Potato and prawn salad

🔪 defrosting prawns if necessary, then 30 minutes plus 1 hour cooling

Serves 4
500 g /1 lb waxy new potatoes
salt and freshly ground black pepper
45 ml /3 tbls mayonnaise
2.5 ml /1/2 tsp dried tarragon
2 hard-boiled eggs, chopped
100 g /4 oz peeled cooked prawns, defrosted if frozen
7.5 cm /3 in piece of cucumber, thinly sliced, to garnish

1 Drop the potatoes into lightly salted boiling water and simmer for 15–20 minutes or until tender. Drain, peel and chop, then mix in the mayonnaise, tarragon and salt and pepper to taste. Leave to cool, about 1 hour.
2 Mix the potatoes with the chopped eggs and prawns. Spoon onto a serving platter or 4 individual serving plates, surround with the sliced cucumber and serve.

Potatoes and beans in mustard sauce

🔪 25 minutes

Serves 4
500 g /1 lb new potatoes, halved if large
salt and freshly ground black pepper
500 g /1 lb French beans
150 ml /5 fl oz thick cream
10 ml /2 tsp tarragon and thyme mustard, or other mild French mustard

1 Drop the potatoes into lightly salted boiling water, simmer for 15–20 minutes or until just tender, then drain well.
2 While the potatoes are cooking, drop the beans into lightly salted boiling water for 8–10 minutes or until they are just tender. Drain well and keep warm.
3 Mix the cream and the mustard and pour over the potatoes. Season with pepper, bring to the boil and boil for 1–2 minutes, until the cream begins to thicken a little. Pour onto a heated serving dish and surround with the beans. Serve at once.

Potato gnocchi

🔪🔪 50 minutes, plus 1 hour chilling

Serves 4
450 g /1 lb floury potatoes
salt and freshly ground black pepper
65 g /2 1/2 oz butter
100 g /4 oz flour, or more if necessary, plus flour for flouring hands
1 small egg, beaten
freshly grated nutmeg
50 g /2 oz freshly grated Parmesan cheese

1 Drop the potatoes into lightly salted boiling water and simmer for about 20 minutes or until tender. Drain, peel, mash and sieve them.
2 Mix the potatoes with 15 g /1/2 oz butter and the flour, egg, salt, pepper and nutmeg to taste. Work the mixture to a firm dough, adding a little extra flour if the dough is wet. Chill for 1 hour.
3 Form into small cylindrical shapes with floured hands.
4 Bring a very large pan of lightly salted water to the boil. Gently lower the gnocchi into the water and simmer for about 5 minutes, or until they rise to the surface.
5 Meanwhile, melt the remaining butter. Lift the gnocchi out carefully using a slotted spoon and place on a heated serving dish. Pour the melted butter over the top, sprinkle with Parmesan cheese and serve.

● Serve this classic Italian first course with a tomato or meat sauce instead of melted butter, if wished.

Potato almond tart

🔪🔪 1 hour 35 minutes plus 1 hour chilling, then cooling

Serves 4–6
200 g /7 oz floury potatoes, peeled and chopped
salt
175 g /6 oz self-raising flour
175 g /6 oz butter
50 g /2 oz sugar
1 medium-sized egg, beaten
50 g /2 oz ground almonds
25 g /1 oz raisins
few drops of almond essence
125 g /4 oz raspberry jam
whipped cream, to serve

1 Drop the potatoes into lightly salted boiling water and cook until tender, then drain well, mash, sieve and leave to cool.
2 Meanwhile, make the pastry. Mix 150 g /5 oz flour with a pinch of salt. Rub 125 g /4 oz butter into the mixture until it resembles fine breadcrumbs.
3 Mix 75 g /3 oz of the sieved potatoes into the pastry with a fork. Shape into a ball, place in a polythene bag and chill in the refrigerator for 1 hour.
4 To make the filling, cream the remaining butter with the sugar. Add the egg with a little of the remaining flour. Beat well. Stir in the remaining potato, the rest of the flour and the ground almonds, then the raisins and a few drops of almond essence. Mix well.
5 Heat the oven to 180C /350F /gas 4. Roll out the pastry to fit the base of a 20 cm /8 in loose-bottomed flan case. Place in the case and work the pastry up the sides with your fingers.
6 Spread the jam over the base of the case, then spoon the filling over the top and smooth flat with a knife. Bake in the centre of the oven for 45–50 minutes, until it is golden brown on top and the pastry is cooked.
7 Leave to cool, then serve with a bowl of whipped cream, if wished.

Unusual root vegetables

Instead of limiting your family to the usual potatoes or carrots, make your menus more exciting by trying a few of these unusual root vegetables.

Salsify and scorzonera, Hamburg parsley and kohlrabi, yam and cassava – all are root vegetables, popular elsewhere, that we should use occasionally to add variety to our family meals.

Salsify and scorzonera

Salsify is sometimes known as oyster plant or vegetable oyster because its slightly smoky flavour reminds some people of oysters. It has carrot-shaped white roots 20–30 cm /8–12 in long. Its grey-green shoots are long and leafy, but these are usually cut off before the vegetable reaches the shops.

Scorzonera is a very close relative of salsify. It looks very similar except that its skin is black instead of white – which is why it is sometimes called black salsify. Many people prefer its taste.

Buying and storing: salsify and scorzonera are available from autumn to early winter. Look for firm, moist roots. Salsify should look shiny and white – brown marks indicate bruising. Handle both vegetables with care; the roots bruise easily.

Cans of salsify in brine can be purchased from specialist shops.

Store salsify and scorzonera in a cool, dark, airy place, where they will keep fresh for up to five days.

❋❋❋ To freeze, scrub the roots, cut them into short lengths and blanch for two minutes. Drain and peel while they are still warm, let cool, then pack into freezer bags and freeze for up to one year.

Preparing and cooking: as soon as they are peeled or cut, salsify and scorzonera turn brown, so drop the prepared roots into a bowl of water with a little lemon juice added.

To boil, it is best to scrub the roots and cut them into short lengths, then boil in lightly salted water for about 25 minutes, or until they are tender. Drain, then skin them as soon as they are cool enough to handle. To steam, peel the roots, then cut into short lengths and steam for 35–40 minutes.

Boiled or steamed salsify or scorzonera can be tossed with butter and lemon juice or chopped herbs, or mixed into vinaigrette and left to cool. Try them coated in a white or cheese sauce and served au gratin, or topped with a tomato sauce.

Peel salsify or scorzonera, slice thickly and sauté quickly in a mixture of butter and oil, or cut into sticks, dip in batter and deep fry. Diced raw salsify or scorzonera can be added to casseroles along with other root vegetables, or add the grated raw root to salads for a nutty flavour.

Scorzonera roots can be well scrubbed, then baked, whole, in their skins in the centre of an oven heated to 180C /350F /gas 4 for 45 minutes. Before serving, cut in half lengthways, dot with butter and sprinkle with freshly grated Parmesan cheese.

Hamburg parsley

Hamburg parsley (also known as parsley root, turnip-rooted or parsnip-rooted parsley) has long been popular in eastern and northern Europe. It looks like a small, white, even-shaped parsnip, and tastes rather like a combination of parsnip, parsley and celery. In Germany, it is a favourite ingredient of stock-pots, soups and stews.

Buying and storing: Hamburg parsley is available all year round, but is difficult to find. It is usually sold in bunches with the leaves attached. The roots should be crisp and white. Avoid any that are discoloured, dry or soft. The leaves, which look like flat-leaved parsley, should be fresh and green.

Store Hamburg parsley in a cool, dry place for up to four days.

❋❋❋ Scrub, dice or slice, blanch for two minutes, drain, cool, pack in freezer bags and freeze for up to three months.

Preparing and cooking: it is not necessary to peel the roots, simply scrub them well and trim away the ends and any rootlets and irregular pieces.

The raw, grated root is good in a salad combined with grated carrot, chopped celery and shredded cabbage.

To cook, slice the roots and boil for 20 minutes or steam for 35–40 minutes. Or braise them with 300 ml /10 fl oz stock and 25 g /1 oz butter to each 500 g /1 lb vegetable for 20 minutes, or until the stock has reduced to a glaze. Hamburg parsley chips are prepared and cooked in the same way as potato chips (*page 215*).

The leaves can be chopped and sprinkled over cooked dishes and salads.

Kohlrabi

Kohlrabi or cabbage-turnip, a member of the cabbage family, consists of a round, bulbous stem, coloured green or purple, from which the leaf stems grow at regular intervals. In texture and flavour, the bulb is similar to the crisp, nutty core of cabbage or cauliflower.

Buying and storing: kohlrabi is available from late summer to early winter. Buy the smallest bulbs – ideally, no bigger than a small orange. The bulbs should be unwrinkled, the leaves fresh and green. Store in the bottom of the refrigerator for up to four days.

❋❋❋ Best for freezing are very small bulbs, no bigger than 25 mm /1 in. Peel thinly, blanch for three minutes and freeze whole. Larger vegetables should be diced, then blanched for two minutes. Freeze for up to one year.

Preparing and cooking: trim off any stalk ends, and peel the thin outer layer of larger bulbs.

Raw kohlrabi can be chopped or very thinly sliced and added to salads. To cook, quarter or slice the bulbs, depending on size, and boil for 20–25 minutes, or steam for 40 minutes. Then toss with butter and herbs or coat with a savoury sauce, or coat with mayonnaise and leave to cool. Sliced kohlrabi can be braised in butter and chicken stock, or the bulbs can be diced and added to stews or sautés (see recipe).

Yams

There are many varieties of yams grown in tropical countries. They can grow very large – more than 20 kg /44 lb – but those available in Western countries usually weigh around 1 kg /2 lb. If larger, they may be cut for sale. They are potato-shaped, with fibrous brown skin and moist, white flesh. The flesh has a high starch content and becomes floury when cooked. Do not confuse them with sweet potatoes, known as 'yams' in the southern U.S. states.

Buying and storing: yams can be found all year round, especially in West Indian and African shops and markets. Smaller ones are sold whole, larger ones in halves or slices. As long as they are quite firm when you buy them, yams will keep well; you can store whole yams for several months in a cool, dark, dry place – so it is not necessary to freeze them.

Preparing and cooking: when preparing yams, peel them and drop them immediately into a bowl of cold water with the addition of a little lemon juice.

Boil yams in water with salt and lemon juice added, and serve diced or puréed, as an accompaniment to meat. A yam purée

can be flavoured with cinnamon and brown sugar, then used as a base for a soufflé.

They can also be sliced and fried, or baked in their skins and served with butter. In tropical countries, diced yam is added to curries and stew. Yam cakes are a favourite in the Caribbean (see recipe).

Cassava

Cassava, manioc or yuca is native to South America. It has become a staple food in many tropical countries, but as it is very low in protein (it is mostly starch), a diet based on it can result in malnutrition. There are about 150 varieties of cassava, but these can be divided into two main groups, sweet and bitter. The bitter varieties can be poisonous when raw, but become edible when cooked.

Cassavas are covered with a scaly bark, and are about 25-30 cm /10-12 in long. They are difficult to buy outside of the tropics; you may be able to obtain them in West Indian markets.

The cassava product best known in the West is tapioca, which is used in milk puddings and to thicken soups.

Preparing and cooking: first, the hairy bark must be peeled away. The flesh can then be grated and made into flat cakes, cut into chips and deep fried, or dried and ground into a meal called *farhina*, which can be made into bread.

The juice squeezed out of the pulp is made into a sweetened syrup called *cassareep*, which in the Caribbean is added to spicy stews and savoury dishes.

Pork with kohlrabi and caraway

🍴🍴 1 hour

Serves 4
750 g /1½ lb lean boneless pork (shoulder or spare rib), in 20 mm /¾ in cubes
500 g /1 lb kohlrabi, in 20 mm /¾ in cubes
25 g /1 oz butter
1 large onion, thinly sliced
1 garlic clove, finely chopped
100 ml /3½ fl oz chicken stock
100 ml /3½ fl oz dry white wine
5 ml /1 tsp caraway seeds
salt and freshly ground black pepper
boiled potatoes or noodles, to serve

1 Melt the butter in a sauté pan or large frying-pan on a high heat. Brown the pieces of pork all over, then transfer to a plate.
2 Lower the heat to medium, add the onion and garlic and cook until they are soft but not coloured. Stir in the kohlrabi, pour in the stock and wine and bring the liquid to the boil.
3 Return the pork to the pan, add the caraway seeds and salt and pepper to taste. Cover and cook over a low heat for 30 minutes, or until the pork is tender and most of the liquid has been absorbed.
4 Turn onto a warmed serving platter and serve, with boiled potatoes or noodles.

Salsify bake

In this easy main dish, anchovies complement the smoky flavour of the vegetable.

🍴🍴 1 hour 15 minutes

Serves 4
500 g /1 lb salsify or scorzonera
salt
6 medium-sized eggs, separated
125 g /4 oz Cheddar cheese, grated
3 anchovy fillets, finely chopped
15 ml /1 tbls freshly chopped thyme or 7.5 ml /1½ tsp dried thyme
butter for greasing

1 Scrub the salsify or scorzonera well. Cut it into 10 cm /4 in lengths. Drop into a pan of lightly salted boiling water and simmer for 20 minutes or until tender.
2 Drain the salsify, peel it and slice into thin rounds. Heat the oven to 200C /400F /gas 6.
3 In a large bowl, beat the egg yolks and mix in the cheese, anchovies and thyme. Fold in the salsify. Stiffly whisk the egg whites and fold them in.
4 Pile the mixture into a deep, buttered ovenproof dish and bake for 30 minutes, until golden brown and well risen. Serve at once, from the dish.

Pork with kohlrabi and caraway

Curried yam cakes

Serve these fried yam cakes as a delicious accompaniment to a curry.

♦♦ 1 hour 20 minutes

Serves 4
1 kg /2 lb yams, peeled and cut in chunks
salt
90 ml /6 tbls oil plus extra for shallow frying
1 large onion, finely chopped
1 garlic clove, finely chopped
5 ml /1 tsp curry powder
5 ml /1 tsp cumin seeds
5 ml /1 tsp ground coriander
25 g /1 oz flour seasoned with a pinch of curry powder

1 Boil the yams in lightly salted water until they are tender, about 20 minutes. Drain and mash them.
2 Heat the 90 ml /6 tbls oil in a frying-pan on a low heat. Add the onion, garlic and

Curried yam cakes with a beef curry

spices and cook, stirring often, until the onion is golden, about 15 minutes. Mix the contents of the pan into the mashed yams and leave to cool.
3 Form the mixture into flat, round cakes about 7.5 cm /3 in in diameter. Coat them with the seasoned flour.
4 Heat oil in a large frying-pan on a medium heat, then fry the yam cakes until they are golden on both sides. Drain on absorbent paper, place on a warmed serving dish and serve at once.

Lamb and Hamburg parsley casserole

Hamburg parsley and orange juice and zest make this warming lamb casserole something out of the ordinary.

♦♦ 2 hours 15 minutes

Serves 4
1 kg /2 lb lean lamb (shoulder or leg), cut in 25 mm /1 in cubes
500 g /1 lb Hamburg parsley root, sliced
25 g /1 oz butter
350 g /12 oz carrots, sliced
1 large onion, thinly sliced
600 ml /1 pt chicken stock
zest and juice of 1 small orange
1 bay leaf
salt and freshly ground black pepper
45 ml /3 tbls chopped Hamburg parsley leaves

1 Heat the oven to 180C /350F /gas 4. Melt the butter in a flameproof casserole over high heat. Add the lamb cubes, brown them quickly and remove them.
2 Lower the heat, add the Hamburg parsley, carrots and onion. Cover and cook gently for 10 minutes.
3 Pour in the stock and bring to the boil. Add the orange juice, lamb, bay leaf and salt and pepper. Cover and cook in the oven for 1½ hours.
4 While the lamb is cooking, cut the orange zest into small, thin slivers. Blanch in boiling water for 2 minutes and drain.
5 Turn the lamb, vegetables and sauce into a warmed serving dish, scatter the orange zest and chopped Hamburg parsley leaves over the top and serve the casserole at once.

Salsify and tomato soup

Salsify gives a creamy texture and unusual flavour to a simply made soup.

♦♦ 1 hour

Serves 4
250 g /8 oz salsify or scorzonera, peeled and thinly sliced
500 g /1 lb tomatoes, blanched and skinned
25 g /1 oz butter
1 medium-sized onion, chopped
600 ml /1 pt chicken stock
1 bouquet garni
1.5 ml /¼ tsp Tabasco sauce
salt and freshly ground black pepper
45 ml /3 tbls thick cream

1 Cut the skinned tomatoes in half. Squeeze the seeds into a sieve over a bowl and press to extract the juice. Reserve the juice and chop the tomato flesh.
2 Melt the butter in a saucepan over a low heat. Stir in the salsify and onion, cover and cook gently for 10 minutes.
3 Add the stock, tomato juice and flesh and bring to the boil. Add the bouquet garni, Tabasco and salt and pepper, cover and simmer for 20 minutes.
4 Cool the soup slightly and remove the bouquet garni. Purée the soup in a blender or food processor or put it through a vegetable mill.
5 Return the soup to the rinsed-out saucepan, reheat, pour into warmed bowls and garnish with swirls of cream over the top. Serve at once.

Celeriac and Jerusalem artichokes

Both under-used vegetables, celeriac and Jerusalem artichokes can do much to enliven and vary your winter menus – use them cooked or raw, in soups, salads, as main courses or as vegetable accompaniments.

Celeriac and Jerusalem artichokes are two vegetables that were popular in the 18th and 19th centuries but for many years after that were almost unheard of. They are now becoming more widely known and are not difficult to find. Chinese artichokes are another, rarer tuber, similar in flavour to the Jerusalem artichoke.

Celeriac

Celeriac, or turnip-rooted celery, is a root vegetable closely related to celery. It was originally native to southern Europe, but is now grown on a small scale in most countries with temperate climates.

Buying and storing celeriac: celeriac is available throughout most of the winter months. In appearance, it is rather like a turnip, but with a much rougher, yellowish-brown skin. Its size varies from 250–750 g /8 oz–1½ lb. When buying celeriac, make sure that the root is hard. If you pick up two of similar size but of different weights, choose the heavier one, as the lighter one may well be hollow and floury-textured in the middle, especially towards the end of the season. Try to find one with as smooth a skin as possible, so you will have less to cut away when you peel it.

Buy 500–750 g /1–1½ lb for four people when you are cooking it, 350–500 g /12 oz –1 lb when you plan to serve it raw. Store celeriac in a dry, cool, dark place, where it will stay fresh for up to two weeks.

✱✱✱✱ To freeze celeriac, slice it, blanch then chill it for 3 minutes each, then pack it in a polythene bag. Freeze it for up to 9 months.

Preparing celeriac: celeriac is very similar in texture and flavour to the nutty inner heart of a head of celery. It can be eaten raw or cooked.

To prepare, slice off the top and the stubby remains of the stems. The root always needs to be peeled; you can sometimes use a potato peeler, but when the skin is really thick it is best to use a sharp knife. To prevent discoloration, drop the peeled celeriac pieces in a bowl of cold water with a spoonful of vinegar or lemon juice added to it, or rub the cut surfaces of the vegetable with a slice of lemon.

Using celeriac: for serving raw in salads, celeriac is best either coarsely grated or very finely chopped. Marinate it in the dressing for about 30 minutes before you add the remaining ingredients. Celeriac goes well with chopped celery in a salad, and chopped apples, walnuts and a few sultanas make it more interesting.

Another way of making a celeriac salad is to cut the root into small julienne sticks and blanch them quickly in boiling water before mixing them, still warm, into the dressing. This type of celeriac salad is often flavoured with Dijon mustard (see recipe).

Celeriac can be plainly boiled or steamed. To boil, cut it into 4 cm /1½ in chunks, drop it into lightly salted boiling water and cook for 20 minutes. Save the water for soup or a stock. Chunks the same size will take about 30 minutes to steam.

Plainly cooked celeriac can be served with a bechamel or hollandaise sauce, tossed with butter and chopped herbs, or coated with a cheese sauce and made into a gratin. Or toss in butter and brown it in a moderate oven for 15 minutes. Bake thickly sliced (about 25 mm /1 in) uncooked celeriac in butter, or sauté small, thin slices in butter.

Small chunks of celeriac can be braised (see recipe) or simmered in a covered saucepan on top of the stove with a little butter, stock or milk, and chopped herbs. Finely chopped celeriac can be added to casseroles and stews. Its celery-like flavour goes very well with beef, veal and chicken.

The flavour and texture of celeriac blend well with potatoes.

● Boil equal amounts of each together, then cream them with butter and milk or cream. Serve the purée with beef, veal, pork, chicken or white fish.

Celeriac can also be puréed and made into an unusual soup, flavoured with a pinch of freshly grated nutmeg and enriched with a few spoonfuls of cream.

Jerusalem artichoke and sausage salad

Jerusalem artichokes

Jerusalem artichokes are the tubers of a tall plant that was first discovered in North America in 1605. The name of this vegetable has a very curious history: it was taken to France by the explorer Champlain. Arriving at the French court at the same time were members of a Brazilian tribe called the Tupinamba, and this name was given to the new vegetable. When the *topinambour* arrived in Holland soon after, it became known as *artischokapeln van Ter Neusen*, after the man who thought it was similar in flavour to the globe artichoke. In Italy someone discovered that it was related to the sunflower, and so it was called *girasole articiocco*, girasole meaning 'follow the sun'. This name in time became corrupted in English to Jerusalem artichoke, although the vegetable has no connection at all with that city. Jerusalem artichokes are now grown in countries with temperate climates.

Buying and storing: there are two types of Jerusalem artichoke, red and white. The white have a better flavour and are far more widely grown. They are not actually white but a light brown colour, about 7.5 cm /3 in long with a rounded base and tapered top. They have several round, knobbly protrusions which are sometimes small and sometimes as large as the main part, making them difficult to peel. The flesh is white, slightly translucent and very crisp when fresh. Raw artichokes have a nutty flavour; when they are cooked they become opaque and soft, and have a slightly smoky flavour. Look for tubers that are firm. As they age

Jerusalem artichoke and lemon soup

they become soft and slightly wrinkled. Buy 750 g /1½ lb to serve four people. Jerusalem artichokes are in season throughout the winter. Store in a cool, dry, dark place. They will stay fresh for about five days.

✷✷✷✷ To freeze Jerusalem artichokes, peel them, then cube or slice and blanch for 2 minutes. Freeze them in a polythene bag for up to 1 year.

Preparing: as soon as the flesh of the Jerusalem artichoke is exposed to air, it darkens. So before you start peeling, have ready a large bowl of cold water to which you have added a dash of vinegar or lemon juice. Use a potato peeler or sharp knife for removing the skin and any long hard ends. Dip the artichokes into the water every so often as you peel them. When peeled, drop them into the bowl and keep them there until you are ready to cook them. This will keep them white.

A quicker method is to cook the tubers in their skins and peel them afterwards. For this they need only to be scrubbed and have any blemishes cut away. They are far easier to peel when cooked.

Using Jerusalem artichokes: cook them in lightly salted boiling water. If they are whole, cook them for 10 minutes if unpeeled, 7 minutes if peeled. If they are sliced or chopped, they will need about 5 minutes. They are done when they can easily be pierced by the point of a sharp knife. They can also be successfully steamed: they will take about 15 minutes if

they are whole and 7 minutes if they are cut into pieces.

Plainly boiled or steamed artichokes can be served with melted butter and chopped parsley or with a tomato or a thick bechamel sauce. They can be puréed, creamed, sliced and sautéed, or made into a gratin (see recipe). Or mix them, as soon as they are cooked, into a salad dressing (see recipe).

You can also make salads with raw Jerusalem artichokes, if they are very fresh. Mix the other ingredients into the dressing first and grate the peeled artichokes directly into them, mixing them in as you go, to prevent browning. They go well with white cabbage, grated carrot, shredded lettuce and curly endive.

Uncooked Jerusalem artichokes can be baked in their jackets in a hot oven for 30–40 minutes, cut into chips or sliced and battered and deep fried (see recipe), or sliced and fried in a mixture of butter and olive oil.

They make soups with a deliciously creamy texture. Good flavourings are tomato, orange, lemon (see recipe) and Dijon mustard.

Chinese artichokes

Chinese or Japanese artichokes (*crosnes* in French) are small tubers which are popular in the Far East, where they originated, and in France. They are creamy coloured and taper off towards the ends, with a series of ring markings along the length.

Preparing and using: Chinese artichokes must be eaten while fresh, or they will lose their delicate flavour. They do not need to be peeled. Wash them well, then cook uncovered in a pan of boiling salted water for 10–15 minutes, until tender but still firm. Drain well, then serve with butter or a cream sauce. Or toss them, still warm, in a vinaigrette and serve. They can be used in any recipe calling for Jerusalem artichokes.

Jerusalem artichoke and lemon soup

This is a thick and creamy soup with an underlying refreshing sharpness.

🍴🍴 1 hour

Serves 4
25 g /1 oz butter
500 g /1 lb Jerusalem artichokes, peeled and thinly sliced
2 medium-sized onions, thinly sliced
850 ml /30 fl oz chicken stock
2 thinly pared strips of lemon zest
1 bouquet garni
salt and freshly ground black pepper
10 ml /2 tsp lemon juice, or more
150 ml /5 fl oz yoghurt
thinly sliced lemon
30 ml /2 tbls chopped parsley

1 Melt the butter in a saucepan over a low heat. Stir in the artichokes and onions. Cover and cook gently for 10 minutes.
2 Pour in the stock and bring it to the boil.

Add the lemon zest and bouquet garni and season to taste with salt and pepper. Cover and simmer for 20 minutes.

3 Discard the zest and bouquet garni. Purée the soup in a blender or put it through a vegetable mill. Return to the cleaned-out pan. Add about 10 ml /2 tsp lemon juice and the yoghurt. Taste and add extra lemon juice if required.

4 Reheat gently, without boiling, and serve garnished with lemon and parsley.

Veal blanquette with celeriac

Serve this creamy, delicately flavoured blanquette with plainly boiled potatoes or buttered noodles.

2 hours 45 minutes
including 1 hour standing

Serves 4
350 g /12 oz celeriac, peeled
4 celery stalks
2 sprigs of thyme
2 sprigs of parsley
2 thinly pared strips of lemon zest
750 g /1½ lb pie veal, in 20 mm /¾ in dice
250 g /8 oz carrots, sliced
1 large onion, thinly sliced
600 ml /1 pt white veal stock or
*   chicken stock*
pinch of ground mace
salt and white pepper
25 g /1 oz butter
45 ml /3 tbls flour
2 medium-sized egg yolks
25 g /1 oz freshly grated Parmesan cheese
chopped parsley, to garnish

1 Cut the celeriac and celery into large, similar-sized pieces. Tie the thyme and parsley sprigs and lemon zest together to make a bouquet garni.

2 Put the veal, celeriac, celery and bouquet garni into a large saucepan with the carrots and onion. Pour in the stock and add the mace, salt and pepper. Bring to the boil over a medium heat, cover and simmer for 1 hour.

3 Strain off and reserve the stock. Discard the bouquet garni. Return the veal and vegetables to the saucepan.

4 Melt the butter in a medium-sized saucepan over a medium heat. Stir in the flour and cook for ½ minute. Stir in 425 ml /15 fl oz of the reserved stock and bring it to the boil, stirring. Simmer the sauce for 2 minutes and take the pan from the heat.

5 Beat the egg yolks with the cheese and gradually add about 100 ml /3½ fl oz of the hot sauce. Stir this mixture back into the rest of the sauce. Reheat very gently, without boiling, so the mixture thickens.

6 Mix the sauce into the veal and vegetables and let the blanquette stand for 1 hour to let the flavours blend.

7 Just before serving, reheat gently – do not allow the sauce to boil – and sprinkle with the chopped parsley.

Veal blanquette with celeriac

Celeriac braised with bacon

50 minutes

Serves 4
500 g /1 lb celeriac
15 g /½ oz butter
125 g /4 oz back bacon, chopped
1 medium-sized onion, thinly sliced
150 ml /5 fl oz chicken stock
4 sage leaves, chopped
freshly ground black pepper

1 Heat the oven to 180C /350F /gas 4. Peel the celeriac and chop it into 20 mm /¾ in dice.

2 Melt the butter in a flameproof casserole over a low heat. Add the bacon and onion and cook until the onion is soft but not coloured. Mix in the celeriac.

3 Pour in the stock and bring it to the boil. Add the chopped sage and season with the pepper. Cover the casserole and put it into the oven for 30 minutes. Serve hot.

Celeriac salad dijonnaise

Serve this salad as a starter or with casseroles and sautés.

20 minutes

Serves 4–6
750 g /1½ lb celeriac
For the dressing
45 ml /3 tbls yoghurt
30 ml /2 tbls olive oil
5 ml /1 tsp Dijon mustard
1 garlic clove, crushed with a pinch of salt
45 ml /3 tbls chopped parsley

1 Peel the celeriac and cut it into match-stick-sized pieces. Drop the pieces into a large pan of boiling, salted water. Boil for 2 minutes and drain.

2 Beat together the yoghurt, oil, mustard, garlic and parsley to make the dressing and fold it into the celeriac while it is still hot. Serve the salad hot or cold.

Jerusalem artichoke fritters

⏱ 45 minutes

Serves 4
125 g /4 oz flour
5 ml /1 tsp paprika
2.5 ml /½ tsp cayenne pepper
pinch of salt
1 medium-sized egg, separated
300 ml /11 fl oz milk
750 g /1½ lb Jerusalem artichokes
oil for deep frying
parsley to garnish
tomato sauce, to serve (optional)

1 Place the flour, paprika, cayenne pepper and salt in a bowl, make a well in the centre and gradually beat in the egg yolk and milk. Leave in a cool place for 30 minutes.
2 Meanwhile, peel the artichokes and cut them into 5 mm /¼ in slices. Leave them until needed in a bowl of water to which has been added a dash of lemon juice or vinegar.
3 Whisk the egg white until stiff, then fold it into the batter.
4 Heat the oil in a deep-fat frier to 190C /375F, or until a cube of bread browns in 50 seconds. Dry the artichoke slices on absorbent paper. A few at a time, dip the slices in the batter and deep fry them in the hot oil until they are golden brown, about 1½ minutes. Lift them out with a slotted spoon, drain on absorbent paper, and keep them hot while you cook the rest in the same way. Garnish with parsley and serve with tomato sauce, if you like.

Jerusalem artichoke and sausage salad

Serve as a main course or as one of a selection of salads on a buffet table.

⏱⏱ 1 hour 45 minutes
including 1 hour cooling

Serves 4
750 g /1½ lb Jerusalem artichokes
1 large orange
350 g /12 oz tomatoes, chopped
1 medium-sized green pepper, seeded and diced
1 medium-sized red pepper, seeded and diced
8 green olives, halved and stoned
250 g /8 oz boiling sausage, in 10 mm /½ in dice
45 ml /3 tbls chopped parsley to garnish
For the dressing
60 ml /4 tbls olive oil
30 ml /2 tbls white wine vinegar
10 ml /2 tsp tomato purée
1.5 ml /¼ tsp Tabasco sauce
1 garlic clove, crushed with a pinch of salt

1 Peel the artichokes, cut them into 10 mm /½ in dice and steam for 7 minutes.
2 Cut the peel and pith from the orange and chop the flesh.
3 Mix together the oil, vinegar, tomato purée, Tabasco sauce and garlic to make the dressing. Fold it into the artichokes while they are still warm. Leave them to get cold, about 1 hour.
4 Mix the orange, tomatoes, green and red peppers, olives and sausage into the artichokes. Put the salad into a serving bowl and sprinkle it with the chopped parsley.

Jerusalem artichoke fritters

Jerusalem artichoke gratin

⏱⏱ 1 hour 5 minutes

Serves 4
750 g /1½ lb Jerusalem artichokes
25 g /1 oz butter
1 small onion, thinly sliced
5 ml /1 tsp mustard powder
30 ml /2 tbls flour
300 ml /11 fl oz milk
175 g /6 oz Cheddar cheese, grated
6 sage leaves, chopped
butter for greasing
45 ml /3 tbls rolled oats
5 ml /1 tsp paprika

1 Heat the oven to 200C /400F /gas 6. Peel the artichokes and cut them into 25 mm /1 in pieces. Steam them for 10 minutes.
2 Melt the butter in a saucepan over a low heat. Add the onion and cook until it is soft.
3 Stir in the mustard powder and flour and cook for 30 seconds. Pour in the milk and bring to the boil, stirring. Simmer the sauce for 2 minutes. Take the pan from the heat and stir in two-thirds of the grated Cheddar and the chopped sage leaves.
4 Place the artichokes in a buttered pie dish and top with the sauce, the remaining cheese and then the oats and paprika.
5 Put the dish into the oven for 20 minutes, until the top becomes brown and crisp. Serve hot, as a lunch or supper dish or with plainly cooked meats.

Sweet potatoes

Sweet potatoes are a slightly exotic vegetable which can be used to enliven menus in many ways – from creamy soups and hearty, colourful stews to desserts, pies and sweet and spicy rolls.

Sweet potatoes are the tubers of a plant native to South America. They were brought to Europe by Christopher Columbus in 1493 and, as they were grown very successfully in Spain, came to be known as Spanish potatoes. They were very popular in Tudor England, where they were regarded as an aphrodisiac. They were used interchangeably with ordinary potatoes, mainly in sweet pies.

Eventually sweet potatoes lost their popularity in Europe, but over the past ten years they have had a small revival, owing to their appearance in ethnic communities. In the U.S. they never lost their popularity. They are often known as yams there, which can lead to some confusion, as African yams are a different vegetable (which are covered on *page 218*).

Sweet potatoes are now grown in most tropical and subtropical parts of the world, as well as the U.S. and around the Mediterranean.

Buying and storing sweet potatoes

There are many varieties of sweet potato, but only two basic types. One has dry, yellow flesh; the other has watery, whiter flesh and is generally sweeter. The flesh of both types becomes yellow when cooked.

Sweet potatoes are about the same size as ordinary potatoes, but they are more elongated and come to a point at each end. Their skins can be light brown, grey, light pink or a deeper, reddish pink. Their texture is similar to that of Jerusalem artichokes, and their flavour is rather like cooked chestnuts. They are generally available from autumn to early spring.

In some countries they are available canned, either in water or in a sugar syrup.

When buying fresh sweet potatoes, make sure they are firm and unscratched. Try to buy whole ones if you can. They will keep for up to 4 weeks in a cool, dark place.

✳✳✳ To freeze sweet potatoes, peel them, cut them into 25 mm /1 in chunks and blanch them quickly. Drain and cool them and pack into covered containers. They will keep for 4 months. Cook them from frozen.

Using sweet potatoes

It is best to boil or steam sweet potatoes in their skins. Scrub them well and cut them into halves or quarters, depending on their size. They take just under 20 minutes to become tender when boiled and about 30 minutes when steamed. Remove the skins as soon as they are cool enough to handle. Or peel and thickly slice them, and steam them for about 20 minutes.

Boiled or steamed sweet potatoes to accompany savoury dishes can be finished in a number of ways. Toss diced potatoes with melted butter, cayenne pepper and chopped parsley. They are also good sautéed, either alone or with onions and peppers or chillies.

Boiled potatoes can be creamed with butter. They are delicious if mixed with an equal quantity of cooked puréed haricot or butter beans and some chopped fresh coriander or parsley leaves. For croquettes, make a purée of sweet potatoes and add 40 g /1½ oz butter and 1 beaten egg for each 750 g /1¼ lb purée. Form it into small balls or croquettes, coat in flour, egg and breadcrumbs or flour alone, and deep fry.

'Candied sweets' are an American favourite often served with the Thanksgiving or Christmas turkey. The potatoes are first boiled and skinned and then cut into dice or thick slices and placed in an ovenproof dish. They are dotted with butter, topped with honey, maple syrup or brown sugar and baked until the top is browned and glazed. Orange or lemon juice, crushed pineapple, or pieces of cooked bacon are sometimes added for flavour.

Boiled and diced sweet potatoes can be served as a salad. Mix them into the dressing while they are still warm, and add something sharp and savoury to the salad, such as thinly sliced raw onion, which will contrast with the sweetness of the potatoes.

Sweet potatoes can also be fried. Peel them, cut them into chips and deep fry them as an accompaniment to pork, ham or poultry, or cut them into 5 mm /¼ in slices and shallow fry on a medium heat in a mixture of oil and butter until they are golden brown and crisp on the outside and soft in the middle. They go well with

Pork, red pepper and sweet potato stew

Sweet potato and bacon kebab

sautéed dishes and cold meats.

To serve with roast meats, peel sweet potatoes, cut them into chunks of about 4 cm /1½ in and roast them in oil or butter. They take only 45 minutes in a hot oven to brown. Either roast them plainly or glaze them by mixing about 15 ml /1 tbls dark brown sugar into the fat before turning the potatoes in it. You can also roast sweet potatoes around the meat so that they will absorb the savoury juices.

Sweet potatoes are delicious baked in their jackets. Scrub them and prick them all over. Place them directly on an oven rack and bake them in a preheated 200C /400F /gas 6 oven for 1 hour. The centres should be soft and and the skins crisp. Split them in half, scoop out the flesh and mash it with butter, salt and black or cayenne pepper and a little chopped parsley. A dash of port will add extra zest on special occasions. Then pile back into the shells and serve.

Use sweet potatoes to make rich and creamy soups. Flavour the soup with tomatoes and chillies or give it a more European flavour with vegetables such as celery (see recipe).

Sancochos are spicy Caribbean stews which feature various meats and vegetables, including sweet potatoes, and both Caribbean and American cooks make delicious sweet dishes with them. Eggs, milk and spices, and often grated coconut, are added to cooked potato purée to make cakes, sweet breads, puddings and pies.

Sweet potato and green chilli bake

Serve this savoury vegetable dish with fish, lamb or poultry.

🔪 1 hour

Serves 4
1 kg /2 lb sweet potatoes
salt
4 green chillies
40 g /1½ oz butter
1 large onion, thinly sliced
10 ml /2 tsp paprika

1 Heat the oven to 200C /400F /gas 6. Scrub the potatoes and cut each into 2 or 3 pieces, depending on their size.
2 Cook them in lightly salted boiling water for 15 minutes. Drain them and, as soon as they are cool enough to handle, skin them and cut them into 6 mm /¼ in slices.
3 Cut the chillies in half lengthways and scoop out the seeds and cores. Melt the butter in a frying-pan on a low heat. Put in the onion, chillies and paprika, and cook until the onion is soft but not coloured.
4 Layer the slices of sweet potato and the chilli mixture in a deep, ovenproof dish. End with a layer of potatoes and brush them with any butter remaining in the pan. Put the dish into the oven for 15 minutes, until the potatoes on top become golden brown.

Sweet potato and bacon kebabs

Serve these kebabs with egg and cheese dishes, or with white fish.

🔪🔪 45 minutes

Serves 4
1 kg /2 lb sweet potatoes
salt
175 g /6 oz streaky bacon slices, in 25 mm /1 in squares
50g /2 oz butter
1.5 ml /¼ tsp cayenne pepper
10 ml /2 tsp Barbados or soft dark brown sugar

1 Scrub the potatoes and cut each one into 3 pieces. Cook them in lightly salted boiling water for 15 minutes. Drain them and, as soon as they are cool enough to handle, skin them and cut into 25 mm /1 in cubes.
2 Thread alternate pieces of bacon and sweet potato on to each of 6 kebab skewers.
3 Melt the butter on a low heat. Remove from the heat and mix in the cayenne pepper and sugar.
4 Heat the grill to high. Brush the kebabs with the butter mixture and grill them, turning often, until they are golden brown on all sides, 8 - 10 minutes.

Sweet potato and beef parcels

These parcels of peppered beef can be served as party snacks or as a main course.

🔪🔪 2 hours, plus 1 hour chilling

Serves 4 as a main course, 8 as a snack
350 g /12 oz sweet potatoes, scrubbed
salt and freshly ground black pepper
125 g /4 oz butter, at room temperature
125 g /4 oz flour
flour for coating
90 ml /6 tbls oil
For the filling
350 g /12 oz minced beef
25 g /1 oz butter
1 medium onion, finely chopped
1 garlic clove, finely chopped
1 green pepper, cored, seeded and chopped
1.5 ml /¼ tsp cayenne pepper

1 Cook the sweet potatoes in their skins in lightly salted boiling water until tender, 20–30 minutes. Drain them and, as soon as they are cool enough to handle, skin them and mash them with 1.5 ml /¼ tsp salt and freshly ground black pepper to taste.
2 Cut the butter into small pieces and beat it into the mashed potatoes. When it has melted, add the flour and beat the mixture with a wooden spoon until it forms a soft dough. Coat the dough with flour and chill it for 1 hour.
3 Meanwhile, place the minced beef in a

bowl. Melt the butter in a frying-pan on a low heat. Add the onion, garlic, green pepper and cayenne pepper. Cook them until the onion is soft but not coloured. Mix them into the beef and let the mixture cool.

4 Heat the oven to 180C /350F /gas 4. Divide the pastry into 8 pieces. Roll them out thinly into 15 cm /6 in rounds.

5 Divide the beef mixture into 8 portions and place one in the centre of each pastry round. Fold over one side of the pastry, then the opposite side, and then the adjacent sides so you have small pastry parcels.

6 Lay the parcels on a floured baking sheet and brush them with the oil, using it all. Bake for 40 minutes, until the parcels are golden brown. Serve them hot.

Spiced sweet potato rolls

These light rolls are best the day they are made, simply buttered or topped with jam and cream. On the second day, toast them on both sides and split and butter them like muffins.

⏲⏲⏲ 2 hours 10 minutes
plus 1 hour 20 minutes rising

Makes 25–30
350 g /12 oz sweet potatoes, scrubbed
salt
25 g /1 oz fresh or 15 g /1/2 oz dried yeast
175 g /6 oz Barbados or soft dark brown sugar
25 g /1 oz butter, melted
200 ml /7 fl oz milk
600 g /1 lb 6 oz flour
10 ml /2 tsp ground mixed spice
butter for greasing
flour

1 Cook the sweet potatoes in their skins in boiling salted water until tender, 20–30 minutes. Drain them, reserving 150 ml /5 fl oz of the cooking water, and peel and mash them as soon as they are cool enough to handle.

2 When the potato water has cooled to lukewarm (10–15 minutes), sprinkle in the yeast and add 5 ml /1 tsp sugar. Let it stand until it froths.

3 Place the mashed potatoes in a bowl and beat in 5 ml /1 tsp salt, remaining sugar, butter and milk. Stir in the yeast mixture.

4 Sift the flour with the mixed spice. Gradually beat it into the sweet potato mixture to make a dough. Turn out on to a floured board and knead until it is smooth.

5 Return it to the bowl and make a cross-shaped cut in the top. Put the bowl into a large, greased polythene bag and leave it in a warm place for 1 hour, or until the dough is doubled in size.

6 Heat the oven to 220C /425F /gas 7. Knead the dough again and form it into small balls, 4–5 cm /1 1/2–2 in in diameter. Place them on floured baking sheets and leave them in a warm place to prove for 20 minutes.

7 Sprinkle the rolls with flour and bake the rolls for 15 minutes, until they just begin to brown. Cool on wire racks.

Pork, red pepper and sweet potato stew

⏲⏲ 1 3/4 hours

Serves 4
2 large red peppers
25 g /1 oz lard
1 kg /2 lb lean hand or shoulder of pork, in 20 mm /3/4 in dice
2 medium-sized onions, sliced
1 garlic clove, finely chopped
15 ml /1 tbls paprika
1.5 ml /1/4 tsp cayenne pepper
500 g /1 lb tomatoes, blanched, skinned and chopped
150 ml /5 fl oz dry white wine
150 ml /5 fl oz chicken stock
750 g /1 1/2 lb sweet potatoes, peeled, in 20 mm /3/4 in dice
6 sage leaves, chopped
salt

1 Core and seed the red peppers and cut them into pieces 5 × 25 mm /1/4 × 1 in.

2 Melt the lard in a large saucepan on a high heat. Add the diced pork, brown it quickly and remove it from the pan with a slotted spoon. Lower the heat. Add the onions and garlic and cook them until they are soft but not coloured.

Spiced sweet potato rolls

3 Add the peppers, cover and cook for 5 minutes. Stir in the paprika and cayenne. Add the tomatoes, cover and cook for a further 5 minutes, until they are very soft.

4 Pour in the wine and stock and bring to the boil. Add the pork, sweet potatoes and sage and season with salt. Cover the pan and cook on a low heat for 45 minutes. Serve immediately.

Sweet potato pone

⏲⏲ 3 hours

Serves 6
500 g /1 lb sweet potatoes, peeled and grated
1 medium-sized egg, beaten
50 g /2 oz butter, melted
90 ml /6 tbls milk
150 ml /5 fl oz maple syrup
65 g /2 1/2 oz flour
5 ml /1 tsp ground cinnamon
1/4 nutmeg, grated
butter for greasing

1 Heat the oven to 170C /325F /gas 3. In a large bowl, beat together the sweet potatoes, egg, butter, milk, maple syrup, flour, cinnamon and nutmeg.

2 Pour the mixture into a 1.1 L /2 pt shallow, thickly buttered pie dish or oven-proof dish and bake for 2 1/2 hours, until it is firm and has a browned, crusty top. Serve hot or cold, as a cake or pudding.

Aubergines

Moussaka and ratatouille are always popular, but why not try the other delicious things that can be made from aubergines. This lovely vegetable can be made into soups, salads, dips, fritters, soufflés and casseroles of all kinds.

Aubergines originated in southern Asia and have been around for quite a long time—even the ancient Egyptians knew about them. In America and Australia they are known as eggplants; other names include *brinjal* in India and *melanzane* in Italy.

Buying and storing aubergines

Aubergines can be long and thin, pear-shaped or completely round. They also vary considerably in size and in colour—they can be yellow or white but the majority range from a pale mauve to a strong purply-black.

A warm climate vegetable, aubergines are exported to cooler areas all year round but are at their best and cheapest in mid-summer. Choose aubergines which are firm, very shiny and uniform in colour. Avoid soft or wrinkled ones, or those with brown marks or bruises on their skins.

Buy only enough for immediate use and cook them as soon as possible, although they can be stored in the salad compartment of the refrigerator for up to three days.

✳✳✳ Aubergines can be frozen either raw or cooked. Choose very fresh vegetables. Peel and slice or cube them, then blanch them for 3-4 minutes. Drain, plunge into chilled water, then drain and dry. Pack in plastic containers, separating the layers. Freeze for up to 1 year. They can be cooked from frozen or defrosted first. Deep-fried aubergines can be packed in the same way and frozen for 2 months: plunge them, frozen, into hot fat to thaw and reheat.

Preparing aubergines

The skin of the aubergine is very tender and, unless the vegetable is very old or very large, it does not really need to be peeled. However, some dishes do look more attractive when the aubergine is peeled.

Always use a stainless steel knife when cutting aubergines as they might otherwise turn black. They will also discolour if left in contact with the air for too long. If you prepare them in advance either *dégorger* them (see below) or leave them in a bowl of water which has lemon juice added.

Aubergines contain a good deal of water and this means that they will absorb a lot of oil when they are fried. One way round this is to sprinkle the vegetable with salt to bring out some of the excess moisture. This process, known as 'degorging', also removes any bitterness that might be present.

To degorge aubergines, cut them into slices or cubes and sprinkle liberally with salt. Place them in a colander and cover with a saucer with a small weight on it. Let stand for 45 minutes or longer, then rinse very well under cold running water to get rid of all excess salt. Press between absorbent paper to dry. Remember that the aubergines will have absorbed some salt, so be cautious when adding salt later.

Cooking aubergines

Aubergines can be sautéed, deep fried, grilled, puréed, baked or stuffed. They can be added to soups, stews, casseroles, pasta dishes, curries, kebabs, soufflés and salads, or used to garnish egg, meat and fish dishes.

Sautéing: slice and degorge the aubergines; rinse well, drain and dry. Dredge with seasoned flour and sauté in olive oil or a mixture of oil and butter on a high heat, until the aubergine is well browned and tender. Serve sprinkled with parsley.

Small quantities of diced aubergine sautéed in butter can be used as a garnish for egg dishes, grilled meats or chicken.

Two famous dishes featuring aubergines are ratatouille and *caponata*. Both include aubergines which are first sautéed and then simmered with either courgettes, peppers and tomatoes, or capers, olives and celery.

Deep frying: slice aubergines fairly thinly or cut into sticks. Degorge, dredge with flour and plunge into hot fat. Fry until golden brown in colour, drain and season with salt. Aubergines can also be deep fried after dipping in a thin batter or in egg and breadcrumbs. Fried aubergines are delicious with Greek garlic sauce (*page 160*).

Grilling: cut the aubergines into thick lengthways slices, degorge, rinse, drain and dry. Brush with olive oil and grill under a gentle heat for about 3-4 minutes on each side. Serve topped with rounds of parsley and lemon flavoured savoury butter.

Puréeing: place a whole aubergine under the grill, turning from time to time, until the vegetable is soft. This takes about 10-15 minutes. Or alternatively bake them in an oven heated to 200C /400F /gas 6 for 40-50 minutes. Cut the cooked aubergine in half and scrape out the flesh with a spoon. Mash with a fork or rub through a sieve. Mix with butter and serve as a vegetable or use for a soufflé. The purée is used throughout the Middle East to make cold salads and dips.

Stuffing: aubergines are often stuffed and baked in their skins. Stuffings include minced beef or lamb, rice, eggs, nuts, breadcrumbs and cheese. The centre of the aubergine is usually cut out, chopped, sometimes degorged, added to the other stuffing ingredients, then piled back into the empty skins and baked in the oven.

The famous aubergines imam bayeldi, a Turkish dish, uses onions and tomatoes in the stuffing. The aubergines are covered with olive oil, baked, then served luke-warm.

Baking: a simple casserole can be made by layering sliced and degorged aubergines with tomatoes in an ovenproof dish. Top with breadcrumbs which have been mixed with crushed garlic and chopped parsley. If wished, add a little grated cheese and finely chopped onion to each layer. Moussaka is a more elaborate casserole using lamb.

Aubergine fritters with piquant sauce

◖◖ 40 minutes

Serves 4
2 medium-sized eggs, beaten
75 g /3 oz cornmeal
2 medium-sized aubergines, cut across into 6 slices each
30 ml /2 tbls seasoned flour
oil for deep frying
fennel sprigs and lemon slices, to garnish
For the sauce
15 ml /1 tbls oil
1 medium-sized onion, chopped
500 g /1 lb tomatoes, blanched, skinned, seeded and chopped
15 ml /1 tbls tomato purée
15 ml /1 tbls wine vinegar
5 ml /1 tsp Worcestershire sauce
few drops of Tabasco sauce

1 First make the sauce. Heat the oil in a small saucepan. Fry the onion for 2-3 minutes, add the remaining ingredients and bring to the boil. Reduce the heat and simmer for 20 minutes, then sieve or purée.
2 Heat the oil in a deep-fat frier to 200C /400F. At this temperature a cube of day-old bread will brown in 40 seconds.
3 Meanwhile place the beaten eggs and the cornmeal in two separate soup bowls. Sprinkle the aubergine slices with the seasoned flour. Dip each slice in the egg and then lightly coat with cornmeal. Deep fry

the aubergine slices for about 2 minutes, or until golden brown on both sides.

4 Remove from the oil with a slotted spoon, drain on absorbent paper, place on a heated serving dish and keep warm.

5 Reheat the sauce, garnish the fritters and serve with the sauce in a sauce-boat.

Aubergine soup

⚑ 1 hour 10 minutes

Serves 4-6
15 ml /1 tbls oil
1 large onion, chopped
15 ml /1 tbls dry sherry
400 g /14 oz aubergines, chopped
250 g /9 oz potatoes, peeled and chopped
1 beef stock cube
15 ml /1 tbls tomato purée
1 bay leaf
2.5 ml /1/2 tsp oregano
salt and freshly ground black pepper
30–45 ml /2–3 tbls milk
croûtons, to serve

1 Heat the oil in a large saucepan. Sauté the onion for 2-3 minutes, then add the sherry and bring to the boil.

2 Add the aubergines, potatoes, stock cube, tomato purée, bay leaf, oregano, salt and pepper and 1 L /1¾ pt water. Bring to the boil, then lower the heat, cover and simmer for 45 minutes.

3 Sieve or purée the soup, return it to the washed-out pan and reheat. Stir in the milk and, when hot, serve with the croûtons.

Lamb and aubergine casserole

⚑⚑ 1 hour degorging aubergines then 1 hour 40 minutes

Serves 4
500 g /1 lb aubergines, peeled and sliced
30–45 ml /2–3 tbls salt
25 g /1 oz butter
700 g /1½ lb boned leg of lamb, in large chunks
2 medium-sized onions, chopped
2.5 ml /1/2 tsp ground cumin
salt and freshly ground black pepper
30 ml /2 tbls oil
4 medium-sized tomatoes, sliced

1 Sprinkle the sliced aubergines with salt and degorge for about 1 hour.

2 Melt the butter in a flameproof casserole. Add the chunks of lamb and fry, turning, until they are well sealed. Add the onions and cook gently for 3-4 minutes. Add 150 ml /5 fl oz water, the cumin and salt and pepper to taste. Bring to the boil and simmer for 1¼ hours.

3 Rinse the aubergines to remove any excess salt and squeeze dry between layers of absorbent paper.

4 Heat the oil in a frying-pan and fry the aubergines until golden on both sides. Remove from the pan with a slotted spoon. Fry the sliced tomatoes and place in the casserole on top of the lamb. Add the aubergines and heat through for 5 minutes. Stir once just before serving.

Aubergine fritters with piquant sauce and Aubergine soup

Curried aubergines

⚑ 40 minutes

Serves 4
25 g /1 oz butter
1 garlic clove, finely chopped
3 cm /1¼ in fresh root ginger, finely chopped
6 black peppercorns
1.5 ml /1/4 tsp caraway seeds
4 cardamom pods
3 cloves
15 ml /1 tbls ground coriander
10 ml /2 tsp turmeric
2.5 ml /1/2 tsp ground cinnamon
2 large onions, sliced
400 g /14 oz potatoes, cut into chunks
500 g /1 lb aubergines, cut into chunks
salt
125 ml /4 fl oz chicken stock or water
4 tomatoes, quartered
juice of 1/2 lemon

1 In a large saucepan, melt the butter and fry the garlic, ginger and whole spices for 2-3 minutes. Add the powdered spices and the onions and cook for a further 5 minutes.

2 Add the potatoes and aubergines, salt and stock or water and stir well.

3 Cover and cook on a low heat for 20 minutes, stirring once or twice. Add the tomatoes and continue cooking for a further 5 minutes. Add the lemon juice, pile into a warmed serving dish and serve at once.

Catalan stuffed aubergines

Serve these stuffed aubergines with salad and crusty bread.

 1 hour

Serves 4
2 medium-sized aubergines, cut in half
 lengthways
oil for greasing
1 medium-sized onion, finely chopped
1 garlic clove, crushed
25 g /1 oz butter
4 medium-sized hard-boiled eggs, chopped
60 ml /4 tbls fresh breadcrumbs
30 ml /2 tbls freshly chopped parsley
salt and freshly ground black pepper
parsley sprigs, to garnish

1   Heat the oven to 200C /400F /gas 6. Oil a shallow ovenproof dish large enough to hold the aubergine halves.
2   In a small pan, fry the onion and garlic in half the butter until lightly browned.
3   Scoop out the aubergine flesh, leaving the skins intact. Chop the flesh and mix with the onion, garlic, hard-boiled eggs, breadcrumbs, parsley and salt and pepper to taste. Pile this mixture into the aubergine skins and arrange in the dish. Dot with the remaining butter, bake in the oven for 45 minutes, garnish with the parsley and serve.

Russian aubergine and meat pie

Serve this unusual 'pie' with mashed or boiled potatoes or boiled rice.

 1 hour degorging aubergines
 then 2 hours

Serves 4
500 g /1 lb aubergines, sliced
salt and freshly ground black pepper
1 large onion, very thinly sliced
15 ml /1 tbls oil
500 g /1 lb minced beef
3 medium-sized green peppers
250 g /8 oz tomatoes, blanched, skinned,
 seeded and sliced

1   Sprinkle the aubergines with salt and degorge for about 1 hour. Rinse well, drain and dry on absorbent paper.
2   Heat the oven to 190C /375F /gas 5. Fry the onion in the oil until it is transparent. Remove the pan from the heat and mix the onions with the minced beef. Season with salt and pepper and shape into a large ball.
3   Slice the peppers into rings, reserving the caps with the stalks attached. Remove the seeds. Line a deep casserole with the green pepper rings and three-quarters of the tomatoes. Add a layer of aubergines. Press the ball of meat into the centre and cover with the remaining aubergines and tomatoes. Top with the green pepper caps.
4   Cover the casserole and bake for about 1½ hours, or until done. Serve at once.

Papal pudding

Serve this dish, invented by the chef of an Avignon pope, with roast meat.

 2 hours

Serves 4
500 g /1 lb aubergines
15 ml /1 tbls oil plus oil for greasing
1 large onion, chopped
2 garlic cloves, crushed
30 ml /2 tbls thick cream
2 medium-sized eggs, beaten
pinch of dried thyme
pinch of freshly grated nutmeg
salt and freshly ground black pepper
2 small tomatoes, blanched, and skinned

1   Heat the oven to 200C /400F /gas 6. Place the aubergines on a baking sheet and bake until they are tender, 40-50 minutes.
2   Heat 15 ml /1 tbls oil in a frying-pan and gently sauté the onion and garlic for about 5-6 minutes, until the onions soften.
3   Remove the aubergines from the oven and reduce the heat to 180C /350F /gas 4. Cut in half, scrape out the flesh and mince or purée it with the onion and garlic.
4   Oil a small soufflé dish. Beat the aubergine purée with the cream, eggs, thyme, nutmeg and salt and pepper to taste. Spoon the mixture into the soufflé dish and smooth it. Thinly slice the tomatoes and cover the top. Place in a roasting tin filled with very hot water and bake for 45-50 minutes, or until set in the centre.

Unusual pods and shoots

Okra, bean sprouts, water chestnuts, bamboo shoots and palm hearts were at one time virtually unknown in Western kitchens but are now increasingly popular. Easy to use, they bring variety and a touch of the exotic to meals.

Okra

Okra is a long delicate pointed pod belonging to the hibiscus family. Okra has many names, the most familiar being ladies' fingers. It came originally from Africa, and from there it was taken to the U.S. and the Caribbean where it is called gumbo. It now grows in many tropical and sub-tropical areas of the world, notably in India, where Hindus call it *bhindi*, and all the way round the Mediterranean. In the Middle East it is called *bamia*.

Buying and storing okra: okra was first exported to northern Europe for its immigrant population, but it has lately become more familiar and can now be bought in many supermarkets and greengrocers. It comes mainly from Cyprus (in the summer) and Kenya (during the winter). Canned okra from Greece is also available and is successful in traditional recipes.

When buying okra, look for the smaller pods – not more than 10 cm /4 in long. They should be crisp and firm. Some pods are ridged and deep green while other varieties are smoother and more yellow. Both types are used in the same ways, although the smoother type is said by some to have the better flavour. Avoid older brownish pods. Store okra, well wrapped in a polythene bag, refrigerated, for up to three days.

✳✳✳✳ To freeze okra, blanch it quickly and pack the pods into plastic containers. It will keep for up to 4 months. Use it directly from frozen.

Using okra: okra is grown in many countries and as a result features in many ethnic dishes. It has a rather glutinous texture which is used to advantage in gumbo (see recipe), a cross between a thick, chunky soup and a stew. It is always spiced with cayenne or chilli pepper, and almost always contains okra, but the other ingredients vary tremendously and gumbos can be made from most kinds of meat and fish.

Okra fritters are another favourite in the southern U.S. The pods are dipped into beaten egg and then into cornmeal and deep fried.

In India okra is made into a vegetable curry, sometimes referred to as a *bhaji*. In the Middle East a meat loaf made by layering spiced minced lamb and okra is very popular, as is a meat and okra stew; and in the Caribbean okra is mixed with a preparation of cornmeal to make a dish which is called *coo-coo*.

Okra can be boiled until tender, about 8 minutes, and served with melted butter, or it can be sautéed in oil with onions and garlic. With tomatoes and aubergines or green peppers it makes a rich, very thick vegetable dish that can be served as a first course or as an accompaniment to meat (see recipe). The smallest pods can be used raw in salads and in some countries they are pickled.

Bean sprouts

Bean sprouts are the 3- to 6-day-old new sprouts of a number of small beans. Most widely sold, however, are mung (moong) bean sprouts.

Buying and storing bean sprouts: bean sprouts were at one time only available from Chinese shops, but they are now sold in supermarkets, health food shops and greengrocers, either loose or in 300 g /10 oz packs. They are also available canned in water, but these tend to be soggy.

If possible, use fresh bean sprouts on the day of purchase. They will be usable the next day, if kept overnight in the refrigerator, but not thereafter. Before using them, rinse them quickly in cold water to clean them.

Preparing bean sprouts: put them into a colander and run cold water through them. This will force the green bean casings to the bottom and you will be able to pick out the sprouts easily. It doesn't matter if one or two casings are left with the sprouts, but too many will give a bitter flavour.

Using bean sprouts: bean sprouts can be added to all kinds of mixed salads; they combine well with many salad vegetables including Chinese cabbage, white cabbage, celery, carrots, watercress, lettuce, cucumber, fennel, avocado and cauliflower.

In Chinese cookery, bean sprouts are

Chicken and ham gumbo

Growing bean sprouts

The most popular kind of bean sprout is grown from the small, green mung bean, and it is very easy to grow your own at home. Put 45 ml /3 tbls mung beans into a 1 kg /2 lb jam jar. Cover the top of the jar with muslin anchored with an elastic band. Pour warm water into the jar, rinse it round and pour it out. Pour in enough warm water to cover the beans and leave them to soak for 24 hours in a warm place. Pour away the water, rinse the beans again and drain well.

Place the jar on its side in a flat dish and put the dish into a brown paper bag. Leave the dish in a warm place for 3–6 days, rinsing the beans twice a day with warm water, then draining well. Eat the sprouts when they have grown to a length of 3–5 cm /1¼–2 in; they should weigh 225–300 g /8–11 oz in total.

often stir-fried, either alone, with another vegetable or with finely cut meat. They are also combined with eggs to make a *foo-yung* (see recipe), a dish which has become very popular in the West. When stir-frying bean sprouts, remember that they cook down considerably.

Water chestnuts

Water chestnuts are tubers, like potatoes and Jerusalem artichokes. They are brown, about 4 cm /1½ in across with a small tuft on top, and they grow in the shallow water at the edges of ponds, lakes and streams in the Far East. Most of those sold in the West come from Taiwan.

Buying and storing water chestnuts: you can occasionally find fresh water chestnuts (use within 4 days, peeled) but more likely you will have to use canned ones, which you can find in Oriental shops, delicatessens and some supermarkets. These come peeled, trimmed and packed in water. They are flattish ovals in shape, 20–25 mm /¾–1 in across.

Once the can is opened, you can keep the unused water chestnuts in a jar of water in the refrigerator, changing the water every day, for several days.

Using water chestnuts: water chestnuts have a similar crispness and nutty flavour to raw Jerusalem artichokes, although in texture they are lighter and more tender and the flavour is more delicate, closer to an almond. When they are cooked they retain their crisp texture and this makes them a delicious contrasting accompaniment to rich meats such as duck (see recipe).

Water chestnuts can be cooked in both casseroles and stir-fried dishes, or they can be finely chopped and added to stuffings, or thinly sliced and used as a garnish for clear soups and consommés. Rumaki is a popular Japanese-style first course, made by marinating chicken livers in soy sauce and then wrapping them with half a water chestnut in a rasher of bacon. The parcel is then skewered and grilled until the bacon is crisply cooked.

Thinly sliced water chestnuts can also be added to salads. Mix them with lighter, leafy salad vegetables such as lettuce and corn salad. Young spinach leaves, sliced water chestnuts and crumbled bacon in a vinaigrette dressing make a delicious salad. They also mix well with bean sprouts.

Bamboo shoots

Bamboo shoots, which are a shiny ivory in colour, are grown in China, Japan and Taiwan. They are the new stems which emerge from the base of the bamboo plant.

Buying and storing bamboo shoots: bamboo shoots are only available in cans. They can be bought from Oriental shops, delicatessens and some supermarkets.

For canning they are either thinly sliced or in 25 mm /1 in pieces, and they are packed in either water or brine. If you do not use all the contents of the can at once, refrigerate the remainder in a jar of water, changing the water daily, for up to 10 days.

Using bamboo shoots: bamboo shoots have a firm, crunchy texture and a slightly bitter flavour. They are most often stir-fried with vegetables or meat in Oriental-style dishes. If they are very thinly sliced they can be added to salads. They go particularly well with bean sprouts in a dressing flavoured with soy sauce, tomato purée and ginger.

Palm hearts

Palm hearts are the tender shoots of certain types of palm tree which grow in tropical and sub-tropical countries. When the shoots are cut off, the tree dies, and this makes palm hearts fairly uncommon. They have a mild taste and a firm texture.

Buying and storing palm hearts: palm hearts are rarely available fresh in the West, but canned ones can be found in delicatessens and specialist food shops. They are ivory in colour and roughly cylindrical in shape, resembling small leeks.

Store any unused palm hearts in their canning liquid for up to 10 days in the refrigerator.

Using palm hearts: palm hearts can be served cold in a vinaigrette dressing or hot with melted butter, hollandaise or bechamel sauce or cooked au gratin. In the Caribbean they are made into fritters or stuffed.

Okra and tomatoes in white wine

Okra makes an unusual first course which can be served either hot or cold.

◁ 40 minutes,
plus cooling if serving cold

Serves 4
2 medium-sized green peppers
60 ml /4 tbls olive oil
1 large onion, quartered and thinly sliced
1 garlic clove, chopped
500 g /1 lb okra, stems cut off
5 ml /1 tsp paprika
500 g /1 lb tomatoes, blanched, skinned, seeded and chopped
150 ml /5 fl oz dry white wine
60 ml /4 tbls chopped parsley

1 Core and seed the peppers and cut them into strips 5×25 mm /¼×1 in.
2 Heat the oil in a saucepan over a low heat. Add the onion and garlic and cook them until they are soft but not coloured.
3 Add the okra and green pepper strips and sprinkle in the paprika. Cover the pan and cook over a low heat for 10 minutes.
4 Add the tomatoes and pour in the wine. Add the parsley, cover and cook over a medium heat for a further 10 minutes. Serve immediately or cool and chill.

Casserole of duck with water chestnuts

🍴🍴 2¼ hours

Serves 4
1.8 kg /4 lb duck, in 4 serving pieces
oil for greasing
300 g /11 oz carrots, thinly sliced
1 large onion, quartered and thinly sliced
1 garlic clove, chopped
150 ml /5 fl oz stock (made from the duck backbone and giblets if possible, otherwise chicken)
100 ml /3½ fl oz dry sherry
30 ml /2 tbls soy sauce
1 small piece star anise (if available)
450 g /1 lb canned water chestnuts, drained and halved
flat-leaved parsley, to garnish

1 Heat the oven to 180C /350F /gas 4. Lightly oil a large, flameproof casserole and set it over a high heat. When it is very hot, put in the duck pieces, skin side down, and brown them on both sides.
2 Remove the duck from the casserole, lower the heat and put in the carrots, onion and garlic. Cover and cook for 7 minutes.
3 Pour in the stock, sherry and soy sauce and bring to the boil. Replace the duck, tuck in the piece of star anise and add the water chestnuts. Cover the casserole and put it into the oven to cook for 1½ hours.
4 Take out the pieces of duck and place them on a warmed serving dish. Remove the star anise. Skim off and discard the fat from the casserole and spoon the juices over the duck, together with the water chestnuts, carrots and onions. Serve immediately, garnished with the parsley.

Bean sprout salad

🍴 20 minutes

Serves 4–6
125 g /4 oz bean sprouts, rinsed and drained
½ medium-sized Chinese cabbage, finely shredded
4 celery stalks, sliced
1 medium-sized green pepper, cored, seeded and chopped
2 crisp dessert apples, cored and chopped
For the dressing
15 ml /1 tbls sesame oil
60 ml /4 tbls sunflower oil
juice of ½ lemon
5 ml /1 tsp honey
2.5 ml /½ tsp ground ginger
1 garlic clove, crushed with a pinch of salt
freshly ground black pepper

1 In a bowl, combine the bean sprouts, cabbage, celery, green pepper and apples.
2 Beat the ingredients for the dressing together and toss with the vegetables.

Okra relish

Serve this hot relish, with its sweet and sour flavours, as an accompaniment to curry or with plainly cooked lamb, chicken or white fish. It will keep for up to 5 days in a covered container in the refrigerator. Reheat it gently before using.

🍴 1 hour 10 minutes

Makes about 600 ml /1 pt
250 g /8 oz okra
250 g /8 oz tomatoes
1 medium-sized green pepper
2 green chillies
1 large onion, finely chopped
1 garlic clove, finely chopped
90 ml /6 tbls oil
150 ml /5 fl oz white wine vinegar
30 ml /2 tbls tomato purée
15 ml /1 tbls molasses or black treacle

1 Trim the okra and thinly slice it crossways. Blanch, skin and chop the tomatoes. Core, seed and finely chop the green pepper and the chillies.
2 Place all the ingredients in a saucepan and set it over a low heat. Bring to the boil and simmer until you have a soft, thick mixture, about 50 minutes. Serve hot.

Casserole of duck with water chestnuts and Bean sprout salad

Stir-fried beef with bamboo shoots

🍴🍴 30 minutes

Serves 4
700 g /1½ lb top rump steak
450 g /1 lb canned bamboo shoots, drained
60 ml /4 tbls oil
1 garlic clove, finely chopped
125 g /4 oz carrots, thinly sliced
1 large onion, finely chopped
5 ml /1 tsp ground ginger
1.5 ml /¼ tsp cayenne pepper
juice of 1 lemon
30 ml /2 tbls soy sauce

1 Cut the steak into small, thin slivers. Slice the bamboo shoots.
2 Put the oil and garlic into a wok or a large frying-pan and set it over a high heat. When the garlic begins to sizzle, add the beef and carrots. Stir-fry them until the meat has browned.
3 Lower the heat and add the onion, bamboo shoots, ginger and cayenne pepper. Stir-fry for a further 2 minutes.
4 Pour in the lemon juice and soy sauce. Bring to the boil, stirring, and remove the pan from the heat. Turn it into a heated serving dish and serve immediately.

● Serve with boiled rice, boiled Chinese noodles or fried rice.

Prawn foo-yung

Chicken and ham gumbo

🍴🍴 1 hour 40 minutes

Serves 6
1.4 kg /3 lb roasting chicken, jointed
750 g /1½ lb aubergines
15 ml /1 tbls salt
60 ml /4 tbls olive oil
1 large onion, finely chopped
10 ml /2 tsp paprika
2.5 ml /½ tsp cayenne pepper
500 g /1 lb okra, trimmed
350 g /12 oz canned sweetcorn, drained
600 ml /1 pt ham stock
1 garlic clove, crushed
30 ml /2 tbls tomato purée
250 g /8 oz lean cooked ham, diced

1 Cut the aubergines into 20 mm /¾ in dice. Put them into a colander and sprinkle them with salt. Leave to drain for 20 minutes. Rinse with cold water and drain on absorbent paper.
2 Heat the oil in a flameproof casserole over a medium heat. Add the chicken, brown quickly on all sides and remove.
3 Lower the heat. Add the onion and cook until it is soft but not coloured. Mix in the paprika, cayenne pepper and aubergines. Cook for 1 minute.
4 Add the okra and sweetcorn. Pour in the stock and bring to the boil. Stir in the garlic and tomato purée. Add the chicken and ham. Cover the casserole and cook it over a low heat for 45 minutes.
5 Take out the chicken pieces, remove the meat from the bones and cut it into 20 mm /¾ in cubes. Return the chicken meat to the casserole and reheat it briefly before serving with plain boiled rice.

Prawn foo-yung

🍴 defrosting if necessary, then 20 minutes

Serves 4
8 medium-sized eggs, well beaten
60 ml /4 tbls soy sauce
60 ml /4 tbls oil
16 spring onions, in 25 mm /1 in lengths
300 g /11 oz bean sprouts
350 g /12 oz boiled shelled prawns,
*   defrosted if frozen*
spring onion tassels, to garnish
tomato wedges, to garnish
flat-leaved parsley, to garnish (optional)

1 Beat the eggs with the soy sauce.
2 Heat the oil in a wok or a large frying-pan over a high heat. Add the spring onions and bean sprouts and stir-fry them until the onions begin to wilt, about 2 minutes.
3 Stir in the prawns, then add the well-beaten eggs. Stir until the eggs set, then serve immediately, garnished with the spring onion tassels, tomato wedges and flat-leaved parsley, if desired.

Celery

Crunchy and crisp when raw, succulent and full of flavour when cooked, celery is delicious raw with cheese at the end of a meal; as a side dish or as a crispy addition to a salad. It is also an essential for adding flavour, texture and variety to stock, soups, stews and casseroles.

Today's celery bears little resemblance to the bitter-tasting weed from which it descends. The Romans used its forebear in cooking, but for centuries its main use was medicinal. It was thought to have cleansing properties and to be an appetite stimulant. Cultivated celery, although not particularly nutritious, is a tasty source of roughage. The juice is rich in Vitamins A and C.

Efforts to turn the weed into a palatable vegetable were rewarded in the 16th century when Italian gardeners earthed up the growing plant, thus blanching the stalks and reducing their bitterness. Nowadays, there is also a form of celery cultivated for its knobbly root, called celeriac (see *page 221*). Celery seeds can be used for flavouring.

Choosing and storing celery

There are many varieties of celery – the white winter varieties, pale green ones which are available most of the year and the pink American varieties. Always choose well-shaped compact heads with firm unblemished stalks. Brightly coloured, feathery leaves are a sure sign of freshness. If the stump is discoloured but not uniformly black the head is fresh. Trimmed celery, with overly large hearts, are usually past their peak. As a guide, the darker the colour of the celery, the coarser its texture.

If you have to buy celery in advance of use, store the unwashed head, loosely wrapped in the crisper compartment of the refrigerator for up to 5 days, or in a cool, well-ventilated place for a day or two. If the celery has begun to wilt when you come to use it, revive it by soaking in ice-cold water for 30 minutes.

✳✳✳✳ Box raw celery scraps for use in stews and soups, freeze leaves in plastic bags, both for up to one month. Chunks of celery should be blanched for 3 minutes, halved hearts for 5 minutes. Keep for 6 months, but do not use for salad.

Preparing celery

You can use just about every bit of celery, so waste is minimal. Trim off the base then separate the stalks. Scrub or rinse them clean under cold running water and pat dry. Cut away any bruised or damaged bits. Slice off the leaves and trim the upper stalks.

The outermost stalks may be too coarse to use raw, so save them for soups and stocks. Store the large bright green leaves together with the outer stalks and use to flavour stuffings, sausage-meat or meat loaves.

Stringing is necessary for older celery and outer stalks. Hold each stalk in turn so that the base end points away from you. With a sharp knife, make a tiny nick at the top end – just inside the rounded edge – but do not cut right through. Pull the knife away from you, towards the base of the stalk: the strings should come away easily. Continue until all the strings are removed. For soup which is to be sieved this is unnecessary.

Preparing hearts: use small, tender green heads as they are less gritty and stringy than the white varieties. Break off the coarse outer stalks to leave a cluster of tightly packed stalks, about 5 cm /2 in thick. Trim the base neatly and cut off the tops so that each heart is about 15 cm /6 in in length. Leave them whole or, to shorten cooking time, halve lengthways. Wash them well.

Using celery

Celery's robust flavour goes well with meat, notably beef, and it has an affinity with nuts, especially chestnuts, and with tomatoes. Use the coarse outer stalks in stocks or puréed soups. The tender inner stems are good in meat and vegetable casseroles as well as in stuffings for poultry.

Braised celery hearts are traditionally served with roast meat, but their flavour and succulence are possibly better appreciated when served as a separate course. Short lengths of celery can be simmered briefly, refreshed and then finished in a tomato, bechamel or cheese sauce.

Sautéing celery preserves the vegetable's character well. Toss thick slices briefly over the heat in some butter, bacon fat or oil until they are just browned but still crisp. Add walnut halves or blanched almonds and you will have a mouthwatering accompaniment for roast poultry or game.

Using celery raw: a tall glass or jug of celery stalks provides the finishing touch to a cheese board: the celery will balance the richness of mature cheeses.

In France the best stalks of white winter celery are included in a mixed *crudités* for a first course or served alone with a thick piquant sauce – such as anchovy or Remoulade. Another French custom is to serve raw celery with a dish of unsalted butter, a mill of coarse sea salt and a basket of very fresh bread. Fill the celery cavities with butter, sprinkle over the salt and eat with bread. Another alternative is to use the sliced central stalks in apple salad.

Short lengths of celery are a natural base for canapés and other party finger food. Fill the cavities with soft mixtures such as fish or liver pâté, blue cheese mashed to a paste with butter or cream, or chopped hard-boiled egg bound with thick, chervil-flavoured mayonnaise.

Garnishes: float the pale feathery leaves from the inner stalks on soups or use them to decorate salads. To make celery curls to garnish moulded rice or jellied salads and savoury mousses, cut the stalks across into 5 cm /2 in lengths. Slit each piece lengthways several times almost to the base. Soak in iced water for 2 hours until the strips curl.

Celery, butter bean and mushroom salad

The attraction of this vegetable salad is the contrast of textures: the softness of butter beans and mushrooms set against the crispness of celery and onion. Serve it with crusty rolls and cheese, or a smoked fish pâté for a light summery lunch.

⏱ 30–45 minutes

Serves 4
*425 g /15 oz canned butter beans, drained and
    rinsed*
*50 g /2 oz button mushrooms, wiped, trimmed
    and thinly sliced*
2 large spring onions, finely chopped
*4 celery stalks, trimmed, stringed and thinly
    sliced*
For the dressing
7.5 ml /1½ tsp wine vinegar
7.5 ml /1½ tsp green peppercorn mustard
45 ml /3 tbls sunflower or safflower oil
30 ml /2 tbls thick cream
15 ml /1 tbls freshly chopped parsley
salt and freshly ground pepper
To garnish
1 bunch watercress, washed and trimmed
black olives, stoned and halved

1 Combine the butter beans, mushrooms, spring onions and celery, then set aside.
2 To make the dressing, whisk together the vinegar and mustard, then whisk in the oil. When the mixture has emulsified, whisk in the cream and parsley and season to taste.
3 Pour the dressing over the vegetables. Gently turn the vegetables until they are evenly coated with the dressing. Leave to stand for 15–20 minutes to allow the flavour of the dressing to penetrate the vegetables. Check the seasoning and serve the salad on a bed of watercress, garnished with olives.

Celery boats

These make excellent buffet fare, or they can be served with pre-dinner drinks. Choose stalks with large cavities.

⏱ 20 minutes

Makes 8 boats
4 celery stalks, trimmed and washed
100 g /4 oz cream cheese
30 ml /2 tbls soured cream
pinch of cayenne pepper
30 ml /2 tbls red caviar-style lumpfish roe

1 Neaten the ends of each stalk and remove any fibrous strings. Cut the stalks in half, each about 7–9 cm /3–3½ in long.
2 Beat together the cream cheese and soured cream until smoothly blended. Beat in the cayenne.
3 Divide the cream cheese mixture equally between the celery boats and pack into the cavities. Smooth the surface and sprinkle over the lumpfish roe.

Celery and Stilton soup

This is a velvety smooth soup with a slight 'bite' to it. Serve it garnished with crisp, butter-fried croûtons or with the pale feathery leaves from the inner stalks.

⏱ 1¾ hours

Serves 4
*1 head of celery, washed, trimmed and the
    leaves reserved*
50 g /2 oz butter
2 medium-sized onions, peeled and chopped
1 L /1¾ pt light vegetable or chicken stock
salt and freshly ground black pepper
100 g /4 oz Stilton cheese
2 large egg yolks
150 ml /5 fl oz thin cream

1 Melt the butter in a large, heavy-based saucepan. Chop the celery and add this, the celery leaves and the onions to the pan. Cover and cook gently, stirring occasionally, for 10 minutes until the vegetables are soft but not coloured.
2 Pour in the stock and season lightly. Bring to the boil then simmer, uncovered, for about 30 minutes until the vegetables are quite tender.
3 Allow the soup to cool slightly, then blend to a purée. Press through a sieve to remove any fibres and return to a clean pan. Reheat gently, but do not allow to boil.
4 Meanwhile remove and discard the cheese rind and mash the cheese to a soft paste. Beat together the egg yolks and cream and to obtain a smooth consistency, blend into the cheese a little at a time.

Celery and Stilton soup

5 Stir 30 ml /2 tbls of hot soup into the cheese and cream mixture. Add the mixture to the pan and cook gently, stirring constantly, until the soup has thickened. Do not allow to boil. Adjust seasoning before serving.

Waldorf salad

This crunchy, slightly sweet salad, invented at the Waldorf hotel in New York, is excellent in winter as an appetizer or as an accompaniment to cooked ham or bacon. Red-skinned apples are traditional, but in autumn try using Golden Russets if you can. To vary the salad, add halved and seeded black grapes.

⏱ 15–20 minutes

Serves 4
3 medium-sized dessert apples, washed
lemon juice
6 celery stalks, scrubbed, trimmed and stringed
50 g /2 oz walnuts, chopped
150 ml /5 fl oz mayonnaise
crisp lettuce leaves
a few walnut halves, to decorate

1 Core, but do not peel, the apples. Cut into dice and turn the pieces in lemon juice to prevent discoloration. Drain and place in a mixing bowl.
2 Thinly slice the celery and add to the apples together with the walnuts. Mix together, then gently stir in the mayonnaise.
3 Line a salad bowl with lettuce leaves. Pile the apple and celery mixture in the centre and decorate with walnut halves.

Sicilian vegetable hors d'oeuvre

Caponata

Usually served as an hors d'oeuvre, *caponata* is a Sicilian vegetable stew. If you omit the tuna fish it makes a good accompaniment to sausages or egg-based dishes. It is also excellent with pasta. Prepare the dish at least 24 hours before required to allow the sweet-sour flavour of the sauce to permeate the vegetables. If pine nuts are unavailable, substitute slivered blanched almonds or, for a more piquant flavour, use two rinsed and chopped anchovy fillets. Good quality, fruity olive oil is essential.

  1½ hours
24 hours marinating

Serves 4
2 large aubergines, diced
salt
30–60 ml /4–6 tbls olive oil for frying
1 small onion, peeled and chopped
400 g /14 oz canned tomatoes
45 ml /3 tbls red wine vinegar
15 ml /1 tbls sugar
freshly ground black pepper
½ head of celery, trimmed, chopped and blanched
15 ml /1 tbls capers
25 g /1 oz black olives, stoned and coarsely chopped
30 ml /2 tbls pine nuts, toasted
200 g /7 oz canned tuna fish, drained
freshly chopped parsley, to garnish

1 Layer the diced aubergine in a colander, sprinkled with salt. Cover with a plate, weight it and leave to drain for 30–40 minutes. Then rinse the pieces and squeeze them dry in absorbent paper. Sauté in olive oil, then drain and reserve.

2 Heat 15 ml /1 tbls olive oil in a large, heavy-based saucepan. Add the onion and cook, stirring, for 5–7 minutes until soft. Add the tomatoes with about one-third of their juices. (Reserve the remaining juices.) Simmer for 5 minutes, then stir in the vinegar and sugar and season to taste. Simmer the sauce for 15–20 minutes, until well reduced and richly coloured.

3 Add the blanched celery to the pan together with the aubergine, capers, olives and pine nuts, stirring well to mix. Cover the pan with a tight-fitting lid and cook gently for 30 minutes, stirring regularly. If the mixture appears too dry and the vegetables show signs of sticking add a little of the reserved tomato juices, but avoid making the stew too wet.

4 Remove the pan from the heat and turn the stew into a bowl. Allow to cool, then cover tightly and chill for at least 24 hours.

5 Bring the stew to room temperature before serving. Correct the seasoning and turn into a serving dish. Flake the tuna into fairly large chunks and scatter these around the edge. Garnish with plenty of freshly chopped parsley.

Beef and celery casserole

 30 minutes then
 1¾–2 hours cooking

Serves 4
700 g /1½ lb chuck steak, trimmed and cubed
250 g /8 oz streaky bacon slices, cut into matchsticks
15–30 ml /1–2 tbls oil
2 medium-sized onions, chopped
1 garlic clove, chopped
4 celery stalks, trimmed and sliced
10–15 ml /2–3 tsp flour
150 ml /5 fl oz red wine
bouquet garni
300 ml /10 fl oz beef stock
salt and freshly ground black pepper
50 g /2 oz chopped walnuts

Sicilian vegetable hors d'oeuvre

1 Heat the oil in a flameproof casserole; when hot, fry the bacon until it browns. Remove the bacon and reserve. Add the cubes of the beef and fry for 5–7 minutes, turning once, until browned. Remove the meat with a slotted spoon and reserve.

2 Reduce the heat, then cook the onions and garlic until the onions begin to colour. Remove the onions and garlic and reserve.

3 Adding more oil if necessary, cook the celery until it colours slightly. Sprinkle in the flour. Cook, stirring, for a few minutes, then gradually stir in the wine.

4 Add the beef, onions, bacon and bouquet garni; pour in just enough stock to barely cover. Season to taste. Bring slowly to the boil, cover the casserole and simmer gently for 1½–2 hours until the beef is tender.

5 Before serving, check the seasoning then garnish with the chopped walnuts.

● This is an excellent recipe for preparing in advance, as it reheats well and the flavour improves with keeping.

Cucumbers

Cucumbers are most often eaten raw in refreshing salads or as an attractive garnish, but this readily available vegetable can be used in a variety of other dishes, cooked or uncooked.

Cucumbers are one of the oldest of cultivated vegetables. There are many kinds, varying in size from the very small pickling cucumber to enormous ones about 45 cm /1½ ft long, and in colour from yellow to the familiar dark green, but they can all be divided into two main types: hot-house cucumbers, which are long and smooth-skinned and are grown under glass, and ridge cucumbers, which are shorter, with tough, knobbly skins, and are grown out-doors on raised ridges of soil. In general, the hot-house cucumber is grown in Britain and northern Europe, while the ridge is grown in warmer countries.

Buying and storing cucumbers

Choose cucumbers that are firm to the touch – check that the stalk end of a plastic-wrapped, imported cucumber has not gone soggy – and regular in shape. A bulbous end indicates an old cucumber, tough-skinned, full of seeds and with yellowing flesh.

Fresh cucumbers are available all year round in Europe – imported during the winter months – and can also be bought pickled: loose from a delicatessen, or in cans or jars. These dill-flavoured pickles are very popular in the U.S. and central and eastern countries of Europe.

Gherkins look like tiny cucumbers but are a different species. They are most often bought already pickled and are used in northern Europe as a garnish.

Eat cucumbers as soon as possible after purchase. They can be stored for a few days in the salad compartment of a refrigerator, the cut side covered with cling film, or in a glass of cold water in a cool place away from direct light. The stalk end should be placed downwards in the glass, and the cut end covered with foil.

✳✳✳ Because they have a very high water content, cucumbers cannot be frozen raw for use in salads. They can, however, be successfully frozen after salting and draining for use in a cooked dish.

Preparing cucumbers

If a hot-house cucumber is fresh and young and to be used in a salad, peeling is unnecessary, as the skin adds flavour and colour. Some people find cucumber indigestible, but removing the skin does nothing to remedy this. Peeling is necessary if the skin is tough or if you are cooking the cucumber. Cucumbers imported from the U.S. are sometimes dipped in wax, which will make the skin tough and unpalatable, and ridge cucumbers should always be peeled, except when they are to be pickled. Peel them with a potato peeler, removing as

little of the cucumber flesh as possible.

If a cucumber is past its prime it will be full of seeds, which should be scraped away with a teaspoon after cutting the vegetable in half lengthways.

Cucumbers are traditionally sliced very thinly in rounds, using a mandolin, the straight-cut blade of a box grater or a food processor. They can also be cut in half lengthways, then quartered or chopped, or grated or cut into small matchsticks.

Usually, before using cucumbers in salads or cooked dishes the excess moisture is removed by 'degorging'. The cucumber is sliced or chopped, sprinkled with salt to draw out the moisture, and left for at least 30 minutes, then drained and dried.

Cucumber garnishes

Pale green, thin slices of cucumber make an extremely attractive garnish for many dishes. Use them to add the finishing touch to a summer soup, or set them in a layer of aspic on top of a salmon mousse. The peeled skin can also be cut into shapes.

Give unpeeled slices an attractive crimped appearance by running the prongs of a fork down the whole cucumber before slicing. Thin slices, peeled or unpeeled, can be made into twists and then arranged around the edge of a pale-coloured egg or fish mousse, or used to decorate glasses for a cool summer drink – slices of cucumber and mint leaves are a traditional garnish for a glass of Pimms.

Make cucumber rings by hollowing out a whole cucumber, stuffing with a suitable mixture, then cutting across. Long strips of cucumber peel can also be tied into bows.

Using cucumbers

Cucumber is most often used as part of a simple mixed salad, but there are many different ways in which it can be presented. Use both hot-house and ridge cucumbers for the following ideas. For the simplest side salad, slice cucumber thinly, dress with oil and white wine vinegar and sprinkle with herbs – chives, dill or parsley.

In the Middle East, cucumber, in small chunks or grated, is combined with yoghurt, garlic and sometimes mint, and

Pretty cucumber garnishes, from the left: for the simple cucumber salad the unpeeled cucumber was scored then thinly sliced and carefully arranged with a radish rose centre. The salmon mousse has a border of cucumber twists and a folded slice in the centre to look like a flower. Make cucumber boats from short pieces halved lengthways: use lemon and cucumber slices speared with cocktail sticks for the sails and fill the boat with taramasalata or other dips. On a cold poached salmon trout paper-thin slices of cucumber look like scales. Other garnishes include chains made from thick slices of hollowed-out cucumber, slit and joined together; flowers made of thin cucumber slices, with hidden cucumber ring bases and a slice of stuffed olive in the centre; and long strips of peel, knotted and placed on a trio of peeled, thin cucumber slices

chilled to make a wonderfully refreshing side dish to eat with kebabs or curries. This salad has many names, including *cacik* in Turkey, *tsatziki* in Greece, *raita* in India, and *salatit khiar bi laban* in Egypt. Increase the quantity of yoghurt to make a cooling summer soup.

In European cookery cucumber is often combined with cream, fresh or soured. Serve a simple hors d'oeuvre of coarsely grated cucumber dressed with soured cream, oil and white pepper, or a dish of chilled, thinly sliced cucumber accompanied by salted whipped cream.

Cucumber combines well with cheese, particularly the soft, creamy varieties. Serve with blue cheese dressing in a salad, or combine with cottage cheese, soured cream, gelatine and herbs for a delicious savoury mould.

A light mousse can be made by mixing finely chopped cucumber with chopped hard-boiled egg, mayonnaise and gelatine. The fresh flavour of cucumber goes particularly well with many fish, from salmon to shellfish to sardines. Blend canned tuna fish, cucumber and cottage cheese together to make a quick fish paté.

Use cucumber in chilled summer soups, or purée it and thicken with potato, a liaison of egg yolks and cream, or a creamy sauce for a rich hot soup. The addition of sorrel or spinach leaves will enhance the colour and flavour.

Hollow out cucumber halves, fill with a minced veal stuffing, top with soured cream and bake, or use a Provençal mixture of garlic, herbs and breadcrumbs and grill. Cucumbers can themselves be chopped, mixed with rice, onion and herbs and used to stuff oily fish such as mackerel.

Hollowed-out cucumbers can be stuffed with a variety of fillings to make cocktail party savouries (see recipe). For a party version of the famous English cucumber sandwich, cut very thin slices of brown bread, butter them, sprinkle with drained grated cucumber, roll up, secure with a cocktail stick and chill overnight. Next day, the cocktail sticks can be removed and the rolls will remain intact.

Do try cooked cucumbers – they taste quite different and should be treated in a similar way to courgettes and marrows. Hot cucumber combines well with all types of fish, chicken and veal, and can be served in a creamy sauce with any of these. Cucumber chunks or balls cut with a melon baller can be boiled in salted water for about 10 minutes, or steamed for 15–20 minutes. Toss them in butter and finely chopped parsley and use as a garnish for fish. They can be fried quickly in butter or baked in the oven with butter or soured cream and dill, and served as a bed for baked brill.

Make a sweet cucumber pickle by combining sliced ridge cucumbers with onion and green pepper and boiling in vinegar with sugar and spices. Serve with hamburgers, barbecued or cold meats.

Pickled whole cucumbers or gherkins can be used as a garnish for cold meats and pâtés, or sliced into a pickled herring salad. Chop gherkins finely and add to mayonnaise to eat with hot boiled beef or tongue.

Sautéed veal with cucumber sticks

⏱ 30 minutes degorging cucumber, then 20 minutes

Serves 4
1 medium-sized cucumber, peeled
salt and freshly ground black pepper
75 g /3 oz butter
1 medium-sized onion, chopped
4 × 100 g /4 oz veal escalopes
30 ml /2 tbls flour
10 ml /2 tsp paprika
150 ml /5 fl oz soured cream (optional)
chopped parsley, to garnish

1 Cut the cucumber in half lengthways, scoop out any seeds, then cut into sticks about 25 mm /1 in long and 10 mm /½ in wide. Sprinkle with salt and leave to degorge for at least 30 minutes.
2 When you are ready to start cooking, melt the butter in a frying-pan on a low heat and soften the onion in it.
3 While the onion is cooking, beat out each escalope thinly. Mix together the flour, paprika and salt and pepper to taste, and dip each escalope in this mixture.
4 Turn the heat up to medium and add the escalopes to the pan, frying until well browned on each side. Place on one side of a warmed serving dish and keep warm.
5 Pat the cucumber sticks dry and add to the pan. Cook until lightly browned, stirring occasionally. Pile on to the other side of the serving dish and, if liked, spoon the soured cream over the veal and cucumber. Sprinkle with the parsley and serve at once.

Cucumber cocktail savouries

Try minced chicken in mayonnaise or ham and cottage cheese as a filling instead of sardines and egg.

⏱ 30 minutes degorging cucumber then 15 minutes

Makes about 15
1 medium-sized cucumber
salt and freshly ground black pepper
100 g /4 oz canned sardines
hard-boiled egg, chopped
15 ml /1 tbls lemon juice
about 30 ml /2 tbls mayonnaise
parsley, to garnish

1 Cut the cucumber into 25 mm /1 in rounds. Hollow out the centres gently to make little containers, being careful not to cut right through the cucumber. Sprinkle with salt and place upside down to drain for at least 30 minutes.
2 Drain some of the oil from the sardines. Mash with the egg, adding pepper, lemon juice and enough mayonnaise to make a smooth, not too runny mixture. Wipe the cucumber rounds dry, fill them with the sardine mixture and garnish with parsley.

Baked salmon with cucumber sauce

This is a luxurious dish which would make a delightful main course for a 'special occasion' summer dinner party. New potatoes are the ideal accompaniment for the hot fish.

⏱⏱ 1 hour 50 minutes

Serves 6
1.4 kg /3 lb piece of salmon
75 g /3 oz butter, melted
sea salt and freshly ground black pepper
fresh dill sprigs (optional)
1 lemon, sliced
30 ml /2 tbls white wine (or more butter)
For the cucumber hollandaise sauce
1 medium-sized cucumber, peeled and thinly sliced
salt
45 ml /3 tbls white wine vinegar
10 white peppercorns
3 large egg yolks
175 g /6 oz butter
lemon juice

1 Heat the oven to 150C /300F /gas 2. Sprinkle salt over the cucumber slices and leave them to degorge in a colander while the salmon is cooking.

2 Line a large roasting tin with a piece of foil big enough to wrap around the fish. Brush the foil generously with melted butter and place the salmon in the centre. Season with sea salt and freshly ground black pepper. Arrange the sprigs of dill, if used, and the slices of lemon around the salmon. Pour the wine over (or dot with butter). Bring the edges of the foil together and parcel up loosely. Bake for 1–1¼ hours, depending on thickness.
3 Meanwhile, make the hollandaise: put the vinegar, 45 ml /3 tbls water and the peppercorns into a saucepan and boil vigorously until the liquid is reduced to approximately 15 ml /1 tbls. Leave to cool.
4 About 15 minutes before the salmon has finished cooking, complete the sauce. Wipe the cucumber slices, chop roughly and set aside. Beat the egg yolks into the reduced vinegar mixture, then pour into the top pan of a double boiler over barely simmering water on a low heat. Stirring all the time, add the butter piece by piece, adding more only when the previous piece has been absorbed. The sauce should be thick and glossy. When all the butter is used, add salt and lemon juice to taste, and fold in the cucumber.
5 Unwrap the salmon, place it on a warmed serving dish and serve immediately with the sauce in a sauce-boat.

Cucumber cocktail savouries filled with ham and cottage cheese

Avocados

A fruit that can be served as a vegetable, that turns up as a starter, main course or dessert – the avocado, with its luscious texture and faintly nutty flavour, has earned a reputation as 'the subtlest of all foods'.

The first Europeans to see the avocado were the Spanish conquistadores when they invaded Mexico at the end of the 15th century, as the *ahuacatl* had long been a staple of the Aztec diet. Unable to pronounce the word, the Spaniards converted it into *aguacate*, and it became 'avocado' in English.

The avocado is an almost sugarless fruit that is rich in vitamins, minerals, protein and fat.

Buying and storing avocados

Continual experiments with cross-breeding and the entry of many African countries into the export market is making the avocado nearly a year-round product, although its most plentiful time remains late autumn, winter and early spring.

There are over 500 varieties cultivated, but the most popular in European markets are the Hass, the Fuerte, the Nabal and the Ettinger. The Hass is small and pear-shaped, with a pebbly skin which turns black when it is ripe. The Fuerte is larger and is also pear-shaped. It has a smooth green skin which becomes brownish when ripe. The Nabal is about the same size as the Fuerte, but has a rounder shape, and a reddish-brown skin when ripe. The Ettin-

ger, the largest of the four, has a smooth, thin skin which stays green. The biggest avocados are about 250 g /8 oz. A new development is a very tiny 'cocktail' avocado, up to 5 cm /2 in long, which has no stone.

It is best to buy avocados before they are ripe and ripen them at home; this way they ripen more uniformly. The avocado dislikes squeezing – if it gives in to light pressure at the top or bottom, it is usually ripe. Dark spots on the skin of green-skinned avocados are another sign of ripeness and, of course, you can also tell by the characteristic colour changes in certain varieties mentioned above.

Very bruised avocados are usually over-ripe. These can be eaten on the day of purchase if you remove any dark brown spots and mash the remaining flesh.

Ripe avocados can be stored in the vegetable drawer of the refrigerator for up to 4 days, but never put hard avocados in the refrigerator. Store cut avocados with their stone still in, wrapped in cling film, for up to 24 hours.

✳✳✳✳ Avocados blacken when frozen whole but can be frozen as a purée, with 5 ml /1 tsp lemon juice added to each 600 ml /1 pt purée.

Preparing avocados

To open the avocado, cut in half lengthways with a knife, touching the centre stone as you go round. Then gently turn the two halves in opposite directions until they come apart. If you want to use the shells, remove the stone and scoop out the flesh with a teaspoon. For avocado slices, make a slit in the skin and gently peel it back. The darker green part near the outer skin is one of the most delicate parts of the avocado and should never be peeled away with the skin.

Rubbing the cut surfaces of an avocado with a wedge of lemon prevents it from turning brown. If you want to prepare an avocado salad or dip ahead of time, keep the stone in until serving – this also helps prevent browning.

Using avocados

At its simplest, half an avocado sprinkled with lemon juice and salt and pepper can begin a meal; sprinkled with sugar it can end one.

One of the classic flavour combinations is avocado and vinaigrette, but other good dressings to try include those made with Roquefort or Cheddar cheese, soured cream or yoghurt, or a simple sauce of crushed garlic, lemon juice and freshly ground black pepper.

Avocado shells can be filled with the chopped flesh mixed with tuna, poached fish (with a curried mayonnaise), cooked poultry, devilled or scrambled eggs, celery and tomatoes, or sautéed mushrooms. Or you can leave the flesh in the shell and

Avocado with prawns

simply fill the centre with any of the above.

Shellfish and avocados go together very well. Try baked avocados with a curried crab mixture, or fill an avocado half with peeled prawns and top with a spoonful of mayonnaise flavoured with a little tomato ketchup.

Avocados blend into fine dips with all kinds of different ingredients. The most famous of all is the Mexican guacamole, which can also be served as a salad or used to stuff eggs.

● Make an avocado-yoghurt dip by blending together the flesh of one avocado, 50 g /2 oz cream cheese at room temperature, 150 ml /5 fl oz yoghurt, and lemon juice, salt and freshly ground black pepper to taste. Chill before serving with raw vegetable sticks or potato crisps.

Sliced or mashed avocado on bread or toast sprinkled with a dash of lemon juice makes a great open sandwich, and to this basic idea you can add anchovy strips, caviar, prawns, bacon, ham, grated cheese, cottage cheese, sliced olives, and all sorts of vegetables including lettuce, tomatoes, cucumbers, green peppers, mild onions or celery.

● Mash two avocados with lemon juice and freshly ground black pepper to taste. Spread on six slices of toast, top with 12 large stoned and halved black olives, criss-cross over the top 12 crisply grilled rashers of streaky bacon, sprinkle with a little chopped fresh parsley and serve at once.

Add sliced or chopped avocado to salads: for example, sliced avocado and egg salad or, for a more unusual combination, avocado, almond and cheese salad. Other salad ingredients that combine well with avocados are lettuce, tomatoes, celery, cucumbers, cabbage, onions, French beans, mangetout, artichoke hearts, cauliflower, mushrooms, spinach, sweetcorn, kidney beans, peanuts, walnuts, olives, rice, oranges or grapefruit.

Avocados can feature in main courses as well. Slices of avocado provide the perfect flavour contrast to sautéed calf's liver, and fried avocado balls go well with chicken in a spicy, creamy sauce (see recipe). A simple sauce for fish, ham or steak is made by mashing the flesh of avocados with lemon juice and a chopped onion or garlic clove.

Combined with fruit the avocado takes on an entirely new aspect – it is delicious with grapefruit, grapes, bananas, oranges, apples, peaches, mangoes and pineapple. Combine several of these to make a fabulous fruit cup. Avocado halves filled with strawberries and sprinkled with icing sugar or mixed with sliced water-melon are two other dessert ideas.

Pour a spoonful of cognac, crème de menthe or Cointreau into the centre of an avocado half, or blend the flesh with soft vanilla ice cream and refreeze for a quick avocado ice cream. Avocado desserts are best made with slightly under-ripe fruit – a good tip for those occasions when your planning or purchasing goes wrong. One word of caution – remove any brown spots first from the avocado flesh; these might give your dessert an unpleasant flavour.

Avocado and garlic soup

The subtle flavour of the avocado, with just a hint of garlic, makes this soup special, but it must first be thoroughly chilled to blend the flavours.

10 minutes,
then 2 hours chilling

Serves 4-6
3 medium-sized avocados, chopped
350 ml /12 fl oz chicken stock
10 ml /2 tsp lime juice
2.5 ml /1/2 tsp salt
1 garlic clove, crushed
350 ml /12 fl oz thin cream
For the garnish
thin slices of lemon or lime
finely chopped parsley

1   Purée the avocados by hand or in a blender with half of the stock, the lime juice, salt and garlic. Thoroughly stir in the remaining stock and the cream. Pour into a soup tureen or individual serving bowls and chill for at least 2 hours, or overnight.
2   To serve, top with the lemon or lime slices and sprinkle with the parsley.

Eggs with avocado sauce

20 minutes

Serves 4
8 medium-sized eggs
25 g /1 oz butter
30 ml /2 tbls finely chopped onion
1 green chilli, fresh or canned, finely chopped
15 ml /1 tbls flour
100 g /4 oz frozen peas
125 ml /4 fl oz milk
2 ripe avocados
salt

1   Hard boil the eggs, run them under cold water to arrest cooking, then peel them and keep them warm in a bowl of hot water while you prepare the sauce.
2   Melt the butter in a saucepan and cook the chopped onion until it is soft. Add the chopped chilli pepper and stir in the flour. When completely blended, add the frozen peas and milk and stir until it thickens.
3   Purée the avocado and stir it in. Season with salt to taste.
4   Halve the eggs, place them on a warmed serving dish, pour over the sauce and serve.

Chicken with avocado sauce

Chicken and avocados blend together beautifully, and especially in this dish which combines them with curry powder and ginger.

1 hour 10 minutes

Serves 4-6
1.8 kg /4 lb chicken, in 6-8 pieces
salt and freshly ground black pepper
15 ml /1 tbls powdered ginger
25 g /1 oz butter
2 medium-sized onions, chopped
15 ml /1 tbls mild curry powder
225 ml /8 fl oz chicken stock
4 small, ripe avocados
30 ml /2 tbls thick cream
pinch of cayenne pepper
flat-leaved parsley, to garnish

1 Pat the chicken pieces dry with absorbent paper. Rub salt, black pepper and ginger into the chicken with your fingers.
2 In a heavy frying-pan over a medium heat, melt half the butter and add the chopped onions. Cook until softened.

Chicken with avocado sauce

3 Add the chicken pieces and cook, turning, until they are lightly browned on all sides. Sprinkle with the curry powder and stir for 1-2 minutes, then pour in the stock. Cook, covered, over a low heat until the chicken is just tender, about 40-45 minutes.
4 While the chicken is cooking, prepare the avocado balls. Reserve the ripest avocado. Cut the others in half and remove the stones. Use a melon baller to scoop out perfect balls. With a fork, mash together the left-over flesh and the flesh of the reserved avocado.
5 When the chicken is almost done, melt the remaining butter in another frying-pan on a very low heat. Add the avocado balls and cook gently, shaking the pan every few minutes, until the avocado balls are heated through; do not stir. Keep warm.
6 When the chicken is cooked, transfer the pieces to a warmed serving dish with a slotted spoon. Add the avocado paste, the cream and the cayenne pepper to the stock remaining in the pan. Heat thoroughly, but do not allow it to boil. Pour over the chicken, garnish with avocado balls and flat-leaved parsley and serve at once.

Avocado pancakes

These hearty pancakes make an attractive first course. If you wish to add a touch of elegance, try a slice of smoked salmon with each pancake.

1 hour

Makes about 16 pancakes
4 medium-sized eggs
15 ml /1 tbls milk
5-7.5 ml /1-1½ tsp Worcestershire sauce
5 ml /1 tsp salt
1 medium-sized onion, chopped
40 g /1½ oz flour
1 large, firm avocado, chopped
1 large potato, peeled and grated
15 ml /1 tbls lemon juice
freshly ground black pepper
butter for greasing
For the sauce
125 ml /4 fl oz soured cream
125 ml /4 fl oz yoghurt
freshly ground black pepper
dash of Tabasco sauce

1 First make the sauce by combining all the ingredients.
2 Put the eggs, milk, Worcestershire sauce, salt and chopped onion into a blender and blend until thoroughly combined. Add the flour, avocado, potato, lemon juice, and black pepper to taste and blend for a few seconds at low speed.
3 Heat a heavy frying-pan on a medium heat, lightly grease with butter and pour in about 50 ml /2 fl oz of the batter. Cook until lightly browned on the bottom, then turn carefully and cook until done. Keep the pancake warm while you make the rest in the same way, then serve at once, with the sauce handed separately.

Fluffy avocado tart

1 hour,
plus 2 hours cooling and chilling

Serves 8
15 ml /1 tbls gelatine
2 medium-sized eggs, separated
275 ml /10 fl oz milk
75 g /3 oz sugar
1 medium-sized under-ripe avocado, peeled and mashed
125 ml /4 fl oz lemon or lime juice
5 ml /1 tsp lemon juice
whipped cream, to serve (optional)
For the biscuit crust
225 g /8 oz digestive biscuits
45 ml /3 tbls ground almonds
50 g /2 oz sugar
100 g /4 oz butter, melted

1 Heat the oven to 150C /300F /gas 2. Crush the biscuits to crumbs in a polythene bag, then make the biscuit crust. Mix the biscuit crumbs, ground almonds and sugar in a bowl. Stir in the melted butter, mix well and press evenly into a 23 cm /9 in flan dish. Bake for 15 minutes, then let cool.
2 Sprinkle the gelatine over 125 ml /4 fl oz cold water in a bowl and leave for 1 minute.
3 In the top pan of a double boiler beat together the egg yolks, milk and 60 ml /4 tbls sugar. Stir over simmering water until slightly thickened, about 5 minutes. Add the gelatine liquid and stir until completely dissolved.
4 Remove from the heat and blend in the mashed avocado and the 125 ml /4 fl oz lemon or lime juice, using a wire whisk or an electric beater. Pour the mixture into a large bowl and chill, stirring occasionally, until the mixture is thick enough to form mounds when dropped from a spoon.
5 In a clean bowl, whisk the egg whites until soft peaks form. Whisk in the remaining sugar and fold into the gelatine mixture. Pour into the cooled biscuit crust and chill until firm. Sprinkle with lemon juice and serve, with whipped cream if wished.

Avocado lemon creams

This rich dessert is also delicious made with limes instead of lemons.

15 minutes

Serves 4
2 ripe avocados, chopped
2 lemons
25 g /1 oz icing sugar
100 ml /3½ fl oz thick or whipping cream, whipped

1 In a blender, purée the avocado flesh, the juice of the lemons and the icing sugar. Divide the mixture between 4 small dishes.
2 Spread the whipped cream over the top of each dish and decorate with a little grated lemon zest. Serve chilled.

Lettuce

Most people use lettuce in a salad and leave it at that; indeed, a bowl piled high with crisp green leaves is very appetizing. But have you ever tried cooking with lettuce? It imparts a delicate flavour to soups, main course dishes and other vegetables, and can be used as a cooked vegetable in its own right.

Lettuce is attributed with certain medicinal qualities: the ancient Romans used it as a digestive and it is still thought of as such by some people – which may explain why a salad is usually served after a meal in France. We do know that it is mildly sedative.

There are basically two kinds of lettuce: the cabbage or butterhead lettuce and the cos or romaine lettuce. Cabbage lettuces have roundish or somewhat flattened heads, and range from the soft 'All the Year Round' to the crisp, solid Webb's Wonderful or the crunchy, tightly packed Iceberg. Cos lettuces have elongated, coarse leaves and a sweeter taste. There is also a new kind of lettuce called a loosehead or cutting lettuce, such as the 'Salad Bowl' variety.

Buying and storing lettuce
Which lettuce you use depends on personal taste and availability; but whichever you buy, always choose carefully. A lettuce should be heavy and feel springy to the touch. Check inner leaves, and avoid any lettuces that look droopy or have slimy or brown patches on the leaves.

A lettuce goes limp because it lacks moisture. To ensure that it stays in prime condition, spray it all over lightly with water, then wrap it in a polythene bag or in a damp cloth and store it in the refrigerator – this will prevent evaporation. Lettuces are best used the day you buy them; in any case they should not be kept for more than two or three days.

✱✱✱✱ Because of its high water content, lettuce loses its crisp texture when it is frozen. However, tender hearts can be blanched for two minutes, then drained, dried and frozen for up to six months. They can then be used to make soups.

Preparing lettuce
Always wash the leaves thoroughly before use to remove all traces of grit or earth, and dry them either in a salad shaker or by patting the leaves gently with a clean tea-towel: water left on the leaves dilutes the dressing and prevents it from coating the leaves when you are making a salad.

Tear a lettuce with your hands; cutting it with a knife can cause bruising and discolouring and will make it wilt much more quickly. When a recipe does call for chopped or shredded leaves, cut them at the last moment.

Using lettuce
Salads, of course, are what lettuce is usually used for, and they range from a simple lettuce and vinaigrette combination to, for example, two kinds of lettuce combined with watercress, hard-boiled egg, Parmesan cheese and herbs.

But lettuces have many other uses as well. They combine successfully with other fresh vegetables: a handful of leaves added to fresh peas or baby carrots will sweeten them as they simmer. Or bake broad beans and lettuce in little foil packets. The outer leaves or the leaves of bolted lettuces – lettuces which have gone to seed – make superb soups (see recipe), or they can be added to a stock pot.

A coat of lettuce leaves wrapped around fish or fowl (see recipe) will flavour it and prevent it from drying out.

Whole lettuce leaves can be used as a casing for timbales or individual mousses set in dariole moulds and as an outer layer for steamed fish mousses. The secret is always to blanch the leaves first; otherwise they will shrink during cooking; they will also give off too much moisture.

Four kinds of lettuce, from the left: cabbage, 'Salad Bowl', Iceberg, cos

Tuna fish bake

If you cannot find a tuna steak, you can substitute thick cod steaks. Likewise, spinach sprinkled with lemon juice can be used instead of sorrel.

🍴🍴 2 hours

Serves 6–8
3–4 anchovy fillets, drained
1.5–1.8 kg /3–4 lb tuna steak
5 ml /1 tsp olive oil
1 round lettuce, outer leaves blanched
450 g /1 lb tomatoes, blanched, skinned, seeded
and sliced
2 medium-sized onions, cut into thin rings
coarsely chopped flesh of 1 medium-sized lemon
225 g /8 oz sorrel, shredded
salt and freshly ground black pepper
175 ml /6 fl oz dry white wine

1   Soak the anchovy fillets in warm water for 5 minutes to remove excess salt, drain and cut into slivers. Spear a sliver with the point of a sharp knife and insert into the tuna steak. Carry on until it is studded with anchovy slivers. Heat the oven to 170C /325F /gas 3.
2   Choose a casserole just large enough to hold the tuna and pour in the oil. Break off the outer leaves of the lettuce and set aside; shred the remainder with a sharp knife. Line the bottom of the casserole with half of the whole leaves, overlapping, then scatter with half of the shredded lettuce, tomatoes, onions, lemon and sorrel.
3   Season with salt and pepper to taste. Lay the tuna on the bed of vegetables and cover with the remainder of the tomatoes, onions, lemon and sorrel and top with the rest of the shredded lettuce. Finish with a final layer of whole lettuce leaves, tucking them down the sides of the casserole so they will not shrink during cooking.
4   Pour over the white wine, cover the casserole and bake for 1 hour, or until the fish is cooked. Cut into wedges and serve directly from the casserole.

Cream lettuce salad

🍴 hard boiling eggs,
🍴 then 10 minutes

Serves 4–6
1 cos lettuce or 2 soft-leaved cabbage lettuces
2 medium-sized eggs, hard-boiled
5 ml /1 tsp freshly chopped tarragon
150 ml /5 fl oz thin cream
10 ml /2 tsp tarragon vinegar
1 garlic clove, crushed
salt and freshly ground black pepper

1   Arrange the torn lettuce leaves in a salad bowl. Separate the whites from the yolks of the eggs and finely chop the whites. Add to the lettuce with the tarragon.
2   To make the dressing, pass the egg yolks through a sieve and stir in the cream, vinegar and crushed garlic. Season to taste, pour over the salad, toss and serve at once.

Lettuce and sorrel soup

🍴 35 minutes

Serves 4
25 g /1 oz butter
1 medium-sized onion, chopped
225 g /8 oz sorrel
225 g /8 oz lettuce leaves (use outer leaves or
bolted lettuces)
1 small bunch fresh chervil or parsley, chopped
850 ml/1½ pt chicken stock
2 medium-sized egg yolks, beaten
salt and freshly ground black pepper
60 ml /4 tbls thick cream (optional)

1   Melt the butter in a saucepan. Cook the chopped onion until it is translucent, but do not let it brown.
2   Meanwhile tear the sorrel and lettuce leaves into large pieces. Add to the pan with the chervil or parsley and simmer for 3–4 minutes, until they are reduced to a pulp. Add the stock, bring to the boil and simmer, covered, for 10–15 minutes.
3   Liquidize the soup in a blender or purée it in a sieve and return it to the cleaned-out pan. Add a couple of spoonfuls to the beaten egg yolks and stir, then pour this mixture back into the pan.
4   Stirring constantly, gently reheat the soup until it thickens slightly. Add salt and pepper to taste and serve at once, swirling a spoonful of cream in each bowl, if wished.

Braised lettuce with tomatoes

Flavour lettuces with tomatoes and ham, and serve them as a cooked vegetable.

🍴🍴 1 hour 5 minutes

Serves 4
4 small cos or soft-leaved cabbage lettuces
salt and freshly ground black pepper
15 ml /1 tbls olive oil
25 g /1 oz butter
1 medium-sized onion, finely chopped
50 g /2 oz ham, finely chopped
225 g /8 oz tomatoes, blanched, skinned,
seeded and coarsely chopped
1 small bunch parsley, chopped
5 ml /1 tsp sugar

1   Plunge the whole lettuces in a large pan of boiling salted water for 1 minute, then refresh in cold water, drain and pat dry.
2   Heat the oil and butter in a stewpan or a sauté pan with a lid and sweat the chopped onion for 2–3 minutes. Add the ham, tomatoes, parsley and sugar and cook, stirring constantly, for about 10 minutes or until the mixture reduces to a thick purée.
3   Add the lettuces, cover and simmer on a low heat for 30 minutes, or until tender. Place in a warmed dish and serve at once.

Walnut and lettuce salad with croûtons and Tuna fish bake

Walnut and lettuce salad with croûtons

⏱ 25 minutes

Serves 4
4 slices white bread, crusts removed
oil for frying
1 large lettuce
100 g /4 oz walnuts, coarsely chopped
For the dressing
90 ml /6 tbls walnut oil
30 ml /2 tbls lemon juice
pinch of powdered rosemary
salt and freshly ground black pepper

1 First prepare the croûtons. Cut the bread into small squares. Heat the oil in a frying-pan and fry the bread until golden brown. Remove with a slotted spoon and drain on absorbent paper.
2 Tear the lettuce leaves into pieces. Place in a salad bowl and scatter with the chopped walnuts.
3 Make the dressing: mix the walnut oil and lemon juice together; add the rosemary and salt and pepper to taste. Pour over the salad and toss. Add the croûtons and serve at once.

Pigeons wrapped in lettuce leaves

🕐 soaking sultanas overnight, then 2 hours 10 minutes

Serves 4
4 small pigeons
salt and freshly ground black pepper
4 cos lettuces
15 ml /1 tbls olive oil
25 g /1 oz butter
1 medium-sized onion, finely chopped
2 slices bacon, finely chopped
100 g /4 oz mushrooms, finely chopped
25 g /1 oz sultanas, soaked overnight, drained and finely chopped
5 ml /1 tsp freshly chopped thyme or 2.5 ml /¹/₂ tsp dried thyme
175 ml /6 fl oz dry white wine
275 ml /10 fl oz pigeon or chicken stock

Pigeons wrapped in lettuce leaves

1 Heat the oven to 180C /350F /gas 4. Blanch the pigeons in boiling salted water for 5 minutes and drain. Blanch the whole lettuces in fresh boiling water for 1 minute, then refresh in cold water, drain and pat dry with absorbent paper.
2 In a small frying-pan, heat the oil and butter and soften the onion. Add the bacon, mushrooms, sultanas, thyme and salt and pepper to taste and cook, stirring occasionally, for about 5 minutes or until soft.
3 Separate the leaves of each lettuce without breaking them off, to make a space in the centre large enough to take a pigeon. Put in a bird, spoon over one-quarter of the mushroom mixture and arrange the leaves to cover the bird. Tie up each parcel with string and place in a casserole.
4 Pour over the white wine and stock, cover and cook for 1½ hours. Using a slotted spoon, lift out the packages onto a warmed serving plate. Cut the strings and unwrap the lettuces to reveal the birds. Keep warm while you boil the sauce quickly to reduce it by about one-third. Spoon it over the pigeons and serve at once.

Cress, chicory and other salad vegetables

Add these vegetables, some unusual and some familiar, to your shopping list to ensure that your table is well provided with salads, every month of the year; learn how to use them in cooked dishes as well.

Watercress

Watercress grows wild in freshwater streams throughout Europe and western Asia, and is cultivated in special water beds throughout the northern hemisphere. Do not eat wild watercress; it may be growing in contaminated water.

Buying and storing: watercress is available throughout the year, although it may disappear during periods of very hot or very cold weather. It is generally sold in bunches, though some supermarkets sell it, ready trimmed, in vacuum packs. The leaves should be dark green and shiny; avoid any that are yellow or wilted. If bought in bunches, the stems should be long and there should not be too many small rootlets attached to them.

Unopened packs of watercress can be stored at the bottom of the refrigerator for up to four days. It can then be rinsed and used without further preparation.

If you intend to eat bunched watercress within 12 hours of purchase, place the bunches, head down, in a bowl of cold water. (This procedure also helps to enliven slightly wilted watercress.) Alternatively, store the bunches in a polythene bag at the bottom of the refrigerator for up to three days. Wash thoroughly before using, and trim away any hard ends of the stems.

Using: watercress can be used in sandwiches and salads; it goes particularly well with tomatoes and also with citrus fruits. It can also be used to garnish meat and poultry. Finely chopped, it can be mixed into savoury butters and creamy dips.

Creamy watercress soup is always popular. Use the leaves chopped like a herb in sautés, or the leaves and stems in simple stir-fried dishes. Watercress also makes a tasty addition to omelettes, sauces and quiche fillings; and buttered watercress is a tasty cooked garnish for lamb or rich poultry such as duck or goose:

● Melt 25 g /1 oz butter in a saucepan over a low heat. Add two trimmed bunches of watercress, with the stems facing in the same direction. Turn over in the butter, cover tightly and cook for 5 minutes.

Salad cress

Salad cress is also called mustard and cress. At one time it was grown from a combination of garden or pepper cress seeds and white mustard seeds, and the cress had to be planted three or four days before the mustard as it is slower to sprout. Now, however, most commercially grown cress is produced from one type of seed only, that of a variety known as salad rape. Cress seed is only rarely mixed with it, mustard never.

Buying and storing: salad cress is available throughout the year. It is grown in most temperate countries, usually in a small block of peat inside a plastic punnet, and sold while it is still growing. Occasionally it is allowed to grow a little taller to be cut and sold in bunches.

A punnet of salad cress will keep fresh for 24 hours in a cool place, or for up to three days in a polythene bag at the bottom of the refrigerator. Store bunches in a polythene bag in the refrigerator.

Growing: salad cress is easy to grow at home. Spread a layer of blotting paper or flannel on a tray and dampen it. Sprinkle on the seeds (which must be fresh) and leave the tray in a light, warm place, watering every day. The cress should be ready to eat in about five days.

Using: salad cress can be tossed into green and mixed salads or used as a garnish for hot or cold dishes and soups. It makes an ideal sandwich filling, and goes especially well with eggs. It can also be used like a herb in some cooked dishes (see recipe).

White chicory

Chicory was originally developed from the wild plant called succory which is native to Europe and western Asia.

White chicory is probably the most familiar and most readily available type of chicory. It was developed in the area around Brussels and has consequently become known as Brussels or Belgian chicory or, in the U.S., Belgian endive. The French also refer to it as *endive*, or sometimes *witloof*, the name used in Belgium. White chicory is produced by cutting off the natural foliage and forcing the roots in the dark to produce the tightly packed, white, spindle-shaped heads, which are usually 10-12 cm /4-5 in long and 4-5 cm /1½-2 in thick.

Buying and storing: white chicory is on sale from autumn to spring, when it is widely available. Chicory is often packed in dark paper, to protect it from the light, which

Rocket, tomato and cucumber salad

makes the vegetable turn green and become bitter. When you are buying chicory, therefore, make sure it is very white and that the leaves have a translucent, fresh appearance. Reject any heads with leaves turning brown at the edges or those that have turned brown at the base of the stem.

Chicory should be eaten as soon as possible after purchase, but can be stored at the bottom of the refrigerator, wrapped in dark paper, for up to two days.

Using: white chicory can be eaten raw or cooked. For serving raw, trim away the stalk end and any withered parts of the outer leaves. Dip the head into cold water, shake dry, then thinly slice the head crossways. If the head is very thick, it can be halved lengthways before slicing. In salads, chicory combines particularly well with oranges, tomatoes, celery, nuts, diced cold meats or cheese. One head per person, or less, is usually enough in a salad.

For cooking, allow two heads per person and trim and wash them as above. To remove bitterness, the heads can be blanched in boiling, salted water to which you have added 15 ml /1 tbls lemon juice or white wine vinegar. Simmer for four minutes, then drain well. Then halve, and either cut the chicory into diagonal slices or cook it whole.

Whole heads can be braised with onions and stock in a moderate oven for 45 minutes, or simmered on top of the stove for the same amount of time. Lemon juice, cream and chopped herbs can be added towards the end of cooking, or the cooked heads can be coated in a cheese sauce and served au gratin. Or try chicory in a casserole with pork or beef.

Other types of chicory

Red chicory, or *radicchio,* was developed in Italy; there are three types. The first is forced, and is shaped like a head of white chicory with dark red leaves. The second is more open, and is streaked with red and cream. This is called *rossa di Treviso*. The third type, *rossa di Verona,* is round, and maroon in colour. All three are similar in flavour and texture to white chicory. Try a red chicory, lettuce and potato salad, or trim, blanch and cook the heads as for white chicory.

Asparagus chicory is an Italian vegetable with long, narrow leaves which can be used in salads. The stalks can also be used in salads, or they can be cooked: shave off pieces with a sharp knife, as though you were whittling a stick, starting from the base and working towards the tip. Blanch the shavings, then finish cooking with butter, garlic and herbs, or with olive oil and lemon juice.

Green chicory is rarely found in shops, but it can be grown in your garden to provide winter salads. The heads are larger and less tightly packed than those of white chicory. The leaves, which are a crisp, translucent pale green, are not blanched or forced. They are more suitable for salads than for cooking.

Magdeburg chicory is cultivated solely for its large roots, which are dried, roasted and ground, then added to coffee. This mixture is popular in France and in the New Orleans area of the U.S. Some health food shops sell instant chicory powder which is used as a coffee substitute.

Minced beef with chicory and orange

Lamb's lettuce

Lamb's lettuce is also known as corn salad, and as *mâche* in France. Occasionally available at specialist greengrocers, it is best from mid to late winter. Its soft green leaves have a slightly earthy taste and the shape and velvety texture of young lamb's tongues. When young they make an excellent salad, on their own or combined with beetroot. They can also be cooked in the same way as spinach.

Rocket

Rocket grows wild in many parts of Europe, but is popular only around the Mediterranean. It is related to the cresses and has deeply cut leaves about 10 cm /4 in long, with a slightly peppery flavour. It grows easily from seed, and some cultivated varieties are milder and more tender than the wild types.

Rocket is best chopped sparingly in salads – green or tomato – to be served as an accompaniment to cold meats.

Celtuce

Celtuce is also called asparagus lettuce or stem lettuce. It has a long green stem topped with a thick fan of pointed leaves and has been grown in western China for centuries. Easy to grow at home, its flavour is rather like a cross between celery and lettuce, hence the name.

Both stem and leaves are eaten. The stem should be pared, then thinly sliced for salads or stir-frying, or cut into short lengths for boiling, steaming or braising. Use the smallest leaves for salad; the larger, outer leaves are best cooked like spinach or added to stir-fried dishes.

Watercress and onion soup

⁑ 45 minutes

Serves 4
25 g /1 oz butter
2 medium-sized onions, finely chopped
15 ml /1 tbls flour
600 ml/1 pt chicken stock
1.5 ml /¼ tsp ground mace
salt and freshly ground black pepper
1 bay leaf
300 ml /10 fl oz dry white wine
75 g /3 oz watercress, stems and leaves,
  finely chopped
4 slices of French bread, toasted
125 g /4 oz Gruyère cheese, finely grated

1 Melt the butter in a saucepan over a low heat. Add the onions and cook, stirring occasionally, until they are golden.
2 Stir in the flour and cook for 1 minute. Stir in the stock, bring to the boil, stirring, then add the mace, salt and pepper and bay leaf. Simmer, uncovered, for 10 minutes.
3 Remove the bay leaf. Pour in the wine and add the watercress. Bring the soup to just below boiling point and remove it from the heat.
4 Put a slice of toasted French bread in the bottom of each of 4 hot, deep soup bowls. Top them with the cheese, pour the soup over and serve at once.

Minced beef with chicory and orange

⌇ 30 minutes

Serves 4
3 medium-sized oranges
15 g /½ oz butter
700 g /1½ lb minced beef
1 garlic clove, finely chopped
4 small heads of white chicory, thinly sliced
7.5 ml /½ tbls freshly chopped parsley
7.5 ml /½ tbls freshly chopped thyme
8 green olives, stoned and quartered
For the garnish
chicory leaves
orange slices
flat-leaved parsley

1 Cut the rind and pith from 2 of the oranges. Cut the flesh into quarters and thinly slice it. Squeeze the juice from the remaining orange.
2 Melt the butter in a large, heavy frying-pan over a high heat. Add the minced beef and break it up. Add the garlic and cook, stirring, until the beef browns, about 5-7 minutes.
3 Lower the heat and mix in the chicory and herbs. Add the orange juice and cook gently, uncovered, for 5 minutes, stirring.
4 Stir in the sliced oranges and the olives. Cook for 1 minute, garnish with the chicory leaves, orange slices and parsley and serve.

Salad cress soufflé

Salad cress and Dijon mustard make unusual flavourings for a slimming soufflé.

⁑ 1 hour 10 minutes

Serves 4
15 g/½ oz butter plus extra for greasing
25 g /1 oz browned breadcrumbs
150 ml /5 fl oz milk
1 bouquet garni
1 slice of onion
1 blade of mace
4 black peppercorns
15 ml /1 tbls flour
10 ml /2 tsp Dijon mustard
4 medium-sized eggs, separated
125 g /4 oz cottage cheese
2 punnets of salad cress

1 Heat the oven to 190C /375F /gas 5. Cut a length of paper 7.5 cm /3 in higher than an 18 cm /7 in soufflé dish. Tie or pin the paper securely around the dish, then butter and crumb both dish and paper.
2 Infuse the milk with the bouquet garni, onion, mace and peppercorns for 10 minutes, then strain it.
3 Melt the butter in a saucepan over a moderate heat. Stir in the flour, cook for a minute or 2, stirring, then add the milk and cook, stirring frequently, until the sauce is thick, about 2 minutes.

Watercress and onion soup

4 Remove the pan from the heat. Beat in the mustard, then the egg yolks, one at a time. Beat in the cheese, then cut in the cress and mix well.
5 Stiffly whisk the egg whites in a large bowl and fold them into the mixture with a metal spoon. Quickly transfer the mixture to the prepared soufflé dish and bake for 35 minutes, until it is risen and golden brown, then serve at once.

Chicken, caper and cress sandwiches

⌇ 15 minutes

Serves 4
225 g /8 oz cooked chicken
15 ml /1 tbls chopped capers
60 ml /4 tbls mayonnaise
butter for spreading
8 slices granary bread
2 punnets salad cress

1 Skin and finely shred the chicken. Mix with the capers and mayonnaise.
2 Butter the bread and scatter half the cress over 4 of the slices. Top with the chicken mixture, then the remaining cress.
3 Cover with the remaining slices of bread, cut the sandwiches into halves or quarters and serve.

Fruit

Fruit is readily available and we know that fruits with their vitamin content and natural sweetness are good for us, yet the main image that fruit conveys is one of luxury.

As with vegetables, the fruits that are available today appeal to the cook on opposing grounds. On the one hand is the sheer variety and choice, the wide range of imported fruit, both exotic, such as lychees and kiwi fruit, and 'staple' to our diet, such as oranges and lemons. On the other hand, the exciting seasonal availability of home-grown fruits provides the wonderful traditional repertoire of home-made fruit puddings and desserts.

Fruits are an immensely versatile ingredient for the cook. Almost without exception they can be served on their own to provide a simple and nutritious conclusion to the meal. Yet these same fruits can be used to make the most eleborate rich concoctions in pies, ices, puddings and cakes. An additional asset is that fruit can be made into jams, jellies and preserves, then used for a variety of winter puddings.

Nowadays fruits are not only served at the end of a meal. Adventurous cooks are building on the traditional combinations such as apple sauce with pork or cranberries to accompany turkey, or using fruit to enhance the flavour of all sorts of fish and meat appetizers and main courses. The tempting recipes in this chapter will help you to make the most of the fruits you buy.

Lemons, limes and citrons

The taste of lemon is instantly recognizable and both zest and juice are used in a variety of ways. For sponges and puddings it is one of the most popular flavours and slices of lemon are regarded as the natural accompaniment to fish and white meat like chicken and veal. Emulsion sauces would not be possible without lemon, while lemonade is one of the best-known soft drinks.

Lemons are thought to have originated in south-east Asia. They were used by the Romans, as an antidote to poison and a moth repellent, rather than as food! The Arabs used lemons in cooking and brought them to Europe where they became popular in the 12th and early 13th centuries. Like other citrus fruit, lemons grow on fairly small trees with glossy, dark evergreen leaves and fragrant blossom. The fruit ripens in winter. Lemons are fairly hardy and will thrive where there is no frost in winter. They are exported, in particular, from Italy, Cyprus, Israel, and California.

Limes prefer a hotter, wetter climate than lemons, and flourish in the tropics where they replace lemons. They are grown in India (where they originated), Mexico, the Caribbean and tropical Africa.

Citrons have a yellow-green colour and resemble lemons, but are rather larger with a thicker skin and a less juicy pulp. They were the first citrus fruit cultivated outside the Far East and are now grown in France and Italy exclusively for making crystallized peel. They are also grown in Israel for use in the Jewish harvest festival of Tabernacles, in which they symbolize autumn fruit.

Lemons and limes are both rich in vitamin C, although the lemon contains twice as much as the lime. Both lemons and limes were found to be very effective in treating scurvy, a disease suffered in the past by sailors deprived of other fresh fruit and vegetables during long sea voyages. A regular ration of limes was handed out; hence the British sailors' nickname 'limeys'.

There is little sugar in natural lemon and lime juice, which is very easily digested. The citric acid it contains has a preservative effect on other food and is used, like vinegar, for pickling fish.

Lemon skin contains an oil which is used in confectionery and perfumery: 20 drops of lemon oil is the equivalent of the juice of an average-sized lemon. This is why the finely grated zest – which is the easiest way of obtaining the oil – is such an effective flavouring. However you can buy lemon oil from specialist shops and herbalists. Lemon 'flavouring', sold for cakes, is synthetic.

Buying and storing

Avoid buying fruit that looks shrivelled. The skins should be glossy and firm to the touch. Small, roundish lemons with smooth skins generally have more juice than the knobbly skinned, larger varieties. Lemons are in season all year round. Limes can also be bought throughout the year, but are easier to obtain in summer. They are always more difficult to find and more expensive than lemons. Citrons are marketed in early autumn but are hard to find.

When whole, lemons and limes will keep for 2 weeks in the refrigerator, but use them immediately when cut, or wrap them in cling film and use the next day, as the vitamin C content is lost when the flesh is exposed to the air.

You are most likely to find citrons crystallized. These may be sold as caps: this is the rind of the squeezed half fruit, preserved in sugar. To use, scrape out the spare sugar from inside and chop the peel. Or they may be in the form of wide, thin crystallized slices (which are mainly pith). These are useful for cutting shapes for decorating desserts and cakes. Store both types in an airtight jar. If you do see fresh citrons, they can be preserved in sugar syrup.

✳✳✳✳ Lemons and limes may be frozen whole, or freeze slices or segments, coated with granulated sugar. The grated zest can be frozen in small bags, and the unsweetened juice in ice cube trays.

Using lemons and limes

To extract the most juice from a lemon do not use it straight from the refrigerator; bring it to room temperature then roll it under your palm for a few minutes. Or pour boiling water over it and soak for 3 minutes. For 75 ml /3 fl oz juice you will need 2 lemons: 1 lemon yields 37 ml /2½ tbls juice, ½ lemon yields 15–20 ml /3–4 tsp juice.

The simplest of lemon drinks, called *citron pressé* in France, is the juice of a lemon plus a teaspoon of sugar topped up with water. The fruit can also be made into lemonade (see recipe) or lemon barley water. The undiluted juice is used in alcoholic drinks, and Russian tea. Concentrated lemon juice is available bottled and frozen.

Lemon juice is a natural bleach: add a few drops to the water when boiling root vegetables, to keep them white, and sprinkle the juice on to the cut flesh of apples, pears and avocados to prevent discoloration. The acid in lemons and limes has a pickling effect on fish, as in the Mexican dish seviche. Lemon juice mixed with salt makes a good scouring powder for kitchen utensils.

Use lemon juice for sharp flavour or to counteract oiliness and greasiness. It can be used in a simple vinaigrette. Its flavour is more subtle and aromatic than vinegar and it is an essential ingredient in mayonnaise and emulsion sauces like hollandaise and béarnaise. Lemon juice brings out the delicate flavour of fish and chicken very well, indeed it is a good rule always to buy a lemon when you buy a fish. In Greece, lemon juice is combined with egg yolk in a delicious creamy soup called *avgolemono*.

Lime juice can be used for almost all the same purposes in cooking as lemon juice, although it has a rather sweeter flavour. It is very good in a marinade for both meat and fish. It goes exceptionally well with rum, and is mixed with wine in the Mexican version of the Spanish wine cup, *sangría*. Commercially manufactured lime juice cordial is excellent diluted with water or used as a mix in alcoholic drinks.

The fragrant lemon oil in the zest is excellent for flavouring. Use it to give a delicious tang to many dishes from a savoury herb stuffing to a sponge cake. One lemon yields 5 ml /1 tsp grated zest. Pare off a strip with a potato peeler to flavour fruit syrups, for adding to a bouquet garni or to stew with dried fruit to improve the colour and flavour. Lemon rind can also be crystallized and is often shredded and added to marmalade.

Lemon pips, tied in a bag lend acidity to jam. This will help fruit low in pectin, such as strawberries, to achieve a set.

Garnishing with lemons and limes

You will find that the fruit cuts more easily if it is chilled first. Always use a very sharp knife. To make wedges, cut the fruit lengthways into quarters. Their colour makes an attractive meat or shellfish garnish; try also dipping the cut centre in paprika to achieve a red line. For lemon or lime rings, slice the fruit fairly thickly and cut away the pulp, leaving a circle of rind. These make an attractive decoration for savouries in aspic. Or groove the fruit in the same way as oranges (*page 257*) then cut thinly into rounds. Use in drinks or to decorate sweet or savoury dishes.

Hollowed out lemon shells make perfect containers for fish pâtés, sorbets or ice

cream (see recipe), but limes cannot be used in this way as their rind is too thin.

Use thinly sliced lemon or lime rings on the rim of a glass. Slices can be quartered, then arranged like a butterfly to make a simple but effective decoration for a dessert. Or cut the ring from the centre through to one side and open it pulling one point forward and one backward, to make a twist.

Thinly pared lemon or lime zest can be parboiled, refreshed in cold water and cut into julienne strips for decorating.

Fresh lemonade

 5 minutes
plus infusing overnight

Makes about 1.1 L /2 pt
500 g /18 oz sugar
juice and pared zest of 8 large lemons
5 ml /1 tsp orange-flower water

1 Pour 2 L /3½ pt water into a large bowl and add the sugar and lemon zest. Refrigerate overnight.
2 Strain the lemon juice into the liquid in the bowl and add the orange-flower water. Strain the liquid through a piece of cheesecloth, and chill. Serve with plenty of ice. Bottled, the lemonade will keep in the refrigerator for 1 month.

● To make lemon barley water, boil the water with the lemon zest and 150 g /5 oz pearl barley for 20 minutes, and leave until tepid. Strain, add the sugar and pour on to the lemon juice. Mix well, then chill.

Soused fish in lime juice

In the original Mexican recipe, the fish is not cooked, but simply marinated for 6 hours and eaten raw as a starter. In this version the fish is cooked, and the quantities given are for a main course.

 30 minutes
then overnight marinating

Serves 4
500 g /18 oz white fish fillets, skinned
juice of 6 limes, strained
15 ml /1 tbls salt
dash of Tabasco sauce
15 ml /1 tbls coriander seeds
30 ml /2 tbls olive oil
1 spring onion, finely chopped
60 ml /4 tbls chopped parsley
2.5 ml /½ tsp dried oregano
250 g /9 oz canned tomatoes with their juice

1 Arrange the fish in a shallow bowl. Pour the lime juice over it and sprinkle it with the salt. Add the Tabasco sauce and coriander seeds. Cover and refrigerate overnight.
2 Heat the oil in a frying-pan with a lid, add the spring onion, parsley, oregano and tomatoes, and cook until the liquid boils. Remove from the heat.
3 Drain the fish, reserving the marinade. Add the fish to the frying-pan. Cover and simmer gently for 20 minutes. Add the strained marinade and heat through. Place fish on a platter and pour marinade over.

Lemons and limes are used in a variety of ways to add colour and flavour to food

Pickled lemons

These can be served with cold meat, or cooked in a casserole (see recipe). Limes can be pickled in the same way.

25 minutes

Makes 4 lemons
8 small lemons
about 250 g /9 oz coarse salt
2 bay leaves
10 allspice berries
10 coriander seeds

1 Cut 4 of the lemons almost into quarters to within 15 mm /½ in of the base. Open out the cut sides and pack some of the salt between each segment. Squeeze the lemons back into shape.
2 Sprinkle half the remaining salt in a layer into a 450 ml /16 fl oz preserving jar, or any other screw-top jar large enough to hold the lemons firmly. Pack in the lemons tightly, pushing them well down, so that they release their juices. Sprinkle on more salt and push the bay leaves down between the lemons. Sprinkle them with the allspice berries and coriander seeds.
3 Squeeze the remaining lemons and pour the strained juice into the jar. Seal it and leave in a cool place for at least 1 month, turning the jar on end once a day if possible. The lemons will keep for a year unopened.

Pickled lemon lamb stew

This is a traditional Moroccan dish and an unusual way of serving lamb.

⏱ 55 minutes

Serves 4
800 g /1¾ lb boned shoulder or leg of lamb, cut into 4 chunks
15 ml /1 tbls oil
25 g /1 oz butter
1 medium-sized onion, sliced
salt and freshly ground black pepper
grated zest of 1 orange
1.5 ml /¼ tsp powdered saffron, dissolved in 30 ml /2 tbls warm water
2.5 ml /½ tsp ground ginger
2.5 ml /½ tsp ground cinnamon
1 dried bay leaf, crumbled
1.5 ml /¼ tsp cayenne pepper
1.5 ml /¼ tsp paprika
rind of 1 pickled lemon, cut in strips (see recipe)
250 g /9 oz green olives, stoned
30 ml /2 tbls chopped parsley

1 Heat the oil and butter in a frying-pan and cook the onion over a medium heat for 5 minutes. Season the meat then add it to the pan with the orange zest. Cook, turning frequently, until the meat is lightly browned on all sides.
2 Transfer the mixture to a flameproof casserole with a tight-fitting lid. Add the saffron, ginger, cinnamon, bay leaf, cayenne pepper and paprika. Cover the casserole and simmer over a very low heat for 35 minutes or until the meat is tender, checking every 15 minutes that the liquid has not dried up. Add a little water if necessary.
3 Add the pickled lemon rind and the olives and cook for another 10 minutes. Sprinkle with chopped parsley and serve with plain boiled rice.

Lemon soufflé

⏱⏱ 50 minutes
plus 2 hours setting

Serves 6
oil for greasing
20 ml /4 tsp gelatine
4 large eggs, separated
150 g /5 oz caster sugar
strained juice and grated zest of 4 large lemons
300 ml /10 fl oz thick cream
To garnish
150 g /5 oz almonds, blanched and split
300 ml /10 fl oz thick cream, whipped (optional)

1 Measure round an 850 ml /1½ pt soufflé dish and cut a 15 cm /6 in wide strip of greaseproof paper to fit round it. Oil the paper and pin it, then drop the dish into the paper ring: it should stand at least 5 cm /2 in above the rim.
2 Put 60 ml /4 tbls warm water in a small bowl and stir in the gelatine.

Lemon soufflé

3 Put the egg yolks and sugar in a large bowl, mix well and place it over a pan of boiling water, making sure the base of the bowl does not touch the water. Beat the mixture until it is smooth and pale yellow and beginning to thicken. Remove it from the heat and continue whisking until it cools. Whisk in the lemon juice and zest.
4 Put the bowl containing the gelatine over a small pan of hot water and stir until the gelatine has dissolved completely. Do not let the gelatine mixture boil. Stir it into the lemon mixture. Chill the lemon mixture in the refrigerator until it is on the point of setting. Watch it carefully; it sets quickly.
5 Whip the cream until it is floppy. Whisk the egg whites until stiff peaks form.
6 Remove the lemon mixture from the refrigerator and fold in the cream, then the egg whites. Pour the mixture carefully into the prepared soufflé dish and refrigerate for at least 2 hours or until set.
7 Meanwhile, dry-fry the almonds in an ungreased frying-pan, stirring frequently until they turn pale brown.
8 When the soufflé has set, run a knife dipped in hot water around the inside of the greaseproof paper band to loosen it, and discard the paper. Chop the almonds, and stick most round the sides of the soufflé above rim of the dish. Garnish with whipped cream and almonds if wished.

Lemon curd

This traditional English preserve, sometimes also known as lemon cheese, is remarkably easy to make. Use it to sandwich a sponge cake or as a filling for lemon meringue pie or tartlet cases.

⏱ 15 minutes

Makes 500 g /18 oz curd
250 g /9 oz sugar
75 g /3 oz unsalted butter
grated zest and juice of 3 lemons
3 large eggs, beaten

1 Put the sugar in the top pan of a double boiler. Add the butter, lemon zest and juice and eggs, and stir well to blend.
2 Put the pan on to the boiler containing simmering water and cook gently, stirring all the time, for about 10 minutes, until the sugar has dissolved and the mixture is thick. On no account allow the mixture to boil, or it will curdle.
3 Pour the lemon curd into clean, dry, warmed jars and cover with discs of waxed paper. When cold, cover with screw-top lids. Eat within 1 month.

✳✳✳ Lemon curd freezes well: it will keep for 3 months.

Sussex pond pudding

This traditional English pudding is still served in the City of London in cold weather. During the steaming, the brown sugar melts with the lemon and dried fruit to make a delicious treacly filling for the suet crust.

 3 hours

Serves 6
2 lemons
75 g /3 oz suet or cold lard, grated
150 g /5 oz self-raising flour
about 100 ml /3½ fl oz milk
75 g /3 oz raisins
butter for greasing
100 g /4 oz butter, diced
50 g /2 oz Demerara sugar

1 Put the lemons in a small saucepan, cover them with boiling water and cook for about 30 minutes until the skins are soft when pierced with a skewer.
2 In a mixing bowl, rub the suet into the flour with your fingertips. Add enough milk to make a smooth, soft dough. Work in the raisins. Divide the dough into 2 pieces, one of them should be twice as big as the other.
3 Roll out the larger piece of dough into a circle and use it to line a well-buttered 850 ml /1½ pt pudding bowl. Dot the dough lining with half the pieces of butter, and sprinkle it with half the sugar.
4 Cut the softened lemons almost through into quarters and put them in the pudding. Sprinkle them with the rest of the sugar and dot with the rest of the butter.
5 Roll out the remaining dough to a circle and use it to make a lid for the pudding, sealing the edges well.
6 Cut out a circle of aluminium foil about 25 mm /1 in bigger than the top of the pudding and make a pleat in it to allow the pudding to expand. With fine string tie the foil securely over the pudding; leave a long end of string and tie a loop in it so that you can easily remove the pudding from the pan.
7 Put the pudding into a large saucepan and pour in boiling water to come halfway up the sides of the bowl. Cover the pan and simmer the pudding for 2 hours. Add more boiling water when necessary.
8 Turn the pudding out on to a dish. Serve with custard if you like, although it is delicious on its own.

Lemon and lime sorbet

Lemon and lime sorbet

 4¼ hours including freezing time

Serves 6
8 lemons
150 g /5 oz granulated sugar
1 large egg white
25 g /1 oz caster sugar
juice of 2 limes
30 ml /2 tbls white rum
mint leaves
maraschino cherries

1 Carefully slice the tops from 6 lemons and scoop out the pulp, taking care not to pierce the skin. Reserve the pulp. Trim a small slice off the bottom of each lemon so that it stands firmly upright.
2 Heat the granulated sugar and 850 ml /1½ pt water in a heavy-based saucepan, stirring all the time, until the syrup boils. Boil, without stirring, for 5 minutes.
3 Meanwhile, strain the reserved lemon pulp and grate the zest from the 2 remaining lemons. Add the lemon juice and zest to the syrup, and bring the pan back to the boil. Remove from the heat and leave until cold.
4 Pour the cold syrup into an ice tray. Freeze in the freezing compartment of the refrigerator for about 1½ hours or until the mixture is frozen at the sides but still liquid in the centre. Transfer to a large bowl.
5 Whisk the egg white until stiff. Fold in the caster sugar and whisk again. Fold the egg white into the sorbet mixture. Stir the lime juice into the mixture with the rum.
6 Spoon the sorbet into the hollowed out lemons, and return them to the freezing compartment. Freeze for at least 2 hours before serving. Garnish with mint leaves and maraschino cherries.

Avocado and lime dessert

This delicious Brazilian dessert is incredibly simple to make.

 10 minutes

Serves 4
2 large, ripe avocados
4 limes
75 g /3 oz icing sugar, sifted
mint leaves

1 Remove all the flesh from the avocados, scraping it from the skins with a teaspoon. Mash the flesh with a fork, then process it in a blender or pass it through a sieve, to obtain a smooth purée.
2 Strain the juice of 3 limes and mix it into the avocado purée. Stir in the icing sugar and mix very thoroughly.
3 Pile the mixture into individual glasses and serve immediately, garnished with slices of the remaining lime and mint leaves.

Oranges and tangerines

These bright, globe-shaped fruit, full of delicious juice, are so well known throughout the world that they have given their name to a colour. Orange is one of the world's great flavours and it is hard to imagine food without it, or drinks without orange juice.

The sweet orange originated in China, but it is now grown throughout the world in the warm areas outside the tropics. Because oranges travel and store well, they are also widely exported. Like the tomato and the potato, however, the sweet orange is a comparative newcomer to Europe.

Bitter oranges have been cultivated in Europe for a thousand years. They are called Seville oranges in Britain, after the Spanish city which first grew and shipped them round Europe, and *bigarade* in France. They are not really attractive to eat raw, so at first oranges were used as a flavouring, like lemons, rather than a fruit in their own right.

Portuguese explorers in the 1400s brought back sweet oranges from China. They reached England in time to be one of the refreshments offered at the Globe theatre when Shakespeare was performing, and their popularity was no doubt helped later when an orange seller, Nell Gwynn, caught the King's eye. Later in the 17th century, Versailles set the fashion of building indoor orangeries on to large houses in France and England, to protect the trees from frost.

Oranges are now grown on a large scale particularly in Spain, Israel, Florida, California, Australia and South Africa. As a result, they are always available and are never really expensive.

Oranges have long been recognized for their high vitamin C content. One orange supplies all your vitamin C needs for a day and is the equivalent to 10 apples. Oranges are also high in potassium and low in calories.

Oranges, tangerines and clementines

Oranges are generally better in the winter, as in summer the heat reduces juice and flavour. European and American oranges are available from November to February, followed by Middle Eastern and North African ones, while the South African, Australian and Brazilian ones are available after May.

There are many new varieties within the orange family, in particular orange and tangerine crosses, but the following are the most popular.

Sweet oranges: Spanish oranges have an easy-to-peel skin and a sharp, refreshing taste; Cyprus and Moroccan oranges are sweeter. Israeli oranges, marketed as Jaffas, are seedless. South African oranges have thicker skins and are very sweet, but with a less pronounced flavour. Two other well-known types are the smaller, sweeter Spanish blood oranges, with the red-tinged flesh, and the navel, which contains a baby orange within it opposite the stalk.

Seville oranges have a short season, usually for 4-6 weeks after Christmas. They are full of pips, which helps marmalade to set.

Tangerines or mandarins are also called satsumas; they too, originated in China. They have all the virtues of the sweet orange plus the additional one of being easy to peel without a knife. Unlike oranges, mandarin segments are sold canned in syrup. They are widely grown in the south-eastern US and south Europe. They are usually eaten raw.

Clementines, known as 'Oh my darlings' in London's East End, are a cross between a tangerine and a North African wild orange. Much smaller than other oranges, they are virtually seedless. When the leaves are attached, they make an attractive table decoration. Use them like tangerines.

Using oranges

For a perfect orange fruit salad, soak sliced rings in syrup flavoured with orange peel or in Marsala together with a spoonful of any liqueur. Or serve orange salad in the Creole way with chopped pineapple; cover the fruit with a white wine and a little sweet sherry.

Oranges combine well with all other fruit: add a few orange segments when cooking rhubarb, pour orange juice over fresh strawberries and include it when cooking apricots. Add orange when making stawberry ice cream – or chocolate mousse – it improves the flavour quite magically.

Oranges make delicious fruit jellies (see recipe), ice creams and sorbets. Put the ices back into their scooped-out shells. For a party, arrange these as Sophia Loren does,

Decorative oranges

For orange slices for garnishing, groove the orange lengthways at intervals before slicing. This gives the slices a frilly edge.

For oranges for stuffing, cut off the tops for lids and scoop out the flesh. Start with a grapefruit knife, then tidy up with a spoon.

For orange baskets, draw a line round the orange with a pen about two-thirds of the way up. Mark the handle and cut out flesh.

---

with sprays of fresh bay leaves between them, or with a border of shiny, flat camellia leaves.

Include orange juice in sweetened, whipped cream for a classic cake filling or add it to cake mixtures, biscuits, mousse or cheesecake. Use chopped candied peel in sweet yeast buns and scones. Experiment with bitter orange juice in mousses or squeeze it over pancakes instead of lemon. Bitter oranges are mainly used to make marmalade, perhaps the world's most celebrated jam.

Oranges help to fill the winter salad bowl. Try rings of orange and raw chicory together, or a Tunisian salad of orange, Spanish onion rings and black olives, well dressed with vinaigrette and black pepper. Serve them with rich meats like duck, lamb and pork sausages. Add tangerine segments to salads and bitter orange juice to dressings. Segments of orange and grapefruit look pretty arranged in alternating circles; dress the salad with chopped mint.

Liven up tomato soup with orange juice or add a little to an iced, mint-flavoured tomato juice cocktail. For a new dressing for a prawn cocktail try orange-flavoured mayonnaise mixed with a dab of tomato purée.

Use orange juice and zest to make seasoned butter for lamb chops. Wrap up orange butter with fish fillets in foil and bake them. Add orange to the pan of roast lamb and veal for a delicious sauce; the meat can also be marinated in the juice. Add orange and cloves to beef and onions for a hearty winter stew.

Orange products.

The zest is the brightly coloured outside of the orange rind. This contains essential oils and is extremely useful for flavouring. Pare off the rind thinly with a potato peeler and simmer in liquid. For a casserole, tie up the strips with any herbs and remove after cooking. For sweet dishes with an absolutely smooth texture, rub sugar lumps

Cut julienne strips from thinly pared zest

against the rind until golden, then use these for cooking. Alternatively, use a fine grater and add pinches of zest with the juice to dishes. One small orange will give 5 ml /1 tsp grated zest. For 15 ml/1 tbls zest, use 2 large oranges.

Peel includes both the coloured zest and the white pith. Inedible raw, it is delicious candied. Peel is included when making marmalade, and is used for baking.

Orange juice can be bought ready-squeezed, while concentrated juice is very useful for ice creams, sorbets and sauces.

Orange-flower water: orange flowers used to be worn by brides for their wonderful scent and the flowers of the stronger bitter oranges are used for a flavouring essence. This is obtainable from chemists and appears in French, Spanish and Middle Eastern recipes. It is used like vanilla; a few drops will flavour creams or pastries.

Decorative tips

For perfect rings, put the oranges in the freezer for 10 minutes to firm up, then slice with a serrated knife.

Whole oranges can be reassembled from

the rings. Keep the rings of one orange together holding it pierced through with a stick.

Julienne strips are the ideal garnish for orange flavoured dishes. Pare off the zest with a potato peeler and cut into 25 mm /1 in lengths. Cut into very thin strips. To make them edible, simmer for 5 minutes in boiling water. Drain, then pour cold water over to refresh them; drain again.

Buying and storing

When buying oranges, look for skins that are bright, plump and glossy and avoid any with brown marks around the stalk ends. As oranges are always available, buy to suit your needs and store in a cool place.

✳✳✳✳ Freeze orange juice in small containers, or in an ice-cube tray with grated zest added, for use as flavouring cubes. Freeze peeled orange segments dry with sugar scattered between. Freeze sliced rings in a medium-strength syrup; allow 2 hours for defrosting 500 ml /1 pt and use within 1 year. The pared zest and empty orange shell cups, for use as containers, can also be stored for a couple of months.

Use frozen orange juice as flavouring cubes

Melon and tangerine salad

Melon and tangerine salad

 20 minutes preparation

Serves 4
1 small to medium-sized honeydew melon
4 tangerines or 300 g /11 oz can
mandarin segments, drained
90 ml /6 tbls natural yoghurt
1 garlic clove, finely chopped
pinch of salt
5 ml /1 tsp ground ginger
1 lettuce
30 ml /2 tbls sesame seeds

1 Cut the melon in half, scoop out the seeds and discard. Use a melon baller, if you have one, to make neat balls from the flesh. Otherwise, cut the melon into 12 mm /½ in slices. Cut off the rind and chop the slices into dice. Peel the tangerines, remove the white membranes and pull them into segments. Mix them or the mandarins with the melon.
2 Put the chopped garlic and salt on a plate and crush with a round-bladed knife until a paste is formed. Mix this and the ginger into the yoghurt.
3 Line a serving bowl with lettuce leaves and pile the salad inside. Pour over the yoghurt and scatter the sesame seeds on top.

● To increase the taste of the sesame, stir 15 ml /1 tbls tahini paste into the yoghurt dressing. This is a creamy-brown paste, made of finely ground sesame seeds. You will find it in some delicatessens.

Spiced beef with oranges

This attractively glazed salt beef is superb on the festive cold table or for buffet parties. Though it means planning well ahead, the recipe is very simple to do. Saltpetre is available from chemists. It is used to add a pleasant, rosy colour to the beef, but can be omitted.

marinating 5 days
2½ hours cooking plus chilling

Serves 12 or more
one 2 kg /4½ lb piece boned brisket of beef
For salting
50 g /2 oz coarse sea salt
5 ml /1 tsp saltpetre
3 bay leaves
12 cloves
12 juniper berries
12 black peppercorns
1 garlic clove, chopped
30 ml /2 tbls Barbados sugar
grated zest of 2 large oranges
For boiling
1 onion, roughly chopped
1 carrot, roughly chopped
1 celery stalk, roughly chopped
bouquet garni
For finishing
approximately 30 ml /2 tbls cloves
juice of 2 large oranges
30 ml /2 tbls clear honey

1 Start at least 6 days before you plan to serve the beef. Open the beef out flat on a large flat china, earthenware or pyrex dish. Put the salt and saltpetre into a bowl and crumble in the bay leaves. Crush the cloves, juniper berries, peppercorns and garlic together and add to the salt. Grate in the orange zest, add the sugar and mix well. Rub the salt mixture all over the beef.
2 Cover the beef and put it in a cool place for 5 days, turning it and rubbing it with the marinade every day.
3 When you are ready to cook, rinse the beef under cold water. Roll it up and tie it with cotton string. Put it into a saucepan with the boiling ingredients. Cover with water, bring to the boil and skim, then let it simmer, covered, for 1½ hours.
4 Lift out the beef and cool it a little. Heat the oven to 200 C /400F /gas 6.
5 Stick the cloves over the surface of the beef at intervals of about 25 mm /1 in. Put the beef into a roasting tin. Put the orange juice and honey into a saucepan and set over a low heat until the honey melts. Spoon the mixture over the beef.
6 Put the beef into the oven for 20 minutes to glaze, basting it half-way through. Lift it out onto a serving dish and leave it until it is completely cold before slicing.

Veal chops with orange

The orange marinade in this recipe flavours the veal chops, and the orange topping makes a festive garnish and a refreshing contrast to the rich meat.

Serves 4
4 large veal chops
2 medium-sized oranges
1.5 ml /¼ tsp cayenne pepper
150 ml /5 fl oz stock
15 ml /1 tbls chopped fresh thyme
For the marinade
grated zest and juice of 1 medium-sized
*   orange*
150 ml /5 fl oz dry white wine
1 small onion, finely chopped
30 ml /2 tbls chopped fresh thyme
1.5 ml /¼ tsp cayenne pepper

1 Mix the ingredients for the marinade in a large flat dish. Turn the chops in the marinade, then leave them for 4-6 hours at room temperature, turning them several times.

2 When you are ready to cook, heat the oven to 200C /400F /gas 6. Cut the rind and pith from the remaining oranges and cut the flesh into rings about 9 mm /⅜ in thick.

3 Brush all the pieces of marinade from the chops and reserve it. Put the chops on a rack in a roasting tin and cook in the oven for 40 minutes.

4 Lay a slice of orange on each chop, or two slices on large chops. Sprinkle a little cayenne pepper over the top. Return the chops to the oven for 5 minutes so the orange slices heat through but remain firm and juicy.

5 Lift the chops onto a serving dish and keep them warm. Pour all the fat from the roasting tin. Strain the marinade into it and add the stock. Set over a moderate heat on top of the stove and bring to the boil. Add thyme and simmer the sauce for 1 minute. Pour it over the chops before serving.

● Substitute 4 large loin of lamb chops or 8 small best end of neck lamb chops for the veal, or use pork chops. Garnish the dish with fresh mint leaves.

Sauce bigarade

Bitter orange sauce

♩♩ 1½ hours

Serves 6
45 ml /3 tbls olive oil
1 small onion, finely chopped
1 small carrot, finely chopped
½ celery stalk, finely chopped
15 ml /1 tbls flour
5 ml /1 tsp tomato purée
1 mushroom, finely chopped
bouquet garni
600 ml /1 pt stock
salt and freshly ground black pepper
15 g /½ oz butter
1 shallot or small onion, finely chopped
150 ml /5 fl oz sherry
1 bay leaf
1 Seville orange
10 ml /2 tsp lemon juice

1 Heat the oil in a saucepan on a low heat. Stir in the prepared onion, carrot and celery

and cook them until they begin to shrink. Stir in the flour and let it brown. Stir in the tomato purée, mushroom, bouquet garni and 300 ml/10 fl oz stock. Season to taste.

2 Return the pan to the heat and bring to the boil. Skim, then simmer for 40 minutes.

3 Add half the reserved stock, bring the sauce to the boil again and skim. Add the remaining stock, boil and skim once more. Simmer for 5 minutes.

4 Strain the sauce, pressing down hard on the vegetables to extract all the liquid. Return the sauce to the rinsed-out pan and simmer for a further 5 minutes. Adjust the seasoning to taste.

5 While the basic sauce is cooking, prepare the flavourings. Melt the butter in a small saucepan on a low heat. Add the shallot or onion, cover and cook for 2 minutes. Pour in the sherry and add the bay leaf and thinly-pared zest of half the orange. Bring the sherry mixture to simmering point and boil until the quantity has reduced by one quarter. Strain the reduced sherry into the basic orange juice.

6 Cut the rest of the orange zest into julienne strips and blanch them in boiling

Sauce bigarade with glazed gammon

water for 5 minutes. Refresh them by pouring cold water over them, then add to the sauce.

7 Cut the pith from the orange and cut out the segments, catching any juice as you do so. Add this juice and the lemon juice to the sauce. Simmer for 5 minutes. Add the orange segments just before serving.

● Serve bigarade sauce with a hot boiled gammon or bacon joint. Boil the gammon for 20 minutes less than usual and finish it in an oven heated to 200C /400F /gas 6. Strip off the rind, score the fat and glaze with 45 ml /3 tbls chunky marmalade, 15 ml /1 tbls Demerara sugar and 10 ml /2 tsp white wine vinegar, basting every 10 minutes. Cook it for 20 minutes.

● Serve bigarade sauce with roast duck garnished with orange segments.

● This sauce makes an excellent accompaniment for hot, boiled, cured silverside.

● Thin slices of cold roast leg of lamb are delicious gently reheated in this sauce.

● This is an excellent sauce for the freezer.

Caramelized oranges

A dessert from Sicily in the Mediterranean, caramelized oranges are the most attractive of all orange fruit salads.

🍴🍴 35 minutes plus chilling

Serves 4
4 large oranges
175 g /6 oz sugar

1 Using a potato peeler, remove very thin strips of zest from 2 of the oranges and reserve. Cut 2 strips from a third orange. Put all the oranges into the freezer compartment of the refrigerator to firm up for 10 minutes. Meanwhile reserve 2 strips of zest and cut all the rest into thin julienne strips with scissors. Simmer the strips in boiling water for 5 minutes. Drain and pour cold water over the strips.
2 Put the sugar, 125 ml /4 fl oz water and 2 orange strips into a small saucepan. Stir over medium heat to dissolve, then boil for 5 minutes to form a syrup. Remove from heat.
3 Take the oranges from the freezer and peel them with a very sharp knife, removing the peel and every trace of pith. Slice one orange into neat rings. Reassemble into an orange and hold in shape by sticking a cocktail stick down through the rings.

Caramelized oranges

Prepare the other oranges in the same way and arrange in a shallow dish.
4 Remove and discard the orange strips. Spoon the syrup over the oranges, spooning it up from the bottom of the dish so that each orange is coated 2-3 times.
5 Transfer the oranges to a serving plate and pour the syrup back into the saucepan. Add the julienne strips, bring to the boil and boil for 2 minutes or until the syrup begins to turn brown round the edges of the pan. Remove the pan from the heat, stir once, then spoon a little heap of strips like a thatch on top of each orange. Chill before serving.

● Add 30 ml /2 tbls of Marsala or Grand Marnier to the syrup before pouring it over the reassembled oranges.
● For an orange salad, do not reassemble the rings. Simply place them in a bowl and pour syrup over them. Decorate with julienne strips or a scattering of flaked, toasted nuts.

Maple syrup and orange mousse

This is a deliciously light, fluffy and refreshing sweet because the yoghurt is much less rich than cream.

🍴🍴 1 hour plus 2 hours setting

Serves 4
3 medium-sized eggs, separated
1 large orange
175 g /6 oz maple syrup
15 g /1/2 oz gelatine
575 ml /1 pt natural yoghurt

1 Put the egg yolks into a double saucepan and add the grated zest of half the orange. Stir over a low heat until they thicken, then take the pan off the heat. Stir in the maple syrup.
2 Squeeze the juice from the orange, then melt the gelatine in the juice in a small pan over a low heat – do not let it boil.
3 Stir this mixture into the egg yolks and leave until it is on the point of setting. Use it when it is syrupy – the consistency of unbeaten egg whites.
4 Whisk the egg whites until they are stiff. Stir the yoghurt into the yolks and maple syrup, then fold in the egg whites. Pour the mousse into a serving dish and leave it in a cool place to set for 2 hours.

Orange jelly baskets

Pretty orange baskets are ideal for serving jelly, orange sorbet, or any fruit salad containing oranges.

🔪 40 minutes, plus 2 hours setting

Serves 4
4 large oranges
15 g /1/2 oz gelatine
50 g /2 oz sugar
30 ml /2 tbls orange liqueur (optional)
150 ml /5 fl oz thick cream
20 ml /4 tsp lemon curd
4 hazelnuts

1 With a pen, draw a line round each orange two-thirds of the way up. Then draw in the handle over the top. With a small sharp knife carefully cut the wedges on either side of the handle and reserve. Run the knife close to the handle to remove the orange flesh from underneath it.
2 Scoop out all the remaining flesh with a spoon or grapefruit knife. Clean out any remaining membrane with a teaspoon. Roughly chop all the orange flesh and rub it through a sieve to extract the juice.
3 Soak the gelatine in a small pan in 60 ml /4 tbls juice. Put the rest of the juice into a saucepan with the sugar and grate in 15 ml /1 tbls zest fom the unwanted pieces of peel. Stir on a low heat until the sugar has completely dissolved.
4 Melt the gelatine on a low heat and stir it into the juice mixture. When it has dissolved, take the pan from the heat and stir in the liqueur. Cool the jelly a little.
5 Place the orange baskets on a flat dish and press them down slightly so they stand upright. Carefully fill them with the jelly and leave them in a cool place for 2 hours to set.
6 Whip the cream and pipe it thinly round the edges of the baskets. Put a rosette of cream in the centre of each basket. Spoon 5 ml /1 tsp lemon curd on each rosette and put a hazelnut on top.

Grapefruit and some unusual citrus fruit

With its distinctive, bittersweet flavour, grapefruit can be used in all sorts of ways – in starters, main courses, salads and desserts, as well as in exotic cocktails and unusual preserves. You can use it to make slimming salads or fattening but luscious chiffon pies.

Grapefruit has a wonderful reputation with nutritionists, although many cooks think of it as boring. However, it can be used in so many ways that it does not have to be boring at all!

Other citrus fruits such as the ugli fruit, the tangelo, the topaz, and the kumquat, which is a close relative of the citrus family, are well worth trying for the variety they will bring to your menus.

The grapefruit is the largest of the popular varieties of citrus fruit. It is so called because its fruits, hanging in clusters on its evergreen tree, look like an outsize bunch of grapes.

Grapefruit made its first appearance in the 18th century in the West Indies, probably as a cross between an orange and a pomelo (also known as a shaddock), which is larger, with a thick rind and dry, bittersweet flesh. It soon spread to Florida, which is now the world's largest grower, and to other parts of the U.S., South Africa, South America, Israel and other Mediterranean countries. These countries now produce most of the world's crop of the 23 varieties of grapefruit grown commercially.

Its high vitamin and mineral content, combined with its low calorie content, have made the grapefruit very popular with dieticians and nutritionists. The claim that grapefruit contains an enzyme which stimulates metabolism and thus 'burns off' fat is still controversial and unproven; however, it is rich in vitamins.

Other citrus fruits

There are many types of crossbred citrus fruit, of which the grapefruit is just one example.

The grapefruit has been crossed with the tangerine to produce the ugli fruit, a rather misshapen specimen with sweet and juicy flesh. Other grapefruit and tangerine crosses are the tangelo, the orlando and the mineola. Ortaniques are tangors, or tangerine and orange crosses, as are topazes and temples. All these fruits are suitable for eating on their own or in salads.

The kumquat (or cumquat) is closely related to the citrus group, with which it is often crossed. Crosses include the limequat, orangequat and citrangequat, as well as the calamondin, which is a cross between a kumquat and a tangerine.

Kumquats, which are tiny, about 25 mm /1 in long, are in season for only a short time in the winter. They are the only fruit in this group with a sweet-tasting peel. They can be eaten raw (peel and all), made into fruit salads, cooked in syrup, made into preserves (see recipe), or pickled, to serve as an accompaniment to pork, chicken and duck.

Buying and storing grapefruit

The skin of the fruit should be smooth and free from marks and blemishes. The grapefruit should not have soft spots, but should feel firm and heavy. A greenish tinge to the skin does not mean that the fruit is unripe; some varieties of grapefruit turn yellow, then begin to produce chlorophyll in their skins again while ripening. In general, there is little difference in sweetness or flavour between the pink- and yellow-fleshed varieties. Some pink-fleshed

From the left, ugli fruit, grapefruit and, in front, kumquats

varieties have pink-tinged skins, but it is safer to ask which ones are pink.

Canned grapefruit is available, packed either in syrup or in grapefruit juice. Grapefruit juice is sold as a frozen concentrate, canned, bottled and in cartons, sweetened or unsweetened.

Fresh grapefruit is available all year round. Keep grapefruit for up to two weeks in the salad compartment of the refrigerator. Opened canned grapefruit can be kept, refrigerated, for up to three days.

❋❋❋ Grapefruit can be open frozen whole: simply wash, dry and freeze the fruit on a tray. However, when thawed it will not look very attractive and is best used in recipes where its appearance is not important, such as marmalade.

Freeze segments, either in a medium syrup in a plastic container, or dip the segments in caster sugar (250 g /8 oz sugar to 500 g /1 lb fruit), wrap in polythene bags and freeze. Store for up to one year.

Preparing grapefruit

To peel the grapefruit, cut a slice from the stem end so that the flesh just shows. With a sawing motion, remove the peel and pith in strips, then remove any remaining pith, which is very bitter.

To serve halved grapefruit, use a grapefruit knife (a flexible, curved-bladed knife with one or two serrated edges) to separate the flesh from the pith. Then slice along the natural line of the segments to make the fruit easier to scoop out. Grapefruit halves are easiest to eat with grapefruit spoons, which have elongated bowls and sharply pointed ends.

Grapefruit can be cut into attractive shapes to be served as they are, to be used as containers for fruit salads or water ices (which can be made with the flesh of the grapefruit), or to garnish other dishes.

Grapefruit peel is very bitter: if it is to be eaten, blanch it (cover with water and bring to the boil) 3 times, then refresh.

Preparing grapefruit

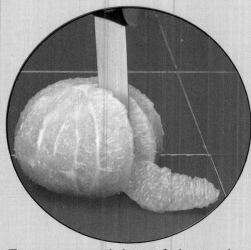

To segment a peeled grapefruit, open it on one side. Cut down the side of the segment, inside the membrane, then again on the other side. Lift out the segment.

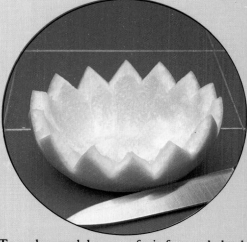

To make vandyke grapefruit from a halved fruit, scoop out the flesh, then snip small 'V' shapes around the edge of each shell, using a pair of kitchen scissors.

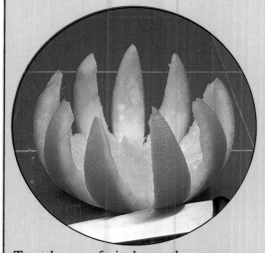

To make grapefruit chrysanthemums, score deep saw-toothed cuts in the peel, leaving about 20 mm /¾ in peel whole at each end. Separate peel from flesh, making two sets.

For an unusual basket, scoop out the flesh from one half, then cut a thin strip around the top, leaving a bit intact in the centre of each side. Tie the two strips together.

Using grapefruit

Serve halved as a starter, sprinkled with sugar, ginger or a few drops of Angostura bitters, if wished.

● For a change, they are delicious grilled: top each half with 15 ml /1 tbls honey, golden or maple syrup, or with 30 ml /2 tbls brown sugar. For a more exotic flavour, add 10 ml /2 tsp coffee liqueur, cherry brandy or vermouth, or sprinkle on some powdered cinnamon, nutmeg or ginger. Place the fruit 7.5-10 cm /3-4 in below a hot grill and cook until the topping bubbles.

Grapefruit go well in both savoury and sweet salads and blend with all the traditional salad vegetables to give an original flavour. Serve with rich meats.

● For an impressive dessert, serve flambéed grapefruit: divide one grapefruit per person into segments, removing all pith and carefully reserving the juice. Pour the juice into a saucepan, add 15 ml /1 tbls honey per grapefruit, bring to the boil and add the grapefruit segments. Spoon the liquid over them for 3 minutes, place in a warmed serving dish, pour over 15 ml /1 tbls warmed white rum or kirsch per grapefruit and set the liquid alight. Serve flaming.

Grapefruit peel can be dried in a cool oven, or overnight in an airing cupboard, and grated to use as a flavouring. Alternatively blanched peel may be candied.

Grapefruit-glazed gammon joint

🍴🍴 2 hours 20 minutes

Serves 8-10
2.3 kg /5 lb middle joint of gammon
For the glaze
60 ml /4 tbls honey
75 g /3 oz sugar
coarsely grated zest of 1 grapefruit
60 ml /4 tbls grapefruit juice
For the sauce
75 g /3 oz sugar
30 ml /2 tbls cornflour
pinch of salt
coarsely grated zest of 1 grapefruit
350 ml /12 fl oz grapefruit juice
1 large grapefruit, peeled and segmented

1 Wash the gammon joint. Put it into a large saucepan, cover completely with cold water and bring it slowly to simmering point. Skim any scum from the water, cover tightly and simmer gently for 1½ hours.
2 Heat the oven to 200C /400F /gas 6. Drain the joint and peel off the rind. Score the fat into diamonds and place the gammon, fat side up, in a shallow roasting tin.
3 Combine the ingredients for the glaze and glaze the gammon. Put it into the oven and cook for 30 minutes, basting with the glaze every 10 minutes.
4 Meanwhile, make the sauce: combine the sugar, cornflour, salt, grapefruit zest and juice, and 200 ml /7 fl oz water in a saucepan. Heat gently, stirring constantly, until it boils and thickens.
5 Transfer the gammon to a warmed serving dish. Add the grapefruit segments to the sauce and reheat. Pour into a sauce-boat and serve as soon as possible.

Grapefruit and prawn cocktail

Serve in grapefruit shells; grapefruit flavour blends surprisingly well with prawns.

🍴 15 minutes

Serves 4
1 large grapefruit, peeled and segmented
100 g /4 oz boiled shelled prawns, defrosted if frozen
100 g /4 oz lettuce leaves, finely shredded
60 ml /4 tbls mayonnaise
chopped parsley, to garnish
pinch of paprika, to garnish

1 Chop the grapefruit segments and mix them with the prawns and lettuce. Stir in the mayonnaise.
2 Divide the mixture into 4 portions and sprinkle with the parsley and a pinch of paprika before serving.

Slimmer's savoury salad

🍴 20 minutes
plus 15 minutes or more chilling

Serves 6
1 large orange
2 grapefruit, peeled and segmented, or 450 g /1 lb canned unsweetened grapefruit segments, drained
250 g /9 oz white cabbage, shredded
75 g /3 oz cucumber, thinly sliced
1 sweet red pepper, seeded and chopped
200 g /7 oz smoked, cooked tongue, sliced into matchstick strips
100 ml /3½ fl oz yoghurt
30 ml /2 tbls cider vinegar

1 Peel and segment the orange and grate the zest. Cut the grapefruit and orange segments into smaller pieces and place them in a large bowl. Add the cabbage, cucumber, red pepper and tongue.
2 In a small bowl, stir the orange zest into the yoghurt and thoroughly blend in the cider vinegar.
3 Pour the dressing over the contents of the large bowl and mix thoroughly. Chill for at least 15 minutes before serving.

Kumquat preserve

🍴🍴 2½ hours

Makes about 1.6 kg /3½ lb
1.1 kg /2½ lb kumquats
1 lemon, roughly chopped (including skin)
800 g /1¾ lb sugar

1 Wash the kumquats carefully, dry them thoroughly and slice each fruit in half lengthways. Remove the pips. Tie the kumquat and lemon pips in a muslin bag.
2 Put the kumquats and lemon into a large saucepan or a preserving pan and add the muslin bag and 600 ml /1 pt water. Heat to boiling point, reduce the heat and simmer, covered, for 30 minutes, or until the kumquats feel tender when pierced with a skewer.
3 Stir in the sugar carefully, making sure you do not break the fruit, and simmer uncovered until the sugar has dissolved, stirring occasionally with a wooden spoon. Then bring to a boil, stirring constantly. Remove any scum from the surface and simmer for 45 minutes, or until the kumquats are translucent and the syrup is thick.
4 Pour into warmed, sterile jars and seal. Store in a cool place for up to 6 months.

263

Grapefruit mint ice

Grapefruit marmalade

25 minutes, then 24 hours, then 1¾ hours

Makes about 2.3 kg /5 lb
3 grapefruit (about 700 g /1½ lb)
1 small lemon
1.4 kg /3 lb preserving sugar

1 Wash and dry the grapefruit and lemon. Squeeze the juice and reserve. Slice the peel of the grapefruit into thin strips about 5 mm /¼ in thick, reserving all the pith, connective tissue and pips, if any. Remove and reserve the lemon pips.
2 Tie the grapefruit pith, connective tissue and pips, and the lemon pips in a cheesecloth bag and reserve. Put the juice and strips of peel into a preserving pan or a large saucepan, add 2.5 L /4½ pt cold water. Stand at room temperature for 24 hours.
3 Put the pan over a medium heat, add the cheesecloth bag and bring to the boil. Boil uncovered for 1 hour, or until the liquid is reduced by half. Remove and discard the cheesecloth bag.
4 Add the sugar, stir to dissolve, then boil for 20 minutes or until the marmalade is set when tested. Pour into warmed, sterile jars and seal. Store the marmalade in a cool, dry place for up to 1 year.

Grapefruit mint ice

25 minutes
plus 2 hours or more freezing

Serves 6–8
2 grapefruit, peeled and segmented
about 250 ml /9 fl oz grapefruit juice
15 g /½ oz gelatine
150 g /5 oz sugar
peppermint essence
2 medium-sized egg whites

1 Purée the grapefruit flesh in a blender, then make up the purée with juice to 700 ml /1¾ pt.
2 Stir the gelatine into one-third of the grapefruit purée; soften for 5 minutes.
3 Put the rest of the grapefruit purée into a saucepan and heat gently, adding the sugar gradually, until it is just below boiling point. Pour the hot liquid onto the gelatine mixture and stir until the gelatine is thoroughly dissolved. Let cool slightly.
4 Stir in a few drops of peppermint essence. Pour into a freezer tray and freeze until it starts to set, about 1 hour.
5 Whisk the egg whites until they form stiff peaks. Remove the ice from the freezer and whisk in the egg whites. Return to the freezer until set.
6 About 30 minutes before serving, transfer to the refrigerator to soften slightly.

● Use 6 grapefruit, make baskets and garnish with cherries and mint.

Grapefruit chiffon pie

40 minutes
plus 3 hours chilling

Serves 6–8
150 g /5 oz shredded desiccated coconut
150 g /5 oz butter
75 g /3 oz soft light brown sugar
coarsely grated zest of 1 grapefruit
For the filling
225 ml /8 fl oz grapefruit juice
15 g /½ oz powdered gelatine
4 medium-sized eggs, separated
150 g /5 oz sugar
1.5 ml /¼ tsp salt
coarsely grated zest of 1 grapefruit
250 ml /9 fl oz thick cream

1 To make the pastry case, toast the coconut in a dry frying-pan, turning constantly with a spatula, until it is lightly browned. Turn it into a bowl. Melt the butter and pour it over the coconut. Stir in the sugar and grapefruit zest. Use the mixture to line a deep 23 cm / 9 in pie dish. Chill the pastry case while you make the filling.
2 Place the grapefruit juice in a saucepan over a low heat. Stir in the gelatine and remove from the heat when the gelatine has softened.
3 Whisk the egg yolks with 100 g /4 oz sugar in the top part of a double boiler. Beat until smooth, then whisk in the gelatine mixture. Continue whisking over boiling water until the mixture begins to thicken, about 10 minutes. Stir in the salt and grapefruit zest. Pour into a bowl, leave to cool, then refrigerate for about 1 hour, or until the mixture begins to gel.
4 Whisk the egg whites with the rest of the sugar until the mixture forms soft peaks. Whip the cream. Fold the whipped cream and egg whites into the grapefruit mixture.
5 Spoon the mixture into the chilled case and chill for at least 2 hours, or until the filling is firm, before serving.

Acapulco gold

This cocktail can be enriched by adding 30 ml /2 tbls coconut cream per serving.

10 minutes plus chilling

Serves 4
125 ml /4 fl oz Jamaica rum
125 ml /4 fl oz tequila
250 ml /9 fl oz unsweetened grapefruit juice
250 ml /9 fl oz unsweetened pineapple juice
sugar to taste (optional)

1 Shake together in a cocktail shaker or a jar with a lid the rum, tequila, grapefruit and pineapple juices. Add sugar to taste, if desired, and shake again to dissolve. Chill.
2 Half fill 4 tall glasses with ice cubes. Shake the cocktail again, pour over the ice cubes and serve at once.

Currants and gooseberries

These summer soft fruit with their beautiful colours and distinctive flavours are delicious in ices, creamy desserts and hot puddings and pies. Their sharp, tangy taste is also exceptionally good with rich meat and you can use them to make your own fruit syrups and cordials, and crystal-clear jellies.

Blackcurrants, redcurrants, whitecurrants and gooseberries all belong to the genus *Ribes*. Blackcurrants and redcurrants were first cultivated in Europe in the 16th century and introduced to America in the early part of the following century. The bushes thrive best in cool, moist, northern climates, and are widely grown in northern Europe and northern and central Asia. They also grow to a certain extent in Australia (Victoria and Tasmania) and New Zealand.

Whitecurrants, which are actually a very pale, translucent green with a pinkish blush, are an albino strain of redcurrants. They are sweeter, with a more delicate flavour, than redcurrants.

Currants grow in clusters – the redcurrant berries are slightly smaller than those of the blackcurrant – and are usually ready for picking in midsummer. They are rich in vitamin C and have a high acid content.

The European gooseberry was cultivated as early as 1600 and in Victorian times its popularity, and the number of cultivars grown, was much greater than nowadays. In the north of England gooseberry clubs were formed, and the members held annual competitions, at which prizes were awarded for the largest berries. The European gooseberry is now grown mainly in northern Europe, Asia, parts of North Africa and to a certain extent in New South Wales.

The gooseberry is oval, of varying size as there are hundreds of varieties, which can be roughly classified into 2 types: cooking and dessert. Cooking gooseberries are usually bright green and are smaller and thicker-skinned than dessert varieties, which may be pink, red, yellow or white as well as green, and smooth-skinned or covered with small hairs. Cooking varieties may be picked as early as April in the Northern hemisphere, and dessert varieties later, in July – August. Dessert gooseberries may also be picked young for cooking.

Processed berries: out of season you can buy dry frozen, canned or bottled blackcurrants and gooseberries and, more rarely, redcurrants. Canned or bottled blackcurrants in syrup are specially good, and cans and bottles of blackcurrant syrup enriched with extra vitamin C are also available: use to make drinks and sauces.

Liqueurs: The French make a delicious blackcurrant liqueur called crème de cassis.

Buying and storing

Currants in clusters or loose are usually sold in punnets (baskets) to protect them from damage. Freshly picked currants should be bright and shiny and should not stick together. Try to check that you do not buy a punnet with any mushy fruit at the bottom. Choose gooseberries that are firm and glossy, and avoid any that are dull, wrinkled or

split. When buying dessert gooseberries make sure they are not squashy. Ideally use the fruit the day you buy it: if this is not possible, keep currants in the refrigerator for up to 2 days, spread out in a single layer on a covered flat plate. Gooseberries are best kept in a cool, dark place for up to 2 days.

✻✻✻ Because of their relatively short season it is well worth freezing currants and gooseberries for use in winter. Open freeze prepared currants or topped and tailed gooseberries without sugar on greaseproof covered trays, then bag. They will keep for 6–8 months. To freeze with sugar, pack currants in dry sugar (200 g /7 oz sugar to 500 g /18 oz fruit) and cover gooseberries with a light-strength syrup before packing into containers. Frozen this way, the fruit will keep for 9–12 months. Cooked and sieved purées keep frozen for 3–6 months if unsweetened, or 6–8 months if sweetened.

Blackcurrant cheesecake

Preparing berries

The picked berries always have the remains of the flower and a piece of stalk attached. Snip these off gooseberries before cooking: this is called 'topping and tailing'. (For gooseberry purée this is unnecessary, as they will be removed by sieving.) The tops and tails of currants are so small that they become unnoticeable once cooked. Remove the berries from the stalks by running the prongs of a fork down the cluster. This is called 'stringing'.

Using currants and gooseberries

The large quantity of seeds in the juicy flesh of blackcurrants and redcurrants and the acidity of the fruit means they are more suitable for cooking than eating raw.

● Frosted clusters of freshly picked raw redcurrants make a very pretty decoration for desserts, particularly with creams or meringues. Dip small bunches of the fruit in egg white, shake off all the excess, then dip in caster sugar and shake off the excess. Leave to dry for about 1 hour.

Currants and gooseberries make wonderfully light fools, creams, mousses and ices, and are also delicious hot in crumbles, pies and latticed tarts. Redcurrants mix well with fruit such as cherries or raspberries, and this combination – to which other fruit like blackcurrants, blackberries and rhubarb, may be added – is the base for the glorious fruity summer pudding.

Blackcurrants make a rich dark purée, excellent as a sauce and a base for mousses or ice creams. Cinnamon goes well with blackcurrants: cook a pinch with the fruit, or use cinnamon-flavoured pastry. Blackcurrant leaves are exceptionally fragrant and can be used to flavour cakes and ices.

Redcurrants and gooseberries are excellent in savoury dishes, cooked together with the meat or fish, or separately in sauces and stuffings. Redcurrants are best with lamb and game, and gooseberries with rich pork and oily mackerel.

Currants and gooseberries are ideal for making jams and jellies as they have a high pectin content. Home-made redcurrant jelly has a beautifully deep red colour, tangy flavour and dense texture; it is a delicious, classic accompaniment to hot or cold roast lamb, and is the main ingredient in Cumberland sauce. Melted redcurrant jelly makes an attractive glaze for a fruit flan. You can also use it to prevent the pastry in sweet flans from becoming soggy or discoloured at the base. After baking the pastry blind, let the baked pastry case cool completely; then brush the base and sides with the redcurrant jelly glaze and leave to set firm before putting in the filling.

Currants and gooseberries are very suitable for home wine-making.

Tenderloin stuffed with gooseberries

ḟḟḟ 1½ hours

Serves 4–6
2 × 500 g /18 oz pork tenderloins
175 g /6 oz green gooseberries
25 g /1 oz butter
1 medium-sized onion, finely chopped
75 g /3 oz fresh wholemeal breadcrumbs
15 ml /1 tbls chopped parsley
15 ml /1 tbls chopped marjoram
pinch of ground cloves
30 ml /2 tbls dry white wine
30 ml /2 tbls clear honey
For the gravy
150 ml /5 fl oz dry white wine
150 ml /5 fl oz ham stock

1 Heat the oven to 200C /400F /gas 6. Slit through each tenderloin lengthways, leaving it uncut down one side. Open each tenderloin out flat, like a book. Beat the meat with a mallet or rolling pin until thin.
2 Top and tail the gooseberries and finely chop 125 g /4 oz of them. Cut the remaining 50 g /2 oz into half lengthways and reserve.
3 Melt the butter in a frying-pan over a

low heat and cook the onion until it is just transparent. Stir in the finely chopped gooseberries and continue cooking until the onion is soft.
4 Remove the pan from the heat and stir the breadcrumbs, herbs, cloves and the 30 ml /2 tbls wine into the onion mixture.
5 Spread the mixture on the open pork tenderloins, reshape each piece and tie up like a parcel with strong thread or cotton string. Lay the tenderloins side by side on a rack in a roasting tin and roast in the oven for 45 minutes.
6 Take the tin out of the oven, remove the rack and put the pork in the bottom of the tin. Spoon the honey over each piece, and arrange the reserved, halved gooseberries on top.
7 Mix together the wine and stock and pour into the tin around the meat. Cook in the oven for a further 15 minutes.
8 Carefully remove the thread or string from the pork without dislodging the gooseberries, before serving. Cut the meat into slices at the table, rather than in the kitchen, so that the gooseberry topping is shown to best advantage.

Venison with port and redcurrant jelly

The port marinade tenderizes the venison, while the redcurrant jelly makes a particularly rich, tasty sauce.

 ḟḟ 24 hours marinating, then 2 hours

Serves 4
1 kg /2 lb joint of lean, boned venison (haunch, leg or shoulder)
350–400 ml /12–14 fl oz game or chicken stock
25 g /1 oz butter
1 medium-sized onion, finely chopped
15 ml /1 tbls flour
30 ml /2 tbls redcurrant jelly
bouquet garni of fresh herbs including 1 strip thinly pared lemon zest
30 ml /2 tbls chopped parsley
For the marinade
150 ml /5 fl oz port
grated zest and juice of 1 lemon
30 ml /2 tbls olive oil
salt and freshly ground black pepper
pinch of grated nutmeg
1 small onion, finely chopped
1 small carrot, finely chopped
1 celery stalk, finely chopped
15 ml /1 tbls chopped parsley
15 ml /1 tbls chopped thyme

1 Mix together all the ingredients for the marinade in a large, deep dish. Turn the venison in the marinade so that it is thoroughly coated. Leave it at room temperature, turning it several times, for 24 hours.
2 Heat the oven to 180C /350F /gas 4. Remove the venison from the dish. Strain the marinade and add it to the stock to make up the liquid to 400 ml /14 fl oz.

Redcurrant jelly

3. Melt the butter in a large, flameproof casserole over a high heat. Put in the venison, turn it all over to brown, then remove from the casserole.

4 Put the onion in the casserole, reduce the heat and cook until softened. Stir in the flour and cook until the mixture is browned. Gradually stir in the marinade and stock mixture, increase the heat and bring to the boil.

5 Stir in the redcurrant jelly. When it has dissolved, put the venison and the bouquet garni into the casserole. Cover and cook in the oven for 1½ hours.

6 To serve, carve the venison into thin slices and arrange them on a warm serving dish. Pour the sauce over the meat and scatter over the chopped parsley; serve with buttered, puréed root vegetables.

Redcurrant jelly

Home-made redcurrant jelly is firmer, with a deeper colour and fruitier taste, than bought varieties, useful though these are.

 1½ hours or overnight then 30 minutes

Makes about 1.25 kg /3 lb
2 kg /4½ lb redcurrants
500 g /18 oz sugar to each 600 ml /1 pt juice (about 800 g /1¾ lb)

1 Heat the oven to 180C /350F /gas 4, or choose the stove top method. String the redcurrants and put them in a casserole which will fit comfortably into a large saucepan. Place the covered casserole in the saucepan, pour round it enough water to come halfway up the sides. Then remove the casserole and bring the water in the pan to the boil. Return the casserole to the pan.

2 Put the pan into the oven, or keep it at simmering point on top of the stove, for about 45 minutes, until all the juice has run from the redcurrants. Stir and mash the fruit with a wooden spoon from time to time during the cooking.

3 Turn the contents of the casserole into a jelly bag, set over a bowl and allow all the juice to drip through, without squeezing the bag: you may have to leave it overnight. Do not be tempted to squeeze the bag, or the jelly will be cloudy.

4 Measure the redcurrant liquid and put it in a preserving pan. Stir in the appropriate amount of sugar. Set the pan over a low heat and stir until the sugar has dissolved. Bring to the boil and boil rapidly for about 3 minutes.

5 Test for setting by pouring 5 ml /1 tsp jelly on to a cold saucer and leaving it to cool. If the surface of the jelly wrinkles when you push it with your finger, setting point has been reached.

6 Pour the jelly into warmed jars and cover the surface of each with a circle of waxed paper. When the jelly is cold, cover with screw-top lids and label the jars. It will keep a year or more in a cool dry place.

Blackcurrant syrup

Serve this syrup as a sauce with hot or cold puddings, stir it into yoghurt, or dilute to make a fruit drink.

 50 minutes

Makes about 700 ml /1¼ pt
1 kg /2¼ lb blackcurrants
200 g /7 oz sugar to every 500 ml /18 fl oz juice

1 Put the blackcurrants in a saucepan with 150 ml /5 fl oz water. Cover and cook over a low heat for 15 minutes or until the fruit is soft and pulpy.

2 Rub the fruit through a fine sieve, to remove the seeds. Measure the juice, return it to the rinsed saucepan and set it over a low heat. Stir in the required amount of sugar and continue to stir until it has dissolved. Heat and boil for 10 minutes.

3 Sterilize a bottle by rinsing it out with boiling water. Pour the syrup while it is still warm into the bottle and cork it tightly.

● The syrup will keep for up to 1 year, unopened, and up to 6 months after opening, if kept in a cool dark place.

Gooseberry fool

This classic, fluffy sweet has a more interesting flavour and darker colour if you use sweet spices and brown sugar.

 1 hour plus 1 hour chilling

Serves 6
500 g /18 oz green gooseberries
50 g /2 oz Barbados sugar
2.5 ml /½ tsp ground cinnamon
pinch of ground cloves
300 ml /10 fl oz thick cream
mint leaves

1 Top and tail the gooseberries. Put them in a large saucepan with the sugar, spices and 60 ml /4 tbls water. Cover and cook over a low heat for 20 minutes or until the fruit is very soft.

2 Put the cooked gooseberries into a bowl and break them up with a fork, but do not reduce them to a purée.

3 Whip the cream until softly peaked, then gently fold it into the gooseberries with a metal spoon.

4 Pile the fool into one large glass bowl or 6 individual bowls. Chill for 1 hour, and garnish with mint leaves before serving.

Currant leaf cake

Aromatic blackcurrant leaves give a delicate flavour to this light sponge cake.

🍴🍴 1½ hours

Makes a 18 cm /7 in cake
8 blackcurrant leaves
125 g /4 oz cream cheese
200 g /7 oz butter, softened
grated zest of ½ lemon
200 g /7 oz caster sugar
200 g /7 oz self-raising flour
pinch of salt
3 large eggs, beaten
75 ml /3 fl oz milk
butter for greasing
For finishing
30 ml /2 tbls caster sugar
45 ml /3 tbls apricot jam

1 Heat the oven to 180C /350F /gas 4. Bruise 2 of the blackcurrant leaves by folding them and crushing them on a board with a rolling pin. Make sure the leaves remain whole. Put the cream cheese in a bowl and mix in the leaves. Set aside.

2 Cream the butter with the lemon zest in a mixing bowl. Beat in the sugar until the mixture is light and fluffy. Sift the flour with the salt and beat it into the butter and sugar mixture alternately with the beaten eggs. Mix in enough milk to make a soft dropping consistency.

3 Butter 2 × 18 cm /7 in sandwich tins and line the base of each with a circle of buttered greaseproof paper. On top of each circle place 3 currant leaves, evenly spaced.

4 Divide the cake mixture evenly between the tins, smooth the tops and bake for 30 minutes in the centre of the oven until they are golden brown and firm and have shrunk slightly from the sides of the tins. Cool for 5 minutes in the tins, then turn on to wire cooling racks. Remove the greaseproof paper and currant leaves from the base of each.

5 Remove the currant leaves from the cream cheese in the bowl, and beat 15 ml /1 tbls caster sugar into the cheese. When the cakes are completely cold, spread the underside of one of them first with the cheese, then with the jam. Place the other cake on top and dredge with the remaining sugar.

● Geranium leaves may be substituted for the blackcurrant leaves.

Redcurrant sorbet

This pink water ice makes a very pretty sweet to end a summer meal.

🍴🍴 4½ hours including freezing

Serves 4
75 g /3 oz sugar
500 g /18 oz redcurrants
60 ml /4 tbls red wine
15 ml /1 tbls icing sugar, sieved
1 medium-sized egg white

For the garnish
caster sugar
redcurrant or mint leaves
maraschino cherries

1 If you are making the sorbet in a refrigerator, turn the temperature to the coldest setting.

2 Make a sugar syrup by dissolving the sugar in 100 ml /3½ fl oz water in a small saucepan over a low heat. Increase the heat, boil the syrup for 3 minutes, then cool and set aside.

3 Put the redcurrants in a large saucepan with the wine. Cover and cook gently over a low heat for 15 minutes or until the fruit is soft and very juicy.

4 Rub the redcurrants through a fine sieve into a bowl, making sure no seeds pass through with the juice. Stir the icing sugar into the purée, then stir in the sugar syrup.

5 Pour the mixture into a freezing tray and freeze – about 1½ hours in a refrigerator, less in a big freezer – until it is slushy.

6 Transfer the mixture into a large mixing bowl, and whisk until it becomes light in colour. Stiffly whip the egg white and fold it into the whisked mixture.

7 Pour the mixture back into the freezing container and freeze for a further 1½ hours, until it is just firm. Whisk up again in the mixing bowl, then pour back into the container and cover with a lid or foil. Freeze again for 30 minutes, this time turning the refrigerator setting back to normal.

8 Meanwhile chill 4 large wine glasses and dip the rims in caster sugar. Spoon the sorbet straight from the freezing compartment or freezer into the glasses, and top each one with a redcurrant leaf and halved maraschino cherries, or mint leaves.

● The sorbet will keep for up to 1 week in the freezing compartment of the freezer, or for up to 2 months in the freezer.
● Whitecurrants, a mixture of whitecurrants and redcurrants, or blackcurrants can be substituted for the redcurrants.

Gooseberry cream pie

Gooseberry pie is a traditional favourite: a cream filling makes it really special.

🍴🍴 1 hour 25 minutes

Serves 6
For the pastry
65 g /2½ oz butter, diced small
65 g /2½ oz lard, diced small
250 g /9 oz flour, sifted
pinch of salt
beaten egg for glaze
For the filling
500 g /18 oz green gooseberries
75 g /3 oz sugar
5 ml /1 tsp ground cinnamon
1.5 ml /¼ tsp ground mace
60 ml /4 tbls thick cream

1 Heat the oven to 180C /350F /gas 4. Make the pastry by rubbing the butter and lard into the flour and salt with your fingertips. Add enough cold water to mix. Chill the pastry while you prepare the rest of the ingredients.
2 Top and tail the gooseberries. Mix them with the sugar, cinnamon and mace.
3 Roll out two-thirds of the pastry and with it line a 20 cm /8 in greased flan tin. Put the gooseberries into the flan and spoon the cream over the top. Cover with the remaining pastry. Seal the edges and brush the top with the beaten egg.
4 Bake the pie for 50 minutes until the top is golden brown.

● Serve this pie hot and hand round extra whipped cream flavoured with vanilla sugar separately, if you like.

On the cake stand is Currant leaf cake; to the right is Gooseberry cream pie and in front, Redcurrant sorbet

Blackcurrant cheesecake

Use canned or bottled blackcurrants to make this rich, attractive cheesecake, shown on *page 265*.

🍴🍴🍴 1 hour plus 1 hour setting

Serves 6
For the base
200 g /7 oz digestive biscuits
75 g /3 oz butter
1.5 ml /¼ tsp vanilla essence
For the topping
375 g /12 oz canned blackcurrants in syrup
15 g /½ oz powdered gelatine
juice of ½ lemon
175 g /6 oz cream cheese
2 large eggs, separated
50 g /2 oz caster sugar
200 ml /7 fl oz thick cream
10 ml /2 tsp arrowroot

1 Heat the oven to 200C /400F /gas 6. Put the biscuits between 2 pieces of greaseproof paper or in a polythene bag and crush them to fine crumbs with a rolling pin. Put them in a bowl.
2 Melt the butter in a small saucepan and stir the crumbs into it, with the vanilla essence.
3 Press the crumb mixture into the base of a deep 18 cm /7 in cake tin with a loose base. Bake the crumb case for 15 minutes and let it cool completely. Line the sides of the cake tin with greaseproof paper oiled on both sides.
4 Drain the blackcurrants and reserve the syrup. Sprinkle the gelatine over the lemon juice and 30 ml /2 tbls water in a small bowl and leave to soak.
5 Put the cream cheese in a bowl and beat in the egg yolks and caster sugar. When the mixture is smooth, gradually beat in the cream and 60 ml /4 tbls of the reserved blackcurrant syrup. Fold in half of the blackcurrants. Stiffly whip the egg whites and fold them into the mixture.
6 Set the bowl containing the gelatine over a saucepan of hot water on a low heat until the gelatine is melted. Then stir it into the blackcurrant and cream mixture. Pour into the prepared cake tin and put it into the refrigerator to set.
7 Mix the arrowroot with 30 ml /2 tbls of the remaining blackcurrant syrup. Put the rest of the syrup into a saucepan and bring it to the boil. Add the arrowroot and cook, stirring all the time, until the syrup is thick and transparent. Remove the pan from the heat and stir in the remaining blackcurrants. Leave to cool.
8 Stand the cake tin on an upturned jam jar and slide away the ring. Transfer the cheesecake from the base of the tin to a serving plate. Carefully pour the thickened blackcurrant syrup evenly over the top of the cake. Serve chilled.

● This cake makes a perfect supper party dessert; it looks pretty on a buffet table.

Strawberries and raspberries

Of all the soft summer fruit, strawberries and raspberries are perhaps the most popular and most eagerly awaited. Jewel-coloured and fragrantly scented, these luscious berries can be served in a delicious variety of ways.

Cultivated strawberries came to Europe from America at the beginning of the 17th century. Plumper, larger and more juicy than the native European strawberries, the fruit range in colour from scarlet to pinkish-orange.

Alpine or wild strawberries are found in woods and shady pastures in Europe; they are also commercially cultivated in France. Their tiny, bright red fruit are highly scented, with an exquisite muscat flavour.

Raspberries may be wild or cultivated. Their exact origin is obscure, but they were cultivated in the 16th century, although not much used in the kitchen until the 1800s – and then mainly for vinegars and syrupy drinks. Usually crimson there are some varieties which bear yellow fruit, as well as black and purple fruiting varieties. Raspberries have a fruity, sharp flavour.

Buying and storing

Both types of berries are usually sold in punnets, but strawberries are sometimes sold loose. Perfectly ripe berries should have bright, fresh-looking leaves. Avoid punnets which are stained with juice – this indicates the fruit is mushy.

Both strawberries and raspberries are perishable so use as soon as possible after picking or buying them. They will only keep for 1–2 days before turning mouldy.

To store, pick over the fruit and discard any mouldy or badly squashed berries. Place the selected fruit in a single layer if possible, in a clean container, cover loosely and keep at the bottom of the refrigerator. If stored in a deep container, the weight of the berries can crush those at the bottom of the container. Allow to stand at room temperature for 1 hour before serving.

Traditional ways of preserving are by bottling or making jam. Nowadays large quantities of strawberries and raspberries are sold canned in syrup or frozen.

❉❉❉❉ Raspberries freeze whole very successfully – they are one of the best frozen fruit. Strawberries can be frozen whole if you wish, but it is not really recommended because they are often mushy when defrosted and lose some flavour, colour, texture and pectin. Alpine strawberries, however, freeze very successfully.

Freeze only firm, ripe berries. Hull strawberries and cut any large ones in half. Wash raspberries only if absolutely necessary. Open freeze until the fruit is firm, then pack in polythene bags or rigid containers; store for up to 9 months. Another method is to layer in rigid containers with dry sugar, using 125 g /4 oz sugar to each 500 g /1 lb fruit; store for up to 12 months. Thaw in containers for 6–8 hours in the refrigerator.

Serve as a dessert when only just thawed.

Puréeing is the most successful method of freezing strawberries. Raspberries can be puréed if too juicy to freeze whole. Pack the purée in 250 ml /10 fl oz containers leaving head space. Use unsweeetened purée within 6 months of freezing, sweetened purée within 8 months.

Preparing the berries

Discard any mouldy ones. Remove the stalks and attached leaves from strawberries and cut large fruit in half. Hull raspberries and remove damaged portions if necessary. Just before using, place the fruit in a colander and dip in cold water a few times, drain and then dry the berries well with absorbent paper.

To purée: crush the fruit with a wooden spoon and press through a nylon sieve, or use a blender and, if you dislike seeds, sieve the purée. As a guide, 250 g /8 oz fresh berries will give 200 ml /6 fl oz purée. Use icing sugar for sweetening as this dissolves most easily. Thawed frozen berries are puréed in the same way as fresh. Frozen raspberries can also be puréed in a blender without defrosting, if you add them a few at a time to the whirling blades.

Using the berries

Lightly sugared fresh, raw strawberries and raspberries make an irresistible dessert. To enhance their flavour, sprinkle the fruit with fresh orange juice or a few drops of lemon juice. For a headier result, use a liqueur – any orange-flavoured liqueur with strawberries; framboise with raspberries; kirsch or maraschino with either. Try also macerating the fruit with Marsala, port or sherry, sweet dessert wine or – best of all – champagne. Some cooks like to perfume strawberries with a sprinkling of rose water; others recommend a grinding of black pepper to bring out the flavour.

Cream – thick, clotted or softly whipped and then flavoured with vanilla sugar – is the classic accompaniment to a bowl of fresh berries. Sour cream, thick natural yoghurt, ice cream or smoothly beaten curd cheese all make a delicious change. The French custom of serving sugared strawberries with portions of cream cheese or fromage blanc (curd cheese) works equally well with raspberries.

Both berries combine well with other fresh fruit. A salad of strawberries and sliced bananas or oranges is delectable. Raspberries go well with cubes of pineapple or melon. For a ruby salad, layer raspberries, redcurrants and sliced strawberries with sugar and leave in a cool place for a few hours until a natural syrup has formed.

Strawberry mille-feuilles, Strawberry shake and a French raspberry tart

Whole raspberries and small strawberries make a luscious topping for cheesecakes or fillings for open tarts and tartlet cases. Glaze the fruit with melted redcurrant jelly to keep it fresh and moist.

Either fruit can be crushed and folded into cream fillings for choux and flaked pastries, sponge cakes and meringues. They may be puréed and used as the base for cream desserts, such as fools, ice cream, mousses and cold soufflés, or refreshing water ices and sorbets. When using raspberries for any of these desserts, add some redcurrant juice or purée for flavour and colour. The classic Melba sauce (see recipe) is simply a slightly sweetened purée of fresh raspberries.

Both raspberries and strawberries lose something when cooked, and are really at their best when served fresh and as soon as possible after picking.

French raspberry tart

2 hours for pastry case plus cooling
then 30 minutes

Serves 6–8
700 g /1½ lb fresh raspberries, washed and
  picked over
225 g /8 oz flour
1 large pinch of salt
75 g /3 oz unsalted butter, diced and left at
  room temperture
25 g /1 oz caster sugar
1 medium-sized egg, lightly beaten
60 ml /4 tbls iced water
For the glaze
100 g /4 oz redcurrant jelly
5 ml /1 tsp framboise or kirsch
For the filling
225 g /8 oz Petit suisse, Demi-sel or other
  medium-fat soft cheese
15 ml /1 tbls framboise or kirsch
15–30 ml /1–2 tbls caster sugar

1 Sift the flour and salt onto a marble slab or pastry board in a mound. Make a large well in the centre and put in the diced butter, caster sugar, egg and half the water. With the fingertips of one hand, blend these ingredients together.
2 Still using one hand, start working the flour into the blended ingredients. When about one-third of the flour has been incorporated, add the remaining water. Gradually work in the rest of the flour.
3 Smooth the pastry by pressing down lightly with the 'heel' of one hand 5 or 6 times. Chill in cling film for 1 hour.
4 Heat the oven to 190C /375F /gas 5. Roll out the pastry and use to line a 25 cm /10 in diameter, loose-bottomed flan tin with fluted sides. Prick the base with a fork then chill the pastry case for 10 minutes.
5 Line the pastry case with foil and beans. Bake the case for 10 minutes then remove the foil and beans. Bake for a further 15–20 minutes until cooked and lightly browned. Remove the case from the tin, place on a

wire rack and leave until completely cold.
6 Not more than 2 hours before serving make the glaze. Put the redcurrant jelly in a small, heavy-based saucepan, breaking up the jelly with a fork. Add the framboise or kirsch and heat gently, stirring until smooth. Brush the inside of the pastry case with a thin layer of glaze.
7 To prepare the filling, beat the soft cheese in a bowl with a wooden spoon until smooth and creamy. Beat the framboise or kirsch and caster sugar to taste. Spread the cheese mixture evenly in the pastry case and smooth the surface.
8 Arrange the raspberries close together in concentric circles over the cheese mixture. (Start with the largest berries in the centre and work outwards.) Re-melt the remaining glaze and brush thickly over the fruit; allow to set before serving.

● The uncooked pastry can be stored, wrapped, for 2–3 days in the refrigerator, as can the baked, unfilled case.

Strawberry shake

If you do not possess an ice cream scoop remember that 1 scoop equals 60 ml /4 tbls. You can decorate the drinks with a few whole tiny strawberries or fan wafers.

🍴 10 minutes

Serves 2
lightly beaten egg white
caster sugar
4 scoops vanilla ice cream
150 ml /5 fl oz cold milk
100 g /4 oz strawberries, hulled and crushed
30 ml /2 tbls strawberry syrup

1 Brush the rims of 2 tall, 250 ml /10 fl oz glass tumblers with beaten egg white, then dip in caster sugar to give a frosted effect. Chill the glasses in the refrigerator while you make the shakes.
2 Put the ice cream, milk, strawberries and strawberry syrup in a blender and blend, covered, at maximum speed for 60–90 seconds until frothy. Pour into the prepared glasses.
3 Serve with 2 straws in each glass.

● For an extra rich, very thick shake replace the milk with an equal quantity of ice cream.
● For strawberry and banana shakes, omit the strawberry syrup and add a small peeled and sliced banana and 1–2 drops red food colouring (to give a good colour).

Strawberry mille-feuilles

A mouthwatering confection of light, crispy pastry, the French name means '1000 leaves'. The cake is layered with whipped cream and topped with glazed strawberries. Crème pâtissière (pastry cream) can be used in place of the whipped cream if preferred and you can pipe a border of cream around the strawberries for extra embellishment, as on *page 271*.

🍴🍴 1¼ hours plus cooling

Serves 4
215 g /7½ oz made weight frozen puff pastry, defrosted for 2 hours
60 ml /4 tbls strawberry jam, warmed and sieved
150 ml /15 fl oz thick cream, lightly whipped
100–150 g /4–6 oz strawberries, hulled

1 Heat the oven to 220C /425F /gas 7. Roll out the pastry to a 25 cm /10 in square. Using a sharp knife, trim the edges and cut the pastry into 3 equal strips. Place the strips on 1 or 2 large dampened baking sheet(s) and prick well with the prongs of a fork. Chill in the refrigerator for 5 minutes.
2 Bake the pastry for 10–12 minutes until well browned. Turn over the strips and return to the oven for a further 3–4 minutes to dry out the undersides. Leave on wire racks until completely cold.

3 Not more than 1 hour before serving, trim the edges of each pastry strip with a sharp knife. Brush the surface of 1 strip very thinly with jam and spread with half the whipped cream, to within 5 mm /¼ in of the edges. Place on a flat serving dish. Lightly brush a second strip with jam and spread with the remaining cream. Place on top of the first strip.
4 Brush the surface of the last strip with half the remaining jam. Cut the strawberries in half and arrange, cut side down, on top. glaze the fruit with the remaining jam. Carefully place the strawberry-covered pastry on top of the other two strips. Leave the mille-feuilles to firm up in a cool place for 15 minutes before serving.

Strawberry ice cream

The simplest form of strawberry ice cream is made by freezing strawberry purée mixed with thick, whipped cream. This strawberry ice cream uses a thick cream-and-egg custard.

🍴🍴 1 hour 50 minutes including chilling, plus 2½–3 hours freezing

Serves 4
700 g /1½ lb strawberries, hulled
30 ml /2 tbls frozen concentrated orange juice
225 ml /8 fl oz thick cream
3 medium-sized egg yolks
75 g /3 oz caster sugar
sweet biscuits, to serve

1 Turn the refrigerator to its coldest setting 1 hour before making the ice cream. Chill a shallow metal container.
2 Purée the strawberries in batches in a blender or through a vegetable mill. Add the frozen concentrated orange juice to the strawberry purée and stir well to mix. Cover and chill in the refrigerator.
3 In a small, heavy-based saucepan, scald the cream over a low heat. Allow to cool.
4 Combine the egg yolks and sugar in the top of a double boiler off the heat and beat vigorously with a wooden spoon. Pour in the hot cream in a thin stream, stirring constantly.
5 Put the top on the double boiler over barely simmering water and cook the custard, stirring constantly, for about 15 minutes until thickened. Strain the custard into a bowl. Cool for about 30 minutes, then chill, covered, in the refrigerator.
6 Stir the custard into the strawberry purée and turn the mixture into the chilled container. Cover and freeze for about 1 hour, or until frozen 25 mm /1 in at edges.
7 Turn the partially frozen ice cream into a chilled bowl and beat thoroughly with a whisk or fork to break down ice crystals. Return to the container and freeze for a further 1½–2 hours until firm.
8 Soften the ice cream in the refrigerator for about 45 minutes before serving. To serve, scoop the ice cream into individual, chilled glass serving dishes and accompany with sweet biscuits.

Strawberry ice cream

4 Divide the paste between the prepared tins. Pat out over the base of the tin and press gently into the fluted sides. Smooth the surface with the back of a metal spoon, then prick well with a fork.
5 Bake the shortcakes in the oven for about 40 minutes, until pale biscuit in colour and just firm to the touch. While still warm, cut one of the shortcakes into 6 equal wedges with a sharp knife and dredge with caster sugar. Cool the shortcakes in the tins for 10 minutes, then transfer to a wire rack. Leave until cold.
6 Reserve a few small, perfect berries for decoration and slice the rest. Whisk the cream with the vanilla essence until fluffy and sweeten to taste with icing sugar.
7 Not more than 1 hour before serving, put the uncut shortcake on a flat serving dish and spread with half the cream. Cover with the sliced strawberries and the remaining cream, heaping it slightly in the centre. Place the wedges of shortcake on top. Decorate with whole strawberries. Serve within 1 hour of filling.

● Remember that you can use any variety of soft fruit as a filling for a shortcake.

Strawberry and cucumber salad

Peppering strawberries really does bring out their flavour. Assemble this summery salad just before needed – if left to stand, the strawberries will 'bleed' unattractively. Serve with delicate fish, such as trout or salmon, or with chicken. Frozen strawberries are not suitable for this dish.

🍴 10–15 minutes

Serves 4
½ medium-sized cucumber
225 g /8 oz fresh strawberries, hulled
1–2 lettuce leaves, shredded
15 ml /1 tbls sunflower oil
7.5 ml /1½ tsp lemon juice
salt and freshly ground black pepper

1 Trim off the cucumber end. Using a cannelle cutter, the sides of a citrus zester or the prongs of a fork, score the cucumber skin lengthways at regular intervals. (This gives each slice a scalloped edge.) Thinly slice the cucumber and reserve. Slice the strawberries lengthways so that the slices are heart-shaped.
2 Spread the shredded lettuce over the base of a large, flat, round serving plate. Arrange alternate rings of cucumber and strawberries over the bed of lettuce, starting with a border of cucumber and finishing with strawberries in the centre.
3 Whisk together the oil and lemon juice and season very lightly with salt and freshly ground black pepper. Sprinkle over the cucumber and strawberries. Grind a little black pepper over the salad and serve.

Melba medley

Slightly tart and brilliantly coloured, Melba sauce is a classic fresh fruit sauce.

🍴 10 minutes plus 1–2 hours chilling for the sauce

Serves 4
For the Melba sauce
225 g /8 oz raspberries, cleaned
45–60 ml /3–4 tbls icing sugar, sifted
For Peach Melba
2 peaches, skinned, halved and stoned
425 ml /15 fl oz vanilla ice cream
toasted slivered almonds to decorate
For Strawberries cardinal
450–700 g /1–1½ lb strawberries, hulled
caster sugar
15 ml /1 tbls kirsch
ratafias to decorate

1 First make the sauce. Crush the raspberries through a sieve into a heatproof bowl.
2 Set the bowl over a very low heat until the purée is just warm, then remove from the heat and beat in the sifted icing sugar to taste. Turn the Melba sauce into a container, cover tightly and chill for 1–2 hours.
3 For Peach Melba, divide the ice cream between 4 chilled glass serving dishes and top with a peach half. Spoon a quarter of the chilled Melba sauce over each portion and spike with toasted slivered almonds.
4 For Strawberries cardinal, divide the strawberries between 4 chilled glass serving dishes and sprinkle lightly with caster sugar. Decorate with Melba sauce and ratafias.

Strawberry shortcake

Using flan tins with fluted sides and loose bottoms is the safest (and easiest) way of achieving a frilly 'petticoat' edge.

🍴🍴 2¼ hours, including baking and cooling time

Serves 6
225 g /8 oz flour
100 g /4 oz fine semolina
100 g /4 oz caster sugar
225 g /8 oz unsalted butter, at room temperature
caster sugar to dredge
For the filling
225 g /8 oz strawberries, hulled
275 ml /10 fl oz thick cream
a few drops of vanilla essence
icing sugar

1 Sift the flour with the semolina and caster sugar into a large mixing bowl. Make a well in the centre and add the butter. Using the fingers of one hand, lightly work the dry ingredients into the butter for 3–4 minutes, until the mixture clings together.
2 Gather the mixture together and knead very lightly and briefly to make a soft, pliable paste. Wrap in cling film and chill in the refrigerator for 10 minutes.
3 Meanwhile, heat the oven to 170C /325F /gas 3. Lightly butter two 20 cm /8 in diameter loose-bottomed flan tins preferably with fluted sides.

3 Place the strawberries in a bowl, sprinkle with the orange zest and orange juice and crush to a pulp with a fork. Set aside. Sprinkle the gelatine over 45 ml /3 tbls warm water in a small heavy-based saucepan and leave to soak.
4 Beat the curd cheese with a wooden spoon until soft and smooth. Gradually beat in the caster sugar, vanilla essence, yoghurt, cream and pulped strawberries.
5 Set the soaked gelatine over a very low heat for 2–3 minutes until completely dissolved, then remove from the heat. Stir a little of the curd cheese mixture into the dissolved gelatine, then pour onto the rest of the cheese mixture in the bowl, stirring constantly to incorporate the gelatine.
6 Allow the cheese mixture to stand for 5 minutes, then fold in the stiffly whisked egg white. Turn the mixture into the tin and gently tilt the tin to level the surface. Cover loosely and refrigerate for 3–4 hours until the cheese mixture is set.
7 Just before serving, remove the sides of the tin and decorate the cheesecake with halved strawberries.

Raspberry soufflé

40 minutes plus cooling
5 minutes to decorate after setting

Serves 4
500 g /1 lb raspberries
15 g /1/2 oz powdered gelatine
3 medium-sized eggs, separated
125 g /4 oz caster sugar
150 ml /5 fl oz thick cream
To decorate
150 ml /5 fl oz thick cream, whipped
a few raspberries (optional)

1 Prepare a 15 cm /6 in or 700 ml /1¼ pt soufflé dish by tying a collar of double thickness foil around the outside so that it stands about 5 cm /2 in above the rim.
2 Pick over the raspberries and rub through a sieve, or blend them then sieve.
3 Put 45 ml /3 tbls water into a small bowl, stir in the gelatine and stand the bowl in a pan of hot water until the gelatine has dissolved. Cool slightly then stir into the raspberry purée.
4 Using an electric mixer, whisk the egg yolks with the sugar at high speed until thick. Alternatively, put the egg yolks into a bowl with the sugar. Stand the bowl over a pan of hot water and hand whisk until the mixture is thick and creamy. Remove from the heat and continue to whisk until cool.
5 Stir the purée into the egg yolk mixture. Whip the cream until it begins to thicken and fold it in.
6 Whisk the egg whites until they form stiff peaks. Using a metal spoon, fold them gently into the mixture. Pour into the prepared soufflé dish and leave to set in the refrigerator.
7 To serve: remove the collar. Pipe the cream into rosettes round the edge. Decorate with raspberries, if liked.

Strawberry liqueur-cream delight

1¼ hours draining and marinating, then 15 minutes

Serves 6–8
1 kg /2¼ lb strawberries
30–45 ml /2–3 tbls icing sugar
100 ml /3½ fl oz kirsch
50 ml /2 fl oz anisette
250 ml /9 fl oz thick cream
100 g /4 oz vanilla-flavoured icing sugar

1 Wash the strawberries in a colander and leave them to drain thoroughly, about 15 minutes.
2 Hull the berries and put them in a large bowl, then dust them with the icing sugar. Pour the kirsch and anisette over the fruit, cover and leave the bowl in a cool place for about 1 hour.
3 Whip the cream until stiff then fold in the vanilla-flavoured icing sugar. Arrange the strawberries with some of their juice in a glass bowl or in individual glass dishes, top them with the cream and serve.

Strawberry cheese-cake

1 hour plus setting

Serves 6–8
100 g /4 oz shortbread biscuits, crushed
40 g /1½ oz butter, melted
225 g /8 oz strawberries, hulled
grated zest of ½ orange
30 ml /2 tbls orange juice
10 ml /2 tsp powdered gelatine
175 g /6 oz curd cheese
75 g /3 oz caster sugar
1–2 drops vanilla essence
30 ml /2 tbls yoghurt
150 ml /5 fl oz thick cream, lightly whipped
1 medium-sized egg white, stiffly whisked
halved strawberries, to decorate
butter for greasing

1 Heat the oven to 180C /350F /gas 4. Lightly butter an 18 cm /7 in loose-bottom cake tin.
2 Add biscuits to butter and stir until evenly coated; spoon into tin and press over base. Bake for 8 minutes until browned.

Blackberries, cranberries and other berries

Sweet, juicy blackberries; sharp-tasting red cranberries; plump blueberries — these colourful little fruits are delicious, blend well with other flavours, and can make your menus more exciting.

Most of us have experienced the thrill in childhood of finding wild blackberries ripening in the autumn sun, for they grow anywhere, from country roadsides to abandoned urban land.

Children seem to be especially tempted by wild berries, often to the horror of mothers who may fear they have chosen an inedible variety – though these are relatively few. Berries in the wild also appeal to adults, perhaps because they represent natural 'food for free'. But today most of the best varieties can also be bought from the greengrocer, though even there, the season is all too short.

Blackberry charlotte

Types of berry

Blackberries are also called brambles. Choose firm black fruits with no brown spots or red patches. Blackberries, which are widely available, ripen in early autumn. The first fruits are the largest, sweetest and most fully flavoured and can be eaten raw. Later berries are smaller, tougher, less juicy and should be cooked. Very seedy ones should be used only for jellies and wine.

Cultivated blackberries have a weaker flavour than wild ones. They are larger, with fewer seeds, and therefore more suitable for making into preserves.

Try crushing raw blackberries with a little red wine and sugar to taste. Cooked, blackberries may be made into blackberry and apple pie, or wine.

Cranberries are small, blood-red berries, very juicy and with a refreshing, sharp taste. They grow in Europe, North America and northern Asia, and are available fresh from autumn to early winter, or frozen all year round. Fresh cranberries can be covered with cold water and stored in jars in the refrigerator for up to 8 months.

Cranberries are too sour to be eaten on their own, but can be made into muffins, cakes, and the classic American cranberry sauce, traditionally served with the Thanksgiving turkey:

● Dissolve 175 g /6 oz sugar in 150 ml /5 fl oz water. Add 225 g /8 oz cranberries, bring to the boil, then simmer gently for about 10 minutes, until the berries are soft. Serve cold. Grated orange zest can be added, if wished.

Blueberries have a thin, blue-black skin with a bloom. Good ones are plump, sweet and juicy, with only a few soft seeds. Blueberries come mostly from North America, but are also grown in some areas of England. They are in season in late summer, but are also available both frozen and canned.

Blueberries are delicious eaten raw – with cream and sugar, with ice cream or in a fruit salad (see recipe), but they also make wonderful pies, cakes, muffins, waffles, steamed puddings and sorbets.

Bilberries: the bilberry (also known as blaeberry, whortleberry or hurtleberry) is frequently confused with its American cousin the blueberry, because they are similar in both name and appearance. However, bilberries are smaller and less succulent than blueberries. They grow wild in Britain, northern Europe and Asia and ripen in midsummer, though they are very rarely available in shops.

Eat them raw with cream and sugar or a vanilla-flavoured custard; or make them into tarts, jams and jellies as they do in France, where they are known as *myrtilles*.

Huckleberries are wild berries found only in North America. They are similar to blueberries, although they may be white or pink instead of blue, and have more pips. They are used in the same way.

Dewberries taste and look similar to blackberries, though they are bluish-grey in colour. They are found in only a few spots in Britain and the U.S.

Loganberries: the loganberry is a hybrid of the blackberry and the raspberry. It resembles the raspberry, but is more elongated and darker in colour, with tougher flesh and a less delicate taste. Loganberries are available fresh during the summer, and in cans all year round, and can be used in any recipes calling for cooked raspberries, boysenberries, wineberries or cloudberries.

Cloudberries are small, orange-yellow fruits like blackberries in shape, found mostly in Scandinavia. They are made into puddings, jam and a liqueur.

Wineberries come from Asia, but are also cultivated in Britain, though only in private gardens. They are small berries, which are deep red when fully ripe, with shiny, translucent skins. They are best raw with sugar and, perhaps, some thick cream.

Boysenberries: the boysenberry is a hybrid of the blackberry and loganberry. The fruits are large and wine coloured, and are used for pies and jams in North America.

Mulberries: black mulberries are a rich wine-red colour, with a sharp, clean flavour, a tight skin and a few soft seeds which contain a great deal of sweet juice. Unlike all the others they are a tree fruit. Pick the berries only when they are completely ripe, in late summer. Cook them briefly in pies and preserves, or use raw in drinks (see recipe), sorbets and ice creams.

The white mulberry is sweet but rather insipid; it is made into Oriental sauces.

Lingonberries: the lingonberry, also called the crowberry, is a small wild berry native to Scandinavia and Russia and less frequently found in Scotland. It is small, and has a vibrant red colour. Make lingonberries into relishes, compotes or fruit soups, or substitute for cranberries in any recipe.

Elderberries grow along country lanes and hedgerows in Europe. They are tiny, purple-black berries which ripen in late summer. Picking them is a messy job as the berries tend to burst; however, as they are never on sale, picking is the only way to obtain them. They can be made into wine, jams and jellies.

Buying and storing berries

Look for well-shaped berries with a good colour, and avoid any punnets with excessive juice stains – these will contain mushy, possibly mouldy fruit. Tip out the berries onto a tray lined with absorbent paper and discard any doubtful ones. Then use them at once, if possible, or pack in airtight containers and store them at the bottom of the refrigerator for up to 24 hours. Most berries do not need washing; if they do, wash them just before using them by placing them in a colander or sieve and dipping in a bowl of cold water. Drain and dry on absorbent paper.

✳✳✳ Pack berries in rigid containers, washing and drying first if necessary. Blueberries, bilberries, boysenberries and huckleberries can be open frozen, then packed in freezer bags, or frozen in heavy syrup for up to 1 year. Thaw at room temperature for 2½ hours if eating raw. If using cooked in a recipe, they can be cooked straight from frozen.

Using berries

With the exception of cranberries, berries are probably at their best eaten raw with a little sugar and cream or yoghurt. Alternatively try a little cream cheese or Ricotta, or a combination of one of these with soured cream. The addition to one of these creamy mixtures of a liqueur, slivered almonds, desiccated coconut or grated citrus zest gives an intriguing flavour: coconut goes well with blackberries or dewberries, orange with cranberries, lime or lemon with blueberries or bilberries.

New Englanders make blueberries, blackberries or bilberries into a steamed pudding called a grunt; Canadians layer cranberries and raisins with suet pastry; the English make a fool with blackberries and apples and the Finns make a blueberry tart.

Mulberry cocktail

This is a refreshing drink to serve on a hot, late summer afternoon. It is also delicious with gin instead of vodka, or you can omit the spirit altogether.

🍴 10 minutes

Serves 4
450 g /1 lb mulberries
30–45 ml /2–3 tbls sugar
15 ml /1 tbls lemon juice
175 ml /6 fl oz vodka
crushed ice
4 mint sprigs, to garnish

1 Purée the mulberries in a blender and strain the juice through a sieve. In a jug, mix the juice with the sugar, lemon juice, vodka and crushed ice.
2 Stir well and pour into chilled glasses. Garnish each cocktail with a sprig of mint and serve at once.

Blackberry charlotte

Using Ricotta cheese and yoghurt instead of cream makes this dinner-party dessert less rich and more unusual, as Ricotta has a taste all its own.

🍴🍴 1 hour 15 minutes, plus 4 hours or more chilling

Serves 4–6
75 g /3 oz hazelnuts
about 24 sponge fingers (2 packets boudoir biscuits)
15–30 ml /1–2 tbls gin
about 15 ml /1 tbls red- or blackcurrant jelly
450 g /1 lb Ricotta cheese
100 g /4oz vanilla sugar
150 ml /5 fl oz yoghurt
zest of 1 lemon, grated
2 medium-sized egg whites
450 g/1 lb blackberries, plus extra for decoration

1 Heat the oven to 190C /375F /gas 5. Place the hazelnuts on a baking sheet and

Serves 4-6
zest of 2 oranges, cut into julienne strips
225 g /8 oz sugar
juice of 1 orange
450 g /1 lb cranberries

1 In a saucepan, bring some water to the boil. Add the orange julienne, leave for 1 minute, then drain.
2 In the pan, combine the sugar with 225 ml /8 fl oz water. Bring to a gentle boil, stirring to dissolve the sugar, and add the blanched orange julienne. Simmer for 1 hour or until the syrup starts to thicken. Remove the julienne with a slotted spoon, place on greaseproof paper and reserve.
3 Add the orange juice and cranberries to the hot syrup. Simmer for 6-10 minutes, until the berries start to pop. Remove the pan from the heat and leave to cool.
4 Remove the berries from the pan with a slotted spoon, reserving the syrup. Press the berries through a sieve, stir to combine with the syrup and pour into a shallow tray. Freeze until mushy, about 1 hour.
5 Transfer the sorbet to a chilled bowl and beat with a fork to break up the crystals. Return to the tray and freeze again until firm but not solid, about 3 hours.
6 Spoon into chilled glasses, sprinkle with candied orange peel and serve.

Exotic fruit and berry salad

This combination of berries and exotic fruits tastes of far-away countries. Serve it with a dessert wine such as Muscat de Beaumes de Venise.

20 minutes
plus 2 hours or more chilling

Serves 6
4 passion fruits
2 mangoes, peeled and sliced
225 g /8 oz blueberries
225 g /8 oz loganberries
225 g /8 oz raspberries
30 ml /2 tbls sugar
juice and grated zest of 1 lime
5 ml /1 tsp angostura bitters
5-7 mint sprigs

1 Cut the passion fruits in half. Using a teaspoon, scoop out the flesh into a sieve placed over a bowl. Push the flesh through the sieve, discarding the seeds.
2 Combine the flesh with the mangoes and berries, sprinkle with sugar, add the lime juice and zest and the bitters; toss.
3 Reserve a few whole mint sprigs for garnishing. Strip the remaining leaves from their stalks and, with scissors, cut the leaves in thin strips. Scatter over the fruit, toss, place the salad in a serving bowl and chill for at least 2 hours.
4 Just before serving, tuck the remaining mint leaves into the fruit and berry salad.

toast them for about 20 minutes, or until the brown skins start to flake off.
2 Let them cool a few minutes, then rub with your fingers to remove most of the skin. Chop the nuts coarsely and return to the oven for 10 minutes, shaking the sheet twice so that the nuts are evenly browned. Remove the sheet from the oven and reserve the nuts.
3 Line the bottom of a charlotte or other cylindrical mould about 10 cm /4 in deep with greaseproof paper.
4 Cut enough of the sponge fingers into wedge shapes to line the base tightly. Dip them quickly in 15 ml /1 tbls gin, if wished, and place them in the mould curved side down.
5 Spread a little jelly on the sides of some of the remaining sponge fingers and use the biscuits to line the sides of the mould, sugared sides out.
6 In a large bowl, beat together the Ricotta cheese and vanilla sugar with a fork. Add the yoghurt, lemon zest and 15 ml /1 tbls gin and beat until the mixture is smooth.
7 Whisk the egg whites until stiff, then

fold a third of them into the cheese mixture. Gently fold in the rest, until well incorporated.
8 Spread a quarter of the cheese mixture in the bottom of the lined mould, top with a third of the blackberries and a third of the nuts. Repeat until all the ingredients are used up, finishing with the cheese mixture.
9 Cover with sponge fingers cut in wedge shapes, curved sides up. Cover the charlotte with foil and chill for at least 4 hours.
10 Turn the charlotte out onto a serving platter and decorate the top and the base with blackberries. Serve at once.

Cranberry and orange sorbet

This vibrant red sorbet has a sharp-sweet flavour which is enhanced by the candied orange peel topping.

1 hour 30 minutes, plus cooling and 4 hours freezing

Melons

Refreshing and light, sweet and juicy, melons have been popular since very early times. They are usually served raw – as a first or last course – but they can also be made into jam or pickled in vinegar. Crystallized melon is made commercially and melon seeds, stripped of their husks, are roasted and salted for savoury snacks in Greece, Central and South America.

Melons came from Asia (from where they spread to France, via Italy) and from tropical Africa. They are now extensively cultivated in hot, sunny areas. Like other members of the *Cucurbitaceae* family (which includes cucumbers, marrows and squashes), melons have a high water content – the flesh is 94% water. Melons contain vitamins A and C, but apart from that they are not especially nutritious: they are lower in calories than many other popular fruit such as apples.

Types of melon
There are many closely related varieties of melon, although watermelons are a distinct genus. Other melons fall into three main groups: cantaloupes, which have the most fragrant flesh, netted or musk melons which have a raised pattern on the outside skin and a scented flesh, and the oval-shaped winter melons.

Watermelons are very large (they weigh up to 30 kg /66 lb) and are extremely juicy. They can be round or oval in shape with a smooth, thick, dark green skin. The flesh is usually crimson, and the dark seeds are distributed through the flesh, which makes them more fiddly to deal with than other melons. They are most frequently eaten raw in wedges. They are, however, ideal for large melon baskets.

Cantaloupe melons are easily recognized by their pinkish-orange, aromatic flesh. They are round and may have rough, warty, dark green or dark gold skin clearly marked in segments. There are also varieties with red and even pale green flesh. Medium-sized cantaloupes are extensively cultivated in Europe and elsewhere.

Charentais (related to the cantaloupe) are small, round, highly scented fruit with light greenish-white skin clearly marked in segments and well-flavoured, deep pink flesh. Half a Charentais melon is just the right size for a single portion for an hors d'oeuvre.

Ogen melons (also related to the cantaloupe) are round, highly scented, honey-sweet and very juicy. They have a smooth, speckled skin divided by stripes of green; the flesh is fine-textured and pale green in colour. Ogen melons were developed on an Israeli kibbutz whose name they take: they can be small or medium in size.

Galia, the newest variety of melon from Israel, is related to the Ogen. Galias have a distinctively netted skin, with rough, bark-like lines raised on the surface. On ripening, the skin turns from green to honey-gold. The creamy-green flesh is soft and mealy, with a strong musky scent. They are usually medium-sized, but small ones are available.

Netted melons are called rock melons in Australia (and cantaloupes in America). They are similar to cantaloupes and may be round or large and oval. They may be green or yellow, segmented or not, but have a raised pattern on the rind. The flesh is orange and has a musky smell, so they are also called musk melons.

Honeydews are a variety of winter melon. They are egg-shaped, ripen late and can be stored for 1 month, so are ideal for export. A true honeydew has a banana-yellow skin which can be smooth or ridged. It has pale yellow, firm, sweet flesh and is not scented. A similar melon, much exported by Spain and also called honeydew, has dark green, deeply ridged skin. A slice of honeydew is a favourite starter for a meal but honeydews can also be served for desserts.

Levan melons are a new variety from Israel. They are medium-sized and egg-shaped, with an opaque white skin tinged with yellow. The creamy-green flesh is very sweet but is not scented.

Buying and storing melons

Ripe melons feel heavy for their size and the end opposite the stalk 'gives' slightly when gently pressed. Aromatic melons should be strongly scented when ripe. If you are buying a half of melon or a wedge, check that the flesh is firm and unblemished.

Ripe whole melons will keep in a cool, dark larder for up to 1 week. Store cut melon, tightly wrapped in cling film, in the crisper compartment of the refrigerator for up to 2 days. Leave the seeds in, as they will help to prevent juices escaping. Never leave cut melon to stand in sunlight or warmth: this makes it tasteless and mushy. To ripen a whole melon, place it in a brown paper bag and leave in a warm, dark place until ready.

✳✳✳✳ Freeze cubes or balls of honeydew or cantaloupe melon in medium sugar syrup for up to 12 months. Alternatively, dry the pieces well and layer in rigid polythene containers, with or without sugar, and freeze for 6–8 months. Thaw, unopened, in the refrigerator for 6–8 hours, and use when just defrosted. Thawed, frozen melon lacks crispness but can still be used for salads and desserts.

Preparing melons

Use stainless steel or silver knives, spoons and cutters to prepare melons. Try using the whole or half melon shell to make a decorative natural container. Chill thoroughly before filling. Chill dishes based on raw melon before serving – chilling intensifies the sweet, yet refreshing character of

the fruit and brings out its flavour.

To clean a melon, cut lengthways or horizontally according to the recipe and discard seeds and any membrane. Before serving watermelon flick out the seeds with the point of a knife after slicing or scooping out the flesh.

Melon slices: cut melon in half lengthways, clean, then cut lengthways into wedge-shaped slices. Spear flesh with a fork and run a knife between flesh and skin, then cut downwards into chunks. Serve on the skin and with a fork.

Melon cubes: slice the melon and cut into chunks as above; discard skin and cube the flesh.

Melon balls: halve the melon and press a parisienne cutter (melon baller) firmly into the flesh, twisting the cutter in a circle. Lift the cutter away and gently shake out the melon ball.

Individual melon cups: cut a small melon in half, horizontally. Scoop out the flesh to leave a shell about 5 mm /¼ in thick, taking care not to puncture the skin. Scrape out any untidy bits of flesh with a spoon. Drain and chill before filling.

Melon 'en surprise': trim the base of the melon, if necessary, so the fruit will stand upright. Cut off the top third of the melon and reserve as a lid. Clean the melon and scoop out all the flesh to leave a shell. Stand the shell upside down to drain, then chill. Replace 'lid' after filling.

Melon basket: level off the base of the melon. With a pen, draw a horizontal line around the middle of the melon, then draw 2 parallel lines either side of the stalk to mark the handle. With a long sharp knife, cut vertically and horizontally along the marked lines, but do not cut through the base of the handle. Lift out the two melon wedges either side of the handle. Cut out the flesh from under the melon handle. Clean the melon, scoop out the flesh and neaten the inside of the basket.

Melon purée: scoop out the flesh, drain well, remove all seeds and reduce to a purée in a blender or by passing through a sieve.

Top: Honeydew
Centre (left to right): Galia, honeydew, Charentais: bottom (left to right): Ogen, Galia, Levan. Ogen.

Melon slices

Using melons

Melon is usually served raw, as an hors d'oeuvre or dessert, but can also be made into a jam or sweet pickle. Melon purée is the base for light iced desserts and a chilled summer soup. Melon balls can be used in place of grapes to garnish fish dishes such as sole Véronique.

Watermelon wedges are as refreshing as a cold drink and a great favourite with children. On hot, sticky days, make a long cool drink by liquidizing cubes of melon flesh with crushed ice or another fruit juice.

Slices of melon accompanied by ground ginger and fine soft brown sugar are delightful dinner party starters. For a change, sprinkle the slices with slivers of preserved stem ginger and spoon over a little syrup from the jar. Pepper also accentuates the delicate flavour: for an elegant first course, serve halves of small melons with wedges of lime, caster sugar and black pepper.

Wedges of honeydew melon with wafer-thin slices of Parma ham is a classic Italian hors d'oeuvre: you could use smoked turkey or another sort of ham. Or serve halved, small melons with port sprinkled in the central cavities, or try sherry, Marsala or a sparkling white wine. The centre may also be filled with curd cheese flavoured with finely chopped fresh tarragon.

For a savoury salad, serve diced avocado and melon tossed in well seasoned vinaigrette with steaks or chops. A salad of melon and orange segments dressed in lemon juice or olive oil goes well with roast poultry. For a light lunch dish, mix cubes of melon with diced cooked chicken meat, finely chopped sweet pepper and coarsely chopped walnuts; coat with mayonnaise and serve on a bed of crisp lettuce.

If the main course is a rich or substantial one, then melon makes a light dessert, as it is refreshing. Try chilled melon balls masked with Melba sauce (*page 273*), or fill small melons with vanilla ice cream and top with a spoonful of clear honey or a ginger-flavoured preserve. Melon is also a delicious base for a fruit salad. Mix cubes of melon with prepared pineapple, grapes, strawberries or cherries and sweeten with a little caster sugar or honey; add a spoonful or two of fresh citrus juice to bring out the fruity flavour and chill well before serving.

Melon basket

Melon, prawn and grapefruit cocktail

Choose melons weighing no more than 700 g /1½ lb each. If using thawed frozen prawns, dry them well on absorbent paper. Serve with thin slices of brown bread and butter to soak up the dressing.

🔪 30 minutes plus chilling time

Serves 4
2 small Ogen or Charentais melons
1 pink grapefruit
60 ml /4 tbls soured cream
30 ml /2 tbls lemon juice
15 ml /1 tbls caster sugar
60 ml /4 tbls chopped chives
100 g /4 oz boiled, peeled prawns
50 g /2 oz cashew nuts
4 unpeeled prawns to decorate (optional)

1   Cut each melon horizontally in half; remove and discard the seeds and seed membrane. With a small melon baller, scoop out as much of the melon flesh as possible into balls and reserve in a bowl. Scrape out the remaining flesh, taking care not to puncture the melon skins, and use for another dish. Place the melon shells in polythene bags and chill.
2   Thickly peel the grapefruit, taking care to remove every bit of white pith. Cut into segments and remove the seeds with the point of the knife. Cut each segment in half and add the melon balls. Cover and chill.
3   Blend the soured cream with the lemon

Melon, prawn and grapefruit cocktail

juice and caster sugar. Season to taste and stir in half the chopped chives.
4   When ready to serve, drain the melon and grapefruit and toss in the soured cream dressing; fold in the peeled prawns, taste and correct the seasoning. Spoon the salad into the chilled melon shells, scatter over the nuts and sprinkle with the remaining chives. Place an unpeeled prawn on each.

Watermelon

🔪🔪 1 hour plus 1 hour chilling

Serves 4
1.5 kg /3 lb watermelon, halved, skinned,
   cut into cubes and seeded
450 ml /16 fl oz sweet white wine
30 ml /2 tbls soft light brown sugar
5 ml /1 tsp ground allspice
15 ml /1 tbls grated lemon zest
225 ml /8 fl oz soured cream

1   Combine the prepared watermelon cubes with the wine, sugar, allspice and lemon zest in a medium-sized saucepan. Bring gently to the boil over a moderate heat, stirring constantly. Then simmer the 'soup', uncovered, for 20 minutes.
2   Strain the soup through a fine nylon sieve. With a wooden spoon, rub the melon through the sieve until only a dry pulp is left. Discard the pulp.
3   Leave the soup until completely cold, then stir in the soured cream. Chill in the refrigerator for 1 hour before serving.

Melon slices with raspberry jelly

🔪 30 minutes plus chilling time

Serves 4–6
225 ml /10 fl oz sieved raspberry purée
1 squeeze lemon juice
icing or caster sugar to taste
10 ml /2 tsp gelatine
1 medium-sized honeydew melon

1   Turn the raspberry purée into a small pan, add the lemon juice and sweeten to taste with icing or caster sugar. Heat very gently until warmed, stirring to dissolve the sugar. Remove from the heat and reserve.
2   Dissolve the gelatine in 22 ml /1½ tbls hot water, then pour into the warm purée, stirring constantly. Turn into a jug and chill for 35–45 minutes until the jelly has thickened but not set.
3   Cut the melon in half lengthways. Scrape out and discard the seeds. With a spoon, scoop out some of the flesh to enlarge the centre cavities. Pour the jelly into the melon cavities. Chill in the refrigerator for about 1½–2 hours until set. To serve, cut each half lengthways into 2 or 3 slices.

Melon glacé

🔪🔪 30 minutes plus chilling time, then 2½–3 hours freezing

Serves 4
50 g /2 oz sugar
1 medium-sized melon (about 1 kg /2 lb 3 oz)
225 ml /8 fl oz unsweetened white grape juice
30 ml /2 tbls lemon juice

1   Turn the refrigerator to its lowest setting point and chill a large ice-cube tray (with dividers removed) or another shallow container 1 hour before you begin making the ice. Refrigerate the grape juice.
2   Combine the sugar and 125 ml /4 fl oz water in a small, heavy-based saucepan. Set over a low heat and stir until the sugar has dissolved. Bring to the boil, without stirring, and boil for 1 minute. Leave the syrup to cool, then chill.
3   Cut the melon in half; remove and discard the seeds and any membrane. Scoop out all the flesh, drain and purée in a blender.
4   Measure out 575 ml /1 pt of the melon purée and place in a mixing bowl. Stir in the chilled sugar syrup, grape juice and lemon juice. Turn the mixture into the chilled container and cover with foil.
5   Place in the freezing compartment of the refrigerator and leave for 1–1½ hours until mushy around the edges. With a fork or wooden spoon, stir the mixture well. Cover and freeze for a further 1½–2 hours, stirring every 30 minutes. The ice is ready to serve when it has reached an evenly granular slushy consistency.
6   To serve, work the ice lightly with a fork then spoon into individual bowls set on ice.

Sunset salad bowl

If you can, use a cantaloupe melon because of its orange-coloured flesh. Sherry or port could replace the liqueur.

⏳ 30 minutes
plus 1–2 hours chilling time

Serves 4–6
1 medium-sized melon, halved, seeded, skinned and cubed
225 g /8 oz prepared fresh pineapple, cubed
100 g /4 oz hulled strawberries or stoned cherries
1 large orange
15 ml /1 tbls caster sugar
30 ml /2 tbls orange-flavoured liqueur
pinch ground ginger

1 Combine the prepared fruit in a bowl. Next peel the orange, taking care to remove every bit of bitter white pith. Cut the orange into segments and remove the pips with the point of a knife. Cut each segment in half and add to the bowl. Reserve any orange juice.
2 Sprinkle the caster sugar over the fruit. Combine the liqueur, ground ginger and reserved orange juice and pour over the fruit. Stir gently to mix, taking care not to crush the fruit.
3 Cover the bowl and chill in the refrigerator for 1–2 hours, stirring occasionally. Just before serving, gently stir the salad to coat the fruit with the juices that have collected in the bowl.

Sweet pickled melon with cherries

Choose a firm-fleshed, slightly unripe melon weighing about 1.5 kg /3 lb before preparation.

 🍴 8 hours brining
then 1¼ hours plus 2 months

Makes 1.1 kg /2½ lb
700 g /1½ lb melon flesh, cut into cubes
22 ml /1½ tbls salt
150 ml /5 fl oz distilled (white) malt vinegar
7.5 ml /3 in stick cinnamon
15–30 ml /1–2 tbls whole mixed spice
10 ml /2 tsp coriander seeds
450 g /1 lb granulated sugar
450 g /1 lb fresh or well drained canned cherries, stoned

1 Dissolve the salt in 1.7 L /3 pt water and pour over the melon cubes in a large bowl. Place a plate on top to keep the fruit immersed. Leave for 8 hours or overnight, then drain well and rinse.
2 Place the vinegar, spices and sugar in a large stainless steel or enamelled pan. Pour in 400 ml /14 fl oz water. Bring slowly to the boil, stirring until the sugar is dissolved. Add the melon cubes and stoned cherries and stir well. Bring to simmering point, and simmer covered, for 30–40 minutes until

the melon is transparent and tender.
3 With an enamelled or stainless steel slotted spoon, lift out the melon and cherries and pack loosely into clean, warmed jars to within 5 mm /¼ in of the tops. Boil the vinegar syrup for 10 minutes until reduced and slightly thickened. Remove the cinnamon stick and pour the syrup into the jars. Discard any surplus syrup. Cover and seal the jars while still hot.
4 Leave the pickle to mature for 2 months in a cool, dry place. After opening keep in a cool place and use within 2 months.

Melon lime mousse

Ogen, honeydew, Galia or Levan melons are all suitable for this pale, delicately flavoured dessert, which can also be served in individual bowls.

⏳ 45 minutes
plus 2 hours setting

Serves 4–6
½ medium-sized, very ripe melon, about 700 g /1½ lb
1 large pinch ground ginger
grated zest and juice of 1 lime
30 ml /2 tbls natural yoghurt
2 large eggs, separated
50 g /2 oz caster sugar
15 g /½ oz gelatine
slices of kiwi fruit and/or lime to decorate

1 Remove and discard the seeds and seed membrane. Scoop out the melon flesh, drain, and reduce to a purée in a blender.
2 Turn the melon purée into a bowl. Add the ground ginger, grated lime zest and all but 5–10 ml /1–2 tsp of the juice and the natural yoghurt, stirring well. Set aside.
3 In a medium-sized mixing bowl whisk the egg yolks and the caster sugar together. Set the bowl over a pan of hot (but not boiling) water and whisk until the mixture is pale in colour and thick enough to retain the impression of the whisk for 3 seconds. Remove the bowl from the heat.
4 Pour the melon purée into the whisked egg mixture, stirring constantly with a wooden spoon to blend. Dissolve the gelatine in 30 ml /2 tbls hot water. Blend a little of the melon mixture with the dissolved gelatine, then pour the mixture back into the bowl, stirring constantly.
5 Lightly cover the bowl and leave in a cool place for 45–60 minutes until the mixture has thickened to a syrupy consistency but not set. In a clean, dry bowl, whisk the egg whites until stiff. With a spatula or large metal spoon, fold the whisked whites into the melon mixture.
6 Pour the mousse into a serving bowl, cover lightly and leave in a cool place for about 2 hours until set. Just before serving, decorate the mousse with slices of kiwi fruit and/or lime and sprinkle these with the remaining lime juice.

Melon lime mousse

Grapes

Add small seedless grapes to breakfast muesli or cook them with fish, poultry or game. Use large grapes to make decorative flans, or purée them in ices, sorbets and creams. And a cluster of two or three grapes is one of the most decorative ways to grace a cheeseboard, garnish a cool drink or a frosted cake – grapes can feature in every course of every meal throughout the day!

Grapes have an aura of elegance and luxury, evoking visions of Roman banqueting tables, silver bowls piled high with the green and black fruits and goblets of sweet wine, the fermented juice of the grape.

Grapes are small fruits which grow in bunches on a vine, and are thought to have been cultivated for at least 6,000 years. They are actually cultivated for four distinct uses: dessert grapes, the 'show pieces' of the family, larger and sweeter than the others, wine grapes, grapes for drying into raisins, currants and sultanas and grapes for processing into non-alcoholic, unfermented grape juice. Some varieties, however, are used for both wine-making and eating.

Grapes are sun-loving fruit and will not fully ripen in open ground without sun. All countries with warm, temperate climates grow grapes; the main producing areas of dessert grapes are Spain, South Africa, Australia and California, while wine grapes are more widely cultivated. Some excellent dessert grapes are produced in hot-houses. Dried fruits come from Greece (currants), Spain (raisins), the U.S. and Australia (raisins and sultanas) and Turkey and South Africa (sultanas).

Grapes consist of about 80% water but, because of their high sugar content, are high in calories. They contain some vitamin C and are rich in minerals.

Grape varieties

'White' grapes in reality vary from green to yellow, and 'black' ones range from deep, rose pink through purple to a velvety black. All the following dessert grapes are varieties of the species *Vitis vinifera*.

Muscat of Alexandria, with its pale amber, muscat-flavoured fruit, is a favourite. Chasselas de Fontainebleu has smaller, golden fruits and the Royal Madeleine, pearly white round fruits. These three white grape varieties are available in the early autumn. More and more of the tiny white seedless grapes, sultanina, are now exported from Greece and Cyprus.

Among the most succulent varieties of black grapes is the Gamay, which has round black fruits ready for eating in the summer. Later in Europe come Rose Chasselas with large, round, reddish pink fruits, and Black Alicante, with elliptical, purply-black fruits. Australia has the Purple Cornichon and the Waltham Cross. One of the best known of the hot-house-cultivated grapes is Black Hamburg, which has large, tender and very sweet fruits.

In Australia and America grapes of the species *Vitis labrusca* are grown; these have a distinct musky or 'foxy' flavour.

Buying grapes

There is no significant difference in flavour between black and white grapes – the flavour is variable according to the season. The skin of good-quality black grapes is usually more tender than white but a contrasting effect is achieved by a mixture of the two – black and white grapes alternating in a wheel pattern topping a flan, for example.

Grapes are a very delicate fruit and bruise easily. Handling should be kept to the minimum to avoid removing the delicate translucent film known as 'bloom'. The best grapes are transported with great care, each bunch carefully laid in crumpled paper. If you are in doubt about the freshness of the fruit, look closely at the grapes. The slightest trace of a ring of bruising around the stalk is a sign of loss of quality.

Health food shops, delicatessens and speciality food stores sell a number of grape products – grape jelly, which is a good accompaniment to poultry, game and pork; white and red grape juice, either still or sparkling, which are pleasant alternatives to wine for people who do not drink alcohol (as well as those who do); and grape juice 'drinks', which contain additives.

Storing grapes

The Romans stored their grapes in huge urns buried underground, or preserved them in jars of thin, clear honey, in new wine or in a pickling solution of brine and vinegar. In mid-18th century England they were preserved in brandy diluted with a little sugar syrup and served after dinner. More prosaically, the Victorians bought bunches of under-ripe fruit and stood the stalks in a jar of water on a cool shelf.

Nun's tart and Grape and wine sundaes

• For jelly, cook crushed grapes in a little water for 10 minutes, strain the juice through a jelly bag and add 200 g /8 oz of sugar to each 500 ml /1 pt of the juice – grapes are a low-pectin fruit and will not set with a high proportion of sugar.

You can store grapes, carefully laid on several layers of crumpled paper, in the refrigerator for up to five days.

✳✳✳✳ To freeze, strip the grapes from the stalks, remove the seeds (see below) and the skins if they are tough, pack them in rigid containers, cover them with a medium sugar syrup and the lids, allowing 25 mm /1 in headroom. Frozen grapes are not suitable for dessert or fruit salad, but are perfect for fruit pies and in sauces.

Preparing grapes

It's up to you whether or not you skin grapes for use in desserts or sauces. Taste one first and then consider whether the undoubtedly slow task is worth while.

To skin grapes, dip them in boiling water for a few seconds, then, using a silver or stainless steel knife, flip back the skin,

Decorating with grapes

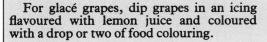

For glacé grapes, dip grapes in an icing flavoured with lemon juice and coloured with a drop or two of food colouring.

For frosted grapes, dip clusters of seedless grapes in lightly beaten egg white, shake off the excess, then dip in caster sugar and dry.

starting at the stalk end. The skin will usually come off in two pieces. Remember black grapes are green under their skins! To create contrast, you can dip some of the skinned grapes in a syrup coloured with a few drops of red or blue food colouring and put them on a wire rack to dry.

To seed grapes, cut a small slit in one side and flick out the seeds, using the eye of a sterilized needle or a fine skewer.

Cooking with grapes

Because of their sweet flavour, moistness and compact shape, grapes are used in a wide range of dishes, as an integral ingredient, as a topping or as a decorative finish.

In medieval times they were always added to the court bouillon in which fish was cooked, and now sole Véronique, in which the fish are served with a wine, cream and grape sauce, is a classic. Grapes have a special affinity with poultry and game, adding flavour to the blandness of chicken and turkey and cutting across the richness of pheasant and partridge. A simple breadcrumb, onion and herb stuffing for poultry is transformed with the addition of halved and seeded grapes, and a cold chicken, tarragon and watercress salad, with grapes folded into the creamy mayonnaise, makes a delicious summer buffet dish.

Grapes can be served as a single-ingredient salad in a lemony vinaigrette dressing, or in a mixed green salad tossed with endive, Chinese cabbage, chicory and watercress.

Grapes go well with cheese – use a combination of black and white grapes to garnish a cheeseboard, or use grapes to make a topping for a rich cooked or uncooked cheesecake or a savoury blue cheese mousse. For cocktail titbits, large grapes can be split, seeded and stuffed with one of several cheese mixtures: a blue cheese filling; a slightly spiced mixture of sieved cottage cheese, yoghurt and paprika; soft cream cheese mixed with finely chopped black olives, or freshly grated Parmesan

cheese folded into stiffly whipped cream.

In Roman times, tiny bunches of grapes were set in wine and lemon-flavoured jelly in fluted moulds – a pretty idea still. With a dash of kirsch or marsala, grapes make a delicious between-courses sorbet, or a cream or ice cream to give any meal a memorable ending.

For a green dessert salad, grapes blend beautifully with cubed melon, sliced kiwi fruit and quartered greengages, while unpeeled black grapes make a similarly striking combination with sliced black figs, watermelon cubes and blackberries.

Also for dessert, open tarts and flans show off grapes to the best decorative effect. In a classic French tart they are arranged in concentric circles or wedges, black and white alternately on a crème pâtissière filling, and in a French country tart they are concealed under a foamy custard.

Decorating with grapes

Grapes can be made into delightful petits fours to serve with coffee and after-dinner mints. Serve them in little sweet cases on your prettiest cake-stand or dish.

● To make frosted grapes, cut them into clusters of two or three, depending on size, and seed them. Dip the grapes in lightly beaten egg white, then shake off the excess. Dip in caster sugar, and spread them out to dry on greaseproof paper. Leave them for at least 2 hours in a warm, dry room – they will not dry properly in a humid atmosphere or a steamy kitchen.

● For glacé grapes with a shiny coating of sugar icing, dip the little bunches in an icing flavoured with a little lemon juice and stand them in sweet papers to dry.

● Make marzipan surprises by rolling out marzipan very thinly, cutting it into small circles and shaping each circle around a seeded black or white grape to enclose it completely. Or slit and seed the grapes and stuff them with a strip of marzipan coated in toasted and coarsely chopped almonds or hazelnuts.

Fennel, grape and orange salad

A crisp combination of vegetables and fruit, this salad is particularly good with cold chicken or duck.

⧗ 25 minutes,
then 1 hour standing

Serves 4
1 bunch watercress
2 fennel bulbs, thinly sliced
2 large oranges, peeled and segmented
10 cm /4 in length of cucumber, peeled and
*   thinly diced*
100 g /4 oz black grapes, seeded
60 ml /4 tbls sunflower oil
15 ml /1 tbls lemon juice
15 ml /1 tbls red wine vinegar
pinch of caster sugar
salt and freshly ground black pepper

1 Remove any yellow leaves from the watercress, wash thoroughly and divide into sprigs.
2 Mix together the sliced fennel, orange segments, diced cucumber and grapes. Reserve a few watercress sprigs for garnish and mix in the remainder.
3 Mix together the sunflower oil, lemon juice and vinegar and season with sugar, salt and pepper. Pour the dressing over the salad and cover. Let the salad stand at room temperature for about 1 hour.
4 Turn the salad into a serving dish, garnish with the reserved sprigs of watercress and serve.

Pigeons with grapes

This makes an impressive party dish yet it requires the minimum of last-minute attention.

⧗⧗ 2 hours 10 minutes

Serves 4
4 young pigeons, cleaned and dressed
100 g /4 oz butter
salt and freshly ground black pepper
8 thin slices of unsmoked streaky bacon
200 ml /7 fl oz chicken stock
450 g /1 lb seedless grapes
15 ml /1 tbls flour
150 ml /5 fl oz thick cream
30 ml /2 tbls brandy (optional)
croûtons to serve (optional)
watercress to garnish

1 Heat the oven to 180C /350F /gas 4. Rub the pigeons all over with butter and put a little into the cavity of each bird, using about 40 g /1½ oz in all. Season the birds inside and out with salt and freshly ground black pepper, wrap them in the bacon slices and tie with fine string.
2 Melt about 40 g /1½ oz of the butter in a flameproof casserole over a medium heat and fry the pigeons on all sides for about 15 minutes, until the bacon is almost crisp.

Pigeons with grapes and Fennel, grape and orange salad

3 Arrange the pigeons neatly, breast side up, in the casserole and pour on the stock. Season with salt and freshly ground black pepper and bring to the boil. Put the lid on the casserole and transfer it to the oven. Cook for 1 hour.
4 Add the grapes and cook for a further 15–30 minutes, or until the pigeons feel tender when pierced with a fine skewer.
5 Remove the pigeons from the casserole and discard the bacon. Arrange them on a warmed serving dish. Remove the grapes with a slotted spoon, arrange them around the pigeons and cover the dish with foil to keep warm.
6 Mix the remaining butter with the flour to make a beurre manié. Place the casserole over a moderate heat, add the beurre manié in small pieces and stir until the sauce thickens. Stir in the cream and, if you are using it, the brandy. Pour the sauce over the pigeons, scatter with the croûtons, if using, garnish with watercress and serve at once.

Veal chops with white grapes

Luscious white grapes make a sparkling and delicious garnish to a simple top-of-the-stove dish, which could be served with boiled white rice.

⧗ 40 minutes

Serves 4
4 veal chops, trimmed of excess fat
20 g /¾ oz butter
15 ml /1 tbls oil
1 small onion, finely chopped
1 garlic clove, crushed
150 ml /5 fl oz orange juice
grated zest of ½ orange
2.5 ml /½ tsp dried rosemary, crumbled
salt and freshly ground black pepper
225 g /8 oz white grapes, skinned and seeded
15 g /½ oz softened butter
5 ml /1 tsp flour

vertical cuts downwards to make spears. To make chunks, cut spears crossways.

The pineapple shell makes an exotic container for a salad, ice cream or water ice, or drink. It can be sliced in half lengthways through the crown and scooped out, or sliced across, scooped out and trimmed top and bottom, to make two cups.

To hollow the whole pineapple shell, cut off the top of the pineapple with a sharp knife. Insert the knife close to the shell and cut completely around the fruit with a sawing motion. Insert the blade of the knife into the base and wriggle it around so that you loosen the flesh from the shell without separating the base from the fruit. You should now be able to remove the cylinder of fruit. Fill the shell with a savoury or sweet salad and top with the crown.

● For pineapple surprise, hollow the pineapple, remove the core and cut into chunks. Toss the cubes in 30 ml /2 tbls Cointreau with 12 halved or whole strawberries, 12 grapes, deseeded, and 1 mandarin orange in segments or 1 banana, sliced. Chill 1 hour then pile back into the shell.

Cut out the 'eyes' from a peeled pineapple

To make a pineapple outrigger, divide the fruit lengthways into quarters, leaving the crown on. Using a grapefruit knife, loosen the flesh from the skin. Remove the fruit from the core and slice the flesh crossways into easy-to-manage pieces. Arrange the pineapple sections in the shell in a staggered pattern, to look like a boat with oars out.

Using fresh pineapple: the fresh fruit contains an enzyme called bromelin which is used commercially as a meat tenderizer. For this reason, fresh pineapple is excellent in meat and fish marinades, as it helps to make them more digestible. However, this enzyme also stops gelatine from setting, so if you want to use fresh (or frozen) pineapple or its juice in a dish containing gelatine, you must first boil the fruit juice for 2-3 minutes. This enzyme also reacts with milk products, so if you plan to combine the two, do so just before serving.

Fresh pineapple is delicious on its own, as a starter or dessert. It combines particularly well with fish and shellfish, pork and pork products, and is delicious with chicken and duck. Grilled pineapple chunks are excellent as one of the ingredients in kebabs. Nuts and pineapple are a good combination – the Chinese make a simple sweet dish consisting of gelatine cubes flavoured with almond essence, mixed with chunks of fresh pineapple. Fresh pineapple spears or chunks give a long cool drink or fruit salad the luxury touch.

Pineapple is delicious in jams, pickles (see recipe), chutneys and preserves.

Preserved pineapple

Buying preserved pineapple: canned pineapple is sold in rings, in chunks or crushed, in a heavy syrup or, unsweetened, in its own juice.

You can buy candied (glacé) pineapple, but it is much more economical to make your own using canned fruit.

Pineapple juice, which can only be extracted commercially, is sold as a liquid or concentrate, on its own or mixed with other fruit juices.

Pineapple essence adds the distinctive flavour of the fruit to drinks and desserts. The essence, as well as a concentrated pineapple syrup, is useful for making milk shakes and flavouring puddings.

Using preserved pineapple: pineapple in syrup is delicious in sweet-and-sour dishes, in cakes such as Pineapple upside-down cake (see recipe), in sauces for milk or sponge puddings and as a filling for cakes.

Unsweetened canned pineapple can be used in the same way as fresh, but it is less acid and therefore some people find it more palatable. It is also lower in calories than pineapple in syrup. Both types of crushed pineapple are good additions to brown breads, bran fruit loaves and buns.

Pineapple juice is delicious on its own or blended with milk and ice to make a pineapple frappé. It is an important ingredient in a variety of tropical long drinks and cocktails, such as the famous Piña colada as it blends so well with rum. It is also a favourite ingredient in hot and cold punches (see recipe).

The French produce a liqueur called *crème d'ananas*, and the Brazilians and West Indians make a mildly alcoholic drink by covering pineapple peelings with water and leaving the mixture to ferment.

Pineapple cheesecake

This is a cheesecake classic. Use a spring-release tin with a removable rim and bottom.

◁ 25 minutes preparation, 1 hour baking, then cooling

Serves 10-12
75 g /3 oz butter, melted
175 g /6 oz digestive biscuits, crushed
15 ml /1 tbls grated lemon zest
300 g /11 oz sugar
250 g /9 oz canned crushed pineapple in syrup, well drained
750 g /1 lb 11 oz curd cheese
5 ml /1 tsp salt
25 g /1 oz flour
45 ml /3 tbls lemon juice
100 ml /3½ fl oz thick cream
4 medium-sized eggs
extra crushed pineapple, to garnish (optional)

1 Heat the oven to 170C /325F /gas 3. To make the crust, stir the melted butter into the biscuit crumbs, then thoroughly mix in 5 ml /1 tsp grated lemon zest and 50 g /2 oz sugar. Use all but 60 ml /4 tbls of the mixture to line a 23 cm /9 in spring-release tin. Cover the crust with 250 g /9 oz crushed pineapple.
2 Sieve the curd cheese. Add the salt, flour, remaining lemon zest, lemon juice and thick cream and beat well.
3 Beat the eggs with the remaining sugar until the mixture is light and fluffy. Fold into the cheese mixture.
4 Pour the filling into the tin and sprinkle the top with the reserved crumb mixture.
5 Bake the cheesecake for 1 hour, then turn off the heat and let the cake stand in the oven for 1 hour. Transfer it to a wire rack and let it cool completely before removing the rim of the tin. Decorate with extra pineapple before serving, if wished.

Mexican pineapple custard meringues

In this dessert, the tart taste of the pineapple enlivens the bland custard. Without the almonds, it makes a perfect dessert for a children's party.

⚓⚓ 1 hour 35 minutes
plus cooling meringues and custard

Makes 8 meringues
For the meringues
2 medium-sized egg whites
100 g /4 oz caster sugar
pinch of salt
1.5 ml /¼ tsp cream of tartar
2.5 ml /½ tsp vanilla essence
For the pineapple custard
250 g /9 oz well-drained canned crushed pineapple
30 ml /2 tbls cornflour
250 ml /9 fl oz milk
4 medium-sized egg yolks, well beaten
60 ml /4 tbls sugar
2.5 ml /½ tsp pineapple essence
For the garnish
halved glacé cherries
toasted flaked almonds

1 Heat the oven to 110C /225F /gas ¼. Cover 2 baking sheets with greaseproof or silicone baking paper.
2 To make the meringues, whisk the egg whites stiffly. Whisk in the sugar, salt, cream of tartar and vanilla essence and continue whisking until the mixture is stiff and glossy.
3 Drop tablespoons of the mixture onto the paper-lined baking sheets to make 8 meringues. Use the back of the spoon to make an indentation in the centre of each, or put the meringue mixture into a piping bag and pipe 8 'nests' onto the paper.
4 Bake the meringues for 50–60 minutes or until set and dry but not coloured. Cool them on wire racks and, if making in advance, store in an airtight container until needed.
5 To make the custard, purée the crushed pineapple in a blender and reserve. Dissolve the cornflour in half the milk. Beat the rest of the milk with the egg yolks, cornflour mixture and sugar.
6 Pour the mixture into the top of a double boiler and stir constantly with a wooden spoon over simmering water until the mixture thickens enough to coat the back of the spoon, about 15 minutes.
7 Remove the pan from the heat and stir in the pineapple purée and essence. Cool the custard to room temperature before using it to fill the meringues, then decorate with halved glacé cherries and toasted flaked almonds. Serve with any extra custard handed separately.

● To make pineapple ninons, place the meringues on slices of fresh pineapple, and decorate with strawberries instead of the glacé cherries and almonds.

Pineapple upside-down cake

⚓⚓ 1 hour,
plus 10 minutes or more cooling

Serves 4-6
25 g /1 oz butter
100 g /4 oz soft light brown sugar
9 pineapple rings canned in syrup, well drained
5 maraschino cherries, halved
75 g /3 oz flour
7.5 ml /1½ tsp baking powder
pinch of salt
2 medium-sized eggs
100 g /4 oz sugar
15 ml /1 tbls pineapple syrup from can
angelica, to garnish (optional)
whipped cream, to serve (optional)

1 Heat the oven to 180C /350F /gas 4. Melt the butter in a heavy 23 cm /9 in square flameproof casserole over a low heat. Alternatively, melt the butter in a saucepan and pour into a 23 cm /9 in square cake tin.
2 Remove the pan from the heat, stir in the brown sugar and coat the inside of the pan evenly with the mixture. Arrange the pineapple rings in the pan, with the halved cherries in the centres of the rings, rounded sides down, and set aside.
3 Sift the flour with the baking powder and salt. Beat the eggs thoroughly until pale yellow and foamy. Gradually beat in the sugar. Beat in the flour mixture and, when well incorporated, beat in the pineapple syrup. Continue beating for a few more minutes until it is thoroughly blended.

4 Carefully pour the mixture over the pineapple rings. Bake the cake for 30 minutes or until a skewer inserted into the centre comes out clean. Remove the cake from the oven and let it stand on a wire rack for at least 10 minutes, so it will be easy to turn out.
5 Loosen the edges of the cake from the casserole or tin with a knife before turning it out, upside down, on to a serving dish. Garnish with angelica shapes, if you wish, and serve the cake warm or cold, with whipped cream if you like.

Brazilian pineapple punch

⚓ 25 minutes plus chilling

Serves 6
1 pineapple weighing 1 kg /2¼ lb
100 g /4 oz sugar
250 ml /9 fl oz dry white wine, chilled
250 ml /9 fl oz red port, chilled
24 strawberries (about 450 g /1 lb)

1 Slice off the top and bottom of the pineapple and remove the skin. Grate the flesh into a bowl, taking care to catch all the juice. Add 1 L /1¾ pt cold water and strain the mixture through cheesecloth, squeezing to extract all the juice. Discard the pulp.
2 Add the sugar, stirring to dissolve, and chill until ready to serve.
3 Just before serving, stir in the chilled white wine and port and garnish with the strawberries, whole or halved.

Sweet pineapple pickle

◔ 45 minutes

Makes about 1 kg /2 lb
1 large fresh pineapple, peeled and cubed
900 g /2 lb sugar
600 ml /1 pt white vinegar
2 cinnamon sticks
30 ml /2 tbls whole cloves

1 In a large saucepan, combine the sugar with 500 ml /18 fl oz water and the vinegar. Tie the cinnamon sticks and cloves in a piece of cheesecloth and add them to the pan. Bring to the boil.
2 Add the pineapple, return to the boil, cover the pan and simmer for 20 minutes, or until the pineapple is tender and translucent. Transfer the pineapple and liquid to sterile jars and seal them. Store in a cool, dark place for up to 1 year.

● This pickle should be left to mature for 4 to 6 weeks before eating.

Pineapple fish stew

This Vietnamese dish is a cross between a soup and a stew. If available, use Vietnamese nuoc-nam or Chinese oyster sauce instead of the soy sauce.

◔ 35 minutes

Serves 4-6
60 ml /4 tbls oil
250 g /9 oz white fish, skinned, boned and cut into bite-sized pieces
2 spring onions, chopped
2 garlic cloves, chopped
250 g /9 oz boiled peeled prawns
5 ml /1 tsp salt
1.5 ml /1/4 tsp freshly ground black pepper
1.5 ml /1/4 tsp aniseed
1.5 ml /1/4 tsp turmeric
1 bay leaf
10 ml /2 tsp grated orange zest
1.5–2.5 ml /1/4–1/2 tsp cayenne pepper
30 ml /2 tbls cornflour
45 ml /3 tbls dry sherry
30 ml /2 tbls soy sauce
250 g /9 oz fresh or drained canned unsweetened pineapple, chopped or crushed.
boiled rice, to serve .

1 Heat the oil in a large deep pan or a wok over a medium heat. Add the pieces of fish, chopped spring onions and garlic and sauté for 2 minutes, stirring constantly. Add the prawns, salt, freshly ground black pepper, aniseed, turmeric, bay leaf, orange zest and cayenne pepper. Turn the heat up to high, add 600 ml /1 pt water and bring to the boil.
2 Dissolve the cornflour in the sherry and soy sauce. Add this to the pan and stir until the liquid thickens, about 2 minutes. Stir in the pineapple and heat through. Serve immediately, with plain boiled rice.

Chicken and pineapple

The Chinese cultivated pineapple as early as 1640. In fact, Oliver Cromwell was presented with pineapples produced from plants brought from China by the East India Company.

◔◔ 1¾ hours

Serves 4-6
1.5 kg /3½ lb chicken, jointed
1 medium-sized onion, sliced
salt and freshly ground black pepper
45 ml /3 tbls oil
100 g /4 oz Chinese or white cabbage, shredded
2 stalks celery, diced
100 g /4 oz Brazil or cashew nuts, chopped
30 ml /2 tbls soy sauce
5 ml /1 tsp sugar
250 g /9 oz fresh or drained canned unsweetened pineapple chunks
Chinese egg noodles or boiled rice, to serve

1 Put the chicken pieces into a deep saucepan and add 600 ml /1 pt water, the sliced onion, and salt and freshly ground black pepper to taste. Bring the water to the boil, cover the pan and simmer for 1 hour or until the chicken is tender. Remove the pieces of chicken and strain and reserve 275 ml /½ pt of the cooking liquid.
2 When it is cool enough to handle, skin and bone the chicken and cut the meat into bite-sized pieces.
3 Heat the oil in a large saucepan or a wok. Add the shredded cabbage, diced celery, and pieces of chicken. Sauté, stirring constantly, for 5 minutes. Then stir in the nuts, soy sauce, sugar and the reserved chicken cooking liquid. Cook, stirring, until the liquid boils.
4 Add the pineapple, bring the liquid back to the boil and cook for another 3 minutes. Serve with plain boiled rice or Chinese egg noodles.

● If you substitute pineapple in syrup for the unsweetened pineapple, omit the sugar.

Chicken and pineapple

Rhubarb

Sharp and tangy to taste, rhubarb is most familiar as a dessert, but the pink and juicy stems can be turned into delicious sauces to accompany savoury dishes and, chilled, rhubarb makes an unusual fruit soup.

Rhubarb, although native to Asia, has become associated with English cookery. It was first cultivated for medicinal use – the root has a purgative property – and later as an ornamental plant. It came to Europe in the 14th century but became popular 500 years later.

Although it is classed as a vegetable, the tall slender stems are cooked and eaten as fruit. It is used in fruit stews, sauces, as pie fillings and to make jams and chutneys. Chilled or hot, it makes a delicious soup and can be used to make rhubarb wine. Never eat the leaves: they contain a large amount of oxalic acid and are very poisonous.

Early rhubarb comes into season in mid-winter in the northern hemisphere. This is forced rhubarb, grown under cover to precipitate growth. The slender, ice-pink stalks of forced rhubarb are very tender and have a slightly tart, refreshing flavour. Unforced rhubarb is ready some months later. The stalks are dark red, usually tinged with green; they have a stronger flavour and are more juicy than the early varieties. As rhubarb matures it becomes progressively more acid and needs more sweetening.

Treat quantities of sugar in recipes therefore, as a guide, and vary the amount according to your taste. If you like, you can blanch mature rhubarb in boiling water before cooking to reduce its acidity.

Picking, buying and storing rhubarb

If you grow rhubarb pick the ripe stalks as you require them: pull them gently from the crowns with your hand, never cut them off with a knife. If you are buying them, look always for firm, fresh-coloured, undamaged stalks.

To store: wrap cleaned, dry stalks loosely in polythene and keep at the bottom of the refrigerator for up to 1 week. Traditional methods of long term preservation (or dealing with a glut) include bottling and making rhubarb into chutney or jam.

✳✳✳ Cut cleaned, trimmed stalks into 25 mm /1 in lengths; pack in rigid plastic containers with or without sugar or in a heavy sugar syrup. Freeze and store for up to 12 months. Frozen rhubarb should be completely defrosted and drained before using or the recipe may be excessively watery. Stewed and/or puréed rhubarb can also be frozen for up to 6 months.

Preparing rhubarb

Because it is so acid, rhubarb is always eaten cooked, never raw. Cut off the the crinkly yellow leaves and trim the base. Simply wipe forced stalks clean with a damp cloth but wash unforced garden rhubarb. Mature stalks have tough skin and can be peeled with a sharp knife, but this results in a loss of colour. Slice prepared stalks into 2.5–5 cm /1–2 in lengths for cooking.

Cooking rhubarb

To stew: use a heavy-based aluminium or enamel-lined pan. Place the sliced rhubarb in the pan and add a large spoonful of water or orange juice, or a lump of butter for each 500 g /1 lb rhubarb to prevent sticking and burning. Add the sugar and any flavourings. Cook, covered, over a low heat, shaking the pan occasionally until the rhubarb is tender but not disintegrating – about 10 minutes for forced rhubarb, 20–30 minutes for mature stalks. Avoid overcooking or the rhubarb will be mushy and lose colour.

Rhubarb and banana pie

To poach: make a syrup with 75 g /3 oz sugar and 275 ml /10 fl oz water for each 500 g /1 lb rhubarb. Pour syrup over rhubarb in an ovenproof dish and add flavourings; cover and cook in the oven at 180C /350F /gas 4 for 20–25 minutes until tender.

To purée: turn cooked rhubarb into a nylon sieve and allow any liquid to drain off so that the purée is not watery. Early season, tender rhubarb can be mashed to a pulp with a wooden spoon; otherwise, press the rhubarb through the sieve into a clean bowl or use an electric blender.

Using rhubarb

Rhubarb mixes well with other fruit, particularly oranges, bananas, gooseberries, apples and pineapple, and with dried fruit such as raisins and dates. It has a special affinity with orange and lemon, ginger, cinnamon and nutmeg. For a special muscat flavour, add a few heads of elderflowers tied in muslin when cooking rhubarb.

Some of the best traditional English puddings – crumbles, sweet pies and charlottes for instance are made with rhubarb. It is also used to make a delicious iced soup.

Stewed or poached rhubarb can be served hot or cold, with pouring cream, egg custard or thick natural yoghurt. Chilled, stewed rhubarb is especially nice, thickly dusted with ground cinnamon and served with shortbread or almond biscuits. For Spring pudding fill a bread-lined bowl with stewed rhubarb instead of the usual soft summer fruit.

Make a delicious compote by adding carefully peeled segments of orange, or drained, canned mandarin oranges to cold, poached rhubarb. Puréed rhubarb can be combined with thick cream to make a very pretty fruit fool. Layer it with crushed ginger biscuits to make a quick pudding for the family. It can also be used to flavour a sweet soufflé. As a change from the usual gooseberry sauce, try serving hot puréed rhubarb with mackerel.

Iced rhubarb soup

Chilled fruit soups are often served in Scandinavian countries as a refreshing first or last course. Use soured cream if the soup is a starter and thick cream if it is a dessert. Served hot, without cream, it is still delicious. Slices of lightly toasted milk bread are a good accompaniment.

 30–40 minutes, plus cooling and chilling

Serves 4
450 g /1 lb rhubarb, trimmed and cut into 5 cm /2 in lengths
100 g /4 oz sugar
grated zest of 1 lemon
1 cinnamon stick
30 ml /2 tbls cornflour
400 ml /15 fl oz medium-dry white wine (such as Riesling)
lemon juice (optional)
a few drops pink food colouring (optional)
90 ml /6 tbls chilled soured or thick cream
ground cinnamon, to garnish

1 Place the rhubarb, sugar, lemon zest and cinnamon in a large heavy-based saucepan with 575 ml /1 pt water. Bring to the boil slowly, then reduce the heat and simmer gently until the rhubarb is very tender and is beginning to disintegrate.
2 Blend the cornflour to a smooth paste with a little of the wine, then blend in the remaining wine. Pour the mixture into the rhubarb, stirring constantly. Bring the soup to the boil gently and cook, stirring for about 5 minutes.
3 Remove the pan from the heat and allow to cool slightly. Remove the cinnamon stick. Reduce the contents of the pan to a smooth purée in batches in an electric blender. Pour the soup into a bowl and leave to cool, stirring occasionally. Chill in refrigerator for 8 hours or overnight.
4 Taste and add a little lemon and/or more sugar as necessary. Stir in a few drops of colouring, if you wish.
5 Just before serving, blend 30 ml /2 tbls of cream with a little of the soup. Gradually blend in the remaining soup. Pour soup into 4 chilled glass serving dishes, and top each portion with 15 ml /1 tbls cream. Decorate each with ground cinnamon and serve.

Rhubarb and banana pie

Two simple, easy-to-get ingredients are combined here to make an unusual pie.

1 hour

Serves 4
shortcrust pastry, made with 100 g /4 oz flour
450 g /1 lb rhubarb, trimmed and cut into 4 cm /1½ in lengths
50–75 g /2–3 oz Demerara sugar
1 large banana
lemon juice
5 ml /1 tsp ground mixed spice
1 medium-sized egg white, lightly beaten
caster sugar
cream or custard, to serve

1 Select an ovenproof pie dish, about 700 ml /1¼ pt capacity. On a lightly floured surface, roll out the pastry about 25 mm /1 in larger all round than the pie dish rim. Using the inverted pie dish as your guide, cut out a pastry lid. From the remaining pastry, cut a strip the same width as the rim of the dish.
2 Brush the rim of the dish lightly with water. Place the pastry strip on the rim and press down lightly. Gather up the pastry trimmings and use to make decorations (see picture). Reserve the pastry decorations with the lid in the refrigerator until required.
3 Heat the oven to 200C /400F /gas 6.
4 Place half the rhubarb in the dish and sprinkle with Demerara sugar. Peel and thinly slice the banana. Toss the slices in lemon juice, then spread over the rhubarb in the dish. Add the mixed spice and pile the remaining rhubarb on top, heaping it at the centre of the dish.

5 Brush the pastry lightly with egg white. Lay the pastry lid on top of the dish; seal, trim and crimp the edges. Brush the undersides of the pastry decorations with the egg white and use to decorate the pie.
6 Brush the pastry crust with egg white and dust with caster sugar. Prick the pie with the prongs of a fork. Bake the pie for about 30 minutes or until the pastry is golden and the rhubarb is tender. Dredge with more caster sugar. Serve hot, warm or cold, with cream or custard.

Rhubarb almond crumble

Serve this delicious old-fashioned pudding with cream or custard. For a traditional crumble, omit the almonds and increase the flour to 175 g /6 oz.

about 1 hour

Serves 4–6
700 g /1½ lb rhubarb, trimmed and cut into 4 cm /1½ in lengths
5 ml /1 tsp grated orange zest
100 g /4 oz sugar
For the crumble topping
100 g /4 oz flour
pinch of salt
50 g /2 oz ground almonds
75 g /3 oz butter, diced small
50 g /2 oz sugar

1 Heat the oven to 190C /375F /gas 5. Combine the rhubarb and orange zest with sugar to taste in a large bowl and reserve.
2 Make the topping. Sift the flour and salt into a mixing bowl and stir in the ground almonds. Add the butter and cut it into the dry ingredients with a palette knife, then lightly rub it in with your fingertips until the mixture resembles fine breadcrumbs. Stir in the sugar.
3 Add 30–45 ml /2–3 tbls of the crumble mixture to the rhubarb and mix well. Then turn the rhubarb into a generously buttered 1 L /2 pt ovenproof dish and level the surface. Sprinkle the remaining crumble mixture over the top.
4 Bake for 30–40 minutes until the topping is golden brown and the rhubarb is tender. Serve hot, warm and cold.

● For a more orange-flavoured version, add the peeled, halved segments of the orange to the fruit in the dish.

Rhubarb amber

A crisp pastry case filled with smooth rhubarb purée and topped with marshmallow meringues makes a lovely dessert or tea-time treat. The pastry case and rhubarb filling can be prepared and stored (separately) a few days ahead. If you want to serve this dessert cold, bake the meringue topping at 150C /300F /gas 2 for 20–30 minutes so it is firmer and dryer, then leave until cold.

chill in the refrigerator for 10 minutes.

4 Line the pastry case with foil and dried beans and bake blind for 10 minutes; remove the foil and beans and return the pastry case to the oven for 5 minutes more. Remove from the oven.

5 Reduce the oven temperature to 180C /350F /gas 4. Make the rhubarb filling: combine the rhubarb purée, lemon zest, melted butter and egg yolks and beat with a wooden spoon until smoothly blended. Pour the filling into the pastry case and bake for 15 minutes until just set.

6 Place the egg whites in a clean dry bowl, add the salt and whisk until stiff. Whisk in half the caster sugar; reserve 5 ml /1 tsp sugar, then fold in the remainder.

7 Pile the meringue over the filling, taking it right to the edges and making sure it meets the pastry rim. Sprinkle over the reserved 5 ml /1 tsp caster sugar. Bake for a further 10 minutes until the meringue is lightly browned. Serve warm.

Rhubarb fool

This classic English dessert will keep for 1–2 days in an airtight container in the refrigerator. You may like to improve the colour of the fool by adding a few drops of red food colouring.

🍴 20 minutes (plus chilling)

Serves 4
700 g /1¹/₂ lb rhubarb, trimmed and cut into
*   25 mm /1 in lengths*
175 g /6 oz soft dark brown sugar
grated zest of 1 orange
15 g /¹/₂ oz butter
10–15 ml /2–3 tsp orange-flavoured liqueur
*   (optional)*
150 ml /5 fl oz thick cream

1 Place the rhubarb, brown sugar to taste, orange zest and butter in a large, heavy-based saucepan and mix well. Set over medium heat and bring to simmering point. Cover the pan, reduce the heat and cook the rhubarb until tender.

2 Turn the contents of the pan into a nylon sieve and allow the liquid to drain away (reserve for another use). Purée the rhubarb in an electric blender or press through the sieve into a clean bowl. Leave the purée to cool completely.

3 Stir the liqueur (if used) into the cold purée. Add more sugar if necessary, but keep the rhubarb slightly sharp and remember that the addition of cream and the chilling will slightly soften the flavour.

4 Whisk the cream until it stands in soft peaks. Using a spatula or large metal spoon, lightly fold the cream through the purée, keeping the marbled effect.

5 Turn the rhubarb fool into a china serving bowl or into 4 long stemmed glasses. Chill for at least 1 hour before serving.

● Thick yoghurt may be substituted for the cream.
● For a different flavour replace the orange liqueur with Pernod.

🍴🍴🍴 65 minutes, including chilling the pastry case, then 30 minutes

Serves 4–6
175 g /6 oz flour
pinch of salt
7.5 ml /1¹/₂ tsp caster sugar
115 g /4¹/₂ oz butter
1 medium-sized egg yolk
2.5 ml /¹/₂ tsp iced water
For the filling and topping
450 g /1 lb rhubarb, stewed with sugar,
*   drained and puréed*
5 ml /1 tsp grated lemon zest
25 g /1 oz butter, melted
2 medium sized eggs, separated
pinch of salt
50 g /2 oz caster sugar

1 Make the pastry: sieve the flour and salt into a large mixing bowl and stir in the

Rhubarb amber, in the foreground, and Rhubarb fool in the individual dishes

sugar. Using a chilled palette knife, or a pastry cutter, cut the butter into the flour until the mixture resembles fine breadcrumbs. Make a well in the centre.

2 Beat together the egg yolk and water and pour into the well. With the palette knife, draw the dry ingredients into the egg. With your fingertips, gather the mixture together to make a soft dough. Turn onto a lightly-floured surface and knead briefly until smooth. Wrap in cling film and leave in the refrigerator to rest for 30 minutes.

3 Heat the oven to 200C /400F /gas 6. Allow the dough to soften for a few minutes at room temperature. Use the dough to line a 20 cm /8 in diameter fluted flan tin, gently pressing it over the base and up the sides. Trim the edges of the pastry and leave to

Rhubarb and orange chutney

End of season rhubarb that is too tough for stewing can easily be turned into a deliciously spicy chutney which you can enjoy later on in the year. Do not peel the rhubarb stalks as the skin gives the chutney colour.

 30 minutes, then 1½ hours cooking

Makes about 1.4 kg /3 lb
2 oranges
700 g /1½ lb rhubarb, trimmed and cut into 25 mm /1 in lengths
2 medium-sized onions, chopped
225 g /8 oz seedless raisins
425 ml /15 fl oz malt vinegar
450 g /1 lb Demerara sugar
8 black mustard seeds
4 white peppercorns
8 coriander seeds
1 large pinch ground allspice

1 Wash and dry the oranges. Thinly peel the zest from the oranges, with a potato peeler. Shred the zest finely and reserve. Squeeze and reserve the juice.
2 Put the rhubarb in a heavy-based pan with the orange zest, juice, chopped onions, raisins, vinegar and sugar. Tie the whole spices in muslin and add to the pan with the allspice.
3 Bring the mixture slowly to the boil, stirring frequently. Reduce the heat and simmer, stirring occasionally, for about 1½ hours until the mixture is thick and pulpy.
4 Remove the chutney from the heat; remove and discard the bag of spices. Ladle the chutney into clean warmed jars to within 15 mm /½ in of the tops. Cover, seal and label the jars. Store in a cool, dry place for 3 months before using.

Rhubarb and crystallized ginger preserve

Blend rhubarb – usually plentiful and cheap in season – with a more expensive ingredient, such as crystallized ginger, to make a really luscious preserve.

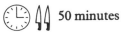 50 minutes

Makes about 2 kg /4½ lb
1.1 kg /2½ lb rhubarb, trimmed and cut into 25 mm /1 in lengths
1.1 kg /2½ lb sugar
grated zest and juice of 2 lemons
4 cm /1½ in piece fresh root ginger, bruised and tied in muslin
50 g /2 oz crystallized or drained preserved ginger, chopped

1 In a large bowl, layer the rhubarb with the sugar, lemon zest and lemon juice.

Cover and leave to stand overnight.
2 Turn the contents of the bowl into a preserving pan and add the root ginger. Clip a sugar thermometer to the pan if you own one. Bring the mixture to the boil and boil briskly for 15 minutes.
3 Remove and discard the root ginger. Stir in the chopped crystallized or preserved ginger. Boil for a further 5 minutes or until the thermometer registers 108–109C /220–222F. To test for set without a thermometer put a small spoonful of the jam on a chilled saucer. Let it stand for 30 seconds, then push the surface with your finger: it should be firm enough to crinkle.
4 Remove the jam from the heat as soon as setting point is reached. Skim off any scum from the surface with a slotted spoon. Pour the jam into clean, warmed jars and cover with a disc of waxed paper.
5 Wipe the rim and outsides of the jars clean with a damp cloth. If using metal screw-top lids, put these on while the jam is still hot. Otherwise, leave the jam until cold, then cover with cellophane and secure with rubber bands.

● For rhubarb and orange preserve, omit the root and crystallized ginger. Add the grated orange zest with the lemon zest. Peel the orange, divide into segments and halve these. Boil them for the last five minutes.

Rhubarb combines well with citrus fruit and spices to make a variety of delicious jams and preserves

Bananas

Bananas are one of the most popular fruits – readily available all the year round, very nutritious and easily prepared. Bananas make an attractive addition to a fruit bowl, and can also form the basis of many delicious dishes, savoury and sweet: curries, salads, moist cakes and creamy desserts.

Bananas originated in Asia – there is even an Indian legend that the 'forbidden fruit' was a banana. Arab traders brought them to Africa, and the Portuguese introduced them to the West Indies although they remained a rarity in Europe until the 19th century. Today, bananas are grown in all parts of the tropics, where they are often a staple element of the diet and a vital export: the main producers are the West Indies, Central and South America, West Africa and the Canary Islands.

Available all year round, bananas are one of the most nutritious fruit, being rich in Vitamins A, B and C.

Cooking bananas, or plantains, are larger than dessert bananas, weighing on average at least 350 g /12 oz, and have a lower sugar content. Their flesh is very firm and they are always eaten cooked, never raw; their flavour is rather like that of parsnips. Plantains feature widely in West Indian and African cooking and in these countries the large banana leaf is also often used as a flavoursome wrapping in which to boil or steam food.

Buying and storing bananas

Dessert bananas can be bought according to requirements at various stages of ripeness, from quite green to blackish-yellow. In general, avoid any with large black spots, as these are a sign of decay. The Canary Island banana is smaller, sweeter and more curved than the West Indian type. The smaller varieties are not really sweet until the skin shows some brown speckles, but the larger ones should be a uniform gold colour.

If you buy a bunch of bananas, do not break them up, as they keep better in the bunch than singly. Leave bananas to ripen gradually at room temperature, do not store them in the refrigerator, where they will deteriorate.

Plantains are most readily available in cities with large West Indian communities, where the local greengrocers and market stalls usually stock them. Like dessert bananas, they are sold at all stages of ripeness, but usually singly rather than in a bunch.

✳✳✳✳ Bananas are not recommended for freezing whole as they will discolour and turn to pulp as soon as they thaw. They can be frozen mashed with a little lemon juice, but there is still a tendency for them to develop an over-ripe flavour.

Dried bananas are available from health food shops. They are delicious and extremely nutritious. Eat them just as they are, use them in baking or chop them into muesli mixtures.

Banana liqueur, which is very sweet, can be mixed with other spirits or with fresh lime or orange juice to make cocktails.

Using bananas in cooking

To prepare bananas, peel, remove strings and cut away any blemishes. The skin of green plantains does not peel off easily and has to be carefully removed by slitting with a sharp knife. As bananas discolour very easily, peel them just before using; the addition of lemon juice to both sliced and puréed bananas helps keep them white.

Sweet ways: bananas are most commonly used in a variety of easily prepared desserts. They are delicious with cream, ice cream and home-made custard, and their slightly bland but distinctive flavour blends particularly well with orange, chocolate, coffee, ginger and rum. Add firm banana slices to a fruit salad shortly before serving, or set them in a clear green or yellow jelly to make banana chartreuse. Split a banana lengthways, add some fresh summer fruit and vanilla ice cream and top with chocolate sauce and nuts for a banana split; for a banana coupe, add ice cream, strawberry jam and a swirl of whipped cream.

For a delicious hot sweet, bake bananas with honey, or fry them with sugar and cinnamon. Fried banana slices make a delicious pancake filling. For a barbecue, slit bananas lengthways with the peel still on, insert a thin bar of milk chocolate, close and bake: children will love scooping out the delicious banana and chocolate mixture.

Coarsely mashed bananas make a popular sandwich filling (a little yeast extract combines well with this). Puréed bananas are used in cake and bread mixtures, giving deliciously moist results, and as the basis of soufflés and ice cream. Banana purée added to a carton of natural yoghurt makes a very quick and nutritious dessert. For a banana milk shake, blend together bananas, milk, vanilla essence, egg and ice cream.

Savoury ways: bananas can be used raw in a variety of salads and hot dishes. They combine well with walnuts, watercress and mayonnaise, or with cottage cheese, lettuce leaves and lemon juice. Serve chilled, sliced bananas with plenty of lemon juice as a refreshing side dish with curries.

Banana fritters are a classic accompaniment to fried chicken, and are also delicious with fried trout or sole. For a change, try fried banana with bacon and eggs. A piece of fried bacon wrapped round a slice of fried banana makes an unusual cocktail savoury.

Plantains can be used in cooking at different stages of ripeness. When green and hard they are boiled in salted water just like potatoes. They can also be sliced very thinly and fried to make a type of crisp. Semi-ripe plantains are fried and mashed with pork crackling and garlic to make a savoury spread. Ripe plantains combine well with spices: they can be curried, filled with a savoury stuffing, or deep-fried.

Chicken Maryland

┦┦ 1 hour

Serves 4
1.4 kg /3 lb chicken, jointed into 4 pieces
30–45 ml /2–3 tbls flour, seasoned with salt, freshly ground black pepper, 1.5 ml /¹/4 tsp cayenne and 2.5 ml /¹/2 tsp mustard powder
2 medium-sized eggs, beaten
60–90 ml /4–6 tbls fine dried breadcrumbs
4 medium-sized bananas
100 g /4 oz butter
lettuce leaves, to garnish
For the sweetcorn fritters
225 g /8 oz frozen corn kernels, thawed, or 350 g /12 oz canned sweetcorn, drained
100 g /4 oz flour
5 ml /1 tsp salt
1 medium-sized egg
100 ml /3¹/2 fl oz milk combined with 25 ml /1 fl oz water

1 Remove the skin from the chicken pieces. Dip each piece first into the seasoned flour, then into the beaten egg and finally in the breadcrumbs to coat. (It is necessary to

press hard to make the breadcrumbs stick.) Refrigerate the coated chicken pieces.

2 Prepare the sweetcorn fritter batter. Sift the flour and salt into a bowl. Make a well in the centre and add the egg and half the milk mixture. Stir until smooth and thick, then beat in the remaining milk. Stir in the sweetcorn. Set aside.

3 Heat 75 g /3 oz butter in a large frying-pan over a high heat until sizzling, and fry the chicken for about 2½ minutes on each side. Reduce the heat and gently fry the chicken for about 10 minutes on each side, or until the meat is tender and the juices run clear when the thickest part is pierced with a skewer. Keep the fried chicken warm.

4 Halve the bananas lengthways, then cut each half in two crossways. Heat the remaining butter in the pan and fry the bananas until lightly browned. Remove from the pan with a slotted spoon and keep warm with the chicken.

5 Drop 15 ml /1 tbls sweetcorn batter at a time into the hot butter in the pan and fry until firm and golden, turning once.

6 Serve the chicken surrounded by the fried bananas and sweetcorn fritters, garnished with lettuce leaves.

Spicy pork with baked plantains

This is a simplified version of a Puerto Rican dish. Serve with boiled red kidney beans and rice.

 50 minutes

Serves 4
2 large ripe plantains
45 ml /3 tbls vegetable oil
500 g /1 lb lean minced pork
1 medium-sized onion, finely chopped
1 green pepper, seeded and finely chopped
5 ml /1 tsp finely chopped fresh chilli
1 garlic clove, chopped
15 ml /1 tbls flour
4 small tomatoes, blanched, skinned, seeded and chopped
salt and freshly ground black pepper
10 ml /2 tsp capers, chopped
2.5 ml /1½ tsp dried sage
2 medium-sized eggs, beaten
butter and oil for greasing
watercress sprigs, to garnish

1 Heat the oven to 180C /350F /gas 4. Lightly butter a shallow ovenproof dish.

2 Peel the plantains and cut each one lengthways into 4 strips. Then cut each strip in half crossways.

3 Heat the oil in a large frying-pan and fry the plantains until golden brown. Drain on absorbent paper.

4 Add the minced pork to the pan and fry gently until lightly coloured, breaking up any lumps that form.

5 Add the onion, green pepper, chilli and garlic to the meat in the pan and fry until soft. Stir in the flour and cook for about 3 minutes until well blended.

6 Add the chopped tomatoes and season with salt and pepper. Simmer until the mixture is thick, then stir in the capers and sage.

7 Remove the pan from the heat and mix the beaten eggs in thoroughly.

8 Pour the meat mixture into the prepared dish and arrange the plantain pieces on top. Lightly brush the plantains with oil.

9 Bake for 20 minutes. Serve garnished with watercress, with boiled red kidney beans and rice handed separately.

Chicken Maryland

Banana-orange flan

 1 hour

Serves 4–6
shortcrust pastry made with 225 g /8 oz flour
For the orange cream filling
2 large egg yolks
50 g /2 oz caster sugar
25 g /1 oz flour
juice and grated zest of 1 large orange
275 ml /10 fl oz milk
2.5 ml /1/2 tsp vanilla essence
5 ml /1 tsp orange liqueur (optional)
For the topping and glaze
2 medium-sized bananas
15 ml /1 tbls orange juice
45 ml /3 tbls apricot jam
juice of 1/2 small lemon

1 Heat the oven to 200C /400F /gas 6.
2 Roll out the pastry and with it line a 20 cm /8 in flan case. Line the pastry case with foil, fill with beans and bake blind for 10 minutes. Remove from the oven and lift out the foil and beans. Reduce the oven heat to 180C /350F /gas 4 and bake the pastry case for a further 15 minutes. Leave on one side until cool.
3 Make the orange cream filling. Cream the egg yolks and caster sugar with a wooden spoon until light, then beat in the flour. Add the juice and zest of the orange to the milk and bring to the boil in a saucepan. Strain into the egg mixture and beat well. Return the mixture to the rinsed-out pan and heat gently, stirring, until smooth and thick. When it comes to the boil, remove from the heat. Stir in the vanilla essence and orange liqueur if using.
4 Pour the cream filling into the baked flan case and leave until cool.

Banana party cake

5 Slice the bananas thinly, dip them in the orange juice and arrange in concentric circles all over the top of the flan.
6 Bring the apricot jam and lemon juice to the boil and simmer for 5 minutes, then strain. Brush the apricot glaze evenly over the orange cream filling. Let stand until quite cold, then serve.

Banana party cake

 1 hour 25 minutes plus cooling

Makes 8 slices
3 large bananas
about 30 ml /2 tbls milk
2 large eggs
100 g /4 oz softened butter, in small pieces
100 g /4 oz sugar
225 g /8 oz flour
20 ml /4 tsp cocoa powder
2.5 ml /1/2 tsp bicarbonate of soda
2.5 ml /1/2 tsp baking powder
5 ml /1 tsp ground ginger
1.5 ml /1/4 tsp salt
100 g /4 oz sultanas
butter for greasing
For the vanilla buttercream
100 g /4 oz unsalted butter
175 g /6 oz icing sugar, sifted
2.5 ml /1/2 tsp vanilla essence
For the topping
1 medium-sized banana
15 ml /1 tbls lemon juice

1 Heat the oven to 180C /350F /gas 4. Grease a 20 cm /8 in cake tin and line it with greased greaseproof paper.
2 Chop the bananas roughly and purée in the blender with the milk, adding more

milk if necessary to make the quantity up to 275 ml /10 fl oz.
3 Add the eggs, butter and sugar. Blend until smooth.
4 Sift the flour, cocoa, soda, baking powder, ginger and salt together into a large mixing bowl and stir in the sultanas.
5 Gradually add the banana mixture from the blender to the dry ingredients. Stir well.
6 Pour the mixture into the prepared tin and bake for about 1 hour 10 minutes, or until a skewer inserted into the centre comes out clean. Remove from the oven, cool slightly and turn on to a wire rack to cool completely.
7 Beat together the butter, icing sugar and vanilla essence until smooth and fluffy. Spread the buttercream over the top of the cold cake.
8 Just before serving, slice the banana and dip each piece in lemon juice. Decorate the top of the cake with the banana slices.

Brazilian bananas

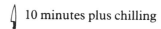 10 minutes plus chilling

Serves 4
225 ml /8 fl oz thick cream
30 ml /2 tbls strong black coffee
15 ml /1 tbls dark rum
4 large bananas, thinly sliced
juice of 1/2 small lemon
15 ml /1 tbls soft brown sugar
15 ml /1 tbls sultanas

1 Whip the cream with the coffee and rum until thick. Arrange the bananas in a shallow dish. Pour over the lemon juice.
2 Sprinkle the sugar and sultanas over the bananas. Spread the coffee, rum and cream mixture on top and chill thoroughly.

Apples

Apples are our most popular and versatile fruit. They can be baked, stewed or poached, puréed or fried, and cooked in pastry dishes, cake mixtures and pancake batter. Apples give a tangy flavour to vegetable casseroles and poultry and meat dishes. They are often used to bulk out fruit and vegetable preserves, but make delicious jams and jellies in their own right. They are also delicious eaten raw with cheese, or chopped into salads.

The apple is one of our oldest known fruits; it is mentioned in the Bible in the account of the origin of the human race. In Europe it has been cultivated for at least 3,000 years. Extensive breeding means that there are now several thousand varieties, each with its own characteristics.

The apple is a useful source of vitamin C, hence the old saying 'an apple a day keeps the doctor away' although, unlike the orange, one apple cannot supply all the vitamin C needed for one day.

Crab apples grow wild in Europe, America and Asia. The common European crab (*Malus sylvestris*) was the original wild apple and the parent of all cultivated varieties. Crab apples are very small with shiny red, green or yellow skin and compact, firm flesh. They are too sour to use raw, and are chiefly made into jelly.

Dessert apples contain a large amount of fructose (natural sugar) and come in an assortment of colours, shapes and sizes. The flesh can be firm and crisp or soft and mealy, and some varieties are more juicy than others. Delicious eaten raw, they are also extremely useful for cooking. Choose them when it is important that the fruit retains its shape – in an open tart, for instance, or dishes garnished with apple rings. The shells of these apples are excellent for stuffing. Use them also when a thick-textured purée or a naturally sweet flavour is required.

Apples which cook to a pulp: some varieties of apple cook to a fluffy pulp or purée. They are more acid and sharper tasting than dessert apples, and usually larger too. In Britain they are specially grown and sold as 'cooking apples', because they are usually too acid to use raw. This type of apple is higher in pectin than the sweet dessert apple, and so it can be combined with low pectin fruit in preserves to achieve a good set.

Cider apples cannot be eaten as they are too bitter: they are grown specifically for their juice which has a good balance of acidity and tannin. The apple is pressed and cider, cider vinegar and apple wine made from the resulting juice.

Apple drinks and products

Cider is made from the fermented juice of apples; it can be still or sparkling, dry or sweet and has an alcoholic content between 3° and 8°.

Cider vinegar makes particularly nice dressings for salads made with cabbage, carrot and fruit.

Apple wine is also the fermented juice of apples, but has a higher alcoholic content than cider, about 9°.

Apple brandy is distilled from cider. The most famous is calvados, taking its name from the renowned apple-growing district of northwest France. It is considered the finest apple brandy and features in many traditional Normandy dishes, both sweet and savoury. It is also delicious in rich fruit cakes and a spoonful or two does wonders for a plain apple pudding. Applejack, a speciality of New England, is another well known brandy.

Natural apple juice is free of preservatives and added sweeteners; some brands contain extra vitamin C. You can also buy concentrated apple squash and a slightly sparkling, carbonated apple juice drink.

Dried apple rings, slices and flakes are delicious casseroled with pork chops, stirred in muesli, stewed for fruit compotes and baked in a variety of cakes.

Canned or bottled apple slices and purée are a useful store-cupboard standby. They can be used for pie fillings or 'instant' puddings and sauces.

Buying and storing apples

Look for unblemished fruit with firm unwrinkled skin. Well-flavoured dessert varieties will smell fragrant when ripe. For jam-and jelly-making choose slightly under-ripe cooking apples as their pectin content is highest at this stage.

Keep apples in a loosely tied polythene bag in the crisper compartment of the refrigerator for up to 2 weeks. Transfer dessert apples to your fruit bowl as needed – they lose their crispness after a few days at room temperature.

Bulk- and long-term storage: store only sound, unblemished apples; wrap individually in newspaper and place close together, but not touching, on trays, with paper or polystyrene between layers. Store in a cool, dark, airy place for up to 6 months. Check periodically and remove any that are rotting or becoming soft.

Apples can also be preserved by bottling and pickling; they can be dried in rings or slices, or they can be made into jelly, jam or chutney.

✳✳✳ Freeze only firm, undamaged, just-ripe apples. Peel and core the fruit and slice or dice them, fairly thickly, straight into cold salted water. Drain, then blanch in boiling water for 2 minutes; cool in iced water for the same length of time, then drain and pat dry. Pack in bags or rigid containers, with or without sugar between layers. Freeze for 9–12 months. Freeze sweetened apple purée for up to 9 months, unsweetened for up to 12 months.

Apple varieties

Variety	Description	Use
Great Britain		
Bramley's Seedling	The most popular and widely used cooking apple. Large, squat shape. Greeny-yellow skin with reddish tinge. Mealy flesh.	Cooks to a pulp
Charles Ross	Large fruit. Shiny, greenish-yellow skin, striped or flushed with red. Soft white flesh.	Dessert, also specially good for cooking
Cox's Orange Pippin	Usually yellowish-green with orange-red flush and russet markings, but skin colour can vary. Fairly crisp, creamy-yellow flesh with superb flavour. Highly scented when ripe.	Dessert, also specially good for cooking
Crispin	Large fruit with bright, yellowish-green skin. Firm, juicy flesh. Well-flavoured.	Dessert
Discovery	Red-skinned. Firm, juicy, creamy-white flesh. A fairly new variety.	Dessert
Egremont Russet	Thick, tawny coloured skin. Very crisp, firm flesh. Well-flavoured.	Dessert
Grenadier	Large fruit. Greenish-yellow skin. Crisp white flesh.	Cooking
Laxton's Superb	Orange-red skin with yellow and green tints. Very sweet flesh.	Dessert
Worcester Pearmain	Red skin streaked with green. Crisp, juicy white flesh. Sweet.	Dessert
France		
Calville Blanche d'Hiver	Large, golden-skinned fruit. Juicy, aromatic and well-flavoured. Difficult to obtain.	Dessert
Golden Delicious	Thin, pale green or yellow skin. Crisp, juicy, fine-textured flesh. Not strongly flavoured.	Dessert
Reine des Reinettes	Yellow skin streaked with russet. Well-flavoured.	Dessert
Reinettes	Similar to Cox's but sweeter and less juicy.	Dessert
South Africa		
Granny Smith	See below	
Rome Beauty	Completely red, or marked with yellow. Soft, juicy, pale yellow flesh.	Dessert and cooking.
Starking	Yellow skin well streaked with red, Crisp, juicy, pale yellow flesh.	Dessert and cooking
Australia and New Zealand		
Cleopatra	Green to lemon-yellow skin. White flesh.	Dessert
Cox's Orange Pippin	See above	
Dunn's Seedling	Pale yellow or green skin. Mealy flesh.	Dessert and cooking
Golden Delicious	See above	
Granny Smith	Glossy, bright green skin. Very crisp flesh.	Dessert and cooking.
Sturmer Pippin	Yellowish-green skin. Firm, crisp flesh.	Dessert and cooking
U.S. and Canada		
Golden Delicious	See above	Dessert
Ida Red	Dark crimson skin. Soft, sweet flesh.	Dessert
Red Delicious	Medium-large fruit. Shiny, dark red skin. Very crisp sweet flesh.	Dessert
Richared	Medium-large fruit. Shiny, dark red skin. Very crisp sweet flesh.	Dessert
Spartan	Dark crimson skin. Soft, sweet flesh.	Dessert
Starking Delicious	Medium-large fruit. Shiny, dark red skin. Very crisp sweet flesh.	Dessert

Preparing apples

Apples can be used whole, quartered, sliced or chopped, cut into rings or grated. Use a stainless steel knife and apple-corer and a nylon sieve to prevent the flesh discolouring. Wipe fruit to be used unpeeled with a damp cloth.

Once cut, apples quickly begin to turn brown. If using the fruit raw, brush all cut surfaces immediately with lemon juice to prevent discoloration. If you are cooking apples and wish to preserve their natural colour, drop the fruit as you prepare it into a bowl of cold water into which you have squeezed a few drops of lemon juice; drain thoroughly before using.

To slice or chop: quarter, core and thinly peel the apples. (If using dessert apples in salads, leave the skins on for added colour.) Cut away any bad parts, then cut the apples lengthways into slices, or chop them.

To grate: rub sections of apple against the coarse holes of a grater.

For rings, remove the core neatly from the whole fruit, using an apple-corer; thinly peel the skin, then slice the fruit across into rings.

For stuffed apple shells, choose medium-sized or large dessert apples. Cut large fruit horizontally into halves and turn the top half over. With a small spoon remove the core and very carefully scrape out the apple flesh without piercing the skin, to leave a shell. Brush the inside with lemon juice. Chop the flesh, combine it with other ingredients such as celery, dates and mayonnaise, and pile the mixture back into the apple shells.

Cooking apples

Apples can be baked, stewed or poached, puréed, shallow-fried in butter or coated in batter and deep-fried in hot oil for fritters. They can be cooked in different kinds of pastry, or added to cake mixtures or pancake batters.

Apples are good 'mixers' and go well in savoury as well as sweet dishes. Their refreshing sharpness offsets the richness of fatty meat, especially pork, and they are often included in stuffings for goose and other poultry. They give an excellent flavouring to red cabbage and root vegetable casseroles.

When combined with raspberries, apples make one of the best garnishes for roast grouse or guinea fowl.

Sweetened and spiced apples can be used for a huge variety of desserts, from a homely apple crumble or pie to a sophisticated strudel.

They also make a delicious filling, either on their own or combined with other fruit such as blackberries, apricots or quinces, for pies, tarts and pancakes.

You can ring the changes by your choice of flavourings: cinnamon, cloves, mixed spice and nutmeg all marry well with apples, as do grated lemon and orange zest, chocolate and vanilla.

To bake, choose even-sized cooking apples. Core the fruit neatly, using an apple corer; with a sharp knife make a slit around the waist of each apple to prevent the skin from bursting during cooking. For a warming pudding stuff the apple cavities with mince-meat, chunky marmalade, honey or syrup thickened with breadcrumbs, or butter and brown sugar. Place the apples in a buttered, shallow ovenproof dish with a little water, fruit juice or wine; dot them with butter and sprinkle with sugar. Bake at 180C /350F /gas 4, basting occasionally with the cooking juices, until tender: ¾–1 hour, depending on size. Serve the baked apples hot with cream or custard.

To stew, place peeled, sliced apples in a heavy-based saucepan or casserole with a knob of butter; add sugar and flavourings to taste. Cover tightly and cook over a gentle heat for 10–15 minutes, or in the oven at 180C /350F /gas 4 for 25–30 minutes. Shake the pan or stir occasionally during cooking to prevent the fruit from sticking. Provided they are not overcooked, dessert apples will retain their shape; cooking apples will disintegrate to a pulp when stewed.

You can omit the butter and add a little liquid instead – water, fruit juice or cider. But do not use more than 60 ml /4 tbls liquid to each 500 g /1 lb apples or the results will be slushy.

To poach: use sliced dessert apples. Place them in a heavy-based saucepan or shallow ovenproof dish with enough sugar syrup to cover. Add flavourings to taste. Cover tightly and cook over a low heat for about 15 minutes, or in the oven at 180C /350F /gas 4 for about 20 minutes, until the apples are tender but not mushy. Serve hot or chilled, for dessert.

To purée: quarter, core and chop, but do not peel, the apples and stew until very soft. (Or use left-over cooked apples.) Drain off all the liquid (reserve for another use) and rub the apples through a fine nylon sieve. Return the purée to a clean pan and stir over a very low heat for a few minutes to allow any excess moisture to evaporate.

Apple purée can be used as a sauce (see recipe), or as the base for a variety of desserts including apple snow, apple fool, apple amber and apple charlotte. It also makes a refreshing filling for pastries, sweet omelettes and sponge cakes.

To grill: use dessert apple rings or slices. Arrange them in a single layer in a buttered, shallow flameproof dish and brush with melted butter. Sprinkle with ground mixed spice and, if liked, top with soft brown sugar for a light caramel finish. Place under a medium heat for 5 minutes until light golden, turning the dish round once. Serve immediately with sausages, pork chops, or veal escalopes, or use to top ice cream.

To shallow-fry: use dessert apples cut into rings or slices. Fry them in a single layer in butter over a high heat for 1½ minutes until browned, turning once. Cook in batches if need be, so as not to overcrowd the pan. Serve as for grilled apples.

For flambéed apples, return all the fried apples to the pan and sprinkle with brown sugar; set light to a small ladleful of calvados or cognac and pour the burning spirit over the fruit. Let the flames die down completely, then transfer the apples to a heated serving dish.

Curried apple soup

Using apples raw

A perfectly ripe, unblemished apple is a treat to eat at any time of day, as well as being good for your teeth; for a snack or to end a meal, just add some cheese – preferably mature Cheddar or another hard cheese.

Sliced or chopped dessert apples are a basic ingredient of a fresh fruit salad. They are also good in savoury salads, adding extra crunch and crispness: combine them with celery and walnuts in a classic Waldorf salad (*page 236*). Try apples, too, in potato, carrot and beetroot salads, in coleslaws, or in salads based on cooked or canned fish, cheese, or cold chicken or ham. Grated raw apple is delicious in muesli. For a nursery sweet, spear small dessert apples on lollipop sticks and coat them with toffee: these are a universal favourite with children.

Curried apple soup

Serve this creamy, spicy soup very cold, for an unusual dinner party first course. Use dessert apples for a sweet flavour, which combines well with the hot spiciness of curry.

🕗 30 minutes plus chilling

Serves 4
500 g /lb dessert apples
a few drops of lemon juice
15 g /1½ oz butter
½ Spanish onion, finely chopped
15 ml /1 tbls mild curry powder
600 ml /1 pt hot chicken or vegetable stock
piece of cinnamon stick
150 ml /5 fl oz cold milk
75 ml /5 tbls thin cream
1–2 wafer-thin slices of lemon or lime, quartered, to garnish

1 Quarter, core, peel and chop the apples. As you prepare them, place them in a bowl of cold water containing the lemon juice.
2 Melt the butter in a medium-sized, heavy-based saucepan. Thoroughly drain the apples and add them to the pan with the finely chopped onion. Cover and cook gently, stirring occasionally, until the apples and onion are soft but not coloured.
3 Add the curry powder and cook over a medium heat, stirring, for 2–3 minutes. Pour in the hot stock and add the cinnamon stick. Bring to the boil, cover the pan, and simmer for 10 minutes, stirring.
4 Purée the soup in a blender or through a vegetable mill. Allow to cool, then stir in the milk and cream; chill, covered, for 2 hours.
5 Just before serving, stir the soup well and garnish with lemon or lime.

Herring and apple salad

Serve this piquant salad with wholemeal rolls and a tomato and herb salad for a light summer lunch.

🍴 15 minutes plus chilling

Serves 4
150 ml /5 fl oz soured cream
60 ml /4 tbls natural yoghurt
1 large, crisp, red-skinned dessert apple
4 pickled herrings, drained and cut into 25 mm /1 in dice
½ Spanish onion, thinly sliced
salt and freshly ground black pepper

For the garnish
watercress sprigs
2 hard-boiled eggs, sliced
snipped chives

1   In a medium-sized bowl, blend together the soured cream and yoghurt. Quarter and core, but do not peel, the apple. Cut the apple into thin slices and fold these into the soured cream mixture. Add the diced herrings and sliced onion and toss gently but thoroughly. Season carefully with salt and black pepper; cover and chill.
2   Arrange the watercress around the edge of a serving plate. Toss the salad again and pile it in the centre of the plate. Arrange the hard-boiled eggs around the edge of the salad. Sprinkle with chives and serve.

Herring and apple salad

Apple brown Betty

🍴🍴 40 minutes,
then 40 minutes baking

Serves 4
175 g /6 oz slightly stale bread, broken into coarse crumbs
50 g /2 oz butter, melted
500 g /1 lb crisp dessert apples, quartered, cored, peeled and thinly sliced
75–100 g /3–4 oz soft dark brown sugar
1.5 ml /¼ tsp ground cinnamon
2.5 ml /½ tsp ground mixed spice
50 ml /2 oz seedless raisins
30 ml /2 tbls lemon juice
butter for greasing
vanilla ice cream, cream or custard, to serve

1   Heat the oven to 190C /375F /gas 5.
2   Add the breadcrumbs to the melted butter. Using a metal spoon, stir until the bread has absorbed the butter. Spoon one-third of the breadcrumbs over the base of a 1 L /2 pt greased ovenproof baking dish. Spread half the sliced apples evenly in the dish.
3   Mix together the sugar, spices and raisins. Scatter half of this mixture over the apples in the dish and sprinkle with half the lemon juice. Cover with half the remaining breadcrumbs. Add the remaining sliced apples, then the rest of the sugar and raisin mixture, and sprinkle with the remaining lemon juice. Top with the remaining breadcrumbs and sprinkle over 45 ml /3 tbls water.
4   Bake the pudding for 40 minutes, until the apples are tender and the top is crisp and golden. Serve warm with vanilla ice cream, cream or custard.

Apple cider butter

🍴🍴🍴 2 hours

Makes about 1.1 kg /2½ lb
1.4 kg /3 lb ripe, cooking apples
about 850 ml /1½ pt medium-dry cider
about 350 g /12 oz sugar
2.5 ml /½ tsp ground cinnamon
1.5 ml /¼ tsp ground mixed spice
1.5 ml /¼ tsp ground cloves

1   Wash the apples and cut away any discoloured parts. Chop, but do not peel or core them.
2   Place the chopped apples in a large saucepan with enough cider just to cover them. Cook gently, stirring occasionally, for about 20 minutes until the apples are disintegrating and pulpy.
3   Rub the apples, with their cooking liquid, through a fine nylon sieve. Weigh the apple purée. Return the purée to the rinsed out pan and add 250 g /8 oz sugar for each 500 g /1 lb purée. Add the ground spices.
4   Stir the mixture over a low heat until the sugar is dissolved, then bring slowly to the boil. Reduce the heat and simmer gently for about 1 hour until the mixture is thick and

toffee-coloured and no excess liquid remains. Stir frequently during cooking to prevent the apple butter from burning. Warm some scalded jars in a low oven.

5 Pour the hot apple butter into the jars. Cover with waxed paper discs, seal tightly and leave to cool. Label and store in a cool, dry place. Use within 3 months. Spread it on bread or use it as a tart filling.

French upside-down apple tart

Choose not-too-juicy apples such as Cox's Orange Pippins for this delectable tart (called *Tarte Demoiselles Tatin* in France).

🍴🍴🍴 10 minutes plus chilling time for the pastry, then 2 hours

Makes 4–6 slices
100 g /4 oz flour
pinch of salt
15 g /1/2 oz caster sugar
65 g /2½ oz chilled butter, diced
sifted icing sugar, to dredge
cream, to serve
For the filling
20 g /3/4 oz butter
50 g /2 oz sugar
500 g /1 lb dessert apples, quartered, cored, peeled and sliced
1.5 ml /1/4 tsp cinnamon

1 Sift the flour and salt into a bowl. Stir in the caster sugar. Add the diced butter and rub it in with your fingertips. Sprinkle over 5–10 ml /1–2 tsp chilled water and mix to a soft dough.
2 Turn the dough out onto a lightly floured surface and knead very briefly and lightly until smooth. Wrap the pastry in cling film and chill for at least 1 hour.
3 Heat the oven to 190C /375F /gas 5. Place a baking sheet in the oven to heat. Select a 700 ml /1¼ pt, round, ovenproof dish.
4 Grease the base and sides of the dish with a quarter of the butter for the filling. Sprinkle half the sugar over the base.
5 Arrange rings of sliced apples in a single layer over the base of the dish. Cover with half the remaining apple slices. Sprinkle over the cinnamon and half the remaining sugar. Top with the remaining apple slices and sprinkle with the rest of the sugar. Melt the remaining butter and pour it over the top layer of apples.
6 Roll out the pastry to a round slightly larger than the top of the dish; trim the edges. Lay the pastry over the apples and tuck the edges inside the rim of the dish. Prick surface in a few places with a fork.
7 Place the dish on the baking sheet and bake for 1 hour. Allow the cooked tart to 'settle' slightly, then carefully turn it out on to a flameproof serving plate.
8 Heat the grill to medium-high. Dredge the top of the tart with icing sugar and place under the hot grill for a few minutes until the apples are lightly caramelized. Serve the tart warm or cold, with cream.

Apple tansy

Crisp, thin ginger biscuits go well with this old-fashioned dessert. A tansy is basically a thick, unpuréed fool, and needs to be made with dessert apples.

🍴🍴 1 hour, plus chilling

Serves 4
500 g /1 lb well-flavoured dessert apples
squeeze of lemon juice
30 ml /2 tbls fresh orange juice
225 ml /8 fl oz milk
piece of vanilla pod
25 g /1 oz caster sugar
5 ml /1 tsp cornflour
2 large eggs, beaten
extra caster sugar (optional)
75 ml /3 fl oz thick cream, lightly whipped
To garnish
chopped walnuts or coarsely grated chocolate

1 Quarter, core, peel and dice the apples. As you prepare them, place them in a bowl of cold water containing the lemon juice to prevent them from discolouring.
2 Thoroughly drain the apples and place them in a heavy-based saucepan with the orange juice; cover and cook gently until tender. Strain off any liquid (reserve for another use) and crush the apples with a potato masher or fork. Stir the apples in a pan over a medium heat for 1–2 minutes to dry them off, then turn them into a large bowl; cool, then chill in the refrigerator.
3 In the top of a double boiler scald the milk with the vanilla pod over a low heat. Remove the pan from the heat, cover and leave to infuse for 10 minutes.
4 Mix together the caster sugar and cornflour and combine with the beaten eggs in a large bowl. Beat with a wooden spoon until the mixture is pale and thick. Remove the vanilla pod from the milk. Pour the milk in a thin stream onto the egg mixture, stirring continuously.
5 Pour the egg and milk mixture into the top of the double boiler and place over barely simmering water. Cook, stirring, for 10–15 minutes until the custard is very thick. On no account allow the custard to boil or the eggs will scramble. Strain the custard into a jug or bowl and cover the surface with a piece of greaseproof paper. Cool, then chill in the refrigerator.
6 Stir the cold custard into the cooked apples. Taste and add extra sugar if needed. Fold the cream into the apple custard. Spoon into glass dishes and chill.
7 Just before serving, sprinkle each tansy with chopped walnuts or grated chocolate.

Pears, quinces and japonicas

Add a Moroccan touch to lamb chops and rice with quinces, bake pears with ginger for a delightfully simple dessert, cover poached pears with a rich butterscotch sauce . . . after all that you might need to try a slimming salad of pears filled with prawns in a herby dressing!

Pears have a shorter season than apples and store less well, though it is possible to buy imported ones out of season. While they can be superb eaten out of hand, they display great versatility in cooking. Quinces and japonicas, related to pears, are autumn fruits, much more difficult to find, but worth trying if you can.

Pears

It is said that there are over 5000 varieties of pear, but only a few are cultivated on any great scale. They are all derived from the common or wild pear, a native of the Middle East and Eastern Europe. The chief growing and exporting countries are France, Belgium, West Germany, Britain, Holland, Spain, Australia, New Zealand and South Africa.

Buying and storing pears: as pears ripen very quickly once picked, most are taken from the tree when they are almost ripe. When you buy them, therefore, they will either be at peak eating condition – slightly yielding when you press the stalk end – or still firm enough for you to use immediately for cooking or ripen at home for eating.

Never buy pears that are soft or have discoloured patches and always handle them very carefully, for they are easily damaged.

Pears that are ready for eating are best eaten the same day, though you can store them at the bottom of the refrigerator for a few days. To ripen firm pears, keep them in a warm, dark place and check every day.

✱✱✱✱ Uncooked pears can be peeled, sliced, dipped in lemon juice and frozen in rigid containers topped up with medium sugar syrup for up to 2 months. The best way to freeze them, however, is to peel, core and halve them, then poach them in a light sugar syrup until just tender. Freeze them in rigid containers in their poaching liquid for up to 8 months.

Types of pear: the Conference pear is elongated, with a thick green and brown skin which can turn yellowish when the pears are very ripe. Conference pears are very good for cooking as well as eating raw. Firm ones can be poached, baked and pickled.

The Williams or Bartlett is a large, oval pear with a bright green skin which turns yellow as the fruit ripens. Under-ripe Williams pears can be poached or baked. Ripe, they are juicy with a melting texture for eating raw; they are excellent for canning.

Beurré Hardy pears are large, conical or round pears with a rough yellowish-green skin covered with large russet patches. Under-ripe ones can be used for cooking and, once ripe, the pink-tinged flesh is very tender and sweet; best for dessert purposes.

The Doyenné du Comice has a pale yellow, russet-flecked skin which is sometimes tinged with pink. With its melting, buttery texture and cinnamon-like flavour it is best eaten raw.

Preparing pears: remove the cores from halved pears with a teaspoon, making a circular movement with your wrist, then use the tip of the spoon to lift out the threads running to the stalk. Cores can be removed from whole pears by working into the pear from the base, only as far as the core, with an apple corer.

Prepared pears should be brushed with lemon juice to prevent discoloration.

Using pears: a sliced ripe pear can be served as a first course with Parma ham; halved pears can be coated with a tarragon or cheese dressing or hollowed out and filled with a savoury salad (see recipe) to start a meal.

Belgians add pears to a red cabbage and sausage stew and the Argentinians make them into *empanadas*, savoury beef turnovers. Chopped firm pears make a good

Prawn and pear salad

addition to side salads – their fresh taste goes particularly well with the tangy flavour of watercress.

After a meal, a sliced pear is delicious accompanied by a soft cheese such as Brie or Camembert. Classic desserts are made with pears: pears poached in red wine, poires à l'impératrice – poached pears topping a creamy rice mould, and pears belle Hélène – pears served with vanilla ice cream and chocolate sauce. Bake pears in pastry and serve them with a sweet cream sauce, fry battered pear slices to make fritters, or add pears to a fruit salad.

All types of pear can be bottled in syrup. Dessert pears are suitable for making sweet chutneys and cooking pears can be pickled in a sweet, spiced vinegar.

Pear products: canned pears in syrup are widely available. Some health food shops stock pear juice.

In England and France, an alcoholic drink called perry is made from pears, much as apples are made into cider. Country wine makers can also produce a pear wine. Pear eau de vie, known as *poire William, poire* or *Williamine*, is made in Switzerland, Germany and Alsace. It can be colourless or light golden. Some varieties have a pear inside the bottle – this is achieved by putting the bottle over the pear almost as soon as the blossom has dropped so that the pear ripens in the warmth inside the bottle.

Quinces

Quinces are hard, golden yellow fruits, which in size and shape can be like either an apple or a fat pear, depending on the variety. The flesh is hard and granular and unpleasant to eat raw, but when cooked it becomes soft, with a distinctive flavour.

Buying and storing quinces: quinces are not widely sold: they are more likely to be found in small greengrocers than in large supermarkets. They are available only in the autumn. Look for firm fruits without brown patches. Store them in a cool, dry place for up to a week and keep them apart from other foods: they have a penetrating aroma.

✳✳✳✳ Quinces do not freeze well raw. Peeled, cored and sliced quinces can be poached in a light sugar syrup and frozen in rigid containers for up to 8 months.

Using quinces: the sharp, pungent flavour of quinces contrasts well with rich meats. Try making a quince sauce for roast pork in the same way as you would an apple sauce. In the Middle East, quinces are added to stews of lamb or chicken.

Peeled, sliced quinces can be made into a compote to be served with cream or yoghurt. They can be mixed with apples to make pies and crumbles, or cooked alone to make purée-based dishes such as mousses and fruit creams (see recipe). They also make good jams and jellies. In the Middle East, France and Spain, quinces are made into a sweet, jellied paste which is cut into pieces and served as a sweetmeat or with semi-hard cheese.

Japonicas

The ornamental japonica (*Chaenomeles*) shrub bears small, round, yellow, white or green fruits which are sometimes called

Japanese quinces. They have a quince-like scent and a slightly lemony flavour and can be used in the same ways as quinces. They are good for preserving and in cooked dishes both sweet and savoury.

Lamb chops with quinces and rice

🍳🍳 1 hour 25 minutes

Serves 4
60 ml /4 tbls oil
8 small loin lamb chops, trimmed of excess fat
1 medium-sized onion, finely chopped
1 garlic clove, finely chopped
275 g /10 oz brown rice
2 quinces, peeled, cored and chopped
5 ml /1 tsp ground cumin
30 ml /10 fl oz dry cider
300 ml /10 fl oz chicken stock
salt and freshly ground black pepper
25 g /1 oz pine nuts
spring onion tassels, to garnish

1   Heat the oil in a large, heavy saucepan or flameproof casserole over a medium heat. Add the chops, brown quickly on both sides and remove them.
2   Lower the heat. Add the onion and garlic and cook until they are soft but not coloured. Stir in the rice, quinces and cumin and cook, stirring, for 1 minute.
3   Pour in the cider and stock and bring to the boil. Season with salt and pepper. Bury the chops in the rice. Cover the pan and cook over the lowest possible heat for 45 minutes.

Lamb chops with quinces and rice

4   While the rice is cooking, toast the pine nuts. Place them in a heavy, dry frying-pan and cook, stirring, over a low heat until they are golden brown.
5   Turn off the heat under the pan and leave, still covered, for 10 minutes.
6   Make a bed of the rice and quinces on a warmed serving platter and top with the lamb chops and pine nuts. Garnish with the spring onion tassels and serve at once.

Prawn and pear salad

🍤 defrosting prawns if necessary, then 20 minutes

Serves 4
4 large pears, ripe but still firm
juice of 1 lemon
60 ml /4 tbls mayonnaise
15 ml /1 tbls tarragon mustard
175 g /6 oz shelled prawns, defrosted if frozen
8 small sprigs of fresh parsley or tarragon

1   Peel the pears and brush the outsides with lemon juice. Cut each pear in half lengthways and remove the core.
2   Scoop out the centres of the pears leaving shells about 6 mm /¼ in thick. Brush the insides with lemon juice. Chop the scooped-out pieces of pear.
3   Mix together the mayonnaise and mustard. Stir in the chopped pear and the prawns. Pile the mixture into the pear shells. Arrange 2 halves on each of 4 serving plates, garnish with fresh herbs and serve.

Poached pears with butterscotch sauce

🔪🔪 1 hour, plus cooling

Serves 4
4 dessert pears, slightly under-ripe
30 ml /2 tbls golden syrup
7.5 cm /3 in cinnamon stick
1 strip of lemon zest
25 g /1 oz walnuts, finely chopped, to serve
For the sauce
60 ml /4 tbls Demerara sugar
30 ml /2 tbls golden syrup
25 g /1 oz butter
15 ml /1 tbls lemon juice
300 ml /10 fl oz thick cream
2 medium-sized egg yolks

1 Peel and core the pears from the bottom, using an apple corer. Put 300 ml /10 fl oz water, the golden syrup, cinnamon stick and lemon zest into a saucepan and set over a low heat until the syrup has melted.
2 Bring to simmering point, add the pears and poach very gently until they are tender and transparent but still firm, about 30 minutes. Remove from the heat and let cool in the syrup.
3 To make the sauce, put the Demerara sugar, golden syrup, butter and lemon juice into a saucepan. Set over a low heat until the mixture has melted. Remove the pan from the heat.
4 Scald the cream and stir it into the sugar and golden syrup mixture.

Poached pears with butterscotch sauce

5 Beat the egg yolks in a small bowl. Beat in about 90 ml /6 tbls of the cream mixture, then stir this back into the saucepan. Set over a low heat and stir with a wooden spoon until it begins to thicken. Take the pan from the heat and cool the sauce completely.
6 To serve, remove the pears from the syrup with a slotted spoon and arrange them on a serving dish. Spoon the sauce over the top and garnish the pears with the chopped walnuts.

Gingered pears

🔪 1–1¼ hours

Serves 6–8
1 kg /2 lb firm Conference pears
4 pieces preserved stem ginger, halved and thinly sliced
60 ml /4 tbls syrup from the ginger jar
275 ml /10 fl oz dry white wine
150 ml /5 fl oz soured cream

1 Heat the oven to 180C /350F /gas 4. Peel the pears. Quarter and core them and cut them into pieces about 3 × 1 cm /1¼ × ⅓ in. Place them in an ovenproof dish.
2 Mix the pieces of ginger into the pears, spoon the syrup over and pour in the wine. Bake, uncovered, for 45–60 minutes, until the pieces of pear are soft and transparent.
3 Serve hot, with the soured cream handed round separately in a bowl.

Quince syllabub

This creamy golden syllabub is similar to the fruit creams of the 18th century.

🔪🔪 1 hour, plus cooling and chilling

Serves 4–6
4 quinces, peeled, cored and chopped
2 medium-sized eggs, separated
125 g /4 oz icing sugar, sifted
200 ml /7 fl oz thick cream
For the decoration
25 g /1 oz almonds, blanched and split
25 g /1 oz glacé cherries, halved
15 g /1½ oz candied angelica, in thin slivers

1 Put the quinces and 60 ml /4 tbls water into a saucepan and cook, covered, over a low heat for about 15 minutes, until they can be beaten to a thick purée.
2 Rub the purée through a sieve and return it to the rinsed-out saucepan. Beat in the egg yolks, one at a time.
3 Set the pan over a low heat and stir until the mixture begins to thicken; it should coat the back of a wooden spoon. Do not boil.
4 Remove the pan from the heat and beat in the icing sugar, then cool the mixture completely.
5 Whip the cream lightly; whisk the egg whites stiffly. Fold first the cream, then the egg whites into the quince purée, using a metal spoon. Pile the syllabub into a serving bowl and chill for at least 1 hour.
6 Just before serving, decorate it with the almonds, cherries and angelica.

Cherries

During the cherry season, make the most of this luscious, colourful fruit. As well as for desserts, try using fresh cherries in soups or salads. Out of season, use preserved or frozen cherries in rich cakes, puddings and sauces. Sample the variety of cherry liqueurs available and experiment with them to add extra interest to almost any sweet or savoury cherry dish.

The cherry (*Prunus* spp) is closely related to the plum. It produces small, round, succulent stone fruit, and is native to the temperate regions of the Northern hemisphere. The Romans discovered cherries in Eastern Europe and Western Asia and introduced them to the countries of Western Europe, where they have been valued in cooking and wine-making ever since.

Types of cherry
Cherries are now grown in orchards in Britain, France, Germany, Italy, Rumania, Australia, the United States and Canada. Their season, which is unfortunately a short one (about 2 months), generally begins in early summer. There are hundreds of varieties of cherry, but most of them are not commercially available as many are light croppers and others do not stand up to the rigours of transport. These varieties can be roughly grouped into 3 types: sweet, sour and hybrid cherries (although when you buy cherries in a shop the only distinction usually is between sweet and sour).
Sweet cherries: excellent dessert varieties are 'Early Rivers' which are large and blackish-crimson with a delicious flavour,

and 'Bigarreau Napoleons', which are a blushing pale yellow, with firm flesh.
Bitter or sour cherries are very much favoured for cooking and most types of preserving. The best are the Morellos which are dark red and juicy, with an acid taste. Amarelles or Griottes have a light, yellow-tinged flesh and are less acid.

Buying and storing cherries
When you are buying fresh cherries, avoid fruit that looks too light in colour, as it will be under-ripe, and split fruit, which indicates that it is over-ripe. Sweet cherries should have the stalks attached, but Morello cherries are usually sold without stalks. Cherries are best eaten on the day of purchase but they will keep in an airtight container in the vegetable drawer of the refrigerator for up to 4 days.
✳✳✳✳ As the cherry season is short, it is a good idea to buy more fruit than you need for immediate use and freeze some of it for the winter. Black cherries freeze best. Always stone them before freezing, since the stones may cause the cherries to develop an 'off' flavour if left in. You can buy a special cherry stoner; or use a small vegetable

scoop, the fine point of a potato peeler or the bent end of a sterilized hairpin, which must be inserted at the stalk end and twisted to draw out the stone. The simplest way is to open freeze cherries individually on trays. Then bag them: they will keep for 6-8 months. Cherries can also be frozen poached in a medium strength sugar syrup and you can buy ready-frozen cherries.
Bottling cherries: cherries can be bottled in syrup, or in brandy for special occasions; or bottle them in a sweetened spiced vinegar to eat as a pickle with cold meats. You can of course buy commercially bottled cherries, but home-bottled ones make very nice and unusual presents.
Canned cherries: you can buy very good canned cherries to use out of season. Most popular are the sweet black cherries, but you can also find canned Morellos and red sweet cherries. It is more convenient to buy cans of stoned rather than unstoned cherries. It is worth remembering that inside a 425 g /15 oz can of stoned cherries there will be 225 g /8 oz of drained fruit.
Cocktail cherries: these are coloured cherries, preserved with syrup and flavourings. The most popular are the small, stoned red ones flavoured with maraschino liqueur. You can also buy bottles of larger maraschino cherries, stoned but with the stalk still attached, so that they can be attractively hung over the side of a glass. Other cocktail cherries are coloured green and flavoured with crème de menthe; yellow ones are flavoured with curaçao, and there are sweet and sour orange ones. As well as being used

Cherry and almond sherry cake

in drinks, cocktail cherries can be mixed into fruit salads or used to garnish grapefruit, melon or pineapple. Maraschino cherries can be speared, with cheese, on to cocktail sticks as an appetizer.

Crystallized, or glacé, cherries are used in cake making, both as part of the basic mixture and as decoration. They are mostly red, but yellow and green ones are also available and the three colours together look very pretty arranged on the top of a rich, uniced fruit cake for a tea party.

Cherry liqueurs

These are delicious to drink and also give extra zest to cherry recipes, both sweet and savoury. Cherry liqueurs are made in many different countries, including France, Denmark (home of Cherry Heering, one of the best-known cherry brandies), Holland, Germany, Italy and Poland.

Kirsch or kirschwasser is a clear, colourless liqueur made mainly in Alsace and the Black Forest region of Germany from fermented wild cherries. Maraschino, also colourless, is made in Yugoslavia and Italy from Marasca cherries and honey. Cerasella is one of the finest Italian cherry liqueurs, flavoured with herbs.

Cherry brandy gets an interesting almond flavour from the kernels extracted from crushed cherry stones.
● Make your own cherry brandy by layering Morello cherries in a bottle with caster sugar and pouring brandy over them. Leave for at least 3 months before using.

Sweet ways with cherries

Raw sweet cherries are an excellent addition to fresh fruit salads, and folded into sweetened, whipped cream they make a delightful topping for a shortbread or light sponge. Cherries make mouth-watering fillings for pancakes, pastries and strudels. They can be puréed and made into frothy snows and creams. You can make cherry tarts, puddings and batters. Perhaps the most popular cherry recipe of all is for Black Forest gateau.

Cherries as sweets: frost cherries by dipping them into beaten egg white and then caster sugar, and leaving them on a rack to dry. Cherries can also be dipped into melted chocolate or filled with halved almonds or small pieces of marzipan. These make an elegant accompaniment to coffee at the end of a dinner party.

Cherry jam: cherries contain very little pectin, but it is still possible to make an excellent jam with them. Use slightly underripe sweet cherries and mix them with redcurrants or apples or lemon juice, and use a relatively large proportion of fruit to sugar. The acid Morellos make a jam that sets particularly well.

Savoury ways with cherries

The fresh flavour of cherries goes beautifully with rich meat such as duck, hot or cold. Or mix cherries with cold chicken or lamb in a French dressing or mayonnaise. A sweet-savoury cherry soup is a favourite starter in Scandinavia, and cherries make an unusual and colourful addition to a mixed side salad in summer.

Cherry and avocado salad

30 minutes

Serves 4
175 g /6 oz sweet red or black cherries
2 small, ripe avocados
30 ml /2 tbls chopped fresh mint
15 ml /1 tbls chopped fresh tarragon
45 ml /3 tbls olive oil
15 ml /1 tbls red wine vinegar
freshly ground black pepper
1 small, crisp lettuce
100 g /4 oz curd cheese

1 Stone the cherries. Peel and stone the avocados, and cut them into cubes. Put the cherries and avocado pieces into a bowl with the mint and tarragon.
2 Mix the oil, vinegar and pepper together and fold the dressing into the cherries and avocados.
3 Make beds of crisp lettuce hearts on 4 small plates and pile a portion of the salad on top of each one. Spoon 25 g /1 oz curd cheese on each salad and serve immediately, to prevent the avocados from discolouring.

Black cherry soup

1 hour if serving hot
plus 1 hour if serving cold

Serves 4
500 g /18 oz black cherries
25 g /1 oz butter
1 medium-sized onion, thinly sliced
15 ml /1 tbls flour
850 ml /1½ pt chicken stock
5 cm /2 in piece of cinnamon stick
2 cloves
2 thinly pared strips of lemon zest
2 medium-sized egg yolks
50 ml /2 fl oz soured cream

1 Stone and quarter 16 of the cherries and reserve for garnish. Stone and chop the rest.
2 Melt the butter in a saucepan on low heat. Add the onion and cook gently until soft but not browned. Stir in the flour and cook for 1 minute. Stir in the stock and bring to the boil, stirring. Remove from the heat.
3 Add the chopped cherries, cinnamon, cloves and lemon zest. Bring the soup back to the boil, reduce the heat and simmer gently, uncovered, for 20 minutes.
4 Strain the soup through a sieve, pressing down hard to extract as much liquid as possible.
5 Lightly beat the egg yolks together in a bowl and gradually work into them 75 ml /3 fl oz of the cherry liquid. Mix the contents of the bowl into the rest of the soup. Return the soup to the rinsed saucepan and reheat gently, without letting it boil.
6 Pour the soup into individual soup bowls, swirl some soured cream on top of each one, and scatter over the reserved, quartered cherries to garnish.

● To serve the soup chilled, gently reheat it after adding the yolks, then cool and chill in a covered bowl in the refrigerator. Add 30 ml /2 tbls cherry brandy if liked, and the soured cream and reserved, quartered cherries to garnish as in step 6.

Roast duckling with cherries

2¾ hours

Serves 4
1.75 kg /4 lb duckling
1 sprig fresh mint
1 sprig fresh marjoram
2 sprigs fresh thyme
1 sprig parsley
½ lemon, sliced
10 juniper berries
6 black peppercorns
5 ml /1 tsp salt
45 ml /3 tbls redcurrant jelly
225 g /8 oz sweet red or 425 g /15 oz canned stoned red cherries in syrup
200 ml /7 fl oz duck giblet stock
150 ml /5 fl oz dry red wine
30 ml /2 tbls chopped fresh mint

1 Heat the oven to 180C /350F /gas 4. Wipe the duck all over with a damp cloth, then pat dry. Put the herb sprigs and lemon inside the cavity, then truss. Prick the skin all over with a fork, crush the spices and salt together and rub them into the skin.
2 Place the duck on a rack in a roasting tin, cover it completely with foil and roast for 1½ hours.
3 Pour away all the excess fat in the tin, remove the foil and spread the duck with 30 ml /2 tbls redcurrant jelly. Continue roasting for a further 30 minutes until the skin is crisp and dark. Meanwhile, stone and halve the fresh cherries, or drain and halve the canned cherries.
4 Take the duck out of the oven and keep it warm. Pour off any further excess fat from the roasting tin and put it on top of the stove on medium heat. Pour in the stock and bring to the boil, stirring and scraping any residue from the bottom and sides of the pan.
5 Pour in the wine and stir in the remaining 15 ml /1 tbls redcurrant jelly and the chopped mint. Add the cherries and let the sauce simmer very gently while you joint the duckling.
6 Arrange the pieces of duckling on a heated serving dish and spoon the cherry sauce over the top.

Clafoutis

You can make this classic dessert from the Limousin district of France with either fresh or canned black cherries.

🍴🍴 1½ hours,
or 2½ hours if using kirsch

Serves 6
550 g /1¼ lb fresh black cherries, or 900 g /2 lb canned stoned black cherries in syrup
75 ml /3 fl oz kirsch (optional)
65 g /2½ oz flour
pinch of salt
50 g /2 oz caster sugar
3 medium-sized eggs
225 ml /8 fl oz milk or 300 ml /11 fl oz if kirsch is omitted
2 drops vanilla essence
30 ml /2 tbls icing sugar

1 Stone fresh cherries or drain canned ones. Heat the oven to 200C /400F /gas 6.
2 Soak the cherries in the kirsch, if using, for 1 hour. Drain, reserving the kirsch. Put the cherries into a lightly buttered flan dish, 25 cm /10 in diameter and 4 cm /1½ in deep.
3 Sift the flour with the salt into a mixing bowl and mix in the sugar. Make a well in the centre and break in the eggs. Add about 75 ml /3 fl oz milk. Beat the eggs and milk with a wire whisk, gradually beating in the flour from the sides of the bowl.
4 Add the vanilla essence to the rest of the milk, then beat the milk mixture into the batter in the bowl. If using kirsch, add it after the milk. Beat until very smooth. Pour the batter over the cherries and bake the clafoutis for 1 hour.
5 Remove from the oven and cool in the tin for 15 minutes. Dredge sifted icing sugar over the top and serve warm.

Cherry and honey strudel

🍴🍴 1¼ hours

Serves 8
For the dough
200 g /7 oz flour, plus extra flour for dusting
pinch of salt
1 medium-sized egg
15 ml /1 tbls olive oil
25 g /1 oz butter, melted
45 ml /3 tbls browned crumbs
30 ml /2 tbls icing sugar
For the filling
450 g /9 oz fresh sweet red cherries or 750 g /1½ lb canned stoned red cherries in syrup
250 g /9 oz cream or curd cheese
50 g /2 oz clear honey
2.5 ml /½ tsp grated nutmeg
finely grated zest of 1 lemon
2 medium-sized egg yolks, lightly beaten
10 ml /2 tsp flour

1 Sift the 200 g /7 oz flour and salt into a bowl and make a well in the centre. Beat the egg, oil and 75 ml /3 fl oz warm water together, pour into the flour and beat with a wooden spoon until the dough is soft and elastic. Put in a warm place for 15 minutes. Heat the oven to 200C /400F /gas 6.
2 Dust a clean tea towel with flour. Put the dough on to it and roll it out till 5 mm /¼ in thick and about the size of the tea towel. Leave it while you prepare the filling.
3 Stone the fresh cherries or drain the canned ones. Put the cheese in a bowl and gradually beat in the honey. Beat in the grated nutmeg, lemon zest and egg yolks, and finally the flour. Beat until the mixture is smooth, then fold in the cherries.
4 Gently pull the dough outwards by putting your hands, palms upwards, under the tea towel, and drawing your fingers towards the edges of the tea towel. Trim the edges straight. Brush the dough with the melted butter and scatter over the crumbs.
5 Put the filling in a long strip about 5 cm /2 in in from one long edge of the dough. Raise one long side of the tea towel and carefully roll up the dough. Roll it on to a buttered baking sheet, curving the roll round if it is too long.
6 Bake the strudel for 30 minutes, or until it is golden brown. Dust it with sifted icing sugar. Serve hot or cold, in slices.

Cherry and honey strudel

Compote of cherries

The best cherries for compote are Morellos, but any firm, not too ripe, cherries will do. This lovely dessert, which may be eaten hot or cold, can also be made with canned black, red or Morello cherries. In this case do not cook them first, just proceed with the recipe from step 2. Serve with whipped cream handed separately.

⚔ 1¼ hours

Serves 4-6
1 kg /2¼ lb fresh cherries, or 1.4 kg /3 lb
  canned cherries in syrup
25 g /1 oz caster sugar
5 cm /2 in piece of cinnamon stick
thinly pared zest of 1 medium-sized orange
juice of ½ orange
150 ml /5 fl oz dry red wine
30 ml /2 tbls redcurrant jelly
10 ml /2 tsp arrowroot, blended with 30 ml
  /2 tbls water
60 ml /4 tbls cherry brandy or kirsch (optional)

1 If using fresh cherries, stone and put in a saucepan with the sugar, cinnamon and a piece of the orange zest. Cover and set on low heat until the juices begin to run (by which time the mixture will be almost at boiling point). Remove from the heat and pour into a bowl. Discard the orange zest.
2 Cut the remaining orange zest into julienne strips, blanch them in boiling water for 5 minutes, then drain.
3 Put the piece of cinnamon into the rinsed saucepan with the red wine. Bring to the boil and cook until the wine is reduced by about one quarter. Take from the heat.
4 Beat the redcurrant jelly with a fork and

Compote of cherries
_____

stir it into the wine. When it has melted, stir in the orange juice. Drain the syrup from the cooked, fresh or the canned cherries and stir into the mixture in the pan with the blended arrowroot. Bring to the boil, stirring. Simmer, still stirring, for 1 minute.
5 Take the pan from the heat and stir in the cooked, fresh or the canned cherries, the cherry brandy or kirsch, if using, and the orange strips. Serve hot or chilled.

Cherry and almond sherry cake

⚔ 2½ hours

Makes an 18 cm /7 in cake
100 g /4 oz flour
100 g /4 oz self-raising flour
pinch of salt
250 g /9 oz glacé cherries
175 g /6 oz butter
175 g /6 oz caster sugar
3 medium-sized eggs, lightly beaten
75 g /3 oz ground almonds
90 ml /6 tbls sweet sherry

1 Heat the oven to 180C /350F /gas 4. Sift the flours and salt together in a bowl. Halve, wash and dry the cherries and toss them with 45 ml /3 tbls of the flour.
2 In a large mixing bowl beat the butter to a cream. Add the sugar and beat until the mixture is light and fluffy.
3 Gradually add the eggs, beating well after each addition. Fold in the flour and almonds with a metal spoon until they are completely mixed with the butter and eggs.

Stir in the sherry and then fold in the cherries.
4 Put the mixture in a buttered 18 cm /7 in diameter deep cake tin and bake for 1¾ hours, or until the cake has shrunk slightly from the sides of the tin and a warmed skewer inserted into the centre comes out clean.
5 Remove the cake from the oven and leave in the tin for 15 minutes. Turn it on to a wire rack to cool.

American cherry pie

Cherry pie is a favourite American dessert which can be made with either fresh, frozen or canned cherries. The self-raising flour makes the pastry very light and short, and the tapioca or sago thickens the cherry syrup to a clear sauce.

⚔ 1 hour 20 minutes

Serves 6
For the pastry
175 g /6 oz shortening, or butter and lard mixed
250 g /9 oz self-raising flour
pinch of salt
For the filling
550 g /1¼ lb fresh or frozen sweet red or
  Morello cherries, stoned, or 900 g /2 lb
  canned stoned red cherries in syrup
30 ml /2 tbls granulated sugar (for fresh
  or frozen cherries)
30 ml /2 tbls caster sugar
30 ml /2 tbls fine tapioca or sago
2 drops almond essence
15 ml /1 tbls lemon juice
20 g /¾ oz butter
For the glaze
1 medium-sized egg white, lightly beaten
15 ml /1 tbls caster sugar

1 Make the pastry by rubbing the shortening into the sifted flour and salt and binding with 45 ml /3 tbls cold water. Chill lightly.
2 If using fresh or frozen cherries, make a syrup: place the granulated sugar in a pan with 300 ml /11 fl oz cold water, and stir over a gentle heat until the sugar has completely dissolved. Increase the heat: boil rapidly for 2 minutes. Add the stoned, fresh or frozen cherries and poach them for 10 minutes. Drain, reserving the poaching syrup, then leave the cherries and syrup to cool. If using canned cherries, drain them, reserving the syrup.
3 Measure 150 ml /5 fl oz of the reserved cherry syrup. Mix with the cherries, sugar, tapioca or sago, almond essence and lemon juice. Leave to stand for 15 minutes. Heat the oven to 200C /400F /gas 6.
4 Roll out two-thirds of the pastry and line a 20 cm /8 in diameter, 4 cm /1½ in deep, greased pie dish. Put in the cherry mixture and dot it with the butter. Roll out the remaining pastry and use to cover the pie, sealing the pastry edges with cold water.
5 Bake the pie for 30 minutes. Remove from the oven, brush the surface with the egg white and dust with the caster sugar. Replace in the oven for a further 10 minutes until the crust is golden brown. Serve hot.

Plums, damsons and greengages

The plum and its many relatives are much loved fruits. Ripe, juicy dessert plums are exquisite raw; sharper varieties make luscious compotes, pies and jams. Greengages are delicious puréed or baked in a flan, while damsons are used for preserves such as damson cheese or spicy chutney.

All types of plum belong to the genus *Prunus* and are closely related to apricots, peaches, nectarines and cherries.

Types of plum

Large plums are all varieties of *P. domestica* which dates back about 2,000 years. They are now widely cultivated in the temperate zones: California, Yugoslavia, Germany, France and South Africa are among the main producing countries. According to the variety, plums may be 3–5 cm /1¼–2 in long. The flesh is always golden-green, the skin may be purple, red, green or yellow.

The sweet, juicy dessert fruit varies considerably in texture and flavour from the sharper, less juicy varieties that are best for cooking and preserving. Some varieties are good for both purposes: they are sharp at the beginning of their season and become sweeter and juicier as they ripen. The best-known dual-purpose plums grown in Britain, where the season is from late July to early October, are in late summer. Look for golden-skinned Early Laxtons; large, dark blue Czars; oval, yellowish-red Burbanks; large, purple Monarchs; the purple Mar-jorie Seedling and the large, oval Belle de Louvain which is red and ripens to purple.

Santa Rosa, huge in size and rounded in shape, ruddy red with a firm skin, is a much exported plum; it comes from South Africa, Italy and the U.S. Switzens, smaller and oval in shape with a dark skin and blue bloom, are exports from Eastern Europe.

For preserving and cooking, look for the small, purple Early Rivers and Yellow Egg, the oval, reddish-purple Purple Pershores, the brownish-red Warwickshire Droopers and the long, claret-coloured Blaisdon Reds. The most popular dessert plum, the large Victoria, which has a pinkish-yellow skin is also superb for cooking; it is in season in Britain late August to October.

Gage plums (*P. italica*) which are all fairly small, very sweet and fragrantly scented, are a distinct group of plums thought to have originated in Armenia. They were first eaten in France in the 16th century. In 1725 a Sir Thomas Gage took a variety known in France as the Reine Claude home to England, where it became known as the green-gage. Greengages, sweet when ripe, are good for eating raw as well as for cooking.

Japanese plums (*P. salicina*) were introduced to Japan from China in the 16th century, and to Australia in the late 19th century; they are also grown in America and South Africa. Japanese plums are heart-shaped, and 5–8 cm /2–3 in long; both cooking and dessert varieties are found, and the fruit can be yellow or red – some are called blood plums because of their dark, ruby-coloured flesh.

Damsons (*P. damascena*) probably date back even further than *domestica* plums and were first found growing in Damascus by the Crusaders, who took them back to Europe. They are small, oval fruit, purple in colour, with a soft, blue bloom, and are in season in Europe in early autumn. The flesh is greenish-yellow and too bitter to eat raw. Damsons should only be used for cooking and preserving; they make excellent home-made wine.

Cherry plums (*P. cerasifera*): these early plums are small, round and resemble the cherry; they have sweet, yellow, flesh and red or yellow skin which can be on the bitter side. Cherry plums are usually kept for cooking and preserving. They are grown widely in Australia as well as in Europe.

Mirabelles are grown in France and Germany, particularly in the border district of Alsace. They are small and round, sweet-scented and a blushing yellow in colour, and are used mainly for cooking and preserving and making brandy.

Bullaces (*P. insititia*) are very small, shiny black fruit not unlike sloes. Their yellow, acid flesh is best suited for cooking and preserving. They are mainly a garden fruit.

Spiced plum flan

Buying and storing plums

Buy plums for immediate use wherever possible. They should be ripe but firm, unshrivelled and with no brown patches.

Ripe plums will not keep for more than about 2 days in a bowl in the bottom of the refrigerator. If you need to shop in advance, buy slightly under-ripe fruit and keep it in a bowl in a cool larder or cupboard.

Plums are excellent bottled – try some in brandy for a special treat.

❉❉❉❉ To freeze plums, wash, halve and stone them. Pack the halves into rigid plastic containers and pour over a sugar syrup made in the proportions of 500 g /18 oz sugar to 1 L /1¾ pt water. They will keep for 9–12 months. An unsweetened purée will keep frozen for up to 3 months, and sweetened for up to 6 months.

Preserved plums

Golden and red-skinned canned plums are a very useful store-cupboard standby, and canned plum juice is also available from some health food shops. Dried plums, called prunes, come from varieties grown mainly in France and California: prunes are covered dried fruit (*page 322*).

Plum brandies

Mirabelle and Switzen plums are the basis of excellent brandies, called mirabelle and quetsch respectively. Both are colourless, like kirsch. Plum brandy is called slivovica in Yugoslavia and slibovitz in Rumania.

Cooking with plums

Plums can be made into pies, tarts and crumbles, and can be added to cake mixtures such as a yeast cake from southern Germany. They can also be poached or baked in a sugar syrup to make a compote, and puréed for mousses, ice creams and sauces. Plums make delicious, melt-in-the-mouth fritters or can be enclosed in pastry for dumplings.

In Germany and Scandinavia plums are often cooked to be used in savoury ways. They are a good accompaniment to rich meats and the dessert varieties can be used in savoury side salads.

Plums make a delicious jam, varying in colour according to the type of fruit used. Damsons and bullaces are excellent for dark coloured jellies and stiff fruit 'cheeses', and their sharpness makes for spicy chutneys. Use plums for home-made wine.

Greengage purée

This purée is a very handy freezer standby: it has so many uses and can be sweetened to taste.

◖ 45 minutes

Makes about 600 ml /1 pt
1 kg /2¼ lb greengages
50 g /2 oz granulated sugar
1 cinnamon stick or a vanilla pod (optional)

1 Halve and stone the greengages. To make a sugar syrup, put the sugar with 450 ml /16 fl oz water in a large, heavy-based saucepan. Add the cinnamon stick or vanilla pod if using. Bring slowly to the boil, then boil rapidly for 2 minutes.

2 Remove the pan from the heat and put in the greengages, skin side down. Return the pan to the heat and let the syrup come up to the boil. Cover and simmer the greengages for 15 minutes, until they are soft and pulpy.

3 Lift out the greengages with a slotted

Wheatmeal plum and sultana cobbler

Plum cobbler with its scone topping is easy to prepare and makes a substantial family sweet.

⏱ 50 minutes

Serves 6–8
2 × 550 g /1¼ lb cans red plums in syrup
For the cobbler topping
250 g /9 oz wheatmeal self-raising flour
5 ml /1 tsp salt
1.5 ml /¼ tsp grated nutmeg
50 g /2 oz lard
50 g /2 oz Demerara sugar
75 g /3 oz sultanas
200 ml /7 fl oz natural yoghurt

1 Heat the oven to 200C /400F /gas 6. Drain the plums and reserve the syrup. Stone the plums and put the fruit in a 1.5 L /2½ pt pie dish. Pour in enough syrup just to cover.
2 Put the flour, salt and nutmeg into a mixing bowl and with your fingertips rub in the lard. Stir in the sugar and sultanas.
3 Make a well in the centre of the scone mixture, pour in the yoghurt, and with a fork mix to a soft dough. Divide the dough into 8 portions and form them into 25 mm /1 in thick rounds. Arrange them symmetrically on top of the plums.
4 Bake the cobbler for 35 minutes or until the scones are golden brown on top. Serve hot, with cream or custard.

Plum and honey mousse

This light, fluffy mousse combines the sharpness of plums with the mellow sweetness of honey.

⏱ 1½ hours
plus 1½ hours setting

Serves 4
juice of 1 lemon
15 g /½ oz gelatine
400 g /14 oz dark cooking plums
75 ml /3 fl oz unsweetened apple juice or water
5 cm /2 in piece of cinnamon stick
1 blade of mace
45 ml /3 tbls clear honey
2 large eggs, separated
150 ml /5 fl oz thick cream
30 ml /2 tbls chopped nuts, to garnish

1 Put the lemon juice in a small saucepan and sprinkle the gelatine on top. Leave to soak.
2 Halve and stone the plums. Put them in a large saucepan with the apple juice or water and the cinnamon and mace. Cover and cook over a low heat for 20 minutes, until the plums are very soft. Rub them through a nylon sieve with the spices.
3 Return the plum purée to the rinsed pan

and set it over a low heat. Add the honey and stir until it has dissolved. Remove from the heat.
4 Gently melt the gelatine in the small pan, without letting it boil, and stir it into the plum purée. Then beat in the egg yolks.
5 Return the pan to a very low heat and stir with a wooden spoon, without letting the mixture boil, until it will coat the back of the spoon.
6 Remove the pan from the heat. Allow the mixture to cool slightly, then chill it in the refrigerator for about 30 minutes, until it is on the point of setting.
7 Lightly whip the cream and whisk the egg whites until stiff. Using a metal spoon, fold first the cream and then the egg whites into the plum mixture.
8 Pour the mixture into individual glasses and chill for about 1 hour in the refrigerator until set. Just before serving, decorate the mousses with the chopped nuts.

Spiced plum flan

⏱ 1 hour

Serves 4–6
For the base
butter for greasing
125 g /4 oz flour
2.5 ml /½ tsp ground mixed spice
125 g /4 oz butter
grated zest of 1 medium-sized orange
125 g /4 oz caster sugar
2 large eggs, beaten
For the filling
350 g /12 oz golden dessert plums
150 ml /5 fl oz sweet white wine
60 ml /4 tbls redcurrant jelly
juice of ½ a medium-sized orange
5 cm /2 in piece of cinnamon stick

1 Butter a 20 cm /8 in sponge flan ring. Heat the oven to 180C /350 F / gas 4. Sift the flour with the mixed spice on to a plate.
2 In a mixing bowl, beat the butter until it is soft. Beat in the orange zest and sugar. Beat in the eggs, alternately with the flour.
3 Pour the mixture into the prepared flan ring. Bake for 25 minutes or until the flan is golden and has shrunk slightly from the sides of the ring. Remove from the oven, cool for 10 minutes and turn on to a wire cake rack to cool completely.
4 Meanwhile halve and stone the plums. Put the wine in a saucepan and boil until it is reduced by half. Remove the pan from the heat and stir in the redcurrant jelly. Continue to stir until it is dissolved.
5 Add the plums, orange juice and cinnamon stick to the pan. Poach the plums gently for 10 minutes. Remove from the heat and leave until completely cold. Discard the cinnamon stick.
6 Arrange the plums, skin side up, symmetrically in the flan base. Spoon over half the poaching syrup, allowing it to sink into the sponge. Just before serving, spoon more of the syrup over the plums to glaze them. Serve with whipped cream.

● Greengages may be substituted.

Greengage purée, Plum and honey mousse and Wheatmeal plum cobbler

spoon and rub them through a nylon sieve. Cool, then chill.
✳✳✳✳ Pour into a polythene container, leaving 10 mm /½ in headspace. Cover, label and freeze.
Storage time: 6 months

● The purée can be sweetened with a little extra sugar syrup to taste and used as a sauce for hot puddings or ice cream.
● For greengage syllabub, fold 150 ml /5 fl oz purée and 60 ml /4 tbls brandy into 400 ml /14 fl oz whipped cream sweetened to taste with caster sugar. Serve in glasses with chopped candied peel and nuts scattered over the top.
● For baked greengage custard, blend together 300 ml /10 fl oz purée, 300 ml /10 fl oz milk and 2 large eggs, beaten, sweetened to taste with caster sugar. Pour the mixture into individual soufflé dishes and stand them in a baking tin with water to come halfway up their sides. Bake at 170C /325F /gas 3 for 1 hour or until they are set and browned on top.

Plum salad

Damson and raisin chutney

This dark, rich chutney will keep un-opened for up to 2 years stored in a cool, dark place. Serve it as an accompaniment to cheese or cold meat and salads.

🍴🍴 2 hours

Makes about 1.4 kg /3 lb
1.4 kg /3 lb damsons
400 g /14 oz raisins
2 large onions, finely chopped
300 ml /10 fl oz distilled malt vinegar
200 g /7 oz Barbados sugar
15 ml /1 tbls mustard seeds
5 ml /1 tsp ground mace

1 Halve and stone the damsons and put them in a preserving pan with all the other ingredients.
2 Bring the contents of the pan to the boil and simmer for 1 hour, stirring from time to time, until the mixture is thick.
3 Pour the chutney into clean, warmed jars and cover immediately with circles of waxed paper. Seal with screw tops while the chutney is still warm.

Almond-flavoured plum jam

Cracked plum kernels give this pinkish-gold jam a light almond flavour.

🍴🍴 1¾ hours

Makes approximately 3.5 kg /7¾ lb
2 kg /4½ lb golden skinned plums
2 kg /4½ lb granulated sugar

1 Halve and stone the plums, reserving 20 stones. Put the plums in a preserving pan.
2 Crack the reserved plum stones with nut crackers, take out the kernels and put them with the plums in the pan. Add 300 ml /10 fl oz water.
3 Set the pan over a low heat and slowly bring the plums to the boil. Simmer for 45 minutes or until you have a thick pulp.
4 Stir in the sugar and continue to stir until it has dissolved. Bring the jam to the boil and continue to boil until setting point is reached. To test for setting, drop 5 ml /1 tsp jam on to a chilled saucer. If the surface wrinkles when you push the jam with your finger, the jam is set.
5 Pour the jam into clean, warm jars and cover immediately with circles of waxed paper. When it is cool, seal the jars with screw tops. Store in the dark.

Plum salad

This salad goes well with lamb, pork or plainly cooked mackerel.

 20 minutes

Serves 4
175 g /6 oz dessert plums
1 medium-sized round lettuce
¼ cucumber
6 spring onions
4 sage leaves, chopped
15 ml /1 tbls chopped tarragon
15 ml /1 tbls chopped parsley
60 ml /4 tbls olive oil
30 ml /2 tbls white wine vinegar
salt and freshly ground black pepper

1 Halve and stone the plums and cut them lengthways into thin slices. Shred the lettuce, cut the cucumber lengthways into 4 long sticks, then across into thin slices. Finely chop the spring onions.
2 Put the plum and cucumber slices, lettuce and spring onion in a salad bowl and mix in the herbs. Beat the oil, vinegar and seasonings together and fold into the salad.

Grilled lamb chops with plums

This dish is easy to prepare, yet unusual and impressive enough to serve at a dinner party.

🍴🍴 1 hour

Serves 4
8 small loin lamb chops
45 ml /3 tbls olive oil
pinch of cayenne pepper
350 g /12 oz purple dual-purpose plums
1 large onion, finely chopped
15 ml /1 tbls chopped thyme
150 ml /5 fl oz dry white wine

1 Trim the chops if necessary and, if they are boneless, wrap the tail round the thick end. Brush the chops with olive oil and sprinkle them on both sides with cayenne pepper. Leave them to stand for 30 minutes. Meanwhile stone and thinly slice the plums.
2 Heat the grill to high. Grill the chops on the hot rack for about 7 minutes on one side until they are a rich brown. Turn the chops and grill them for 1 minute more.
3 Scatter the onion over the chops and continue to grill until the onion begins to brown. Pour off any fat that has collected in the grill pan.
4 Remove the rack and set the chops in the bottom of the grill pan. Arrange the plum slices over the chops, scatter with thyme and pour the wine into the pan.
5 Grill the chops for a further 5 minutes, or until they are cooked through. Serve with French beans and creamed potatoes.

Peaches, nectarines and apricots

Fill ripe peaches with an almondy stuffing and bake them, cool down with a creamy apricot ice, or make a simple but deliciously alcoholic trifle with nectarines – these fragrant fruits add a taste of high summer.

Peaches were introduced into Europe from Persia over 2,000 years ago, although they originally came from China. Apricots, also originating in China, are a much more recent arrival in Europe.

Both fruits have a single stone and, generally, a roughish, hairy skin. The nectarine is, in fact, a type of peach with a smooth skin and a sharper flavour.

Nectarines, apricots and peaches

Buying and storing

Peaches can be divided into clingstone and freestone types. The flesh of clingstone peaches is difficult to separate from the stone. The flavour is rather tart. Freestone peaches have sweet, juicy flesh; the stone comes away from the flesh easily. Unfortunately, there is no outward difference between the two, and as even your greengrocer might not be sure which type is on sale, which type you buy is a matter of luck.

The flesh of peaches can be white or yellow. The white varieties mature earlier, have less tawny skins and are more fragrant and flavourful. Yellow peaches are larger and travel better than white ones.

Peaches are available all year round but at their best during the summer. Feel the fruit, if possible, to test for ripeness – they should be firm; if they are too soft they will be woolly. They should be free from bruises, with cream-to-yellow skins tinged with red. Peaches with a greenish tinge will never ripen. Handle peaches with great care; they bruise easily.

Peaches kept at room temperature should be eaten within two days, but they will keep for up to five days in a paper bag at the bottom of the refrigerator.

Nectarines should be firm and blemish-free, with shiny skins. Reddish varieties should be quite red; lighter-skinned ones (which taste better) should not be at all greenish. Store as for peaches.

Apricots range in skin colour from pale yellow to a deep red-orange; flesh colour is white to orange. They should be firm, free from blemishes and have velvety skins. Apricots are an early summer fruit, but may be imported in winter.

Ripe apricots quickly become mushy and mouldy, so if you don't plan to eat them the same day, buy slightly under-ripe fruit and ripen them at room temperature. Store the ripe fruit at the bottom of the refrigerator and eat within two days, but bring the apricots to room temperature before eating.

✳✳✳✳ Peel, halve and stone peaches and apricots. Slice if wished, brush immediately with lemon juice and pack in a medium sugar syrup. Halve and stone nectarines; pack in heavy syrup. Freeze for up to 1 year.

Peach and apricot products

Canned peaches and apricots are a good store-cupboard stand-by in winter. They are available in heavy syrup or, less commonly, in fruit juice, whole or halved or, in the case of peaches, sliced.

Dried apricot halves are widely available. Bright orange ones have usually been treated with sulphur dioxide to prevent discoloration and spoilage. Whole Hunza apricots – wild apricots from Afghanistan – have not, and have a superior flavour, but are more difficult to find (try health food shops) and must be picked over carefully – discard any that have holes. Dried peach halves can be found in health food shops, or in dried fruit assortments in some supermarkets.

There are both peach and apricot jams; apricot is more often used in cookery.

Both brandies and liqueurs are made from these fruits. The best apricot brandy is said to come from Hungary. Amaretto is a distinctive, almond-flavoured liqueur made from apricot kernels, Ratafia is a liqueur from the juice and kernels of peaches, apricots or cherries, while noyau is flavoured with the kernels alone.

Apricot kernels are also used to make *amaretti di Saronno*, also called ratafia biscuits, little almond-flavoured biscuits available in Italian delicatessens.

Preparing the fruit

To peel peaches or apricots (nectarines do not need to be peeled), submerge the fruit in boiling water for 30 seconds (15 seconds if the fruit is very ripe), then plunge in cold water. The skins should come off easily. As soon as the flesh is exposed to the air, brush it with lemon juice to prevent discoloration. To stone the fruit, cut it in half at its natural indentation and twist.

Apricot kernels have an almondy flavour. To obtain them, use a nutcracker or hammer to break open the stone. Slip off the brown skin and split the kernel in half lengthways with a sharp knife. These kernels are poisonous when eaten raw; they must be blanched or toasted.

To cook dried apricots or peaches, soak them overnight in cold water to cover, then transfer, with the soaking liquid, to a saucepan, add sugar if wished, and bring slowly to the boil, stirring. Simmer until tender, then cool in the syrup.

Using the fruit in cooking

Peaches: the flavour of peaches goes well with rich duck dishes and in South American countries they are often combined with beef.

Make peach compote by poaching peach halves in a vanilla-flavoured syrup, then cooling in the liquid. Add a little orange juice or Grand Marnier before serving. In the classic peach Melba (*page 273*), poached peaches are served with vanilla ice cream and raspberry purée.

Toss sliced peaches with a little cornflour and sugar and bake in a double-crust pie. Serve this warm with ice cream. Or coat a flan base with pastry cream flavoured with crushed macaroons, cover with a layer of sliced peaches and top with an apricot glaze.

The Italians often stuff halved peaches with crushed almond macaroons and bake them for a light summer dessert (see recipe). They also make an elegant tart.

Raw sliced peaches are a luxurious addition to fruit salads – try adding a little kirsch to the syrup before chilling, or mix peach slices with melon balls, add lemon juice and sugar and chill. Perhaps one of the best ways to eat ripe peaches is sliced, sprinkled with a little caster sugar and topped with red or white wine, port, a medium dry sherry or a liqueur. Chill for an hour or so before serving.

Chop raw peaches roughly and combine them with whipped cream for a delicious sponge cake filling.

Canned peaches are good for quick desserts with ice cream and some spicy flavouring, or for spiced peaches, a sweet-sour accompaniment to meat.

Nectarines can be used instead of peaches in any recipe, or you can make a water ice from them.

Apricots, both fresh and dried, combine surprisingly well with meat, especially lamb, chicken and pork. Try serving a roast chicken surrounded by baked apricot halves filled with bread sauce, or add chopped apricots to stuffing mixtures.

Poach fresh whole apricots in syrup flavoured with lemon or vanilla for a com-

Nectarine syllabub trifle

Nectarine syllabub trifle

Nectarines, which do not need peeling, make a delicious and very easy dessert.

2 hours macerating,
then 15 minutes, plus chilling

Serves 4
4 trifle sponges
30 ml /2 tbls sweet sherry
6 nectarines
300 ml /10 fl oz thick cream
25 g /1 oz caster sugar
45 ml /3 tbls orange juice
45 ml /3 tbls brandy
60 ml /4 tbls lemon juice
4 sprigs of mint, to decorate

1 Arrange the trifle sponges over the base of a flat dish. Pour the sherry over and leave to soak for at least 2 hours.
2 Whip the cream with the caster sugar until very thick. Beat in the orange juice and brandy.
3 Stone 4 nectarines and cut up the flesh roughly. Cube the sponge cakes. Put a little of the syllabub mixture into the bottom of each of 4 stemmed glasses. Divide the cake cubes and chopped nectarine between the glasses, then top with the remaining syllabub. Chill for at least 3 hours.
4 To serve, slice the remaining nectarines and toss them in the lemon juice to prevent discoloration. Decorate each dessert with fruit slices and a sprig of mint.

Nina's cream mould with peaches

In this attractive dessert, a vanilla cream mould based on semolina is surrounded by whole poached peaches.

1 hour plus chilling

Serves 6–8
575 ml /1 pt milk
75 g /3 oz semolina
50 g /2 oz caster sugar
15 g /1/2 oz gelatine
2 medium-sized egg yolks
5 drops vanilla essence
150 ml /5 fl oz thick cream
6–8 peaches, blanched and peeled
For the glaze
30 ml /2 tbls apricot jam
15 ml /1 tbls sugar
For the decoration
angelica, cut into leaf shapes
glacé cherries, halved

1 Pour the milk into a saucepan, add the semolina and 25 g / 1 oz sugar and place over a low heat. Cook, stirring, until the mixture is thick, then remove from the heat.
2 Meanwhile sprinkle the gelatine over 150 ml /5 fl oz water in a saucepan, then heat gently to dissolve. When the semolina

mixture has cooled a little, stir in the egg yolks and the gelatine mixture. Leave for 15 minutes, then add 3 drops of vanilla essence and stir in.
3 Whip the cream until stiff and fold in. Pour into a dampened 850 ml /1½ pt souffle dish or other mould and chill.
4 Put the peeled peaches into a saucepan with enough water to just cover, the remaining sugar and 2 drops of vanilla essence. Cover and simmer for about 10 minutes, or until the peaches are tender, then cool and chill.
5 About 30 minutes before serving, turn out the semolina cream onto a serving platter and surround with the peaches. Make the glaze by beating the jam, sugar and 15 ml /1 tbls water until smooth and runny, then sieving. Coat the peaches with this and leave to cool.
6 Just before serving, decorate the semolina cream mould with the angelica shapes and glacé cherry halves.

Apricot ice cream

Serve this fresh-flavoured ice cream as an accompaniment to a summer fruit salad or on its own with crisp sweet biscuits.

1 hour
plus chilling and freezing

Serves 6
100 g /4 oz caster sugar
3 medium-sized eggs, separated
10 ml /2 tsp flour
275 ml /10 fl oz milk
450 g /1 lb apricots, halved and stoned
juice of 1/2 lemon
few drops of vanilla essence
150 ml /5 fl oz thick cream

1 In a mixing bowl, combine 75 g /3 oz sugar with the egg yolks. Sift in the flour and stir well. Gradually pour in the milk, whisking.
2 Place the bowl over a pan of simmering water and stir until the mixture begins to thicken. Remove from the heat and continue stirring for 5 minutes. The custard will not be very thick. Let cool, then chill in the refrigerator.
3 Meanwhile, place the apricots in a saucepan with the remainder of the sugar and the lemon juice. Add water barely to cover. Bring to the boil, then simmer until the apricots are soft.
4 Drain the apricots, reserving the syrup, and push through a sieve to make a smooth purée. Add enough of the reserved syrup to make 575 ml /1 pt. Cool, then chill.
5 Add the vanilla essence to the chilled custard, then stir in the chilled fruit purée. Whip the cream and stir in. Pour into a freezer container, cover and freeze.
6 After 2 hours, remove the ice cream from the freezer and beat thoroughly until smooth. Whisk the egg whites until stiff peaks form, then fold into the soft ice. Return to the freezer and freeze until firm.
7 Transfer the ice cream from the freezer to the refrigerator 45 minutes before serving to allow it to soften.

pote, or use them to decorate a rice cream mould for apricot condé. Combine a purée of cooked apricots with cream and custard to make a fool, or thicken the purée with egg yolks, pour into a pastry shell, top with meringue and bake for apricot amber. Apricot purée flavoured with a liqueur makes a good sauce for fruit puddings such as apple charlotte.

Apricots are much used in *pâtisserie*. For an apricot cream tart, arrange peeled apricot halves, rounded side up, in a pastry case, pour in a mixture of cream and egg yolks and bake.

Apricot glaze is made by heating apricot jam with water or lemon juice, then sieving. It is used to coat fruits to prevent discoloration, to spread between the layers of a cake before the filling is added or over the base of a flan case or pastry shell to prevent the filling seeping through. It is also used to coat a fruit cake before sticking marzipan on the surface.

Apricot toasts

Cream and apricots contrast surprisingly well with the crispness of fried bread.

🍴🍴 35 minutes

Serves 4
150 ml /5 fl oz thick cream
30 ml /2 tbls apricot brandy
15 ml /1 tbls orange juice
8 ripe apricots
175 ml /6 fl oz dry white wine
75g /3 oz caster sugar
100 g /4 oz butter
8 slices white bread, crusts removed

1 In a bowl, whip the cream until stiff, then add the brandy and orange juice and chill in the refrigerator while you finish the dessert.
2 Peel, halve and stone the apricots. Crack the stones to obtain the kernels. Put the wine, 275 ml /10 fl oz water and the sugar in a saucepan and heat gently, stirring to dissolve the sugar. Bring to simmering point, then add the apricots and kernels and simmer for 3–4 minutes.
3 Melt the butter in a frying-pan and, when it is bubbling, add the bread. Fry, turning once, until golden brown. (You will probably have to fry the bread in two batches, so keep the first batch warm while you cook the second.)

4 Arrange 2 slices of fried bread on each of 4 warmed plates. Place 2 apricot halves on each piece of bread, one half cut side up with an apricot kernel placed in its centre, the other half rounded side up. Spoon a little of the syrup over each apricot toast. Spoon some whipped cream on each plate and serve at once.

Stuffed peaches

🍴 45 minutes

Serves 4
4 peaches, blanched, peeled, halved and stoned
75 g /3 oz almond macaroons, crushed
25 g /1 oz sugar
25 g /1 oz softened butter, plus butter for greasing
2 medium-sized egg yolks
pouring cream, to serve

1 Heat the oven to 180C /350F /gas 4. Scoop out a little flesh from each peach half to make a hollow.
2 Put the scooped-out flesh in a bowl and add the crushed macaroons, sugar and butter. Mix well, then stir in the egg yolks. Divide this mixture between the peach halves.
3 Butter a baking tin and arrange the stuffed peach halves in it. Cook for 30 minutes, then serve warm accompanied by a jug of pouring cream.

Apricot toasts

Spiced peaches

Serve these peaches with cold meats, especially ham, pork or turkey.

🕐🍴 20 minutes, cooling, then overnight chilling

Serves 4
425 g /15 oz canned peach halves in heavy syrup
75 ml /5 tbls white wine vinegar
50 g /2 oz brown sugar
7.5 cm /3 in piece of cinnamon stick
10 allspice berries
6 black peppercorns
6 cloves
5 ml /1 tsp ground ginger

1 Drain the peaches, reserving the syrup. Pour the syrup into a saucepan and add the remaining ingredients. Bring to the simmer over a low heat, stirring, then simmer, uncovered, for 10 minutes.
2 Add the peaches and simmer for a further 5 minutes, then pour into a bowl and leave to cool. Cover and chill overnight.
3 To serve, lift out the peaches with a slotted spoon and place in a serving dish. Strain the juice over.

● This can be kept in a covered container in the refrigerator for up to 3 days.

Tropical and other fruit

Fruit familiar in one part of the world may be a rarity in another. Kiwi fruit, so familiar in New Zealand, and Cape gooseberries, prolific in South Africa, are luxuries in Europe. In this section we look at numerous fruits, many of them from tropical countries, which are less universal than the ubiquitous banana.

Do not be afraid to experiment with unfamiliar fruit. Tropical fruit are often expensive outside their native lands as they deteriorate quickly and you are paying shipping costs, but even a small quantity, added to a mixed fruit salad, will give you a chance to sample a new taste.

Choose unblemished, ripe (but not over-ripe) fruit, though many will ripen if kept in a paper bag at room temperature. Refrigerate ripe fruit, but eat as soon as possible.

Dates

Among the oldest known fruit, dates grow on a tall palm. Each firm, brown, oblong date is about 5 cm /2 in long with a single cylindrical stone. Soft dates may be sold fresh — European imports come from Israel. More familiar are semi-dried dessert dates, sold in boxes, with or without stones. These wrinkled, semi-dried fruit come from Iraq, North Africa and the southern U.S. as well as Israel. Fresh and semi-dried dates can be bought in all seasons. Dates for cooking are compressed into blocks or cut into pieces and rolled in sugar.

A traditional Arab sweetmeat is made by stuffing stoned dates with almond paste, but they are also delicious as savouries, stuffed with cream cheese mixed with liqueur, chopped nuts or crisp bacon bits. The high sugar content of dates makes them excellent in puddings, sweet breads, and chutneys.

Figs

Another Biblical fruit, figs flourish in Mediterranean climates. The shape may be elongated or almost round, and the skin colour of the fresh fruit varies from white to green to purple to black; the flesh colour is often rich pink. Fresh figs can be bought throughout the summer; they are ripe when soft, and should be eaten as soon after purchase as possible, as they are highly perishable. Peel them and eat them on their own or with prosciutto or cheese.

Dried figs are usually brown, though they may be covered with a white sugary deposit. They may be eaten as they are, stewed, made into jam, added to savoury meat dishes or sweet puddings.

Canned green figs are widely available, and can be made into a delicious sorbet. Figs are a mild laxative and syrup of figs is sold for this purpose.

Kiwi fruit

New Zealand is the main grower of this oval fruit, about 10 cm /4 in long, with a fuzzy, brownish skin. As they store well under cold conditions, kiwi fruit are available summer and winter.

The thin skin is peeled to reveal thick, succulent flesh of a brilliant green, with minute black seeds arranged in an elegant pattern in the centre. The kiwi fruit's spectacular appearance makes it an excellent garnish, and it is much used in *nouvelle cuisine* dishes such as guinea fowl garnished with fresh fruits. It also adds colour to fruit salads (see recipe).

Lichees

The lichee or litchi is a tree fruit originating in China, but now grown in India, South Africa and elsewhere. The round fruit, smaller than a plum, has a rough brittle skin, which is reddish when first picked, but turns brown later. When peeled it reveals translucent, greyish white flesh surrounding a large, brown, shiny stone. Lichees are available in early summer, but can be kept in the refrigerator for up to three months. Eat the chilled flesh in Chinese-style sweet and sour dishes, and in

Tropical ambrosia

fruit salads such as tropical ambrosia (see recipe).

Canned, stoned lichees are well known. Lichees are also available dried in Oriental food shops. The longan is related to the lichee, but it is smaller and inferior in flavour.

Mangoes

Mangoes have been cultivated in India since ancient times, and are now grown in many tropical countries. The fruit is available from midwinter to autumn. The skin of the oval, flattish fruit can be many colours — often mottled green, yellow or red. The flesh is bright orange surrounding a large flat stone. In general, price is an indication of quality; a good mango has an exquisite flavour.

A ripe mango should be soft all over, and should be eaten chilled, on its own, or 'stretched' with vanilla ice cream. Eating a mango can be very messy: the best way is to make downward cuts on either side of the stone, strip the skin off the three resulting pieces, then cut off as much of the flesh surrounding the stone as possible.

Mangoes can be made into mousses or ice creams, or sautéed with chicken breasts. Sliced mangoes and mango nectar are available canned. Dried mango powder is often used in traditional Indian cookery, while mango chutney is a popular accompaniment to curries.

Passion fruit

The passion fruit or purple granadilla is a vine fruit from Brazil, now grown in hot countries around the world. The size of an egg, its thin purple skin turns brown and wrinkled as it ripens. Inside is yellow pulp full of tiny seeds. The yellow granadilla, also called a water-lemon, is rather larger with a thicker skin and whitish pulp.

Cut off the top of fresh fruit and eat the fruit with a teaspoon, seeds and all. Or use

the pulp to top a classic Australian Pavlova meringue or a fruit salad. Sieved, the flesh can be added to a salad, ice cream or posset; canned pulp or concentrate can also be used for these.

The largest fruit of the passion flower family is the yellowish-green giant granadilla. Up to 25 cm /10 in long, it looks square-sided and has thickish skin and hard flat seeds. The taste is somewhat insipid.

Persimmons

Persimmons or kaki are a deciduous tree fruit grown throughout the Mediterranean and sub-tropical regions of the world. Ripe in late autumn and winter, they resemble large, waxy-skinned, orange-coloured tomatoes with a prominent calyx on top. Wait until they are very soft before you eat them, then cut off the tops and eat the pulp with a spoon, adding cream if you like.

The Israelis have developed a new variety called the Sharon persimmon. Its flavour is less exciting, but it can be sliced and eaten when firm, and makes a good addition to fruit salads (see recipe).

Pomegranates

The small pomegranate tree is found in Mediterranean climates throughout the world. The size of a large apple, the round fruits have hard red and yellow skins with the end opposite the stalk shaped like a crown and revealing old stamens. Inside the fruit, the translucent pink capsules each contain a black seed. Cut the fruit in half lengthways and scoop out the flesh with a teaspoon. Spit out the hard seeds. To extract the juice, squeeze the halved fruit on a lemon squeezer. Pomegranate seeds make a beautiful decoration for puddings and salads, and are especially effective against a white background.

Pomegranate syrup is called grenadine and is used for making drinks and cocktails.

Other exotic fruit

Ackees: these delicately flavoured scarlet fruits have creamy flesh and black seeds. In Jamaica they are eaten as a vegetable with salt cod. Ackees are available in cans.
Breadfruit is a staple in some tropical countries, where it is eaten as a vegetable. Grown on a tall tree, the fruit is roundish, up to 20 cm /8 in in diameter, covered with a rough, rather waxy skin which may be yellowish green or brown. Inside, a yellowish white pulp surrounds a single central core; the best varieties are seedless. Breadfruit consists largely of starch and is usually roasted; the smell resembles baking bread. The pulp is sometimes canned.
Cape gooseberry, physalis, Peruvian cherry or golden berry: a bush fruit from South America bearing marble-sized berries, Cape gooseberries have been naturalized in South Africa, which is the main exporter. Orange when ripe, the berries are encased in a brown, papery calyx (like a Chinese lantern) when fresh, but are obtainable canned. The berries can be eaten raw, stewed or made into preserves. Fresh fruit can be dipped into fondant icing. Fold the calyx back above the fruit, like wings, and hold these during dipping.

The carambola is a waxy yellow fruit, up to 12 cm /5 in long, with five distinct ribs, so that a cross-section is star-shaped. The sour-sweet flesh can be eaten raw or stewed. Use it for fruit salads, drinks and jams.
Custard apples: cherimoyas, sweet-sops, sour-sops and bullock's hearts all belong to the family *Anona* and are native to the American tropics, though now grown elsewhere. The best of them, the cherimoya, is the size of a large apple, with a greenish-grey skin with a darker scaled pattern, like a pine-cone. The flesh is like a sweetly scented, rather grainy custard, with neat rows of flattish seeds. Eat the flesh raw, scooping it out with a spoon, or make into sorbets or ice creams.

Sour-sops are kidney shaped and much larger — as much as 3.5 kg /8 lb in weight. The thin skin has rows of dark green spines. The shape and appearance of the bullock's heart is suggested by its name. The fruit is buff or reddish with a scaled surface and it may be as much as 12 cm /5 in in diameter.
Durian: this fruit, about the size and shape of a rugby ball, is covered with pointed projections on a scaly-patterned, woody skin. It is dull yellow when ripe and is famous both for its delicious flavour and its nauseating, all-permeating smell. The pulp is rich and creamy, containing two to six seeds the size of large chestnuts. The fruit is rarely found outside Malaysia.
Feijoa or pineapple-guava: this small sub-tropical fruit has a thin green skin and ivory-coloured granular flesh surrounding a jelly-like pulp with tiny seeds. With its pineapple scent and slightly tart flavour, it can be added to fruit salads, stewed or made into jams and jellies.
Guavas, which came originally from tropical America, are the size of an apple or smaller, plum or pear-shaped, with pink, cream, yellow or green skins. The colour of the pulp also varies, but it is juicy and very aromatic, with many seeds in the centre. Guavas are available in spring and summer.

They can be peeled and eaten raw (eat the seeds if you wish), but are more often made into preserves. Use canned guavas, which are often pink, to make a water ice.
Loquat: also known as the Japanese medlar, this orange, waxy-skinned tree fruit, plum-sized but pear-shaped, is picked with the fuzzy brown stalk still attached. At the wide end is a hard brownish eye. Inside, the brown stones fit neatly into soft orange flesh. Eat loquats raw, poach them with lemon juice, or make them into preserves.
Medlar: the size of a golf ball, this brown skinned tree fruit is open at the end opposite the stalk, like a cup, revealing five internal sections. In colder climates the fruit is not palatable until half rotted — called 'bletted'. Eat medlars raw or make jelly.
Mangosteen: a dark brownish-purple fruit, rather larger than a golf ball and flattened on the top and bottom, the mangosteen is distinguished by the prominent calyx, which remains attached to the stalk, and the hard eye on the opposite side. Inside the tough rind the white flesh is divided into five to seven segments. Slice the skin round the fruit and eat the segments individually, or cut off the top and spoon out the flesh.

1 guavas, 2 mangoes, 3 cherimoya, 4 fresh dates, 5 persimmons, 6 fresh figs, 7 tamarillos, 8 kiwi fruit, 9 papayas, 10 passion fruit, 11 lichees, 12 prickly pear, 13 pomegranate, 14 Cape gooseberries.

Mexican green sauce with steamed cod

Papayas or pawpaws: this fruit from a tall tree originated in tropical America. Papayas contain an enzyme called papain, which is used as a meat tenderizer. Papayas vary in size and shape, being comparable to melons. Some varieties are still green when ripe, but most are yellow or orange. The succulent pink or orange flesh surrounds a cavity full of black seeds, which are discarded.

Eat the raw flesh with a squeeze of lime juice or use it to make a breakfast juice. Sprinkled with sugar and lemon juice, papaya goes well with prosciutto; add it to a fruit salad (see recipe) or make into preserves. Green or unripe fruit can be cooked like squashes or made into pickles. You can also buy canned papaya chunks and papaya nectar.

Prickly pear: also called the Indian fig or Barbary pear, this coral-coloured, egg-shaped fruit grows in rows on the lobes of a fleshy cactus. It is covered with groups of prickly spines. Hold the fruit with a fork and peel it with a knife. Eat the juicy flesh sprinkled with lemon or lime juice and zest.

Rambutan: about the size of a plum, rambutans are covered with dark brown soft spines which make them look hairy. The white flesh is attached to a brown seed and is similar to a lichee, to which it is related.

Sapadilla or chico, from tropical America, is the source of chicle, the chewing gum ingredient. The roundish, egg-sized fruit has a rough brown skin and, when fully ripe, a luscious pulp tasting of brown sugar.

The tamarillo, jamberry or tree tomato is grown in New Zealand and Kenya, among other places, on a small tree. The egg-shaped red fruit has tart orange flesh and a tough skin. Eat raw or stewed, made into desserts or chutneys.

Mexican green sauce

🔪 20 minutes

Makes about 200 ml /7 fl oz
100 g /4 oz green Cape gooseberries, papery
*   calyxes and stems removed*
1-2 small green chillies, seeded and chopped
½ small onion, finely chopped
1 garlic clove, finely chopped
1.5 ml /¼ tsp salt
5 ml /1 tsp freshly chopped coriander

1 Put the Cape gooseberries into a small saucepan with water just to cover. Bring to the boil, lower the heat and simmer gently for 5 minutes, until the fruit is soft.
2 Put the chillies, onion, garlic, salt and coriander into a blender or food processor. Add 60 ml /4 tbls of the cooking liquid and blend, then add the cooked fruit and blend briefly. The sauce should be coarse.
3 Cool the sauce completely, then serve.

● This hot spicy sauce is usually made with *tomatillos* (Mexican green tomatoes).

Almond fig tart

🔪🔪🔪 4½ hours
plus chilling

Serves 8
350 g /12 oz dried figs
500 ml /18 fl oz dry red wine, more if needed
15 ml /1 tbls cornflour
150 ml /5 fl oz milk
5 ml /1 tsp sugar
100 ml /3½ fl oz thick cream
45 ml /3 tbls redcurrant jelly

For the pastry
100 g /4 oz flour, plus extra for dusting
200 g /7 oz ground almonds
50 g /2 oz sugar
150 g /5 oz cold butter, in small dice
1 small egg yolk, lightly beaten
iced water, if needed
For the almond paste
75 g /3 oz ground almonds
15 ml /1 tbls sugar
1 small egg white, lightly beaten

1 Soak the figs in wine to cover for 2 hours.
2 Meanwhile, prepare the pastry: mix the flour, ground almonds and sugar in a large bowl. Make a well in the centre, add the diced butter and cut in, using a pastry blender or 2 knives, until the mixture resembles coarse breadcrumbs. Then rub the mixture through your fingertips until it resembles fine breadcrumbs.
3 Add the egg yolk and work lightly with your fingertips, adding a few drops of iced water if necessary, until the pastry binds together. Form into a ball, wrap in grease-proof paper and then a polythene bag and let rest in the refrigerator for at least 1 hour.
4 On a lightly floured surface, roll out the pastry 3 mm /⅛ in thick and use to line a 24 cm /9½ in loose-bottomed tart tin. Chill in the refrigerator for 30 minutes.
5 While the pastry is chilling, make the almond paste: mix the ground almonds with the sugar, then add enough of the lightly beaten egg white to bind. Knead until the mixture is smooth and reserve.
6 Put the cornflour in a small bowl. Stir in a little of the milk to make a thick paste. In a saucepan, bring the remainder of the milk just to boiling point, then pour onto the cornflour mixture, stirring.
7 Return to the saucepan and bring to the boil, then lower the heat and simmer for 2-3 minutes. The mixture will be thick. Stir in the sugar and let it cool. Heat the oven to 190C /375F /gas 5.
8 Line the pastry with greaseproof paper and baking beans and bake blind for 10 minutes. Remove the paper and beans and return to the oven for another 10-15 minutes, or until the pastry is set and golden. Remove from the oven and let it cool.
9 In a saucepan, bring the figs and their soaking liquid to the boiling point, then lower the heat and simmer gently, partially covered, for about 30 minutes, or until the figs are tender, adding more wine if necessary to keep the figs covered with liquid. Drain the figs and let them cool. Strain and reserve 45 ml /3 tbls of the wine.
10 Trim off the hard stems of the figs and slice the fruit in half lengthways. Stuff each half with a small piece of almond paste.
11 If the cornflour mixture has stiffened, beat it lightly. Whip the cream until it is stiff, then fold it into the cornflour mixture. Spread over the pastry case, then arrange the stuffed figs, cut sides downwards, in concentric rings to cover the cream.
12 Combine the redcurrant jelly and the reserved wine in a saucepan. Heat gently, stirring constantly, until the jelly melts. Cool slightly, then glaze the top of the tart with the mixture, using a pastry brush. Refrigerate the tart and serve it chilled.

Chicken with pomegranate sauce

🍴🍴 1 hour 40 minutes

Serves 3-4
30 ml /2 tbls oil
1 large onion, finely chopped
200 g /7 oz walnuts, coarsely ground
juice of 2 oranges, strained
juice of 6-8 pomegranates, strained
5 ml /1 tsp salt
2.5 ml /1/2 tsp cinnamon
15 ml /1 tbls sugar
1.5 ml /1/4 tsp powdered saffron
50 g /2 oz flour
1.5 ml /1/4 tsp turmeric
1.1 kg /21/2 lb chicken, jointed
100 g /4 oz chicken fat or hydrogenated fat
*1.5-2.5 ml /1/4-1/2 tsp freshly ground black
    pepper*
boiled rice, to serve
watercress sprigs, to garnish

1 In a large saucepan, heat the oil and sauté the onion until it is golden. Add the ground walnuts and cook over a medium heat, stirring constantly, for 5 minutes, being careful not to let the nuts burn.
2 Add 250 ml /9 fl oz water, orange juice, pomegranate juice, salt, cinnamon, sugar and saffron. Simmer while you brown the chicken.
3 Combine the flour and turmeric on a plate and dredge the chicken pieces. Heat the fat in a large frying-pan over medium heat and sauté the chicken until it is golden brown on all sides.
4 Add the chicken to the walnut sauce and continue simmering for about 30-40 minutes, or until the chicken is tender. Grind in the pepper and serve on a bed of boiled rice, garnished with watercress.

Tropical ambrosia

🍴🍴 1 hour 10 minutes
plus cooling

Serves 8-10
*1 medium-sized canteloupe or 2 charantais
    melons, peeled, seeded and cubed*
1/2 small watermelon, peeled, seeded and cubed
1 large mango, peeled, seeded and sliced
*1 medium-sized papaya, peeled, seeded and
    cubed*
8 lichees, peeled and seeded
2 Sharon persimmons, peeled and sliced
4 kiwi fruit, peeled and sliced
*25 g /1 oz desiccated sweetened coconut, to
    garnish*
For the sauce
250 g /9 oz desiccated sweetened coconut
350 ml /12 oz canned passion fruit nectar

1 Put the prepared fruit into a serving bowl, cover with cling film and refrigerate while preparing the sauce.
2 In a saucepan, combine the coconut and 250 ml /9 fl oz water. Bring to the boil and simmer uncovered, stirring occasionally, for

10 minutes. Strain the liquid through cheesecloth, then wring out the cloth to extract all the liquid.
3 Let the coconut milk cool to room temperature, then combine it with the passion fruit nectar. Pour the mixture over the chilled fruit and place the salad in a serving bowl.
4 Sprinkle the salad with the desiccated coconut for the garnish, and serve.

● If any fruit is not available you can make the salad without it, or substitute bananas or pineapple.

Date roll

🍴🍴 1 hour 45 minutes
plus cooling

Serves 10-12
700 g /11/2 lb dates, stoned and finely chopped
juice of 2 lemons
175 g /6 oz sugar
For the biscuit dough
100 g /4 oz butter, plus extra for greasing
50 g /2 oz soft brown sugar (light or dark)
100 g /4 oz sugar
250 g /9 oz flour, plus extra for dredging
2.5 ml /1/2 tsp bicarbonate of soda
1.5 ml /1/4 tsp salt
2 medium-sized eggs, beaten
50 ml /2 fl oz milk
For the topping
1 medium-sized egg
30 ml /2 tbls milk
50 ml /2 fl oz honey
10-12 walnut halves

1 To make the filling, combine the dates, lemon juice, sugar and 150 ml /5 fl oz water in a saucepan. Bring to the boil, stirring constantly with a wooden spoon, and simmer for 5 minutes, or until the mixture forms a smooth mass. Let it cool.
2 To make the biscuit dough, cream the butter with the sugars in a large bowl. Sift together the flour, soda and salt in another bowl. In a third bowl, beat the eggs with the milk. Add the eggs and flour mixture alternately to the creamed butter mixture, beating until the dough is smooth and stiff.
3 Knead the dough briefly, then dust a sheet of greaseproof paper about 40 × 30 cm /16 × 12 in with flour. Roll out the dough to cover the paper. Spread with the date filling, leaving 15 mm /1/2 in border all round.
4 Roll up the dough along the long side and transfer the roll carefully to a buttered baking sheet. Arrange the roll in a ring. Heat the oven to 190C /375F /gas 5.
5 Beat the egg and milk for the topping together and brush over the roll with a pastry brush.
6 Place the honey in a small saucepan and warm it gently over a low heat. Dip the walnut halves in the honey to coat them, then place them at intervals on top of the roll.
7 Bake the roll for 30-40 minutes, until it is golden brown. Leave it on the baking sheet for 5 minutes before transferring it to a wire rack to cool completely.
8 To serve, slice the roll into 10-12 slices, each topped with a walnut half.

Chicken with pomegranate sauce

Dried fruit

Dried fruit makes glorious winter puddings, and moist fruit cakes are associated with festive occasions such as weddings. But dried fruit can also be eaten on its own as a dessert, and adds a subtle interest to Middle Eastern savoury dishes.

Grapes left hanging on the vine or spread out on terraces, in the heat of the sun, dried and so were preserved, to make man's first convenience food. The chemistry of this method of preserving is simple. Drying draws off the moisture and this inhibits the growth of enzymes, mould and bacteria. With most of the water content gone, the fruit is left energy-packed with sugar (calories, too, unfortunately) in the form of glucose. Without any further processing it can safely be stored in a cool, dry place for a year or more – round to the next harvest.

In some regions fruit is still dried naturally, in the sun, but artificial heat is increasingly employed. This can be in the form of hot, dry air streams, in ovens, or by freeze-drying.

Buying and storing dried fruit

The most popular dried fruits are sold in supermarkets and grocers ready-washed and conveniently packed. Health food shops have an even wider range, including bananas, and often specify that their products are 'natural'. This means that they have not been sulphurated: a small amount of sulphur dioxide, which vanishes on exposure to air, water and heat, is permitted in processing to preserve colour. Always choose plump, unblemished, supple fruit – no dried fruit should be as hard as leather. Currants, raisins and sultanas, the 'vine' fruits all dried from grapes, are sold separately or mixed together with added chopped peel. The 'orchard' fruit, apples, apricots, peaches and pears, can be bought ready-mixed, often with figs, to make delicious hot or cold fruit salads or compotes.

Once the packets are opened, tip the contents into airtight containers such as screw-topped jars where they will keep for a year or more.

Vine fruit

Currants: since ancient times, currants have been dried in Greece from the small black seedless grapes cultivated along the Gulf of Corinth – their name is a corruption of this. Greece is still a prime producer of currants but Australia is now another large producer. With a high sugar content, which consti-

tutes about 70% of their weight, 100 g /4 oz of currants contain about 240 calories. Famous currant-packed specialities are Dundee cake and Eccles cakes.

Raisins: dessert raisins come from the purplish Muscatel grape from the Malaga area of Spain. Because they contain so many pips they are rarely used for cooking. Seedless raisins, produced mainly in Spain, the U.S. and Australia, vary in size according to the variety of grape.

Raisins combine well with nuts, not only in chocolate bars, but in traditional Westmorland pie, in moist teabreads – sometimes first steeped in tea – and in coleslaw-type salads of grated cabbage and carrot. Raisin purée, made from pre-soaked fruit, is a Finnish speciality, served with porridge on feast days.

Sultanas: dried from small, white, seedless grapes, sultanas are produced in Turkey, Australia, the U.S. and South Africa. They are added raw to some salads but are usually cooked. Their pale colour and delicate flavour are specially appreciated in cheesecake and custard-based desserts, and in apple cake and saffron cake.

Tree fruit

Apples: dried apples are one of the few fruits that do not lose any vitamin C in the drying process. Soaked apple rings can be dipped in a light batter and fried – like bananas – to make delicious fritters.

Apricots: exported mainly by South Africa, Australia and Turkey, dried apricots are deep golden-coloured and the best ones are soft and supple. Wild Turkish apricots can occasionally be bought, whole or halved, in health food shops. They have an even stronger, sweeter flavour.

Soak the fruit in orange juice to emphasize the flavour. Add a few apricots to fresh fruit salads or oranges soaked in wine or liqueur. Apricot purée sweetened with honey makes a beautiful glaze for baked ham or grilled chicken pieces.

Bananas: this fruit from the tropics, West Indian and Latin American countries, is sold dried, loose or packaged, in health food shops. Soak the banana halves in warm water for 30 minutes, dry them, then dip them in batter or egg and breadcrumbs, and fry. Serve these golden fritters with

whipped cream and raisins. Or try them baked in natural brown sugar, butter and a dash of rum.

Dates: three-quarters of the world's dates come from Iraq, with other producers being Israel, North Africa and the U.S. Dates are rich in vitamins A and B, and two-thirds of their content is sugar.

Dried dates are sold stoned and compressed in transparent packets; they are convenient for chopping for cakes and biscuits. Sold whole in boxes or tubs, they make the perfect winter sweetmeat. Whole dates can be stuffed with cream cheese or Brazil nuts as cocktail snacks or coated with melted chocolate for quick-to-make bonbons to serve with coffee.

Figs have been cultivated in all the Mediterranean countries for thousands of years and, together with olives, symbolize peace and plenty. Turkey is a major exporter of Smyrna figs, compressed in packets, decoratively strung in loops, or loose.

Dried figs, which contain 50% sugar, have a powdery sugar deposit on their skins. They are high in protein, B vitamins, iron and dietary fibre – and so serve as a gentle laxative. Syrup of figs is given to children for this reason.

Dried figs are a delicious sweetmeat. In cooking, they are used in biscuits, scones, cakes and steamed puddings.

Peaches are usually sold as part of a dried fruit mix. Dried peaches – unlike apricots – lack much of the flavour of the fresh fruit.

Pears: resist any temptation to eat dried pears by the handful, as they contain six times as many calories as fresh pears.

Prunes: the Californian prune industry owes its origins to the early European settlers, who took their favourite, extra-sweet plum varieties with them. Prunes are dried both with and without the stones, and sold packaged, loose or canned in syrup. Prune juice is popular in the U.S.

Prunes contain only half as much sugar, and half as many calories, as dates and figs, so slimmers may enjoy them more freely. They are also a mild laxative.

Prunes are the 'plums' in old-fashioned plum pudding. They can also be stuffed with blanched almonds, wrapped in bacon and grilled – the traditional English devils on horseback. This savoury can be served at the end of a meal or as a cocktail snack.

Prunes can be macerated (steeped) in gin or brandy to make an exquisite liqueur.

A mixture of dried fruits
Left to right: jars of macerated fruit, dried apricots, apple rings, sultanas, bananas, dates, prunes, figs and pears.

Drying fruit at home

You can successfully dry apples and pears in your own kitchen. Apples should be peeled, cored and sliced into 5 mm /¼ in thick rings. Pears should be peeled, cored and halved. To prevent the fruit discolouring, place the pieces immediately in cold salted water for a few minutes. Lift out and pat dry with absorbent paper. Spread the fruit out on wire racks, pears with cut sides uppermost. Dry for several hours in the oven at the lowest setting with the door slightly ajar or in the cooling oven when you have finished cooking. To test that they are completely dry press two or three of the pieces of fruit together; they should feel rubbery and springy. Remove the racks from the oven and leave for twelve hours before putting the fruit in sealed, air-tight jars or containers.

Using dried fruit

Nibbled raw straight from the packet or reconstituted in water or wine, dried fruit can be enjoyed in a variety of ways.

Currants, raisins and sultanas are most often used raw, in baking. They may need washing before they can be used; if so, put them in a colander, rinse under cold, running water and drain well. Toss them on crumpled absorbent paper to dry, then in a light dusting of flour. If the fruits are not properly dried, they will sink to the bottom of the dough or batter.

Sultanas are especially good added to a curry sauce because they soak up and retain all the different spice flavours. Raisins simmered in cider make a delicious sauce to accompany poultry.

Apples, apricots, peaches, pears and prunes can be added unsoaked to casseroles. Lamb or chicken with apricots, for example, is a typical North African dish which combines the sweetness of fruit with meat. Apple rings served with braised pork chops or peaches with duck not only taste delicious but the dried fruit helps to break down the richness of the meat.

Chopped dried fruit mixed with herbs and breadcrumbs and bound with a little melted butter or beaten egg makes moist tasty stuffings or forcemeat balls, again ideal with rich meat and poultry. Try apricot stuffing with duck, prune with goose and apple and raisin with chicken. Finely chopped dried apricots, stirred with some toasted almonds into boiled rice, makes a perfect party accompaniment for meat and chicken.

Many Middle-Eastern recipes call for apricots, prunes and raisins soaked in orange-flower water or rose-water. Prunes and apricots are threaded on kebabs with pork. Since medieval times dried fruit has been soaked and incorporated into European meat dishes – for example, traditional English mincemeat, which is now a sweet stuffing containing no meat whatever.

Dried fruit goes particularly well with spices such as cinnamon, in sweet dishes like pies, flans and crumbles. Dried fruit purée, made in a trice from stoneless soaked fruit, is a marvellous stand-by which can be used as a base for fruit ice creams, mousses, fools and as a filling for sponge sandwiches.

Christmas pudding

Make this traditional pudding well ahead of other Christmas chores – it will improve with keeping. It is very rich, so a little will go a long way.

🕐 🍴🍴 6½ hours, plus 4 weeks maturing then up to 4 hours reheating

Makes 2 × 1.4 kg /3 lb puddings
225 g /8 oz wholemeal flour
5 ml /1 tsp salt
100 g /4 oz wholemeal breadcrumbs
225 g /8 oz shredded suet
225 g /8 oz soft dark brown sugar
2.5 ml /½ tsp ground cinnamon
1.5 ml /¼ tsp grated nutmeg
1.5 ml /¼ tsp mixed spice
500 g /1 lb seedless raisins
350 g /12 oz sultanas
350 g /12 oz currants
175 g /6 oz mixed candied peel, chopped
25 g /1 oz sweet almonds, blanched and chopped
25 g /1 oz bitter almonds, blanched and chopped
3 medium-sized eggs, beaten
275 ml /10 fl oz milk
125 ml /4 fl oz brandy, to serve

1 In a large bowl, mix together the flour, salt and breadcrumbs. Stir in the suet, sugar and spices and mix thoroughly. Stir in the dried fruit, peel and almonds.

2 Beat in the eggs and milk. The mixture will be very stiff. Stir well and, if possible, cover the bowl and leave to stand for several hours, or overnight, stirring occasionally.

3 Prepare two pudding bowls. Grease them thoroughly and have ready greased greaseproof paper and scalded pudding cloths large enough to cover them.

4 Turn the pudding mixture into the prepared bowls. Cover each one with a double thickness of the greaseproof paper, pleated in the middle to allow for the pudding to rise. Cover with scalded cloth, also pleated. Tie the cloth securely over the paper with string.

5 Place the bowls on trivets in large saucepans. Pour in enough boiling water come half-way up the sides of the bowls. Cover the pans and steam for 6 hours, topping up the level of the water as necessary with more boiling water. When cooked remove the bowls from the water, remove the cloths and paper when they are cool enough to handle and replace with fresh covers.

6 Store in a cool, dry, airy place, checking from time to time that the puddings have not become damp. They should store for 1–2 years.

7 To reheat the pudding when needed, place on a trivet in boiling water in the same way and steam for 4 hours. Remove the covers, run a knife between the bowl and the pudding and invert on to a heated serving dish.

8 To serve, warm the brandy in a saucepan. Pour it over the pudding, and set alight. Spoon the flaming liquid back over the pudding and serve it flaming.

Dundee cake

Dundee cake

This famous Scottish fruit cake is rich, dark and moist and full of plump sultanas and currants.

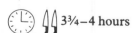 3¾–4 hours

Serves 8
175 g /6 oz butter
175 g /6 oz soft light brown sugar
3 medium-sized eggs, beaten
50 g /2 oz ground almonds
150 g /5 oz currants
150 g /5 oz sultanas
25 g /1 oz mixed candied peel, chopped
175 g /6 oz flour
5 ml / 1 tsp baking powder
15 ml /1 tbls milk
50 g /2 oz blanched almonds

1 Grease an 18 cm /7 in deep cake tin, line the base and sides with two thicknesses of greaseproof paper and grease the paper. Heat the oven to 150C /300F /gas 2.
2 Cream together the butter and sugar until light and fluffy. Gradually beat in the eggs. Stir in the ground almonds, currants, sultanas and peel.
3 Sift together the flour and baking powder and, using a large metal spoon, fold into the mixture alternately with the milk.
4 Turn the mixture into the prepared tin and level the top, making a slight depression in the centre. Arrange the almonds over the top in concentric rings. Lightly press them into the mixture.
5 Put in the oven and bake for 3¼–3½ hours or until cooked. Test by piercing the cake through the centre with a skewer. The skewer should come out clean.
6 When the cake is cooked remove the tin from the oven and stand it on a wire rack to cool for 30 minutes. Turn out the cake, peel off the paper and leave to cool thoroughly. Store in an air-tight tin and let the cake mature for 2 days before eating.

Prune mousse

about 1 hour
plus 2 hours setting time

Serves 6
350 g /12 oz prunes, stoned
300 ml /10 fl oz red wine (or cold tea)
50 g /2 oz sugar
15 ml /1 tbls lemon juice
20 g /¾ oz gelatine
150 ml /5 fl oz thick cream, softly whipped
2 medium-sized egg whites
150 ml /5 fl oz thick cream, whipped, for decoration

1 Put the prunes in a pan with the wine or tea and sugar and bring to the boil. Simmer for 20 minutes. Push the prunes through a sieve or purée in a blender. Measure the purée and make it up to 600 ml /1 pt with water if necessary. Stir in the lemon juice.
2 Put 45 ml /3 tbls water into a cup or small bowl, sprinkle on the gelatine and stand in a pan of hot water, stirring occasionally, until the gelatine has dissolved, about 5 minutes. Stir into the prune purée, and set aside to cool.
3 When the mixture is on the point of setting, about 20 minutes, fold in the softly whipped cream. Whisk the egg whites until they are stiff but not dry and, using a large metal spoon, fold them into the mixture.
4 Rinse a 850 ml /1½ pt mould in cold water and pour the mixture in. Set aside to chill in the refrigerator for 2 hours.
5 To serve, run a knife round the inside of the mould. Hold a serving plate over the mould, invert it and give the mould a gentle shake. If the mousse will not slide out, wring out a tea-towel in very hot water, and wrap it round the base of the mould for a few seconds, and then repeat the process. Serve the mousse decorated with whipped cream.

Apricot cream pudding

Smooth, sweet layers of golden apricot purée and crunchy layers of crumbs make a pudding that is interesting in both texture and flavour.

1 hour soaking,
30 minutes, then chilling

Serves 4
225 g /8 oz dried apricots, soaked in warm water, to cover, for 1 hour
45 ml /3 tbls orange juice
1 large cooking apple, cored and chopped
150 ml /5 fl oz thick cream
100 g /4 oz butter
100 g /4 oz fresh white breadcrumbs
50 g /2 oz Demerara sugar
pinch of ground cinnamon
25 g /1 oz blanched almonds, toasted

1 Drain the apricots and put them in a pan with the orange juice and chopped apple. Slowly bring to the boil and simmer for about 10 minutes or until the apple is tender. Purée in a blender or rub through a sieve. Allow the purée to cool. Lightly whip the cream and fold in all but 45 ml /3 tbls.
2 Meanwhile, melt the butter in a frying-pan, stir in the crumbs, sugar and cinnamon and stir over low heat for about 5–7 minutes, until the crumbs are golden brown. Remove from the heat and allow to cool.
3 In a glass bowl, make a layer of apricot purée, sprinkle with a layer of crumbs, and so on, finishing with the fruit. Cover the pudding with the remaining whipped cream and put in the refrigerator to chill thoroughly for about 1½ hours. Arrange the almonds in a pattern on top to serve.

Macerated fruit

Fruit layered in a jar with nuts and sprinkled with orange-flower water and rose-water captures all the exotic quality of the East.

 10 minutes preparation
1 week maturing

Serves 8–10
500 g /1 lb dried apricots
100 g /4 oz prunes
100 g /4 oz seedless raisins
100 g /4 oz blanched almonds, halved
25 g /1 oz pine nuts
100 g /4 oz caster sugar
15 ml /1 tbls orange-flower water
15 ml /1 tbls rose-water
To serve as dessert
soured cream with pinch of grated lemon zest or cinnamon (optional)

1   Choose a large jar with a well-fitting stopper, about 1 kg /2 lb capacity.
2   Arrange the fruit in the jar in layers; apricots, prunes, apricots, raisins and so on, sprinkling each layer with almonds, pine nuts, sugar and a few drops of the flower waters. When all the fruit is used up, pour on just enough water to cover the fruit, and seal the jar. Leave it in a light, sunny place, if possible, for at least 1 week while the syrup deepens in colour and thickens.
3   The fruit is very sweet and rich and can be drained and served as a sweetmeat. Alternatively serve as a dessert; accompany it, if you like, with whipped soured cream with a little grated lemon zest and cinnamon stirred in, or with natural yoghurt.

Fig cookies

20 minutes

Makes about 36 cookies
100 g /4 oz butter
100 g /4 oz soft light brown sugar
1 medium-sized egg, beaten
15 ml /1 tbls clear honey
225 g /8 oz self-raising flour
100 g /4 oz dried figs, chopped
flour and butter for baking sheets

1   Heat the oven to 180C /350F /gas 4 and grease and flour 2 baking sheets.
2   Cream the butter and sugar until light and fluffy. Gradually beat in the egg and the honey. Sprinkle on the flour and fold in, a little at a time, to make a soft paste. Stir in the chopped figs.
3   Place teaspoonfuls of the mixture on the baking sheets, spaced well apart to allow room for spreading. Gently press down each cookie to flatten it.
4   Bake for 10–12 minutes, until the cookies turn light brown at the edges. Leave on the tray to cool before removing to a wire rack. When the cookies are completely cold, store in an airtight tin.

Glazed chicken with apricots

Fish and prune kebabs

30 minutes marinating time then 30 minutes

Serves 6
700 g /1½ lb white fish such as fresh cod or haddock, skinned
18 prunes, stoned
30 ml /2 tbls olive oil
juice of 1 lemon
salt and freshly ground black pepper
15 ml /1 tbls chopped fresh mint or parsley
6 bay leaves
6 small tomatoes, halved
1 lemon cut into 6 wedges, to serve

1   Place the prunes in a bowl and cover with warm water. Set on one side.
2   Trim the fish, remove the bones and cut the fish into 4 cm /1½ in squares.
3   Mix together the olive oil, lemon juice, salt, pepper and herbs. Put the fish into a small, shallow container, pour over the marinade and toss well. Cover and refrigerate for about 30 minutes, stirring occasionally.
4   Heat the grill to medium and drain the prunes. Divide the fish between 6 skewers, alternating it with the prunes, bay leaves and halved tomatoes.
5   Brush the kebabs with the remaining marinade and grill them for 5–7 minutes on each side, until the fish is firm. Serve the kebabs on a bed of rice, garnished with the lemon wedges.

Glazed chicken with apricots

This combination of chicken and dried fruit is in the Moroccan tradition.

30 minutes marinating time then 50 minutes

Serves 6
1.4 kg /3 lb chicken, cut into 6 serving pieces
salt and freshly ground black pepper
30 ml /2 tbls seedless raisins
300 ml 10 fl oz orange juice
30 ml /2 tbls lemon juice
45 ml /3 tbls clear honey
100 g /4 oz dried apricots, soaked and drained
orange slices, to garnish

1   Heat the oven to 190C /375F /gas 5. Season the chicken pieces well with salt and pepper and arrange them in a shallow ovenproof dish. Sprinkle over the raisins.
2   Mix together the orange juice, lemon juice and honey and pour it over the chicken. Set aside to marinate for 30 minutes, turning the chicken once or twice.
3   Bake the chicken uncovered for 15 minutes. Add the apricots, turn the chicken and continue baking for 30 minutes, or until the chicken is tender. Test with a fine skewer pierced through a thigh portion; the juices should run clear when cooked. Remove the chicken pieces and transfer to a heated serving dish. Season the sauce to taste and spoon over the chicken.
4   Serve garnished with the orange slices.

Herbs and Spices

Herbs and spices have played an extremely important part in cooking for centuries and are used to enhance or complement the flavour of a dish. In earlier times herb gardens were commonplace and the herbs were used for medicinal purposes as well as in the kitchen. Spices were an extremely valuable commodity – it was partly the merchants' quest for sea routes to India and the spice islands that led to the discovery of the New World.

Today there is a revival of interest in these flavourings. The popularity of gardening has inspired people to grow all sorts of different herbs, realizing that many of the plants look attractive in the garden as well as being a practical asset in the kitchen. If you want to use the less common herbs, or even to use the common ones in any quantity, the only answer is to grow them for yourself, and this is not difficult as most herbs will thrive in poor soil or in window boxes.

Fifteen years ago few of us would have dreamt of making a curry with anything but curry powder. Now, the growing interest in ethnic cooking and culinary styles means a search for greater authenticity and subtlety in the kitchen. Western cooks have learnt that different spices can be blended together to make a host of tasty dishes, and we are now being reintroduced to the exciting range of spices that come from the East.

While this introduces us to exciting new dishes, do not forget the traditional use of spices such as nutmeg and ginger as flavouring for classic puddings. This chapter provides a wide range of recipes to help you make the fullest use of all the aromatic herbs and spices.

Bouquet garni and mixed herbs

Basil, bay, marjoram, sage, thyme, oregano and rosemary can each be used very effectively to bring out the flavour of 'bland' food, such as white fish, chicken or courgettes. Used singly or in combinations, they also offset the heavy richness of meat, such as pork and offal, and the oiliness of certain fish. From pizzas to cool custards our meals are transformed by these herbs.

Pungent and aromatic, robust herbs are particularly associated with country-style soups, slow-cooked meat and fish dishes, hearty sauces and, in some cases, with baking and flavouring sugars for cakes, puddings and ice creams. They may be combined with parsley to make a flavour bundle – nowadays often a sachet – which predates all modern flavouring cubes.

Basil, bay, marjoram, sage, thyme, oregano and rosemary can also be used for making herb butters, teas and tisanes and to flavour oils, vinegars and marinades. All these herbs can be grown at home; they tend to be sun-loving and dry better than *fines herbes*.

Fresh or dried, these strong flavoured herbs are especially associated with the *bouquet garni*. This is a bunch of fresh herbs (or sachet of dried), which is used to flavour food ranging from stocks and soups to stews, casseroles and sauces: it is discarded at the end of cooking. The basic herbs usually included in the bouquet garni are a bay leaf and a few sprigs of both thyme and parsley: the number and size of the sprigs can be varied according to the nature of the dish. Other herbs such as rosemary, marjoram, basil or tarragon (particularly for fish and chicken dishes) are sometimes included, as well as celery stalks with the leaves and pared lemon or orange zest.

Types of herb

Basil originally came from India, where it was revered as a sacred herb and regarded in particular as symbolizing the protection of the poor. In Italy it symbolized love, and the Jews believed that holding a sprig gave moral support on fast days. Medicinally, the herb was used to treat digestive disorders and headaches, and it was also grown indoors as an insect repellent.

Of the 40 or so types of basil, the most common are sweet basil (*Ocimum basilicum*), whose large, shiny, bright green leaves give off a heady scent at the slightest touch, and bush basil (*O. minimum*), which in fact grows to a height of only 15–30 cm /6–12 in, and has tiny, scented leaves. In cooking, basil is particularly associated with hot or cold tomato dishes: the chopped raw leaves make tomato salad a delicacy, and fresh or dried basil is delicious in tomato sauce. With Parmesan cheese, pine nuts and olive oil, basil is a basic ingredient of *pesto*, the superb green sauce the Italians often serve with pasta. You will also find that the flavour of basil enhances egg dishes of all kinds, and goes specially well with vegetables such as beans, peas, marrows and courgettes. Cream cheese pounded with a few basil leaves makes a delicately flavoured sandwich spread.

Basil dries and freezes well (for instructions on drying and freezing, see *page 332*). Freeze a few basil sprigs in cubes of concentrated stock to flavour soups and sauces, and in cubes of syrup for fruit salads. Basil can be part of a bouquet garni.

Bay: whether grown as an evergreen shrub in the open ground, or clipped to a neat round shape in a tub, a well-tended bay is a great delight. Bay is native to Mediterranean countries, and the ancient Greeks honoured their poets and other heroes with wreaths of bay leaves – hence the title 'poet laureate', from *Laurus nobilis*, the Latin name for bay.

The tough, oval bay leaves are dark green and have a strong, almost sweet scent; fresh or dried, a bay leaf is an essential part of a bouquet garni. Add a bay leaf to the cooking liquid when poaching fish or casseroling meat, or to the milk when you are making a bechamel sauce. A bay leaf is a good addition to the brine when salting or pickling meat or fish. Bay leaves were traditionally infused in milk for making custards and other desserts. A sprig of bay makes a very attractive decoration for the top of a pâté, meat loaf or savoury flan.

There is little point in freezing bay leaves as they dry so well. Strip the leaves from their stems after drying and store them in an airtight container away from the light. Like this, they will keep their fragrance for a very long time. You can also buy powdered bay, which makes a tasty garnish for cream soups and quiches.

Marjoram is native to Asia, southern Europe and North Africa. It was traditionally used as a dye, a strewing herb and, medicinally, for cramp and rheumatism, stomach ailments, toothache, headache and nervous disorders. In Greece, where marjoram grows wild on the hillsides, it is the clusters of white or purple flowers, called *rigani*, rather than the soft grey leaves, that are valued. Sprinkled over lamb or beef

Fish and courgette casserole, with bunch of basil and bouquet garni.

Making a bouquet garni

Tie herbs in a piece of scalded and dried muslin. Use for any dish in which broken leaves would be undesirable.

Tie bay leaf, thyme, parsley sprig and orange zest with fine string. Leave a long end of string to attach to pan handle.

kebabs or spit-roasted pork or goat, they impart an aroma slightly reminiscent of lavender. Sweet or knotted marjoram (*Origanum marjorana*) is the type that features most in cooking generally, particularly to flavour poultry, veal, sausages and pulses. Like basil, marjoram has a special affinity with tomatoes, and with mushrooms as well. It is very good baked in bread and scones, and makes excellent tea and jelly. It can be included in a bouquet garni; with thyme and sage it is one of the traditional mixed herbs.

Marjoram freezes and dries well: cut the stems just before they flower if drying.

Oregano (*Origanum vulgare*) is a form of wild marjoram and shares many of the marjoram's characteristics, but its small, roughish leaves are much more pungent than those of any other marjoram – almost spicy-hot and sweet at the same time. With the popularity of Italian cooking and pizza restaurants, oregano is perhaps best known for the piquancy it brings to pizza toppings and pasta sauces. It is also good with grilled meat and, in moderation because it is so strong, in fish, egg and cheese dishes. Oregano freezes and dries well.

● For an appetizer with an unusual flavour to serve with drinks, steep some black olives in oregano-flavoured oil. First prick the olives with a sterilized needle, then pack them into a screwtop jar. Add 5 ml /1 tsp lightly crushed black peppercorns and 15 ml /1 tbls fresh chopped oregano if available (or half that quantity of dried). Fill the jar with olive oil, cover, shake well and leave for about 2 weeks, shaking the jar from time to time.

Rosemary is a native of the Mediterranean that thrives particularly well by the sea. Mentioned in ancient Greek, Roman and medieval legends, it has been valued medicinally as a tonic and, because of its abundance of natural oils, as an ingredient in skin fresheners, hair rinses and perfumes. There are a number of varieties of rosemary available, with white or light mauve flowers,

and arching or erect habit of growth, but no cottage or garden kitchen is complete without a thick sprawling bush of the ordinary form, *Rosemarinus officinalis*, which has thin, spiky green leaves, grey underneath, and small mauve flowers.

Tuck a sprig of rosemary inside a chicken for roasting or boiling, against the bone in loin of lamb, pork or veal for roasting, or on top of chops and fish for braising or grilling. Remove the herb before eating. When rosemary is an integral part of a dish, snip the leaves very finely, several at a time, with sharp kitchen scissors. Include a sprig of rosemary in a bouquet garni, or push a few sprigs of the fresh herb into a jar of sugar to lend an interesting flavour to sweet dishes. Rosemary is often associated with baking, and in Mediterranean countries bakers use bunches of rosemary to sweep out their ovens, leaving behind some of the herb to lend a sweet aroma.

Rosemary does not freeze well; for drying, cut the stems when the plant is just coming into flower. The dried leaves can be easily crumbled between the fingers.

Sage, another native of the Mediterranean, is used medicinally as a mouthwash, and is also considered to be beneficial in warding off winter ills and curing failing memory. There are a large number of garden varieties, differing in the shape and colour of the leaves. The type most frequently used in cooking, *Salvia officinalis*, has furry, greyish-green leaves and purple flowers. Sage helps to make rich meat and oily fish more digestible: sage and onion is a traditional stuffing for duck, goose and pork. Sage is also cooked with eel and mackerel and used in spicy sausages and pâtés. The Italians cook fresh sage leaves with liver – a delicious combination (see recipe). Sage freezes and dries well.

Thyme, of Mediterranean origin, has had a chequered history – traditionally favoured by fairies in folklore, considered a symbol of courage in ancient Greece, burnt as incense in Roman times and used medicinally as an

antiseptic and for bronchial complaints. There are numerous types, but the ordinary garden thyme (*Thymus vulgaris*), with tiny, round, greyish green leaves and pale pink flowers, is most often used in cooking. A sprig of thyme is one of the basic herbs in a bouquet garni and in that role flavours soups, stews and casseroles. Combined with parsley and grated lemon zest, it also makes particularly tasty flavourings for stuffings for meat and poultry, and is good in fish and cheese dishes and with root vegetables. The tiny leaves are very highly scented and a little goes a long way, whether in herb butter, bread or a salad.

Lemon thyme (*T. citriodorus*), with softer leaves than garden thyme and a delicate lemon scent, is particularly good with fish and chicken and in custard-based dishes.

Thyme freezes and dries well. You can dry the flowers and rub them on grilled meat and use them in marinades, as the Greeks do.

Making your own mixed herbs
Traditionally mixed herbs consist of marjoram, thyme and sage, usually 1 part of each of marjoram and thyme and 2 parts of sage. Try making your own blend from dried home-grown herbs, varying the proportions to your personal taste; store in small screwtop jars in a dry, dark place.

Herb soda bread

Thyme, oregano, rosemary or a mixture of herbs are all suitable for this bread.

🕐 55 minutes

Makes 2 × 18 cm /7 in loaves
500 g /18 oz wholemeal flour
5 ml /1 tsp bicarbonate of soda
10 ml /2 tsp salt
30 ml /2 tbls chopped fresh herbs, or 15 ml /1 tbls dried herbs
275 ml /10 fl oz buttermilk or milk soured with 5 ml /1 tsp lemon juice

1 Heat the oven to 230C /450F /gas 8. Sift the flour, bicarbonate of soda and salt into a mixing bowl and add the bran that remains in the sieve. Stir in your chosen herb or herbs.

2 Add the buttermilk or soured milk and mix well, adding a little tepid water (up to 45 ml /3 tbls) if necessary, to make a firm but not sticky dough.

3 Divide the dough into two, shape each piece into a 6.5 cm /2½ in thick round, about 15 cm /6 in in diameter. Score the top of each round into 4 sections. Place the dough rounds on floured baking sheets and cover with 20–23 cm /8–9 in inverted deep cake tins. Using the tins means the bread is steamed for the first part of cooking, with a really moist result.

4 Bake the dough rounds slightly above the centre of the oven for 30 minutes. Remove the covering tins and bake for a further 10–15 minutes, until the loaves sound hollow when rapped on the base with the knuckles. Cool on a wire rack.

Liver with sage and Madeira sauce

Liver with sage is a classic North Italian combination.

🥄 20 minutes

Serves 4
450 g /1 lb calf's liver, sliced
22.5 ml /1½ tbls flour
2.5 ml /½ tsp dried sage
salt and freshly ground black pepper
40 g /1½ oz butter
about 20 fresh sage leaves
60 ml /4 tbls chicken stock
60 ml /4 tbls Madeira or medium-dry sherry
a few sprigs of sage to garnish

1 Cut the slices of liver into very thin strips (about 10 mm /½ in). Shake the flour and dried sage together in a polythene bag, empty out onto a plate and season with salt and pepper. Coat the liver strips in the seasoned flour and shake off the excess.
2 Heat the butter in a frying-pan. Fry the liver pieces for 2 minutes, turning them to brown on all sides. Add the sage leaves and continue to fry the liver, turning once or twice, for 1–2 minutes more, or until it is just cooked: be careful not to overcook it; it should be slightly pink inside.

3 Pour in the stock and Madeira or sherry, stir to take in all the pan juices, and bring to the boil. Adjust the seasoning if necessary. Turn the liver onto a heated serving dish and garnish with sprigs of sage.

Pork chops in cider

Apples, rosemary and sweet cider give a delicious tang to pork.

🥄🥄 1 hour

Serves 4
4 pork chump chops
salt and freshly ground black pepper
15 ml /1 tbls vegetable oil
25 g /1 oz butter
1 medium-sized onion, finely chopped
1 clove garlic, crushed
300 ml /10 fl oz sweet cider
2 sprigs rosemary
2 dessert apples, cored but not peeled
15 ml /1 tbls flour

1 Heat the oven to 180C /350F /gas 4. Trim most of the fat from the chops and season them with salt and pepper.
2 Heat the oil and half the butter in a

Pork chops in cider, garnished with a sprig of rosemary.

flameproof casserole and fry the chops over a moderate heat for 3–4 minutes, turning them so that they brown on both sides.
3 Stir the onion and garlic into the casserole and cook until the onion is lightly coloured. Pour over the cider, add one sprig of rosemary and bring the sauce to the boil. Cover and cook in the oven for 30 minutes.
4 Slice the apples into rings, add to the casserole and stir to coat them with sauce. Cook for a further 10 minutes. Discard the rosemary.
5 In a small bowl, beat together the remaining butter and the flour to make a beurre manié. Using a slotted spoon, transfer the chops and apples to a heated serving dish and keep warm. Stir the beurre manié into the sauce in the casserole and whisk over a high heat until the sauce thickens and becomes glossy.
6 Pour the sauce over the chops and garnish with the reserved sprig of rosemary.

Fish and courgette casserole

This is a good dish to make in summer, when courgettes are plentiful.

🥄🥄 1 hour

Serves 4
700 g /1½ lb cod fillet
75 g /3 oz butter
1 large onion, sliced
350 g /12 oz courgettes, sliced
15 ml /1 tbls flour
5 ml /1 tsp paprika
2 large tomatoes, blanched, skinned and sliced
225 ml /8 fl oz dry white wine
5 ml /1 tsp chopped fresh basil or thyme, or 2.5 ml /½ tsp dried herbs
a fresh bouquet garni including a strip of thinly pared orange zest
salt and freshly ground black pepper
8 thin slices French bread

1 Heat the oven to 170C /325F /gas 3. Skin the fish and cut it into 5 cm /2 in pieces.
2 Melt 25 g /1 oz of the butter in a flameproof casserole, add the onion and courgettes and cook over a moderate heat for 2 minutes, stirring so that the vegetables become thoroughly coated. Stir in the flour and paprika and cook for a further 3 minutes, stirring continuously.
3 Add the tomatoes to the casserole with the wine, basil or thyme and the bouquet garni and season with salt and pepper.
4 Bring the contents of the casserole to the boil. Stir well, add the fish pieces, cover and cook in the oven for 35–40 minutes, until the fish is just tender. Adjust the seasoning if necessary and discard the bouquet garni.
5 Heat the remaining butter in a large saucepan and briskly fry the bread slices on both sides until they are crisp and golden brown. Drain on absorbent paper.
6 Arrange the fried bread slices to stand up round the rim of the casserole, so that they do not get soggy. Serve at once.

Fines herbes

It is impossible to imagine our kitchens without the variety of flavours that herbs offer: for tasty soups, delicious sauces to accompany meat, poultry and fish; golden savoury flans and omelettes lightly speckled with fresh green herbs; sparkling herb jellies and refreshing and invigorating herbal drinks. Herbs are nature's ingredients that transform everyday cooking into an art.

The leaves and sometimes the seeds of herb plants have been used since time immemorial for flavouring food in different ways. Wild plants, herbs among them, were man's first food. Over the centuries herbs were additionally valued for their soothing and healing properties; some were used as preservatives and in making dyes, cosmetics, perfumes and essences. Herbs were also used in fragrant pot-pourris and strewn on floors to sweeten the air. Indeed, our early ancestors were so dependent on herbs that they even believed them to have magical powers, and included them in many a recipe for a witch's brew or magical love potion.

The first formal herb gardens were established by the monks in their monasteries and by the nobility in their castle grounds; these beautifully laid out gardens brought together herbs imported in the course of trade with the spice lands, as well as those planted centuries before by the Romans. In the monastery gardens there was strong emphasis on the medicinal herbs the monks needed to tend the sick: chervil and mint to combat stomach ailments; dill for insomnia; parsley and savory as digestives; tarragon for heart and liver disorders, and so on. The monks dispensed not only herbal medicines but the plants and seeds themselves, which then became established in cottage gardens.

Fines herbes: this is a term you will come across in classical French cookery. It refers to a mixture of fresh chervil, chives, parsley and tarragon, which is used in savoury flans and omelettes and with bland poultry and fish dishes to give a delicate mixed herb flavour. Together or individually, these herbs must be used with particular care to achieve subtle results. The following section describes each of the *fines herbes* and dill, mint and savory, which also require delicate treatment in cooking.

Types of herb and their use

1 Chervil (*Anthriscus cerefolium*) is more widely used in France than elsewhere. It is rather like parsley with delicate cut leaves. Its very slightly aniseed flavour complements other herbs well. One of the first fresh herbs of springtime, it is traditionally used in Easter cookery. Chop fresh leaves into green salads, mix with mayonnaise or soured cream dressing for potato or cucumber salads, or sprinkle on to soups as a garnish. Use sparingly in egg and cheese dishes and with beef and fish. *Sauce messine*, combining cream, egg yolks, chopped shallot and equal quantities of chervil and tarragon, is a classic dressing for turbot. Chervil is best added towards the end of cooking – long cooking makes it slightly bitter. The leaves can be dried or frozen.

2 Chives (*Allium schoenoprasum*) have long been cultivated as herbs; they were used in China as early as 3000 BC, but not introduced to Europe until the 16th century. Chives belong to the same genus as garlic, leeks and onions and grow from bulbs. They have pretty, clover-like mauve flowers and long, straight, grass-like leaves with a mild onion flavour, which can be used in many different ways. Snip the leaves very finely with sharp kitchen scissors to garnish soups and salads, particularly tomato and egg, cucumber and potato. Blend snipped chives with soured cream as a filling for baked potatoes, beat them into cream cheese, or use them to flavour omelettes and fried potato cakes. Chives do not dry well, but snipped small, can be frozen.

3 Dill (*Anethum graveolens*) has fine, feathery leaves, which grow in sprays and have a faintly aniseed flavour; it is particularly associated with Scandinavian and Russian cooking. When dried, dill is sold as dillweed. Dill seeds make a good *tisane*. Use the leaves or seeds to flavour vinegar, which you will find excellent for pickling vegetables and fish. Dill seeds give piquancy to soups and stews, especially beef, and are delicious in cole slaw and with cooked cabbage. Cooked dill leaves combine well with bechamel sauce to serve with fish and poultry. Dry or freeze the leaves; dry the seeds.

4 Mint (*Mentha* spp.), of which there are many varieties, is among the oldest of European herbs. Spearmint (**4a**), with its long, oval, greyish-green leaves, is the best for the sweet-sour mint sauce that is such a favourite with lamb.

● For mint sauce, mix together 30 ml /2 tbls chopped mint, 30 ml /2 tbls vinegar, 5 ml /1 tsp sugar and 15 ml /1 tbls boiling water. Leave to infuse for 1 hour.

Other varieties are applemint (**4b**), which has round, variegated leaves, and peppermint, which is good for drinks and some dessert dishes. Experiment with the different mints: cook mint with new potatoes, peas and other spring and early summer vegetables, chop it into green salads or stir it into yoghurt to dress cucumber salad. Use it in tea and alcoholic drinks like wine cup or julep (see recipe) or chopped with cream cheese as a sandwich filling. The leaves make pretty garnishes, and dry and freeze well.

5 Parsley (*Petroselinium* spp.): there are many different varieties and the most common are curly and crisp, and (**5b**) a flat-leaved type. Parsley is rich in Vitamin C and is a good digestive. Chew it to be friendly, after eating garlic! Sprigs of the bright green leaves are a most popular garnish, and chopped parsley is used in sauces, stuffings and breadcrumb toppings for poultry, fish and vegetable dishes, as well as in meat, fish, egg and cheese dishes of all kinds. Parsley stalks and roots are highly flavoured and lend piquancy to soups and stocks. Freeze large parsley sprigs on the stems. Dried parsley is not particularly successful.

6 Savory: there are 2 main types of *Satureia* – summer and winter. Summer savory has a slightly more subtle spiciness than the winter variety, which is stronger and more pungent. Savory is sometimes known as the 'bean herb' as it is traditionally cooked with fresh beans of all kinds, in the same way that mint is with peas. Use small quantities of the long, pointed leaves to flavour, or chop and add to stuffings, soups, casseroles, salads, fish dishes or herb butter – whenever a slightly peppery flavour is required.

7 Tarragon (*Artemisia dranunculus*) is a classic accompaniment to chicken; it is equally good with veal, pork, lamb, white fish, shellfish and eggs. Be sure to use the true French tarragon, prized by cooks, not the Russian variety, which is coarser and more bitter. Chop the long, thin leaves into salads, stuffings and sauces, especially bearnaise, tartare and mustard sauce. Tarragon leaves dry and freeze well.

Using herbs

Try growing your own herbs in the garden, in window boxes, indoors or on a patio. As well as enlivening all kinds of dishes and sauces, fresh herbs offer you the added delight of their fragrance and sometimes their flowers: enjoy their beauty and keep them fresh by arranging them in a jar of water. Cut herbs can be bought in season and will keep fresh for several days in a covered container in the refrigerator.

✳✳✳✳ You can freeze herbs on the stem, tied tightly in plastic bags or packed into small containers, then strip off the leaves as you need them. You can save space and freeze just the leaves, which crumble at a touch when frozen, or chop the herbs, pack them into ice-cube trays, fill with water and freeze, so that you can add a whole cube of flavour to a soup or stew in moments. For a luxury touch, freeze tiny sprigs of mint in ice cubes and then float them in long summer drinks.

Dried herbs: there is nothing to beat the flavour of fresh herbs, but for longer-term storage, try drying your own. Cut the herbs on a dry day, when there is no excess moisture on their leaves. Hang them in bunches in a warm, dark, airy place – not the kitchen – until the leaves feel papery. By then the water content will have evaporated, leaving the aroma and flavour intact. Strip off the leaves, gently crumble or snip them and store them in labelled, screw-top jars in a cupboard. Leave herb seeds such as dill to ripen on the plants. Cut the heads when they turn brown and hang them upside-down in a paper bag until the seeds drop, then store in the same way as leaves.

You can buy a wide range of individual or mixed dried herbs. Whenever you use dried herbs, your own or commercially prepared ones, use half, or a little less than half, the quantity of fresh herbs listed in the recipe ingredients.

Herb oils and vinegars: another way to capture the aroma of herbs is to flavour vegetable oil or wine vinegar with them, for making delicious salad dressings and marinades. Experiment with tarragon, mint or dill.
● Add 60 ml /4 tbls lightly bruised leaves to 600 ml /1 pt oil or vinegar and cork tightly. Leave oil to infuse for 3 weeks, and vinegar for 10 days, shaking occasionally. Strain, pour into fresh bottles and add a fresh herb sprig before corking.

Herb teas: to chase away the winter blues, or as a cooling drink on a summer day, use herb leaves or seeds to make hot or iced teas: mint and dill seeds make specially good teas. Mint tea is very popular in the Middle East, and in France herb tea or *tisane* is often drunk after a meal.
● To make tea allow 15 ml /1 tbls fresh or frozen leaves or 5 ml /1 tsp dried herbs to each teacupful of boiling water, infuse for 5–10 minutes, sweeten if you like with a little honey, reheat or chill, and garnish with a thin slice of lemon.

Herb jellies are a traditional delicacy to serve with roast, grilled or cold meats. Parsley and mint jellies are favourites.

Herb butters stored in the refrigerator or freezer are useful in many ways, melted onto freshly cooked young vegetables or baked potatoes, as a topping for grills, or spread in sandwiches. Butter made with parsley is called *maître d'hotel* butter.
● To make herb butter beat about 10 ml /2 tsp chopped individual or mixed herbs into 125 g /4 oz unsalted butter, season with a dash of lemon juice and salt and pepper to taste. Shape into a roll, wrap closely in foil, and chill or freeze.

Herb bread: make evenly spaced diagonal slits along the length of a loaf of French bread. Spread the herb butter of your choice in each slit, wrap in foil and heat in a moderate oven for 15 minutes until the butter has melted and the bread is crisp.

Herb pâté

Serve this delicious pale green pâté as a starter, or as a main course with a tomato and onion salad and plenty of hot French bread.

2½ hours, including standing time

Serves 6 as a starter, 4 as a main course
1 kg /2 lb courgettes
15 ml /1 tbls salt
50 g /2 oz butter
4 medium-sized eggs
300 ml /10 fl oz thick cream
30 ml /2 tbls chopped mixed fresh herbs, such as chervil, parsley, mint and tarragon
pinch of cayenne pepper
freshly ground black pepper
For the garnish
45 ml /3 tbls thick cream
extra chopped mixed fresh herbs
sprigs of fresh herbs
lettuce leaves
tomato slices

1 Coarsely grate the courgettes into a colander. Sprinkle in the salt, stir well and set aside for 1 hour. Then strain, discarding the liquid which will have formed. Rinse the courgettes under cold running water and leave to dry.

2 Melt the butter in a saucepan, add the courgettes and cook over a low heat for about 10 minutes, stirring occasionally, until they are soft. Leave to cool.
3 Meanwhile heat the oven to 180C /350F /gas 4. Line a 1.5 L /3 pt loaf tin with greased greaseproof paper.
4 Mix together the eggs and cream in a bowl. Add the courgette and butter mixture and the herbs. Stir well and season with a pinch of cayenne pepper, and black pepper to taste.
5 Pour the mixture into the prepared tin, cover with foil and stand in a roasting tin. Pour enough cold water to come halfway up the sides of the loaf tin.
6 Bake in the centre of the oven for 1¼ hours, until the pâté is firm. Leave to cool in the tin, then turn out on to a serving dish.
7 Whip the cream and spread it over the top of the pâté. Scatter with chopped mixed fresh herbs and decorate with herb sprigs. Arrange lettuce leaves and tomato slices round the edge of the serving dish.

Spinach and chervil soup

Top this rich, green soup with soured cream for a striking colour contrast.

50 minutes

Serves 4
500 g /1 lb fresh spinach leaves or 375 g /12 oz frozen spinach, thawed
50 g /2 oz butter
1 medium-sized onion, thinly sliced
850 ml /1½ pt chicken stock
salt and freshly ground black pepper
30 ml /2 tbls lemon juice
1 bay leaf
15 g /½ oz flour
30 ml /2 tbls chopped fresh chervil or 10 ml /2 tsp dried chervil
30 ml /2 tbls soured cream

1 Thoroughly wash the fresh spinach, if using, and discard the stalks.
2 Melt half the butter in a large saucepan. Add the onion and cook over a moderate heat for 3–4 minutes, stirring occasionally, until it is soft but not coloured.
3 Add the fresh or thawed frozen spinach to the pan and cook for 5 minutes, stirring frequently. Add the chicken stock, salt, pepper, lemon juice and bay leaf, reduce the heat, cover the pan and simmer for 20 minutes.
4 Discard the bay leaf. Blend the soup to a purée in a liquidizer, or sieve it.
5 Melt the remaining butter in the rinsed pan, add the flour and stir over a low heat to form a roux. Gradually pour on the soup, stirring continuously. Add the fresh or dried chervil, and simmer over a low heat for 5 minutes.
6 Pour the soup into a heated tureen or individual bowls, top with soured cream and serve very hot.

Herb pâté

Mint julep

This is a wonderfully refreshing drink on a hot summer evening.

10 minutes, plus chilling time

Serves 4
30 ml /2 tbls caster sugar
a strip of thinly pared lemon zest
crushed ice
125 ml /4 fl oz whisky
16 fresh mint leaves
4 fresh mint sprigs

1 Chill 4 tall glasses in the refrigerator.
2 Put the sugar and 125 ml /4 fl oz water into a small saucepan with the lemon zest. Stir over a low heat until the sugar has dissolved. Bring to the boil, remove from the heat and allow to cool. Remove the lemon zest.
3 Spoon crushed ice into the glasses, to quarter fill them. Add the whisky, cold sugar syrup and mint leaves, and stir well. Decorate each glass with a mint sprig.

Veal chops with chervil and parsley

45 minutes

Serves 4
4 veal loin chops
salt and freshly ground black pepper
10 ml /2 tsp chopped fresh chervil or 5 ml /1 tsp dried chervil
100 g /4 oz butter
1 small onion, finely chopped
1 garlic clove, crushed
250 ml /8 fl oz dry white wine
50 g /2 oz fresh parsley sprigs
a few extra fresh parsley sprigs, to garnish

1 Season the chops with salt, pepper and the fresh or dried chervil, rubbing the seasoning well into the meat.
2 Melt half the butter in a large, heavy-based frying-pan over a moderate heat. Add the onion and garlic and cook for 3–4 minutes, stirring occasionally, until the onion is soft but not brown.
3 Add the chops to the pan and fry them for 3 minutes on each side.
4 Pour the wine over the chops, check the seasoning, bring to the boil, reduce the heat and simmer for 25–30 minutes, or until the chops are tender.
5 Using a slotted spoon, transfer the chops to a heated serving dish. Pour over the sauce, cover and keep warm.
6 Just before serving, melt the remaining butter in a small saucepan until it sizzles, but do not allow it to turn brown. In it toss the 50 g /2 oz fresh parsley sprigs and fry briskly for about half a minute, until they are crisp but still bright green.
7 Garnish the chops with the extra fresh parsley sprigs and serve the fried parsley separately in a small, heated dish.

Quiche aux fines herbes

This classic savoury flan has a deliciously creamy filling. It is essential to use fresh herbs for the right delicate flavour.

🍴🍴 45 minutes, plus chilling time

Serves 4
300 g /10 oz flour
1 medium-sized egg
90 ml /6 tbls vegetable oil
2.5 ml /½ tsp salt
iced water
For the filling
600 ml /1 pt thick cream
4 medium-sized eggs
salt and freshly ground black pepper
60 ml /4 tbls chopped fresh fines herbes (mixed chervil, chives, parsley and tarragon)

1 Tip the flour on to a pastry board, make a well in the centre; add the egg, oil and salt.
2 Using your fingertips, draw the flour over the centre and work all the ingredients together to form a dough. Add enough iced water to bind – about 30 ml /2 tbls – but do not let the dough become sticky. Form the dough into a ball, wrap tightly in cling film or foil, and leave to rest in the refrigerator for 2–3 hours.
3 Heat the oven to 220C /425F /gas 7.

Lightly grease a 20 cm /8 in flan tin.
4 Lightly flour a board and roll out the pastry on it with a floured rolling pin. Wrap the rolled pastry loosely over the rolling pin. Lift onto the flan case, ease the pastry into the case and trim the edges. Prick the base all over with a fork.
5 Line the pastry case with foil and baking beans and bake blind in the centre of the oven for 10 minutes.
6 Meanwhile mix together the cream and eggs in a bowl, season with salt and pepper and stir in the herbs.
7 Remove the baking beans and foil from the partly baked pastry case, pour in the filling and return to the oven for 15–20 minutes, or until the custard is just set. Serve the quiche warm.

Parsley and apple jelly

Serve this parsley-flavoured apple jelly with ham, pork and veal dishes.

🕐🍴🍴 50 minutes, plus overnight draining and cooling time

Makes about 1 kg /2 lb jelly
500 g /1 lb cooking apples
about 600 g /1lb 6 oz sugar
45 ml /3 tbls lemon juice
75 g /3 oz chopped parsley
a few drops of green food colouring (optional)

Parsley and apple jelly

1 Wash and roughly chop the apples without peeling or coring them. Put them in a saucepan with 600 ml /1 pt water and simmer until soft and pulpy.
2 Scald a large piece of muslin or cheesecloth by immersing it in boiling water, or use a jelly bag if you have one. Hang the material or jelly bag over a bowl, tip in the contents of the pan, and leave undisturbed overnight to drain. Do not squeeze the bag or the jelly will be cloudy.
3 Measure the apple juice, and to each 600 ml /1 pt allow 500 g /1 lb sugar. Put the juice and sugar in a large saucepan, stir over a low heat until the sugar has dissolved, then bring to the boil. Boil for 15–20 minutes until 5 ml /1 tsp of the syrup will set on a saucer when left to cool. Remove the pan from the heat each time you test the syrup, to avoid overcooking it.
4 When setting point has been reached, remove the pan from the heat and stir in the lemon juice, parsley, and food colouring if using. Set aside for 10–15 minutes to cool.
5 Stir well to distribute the parsley evenly through the jelly, pour into small, sterilized jars and cover with discs of waxed paper and then cap tightly. Label and store in a cool, dark, dry place. The jelly will keep for 1 year. If a slight mould develops on top after opening, scrape it off with a spoon.

● You can substitute other herbs for the parsley: try mint, savory or tarragon.

Sole fillets with dill and cucumber sauce

This interestingly flavoured sauce is surprisingly quick and easy to make.

 45 minutes

Serves 4

2 large lemon soles, filleted, with the trimmings (bones and skin) reserved
1 onion, sliced
1 bay leaf, crumbled
a few sprays of fresh dill or 2.5 ml /1/2 tsp dillweed
a few black peppercorns
pinch of salt
butter for greasing
juice of 1/2 lemon
For the sauce
1/2 small cucumber
25 g /1 oz butter
25 g /1 oz flour
300 ml /10 fl oz milk
salt and freshly ground black pepper
30 ml /2 tbls chopped fresh dill or 10 ml /2 tsp dried dillweed
2.5 ml /1/2 tsp caster sugar
30 ml /2 tbls thick cream
a little extra dill or dillweed, to garnish

1 Put the fish trimmings in a large saucepan with the onion, bay leaf, dill or dillweed, peppercorns and salt. Pour on just enough water to cover. Bring to the boil, reduce the heat and simmer for 20 minutes.

2 Meanwhile, heat the oven to 180C /350F /gas 4 and grease a shallow baking dish. Roll up the fish fillets, skin side inwards, and arrange them close together in the dish.

3 Remove the pan of fish stock from the heat, strain off the trimmings and reserve the stock. Mix 60 ml /4 tbls of stock with the lemon juice and pour over the fish in the baking dish. Cover the dish with foil.

4 Poach the fillets in the oven for 20 minutes. When they are cooked, remove them from the dish with a slotted spoon and keep them warm on a heated serving dish.

5 To make the sauce, peel the cucumber, cut it in half lengthways, scoop out and discard the seeds and chop the flesh coarsely.

6 Melt the butter in a saucepan, add the cucumber pieces, cover and cook over a low heat for 5 minutes, or until the cucumber is soft.

7 Stir the flour into the pan and gradually pour on the milk, stirring continuously. Bring to the boil, reduce the heat and simmer for 3 minutes, stirring.

8 Remove the pan from the heat, season the sauce with salt and pepper, and stir in the dill or dillweed, sugar and cream.

9 Pour a little of the sauce over the fish on the serving dish and sprinkle with the extra dill or dillweed. Serve the remaining sauce separately in a heated sauceboat.

● Arrange grilled mushrooms or small grilled tomatoes round the edge of the serving dish if you like.

Mint ice cream with chocolate sauce

 45 minutes preparation, plus 2½ hours cooling and freezing time

Serves 4

50 g /2 oz mint leaves
125 g /4 oz caster sugar
juice of 1/2 lemon
300 ml /10 fl oz thick cream
a few drops of green food colouring (optional)
4 mint leaves to garnish
For the chocolate sauce
125 g /4 oz plain chocolate
75 g /3 oz sugar

1 If you are using the freezer compartment of your refrigerator, turn the refrigerator to its coldest setting.

2 Put the caster sugar and 150 ml /5 fl oz water in a small saucepan, stir over a low heat until the sugar has dissolved, then bring to the boil.

3 Wash and dry the mint leaves, add to the syrup in the pan as soon as it boils, remove immediately from the heat and set aside to cool.

4 Strain the syrup through a sieve into a bowl, crushing the mint leaves with a wooden spoon to extract as much flavour as possible. Add the lemon juice to the strained syrup.

5 Lightly beat the cream and stir it into the syrup in the bowl. Beat the mixture to blend thoroughly. Add a few drops of food colouring if you like, to improve the appearance (the ice cream will otherwise be slightly grey-green).

6 Spoon the mixture into a freezer tray if using the freezing compartment of your refrigerator, or into a metal or strong plastic bowl if using a freezer. Leave for 30–40 minutes, or until the mixture is beginning to freeze around the edges. Tip the mixture into a chilled bowl and whisk well, then return to the freezer tray or bowl, cover and freeze until firm (at least 2 hours).

7 Transfer the ice cream to the main part of the refrigerator and allow to stand for 30 minutes before serving. This makes the ice cream easier to serve and mellows the flavour.

8 Meanwhile, make the chocolate sauce. Break the chocolate into a bowl and rest it over a pan of hot but not boiling water. Make sure that the bottom of the bowl is not touching the water. Stir the chocolate gently until it has completely melted. Keep the bowl standing over the pan of hot water.

9 Put the sugar and 450 ml /15 fl oz water into a small saucepan, stir over a low heat until the sugar has dissolved, then bring to the boil and boil gently for 5 minutes.

10 Remove the pan containing the sugar syrup from the heat and gradually pour the syrup into the melted chocolate in the bowl, beating well.

11 Pour the chocolate sauce back into the pan, return to the heat and simmer for 10 minutes, or until the sauce thickens enough to coat the back of the spoon. Either use the sauce hot, or allow it to become cold before serving.

12 Scoop the ice cream into individual glasses. If wished, spoon 5 ml /1 tsp of chocolate sauce on top of each portion, decorate each with a mint leaf and serve the remaining chocolate sauce in a jug, or pour all the sauce into a jug and serve separately.

Mint ice cream with chocolate sauce

Unusual herbs

Elderflower, lemon balm, salad burnet, borage – all were once common in gardens and kitchens, grown for their usefulness in lotions and potions, their decorativeness and sweet aromas in dishes of all kinds.

Sadly, today, these herbs along with fennel, bergamot, lovage, coriander and angelica, are considered unusual and will not be found in convenient little packages on supermarket shelves. But all are easy to grow, and it is well worth setting aside a part of your garden to grow them.

Many of these herbs were grown and used thousands of years ago. The ancient Egyptians, Hebrews, Greeks and Romans were all familiar with herbs and their uses, both medicinal and culinary, and in Europe and America the heyday of the herb was reached in the 17th and 18th centuries, with many a lady of the manor being an expert herbalist.

The 20th century and scientific progress brought with it bottles of synthetic flavourings and little pills to provide instant flavours and cures, and the delicacy of fresh herbs was lost to many. But a walk in the country, or a few plants in a windowbox, can provide you with some new, delicious and unusual tastes in the kitchen.

Types of herb and their uses

Angelica (*Angelica archangelica*): a sweet-smelling plant with large leaves, thick stalks and creamy white flowers, it grows up to 2 m /6 ft tall. It likes a rich, moist soil and partial shade, and can be grown from fresh seed in late summer.

Every part of the plant has some use: the distilled oil from the seeds and roots flavours liqueurs and wines; tea can be made from the leaves – it calms the nerves and helps insomnia, it is said, but it should not be drunk by diabetics; and the stems are well known for being candied and used decoratively. The young leaf tips add a sweet flavour to stewed rhubarb or gooseberries, marmalade and salads, and are a delicious flavouring for trout.

Bergamot (*Monarda didyma*) is also known as bee balm owing to bees' love of its fragrance. The most popular bergamot is the bright red Cambridge Scarlet. Reminiscent of mint in taste and smell, it likes similar growing conditions – cool and moist at the roots with a bit of morning sun. It will rapidly grow to 45 cm-1 m /18-40 in, the spidery flowers appearing at the beginning of summer.

Add sprigs to claret and ginger ale to make a delicious punch or make a tisane with the leaves. The shredded petals add a delicate honey taste to a green salad, while the dried leaves and flowers lend colour and fragrance to pot pourris and herb pillows.

Borage (*Borago officinalis*) is one of the most beautiful of herbs, growing up to 50 cm /20 in, with hairy leaves and vivid blue, star-like flowers in clusters. It was steeped in wine by the ancient Greeks to dispel melancholy. Nowadays it adds a cool, cucumbery flavour to Pimm's No 1 Cup or to a white wine punch.

Sow the seed in spring; once established, you will always have borage, for it self-sows profusely and, although it is an annual, it will often flower right through a mild winter. The leaves can be dipped in batter and deep fried, or finely chopped and added to sandwiches – they are especially delicious combined with either cream cheese or natural yoghurt.

● The leaves may be gently heated in butter, then liquidized and added to a light chicken stock with salt and freshly ground black pepper. Use about 10 leaves to 600 ml /1 pt stock. Serve this simple-to-make soup with a few borage flowers floating on top of each bowl.

Crystallized like violets, the attractive flowers make a beautiful addition to fruit salads or they can be used as cake decorations.

Coriander (*Coriandrum sativum*) is an annual, growing up to 60 cm /2 ft, with fine, feathery leaves which resemble those of flat-leaved parsley; its delicate, lacy pink flowers are followed by round, aromatic seeds, well known as a spice. The leaves, highly regarded in the Oriental kitchen – indeed coriander is sometimes called Chinese or Japanese parsley – are less commonly used in the West. They have a bitter, spicy flavour and are one of the oldest herbs known to man – Hippocrates used coriander as a medicine and the Hebrews included it among the bitter herbs eaten at the Passover Seder. The seeds are also used for cooking, especially in Indian and Middle Eastern dishes.

Coriander can sometimes be bought in Oriental and Middle Eastern shops, but it flourishes easily if sown in a rich, well-drained soil in full sun. Cut the leaves when young and add to salads, or chop them finely and sprinkle over new potatoes for a sharp tang. Coriander gives a delicate but unmistakable flavour to fish (see recipe) and is an essential ingredient in many Oriental and South and Central American dishes, as well as being useful as a garnish for curry-type dishes.

Elder (*Sambucus nigra*) is a hardy, deciduous shrub, 3-7 m /12-22 ft tall, with clusters of white flowers which are followed, in the autumn, by dark purple berries, much used in wine making. The flowers, with their sweet, heady scent, can be used to make an infusion which softens the skin and lightens the complexion; in cookery they have a variety of uses – elderflower fritters were a favourite Victorian delicacy, as were elderflower ice creams and sorbets. Several flowers, infused in cream for 2-3 hours, will impart a light, honeyish taste to the cream – delicious with strawberries or raspberries. If they are cooked with gooseberries (see recipe) they give an exotic flavour of muscat grapes.

Fennel (*Foeniculum vulgare*) is a tall (up to 2 m /6 ft), feathery, perennial plant with a mass of golden flowers in the autumn. It grows wild on many European coastlines but will do well even in a pot, provided it is given good drainage and sun. Made into a compress it soothes inflamed eyes; the ancient Greeks believed it made fat people lean. Wild fennel has a bitter taste, unlike Florentine, sweet or Roman fennel, which is aniseed-like. This latter variety is grown for the swollen base, which is used as a vegetable, although its fronds can be chopped and used as a herb.

Dried fennel stalks can be bought at delicatessens: in Italian shops they are sold as *finocchio* and look like shreds of white wood. They give a unique flavour to grilled fish, such as sea bass or fresh mackerel; the herb also goes well with pork, mange-tout, cabbage, lentils and potatoes (see recipe).

Lemon balm (*Melissa officinalis*) is a fragrant, lemon-scented perennial growing to 45-60 cm /1½-2 ft. It is very easy to grow from seed or root division in spring or autumn, liking a rich, moist soil and a sunny, sheltered position.

Delicious with fruit juices, wine cups, iced tea, salads, eggs and milk dishes, it adds natural sweetness and a lemony taste to stewed fruits. It is also good with chicken, veal, fish and vegetables and makes an unusual addition to hollandaise sauce (see recipe).

Lovage (*Levisticum officinalis*) is one of the giants of the herb garden, growing to 2.75 m /7 ft. Divide the roots in the spring, plant at the back of the border in a sunny position and you will be rewarded with an abundance of finely divided leaves tasting of celery. Use it sparingly in soups, stews and salads; it sets off the richness of pork perfectly (see recipe) and also goes well with tongue.

Salad burnet (*Sanguisorba minor*) is a small plant growing about 30 cm /1 ft high which will keep its fresh green rosettes of leaves right through the winter. Sow it in the spring or autumn – although it is an annual it is a prodigious self-sower – and use it chopped in salads, as a flavouring for vinegar or with cream cheese (see recipe) to give a fresh, cucumbery flavour.

Storing unusual herbs

As with all herbs, these are better if you can use them freshly gathered, and some, like elder, cannot be stored at all. Bergamot and borage must be used fresh in cookery, although you can dry the flowers for making pot-pourris; angelica stalks can be candied and stored, but the young leaves should be used fresh.

Coriander, fennel and lovage may be dried (see *page 332*) for use in stews, soups and curries, but are too strong when dried to be used uncooked.

✳✳✳ Lemon balm and salad burnet may be frozen: gather the leaves when they are dry, pack them in freezer bags, expel all air and freeze for up to 2 months (lemon balm) or 8 months (salad burnet). They may be used straight from the freezer in cooked dishes or defrosted and chopped for use in sauces, soups and salad dressings.

Veal with lemon balm hollandaise and Mixed herb and lettuce salad

Veal with lemon balm hollandaise

Lemon balm gives a sweet, lemony taste to hollandaise sauce – ideal with veal or trout.

⏲⏲ making the hollandaise sauce, then 15 minutes

Serves 6
6 veal escalopes, 175 g /6 oz each
freshly ground black pepper
50 g /2 oz butter
175 ml/6 fl oz hollandaise sauce (page 163), kept warm
10 lemon balm leaves plus extra to garnish
lemon slices, to garnish

1 Season the escalopes with pepper. In a large frying-pan, melt the butter over a low heat. Add 3 escalopes and sauté for 3-4 minutes each side or until cooked. Remove and keep warm while you cook the rest.
2 Using a pestle and mortar, pound 10 lemon balm leaves until thoroughly pulverized. Add to the hollandaise sauce, scraping the sides of the mortar clean with a spatula. Mix well, pour over the veal, garnish with lemon balm leaves and lemon slices and serve at once.

Pork fillets with lovage sauce

The sharp taste of lovage combines with mustard to make this delicious sauce.

⏲ 30 minutes

Serves 4
550 g /1¼ lb pork fillet, in 5 cm /2 in slices
50 g /2 oz butter
12 lovage leaves, finely chopped
30 ml /2 tbls dry white wine
5 ml /1 tsp Dijon mustard
salt and freshly ground black pepper

1 Pound the slices of pork with a meat bat to flatten them.
2 Melt 25 g /1 oz butter in a large frying-pan over a medium heat and sauté the pork for about 2 minutes each side or until done right through. This will have to be done in batches so keep the cooked meat warm while you cook the rest.
3 Add the remaining butter to the pan and sauté the lovage leaves until they are soft and very dark green, about 3 minutes.
4 Add the wine and let it bubble for a minute before stirring in the mustard. Season with salt and pepper, pour the sauce over the pork and serve at once.

Salad burnet cheese mould

Salad burnet cheese mould

⏱ 15 minutes,
plus 30 minutes chilling

Serves 6
225 g /8 oz cream cheese
30 ml /2 tbls thick cream
5 cm /2 in piece of cucumber, peeled and
  very finely chopped
salt and freshly ground black pepper
pinch of cayenne pepper
60 ml /4 tbls very finely chopped salad
  burnet leaves, or a combination of tarragon,
  basil, mint and parsley
50 g /2 oz raspberries, to garnish
toast, to serve

1   Beat the cream cheese and cream in a
large bowl until soft. Add the cucumber,
salt and black and cayenne peppers and mix
thoroughly.
2   Pile the mixture onto a flat dish and pat
it into a circular, dome-shaped mound with
a spatula, smoothing the sides flat.
3   Sprinkle the salad burnet leaves over the
mixture and press down with a palette
knife. The dome should be covered.
4   Surround the dome with the raspberries
and chill for 30 minutes or longer before
serving with toast.

Cucumber and borage soup

**This pale green soup with its bright blue
garnish makes a pretty and delicate
starter.**

⏱ 30 minutes,
plus 1 hour or more chilling

Serves 6
15 ml /1 tbls olive oil
1 large cucumber, peeled and chopped
½ Spanish onion, chopped
12 borage leaves, finely chopped
850 ml /1½ pt chicken stock
150 ml /5 fl oz thin cream
12-18 borage flowers

1   In a large saucepan, heat the oil gently.
Add the cucumber, onion and borage leaves
and sweat gently for 5 minutes, stirring
occasionally.
2   Add the chicken stock, bring to the boil
and simmer for 10 minutes, or until the
cucumber is soft and the onion is cooked.
Remove the pan from the heat and cool
slightly.
3   Liquidize the soup in a blender, pour
into a bowl and stir in the cream. Refrigerate for at least 1 hour or until chilled.
4   Just before serving, pour the soup into 6
chilled individual bowls and garnish each
with 2-3 borage flowers.

Fennel baked potatoes

**These potatoes are delicious with a bar-
becue or a platter of cold meats.**

⏱ 1½-2 hours

Serves 6
6 large floury potatoes
coarse salt
175 g /6 oz butter
180 ml /12 tbls finely chopped sweet fennel
75 g /3 oz Austrian smoked cheese, grated
salt and freshly ground black pepper
12 small sprigs of sweet fennel, to garnish

1   Heat the oven to 170C /325F /gas 3. Rub
the potatoes in coarse salt. Put them on a
baking sheet and cook for 1-1½ hours, until
a thin-bladed knife pierces them to the
centre easily.
2   Remove them from the oven and cut
each potato in half. Scrape out the flesh,
being careful not to pierce the skin, and put
it into a large bowl. Add 150 g /5 oz butter,
the chopped fennel, grated cheese and a
little salt and pepper and mix well.
3   Pile the stuffing back into the skins, dot
each with a little of the remaining butter and
return to the oven for 5 minutes.
4   Garnish each potato half with a sprig of
sweet fennel and serve at once.

Coriander halibut steaks

Wrapping fish steaks in coriander leaves and baking them in foil gives a very unusual spicy flavour. Cod steaks can be used instead of halibut.

⏱ 50 minutes

Serves 6
6 halibut steaks, 225 g /8 oz each
40 g /1½ oz butter, plus butter for greasing
24 coriander leaves
salt and freshly ground black pepper
30 ml /2 tbls dry white vermouth
1 lime, cut into 6 slices

1 Heat the oven to 190C /375F /gas 5. Line a roasting tin large enough to take the steaks in 1 layer with foil, leaving enough foil all round to seal the package. Butter the foil; line with half the coriander leaves.
2 Season the halibut steaks with a little salt and pepper and place them side by side in the tin. Top each one with 7 g /¼ oz butter, 5 ml /1 tsp vermouth and a slice of lime. Cover the fish with the remaining coriander leaves and seal the foil. Bake for 30 minutes.
3 Remove the tin from the oven, unseal the foil and remove and discard the top layer of leaves. Put each steak on a warmed serving dish with its slice of lime on top and pour over the juices that have accumulated, discarding the remaining coriander leaves. Serve the fish steaks at once.

Mixed herb and lettuce salad

If you don't have all these herbs, you can still make this salad, using the herbs you do have. Add parsley, chives or a little mint, if you wish.

⏱ 15 minutes

Serves 4-6
12 lettuce hearts
6 lovage leaves, finely chopped
8 lemon balm leaves, finely chopped
16 salad burnet leaves, finely chopped
¼ Spanish onion, very finely chopped
125 ml /4 fl oz vinaigrette dressing
12 borage flowers, whole
6 bergamot flowers, petals only

1 Put the lettuce hearts into a large salad bowl with the lovage, lemon balm and salad burnet.
2 Add the finely chopped onion to the vinaigrette, mix well and pour over the salad. Toss with your hands to make sure it is evenly coated with the dressing.
3 Scatter the borage flowers and bergamot petals over the salad and serve at once.

Gooseberry and elderflower soufflé

Gooseberry and elderflower soufflé

This refreshingly light concoction has a definite taste of muscat grapes imparted by the elderflowers.

⏱ 1½ hours, plus 3½ hours

Serves 4
225 g /8 oz gooseberries
8 elderflower heads
25 g /1 oz sugar
15 g /½ oz gelatine
150 ml /5 fl oz thick cream
5 medium-sized egg whites

1 Put the gooseberries into a large saucepan and add 40 ml /1½ fl oz water. Tie the elderflowers in muslin or cheesecloth and bury them in the gooseberries. Bring to the boil and simmer gently for 20 minutes or until the gooseberries are very soft, then let them cool for about 20 minutes, leaving them in the pan.

2 Remove the elderflower bouquet and discard. Push the gooseberries through a sieve to make a purée and sweeten with the sugar.
3 Pour 45 ml /3 tbls water into a cup, add the gelatine and put the cup in a pan of barely simmering water until it dissolves. Remove it from the heat and allow it to cool, then stir it into the gooseberry purée and leave until it is almost set.
4 Meanwhile, tie or pin a double thickness of greaseproof paper around each of 4 small ramekin dishes to stand 5 cm /2 in above the rims.
5 Whip the cream until it forms soft peaks, then mix into the purée.
6 Whisk the egg whites until they form soft peaks, fold into the gooseberry mixture and pour into the ramekins. Refrigerate for at least 3 hours.
7 Remove the ramekins from the refrigerator 30 minutes before serving. Remove the strings or pins from the paper. Dip a knife into hot water and, holding it with the back of the blade against the paper, carefully ease off the paper. Let the soufflés rest at room temperature for 20 minutes before serving.

Hot spices

Colourful, pungent and aromatic, hot spices are some of the most powerful ingredients available to the cook. Although these hot spices are mainly associated with the food of India and South America, they can be used to enhance and enliven a wide range of dishes.

The effect of a spice varies enormously according to the quantity used, so that when people say that they do not like spices, it is probably because they associate them with hot, strongly flavoured dishes. However, used sparingly, many of the hot spices are quite subtle and can give a lift to food without being at all obvious or fiery.

Many of these spices have other intriguing properties besides their flavour. Chilli, for instance, stimulates the flow of gastric juices, while paprika contains more vitamin C than citrus fruit. Fenugreek acts as an emollient and used to be administered for inflammations of the digestive tract. Cumin seeds contain up to 5% essential oil which is used in perfumery and to flavour liqueurs and some medicines. Turmeric also has medicinal properties. In Asia it is used to impart a golden glow to the skin!

Hot spices

1 Cardamom, the most expensive of this group of spices, has a warm, slightly pungent, but highly aromatic flavour. It is the pod of *Eletaria cardamomum*, a leafy member of the ginger family. The plant is a native of the moist forests of India, Sri Lanka and Guatemala. The pods are bleached to a creamy or pale green colour and contain numerous dark seeds. Black cardamom is a different variety, with large, dark, hairy pods. It is slightly cheaper but less aromatic.

Buy cardamom in the pod and add the whole pod to a recipe, or extract the seeds and crush them lightly before use. It is a very important ingredient in many Near and Far Eastern recipes, and it enhances any curry or rice dish in which it is used. It is also used in meat dishes in northern Europe.

2 Cumin is the seed of an annual herb, *Cuminum cyminum*, a member of the parsley family. Although native to the Mediterranean, cumin is more important in the cooking of North Africa, the Far East and South America.

The thin, yellowish-brown seeds are about 5 mm /¼ in long and have a strong, aromatic flavour. They can also be bought ground, as a light brown powder. It is useful to have both seeds and powder available, for while the powder is more convenient for most purposes, the whole seeds are very pleasant in curries, rice dishes, pickles and chutneys. They are also sprinkled on top of loaves of bread. Always warm the seeds or powder before use, as this helps to release the aromatic oils and bring out the flavour.

3 Fenugreek is the seed of *Trigonella foenum-graecum*, an annual belonging to the pea family. The plant is indigenous to the Mediterranean but is overwhelmingly important in India. You can buy it in seed or powder form. The seeds, small, flat and

yellowish-brown, are difficult to crush, so buy fenugreek in powdered form.

Bittersweet in flavour, fenugreek is mainly used in curries, chutneys and spicy vegetable mixtures. It is the dominant taste in commercial curry powder. Combined with cumin and mango chutney, fenugreek will give a spicy but not too hot flavour to stuffed eggs (see recipe).

4 Tamarind, which looks like a lump of dark brown sticky fibres, is actually the pulp from the pods of an evergreen tree, *Tamarindus indica*, a member of the pea family. It can be obtained from Indian shops and will keep for several months, stored in a screw-top jar in a cool dark place. To use tamarind, break off about 25 g /1 oz, steep it in a little boiling water for about 30 minutes, then press it through a sieve and use the liquid. Added to fish dishes, curries and vegetable mixtures, tamarind imparts a pleasantly sour, citrus-like flavour. Use a little lemon juice as a substitute.

5 Turmeric is the dried root of a perennial plant, *Curcuma longa*, belonging to the ginger family. It is normally bought as a powder, bright mustard yellow, and has a peppery smell and warm, slightly bitter taste. Added to pickles, relishes, rice, egg and fish dishes, turmeric gives colour as well as flavour: it can be used as a cheaper substitute for saffron, although the flavour is not the same.

Try blending a little turmeric with butter and lemon juice, and serving with plainly cooked vegetables. Use turmeric for flavour as well as colour in the famous Anglo-Indian breakfast dish of rice and smoked haddock, golden kedgeree (see recipe).

6 Chilli is the fruit of a variety of capsicum or pepper, *Capsicum frutescens*, which is a native of tropical America. The small pointed fruit may either be red or green and can be bought in various forms: fresh or dried and whole, flaked or powdered.

One of the hottest spices known to man, chilli is used extensively in South American cookery. The powder is an important ingredient of curry powder. Use discreetly in dishes, particularly those containing cheese. There is also something called chilli seasoning which is a milder form.

7 Chilli sauce and Tabasco sauce are flavouring liquids made from chillies. They are very hot and only a few drops are needed. The sauces are convenient to use because they blend in easily. Try adding a dash of chilli sauce or Tabasco to tomato juice, cream cheese, or to the dressing served with avocado.

8 Cayenne pepper is made from pulverized red capsicums which are mixed with wheat flour, made into hard biscuits and ground to a powder. Although hot, cayenne pepper is not as fiery as chilli powder. It is

added to some curry powders and used in many traditional Mexican dishes. Cayenne is often the ingredient which makes devilled dishes hot and is traditionally served with first course dishes such as smoked salmon and potted shrimps. Try adding a pinch of cayenne pepper to a cheese or leek soufflé or to a quiche. It gives a spicy flavour to egg mayonnaise or scrambled eggs.

9 Paprika pepper is a scarlet powder made from the dried sweet peppers of the capsicum family. It is chiefly made in Hungary and is widely used there and in Central Europe. Several grades of paprika are produced: the best quality is called 'rose' paprika and this has a full, sweet, slightly smoky flavour and glowing colour.

Paprika is the essential flavouring for goulash and in Hungary is included in many other stews and casseroles. Unlike peppers and chilli powder it can be used in generous quantities. Many dishes can be enhanced both in flavour and colour by the use of a little paprika. Try adding a teaspoonful to tomato soup or sauce; sprinkle it over mashed potatoes, potato or onion soup, creamed fish or chicken dishes, vegetables in cream sauce and hard-boiled eggs.

10 Garam masala is the Indian name for a special blend of spices. A typical mixture would be three parts each cardamom and cinnamon, 1 part cloves and 1 part cumin. Some mixtures have black pepper added but the overall flavour is meant to be mild rather than hot. In India there are numerous combinations as each cook makes up an individual favourite blend. If you are very enthusiastic about making curries, you might find it worthwhile making your own, but the tinned ones are satisfactory for most purposes. Unlike other curry spices, garam masala is added towards the end of the cooking time, to deepen the flavour.

11 Curry powder is another spice blend. Though not used in traditional Indian cookery it is useful for making Western-style curry. A pinch added to gravy or mayonnaise will give them a subtle lift. If you are adding curry powder to an uncooked mixture, warm the powder first in a small saucepan to release the maximum flavour.

Golden kedgeree

🔪🔪 1 hour 10 minutes

Serves 4
500 g /1 lb smoked haddock
1 bay leaf
50 g /2 oz butter
200 g /7 oz long-grain rice, washed and drained
5 ml /1 tsp turmeric
salt and freshly ground black pepper
10 ml /2 tsp lemon juice
3 hard-boiled eggs, coarsely chopped
30 ml /2 tbls chopped parsley

1 Poach the haddock gently in 600 ml /1 pt water with the bay leaf for about 15 minutes, until tender. Drain the fish, reserving the water; then skin, bone and flake the fish.
2 Melt half the butter in a medium-sized saucepan and add the rice and turmeric, stir for 1–2 minutes, then add the reserved water, making it up again, as necessary, to 600 ml /1 pt. Add 2.5 ml /½ tsp salt and a grinding of pepper. Bring to the boil, cover and simmer over low heat for 20 minutes, until all the liquid has been absorbed and the rice is tender.
3 Using a fork, add the flaked fish, lemon juice, hard-boiled egg and remaining butter to the rice. Check the seasoning, then re-heat gently, stirring so it doesn't stick to the bottom of the pan. Serve sprinkled with the chopped parsley.

Leeks vinaigrette

🔪🔪 40 minutes, plus 3 hours chilling and marinating

Serves 4–6
12 slim leeks, trimmed and washed
1.5 ml /¼ tsp cayenne pepper
30 ml /2 tbls red wine vinegar
90 ml /6 tbls olive oil
salt and freshly ground black pepper
5–10 ml /1–2 tsp paprika pepper
a few sprigs of watercress or
*   parsley, to garnish*

1 Trim the leeks, removing the roots and most of the green part. Wash them very thoroughly in cold running water. Cut them into 5 cm /2 in lengths.
2 Cook the leeks in boiling salted water in a large saucepan until they are just tender. Drain them very well.
3 While the leeks are cooking mix together the cayenne pepper and vinegar, then stir in the olive oil and a little salt and pepper. Mix really well to blend.
4 Place the hot, drained leeks in a shallow dish and pour the oil and vinegar mixture over them, turning them to make sure they are all covered. Leave for several hours, turning the leeks in the dressing from time to time.
5 To serve, sprinkle paprika pepper over the top of the leeks and garnish round the dish with a few sprigs of fresh watercress or parsley.

Spicy stuffed eggs

🔪 20 minutes

Serves 4–6
8 hard-boiled eggs
25 g /1 oz butter
5 ml /1 tsp powdered fenugreek
5 ml /1 tsp cumin seed or powder
1 medium-sized onion, finely chopped
15 ml /1 tbls mango chutney
salt and freshly ground black pepper
sprigs of watercress, to garnish
thin brown bread and butter, to serve

1 Halve the eggs lengthways and scoop out the yolks into a medium-sized bowl.
2 Melt the butter in a small saucepan and add the fenugreek and cumin. Cook over a gentle heat for 1–2 minutes, stirring all the time.
3 Add the butter and spices to the egg yolks and mash well with a fork to make a smooth mixture. Stir in the onion, mango chutney and salt and pepper to taste.
4 Arrange the whites on a serving dish. Fill the cavities with the yolk mixture, using a piping bag fitted with a 5 mm /¼ in shell nozzle. Or use a teaspoon to heap up the filling in the whites and then mark attractively with the prongs of a fork.
5 Garnish the dish with watercress sprigs and serve with thin brown bread and butter.

Golden kedgeree

Festive curried chicken salad

In this recipe the curry powder is used to give the creamy sauce a warm tang and to cut the richness. It is a twentieth century English classic, as it was served for the Jubilee of George V and re-created for the guests after Queen Elizabeth II's coronation. This version is a beautiful mixture of flavours and textures.

 1 hour 30 minutes

Serves 6
1.8 kg /4 lb roasting chicken
bouquet garni
1 carrot
1 onion
salt and freshly ground black pepper
15 ml /1 tbls cooking oil
1 small onion, peeled and choppped
1 garlic clove, peeled and crushed
10 ml /2 tsp curry powder
5 ml /1 tsp tomato purée
75 ml /3 fl oz red wine
15 ml /1 tbls apricot jam
300 ml /11 fl oz mayonnaise
50 ml /2 fl oz thick cream, whipped
5–10 ml /1–2 tsp lemon juice
To serve
cold boiled rice
a little paprika pepper

1   Put the chicken into a large saucepan, with the bouquet garni, the carrot, onion, a little salt and a good grinding of pepper. Cover with water and simmer gently for 50–60 minutes, until tender. Leave to cool in the liquid, then drain well, remove skin and slice off the meat.
2   Heat the oil in a small saucepan and fry the onion and garlic for 10 minutes until softened but not browned. Add the curry powder and cook for 1–2 minutes, then stir in the tomato purée, red wine and 50 ml /2 fl oz water and simmer gently for about 10 minutes. Add the apricot jam and cook for a further 2–3 minutes. Cool completely.
3   Put the mayonnaise into a bowl and sieve the curry mixture into it. Add the whipped cream, mix well, and season to taste, adding enough lemon juice to sharpen the flavour pleasantly.
4   Place the chicken on a serving dish and spoon the mayonnaise mixture on top, so that it is covered. Surround with a border of cold boiled rice. Sprinkle a little paprika pepper over the top of the mayonnaise.

Mixed vegetable curry

The flavour of garam masala goes particularly well with vegetables. With the accompaniments suggested here, this curry makes a complete main course.

 40 minutes

Festive curried chicken salad

Serves 4
500 g /1 lb potatoes, cubed
500 g /1 lb leeks, trimmed and washed
1 small cauliflower, in florets
100 g /4 oz shelled peas
60 ml /4 tbls oil
1 clove garlic, peeled and crushed
1 onion, peeled and chopped
15 ml /1 tbls ground cumin
2.5 ml /½ tsp turmeric
2.5 ml /½ tsp powdered fenugreek
2.5 ml /½ tsp white mustard seed
1 bay leaf
250 g /9 oz canned tomatoes
10 ml /2 tsp garam masala
salt and pepper
To serve
hot, boiled rice
salted peanuts or cashew-nuts
4–6 hard-boiled eggs, chopped
mango chutney or lime pickle
poppadoms

1   Cook the potatoes in a little boiling salted water for 15 minutes. Meanwhile cut the leeks into 10 mm /½ in pieces. Add the leeks, cauliflower florets and peas to the potato. Continue cooking until all the vegetables are just tender.
2   Heat the oil in a large saucepan and add the garlic and onion. Cook gently for 10 minutes, then stir in the ground cumin, turmeric, fenugreek and mustard. Cook for 2–3 minutes, stirring often.
3   Add the bay leaf, tomatoes and 400 ml /14 fl oz water to the onion and spices. Let the mixture simmer gently for 15 minutes, stirring from time to time.
4   Stir in the garam masala and add the drained vegetables, being careful not to break them. Taste and season with salt and pepper. Serve at once.

Festive curried chicken salad

Paprika and red wine sauce

Paprika and red wine add sparkle to this quick and simple-to-make sauce. Sieve the sauce after liquidizing if you want a really smooth texture.

 30 minutes

Serves 4–6
1 medium-sized onion, finely chopped
25 g /1 oz butter
400 g /14 oz canned tomatoes
60 ml /4 tbls red wine
2.5–5 ml /½–1 tsp paprika
pinch of sugar
salt and freshly ground black pepper

1   Melt the butter in a small saucepan and fry the onion gently for 10 minutes; do not let it brown.
2   Stir the tomatoes and red wine into the onions then purée in a blender. Return the tomato mixture to the rinsed-out saucepan, pressing it through a sieve if you want a really fine texture without pips.
3   Re-heat the sauce and add the paprika, a very little sugar and some salt and pepper to taste.

● Pour the sauce over grilled pork chops, use it to reheat cooked lamb.
● Whole small carp could be poached and served in this piquant sauce.
● Use the sauce for reheating cold cooked turkey; it is a change from white sauce.

Jewelled Danish loaf

You may be surprised to find cardamoms, which are often associated with curry, in a sweet bread dough, but they add fragrance to it. Jewelled Danish loaf is traditionally served at Christmas, but it makes an impressive accompaniment to coffee at any time of the year. Choose a mixture of different coloured candied fruit for the most attractive result.

3 hours including 1½ hours rising time, plus cooling

Makes 1 large loaf
100 ml /3 fl oz milk, lukewarm
25 g /1 oz fresh yeast
500 g /1 lb 2 oz strong flour
50 g /2 oz soft brown sugar
100 g /4 oz butter, diced
2.5 ml /½ tsp cardamom seeds, slightly crushed
10 ml /2 tsp vanilla essence
grated zest of ½ lemon
225 g /8 oz mixed candied fruit, chopped
2 medium-sized eggs, beaten
a little icing sugar, to dredge

1 Grease a 1.7 L /3 pt loaf tin with butter. Put the milk into a small bowl, crumble in the yeast and leave for 10 minutes until very frothy.
2 Meanwhile put the flour and sugar in a large bowl, and using your fingertips, rub in the butter. Mix in the cardamom seeds, vanilla essence, lemon zest, fruit and beaten eggs.
3 Make a well in the centre of the flour mixture and pour in the milk and yeast, mix to a dough, adding a very little more milk if necessary to make a medium-soft consistency. Knead the dough for 10 minutes.
4 Place the dough in an oiled bowl which is large enough to allow it to double in size; cover with a piece of oiled polythene and leave in a warm place for 45–60 minutes, or until it has doubled in bulk.
5 Punch down the mixture with your fist and knead the dough again for 2–3 minutes. Then form it into a loaf shape to fit the prepared tin. Place the dough in the tin, pressing it well into the corners. Cover the tin loosely with greased polythene and leave in a warm place to rise.
6 Heat the oven to 180C /350F /gas 4. When the loaf has risen to the top of the tin, bake in the centre of the oven for 1 hour, until golden and crisp. When turned out of its tin and rapped with the knuckles on its base the loaf should sound hollow, like a drum. Cool the loaf on a wire rack.
7 Dust the loaf with a little icing sugar, or if you prefer serve it sliced and lightly buttered.

● You can use chopped mixed peel in this cake, but for the colour effect use a selection of glacé fruit, such as apricots, pineapple and red, yellow and green cherries. Wash them first to remove excess sugar (or they will sink in the cake), pat them dry and chop coarsely.

Sweet chilli tomato chutney

Hot and spicy, this chutney is delicious with curry and particularly good with cheese. You could omit the whole mustard seeds if you have trouble getting them, but they give an interesting texture.

 1 hour 20 minutes

Makes about 1 kg /2¼ lb
500 g /1 lb cooking apples, weighed after peeling and coring
500 g /1 lb tomatoes, skinned
2 large onions
1 bulb of garlic, peeled
10 ml /2 tsp salt
200 g /7 oz stoned pressed dates
100 g /4 oz brown sugar
300 ml /11 fl oz malt vinegar
30 ml /2 tbls black mustard seed
50 g /2 oz dried root ginger
5–10 ml /1–2 tsp chilli powder

Jewelled Danish loaf

1 Cut the apples and tomatoes into small pieces; peel and chop the onions. Crush the garlic cloves in the salt. Chop the dates.
2 Put the apples, tomatoes, onions, garlic and dates into a large saucepan and add the sugar, vinegar and mustard seed.
3 Bruise the ginger by banging it several times with a rolling pin, then tie it in a small piece of muslin and put it into the saucepan with the other ingredients.
4 Bring to the boil, then simmer gently for 45 minutes. Add the chilli powder, a little at a time, tasting after each addition, until the chutney is 'hot' enough.
5 Cook the mixture for a further 15 minutes, until fairly thick, stirring frequently towards the end. Remove the bag of ginger, pressing it against side of pan with a wooden spoon to extract all the juices.
6 Let the mixture cool a little, then put into warmed, sterilized jars. Label and store in a cool dark place.
7 Mature for 3 months, if possible, in a cool, dark, dry place before eating. The chutney will keep for 1 year or more.

Sweet spices

Cloves, cinnamon, nutmeg, vanilla – these are all familiar spices in the kitchen. Today when spices are easy to buy and most people have a rack of them in the kitchen, it is surprising to realize that in the past men have risked their lives to discover spices, wars were fought over them and the wealth of nations has depended on them.

It is difficult to imagine custards and ice cream without vanilla, fruit cake without mixed spice or milk pudding without nutmeg. Yet these everyday ingredients were once precious and rare commodities, and spices were valued as much for medicine as for cooking.

In past centuries spices added interest to what would otherwise have been an intolerably dull, repetitive diet, and helped to disguise the flavour of stale or salted food. Spices were also used in preserving. Both cinnamon and cloves have some preservative properties; cinnamon contains phenols which help to discourage decay in meat. Present-day recipes for British mincemeat, a name which always confuses visitors from abroad, developed from a way of preserving meat with spices, although the only reminder of the meat still included in the modern recipe is the suet.

Spices had other uses beside culinary

Popular and useful in the kitchen, sweet spices are available whole or ground. Clockwise from the lidded jar are ground and whole cloves, ground mixed spice, vanilla pods, whole allspice, ground and whole nutmeg, whole mace in the sack, ground mace, cinnamon sticks and ground cinnamon. In the centre container is ground allspice.

ones; they were highly prized for use in perfumes, and as medicines. Cloves have a powerful antiseptic action. In Tudor times the upper classes carried pomanders, oranges stuck with cloves and dried, to sniff when visiting squalid areas of the city to ward off unpleasant smells.

Sweet spices

Cloves are pungent and aromatic, and are the best known of all spices. They are the flower buds, pink when picked, of *Eugenia caryophyllata*, a tree belonging to the myrtle family. It grows on tropical islands such as Zanzibar and the West Indies. Cloves have been imported into Europe for over 2,000 years. When freshly dried, cloves contain up to 18% oil. They can be bought whole or powdered and it is worth buying both types as they are difficult to grind at home.

Whole cloves are pungent and should be used sparingly. Stick them into apples or onions, or into an orange for a mulled wine, in order to find and remove them before serving. They are used generously in apple pie, bread sauce and in the topping for a

glazed ham. Use one or two to add interest to a beef stew or a spicy rice dish, or to give a lift to dried pulse dishes, such as pease pudding or lentil soup. They are also added to curries and pickles. Powdered cloves are added to fruit cakes and pudding and buns.

Cinnamon is the bark of a small evergreen tree, *Cinnamon zeylanicum*, which belongs to the laurel family. It grows in Ceylon and South India. There is also a related but inferior spice called cassia. Like cloves they have been traded for thousands of years. Paper thin strips of the bark are peeled off, rolled into thin sticks and left to dry. Cinnamon can be bought in this form, as stick cinnamon, or ready-ground as a powder. It is not worth trying to grind cinnamon at home, as the bark is very hard.

It is useful to have both forms of cinnamon in your store cupboard. Break off a piece of cinnamon and add it to milk puddings. Stewed fruit, spiced rice, curries and mutton stews are enhanced by the addition of stick cinnamon. Powdered cinnamon is useful for sprinkling on top of milk puddings, for adding to cakes and biscuits or even cheese pastry for cheese straws. Sprinkle it on hot buttered toast to make that old favourite, cinnamon toast.

Cinnamon goes well with chocolate; try adding a pinch to a hot cocoa drink. From Greece eastward round the Mediterranean, cinnamon is an essential element of meat cookery. It is one of the spices contained in curry powder.

Nutmeg is the kernel of a yellow, plum-like fruit of an evergreen tree, *Myristica fragrans*. Nutmegs are extracted after a long and complicated drying process and are mainly exported from Indonesia and the West Indies. Whole nutmegs are dark brown, oval and about half the size of walnuts.

Although powdered nutmeg is available, it is not really worth buying as nutmeg is easy to grate and the flavour of freshly grated nutmeg is far superior. In many parts of Europe, nutmeg is used in much the same was as salt and pepper and, in the 18th century, British travellers carried their own nutmeg graters for flavouring food. Nowadays the fine holes of an ordinary grater are equally effective for grating.

Grated nutmeg is delicious with many vegetables, necessary for proper mashed potato and much used in Italy with spinach for pasta fillings. Try a pinch with cauliflower, cabbage and all root vegetables. It is excellent with cheese; a pinch improves cream soups and sauces and is delicious with scrambled eggs. It also livens up mixtures containing sausage meat. It is the traditional garnish for milk puddings and egg custards and is often added to fruit cakes and Christmas pudding.

Mace is the husk round the nutmeg kernel, scarlet when fresh but orange-brown when dry. It is called blade mace and comes in spiky pieces too hard and brittle to grind at home. It was much more used in Britain between the 16th and 18th centuries than it is today. A blade of mace can be included in a bouquet garni for flavouring stews and its delicate flavour goes well with fish and chicken. Ground mace is a traditional flavouring for potted shrimps and meat dishes, and is also good with eggs, and in ketchups and white sauces.

Allspice is the dried unripe berry of a small tree, *Pimenta officinalis*. It is also known as 'pimenta' or 'pimento' and 'Jamaican pepper', since it grows abundantly there. It tastes rather like a mixture of cloves, cinnamon and nutmeg, although not identical. Buy it whole; as it is easily ground at home it makes a fresher substitute for bought mixed spice. Add whole crushed allspice to chutneys and spiced fruit and vegetable mixtures, or use in marinades for meat. Crushed berries add interest to a fruit compote. Powdered allspice is especially good in rich fruit cakes, and will pep up mashed root vegetables or tomato soup.

Mixed spice is a combination of ground spices, usually nutmeg, cinnamon, cloves and allspice. This is a useful way to buy spices when you want to add a small quantity of several spices to dishes. Use the mixture in fruit cakes, puddings and buns, or add a pinch to vanilla ice cream.

Vanilla looks like a long black bean – and that is precisely what it is – the bean or pod of a climbing tropical orchid, *Vanilla planifolia*. The pods are gathered before they are fully ripe and are dried. Madagascar and Mexico are the main exporters.

By using the whole pod you will get the most delicate flavouring. Vanilla is also available as a liquid extract, which is genuine vanilla and as an essence. Vanilla essence contains some synthetic flavouring, but vanilla flavouring is totally synthetic.

To use vanilla pods, steep them in the hot liquid, for instance in the sugar syrup you will use to poach fruit, or in the milk needed to make custard. This is the classic way of flavouring an egg custard. After use wash and dry the pod and store it for re-use. A

Cinnamon plum crumble, Vanilla ice cream

vanilla pod stored buried in a jar of caster sugar will impregnate the sugar with a delicate vanilla flavour. Use this vanilla sugar to sprinkle over deep-fried, battered fruit (sweet beignets), or for making cakes and biscuits. This is the classic flavouring for all sponge mixtures.

Experimenting with spices

Although there are certain traditional uses, there are no set rules for using spices, so they offer a wonderful opportunity for experiment in the kitchen. Try adding a pinch of spice to a well-known and favourite dish for a subtly different flavour. Taste a little spice on your fingertip when you can smell the aroma of the dish. This way you can match the smell and taste and decide if it is likely to be a successful addition, before adding a little.

Buying and storing

When buying spices, go to a specialist shop which has a rapid turnover, as spices lose their flavour during prolonged storage. Buy spices packaged in opaque drums not glass bottles, as the light can spoil them.

Keep your spices in small airtight containers. Spice racks filled with small glass bottles look decorative on a kitchen wall, but it is better to keep them in a cupboard out of the light, in a cool dry place. Although some spices will keep for several years, in general their flavour and fragrance deteriorate. It is a good thing to buy spices in small quantities and use them up within three months if possible.

Cinnamon plum crumble

Here is a favourite pudding with a difference; the addition of cinnamon to plum crumble gives it an exciting, spicy flavour, while adding oats to the topping makes for an interesting new texture.

1¼ hours

Serves 4
500 g /1 lb cooking plums
50 g /2 oz sugar
2.5 ml /½ tsp cinnamon powder
For the crumble topping
100 g /4 oz flour
100 g /4 oz rolled oats
5 ml /1 tsp cinnamon powder
100 g /4 oz soft margarine
50 g /2 oz sugar

1 Heat the oven to 170C /325F/gas 3. Wash, halve and stone the plums; place them in a shallow, ovenproof dish and sprinkle with the sugar and cinnamon.
2 To make the topping, place the flour, oats and cinnamon in a bowl and rub in the fat with your fingertips until the mixture resembles fine breadcrumbs, then stir in the sugar. Spoon the crumble mixture lightly over the plums and smooth the top.
3 Bake for about 40 minutes, or until the topping is crisp and golden and the plums tender when pierced carefully with the point of a knife. Serve with custard, thin cream or vanilla ice cream.

Vanilla ice cream

 30 minutes preparation
plus cooling and freezing

Serves 4
200 ml /7 fl oz milk
vanilla pod
3 large egg yolks or 4 smaller ones
50 g /2 oz vanilla sugar or caster sugar
200 ml /7 fl oz thick cream

1 Turn the refrigerator to its coldest if you are not using a domestic freezer.
2 Put the milk and vanilla pod into a medium-sized saucepan and bring to the boil. Turn off the heat. Whisk the yolks in the top of a double boiler with the sugar.
3 Pour the hot milk (and the vanilla pod) onto the beaten yolks, then cook in the double boiler over very gently simmering water, stirring all the time with a wooden spoon, until the mixture thickens and your finger leaves a mark on the back of the coated spoon – about 15 minutes. Leave to cool completely, then remove the vanilla pod. (Wash, dry and store this, as the pod can be used for flavouring again.)
4 Whisk the cream until it has thickened slightly, then fold into the cold custard.
5 Spoon the mixture into a metal container. Cover and place in a deep freeze or the ice-making compartment of your refrigerator. Leave for 30–45 minutes, or until the mixture is beginning to set around the edges. Tip the mixture into a bowl and whisk well, then return, covered, to the deep freeze and freeze until firm.
6 Allow the ice cream to stand 30 minutes in the refrigerator before serving.

Honey bread and Easter biscuits

Honey bread

This enriched bread is from France, where it is called *pain d'épice* – spice bread.

1¾ hours
then 2 days maturing

Makes 10 slices
300 g /11 oz honey, warmed to liquid
150 g /5 oz sugar
50 ml /2 fl oz boiling water
300 g /11 oz light rye flour
pinch of salt
15 ml /1 tbls bicarbonate of soda
30 ml /2 tbls dark rum
15 ml /1 tbls ground aniseed
2.5 ml /½ tsp ground cinnamon
1.5 ml /¼ tsp ground mace
1.5 ml /¼ tsp almond essence
50 g /2 oz ground almonds
125 g /4 oz chopped crystallized peel

1 Heat the oven to 180C /350F /gas 4. Grease a 2 L /3 pt loaf tin, line it with greaseproof paper and grease again.
2 Measure the honey first, by pouring it into the mixer bowl of your electric mixer or a large mixing bowl, on the top of the scales. Add the sugar and boiling water and beat until the sugar has dissolved.
3 Measure together the flour, salt and soda. Add enough flour to the honey mixture to make a stiff heavy dough, but one that can still be beaten. Beat 5 minutes.
4 Beat in the remaining ingredients and any left-over flour. Turn the mixture into the prepared tin. Smooth the top with the back of a spoon dipped in water, doming it slightly in the middle.
5 Bake in the middle of the oven for 1½ hours. Do not open the oven door during this time, as the wet, heavy dough sinks easily if the temperature drops suddenly.
6 When the bread is cooked it will shrink away from the sides of the tin. Allow the bread to cool in the tin for 15 minutes, then unmould it onto a rack. Immediately peel off the paper and turn the bread right side up. When cold – about 2 hours' time – wrap it tightly and keep for 48 hours before cutting, to allow to mature.

Easter biscuits

40 minutes

Makes about 24
150 g /5 oz flour
pinch of salt
5 ml /1 tsp mixed spice
75 g /3 oz softened butter or margarine
50 g /2 oz caster sugar
25 g /1 oz currants, cleaned
finely grated zest of ½ lemon
15 ml /1 tbls beaten egg

1 Set the oven to 170C /325F /gas 3; lightly grease a baking sheet. Sift the flour, salt and mixed spice onto a clean plate.
2 In a large bowl, cream together the butter or margarine and the sugar. Add the sifted flour and spice to the creamed mixture, together with the currants, lemon zest and egg. Mix to a smooth dough.
3 On a lightly floured board roll the dough out to a thickness of 5 mm /¼ in and cut into rounds using a 5 cm /2 in cutter.
4 Place the biscuits on the prepared baking sheet and bake for 20–25 minutes, until golden brown.
5 Carefully transfer the biscuits from the baking sheet to a wire rack and leave them to cool before serving.

Ginger

Fresh, dried whole or powdered, preserved in syrup or crystallized in sugar, ginger is one of the most versatile of spices. Add it to Chinese-style stir-fried dishes, make ginger marmalade or bake a sticky gingerbread.

The origins of ginger go back far beyond recorded history; later it was one of the first spices to be brought to Europe from Asia by Arab merchants, and was used as a medicine and as a flavouring. Indigenous to southern Asia, it is now grown in many tropical countries including India, China and Japan.

Buying and storing ginger
Fresh ginger: fresh 'green' root ginger has a soft brown skin and is very knobbly – rather like a Jerusalem artichoke. A whole piece, sometimes referred to as a 'hand' or a 'race', weighs perhaps 350–450 g /12 oz–1 lb, but it is usually sold in smaller pieces. Buy it in vegetable shops and Oriental food stores, and look for plump pieces with solid, firm flesh and smooth skin.

Store fresh ginger closely wrapped in foil, in the lowest part of the refrigerator, for up to three weeks, or in the freezer for up to a year – simply grate some off when you need it, then return the root to the refrigerator or freezer. Or scrape off the skin, slice the ginger thinly and cover it with dry sherry or good-quality olive oil. In a screw-topped jar it will keep for up to a year in the refrigerator, losing only a little of its flavour. 'Fresh' ginger is also sold, peeled and sliced, in cans in speciality and Oriental food shops.

Dried root ginger retains only 25% of its original weight, so has a more concentrated flavour. It is prepared from the fresh root in one of two ways: it may be simply washed and sun- or kiln-dried, in which case it still has its brown, wrinkled skin, or it may be boiled, peeled and (sometimes) bleached, when it will be cream-coloured or white.

Buy it, loose or in containers, in Oriental food shops, and store it loosely wrapped or in a stoppered jar in a dark, cool place. For maximum flavour, use it within three or four months.

Ground or powdered ginger is ground from the dried root. Jamaican ginger, lightest in colour, is considered the most delicate in flavour and most suitable for use in baking, while African ginger has a harsher, more peppery taste.

Buy ground ginger in small quantities and store it in a small, tightly capped jar in a dark place. Use it within three months, if possible.

Preserved or Chinese ginger is produced from young and tender roots, cleaned, peeled, partly dried and simmered in a heavy syrup that takes on the delicious aroma and flavour of the spice. The best is called 'stem' ginger.

Chinese ginger jars were made in exquisitely patterned porcelain to export this delicacy and are now collectors' items.

Many present-day jars still retain the characteristic bulbous shape. Ginger in syrup may be bought in speciality and Oriental food shops and stored for a year or more. The flavoured syrup from the jar is also useful in cooking.

Crystallized ginger, another sweetmeat made from the fresh root, is boiled in heavy syrup, cooled and reboiled several times, then dried with a hard, white, sugary coating.

It is sold loose by weight, or prepacked, in chunks or sticks. You can find it in speciality food shops. Store it in an airtight jar in a cool, dark place for up to one month: it tends to shrink and harden when stored for a long time.

Other ginger products: there are two liquid ginger flavourings. One is the genuine essence or extract of the root, which is superior in flavour to the cheaper imitation product. Buy them in speciality food shops.

Ginger beer and ginger wine, both favourite drinks of the Victorian era, and the non-alcoholic ginger ale, particularly good with whisky, are refreshing spiced drinks that can also be used for flavouring.

Using ginger

Fresh ginger is invaluable as a flavouring in Oriental dishes. In Chinese cookery it is peeled and very thinly sliced or shredded, then heated in the oil to flavour it before stir-frying, sliced and scattered over meat or fish for steaming, or quick-fried, for example with duck, pepper and leeks. To make a spice paste for Indian curries, fresh peeled ginger is ground to a pulp with other spices or grated with onions and garlic.

To give a subtle hint of ginger, rub a cut piece of the root round a salad bowl or over the skin of duck or chicken; place a couple of slices inside a whole fish – trout or mackerel, for example – before baking or steaming, or steep one or two slices in vinegar or oil for salad dressings, or in syrup for fruit salads.

Dried root ginger should be peeled, if necessary, then lightly crushed or bruised to extract the full flavour: the best way to do this is a gentle tap with a hammer or rolling pin, just enough to separate the fibres, is all that's needed.

Bruised dried ginger is well suited for flavouring marinades for meat, poultry and fish, casseroles and salad dressings. Infusion over several hours or even days allows time for the flavour to mellow. Ginger can also be infused in water, syrup or milk to flavour puddings. Or add it to the spice blend when pickling onions, red cabbage, gherkins or – particularly tasty – with fruits such as peaches or apricots.

You can grind peeled and bruised dried root ginger to make ground ginger, which will have a much less musty taste than the commercially prepared product. Cut the ginger into small pieces and pound them with a pestle and mortar or grind them in a coffee grinder. If any tough fibres remain after pounding or grinding, sift the powder through a fine sieve.

Ground ginger: whether home-ground or bought, ground ginger is immensely versatile. In baking, it combines well with other spices – cinnamon, cloves, allspice and nutmeg – in American pumpkin pie or, for example, gingerbread men, and is also delicious on its own, in homemade gingerbread or ginger biscuits.

A little ground ginger gives a surprise lift to a scone mixture for cobbler toppings, especially for fish; crumble mixtures for plums, apples and quinces, and coatings such as oatmeal and ginger for belly of pork or rolled oats and ginger for fried herrings. It is often served as a condiment with slices of fresh melon; but remember – a little goes a long way, and too much induces sneezing!

Preserved ginger: straight from the jar, with or without cream, preserved ginger makes a perfect ending to a highly spiced meal. Pieces of chopped or sliced ginger with the syrup make an instant topping for ice creams and other puddings, and a little of the syrup peps up canned fruits, especially peaches and pears. It's also delicious in a glaze for baked ham or, for a change, try a ginger-glazed roast shoulder of lamb.

Ginger marmalade

Chopped preserved ginger added to gingerbreads, ginger cakes, teabreads, scones and buns helps to keep them moist for longer; besides providing deliciously spicy, chewy morsels!

Crystallized ginger can, in many cases, replace preserved ginger. For baking, the hard sugary coating should be cracked or washed off, or the ginger may sink to the bottom.

Try adding a few pieces of crystallized ginger to an apple pie or crumble, to a hot salad of mixed dried fruits, or to rhubarb in a preserve.

Ginger essence must be used very sparingly if it is not to overwhelm a dish; try it in ginger honey fudge (see recipe) or stir a few drops into the custard for ice cream, a fruit mousse or jelly – though this is best saved for times when other forms of the spice are not available.

Ginger marmalade

You can use windfall apples for this economical preserve, which is specially good with toasted teacakes or hot buttered scones.

2½ hours

Makes about 2.3 kg /5 lb
3 Seville or sweet oranges
750 g /1 lb 10 oz cooking apples
4 cm /1½ in piece of dried root ginger, peeled and bruised
1.5 kg /3 lb 5 oz sugar
100 g /4 oz preserved ginger, drained and chopped

1 Peel the oranges and finely chop the peel. Slice the flesh thinly, reserving the pips. Peel, core and slice the apples, reserving peel, cores and pips.
2 Tie the orange pips, apple peel, cores and pips and the root ginger in a piece of muslin or cheesecloth.
3 Put the orange peel, orange and apple flesh and the muslin bag into a large pan and add 1.4 L /2½ pt water. Bring to the boil and simmer, stirring occasionally, for 1½ hours, or until the liquid has reduced by half.
4 Remove the muslin bag, squeezing it to extract as much liquid as possible. Add the sugar and stir over low heat until it has dissolved. Stir in the chopped preserved ginger.
5 Bring to the boil and boil rapidly for 10–15 minutes or until setting point is reached. To test for set, remove the pan from the heat and put 5 ml /1 tsp of the pulp on a saucer. When the pulp has cooled, push a finger across the surface. If it has reached setting point, the surface will wrinkle. If it does not, bring back to the boil and boil the fruit pulp quickly for a few minutes more.
6 Pour the marmalade into sterilized, warmed jars. Cover them at once with waxed paper circles and transparent covers. When the marmalade is cool, label the jars and store in a dry, airy place.

Ginger melting moments

⏱ 40 minutes
plus cooling

Makes 20
100 g /4 oz butter plus extra for greasing
75 g /3 oz caster sugar
1 medium-sized egg yolk
5 ml /1 tsp grated orange zest
150 g /5 oz self-raising flour plus extra for dredging
7.5 ml /1½ tsp ground ginger
45 ml /3 tbls bran breakfast cereal flakes, crushed

1 Heat the oven to 190C /375F /gas 5. Grease and flour 2 baking sheets.
2 Cream together the butter and sugar, then beat in the egg yolk and orange zest. Sift together the flour and ground ginger and stir into the butter mixture. Beat until smooth.
3 Divide the dough into balls the size of a large walnut and roll each one in the crushed cereal. Place them well apart on the baking sheets.
4 Bake for 15–17 minutes, until they are golden brown. Let them cool on the sheets for a few minutes, then transfer them to a wire rack to cool completely.

Ginger pudding

🍴🍴 2 hours 10 minutes

Serves 4–6
100 g /4 oz self-raising flour
5 ml /1 tsp baking powder
10 ml /2 tsp ground ginger
100 g /4 oz caster sugar
100 g /4 oz soft tub margarine plus extra
2 large eggs
5 ml /1 tsp grated lemon zest
5 ml /1 tsp lemon juice
100 g /4 oz crystallized ginger, rinsed and roughly chopped
30 ml /2 tbls ginger syrup (from a jar of preserved ginger)
chopped preserved ginger, to garnish
For the sauce
60 ml /4 tbls clear honey
30 ml /2 tbls ginger syrup
30 ml /2 tbls lemon juice
50 g /2 oz preserved ginger, chopped

1 Grease an 850 ml /1½ pt pudding bowl. Sift together the flour, baking powder and ground ginger. Beat together the sugar, margarine and eggs until the mixture is light. Stir in the lemon zest, lemon juice and chopped ginger, then the flour mixture. Beat until the mixture is smooth.
2 Spoon the ginger syrup into the bowl, pour in the sponge mixture and smooth the top. Cover with greased foil and tie down.

3 Stand the bowl on a trivet in a large pan with boiling water to come half-way up the sides. Cover the pan and steam for 1½ hours, topping up with more boiling water as needed.
4 To make the sauce, put all the ingredients into a small saucepan, add 60 ml /4 tbls water and heat gently.
5 When the pudding is cooked, run a knife around the inside of the bowl. Cover the bowl with a heated serving plate, invert the two and give a sharp shake to release the pudding. Spoon a little of the sauce over the pudding, garnish with the chopped preserved ginger and serve at once, with the rest of the sauce handed round separately.

Ginger honey fudge

⏱ 30 minutes
plus cooling

Makes about 500 g /1 lb
350 g /12 oz sugar
100 g /4 oz honey
50 g /2 oz butter plus extra for greasing
150 ml /5 fl oz milk
150 ml /5 fl oz evaporated milk
a few drops of ginger essence
100 g /4 oz preserved ginger, well drained and finely chopped

1 Grease a tin measuring 18 × 12.5 cm /7 × 5 in. Put the sugar, honey, butter, milk and evaporated milk into a large, heavy-based saucepan and cook over a low heat until the sugar has dissolved, then stir well.

2 Bring the mixture to the boil and boil, stirring occasionally, until it reaches 115C /240F – the soft ball stage.

3 Remove the pan from the heat, stir in the ginger essence and the chopped ginger and beat until the mixture is smooth. Pour it into the tin at once.

4 Let the fudge cool for about 20 minutes, then mark the top in squares. Cut it up when cold and store in an airtight container.

Veal with ginger cream sauce

⧗ 25 minutes

Serves 4
450 g /1 lb veal escalopes, in very thin strips
75 g /3 oz butter
1 small onion, finely chopped
2 green peppers, thinly sliced
225 g /8 oz button mushrooms, thinly sliced
salt and freshly ground black pepper
75 g /3 oz preserved ginger, well drained and very thinly sliced
150 ml /5 fl oz thick cream
1 orange, thinly sliced, to garnish
boiled white rice, to serve

Chinese-style fish with ginger

1 Heat half the butter in a heavy-based pan over moderate heat, add the onion and green peppers and fry for 2 minutes, stirring occasionally.

2 Add the mushrooms and stir until they are well coated with butter. Cook for 1 minute, then remove the vegetables with a slotted spoon and keep warm.

3 Add the remaining butter to the pan. When it is hot, add the veal and fry, stirring frequently, for 4–5 minutes, until it is just cooked. Return the vegetables to the pan, season with salt and pepper and stir in the ginger.

4 Pour in the cream, stir well and lower the heat. Bring just to simmering point but do not boil. Taste the sauce and adjust seasoning if necessary.

5 Turn the contents of the pan onto a heated serving dish, garnish with the orange slices and serve at once, accompanied by boiled white rice.

Chinese-style fish with ginger

In this quick stir-fried dish, the fish is coated with ground ginger and cooked in a sauce flavoured with fresh ginger. It is hot, so serve it with lots of rice.

⧗ 20 minutes marinating, then 15 minutes

Serves 4
700 g /1½ lb haddock, cod or other white fish fillets, skinned, in 4 cm /1½ in squares
5 ml /1 tsp salt
2.5 ml /½ tsp ground ginger
20 ml /4 tsp cornflour
50 g /2 oz fresh root ginger, peeled and very thinly shredded or sliced
4 spring onions, very thinly sliced diagonally
15 ml /1 tbls red wine vinegar
30 ml /2 tbls dry sherry
45 ml /3 tbls soy sauce
5 ml /1 tsp sugar
45 ml /3 tbls orange juice
45 ml /3 tbls oil
boiled white rice, to serve

1 Mix together the salt, ground ginger and cornflour. Toss the fish in this mixture and set it aside for 20 minutes.

2 Mix together half the shredded root ginger and half the spring onions. Add the vinegar, sherry, soy sauce, sugar and orange juice. Reserve.

3 Heat the oil in a wok or a large, heavy-based frying-pan. When it is hot, add the remaining ginger and onion and stir-fry over high heat for 1 minute.

4 Add the fish and fry for 3 minutes, using tongs to turn the pieces frequently to seal.

5 Pour on the vinegar mixture, bring to the boil and cover. Lower the heat and simmer for 3 minutes. Turn into a heated serving dish and serve at once, accompanied by boiled white rice.

The Wine Guide

For the first time in history there are now more Britons regularly drinking wine than there are drinking beer, though even now our consumption of wine is modest when compared with the annual intake of our wine-producing Continental neighbours. We are still taking our first tentative and timid steps in wine appreciation, and as yet we are mostly missing out on much of the marvellous fun that wine affords. That is because, for many of us, the vinous repertoire is still restricted to just a few tried and tested popular brands which we know we like.

By playing it safe with just a handful of commercial blends we deny the whole point about wine, which is its diversity and infinite variety. If we wanted to be absolutely safe we should no doubt stick to water, an innocuous drink which goes pretty unobjectionably with anything and everything. Wine has a bit more to say for itself. It can, accordingly, argue or be difficult to accommodate. But it can make a powerful positive contribution. Water we drink to survive. Wine is for pleasure, excitement, delight.

'The Wine Guide' is a complete wine primer, easy to understand and full of useful information for those who are introducing themselves to the wonderful world of wine. But it is also a collection of thoroughly tested and mouthwatering recipes. Every dish is paired with a carefully considered wine suggestion, so that you can use your choice of food to guide your exploration of the huge choice of wines available.

Used properly, wine is the most exciting and stimulating condiment of all – a spur to the appetite, a relish to the meal, an aid to the digestion and a health-giving food in its own right. Plenty of wines are delicious alone and served at any time, but most are at their best when properly partnered in a perfect marriage with food. Wines not only taste different from each other; the same wine will taste different according to what it accompanies. 'The Wine Guide' shows you the way.

In addition, for every wine you choose, you will find a page of the guide devoted to the area from which it comes, with pictures that capture the atmosphere and spirit of the place. It makes every mealtime a mini-holiday!

Robin Young

Wine Know-How

Learning to fully appreciate wine demands some attention to detail. Of course, reading about the varieties of grape and national or regional characteristics of wines is important. But there are more practical points to take into account. Whether a particular wine should be served chilled or at room temperature, and the best corkscrew to use, are very basic. But even these considerations, together with partnering the right wine with the right glass, come just before you raise the wine to your lips for that moment of pure enjoyment. The more you know about how wine is actually made, so that you can make an informed choice from the styles of wine on offer, and the more you know about storage requirements – position, temperature and putting down – the more you will enjoy that moment of truth.

Finally, learning how to savour a glass of good wine – to roll it around your tongue and inhale its bouquet – is not the mark of a *poseur*. Done unostentatiously, it need never be noticed, and will give you much more pleasure than simply gulping it down. Good wine deserves to be treated with respect – from the moment you buy it to the moment you proudly serve it with food you know will complement it.

Serving wine

Just as important as understanding vintages and wine regions is the correct way to prepare wine for the table. Is it best brought to room temperature or served chilled? How long should it be allowed to breathe? Here are a few guidelines to make your enjoyment as perfect as possible.

Whatever wine you are serving, whether it is red, rosé or white, cheap or expensive, it is worth making sure that it is at its best when it arrives in the glass. This need not be a complicated ritual, just a matter of ensuring that the bottle is opened at the right time and the contents poured at the right temperature into an appropriate glass.

Temperature
The rules about the temperature for serving wine are basic and easy to remember. It is common knowledge that white wines and rosés should be served chilled and the red wines at room temperature, but over-enthusiasm can lead to white wines that are frozen into tastelessness and red wines that are almost as warm as the soup! This is a waste of wine however low the price.

As a general rule, the cheaper or sweeter the white wine, the cooler it should be, but about 7°C /45°F should be cold enough for any wine. Better quality white wines, champagne and other sparkling wines, as well as rosés, need only be as cool as the ideal cellar – 10° /50°F or, more realistically for most of us, the temperature of the bottle after an hour in the refrigerator.

A quicker way to chill white wine is to plunge it into a bucket filled with water and a handful of ice-cubes. A few minutes in the freezer or a couple of ice-cubes in the glass are acceptable emergency measures for ordinary wines.

The chemicals that give red wine its bouquet and flavour come alive at higher temperatures than those in white wine, so it makes sense to serve red wine rather warmer. Think of 'room temperature' as a term coined in the days before central heating – 15°C /60°F is quite warm enough for red wine, if not for living rooms. Allow the bottle to warm up gradually, perhaps in the

The bubbles in champagne look best in tulip-shaped glasses.

kitchen as you cook, but not next to the cooker or on a radiator. If you are buying a bottle of red wine and do not have time to bring it to the right temperature, look for a beaujolais or a red Loire wine, or perhaps an Italian Valpolicella, all of which can be served cool.

Most red wines improve with being allowed to 'breathe' for an hour or two before they are drunk, whether you simply draw the cork to let the air in or pour the wine into another glass container (a process known as decanting, even if you are using an old jug rather than an antique decanter). Before wine-making techniques improved, decanting was essential to get rid of all the sediment; nowadays most wines are crystal clear in their bottles and only fine claret, old burgundies and vintage port are likely to need decanting. For most purposes, therefore, decanting is just a useful way of getting air to the wine and an equally useful way of disguising its possibly humble supermarket origins. All in all it is a matter of personal choice. Similarly the wicker baskets that are designed to stop the sediment being shaken up as the wine is poured, are, in the vast majority of cases, an unnecessary affectation.

Opening a wine bottle
Opening the bottle is often the most difficult part of serving wine, particularly if you are confronted with a plastic covering which has to be sliced with a knife. A conventional lead covering (the capsule) should be scored with the point of a knife and then peeled off. Any mould should be wiped away from the rim of the bottle with a clean cloth.

The best corkscrew is a simple, sturdy spiral with a good sharp point. Avoid gimmicky contraptions, particularly those that operate by pumping gas into the bottle. If a cork refuses to budge, run hot water over the neck of the bottle until the glass expands and allows the cork to be eased out with a corkscrew.

The best way to open sparkling wine is to take off the wires, hold the cork wrapped in a clean cloth in one hand and twist the bottle in the other until the cork eases out. There is no need for dramatic explosions.

Pouring the wine into a glass is, of course, the final stage of serving wine. The colour and clarity of the wine is (or should be) something to be appreciated, and coloured or ornate glass make this difficult. Fine, thin wine glasses are an enjoyable luxury but uncut, plain bowl or tulip-shaped glasses with a stem are cheap, easily obtainable and quite adequate for all table wines including champagne. The traditional saucer-shaped champagne glasses are not the best glasses for serving champagne, as they allow the bubbles to escape too quickly. Fortified wines are usually served in small glasses. The one point that all glasses should have in common, is that they are sparkling clean and free of cupboard smells and any trace of dust.

Last of all, the glass should not be overfilled. A third to half full is generous enough. The vapours from the wine will collect in the upper half of the glass and will increase the pleasure of drinking the wine.

Glasses

Just as you use a different sort of knife for meat or for cheese, so there are different glasses available to suit the particular drink you intend to serve. A whole array of gleaming glasses in the drinks cupboard may look inviting but unless you know how to select and use glasses to best advantage, they will add little to the pleasures of drinking.

General points
The three remarkable qualities of any drink are its colour, bouquet and taste. Consequently, the best glasses are always clear, to show the real colour without any distortion. This is especially valuable in the case of wines and fortified wines, which reveal a lot about their age, style and freshness through their colour.

With the exception of tumblers, the best glasses are bowl shaped, tapering towards

Traditional shapes: the Paris goblet, Alsace hock glass and champagne flute.

the rim to contain and concentrate the bouquet for you to inhale. Bowl-shaped glasses should also be large enough to hold a good measure without being more than a third to half full. This is because, before you take the first sip, you should swirl the wine around in the glass to fill the glass with the bouquet.

All wine and fortified wine glasses also have stems, so that you can hold the glass by the stem, not the bowl. This is so that your hand does not affect the temperature of the wine. Holding the glass by its stem will also prevent you from smearing the glass. There are three primary sizes and shapes of glasses which, between them, are quite adequate on their own. The three types are: a small stemmed glass which narrows towards the rim for sherry, port, Madeira or liqueurs; a bowl or tulip-shaped stemmed glass for white or red wine; and a tumbler for spirits and long drinks. This, however, is really the bare minimum, and over the years it can be rewarding to collect a much wider range. Some people say that wine actually tastes – as well as looks – better in a thin glass. This is just psychological – but then psychology does play its part in the enjoyment of wine. Certainly it is true that delicate glass rests more lightly on the lips and guides the bouquet artfully to the nose, because its shape too is usually more carefully designed. But do not let lack of fine glassware mar your pleasure. Vineyard owners in France drink their wine from mustard glasses, washed and kept for everyday drinking. No one enjoys their wine more than they!

There are many designs of glasses associated with wines from different regions and individual shapes have developed for mixed drinks and cocktails. Here we describe some of the more common types.

Table wine glasses
Champagne: the best glass to use for champagne or sparkling wine is the tall, slim flute which preserves the 'mousse' or bubbles for as long as possible. The common wide-brimmed saucer became popular in Victorian times, but it is a very poor substitute for the classical flute design; it encourages the bubbles to die quickly in the glass besides being easy to spill.

Paris goblet: This round bowl-shaped glass is the commonest wine glass available. It is best suited to red wines, although if you have a limited choice of glasses it will do for white wine too.

Alsace: the glass traditionally used for the delicate young white wines made near the eastern border of France has an extra long stem of green glass, supporting a wide bowl. The wines of the area are very fresh and are complemented by the greenish reflection.

Anjou: a long stem is also a feature of the typical straight-sided glass used for the white wines of Anjou and the Loire. The extra long stem is not merely for elegance, but also keeps the wine well clear of any warmth transmitted by your hand.

Moselle: cut glass is frowned upon by purists and wine buffs as distorting the appearance of wine. However, in the Moselle area, cut glass is entirely typical and gives an added glint to white wines.

Hock or Rhine: hock was a Victorian name for the German wines of the Rhine. In their homeland, these aristocratic white wines are served in an unwieldy glass with a thick bobbly stem. However, it is unlikely that you will come across these unusual, old-fashioned glasses outside Germany.

357

Drinking wine

In order to get the utmost pleasure out of drinking wine, it is worth knowing a bit about the way the wine should look, smell and taste. The best method of assessing these points is to follow the procedure used by professional wine tasters. Here is a simple guide on how to judge wine.

Before drinking any wine, it is vital that the wine is at the right temperature and that it is served in clean wine glasses. If you are really seriously trying to assess the wine, the room should not have an off-putting smoky or scented atmosphere and you should not have recently eaten strongly-flavoured food, such as peppermint.

The routine for tasting a wine is to start by pouring two or three mouthfuls of wine into a glass. The clarity of the wine is the first thing to examine. Raise the glass to eye-level and look straight through it to see how clear the wine is. You should hold the glass by its stem, not by its bowl or your fingers will smear the glass and affect your judgement of the wine's clarity. All wine, whether red or white, should be clear. 'Star-bright', 'brilliant' and 'clear' are the terms usually used for good wine, but if you find that 'murky' or 'muddy' is a closer description of the wine you are looking at, it will not be at its best.

Looking at the colour

A wine's colour can tell you a great deal, and its importance should not be underestimated. It is claimed that daylight from a north-facing window is the ideal source of light by which to judge colour, but obviously this is not always available. Normal artificial lighting can be used but you should make allowances for its slight distortions. Fluorescent lighting is the worst light by which to judge wine, since it is often very blue – it tends to make red wines look strangely browny-purple and sometimes almost blue! Candles give off a yellowish light. Electric lightbulbs are probably the next best pure source of light, after natural daylight, although even they can add some blue or yellow to the wine's colour.

Hold the glass over a white surface, tilt it slightly and look at the colour of the wine. You will see that in a red wine the colour is most intense at its deepest part and palest at its shallowest. Young red wine is purple but changes to red as it ages, and later becomes almost brown. It is easiest to judge a wine's age by looking at the paler edge where any browning will be more evident.

Generally, wine of a good vintage will have more colour, and will turn brown more slowly than the same type of wine from a bad year. For instance, clarets of 1970 are deeper and redder than the clarets of 1972, a bad year. Quite often Beaujolais has a purple hue to it. Burgundies are noted for having a velvety-red colour, while red Rhône wines, especially Châteauneuf du Pape, are often so intensely red that they seem almost black.

White wines are judged in the same way but because they are naturally pale, the gradation of colour is much harder to detect. However, you will see that sweet white wines, such as Sauternes, are yellow-gold when young, becoming gold or even burnt gold with age. They also have a thicker texture than dry white wines.

Of the dry white wines, Chablis is known for having a very faint greenish tinge, as do German wines from the Mosel. The dry white wines of the Loire have a touch of yellow to them, while Alsatian wines are definitely yellow.

Smelling the wine

Having examined the colour, you then have to assess the smell or 'nose'. Just as the wine should look good, so it should smell good. Your first sniff will tell you most about the wine – take a good deep sniff and concentrate on it.

Surprisingly, grapes do not figure very highly in people's descriptions of the smell of wine. Clarets often smell of blackcurrants or even cedar wood, pencils and antique shops. Beaujolais and Côtes du Rhônes are often said to smell of freshly dug earth or raspberry sorbet.

White wines come closest to smelling like grapes, especially those from Germany, although 'melon' often crops up in descriptions of white wines. Sweet white wines from Germany, Sauternes and the Loire valley will usually have a honey-like nose. Meursault, a white from Burgundy, is famous for smelling of asparagus and wines made from the Riesling grape have a curiously petrol-like bouquet. Probably the most distinctive white wine, easily identified by its aroma, is the Alsatian Gewürztraminer. This has a very spicy smell. Champagne is said to smell of fresh bread, or even toast!

Tasting the wine

Once you have examined the sight and smell of the wine, you are ready to actually taste it! Take enough into your mouth to allow you to swirl it about and chew it, so that it reaches every part of your mouth. Keep it there for at least 5 seconds before swallowing.

Your taste buds register sweetness (at the tip of the tongue), acidity (at the sides of the tongue), saltiness (towards the back) and bitterness (at the back). As a result of the positioning of these taste buds, wines usually begin by tasting sweet or rich and end with an impression of acidity. All other sensations are those of touch. These include the density or weight of the liquid – sweet wines are usually 'thicker'. With red wine the tannin, which gives the sensation that your gums and cheeks are puckered, is most evident in young clarets – this effect lessens with age.

In a good wine the sensation of sweetness or richness should be equally proportioned with acidity, so that neither appears to be in excess. An equally proportioned wine is known as a balanced wine.

Having swallowed the wine, you should still be able to smell and taste it – the length of time that these sensations remain with you is the best guide to the quality of the wine. A minor wine will be forgotten in 2–3 seconds, but a great wine will last for 10 seconds or more. Don't confuse this with the length of time your tongue registers the presence of acid in your mouth, as this will probably last for longer than 10 seconds.

Gently swirl the wine in the bowl of the glass. Breathe in to assess the 'nose'.

Storing wine

Cheap, everyday wine is nowadays ready to drink as soon as it it bottled, so there is not much to be gained from filling up a wine cellar with it. Buy it and drink it as and when you need it. However, better quality wines, even quite modest ones, do benefit from 'laying down'.

How and where

The first question for most wine drinkers is how and where to store even a limited number of bottles. The ideal, of course, is a cool dark cellar with a steady temperature of about 10°C /50°F. But very few modern houses have cellars, so the alternative is to look around for a dark place where the bottles can lie undisturbed.

The storage place must be dark – because light can affect the colour of the wine – and free from strong smells (paint or detergent), that could penetrate the cork. There should also be no local vibrations that might shake up the bottles and stir up the sediment.

The temperature of the 'cellar' is crucial too, although it is more important that it should be constant rather than particularly cool. Anywhere free from draughts that is not near a radiator, central heating boiler or hot water tank should be adequate – in practice this means the back of a broom cupboard or a recess under the stairs. A shed or garage may be suitable, but it is vital that it is well enough insulated for there to be no risk of the bottles freezing in winter. It should, of course, also be kept securely locked.

Wine bottles should be stored lying horizontally. This is to ensure that the corks are kept in contact with the wine, so that they do not dry out and let in too much air. Wine merchants' cardboard boxes lying on their sides will just about do for a limited number of bottles, but for a more serious cellar, wine racks are essential. Do-it-yourself enthusiasts can make their own built-in racks, and most good department stores sell quite cheap and perfectly adequate racks that will hold 12, 24 or 48 bottles. Some types are collapsible, which is useful for itinerant flat dwellers.

As your cellar fills up, keep it well organized. Store whites below reds because they like to be cooler and heat rises. Keep all necks pointing outwards, labels uppermost so that you can see what is where without too much rooting about. You may even find it fun to keep a 'cellar book', with the dates of purchases and comments on the wines as you drink them. Wine accessory shops often sell smart, leather-bound ones, but an exercise book does just as well.

What to store

Fine clarets and red Burgundies, classy white Burgundies, Sauternes and vintage port used to be the staples of the traditional cellar, laid down to mature for a decade or so, much longer in the case of very great wines. During these years, tiny amounts of air seep in through the cork and combine with the wine. Gradually the raw elements knit together and the marvellous bouquet builds up, to be savoured when the bottle is eventually opened and drunk.

For those who can afford to buy fine wines when they first come on the market and are able to lay them down until they are ready to drink, it is a major and highly important financial investment. However, right at the other end of the scale, for those of us who can only afford to buy a few modest bottles at a time, it still makes economic sense to bulk buy and lay down.

The most important reason for storing wine is that certain wines improve dramatically with keeping. Some cheap young reds will taste much better after six months or a year. Big red wines like those from the northern Rhône, Italian Barolos, Chiantis and Barbarescos, Spanish red and white Riojas, and meaty Californian and Australian reds (made from Shiraz, Pinot Noir and Cabernet Sauvignon grapes) will benefit from keeping considerably longer. Better quality heavyweight Chilean, Argentinian and South African reds, too, deserve to be stored for a couple of years. Look out for any wines from these areas that you particularly like, with a view to laying down. Of course, if you are going to invest money in a large volume of wine, make sure you taste it carefully before you buy it.

Lighter reds, anything that says 'fresh and fruity' to you when you taste it, may well benefit from just a few months 'rest' in their bottles, but need not be kept any longer. Southern Rhône wines, vins de pays, Valpolicella and Beaujolais fall into this category. As a general guide, the 'bigger' and 'heavier' a wine tastes, the longer it needs to mature.

Generally speaking, most of the more ordinary white wines will not benefit from more than a very few months 'rest'. Drink light, dry whites such as Muscadet, Mâcon, any Sauvignon and the Italian whites as soon as you like. Sweet dessert white wines, however, do improve with keeping. Non-vintage champagne does not need laying down – just buy it when you need it. Vintage champagne does benefit from laying down, however.

Apart from the definite improvement in taste, there are two or three other good reasons for buying wine in bulk and keeping it in your cellar. Wine prices are rising all the time, and what is cheap now will not be any cheaper in a year's time. Wine merchants will often give a discount of a few per cent on 'bulk' purchases too – generally a case or more, sometimes a mixed case of several different wines. Finally, if you have a comfortably stocked cellar, there is no chance of running out of wine in the middle of a particularly thirsty dinner party!

Wine should be stored on its side, necks pointing outwards, label uppermost.

Wine as an aperitif

The most important function of an aperitif is to stimulate the appetite gently, and wine fulfils this purpose admirably. Spirits and strong cocktails may be fashionable and more popular, but they tend to deaden the tastes of the food and wine to come. Many people also find spirits too much to cope with on an empty stomach, particularly at the end of a long day.

Wine is not only cheaper and gentler as an aperitif than spirits, but it can also have the advantage of being a much more original choice, especially if it is chosen with care, bearing in mind the subsequent meal.

Whatever wine you choose to offer your guests as an aperitif, remember everyone will be hungry, or at least empty, so it is considerate and sensible to offer them something to nibble at the same time. A bowl of olives, some nuts or cocktail biscuits are all that is really necessary; avoid over-salty tit-bits, however, because these simply increase the thirst.

Champagne is definitely the king of aperitifs. The festive sparkle is guaranteed to break the ice and lift everyone's spirits – invaluable if your guests do not know each other well. As only a glass each (two at the most) is necessary at the aperitif stage, it need not be too expensive a choice either, particularly as a non-vintage or the house champagne of one of the big merchants is perfectly good for this sort of drinking.

A cheaper alternative with the same effect might be a non-champagne sparkler such as sparkling Moselle or hock from Germany (also known as Sekt), or Asti Spumante from Italy. Astis are usually sweet, but there are dry ones too and these make particularly good aperitifs. Other possibilities would be a dryish sparkling Vouvray or Saumur from the Loire, or one of the Spanish sparklers that are made by the *méthode champenoise*.

For a popular and economical aperitif, still white wine is the most obvious choice. It is refreshing, and if you are not offering any alternatives it is the most widely acceptable drink. Bear in mind that very dry whites that are high in acidity are rather hard to drink without food – light wines with fragrance and plenty of fruit are the ones to go for. In Europe the wines of Alsace fit this bill perfectly. Look out for those made from the Riesling or – cheaper – Sylvaner grapes. A Muscat from Alsace would be a more unusual choice – elsewhere the Muscat grape makes sweet wines but these are dry, distinctively perfumed, and mouth-wateringly spicy.

Other white wines that would make suitable aperitifs are Sancerre or Pouilly from the Loire (these can be expensive though), a fresh and fruity Saumur from the Anjou district, a good white Mâcon from Burgundy or a dry white Graves from Bordeaux. Outside France you might choose an Italian Soave or a Frascati, a German Kabinett or a Qualitätswein, a Yugoslavian Riesling or – to be slightly unusual – a Portuguese *vinho verde* with its slight tingly 'prickle'. All these white aperitif wines should be served cool.

Do not feel, however, that aperitif wine must be white. One of the drier rosés can be an excellent choice. Look out for the pale pink wines of Saumur.

It is more difficult to start off an evening's drinking with red wine, just because the majority of them tend to be heavier than whites, and full-bodied enough to demand food. However, if you think that red wine would suit your guests or your menu there is no reason why you should not serve it. Try a Bourgeuil, a delicate, fruity wine from Touraine, or perhaps a light young Beaujolais. With a little careful planning, any of the above wines can go on from the aperitif stage to be drunk with the first course.

More unusual choices

If you are looking for an idea that is a little more special than serving plain wine, the answer might be one of the wine cups or cocktails. Buck's Fizz (champagne mixed half-and-half with fresh orange juice) is wonderful at lunchtime, and some people swear by it as a morning-after hangover cure. Vin blanc cassis is popular for summer drinking – make it from any dry white wine mixed with the blackcurrant syrup in the proportions five of wine to one of syrup. More exotic is a similar drink made with raspberry syrup instead of blackcurrant.

Hock and seltzer is refreshing and can be made with any sweeter white wine (not necessarily hock) with an equal splash of soda. Many books of cocktails also give recipes for more elaborate concoctions, often mixing wine with brandy or other spirits. These can look very innocent with their decorations of fresh fruit, and they can taste exciting, but they are deceptively potent, so pour them sparingly.

If you are aiming at real originality you could serve either a white port or a Muscat de Beaumes de Venise. White port is a succulent golden colour, although it is now more often dry than sweet. As such it is a stimulating aperitif although, because it is a little heavy, most people will probably not want more than one glass.

Muscat de Beaumes de Venise is most unusual. A sweet wine, made from the Muscat grape in the southern Côtes-du-Rhône, with a beguiling tang of herbs, it is best known as a *digestif*, but if it is served lightly chilled it is delicious as an aperitif.

Serve sparkling wine to start your party with a swing.

Wine and food

Although it is perfectly possible to drink any wine with any food, it is worth at least considering general guidelines accumulated from the experience of others, over the years, of eating and drinking. These may help to avoid real disasters and increase the combined enjoyment of food and wine.

When trying to match wine to food there are a few sensible points that are worth remembering. One is that it is best to balance the type of wine to the type of food, so that neither overpowers the other – a light meal requires a light wine, whilst richer, heavier fare calls for a more robust wine. The way in which the food has been prepared may influence the balance. For instance, a white or light red wine will happily complement a plain roast chicken, but if the bird has a rich stuffing, a fuller-bodied red wine would taste better.

Food from a particular region will often match a type of wine from the same region. Bear in mind that if you use a particular wine in the making of a dish, it is likely to be the best one to drink with the dish.

The order in which wines are generally served is also based on practical experience and common sense. If you are serving two wines in succession, or even an aperitif and then a wine at dinner, take care that the first one does not spoil the effect of the second. Make sure that you serve dry before sweet, light-weight before full-bodied, delicate before spicy, fruity or intensely flavoured white before red, young before old and a cheaper wine before a better quality one. Like all rules, there are some exceptions, such as serving sweet white wines with a slightly tart dessert.

Difficult combinations

Although, in general, food and wine are natural partners, there is some food which clashes or is difficult to combine with wine. Try to avoid drinking good wine with food that contains vinegar. Acidic fruit, like oranges, lemons and pineapples, react badly with wine, as does chocolate.

If you do serve a dressed salad as a side dish, try to keep the dressing light (preferably made with lemon juice rather than vinegar) and serve something bland, such as bread, to act as a barrier between the salad and the wine. Salad as a main course can be partnered by one of the dry, stronger rosés such as Tavel, a light Provençal red wine or a light Italian red wine such as Valpolicella.

Eggs and egg dishes mask wines so there is no point serving them with one which is fine or delicate. Keep the wine simple and on the robust side, for example a Côtes du Rhône or a dry sherry. Highly spiced food, and curries which are not too hot, may be served with fuller-flavoured white wines such as Gewürztztraminers, while Chinese food only requires a light, sweetish rosé (Mateus or Rosé d'Anjou) or a Riesling.

Although cheese and wine are the classic companions, really strong cheese can overpower all but the most robust of wines (such as a Rhône) or dessert or fortified wines.

If possible, avoid serving full tannic red wines with fish – not only do these wines 'swamp' delicate fish, but they tend to make the fish taste metallic. However, very light red wines, which have acidity rather than tannin, like red vinhos verdes, can be drunk with fish such as salmon, especially when it is served hot. Red wines do not combine well with rich puddings either. Although combinations of red wine with some fruit (such as strawberries, peaches and pears) can work well, the dryness and tannin of a red wine will clash with a rich pudding.

Good Combinations

There are certain combinations of food and wine that are particularly good, when the food and wine can improve each other.

White meat, such as chicken or veal, should be served with fairly 'full', not too dry, white wines – for instance, southern burgundies, white Rhône, Frascati and Riesling. Stronger rosés like Tavel, or light reds, such as Bordeaux, Chianti or Italian Merlot also go well with white meat.

Red meat cooked plainly, and white meat cooked in a rich sauce or with a stuffing, call for the classic accompaniment of claret or medium-bodied reds like Chianti classico, Bardolino, Barbaresco and Dão.

Game and rich beef dishes are best served with Burgundy or Rhône wines – especially Châteauneuf du Pape – or with full-bodied red wines, such as Argentinian, Chilean, Barolo, Riojas, South African Pinotage or Australian Shiraz.

Light fish, simply prepared, goes well with any dry white wine – try a white burgundy, Australian Chardonnay, South African Chenin Blanc or Steen. Pouilly Fuissé or Fumé, Sancerre, Soave or a Mosel wine. Richer fish dishes need a fuller flavoured white wine such as Graves, Orvieto or white Penedes, while shellfish calls for light, crisp white wine (a Muscadet or Mâcon would be an excellent choice).

Light red wines combine pleasantly with dishes made with rice, pasta, pizzas, pastries and bread. Where these are 'national' dishes, as quite a few are, the natural thing to drink is the wine of the area. For example, drink chianti with a pizza.

With gateaux and not too creamy desserts, it would be appropriate to serve a sweet white wine. Sauternes, Muscat de Beaumes de Venise, Monbazillac, Bonnezeaux and sweet sparkling wines are suggestions.

A wedding reception, Portuguese style: local wine to accompany local dishes.

The geography of wine

The grape vine is a plant which is traditionally associated with the Mediterranean – the mild damp winters and hot dry summers of that region provide ideal conditions for it to flourish. However, the climate described as 'Mediterranean' is also found outside Europe, most notably in California, South Africa, southern Australia and parts of Chile and Argentina. Vines are cultivated in all these areas and their wines, previously drunk locally, are now gaining wider recognition in other parts of the world.

Climate

Of the three main geographical factors in the production of wine – climate, soil and site – climate is the most important. There must be sufficient rain at the right time of year to sustain growth and a period of at least a hundred warm sunny days after flowering to enable the fruit to ripen. In Europe these conditions are normally only found below latitude 50°N.

Producing wine can never be a straightforward business, in that even a 'reliable' climate is subject to occasional extremes. It is also a strange fact that the greatest European wines come not from the areas around the Mediterranean itself where conditions would appear to be most suitable, but from the northern fringe areas of Bordeaux, Champagne and Burgundy in France and the Rhine and Mosel valleys in Germany. The vine may be a sensitive plant but it seems that it also needs an element of challenge to bring out the best in it.

Of all the extremes of weather which affect these growing areas, drought is the least likely to do damage. The roots of the wine go very deep, and even the prolonged dry heat of 1976 did little harm – on the contrary, most regions produced an outstanding vintage.

Frost is another matter; sharp springtime frosts which attack the budding plants can severely limit the year's output, as happened in Bordeaux in 1977. Deep penetrating winter frosts are even worse, for they can kill the entire plant, as occurred widely in France in 1956 and 1963. Hail is another great hazard, though usually a local one, which can ruin an unfortunate grower's entire crop.

Even rain can be harmful if it comes at the wrong time. A cool damp flowering period will mean a small crop, though if the weather later improves, the quality is not necessarily affected. The year 1961 followed this pattern in Bordeaux, and the resulting vintage was very fine.

A wet harvest period is more serious, as many grapes may become mildewed and rot on the vines. This is a particular problem in Germany where a portion of the crop is traditionally harvested late, when the grapes have the maximum possible sugar content, to produce the rich 'Spätlese' and 'Auslese' wines. If the weather breaks too soon, the grower may not be able to produce any of these wines at all.

Even when there are no major disasters, persistent cool, cloudy weather can result in an inferior crop of unripe grapes. These give an unbalanced wine with too much acidity and too little alcohol.

As a result of all these possible variations in climate, vintage charts can be a useful guide as to when the best growths occurred. However, it would be a mistake to regard the charts as gospel, for a number of reasons. In the first place, weather can vary significantly from place to place within a small area – one slope may be exposed to rain or cold winds from a certain quarter while another is sheltered. One village may be more susceptible to summer storms than another a few miles away. These local variations, or 'microclimates', can mean that even in a bad year one estate or chateau may be able to produce a much better wine that its neighbours.

Soil and site

Not only do vines produce their finest results in areas where the climate is least predictable, they can also flourish on soils and sites which appear very unpromising. Appearances can be deceptive – a stony topsoil, which anyway has the advantage of efficient drainage, may conceal rich subsoils beneath. However, it seems that vines struggling to extract the maximum benefit from the soil, producing vigorous root growth, achieve the best results in quality of fruit – provided, of course, that the plants themselves are skilfully pruned and tended.

The steep-sided hill slopes of the Mosel valley, for example, with their thin slaty soil, produce some of the finest results from the Riesling grape. Farther south in the Rhine district of the Palatinate, better wines are made on the hills of the Haardt Mountains than on the rich alluvial plains of the valley floor.

Soil conditions vary from area to area as with microclimates. In Burgundy, for example, some of the most spectacular – and expensive – wines in the world, with names like Romanée-Conti and Le Montrachet, come from very small and unspectacular-looking patches of ground only a few acres in extent.

Of course, for every bottle of Romanée-Conti there will be millions of bottles from more humble and probably more easily cultivated vineyards whose uncomplicated table wines provide the staple of wine-drinking the world over. Greatness, however, is less easily achieved, depending as it does on several factors still imperfectly understood, and containing always an element of mystery.

A vineyard in Germany

Grape types

It is an obvious enough fact that grapes do not all look or taste the same: aside from the basic division into black and white, there are all sorts of subtle differences in appearance and flavour. These differences will naturally also appear in the fermented juice of the grape (the wine) and are largely responsible for the many varied styles of wine available today.

Colour
Many people think that black grapes produce red wine, and generally speaking this is so; it is the broken grape skins present in the vats during fermentation that give colour to a wine. However, the juice of any grape, even a black grape, is pale yellow – and if the black skins are carefully removed before the juice ferments, a white wine will result. Champagne, for example, is made mainly from a black grape which, by a different process of fermentation, also produces the great red wines of Burgundy.

Grape varieties
There are over 5000 varieties of the one species of vine, *Vitis vinifera*, from which wine is made. Sometimes several names are given to one variety. For instance, the variety Syrah, the best red grape of the Rhône and the one which produces Hermitage, is known in Australia and South Africa as Shiraz.

Some closely related grape varieties come under a family name. One family which is encountered again and again in the making of wine is the Pinot family – Pinot Noir (the

Pinot Noir – the burgundy grape

red burgundies); Pinot Chardonnay (Chablis and the great white burgundies); Pinot Gris (full-bodied whites); Pinot de la Loire (the name often used for the classic white grape of the Loire); Pinotage (a South African grape crossed with the Pinot Noir) and so on.

Grape regions
Most of the good European wines are named after the château or estate, or at least the region, from which they come, so you do not really need to know the grape from which they are made.

However, certain grape types are best suited to certain areas, and in order to maintain the quality and reputation of a wine, the independent governing bodies which control wine-making will usually specify which varieties are to be used. For example, in the area of Bordeaux there are only six grape types authorized for red wines, and of these Merlot, Cabernet Franc and above all Cabernet Sauvignon make up the bulk of the crop. Unless these varieties are used, the wine will not qualify for the *Appellation Contrôlée* which is the mark of the finest French wines.

In Germany and Italy similar controls are applied: an approved wine will be labelled *Qualitätswein* or *Denominazione di Origine Controllata* (D.O.C.).

Varietal wines
Some wines are, however, known by the grape rather than the place of origin. These are called varietal wines. The French district of Alsace, for example, traditionally names its white wines in this way as Riesling, or Sylvaner, or Gewürztraminer.

Riesling is a particularly familiar grape name to be found on labels. True Riesling is regarded as the king of grapes in Germany and Alsace, where it produces magnificent, fragrant and fruity wines. This true Riesling is also grown successfully in Austria, Australia, South Africa, California and parts of Europe, when it is usually called Rhine, White or Johannisberg Riesling depending on the country of origin.

The true Riesling grape has a doubtfully related cousin that is grown in northern Italy and all over Eastern Europe. It produces a lighter, cheaper wine and will often be labelled as Laski Riesling, Olasz Riesling, Welschriesling or Italian Riesling.

The Muscat wines are another good example of varietal wines. Muscat wine is easily recognizable as it has a distinctively fragrant, grapy smell. The naturally high sugar content of the grape results in the dessert wines of southern France, such as Muscat de Beaumes de Venise, as well as the sweet sparkling Italian wine, Asti Spumante. However, in Alsace, it produces a wine that is surprisingly dry.

Quite different from Muscat is Muscadet, which many people probably do not think of as a grape because it is always associated with the small area around the mouth of the Loire where it is grown. The white wine Muscadet produces is refreshingly dry.

The Gewürztraminer grape is by far the easiest grape to identify as it has a very strong and spicy flavour. It is at its best in the fruity, dry wines of Alsace but it also makes good wine in Germany, Australia, California and Eastern Europe.

The Cabernet Sauvignon grape, aside from its reputation in the making of claret, is a name increasingly seen on labels from many countries such as Australia, Argentina, Chile, South Africa and California. In fact the Cabernet Sauvignon grape is the pride of California and while in Bordeaux this grape is almost always blended with others, some of the best Californian wines are pure Cabernet Sauvignon. There is also America's own variety, Zinfandel, which produces a fruity red wine.

Shopping around among varietal wines is a good way of discovering just how many different flavours there are to be enjoyed. It can also be interesting to compare wines of the same grape type, but from different areas – a Chardonnay from California is obviously going to share certain basic characteristics with a Chardonnay from Burgundy, but soil, climate and the wine-making method differ from place to place and year to year, affecting the finished product. This is a discouraging thought for those who want their wine always to taste the same, but not for those who enjoy variety.

How wine is made

The natural process of fermentation, which transforms crushed grapes into wine, is as old as time. In very simple terms, fermentation means that the sugar in the sun-ripened grapes is converted by substances in the wine called yeast enzymes, into alcohol and carbon dioxide. Modern wine makers prefer to leave nothing to chance and so their techniques are very sophisticated, but at the heart of all their high-powered technology lies the same ancient equation that has been used since wine was first made.

An old-fashioned manual wine press from the Beaujolais region

Fermentation

Once the grapes are ripe (which in the northern hemisphere happens sometime between August and November, depending on the weather and the latitude), they are picked by hand or by machines and brought into the winery in lorry-loads.   The grapes are then crushed, and the stalks removed – in a modern mechanized winery this is done at the same time in a stemmer-crusher. The ancient method of crushing the grapes with the feet is rarely seen today, except perhaps on a few small farms in some parts of France, Spain, Portugal and Italy.

The traditional method of making wine was to press the grapes in a manual press and then leave the juice to ferment. Nowadays, however, red wine is made by pumping the crushed grapes, with their skins and pips, into huge fermentation vats. It is the skins that give red wine its colour so the grapy mixture may be left on the skins for as long as three weeks. The newly-fermented alcohol sucks up colour, and also the tannin that will make the wine powerful and long-lasting.

White wines may be made from red or white grapes, or a mixture. The juice is usually pressed out of the grapy mixture and the skins and pips are left behind when the juice is put into vats to ferment. Rosé wines always include some red grapes. The juice is removed ('racked off') from the skins after only a day or so, when it is delicate pale pink. The pale pink grape juice is then left to ferment.

Before fermentation is allowed to begin the wine maker often removes the yeasts that are naturally present on the grape skins and substitutes a more effective strain of his own. The amount of sugar in the grapes is critical too. If there has been too little sun during the summer it may well be in short supply, so the wine maker is allowed to add a specified amount to raise the future alcoholic strength (this is known as 'chaptalization'). Another crucial factor is temperature. Fermentation will not happen at all if the vats are too cool. On the other hand, if there is too much heat, the fermentation will be over-vigorous and the resultant wine will be short on subtlety.

Once under way, fermentation of red wine is allowed to go on happily until all the sugar has been converted into alcohol. The new wine (known as *vin de goutte*) is then run off the used-up skins and pips and left in vats so that it can settle. The remaining used-up skins and pips are sometimes then pressed, resulting in a rough wine (known as *vin de presse*) which is extremely harsh and very dark.

Ageing

The next stage is to transfer the new wine to the casks to acquire some 'age'. These casks are traditionally wooden, but nowadays they are often made of something less picturesque, such as stainless steel. The time that red wines are left in barrel varies widely, depending on the quality of the wine – it can be anything from several years to just long enough for the lingering deposits to settle.

For white wines the procedure is slightly different because fermentation may be stopped artificially so that some sugar remains, resulting in a sweeter wine. White wines are not usually aged in barrels, being left instead in stainless steel tanks for up to a year until the deposits settle.

Final stages

Before bottling, the wine is filtered and 'fined' – treated with chemicals to make it completely clear. In some cases there is yet another piece to be fitted into the puzzle – blending. This is a highly skilled operation by the wine maker, who may take wine from different grapes and different vineyards and even different years and vinify them together to produce his individual end product – the cuvée. Blending can improve the quality of even the greatest wines, or it can simply produce an acceptable table wine. It all depends on the type of wine the wine maker is aiming for. It is not, as some people think, a shady procedure to be frowned on by purists, but one of the most important operations in the winery.

Bottling, corking, capsuling and labelling are the last stages in the process, nowadays done almost exclusively by huge machines. Finally, the wine may be left for years to acquire 'bottle age', or it may be shipped straight off to appear on the supermarket shelf within days.

Wine Regions

Wine is now grown the world over, on every continent. In some areas, like South Africa, South America and Australia, it is a relatively new industry, with young vines and the benefit of expertise brought over from older European viniculture. In other areas – like Greece, Turkey and the Balkan States – wine has been produced for hundreds, even thousands, of years for a mainly local market, and is only recently beginning to compete with more established exporters for world attention. North America – particularly California – is a case apart. There vines have been grown since the time of the Spanish missions, but the last twenty-five years have seen enormous growth, both in the number and acreage of wineries, and in the interest of wine connoisseurs everywhere. The new processing techniques being pioneered in California's Napa Valley are being brought back for incorporation into the Continent's long-established industry. Here, in Europe, France is the undisputed king, producing the best-known and most respected red, white and rosé wines – and, of course, champagne. But Germany, Italy, Spain, Portugal, Austria and Hungary all have venerable traditions of wine-making, and England too has recently revived a history of white wine-making begun with the Romans and carried on by the monks until the supression of the monasteries by not-always-good King Henry. The styles of wine – from sweet to dry, from sparkling to still, in red, white or rosé – may vary from region to region within a country, but all growers and winemakers share a proud common heritage that ensures they learn from one another and exchange new ideas – for wine-making is more than an industry. It is a way of life.

France

France's reputation as a wine producer rests firmly on her greatest wines, which continue to set standards for all other countries. Her two best-known regions, Bordeaux and Burgundy, have become by-words, but the variety and richness of her wine heritage extends far beyond these two.

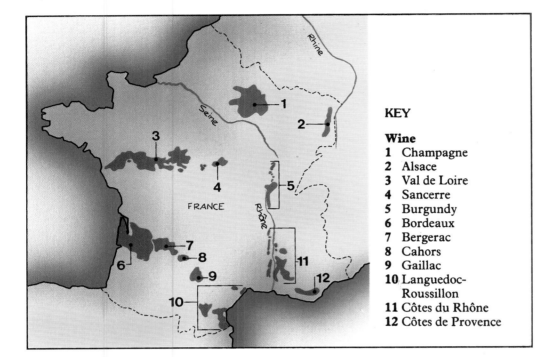

KEY

Wine
1 Champagne
2 Alsace
3 Val de Loire
4 Sancerre
5 Burgundy
6 Bordeaux
7 Bergerac
8 Cahors
9 Gaillac
10 Languedoc-Roussillon
11 Côtes du Rhône
12 Côtes de Provence

Despite her large land area, France is not the most productive of wine-growers, but she produces more quality wines than any other country. A quarter of the 75 million hectolitres which flow annually from French wineries are *Vins de Qualité produits dans les régions determinées* – the official EEC designation for fine wines. This proportion is likely to increase, as many growers in the lesser-known areas are ambitious to achieve a higher status for their wines, and land is being set aside for the cultivation of classic grape varieties.

The demand for these fine wines exceeds even France's capacity to supply them, so that many have become expensive and some prohibitively so. The greatest red wines from Bordeaux and Burgundy are now more often bought as an investment than for drinking; over the past twenty years, they have proved good inflation-beaters. But it seems a pity that after all the hard work, patience and skill which goes into making such a wine, it should end up not in a glass but on a balance-sheet. Fortunately, most of the wines even from these classic regions do not have to be considered in this light and are, if not everyday drinking, at least an affordable luxury.

Why are the best French wines so good? There is no complete answer to that question. In the first place, there is a tradition of wine-making extending back for hundreds of years, even to the Roman occupation; given enough time and practice, skills will develop and be handed on. There has also been an enthusiastic and sophisticated market for the product, not only in France but abroad; the English court developed a taste for Bordeaux wines after the region fell under control of the Crown in the Middle Ages, and at the end of the eighteenth century Thomas Jefferson was there, arranging for cases of his own favourites to make the trans-Atlantic crossing. Geography too is significant; the right combination of soil and site for particular vines, and a climate which is equable but with just enough variation of temperature and rainfall to test their toughness and flexibility. Then in recent years there has been a stringent set of government regulations, controlling the types of grape grown in each region, the maximum yield allowed, and permitted alcoholic strength.

French wines are outstanding not only for their quality but also for their variety. Somewhere in France there should be a wine for every palate. If you like dry wines, then there is a Muscadet from the Loire, Entre deux Mers from Bordeaux, or one of the White Burgundies. Something with a little more fruit? Try a Riesling from Alsace. For red wine, Bordeaux and Burgundy are unrivalled, or if you prefer a lightweight, Beaujolais. Pink perhaps? Then there is a choice between the light rosés of Anjou and the fuller-flavoured ones from Provence. As for sparkling, what could be better then Champagne? We shall be looking at all these – and many others – in the following pages.

The Pinot Noir vendage in Cahors.

French wine labels

In order to get the best value for money, it is essential that you understand the labels on bottles of wine. Once you are familiar with the technical details and sometimes flowery language, you can gather a surprising amount of information from them as to the quality of the wine inside.

Table wine
In the case of French wines, just under three-quarters of the two billion gallons produced every year is ordinary table wine (*vin de table*). The 'Chasse Royale' pictured here is a typical example and, as always, it is the small print on the label that counts. 'Produce of France' means that the wine is made from a blend of French-grown grapes, and 'vin de table' indicates that it is the most basic quality. '*Mise en bouteille par . . . négociant à F. 21700*' indicates which shipper blended and bottled the wine, and where – in this case the French département 21700. The wine's commercial or brand name, and the flowery descriptions like 'La Bonne Bouteille du Patron', are colourful and eye-catching but, in fact, do not tell you anything about the wine.

Ordinary graded wine
Moving further up the scale, the remaining quarter or so of French wine is governed by a complex system of laws designed to stop ordinary wine being passed off as something more special. There are three grades to watch out for. The lowest is '*vins de pays*'. These are really table wines, mostly from the south, made with a little more care by producers conscious of their reputation. Next comes VDQS wines, *Vins Delimité de Qualité Supérieure*. The rules applying to these are less stringent than those governing the next class up, but they do set certain standards and wines in this category can be good value for money.

AC wines
At the top of the pyramid, making up about 20% of the total, are AC or *Appellation Contrôlée wines*. When you look at the label of an AC wine, remember that the more specific the appellation (in geographical terms) the better the quality of the wine. An AC Bordeaux or an AC burgundy will be a decently made wine, but could come from anywhere in a big area. If the wine all comes from a particular area within the region (Médoc, say, in Bordeaux or Côte de Beaune in Burgundy) the label will say so, and likewise if it comes from an even more specific source, whether it is a particular commune, group of villages, area of hillside or even individual château or vineyard, the label will proudly declare it.

So, when you are checking the pedigree of your wine, one of the things to watch out for is brand-name wines with smart labels that are trying to look like, say, château-bottled claret. Look for the give-away words 'AC Bordeaux' (the lowest possible claret appelation). These may be perfectly acceptable wines – Mouton-Cadet is the best-known example – but they are nothing like as good as the producers would like you to think. Remember too that more specific descriptions like '*Côtes de X*' '*Coteaux de X*' (hillside(s) of) and '*X Villages*' indicate a slightly better quality wine than one entitled to give itself only the basic place name.

The label can tell you many important things about the wine you are buying.

Thus AC Beaujolais-Villages is superior to plain AC Beaujolais. The Mâcon-Villages illustrated below comes from certain designated villages within the Mâcon area, and is also bottled by the established négociant Loron et Fils. One qualifying word to be wary of is '*supérieur*'. It is not necessarily superior – this designation simply means over 10.5% alcohol and most wines in a good year reach this anyway.

At the top end of the AC system, wines from certain of the best vineyards (in the Médoc, Côte d'Or and Chablis, for example) may be described as *cru classé* or classed growth. These classes range from *grand cru* down through *premier cru* to *cinquième cru* (first to fifth growth, in the case of the Médoc) with *cru bourgeois* below that: the latter is often good value. The claret shown here, from the property Lamothe Bergeron, is a château-bottled cru bourgeois, entitled to the appelation Haut-Médoc – the most prestigious region of Bordeaux.

Bottling
Where the wine was bottled and who shipped it are important clues to quality. The best wines are '*mise en bouteille à la propriété*', '*. . . au château*' or '*. . . à la domaine*', which means that the grower bottled them himself at the individual property with due care and attention. '*Mise en bouteilles dans nos caves*' or '*. . . nos chais*' is gently misleading. It means *not* bottled at the property. '*Nos caves*' (our cellars), after all, could be almost anywhere. '*Mise par le négociant*' or '*mise par Monsieur X*' means that a shipper bought the wines from the grower(s), blended them and arranged the bottling. 'Shipped and bottled *by*' is more encouraging than 'shipped and bottled *for*', whether the words are in French or English. If you have any choice go for a shipper whose reputation you know and trust.

Vintage
The vintage date may also be important. Few people can carry around in their heads all the information about every vintage of wine, and there are plenty of books that set it all down. On the other hand, it is worth having a rough idea of what years are best.

Varietal wines
From time to time you may come across a wine that is labelled according to the grape variety rather than where it was grown – the so-called 'varietal' wines. These are most likely to come from California or Australia and will be labelled accordingly, but French examples might be 'Gamay' or 'Sauvignon de . . .'. Read the rest of the label, and choose a trustworthy négociant or shipper.

Degree of sweetness and sparkle
Brut: bone dry
Sec: dry
Demi sec: medium sweet
Doux: sweet
Champagne: made by the méthode champenoise in the Champagne area of France
Mousseux: sparkling
Crémant: less sparkling than Mousseux
Pétillant: with a tingly fizz
Perlant: just a touch of fizz

PRODUCE OF FRANCE
LA BONNE BOUTEILLE DU PATRON
Chasse Royale
VIN DE TABLE
mis en bouteille par
JEAN-CLAUDE BOISSET
négociant à F. 21700
70 cl   12% Vol.

PRODUCE OF FRANCE
De Père en Fils
depuis 1821
Mâcon-Villages
APPELLATION CONTROLEE
Mis en bouteille par E. Loron & Fils
PONTANEVAUX
(Saône-s-Loire)
70 cl

PRODUCE OF FRANCE
CRU BOURGEOIS
CHATEAU LAMOTHE BERGERON
HAUT-MEDOC
APPELLATION HAUT-MEDOC CONTROLEE
11.5% Vol.   1978
SCGPD PROPRIETAIRE A CUSSAC (GIRONDE)
MIS EN BOUTEILLE AU CHATEAU   75cl

Introducing Burgundy

Most wine experts are agreed that the best of Burgundy's wines are among the greatest in the world. Almost all burgundy is very expensive nowadays and the famous single-vineyard or even top commune wines are way beyond the reach of the ordinary wine-buyer. But it is still possible, armed with a little knowledge, to find acceptable cousins or cousins-twice-removed from the fringes of the area, that retain some characteristics of the best burgundies.

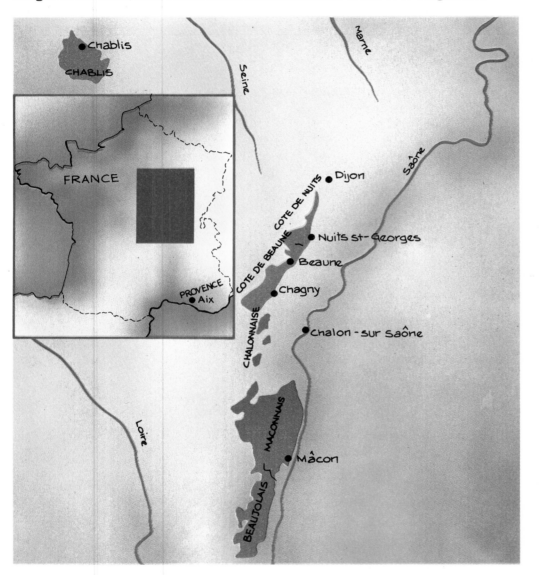

What are the characteristics of a good burgundy – red or white? The incomparable whites make up less than a quarter of the area's total output. As a rough description they are firm and balanced and are powerfully suggestive of the noble Chardonnay grape. They can be laid down for several years, as they have exceptional staying power. Well-made reds are full in the mouth, fruity and emphatic, but not heavy or 'soupy'. The adjective most often used to describe red burgundy is 'velvety'.

Burgundy costs so much because the total area producing wine entitled to bear one of the 114 burgundy appellations is small. The best burgundies come from the vineyards of the Côte d'Or. They lie along a south-east facing strip of gentle hillside no more than 50 kilometres long and often as little as 200 metres wide. The very best vineyards, which produce the *grand crus* (best growths), lie in the centre of this strip. Some of these vineyards, with world-famous names, are no bigger than large gardens. Romanée-Conti, for example, generally thought of as the peak of burgundy, covers a mere 1.8 hectares. Bad weather often dramatically reduces the potential yield, and then a large percentage of what is eventually produced is sold direct to individual buyers. In some years it is remarkable that any burgundy reaches the market at all and what little there is has to satisfy a burgundy-thirsty world.

Burgundy is said to be very variable in quality. In the past 'burgundy' was often doctored with heavy reds from Midi, or even Algeria, to give it the weight that the customers expected. Now, with the law tightened up, any wine with a burgundy Appellation Contrôlée label must be made entirely from grapes grown in the area.

Variability still remains, however, but this is partly because, unlike Bordeaux where large properties often belong to a single owner, burgundy vineyards may have dozens of owners, each responsible for a tiny parcel of land. Even wine made from grapes in adjoining rows may taste quite different because the grapes may have been differently tended and harvested. The grapes are then sold to different middlemen, *négociants*, each of whom will blend wines according to his own house style and bottling standards. The wines will then be marketed with his name on the label.

When buying great burgundy, a careful scrutiny of the label is the best guide. A top-ranking Gevrey-Chambertin or a Montrachet made and bottled by the grower at the property is the best choice; this is indicated by the words, *mise en bouteilles par le proprietaire*. Otherwise opt for a shipper whose reputation you can trust. Reliable names to look for on the label include Louis Jadot, Louis Latour, Joseph Drouhin, and Bouchard Pere et Fils. Beware the misleading *'mise en bouteilles dans nos caves'* ('in our cellars' means bottled almost anywhere.)

Grades of burgundy

The appellation system which governs the way Burgundy's wines are labelled and sold is complex. The most basic appellation is Bourgogne Grand Ordinaire. Next in price and quality comes the red Passe-tout-grains; this means 'all grapes included' and in practice the wine will be a mixture of two-thirds from the Gamay grape, the more prolific grape of the area, and one one-third the superior grape Pinot Noir.

The second grade for white wine is Bourgogne Aligoté; this is made from the Aligoté grape, the lesser of the two grapes used in the region for the white wine. AC Bourgogne comes next, the red made entirely from the noble Pinot Noir grape; the white from the Chardonnay. AC Bourgogne from a reliable shipper is often a good buy.

From the hilly countryside beyond the main slopes come two more basic appellations – Hautes Côtes de Beaune and Hautes Côtes de Nuits. These wines can also be very worthwhile, particularly in good years, when the grapes have plenty of sun, they will compare favourably with their aristocratic relatives.

From the Côte d'Or, the heartland of Burgundy come the three topmost appellations of the region. At the very top are the thirty grands crus, the best vineyards with famous names like Chambertin, Les Musigny and Le Montrachet. *Premier cru* is the grade immediately below. The third rank is *appellation communale*, in other words having the right to use the name of the commune. Examples are AC Vougeot, or AC Chambolle-Musigny. These are still fine wines, although not in quite the same exalted class as those from grand cru or premier cru vineyards.

The individual wine-producing areas will be discussed on the following pages.

Côte de Nuits

The Côte d'Or 'golden slope' stretching between Dijon in the north and Santenay in the south, has been producing legendary wine for hundreds of years. The narrow strip of hillside falls naturally into two parts, of which the northern one is known as the Côte de Nuits.

In the Côte de Nuits vineyards, the Pinot Noir grape produces the finest red burgundies, which all share a powerful family likeness but also display a rich variety of individual flavours and bouquets. Only a small quantity of white wine is made on the Côte de Nuits, but what there is, is of equally fine quality.

The main communes

There are eight important wine communes in this Côte and they take their names from the villages dotted along the length of the slope. For the commune appellation titles some proudly hyphenate the names of their most famous vineyard to the village name, giving resounding combinations like Chambolle-Musigny and Nuits-St Georges.

The two northernmost communes are Fixin and Gevrey-Chambertin. Gevrey-Chambertin is often described as the typical, red burgundy – rich, mouth-filling and long-lasting. Sadly, the description is the closest that most wine-drinkers can get while fine burgundy prices are at their current level. The commune has no fewer than nine *grand cru* vineyards including Chambertin, and Chambertin Clos de Bèze where the monks of the Abbey of Bèze were making wine in the seventh century. The *appellation communale* wine of Gevrey has a high reputation and therefore a high price. The wines from Fixin, north of Gevrey are dark red, strongly perfumed and age well, but the name is less famous and so they are a little cheaper.

Beyond Gevrey-Chambertin lies Morey-St Denis, another of the Côte's less well-known names where prices are still within the realms of possibility. Morey-St Denis wines are big and sturdy like the Gevrey-Chambertin wines, but they also have a trace of softness that makes them the 'bridge' between their northern neighbour and Chambolle-Musigny just to the south.

Chambolle-Musigny is elegant and perfumed, but very full-bodied. The great vineyard in this commune is Les Musigny which also produces a small quantity of white wine. Among the *premiers crus* (first growths) are the prettily named Les Amoureuses and Les Charmes. Next door lies the small commune of Vougeot. Almost all of it is taken up by the single vineyard Clos de Vougeot.

Within the stone walls of the Clos the problems that affect Burgundy as a whole can be seen on a smaller scale. Clos de Vougeot is the biggest vineyard in Burgundy, but it is divided up between sixty-odd separate owners, whose holdings are all at different levels. The best wine comes from the top of the slope and the poorest from the low land bordering the road. Each grower has different methods, and the wine may well be sold to négociants with different standards. Although there is no guarantee of consistency, all the wine still ends up on the market as grand cru Clos de Vougeot. There will also be a price to match the grand cru reputation, and the wine may be worth every penny of that price or it may be a sad disappointment. As a result criticism is often directed at burgundy as a whole, when it should in fact be directed at the multiple-ownership system. The only guarantee of quality for the ordinary buyer is the shipper's reputation.

Between Vougeot and Vosne-Romanée lies Flagey-Echézaux. Most of the wines from this commune are sold as Vosne-Romanée. The commune of Vosne-Romanée itself is almost hallowed ground. Amongst its five grands crus is Romanée-Conti, thought by some of those who can afford it to be the very greatest red wine of all. The other equally famous names here are la Romanée, Romanée-St Vivant, le Richebourg and la Tâche.

The last important commune of the Côte is Nuits-St Georges, centred on the town of Nuits. The wines of Premeaux, the neighbouring commune, are also sold as Nuits-St Georges. These are big wines, typically Côte de Nuits, firm and tannic and with a deep colour. They take time to mature, but are worth waiting for. Nuits has no grand crus, but the quality in general should be high although its reputation in the past has been damaged by the fraudulent passing off of 'Nuits-St Georges' that bore no relation to the real thing. Tightening up the appellation laws has ended this abuse.

Other wines

Certain inferior vineyards along the length of the Côte are only allowed to sell their wines as Côte de Nuits-Villages. (Remember that 'inferior' is a relative term when talking of the Côte d'Or.) These are still of a higher standard than AC (*Appellation Controlée*) Bourgogne, and are worth looking out for. Along the fringes of the busy main road, RN 74, marking the boundary of the Côte proper, are low-lying vineyards of a poorer standard. From these, and from the vineyards across the road comes the bulk of plain AC Bourgogne. However, this is still the Côte d'Or. An honestly-made AC Bourgogne embodies some – even if only a trace – of the great burgundy taste.

Large baskets of Pinot Noir grapes.

Côte de Beaune

Burgundy's southern half, the Côte de Beaune, is world famous for its white wine. To many people the white wine from this region is the greatest in the world, and the many classic wines from the area, with their distinctive dry but lusciously rich flavours command high prices.

The Côte de Beaune produces excellent red wines, as well as classic white. They differ from the wines produced by their neighbours on the Côte de Nuits to the north in that they are usually softer, lighter, and quick to mature.

White Côte de Beaune wines

The neighbouring communes of Puligny-Montrachet and Chassagne-Montrachet at the southern end of the Côte de Beaune are the best known. As in the Côte de Nuits, these communes take their names from the villages with the name of the most illustrious vineyards tacked on. Le Montrachet is the greatest of the white *grands crus* vineyeards. It is split between the two communes of Puligny and Chassagne, with its only marginally less illustrious grand cru neighbours – Chevalier-Montrachet, Bâtard-Montrachet, Criots-Bâtard-Montrachet, and Bienvenues-Bâtard-Montrachet – clustered around it. These wines are intense, succulent and golden and for most wine-drinkers are a once-in-a-lifetime experience. As even Appellation Contrôlée commune wines from this area are very expensive, it is wise to take a look at wines from the neighbouring commune at St-

Vineyards surrounding Meursault

Aubin. Its wines, white and red, are dependable and much cheaper while still providing an echo of the Montrachet distinction.

Next to Puligny-Montrachet lies the commune of Meursault, producing soft white wines with a distinctive flavour described as either 'mealy' or 'buttery'. The single-vineyard wines – les Genevrières, les Charmes, les Perrières – are excellent but the commune AC wines can be disappointing if they come from the low vineyards bordering the main road. As always, it pays to choose a reliable shipper – the Patriarche company is good in this area. Meursault is popular and sometimes overpriced; neighbouring Auxey-Duresses is a cheaper alternative. Red wines from Meursault are generally sold as Volnay, and Volnay's whites as Meursault.

Red Côte de Beaune wines

North of Meursault lie the famous red wine communes of the Côte – Volnay, Pommard and Beaune. Pommard is the most expensive and imitated. Volnay's reds are attractive, short-lived but with a delicate roundness and a fragrant bouquet. A cheaper alternative to these red wines can be found in Auxey-Duresses or Monthélie.

Beaune is a large commune centred on the town of Beaune, the administrative centre of the Burgundy wine trade. It is a famous name and almost all the wines from the commune get *premier cru* rating. AC Beaune is the lowest appellation and tends to be overpriced for its variable quality – better buys are to be found amongst the reds of Savigny-lès-Beaune, or Santenay. The commune of Santenay is at the southern end of the Côte and produces lower priced wines. These may be either light and fruity, or powerful and long-lived - more like a Côte de Nuits red – according to the variability of the soil.

In the town of Beaune is the picture-postcard symbol of Burgundy, the Hôtel-Dieu or, as it is much more widely known, the *Hospices de Beaune*, a charity hospital for the elderly. Over the years, since the first bequest in the fifteenth century, Burgundian vineyard-owners have traditionally bequeathed land to the Hospices. The foundation now owns parcels of vineyards scattered through the Côte de Beaune and the wines of the Hospices are auctioned every November. They command high prices, partly because of the charitable tradition and a certain prestige, but also because they usually are well-made.

At the northern end of the Côte is the village of Aloxe-Corton with the hill of Corton rising above it. On the slopes of this hillside lie a wonderful concentration of grads crus vineyards, both red and white. The red wines of Le Corton rival the very best of the Côte de Nuits. Corton-Charlemagne – legend has it that this land was once the property of the Emperor Charlemagne – produces superb white wine. As prices for AC Aloxe-Corton are very high, AC Pernand-Vergelesses is a less expensive substitute.

The Côte de Beaune is much larger in area than the Côte de Nuits, so its basic wines are more plentiful and therefore cheaper. Immediately below commune level is AC Côte de Beaune-Villages, from several of the villages around the town of Beaune. Some of these villages are also entitled to their own individual appellations. Plain AC Côte de Beaune is the product of sixteen villages on the edges of the Côte proper. If the blending is done by one of the big *négociants* these wines can also be good value. Finally there is Bourgogne Hautes Côtes de Beaune, from the country over the hill beyond the Côte d'Or itself. If they are carefully made in a good year, generic wines like these are excellent and can provide the only really accessible burgundies for the average drinker.

The following Burgundian négociants have well established reputations. One of these names on the label of your bottle should provide a fair guarantee of the quality of the wine inside the bottle. Louis Jadot, Louis Latour, Patriarche, Bouchard Père et Fils, Chanson, Joseph Drouhin, Prosper Maufoux, Marcel Amance, J. Faively and Remoissenet. Remember, when ordering burgundy from a restaurant wine list, check for these names on the wine list.

Côte Chalonnais and the Mâconnais

After the classic names and prices of the Côte d'Or it is a relief to turn southwards to the humbler country of the Côte Chalonnais and the Mâconnnais, where you can find interesting everyday wines, that still have some of the characteristics of the finer ones from the Côte de Beaune.

Côte Chalonnais

The Côte Chalonnais is a tiny area lying to the south of the village of Chagny. It is really a continuation of the Côte d'Or although the countryside in this area is rougher and hillier and the vineyards are broken up between patches of farmland. The Côte produces both red and white wine, and its commune wines are good value especially when compared with the prices commanded further north.

The four Chalonnais commune appellations to watch out for are Mercurey, Montagny, Rully and Givry. Montagny's whites are particularly good, clean-tasting and with a tinge of greenish-gold colour that tells of their closeness to Mâcon. The reputation of these commune wines is growing fast, helped along by the presence of top *négociants* like Louis Latour. In fact a Louis Latour Montagny can command a price nowadays that wouldn't shame a top commune wine from the Côte de Beaune.

Rully is also beginning to be known for its whites. These are dry and quite full-bodied, with a certain sharpness due to the high level of acidity. Both Rully and Montagny are wines for drinking while they are still young and fresh, although a year or two in the bottle will do no harm.

The best known reds of the Côte are from the vineyards of Mercurey. They are light, but with a subtlety that can be reminiscent of a Pommard or a Beaune from a lightweight year. Givry and Rully also produce reds with slightly more body but less finesse than Mercurey; Givry is the better of the two. Do not leave any of these fresh wines lying about for too long, and be wary of any that are more than five years old.

Mâconnais

South of the Côte Chalonnais is the much bigger area of the Mâconnais, best known for its white wines – and for Pouilly-Fuissé in particular. In fact the villages producing Pouilly-Fuissé – Vergisson, Chaintré, Soluré, Pouilly and Fuissé – are so far to the south of the Mâconnais that they overlap with the Beaujolais area. They lie on an isolated pocket of soil that gives the wines a distinctive earthy character, known as the *goût de terroir*.

Pouilly wines are praised for being dry and full-bodied, as well as fruity and soft like a good white burgundy. Unfortunately Pouilly-Fuissé is a famous and fashionable name which has suffered from being too much in demand. When looking for the characteristic Pouilly taste, it would make economic sense to choose from one of the other three appellations in the area, Pouilly-Loché, Pouilly-Vinzelles or Saint-Véran. (Remember that Pouilly-Fuissé is not to be confused with Pouilly-Fumé, made from the Sauvignon grape at Pouilly-sur-Loire on the other side of France.)

Wine from the villages around Chaintré and Saint-Véran may also appear under the label 'Beaujolais blanc'. The appellations here are interchangeable, and the producers are presumably keen to take advantage of the booming fashion for beaujolais – whatever colour their wine happens to be.

The rest of the Mâconnais produces less distinctive but perfectly good, rounded white wines made from the noble Chardonnay grape. The reds generally do not reach the same standard because they are made from the prolific and not at all noble Gamay (the beaujolais grape). Both whites and reds are sold as Appellation Mâcon Controlée if they reach a certain standard.

Apart from Pouilly, where the individual grower predominates, Mâconnais grapes tend to be sold by the grower direct to the local co-operatives, who then turn the grapes into wine. There are about twenty co-operatives in the area, at village centres like Chaintré, Clissé and Viré. Once the wine is made it is sold to a shipper who arranges the bottling. So it is worth being aware when choosing a Mâcon that there are *two* factors likely to affect the quality – the co-operative as well as the shipper.

A cut above plain white AC Mâcon is Mâcon-Villages, from certain designated villages. About forty villages producing white wine of this standard are allowed to hyphenate their names on to the basic appellation title – the best known are probably Mâcon-Prissé, Mâcon-Viré and Mâcon-Lugny.

Another local appellation, and one that can sometimes be puzzling, is Pinot Chardonnay Mâcon. This is a so-called 'varietal' wine, named in the Californian style after two grape varieties, and it can be particularly good value. It may be made from the Chardonnay grape or from its close relative the Pinot Blanc, and it is so called to set it apart from the other Mâconnais whites made from the Aligoté grape. These poorer cousins, which can taste thin and sharp beside the rich depth of the Chardonnay, will be identified as such on the label. Quite large areas of the Mâconnais and Chalonnais are planted with Gamay and Aligoté which will find their way into AC Bourgogne Passe-tout-Grains (or AC Mâcon, of course) and AC Bourgogne Aligoté, or into declassified *vin de table*.

Most of the wines from these two areas (except the Pouillys and the products of the grand *négociants*) are cheap enough to allow room for experiment. Watch the liquor store shelves or your wine merchant's list for the lesser-known names. Once you have found a particular Mercurey, Montagny or Mâcon-Villages that you like it would be well worth investing in a supply to draw on over the next couple of years. They are not the kind of wines to lay down with a view to a profit in ten years' time, but they will benefit from a year or two resting in the bottle, and will then appear at their fresh and economically appealing best.

Celebrating the end of a Mâcon harvest

Beaujolais

Light and fruity, beaujolais is a popular and well-known red wine and a very versatile one – suitable for most social occasions and as an accompaniment for many dishes. It comes from an 80 kilometre stretch of country between Mâcon and Lyons, at the southern end of the Burgundy vineyards. The region is attractive, with rolling hills and small villages, which epitomize rural France.

Grape pickers in a beaujolais vineyard

Until the 1960s much of the 'Beaujolais' exported was a soupy blend of cheap red wines, concocted by blenders from a number of sources; it bore no relation to true beaujolais. Fortunately, the situation has changed: former blending practices are now illegal and there has been a tremendous surge of enthusiasm for the genuine article – a light, refreshing, fruity red wine made exclusively from the Gamay grape, grown within a limited area and intended to be drunk young.

This is not to say that the quality of beaujolais is uniform. It comes from a large area which produces, in a good vintage, over 150 million bottles of wine. A lot of this comes from the lower-lying area in the south of the region, known as the Bas Beaujolais. This area has been extensively planted with new vines in recent years but the Gamay vine here makes a less interesting wine than it does on the granite hills in the north of the region.

How to choose a good beaujolais
Generally speaking, the more precisely a bottle of wine is defined by its label, the better it should be. A wine described simply as A.C. Beaujolais is guaranteed to come from the area, to be made from the Gamay, and to contain at least 9% of alcohol.

Beaujolais Supérieur is the same, but 1% stronger, over 10% (though it is not necessarily better wine). In the heart of the Beaujolais country there is a group of some 35 communes, or villages, whose product is entitled to be known as Beaujolais Villages. This wine has the same strength as Beaujolais Supérieur but because it comes from a region where the conditions of the soil and climate are especially suited to the Gamay grape, it should have more character.

Moving on, in terms of quality, there are nine communes in the area, the Grand Crus, which are entitled to their own *appéllation*, that is, a special wine label of their own. Their names are St. Amour, Juliénas, Chénas, Moulin-à-Vent, Chiroubles, Fleurie, Morgon, Brouilly and Côte de Brouilly. These wines are undoubtedly the best beaujolais, and a beaujolais expert will tell you that each of them has its own distinctive qualities. As a general guide, Fleurie is perhaps the most immediately appealing – bright, translucent and appetizing. Brouilly and Côte de Brouilly are usually the fruitiest of the group. Morgon is harder and longer lasting and Moulin-à-Vent, the biggest and deepest in flavour, sometimes needs several years to develop its full potential.

As a general rule, even Grand Cru Beaujolais is at its best within 2 or 3 years of bottling. Beaujolais also breaks the other rule usually applied to red wine because it can be served slightly chilled, at 'cellar' rather than room temperature.

Merchants
Most beaujolais is bought from individual growers or co-operatives by local négociants or merchants. They will blend the wines according to the traditions of their firms and the name of the négociant will appear on the label. The Beaujolais of Piat is a well-known label marketed in a distinctive rounded bottle with a small lip at the top. Other merchants' names worth looking for are Antoine Dépagneux of Villefranche and Georges Duboeuf of Romaneche-Thorins.

Prices
Beaujolais is a more reasonably priced wine than burgundy, but it has become a lot more expensive in recent years. This is in spite of the great amount produced, as verified by the saying that three rivers flow into the neighbouring town of Lyons: the Rhône, the Saône and the Beaujolais. Among imported wines a good A.C. Beaujolais is not markedly more expensive than unnamed cheap plonk. A Beaujolais Villages will be slightly more expensive than an A.C. Beaujolais. A Grand Cru from a good vintage will be about twice the price of the A.C. Beaujolais which is considerably less than you would pay for a bottle from a limited area in other parts of France.

Beaujolais nouveau
Beaujolais nouveau is newly made wine which is rushed from grape to bottle within the space of about six weeks and traditionally appears on the market around 15 November. It should be drunk immediately. Opinions are divided on its merits. It is very light, with the purplish colour characteristic of young wine, and with a pleasant scent and fruitiness. It is certainly fun to drink, but until quite recently you would have been lucky to find it outside the region of origin. Suddenly, through a combination of shrewd marketing and the whims of fashion, it has become a cult.

'The Beaujolais race' is now a social event in countries near France with merchants trying to get the wine into shops and restaurants at the first possible moment and at the most competitive price. It is at best a six weeks' wonder – by Christmas the fuss is all over for another year.

No other wine is subject to such intense short-lived demand. The effect on the beaujolais market has been colossal. It can be relatively easily and cheaply produced, and the grower and négociant see a quick return on their investment. It is therefore hardly surprising that in 1983, 40% of all the A.C. Beaujolais produced was sold as Beaujolais Nouveau or Primeur, and producers throughout the region feel mounting pressures to jump on the bandwagon. This would be a pity, for beaujolais nouveau is made to be drunk within weeks rather than months, and when it is all gone there is less of the more worthwhile wine to go round.

Chablis

Chablis is the best known of the white burgundies, and could even be described as the most famous white wine of all. It is one of the most widely imitated and debased names in the wine world, and as a result the reputation of authentic chablis has suffered unfairly.

It is quite common to find undistinguished dryish white and sometimes pink wines cheerfully dignifying themselves with the Chablis label when they really come from almost anywhere in the world except the proper place.

Only a limited amount of genuine Chablis is made each year. Real Chablis comes from an isolated little pocket of northern vineyards, a mere 160 kilometres south-east of Paris. It is one of the smallest fine wine-producing areas, comprising only 2000 hectares of vines. The local conditions demand that the land has to be 'rested' from time to time, so that even this small area is not always under cultivation.

The area's geographical situation is a major factor in determining quantity produced. Damaging spring frosts are a recurrent problem, not entirely solved by the elaborate heating devices in the vineyards. In bad years, too, there may just not be enough sun to ripen the grapes and bring the wine up to the required strength to meet *Appellation Contrôlée* requirements.

Yet when the conditions are favourable, Chablis is a great wine that more than deserves its widespread fame. Although

The rolling countryside around Chablis

Chablis is made from the same grape as the great white burgundies, the Chardonnay, its taste is very different from a Côtes d'Or wine. The crucial factor is the mixture of chalk and limestone in the soil ('Kimmeridgian clay', to give it its technical name). It gives the wine a hard and stony taste which is sometimes described as 'flinty', or, in the French version, as having a '*goute de pierre à fusil*'.

Whatever the description, at its best Chablis is an elegant wine that combines fruitiness with a striking steely strength. The bouquet is fresh and clean but comparatively light, and the colour is particularly attractive, pale strawy gold with distinctively gleaming greenish highlights. Traditionally Chablis is paired with oysters or any shellfish, and with more plainly-cooked fish. It might be overwhelmed by heavy sauces.

Classifications

Chablis has its own fairly simple system of classification. The best (and very expensive) wine comes from the seven *grand cru* vineyards. These lie in the best position on the south-facing slope across the river Serein from the little town of Chablis itself. They are instantly recognizable from their labels, on which they will be described as

'Chablis Grand Cru' followed by one of the seven vineyard names: Bougros, Les Preuses, Vaudésir, Grenouilles, Valmur, Les Clos and Blanchot.

As with Côte d'Or wines, the level immediately below grand cru is *premier cru*. These wines will be labelled 'Chablis Premier Cru', which may or may not be followed by a vineyard name. After recent amalgamation there are now about a dozen premier crus, and the label may indicate that the wine is from just one of these, or it may be a blend from several of them. Amongst the better-known names are Les Fourneaux, Montée de Tonnere, Beauroy, Fourchaume, Vaillons, Vosgros, Vaulorent, Monts de Milieu and Montmains.

The Chablis appellation laws state that grand cru wines must reach a level of 11° of alcohol and premier cru must reach 10.5°, so premier cru Chablis will be just a little less powerful than its grander relative both in bouquet and flavour. It is still fine wine however, and is likely to be expensive.

The appellation laws also set out the maximum yield per hectare for grand cru and premier cru vineyards. It is a strictly limited output, so it is hardly surprising that there is not enough of the best Chablis to go round. Prices, of course, reflect scarcity. Because of the climatic problems, the quality of even the best of the region's wine varies radically from year to year. In bad years the wine may not reach the required minimum strength, in which case it has to be sold off as Petit Chablis, the lowest of the local appellations.

Fortunately plain AC Chablis is rather more accessible. This wine comes from the less well-placed slopes of any of the twenty communes in the region, and the bulk of it is handled by *négociants*. As always, it pays to choose a reliable one. To qualify for this appellation the wine need only reach a level of 10°, so it is relatively light, but it should still have the authentic Chablis steely 'bite'.

At the bottom of this classification ladder is Petit Chablis, mainly from the outer fringes of the area (except in bad years, when even the best vineyards' wine may only reach this standard). In general these are very light wines, often disappointingly colourless and thin. They need only reach a minimum strength of 9.5%, and so are a long way removed from the flavourful potency of the top Chablis. They still carry the big name, however, and can often be rather overpriced as a result.

The lighter wines of the Chablis region should not be left too long before they are drunk. A year or so in bottle is plenty for Petit Chablis and the ordinary AC wines. Premier cru wines are ready to drink after two years and most grands crus can be drunk after three years in the bottle. The best Chablis does have remarkable staying power, however, and can go on giving of its best for ten years, or even longer for the great years.

Chablis is never cheap but it is a remarkable and memorable wine. A good bottle might mark a special occasion or celebration meal, but for everyday white wine-drinking there are better and cheaper alternatives to mediocre AC Chablis or Petit Chablis.

Introducing Bordeaux

Bordeaux is the largest fine wine-producing area in the world – Burgundy may rival it for quality, but cannot compete with the wonderful quantity of wine that is produced by the 50,000 Bordeaux growers. Nor can such a wide variety of wines, from the cheerful and easily drinkable to the highest-ranking aristocrats, be found anywhere else in the world. Since there is no shortage of Bordeaux wine, prices are usually reasonable, for all but the great wines.

There are striking differences in the wines of Burgundy and Bordeaux and in the way they are made. While all the great red Burgundies are made from one variety of grape, the Pinot Noir, the Bordeaux reds are made from a blend of three main varieties: Cabernet Sauvignon, Cabernet Franc and Merlot.

Bordeaux wines generally have more finesse, a more individual bouquet and seem a little austere, compared with the fullness and opulence of Burgundy. Although they are quite recognizably from the same family, Bordeaux wines differ tremendously from one another. They range from the light, dry reds and whites, to the honeyed white dessert wines of Sauternes and Barsac, with all the subtle variations in between. The red wines are often referred to as claret – an wholly English term.

As well as the different grapes, the soil, too, accounts for much of Bordeaux's rich variety. It is poor soil, consisting largely of clay, sand, pebbles and gravel – just what the vines need to produce the best grapes.

The weather is equally crucial to the variety of wines available. Bordeaux is famous for its micro-climate. The area of St Emilion, for instance, is warmer than the Médoc area, so that the grapes flower earlier. A sudden hailstorm in one area, causing great damage to the grapes, may leave the rest of Bordeaux unscathed.

Labelling

If the wide range of Bordeaux wines sounds daunting, the clear and simple labelling of bottles is a useful guide. The top grades of all French wines are designated Appellation Contrôlée. In Bordeaux, about 70% of the wines come into this category, which gives some idea of the high standards of wine-making. Between these two words, you often find the name of a region. Appellation Bordeaux Contrôlée indicates an ordinary wine, but nevertheless deserving of the Appellation Contrôlée label. Appellation Bordeaux Supérieur Contrôlée still indicates an undistinguished wine, but it must have an alcoholic strength higher than 10.7%.

After these two lowest grades, successively higher-quality wines are labelled with a district name, then with the name of a precise area within that district, or with a village name. The more precisely the origin of the wine is pin-pointed, the higher the quality, for instance, 'Appellation Haut-Médoc Contrôlée' indicates that the wine comes from the great wine-producing area of Haut-Médoc in Bordeaux. Alternatively, a bottle may be labelled with one of the districts of the Haut Médoc, where giants such as Château Lafite are produced.

A little knowledge of the different areas that make up the huge family of Bordeaux wines comes in useful when you are buying.

The name of the château on a label, unless it is a famous one, does not mean very much. There are about 10,000 châteaux in Bordeaux. Anyone who owns a vineyard and a *chai* (cellar) can call his estate a château and give the bottle a fancy label. Of the 10,000 châteaux, about 200 produce a wine of special reknown, which will naturally cost more.

Classified growths

In 1855, an official classification was drawn up for the best Bordeaux wines. Each of the 60 Médocs and the one red Graves chosen, were solemnly graded in order of excellence: First, Second, Third, Fourth or Fifth Growth, or *cru*. The system gives a roughly accurate guide to the 60 top châteaux in Bordeaux, though many more, especially from St Emilion and Pomerol, would be included if the league table were ever brought up to date. When a wine is referred to as 'Fifth Growth' in Bordeaux, it does not indicate a fifth-rate wine, but a high-class one that was privileged to enter the old 1855 classification.

Classified growths can be very expensive, but below them is a huge range of wines known as *Cru bourgeois*, often wines of real quality that cost much less. Well-made wines from the less highly regarded parts of Bordeaux, such as Blaye, Bourg and Fronsac, can often give more pleasure than the wine of a well-known château in a poor year.

Vintage

When they are young, Bordeaux wines have so much tannin in them that they are not very drinkable. After a few years in bottle, however, they develop in a fascinating way, becoming smoother and more complex. Some are good after three or four years, others are better left much longer.

Vintage dates give the wine buyer some useful hints, but are not always infallible since the weather pattern, as already explained, differs widely.

A	Médoc-Maritime
B	Haut-Médoc
C	Graves
D	Sauternes
E	Premières Côtes de Bordeaux
F	Entre-Deux-Mers
G	Blayais
H	Bourgeais
I	Fronsac
J	Pomerol
K	St Emilion

Haut-Médoc: St Estèphe and Pauillac

The Médoc is the most famous red wine district in Bordeaux. One-third of it, lying to the north, is known simply as the Médoc, or Bas-Médoc, and has a proliferation of small châteaux making sound wine at reasonable prices. The Haut-Médoc, to the south, is in a different league altogether – here the very greatest red wines are made.

Château Lafite

The countryside of the Haut-Médoc is not exciting. To the west, sand dunes and pine forests roll away monotonously; to the east the precious slopes are covered in vines which are beautifully trellised in straight, regimental lines. The overall effect is oddly undramatic.

The wines, too, are unassertive at first and almost have to steal up on you before you appreciate them properly. They are difficult to judge when young. They have to be allowed time to mature, especially a great wine, which should never be opened until it is at least five years old. But once you have begun to recognize the distinction and the depth of flavour of fine Médoc wine, you will be certain to return to it again and again.

A parish in Bordeaux is known as a commune and every commune in the Haut-Médoc has more world-famous vineyards and châteaux than there is space to mention here in this chapter.

St Estèphe

St Estèphe, the northernmost commune in the Haut-Médoc, has sturdy, slightly 'harder' wines than the other communes. They contain a great deal of tannin. Bought young, they need to be kept for 10–15 years before they are at their peak.

Anyone prepared to be patient can disprove the old 1855 classification (see *page 374*), which listed no St Estèphe wines as 'first growths'.

One of the best vineyards of St Estèphe is Château Cos d'Estournel, which has a series of cellars built in an eccentric Chinese pagoda style. The wine from here is a second growth wine. Following closely for quality are the dark-coloured Château Montrose (second growth) and Calon-Ségur (third growth). Even these lesser greats are better known than you might imagine when you consider the prices: only a very special occasion can justify the purchase of, say, the classic 1970 vintage.

However today's buyer can also find good *cru bourgeois* wines from the area to the north of the town of St Estèph itself. Many are produced in rambling, old-fashioned cellars. A knowledgeable wine merchant should be able to hunt out several that are reasonably priced and worth keeping.

From farther south, wine from Château de Pez, although humbly classed as *cru bourgeois supérieur*, is well worth looking out for. Every year Château de Pez makes 400 hogsheads (large casks) of excellent wine. There is also the *cru bourgeois* of Château Meyney, made in a beautifully kept farmhouse: this is a wine that seems to improve year by year.

Pauillac

Adjoining Cos d'Estournel in St Estèphe is the first growth Château Lafite vineyard in the commune of Pauillac, but the two wines have totally different characters. The sturdy, hard quality of St Estèphe gives way to a wine that has sometimes been described as slightly 'feminine'. Château Lafite has been classed, by some, as the greatest claret in Bordeaux; and when you realize that Pauillac also includes Château Latour and Château Mouton-Rothschild – the first two heading the 1855 classification, with Mouton-Rothschild joining their lead in 1973 – there can be no question that this is the greatest of the Bordeaux communes.

In Pauillac the country is hillier and the vines have to work harder to produce their grapes – leading to heightened quality. Even the landscape, like the wine, is a little more sumptuous, with whole hillsides belonging to one rich owner, instead of being confusingly sub-divided, as in Burgundy.

The great wines are all individuals in their own right. Château Latour, produced from soil full of egg-sized stones, is a really big wine. It is strong and full, compared with the perfumed finesse of Château Lafite wines. Château Mouton-Rothschild, on the other hand, is a wonderful, dusky red wine with great concentration of flavour.

Coming a little down the scale, but still in the realm of fine wines, there is Château Pichon Lalande, half in Pauillac and half in the commune of St Julien. Equally well known is the slightly heavier wine of Lynch-Bages. The attractive Château Pontet-Canet has a big production of 1500 barrels a year which means that the wines can sometimes be bought at reasonable prices. Farther inland are the much smaller Château Batailley and Château Haut-Batailley, the latter producing wine that is considered the better claret of the two.

All these châteaux in the Pauillac commune – and many others – cater for connoisseurs who have 'worked their way up' from lesser wines to the great gourmet bottlings. Luckily, there are ways of sampling Pauillac without distressing one's bank manager. Château Latour makes a second wine, Les Forts de Latour, as does Château Lafite, Moulin des Carruades; both make outstanding drinking. From Mouton, there is Mouton-Cadet, a popular branded Bordeaux. There is even a co-operative of some 200 farmers in Pauillac, bottling under the name of La Rose Pauillac. The quality of the wine remains consistently good.

Haut- and Bas-Médoc

Here we look at the well-known Haut-Médoc communes, St Julien and Margaux, together with the lesser-known Bas-Médoc.

St Julien is a small commune on the west bank of the River Gironde. It produces less than the other three great red-wine communes of the Haut-Médoc – Pauillac, St Estèphe and Margaux. There are no first-class growths in St Julien, if you go by the somewhat outdated 1855 classification, but it has a higher proportion of 'classed' growths than anywhere else – five second classes, two thirds and five fourths, although Pauillac has more fifth growths. There are so many good wines that you would be unlucky to buy a bottle of St Julien that fell below a high standard.

The experts tend to say that St Julien is a kind of breathing space between the brilliant but sturdy Pauillac wines to the north and the more refined and elegant offerings from Margaux. They are wonderful wines to lay down, maturing sooner than the Pauillac 'greats', and acquiring a gentle, smooth texture detected easily in the wines of Château Talbot or Gruaud-Larose.

Château Léoville Las Cases is the most revered name in St Julien, closely followed by two other famous châteaux, Léoville Barton and Léoville Poyferré. For sheer aristocratic finesse, Château Beychevelle is a wine to buy in a good vintage year, when it outclasses its rivals. But in a poor year, it can be a disappointing buy.

Château Ducru-Beaucaillou (named after the 'beautiful pebbles' that make up so much of the soil of these riverside vineyards) and Château Gloria are situated next door to each other. It used to be possible to buy the latter cheaply because it is only classed as *cru bourgeois*. However, if a new classification were made now, it would never be so overlooked. Indeed, even without this recognition, so many people seem to know about Château Gloria, with its splendidly dark colour and full taste, that it seems unlikely the wine will ever be sold at a bargain price again.

The two small villages of Moulis and Listrac, situated to the south of St Julien and farther inland, produce cheaper *cru bourgeois*. The well-respected Château Chasse-Spleen is in Moulis, while Listrac has the highly regarded Châteaux Fourcas-Dupré and Fourcas-Hosten. Other good *cru bourgeois* from nearby areas are Châteaux Dutruch-Grand-Poujeaux, Pierre-Bibian, Duplessis and Maucaillou.

Margaux

From farther south comes the magnificent fruity red wine of Château Margaux, a famous first growth of the Margaux area, which can boast another eleven in the hallowed classified list. Choose a Château Margaux from a good vintage year to get full benefit of the marvellous bouquet. Château Margaux also produces a dry, rather individual white wine, Pavillon Blanc, which is by no means over-priced.

You can even find a distinctive dry rosé from these parts, Rosé de Lascombes. This is made by Château Lascombes, whose fine second-growth claret is delicate and perfumed in typical Margaux style, like the sought-after wines of Château Palmer.

For classed growths that are at middle-range prices, but with sound quality, look for the Châteaux Cantenac-Brown, Brane-Cantenac, Malescot, Marquis d'Alesme and Kirwan. Watch out for Château Giscours, a wine that has improved greatly recently, thanks to an energetic proprietor.

Bas-Médoc

The Bas-Médoc has now officially been renamed Médoc-Maritime, because 'bas' suggests inferiority. Sadly, for those who hope to find some undiscovered châteaux selling their wines at giveaway prices, the flat country of the Médoc-Maritime produces only 25% of the wines of the Médoc – and most of these seem to be kept for local consumption.

Few are exported, with the shining exception of Château Loudenne. Apart from producing fine claret, this château also produces a good, inexpensive Appellation Médoc Contrôlée, La Cour Pavillon, made from a careful blend of local wines. Even their Bordeaux Blanc is crisper and fresher than many others in Bordeaux and is worth trying to find.

Two exemplary wines of the Haut-Médoc

Sweet wines of Bordeaux

The rich, sweet wines of Bordeaux are one of its greatest glories. The best of them, Sauternes and Barsac, come from the most southerly area of Bordeaux. They are probably the most undervalued Bordeaux wines, simply because of the recent trend to drink dry wine rather than sweet. But with a dessert or fresh summer fruit nothing can compare with a honeyed glass of Sauternes.

Sauternes

Sauternes is made by a few hundred growers centred on five tiny communes on the banks of a stream 30 miles south of the city of Bordeaux. The five communes are: Sauternes, Bommes, Fargues, Preignac and Barsac. Only they are allowed, under French law, to put the Sauternes label on their wines; Barsac, the largest commune, has the choice of calling its wines either Sauternes or Barsac.

The wine is made from the golden Sauvignon and Sémillon grapes, which are ready for picking by the end of September. However, for producing Sauternes, they are deliberately left on the vine until they are over-ripe and have been attacked by a mould known as the 'noble rot'. As long as October stays mild, the fruit will lose its colour, take on a reddish tinge, then fade to a wizened grey. Every morning the pickers take the grapes with 'noble rot' and press the tiny harvest that evening.

The wine that results from these specially picked grapes is naturally sweeter and has a more concentrated taste than any other in the world. In view of the risk of total failure if the weather fails, coupled with a very small yield and high labour costs, the wine is comparatively moderately priced. The only exception is Château d'Yquem, where the wine is in a class of its own and is highly prized. The château itself is one of the most striking in all Bordeaux, and is the only place where the entire wine-making plant is made of wood. No metal ever comes into contact with the wine in case it affects the taste.

Yquem is in the commune of Sauternes, which also has Châteaux Guiraud, Filhot and Lamothe. The commune of Fargues has just one great name, Château Rieussec, considered second only to Yquem, while Preignac has Château Suduiraut. Châteaux Rayne-Vigeau, Lafaurie-Peyraguey and La Tour Blanche are all in Bommes. All these wines keep beautifully and are worth laying down.

The largest commune, Barsac, makes a slightly different wine from the others. It is a fraction less sweet and not quite so rich. The two outstanding châteaux of Barsac are Climens and Coutet, both of which have changed hands in recent years. Châteaux Doisy-Védrines, Doisy-Daëne and Nairac, just a little lower down the scale, are correspondingly cheaper.

It is important to check that the label on a bottle of Sauternes bears the name of the commune. The term Haut-Sauternes means nothing at all. Any wine calling itself Sauterne, without the concluding 's', is not the genuine article. The best Sauternes should not be highly chilled, otherwise the wine will lose its intensity and depth of flavour.

Other sweet Bordeaux

A district to remember is Cérons, where the wines come halfway in sweetness between Sauternes and Graves. They are half a degree less in alcoholic strength than Sauternes and are more modestly priced. Those who find Sauternes too rich and heavy, should sample Cérons wine.

Equally inexpensive are the sweet wines of Ste Croix du Mont and Loupiac. Both are in the area of the Premières Côtes de Bordeaux, on the right bank of the Garonne river, opposite Sauternes and Barsac. The wines, a little heavier than Cérons are not easy to find because both are prone to frost and produce little in a poor year. In good years, however, they can be a wonderful buy.

Between the Garonne and Dordogne lies the attractively-named Entre-Deux-Mers, an enormous tract of land that at one time produced some quite drinkable sweet wines.

Nowadays, these wines tend to be dry, following the fashion. However, if a wine merchant has an acceptable sweet Entre-Deux-Mers, it might be half the price of a Sauternes.

Finally, there is Monbazillac, which is outside the Bordeaux area altogether. It lies near Bergerac, in the Dordogne valley. Its lovely sweet wines are reminiscent of Sauternes and are fairly cheap. The principal difference is the taste of the Muscat grape.

There seems little demand for it which seems odd with prices so consistently low. Those who develop a palate for it can drink a quality dessert wine fairly cheaply.

Two delicious, yet very different, sweet white wines of Bordeaux

Pomerol and North East Bordeaux

Pomerol, situated to the north-west of St Emilion, is a relative newcomer as a wine area in Bordeaux — it is the place to look for undiscovered red Bordeaux wines. On the other hand, the areas of Fronsac, Bourg and Blaye, to the north-west of Pomerol, are well-established wine areas, offering a more modest, everyday type of wine.

Pomerol

The wines of Pomerol are often grouped with St Emilion, because the best wines of both areas are near their shared border. Yet there is a marked difference in the wines, which is attributed to the extraordinary soil difference. Pomerol consists of a large gravel bank, held together by clay, with the best wines growing on a mixture of quite deep clay and a thin layer of gravel.

The fact that Pomerol is a relative newcomer as a wine area is a great attraction: there is no official classification, nor is there a long history of buying and selling. The wine of Pomerol has an instant appeal, with its full, slightly exotic flavour that turns into a gentle richness in the mouth. The scent is very distinctive, with a faint earthiness.

A small château in Bourg

Even without any official classification, there is no argument about the top wines of Pomerol. They come from Château Pétrus, whose prices regularly fetch as much as the great first growths of the Médoc. This tiny vineyard produces a wonderfully fruity wine but it is very expensive.

Château Trotanoy is said to come second to Château Pétrus in reputation. Its name derives from the mixture of gravel and deep clay that becomes so hard in summer that it is '*trop ennuyeux*', or too much like hard work! Sadly, the vineyard is a tiny one, so demand greatly exceeds the supply of this velvety, fruity wine.

Vieux-Château-Certan, next door to Château Pétrus, is also held in high regard. Other good names include L'Evangile, Certan-de-May, La Conseillante, La Fleur-Pétrus and Petit-Village. Look too for Château Le Gay, Château Rouget, Château Plince, Château Clos René and Château de Sales — they are all reliably consistent.

Pomerol wines need not be hoarded for a great many years, like some of the great Médoc wines, before they are drinkable. Made mostly with the soft Merlot grape, they lack the tannin for laying down. Four or five years after the vintage, they make the most acceptable drinking.

Fronsac, Bourg and Blaye

Fronsac, Bourg and Blaye are situated on the right bank of the Dordogne and Gironde rivers, where the soil is a little too rich to make wines of real distinction. However, they are good enough for all but the grandest dinner party.

Of the three areas, Fronsac makes the liveliest wines with the Cabernet Franc grape much in evidence. There are two appellations here: Côtes de Fronsac and Canon-Fronsac, both producing big, fruity wines that slip down very easily.

Château Canon in the Canon-Fronsac area is a well-known château but is easily confused with a St Emilion wine of the same name. A great deal of Château de la Rivière finds its way abroad and improves with keeping as long as ten years, for a good vintage. Château Rouet, beautifully set high up in the village of St Germain-la-Rivière, makes good, honest wines. Others worth sampling are Châteaux Bodet, Junayme, Mayne-Vieil, Toumalin and La Valade.

The districts of Bourg and Blaye also supply good value wines which are at their best when young. Most are made with a blend of Merlot and Cabernet Franc grapes.

Bourg produces more wines than Blaye. The best of them, such as Château de Barbe and Château Guerry, come from the slopes near the Gironde river. Here the thinner soil produces rather better grapes. Other names to investigate include Du Bousquet, Guionne, Mille-Secousses, Tayac and Rousset.

In Blaye, it is difficult to go far wrong, now that so many small châteaux have improved their standards. Haut-Sociondo and Le Menaudat are châteaux of repute and so are Mondésir-Gazan and Segonzac. They produce a lighter wine than Bourg, that is mellower and even easier to drink. There are also some pleasant, dry, white wines that go well with fish.

St Emilion

St Emilion produces more claret than any other wine district in Bordeaux, simply because it is the largest district. The wines are richer and redder than most other clarets, falling halfway between the fullness and depth of Burgundy and the more usual dry, austere-style Bordeaux.

The wines of St Emilion have a different character from that of other Bordeaux wines for two reasons: the soil is richer and the grapes used are different from the other Bordeaux wine districts. The Cabernet Sauvignon, the king of Bordeaux grapes, is little used in St Emilion. It largely gives way to Merlot which is softer, ages sooner and imparts a certain richness.

The French make a distinction between the wines grown on the hillsides, known as Côtes-St-Emilion, and those grown on the plain, known as Graves-St-Emilion. Although these terms are not used on labels, they are worth remembering when buying a particular château wine. If you know the area it comes from, you will have a good idea of the character of the wine in the bottle.

Côtes wines are 'rounder' with more body and the great name here is Château Ausone. The cellars are cut from the solid rock of the hillside with pillars left to support the roof. The vineyards are situated under the brow of the hill, sheltered from the north wind. The wines of Château Ausone, together with those of Cheval Blanc, top the St Emilion classification list and are designated *Premiers Grands Crus Classés*. St Emilion was left out of the 1855 classification (see *page 374*), so it drew up its own league table 100 years later. Unfortunately, the classifications of the various districts cannot be compared because there is no agreed definition of *grand cru* or *cru classé*. The term may not indicate a wine that is up to a Médoc classified growth and, as the list is always being revised, it is best ignored.

The proprietors of Château Ausone also own Château Belair, a lesser wine that is widely distributed. Farther down the steep slopes are the vineyards of Château La Gaffelière-Naudes, while across the road and running all the way to the top of the plateau are those of Château Pavie. As these are well-known names, and priced accordingly, it is worth looking out for some of the lesser châteaux that are so often overlooked – for instance, Troplong-Mondot, Grand-Pontet, La Clotte, L'Angélus, Clos des Jacobins. These are still good value.

The 'Graves' wines (not to be confused with the Graves district) are mostly grown from vineyards standing partly on heavy clay, partly on light gravel. The velvety, aristocratic wines of Château Cheval Blanc, with their charming softness and perfume, are one example. Since Cheval Blanc is usually mentioned in the same breath as the Médoc first growths, it is best left to the wealthy buyer. However, again, there is a host of not-so-famous châteaux making good wine for much less, notably Châteaux Figeac, Latour-Figeac and Latour-du-Pin-Figeac, Croque-Michette, Corbin and Ripeau.

As if the choice was not already wide enough, the St Emilion name is also shared by seven small communes to the south and east, extending down to the right bank of the Dordogne. The winegrowers here are fiercely independent, making wine of widely different quality. The communes are St Christophe-des-Bardes, St Laurent-des-Combes, St Hippolyte, St Etienne-de-Lisse, St Pey-d'Armens, St Sulpice-de-Faleyrens and Vignonet. Sound château wines can be found in these much overlooked areas.

Finally, there are five more St Emilion communes to the north-east on slightly higher ground, namely St Georges, Montagne, Lussac, Puisseguin and Parsac. They make pleasant wines and stand in relation to St Emilion as Beaujolais villages does to Beaujolais.

Those who would rather not pick and choose from small growers could settle for one of the co-operative wines. The largest, with a total of 400 members, is the Union de Producteurs de St Emilion. Most of its wine is sold as Côtes Rocheuses or Royal Saint Emilion. No fewer than 20 members also have their own *Grand Cru* wines. They use the co-operative to dispose of good St Emilion that is over and above the legal production limit. This information is useful to bear in mind when buying St Emilion co-operative wines.

The town of St Emilion

379

White Graves

For most people, the name Graves conjures up a white wine, pale gold in colour and rather sweet. But things have changed in recent years and nowadays the Graves district offers a whole new range of lighter drier whites as well as several excellent red wines. On this page we look at the different types of white Graves.

The Graves district is a large flat area stretching from the city of Bordeaux along the left bank of the Garonne to the foothills of the Pyrenees in the south-west. The area takes its name from its soil which is a mixture of gravel and sand. Although many of the Graves estates make both red and white wines, it will be easier to look at them separately.

Only white wines may be called simply 'Graves', although red wines may have the appellation on the label. Many of these whites are full-flavoured, with a hint of vanilla in the after-taste which comes from ageing in oak casks. Don't be misled by the term Graves Supérieur on a bottle: it is no guarantee of quality, and simply means that the alcoholic strength is above 12%!

For some years now Bordeaux has been making a strong push with dry white wines from the Sauvignon and Sémillon grapes, sometimes with a little Muscadelle added.

Many growers from the Graves area have followed suit. As a result, the whole spectrum of tastes – from the very dry to the sweet – is available and the choice is wider than ever.

Starting at the top end of the range, there is Haut-Brion Blanc, rarely seen and extremely expensive. It is fresh and full-bodied and connoisseurs think it well worth the price. It comes from Château Haut-Brion, in the commune of Pessac in the suburbs of Bordeaux. One of its great rivals, Laville Haut-Brion, comes from the estate over the road, Château La Mission Haut-Brion. Laville Haut-Brion is another great treat for those who can afford it. If kept for a few years, it acquires an opulent and subtle taste. Another great white wine comes from the Domaine de Chevalier, a very modern establishment with a huge production of excellent wines. These wines have a clean-cut taste.

Choosing the right white Graves

Leaving Bordeaux to the north and travelling south, white wines seem to take over. Generally speaking, they are more difficult to make than the reds. There is an increased risk of oxidation, called *madérisation*, which darkens the colour of the wine and leaves a stale taste in the mouth. Sulphur is the best remedy, but it also leaves its traces which are particularly noticeable when you open the bottle and pour the first glass. The art of buying white Graves is to find the wines that avoid both hazards. It may mean choosing one of the new, drier, delightful wines that are more like Loire whites than traditional Graves. Try Château Carbonnieux – crisp, light, easy to drink, and made mostly with the dry Sauvignon grape.

The commune of Villenave-d'Ornon in the south east also produces several drier, lighter whites in the Loire style, even though this means giving up oak barrels and losing the traditional Graves taste.

If you want an old-fashioned Graves, with its traditional taste, try Graves de Portets. It is a medium dry white, with a fruity flavour which many people enjoy, especially during the winter months. The same goes for Château Millet, which is full of flavour, keeps well and sells briskly to Britain and the U.S.

Château Haut-Brion

Red Graves

Red wines from the Graves area are underestimated: less well known than the local whites, they have improved enormously since the 1960s and are usually good and sometimes excellent.

Graves reds are a good introduction to Bordeaux wines like St Emilion and they are much easier to get to know than any of the Médoc reds. If kept for a few years, they become satin-smooth, with great fullness and richness, and go very well with a creamy cheese. Many experts rate them above the whites of the area. In the official 1959 classification, 13 red wines had the right to call themselves Appellation Graves Controlée, compared to only 8 whites.

The best reds come from the north of the Graves area, very near the city of Bordeaux. The greatest is probably Château Haut-Brion, the only red Graves to be called a First Growth in the original classification of 1855. The vines are grown in very favourable conditions, on a thick layer of pebbly gravel that reflects the heat and allows rainwater to drain away rapidly. The Haut-Brion reds have a marvellously rich aroma, and a smooth velvety taste, with an intense concentration of different flavours. They easily compete with the best reds of Pauillac and Margaux.

Other excellent red wines from the area include Château La Mission Haut-Brion, and Château Pape-Clément, named after the pope who moved the papacy to Avignon in the 14th century. Château Pape-Clément is fragrant, earthy and full, and produced by one of the oldest vineyards in Bordeaux, in the commune of Pessac. Pessac is actually in the suburbs of Bordeaux: in the Middle Ages, the vines grew all around the city. They are now fighting a constant battle against encroaching roads and houses. The Château Pape-Clément vineyards were completely replanted in the 1950s. They now make what is known as a 'big' wine, a blend of Cabernet Sauvignon and Merlot grapes.

A few miles south of Pessac, the commune of Léognan produces extremely fine reds: Château Haut-Bailly, Château Carbonnieux, Domaine de Chevalier and Château Malartic-Lagravière, with its fresh and spicy wines.

Next to Léognan is Martillac, which is the home of a number of well run estates, including two chosen for the 1959 classification: Smith-Haut-Lafitte and La Tour-Martillac. The Smith-Haut-Lafitte wines offer good buying opportunities for people who want to enjoy the classic Graves taste — elegant and full of flavour. A little further south is another Château worth remembering, Château La Garde, which produces a soft red wine, with a pleasant dry finish characteristic of red Graves.

Most of the wines just mentioned are expensive. A more reasonably priced but still good red Graves is Château Bouscaut, well known in the United States as a result of having had an American owner. The Château Bouscaut vineyards have been largely replanted since World War II and produce sound red wines, which are supple, easy to drink and with good lasting qualities, just like their whites.

Red Graves wines are well worth looking for: they have a distinct character, and they are robust and generous.

The satin-smooth reds of the Graves region are a good introduction to claret.

Dry white wines of the Loire

The Loire is the longest river in France and for much of its length it is flanked by vineyards producing a great variety of wines. Few have the distinction of fine Burgundy or Bordeaux wines, but they have more immediately appealing qualities of charm, delicacy and freshness, with the additional advantage – in most cases – of being good value for money.

The chateau of Azay-le-Rideau

The majority of wine produced in the Loire valley is white and most of it is dry. The best known comes from two distinct areas, the region of Sevre et Maine at the Atlantic end of the valley near Nantes, and the area to the East of Orleans, about half-way up the river, around the towns of Sancerre and Pouilly. The district of Touraine in the middle of the Loire also produces some dry white wine.

Sevre et Maine

The best wine from the Sevre et Maine district is Muscadet, named after the grape from which it is made. Pale gold, very dry and slightly acidic, it is traditionally thought of as a 'fish' wine. In fact it is more versatile than this; its refreshing qualities make it the ideal thirst-quencher for hot summer days and it can be a pleasant aperitif.

The reputation of Muscadet outside its own home area is a comparatively recent event. With the greatly increased demand, vineyard area has doubled in recent years and this can mean variable quality. Even the best Muscadet is not expensive by French standards and you would be advised to look for a wine from a single estate or château, which will usually be bottled by the grower. Some good names are Château de la Galissonière, Château la Noë and Château de l'Oiselinière.

Another variable factor, and one which applies to the whole of the Loire, is the weather. Frost, rain and lack of sunshine are obvious enemies, but a very hot summer like 1976 can produce an uncharacteristic wine with too little acidity. The qualities which make Muscadet attractive and appealing will not improve with keeping. It is essentially a wine to be drunk young, certainly within two or three years of bottling.

Some growers do not filter and bottle all their Muscadet immediately after fermentation, but leave some in the vats for another few weeks in contact with the deposit known as the 'lees'. A wine which has been treated in this way will have the additional description *sur lie*. It is considered to have a little extra body and flavour and will also pick up a slight tingle resulting from retained carbon dioxide.

Another rather coarser white wine from the same area is Gros Plant. This is again named after its grape and is sold almost exclusively as the local *vin de pays*.

Sancerre and Pouilly

The most distinguished, and expensive, dry white wines of the Loire come from around Sancerre and Pouilly. These are made from the Sauvignon Blanc grape. Somewhat confusingly, a wine described as Pouilly-sur-Loire will contain at least a proportion of the inferior Chasselas grape; the Sauvignon is known locally as Blanc Fumé and the best wine from Pouilly is called Pouilly Blanc Fumé.

Both Sancerre and Pouilly Fumé are slightly fuller bodied wines than Muscadet. They have a characteristic bouquet usually described as 'gun-flint', because it is reminiscent of the smoke from struck flints. They have been widely adopted as alternatives to Chablis and other very expensive white burgundies. However, the production area is small, demand has recently raced ahead of supply, and this state of affairs, particularly in the case of Pouilly Fumé, has been reflected in much higher prices. The district is also very susceptible to poor weather. Both quality and quantity of vintages have been badly affected by frost and hail in the past. Like all dry Loire whites, Sancerre and Pouilly Fumé should be drunk young; the delicate balance of fruitiness and acidity which gives them their charm will be lost after a few years in bottle.

The seriousness with which Sancerre and Pouilly Fumé have come to be regarded in recent years is really a little inappropriate in wines which used to be considered the white equivalent of Beaujolais. There are good Sauvignon wines produced at a more reasonable price in the neighbourhood of Reuilly, Quincy and Ménétou-Salon to the south-west of Sancerre.

Middle Loire

Sauvignon Blanc is also grown widely in the middle Loire district of Touraine – Sauvignon de Touraine is a good bargain, if you can find it. The main white grape of Touraine is the Chenin Blanc, and the best-known dry wines made from this grape come from the towns of Vouvray and Montlouis. Vouvray is generally reckoned the better.

The Chenin Blanc is chiefly used for producing sweet wines, so the dry Vouvrays tend to have a distinct fruitiness of flavour, but this is balanced by refreshing acidity. They are wines for swigging rather than sipping and have all the straightforward, easy appeal which has made Loire wines so popular.

Other dry white wines from the middle Loire which you may be able to find outside France are Touraine-Azay-le-Rideau and Touraine-Amboise.

Other Loire wines

Although the Loire is best known for its dry white wine, the area is large and productive and a great diversity of wines is to be found there. Unfortunately, it can still be a problem obtaining the lesser known wines outside France.

Rosé

Rosé is one Loire wine that is widely available. The most basic is called simply Rosé de la Loire. More specific, but familiar, names are Rosé d'Anjou and Rosé Cabernet d'Anjou. The latter is made from the Cabernet grape and is generally drier and slightly more scented than plain Rosé d'Anjou. Both are light, attractively pale in colour and ideal summer picnic wines.

Rosé wines are also made in the region from the Pinot Noir, especially in the area around Sancerre and Ménétou-Salon. Some of these, especially those from single estates, are more than just a pretty glassful, but they are correspondingly more expensive. Good examples are the Gold Medal winning Ménétou-Salon of Georges Chavet and Sancerre Clos du Chêne Marchand.

A light Rosé d'Anjou and a sweet dessert wine, Moulin Touchais

Red wine

The main centre of red wine production is the region of Touraine. A variety of grapes are grown here, producing wines of contrasting character. The Gamay, the grape of Beaujolais, yields a pleasantly light red wine for early drinking. It has rather less fruitiness and higher acidity than Beaujolais itself; some is even marketed within a few weeks of harvest as *Touraine primeur*.

Other red wines are mainly made from Cabernet Franc—known locally as Breton, probably because it was introduced to the region from Bordeaux via the Breton port of Nantes—Cabernet Sauvignon and Malbec, known in the area as Cot. These are all grapes traditionally associated with claret, but in the Loire the wine which results is softer, less tannic and faster maturing, with only a relatively brief spell in barrel.

The towns chiefly connected with red wine are Chinon, Bourgueil and St Nicolas de Bourgueil. Some growers aim for a more robust and long-lasting wine in the Bordeaux style. These wines will usually be from a single estate, called a *domaine* or *clos*, which, strictly speaking, is a vineyard enclosed by a wall to give added protection from wind and frost. These wines are also frequently bottled by the grower, in which case the words *propriétaire récoltant* will be on the label. They will be a lot more expensive than wines labelled simply 'Chinon' or 'Bourgueil', but will have more body and distinction. A good vintage may develop for up to twenty years.

Sparkling wines

Another increasingly popular Loire wine is the sparkling wine or *vin mousseux*. Made mainly from the Chenin Blanc or Sauvignon Blanc grapes, sometimes with the addition of Pinot Noir, these are true *méthode champenoise* wines which have undergone their second fermentation in bottle. The best of them have a good rich flavour and, as they are much cheaper than champagne, they must be considered quite a bargain. Saumur and Vouvray are the main centres of production. There is also a lighter, less fizzy sparkling wine from the region called Vin Crémant de Loire.

Sweet dessert wines

Sales of the popular wines, the sparkling wines of Touraine and the rosés of Anjou, enable growers in these areas to continue small-scale production of the wines they consider their greatest achievement, the fine sweet dessert wines. The Chenin Blanc gives a naturally fruity wine and, if the grapes are allowed to ripen through a long fine autumn, they will eventually become affected by a fungus called the noble rot, or *pourriture noble*. The fungus attacks the skins, shrivels the fruit and concentrates the natural sugars. It is difficult to make this process sound attractive, but it is responsible for all the world's greatest sweet wines, the Château d'Yquem of Sauternes, the Trockenbeerenauslen of the Rhine and the Tokay aszu of Hungary. The grapes for such wines have to be carefully selected when they have reached just the right stage of ripeness and a large quantity will yield relatively little juice. These factors, and the long storage period needed before the wines reach full maturity, inevitably make them expensive.

Traditionally these sweet wines are drunk at the end of a meal, though in France it is the current trend to drink them as aperitifs. Ideally, they should be drunk on their own and simply enjoyed for what they are, a glorious mouthful of flavour. It you feel like indulging yourself in one of these luscious wines, the best names to look for are Bonnezeaux, Quarts de Chaumes and Moulin Touchais from the Côteaux du Layon. The vineyard of Moulin Touchais was the only one on the Loire to escape the phylloxera plague of the last century, and until 1959 this extraordinary wine was made only from pre-phylloxera stocks. Look too for the Vouvrays described as *moelleux*, especially those from good growers such as Gaston Huet and Marc Brédif.

Champagne

Champagne has a happy reputation as the wine to drink when it is time to celebrate a memorable occasion or at a romantic moment.

There are good reasons for the high price of champagne—it is not mere snobbery. The quality of the grapes themselves, the length of time the wine must be kept before it can be marketed, the skilled labour involved throughout the making, all contribute to the final cost. However, the quantity produced is never sufficient to satisfy world-wide demand.

The name champagne can only be applied to a drink produced by the *méthode champenoise* in the Champagne area near Reims in France. Wine has been made there, north-east of Paris, for centuries, but until the 17th century the best known wines of Champagne were still reds and whites, not sparkling wines. These wines were highly thought of and rivalled those of neighbouring Burgundy.

The art of making sparkling wine was perfected in Champagne by Dom Pérignon, a Benedictine monk, cellar-master of the Abbey of Hautvilliers. It was seen that sometimes in the spring, wine bottled after the harvest began a second fermentation; warmer weather restarted the fermentation of the sugar—giving the bubbles to the champagne. The second fermentation resulted in many broken bottles and lost wine. Dom Pérignon originated the use of corks to stopper the bottles—rags had been used before—and stronger bottles were made. Dom Pérignon also devised a system of blending wines from different vineyards to produce the fine balance essential to champagne. The champagne produced then was delicious to drink but not pretty to look at. A side-effect of secondary fermentation is the breaking down of yeast particles, which form a sediment and make the liquid cloudy. To hide this, champagne was served in glasses which were frosted.

In the 19th century, Madame Clicquot, founder of the firm Veuve Clicquot in Reims, was responsible for finding a practical way to make champagne clear and bright, as well as sparkling. Holes were cut in tables and the bottles placed in the holes, necks downwards. To make sure that all the sediment moved to just behind the cork, the bottles were moved carefully – a process known as *remuage*. The sediment was removed (*dégorgement*) by opening the bottle, taking the deposit out and topping up, then re-corking, very quickly. These processes have been refined over the years and now the sediment which collects is removed by freezing the neck of the bottle. When the cork is removed the sediment pops out and the wine is topped up with a small amount of wine and sugar. All the sugar in champagne is used up in secondary fermentation, so the sugar added now will give the champagne a dry or sweeter character. Less

than 2% is added for Brut; 1.5-2.5% for Extra Dry; 2-4% for Sec; 4-6% for Demi-Sec and over 6% for Doux. Although most champagne is white, it is usually made from a blend of black and white grapes, with black predominating. The grapes used are Pinot Noir, Pinot Meunier and Chardonnay. During the vinification process the black grape skins are carefully separated from the juices when pressing begins.

Vintage and non-vintage

On wine lists champagne is classified into Non-Vintage (NV) and Vintage. Non-vintage champagnes have to be matured in the cellars for a legal minimum period of 18 months and are blends of wines from several different years. In fact, the NV champagnes exported by the leading champagne houses are usually 3 years old. When allowed to mature longer in a cool cellar or cupboard NV champagnes will improve greatly.

Vintage champagnes, selected from a particularly good year, must by law remain in the producer's cellars for at least three years, often more, and may mature well for up to ten years. The leading champagne houses are known as Grande Marques and all are proud of their individual house styles, which have been evolved over many years of production.

Serving

Most important—never try to pull the cork from the bottle. Remove the foil and wire from the cork. Then lever the cork upwards with your thumbs, turning the bottle, as you gain leverage. When the cork starts to loosen, cover it with a cloth and with the other hand gently turn the bottle away from the cork. The cork should be held back against the escaping gas, to avoid a loud pop, and gush of wine. If opened correctly the only noise should be a soft sigh!

Depending on the temperature at which the bottle has been stored, it will only need an hour or two in the refrigerator.

Styles of champagne

Bollinger: deep, golden colour with an intensity of flavour, dry with great finesse
Charles Heidsieck: traditional, full-bodied and fruity, not very dry
Georges Goulet: a racy, youthful wine, very fruity, medium dry
Krug: subtle bouquet and flavour, silky and well-balanced, dry
Louis Roederer: great elegance, pale golden with a delicate flavour. Notably dry
Laurent Perrier: light gold, brisk and youthful with a 'leafy' bouquet
Mercier: slightly flowery bouquet, dry with a good finish
Moët & Chandon: straw gold in colour, light, well-balanced and not very dry
Mumm: pale and sprightly with a nice finish, medium dry
Pol Roger: very light gold in colour, with an extremely fine bouquet, dry and elegant
Veuve Clicquot: pale, nicely balanced, dry, bright and lively to taste.

Removing the sediment from champagne in the Veuve Clicquot caves, Reims

Alsace

Alsace is the French wine region geographically closest to Germany, and as a result the wines from the area have characteristics of both countries. Although a small amount of light red and rosé wines are made here from the Pinot noir grape, almost all the wine produced is white – fragrant, full-bodied and dry.

Although Alsace is in France, it has spent long periods under German control. Between the Franco-Prussian War and the First World War, Alsace was treated as a poor relation of the great Rhine and Mosel vineyards, planted with inferior vines and used mainly for the bulk production of lower grade wine. A period of recovery during the 1920s and 1930s was halted by the Second World War when some towns were almost totally destroyed. But others were hardly touched – Riquewihr and Kaysersberg for example have an authentic medieval appearance – and enough grapes were still grown to make a memorable vintage in 1945. Since then the reputation of Alsace as a producer of quality wines has been firmly established, though even now the area has no appellation more specific than 'Alsace', and this was only granted in 1962.

The best vineyards lie in a narrow strip on the lower slopes of the Vosges mountains, looking East towards the River Rhine. Growers and merchants may sometimes use village or estate names on their wine labels, but these have little significance outside the area, if at all, because the wines are traditionally 'varietal'. This means that they are labelled with the type of grape used not by the place of origin.

The finest wines, Riesling, Gewürztraminer, Tokay (or Pinot Gris), Muscat and Sylvaner are made from one of five grape types, known as *cépages nobles*. If these are blended the result is known as *edelzwicker* (noble mixture). Although there are about 50,000 individual growers in Alsace, most belong to co-operatives or sell their grapes to the handful of famous merchants in the area, such as Hugel, Dopff, Trimbach and Schlumberger, whose names on a label should guarantee quality.

The wine most usually associated with Alsace is Gewürztraminer; *gewürtz* means spicy and Gewürztraminer is known for its remarkably powerful and spicy flavour, coupled with a strong-scented nose. It is a big wine, designed to complement the rich foods of the region such as *choucroute* (sauerkraut) and *foie gras* (goose liver pâté). But in spite of its fullness it is a dry wine, as the French winemakers prefer strength and dryness to the delicate sweetness of residual grape sugar which is so characteristic of German wines. Gewürztraminer is memorable and attractive, but it lacks subtlety.

The local growers, like their German neighbours, will usually claim pride of place for the Riesling, a vine which never bears heavy crops and also presents more of a challenge to the winemaker. In a good year it is well worth the extra effort; what it lacks in power it makes up for in elegance and delicacy of flavour. The Tokay, or Pinot

Gris, from Alsace is a full-flavoured wine more in the style of the Gewürztraminer but without its pronounced fragrance – do not confuse this with Tokay from Hungary, which is a rich sweet dessert wine.

The Muscat has a heady aroma usually associated with that grape but without its usual sweetness of taste. The Sylvaner, the least interesting of the five, is a reliable but rather bland medium-dry wine, and is now produced less and less.

Unlike most French quality wine-growing areas, Alsace has room for further expansion and in recent years new plantings have been made, particularly with the Pinot Blanc grape, which in 1984 accounted for over 17½% of the total acreage under vines – this should be an interesting wine to watch out for in the future.

Because the French prefer wines suitable for drinking with food rather than on their own, many of these wines are purposely made less sweet than their German counterparts. The merchants and co-operatives do sometimes produce rich wines in the style of German *auslese* (selected bunches) or *beerenauslese* (selected grapes). These are made from late-gathered grapes whose juice, even after fermentation, retains a high sugar content. These are described in French as *vendage tardive* and *sélection de grains nobles*. They are full golden wines with great depth of flavour and repay laying down for a number of years.

Conditions are not suitable for these sweeter wines to be made every year; 1977, for example, was a year of late flowering and a poor, rather chilly summer in which the grapes had no chance to achieve the necessary over-ripeness. The previous year on the other hand, with its prolonged dry heat, produced record levels of natural sugar in many of the grapes and some outstanding late-harvest wines were made which will have a life of at least 20 years.

In general, like other dry whites, Alsace wines should be drunk fairly young. Compared with other French wines of quality, they still represent good value and also offer a variety of distinct flavours to try from dry but fruity to richly sweet.

The wines of Alsace are immediately recognizable in their slim green bottles.

Northern Rhône

The wines of the Rhône Valley include some of the most distinguished in France but, surprisingly, many of them are little known outside France. Most are red, although whites and rosés are made, mainly in the southern region.

Most Rhône wines are full-bodied and improve considerably with age. They are produced by over 100 parishes or domaines under the general label of Appellation Contrôlée Côtes du Rhône. Côtes du Rhône-Villages is only applied to 14 specific communes in the southern part of the valley. Fifteen areas have their own appellations. Here we discuss the main appellations in the northern Rhône Valley, which stretches from Vienne to Valence. On the next page the southern Rhône Valley will be discussed.

Rhône wines fall into two quite separate regions of north and south, but the same robust characteristics apply to both.

In the northern Rhône Valley the sharp, granite-based hills press against the river and the vines are grown on both banks on almost vertical, steep hillsides. The plots are very restricted and the long low walls of each plot retain the soil of the sharply-angled slopes. The climate is ideal for vines: the summers are long and hot and, as the weather is consistent, the vines have a head start. The relentless Mistral wind blows down the valley from the north but it serves a purpose, often drying the grapes after rain, lessening the chance of any mould developing. The red Syrah grape is predominant in the northern Rhône Valley.

The top appellations

On the Côte Rôtie the Syrah grape is mixed with a little wine from white grapes. This rare red wine contains 80% Syrah, which gives it a deep and powerful flavour, and 20% of perfumed Viognier grapes, which softens the flavour. The result is a big gutsy wine rarely at its best before ten years.

The Côte Rôtie, or 'Roasted Hill' has two well-known slopes, the Côte Brune and the Côte Blonde. A blended wine labelled Brune et Blonde can also be found occasionally, but you are more likely to find straightforward Côte Rôtie. The biggest growers are Vidal-Fleury and Chapoutier, with Côte Rôtie Les Jumelles of Paul Jaboulet Aîné, a wine of great distinction. Just south of Côte Rôtie are the vines of Condrieu, a dry white wine made from the Viognier grape. Considered one of the best white wines of the Rhône Valley, it may reach its peak after five or six years of bottle age. Not much is made because of the nature of the terrain on which it is grown.

Within the Condrieu vineyards is a small vineyard, Château Grillet, which has its own appellation contrôlée. It is the smallest individual appellation in France. There are not more than 2 hectares of vineyards and the very few bottles produced have to be rationed out among a few fortunate wine merchants. Château Grillet is a white wine, full and subtle with great finesse.

Hermitage

Hermitage is another of the main appellations further down the east bank of the river. Here on the Hermitage hillside both red and white wines are grown on granite slopes which catch the sun all day. The reds are burly and deep, and last a long time. A fine old Hermitage is for buying and keeping, as they are rarely drinkable in less than ten years. Some will go on improving for 30 years, with the bouquet becoming fuller and the wine softening.

Hermitage la Chapelle, grown on the top of the slopes, is a rich intense red wine that goes well with game or pheasant, and should be kept for special occasions. White Hermitage, excellent with salmon, is made from two grapes, Marsanne and Roussanne. Chante Alouette is one of the best-known wines. It is full and golden and often more powerful than a white Burgundy.

Around the Hermitage hill are the vineyards of Crozes-Hermitage. These wines are not so concentrated as Hermitage and do not last as long but, as they are considerably cheaper, they are often the best buys of the Rhône Valley. Those from Gervans, a small village with the best and steepest slopes, are especially good buys.

On the other side of the river are the St Joseph vineyards. On the bank, opposite the Hermitage vines the St Joseph vines encircle the castle terraces of Tournon. Here there is another range of outstanding red and white wines. The reds have a pleasant earthy flavour and are almost mauve; the whites are fresh and fruity.

Further south are the vineyards of Cornas, where a fine selection of red wines from the Syrah grape are made. These wines take 10–15 years to mature.

St Peray is the most southerly of the northern Rhône vineyards and it produces a sparkling white wine made by the méthode champenoise, excellent as an aperitif.

Sparkling wines are also made at Die, where the production of Clairette de Die has increased rapidly to meet demand. Clairette Brut is made solely from the Clairette grape and is an ideal thirst quencher on a hot day. Clairette de Die Tradition is a blend of Clairette and Muscat. These wines are less dry and sometimes are semi-sweet. It is difficult to be sure of the degrees of sweetness, since the ideas of many individual growers vary, but some Tradition wines are sweet enough to drink with desserts.

Map of the Rhône Valley showing: Côte Rôtie, Château Grillet, Condrieu, St Joseph, Crozes-Hermitage, Hermitage, Cornas, St Péray, Côtes du Rhône, Coteaux du Tricastin, Cairanne, Rasteau, Vacqueyras, Gigondas, Côtes de Ventoux, Beaumes de Venise, Lirac, Tavel, Châteauneuf-du-Pape, Avignon, Côtes du Luberon. Inset map of FRANCE.

Southern Rhône

Wine from the hot, sunny southern part of the Rhône Valley could be described as bottled sunshine. It is ideal for drinking in a cold climate to warm the deepest winter.

The most famous of these southern Rhône Valley wines is Châteauneuf-du-Pape. This is a dark and glorious red wine. It is strong and fruity and matures faster than the wines of Côte Rôtie to the north. Châteauneuf-du-Pape is usually full-bodied with a powerful bouquet and has a higher alcoholic content than any other unfortified wine in France.

The vineyards where this wine is grown are covered with pebbles and stones which, like the slate in the German Rhine vineyards, reflect the sun's heat long after sunset, while the rich soil beneath them stays cool and moist. Unusually, for a great wine, Châteauneuf is made from many different grapes. As many as 13 varieties are permitted, but individual growers know the blends most suitable to their vineyards. The key varieties used for Châteauneuf are Grenache, which gives alcohol and roundness, and Syrah for body and deep near-purple colour.

Châteauneuf is produced under some of the strictest wine quality controls in the world. The best, such as La Solitude, Château de Fines Roches, Domaine du Mont Redon and Château Rayas are usually domaine-bottled.

To the east of Châteauneuf-du-Pape is Gigondas, the southern Rhône's other full-bodied, single appellation wine. The vineyards march up the jagged Dentelles de Montmirail hills and the wine produced is rich and mellow. A good bottle of Gigondas has great depth of flavour and a strongly recognizable bouquet that is nicely earthy. It reminds some drinkers of the scent of blackberries and others of black truffles. It is a very assertive wine, but not always well balanced. It is at its best drunk between eight and nine years old, when the flavour is at its peak.

Near to Gigondas is the area which produces Beaumes de Venise, a delicious, heavily sweet Muscat wine. It is halfway between a dessert wine and a liqueur. There is no escaping the potency of the Muscat, which makes a wine of ample flavour with a long, rich aftertaste. It can be a great after-dinner treat with raspberries or a ripe peach.

Across the Rhône from Châteauneuf is Tavel, where the best-known rosé of France is produced. Tavel is a clear, reddish-pink wine, drier than most rosés and with more backbone. It is made largely from the Grenache grape, which changes character depending on whether it is grown on sandy, chalky or stony soil. Many growers blend wines grown on three types of soil to get a balanced wine.

As the vineyards here are small, most of the grapes go to a modern co-operative, so there is little to be gained by looking for vineyard names. Tavel is Tavel, a sound, all-round wine to be drunk with most white meat and poultry, or served, well-chilled, as an original summer aperitif.

Lirac, next door to Tavel, has a pleasant rosé, which is delicious drunk young. It is just as versatile but much cheaper than its famous neighbour, Tavel. Lirac also produces some noteworthy red wines, with plenty of fruit in them. They are at their most beguiling after six or seven years in the bottle.

Côte du Rhône Villages

This appellation covers 17 communes or villages, not including Gigondas, which now has a full appellation of its own. Of the 17, there are several southern Rhône village wines that are well above average and worth looking out for. Vacqueyras is one of the best with a fine red wine that achieves both depth and balance.

Many of the Vacqueyras vineyards share a border with Gigondas. It is no surprise that in the area there are more private bottlers, making their own individual wines, than in any other of the Rhône villages. Two outstanding domaines are La Fourmone and Pascal Frères.

Cairanne is another southern Rhône name to remember. This hilltop village has a modern co-operative, one of the best in the Rhône Valley, that bottles all the local wine. Half the Cairanne vineyards are planted on clay slopes and the rest on stony slopes. The wines are blended together to make a warm, sturdy red that lasts well in the bottle, up to six or seven years.

Rasteau is famous locally for its fortified white Vin de Liqueur, mostly made from Grenache grapes. Drunk young, this is rather crude and a bit too heavy for most palates. A sweet wine is also made which is usually left in cask for a year or two and improves noticeably with age.

Another village wine to remember is Chusclan rosé. The pinky-orange Chusclan rosé, made from Grenache and Cinsault, should be drunk young to appreciate its fruitiness and pleasant dry aftertaste. The best of them can equal Tavel and Lirac.

A village called Laudun makes red, white and rosé wines. The white is quite outstanding. Fresh and full, it is a natural partner for a fish dish. At Rochegude, the red produced has a softness not usually associated with Rhônes. The red wine from Vinsobres has a great length of taste and lasts in the bottle for eight years but is high in alcohol.

The bigger, more generous Rhône wines are always at their best with hefty, well-flavoured or spicy dishes, such as game, pâté and rich stews.

Making wine in the Rhône

Tricastin, Ventoux and Lubéron

The wines from Tricastin, Ventoux and Lubéron, newer Rhône vineyards, are rarely for serious wine connoisseurs, but are cheap and cheerful wines of the warm south, ideal for holiday and home drinking.

Tricastin

One of the fastest-growing wine areas is Côteaux du Tricastin. In the 1960s little more than pines, bracken and gorse grew here. The new vineyards are south of Montélimar, with the village of Les Granges-Gontardes as the centre. The area was derelict until the early 1960s when the French settlers, expelled from North Africa, set up their base in the village.

Many of the returning French had been wine-growers in Algeria. They found the parched Tricastin terrain very similar to Algeria. They uprooted the existing vegetation and planted huge vineyards which, like those of Châteauneuf-du-Pape, are covered with smooth round stones, that reflect the sun's heat.

Tricastin is red wine country and the grapes which are grown here, Grenache, Cinsault and Syrah, are well able to withstand the heat. Harvests last from the end of September to the end of October and the wines are vinified quickly. Many go to huge co-operatives such as Cellier des Dauphins or Cellier des Templiers. Most Tricastin reds are dark in colour, full-bodied, smooth and eminently drinkable. The better wines, such as Domaine de Grangeneuve, are kept in modern, water-cooled vats that control the temperature of the fermenting wines.

Domaine de Grangeneuve is a wine which has improved from being graded Vin de Table, to VDQS (Vins Délimités de Qualité Supérieure) to Appellation Contrôlée in the course of 15 years. It is a fruity and soft wine.

Equally rapid progress has been made by wines of Pierre Labeye of the Domaine de La Tour D'Elyssas. The high quality of his wine made from recently planted grapes is only just becoming apparent. Try the Cru de Meynas and the Syrah.

Other Tricastins worth noting are Domaine de St. Luc which is very fruity and bold, and Domaine de Bois Noir, which has a velvety smoothness. Domaine de Serre Rouge is slightly perfumed and very drinkable. A little Tricastin rosé is made though the rosés do not match up to the reds. They are best drunk young and well chilled.

Côtes du Ventoux

Côtes du Ventoux is another relatively new wine area which gained its Appellation Contrôlée status as recently as 1974. Its wines are mainly red and rosé, with a little white.

Ventoux wines are very different in character to any other Rhône wines. They are light and summery, low in alcohol and at their most attractive when drunk locally. The vineyards are dotted around the south flank of Mont Ventoux and the wines produced are pale in colour.

Most Ventoux wines are processed by co-operatives but there are several private growers making individual wines of higher quality. Those from the Domaine des Anges and Domaine St. Saveur are fragrant and stylish, with a great deal of charm. The Domaine de Champ-Long makes a rather ordinary rosé and an outstanding Cuvée Speciale red that would well repay keeping.

Lubéron

Whether the wine from Lubéron, a very beautiful area of rolling hills and gorges, inland from Marseilles, counts as Rhône or Haute Provence is a matter of debate. For most wine lovers it is simply a happy hunting-ground with a number of new wines that are proving to be remarkably good value for money.

Lubéron has Vin de table and a VDQS rating, which accounts for its low prices. The 17 co-operatives in the area have a complete wine-making monopoly. They send their wines to the huge new Union des Vignerons de Lubéron for final bottling and packaging. Luckily for the discriminating drinker, the wines are not standardized. The Union des Vignerons treats them all individually so that they have a varying appeal.

One of these, the Vin de Pays de Vaucluse, both red and white, is pleasantly dry and unassuming, with an aromatic bouquet. The ruby red Côtes du Lubéron has a bit more weight to it and lasts longer in the mouth.

The best co-operative wine is Cellier de Marrenon, which is a VDQS wine. The red has an ample bouquet and just the right amount of fullness and depth. The white is flowery and quite subtle, a perfect accompaniment to a bouillabaisse.

The Lubéron wine most likely to attract serious wine drinkers comes from Domaine de L'Isolette, near the town of Bonnieux. These wines are red, white and rosé, and are not cheap, but the red especially, with its depth, subtlety and concentrated flavour is well worth its price.

Wines from the new Rhône vineyards of Ventoux, Lubéron and Tricastin

Languedoc and Roussillon

The vineyards of the Languedoc-Roussillon are to wines what the Middle East is to oil! From this huge wine-growing area, which consists of 35% of the area under vines in France, comes almost a billion gallons of wine a year – enough to provide every man, woman and child in Britain, France and America with a dozen bottles each annually.

Grape pickers in Carcassonne

The vineyards of the Languedoc-Roussillon, or Midi area of France, stretch from the French Pyrenees inland from Banyuls on the Spanish border, in a broad band to the mouth of the Rhône. If the wines from this area are not well known, it is because more than 95% of them are not of Appelation Contrôlée status. They belong to the ordinary table wine category.

However, the number of wine shippers and merchants listing a selection of wines from the Midi demonstrates the growing interest in these wines.

In the Midi there are four *départements,* from which the ordinary *vins de pays* come: the Gard, Hérault, Aude and Pyrénées Orientales. You may find these wines labelled according to the commune in which they are produced. The exact zone of production is not of great importance to the buyer looking for a cheap and cheering wine.

For wines one grade up on the quality scale look out for the VDQS (Vins Délimités de Qualité Supérieure) wines which come from four areas in the Midi. Try the reds, rosés and dry white wines from Corbières, Costières du Gard, Côteaux du Languedoc and Minervois districts.

Languedoc area

Corbières: in the middle of the Corbières district is Château Les Palais. The vineyards here are hemmed in by the Pyrénées Orientales to the south and the valley of the Aude to the north. This VDQS wine, which is fermented by a process called *macération carbonique,* is well up to dinner party standard and goes well with rich dishes like cassoulet or roast duck.

The grapes, including stalks, go straight into the vat without being crushed. Fermentation starts naturally within the grape and then is continued in a process in which carbon dioxide is retained under slight pressure. This helps to produce a wine which needs a shorter maturation period. Château Les Palais is a big and fruity wine with a vivid deep colour and powerful bouquet. It is at its best a year after the vintage, but after three years begins to fade.

Costières du Gard: the wines from this area, around the Roman Pont du Gard, are strong red wines of VDQS level, although some whites and rosés are produced.

Coteaux du Languedoc: Vins Delimites de Qualité Superieure come from a large area between Nimes and Beziers. There are no fewer than 13 communes entitled to add their own names to the overall title. One of them, Faugeres, makes a fine, assertive red wine, while St Chinians's red is well made with a scented bouquet.

St Saturnin is another commune name to remember. It has a good co-operative wine and a Vin d'Une Nuit, a light, fruity red wine, which is achieved by the overnight maceration of the grapes. St Saturnin also has a delicious rosé, which is pleasant chilled and served as an aperitif.

Minervois: there are no Appellation Contrôlée wines in this area. All the wines from the Minervois area are classified as VDQS. The reds which form the bulk of the production are vigorous and sometimes slightly peppery. They are strong in alcohol and much of it is sold in the typical occitan bottle, which is half way between a Burgundy and a Champagne bottle in shape.

Vins des Sables: from the Camargue there are the Vins des Sables, which are neither VDQS nor Appellation Contrôlée but are cheap and drinkable.

Roussillon

Roussillon is the eastern part of the Midi wine area. In the northern part of Roussillon is Latour de France, part of the Côtes d'Agly, whose wines have AC status. Latour de France is full-bodied and strong and is a good choice for rich meat dishes.

Other Roussillon appellations are Côtes du Roussillon, Côtes du Roussillon Villages and Collioure. The best commune names to look for are Maury, Estagel, Rasiguères and Caramany. The reds are bold and straightforward while the whites are mostly dry and fresh. Both should be drunk young. Look out for Vin Vert, a notable white, made from early-picked grapes. It is a lively wine with a pleasant degree of acidity

Other AC wines and muscats

Fitou is an AC area of note producing a red wine made mainly from Carignan and Grenache grapes, with up to 25% of other varieties added. Fitou spends at least nine months in wood before being released. Château de Nouvelles at Tuchan is a good Fitou red. The best white of the region is probably the sparkling AC Blanquette de Limoux. Made by the Champagne method from the Mauzac grape, it is every bit as good as the best sparkling Loire wines.

Do not overlook AC Clairette de Bellegarde from just south of Nîmes. It is a dry white wine made entirely from the Clairette grape and will make a good accompaniment to starters or fish dishes. Another sweet white wine is AC Clairette du Languedoc from west of the Costières du Gard area.

To crown the versatility of Languedoc-Roussillon wines, there are the fortified, *Vins-Doux-Naturels,* which are all AC wines. These wines are made either from the Grenache or Muscatel grapes. From Banyuls, Rivesaltes, and Maury, these wines, lush and honeyed on the palate, are the perfect choice with dessert or fresh fruit to round off a good meal.

Provence

Provence is one of the happiest hunting grounds for lovers of rosé – an uncomplicated and easy wine, which can be drunk at any time and with any food. A small amount of red and white wine is also produced in Provence, so a trip through the area will produce some good drinking.

Côtes de Provence is a wine area which was promoted to *Appelation Contrôlée* status in 1977. It covers an area stretching for 80 kilometres like a half-moon across the Maures plateau, from Toulon to St. Raphael. Within this area is a coastal zone between the Massif des Maures and the sea, with a wide inland strip between Toulon and Fréjus. Here there are particularly good reds to be found at Pierrefeu, Puget-Ville and Cuers. Further inland, there are sound white wines round Correns and reds near Cotignac.

St. Tropez is thought of as the wine capital of the area and is the natural centre for many of the best rosés. The wines are cultivated along the seaward slopes of the hills, where they are sheltered from the fierce mistral winds which blow from the north. These rosés are eminently drinkable and of direct, simple appeal. Just behind St. Tropez is Château de Minuty, with its expensive Cuvée de l'Oratoire, sought after by connoisseurs.

Otherwise the range of tastes and individual bouquets is not very wide. Most growers concentrate on the primary appeal of cheerful, clean, refreshing wines, made to a standard formula in a highly reliable climate, where vintages barely differ from one year to the next.

With so many growers and so many names jostling for attention on the shelves, one can only pick out a few for special recommendation. Châteaux de Selle and de Roseline, Clos du Relais and Domaine de Saint-Martin are well-known for all-round consistency. So, too are Domaine de l'Aumerade, Clos Mirelle, Côte au-du-Ferrage, Domaine de Noyer and Domaine de Mauvanne. The Domaine de la Croix is highly regarded as are Domaine des Féraud, Domaine de la Clapière, Castel-Roubine and Château Grand 'Boise.

Just outside the Côtes de Provence area is Côteaux d'Aix-en-Provence, a VDQS wine area. One outstanding property here is Château Vignelaure, 30 kilometres northeast of Aix, at Rians. From here comes a highly palatable red wine made from a blend of Cabernet Sauvignon, Grenache and Syrah grapes. The soils here are chalky and the wines, made without any chemical treatments, are refined and elegant.

Some other above-average wines in this area include Domaine de la Crémade, the Mas de la Dame, Château La Coste and Château de Calisanne.

AC Palette

To the south of Aix is the tiny appellation of Palette, which enjoys a micro-climate all its own. The only name of note, but a good one, is Château Simone, famous for red wines that are aged in wood until they acquire all sorts of subtle nuances. The rosés and whites are also of fine quality.

Clinging to the coast near Marseilles is the tiny appellation of Cassis. Its white wine is a perfect partner for *bouillabaisse*, the delicious fish stew of Marseilles. Names to note in this area are Château de Fontblanche, Clos Ste-Magdeleine and Domaine du Paternel.

Further along the coast from Cassis is Bandol, the best-known specific AC wine area in the region. There are 200 growers making as much red wine as rosé and the red is usually the better choice.

Domaine Tempier's reputation for making a rich red wine of depth that ages well, has never been surpassed. Domaine du Val d'Arenc and Château des Vannières and the Mas de la Rouvière are not far behind. Some of these reds can take three to six years in the bottle before they are ready.

In general, when buying Provence rosés, avoid those exported in fancy bottles bearing florid labels. They have often been sweetened up for easy marketing and in the process may lose much of their original charm and vigour.

These wines are unbeatable for drinking at picnics, barbecues and other outdoor meals, where they will almost certainly bring to mind the Mediterranean.

Typical village vineyard in Provence

South-West France

Apart from the renowned wines of Bordeaux, the south-west of France also has an extraordinarily wide range of relatively unknown wines for delicious drinking, at reasonable prices.

Inland, to the east of Bordeaux, and in the districts to the south are produced a number of modest drinkable wines.

Bergerac and Cahors

Bergerac produces pleasant, fruity red and white wines, reasonably priced and best drunk when they are young. The dry white Bergerac Sec is made from a trio of grapes: Sauvignon, Sémillon and Muscadelle. These same grapes are used in different proportions to produce the sweet white wines of Monbazillac. A Monbazillac is a first-class choice to serve with a dinner party dessert or with fresh fruit and cheese at the end of a meal. Similar to Sauternes, which is at least double the price, Monbazillac has its own fragrance, lusciousness and peachy charm.

Wines from south-west France

Cahors, further west, used to produce 'the black wine of Cahors' before the days of quality control. This was used to fortify poorer Bordeaux wines. Made largely with the Malbec grape, it is now recognized as a delightful red wine in its own right, and is not as heavy a wine as it once was. Cahors wine goes well with casseroles and red meat, and is a warming winter red. It has the ability to age for many years. Quality varies depending on the grower, but Château de Cayrou, Domaine de Pailhas, Domaine du Cèdre and Clos Triguedina have all proved their worth in the past. A big co-operative, Les Caves d'Olt at Parnac, makes a sound Vin de Cahors, worth trying.

Marmande and Buzet

From the Côtes du Marmande, up the river to the south of Bordeaux, come soft and beguiling red wines, made with a blend of Merlot, Cabernet and Malbec grapes. There is also a delicious rosé. Most Marmande wines come from co-operatives, and carry a VDQS rating.

Côtes de Buzet wines are AC. The reds, made from the usual Bordeaux blend of Cabernet Sauvignon, Cabernet Franc and Merlot, are aged in oak and will improve for a year or two, if left in the bottle. Cuvée Napoleon is the best co-operative wine from the area, while Château de Padère at Ambrus is always a reliable buy.

Gaillac and Madiran

AC Gaillac district lies in the Tarn valley to the south and is a good source of bargain-priced sparkling white wines. Some are made with the local grape, Len de l'El, and some with the Mauzac grape, which is also used for the traditional Gaillac sweet white wines. Red Gaillacs are made from Gamay, the Beaujolais grape, generally blended with Syrah or Merlot to make agreeable wines, suitable for casual drinking.

For serious red wine drinkers, Madiran is the name to remember. It is a rich, full-bodied wine that rates as one of the best reds from the Pyrenees. The local Tannat grape is mixed with Cabernet to make a wine of real staying power. Château de Peyros always seems to have the blend of red grapes absolutely right. Vignobles Laplace, Domaines Barréjat and Lalenne are well regarded Madiran reds.

West of Gaillac, to the north of Toulouse, is a local red wine, Côtes du Frontonnais, which is now being exported and is worth looking out for. It should get better and better, as the new vines mature. Château Bellevue-La Forêt is particularly good.

Jurançon and Béarn

Jurançon, from the foothills of the Pyrenees, is sweet and spicy, and drinking it is an acquired taste. These wines are made from a wide selection of unusual grapes with Courbu, Petit Manseng and Gros Manseng, the most important. Because of the climate, which is affected by the Pyrenees and the sea, these impressive sweet wines are not harvested until mid-October. At this time the effects of the sunshine and night frosts combine to concentrate the sugar in the grape juice, raising the resulting alcohol level to 16%.

The taste of Jurançon wine is sometimes compared to carnations, honey or grilled hazelnuts – all these comparisons, like the wine, are highly individual. Little of this wine is made and it is strictly for the connoisseur. Plenty of Jurançon dry white is made but apart from Clos de la Vierge, it is rather undistinguished.

To the north of the Basque country is Béarn, whose wines are good enough to gain an Appellation Contrôlée. Most of it is red and rosé and much of it comes from the co-operative at Bellocq. A few kilometres nearer the sea than Béarn is the tiny appellation of Irouléguy, which has a light rosé version of typical Pyrenian foothill wines that goes with almost any food.

Germany

The most northerly of the world's great vineyards lie in Germany – in the complex of valleys made up by the Rhine (or Rhein) river and its tributary the Moselle (or Mosel). The wines produced vary from light fruity whites to rich, golden dessert wines.

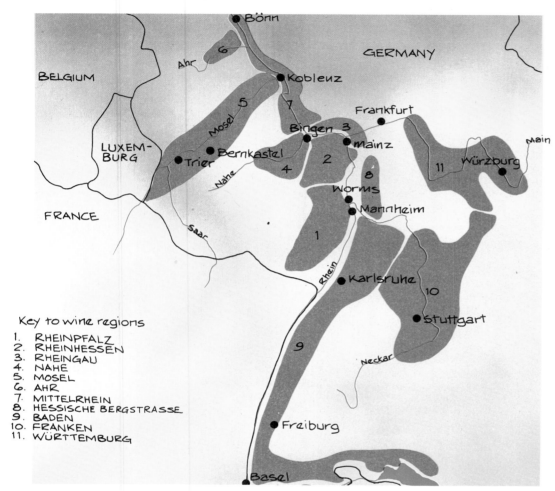

Key to wine regions
1. RHEINPFALZ
2. RHEINHESSEN
3. RHEINGAU
4. NAHE
5. MOSEL
6. AHR
7. MITTELRHEIN
8. HESSISCHE BERGSTRASSE
9. BADEN
10. FRANKEN
11. WÜRTTEMBURG

Known once as 'Rhenish', and more recently as 'Hock', the white wines of Germany have been appreciated in Britain for centuries. We are still the greatest drinkers of exported German quality wines, taking over one third of the total, mostly in the form of Liebfraumilch.

Liebfraumilch is one German wine that everybody knows. But what exactly is it? The name is imprecise by the rigorous standards of German wine law, which will usually see to it that you have an almost embarassing amount of information about what you are drinking. It was originally called after the Liebfrauenkirch, or Church of our Lady, in the Rheinhessen town of Worms. It means literally 'Our Lady's Milk', though it is possible that the 'milch' is a corruption of 'minch', the German word for monk, as the vineyard used to be in the care of the local monastery. Be that as it may, the picturesque title was soon being applied to other Rhine wines, and there is still a certain vagueness about it today, though it must originate from one of the four main Rhine regions, Rheinhessen, Rheinpfalz, Nahe and Rheingau – and be

made chiefly from one or more of the three main grape types – Riesling, Sylvaner and Müller-Thurgau. It must also have been tested to the standard of German quality wine, and will therefore have the letters *Qba* on the label. This is roughly the equivalent of the French AC and Italian DOC designations. All quality wine must also have a control number to prove that it has passed the rigorous tests required; this number is printed on the label.

As a general description, Liebfraumilch is a light, fruity wine, with a pleasantly fragrant bouquet, but the regulations leave some scope for the individual producer to create his own style. Most is sold under a brand name associated with a particular company; two of the better known ones are Blue Nun from Sichel and Hans Cristof from Deinhard.

All wines from the Rhine are traditionally marketed in brown bottles; German wine in a green bottle will come from Moselle. Some blended wines from Moselle appear under brand names; the best known is Moselblumchen. This does not have to satisfy the same quality testing as Lieb-

fraumilch and is of the lower Deutsche Tafelwein status, but it can still be a very pleasant drink; Moselles are generally slightly drier and fresher-tasting than the Rhine wines and often have a penetrating flowery bouquet.

The practice of blending is sometimes regarded by the layman as a slightly suspect activity, but in fact it is an essential part of the winemaker's skill. German wine has a reputation for sweetness, but the main problem in many vintages is a lack of natural sugar, as the vineyards are among the most northerly in Europe and do not always have enough warm sunshine to ripen the grapes. The German Wine Institute at Geisenheim has developed sophisticated techniques for making the most of what is available. For any wine up to and including *Qba* status, it is permitted to add small quantities of grape sugar – *süssreserve* – after fermentation is complete. But for the very best wine – labelled *Qmp* – this is strictly forbidden, as the grading of wine is closely linked to the amount of natural sugar in the unfermented grape juice. It is a temptation – not always resisted – to break this law, as the top wines command much higher prices; hence the recent scandal concerning diethylene glycol, which can give a very ordinary wine a deceptive sweetness and viscosity. Fortunately only a handful of unscrupulous producers have been involved, but the publicity has been disproportionately damaging.

In spite of the best efforts of the legislators to bring order and simplicity to the German wine scene, there are still some terms in use which may be misleading. For instance, a wine which is labelled simply 'Tafelwein', as opposed to 'Deutsche Tafelwein', will almost certainly come from more than one country within the EEC; this label information is likely to be in German and is often inconspicuous. Then there is the word 'Bereich'. This means 'district', so that a wine named Bereich Bernkastel will come from the small neighbourhood of Bernkastel in the Moselle. But Bereich Johannisberg, for example, can come from anywhere in the 7000 acres of Rheingau. Again, vineyard names can refer either to 'einzellagen', individual vineyards, or to 'grosslagen', vineyard areas, and there is no way of telling which is which, except by carrying a reference book around with you or learning from experience. Finally, there is the description 'erzeugerabfullung' which means 'estate-bottled' and was once almost a guarantee of a fine wine in the same way that 'mis en bouteilles au Château' is indicative of good claret; under the new wine law, this can be used not just by individual growers, but by wine co-operatives, for any wine, however cheap.

All of which may make you feel that you would sooner forget the whole business of getting to know the better German wines and just stick to Liebfraumilch. But this would be a pity. As we shall see, German wine labels do give a great deal of genuinely helpful information and can point you in the direction of some very enjoyable drinking.

German wine labels

To fully appreciate German wines you will need to understand the German labelling system. German wine is actually easier to choose than its French counterparts, since the label of a German bottle tells you, in simple terms, how good the wine is.

The German labelling system is strictly controlled according to a major reforming law passed in 1971. This defines exactly what the label must and must not say about the wine. Any indication of the quality of the wine must fall into strict categories and a wine may only be proclaimed as of a certain standard and type after rigorous official testing. There are two basic categories: *Tafelwein* and *Qualitätswein* – table wine and quality wine.

Table wine

To even use the word Tafelwein, the wine must come from one or more E.E.C. countries. Deutsche Tafelwein (German table wine) must be a blend of wines of German origin only – there are five German Tafelwein areas. A Deutsche Tafelwein is likely to be inexpensive and suitable for everyday drinking. Much Tafelwein for export is sold under general brand names.

Quality wine

Qualitätswein is another matter, although it will not necessarily be more expensive. Here, the producer of the wine in one of 11 specified traditional wine growing areas has applied for the wine to be given official approval. This involves the scientific testing of the wine to see if the levels of sugar, alcohol and acidity are correct and that there is no foreign matter in the wine indicating improper cellar techniques.

A great part of the German wine that is sold abroad comes into this category, bearing the designation *Qualitätswein bestimmter Anbaugebeite* (usually QbA on the label) – quality wine from a registered region. The region will be named prominently on the label, together with the registered place of origin, vintage and perhaps the grape type and shipper or bottler. QbA wines are sometimes exported under brand names, like Tafelwein. Look out for QbA on the label – it is an adequate guarantee.

All Qualitätswein is also allocated an official coding – the A.P. number, which gives, in 11 digits, a full record of what it is and when and where it was tested.

Special distinction wines

If a producer feels his wine is of even higher quality, he may submit it for a further level of testing before a panel of experts representing the growers, the state and the wine trade. To be awarded the designation *Qualitätswein mit Prädikat* (QmP – quality with special distinction) the wine must be accepted as having reached a high state of excellence, without the addition of sugar in its fermentation. It will still not be necessarily expensive.

Tafelwein, Kabinett and Auslese labels

There are five categories of QmP:
Kabinett: the basic QmP category.
Spätlese: the grapes were late picked and fully ripe, indicating a rich wine.
Auslese: grape bunches were selected as ripe and in perfect condition. The sweetness and quality of the wine will be high.
Beerenauslese: the grapes were picked only after the 'noble rot' fungus had begun to attack the grapes on the vine. The wine will be even more concentrated in flavour.
Trockenbeerenauslese: wine of superlative quality, made from grapes that had begun to dry to sultana form on the vine.

A final category is Eiswein, a rare and expensive wine made from grapes pressed during a severe frost so that the water in them, still frozen solid, can be separated.

Place of origin

German wine labels are very precise about the place of origin. About 3,000 place names are included in the official list, the *Weinbergsrolle*. The most significant names are the five Tafelwein areas and the 11 Qualitätswein areas. The Tafelwein areas are Rhine, Mosel, Main, Neckar and Oberrhein. Of the 11 Qualitätsweins, seven are in the region covered by Rhine in the Tafelwein classification: Ahr, Hessische Bergstrasse, Mittelrhein, Nahe, Rheingau, Rheinhessen and Rheinpfalz. The others are Mosel-Saar-Ruwer, Franken, Württemberg and Baden, each again occupying the central portion of a larger Tafelwein region. The most important areas are Mosel-Saar-Ruwer, Nahe, Rheingau, Rheinhessen and Rheinpfalz, and most good wines will have one of these names on the label.

The remainder of the 3,000 registered names are villages and parcels of land, from whole areas down to just single vineyards. Generally the first part of the wine's name is most useful – indicating the village from which the wine comes. Bernkastler Doctor, for example, means that the wine comes from the Bernkastel area and from a smaller parcel of land signified by 'Doctor'.

Other information

Vintage: the year in which a quality wine was produced will always appear on the bottle. Refer to vintage charts if you want to know whether a year was good or bad. The categorization system helps here.

Grape types: German wines use many different types of grape and the type will often be mentioned on the label. There are three to look out for among white wines: Riesling is the best; Müller-Thurgau is a newer type, growing in production and reputation; and Sylvaner is grown more in southern regions.

Shipper and bottler: because the German government has taken such a positive role in protecting the reputations of its wines, you will need to rely less on the good names of the traders involved than formerly. But the established shippers do have some of the best growers on their books.

Rheinpfalz – the Palatinate

It is the most productive area of all Germany, home of the most northerly of the world's great vineyards. From its vines come many quality wines – and some of the country's greatest ones.

Riesling grapes in a Rheinpfalz vineyard

The wines of Germany are predominately white. They are sweet in character, but balance their high sugar content with a clear fruitiness that makes the term 'sweet' wholly inadequate. Simple, fresh wines share the market with the traditional giants of German viniculture, much of which comes from the rocky-topsoiled land of the Rhine.

The most productive area of all, making almost 25% of German wine, is the Rheinpfalz – the Palatinate. Wine has certainly been produced here since Roman times. The Rheinpfalz is the warmest and driest area in Germany, hence the huge scale of its wine yield. The other great wine districts of the Rhine valley perch on the slopes of the valley itself, but the Rheinpfalz to the south occupies a strip of land some 15 kilometres to the west of the river, running for about 80 kilometres from north to south. From the French border to the south west, towards the town of Worms in the north, winds the famous *Weinstrasse* – the wine road. Along its twisting course through the Haardt hills it is thickly lined with vineyards.

In the central portion, known as the Mittelhaardt, lie some of Germany's most famous vineyards. And in the south is the Oberhaardt, which does not have the pedigree of the Mittelhaardt but is growing in reputation. To the north of the Mittelhaardt, is an area known as Unterhaardt. Its wines are not highly regarded and not often sold outside Germany.

The Oberhaardt

The southern area, known as the Oberhaardt, is responsible for the greater quantity although it is not renowned for great wines like its neighbouring region, the Mittelhaardt, to the north. In the past, almost all the wine produced here was drunk locally, as carafe wine or as the heady, milky *Federweisser* (feather-white). This is drunk when so young that it is still half grape juice. The better wines that were not drunk by local farmers were often used in blended wine – Liebfraumilch, for example – and this was the only way it was likely to be drunk outside Germany. Now, however, the region is changing and many wines are bottled with the name of their particular places of origin and reputations are being established. Many quality wines are produced, and *Spätlese* and even *Auslese* can be found proudly inscribed on the label.

One reason for this is the growing popularity of the Müller-Thurgau grape variety, gradually replacing the older Sylvaner in the area. While Sylvaner vines ripen early and produce high yields, their wine has none of the character of the Rieslings from which all the great German wines are derived. Müller-Thurgau, however, is a cross between the two types, and combines the efficient qualities of Sylvaner with some of the richness of Riesling. Wines from this vine are often identified on the label. The vine is grown in the southern part of the Rheinpfalz and these wines are an ideal way to become acquainted with German wine style. Pale, fruity and light, they make a better accompaniment to food than the more powerful wines of the Mittelhaardt.

Names to look out for are Rhodten Ordensgut and Berzaberner Kloster Liebfrauenberg – these are the very best.

The Mittelhaardt

To the north of the town of Neustadt, on the *Deutsche Weinstrasse* proper, are a group of villages producing some of the greatest wines of all. Three large owners have properties in the district and their names often appear on the labels of these esteemed products: von Buhl, Bürklin-Wolf and Bassermann-Jordan. These names all indicate superb quality. The four most distinguished villages are Deidesheim, Forst, Ruppertsberg and Wachenheim. Königsbach nearby is also highly thought of, although its output is small. Any wine bearing one of these names (as the first part of the wine's name, as in Deidesheimer Hohenmorgen) will be fine indeed, and will be quite expensive. This area favours the Riesling grape and the wine is much deeper in colour than those from farther south.

The wine from Forst is reputedly the sweetest in Germany. Near the village is an outcrop of black basalt, a rock rich in potassium which contributes to the fine character of the wine. In consequence stone from local quarries is crushed and spread on the vineyard of other districts to impart some of the quality of Forst wine to their products. Next to the church at Forst, almost in the centre of the village, are two of the most famous vineyards in Germany – Jesuitengarten and Kirchenstück. A short distance away is Deidesheim, a charming little village surrounded by famous vineyards such as Grainhübel, Hohenmorgen, Leinhöhle and Kalkofen. Wachenheim, too, has its famous names – Böhlig, Gerümpel, Goldbächel and Rechbächel among others. But these are truly great wines, hard to come by and to be reserved for a special occasion.

To the north is the small town of Bad Dürkheim, Germany's largest wine commune. Here, the famous *Wurstmarkt* (sausage fair) is held annually in September. This fair is a marvellous celebration of wine and sausage. A few local place names, including Bad Dürkheim itself, signify good wine, Kallstadt and Ungstein, in particular.

Rheingau

The Rheingau is the outstanding wine-producing area of the Rhine valley. On the right bank, roughly between the bridges across to Mainz and Bingen, it produces the rich dessert wines for which Germany has no rival.

The site of the Rheingau is unique among the Rhine regions, in that the river, which generally flows from south to north, at this point turns, blocked by the Taunus mountains, and flows slightly to the south. The slopes of the Taunus hills face to the south and receive the maximum amount of sun making them ideal for vines. Furthermore the thickly wooded Taunus mountains form a natural wind-break, keeping off the cold winds from the north and east. It is also believed that the river, with its broad surface, reflects the sun back up on to the slopes, increasing their warmth – an especially important factor when the grapes are ripening. In addition, the great size of the river imparts moisture to the air, favouring the growth of the vines. In autumn the damp mists gathering over the river help the 'noble rot' which attacks the grapes and helps create the fine Auslese, Beerenauslese and Trockenbeerenauslese wines.

The soil is also a contributory factor. On the high slopes, there is quartzite and weathered slate, and closer to the river there are clays, loess and loam. All these advantages make possible the predominant use of the Riesling grape: in Rheingau 83% of the crop is Riesling with 9% Müller-Thurgau and under 5% Sylvaner.

Rheingau produces only 2% of the total German wine production, but because much of this is of the highest quality, the name Rheingau on a wine label will often suggest that the product is amongst the aristocrats of German wine. The good wines from Rheingau age remarkably well.

Rüdesheim and western Rheingau

Lorchhausen and Lorch, the villages furthest downstream and furthest west, are the least distinguished in the region. Some good wine is made, but it has more in common with the lighter, more commonplace wines of neighbouring Mittelrhein. The next village, Assmannshausen, is also an exception. Here, red wines are produced from the blue Spätburgunder (or Pinot Noir) grape.

Just beyond Assmannshausen, on the bend in the river, is Rüdesheim – a town producing characteristic and excellent Rheingau wines. The hill to the west of the town, the Rüdesheimer Berg, produces much of the very best wines – golden in colour, strong in alcohol and in flavour. Paradoxically, the great years for the rest of the Rheingau are not necessarily always the best here, because the soil of the higher slopes tends to dry out in long, hot summers, with the result that the wines, already strong in flavour, become overpowering. Great vineyard names to look out for are Berg Roseneck, Berg Rottland, Berg Schlossberg, Bischofsberg and Klosterberg.

East of Rüdesheim on the river is Geisenheim, and the revered Johannisberg a short distance inland. The official German school of winemaking is at Geisenheim, and the wines of the area are good. Johannisberg, however, is in another class and is perhaps the greatest of Rheingau, or even of Rhine, areas. Schloss Johannisberg is incomparable, immensely subtle in flavour – and very expensive. Other Johannisberg vineyards are Goldatzel and Hölle.

Next along the river, come Winkel, Mittelheim and Östrich, with Hattenheim and Hallgarten in the hills behind. At Winkel is Schloss Vollrads, rivalling even Schloss Johannisberg. Its wines are said to be beyond praise. At Hattenheim is another famous estate, Steinberg, with the monastery of Kloster Eberbach, where wines have been made for at least 700 years.

Eltville and eastern Rheingau

Erbach, along the river from Hattenheim, has another famous vineyard. Named Marcobrunn, the vineyard has been the subject of a legendary dispute between the villages, but it is now officially in Erbach.

Eltville, next along the river, is one of the larger vineyard towns of Rheingau, providing a centre for the wine trade and the manufacture of sparkling Sekt. Its wines are good, and may be less expensive than the more famous villages in the hills behind: Kiedrich, Rauenthal and Martinsthal.

Wiesbaden and Hochheim

On the bend in the river that marks the end of the Rhine part of Rheingau lies the major town of Wiesbaden. Although an attractive old spa resort, its own wines are not up to the high standards of its illustrious neighbours flanking its east and west sides. There are four groups of Wiesbaden vineyards: Wiesbaden itself, Schierstein, Frauenstein and Dotzheim.

Just beyond Wiesbaden, the river Main joins the Rhine. About 3 kilometres up the river Main is the town of Hochheim, forming the eastern edge of the Rheingau. Although not on the Rhine itself, it has given its name to all the wines of the Rhine regions in English usage – 'hock'. Hochheim's wines are certainly Rheingau in character, and are among the first rank in quality. The best vineyards, Kirchenstück and Domdechaney, are close to the centre of the town. Less good, although as famous, is Königen Viktoria Berg, named after Queen Victoria, who showed an idiosyncratic taste in wine by naming it her favourite vineyard on a visit in 1850. The best Hochheim wines are excellent, soft and fruity, but experts complain of an earthy taste in the less than perfect ones.

Rheingau is an area for those who want to start at the top. Its wines are fine indeed – and famous. There is almost no such thing as a bargain, for its products are carefully graded and bought at auction by those who know precisely which wines are the best. This, of course, makes it easier for the beginner. If you want to sample Rheingau, find a good wine merchant and choose a wine at the price you want to pay.

Vineyards around Assmannshausen

Rheinhessen

Rheinhessen produces some of the most famous wines in the world, as well as huge quantities of pleasant but undistinguished table wines. Bingen and the Rheinfront are two centres which export wines of unassailable quality.

Up to 300 million litres of wine are produced in the Rheinhessen annually. Rheinhessen is situated in the bend in the River Rhine known as the Rheinknie (the Rhine knee). Three of the roughly square-shaped region's corners are marked by towns on the river: Bingen, Mainz and Worms. To the west lies the River Nahe and to the south the Rheinpfalz, both areas of quality wines. Rheinhessen has a mild climate and is protected from cold winter winds by hills of the western Black Forest. The rolling, open countryside is not the prettiest in Germany but, because it is so fertile, is known as 'God's garden'. The different sedimentary soils here account for the difference in stature of the wines. The best wines come from grapes grown on the red sandstone along the Rhine, particularly to the south of Mainz. The poorest – in quality if not in quantity – come from the fertile clay soils in the centre of the region.

The Sylvaner grape was for a long time the dominant type in the region. Ripening early and giving high yields, Sylvaner pro-duces wine with a light fragrant character. Recently, Sylvaner has been pushed into second place by the Müller-Thurgau grape – at present about 27% of the production to Sylvaner's 15%. To the grower, Müller-Thurgau has the advantage of high efficiency with a fuller flavour. Other, newer grape varieties are also gaining ground, but it is the most traditional of grape varieties that is grown on the best sites and yields the most famous wines. The Riesling grape is used to produce only 5% of the region's wine, but it has great depth and spiciness.

Bingen

Behind the town of Bingen rises the Schalachberg or 'scarlet hill', although it is brick-red rather than scarlet. Here is the famous chapel of St Rochas, from which the collective name for the vineyards of the area comes – Sankt Rochuskapelle. The best wines from this region are strong and full of flavour, with a smoky taste imparted by the soil. The famous vineyards are Schlossberg, Schwätzerchen and Scharlachberg.

The Rheinfront

The town of Mainz is one of the main centres of the German wine trade, although little wine is actually grown here. To the south is the Rheinfront. Red sandstone soils cover the east-facing slopes of the river banks which are packed with vineyards. The first Rheinfront village, Bodenheim, produces mild wines, known for their bouquet and quality. Nackenheim does not produce much wine, and is not well known outside Germany, but to wine experts, this is a special place. Its wines are now largely sold under the village name and not used in blends. The best vineyard is Nackenheimer Rothenberg; producers to look for are Gunderloch-Lange, Gunderloch-Usinger and the state-owned Staatsweingut.

Further south is Nierstein, important for the quality and quantity of its wine. The sun reflecting off the Rhine on to the vineyard slopes is said to help ripen the grapes. Nierstein's wine production is massive, and less than 20% is bottled as wine of high quality under the name of the place where it was produced. The majority goes into the well known blended wines. However if the wine is labelled 'Niersteiner' with the name of the vineyard it must be a great wine. The most famous Niersteiner vineyards are Floss, Glock, Hipping, Orbel, Pettental and Rehbach. There are also producers of considerable fame whose names will appear on the label, including Freiherr Heyl zu Herrnheim, Rheinhold Senfer, Franz Karl Schmitt and, again, the Staatsweingut.

Oppenheim, the next village up the river, produces wine almost as good as Nierstein. The best vineyards include Daubhaus, Herrenberg, Kreuz, Sackträger and Steig.

The Rheinfront ends with the village of Dienheim. The wine is still good, although not of the superlative quality of Nierstein or Oppenheim. Watch for these vineyard names: Goldberg, Guldenmorgen, Kröttenbrunner and Rosswiesse.

The Worms region

In the ancient town of Worms is a church called Liebfrauenkirche (the church of Our Lady). Though the small vineyards nearby produce average wine, the huge reputation of Liebfraumilch (Our Lady's milk) started here. Now, of course, the name Liebfraumilch is applied to wine produced all over Rheinhessen, and Rheinpfalz as well. The fertility of the soil and the skill of the growers have led to this being one of the most exported wines of all. Liebfraumilch is pleasant, sweet, and reliably fresh, but totally lacking in the distinction of the wines of Nierstein or Oppenheim, or even the individuality of less well-known local types.

Rhine red wines

One final wine of importance comes from Ingleheim, a village situated between Bingen and Mainz. Made from blue Spätburgunder grapes, this is a red wine – one of the best made in Germany. Other Rheinhessen reds are made from the Portugeiser grape, but these are as well left for local consumption. Ingleheim wines, however, are worth looking out for – but little is produced and they are not often found outside Germany.

The Nahe

Situated on a tributary of the Rhine, the Nahe region is less well-known than the other famous Rhine wine regions of Germany, but it ranks very highly since it produces some of the greatest dessert wines as well as good quality wines for everyday drinking. The region is small and only provides about five per cent of the total amount of German wine produced each year.

Although officially Nahe wines are categorized as Rhine wines (hocks), these wines unjustifiably suffer from the reputation that they fall midway between Moselles and hocks. The truth, however, is that the Nahe produces wines of quite individual character, combining the clarity and liveliness of Moselles with the strength and fruitiness of hocks. Its wines vary from place to place and from soil type to soil type. The best Nahe wines rank very high indeed, and the region fully qualifies among the five greatest areas of the eleven officially classified. Because the wines of the Nahe are often underestimated, this means that its better products are available at more acceptable prices than its illustrious neighbours.

The river Nahe is a tributary of the Rhine, flowing in from the west at the town of Bingen, which is in the Rheinhessen wine region, with Rüdesheim in the Rheingau opposite. Many of the Nahe vineyards are on the slopes of the Nahe valley itself, but they also stretch up the tributaries of the Nahe, the Glan and the Alsenz. Some vineyards are also scattered far back into the hills, particularly to the north and west of Bad Kreuznach, the region's central town. The vineyards are protected from the frosts by the range of forested hills – the Soonwald – to the north.

The soils are varied; the best for wine is the sandstone of the central portion of the river valley. The loams and weathered clays found mixed in with the sandstone around the Bad Kreuznach area also produce good wines. Over 80% of the grapes grown are Müller-Thurgau, Riesling and Sylvaner – Germany's great white wine grapes – though Riesling tends to produce the best wine.

This is not an area of great aristocratic producers like the Rheingau and alongside the important state domains there are numerous small and medium estates. The co-operatives which market about 20% of the wine maintain high standards. The Nahe typifies the care and industry with which German wine is produced, combining tradition with the most modern methods. This approach enables German wine production to keep pace with the huge growth in demand for fine wines.

Bad Kreuznach

The most famous centre of the Nahe is Bad Kreuznach, a picturesque old spa with a 600 year-old bridge. Roman artifacts and mosaics found in the area support the claim that viniculture was started here by the Romans, although it may go back even earlier. Some vineyards are quite close to the town centre – Rosengarten, Kahlenberg, St. Martin and Brückes, are names worth looking out for. Bad Kreuznach wines are typical of the Nahe area and are of very good, although not exceptional, quality. There are some good vineyards across the river, notably Höllenbrand, Galgenberg and Rosenberg.

To the north and west, scattered back into the hills, there are a number of well reputed wine villages. Roxheim, Windesheim and Bretzenheim are particularly famous, but there are other lesser-known villages. The best of these produce wines with strongly individual character and a distinctively powerful fruitiness.

Schloss Böckelheim

The most significant name in Nahe wine production is Schloss Böckelheim, which lies further upstream from Bad Kreuznach. Between the two centres are a number of villages on the left bank of the river. Just south of Bad Kreuznach is the huge red rock of the Rotenfels with the village of Bad Münster below. Vineyards clustering at the foot of this giant sun trap (such as Rotenfelser im Winkel, Höll, Steigerdell and Bastei) are also on ideal soil. They produce some of the best Nahe wine, especially Bastei. Opposite Bad Münster, the Alsenz, a tributary of the Nahe, enters the river. Several good wines come from this valley, particularly from the villages of Ebernburg and Altenbamberg.

A little further along the Nahe is Norheim, again producing wine of the first rank. Vineyards include Dellchen, Kafels and Kirschheck, all close to the river, with Klosterberg and Sonnenberg behind. The next riverside village is Niederhausen. Vineyards such as Felsensteyer, Kertz, Rosenheck and Steinwingert cover the slopes leading down to the river and produce fine wines.

The next section of the river front belongs to the village of Schloss Böckelheim itself, beginning with the most famous Nahe vineyard, Kupfergrube or 'the copper mine'. Copper was indeed mined here and the traces in the soil give the wine a strong flavour – its taste has been compared to blackcurrants. The neighbouring Felsenberg, Mühlberg, Königsfels and In den Felsen vineyards also produce excellent drinkable wine.

There are scattered vineyard areas further up the Nahe valley and in the hinterland, many producing notable wines. Village names to look out for include: Waldböckelheim, Monzingen, Martinstein and Merxheim. All these produce above-average wines that are well worth trying.

Left: a Bad Kreuznach wine, and Right: a wine from the famous Schloss Böckelheim region

Moselle: Saar and Ruwer

Moselles are among the most highly prized of all wines. Their very individual style is as recognizable as the slim green bottles the wine comes in. Moselles are paler in colour than the wines of the Rhine.

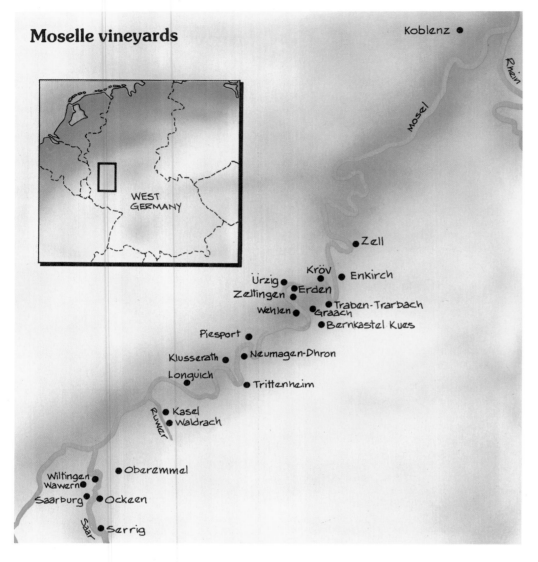

Moselle vineyards

vineyards that can be declared on labels, so it may take a while to discover them all! The key to understanding names is that the first word, ending in 'er' is the possessive adjective from a registered village. The second word is the name of the vineyard, which may be a tiny and famous plot or a major collective which means that the wines are blended from a particular area. The important names to look out for are in the central area of the Moselle or in the valleys of its tributaries, the Saar and Ruwer.

The Mosel rises in France and then flows into Germany near Luxembourg. It then flows north-east from Trier to join the Rhine at Koblenz. The river follows a twisting course past towns and villages, with castles topping the hills that slope down to the water. On the south-facing slopes, with sunshine at a maximum, vineyards are planted precariously, often so steeply that ladders have to be laid on the ground to work the vines. The river is best considered divided in two around the town of Trier, where the Romans first began cultivating the vine in Germany. On either side of Trier are the tributaries, the Saar and the Ruwer. Downstream, to the north-east are the Middle and Lower Moselle areas discussed on the following page

Upper Moselle and Saar wines

Wine is made on the French Moselle and in Luxembourg, but none of it offers the splendour of the German product. It is thin, pale and of local interest only. The Upper Moselle in Germany is similar and the wine from here is drunk locally or used in the manufacture of the sparkling wine Sekt.

To the west of Trier are 30 kilometres of the Saar, included in the Mosel-Saar-Ruwer and in good years its wines are reckoned to be the best in Germany. In bad years they can be disappointing. There are seven great Saar villages and a number of famous vineyards, given in brackets: Serrig (Vogelsang), Saarburg (Klosterberg), Ockfen (Herrenberg, Bockstein), Ayl (Herrenberger, Kupp), Wiltingen (Rosenberg, Scharzhofberg), Wawern (Goldberg, Herrenberger) and Oberemmel (Rosenberg). The name given to wine blended from the whole Saar region is Wiltinger Scharzberg, which is confusingly close to the most famous individual vineyard in the area, Wiltinger Scharzhofberg.

Ruwer wines

The Ruwer, to the east of Trier, is more like a stream than a river. Like the Saar it has wines which are good and very popular. The quality is again recognized to be variable depending on whether it is from a good or bad year. The most famous villages and vineyards, given in brackets are: Waldrach (Krone, Muisenberg, Jesuitengarten), Kasel (Herrenberg, Nieschen, Hitzlay) and Mertesdorf (Felslay).

Trier

Several good wines are made around the town of Trier, east of the confluence of the Saar and Moselle. The most famous vineyards here are Thiergarten, Rotlay, Hammerstein and Kupp.

Whether you are new to German wines or already know them well, you can be sure that every bottle of Moselle holds the promise of a delightful discovery. Moselle wines have a fresh aroma, rich with the perfume of grapes, which is combined with a crisp light flavour.

Moselles are instantly recognizable among German wines by their tall and slender green bottles. The main Moselle characteristic of crispness is the result of the combination of grape type and the soil on which it is grown. Riesling vines are planted on the steep, slate-covered slopes that line the valley of the River Mosel.

The Moselle area is of course, included in, and protected by, the precise but complicated German system of wine laws. If you see the word *Mosel* printed alone on a label

it means that the wine is a *Deutsche tafelwein*, a blended German table wine, from the Moselle region. Mosel-Saar-Ruwer on a label signifies a quality wine, a Qualitätswein, from the same region. QbA is the basic quality grade while QmP indicates even better wines. Both QbA and QmP wines need not be expensive and Moselles of this standard are likely to be very pleasant.

Moselblümchen or 'little flowers of the Moselle' is sometimes used on labels to describe tafelwein. Other blended Moselles are sold under proprietary names. Dienhard's Green Label, for example, is an excellent and inexpensive introduction to the charms of Moselle wines. It is widely available and is preferable to the cheaper Qualitätsweins with complicated names.

There are actually over 500 Moselle

Middle and Lower Moselle

From the narrow, winding, steep-sided river valley of the Middle Moselle come some of the finest and most famous Moselle wines.

Here the river cuts between the Hunsrück and Eiffel mountains and begins its meandering course to the east of the ancient wine town of Trier. The area known as the Middle Moselle ends at the village of Zell. In between Trier and Zell is a valley of incomparable loveliness, centring on the small town of Bernkastel, which is as important to German wine as Bordeaux is to France.

The great wines from the Middle Moselle are exquisite and expensive and should be reserved to enjoy on exceptional occasions. However, there are wines from this area to suit all tastes and from every price level. Many are cheap enough for everyday drinking but still good enough to give great pleasure.

The first stretch of the Middle Moselle consists of a broad valley as far as the town of Klüsserath. Here the vineyards are set well back from the river. The wines are worthwhile but undistinguished. Longuich is the main village and Probstberg is the designated name of the collective. Longuicher Probstberg is a wine you will encounter often but do not expect too much from it.

After Klüsserath, the valley begins to narrow and the slopes overlooking the river, warmed by the sun reflecting back from the river, produce better wines. Klüsserath, Trittenheim and Neumagen-Dhron are the main village names and the collective vineyards enjoy considerable reputations especially in good years. Look out for Klüsserather Bruderschaft, Trittenheimer Apotheke or Altärchen and Neumagen-Dhroner Hofberger.

Next the river takes a long slow bend with steep south-facing slopes above the village of Piesport. This is one of the main centres and wines from here are sought after. Goldtröpfchen, then Falkenberg and Günterslay are the best vineyards. The collective vineyard is Michelsberg, so if you buy a Piesporter Michelsberg, the wine will be from a wide area and will not have the outstanding quality of the great vineyards, although it may be good.

After a sharp bend at Minheim the river flows down to Bernkastel. On the way are Wintrich and Kesten, Brauneberg and Lieser. These villages all make good wine, but it is not in the highest class. These wines are softer than other good Moselles and do not have their unique piquancy.

At the next large bend of the river is the town of Bernkastel-Kues. Here in a single 7 kilometre slope the greatest Moselles of all are produced. Bernkastel-Kues, Graach, Wehlen and Zeltingen-Rachtig are the villages, and all produce fine wines. Bernkastel is the name given to the whole of the Middle Moselle, so Bereich Bernkastel means wine blended from any part of the area. Wine labelled Bernkastler Kurfürstlay signifies wine from the Bernkastel region rather than from a particular famous vineyard. It could be a perfectly acceptable wine but should not be too expensive.

Just above the town of Bernkastel-Kues are the slopes of the most famous Bernkastel vineyards: Doktor and Graben. Other vineyards with good reputations are Johannisbrünnchen, Bratenhöfchen, Mattheisbildchen and Lay. Further downstream are names just as well known: Gracher Domprobst or Himmelreich, Wehlener Sonnenuhr and Zeltingen-Rachtiger Sonnenuhr or Himmelreich. On the opposite bank is the less good but still worthwhile vineyard of Nonnenberg. Gracher Munzlay on a label indicates a cheaper wine from this stretch of the river in general. Beyond Zeltingen the river turns east and another series of south-facing slopes producing good wines begins. These wines are highly recommended as they are less expensive but as good as their Bernkastel counterparts. The villages are Ürzig, Erden, Lösnich, Kinheim and Kröv. The name given to wine from the area is Ürziger Schwarzlay. Beyond here there are good wines from Traben-Trarbach and Enkirch.

Lower Moselle

The Lower Moselle from Zell to the junction with the Rhine at Koblenz, produces wine from vineyards scattered along its whole length. Most are used in the blending of Moselblümchen or other lesser wines of the region and are unlikely to be encountered in named form.

Watch tower at Zell on Lower Moselle

Italy

Italy is a wonderful hunting ground for the newcomer to wine, since it offers a vast range of different types of wine – from full-bodied reds to sparkling whites. The wines are generally extremely good value for money, making them perfect for the enthusiastic wine drinker who has a limited budget.

Most areas of Italy produce wine. In fact, Italy now produces more wine annually than any other country in the world. Her finest wines are powerful reds, but Italy is also the source of lighter fresh reds and clean young whites. These lighter wines make fine everyday drinking.

The great benefit of drinking Italian wine is that it is still possible to taste widely and compare different wines without spending large amounts of money. Italian wines, except the very finest, remain cheap. This is partly because of their abundance, and the Italians' attitude to wine as a happy drink, to be drunk with food and then forgotten about. It is also partly a legacy of the days when 'Italian wine' all too often did mean coarse, heavy reds from the far south, or tired oxidized white from almost anywhere.

Today, production standards have improved to the extent that almost any bottle of Italian wine will be acceptable. It might possibly be dull, in which case the answer is to move on and try something else next time. But the days of the very rough are past. Yet, luckily for the consumer, Italian producers still cannot command the high prices expected by France, for example.

Unfortunately, the very abundance and variety of Italian wine is also its major drawback for the drinker. Confusion reigns: the grading system is, as yet, much less organized than the neat system that applies in France and the many names that appear on the labels are baffling. As a start to penetrating the jungle, the opposite page explains the DOC grading system and Italian label-language in general.

Italian wine labels

Italy is the world's biggest wine producer, turning our some 8 billion bottles of wine a year, varying from tiptop quality down to the everyday blend. There is such a profusion of Italian wine names, labels, producers and styles, that at first the Italian wine buyer can feel baffled when trying to penetrate the jungle. There are however some basic guidelines that are easy to remember, and as always the label provides almost all the clues.

Names

The name of the wine itself is the first pointer to look for when reading the label. Confusingly, an Italian wine may take its name from its geographical home area, from historical tradition or from folklore connected with neither of these. Lacrima Cristi (meaning 'The tears of Christ') is a good example of the latter. Many wines, particularly the best, take their names from their grape variety. Among these are the long-established Italian names like Barbera and Sangiovese, as well as the more familiar European ones like Merlot and Riesling.

Classification

Once past the name, the next most important clue is the classification. In theory, the best ten percent or so of Italian wines are 'DOC': in other words, bear the official quality guarantee *Denominazione di Origine Controllata*. This is roughly equivalent to the French *Appellation Contrôlée* system. Unfortunately the theory is more clear-cut than the reality. The 200 or so DOC zones produce just over 450 types of wine, amongst which are some indifferent ones. So although the letters DOC appear on the label, the wine may still be disappointing.

At the same time, a handful of Italy's very best wines go to market with only the words *vino da tavola* (the lowest official category) on the label. This may be because, as a result of a production technicality, they do not qualify for the local DOC. Alternatively, the producers may simply have decided not to participate in the system. Some of these fine wines – for example Sassicaia and Tignanello – stand on their reputation alone and need no other classifying. They are recognizable by the price they command. Others, less well known, are cheaper and can be excellent bargains.

It is difficult to give specific examples, but it is worth remembering that DOC and *vino da tavola* are indications of quality, not infallible guidelines. You may encounter some *vini da tavola* with a geographical label tacked on too, and these tend to be of higher quality than the basic wine.

DOCG (*Denominazione di Origine Controllata e Garantita*) has now been introduced for a limited selection of the best wines, including Vino Nobile di Montepulciano, Barolo, Barbaresco, Brunello di Montalcino, and – most recently – Chianti. *Vino tipici* is being introduced for table wine. Both new categories are not fully operational. Standards are, however, rising all the time, as the big co-op wineries (watch for *Cantine Sociale* on the label) and large-scale private organizations take over from individual producers.

Vintage

Yet another factor to be considered is the vintage date – the *vendemmia*. It is difficult to be specific when discussing such a variety of wines, but if you follow the golden rule of choosing the 'youngest white and oldest red' available – with the notable exception of the light reds such as Valpolicella and Bardolino – you should not go far wrong.

Some fine red wines may be labelled *vecchio*, *riserva*, *riserva speciale* or *stravecchio*. These terms are legally controlled and relate to specific lengths of time that the wine has been aged in barrel.

Other terms

Superiore is another frequently-met term which appears on the label. It means that the wine conforms to certain production methods and standards, has a higher alcohol level and has been aged for a required amount of time.

If a wine is described as *classico* this means that it comes from the central, and so usually best, area of that particualr wine region. Chianti Classico is an example. The terms *superiore* and *classico* are generally a reliable mark of quality.

Many bottles of Italian wine also carry an exuberant profusion of colourful information, pictures and extraneous decoration. All this is fun but is more an indication of the producer's enthusiasm than his wine-making skills. Take everything but the legally-defined terms with a pinch of salt. Remember too that *Imbottigliato . . . all'origine* means bottled by the producer, and *. . . nella zona di produzione* means that the wine was not estate bottled.

Quick wine terms guide

Bianco: white
Rosso: red
Rosato: pink
Spumante: sparkling
Secco: very dry
Asciutto: dry
Amaro: bitter
Abboccato: semi-sweet
Amabile: sweeter than *abboccato*
Dolce: sweet
Liquorosco: strong, and usually very sweet
Gradi: degrees of alcohol

From the left, good-quality chianti, straight DOC and vino tavola labels

Chianti

Chianti appears the most Italian of Italian red wines. The familiar straw-covered flask is a symbol of Italy in 'Italian' restaurants all over the world and one sip of a fresh young Chianti instantly brings back the memory of Florence for anyone who has ever visited the city.

The changing face of Chianti

Surprisingly, Chianti's image is changing fast, and the present time is one of the most interesting in the wine's long history. Almost all the changes are for the better, but they do mean that the 'traditional' Chianti is fast being left behind. To begin with, the evocative, straw-covered bottle is becoming less and less common. It is labour-intensive and costly to make, and some producers, anxious not to seem too traditional and with an eye to the up-market appeal of Bordeaux, have opted for a high-shouldered claret-style bottle.

Modern technological advances throughout the process mean that the wine is more reliable and there is less chance of buying a bad bottle. The introduction of the DOCG system has improved the quality too, since it ensures that wine labelled Chianti actually comes from Chianti country. In the past, Chianti producers have taken advantage of the rule that allows them to add up to 15% of grapes from outside the region to add a strengthening dose of heavy southern wine.

This often resulted in a sweetish and rather dull brew, but it was thought to be what the customer wanted. However, the practice is less common now and the correction is made with good-quality grapes that do not detract from the characteristic vigorous Chianti flavour.

How Chianti is made

The main Chianti grape is the red Sangiovese, but it may be softened by the addition of 25% of other grapes, including some white. The exact blend is up to the individual winemaker. This flexibility in the make-up means that different Chiantis can be surprisingly varied in style. As a mark of this, the colour can vary from a light, bright ruby-red to a rich deep crimson.

Wine making methods can be very different too. To make a broad generalization, there are two main types. One group is fresh and fruity, rather in the style of a young beaujolais. These wines often have a slight refreshing 'prickle' that is the result of a secondary fermentation known as *governo*.

The other type is barrel-aged wines. These are not usually subjected to *governo*, are distinctly perfumed, powerful and subtle. The wines marked *riserva* have been aged for at least three years in oak barrels while those marked *vecchio* have been aged for at least two years. The best of them benefit from further ageing in bottle, and a ten-year-old Riserva can be a very fine wine indeed.

Again the style of wine that is made is the choice of the producer. Happily, many of them make both kinds.

Types of Chianti

Perhaps the best-known name in the area is Chianti Classico, the senior Chianti from the heart of the beautiful Chianti countryside. The black cockerel on the neck label is the trademark of the 700 members of the Chianti Classico consortium and is one of the most reliable guarantees of quality in the area. Classico Riserva must reach at least 12.5% of alcohol as against the 12% of Chianti Riserva from outside the central region.

It is important to remember, however, that Classico is not necessarily superior to every other Chianti. Chianti Putto is the mark of another giant consortium of growers from outside the central Classico zone. It is recognizable by the pink and white cherub on the neck label. The wine is often of high quality, and the growers have wisely set themselves the same standards as those of the Classico consortium. Other reputable growers choose not to belong to the consortia at all, yet still produce admirable, individual wines. Encircling the Classico zone are six other Chianti regions, together making up the biggest DOC group in Italy. The names to look out for are Montalbano, Colli Fiorentini, Colli Aretini, Colli Senesi, Colline Pisane and Rufina. Rufina is the smallest of the six, but it makes some of the finest wines; Marchesi de' Frescobaldi and Spalletti are the most important names here to remember.

Vintage

In vintage terms, ordinary Chiantis are cheerful, straightforward wines made for drinking young in much the same way as beaujolais. The wines you are most likely to encounter in wine shops will probably be two or three years old and this is quite mature enough. Riserva, of course, has already been aged in oak and a reputable wine of this category deserves a little longer in bottle.

Drinking Chianti

Chianti makes an excellent partner with all kinds of not-too-elaborate food. It is a suitable choice for any meal that requires a vigorous red. Whatever you eat with it, do not treat Chianti with too much ceremony unless it is a very aged and special one. It is basically a reliable red-wine standby that is cheap enough to experiment with, but is still varied enough to be interesting and rewarding.

A familiar Italian sight – Chianti in a straw-covered flask

North-West Italy

North-west Italy is best known for its powerful red wines that are the perfect partners for rich meat dishes. Piedmont is the largest wine region; apart from producing the best reds, it is also the home of the famous, sparkling white Asti Spumante.

Barolo and Barbaresco

As a region, Piedmont has more DOC and DOCG zones (thirty six in all) than any other in Italy. The noble wines of this prosperous corner of Italy are the twin reds Barolo and Barbaresco. At their best, these are complex wines that are fine enough to hold their own with the big names of Bordeaux, Burgundy or anywhere else.

The acknowledged prince is Barolo, although it is admittedly a difficult wine for the beginner, with its high level of alcohol and tannin bite. Made from the intense purplish Nebbiolo grape, Barolo is said, variously, to have the flavour of truffles, violets, raspberries and even tar. Whatever taste seems appropriate to the individual judgement, there is no doubt that wine of this strength may need as much as ten years ageing to make it sufficiently mellow and inviting. A good Barolo is an unforgettable wine and the Piedmontese are justly proud of it. It is not for everyday drinking however.

Barbaresco, Barolo's peer, is also made from the Nebbiolo grape under very similar conditions, but it is a subtly different wine. It has a lower minimum alcoholic content – 12.5% against 13% – and under DOC rules it requires a year's less ageing in barrel. The real effect of these differences is to make a wine that is smoother and more delicate than the intense Barolo. It is an easier introduction to the great Piedmontese reds.

The finest Barolos and Barbarescos are by no means cheap, but fortunately they do not command anything like the dizzy prices of a tiptop claret or burgundy. Both Barolo and Barbaresco should be brought gently to room temperature before serving. The cork should be removed at least a couple of hours beforehand too and the wine may even need to be decanted gently.

Other red wines

Sometimes, perhaps because of overproduction or failure to meet the minimum alcoholic levels, wine from the classic regions of Barolo and Barbaresco does not qualify for the big names on the label. In this case it goes on sale as *Nebbiolo vino da tavola*. This is often good-value drinking if you can find it. Some progressive wine-makers have been experimenting recently with Nebbiolo as a young wine, rather in the Beaujolais style. This known as *da pronta beva*. Interestingly, the result can be a refreshing fruity red that makes palatable drinking as little as a few months after the harvest.

In contrast to Barolo and Barbaresco, the everyday drinking wine for the Piedmontese is Barbera, named after the widely planted grape variety. When it is coupled with a place name, as in Barbera d'Asti, it implies a limited production area and, probably, superior quality. The trend now is to make Barbera dry, light and fresh, definitely for drinking young. Yet, typically for Italy, the wine can still vary dramatically according to the area and the wine-maker responsible. Since Barbera is widely available and cheap, the best way of testing it is to sample a range of bottles.

Another red that may be encountered from this north-western corner is Dolcetto, not a sweet wine despite its name, but a dry red wine with a touch of bitterness. Carema is another wine to watch out for. This is a softer version of Barolo, from the Valle d'Aosta at the fringe of the Alps. The Nebbiolo grape (confusingly also called Spanna locally) also makes easier wines from the north-east of Barolo heartland under the names of Gattinara and Ghemme. Any of these wines are well worth tasting if you come across them.

Harvesting grapes in Piedmont

The white wines

The white wines of the north-west are far less numerous, but they include one of Italy's most famous wines, Asti Spumante – literally meaning foaming wine of Asti. In the past, Asti has been regarded as a sweet budget alternative to champagne, but this is not justified now. To begin with, it is no longer particularly cheap. Although it is not usually made by the classic *méthode champenoise*, its successful production still calls for expensive technology and a great deal of care to preserve the elusive quality of the Moscato bianco grape. Secondly, the almost universal demand for drier wines has meant that its makers have turned their attention to creating a more elegant, fresh wine with a sweet tinge. This is often a less demanding drink than a heavyweight champagne. For these reasons Asti should be regarded as a pleasing sparkling wine in its own right.

The interest in drier sparkling wines has led to the production of other spumantes, made from the Pinot and various other grapes. For some reason, these are more widely exported than drunk in Italy itself.

Asti and its relatives apart, there are few notable wines from the area. Three names that just might be encountered though are Cortese di Gavi and Erbaluce di Caluso from Piedmont and Cinqueterre from Liguria (a region which is more familiarly known as the Italian Riviera).

North-East Italy

The north-eastern corner of Italy follows a pattern that is familiar throughout Italy – it produces a huge volume of wine of all degrees of quality. In fact , many of Italy's best known wines, such as Soave, Bardolino and Valpolicella are from this area.

Sorting grapes in the north-eastern region of Italy

The Veneto

The Veneto region stretches from the shores of Lake Garda eastwards in a wide arc to Venice and beyond. It produces good, abundant wines at accessible prices. Among them are three of Italy's most famous wines – Soave, Bardolino and Valpolicella.

Soave, from the hills around Verona, is the archetypal Italian white. The slim green bottle is a familiar sight on the shelves of many wine merchants and it remains popular for its reliability and low price. If Soave is drunk young enough – anything more than two years old is too old – it is almost always fresh and crisp with a pleasing hint of almonds. The worst criticism that could be made of Soave is that it can be a shade characterless.

Another local big name is Bardolino, which is mainly red although some rosé is produced too. It is made from a combination of different grapes and is another uncomplicated wine to be drunk young. Serve it cool, too. Cellar temperature is best, and most flattering to the hint of bitterness that is characteristic of the wine. *Superiore* means that the wine is aged longer

and has a higher alcoholic strength, and consequent depth, but *classico* is not necessarily any better than straight Bardolino.

The third famous name is Valpolicella. The grape combination is the same as Bardolino's, and it is still a light, fresh wine. However, Valpolicella tends to have more colour, depth and taste, particularly the *superiore*. Some producers also make Recioto della Valpolicella, a strong sweetish wine which may have some sparkle. Another type is Recioto Amarone della Valpolicella in which all the sugar in specially selected grapes is fermented into alcohol. The resulting dry, powerful wine may have up to 16% of alcohol, but it is surprisingly easy to drink when compared with the other big Italian reds, such as Barolo.

Two white wines that make a change from Soave are Gambellara and Bianco di Custoza. Other wines from the Veneto region may be named after their more familiar-sounding grape variety. Merlot is the most widely planted, but Cabernet,

Pinot Bianco, Sauvignon and Chardonnay Riesling also hold their own.

Friuli-Venezia Giulia

Positioned right up in the north-eastern corner of Italy, bounded by Austria and Yugoslavia, this region has begun to be of interest only recently to Italian wine exporters. Now, however, it is gaining a reputation for interesting and reliable varietal wines. It is refreshing too, amid the confusion of Italian wine designations, to find six well-defined geographical DOC zones. Collio, Colli, Orientale del Friuli and grave del Friuli are the best-known zones.

From Collio come the wines labelled by the grape variety Cabernet, Merlot, Pinot Bianco and Sauvignon, and Tocai (no relation to the Hungarian Tokay). Colli Orientale has its varietals too, but its first claim to fame is Picolit. Picolit is a fine dessert wine sometimes (unhelpfully) described as Italy's Château d'Yquem. The most popular grape choice for the growers of Grave is Merlot, which makes soft red wines that are perfect for drinking young under undemanding conditions.

Wine from any of these DOC zones, or the neighbouring Isonzo, Aquilea and Latisana, are likely to have been carefully chosen for export. They often provide rewarding and interesting drinking at close to bargain prices.

Trentino-Alto Adige

The northern position of another region, Trentino-Alto Adige, is reflected in the German names on the wine labels. Even the region itself has the alternative name of the Süd Tirol. Confusion is increased, for the wine buyer, by the fact that the same wines may be labelled in either Italian or German, according to the maker's choice. One of the best known local products, for example, is a widely exported fruity red that may appear as Kalteresee or Lago di Caldaro.

More interesting is Santa Maddalena, once ranked by Mussolini as one of the top three Italian reds. The wine's popularity declined with its admirer's, and while it is not in the same class as the big Piedmont reds, it is a fragrant and supple wine that is frequently undervalued.

White wines make up only a quarter of the Alto Adige output, and those that do appear are most likely to have German names like Sylvaner or Weissburgunder.

Emilia Romagna

From the vineyards of the flatlands around the river Po come huge amounts of wine, much of it low grade for blending, vinegar making and industrial use. True to Italian form, some good wine is made, but Emilia Romagna is best known for one of America's favourite wines, Lambrusco. This purplish red wine froths up in surprising pink bubbles when it is poured: it is sparkling and usually sweet to taste. The Italians themselves belittle it as a wine for non-wine drinkers, and it is true to say that it is a wine that is either liked or immediately disliked. Yet a well made Lambrusco, in one of its drier versions, is a partner with a difference for robust and uncomplicated meat dishes.

Central and Southern Italy

In the area that stretches from Florence down to the toe of Italy, the dominant wines are white – Orvieto, Verdiccho and Frascati are perhaps the most famous names. There are red wines of course, among which are some of Italy's finest wines – Chianti is the best known.

White wines

Orvieto is the most famous wine of Umbria. Classically, this is a smooth, rich wine, golden in colour with a fragrant delicacy that offsets the natural semi-sweetness. Because of this lightness, Orvieto is not a dessert wine, even in the old *abboccato* versions that are slowly being replaced by the more fashionable *secco*. The dry wine the producers prefer to sell nowadays is crisper and paler than the old country wine. It is still perfectly palatable, but less interesting than it once was. However, whether it is secco or abboccato, Orvieto should be drunk young to make the most of its freshness.

Verdicchio is another famous white wine with a long history. It is produced in the region of the Marches, on the Adriatic coast of central Italy. The wine is easily recognizable by the shape of the bottle, a tall vase reminiscent of the two-handled vessel of classical times – it is claimed that the ancient Etruscans enjoyed the delicate Verdicchio

The terraced slopes of Umbria – the region that produces the famous Orvieto

wines. Whatever its illustrious history, this light wine is now a reliable accompaniment to fish or poultry. Many producers do not state the vintage date on the label, and this is because Verdicchio is at its best a year, or at most two years, after the harvest. For this reason you should distrust cobwebby bottles from suppliers who might not have a high turnover of stock.

Frascati, another deservedly popular wine, comes from Rome and its country environs. DOC regulations have brought the end of an era when any flask of cheap white wine from somewhere around Rome could call itself Frascati. Now anything labelled as such is likely to be a pleasantly reliable, golden white wine with a strong taste of the whole grape. The extra grapy flavour is achieved by keeping the must (the grape pulp in the process of fermentation) in contact with the skins, and is distinctive among Italian whites. Frascati is usually dry now, labelled either *asciutto* or *secco,* but it may also be found in softer, sweeter styles called *amabile* or *cannellino* (the latter is the sweetest). Frascati *superiore* has a higher level of alcohol. Thanks to heavy investment in new

vines and equipment by both large and small-scale producers, this wine is remarkably consistent in quality. Frascati is definitely a wine for drinking young – six months is fine, but two years old is the maximum.

Est! Est! Est! from Lake Bolsena, to the north of Rome, is yet another famous white, as renowned for its name as for its taste. Legend has it that a bishop sent his servant ahead to mark the doors of inns serving good wine with the word *Est!*. When he stopped at an inn in Montifiascone, he was so impressed with the wine that he wrote *Est!* three times on the door. It is a soft white wine in the Orvieto style, once lush and golden but now, like its more impressive neighbour, fashionably drier and paler.

Other white wines: These household names apart, central Italy makes numerous other reliable white wines, usually from the Trebbiano grape. Trebbiano di Romagna is excellent value, and other name to look out for is Montecarlo, a splendid Tuscan white that is well balanced between dry and fruity. Contrary to the usual rule, it can stand several years' ageing.

Vernaccia di San Gimignano is a highly-flavoured white that is supposed to have been Michaelangelo's favourite. It makes an unusual aperitif, or a partner for more robust fish dishes.

From the area around Mount Vesuvius comes the famous Lachryma Christi (meaning the tears of Christ). Most of it is an acceptable white wine; the best is dry.

Do not confuse Vernaccia di San Gimignano with Vernaccia di Oristano from Sardinia: Sardinian wines in general are a little too heavy and alcoholic, and sometimes too sweet, to appeal widely, but the Vernaccia has a sherry-like taste that is both unusual and interesting; the *superiore* has a hefty 15.5% of alcohol. Nuragus is another interesting Sardinian wine, lighter and more acid than most Sardinian wines.

Red wines

Chianti apart, there are some excellent red wines from the central region. There is the legendary Brunello di Montalcino from Siena, a long-lived red made from the Sangiovese grape. This wine commands prices as rarefied as any first-growth claret. Sassicaia is an unusual and excellent wine made from 100% Cabernet Sauvignon, and Tignanello is in the Chianti mould, but with more body, flavour and staying-power. These are all connoisseurs' wines. It is worth remembering their names, but for ordinary drinking Sangiovese di Romagna, from the most widely cultivated red grape of the region, is often a rewarding buy. The wine improves with age, so opt for the oldest bottle, within reason. Rosso Conero and Rosso Piceno are two more reds, also from the Adriatic coast, that are worth a try if encountered.

The wines from the far south tend to be strong and alcoholic, intended for local consumption. Some however are used for blending. One of the most interesting reds from this area is Aglianico del Vulture. Ravello Rosso is another red wine from the south worth watching out for.

Spain

Wine is very much a feature of everyday life in Spain, where it is looked on in the same way as the English look on their pint of beer – it is an agreeable way of quenching thirst, not a sophisticated experience.

Although Spain has the largest area under vines of any country in Europe, most of its produce goes into the making of ordinary table wine, *vino corriente*, the Spanish equivalent of *vin ordinaire*. The climate and the unsophisticated, easy-going drinking habits of the Spanish are the two main reasons for the high proportion of ordinary table wine.

The heat of the summer sun, especially in the south of Spain, produces grapes with very high levels of sugar. This ferments out to give wines which are strong in alcohol – sometimes up to 18% – but which are very unsubtle in taste.

This does not mean that Spanish wines of quality do not exist, though with the exception of sherry and Rioja they are not well-known outside Spain. In recent years Spanish authorities have taken determined steps to correct the impression that their country's produce is only fit for bulk export or blending. The *Estatuto de la Vina, del Vino y de los Alcoholes*, a Government Statute of 1970, laid down a strict code of practice for all connected with wine production and distribution. In the Statute, 18 limited areas entitled to a *Denominacion de Origen* (similar to the French A.C. and Italian D.O.C.) were defined and a network of local authorities – *Cosejos Reguladores* were set up to enforce standards within these areas.

Northern Spain

Penedés, a wine region on the north-east coast not far from Barcelona, seems most likely to follow the success of Rioja. In particular, the wines of Torres of Villafranca have been available outside Spain, and have a deserved reputation for honesty and good quality.

The wine which has brought them most prestige is the 1970 Gran Coronas Black Label, a fine red which at a grand wine-tasting occasion in Paris was judged superior to the 1970 Chateau Latour, a first-growth Claret from the Medoc – and at less than a fifth of the price!

At a less rarefied level, Torres of Villafranca market a number of sound red wines of varying fullness and alcoholic strength under such names as Tres Torres, Coronas and Sangre de Toro. They also produce white wines which are unusually fresh and dry by Spanish standards – their Vina Sol is particularly good value. Miguel Torres is a very skilful winemaker and in addition to the established Spanish growths he has introduced and acclimatized vines from France and Germany, to give wines a wide variety of flavours.

Penedés is also the centre of production of Spanish sparkling wine. It is forbidden by law to call this wine champagne, but that is what it is in all but name. The best of the *espumosos*, as they are called, are made by the *méthode champenoise*, which involves a second fermentation in the bottle and is a lengthy and labour intensive business. These wines are made from white grapes, chiefly Sumoll, and are similar to a French *blanc de blanc*. The quality is high, though unless you share the Spanish preference for sweetness, it is best to look for the bottles marked *bruto* or *seco*. The most famous wineries are Cordoniu and Freixenet.

Still in the North of Spain, but well to the West in the upper valley of the river Douro, is the estate which produces one of Spain's most remarkable and expensive red wines. It is called Vega Sicilia. The wine comes from the fruit of the native Spanish and acclimatized French vines. Like Rioja, it is made by traditional Bordeaux methods involving lengthy fermentation in oak barrels. A lesser but still excellent wine from the same estate, bottled after a shorter maturation period, is called Valbuena. Unfortunately, very little of each is produced and they are almost unobtainable outside Spain.

Other northern Spanish wines of quality are the reds from Navarre and both reds and whites from Galicia in the north-west. The Navarre wines, as might be expected, are rather similar to the fuller-bodied Riojas. Galicia produces some pleasant reds from Valdeorras and light, slightly pétillant (a faint fizz) reds and whites in the style of the Vinhos Verdes of Northern Portugal. Some very good still white wines are also made from the Albarino grape – tradition has it that the vines were brought from Germany many hundreds of years ago. The wines have been compared to Moselle in their delicacy and pronounced bouquet.

Central and Southern Spain

Across the great plateau of Central Spain to the wine-growing areas of the south, we are more definitely in 'bulk wine' country. La Mancha and Valdepeñas, and regions to the east as far as Valencia and the Levante, produce more wine than any other part of Spain and a good deal of it is exported. In earlier days, when the English had a taste for fortifying the light red wines of Bordeaux with something stronger, this area frequently supplied the necessary ingredient. Today, it appears under brand names in stores and supermarkets, and many people have probably drunk it at one time without being aware of its origins.

In the far south, the region around Malaga produces a sweet, fortified wine made mainly from the Pedro Ximenes grape. More interesting is the wine from the small region of Montilla-Moriles in Andalucia. The area has always lived in the shadow of Jerez, which has traditionally bought much of its produce for blending. Wines sold under the name of Montilla can be found, ranging like sherry from pale, delicate finos to full-bodied olorosos. Unlike sherry, they are never fortified but the method of production is quite similar and they are good value.

Rioja

Rioja is probably the best-known wine region of Spain – and a really good red Rioja compares very well with chateau-bottled claret – at half the price!

Two excellent examples of Rioja – white Rioja is less common than red.

Until recently, Spain was quite unfairly represented by just about the worst it had to offer – inky reds of doubtful parentage and imitation French whites such as 'Spanish Sauternes' or 'Spanish Chabilis'. Unfortunately there is still some of this about, but Spain not only produces a lot of wine – the area under vines is, in fact, the largest in Europe – but a lot of very good wine too. As usual, the label is your best guide, so it pays to know a little about the names of regions and shippers.

The name Rioja is an abbreviation of Rio Oja, a tributary of the river Ebro, but the Rioja district extends along both banks of the main river for a stretch of almost 100 kilometres. It is where the wild mountainous country of the North meets the great plateau of central Spain, on the borders of Navarre and Castile.

The wines of Rioja have been praised in Spain for centuries, but it is only within the last hundred years that they have found a wider reputation. At the end of the last century the vineyards of France were attacked by a pest called phylloxera which for a time threatened the whole future of wine production. Many growers from Bordeaux, in search of new vineyards, travelled south and settled in Rioja where they added their own knowledge and techniques to native wine-making methods. As a result, Rioja wines are still being made today following the former Bordeaux methods with a lengthy period of ageing in oak which

gives the red wines in particular a very distinctive bouquet and taste.

The French settlers found the area itself very different from home. The North and West, the Rioja Alta and Rioja Alavesa, are regions of upland valleys with plentiful winter rains and, sometimes, snow and frost as well. As the Ebro descends eastwards into the Rioja Baja, the country becomes more arid and summers can be fiercely hot. The vines too are different from the French vines, not only in variety but in the way they are grown. They are not trained on wires in ordered rows or hedges, as in France, but grow as individual bushes, sometimes alternating with other crops, sometimes covering whole hillsides. Nor are the wines named after individual vineyards. Instead the entire produce of the region is sold to the proprietors of the great wineries, or bodegas, who create blended wines with their own distinct character. These are then marketed under brand names.

Red Rioja

Most of the bodegas are to be found in Rioja Alta, in the stretch of country between the traditional wine centre of Haro and the provincial capital of Logrono 40 kilometres down river. This is also the area which produces the best crops of grapes, despite the more mountainous terrain and the more

uncertain climate. Wines often give the best results when they have to fight a little against the climate.

Mediterranean countries can produce rather fat, bland-tasting wines, high in alcohol but lacking acidity, which would give them balance and interest. The red wines of Rioja Baja tend to be like this – very full-bodied with an alcoholic strength of 14–16% and a rich, rather sweet taste. The reds of Rioja Alta on the other hand are lighter, both in colour and body, have an alcoholic strength of 10.5–12%, and greater delicacy of bouquet and flavour.

The grapes grown in this region for the production of red wine are the Tempranillo, the Graciano, the Mazuelo and the Garnacho, which has a relation in the Grenache of Southern France. No wine made from one type alone would be satisfactory, so the Riojas we drink are the result of skilful blending in the bodegas, with Tempranillo being the dominant grape.

Red Riojas respond well to ageing. Most are given a minimum of 2 years in oak casks, whose size is limited to 225 litres so that there is satisfactory contact of the wine with the wood. This gives Riojas their characteristic 'oaky' nose and smooth texture. Wines from particularly good vintages are known as Reserva or Gran Reserva wines and are set aside for longer ageing of up to 8 years in cask. They will then spend perhaps an equally long period in the bottle before being ready to drink. At the end of this time they have the distinction of fine claret at less than half the price. There is no doubt that for a non-wine producing country like the U.K., Rioja currently represents one of the best wine bargains. Though as exports increased fifteenfold in the 1970s, it seems only a matter of time before demand exceeds supply, with the inevitable effect on prices.

Since around 40 different bodegas are now shipping wines abroad there is plenty of scope for shopping around to discover a favourite brand. Among the more widely available wines are the Banda Azul and Vina Vial of Federico Paternina, who also have Gran Reserva at an appropriately higher price. Marques de Riscal and Marques de Murrieta are other respected names. Bottles from the Marques de Riscal are usually covered in wire mesh (supposedly an extra insurance against illegal tampering with the wine). The finest old wines from the Marques de Murrieta are marketed as Castillo Ygay. There are also excellent wines to be found from the Bodegas Bilbainas, Berberana, Olarra and Domecq.

White Rioja

White wines are also made in more limited quantities in Rioja from the Malvasia and Viura grapes; the traditional methods, again involving ageing in oak, produce a mellow wine of 10–12% alcohol, but the flavour is not so popular abroad as it is in Spain. Most bodegas are now concentrating on the production of a fresher, lighter wine which has spent little or not time in wood; Paternina's Banda Dorada and the dry wines from Marques de Caceres and Olarra are good examples of White Rioja.

The rest of Europe

The wines of France and Germany, and more recently Italy and Spain, are known the world over. But wines from the rest of Europe are only just becoming familiar. Many countries offer reasonably-priced, good quality wines to the consumer – what they lack are enterprising merchants to bring them to our attention.

now widely available abroad. Bulgaria also produces good Chardonnay, not as distinguished as the great white wines of Burgundy which are also made from it, though they are recognisably of the same breed. One grape about which you need to take a little more care is Riesling; this produces marvellous wines in Germany and Alsace, but Eastern Europe Rieslings are usually made from a related but inferior strain, the

The blue-black grapes of the Cabernet Sauvignon promise rich red wine; the green Riesling grape of a light white.

Welsch or Laski Riesling, which is pleasant but unexciting.

Another way in which unfamiliar wines can gain notice is by competitive pricing. The Bulgarian wines have this to recommend them too, and so do those from Yugoslavia, Roumania (when you can find them) and especially Portugal. Their vinhos verdes, which although called green are actually red or white, are refreshing and increasingly popular, and the reds such as Dão, many of them well aged before they appear in the shops, can be very good value. The dessert Muscat from Setubal is also worth trying.

We must not forget that England too is now a wine-grower. There are a large number of commercial vineyards scattered about the country, and many of them welcome visitors, so what better way of increasing your wine knowledge than a trip to your very own local producer?

There are a number of reasons why the rich wine country of the rest of Europe has gone unappreciated for so long. Traditional methods have favoured small-scale production with few quality controls. People in countries where the grapes are grown tend to be eager drinkers of their own product, which leaves less for export, and it is not easy to sell strange names to a conservative market. Wine-drinking in England, for instance, is a comparatively new habit and people who have only just acquainted themselves with Pinot Grigio may be resistant to

the charms of Szurkebarat, though it is in fact the same grape.

A little knowledge of grape types can help greatly to guide you through unfamiliar wine territory, as many countries sell varietal wines, named after the grape variety rather than the region of origin, and although there will be subtle differences in flavour from place to place the basic character should remain the same. For example, Cabernet Sauvignon, the grape which is the basis of much fine claret, makes a full, dry blackcurrant wine in Bulgaria which is

Portugal

The abundant vineyards of Portugal, which cover much of the country's finest agricultural landscape, produce a variety of wines to suit every palate. They range from the frisky, slightly sparkling Vinho Verde of the north, to the voluptuous moscatels of the south. There are many styles of red wine too and of course Portugal is the home of the world famous rosé, Mateus.

Vinho Verde

As an aperitif, party drink or accompaniment to a summer buffet meal, Vinho Verde is incomparable. It comes from the Minho, the largest of all the country's wine regions, which extends from the northern frontier with Spain and spreads out beyond Oporto. The name literally means 'green wine' – it does not refer to the colour, which is usually almost platinum blonde, but indicates its youthful freshness. Nobody ever drinks a 'mature' Vinho Verde.

Vinho Verde is grown in an area where the vines climb along trellises, on pergolas and up branches of trees. It must be one of the few places in the wine world where grape pickers can be seen climbing trees to reach some of the grapes.

Although Vinho Verde is a delightfully frivolous wine, it is also one of a restricted number from Portugal which receive the EEC classification VQPRD (which means a quality wine from a designated region). It is now widely exported. If you prefer very dry wines, the Verdes which should appeal are those of 'classic' style. These are usually most popular in Portugal and are drunk with rich and spicy food. One of these is the delicious fruity Gatão: others to note are the very brisk and dry Casalinho and the deeper golden Alvarinho, which comes from the extreme north of the Minho. Look, too, for the more delicate, fruity Verdegar and the not so dry Ribalonga. Aveleda is another name to remember – this is medium dry, and very light on the palate.

On Portuguese wine lists tourists are often baffled to find 'Vinho Verde Tinto' – how can green wine be red, they may well ask! In fact it is a glorious light crimson, slightly sparkling like the white, with an astringency which comes as a shock at the first sip! It is a taste which can be acquired, for it goes very well with highly spiced meat dishes or even curry.

Dão wines

No contrast could be greater than that between Vinho Verde and the glowing rich reds for which the mountainous region of the Dão in the north has become famous. These, at their best, can fairly be compared with wines from the Rioja in Spain and from the Côtes du Rhone in France. The vines, which also produce good white grapes, flourish in rocky, granite-studded soil and produce wines of great stamina and character. When very young, they can be rough, but vastly improved methods of vinification and patient maturing tame their harshness. Among those to look for is the smooth, fairly light and dry Grão Vasco, the white version of which is golden, smooth and not aggressively dry.

Others to note are Terras Altas – the red is deep ruby and rather earthy, while the white is silky, golden and dry; Dão Ribalonga red is softer and lighter in colour; and Cavas Velhas red is subtle and long maturing. The Cavas Velhas white is dry, greeny gold and rather 'steely' – a characteristic of many white wines of this region. The 'steely' quality of the whites makes them particularly suitable to serve with all kinds of fish, while the reds go best with roast meat. Like the Vinho Verde, Dão is one of the larger demarcated regions in Portugal.

Douro

Although the Douro region in the north is best known as the home of port, its vineyards in the mountains and the foothills also produce good, generally full-bodied, red wines. It is also the home of the famous Mateus Rosé. This medium-dry, slightly sparkling pink wine is most popular as a versatile companion for many different kinds of food or as an attractive aperitif.

Another famous medium-sweet rosé is Lancers. This is made by the venerable house of Fonseca, whose original cellars date back to 1834. They are also producers of the rich and luscious golden Moscatel of Setubal. This wine's fame goes back many centuries. It was one of those beloved by Louis XIV of France, who served it regularly at state banquets. It is made in an unusual way – after the grapes are picked, they are pressed very quickly and the fermentation is halted by the addition of brandy. Some of the fresh grape skins are added to the must and are left in until the spring following the vintage. This greatly intensifies the perfume. Connoisseurs like to drink very mature Setubal wines, which are darker, richer and dryer than the younger version.

Bucelas

Another notable wine of Portugal is Bucelas. This comes from the area of that name, situated about 30 kilometres north of Lisbon. Sometimes spelt 'Busellas' on antique English silver wines labels, this used to be called 'Lisbon Hock' and was a favourite of the Duke of Wellington and his officers when they fought in Portugal during the Peninsular Wars. In those days it was a much sweeter wine; now it is a golden, dry wine with a fruity bouquet and a hint of honey. It makes a good aperitif and goes well with fish in rich sauces.

Grape pickers of Pinhâu

Hungary

Hungary has for hundreds of years produced one of the world's great dessert wines – Tokay Aszu – but many parts of the country make excellent red and white table wines, which are well worth trying. The description given to wines of quality is Minosegi bor – the equivalent of the French Appellation Côntrolée.

Hungary is a major wine-producing country, ranking eleventh in the world for quantity. Forty per cent of the production is exported and this goes mainly to Scandinavia and other North European countries.

White table wines

The Hungarian white wine known best outside Hungary is probably the Riesling, made from the Olasz or Italian Riesling grape. This grape is widely grown, especially in the Great Plain of central Hungary, and produces a pleasant, fragrant, medium-dry wine. A particularly good example is made around the town of Pecs in the southwest of the country.

The wines of Hungary taste as exotic as their labels look. Bottle shapes vary too.

More interesting wines, however, are made from native grape varieties, such as the Furmint, Harslevelu and Keknyelu. The wines produced from these native grapes tend to be full-flavoured, aromatic and spicy – the ideal accompaniments to the traditional foods of the country.

Good quality white wines are produced in the regions of Somlo and Mor and especially around Lake Balaton in western Hungary. On the north side of the lake, a range of hills slopes gently down to the water. Villages and towns on these favoured south-facing slopes have been making wine for hundreds of years. The town of Badacsony has the best reputation, producing fragant golden wines of varying sweetness from the Olasz Riesling, Rizlingszilvani (Müller-Thurgau), Keknyelu, Zoldszilvani (Sylvaner) and Szurkebarat (Pinot Gris) grapes.

Tokay Aszu

The Hungarians prize above all the sweet white wines. These are served with dessert, or on their own for they are a delicious drink in their own right. The supreme example of this type of wine is Tokay Aszu.

Tokay is a little town in northeast Hungary on the Bodrog river. The slopes of the nearby hills, with their volcanic soils and favourable exposure to the sun, are ideal sites for vine cultivation. Summers are hot, autumns long, and, in particular, the mists from the nearby river encourage the development on the grapes of a fungus known as the 'noble rot' (*Botrytis cinerea*) which penetrates the skin of the grape, shrivelling it and concentrating the natural sugars. The grapes may not look very attractive, but they produce spectacular results.

The 'noble rot' does not attack the grapes until late in the season and picking is delayed until the end of October, sometimes continuing into December if conditions allow. Grapes which are harvested earlier produce a more conventional white wine, described either by its grape type – usually Furmint or Harslevelu – or, in more general terms, as *Szamorodni* (which means 'as it comes'). Only the wine made from shrivelled grapes is known as Tokay Aszu.

The method of making Tokay Aszu is unique. The grapes are first loaded into tubs where they are allowed to stand while their own weight produces a rich juice known as *Tokay Eszencia*, or essence. This is drawn off from the tubs and used for blending; it has a very high sugar content and ferments extremely slowly. The compressed grapes are then added in varying measures to existing one-year-old wine. The measures – 32 litres /7 gallons each – are known as *puttonys* and the quality of the finished wine is assessed by the number of *puttonys* (up to five) which are used. After a few days this mixture is pressed and allowed to ferment in the usual way. It then matures in barrels in the town's ancient rock cellars. Traditionally brandy was added to Tokay Aszu to give it added stability; this is now achieved by 'cooking' the wine briefly at a high temperature. This is said to give the wine a slightly caramelized flavour.

Red Wine

Hungary does, of course, also produce red wine. Much comes from the warmer south, but the most famous is made around the town of Eger in the north. Called Egri Bikaver, or Bull's Blood – a name supposedly coined by invading Turks hundreds of years ago – it is a full-bodied rich red. It is made from a blend of Kadarka (Hungary's main red wine grape), Kekfrancos and Medoc Noir (Merlot), sometimes with the additions of Cabernet and Oporto. If allowed to mature and develop, it can be a fine wine, comparable to a good Chianti.

Yugoslavia

Yugoslavia is notable in the wine world both for the wide diversity of its products – the contrasting vineyard terrains reflect this variety – and for reaching tenth place among the producing countries.

White wines

The better quality white wines are a most important export of Yugoslavia, particularly to Britain. The finest white wines come from Slovenia, the northern province which extends to the Italian, Austrian and Hungarian borders.

In Slovenia, as in other regions, extremely well-equipped modern wineries have been built to receive the produce of many thousands of small growers, who continue to cultivate their vineyards privately. Much has been done to improve the quality of traditional wines, as well as introducing new varieties of vines and modern methods of cultivation and vinification.

The best Slovenian wines come mostly from the Drava zone in the north-east, near the borders with Austria and Hungary. Here the beautifully terraced vineyards not only yield excellent grapes from the Laski Riesling vine, but also from Rhine Riesling (known locally as Renski Riesling), Sylvaner, Traminer, Sauvignon and Pinot Blanc, among others. The finer mature wines are often molten gold, voluptuous but never cloying. Some of the best come from the area called Jeruzalem. It is said that this area got its name from the Crusaders who, on halting there during their long journey south, imbibed so happily that they said they wished it were their journey's end!

The most notable of the white wines of Slovenia is the medium dry Lutomer Laski Riesling. The most popular of all dryish table wines exported, it is light pale golden, and fragrant with a slightly flowery bouquet. One of the finer versions is called Slamnak, named after its individual vineyard on the Lutomer estates. It is intensely fruity, yet dry with a lovely greeny gold colour. While Lutomer Laski Riesling is equally good as an aperitif, party or picnic drink, Slamnak goes well with fish, chicken or veal, especially in rich sauces.

Amongst the other Slovenian wines, the very pale blonde, dry Lutomer Sauvignon makes a delicious aperitif as well as being most suitable to serve with all kinds of fish. The Rhine (or Renski) Rieslings are more stately wines – golden, dry and fruity. In total contrast there is the pale topaz, very flowery medium dry Gewürztraminer. This is made from the grape so famous in Alsace, but is much cheaper, and less flamboyant.

Some delightful white wines come from the Fruska Gora zone in the Vojvodina region of Serbia, north-west of Belgrade. The name Fruska Gora comes from the wooded mountain range, much visited by tourists for the ancient monuments and monasteries there. The Fruska Gora wines are made using the most advanced modern methods, and the platinum blonde, very dry, Sauvignon is worth seeking out. It is not so astringent as its French counterpart. They also produce a delicately aromatic Traminer, which is medium dry, with a very distinctive bouquet.

On the south bank of the Danube the town of Smederevo is a notable centre for viticulture and fruit. A famous native vine is the Smederevka, which produces an attractive dry white wine.

One of Yugoslavia's most distinctive whites is Žilavka, named after the grape which grows best in the vineyards of Hercegovina, near the historic old town of Mostar. It has a rather 'leafy' subtle taste, is greeny gold and dry. This makes it a good aperitif and compatible with smoked fish, pâtés or mousses, as well as with poultry or the more delicate cheeses.

Red wines

Serbia's most popular red wine is the powerful, deep ruby Prokupac, named after its grape variety. More likely to appeal to Western palates is the delightful Milion Cabernet Sauvignon. This dry, deep garnet-coloured wine is made in the fine cellars at Oplenac which used to belong to the last sovereign, King Peter.

Good Cabernet Sauvignon wines are also made now in the southern region of Kosovo, where viticultural tradition goes back to the era of ancient Greek colonists. Many vineyards are planted with a native vine called Burgundac Crni – the resultant wine is a deep rich dry red.

The smallest Yugoslav region, Montenegro, produces a very different red wine, called Vranac. This is fresh, brisk and as instantly attractive as a good young Beaujolais. It is best served slightly chilled. Nothing could be more different from the long-established Dalmatian favourite, Dingač, which comes from vineyards on the mountainous Pelješac peninsula. You need a strong head to drink Dingač – it is a powerful robust red, on the sweet side. From another Dalmatian holiday place, the island of Hvar, comes Faros. This rather perfumed wine is named after the Greek word for 'lighthouse' and refers to ancient Greek settlements there.

Brandy

It would be a pity to omit Yugoslavia's other celebrated drink – *slivovic*. This is a very potent plum brandy which the locals toss back with ease but novices should sip with respect. It is at its best with black coffee.

Two examples of Yugoslavian wine

Austria

Until a few years ago, Austrian wine was rarely seen outside its native country. However, wine production has now become a serious business in Austria. The recent scandal involving adulterated wine has dealt a blow to the market, but given time reputable growers should re-establish the reputation, particularly of the dessert wines.

There are four principal wine regions in Austria – Lower Austria, Styria, Burgenland and Vienna (probably the only capital in the world with its own vineyards). These regions are again sub-divided into fourteen different areas.

Most of the Austrian wines are sold labelled according to the grape from which they are made. Therefore, it is useful to get acquainted with important grape names.

The grapes and their wines

Grüner Veltliner: over 80% of the wine produced in Austria is white and of this by far the most popular grape is the Grüner Veltliner. It produces a typically Austrian wine, light and spicy with an almost 'peppery' taste – good both with food and as an aperitif. Grüner Veltliner is delicious, too, if drunk in true Austrian-style as a *G'spritzer*: half wine, half soda water. The colour of Grüner Veltliner was once described as 'light gold with green lights' and nothing could be more appropriate.

Müller-Thurgau is an early-ripening grape

From left: Beerenauslese, St Laurent, Grüner Veltliner, Traminer and Weisser Burgunder.

which produces a mild wine with a fruity bouquet and a surprising Muscat flavour. It has a lovely light, green-gold colour and although it has the general reputation of not ageing well, there are some notable exceptions, particularly in the Burgenland.

Rheinriesling: wine pressed from this grape matures slowly and usually reaches its peak only after two to four years in storage. It has a delicate fruity bouquet, faintly reminiscent of peaches.

The Neuburger grape is an Austrian speciality and the wines produced from it are full-bodied yet mild with a pleasant, fresh aroma.

Weisser Burgunder is an interesting wine with a deliciously fragrant bouquet and a flavour of fresh walnuts.

Traminer (or Gewürztraminer) produces an elegant wine which is golden in colour. The wine has a pronounced bouquet which has been likened to roses by some, violets by others. With a spicy, rich flavour, Traminer is usually rich in alcohol and is at its best when grown in Styria and Burgenland.

Muskat-Ottonel is a mild golden wine typical of the province of Burgenland, with an exceptionally strong bouquet of Muscat. According to where the grapes were grown,

the wine can vary from sprightly elegance to mellow fullness.

Welschriesling is not the real Riesling; 'Welsch' in this particular case meaning 'imposter'. However, it is a fresh, spicy wine which keeps well and can vary in colour from palest yellow to deep gold.

Zierfandler and Rotgipfler are two typically Austrian grapes, grown mostly in the Lower Austrian regions of Gumpoldskirchen and Baden near Vienna. They produce similar wines – rich and robust, with a fine fruity bouquet – which are often blended together and sold as Zierfandler/Rotgipfler. This wine is excellent if allowed to mature.

Blaufränkische produces the most popular Austrian red wine. Fruity and full-bodied it has a glowing colour which matures well.

Blauer Portugieser on the other hand, produces a red wine that should be drunk when young – it is velvety and mild with a faint spiciness.

St Laurent, named after St Lorenz because the grape usually starts to ripen around this particular 'saints day', produces a robust wine, deep red in colour. It has a slight, yet delicious, fragrance of raspberries.

Blauer Burgunder gives an elegant red wine, smooth, velvety and rich.

Special dessert wines

The Austrian Auslese, Beerenauslese, Ausbruch, Trockenberenauslese and Eiswein score very highly indeed. These 'special' wines are of truly superior quality, yet are still sold at prices well below those of similar wines from other countries. They have a mellowness about them – like liquid honey spiced with pine and scented with lime blossom – which can be wonderful.

Romania and Bulgaria

Though Romania and Bulgaria have claims to an ancient wine-growing tradition, until recently their wine-making techniques have bordered on the medieval. But a scientific approach and modern production methods have put the wines of these two countries into the forefront in the wine world. Both the red and white wines from these two countries are well worth seeking out.

The wines of Romania and Bulgaria tend to be underestimated because they do not have the hallowed reputations of France, Italy or Germany. In reality, the modern approach Bulgaria and Romania have taken towards wine production has made them the leaders of a revolution taking place in this field. The traditional wine rulers of the world have a tendency to sit on their laurels, benefitting too easily from increased prices for their products resulting from a much greater demand for quality wine around the world. There are many poor French wines, for example, selling in the middle price range purely by virtue of being French. A Bulgarian wine selling in a supermarket for half the price might be much better.

Romanian wine

Romania is situated by the Black Sea, sandwiched between Russia and the Danube. In the centre of the country rise the great Carpathian mountains, with the high Transylvanian plateau. Vineyards are dotted all over the country in pockets – in Carpathian valleys, in Transylvania and on the rolling plains stretching down towards the Danube and the Black Sea. A high proportion are still in private hands, despite a communist government, and are consequently varied, with old methods surviving alongside the new – the latter tending to be promoted on state properties.

Romania has an ancient wine growing tradition, but little reputation in the West. Its wine has historically graced the tables of Eastern Europe and much finds its way to the Soviet Union and East Germany. One light dessert wine, Cotnari, used to be famous world over. Cotnari comes from Moldavia in the north-east, but much of this land was ceded to Russia after the Second World War and the wine is now rarely seen. Although Cotnari is now fairly obscure, the Romanians are waking up to the possibilities of earning foreign exchange from wine exports. Wine production now features more importantly and more varied and better wines are appearing in our shops.

The whites are on the whole better, using some traditional grapes and some, famous from France and Germany, that have been introduced. Romanian whites are well worth trying, especially the Perla from the Tîrnăve region of Transylvania, which you will find labelled *Tarnave*. It is light and slightly sweet, with a hint of the German style, although really quite distinctive – a most pleasant wine for warm summer days and by no means expensive. Other cheaper whites are available, but tend to be sweeter.

A powerful red made from the Merlot grape is on sale from the Dealul Mare region in the Carpathian foothills. This is a hefty, slightly sweet (although that does not mean sugary) wine for drinking with roast meat or spicy casseroles. Again, it has more body and character than its price suggests, and should certainly be tried.

There are also good wines, red and white, from the Murfatlar region near the Black Sea and from Banat in the far west.

Bulgarian wine

Bulgaria, just south of the Danube from Romania, has a very different wine past – and present. Although claims are made of a tradition stretching back thousands of years to the ancient Thracians, 500 years of Muslim law when Bulgaria was dominated by the Turks have had more effect. During this period wine was outlawed and production survived only on a small and local scale. Since the Second World War, however, enormous strides have been made. Bulgaria is now a major wine producer in terms of both volume and quality.

The state monopoly, called Vinimpex, enjoys total domination and has brought the benefits of modern technology to bear in a big way. The vines are cultivated with the maximum mechanization, and viticulture is the subject of a great deal of research. The result is a substantial quantity of good wine to a consistently high standard, selling at astonishingly low prices in the West.

Like Romania, Bulgaria has widely scattered wine areas, although there tends to be a greater concentration in the central and southern plains, and again to the north. The vines are usually grown in flat terrain, facilitating mechanized cultivation.

Of the wines likely to be encountered, Cabernet Sauvignon is best known and often the best in quality. The great Bordeaux grape from which it gets its name seems to do well in Bulgaria, producing mellow wine with considerable body. It should be pointed out, however, that although the general standard is high it is not uniformly excellent. Look out for Cabernet coming from the northern Sukhindol region for a reliable introduction.

Another Bulgarian red, in a more expensive category but more individual with it, is Mavrud. It comes from the south and is darker, heavier and richer than the Cabernet. A currently available example comes from Asenovgrad. It should be drunk in small quantities with a good meal – the Cabernet is for drinking at any time that wine appeals.

Bulgarian whites, although good, are less impressive than the reds. A Pinot Chardonnay from the Shuman area in the north, using the great white Burgundy grape, is a worthy example. It is strong and fruity, but perhaps without the subtleties of the reds. The Misket from Karlovo in the middle of the country is worth a try. It is a lively Muscat and not particularly sweet.

Weighing harvested grapes

Switzerland

Swiss wines are fresh, lightish wines and reliably good. However, outside Switzerland, they are unlikely to be cheap. High production costs, due to the mountainous terrain and unpredictable climate, influence the export price. The Swiss' fondness for good wine also affects the price, in that they understandably keep the best for their own consumption.

A vineyard on the slopes of a Swiss valley

There are five principal wine-growing areas in Switzerland. The biggest and most important are the south-facing slopes of the upper Rhône valley, the area known as the Valais; the shores of Lake Geneva, known as the Vaud; and the environs of Geneva itself. The south-facing shores of Lake Neuchâtel are also under vine; lastly, there are large wine-growing areas in Ticino, in Italian Switzerland.

Rather confusingly, Swiss wines may be labelled in a variety of ways. They may be called after the village or area where they were produced or simply named after the grape variety. Alternatively, they may be given a legally-controlled name that does not relate to either the area or the grape. The profusion of growers and brand names also adds to the confusion. However, the most important wines are easy enough to identify; once you know a little about them, you can buy them with confidence.

Valais and Vaud

By far the largest proportion of the wine produced in the regions of Valais and Vaud is white. Most of it is made from the high-yielding Chasselas grape. The Chasselas is not regarded as a distinguished grape in France but in the Valais and Vaud it takes on a great deal of local character. In the Vaud the wine is known as Dorin, and in the Valais as Fendant, where it tends to have a riper, stronger flavour. Sion is the centre of the Valais region and produces Fendant of the highest quality. Both Dorin and Fendant are light and dry, and should be drunk young.

The red wine grapes of these areas are the Gamay of Beaujolais and the Burgundian Pinot Noir. Dôle is the red wine of Valais, made from either of the grapes or from a mixture of the two, rather like the Passe-tout-Grains of Burgundy. Dôle must reach a certain level of quality and alcoholic strength before it may bear the name. (Wine that does not reach the required level, is sold under the label of Goron.) The red Vaud equivalent is Salvagnin. Again these are light wines, although they tend to be sweeter than the whites. They should not be left lying for too long.

Another name that you may come across is Chablais, which is the area between the Vaud and Valais, where the Rhône leaves Lake Geneva. Look, too, for the name Aigle, the principal town of Chablais. Aigle produces dry white wine with some of the style of both Valais and Vaud. Other names to watch out for are Lavaux, which is the eastern section of the Vaud, and La Côte, the western shore of the lake, between Geneva and Lausanne. The wines from these areas will be pleasant, if lightweight, white Dorin and red Salvagnin.

A name well worth looking out for is Johannisberg. This is the local Valais name for the Sylvaner grape. Here it makes a soft but robust white wine with much more flavour to it than the Chasselas.

The interestingly named Vin du Glacier, a speciality of Switzerland, is sadly no longer made. This was a long-matured white wine, stored at high altitudes until it possessed heroic strength. Its modern equivalent is just an ordinary, branded white wine.

Geneva

The most significant wine-producing area around Geneva is the district of Mandement. This district produces very light reds from the Gamay grape, as well as white Perlan, which is from the Chasselas grape at its palest and least distinguished.

Neuchâtel

To the north, the canton of Neuchâtel produces both red and white wine, as well as a rosé. The rosé is made from the Pinot Noir grape and has the evocative name of Oeil de Perdrix — evocative, at least, to those who have come close enough to the eye of a partridge to recognize the same pink! The Pinot Noir grows well along the sheltered north side of Lake Neuchâtel, and also makes a pale red wine which may be called Cortaillod after the principal village.

Neuchâtel whites from the Chasselas grape sometimes have the distinction of being slightly fizzy because the wine is bottled while still on its yeasty sediment. If the process is taken further, an attractive fully sparkling wine results.

Ticino

To the south, in Italian-speaking Switzerland, the Ticino area has been producing wine for export for only a relatively short time. However, the Merlot, the lesser red wine grape of Bordeaux, grows well here as it does in neighbouring Italy and Yugoslavia. The Swiss Merlots are soft, full, well-rounded wines with more body than most of their national relatives to the west. The better quality reds from the Ticino areas are now called Viti — they must reach at least 12% alcohol and are quite powerful.

England

For many people England seems too far north, too cool and too wet to produce wine. But her northern position does not make wine production impossible, as the existence of 300 commercial producers with almost 430 hectares of land between them under vines shows.

Wine was introduced to England by the Romans who established a small number of vineyards. In the Middle Ages the vine became more widespread, especially at monasteries. The decline of English wine production began in the 12th century, when the English crown came into possession of large parts of south-west France, including Bordeaux, and wine began to appear in quantity across the Channel. The dissolution of the monasteries by Henry VIII finished off large-scale production, although small vineyards continued to be cultivated in the parks of country houses right up to the early 20th century.

After the Second World War, a number of experimental vineyards sprang up, including the famous Hampshire establishment of Hambledon, founded in 1952 by Sir Guy Salisbury-Jones. There was a period of great expansion in the 1970s, powered by a heady enthusiasm which waned with the poor harvests at the end of the decade. The expansion seems to have been haphazard, even reckless, and a number of concerns collapsed or were commercially unsuccessful. Poor sites were chosen and the wrong types of vine were often planted. It has to be said that, whatever the enthusiastic claims of the English wine-producers, the climate does not actively favour grapes.

Great care has to be taken for the vines to have a chance to flourish. With protected, south-facing slopes, the hardier, early-ripening varieties of grapes can do very well. On the right soil these grapes will produce a harvestable crop every year.

At its best English wine is very good and deserves to be tried and appreciated on its own merits, as a distinctive type of wine with its own special qualities. At its worst, it is thin and uninspiring.

The favoured grape type is the Müller-Thurgau, which does well on less than perfect sites in Germany. Other German vines, particularly Reichensteiner, also do well, as do the French Seyval and Madeleine Angevine.

With a few exceptions, English wines are white. The most common style is like light German wine, although English wine is usually less sweet than German. There is often a flowery bouquet and a fresh lively flavour, but rarely much body. The difficulties experienced in producing these wines mean that they are relatively expensive, and the taxman adds a high percentage.

Whatever you buy, choose carefully and make the distinction between English and British wine. The latter is made from imported grape juice and should be avoided. Some English vineyards make the error of marketing British wine as well as their home-grown product. The association can only give English wine a bad name and it negates the whole point of making real English wine in the first place. Another unfortunate practice is the addition of unfermented grape juice to give less successful vintages body and sweetness. This is fine if the additive comes from the same vineyard, but when it is imported from Germany, the wine's Englishness is again called into question. There seems no reason to pay a high price for manufactured wine of this kind. English wines are not widely marketed, as the overall level of production is not great enough for that, nor is it likely to grow substantially. Less productive vineyards will fall by the wayside while those that succeed will grow and consolidate. Treat English wine as an occasional pleasure or experiment – interesting wine for warm summer afternoons and strawberries.

The vineyards are mostly in the south of England, but are widely scattered. Kent, Somerset, Suffolk and Norfolk seem to favour wine-production. One of the most famous sites is Adgestone on the Isle of Wight. Look out for Schönburger from Wootton Vines — the 1981 vintage won the 1982 Gore Browne Trophy for the best English wine. From Kent try wines from prize-winning Lamberhurst Priory. This vineyard produces on average 30,000 bottles a year. Among the grapes they use are Müller-Thurgau and Seyval. Other Kentish wines of particular note are Biddenden Müller-Thurgau and Penshurst, which is a blend of Müller-Thurgau, Seyval and other varieties.

A major Gloucestershire producer is Three Choirs, which produces around 20,000 bottles a year. Müller Thurgau is their major grape, but they also use the Reichensteiner grape. These two grapes are blended, with the addition of Seyval for sharpness, to make the already mentioned Adgestone wine from the Isle of Wight.

Westbury in Berkshire is an exceptionally successful producer with 30,000 bottles on average each year. Try their Reichensteiner and their red wine made from Pinot Noir.

East Anglia has a number of successful vineyards. The main ones are Bruisyard St. Peter in Suffolk and Magdalen in Norfolk. Both rely heavily on Müller-Thurgau. Elmham Park in Norfolk makes an attractive dry white, which is rather German in character.

From Sussex come several wines from the firm of Carr Taylor, including a *méthode champenoise* sparkling white. Finally from Essex comes Felstar and New Hall wines.

Vine-spraying at Wootton Vineyards, Somerset

Greece

The first of European countries to cultivate the vine, Greece has been producing wines for hundred of years. The wines vary considerably in style and include the famous and popular resinated wine, Retsina.

A mellow red wine and a white retsina – Greece's famous resinated wine.

Today a little over half of the vines which are grown in Greece are for wine production; the rest are for the provision of dessert grapes and raisins. The climate is favourable for growing vines – dry sunny heat can be relied upon in summer – but local strong winds occur and the variable nature of the terrain results in microclimates giving strongly contrasting conditions for growth within quite limited areas. Soils are generally rather poor but this is seldom a bar to the production of good wine.

There are of course many local wines produced in Greece which are never tasted outside their immediate areas. Even those which qualify for 'appellation of origin' status, under the laws which now apply throughout EEC wine-producing countries, seldom find their way to other countries – except in the baggage of returning holiday makers! These 'typical' wines are marketed under a regional place name and must be made from approved grape types, by methods traditionally associated with the area. They make up about 12% of the total Greek wine production and often reach a high standard of quality.

The bulk of the wine which Greece produces annually consists of commercial blends from various regions. These are marketed under brand names. Some of these, such as Demestica and Pendeli, are quite well known. But the most familiar of all Greek wines, certainly to those who have travelled to Greece, is Retsina.

Retsina

Hundred of years ago, when wine was stored in jars or amphoras, it was found that the wine kept better if the jars were sealed with a mixture of plaster and resin. We now know that this was because the seals kept the jars airtight, but before it was realized that air was the great enemy of stored wine, the improved quality was attributed to the resin. Hence the tradition of resinated wine. The Greeks have now acquired a taste for it and have given it the name of Retsina.

More Retsinas are consumed than any other native wines. They are entitled to their own *appellation traditionelle*. Today they are made in a similar way to other wines, but during fermentation a small quantity of resin from the native Alep pine is added to the must. This is drawn off with the lees at the first filtering or 'racking'.

The amount of resin added is only 1% of volume, but it results in a distinctive flavour usually, though perhaps unkindly, compared to turpentine. Most Retsina is made from the white Savatiano or red Rhoditis grape. The latter produces a variety of Retsina called Kokkinelli. The real home of Retsina is the region around Athens known as Attica, but wine shops and tavernas throughout the country will have a resinated wine on offer, often made on the premises. The bigger merchant houses all have their own Retsina and large quantities are exported, so commercial examples are not too difficult to find.

Main wine regions

The most important of the Greek wine producing areas, accounting for a third of the total area under vines, is the Peloponnese. Over such a large region there will of course be a great variety of wines, but worth a special mention are the red wine of Nemea, known as 'Blood of Hercules', which is made from the St George or Agiorgitiko grape, and the dry white wine of Mantinea made from the Moschofilero. The region around Patras and the neighbouring Ionian island of Cephalonia are also the sources of famous dessert wines, the white Muscat and the red Mavrodaphne.

The large island of Crete, with its particularly hot climate, produces strong full-flavoured red wines. From the regions of Sitia and Daphnes comes a fine liqueur wine in the tradition of the legendary Malvasia. This was supposed to be made in the palace of Minos from a recipe given to the Cretan King by the Delphic oracle.

The smaller Greek islands have their own distinctive wines, the most widely known outside Greece being the white wines of Samos. The vineyard is extensive and is planted exclusively with the Muscat grape.

The Northern mainland areas of Greece produce a variety of regional wines from native stocks. A fine vigorous red wine is made at Rapsani in Thessaly from three local varieties, the Xynomavro, Krassato and Stavroto. Also famous are the Naoussa and Amynteon vineyards of Macedonia.

In addition to the native grape types, some stocks from other countries are now being used in the north. An excellent red wine called Château Carras is made in the Halkidiki region from Cabernet Sauvignon, Cabernet Franc and Merlot – grapes usually associated with Bordeaux. Vinification is by traditional methods, involving a lengthy spell in oak casks. The 1975 vintage is certainly rival to a good claret. The same growers also produce a very palatable dry white from the Sauvignon Blanc and Ugni Blanc known as Domaine Port Carras, Côte de Meliton. In Epirus, a robust scented red wine is made at Metsovo from the Cabernet Sauvignon, introduced to the area after native stocks were destroyed by phylloxera.

The next few years should see a growth market for improving Greek table wines.

East and South Mediterranean

Wine has been made and drunk in the hot climates of Cyprus, the Middle East and North Africa since the earliest times. There is a strong tradition of wine-making therefore, but much of what is produced is consumed locally.

Cyprus

Cyprus is best known for its successful 'sherry', but the island also produces table wines of all types. The ones you are most likely to come across will be the products of big modern wine firms like KEO and SODAP which have made admirable advances in the production of reliable, everyday reds and whites. Among the the reds, Othello and Afames are the best-known names, rather in the same way as the Demestica of Greece. They are not intricate wines, but they have plenty of fruit and staying power.

Domaine d'Ahera is another pleasant, fruity red wine. Arsinoe is a dry white wine, while Aphrodite is fuller and sweetish. There is a white with a slight sparkle also available under the name of Bellapais.

Perhaps the best-known Cypriot wine is Commandaria. It certainly has the longest history – legend has it that it was enjoyed by the Crusaders. It is made on the southern slopes of the Troodos mountains and, when traditional methods are followed, it is intensely sweet, pungent and concentrated. It is probably quite close in taste to the ordinary wine of ancient Greece and Rome. The modern winery product sold under the same name is a sweet dessert wine.

Turkey

Turkey grows vast amounts of grapes but only a small percentage of them are made into wine – the rest are eaten. The wine in Turkey is produced by a state-controlled monopoly and very little of it is currently exported. What is available is usually well made if not particularly exciting. Buzbag is one red wine of fairly good quality.

Lebanon

The wine makers of Lebanon are doing a very worthwhile job against the climatic odds. Quality is generally good and prices are low, considering the technical expertise involved in production here. Red wines are best, but there are some good dry whites.

Look out especially for a newly fashionable wine called Château Musar. It is not the cheapest of the Lebanese wines but both reds and whites are carefully made from traditional French grape varieties. Château Musar improves with keeping, and the mature red has been called a fascinating cross between a Burgundy and a claret.

Israel

Israel produces table wines of all colours, fruity reds and sweet whites in particular. Small quantities of wine are made from traditional grape varieties and are exported under brand names – Carmel is a reliable one. There is also a huge market within Israel for kosher wine.

North Africa

Tunisia, Algeria and Morocco are the most important wine countries of North Africa.

Algeria, the biggest producer, was once the source of huge volumes of the most basic wine, high in alcohol, which was shipped off to France for blending. Much of it was used to bring thin *vin ordinaire* up to 11%, and as such it had a useful role to play. However, changes in French wine law meant that this was no longer possible. Algerian growers were left with a huge surplus that was useless for the home market because wine is forbidden for Moslems. Other markets were found, notably the USSR, but another solution was to move the focus of wine growing from the mass production of the flat coastal plain to the less productive but higher quality slopes of the inland hills. Much better wines are now produced here, notably reds with a satisfying richness.

Algerian wine is cheap and it has to compete hard at the bottom end of the market with similar wines from France's Midi. But it is no longer invariably plonk.

Tunisia produces some drinkable reds and some pleasant sweet whites made from the ubiquitous muscat grape. Morocco is the newest producer of the three, and her wines are generally of higher quality. Holidaymakers there often enjoy the dry light rosé and meaty reds, and knowledgeably search them out on their return home. Among the reds, Sidi Larbi and Dar Bel Amri are good and are well distributed.

Berber women tending vines in Tunisia

America

With the exception of Australia, the United States – and California in particular – is the most exciting modern wine region in the world. Not only is there a great quantity and variety of good, drinkable wine, but the quality is improving all the time.

Wine growers and chemists from the older wine-producing countries of the world make constant studies of American vineyards, where some of the most far-reaching experiments in grape-growing and wine chemistry are taking place.

The extraordinary variations in soil and climate, and the incidence of so many micro-climates, combine to make wine-growing in America both a fascinating and commercially rewarding business.

Although wine is made in 29 of the American states, California is by far the largest producer. New York State's wines, which are rated as a poor second, are made 'upstate' around the Finger Lakes. These wines are made from American grape varieties or American/European hybrids. Most of them have the typical foxiness of the *labrusca* Concord grape, indigenous to America. It is a difficult taste to acquire for those brought up on European wine styles. Vineyards in other states, such as Oregon, are often small, but make good-quality wine. Oregon wines are thought to be closer in style to European wines.

California

Already one of the areas in California, the Napa Valley, is spoken of as a classic wine-producing area. This might seem odd when its relatively short history is taken into consideration. Vines were first planted in California by a Franciscan, Father Juniper Serra, at San Diego in 1796, using a Spanish grape, known as the Mission grape. This was used for sacramental wine and never intended for large-scale wine production.

Jean Louis Vignes, the son of a Bordeaux wine family, fared better with the vineyard he planted in 1831, in what is now the centre of Los Angeles. The real beginning of vine growing in California was in 1849 with the coming of the gold rush.

One of the 'forty-niners' was a Hungarian nobleman, Agaston Haraszthy. Dissatisfied with the wine from his planting of Mission grapes, he set off for Europe to buy vines. Five months later he returned to Buena Vista Estate in Sonoma, with 100,000 cuttings of some 300 varieties.

Many were sold to growers in lots of 10 and 20, but often bearing identity labels from which the names had vanished. Many of these imported vines brought with them the pest phylloxera and by 1861 Californian vineyards were all but decimated. Phylloxera was finally dealt with by the grafting of the *vinifera* vines onto the native American *labrusca* root stock, which is disease resistant.

No sooner was the wine industry under reconstruction when, from 1922-1936, Prohibition took its toll. When Prohibition was repealed there followed a period when great strides in technology and research took place, and the wine industry in America came into its own. In California many felt that after phylloxera and Prohibition, they were starting from scratch.

The most popular red wine is the Cabernet Sauvignon, made from the famous Bordeaux grape. It is usually fuller and lacks the subtlety of a good Bordeaux. Both the Cabernet Sauvignon and another famous European grape, Pinot Noir, in California have less acidity and more alcohol than their European counterparts.

The native grape, Zinfandel, found hardly anywhere else in the world, produces a dry red wine with a flavour all its own. The Gamay grape produces an attractive red wine, which is similar in style to Beaujolais.

Amongst the white wines, Californian Chardonnay is often delicious. Equally good results have been achieved with the Sauvignon grape, the wine of which is sometimes called Fumé Blanc. Johannisberg Riesling, which is the name given to the Rhine Riesling, also produces a good white wine – the late-harvest Riesling makes a very sweet, luscious wine. Light fruity wines from the Chenin Blanc and Semillon are generally well made and a number of the Gewürztraminers have matched those in Alsace.

Californians drink far more white than red because of the warm climate. This has led to the produce of a white wine, known as Blanc de Noir, which is made from black grapes without their skins.

American wines are rewarding to explore, so a good understanding of the labelling system and a greater knowledge of the main wine regions is worthwhile.

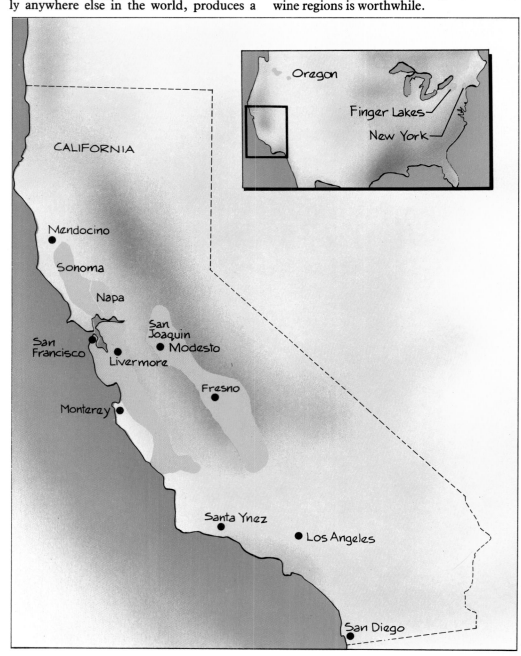

American wine labels

If you are planning to try American wines you will have to make a clear distinction between generic wines – those borrowing European wine names – and varietals – those named after individual grape varieties.

In the U.S. wine labelling is controlled by Federal law. State regulations about content and the words used to describe the wines have to be considered. Generally state regulations do not add anything to the label, except in California and Oregon, where they are stricter than Federal laws.

Generic labels

A generic or proprietary wine may be made from virtually any grape variety and is of little value to the serious wine buyer. Seventeen of these names are permitted on U.S. labels including: claret, chablis, champagne, chianti, moselle, port, rhine wine, hock, sauterne and tokay. These names offer no more than the roughest guide to the wine's characteristics, which are interpreted as the grower sees fit. Worse still, a winery may label the same wine burgundy or claret, depending on which names appeal.

Generic wines are usually cheap, mass-produced blends, or jug wines, but usually quite drinkable. It is merely the slapdash labelling which is at fault. Oregon is an exception here – no generic names are allowed on wines from this state.

Varietal labels

California more than any other wine-producing area has concentrated on the individual varieties of wine. The names of Cabernet, Pinot, Sémillon, Chardonnay and Sauvignon are strictly covered by wine laws and cannot be misused.

A varietal wine must contain 75% of that grape in the wine. Varietals are sometimes referred to as premium wines, which is the buyer's first indication of quality.

Vintage dating

If a wine is vintage-dated, 95% of it must be from the year stated on the label, though Californian State regulations insist on 100%. If there is no vintage date, the wine has been blended from several years' vintages. Some wineries give a bottling date rather than a vintage date; some add the harvest date.

The producer

In the U.S. there are no shippers as such, so the producer's name is all-important. As it is usually very prominent on the label it cannot be missed. Large wineries are allowed to market under different trademarks, but they can no longer use geographical names as brand names unless certain requirements are met.

Geographical names

The use of geographical names is tightly controlled. Wines may obtain a regional designation if at least 75% of the volume of the wine is derived from the district claimed, 85% if the district is a recognized viticultural area. California goes further still, insisting that wine claimed to be Californian, must be from 100% Californian grapes. There are regional designations on some labels. 'North Coast Counties' on a bottle of Californian wine refers to the counties of Napa, Sonoma and Mendocino. Specific vineyards are on some labels.

Bottling information

The name of the company that bottled the wine and its address must appear on the label. 'Grown, produced and bottled by' means exactly that, but 'cellared', 'blended' and 'bottled by' indicate the wine was bought, aged or bottled by a firm other than the grower.

If the wine is estate bottled it must have come entirely from grapes 'owned and controlled' by the producing winery and 'in the vicinity' of the winery. The control requirement may be met by long-term leases or contracts with independent growers.

Alcoholic content

If labelled table wine or light wine, the alcohol content will average 8–14%. Dessert wines are normally over 14% with most in the 18–20% category.

Sparkling wines produced in the U.S. and marketed under the generic name of champagne always carry a qualifying adjective, such as New York State Champagne. Those who make their sparkling wine according to the *méthode champenoise* label the product 'fermented in this bottle' rather than 'fermented in the bottle'; the latter means the wine left the bottle for disgorging and was then re-bottled.

The equivalent of *Spätlese* and *auslese* white wines is Late Harvest and Selected Late Harvest. The percentage of sugar in the grapes at harvest and the residual sugar in the finished wine must both be included on the label.

Back labels

The American passion for detail spurred the winemakers into putting back labels on bottles. Full descriptions cover the grower, the area, the vintage and the food that best accompanies the wine. Sometimes a small map of the area is added.

A selection of American wine labels

Napa Valley – South

The Napa Valley is the most famous wine-producing area of the United States. It lies north and slightly east of San Francisco Bay and is blessed by both its climate and excellent soil conditions.

Some of the Napa Valley vineyards cluster along the flat valley floor while others climb the hillsides and extend into the mountains. Those tucked into hollows often enjoy their own favourable micro-climates. The soils of the Napa Valley are mostly volcanic and well-drained, although rain is unusual during the growing season.

Many new vines have been planted during the last twenty years and and not all of them are mature yet, but fine red and white wines are available from established stocks. In California, the location of the vineyard is not so significant as the variety of grape used, which will indicate the typical style of the wine, and the name of the producer, which is usually the buyer's best guarantee of quality.

Robert Mondavi

The most famous producer in the South of the Napa Valley is Robert Mondavi. He is elder son of Cesare Mondavi, an Italian immigrant who after twenty years as a

A selection of white and red wines from Christian Brothers and Robert Mondavi

wholesaler of table grapes purchased the Charles Krug winery in 1943. Robert worked as his general manager, introducing a number of classic grape varieties and sophisticated production techniques, before leaving to start his own winery at Oakville in 1967. He was one of the first to use cool fermentation in stainless steel vats and ages his red wines – and some whites – in small oak barrels in the French style. He made his reputation with a Fumé Blanc, a dry white Sauvignon wine in the style of the French Sancerre and Pouilly Fumé, and has since made excellent Chardonnay, Cabernet Sauvignon and Pinot Noir; his Pinot Noir Reserve is an outstanding example of a wine which is rarely successful outside its native Burgundy.

In 1980 he purchased and modernised a winery at Woodbridge in the hot central valley of California where he makes large quantities of jug wines for everday drinking, but his premium wines are all from the Napa.

He recently went into collaboration with Baron Philippe de Rothschild, of Chateau Mouton – Rothschild in Bordeaux, and the result of this joint venture is a remarkable and very expensive red wine, mainly Cabernet Sauvignon, called Opus One. This is the top of the Mondavi range, but it is safe to say that any wine with his name on the label will be scrupulously made and a good example of its type.

Other producers

The Rothschilds are not the only European wine dynasty to take an interest in California; not far from Oakville is the Domaine Chandon, financed by the famous French champagne house Moet et Chandon. Though not permitted to call their product champagne, they make fine sparkling wines in the traditional style from classic Pinot Noir, Pinot Blanc and Chardonnay grapes.

Other small but reputable producers in the South are Stag's Leap, Trefethen and Mayacamas. Stag's Leap made their name with Petite Syrah and Chenin Blanc, but have gone on to make excellent Chardonnay and Cabernet.

Trefethen produce very good Chardonnay, Cabernet and Pinot Noir, and also make superior non-varietal red and white wines which are sold under the brand name Eshcol.

Mayacamas, in the mountains to the west of the Valley, are again famous for Cabernet and Chardonnay, which seem to flourish particularly well in the cooler climate; the wines are deep and long-lasting. Mayacamas also make a powerful late-harvest red from the Zinfandel grape.

Napa Valley – North

The Napa Valley, part of the young wine country of California, produces some of the best American wine. It is worth getting to know the different styles of the wineries in this area of rugged individualists.

Most of the Napa Valley wineries are concentrated at the Northern end of the valley. The climate is very warm and dry, much more so than in the classic European wine-growing areas, and this affects the character of the wines which are fruitier, less acidic and higher in alcohol than their European counterparts. Some might also say less subtle, though this is in part due to the habit of producing straight varietals, with less blending than is usual elsewhere; Cabernet Sauvignon, for example, unless softened with Merlot, Cabernet Franc or Malbec as is done in Bordeaux, will be almost overpowering on the nose and palate. But the large number of small producers, all competing with one another in true American style to produce the best, ensures a wider variety of flavours than you might imagine and encourages constant experimentation and development.

Long-established Wineries

In the face of all this competition, the traditional Napa wineries have been unable to sit still and rely on past achievement. The Charles Krug winery, founded in 1861, was revolutionised after its takeover by the Mondavi family; still run by Robert's

Schramsberg vineyard in the Napa Valley

brother Peter, it retains a high reputation for its red wines, especially the Vintage Selection Cabernets, which are sold under a distinctive label bearing the signature of the late Cesare Mondavi. They are among the best produced anywhere but they should be laid down for a few years to enjoy them at their best.

Beringer is another long-established name, dating back to 1879, but the premises were much in need of modernisation when taken over by Nestlé in 1971. Since then it has put its Cabernets and Chardonnays back on the wine map and has also acquired a reputation for late-harvest Johannisberg Rieslings in the German style.

The fortunes of Freemark Abbey, founded in the 1880's, were also restored by an outstanding Johannisberg Riesling in 1973. Called Edelwein, it was a rich, full flavoured wine very like a Rhine Beerenauslese, and made the name of its creator, Jerry Luper, who has since moved on to the small but very prestigious Chateau Montelena. Though in existence since 1881, Chateau Montelena was also in decline until purchased by wealthy new proprietors in 1972;

their Chardonnay subsequently won a competition against the best French White burgundies at a blind tasting in Paris, and they also make particularly good Cabernet, though all their wines are expensive.

Another traditional producer of sound red and white wines is Christian Brothers; originally members of a religious teaching order dating back to the 17th century, they progressed from altar wine to commercial production in the 1930's and are particularly well known for a sweet white Muscat called Chateau la Salle.

Another great favourite in this style is the delicate, slightly sparkling Moscato Amabile of Louis M. Martini, a firm otherwise noteworthy for its range of reliable and reasonably priced reds.

Beaulieu Vineyard is famous for its Private Reserve Cabernets, which have been among the most consistent in Napa; This is largely thanks to the skills of Andre Tchelistcheff, known as 'The Dean of California Winemakers', who was at Beaulieu for 35 years until leaving to set up his own consultancy in 1973.

Newer producers

A number of the most successful Napa Valley producers have started from scratch within the last twenty five years. Joe Heitz is an example. A graduate of the University of California at Davis, he was briefly Tchelistcheff's assistant at Beaulieu before teaching oenology at Fresno State College. In the 1960's, with very limited capital but a good deal of technical know-how, he bought a tiny vineyard and began making his own wine.

In the early years he purchased grapes from other growers, notably Chardonnay from the Hanzell vineyards in Sonoma County, and he is still a producer rather than a grower, but his wines are excellent. In addition to the Chardonnay, look out for his Martha's Vineyard Cabernet.

A neighbour of Heitz is Joseph Phelphs, who came from bridge-building to winemaking in the 1970's. His is one of the most modern and experimental of all wineries and in addition to having great success with the richer white wines such as Gewürztraminer and late-harvest Johannisberg Riesling, he markets a fine blended red, made from Cabernet Sauvignon, Cabernet Franc and Merlot, under the brand name Insignia.

Two other Napa names to remember are Stony Hill and Schramsberg. Stony Hill specialises in white wines and has a reputation for producing the finest of all the region's Chardonnays. The mountain location, with its appropriately stony soil, gives the wine great resonance and potential for ageing. The vineyard also produces good well-balanced Gewürztraminer which is halfway between the austere and the fruity, with a fine, crisp flavour. A dry, distinctive white Riesling is also produced, clean and refreshing to the taste.

Schramsberg is equally distinguished for its sparkling wines, made by the traditional Champagne method; the two main styles are Blanc de Pinot, made principally from Pinot Noir grapes, and Blanc de Blancs based on Chardonnay.

Sonoma and Mendocino

Sonoma county, north of San Francisco, is where winemaking began in northern California; it is now recognised as one of the three top wine-producing areas.

Sonoma is second only to the Napa Valley in terms of the amount of wine produced. Most of the vineyards are to be found in the three principal valleys, Alexander, Sonoma and Dry Creek.

The old-established Sonoma wineries, like others in California, have had a chequered history. No sooner had they recovered from the depredations of phylloxera at the end of the last century than Prohibition put a stop to production. Most were forced to close down or – if they owned their own land – to turn it over to table grapes or some other crop until the notorious Eighteenth Amendment was repealed. Even then there was a long wait until the wine boom of the 1960's brought their product back into favour.

Sonoma's first vineyard and winery was Buena Vista, founded by the father of Californian viticulture, Agaston Haraszthy, in 1857. After fluctuating fortunes, including a period of closure, it is now under German ownership and enjoying a real renaissance. Their white wines are particularly noteworthy and include a unique blend of Riesling and Gewürztraminer called Spiceling.

One company which has maintained continuous production since its foundation in 1904 is Sebastiani; it survived the prohibition by making sacramental wine. Now under the control of the founder's grandson, Sebastiani are best known for big gutsy reds like Barbara and Zinfandel.

Another winery famous for strong Zinfandel is J. Pedroncelli. Originally producers of generic jug wines, they have recently concentrated on varietals with the emphasis on the more robust reds, which are given plenty of wood ageing.

Some producers offer a wide range of varietal wines from small individual plots; the variety of soils and microclimates in the area make this possible, and the approach is encouraged by the general mood of experiment in Californian winemaking. The company called simply Sonoma Vineyards is one of the largest – owning 1200 acres – and offers an excellent selection of these single vineyard wines; outstanding are their Chalk Hill Chardonnay and Alexander's Crown Cabernet Sauvignon. The French Champagne house Piper Heidsieck has recently taken an interest in the property and is part-financing the production of sparkling wines under the label Piper-Sonoma.

Chateau St. Jean is another winery specialising in single vineyards wines, with the emphasis on whites. They have been remarkably successful with rich late-harvest wines in the German style, made from Johannisberg Riesling and Gewürztraminer. They are also making sparkling wines.

Another highly individual company is Hanzell. It was started in 1952 by James Zellerbach, a former U.S. ambassador to Italy, who was passionately fond of Burgundy; he planted 19 acres with the classic Burgundy grapes, Pinot Noir and Chardonnay, waiting until the vines were mature before constructing an ultra-modern winery. The wines were superb, but after his death in 1963 winemaking temporarily ceased and the grapes were sold off to other producers. Production is now under way again and the new owner, being an enthusiast for Bordeaux wines, has added a few acres of Cabernet Sauvignon.

Three other names worth remembering in Sonoma are Korbel, famous for sparkling wines, Dry Creek, who make excellent Chardonnay, Fume Blanc and Chenin Blanc in a clean style, and Jordan Winery, who concentrate on Chardonnay and Cabernet.

Mendocino County

In the neighbouring county of Mendocino, winemaking is only a recent event. The oldest and best-known winery is Parducci, and they are very experimental in their approach. John Parducci has controversial ideas about maturing wine, believing that the use of wood masks the distinctive varietal flavours, and preferring stainless steel, even for his reds. These ideas have not been fully tested yet, but most people seem to prefer his whites, especially the Chardonnay, Chenin Blanc and French Colombard.

Fetzer offer three good jug wines and a limited range of varietals; they have gained particular recognition for their Zinfandel, which combines a full blackberry flavour with depth from wood ageing. Cresta Blanca have a reliable selection of table wines at reasonable prices.

Wooden barrels in the Sebastiani cellars

Central Coast

Change and growth are the watchwords in the Central Coast wine-producing region. The growers are improving their technical knowledge and at the same time the quality of the wine, making this one of the most exciting new wine regions in the United States.

For the past twenty years sales of table wines in California have increased at a rate of between 10 and 25% annually, and the number of wineries has more than doubled.

Demand has been for quality as well as quantity, and the Californian wine industry is now the most technologically advanced in the world. At the same time, California has seen great population growth, with cities such as San Francisco sprawling outwards into what was once agricultural land, so there is a constant search for new vineyard territory, much of which has been concentrated on the Central Coast region.

Livermore Valley
Some of the oldest established wine producers are to be found in the Livermore Valley.

At Concannon, founded in 1883, there is a long tradition of altar wine – but they also produce a good range of varietal table wines. Their red Petite Syrah and white Sauvignon have won particular attention.

Just across the road from Concannon is Wente Brothers, founded in the same year by a German immigrant who learned his winemaking from Charles Krug in the Napa Valley. Wente were producing good white varietals long before it became the fashion. Their soft and fruity Grey Riesling has always been a great favourite, and so now are Pinot Blanc, Sauvignon and Chardonnay, made in a light and restrained style with little wood ageing. There is also a fine sweet Semillon with the character of French Sauternes.

Another well-known Livermore Valley operation is Weibel Champagne Vineyards which, under the direction of the Swiss Rudolf Weibel, produces a wide selection of sparkling wines, some with remarkable names such as Sparkling Green Hungarian, Crackling Rosé and Crackling Duck.

Santa Cruz Mountains
In the nearby Santa Cruz mountains is the Ridge Vineyards Company which, during its twenty year existence, has made a great reputation for itself with big, rich reds, mainly Zinfandel and Cabernet Sauvignon. Their grapes come from a wide area, but the house style is distinctive, as is their tradition of precise labelling. On their bottles you will find the exact percentage of each grape variety, as well as the vineyard name, alcohol content and date of bottling.

Santa Clara County
The headquarters of Central Coast wine production has always been Santa Clara County. Almaden, Masson and Mirassou, three of the largest and most famous Californian companies, all have their roots here, though all have been forced to expand outside the area.

Almaden owns 4500 acres of vineyards, but few remain on the original site, which is now hemmed in by San Francisco suburbs. Although they have a range of high quality varietals sold under the name of their founder, Charles le Franc, Almaden are best known for sound and reasonably priced jug wines. They are also credited with the introduction to California of the 5 gallon bag-in-a-box dispenser.

Monterey
Both Masson and Mirassou have established vineyards in neighbouring Monterey. The expansion in this county has been astonishing, from 35 acres under vines in the 1960's to 35,000 today.

Of these, 5000 are owned by Paul Masson; their best wines come from the Pinnacles region and are marketed as varietals with the additional description Pinnacles Estate. But the company is more familiar to wine drinkers as the maker of good commercial blends, especially the California Carafes. Mirassou, the oldest wine-making family in the United States, operate on a similar basis. The oldest and most distinguished winery in Monterey is the much smaller Chalone Vineyard. Occupying 125 acres of a limestone ridge, with soils similar to Burgundy, they are said to produce California's finest Chardonnays, as well as excellent Pinot Blanc and Pinot Noir; some of their wines are sold under the secondary label Chapparal.

Other regions
The area around San Luis Obispo, an old mission town, includes scattered vineyards towards the hills of Paso Rables. It is early days yet, but some of the first results are promising. The Firestone Vineyards, near Santa Barbara, are fast building a reputation for themselves.

Paul Masson Winery in Monterey

South America

Although Chilean wines are considered to be the best wines of South America, wine is produced in the neighbouring countries of Argentina, Uruguay and Brazil, where wine-making is a growth industry.

Vines were first introduced to most South American countries in the 16th century by the Spanish. The industry was given a boost in the 19th century by the arrival of European immigrants with new varieties of vines and up-to-date techniques. Also the arrival of the railway systems gave access to wider markets.

Argentina

Vines do best in the Andean foothills, some 1000 kilometres from Buenos Aires in the provinces of Mendoza and San Juan. Both provinces have Mediterranean climates with dry clear air, prolonged sunshine and a low rainfall. Irrigation is necessary but the Andean rivers prove a good water supply, which is supplemented by water from wells.

In Mendoza, red and rosé wines are made from a variety of grapes. San Juan, which has a hotter climate, concentrates more on white wines with high sugar content and low acidity. These wines form the base for vermouths, sherries and brandies. Up to half of the crop is set aside for the production of raisins. In both provinces some wines are made from the classic French white wine grapes and from the Rhine Riesling. Sparkling wines are made by both méthode champenoise and cuvé clos. Vines are also cultivated in the neighbouring provinces of Neuguen and Rio Negro to the south and La Rioja, Catamarca, Salta and Jujuy to the north, but to a lesser degree.

In the 1980s Argentina is the largest producer of wine in the southern hemisphere and fifth in the world. Wine drinking is very much a part of everyday life in Argentina – around 75 litres per head of population are drunk every year. The wine industry has concentrated on producing blended table wines of good quality to meet the demands of this substantial home market. Exports are made to Russia, the United Kingdom and the United States, as well as to other South American countries. Look out for Franchette and Parral.

Fine wines from classic individual growths are also appearing abroad. Cabernet Sauvignon and Chardonnay from the Andean Range of Bodegas Penaflor are two examples. Look out for the ten-year old Chäteau Montchenot from Bodegas Lopez; the Cabernet and Pinot Blanc from José Orfila; the Pinot Blanc 'Oro del Rhin' from Greco Hermanos and Cabernet Sauvignon 'Eminencia' from Bodegas Gargantini. They are good quality wines and are relatively inexpensive.

Brazil

The province of Rio Grande do Sul in the far south of Brazil has become the centre of wine-production in this country. In the early plantings European varieties were tried but were not as successful as an American grape, the Isabella, which accounted for 90% of production. However in the 1980s many leading wine companies are re-introducing the classic European vines, mainly on an experimental basis.

There is no reason why Brazil should not assume more and more importance as a wine producer in the future as it has an enormous, largely untapped home market. Wine consumption is a mere 2½ litres per head of population annually, and international companies like Moët and Chandon and Martini and Rossi are investing here.

Moët, together with Cinzano and the Brazilian Monteiro Aranho Group, have set up the Brazilian company, Provifin, and are now producing 30,000 cases of 'champagne' and 80,000 cases of table wine annually. Martini and Rossi produce a 'Champagne de Greville', an Italian-style spumante and a range of table wines, Baron de Lantier.

Although the emphasis is mainly on good blended wines for domestic consumption, some quality Brazilian wines are finding their way abroad. One of these, the Granja União Cabernet of Rio Grandense, beat Chilean and Argentinian wines at a blind tasting in New York.

Other producers

Uruguay also possesses a flourishing wine industry, mainly around Montevideo, but no wine is exported. The equatorial climate of the rest of South America is not suited to vine cultivation. However it does occur on a small scale in Paraguay, Peru and Venezuela; production in these countries is not sufficient to satisfy home demand, and is therefore not exported.

Vines in the Argentine province of Mendoza

Chile

The wines of Chile are not very well known outside South America, but the country is among the world's major wine producers and has a history of wine-making stretching back over 400 years.

Vines were introduced to Chile by the Spanish conquerors in the 16th century, and cultivation was encouraged by the Catholic Church, initially to produce wine for the Mass. The vines flourished so well that the main problem was soon over-production.

Easy access to the coast meant that Chilean wines were being exported to other parts of South America over 200 years ago, and more and more emphasis is now being placed on the export of wine overseas.

The climate of Chile varies enormously from one region to another. In the north, there is arid desert where it sometimes does not rain for years, while in the south, there are heavy rains and violent gales. Lowland areas are restricted because Chile is hemmed in between the Andes Mountains to the east and the Pacific Ocean to the west. This may sound an unpromising location for the growing of grapes, but there is a small area in the centre of the country, around Santiago, where conditions are almost ideal.

In Chile's colonial days, most wine was made from a grape called the *pais*, which is similar to the *criolla* of the Argentine and the Mission of California. Some sweet dessert wines and fortified wines were also made from the *moscatel*. However, in the middle of the 19th century, at the instigation of Silvestre Ochagavia – the father of Chilean viticulture – a whole new range of classic European vines was introduced, and European wine experts were contracted to supply up-to-date knowledge. This was shortly before the phylloxera plague which devastated European vineyards in the late 1800s and which has attacked European vines in other parts of the world. So far, Chile has remained immune and would appear to have the only vines in existence still grown from ungrafted stocks.

Modern wine-making

The modern Chilean wine industry is based upon these classic grape types and many wines are named after them, like Riesling, Chardonnay, Sauvignon, and so on. The reds made from the Cabernet Sauvignon grape are particularly outstanding. This is the classic Bordeaux grape and Chilean cabernets have won prizes at blind tastings when set against venerable clarets selling at several times the price.

Although there are over 30,000 vineyards in Chile, most of the production is in the hands of a few major bodegas – literally meaning cellars – but now used to mean wine merchants or houses. Wine labels will carry their names rather than the name of a particular vineyard or district. Some of them are now becoming more familiar in Europe as their wines have retail outlets in certain of the main wine shops.

The biggest wine company, Concha y Toro, has more than 1,000 hectares of vines in the favoured Maipo valley. The climate here is more reliable than in most European vineyards and the standard of the wine is therefore less variable from vintage to vintage. Their 1976 Santa Emiliane red (Cabernet Sauvignon) won a double gold award at the 1980 International Wine and Spirits Competition. Other Cabernet Sauvignon wines from Concha y Toro include Casillera del Diablo and Marques de Casa Concha, Gran Vino (gran vino being the general designation for a wine six years old or more). All these wines are matured in oak for at least 2 years and, like all good Cabernets, needs several more years in bottle before they reach their best. Concha y Toro also produce a lighter red Reservado made from a blend of Cabernet Sauvignon and Merlot, and a medium-dry white Reservado made entirely from Riesling. Other major bodegas include Cousino Macul near Santiago, which markets reds under the names Don Luis and Don Matias; Undurrago, which has a variety of old-style and modern white wines; San Pedro at Lontue in Talca district and José Canega at Valparaiso, which handle wines from many areas.

An important new addition to Chile's producers in Miguel Torres, who has opened a winery in the Maule valley, Talca district. As in Spain, he has introduced a range of fresh-tasting, modern-style white wines (such as Santa Digna Sauvignon), probably the best currently available. He has also produced distinguished reds.

In addition to table wines, Chile continues to produce some fortified wines made mainly from the muscat grape, and a native brandy called *pisco*. By law, this can only be made from grapes grown in a limited area of the north where there is a hot, semi-desert like climate: the resulting wine is high in alcohol and low in acidity. Although 20 million litres of pisco is produced annually, almost all of it is consumed at home.

All in all, however, the present almost unique combination of high quality and low price seems unlikely to last for long, and wine drinkers would be well advised to search out and sample Chilean wines while conditions are so much in their favour.

A selection of Chilean red wines

Australia

Australian wine-making is as old as her European settlement. Today Australia makes both red and white high-quality wines, as well as some rich dessert wines, fortified wines and brandies.

Australia is a vast continent, but large areas of it are quite unsuitable for vine cultivation. The best vineyards lie between the 34th and 38th parallels of latitude, in the states of New South Wales, Victoria, South Australia and Western Australia.

These areas are roughly the same distance from the Equator as North Africa in the Northern hemisphere, and the climate is much hotter and drier than in most European vineyards. Because of this, Australia's early wines were stronger, alcoholic, full of sugar, lacking acidity and quick to mature. Much of the country's produce went for distilling or for making rich dessert and fortified wines. Australia's restricted licensing laws encouraged the drinking of these strong wines, sherries and ports.

Australia's wine revolution

Today the situation is quite different. Production of table wines has grown more than tenfold in the last 25 years and now accounts for over three quarters of the total; many of these are of the higher quality. How has this happened? The trigger was the new mobility brought about by air travel. Australians found it easier to get to other parts of the world, and especially Europe, where they discovered other styles of wine. At the same time, Europeans were emigrating to Australia, where many of them set themselves up in the catering or wine trades, and some introduced new or improved vine stocks.

The new interest in wine was encouraged by informed wine journalism and the promotional efforts of the Australian Wine Board. In the industry itself, new techniques of wine-making such as temperature-controlled fermentation in stainless steel vats, the use of small oak barrels for maturing, and vacuum bottling to minimise the risk of oxidation, have all greatly improved the quality of the product. The money from increased sales has made these methods widespread and has also led to extensive irrigation schemes, which in turn have increased the acreage under vines. And so the bandwagon keeps on rolling.

The style of wine

What are these new Australian wines like? Well, no amount of sophisticated equipment can alter their basic character, and both reds and whites are still bigger, fruitier and more alcoholic than European wines made from the same grapes.

They are made from five main varieties, Cabernet Sauvignon and Shiraz for red, Semillion (also called Hunter Riesling), Rhine Riesling and Chardonnay for white. Other strains are increasingly used to modify their varietal character – Pinot Noir, Merlot and Malbec for red, Sauvignon, Chenin Blanc and Colombard for white.

The whites do best in cooler summers, or in high-altitude locations, and, with the exception of some Semillons and special late-harvest sweet wines, should be drunk within two or three years of the vintage. The reds mature sooner than they would in Europe and are full of fruity flavour even when young, but they still benefit from ageing, the best for ten years or more.

Labelling

Along with the new wines has come a new system of labelling. Traditionally, Australian wines were called by generic names such as claret, burgundy, hock and chablis, which could mean widely different things to different producers. Sometimes they were even less specific and called for local knowledge – what would a European make of Yarra Yarra or Mudgee Mud? Now that the business is being taken more seriously, and the wines exported to countries with strict legislation, changes have had to be made.

As in California, wines are now usually identified by the grape type. A single varietal, for example Chardonnay, must contain at least 80% of wine from that grape; if more than one variety is named, for example Cabernet Shiraz, the first must be dominant.

Except in two small areas, Mudgee and Margaret River, there is no geographical system of quality control similar to the French Appellation Contrôlée; indeed, grapes are still often carried long distances, sometimes across state boundaries, for blending by producers. In these circumstances, the reputation of producers is important and it is useful to know their names; these will feature later when we come to look in more detail at the main red and white wines.

If a region of origin is named on the label, 80% of the wine in the bottle must come from that region. Vintages will be shown, but where the climate is so reliable, and wines from different areas so frequently blended, they are not very significant, except to let you know simply how young or old the wine is.

Finally, many Australian bottles also have a back label; this may do no more than tell you the last time the Prince of Wales came to dinner, but it can be a source of more relevant information about grapes, vineyards or producer, fermenting periods, soil and serving temperature. Statistics like bin numbers and prizes in shows are also there, not merely to impress. Bin numbers should be noted for future orders and/or comparison; as for the accolades, with new-world wine production becoming as competitive as it is, makers – and Australian buyers – take them very seriously.

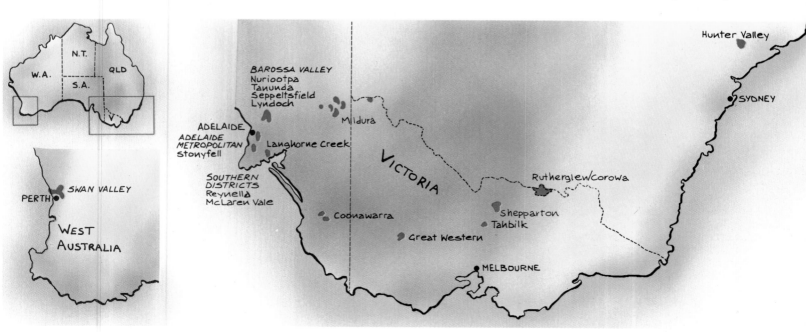

Red wines of Australia

Australian red wines have come a long way since the days of 'bloody kangaroo' and 'sweaty saddle'; Australians now produce many fine red wines which are exported all over the world.

Most Australian red wines come from two French classic varieties, but because of the different climate and soils, the wines made from them will not taste the same as they do in France. Their names are Cabernet Sauvignon and Shiraz.

Australian Cabernets are different again; they vary quite a lot in style according to region and producer, but lean more towards Californian fruitiness, though less heavy and with a shorter, drier finish. Shiraz is the same as Syrah, grown in the Rhône Valley to make the big, warm-hearted wines of Côte Rôtie and Hermitage; another name for the grape in Australia is Hermitage. Australia Shiraz can be an even more deep and concentrated wine, and for this reason it is often blended with Cabernet Sauvignon. Cabernet Shiraz is a great invention and an excellent introduction to Australian red wine.

Other red varieties, Pinot Noir, Merlot and Malbec, are used mainly in blending – though an Australian Pinot Noir defeated all comers at the 1979 Paris Wine Olympiad.

Traditionally, Australian wines have been producer's blends from a number of areas, and plenty of these are still made and sold either under brand names or a bin or vat number. McWilliams Inheritance Dry Red is an example, and so is Australia's most expensive red, Penfolds Grange Hermitage. But winemakers are now giving greater attention to the characteristics of individual regions and so, in addition to grape variety, vintage and producer's name, Australian wine labels often include the place where the grapes were grown. A typical wine description might be Yalumba (the name of the producer) Cabernet Shiraz (the grape blend), 1982 (the vintage), Barossa (the vineyard area).

Hunter Valley

One of Australia's oldest and most famous red wine regions is the Hunter Valley of New South Wales. The fortunes of the valley have followed a boom-bust pattern; thriving in the last century, they went into a long, slow decline until by 1960 only 7 companies were in operation, working less than 800 acres of land. Now there are over 40, and the acreage has increased to 20,000.

Two of Australia's biggest companies have vineyards here, Lindeman's Ben Ean and McWilliams Mount Pleasant, both producing good quality wines. A great favourite is McWilliams Mount Pleasant Philip Hermitage, a long-lasting wine with a distinctive smokey bouquet. A more recent company, founded in 1968, is Rothbury Estate, whose Chairman is one of the great authorities on Australian wine, Len Evans. All the wines sold under the Rothbury label must come from vineyards owned by the company, and at the top of their range they have Individual Paddock and Individual Vineyard wines with particularly outstanding qualities.

Another modern, highly efficient and well-advertised operation is Rosemount Estate; they are keen exporters, and both single varietals and blends are widely available. Other names to remember from this area are Wyndhams, Australia's oldest operating winery, Allandale and Tyrrells.

Victoria

Victoria has a number of red wine regions. In the North-East, near the border with New South Wales, the best known company is the family firm of Brown Bros., run by father and four sons, each of whom specialises in one aspect of the business. They are enthusiasts for single varietal wines, including the more unusual Pinot Noir and Merlot, which are made in an elegant, restrained style. Other respected wineries in the region include Bailey's, Campbell's of Rutherglen and Seppelt, which has other vineyards in Victoria.

In the Goulburn Valley, is the old-established winery of Château Tahbilk, run by the same family for over 50 years; their reds, especially the Shiraz, are substantial, long-lived wines. Further south, in the Bendigo – Ballarat, Yarra Valley and Geelong areas, Balgownie, Virgin Hills, Idyll Vineyard and Taltarni all make red wines of great character and refinement, especially from the Cabernet Sauvignon grape.

South Australia

South Australia produces more wine than any other state and is the home of a number of large companies. Thomas Hardy & Sons in McLaren Vale are famous for a wide range of blended wines as well as vintage ports made from Shiraz. They also have vineyards at Keppoch, further to the south, which produce good regional Cabernet Sauvignon and Cabernet Shiraz.

Yalumba, founded in the last century by the Dorset brewer Samuel Smith, is one of the most reliable names of all. Their traditional style reds, matured in small oak barrels, are full, smooth and reasonably priced. Their best wines are to be found under the Signature Series label.

The Barossa Valley, near to Adelaide, boasts several of Australia's finest growers. Penfolds were started at Magill in 1844 by an immigrant doctor from Sussex. In addition to the Grange Hermitage, named after the founder's cottage, they offer other excellent red wines at rather lower prices, notably the Bin 389 and St. Henri, both Cabernet Shiraz. Penfolds also have a holding in what is perhaps the most extraordinary and isolated of all Australian vineyard sites, Coonawarra. Only a restricted strip of soil, known as Terra Rossa, is suitable for cultivation, but yields and quality are outstanding for both Cabernet Sauvignon and for Shiraz. Other companies with an interest here are Brand's Laira, Lindemans, Petaluma, Wynn's and Mildara.

Tilling a vineyard, South Australia

White wines of Australia

In the early days of Australian wine-making, white wines were rich and fat; later with new refrigeration techniques and a more sophisticated drinking public to satisfy, Australian wine companies began producing lighter and drier white wines. These are now well-established with reputations as good as the best of European and American table wines.

A selection of Australian white, sweet and sparkling wines

The hot climate of the Australian vineyards suits red wine production better than white. But that same climate makes Australians thirsty for cool, refreshing drinks, and white wines are always much in demand; sales are currently six times those of red. Fortunately the Australian wine boom has been able to cope. New vineyards have been planted, many of them in cooler locations enjoyed by white grapes, and production has grown by leaps and bounds.

Grape types

Traditionally most Australian white wine comes from two European varieties, Rhine Riesling and Semillon. Rhine Riesling produces a light, medium dry, fruity wine, which has improved greatly in the last twenty years with the introduction of new fermentation techniques. Semillon gives an altogether bigger, longer lasting wine with a distinctive flavour all its own. Some sweet wines are made from both these grapes, by waiting until late in the vintage before picking. So that the fruit contains plenty of natural sugar. A rich, sweet wine which had long been an Australian speciality is the fortified liqueur Muscat, made from the Frontignan grape.

The range of Australian whites has been greatly extended in recent years by the introduction of other European varieties, notably Chardonnay, which at its best gives a fine full dry wine, though the heat can make it overblown. And it lacks the backbone and austerity which gives the best French Chardonnays their unique distinction. Other varieties you are likely to find are Chenin Blanc, Sauvignon (also called Fumé Blanc), Traminer, Gewurztraminer, Crouchen and Colombard. Many Australian white wines, like the reds, are varietals, so these grape names will appear on the label, but producers are also quite specific about the contents of their commercial blends, as Australians like to know what they are drinking and have no qualms about blending, which is rightly seen as evidence of the winemaker's skill. As in California, these new growers are using methods which can teach European 'experts' a thing or two.

South Australia to Hunter Valley

A lot of Australia's white wines come from the state of South Australia, and especially the Barossa Valley, which was settled by Silesian immigrants in the middle of the last century. Some of the state's most famous wineries were founded by these immigrants; Buring, now under the control of Lindemans, with a fine reputation for Rhine Rieslings; Seppelt, who are chiefly known for the sparkling wines produced at Great Western in Victoria; and Orlando, the first of all the Barossa companies, founded in 1850 by Joseph Gramp, and still a leader for standard and late-picked Rieslings and Traminers, many coming from individual vineyards.

The Barossa Co-operative Winery, which produces something of almost everything, sells under the label Kaiser Stuhl. Other South Australian wineries with a particular reputation for whites are Petaluma, who make very good Chardonnay; Quelltaler, for fine full-flavoured Rieslings; Lindemans, for Padthaway Chardonnay; De Bortoli, who specialise in rich botrytis affected wines made from Semillon, Rhine Riesling and Traminer; and Wolf Blass, who have excellent blended whites sold under Yellow, Grey, or Black labels.

The finest Semillon wines have traditionally come from the Hunter Valley, where for years the grape had confusingly been called the Hunter Riesling. Fine examples are made by McWilliams, Tyrrells, Rosemount and Rothbury, though the younger companies seem more interested in new arrivals such as Chardonnay and Fumé Blanc. McWilliams make a very reliable range of white varietals at their Riverina wineries in the Murrumbidgee Irrigation Area of New South Wales; the Riesling-Traminer blend is especially popular.

The hot climate of north east Victoria is not ideally suited to white wines, but this is the centre of production for the fine liqueur Muscats, similar to the vins doux of Southern France, also made from the Frontignan grape.

Fine examples come from Morris Wines of Rutherglen and Brown Bros. of Milawa. Brown Bros. also have higher altitude vineyards at Koombahla and Whitlands, and with a reputation as varietal specialists make a range of good white wines, especially Sauvignon, Semillon and Chardonnay. Look out too for the remarkable Mt. Helen Chardonnay from Tisdall, a small new company who have also been successful with late-picked Rhine Rieslings.

Western Australia

Some of the best white wines of Western Australia come from the old-established firm of Houghton, which has now been taken over by Hardys. They make an outstanding blend of Chenin and Muscadelle, which won fame for its creator Jack Mann and sold for years under the label Houghton's White Burgundy.

Further South, in the Margaret River region, Moss Wood are making a name with their Semillon, and Leeuwin Estate offer two styles of Rhine Riesling as well as fine Sauvignon and Chardonnay.

New Zealand

New Zealand is a latecomer to the ranks of large scale wine-producing nations, but is making up for this fast with high-quality wines. It is only in recent times that New Zealand producers have found a market for the light, elegant, fruity wines to which their climate and soil conditions are best suited.

Vines were introduced to New Zealand by a missionary, Rev. Samuel Marsden, who brought a selection with him from Australia and planted them at Keri Keri and Waimate on the North Island in 1819. Not long afterwards James Busby, who had made a success of wine-growing in the Hunter Valley of New South Wales, came to New Zealand as the first Official Queen's Representative. He planted cuttings of French and Spanish vines in the Bay of Islands, and by 1840 had a commercial crop.

During the course of the next century the industry developed spasmodically in the hands of European immigrants. They had to fight against phylloxera and a vigorous temperance movement, and by 1960 there were still only 1000 acres under cultivation. There are now 14,000, many of them given over to classic grape varieties, and the wineries are among the most pioneering in the world.

The revolution which has taken place over the past 25 years is largely due to the greatly increased interest in table wines world-wide which began in the 1960's. Not only were more people drinking more wine, they demanded quality and variety. New Zealand growers sought advice from experts overseas, such as the German Wine Institute at Geisenheim, who were enthusiastic about the potential of European White Grapes, and especially Müller Thurgau. Often called Riesling Sylvaner, this is the dominant grape in large areas of the Rhineland, and for a while it looked as if New Zealand would be known chiefly as the producer of Down Under Liebfraumilch.

A lot of light, fruity wines in this style are still made, but it is French varieties such as Sauvignon, Chardonnay and Pinot Blanc which have lately won most acclaim, and good red wines are now also being produced from Cabernet Sauvignon, Pinot Noir and a South African grape called Pinotage.

The cooler, wetter climate of New Zealand is more reminiscent of the North European vineyards than other Southern Hemisphere countries, and the wines have a more European character. Compare, for example, an Australian and New Zealand Chardonnay; the New Zealand wine is likely to be less full of obvious fruit and lower in alcohol, but refined and subtle, with refreshing acidity.

There are as yet no laws in New Zealand corresponding to the French Appellation Controlée so, as with Californian and Australian wines, the name and reputation of the producer are all-important. Most New Zealand wines are made by a handful of large companies.

Montana

Montana wines were started in 1943 by a Yugoslav immigrant, Ivan Yukich, whose family had been making wine in Europe for 300 years. They began with a modest plot near Auckland, but soon expanded into the Gisborne area – the estate is now called Ormond. In 1973 became the first commercial growers on the South Island, where they purchased some 4000 acres in Marlborough with financial backing from the giant American company, Seagram.

Montana now make almost half of New Zealand's table wines; their Sauvignon Blanc and Cabernet Sauvignon are outstanding, but look out too for their Rhine Riesling, Gewurztraminer and Chardonnay, which are good.

Cooks

The other big name in New Zealand winemaking is Cooks. Vines have been grown at Te Kauwhata, south of Auckland, since the last century, but it was not until the 1960's that Cooks began serious planting of classic varieties, following advice from the Californian expert Professor Petrucci. They also built a modern winery, which is among the most technologically advanced anywhere.

By 1974 the gold medals were coming in, and they subsequently bought estates at Riverhead and Gisborne. Most of their wines are marketed as varietals, and they have won particular attention with their Chardonnay, rich and full by New Zealand standards, and Cabernet Sauvignon, which has plenty of blackcurrant fruit. There is also a good blend of Cabernet Sauvignon and Pinot Noir which sells under the name Cooks New Zealand Dry Red.

McWilliams

The Australian company McWilliams have had an interest in New Zealand since the 1940's and now have a number of vineyards and wineries in the Hawkes Bay area. They produce good Cabernet Sauvignon and Chardonnay in addition to fortified wines and a range of commercial blends – the red Bakano, white Cresta Dore and sparkling Marque Vue.

Corbans, founded over eighty years ago and now largely under the control of Rothmans, have all the latest equipment and offer good varietal wines, generic blends and flor sherries.

Of the small private companies, for future reference, Villa Maria, Matua Valley, Babich and Delegats are names to bear in mind.

A selection of Montana wines

The Cape

South African table wines have improved dramatically over the last few years. In the early 1970s the whites were dull and the reds, though better, were lacking in character. Now, so many advances have been made it is hard to believe the fine Cape wines of today had such predecessors.

Thanks to new wine laws and modern vinification methods, coupled with the enthusiasm of the growers, the wines are now consistently well made. Weather and soil may not provide for the production of the equivalent of a Château Latour, but you can be confident that almost any bottle of South African wine will be eminently drinkable and not over-priced.

The vineyards were started by the early Dutch settlers, who planted the first vines in 1655. The Huguenots followed in 1688 and then the British in 1806. Exports boomed when the British occupied the Cape, but problems followed with the abolition of preferential tariffs and a massive wine glut. For a time the wine industry faced ruin.

It was rescued in 1918 with the formation of the Co-operative Wine Growers' Association (KWV). The KWV pioneered the development of the whole industry, offering technical expertise and assistance throughout the Cape. KWV is now the central controlling body of the wine industry at producer level. All wine farmers are members and their surplus is held by KWV and then exported.

In 1972 the Wines of Origin Laws were passed and quality control came in. Every one of the thousands of wine farms within a demarcated area are now registered. Bottles of wine carry a guarantee stating not only the wines' place of origin and vintage year, but also its cultivar, or grape variety. Gradings are for Wine of Origin, Wine of Origin Superior and Estate Wine of Origin.

Wine regions

The wines come from two distinct regions. From the coastal belt between the sea and the first towering range of mountains come delicate white table wines and some of the best reds, as well as some of the lighter sherries. From the Little Karoo, beyond the Drakenstein mountains, come the sweet dessert wines, the carafe wines, South African sherries and the best muscatels.

The wine estates, whose wines are labelled Estate Wine of Origin, are to South Africa what the classified growths are to Bordeaux. There are approximately 43 classified estates. Estate wines of origin are made only from grapes grown on the estate, and are produced and bottled on the estate.

Many non-estate wine farms do have their own cellars and bottle their own wine, but most send their wines to the many co-operative wineries. Once a wine, even one from a well-known estate, has reached maturity, it is usually bought by one of the large wine companies, such as Nederburg. In general white wines tend to go to the big companies almost as soon as the grapes are harvested.

The reds are often kept in wood by the growers for two or three years before they are blended and bottled by the large companies. The system works because the grower is left free to make an individual wine that is backed by the big groups, who relieve him of all marketing worries.

Grape varieties

Of the white grapes, which account for over three-quarters of South African wines, the Steen is the most popular and is the Cape version of the Chenin Blanc. Most Steen wines are medium-dry, fruity and wonderfully refreshing. They make delicious summer aperitifs. There are also dry Steens and late-picked Steens, which are sweet enough to accompany desserts.

The Riesling grape from the Rhine, once rare in South Africa, is now planted in many of the best vineyards. Notable Riesling vineyards are at Paarl, Stellenbosch and Tulbagh. A Cape Riesling is always clean and flowery and goes well with both fish and white meat.

The red Pinotage, like Steen, is a grape variety first bred in the Cape. It is a cross between the elegant Pinot Noir and the hearty Hermitage or Cinsaut. The result is a smooth, substantial red wine with a fragrant bouquet and a fine finish.

Like Australian Cabernets, red South African Cabernets tend to be dark and full of flavour. They could well replace a French Rhône wine for fireside drinking in the depths of winter.

To these wines add a red wine of great flavour, KWV Roodeberg, a range of slightly sparkling rosés, a variety of South African sherries and brandies, and a tangerine liqueur, Van der Hum, and you will have the taste of one of the great wine countries.

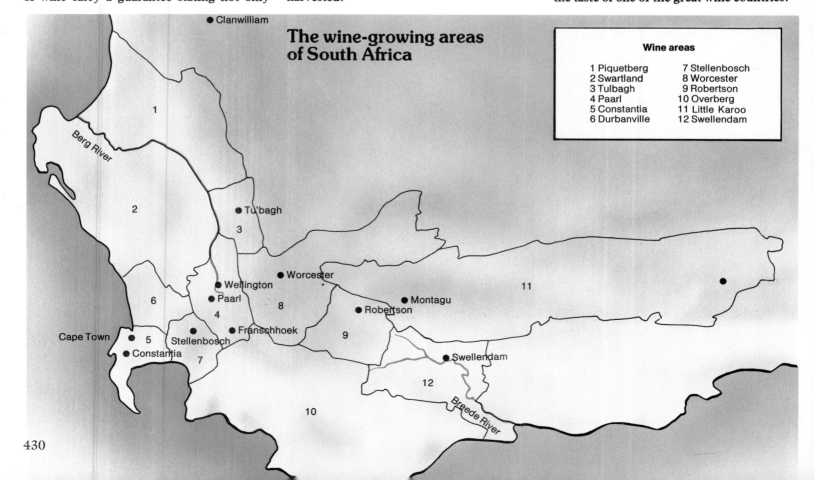

The wine-growing areas of South Africa

Wine areas

1 Piquetberg	7 Stellenbosch
2 Swartland	8 Worcester
3 Tulbagh	9 Robertson
4 Paarl	10 Overberg
5 Constantia	11 Little Karoo
6 Durbanville	12 Swellendam

Clanwilliam

Berg River

Tu'bagh

Worcester

Wellington

Paarl

Montagu

Robertson

Cape Town

Franschhoek

Stellenbosch

Constantia

Swellendam

Breede River

White wines of the Cape

The best South African wines come from the coastal region of the Cape Province, which has a climate ideal for vines. And like Portugal, with its exposure to the west and the influence of the sea, the Cape is best known for its white wines—all reasonably priced and very drinkable.

On the sandy plains with low rainfall, the stunted vines make a poor wine, much of which goes for distillation. But in the green foothills, in the shadow of the mountains, the soil is deeper, the rainfall more generous and the wines of high quality, made by the descendants of Dutch and Hugenot settlers.

The best white wines are to be found on the individual estates along the Stellenbosch Wine Route. This takes in 15 estate wineries and four co-operatives producing the cream of Cape white wines, particularly worth buying for inexpensive summer drinking.

Delheim and Simonsig

The Delheim estate near Koelenhof is perched on the slopes of the Simonsberg mountains. These mountains give the Delheim vineyards an average of 90 cm of rain per year, while Paarl, 15 km away, gets no more than 20 cm.

Look out for the dry Delheim Riesling which has the crisp flavour of a newly pickled apple and a slight sparkle. The same estate produces a dry Steen, a uniquely South African wine, with a flowery, delicate flavour, so refreshing in warm weather.

In the modern cellars of the nearby Simonsig Wine Estate there is a full range of table wines, red, white and rosé. The Simonsig Rhine Riesling has often been mistaken for its German counterpart – it is not only equally dry and silky, with a nice long finish, but it also undercuts German Riesling in price in much of Europe. Simonsig also makes a sparkling wine by the méthode champenoise.

The soft Gewürtztraminer wine from Simonsig is nearly as fruity and spicy as an Alsace Gewürztraminer, and considerably cheaper. If you have never tasted a white Cape Colombard, one of the best varietals comes from Simonsig. It is a big wine, which will go well with shellfish and creamy pasta dishes. It has ample flavour and travels well.

Overgaauw

Overgaauw, one of the oldest Cape estates, has been completely modernized. Its white wines are cold-fermented to bring out freshness and flavour. Try the crisp, concentrated Sylvaner for summer drinking. The Steen from Overgaauw is dry enough to go well with almost any variety of fish.

Blaauwklippen

Blaauwklippen is a beautiful Cape property which dates back to 1692. It produces a bone dry Chenin Blanc and a number of white varietals of good repute such as Chardonnay and Sauvignon. Its Rhine Riesling (called Weisser Riesling in South Africa) is light, with a sweet edge.

Backsberg and Tulbagh

A very versatile winegrower is Sydney Back of the Backsberg Estate. The winery here is as modern as any in the Southern Hemisphere. Backsberg is among the few private estates to bottle and age their own wines. Sauvignon Blanc, Rhine Riesling and Chardonnay predominate, with the Blacksberg Cabernet Sauvignon, a treat for lovers of red wine.

Twee Jongegezellen produces many award-winning white wines, such as the Grand Prix TJ 39, which is a blend of this estates' very best dry wines. It has a distinctive golden colour and is fragrant with plenty of fullness and depth.

Chenin Blanc from Tulbagh is lighter, with more finesse, than those from anywhere else, except Stellenbosch. The Clairette Blanche from this area is recommended.

Theuniskraal

Here there are plantations of both Rhine and South African Riesling, Gewürztraminer, Sémillon, Sauvignon and Pinot Noir. These can be outstanding.

Nederburg

Gunter Brözel, winemaker at Nederburg, thanks to his German expertise, has produced some of the Cape's finest wines. For the lightness and cheerfulness of the muscatel grape do not miss a Nederburg Fonternel. Nederburg Riesling is fresh and buoyant, while the Steen is rich and fruity. Try also the famous Paarl Edelkuer, a golden, sweet dessert wine. Made from the Chenin Blanc grape infected by noble rot, it is luscious and every bit as good as a top-quality Sauternes.

Cape vineyards near Franschhoek

Red wines of the Cape

Cape red wines represent less than a quarter of the total production of wine in South Africa. They are less popular in their home country than white wine because of the consistently warm climate, but are better appreciated in Europe where they cost less than almost any other comparable red wine.

Many of the finest examples of Cape reds come from the vineyards on the slopes of the mountains on the coastal belt. The best area is around Stellenbosch which has 24 different estates and six co-operatives making outstanding red wines.

The Pinotage and Cabernet Sauvignon are two outstanding examples of these wines. Pinotage results from the cross of the Pinot Noir and Hermitage vines. This made a grape variety unique to South Africa, but in 1922 its inventor was unimpressed with the result. Thirty years later the Pinotage was planted in a vineyard and was an immediate success. It ripens earlier than other reds and produces a full, rich wine with a noticeable flowery aroma. Deep red in colour, it is soft and round on the palate.

In inland areas like Malmesbury, the wine is fuller-bodied. In South Africa wine is generally drunk young, but most of them will improve after a few years in the bottle. Cape red wines are perfect with grills, stews, or steak and kidney pudding.

Cabernet Sauvignon, the famous grape of Bordeaux, is the other great grape of South Africa. The best Stellenbosch cabernet wines are full and elegant and need several years in cask and a few more in bottle to attain their peak. The Alto Estate makes a stylish and robust cabernet, which has been shipped to London for 40 years.

From the stunningly beautiful Constantia area, on the coast to the south of Cape Town, come quality cabernets, lighter and fruitier than those from other areas.

Another French red grape which thrives in the Cape climate is the Shiraz of the Rhône Valley. In the drier areas of Constantia, Faure and Durbanville, it yields a dry, smoky-flavoured wine of middle weight. Serve Shiraz wines with veal and lamb and remember they will be better if kept a few years after purchasing.

The only Cape wine to avoid is Cinsaut or Hermitage. As a prolific producer it accounts for 75% of local South African red wine, but it has little individual character. It comes into its own only when blended to make Pinotage.

Dotted further inland are the privately-owned wine estates producing mostly whites with a few red wines, often of surprising character and finesse. Uitkyk produces a quality cabernet and Blaauwklippen, known for its white wines, boasts one of the two Cape plantings of Californian Zinfandel. The Kanonkop Cabernet Sauvignon and Pinotage wines have a well-earned reputation for consistent quality. Meerendal produces nearly every variety of red, with Pinotage singled out for a number of awards in recent years. Meerendal Shiraz can be a huge, deeply-flavoured red which will make good winter drinking.

Another red wine to note is the Meerlust Cabernet Sauvignon. It is one of the few Cape cabernets to which, Bordeaux-style, Merlot is added, to make a more balanced wine. It is velvety and full of character after maturation in oak.

South African red wines tend to be spicier and more robustly flavoured than their French or Italian counterparts. They are delicious with some of the peppery Cape dishes, Irish stews, casseroles and game.

Cape sherry

South African sherry is produced by methods similar to those used for Spanish sherry. In the 1930s research showed that flor, the yeast that is the basis of sherry, is also present in South Africa.

There are few very dry and delicate Cape sherries and there are none of the old, nutty varieties for which Spain is celebrated. Mymering is a pale, extra dry Cape sherry of some renown and KWV Paarlsack have a trio of extra dry, medium dry and cream, with the medium dry the most acceptable. The excellent medium dry Onzerust and the richer Golden Acre are well made and good value for money. Those who prefer a delicate sherry should buy those made in Paarl, Stellenbosch or Tulbagh. Heavier ones come from the Robertson, Montagu and Worcester districts. Other sherry ranges offering sound value are Ravendrost, Marievale, Cape House and RSL. The nearest to the delicate Spanish dry fino is probably Cape Cavendish Extra dry. This goes well with soup or a fish course.

Port and brandy

South African tawny ports are lighter in colour and a little raisiny in flavour, compared to the Portuguese ports. One of the best is made on the Allesverloren Estate.

South Africans are generally fonder of their brandies than their wines. By law, young brandies must mature in oak casks for a minimum of three years to achieve mellowness and the desired amber colour. They may seem a bit rough to an American or European palate and rarely enter the same class as a French cognac or armagnac.

However, the mandarin-flavoured liqueur, Van der Hum, is a splendid alternative to Cointreau or Grand Marnier. This liqueur was first made by Dutch settlers at the Cape of Good Hope.

South African port, red wines and sherry.

Dishes for Wine

The earlier pages of this guide have provided a thorough mini-course in the appreciation of wine. But experience is inarguably the best teacher. Drinking wine on its own, at a professionally conducted tasting or in the relaxed company of friends, is one way to learn more and allows real freedom to choose and experiment. But nothing is more enjoyable than sharing the pleasure of wine with a good meal. A fine claret is truly set up by a good cut of beef, and what is more fun than eating outside on a warm summer's day, washing down olives, fresh, crisp salads, and perhaps a marinated, barbecued chicken, with a clear, clean rosé – wishing you were in the south of France or the Algarve? But with that to enjoy, why wish you are anyplace else?

Wine and food go together – but certain wines complement particular foods. It is a form of matchmaking and, while many wines adapt adequately to a number of foods, when you make that perfect marriage, the "rightness" of the two together is immediately apparent. Light crisp white wines with spicy dishes, a luxuriant white burgundy with rich fish such as lobster or salmon, Chianti with spaghetti Bolognese, young red burgundy with casseroled chicken, a fine elegant sauternes with a fruit flan or crème brûlée – these combinations are matchless. At the same time, such partnerships are not rigid. Personal taste, the time of year, the importance of the occasion, family finances – all can influence your choice. On the following pages are a selection of delicious recipes with suggested wines to go with them. Try the suggestions or introduce your own – eat, drink and be merry!

Starters

Turnip soup
Leek and asparagus soup
Terrine of pork and veal
Terrine of hare
Gin pâté
Tuna mousse
Creamed aubergine salad
Creamy vegetable casserole
Avocado mousse
Stuffed courgettes
Montpellier appetizer
Baked scallops
Cheese and ham soufflé
Smoked salmon cones
Californian avocado
Prawn bouchées
Avocado with crab
Cocktail cheese puffs
Savoury mille-feuille

Turnip soup

This is a simple recipe ideal for baby turnips which are full of flavour and have no coarse fibres. It could also be made equally well with tender young carrots. A dry white Loire would make a good partner to the soup.

Serves 4
500 g /18 oz baby turnips, peeled
850 ml/1½ pt chicken stock,
  fat removed
50 g /2 oz butter
2 garlic cloves, crushed

salt
freshly ground black pepper
100 g /4 oz Gruyère cheese, grated
For the croûtons
4 slices of bread
50 g /2 oz butter for frying

1   Cut the turnips into small sticks, slightly larger than matchsticks. Blanch them in boiling salted water for 2 minutes. Drain well. Put the stock on to heat through.
2   Heat the butter in a heavy-bottomed saucepan over medium-low heat until it foams. Fry the garlic in the butter for 1 minute. Add the turnip sticks and cook for about 4 minutes, turning them occasionally until golden and tender.
3   To make the croûtons, remove the crusts from the bread and cut the bread into cubes. Melt the butter in a frying-pan over

medium-low heat and sauté the cubes until brown on all sides, about 2 minutes. Drain the cubes thoroughly on absorbent paper.
4   Divide the croûtons between the 4 bowls. Season the hot stock with salt and pepper and pour into the bowls. Spoon the turnip sticks into the bowls and sprinkle with the cheese. Serve the soup immediately.

making chicken stock,
then 15 minutes

Leek and asparagus soup

This is a light and delicious soup, simple to make and equally good hot or cold. The asparagus gives a subtle and unusual taste. Serve with a chilled blended Moselle.

Serves 4
500 g /1 lb leeks
50 g /2 oz butter
300 ml /10 fl oz milk
1 bay leaf

850 ml /1½ pt chicken stock
250 g /8 oz canned asparagus tips
salt
freshly ground black pepper
5 ml /1 tsp dried chervil

1 Wash and finely chop the leeks, including the tenderest parts of the green tops. Melt the butter in a large saucepan over moderate heat and sauté the leeks for 10 minutes or until soft.
2 Meanwhile in a small saucepan bring the milk with the bay leaf almost to boiling point over low heat.
3 Add the chicken stock to the pan of leeks. Remove the bay leaf from the infused milk and add the milk and asparagus tips to the leeks. Stir well, remove from heat and leave to cool.

4 Pour the cooled soup into a blender and blend thoroughly. Return to the large pan and heat through. Check for seasoning, adding salt and freshly ground black pepper if necessary, and transfer to individual warmed soup bowls or a warmed soup tureen. Garnish with the chervil and serve immediately.

30 minutes

Terrine of pork and veal

A light pâté makes the perfect lunch, served with green salad, crusty French bread, and inviting Anjou rosé wine.

Serves 8

500 g /1 lb lean pork, minced
500 g /1 lb pie veal, minced
250 g /8 oz pork fat, minced
1 medium-sized onion, finely chopped
1 garlic clove, crushed
25 g /1 oz butter
150 ml /5 fl oz brandy or dry white wine
1 medium-sized egg, beaten
10 ml /2 tsp salt
1.5 ml /¼ tsp freshly ground pepper
pinch of allspice
2.5 ml /½ tsp dried thyme
500 g /1 lb streaky bacon slices
lettuce, tomato and gherkins to garnish

1 Combine the minced pork, veal and pork fat in a large mixing bowl. Heat the oven to 180C /350F /gas 4.
2 In a frying-pan, sauté the onion and garlic in the butter until soft. Remove the onion and add to the bowl of minced meat. Rinse the pan with brandy or wine and pour on to the meat and onion.
3 Mix in the egg. Season the meat mixture with salt, pepper, allspice and thyme and beat well.
4 Remove the rinds from the bacon slices. Use two-thirds of the slices to line a 1.5 L /2½ pt mould or rectangular ovenproof container. Press the meat mixture into the bowl or tin and cover with the remaining bacon slices.

5 Cover the terrine tightly with foil and a lid. Stand the bowl in a baking tin of water and bake in the oven for 2 hours. It is ready when a skewer stuck into the terrine comes out clean.
6 Remove the lid and place a weight on top of the foil. Leave to cool overnight, then chill for at least 8 hours.
7 Run a knife around the dish to loosen the bacon lining from the sides, if the pâté has not shrunk. Turn the terrine out on to a plate. Surround with small lettuce leaves; garnish the top as shown.

2½ hours,
plus 8 hours chilling

Terrine of hare

This is an ideal way of cooking an older hare, especially if you do not plan to eat it immediately, as the terrine keeps for up to a month if refrigerated. Try serving it with a German red wine.

Serves 8

450 g /1 lb cooked hare meat, finely minced
5 ml /1 tsp freshly grated nutmeg
5 ml /1 tsp ground ginger
salt and ground black pepper
275 ml /10 fl oz strong stock
225 g /8 oz sausage-meat
10 ml /2 tsp freshly chopped parsley
5 ml /1 tsp dried thyme
5 ml /1 tsp dried sage
1 garlic clove, cut in half
25 g /1 oz butter
30 ml /2 tbls brandy
8 streaky bacon slices, 6 of them chopped
175 g /6 oz canned chestnuts, drained and chopped
175 g /6 oz clarified butter
hot buttered toast to serve

1 Mix the hare with the nutmeg and ginger in a bowl. Season highly with salt and black pepper, then moisten with the stock: add enough to make the mixture wet without being slushy.
2 In another bowl, mix the sausage-meat with the parsley, thyme and sage. Season with salt and black pepper. Heat oven to 180C /350F /gas 4.
3 Rub a 2 L /3½ pt mould all over inside with the cut sides of the garlic and then grease well with the butter. Spread half the minced hare mixture on the bottom, pressing it well down, and sprinkle with 10 ml /2 tsp brandy. Cover with half the chopped bacon, then half the chestnuts. Put all the sausage-meat and herb mixture over the chestnuts, again pressing well down, and sprinkle with 10 ml /2 tsp

brandy. Cover with the remaining chestnuts, then the bacon, finishing with a layer of hare. Sprinkle with the rest of the brandy. Lay 2 whole bacon slices on top and cover tin with buttered foil.
4 Place the mould in a roasting tin half filled with boiling water and bake for 1¾ hours or until the mixture has shrunk away from the sides of the tin. Remove from the oven and cool.
5 When the terrine is cool, remove the bacon slices from the top and pour the clarified butter over. Refrigerate and serve well chilled with hot buttered toast.

 2¾ hours

Gin pâté

Gin and its flavouring, juniper berries, give a lift to this smooth chicken liver pâté. Serve with an Alsace Gewürtztraminer.

Serves 4–6

250 g /8 oz chicken livers, trimmed
15 g /½ oz butter
1 garlic clove, finely chopped
30 ml /2 tbls gin

4–6 juniper berries, crushed
salt and freshly ground black pepper
50 g /2 oz curd cheese
juniper berries and parsley to garnish

1 Pat the chicken livers dry with absorbent paper. Melt the butter in a frying-pan over moderate heat. When the foaming subsides, add the chopped garlic and cook for 1 minute. Then add the livers and fry for 2–3 minutes, stirring, until cooked but still pink inside.

2 Transfer the livers with a slotted spoon to the goblet of a blender. Blend to a smooth purée.

3 Add the gin and crushed juniper berries to the frying-pan and heat through, stirring to incorporate all the crusty bits from the pan. Add the liquid in the frying-pan to the liver purée in the blender and blend once more. Season with salt and pepper.

4 Add the curd cheese and blend again. Transfer the pâté to a 250 ml /10 fl oz earthenware terrine and smooth the top of it with a round-bladed knife. Chill in the refrigerator for 2 days to let the flavour mature.

5 Before serving, decorate the chilled pâté with both juniper berries and parsley. It can be served, cut into thin slices, accompanied with hot toast and butter curls.

 30 minutes
plus 48 hours maturing

Tuna mousse

This is a deliciously light and creamy mousse which would be perfect for lunch on a hot summer's day, or, set in a fish mould, would make a simple but spectacular appetizer for a grand dinner party. Serve with a dry Australian white wine.

Serves 4–6
350 g /12 oz canned tuna fish
15 ml /1 tbls gelatine powder
30 ml /2 tbls lemon juice
5 ml /1 tsp cayenne pepper
5 ml /1 tsp horseradish sauce
90 ml /6 tbls thick cream
2 large egg whites

For the garnish
1 medium-sized cucumber
10 ml /2 tsp grated onion
1 small chilli, finely chopped
10 ml /2 tsp fresh chervil, finely chopped
15 ml /1 tbls lemon juice
salt and ground black pepper
celery leaves and flat-leafed parsley

1   In a small bowl sprinkle the gelatine powder over 30 ml /2 tbls cold water. Place the bowl in a small pan of simmering water and stir to dissolve the gelatine.
2   Drain the tuna and in a large bowl mash it thoroughly. Add the lemon juice, cayenne pepper and horseradish sauce. Season to taste with salt and freshly ground black pepper. Mix in the cream. Add the dissolved gelatine, stirring well.
3   In another bowl, whisk the egg whites until stiff peaks form. With a large metal spoon, carefully fold the whites into the fish mixture. Turn the mousse into a 575 ml /1 pt soufflé dish or a

fish-shaped mould and leave to set in the refrigerator.
4   Ten minutes before serving make the garnish. Cut the cucumber, unpeeled, into fine julienne strips. Place in a bowl and mix with grated onion, green chilli, chervil and lemon juice. Season with salt and pepper. Take the mousse out of the refrigerator, turn out onto a plate if using a mould, and garnish with cumber, celery leaves and parsley. Serve immediately.

40 minutes,
plus setting time

Creamed aubergine salad

Finely chopped aubergine in a mayonnaise and yoghurt dressing makes an interesting and delicious salad to go with a plain grilled meat dish. Alternatively it makes an unusual vegetable appetizer – serve with a Retsina to set off the richness of the aubergines.

Serves 4
1 large aubergine
45 ml /3 tbls olive oil
700 ml /7 fl oz Mayonnaise
700 ml /7 fl oz yoghurt
1 small onion, finely chopped
7.5 ml /1½ tsp dried marjoram

5 ml /1 tsp honey
5 ml /1 tsp horseradish sauce
5 ml /1 tsp lemon juice
salt
freshly ground black pepper
pinch of cayenne pepper
pitta bread to serve

1 Wipe the aubergine with a damp cloth but do not peel. Cut it in half and chop each half into very fine strips. Put on a plate, sprinkle liberally with salt and leave to drain for 30 minutes.
2 Put the aubergine strips into a colander and thoroughly rinse under running cold water. Shake well to drain.
3 Put 45 ml /3 tbls olive oil in a large frying-pan over medium heat and, when nearly smoking, add the aubergine. Cook for 10 minutes stirring occasionally. Remove from pan and drain on absorbent paper. Leave to cool.
4 Mix the mayonnaise with the yoghurt in a large bowl. Add the

onion, marjoram, honey, horseradish and lemon juice and mix thoroughly. Add the cold aubergine, season to taste with salt and freshly ground black pepper, mix well and put in the refrigerator to chill for 30 minutes.
5 Pile on to a serving dish, sprinkle a pinch of cayenne pepper over the top and serve immediately with crisp, piping hot rounds of pitta bread.

draining aubergines
then 30 minutes plus chilling

Creamy vegetable casserole

Serve this luxurious-looking yet economical starter with a well-chilled Californian wine, such as Gallo's Chablis Blanc, at an informal party.

Serves 6
900 g /2 lb small courgettes
150 ml /5 fl oz Chicken
   stock
450 g /1 lb carrots, cut lengthways
   into 10 mm /⅓ in batons
90 ml /6 tbls aspic powder
425 ml /15 fl oz boiling water
105 ml /7 tbls thick cream
105 ml /7 tbls mayonnaise

15 ml /1 tbls white wine vinegar
5 ml /1 tsp lemon juice
30 ml /2 tbls finely chopped
   fresh parsley
salt
freshly ground black pepper
2 canned pimentos, drained
   and thinly sliced
fresh herbs, to garnish
sliced tomatoes, to garnish

1 Steam the courgettes, whole, for 10 minutes. Cool them quickly and slice them lengthways into 10 mm /⅓ in thick batons.
2 Bring the chicken stock to the boil in a saucepan, add the carrots and simmer for 5–6 minutes or until they are just tender. Drain, discarding the stock, and cool the carrots quickly.
3 Put the aspic into a bowl, pour on the boiling water and stir to dissolve. Let stand for 10 minutes.
4 Stir in the cream, mayonnaise, vinegar, lemon juice and parsley. Season with salt and pepper. Beat the mixture until all the ingredients are well-blended. Chill in the refrigerator for about 20–25 minutes, until it has the consistency of unbeaten egg white.
5 Rinse a 1.5 L /3 pt loaf tin with cold water. Arrange a layer of courgette strips on the base, along the length of the tin. Then place a layer of carrot strips across the tin. Add four layers of courgettes and three of carrots, in the same way. Then add all the pimentoes in one layer. Finish with one more layer each of courgettes and carrots.
6 Pour the aspic cream over the vegetables and rap the sides of the tin so that the cream penetrates all the layers and there are no air bubbles trapped inside. Cover the tin and refrigerate for at least 2 hours, so the aspic cream firms up.
7 To turn out, run a knife around the edges of the terrine. Invert a serving platter over the top, turn over the tin and platter together and give a sharp shake. Garnish and serve sliced.

making stock,
then 1 hour, plus chilling

442

Avocado mousse

This luxurious mousse makes a light starter to a summer dinner party, if served with a fresh white wine, such as a Vinho Verde.

Serves 6
2 large ripe avocados
30 ml /2 tbls lemon juice
10 ml /2 tsp onion, finely chopped
2.5 ml /1/2 tsp Tabasco sauce
250 ml /10 fl oz chicken stock
15 g /1/2 oz gelatine powder
150 ml /5 fl oz thick cream
2 medium-sized egg whites

150 ml /5 fl oz thick mayonnaise
salt
freshly ground black pepper

For the garnish
lemon slices, halved
cucumber slices
150 ml /5 fl oz vinaigrette

1 Peel, stone and chop the avocados. Blend them with the lemon juice, onion, Tabasco sauce and chicken stock until smooth.
2 Place the gelatine in a small pan with a little water and heat until the gelatine has dissolved. Pour the gelatine into the avocado mixture in a thin stream, stirring constantly. Chill for about 15 minutes, until the mixture is just setting.
3 Meanwhile, whip the cream so that it just holds its shape but is not stiff. Whisk the egg whites until they form stiff peaks.
4 Carefully fold the cream into the avocado mixture, followed by the mayonnaise and the egg whites. Season with salt and pepper.
5 Rinse out a 1 L /2 pt charlotte mould. Turn the avocado mixture into the mould. Cover and refrigerate to set for about 2 hours.
6 Turn out onto a plate 30 minutes before serving. Garnish the top with halved lemon slices and cucumber slices. Surround with cucumber twists; dribble the vinaigrette over the garnishes.

1 hour, plus chilling time

443

Stuffed courgettes

Courgettes, filled with a tasty stuffing and served with a smooth cheese sauce, make an interesting vegetable starter. Accompany the dish with a light white wine, such as a Swiss Fendant or a Muscadet de Sevre et Maine, that can happily be served through the rest of the meal.

Serves 4
8 large courgettes
salt
45 ml /3 tbls oil
1 small onion, finely chopped
100 g /4 oz ham, finely chopped
100 g /4 oz fresh white breadcrumbs
30 ml /2 tbls freshly chopped parsley
5 ml /1 tsp dried thyme
15 ml /1 tbls lemon juice
freshly ground black pepper

1 medium-sized egg, beaten
butter for greasing
parsley sprigs to garnish
For the cheese sauce
25 g /1 oz butter
25 g /1 oz flour
275 ml /10 fl oz milk
100 g /4 oz Cheddar cheese, grated
a pinch of grated nutmeg
salt and freshly ground pepper

1 Hollow out the centres of the courgettes by pushing an apple corer into each end. Heat the oven to 190C /375F /gas 5.
2 Boil the hollowed-out courgettes in salted water for 10 minutes, to blanch them. Drain thoroughly and pat dry with absorbent paper.
3 Heat the oil in a frying-pan, add the onion and fry for 5 minutes until soft. Remove from the heat and stir in the ham, breadcrumbs, parsley, thyme, and lemon juice. Season to taste with salt and freshly ground black pepper, then bind all the ingredients together with the beaten egg.
4 Carefully stuff the hollowed-out courgettes with the filling. Arrange the courgettes in a lightly buttered dish, cover with foil and bake for 30 minutes.

5 Meanwhile, make the cheese sauce. Melt the butter in a saucepan and, using a wooden spoon, stir in the flour. Cook over moderate heat for 2 minutes, then remove from the heat. Add the milk gradually, stirring until thick and smooth. Add the cheese, a pinch of nutmeg and salt and pepper to taste. Heat until the cheese has melted into the sauce.
6 Remove the courgettes from the oven and divide them between 4 small plates. Pour a little of the sauce over each serving and garnish with parsley sprigs. Serve immediately.

 1 hour

Montpellier appetizer

Montpellier, in the Languedoc, is famous for its green, herby butter mixed with mustard and anchovies. The butter gives a deliciously piquant flavour to the mushrooms and tomatoes in this appetizer. Serve with crusty French bread and a light and fruity Côteaux de Languedoc red.

Serves 6
3 large tomatoes
450 g /1 lb large button
* mushrooms*
30 ml /6 tsp fresh white
* breadcrumbs*
salt
freshly ground black pepper
crusty French bread, to serve
* (optional)*

For the butter
225 g /8 oz butter, softened
45 ml /3 tbls finely chopped parsley
30 ml /2 tbls finely chopped fennel
45 ml /3 tbls finely chopped
* tarragon*
2 garlic cloves, crushed
6 canned anchovy fillets, pounded
15 ml /1 tbls mustard

1 Cut the tomatoes across in half, scoop out the seeds, being careful not to break the flesh, turn the tomato halves upside down and let them drain.
2 Peel the mushrooms and cut off the stalks. Finely chop these and reserve.
3 Put the herbs in a mortar and pound them well with the pestle. Add the crushed garlic, anchovy fillets, mustard and mix well. Whisk the herb mixture into the softened butter in a large bowl, making sure that it is thoroughly and evenly distributed.
4 Divide the butter mixture into 2 and mix the chopped mushroom stalks into one half of the mixture.
5 Heat the oven to 190C /375F /gas 5.
6 Grease a large roasting pan with some of pounded butter mixture (the half without the mushrooms) and lay the tomatoes in the pan.

7 Fill the tomatoes with the mushroom stalk and butter mixture and sprinkle 5 ml /1 tsp breadcrumbs over the top of each one. Put in the oven and bake for 25 minutes.
8 Remove the pan from the oven and add the mushroom caps. Spread the plain butter mixture over the mushrooms, sprinkle them and the tomatoes with salt and freshly ground pepper and return to the oven for a further 10 minutes.
9 To serve, carefully transfer a tomato half to each of 6 individual plates. Place 6 button mushrooms on each plate and pour over some of the juice. Serve immediately, accompanied by crusty French bread, if wished.

1¼ hours

Baked scallops

Serve these delicate shellfish as the starter for an outdoor evening meal. A Moselle from the Saar region, lightly chilled, would make a perfect accompaniment.

Serves 4
8 large scallops
2 garlic cloves, finely chopped
25 g /1 oz parsley, finely chopped
2 medium-sized onions, finely chopped
1 pinch of ground cloves

1.5 ml /¼ tsp freshly grated nutmeg
salt
freshly ground black pepper
50 g /2 oz fresh white breadcrumbs
olive oil
sprigs of watercress, to garnish
lemon wedges, to garnish

1 Heat the oven to 200C /400F /gas 6. Prepare the scallops: clean away the beard, which appears in a black translucent line behind the coral. Ease the scallop away from its shell and wash and dry the scallops and 4 rounded shells.
2 Chop the scallop meat and corals and place them in a mixing bowl. Add the garlic, parsley and onions. Add cloves and nutmeg, season with salt and freshly ground pepper and mix the ingredients until they are well blended.

3 Divide the mixture into portions and pile it into each of the shells. Cover with the breadcrumbs and sprinkle over a little olive oil.
4 Place the shells on a baking sheet and bake for 20 minutes or until lightly browned on top. Garnish, then serve.

∆ 30 minutes

Cheese and ham soufflé

This soufflé makes a showy starter for 6 people or a main course for 4, accompanied by a green salad and crusty French bread. Serve it with a clean, refreshing Nahe wine.

Serves 4-6

50 g /2 oz butter
50 g /2 oz flour
425 ml /15 fl oz milk
6 medium-sized eggs
1 extra egg white

5 ml /1 tsp mustard
100 g /4 oz ham, cubed
150 g /5 oz Cheddar, grated
25 g /1 oz Parmesan, grated
salt and freshly ground black pepper
butter for greasing

1 Heat the oven to 180C /350F /gas 4. Melt the butter in a medium pan. Off the heat stir in the flour until smooth. Very slowly add the milk, stirring constantly. Return to the heat and cook slowly until the sauce is thick and smooth. Remove the pan from the heat.

2 Separate the eggs and add the extra white to the other 6. Lightly mix the egg yolks together then stir them quickly into the sauce with a wooden spoon.

3 Add the mustard, cubed ham and the grated cheeses, and salt and pepper to taste. Mix everything in well. Lightly butter a 2 L /3½ pt soufflé dish.

4 Whisk the egg whites until they are very stiff, then gently fold them into the cheese mixture with a metal spoon.

5 Turn the soufflé mixture into the prepared dish. With a knife mark a circle round the top of the soufflé about 25 mm /1 in from the edge. (The centre of the soufflé inside this line will rise higher than the edge.) Bake for 40 minutes.

6 Test the soufflé with a clean knife inserted into the centre to see if it is ready. If the mixture is still runny, cook for 5 minutes more. Serve at once.

🔪 1 hour

Smoked salmon cones

Serve this beautiful luxury canapé with champagne or a sparkling
Saumur wine. Everyone will remember it.

Makes about 30 canapés

125 ml /4 fl oz thick mayonnaise
15 ml /1 tbls yoghurt
1.5 ml /¼ tsp horseradish relish
100 g /4 oz boiled, peeled prawns, chopped
pinch of salt

several drops of lemon juice
freshly ground black pepper
about 600 g /1¼ lb smoked salmon cut in 8 long slices
parsley sprigs, to garnish (optional)
lemon slices, to garnish

1 The day before the party, mix the mayonnaise, yoghurt,
horseradish relish and chopped prawns together and season the
mixture with salt, lemon juice to taste and a generous amount of
freshly ground black pepper.

2 Cut the salmon slices into triangles, measuring approximately
7.5 × 6.5 × 6.5 cm /3 × 2½ × 2½ in. Fold the 2 shorter sides
around your index finger, pressing the edges together to make a cone
shape. It is easy to 'patch' any cones and make up any other cones
with unused bits of salmon.

3 Use a teaspoon to fill the salmon cones with the mayonnaise
mixture, then arrange the cones carefully on the serving dish,
overlapping them slightly.

4 Cover the dish with cling film and refrigerate overnight.

5 Remove the cling film just before serving, garnish with the
parsley sprigs and thin slices of lemon, if wished, and serve.

🕐 🍴🍴 **40 minutes**
plus overnight chilling

448

Californian avocado

This simple-to-prepare starter combines some of the best of Californian produce. Large ripe avocados, sliced thinly, are delicious in combination with egg and succulent fresh prawns. Serve it with a chilled Californian Chardonnay.

Serves 4-6
2 large ripe avocados
juice of 3 lemons
6 hard-boiled eggs
225 g /8 oz boiled, peeled prawns

salt
freshly ground white pepper
150 ml /5 fl oz mayonnaise
8-12 large prawns, tail shells
  intact, to garnish

1 Halve, stone and peel the avocados. Slice each half into 3 lengthways. Sprinkle the slices with lemon juice, using 2 lemons, to prevent discoloration. Arrange 2 slices on individual plates in a slightly overlapping shape.
2 Reserve 2 of the hard-boiled egg yolks. Slice the remaining eggs and the egg whites lengthways and place them on the plates.
3 Season the prawns with salt and freshly ground white pepper and pile onto the plates, on the egg.

4 Add the remaining lemon juice to the mayonnaise and blend well. Fit a piping bag with a star nozzle and fill with mayonnaise. Pipe the mayonnaise on top of the prawns.
5 Sieve the reserved egg yolks through a nylon sieve over the mayonnaise. Garnish each plate with 2 prawns.

boiling the eggs,
then 20 minutes

Prawn bouchées

Savouries to serve before dinner not only stimulate the appetite but also help solve the problem of drinking on an empty stomach. Choose types that are not too heavy – these prawn bouchées fit the bill perfectly and marry well with a dry white Mâcon.

Makes 36

500 g /1 lb frozen puff pastry, defrosted
1 beaten egg, for glazing
40 g /1½ oz butter
30 ml /2 tbls finely chopped onion
30 ml /2 tbls flour
425 ml /15 fl oz hot milk
½ bay leaf
6 black peppercorns
good pinch of freshly grated nutmeg
2 shallots, finely chopped
150 ml /5 fl oz dry white wine
15 ml /1 tbls finely chopped parsley
30 ml /2 tbls thick cream
15 ml /1 tbls cognac
Tabasco sauce
175 g /6 oz peeled prawns
salt
freshly ground black pepper
To serve
lettuce leaves, shredded
a few whole prawns, to garnish

1 Using a lightly floured rolling pin, roll the pastry with light, even strokes in one direction to an even thickness of 5 mm /¼ in. Use a sharp 4 cm /1½ in fluted metal cutter, lightly coated in flour, to cut circles of pastry.

2 Using a palette knife, transfer the circles to a damp baking sheet. Mark 20 mm /¾ in rounds in the centre of each circle but do not cut right through. Brush with beaten egg and leave to rest in a cool place for 15 minutes. Heat the oven to 200C /400F /gas 6.

3 Bake the bouchées in the centre of the oven for 20 minutes until risen and golden. With the point of a sharp knife, gently ease away the centre circle. Reserve the caps. With a teaspoon carefully scrape away any soft pastry and return the cases to the oven for 2–3 minutes to dry out. Transfer to a cooling tray.

4 Melt the butter in a small saucepan over a moderate heat. Add the onion and sauté gently, until soft and transparent.

5 Add the flour and cook gently, stirring constantly, for 2–3 minutes. Remove from the heat and gradually stir in a quarter of the hot milk. Return to the heat and gradually bring to the boil, stirring constantly. Still stirring, gradually add the remaining milk and bring to the boil.

6 Add the bay leaf, peppercorns and nutmeg. Pour the sauce into the top of a double boiler or a heatproof jug in a saucepan of gently bubbling water and cook, stirring occasionally, for about 30 minutes until reduced to 275 ml/10 fl oz. Sieve and return to the boiler.

7 Place the chopped shallots, in a small saucepan with the wine and reduce to 15 ml /1 tbls. Add to the sauce with the parsley, cream, cognac and a dash of Tabasco.

8 Roughly chop the prawns and add to the sauce. Add salt and freshly ground black pepper.

9 Ten minutes before serving, heat through the bouchée cases and caps in a 180C /350F /gas 4 oven. Then fill with the hot sauce and replace the caps. Arrange the lettuce around the bouchées and dot with the whole prawns. Serve immediately.

1½ hours

Avocado with crab

A light, fruity Moselle would make an excellent accompaniment to this colourful avocado starter.

Serves 4
2 ripe avocados
juice of ¹/₂ lemon
75 g /3 oz canned crabmeat,
  drained
¹/₂ red pepper, seeded and finely
  chopped
salt
freshly ground black pepper
lettuce heart leaves to garnish

For the dressing
15 ml /1 tbls lemon juice
45 ml /3 tbls olive oil
2.5 ml /¹/₂ tsp French mustard
¹/₂ garlic clove, crushed
30 ml /2 tbls tomato chutney
15 ml /1 tbls finely chopped parsley
salt
freshly ground black pepper

1 Divide the lettuce leaves among 4 individual plates. Cut the avocados in half, remove the stones and sprinkle each half with the lemon juice. Arrange each half on a plate of lettuce.
2 Flake the crabmeat with a fork in a bowl and add the red pepper. Mix gently with the fork.
3 To make the dressing, mix together the lemon juice, olive oil, French mustard, garlic, chutney and parsley and season.
4 Gently stir the dressing into the crabmeat and pepper mixture, then spoon into the avocado halves. Serve immediately.

 15 minutes

Cocktail cheese puffs

Champagne makes the perfect aperitif, but it calls for something really stylish in cocktail party food. Serve these little cheese choux puffs, freshly baked, with a choice of two special fillings, one made with cream cheese and the other with smoked salmon.

Makes 40 puffs
75 g /3 oz butter
5 ml /1 tsp salt
pinch of white pepper
pinch of nutmeg
100 g /4 oz flour, sifted
4 medium-sized eggs, beaten
100 g /4 oz Gruyère cheese, grated
1 medium-sized egg, beaten for
  glazing

For the fillings
225 g /8 oz full fat cream cheese
60 ml /4 tbls thick cream
60 ml /4 tbls chives, finely chopped
freshly ground black pepper
225 g /8 oz smoked salmon
  trimmings
125 ml /4 fl oz soured cream
10 ml /2 tsp lemon juice
sprigs of parsley

1 Heat the oven to 200C/400F/gas 6. Butter 2 baking sheets. Sift the flour ready to use.

2 Bring 275 ml /10 fl oz water to the boil. Add the butter and seasonings and boil until the butter has melted. Quickly remove from the heat and immediately stir in all the flour at one go. Beat with a wooden spoon or hand-held mixer until smooth.

3 Return pan to a low heat and beat vigorously for 1–2 minutes until a smooth ball is formed which leaves the sides of the pan without sticking.

4 Remove the pan from the heat and make a well in the centre. Pour a little of the eggs into the well and beat to incorporate. Continue to beat in the rest of the eggs a little at a time, until the mixture is smooth.

5 Beat the cheese into the choux pastry and season to taste. Fit a piping bag with a medium-sized plain nozzle and fill the bag with the cheese choux pastry. Holding the bag vertically, pipe out small bun shapes, about 1 tablespoonful in size, onto the buttered sheets, 2.5 cm/1 in apart. Brush the puffs with the beaten egg to glaze.

6 Bake the choux puffs for 15 minutes, then reduce the heat to 190C /375F /gas 5 and cook for a further 10 minutes. Remove from the oven and make very small slits in the puffs to allow the steam to escape, and cool completely on racks.

7 Meanwhile, make the two fillings. Beat the cream cheese until it is light and fluffy, then beat in the thick cream. Add the chives and season to taste with black pepper. Set aside.

8 Pound the salmon trimmings to a smooth paste and stir in the soured cream. Add the lemon juice and season to taste with black pepper.

9 Not long before serving, split open the cold puffs and fill half of them with the cream cheese filling and half with the smoked salmon filling. Garnish the dish of puffs with sprigs of parsley.

1 hour

452

Savoury mille-feuille

Served with a medium red wine such as Costières du Gard, this melt-in-the-mouth pastry makes a delightful dish to serve at the start of a dinner party. It can be made a couple of hours in advance and reheated at the last moment. The name, mille-feuille, means thousand leaves in French, and refers to the way the pastry separates into many paper-thin layers, one on top of the other, when cooked.

Serves 8

200 g /7 oz ready-made puff pastry
100 g /4 oz blue cheese
50 g /2 oz butter, softened
15 ml /1 tbls freshly chopped
   parsley

1 egg yolk
30 ml /2 tbls thin cream
freshly ground black pepper
beaten egg mixed with milk to
   glaze

1 Divide the pastry into 3 and roll each piece into a rectangle 10 × 20 cm /4 × 8 in. Carefully roll each piece of pastry over the rolling pin and unroll on to a dampened pastry sheet. Prick 2 of them with a fork. Place in the refrigerator for 30 minutes.
2 Meanwhile, heat the oven to 200C /400F /gas 6 and make the filling: beat the cheese until soft and then beat in the softened butter and parsley. Beat the egg yolk with the thin cream and mix into the cheese mixture. Season with the pepper.
3 Remove the pastry rectangles from the refrigerator and brush the unpricked rectangle with the beaten egg and milk glaze. Bake the pastry for 20 minutes or until lightly golden and puffy. Cool the rectangles on a wire rack until cold.
4 Heat the oven to 190C /375F /gas 5. Spread 1 unglazed rectangle with half the blue cheese mixture. Cover with the other unglazed rectangle and spread that with the remaining cheese mixture. Finally top with the egg-glazed rectangle. Return to the oven for 5–10 minutes, until heated through.

〖 1 hour, plus cooling time
  and 5–10 minutes reheating

Main dishes with red wine

Beef bordelaise
Roast wing rib of beef
French beef casserole
Tournedos with artichoke hearts
Rump steak special
Steak pastry parcels
Pepper and anchovy beef
Crown roast of lamb
Amaretto roast lamb
Hearty hot pot
Barbecued riblets
Pork noisettes with prunes
Pork with pepper
Pork and chick-pea stew
Chicken with tarragon
Roast duck with peaches
Duck with olives
Glazed bacon
Gammon with Madeira sauce
Burgundy ham
Mullet provençale

Beef bordelaise

Pot-roasted fillet of beef, in a sauce enriched with marrow-bone jelly, makes a succulent dinner party dish. Order your marrowbones well in advance from the butcher as they are not always available, and they make all the difference. Serve with a full-bodied claret, or a Cabernet Sauvignon from South Africa or California.

Serves 8-10
1.5-1.7 kg /3 lb 5 oz – 3lb 12 oz
* fillet of beef in one piece*
2 large marrowbones, chopped
50 g /2 oz butter
2 large onions, finely chopped
15 ml /1 tbls brandy
575 ml /1 pt claret

15 ml /1 tbls thyme
5 ml /1 tsp freshly grated nutmeg
15 ml /1 tbls tomato purée
1 garlic clove
salt and freshly ground black pepper
7.5 ml /1/2 tbls beurre manié
7.5 ml /1/2 tbls Dijon mustard
watercress, to garnish

1   Heat the oven to 100C /200F /gas low. Put the marrowbones, standing them upright if possible, in a large ovenproof casserole. Cover, using foil, if necessary, as some of the bones may protrude above the dish. Place in the oven for 3-3½ hours until the marrow is soft.
2   Remove from the oven, and with a marrow spoon, or long thin flat knife, extract all the marrow jelly from the bones. Strain through a fine sieve to remove the excess fat and reserve the jelly.
3   Turn up the oven to 220C /425F /gas 7. Melt the butter in a flameproof casserole and sauté the onions for 15 minutes until soft and golden. Remove from the pan and reserve, keeping warm.
4   Add the beef and brown it all over, quickly.
5   Flambé the beef with brandy, then add the marrowbone jelly, wine, thyme, nutmeg, tomato purée, garlic, salt and freshly ground black pepper. Cover the casserole and put it in the oven for 45-55 minutes. Baste it once, half way through the cooking. If you prefer beef to be well done, add a further 20-25 minutes to the cooking time.
6   Remove the beef from the casserole, place on a warmed serving platter and carve it into thick slices. Keep warm.
7   Stir the beurre manié into the sauce, whisking it well to thicken it, then add the mustard, stirring it in well. Pour the sauce over the beef, garnish with watercress and serve immediately.

preparing the marrowbone jelly,
then 1 hour 10 minutes

Roast wing rib of beef

This cut of beef, cooked on the bone, is generally reckoned to be one of the tastiest joints you can buy. Serve it with roast potatoes and Yorkshire puddings, and a full-bodied Pomerol.

Serves 6–8
2.3 kg /5 lb wing rib of beef
   on the bone
freshly ground black pepper
45 ml /3 tbls Dijon mustard
15 ml /1 tbls dried oregano

30 ml /2 tbls flour
300 ml /10 fl oz beef or other stock
salt
To serve
roast potatoes
Yorkshire puddings

1 Remove the beef from the refrigerator at least 2 hours before cooking and leave to come to room temperature.
2 Heat the oven to 200C /400F /gas 6. Sprinkle the beef with freshly ground black pepper. In a small bowl, mix together the Dijon mustard and dried oregano.
3 Place the joint in the oven and cook, basting and turning as necessary. Allow 33 minutes per kg /15 minutes per lb plus an extra 15 minutes, if you like your beef rare. If you prefer your meat well done allow up to 55 minutes per kg /25 minutes per lb plus 20 minutes extra. About 30 minutes before the meat is done, spread the mustard mixture over the fat.
4 Remove the beef from the oven, transfer to a carving board and leave to stand in a warm place for 15–20 minutes.
5 Meanwhile, strain any excess fat from the roasting tin, leaving about 30 ml /2 tbls of the juices. Add the flour and stir well over a low heat for 3–4 minutes to form a roux. Gradually add the stock, stirring, and bring to the boil. Season with salt and freshly ground black pepper and simmer.
6 To carve the beef, rest the joint on its rib bones. Run a sharp knife down the backbone and then along the ribs to free the meat from the bones. Remove the meat from the bones and place it, fat side up, on the carving board. Carve downwards into thin slices and arrange the slices on a heated serving dish. Pour the gravy into a heated sauceboat and hand it round separately. Serve the beef with roast potatoes and Yorkshire puddings.

2 hours standing,
then 1½–2½ hours

French beef casserole

The French Mediterranean feel of this delicious dish is enhanced if you serve it with a rich St Emilion wine.

Serves 6

1.2 kg /2½ lb braising or stewing steak cut into 5 cm /2 in cubes
30 ml /2 tbls olive oil
salt
freshly ground black pepper
2 medium-sized onions, sliced
2 garlic cloves, crushed
600 ml /1 pt red wine
2 large strips orange zest

1 bouquet garni
1 bay leaf
175 g /6 oz black olives, stoned
100 g /4 oz mushrooms, quartered
15 ml /1 tbls flour
25 g /1 oz butter
15 ml /1 tbls freshly chopped parsley
croûtons

1 Heat the oven to 170C /325F /gas 3. Heat the olive oil in a frying-pan and fry the meat in the oil in batches until browned on all sides. With a slotted spoon, transfer the meat to an ovenproof casserole and season with salt and pepper to taste.
2 Sauté the onions in the remaining oil in the frying-pan until golden. Add the garlic and cook for a further minute. Transfer the contents of the pan to the casserole, then add the red wine, orange zest, bouquet garni and bay leaf.
3 Cover the casserole and cook in the oven for 2½ hours. Remove the orange zest bouquet garni and bay leaf from the casserole, then stir in the olives and mushrooms. Blend the flour and butter together to make a beurre manié paste and stir into the casserole. Return the casserole to the oven for 15 minutes. Meanwhile, make the croûtons.
4 Serve sprinkled with chopped parsley and garnished with croûtons.

🔪🔪 3¼ hours

457

Tournedos with artichoke hearts

A fine claret from the Médoc would be a fitting accompaniment to this extremely elegant dinner party dish.

Serves 4

4 tournedos steaks, about 3 cm /1¼ in thick, with a thin band of fat tied round each
150 g /5 oz butter, plus extra for greasing
8 canned artichoke hearts, drained
4 slices white bread, cut into rounds slightly larger than the tournedos

salt and ground black pepper
125 g /4 oz frozen petit pois
30 ml /2 tbls vegetable oil
5 ml /1 tsp arrowroot
75 ml /3 fl oz Madeira
15 ml /1 tbls freshly chopped parsley
15 ml /1 tbls freshly chopped tarragon
sprigs of parsley to garnish

1 Heat the oven to 170C /325F /gas 3. Melt 50 g /2 oz butter in a flameproof casserole over medium heat. When frothing, remove from the heat and add the artichokes, upside down. Baste with the butter, cover with buttered greaseproof paper and place in the oven for 20 minutes. When cooked, keep warm.

2 In a frying-pan, sauté the bread rounds in the remaining butter over medium heat, until golden and crisp on both sides. Remove with a slotted spoon, drain on absorbent paper and place on an ovenproof serving dish. Keep warm in the bottom of the oven.

3 Bring a pan of salted water to the boil, add the peas and simmer for 3 minutes. Drain and keep covered.

4 Meanwhile, add the oil to the frying-pan. Put over medium heat and when hot, add the tournedos. Fry for 3–4 minutes per side.

Discard the strings and strips of fat from the cooked tournedos. Season the tournedos with salt and pepper, then place each one on a fried-bread round and keep warm in the oven.

5 Pour the excess fat from the frying-pan. Bring the remaining juices to the boil, mix the arrowroot with the Madeira and add to the pan. Boil rapidly, stirring, for 1 minute, to thicken the sauce. Adjust the seasoning and pour over the tournedos. Sprinkle with the chopped parsley and tarragon. Divide the peas between the hollows of the artichoke hearts and arrange around the tournedos. Garnish with parsley sprigs and serve immediately.

1¼ hours

Rump steak special

Accompany this rich dish with a Rioja, a full-bodied wine.

Serves 6
2 rump steaks, one just over
   700 g /1½ lb and one just under
freshly ground black pepper
Meaux mustard
6 thick bacon slices, rindless
25 ml /1 fl oz vegetable oil
60 ml /4 tbls red wine
1 onion, finely chopped
For the filling
175 g /6 oz full-fat soft cheese,
   flavoured with garlic and herbs

75 g /3 oz full-fat soft cheese
5 ml /1 tsp dried tarragon
1 onion, finely chopped
1 large egg, beaten
45 ml /3 tbls dried breadcrumbs
salt and ground black pepper
For the garnish
1 ham slice, cut into strips
stuffed olives, sliced
2 tomatoes, skinned and chopped
18 large mushroom caps, sautéed
parsley sprigs

1 Heat the oven to 190C /375F /gas 5. Thoroughly mix together the filling ingredients. Trim the steaks and season with pepper.
2 Spread a thin layer of mustard on one side of each steak and cover the larger piece with half the bacon. Spread the filling over the bacon and cover with the remaining bacon.
3 Place the smaller piece of steak, mustard side down, on the bacon and tie securely at 25 mm /1 in intervals along the length, then tie longitudinally. Brown the meat in the oil in a frying pan.
4 Place a piece of foil large enough to enclose the meat on a baking sheet. Place the meat on the foil and fold up the sides like a bowl.
5 Pour the wine into the frying-pan and stir to dislodge the sediment. Pour the wine over the meat. Sprinkle on the onion.

6 Fold over the foil to make a parcel. Cook in the centre of the oven for about 1 hour until the juices nearly run clear when a skewer is inserted in the centre (the time will depend on the thickness of the meat). Open the foil and continue to cook for 15 minutes.
7 Remove the meat from the oven and let it stand for 2–3 minutes. Place on a serving dish; remove the string. Pour over the juice.
8 Arrange the ham strips in a criss-cross pattern on the meat and dot with sliced olives. Fill the mushroom tops with chopped tomatoes and arrange around the meat. Garnish with parsley.

 1½ hours

Steak pastry parcels

Fillet steak wrapped in pastry not only looks impressive but is, in fact, a most economical way to serve meat. The smoothness of a claret would combine perfectly with the succulence of the beef.

Serves 4

4 fillet steaks, each weighing 125 g
/4 oz
25 g /1 oz butter, melted
freshly ground black pepper
10 ml /2 tsp freshly chopped mixed
herbs
250 g /8 oz made-weight frozen
puff pastry, defrosted
4 large tomatoes, blanched, peeled,
seeded and chopped
1 medium-sized egg, beaten
lettuce and tomato wedges

For the sauce
2 shallots, finely chopped
2.5 ml /1½ tsp freshly chopped
thyme
2.5 ml /1½ tsp freshly chopped
tarragon
1 bay leaf
175 ml /6 fl oz red Bordeaux wine
275 ml /10 fl oz beef stock
salt
freshly ground black pepper
15 ml /1 tbls tomato purée

1 Put all the ingredients for the sauce in a saucepan and boil until reduced by a third. Leave to cool.

2 Brush the steaks with the melted butter. Heat the grill and when it is very hot, sear the steaks for 1 minute on each side. Season well with black pepper, and sprinkle with the chopped mixed herbs. Leave until cold.

3 Divide the pastry into 4 and roll each piece to about 4 cm /1½ in larger than each steak. Divide the chopped tomatoes between the pieces of pastry and place a steak in the centre of each. Dampen the edges of the pastry and fold over to encase the meat completely. Trim the edges and press firmly together. Using a fish slice, transfer to a damp baking tray with the seam underneath.

4 Re-roll the trimmings and cut into flowers and leaves. Mark the veins with the point of a sharp knife, place on the pastry parcels and brush the surfaces with beaten egg. Refrigerate for 30 minutes. Meanwhile, heat the oven to 200C /400F /gas 6.

5 Remove the pastry parcels from the refrigerator and brush again with beaten egg. Cook in the oven for 15–20 minutes until the pastry is golden.

6 Serve the parcels on a bed of lettuce, garnished with tomatoes. Reheat the sauce, strain into a sauceboat and pass separately.

defrosting pastry, then
1½ hours

Pepper and anchovy beef

The anchovy-stuffed olives add a distinct flavour to this delicious casserole. Cook it a day ahead if you wish, adding the peppers, mushrooms and olives about 30 minutes before the meal. Serve with a sunny red Côtes du Rhône.

Serves 4–6

1 kg /2¼ lb braising steak, trimmed and cut into 4 cm / 1½ in cubes
30 ml /2 tbls olive oil
1 large Spanish onion, finely chopped
25 ml /1½ tbls flour
200 ml /7 fl oz dry red wine
400 g /14 oz canned tomatoes
2 large cloves garlic, crushed
5 ml /1 tsp dried thyme
1 bay leaf
salt
freshly ground black pepper
1 small red pepper, cut into thin rings
1 small green pepper, cut into thin rings
100 g /4 oz finely chopped mushrooms
65 g /2½ oz anchovy-stuffed green olives, halved

1 Heat the olive oil in a large flameproof casserole. Sauté half the cubes of beef until evenly browned. Transfer to a plate with a slotted spoon and repeat with the remaining cubes.
2 Add the chopped onion to the fat in the pan and cook over a low heat for about 10 minutes, or until soft.
3 Return the brown beef to the pan. Sprinkle in the flour, stirring well to coat. Add the wine, canned tomatoes and their liquid, crushed garlic, dried thyme and bay leaf. Season to taste with salt and freshly ground pepper. Stir well and bring to simmering point.

Cook, covered, over a low heat for 1¾ hours, stirring occasionally.
4 Add the pepper rings, finely chopped mushrooms and halved anchovy-stuffed olives and cook for a further 30 minutes, or until the pepper rings are tender.
5 Remove the bay leaf from the beef, check the seasoning and correct if necessary. Serve hot.

2½ hours

Crown roast of lamb

A good claret is an excellent accompaniment for this elegant lamb dish. The stuffing combines a slightly sweet fruitiness with a hint of sharpness, to complement both the wine and lamb.

Serves 6–8

2 best end joints, each with 6–8 cutlets
salt and ground black pepper
30 ml /2 tbls rosemary crushed
25 g /1 oz butter
watercress and 1 segmented orange
For the stuffing
425 g /15 oz canned apricot halves, drained

grated zest and juice of 1 orange
2 oranges, peeled and segmented
grated zest and juice of 1 lemon
225 g /8 oz cooked rice
100 g /4 oz white breadcrumbs
1 medium-sized onion, finely chopped
2.5 ml /1/2 tsp ground cinnamon
salt and freshly ground pepper

1 Cut off the skin from the best ends, then trim the meat from the tops of the bones. Weigh the joints and calculate the cooking time at 44 minutes per kg /20 minutes per lb.

2 Sew one end of each joint together, sewing around the last bone of each joint. Stand the tied joints upright and bend them round until the other ends meet. Stitch these together to form a crown. Then tie around the base to hold the crown in shape. Season the lamb inside and out with salt and pepper and sprinkle a little of the rosemary inside. Heat the oven to 190C /375F /gas 5.

3 Reserve 12 apricot halves. Chop the rest and mix with the rest of the stuffing ingredients; season with salt and pepper.

4 In a roasting tin, melt the butter with rest of the rosemary, then place the lamb in the tin. Spoon the stuffing loosely into centre of the crown. Cover bone ends with foil and roast for the calculated time basting occasionally and covering stuffing with foil if it becomes too brown.

5 Place the lamb on a warmed serving dish. Remove string and foil and place cutlet frills on the bones. Garnish with reserved apricot halves, watercress and orange segments.

45 minutes
plus roasting time

Amaretto roast lamb

Amaretto liqueur and apricots flavour the stuffing for this succulent lamb dish. Serve the dish with new potatoes, sprinkled with freshly chopped parsley, and a fine Barolo.

Serves 6-8
1½–2 kg /3½–4 lb shoulder of
  lamb, boned
150 ml /5 fl oz Amaretto di Saronno
100 g /4 oz dried apricots, chopped
1 small onion, chopped
15 g /½ oz butter
75 g /3 oz fresh breadcrumbs
15 ml /1 tbls freshly chopped parsley

50 g /2 oz walnuts, chopped
2.5 ml /½ tsp ground cinnamon
salt
freshly ground black pepper
30 ml /2 tbls lemon juice
juice of 2 oranges
300 ml /10 fl oz stock
15 ml /1 tbls cornflour
sprigs of watercress to garnish

1 Pour 50 ml /2 fl oz Amaretto over the chopped apricots, stir well and leave to soak for 2 hours.
2 Lightly sauté the onions in the butter, then mix with the apricots, breadcrumbs, parsley, walnuts and cinnamon. Season to taste with salt and pepper and heat the oven to 200C /400F /gas 6.
3 Lay the boned shoulder, skin side down, on a board and season well. Spread the stuffing over the meat. Roll up and tie securely with string at about 5 cm /2 in intervals. Place in a roasting pan.
4 Mix the lemon and orange juice with a further 50 ml /2 fl oz Amaretto and pour this over the lamb. Roast, uncovered, for 30 minutes, basting occasionally.
5 Reduce the heat to 180C /350F /gas 4 and continue cooking for

1½ hours, basting every 15 minutes.
6 Lift the lamb on to a warmed serving dish and remove the string. Pour off the fat from the pan juices, add the stock and the remaining Amaretto. Blend the cornflour with a little water and stir this into the liquid in the pan. Adjust the seasoning to taste and bring to the boil over medium heat. Boil the sauce, stirring, until clear, then pour into a sauceboat.
7 Garnish the lamb with watercress and serve accompanied by the sauce.

2 hours soaking,
then 2¾ hours

Hearty hot pot

Sweet-tasting neck of lamb is the basic ingredient of traditional Lancashire hot-pot. This version has a flavouring of kidney and mushrooms and is topped with a layer of potato slices. Serve it with an equally hearty wine, such as Bull's Blood.

Serves 4

*1 kg /2¼ lb middle neck of lamb,
    chopped*
30 ml /2 tbls flour
salt
freshly ground black pepper
25 g /1 oz dripping or lard

*3–4 lamb's kidneys, trimmed and
    thickly sliced
    quartered if large*
100 g /4 oz mushrooms, quartered
450 ml /15 fl oz beef stock
750 g /1½ lb potatoes, sliced

1 Heat the oven to 170C /325F /gas 3 and wipe the meat with absorbent paper. Season the flour with salt and pepper, then coat the meat in the seasoned flour. Reserve the left-over flour.
2 Heat the fat in a large saucepan and fry the meat, in batches, until lightly browned and sealed. Transfer the meat to a hotpot or deep casserole. Scatter the kidney and mushrooms over the meat.
3 Fry the sliced onion gently in the fat left in the saucepan for a few minutes, then transfer to the hotpot with a slotted spoon. Add the remaining seasoned flour to the pan and stir until lightly browned.

Stir in the stock and bring to the boil. Check the seasoning and simmer for a few minutes, until slightly thickened.
4 Cover the meat with overlapping potato slices. Pour the sauce over the potatoes, cover the hotpot and cook in the oven for 1½ hours. Uncover the pot and cook or a further 30 minutes to brown the potatoes. Serve from the pot.

 2½ hours

Barbecued riblets

Divide breasts of lamb into riblets and cook them in tangy sauce to serve as finger food for an informal summer lunch or dinner party. A medium New Zealand wine like Nobilos Pinotage would bring out their fruity flavour.

Serves 4
2 breasts of lamb
30 ml /2 tbls vinegar
boiling water, to cover
For the sauce
30 ml /2 tbls tomato ketchup

30 ml /2 tbls clear honey
30 ml /2 tbls soy sauce
30 ml /2 tbls plum jam
15 ml /1 tbls dry mustard
10 ml /2 tsp Worcestershire sauce

1 Remove and discard the skin and excess fat, then put the breasts into a saucepan large enough to hold them both. Cover with boiling water and add the vinegar. Cover the saucepan and simmer for 15 minutes.
2 Mix all the sauce ingredients together in a saucepan and heat gently, stirring until all the ingredients are combined.
3 Heat the oven to 180C /350F /gas 4. Drain the breasts, then cut between the ribs into 25 mm /1 in wide strips.
4 Arrange the riblets close together in a roasting tin, pour the sauce over to coat them and cook for 30 minutes. Turn the riblets over once during the cooking time.
5 Baste thoroughly, then increase the heat to 200C /400F /gas 6 and cook for a further 15–20 minutes until the riblets are crisp.
6 Serve the riblets with any remaining sauce as a main course, allowing about 3–4 riblets per portion. Or serve as finger food for an informal party, where sticky fingers are acceptable. Remember to provide finger bowls.

 1½ hours

Pork noisettes with prunes

A delicious prune and onion sauce goes well with this prime cut of pork. Serve Pork noisettes with prunes with a dark, full-flavoured, fruity red wine from Cahors.

Serves 4–6

1.4 kg /3 lb loin of pork, skinned,
*   boned and rolled*
500 g /1 lb prunes, stoned
425 ml /15 fl oz red wine
salt

freshly ground black pepper
50 g /2 oz butter
30 ml /2 tbls olive oil
2 small onions, finely chopped
watercress, to garnish

1 Soak the prunes, preferably overnight, in 300 ml /10 fl oz of the red wine.
2 Heat the oven to 170C /325F /gas 3. Cook the prunes, covered, in the oven for 1 hour. Remove and reserve.
3 Meanwhile, cut the loin of pork into noisettes, approximately 25 mm /1 in thick. Season them well with salt and freshly ground black pepper. In a frying-pan heat 25 g /1 oz of the butter and the olive oil and sauté the noisettes for 2–3 minutes on each side or until golden brown. Transfer the noisettes to a flameproof casserole.
4 Pour off any excess fat from the frying-pan and use 30 ml /2 tbls red wine to deglaze it. Pour these juices over the pork, cover the casserole tightly and cook in the oven for 1 hour.
5 Meanwhile, melt the remaining butter in a saucepan and cook the finely chopped onions, stirring occasionally, for 3–4 minutes or

until transparent. Blend the onions to a purée with 6 of the cooked prunes and 60–90 ml /4–6 tbls of the red wine.
6 Add the cooking liquid from the prunes to the casserole and cook for a further 15 minutes. Warm the prunes in the oven.
7 When the pork is cooked transfer it to a heated serving dish with the prunes. Put the casserole over a high heat and bring the liquid to the boil and boil for about 6–8 minutes, or until the liquid is reduced to about one-third of its original quantity. Add the onion and prune purée and cook, stirring, for 1–2 minutes more.
8 Pour the sauce over the pork noisettes, garnish with watercress and serve immediately.

Overnight soaking,
then 2½ hours

Pork with pepper

This pork dish with its spicy marinade is unusual in being cooked under a low grill instead of in the oven. It can be prepared well in advance. Serve with saffron rice and accompanied by a Cabernet Sauvignon.

Serves 4–6
900 g /2 lb boneless pork steaks
3 garlic cloves
2.5 ml /½ tsp cumin seeds
2.5 ml /½ tsp coriander seeds
2.5 ml /½ tsp turmeric
2.5 ml /½ tsp chilli powder
1.5 ml /¼ tsp salt
75 ml /5 tbls olive oil
1½ Spanish onions
1 large green pepper
1 large red pepper
4 large tomatoes, blanched and skinned
freshly ground black pepper
flat-leaved parsley to garnish

1 Cut the pork into 2 cm /¾ in cubes and put in a large shallow flameproof dish.

2 Using a mortar and pestle, pound the garlic with the cumin and coriander seeds. Add the turmeric, chilli powder and salt. Stir in 45 ml /3 tbls oil. Pour this mixture over the pork and mix well so that all the pieces are well coated. Marinate for at least 1 hour.

3 Heat the grill to low. Coarsely chop onions, peppers and tomatoes. Add the onion and peppers to the pork. Pour in the remaining oil, season with salt and freshly ground black pepper and stir well to distribute the seasonings. Grill for 30 minutes on a low heat, basting and turning the meat and vegetables every 10 minutes and turning the dish as well to cook evenly.

4 Add the tomatoes to the dish and grill for another 20–30 minutes or until the meat is cooked through. Garnish with parsley and serve immediately with saffron rice.

marinating for 1 hour, then 1¼ hours

Pork and chick-pea stew

This hearty stew is perfect for a cold winter meal. Cook and serve it with a full-bodied Argentine Cabernet Sauvignon.

Serves 4

800 g /1¾ lb shoulder of pork,
* cut into 25 mm /1 in cubes*
30-45 ml /2-3 tbls olive oil
100 g /4 oz dried chick-peas,
* cooked and drained*
2 medium-sized onions, halved
* and thinly sliced*
100 ml /3½ fl oz red wine
3 medium-sized tomatoes,
* blanched, skinned, seeded*
* and chopped*

1 bay leaf
1 large red pepper, sliced
sautéed aubergine slices, to
* serve*
freshly chopped parsley, to
* garnish*

For the marinade

7.5 ml /1½ tsp salt
freshly ground black pepper
large pinch ground allspice
1.5 ml /¼ tsp dried marjoram
2 large garlic cloves, crushed

1 Place the cubed pork in a bowl with the marinade ingredients and mix well with your hands, making sure the marinade is evenly distributed. Cover and refrigerate overnight, stirring once or twice, if convenient. Soak and cook the chick-peas.

2 Dry the meat on absorbent paper, reserving any juices. Heat 15 ml /1 tbls oil in a large frying-pan over moderate heat. Add half the pork and fry, stirring, until it changes colour. Transfer the meat to a flameproof casserole, using a slotted spoon. Fry the second batch of pork, adding more oil as needed.

3 Add more oil to the pan, if necessary, then add the onions and cook for a few minutes, until they are softened. Transfer them to the casserole. Deglaze the pan with the wine, stirring in the crusty bits.

4 Pour the wine into the casserole and add the tomatoes, bay leaf and reserved meat juices. Bring to simmering point, then lower the heat, cover and simmer gently for 30 minutes, stirring occasionally.

5 Add the sliced pepper and chick-peas. Continue to cook, stirring occasionally, for a further 1-1½ hours until the meat is very tender.

6 Transfer the meat and vegetables to a heated serving platter with a slotted spoon. Boil the remaining juices quickly until they thicken slightly. Taste and adjust the seasoning, then pour over the pork. Surround with aubergine, sprinkle with parsley and serve.

 overnight marinating, cooking chick-peas, then 2–2¼ hours

Chicken with tarragon

Tarragon is a wonderfully delicate herb which goes particularly well with chicken. If you cannot find fresh tarragon, try frozen, which is excellent. Serve with a colourful vegetable such as carrots. The fresh, bold flavour of a Beaujolais Villages should match this dish admirably.

Serves 4–6
1.8 kg /4 lb chicken
50 g /2 oz butter
30 ml /2 tbls chopped fresh (or
    frozen) tarragon leaves or 30 ml
    /1 tbls dried tarragon

1 garlic clove, crushed
salt and freshly ground black
    pepper
15 ml /1 tbls oil
50 ml /2 fl oz brandy
75 ml /3 fl oz thick cream

1 Heat the oven to 190C /375F /gas 5. Mash together the butter, tarragon, garlic, salt and pepper. Divide the mixture into three.
2 Gently push your fingers between the skin and the breast of the chicken and insert one third of the butter mixture on each side of the breast, under the skin. Flatten the butter slightly by patting the skin. Put the remaining piece of butter into the cavity of the bird.
3 Rub a little oil on the outside of the bird. Arrange the chicken so it rests on one breast on a rack in a roasting tin and roast for 35 minutes. Turn it onto the other side and roast for a further 35 minutes.
4 Remove the tin from the oven, lift off the bird, take out the rack and return the bird to the tin.

5 Put the brandy into a soup ladle and warm it gently. Set a match to it and pour it over the chicken. When the flames subside, carefully remove the chicken, tipping the juices from the cavity into the tin. Place the bird on a serving dish and keep warm.
6 Add the cream to the pan and warm it through gently, stirring well to incorporate all the juices. Pour the sauce over the chicken and serve immediately. There will not be a great deal of sauce, but it is very rich. If you prefer more sauce, add some chicken stock to the pan before the cream.

1½ hours

469

Roast duck with peaches

A Mercurey or Givry from the Chalonnais will complement this succulent dish perfectly.

Serves 4

2.25 kg /5 lb oven-ready duck
800 g /1 lb 13 oz canned peach slices, drained
salt and freshly ground pepper
30 ml /2 tbls lemon juice
225 ml /8 fl oz port
45 ml /3 tbls brandy (optional)

45 ml /3 tbls sugar
75 ml /5 tbls red wine vinegar
425 ml /15 fl oz duck stock, made from the giblets
15 ml /1 tbls arrowroot
sprigs of watercress

1 Heat the oven to 220C /425F /gas 7. Prick the duck skin all over and rub it with salt and pepper. Place the duck, breast-side up, in a roasting tin and roast for 15 minutes, to brown slightly. Reduce the heat to 180C /350F /gas 4 and continue to roast for 1 hour 10 minutes. Turn the duck over, breast-side down, and roast for a further 15 minutes, then turn it breast-side up again for a final 5 minutes' roasting.

2 Place the peach slices in a pan and pour over the lemon juice and 45 ml /3 tbls port, or brandy if you prefer. Set aside until needed, but baste occasionally.

3 Meanwhile, dissolve the sugar in the vinegar, then boil it for 5 minutes until a caramel syrup is formed. As soon as it is dark brown, remove from the heat, pour in 150 ml /5 fl oz stock and stir over low heat to dissolve the caramel. Add the rest of the stock. Mix the arrowroot with 30 ml /2 tbls port and add to the pan. Simmer for 3 minutes and set aside.

4 Remove the duck from the oven. Remove the trussing, place on a dish and keep warm.

5 Tip off the fat from the roasting tin. Add the remaining port, then boil to reduce to 45 ml/3 tbls. Strain into the reserved sauce and simmer for 1 minute.

6 Pour the sauce over the peaches. Heat for 3 minutes, then remove the peaches with a slotted spoon and arrange around the duck.

7 Boil the sauce to reduce it slightly. Adjust the seasoning. Pour into a warmed sauceboat and spoon some over the duck. Garnish with sprigs of watercress.

1¾ hours

Duck with olives

The olives enhance the flavour of the duck in this dish, which is delicious with plain brown rice and an inviting red Graves.

Serves 4
2 kg /4½ lb oven-ready duckling
salt
30 ml /2 tbls oil
25 g /1 oz butter
1 medium-sized onion, chopped
15 ml /1 tbls tomato purée

2.5 ml /½ tsp dried thyme
2.5 ml /½ tsp dried rosemary
1 bay leaf
freshly ground black pepper
275 ml /10 fl oz dry white wine
250 g /9 oz green olives, stoned
200 g /7 oz mushrooms, halved

1 Prick the skin of the duck all over and sprinkle with salt.
2 Heat the oil and butter in a flameproof casserole. Brown the duck evenly on all sides for about 20 minutes until the skin is coloured and crisp.
3 Remove the duck from the casserole, put it on a heated plate and keep it hot. Drain off the excess fat from the casserole, keeping only 15 ml /1 tbls.
4 Fry the onion in the reserved duck fat until soft. Then add the tomato purée, thyme, rosemary, bay leaf, pepper and 225 ml /8 fl oz of the white wine. Cook until the mixture reduces and thickens.

5 Return the duck to the casserole, cover and simmer for about 1¼ hours, turning and basting it occasionally. Add the olives and mushrooms and cook for a further 30 minutes, adding a little water if necessary.
6 Joint the duck and arrange on a serving dish with the olives and mushrooms. Add the rest of the wine to the casserole, stir and bring to the boil. Reduce the heat, strain the sauce and serve it separately.

⚔ 2¼ hours

Glazed bacon

Serve this delicately-flavoured joint with a light red wine such as Beaujolais.

Serves 8
1.8 kg /4 lb middle gammon or bacon joint,
*   rolled and tied*
5 whole black peppercorns
100 g /4 oz brown sugar

20 cloves
15 ml /1 tbls flour
275 ml /10 fl oz cider
salt and freshly ground black pepper
12 apple rings, fried in butter

1   Place the joint in a large pan and add enough water to cover. Add the peppercorns and bring to the boil. Then reduce the heat, cover and simmer for 30 minutes.
2   Heat the oven to 180C /350F /gas 4. Wrap the joint in foil and place on a rack in a roasting pan. Add enough water to the pan to cover the bottom and place in the oven.
3   Roast for 1 hour, then remove from the oven and open the foil. Discard the water in the pan. Increase the oven heat to 200C/400F /gas 6. Remove the string and rind from the joint and, using a sharp knife, lightly score the fat in a criss-cross pattern.
4   Cover the fatty surface with brown sugar, pressing it down on to the fat. Stud the sugared surface with the cloves, following the criss-cross pattern cut into the fat.
5   Leaving the foil open and only loosely covering the lean meat surface, return the joint to the oven for a further 30 minutes. Remove from the oven and transfer to a serving dish. Keep warm.
6   Pour the juices left in the foil into the roasting pan. Stir in 15 ml /1 tbls flour and cook over a moderate heat for 2 minutes. Remove the pan from the heat and stir in the cider. Bring to the boil, stirring.
7   Season to taste, then pour into a sauceboat. Garnish the dish with the fried apple rings and parsley sprigs.

2¼ hours

472

Gammon with Madeira sauce

Madeira and gammon marry here to produce this melt-in-the-mouth dish. Serve with a Rosé from the Loire or Ventoux.

Serves 4

4 gammon steaks, 15 mm /½ in
  thick, with the fat slashed
25 g /1 oz butter
15 ml /1 tbls oil
1 small onion, finely chopped
100 g /4 oz button mushrooms,
  sliced

25 g /1 oz flour
175 ml /6 fl oz ham or brown stock
150 ml /5 fl oz dry Madeira
15 ml /1 tbls tomato purée
salt
freshly ground black pepper
150 ml /5 fl oz thick cream
braised spinach to serve

1 Heat the butter and oil in a heavy-based frying-pan over moderate heat. Add the gammon and fry each side for 4 minutes, until golden brown. Transfer with a slotted spoon to a plate and keep warm.

2 Add the chopped onion and mushrooms to the pan and cook until softened. Stir in the flour with a wooden spoon and cook for 2 minutes stirring continuously.

3 Remove the pan from the heat and stir in the stock and Madeira. Stir in the tomato purée and season to taste with salt and pepper.

4 Return the pan to the heat and bring the sauce to simmering point, stirring continuously. Then add the cream. Simmer for 5 minutes, until the sauce has reduced slightly.

5 Return the gammon to the pan and simmer for 10 minutes until tender. Arrange the gammon on a bed of braised spinach and pour the sauce over the steaks.

🍴 40 minutes

Burgundy ham

This is a traditional Eastertide dish in Burgundy. Its pretty green and pink marbled appearance makes it a spectacular centrepiece for a buffet party or cold luncheon. Serve it with a chilled Pinot Noir rosé, such as Bourgogne-Marsannay-la-Côte.

Serves 6-8

1.4 kg /3 lb piece of gammon
* or ham*
veal knuckle or beef marrow
* bone, chopped in 2–3 pieces*
2 calf's feet or 4 pig's trotters
5 ml /1 tsp dried chervil
5 ml /1 tsp dried tarragon
2.5 ml /½ tsp dried marjoram

2 bay leaves
5 ml /1 tsp dried thyme
4 sprigs fresh parsley
12 black peppercorns
75 cl bottle dry white wine
15 ml /1 tbls finely chopped parsley
green salad, to serve
garlic bread, to serve

1 Place the gammon or ham in a large saucepan, cover with cold water and bring to the boil over a medium heat. Taste the water and if it is very salty, pour it away and cover the gammon with fresh cold water.
2 Bring to the boil again and then simmer very gently for 45 minutes. Remove the gammon or ham from the pan and discard the cooking liquid.
3 Chop the meat into sizeable chunks, removing and discarding any rind or very fatty pieces. Return the chopped meat to the rinsed-out pan and add the veal knuckle or beef marrow bone, the calf's feet or pig's trotters, the herbs and the peppercorns. Pour in the wine and top up with cold water, if necessary, so that everything is covered with liquid. Bring to the boil over a low heat, skimming off any fat as it rises. Simmer for 2½-3 hours.
4 Remove the bone and feet or trotters and discard them. Transfer the ham with a slotted spoon to a large bowl and let it cool slightly.

5 Strain the cooking liquid through a fine sieve and pour it into a jug. Plunge the jug into a bowl of iced water to cool it quickly. Any fat that forms can then be easily removed from the top with absorbent paper. Put the stock aside for the jelly to set slightly.
6 With 2 forks flake the ham but do not mash it too much.
7 Add the finely chopped parsley to the jelly, stirring it well in, then pour over the ham and mix everything well together.
8 Put the mixture into a wetted 1 L /1¾ pt mould, and leave overnight in the refrigerator to set.
9 To turn out the mould, put a tea-towel soaked in hot water round the bottom of the mould for about 1 minute. Put a plate over the mould, invert the two and the ham should fall out onto the plate. Serve with a green salad and garlic bread.

4½ hours plus cooling,
then overnight setting

Mullet provençale

Serve this cold mullet dish for an outdoor luncheon. A Provence rosé would be a delicious wine to accompany it.

Serves 4–6
1.6 kg /3½ lb grey mullet, cleaned
15–30 ml /1–2 tbls dry white wine
juice of ½ lemon
15–30 ml /1–2 tbls olive oil
sprigs of thyme
salt and ground black pepper
25 g /1 oz butter
30 ml /2 tbls olive oil

2 medium-sized onions, sliced
2 green peppers, cut into
  25 mm /1 in squares
500 g /1 lb tomatoes, quartered
125 g /4 oz black olives, stoned
150 ml / 5 fl oz French dressing
For the garnish
lemon slices
sprigs of thyme

1 Heat the oven to 170C /325F /gas 3. Cut a piece of foil large enough to enclose the fish completely. Place the fish on the foil and sprinkle with the white wine, lemon juice and olive oil. Add the sprigs of thyme and season. Wrap the foil around the fish, sealing it tightly. Cook in the oven for 1 hour.
2 Remove the fish from the oven and leave to cool a little. Remove the skin carefully leaving the head and tail in place. Leave to cool.
3 Meanwhile, heat the butter and olive oil in a frying-pan and cook the onions for 3–4 minutes or until transparent. Remove with a slotted spoon and leave to cool.

4 Cook the peppers in the remaining fat for 5 minutes, stirring occasionally. Remove and cool.
5 Mix the onions, pepper, tomatoes and black olives together carefully. Season with salt and freshly ground black pepper to taste and toss with the vinaigrette. Spoon onto a serving dish.
6 Arrange the mullet on top of the vegetables, garnish with the lemon slices and sprigs of thyme and serve.

1¾ hours including cooling

475

Main dishes
with white wine

Turkey escalopes chasseur
Almond chicken puffs
Chicken with port
Pork paprika
Pork with soured cream
Juniper pork
Watercress veal
Normandy veal escalopes
Stir-fried beef with corn
Sardines in white wine
Plaice meunière
Salmon with fennel
Cold seafood platter
Monkfish salad
Buttered lobster
Italian-style scampi
Crawfish with asparagus

Turkey escalopes chasseur

Sautéed mushrooms and shallots are the classic ingredients of a dish cooked *au chasseur*. Here they are combined with light-textured turkey escalopes – delicious served with a dry white Graves.

Serves 4
4 × 125 g /4 oz fillets of turkey breast
40 g /1½ oz butter
15 ml /1 tbls olive oil
3 shallots or 1 medium-sized onion, chopped
350 g /12 oz tomatoes, blanched, skinned, seeds and juice removed
½ garlic clove, finely chopped
salt and freshly ground black pepper
10 ml /2 tsp arrowroot
50 ml /2 fl oz meat juice from beef or good beef consommé
125 ml /4 fl oz dry white vermouth
2.5 ml /½ tsp chopped fresh basil or tarragon (optional)
350 g /12 oz button mushrooms, sliced
chopped parsley to garnish

1 Flatten the turkey breasts slightly with a rolling pin. Dry the surfaces with absorbent paper. Heat 15 g /½ oz butter with the oil in a frying-pan over moderate heat until the butter foams. Put in the escalopes. Fry for 4–5 minutes on each side to seal and brown. Remove from the pan and keep warm.
2 Fry the shallots or onion in the pan for 1 minute, scraping up the sediment from the bottom of the pan. Chop the tomato flesh and stir it into the pan with garlic and seasoning. Cover and simmer for 5 minutes.
3 Mix the arrowroot with a little of the beef juice or consommé. Add the vermouth, arrowroot mixture and remaining beef juice or consommé to the pan and boil rapidly until it is reduced by half.
4 Season the escalopes and return them to the pan. Sprinkle with the herbs if available. Cover with a lid and simmer very gently for 4–5 minutes.
5 Meanwhile, melt 25 g /1 oz butter in a separate pan and sauté the mushrooms for 4 minutes over moderate heat, tossing them until they are brown. Season with salt and pepper.
6 Transfer the escalopes and sauce to a heated serving dish. Spoon over the sautéed mushrooms and serve garnished with parsley.

🕭 30 minutes

Almond chicken puffs

These 'pillows' of puff pastry, encasing chicken breasts poached in white wine and served with a delicate almond and orange sauce, make an impressive main course. Serve with an Australian dry white wine, well chilled.

Serves 4

4 chicken breasts, boned and
  skin removed
225 g /8 oz frozen puff pastry,
  defrosted
150 ml /5 fl oz dry white wine
10 white peppercorns
1 small onion, coarsely chopped
4 sprigs of parsley
1 garlic clove

4 large oranges
175 g /6 oz butter
50 g /2 oz fresh breadcrumbs
100 g /4 oz ground almonds
1 egg yolk, beaten
50 g /2 oz blanched whole almonds
salt
100 g /4 oz thick cream
butter for greasing
flour

1   Put the wine, white peppercorns, onion, parsley and whole garlic clove into a large saucepan and add 1.1 L /2 pt cold water. Bring to the boil. Add the chicken breasts and simmer gently for 15–20 minutes until the breasts are almost cooked through.

2   Remove the chicken and cool.

3   Add the grated zest of one orange to the stock in the pan. Boil the stock hard until reduced to 275 ml /10 fl oz, then strain.

4   Melt 125 g /4 oz butter in a large frying-pan and add the breadcrumbs, stirring so that all the crumbs are coated with butter and evenly browned. Put into a blender together with the ground almonds and the stock and blend thoroughly.

5   Squeeze the juice from 3 oranges and add to the sauce, which should be quite thick. Heat the oven to 220C /425F /gas 7.

6   Divide the pastry into 4 and, using a lightly-floured rolling pin and board, roll out each portion into a 15 cm /6 in square. Place a chicken breast in the centre of each portion and spoon 10 ml /2 tsp of the sauce over each breast. Fold over the pastry to form an envelope

and firmly seal the edges. Brush the edges with beaten egg yolk and place the chicken envelopes on a lightly greased baking sheet. Bake for 20–25 minutes until golden and risen.

7   Melt the remaining butter in the frying-pan and sauté the blanched almonds until evenly browned. Drain on absorbent paper and sprinkle with salt.

8   Peel the remaining orange, removing all the pith, and cut into 8 thin slices. If there is any orange juice on the plate add it to the sauce and stir to blend thoroughly.

9   Put the chicken puffs on a serving platter and keep warm while finishing the sauce.

10   Add the cream to the remaining sauce, stir well and then pour immediately over the chicken. Put 2 orange slices on each envelope, sprinkle with the whole almonds and serve at once.

⚬⚬ 1½ hours

509

511

Index: Wine

Dep. Leg. B-40416-87

Mixed melon salad

A refreshing way to end a meal, this fragrant salad should be served with a wine that is neither too overpowering nor too distractingly dry or sweet – a medium Cabernet d'Anjou would fit the bill perfectly.

Serves 6–8
1 small honeydew melon
1 cantaloupe or Charentais melon
250 g /8 oz black grapes

1 medium-sized orange
600 g /1¼ lb canned, stoned
*   lichees in syrup*

1 Cut the melons in half and scoop out the seeds. Use a melon ball cutter to cut the flesh into small balls, then place them in a large bowl.
2 Seed the whole grapes by cutting half way into them with a sharp knife and removing the seeds with the point of a knife. Add the seeded grapes to the melon balls.
3 Using a sharp knife, cut the peel and all the pith from the orange. Carefully cut out the segments from between the membranes and extract any pips from them with the point of the knife. Place the

segments with the other fruit in the bowl. Squeeze the orange membranes over the bowl to extract any remaining juice.
4 Pour the lichees together with their canned syrup into the bowl. Stir the fruit to mix well and transfer to individual glass bowls. Leave to chill in the refrigerator for 1–2 hours before serving.

🔪 45 minutes, plus chilling time

Ice cream stripe

This cool, delicious dessert is perfect for hot summer days or warm balmy evenings. Serve it with a well-chilled Californian dessert wine – it makes a memorable end to any meal.

Serves 6

700 ml /1¼ pt chocolate ice cream
700 ml /1¼ pt vanilla ice cream
700 ml /1¼ pt coffee ice cream
oil for greasing

125 g /4 oz sugar
50 g /2 oz almonds, unpeeled
whipped cream and chopped nuts, to decorate

1 Put the ice cream in the main part of the refrigerator to soften. Chill a 2 L /3½ pt loaf tin and grease a baking sheet.

2 To make the praline, put the sugar and nuts in a heavy-based saucepan and melt the sugar over a very low heat. Do not stir.

3 Once the sugar has dissolved, turn the heat up a little and stir the nuts in the caramel. Cook carefully until the syrup turns a deep golden colour. Turn the praline out onto the baking sheet and leave to harden.

4 Once the praline has set, remove it from the baking sheet and crush it to a fine powder, either in a blender or using a pestle and mortar.

5 Remove the chocolate ice cream from the refrigerator and spoon it into the loaf tin, level it off and sprinkle with half the praline. Put in the freezer for a few minutes to firm up a little. Repeat with the vanilla ice cream and the remaining praline. Again put in the freezer to firm up and finally add the coffee ice cream. Put in the freezer for at least 3–4 hours to harden.

6 To serve: unmould the ice cream about 15 minutes before serving and leave in the refrigerator to soften slightly. Either serve whole, decorated with whipped cream and chopped nuts, or serve in slices decorated with cream and nuts.

🔪🔪 1½ hours plus chilling

Peach shortcake

Serve this mouth-watering treat with a luscious Muscat dessert wine to make a special end to a dinner party.

Serves 4–6
100 g /4 oz flour
65 g /2½ oz butter, diced
40 g /1½ oz icing sugar
1 large egg yolk
a few drops of vanilla essence

350 g /12 oz fresh or canned peach slices
45 ml /3 tbls redcurrant jelly to glaze
150 ml /5 fl oz thick cream, whipped

1 Sift the flour on to a smooth surface. Make a well in the centre and add the butter, icing sugar, egg yolk and vanilla. Work the ingredients together with your fingers to form a smooth paste. Chill for 30 minutes.

2 Heat the oven to 180C /350F /gas 4. Roll out the pastry to a large round, 5 mm /¼ in thick. Prick all over with a fork and bake in the oven for 20 minutes. Cool on a rack.

3 Melt the redcurrant jelly in a small saucepan over gentle heat. Arrange the peach slices in a pattern to cover the shortcake, then brush with the melted redcurrant to glaze. Decorate with rosettes of whipped cream.

45 minutes plus cooling, then decorating

Grapefruit and vermouth granita

An unusual way of using vermouth, this sorbet makes a distinctive end to a meal, before or after the cheese course. Serve with a light Vinho Verde.

Serves 6

175 g /6 oz caster sugar
2 large juicy grapefruit

75 ml /5 tbls dry vermouth
orange tuiles or wafers, to serve

1   Put 300 ml /10 fl oz water and the sugar in a pan and bring to the boil. Then simmer gently for 5 minutes, remove from the heat and leave to cool.
2   Peel the grapefruit and divide up the segments, removing all pips with the point of a knife. Blend the grapefruit flesh and vermouth in an electric blender or food processor until liquid. Mix with the sugar syrup, pour into a tray and freeze overnight.

3   Remove the sorbet from the freezer and thaw for 10 minutes. Blend again in the blender until pale yellow and fluffy.
4   Refreeze. Serve straight from the freezer, scooping the sorbet into glasses, with orange tuiles or wafers.

25 minutes, plus freezing and 10 minutes thawing

Wine jelly in melon

A delectable combination of wine-flavoured jelly and sweet melon, this dessert is quite delicious served with a light fruity wine, such as Vouvray.

Serves 4
2 small sweet melons
25 g /1 oz powdered gelatine
100 g /3½ oz sugar

500 ml / 18 fl oz dry white
 wine
juice of 1 lemon
30 ml /2 tbls slivovitz or kirsch

1 Using a very sharp knife, cut the melons in half, across the middle, in a zig-zag pattern. Carefully remove the seeds with a spoon and refrigerate the prepared melon halves.
2 Soften the gelatine in 50 ml /2 fl oz cold water. Put the sugar, wine, lemon juice and 350 ml /12 fl oz cold water in a medium-sized pan and heat gently. Add the softened gelatine and stir over a low heat until the gelatine has dissolved completely. Set the mixture aside to cool.
3 When the mixture is just beginning to set – it should be of an

almost syrupy consistency – pour all but about 225 ml /8 fl oz into the melon halves. Put the melons and remaining 225 ml /8 fl oz jelly into the refrigerator to set.
4 Just before serving, whisk the reserved 225 ml /8 fl oz jelly with the slivovitz or the kirsch, until frothy. Pile a little of this mixture on top of each melon half.

15 minutes plus chilling time

Tequila cream

Save this special cream dessert for when you are feeling extravagant. Rich in taste and texture it should satisfy anyone's wish for luxury. Serve with a chilled Californian dessert wine such as a Simi Trockenbeerenauslese Gewürztraminer.

Serves 4

425 ml /15 fl oz thick cream
2 large lemons
150 ml /5 fl oz tequila

icing sugar to taste
3 large egg whites
mint sprigs, to garnish

1 Pare the zest thinly from one of the lemons and cut it into julienne strips. Bring a saucepan of water to the boil and add the julienne strips. Boil for 2–3 minutes until soft and then drain. Refresh under cold running water and drain again.
2 Put the thick cream in a large bowl and add the grated zest of the second lemon. Whip the cream until it stands in soft peaks; be careful not to overwhip at this stage. Gently fold in the tequila and the juice from both lemons. Add icing sugar to taste.

3 In a clean dry bowl whisk the egg whites to stiff peaks, then fold them into the tequila cream. Spoon the mixture into individual glass dishes and chill in the refrigerator for at least 2–3 hours.
4 Just before serving stir each tequila cream and sprinkle the julienne of lemon on top. Garnish and serve immediately.

30 minutes,
then 2–3 hours chilling

Caramel bavarois

Serve a luxurious Sauternes with this creamy dessert, which is
one of the French classics.

Serves 4
oil for greasing
100 g /4 oz sugar
275 ml /10 fl oz milk
3 medium-sized egg yolks

165 g /5½ oz caster sugar
15 ml /1 tbls gelatine
150 ml /5 fl oz thick cream
ice for chilling

1 Lightly oil a 600 ml /1 pt mould. Put the sugar with 75 ml /3 fl oz
water in a medium-sized saucepan. Place over low heat and dissolve
the sugar. Then turn up the heat and boil steadily to form a dark
brown caramel.

2 Carefully pour 50 ml /2 fl oz water into the pan and stir with a
wooden spoon, until the caramel has dissolved. Add the milk and
bring back to boiling point. Remove from the heat.

3 In a heatproof bowl, beat the egg yolks with 40 g /1½ oz caster
sugar until light-coloured, then pour the caramel milk on to this
mixture. Stir and return to the saucepan. Place the pan over low heat
and stir, without boiling, until the custard is thick. Strain into a
bowl and cool.

4 Put the gelatine in a small saucepan and add 75 ml /5 tbls water.
Allow to soak for a few minutes then dissolve over low heat. Whip
the cream until thick and set aside.

5 Gradually add the dissolved gelatine, in a stream, to the custard.
Place the bowl over ice and stir until the custard has thickened.
Then quickly fold in 30 ml /2 tbls whipped cream.

6 Immediately pour into the prepared mould and leave to set for
about 1½ hours.

7 To make the caramel chips, put rest of the caster sugar with 45
ml /3 tbls water in a small heavy-based saucepan over a low heat.
Dissolve, stirring continuously. Then boil until the sugar turns a
golden brown and turns to a golden-brown caramel – 170C /325F on
a sugar thermometer.

8 Line a baking tray with foil and grease well. Pour the caramel
into the baking tray and allow to become completely cold. Remove
the foil from the tray and break the caramel in half. Remove one
half, and fold the foil over the remaining caramel. Beat the
foil-covered caramel with a rolling pin to break into chips. Repeat
with the other piece of caramel.

9 Turn the mould out on to a serving dish and decorate with the
remaining cream and caramel chips.

◁◁ 45 minutes
▷▷ plus cooling and setting

Pansy jelly

Serve this traditional English dessert – both lovely to look at and delicious to eat – after a rich main course. A well-chilled English wine with a flowery bouquet would be a perfect accompaniment.

Serves 8
50 g /2 oz gelatine
225 g /8 oz sugar
thinly pared zest of 4 lemons
300 ml /10 fl oz lemon juice
1 stick of cinnamon

whites and finely crushed shells of 3
  eggs
125 ml /4 fl oz medium-dry sherry
  or sweet white wine
8 pansy flowers, washed and dried
16 small meringues, to serve

1 Sprinkle the gelatine over 45 ml /3 tbls cold water in a small bowl. Leave to soften, then dissolve by standing the bowl in hot water.
2 Pour 850 ml /1½ pt water into a large pan (do not use an aluminium one). Add the sugar, lemon zest and juice and cinnamon stick.
3 Stir over medium heat until the sugar is dissolved. Remove the cinnamon stick and leave the pan on the heat. Stir in the dissolved gelatine.
4 Beat the egg whites and crushed shells together until they are frothy. Pour them into the pan, add the sherry or wine and whisk until the mixture boils. Remove the pan from the heat and leave until the froth sinks.
5 Bring to the boil again and set aside, twice more. Leave the mixture to cool for about 15 minutes.

6 Line a sieve with a double thickness of scalded muslin or cheese-cloth and place over a bowl. Pour in the liquid jelly, leaving the frothy sediment in the bottom of the saucepan. Roll the sediment very gently into the sieve then strain the liquid again, pouring it through the sediment.
7 Reserve 275 ml /10 fl oz of the jelly mixture. Divide the rest equally between 8 old-fashioned champagne glasses. Float a pansy, face upwards on top of each jelly. Place in the refrigerator to set.
8 Melt the remaining jelly, if it has begun to set, and pour some over each pansy. Place the jellies in the refrigerator to set.
9 When ready to serve, stand each glass on a small plate with 2 small meringues.

30 minutes,
then 4 hours setting

Malakoff dessert

A lovely way to end a dinner party, this mouth-watering dessert would be set off well by a sweet Muscat wine such as Muscat de Beaumes de Venise.

Serves 6–8
225 g /8 oz fresh strawberries,
  washed and hulled
100 g /4 oz butter
75 g /3 oz caster sugar
75 g /3 oz ground almonds

150 ml /5 fl oz thick cream
90 ml /6 tbls orange liqueur
24 sponge fingers
For the decoration
150 ml /5fl oz thick cream
toasted flaked almonds

1 Line an 800 ml /1½ pt loaf tin with greaseproof paper, then grease it lightly.
2 Cream the butter and sugar together until pale and fluffy. Beat in the almonds. Gradually stir the cream into the almond mixture being careful not to overstir to avoid curdling.
3 Arrange a layer of sponge fingers in the base of the tin. Sprinkle the fingers with 30 ml /2 tbls liqueur. Halve the strawberries, reserving eight whole ones for decoration, and arrange half of the strawberry halves in a layer upon the fingers. Carefully cover the layer of strawberry halves with half the almond mixture.
4 Cover with another layer of sponge fingers and sprinkle the fingers with 30 ml /2 tbls liqueur. Cover with the remaining strawberry halves and spread the remaining almond mixture on top of that. Finish with a layer of sponge fingers, sprinkled with the remaining 30 ml /2 tbls liqueur. Chill for 6 hours or until firm.
5 Remove from the refrigerator, turn out on to a serving plate and peel off the greaseproof paper. Whip the cream for decoration. Spread two-thirds of it on top of the dessert and pipe the remaining cream just inside the edge. Arrange the reserved strawberries on the piped cream and sprinkle the centre with the toasted almonds.

45 minutes,
plus chilling time

500

Caramelized grapes

This is a rich but refreshing dessert that would make a pleasant end to a dinner party. Serve with a chilled sparkling white wine.

Serves 6–8

450 g /1 lb large, sweet, white grapes
125 ml /4 fl oz maraschino

275 ml /10 fl oz thick cream
175 g /6 oz brown sugar

1 Skin and seed the grapes and put them into a flameproof dish 18 cm /7 in in diameter or in individual ramekins. Sprinkle over the maraschino.

2 In a bowl, beat the cream until it is thick but not buttery and spread in a thick layer over the grapes. Put in the refrigerator overnight to chill.

3 Heat the grill to high about 10 minutes before you are ready to serve the dessert. Cover the cream with an even layer of sugar and grill for 5–8 minutes until the sugar melts. Serve immediately.

 overnight chilling, then 30 minutes

Striped soufflé glacé

With its flavourings of apricot, pistachio and almond, this multi-tiered dessert would complement a luscious sweet wine such as a Monbazillac.

Serves 6-8
350 g /12 oz dried apricots
100 g /4 oz shelled pistachio
   nuts, blanched and skinned
9 large egg yolks
250 g /8 oz caster sugar

750 ml /1¼ pt thick cream
3 drops each of orange and green
   food colouring
100 g /4 oz ground almonds
8-16 langues de chat biscuits or
   fan wafers

1 Simmer the apricots with enough water to cover for 25 minutes. Drain, reserving the cooking liquid. Purée the fruit with 75 ml /3 fl oz of the liquid. Measure 275 ml /10 fl oz purée into a jug and add 75 ml /3 fl oz cooking liquid. Stir, then set aside for the sauce. Reserve the remaining thick purée for one coloured layer of the dessert.

2 Reserve 9 pistachio nuts for decorating and blend the rest to a coarse paste. Halve the reserved nuts.

3 Wrap a collar of double-thickness greaseproof paper around a 12.5 cm /5 in soufflé dish, so that the collar extends 10 cm /4 in above the rim. Secure with an elastic band and paper clips.

4 In a large bowl set over a pan of simmering water, whisk the yolks and sugar, preferably with a hand-held electric whisk, until the mixture is pale and thick and doubled in bulk, about 10 minutes. Stand the bowl in a larger bowl containing crushed ice and continue to whisk until cold.

5 Whip the cream to soft peaks then fold it into the yolk and sugar mixture. Divide the mixture equally between 3 bowls. Stir the thick apricot purée and orange food colour into one of the bowls. Stir the pistachio paste and green food colour into the second, and the ground almonds into the third.

6 Put half the apricot mixture in the soufflé dish and transfer it to the freezer; put the bowls in the refrigerator to chill. When the apricot layer has set (about 45 minutes), add a second layer using half of the almond mixture; freeze until set. Add a third layer using half of the pistachio mixture; freeze again. Continue in this way until the layers are complete. Freeze for 4 hours or until firm.

7 Transfer the soufflé glacé to the refrigerator 30 minutes before serving. Just before serving, slip a knife between the paper and the soufflé all round, then peel off the paper collar. Decorate with the reserved pistachio nuts. To serve, cut the top trio of layers into quarters, then cut horizontally across the soufflé. Cut the second trio of layers into quarters and serve, accompanied by the apricot sauce and biscuits or wafers.

1½ hours plus chilling

498

Sherry surprise

This is a light but very rich pudding ideally accompanied by a Cape dessert wine. Do not be tempted to add more sherry to the pudding as the chilling brings out the full flavour.

Serves 4–6
275 g /10 oz sponge cake
100 ml /4 fl oz sherry
275 ml /10 fl oz custard

60 ml /4 tbls raspberry or
strawberry jam
275 ml /10 fl oz thick cream
rose petals, to garnish

1 Cut the sponge into slices and put in a large bowl. Pour over the sherry and mash the sponge with a fork.
2 Add the custard and the jam and whisk everything together thoroughly so that there are no lumps of sponge or jam in the mixture.
3 In another bowl, whisk the cream until soft peaks form. Add half of the cream to the sponge mixture, mixing well in. Transfer the mixture to a glass serving dish, 18 cm /7 in in diameter.

4 Spread the remaining cream over the pudding, smoothing the top flat with a spatula. Put in the refrigerator and chill for at least 2 hours.
5 Just before serving, sprinkle the rose petals over the surface to garnish.

making the custard,
then 25 minutes plus chilling

Old-fashioned trifle

This is trifle like your grandmother used to make. Complement it with a fine dessert Barsac.

Serves 6
6 trifle sponge cakes
100 g /4 oz raspberry jam
50 g /2 oz ratafias or small
   macaroons
150 ml /5 fl oz medium-dry or
   sweet sherry
4 medium-sized eggs

50 g /2 oz caster sugar
10 ml /2 tsp cornflour
600 ml /1 pt milk
1.5 ml /¼ tsp vanilla essence
6 large, fresh peaches
425 ml /15 fl oz thick cream
For the decoration
diamonds of angelica

1 Split the trifle sponge cakes in half, spread the cut sides thinly with the jam, then sandwich them together again. Cut each sponge cake sandwich into 3 pieces and arrange them in a glass bowl.
2 Crumble the ratafias over the sponge, then sprinkle with the sherry. Cover the bowl and leave to stand overnight.
3 Make the custard: place the eggs in a bowl with the sugar and cornflour and whisk lightly. Heat the milk to just below boiling point then pour it on to the egg mixture, stirring well. Return the mixture to the pan and cook over a very gentle heat, stirring constantly with a wooden spoon until the custard has thickened, and coats the back of the spoon.

4 Strain the custard into a bowl, stir in the vanilla essence. Cover with a piece of dampened greaseproof paper and leave to cool.
5 Skin, halve and stone the peaches. Cut each half into 3 slices and arrange them over the soaked sponge. Remove the paper from the custard and pour the cold custard over the fruit.
6 Softly whip the cream. Spread two-thirds of it over the custard then pipe the remaining cream in swirls around the edge. Decorate with diamonds of angelica and serve.

15 minutes, plus overnight soaking,
then 45 minutes plus cooling

Desserts

Sherry surprise
Old-fashioned trifle
Caramelized grapes
Striped soufflé glacé
Pansy jelly
Malakoff dessert
Tequila cream
Caramel bavarois
Grapefruit and vermouth granita
Wine jelly in melon
Ice cream stripe
Peach shortcake
Mixed melon salad

Crawfish with asparagus

This luxurious but delicate dish is perfect for that special dinner for two or makes a delicious appetizer for 4 people for a grand dinner party. A very lightly chilled, Cape white wine would be an ideal accompaniment.

Serves 2
450 g /1 lb asparagus
salt and freshly ground black pepper
1 kg /2 lb female crawfish or rock
*   lobster with roe, boiled*

olive oil to polish (optional)
25 g /1 oz butter
30 ml /2 tbls finely chopped parsley
125 ml /4 fl oz dry white wine
150 ml /5 fl oz thick cream

1 Trim off the ends of the asparagus to make them an even length and scrape off any leaf scales on the stalks. Tie firmly into a bundle with string. Bring a large pan of salted water to the boil, place the bundle of asparagus standing upright in it, and cover the tips loosely with a cap of foil, crimping this round the top of the saucepan. Cook for 30–40 minutes or until the tips are tender but still firm.

2 Meanwhile prepare the shellfish; remove the roe from under the tail, cut the body into 2 pieces lengthways with a cleaver or sharp, heavy knife and remove the stomach bag and dark vein. (Cut the shell in half again, crossways above the tail, if serving 4.) Carefully remove the white meat from the tail, cut into chunks and put on a plate. Put the soft head meat and any leg meat with the roes. Rinse the body shells, and polish with a little olive oil if wished.

3 Melt the butter in a large frying-pan and add the tail meat. Sauté for 2–3 minutes, remove with a slotted spoon and keep warm.

4 Add the roes and remaining meat to the pan and sauté for 2 minutes. Remove, keep warm but do not mix with tail meat.

5 Add the parsley to the pan and stir-fry for 1 minute. Add the wine, bring to boiling point and boil for 2 minutes. Turn down the heat and simmer to reduce by half, about 5 minutes.

6 Pour in the cream, season with salt and freshly ground black pepper and stir for 3–4 minutes but do not allow to boil. Check the seasoning, adjusting if necessary.

7 Pile the tail meat into the shells, top with the remaining meat and the roes. Place the shells on a warmed plate, drain the asparagus and put some spears on either side of each helping. Pour some sauce over each portion and serve immediately.

40–50 minutes

Italian-style scampi

This delicious dish is reminiscent of hot, exotic settings – perhaps a terrace overlooking the Adriatic. Complete the scenario with a crisp, dry white wine – a Soave would be the ideal choice.

Serves 4

*1 kg /2 lb frozen peeled scampi,
    thawed and drained*
60 ml /4 tbls olive oil
2 garlic cloves, finely chopped
15–20 ml /3–4 tsp lemon juice

*90 ml /6 tbls freshly chopped
    parsley*
30 ml /2 tbls capers, drained
boiled rice to serve
lemon slices to garnish

1 Pat the scampi dry with absorbent paper. Heat the oil in a large heavy-based frying-pan and cook the scampi very gently over low heat, turning them now and then, for 7–8 minutes, until almost cooked.

2 Stir the garlic, lemon juice, parsley and capers into the frying-pan and cook, stirring, for a further 1–2 minutes.

3 Spoon the scampi and cooking juices over a bed of plainly boiled rice arranged on a large serving platter. Garnish the edge of the platter with lemon slices. Serve immediately.

15 minutes

Buttered lobster

For an intimate and rather special dinner for two, try this extravagant lobster dish. As you will have splashed out on the food, serve it with a good Chablis. Baking in the oven is easier than grilling lobster as you do not have to watch it.

Serves 2
1 fresh uncooked lobster, weighing
  700–900 g /1¹/₂–2 lb
butter for greasing
salt
freshly ground pepper
juice of ¹/₂ lemon

75 g /3 oz unsalted butter
lemon wedges for garnishing
watercress sprigs for garnish
For the butter sauce
100 g /4 oz clarified butter
juice and zest of ¹/₂ lemon
30 ml /2 tbls chopped parsley

1   Heat the oven to 180C /350F /gas 4 with a baking tray in it. Plunge the lobster into boiling water, cover and boil for 1 minute to kill it. Starting at the head end, split the lobster in half lengthways with a knife. Discard the stomach sac (which is in the head), and the dark intestinal cord (which runs along its back). Crack the claws with a blow from a hammer or with nutcrackers.
2   Grease a gratin dish with butter and, using buttered paper, lightly rub the lobster shells all over until they gleam. Place the lobster on the gratin dish. Sprinkle the flesh with a little salt, a generous sprinkle of black pepper and 5 ml /1 tsp lemon juice.
3   Cover the flesh completely with dots of the unsalted butter. Place the gratin dish on the warm baking tray and bake in the oven for 15

minutes. Remove from the oven and baste with the buttery juice, adding another 5 ml /1 tsp lemon juice. Return to the oven and cook for 15 minutes longer.
4   Meanwhile, make the butter sauce. Heat the clarified butter, lemon juice and zest in a small saucepan until very hot. Remove from the heat, stir in the parsley and pour into a warmed sauceboat.
5   Remove from the oven, baste with the juices and serve immediately, garnished with the watercress and lemon wedges and accompanied by the butter sauce.

🕐🕐 1 hour

Plaice meunière

Plaice meunière would make a delightful dinner party main course, accompanied by new potatoes and steamed asparagus or broccoli. A Sauvignon Blanc would go very well with this meal.

Serves 4
8 fillets of plaice
parsley sprigs
30 ml /2 tbls seasoned flour

100 g /4 oz butter
15 ml /1 tbls lemon juice
oil, for deep frying

1 Skin any dark-skinned fillet, then rinse all the fillets and pat dry. Remove the stalks from the parsley sprigs, then wash the sprigs and dry thoroughly. Spread the seasoned flour on greaseproof paper and press the fillets into the flour. Shake off the surplus flour.
2 Heat 50 g /2 oz butter in a large frying-pan. When the butter is foaming, add the fillets to the pan. Fry for about 3–4 minutes on each side or until both sides are golden. Arrange the fillets on a hot serving dish and keep hot.
3 Heat oil in a deep frier to 185C /360F. Wipe out the frying-pan

and put in the remaining butter. Heat rapidly until the butter is golden brown. Pour the butter promptly over the plaice, then pour over the lemon juice. Keep hot.
4 Put the parsley sprigs into the deep frier basket and plunge the basket into the hot oil for 30 seconds, or until the parsley is bright green and crisp. Garnish the plaice with the fried parsley and serve.

30 minutes

Salmon with fennel

Delicious pink salmon steaks are ideal for a special summer occasion, especially with this rich but subtly flavoured fennel sauce. Serve the salmon steaks with a crisp, green, summery salad and a fine Pouilly Fumé.

Serves 4

*4 salmon steaks, about 175 g
    /6 oz each
150 ml /5 fl oz dry white wine
1 small onion, chopped
1 bulb fennel, quartered
1 bay leaf*

*2-3 parsley stalks, crushed
2 egg yolks
125 g /4 oz unsalted butter
salt
freshly ground black pepper
sprigs of fennel, to garnish*

1 Heat the oven to 180C /350F /gas 4.
2 Place the salmon steaks in a shallow ovenproof dish. Pour the dry white wine over and add the chopped onion, fennel, bay leaf and parsley stalks. Cover tightly and cook in the oven for 15 minutes.
3 Remove from the oven and strain off 60–75 ml /4–5 tbls of the poaching liquid into a small saucepan. Reserve one of the quarters of fennel, chop it finely and measure out 10 ml /2 tsp. Turn the oven down to 150 C /300F /gas 2 and return the fish to the oven.
4 Over a high heat reduce the poaching liquid to 15 ml /1 tbls, about 5 minutes. Remove from the heat and leave to cool.
5 In the top pan of a double boiler, put the cooled reduced poaching liquid, egg yolks and 25 g /1 oz butter. Season with salt and

freshly ground black pepper. Over gently simmering water whisk the mixture until the butter has melted. Gradually add the remaining butter, whisking between each addition until the sauce is thick. Do not let the water boil or the sauce may curdle. When the sauce is thick, add the reserved chopped fennel and allow to heat through in the sauce.
6 Remove the salmon steaks from the oven and with a slotted spoon, transfer them to a warmed serving dish. Spoon the fennel sauce over and serve garnished with sprigs of fennel.

1 hour 10 minutes

Cold seafood platter

Serve this delicious mixture of seafood as a dinner party starter or as the main course for a special supper for two. The texture and taste of steamed seafood contrast well with the spicy sauce, and are perfect with a Yugoslav Fruska Gora Sauvignon.

Serves 2
500 g /1 lb or 1 pt mussels,
  scrubbed
150 ml /5 fl oz dry white wine
8 raw scampi, with heads and
  shells on
8 large scallops
For the sauce
25 g /1 oz butter
15 ml /1 tbls oil
1 onion, finely chopped

1 garlic clove, crushed
1 green pepper, finely diced
500 g /1 lb tomatoes, blanched,
  skinned and chopped
10 ml /2 tsp lemon juice
1.5 ml /¼ tsp ground coriander
2.5 ml /½ tsp paprika
2.5 ml /½ tsp cumin
salt
freshly ground black pepper

1 To make the sauce, in a saucepan, heat the butter and oil and sauté the finely chopped onion until soft, about 5 minutes. Add the crushed garlic and the finely diced pepper and continue cooking, stirring occasionally, for 5 minutes. Add the tomatoes, lemon juice, coriander, paprika and cumin. Stir well and season with salt and freshly ground black pepper. Simmer the sauce gently for 20 minutes, stirring occasionally.

2 Meanwhile, put the mussels in a large saucepan with 150 ml /5 fl oz water and the dry white wine. Cover the pan tightly and steam over a high heat, shaking the pan occasionally, for about 5 minutes or until the mussels have opened. Strain the mussels, reserving the liquor, discard any that have not opened and set the remainder aside to cool.

3 Bring the reserved liquor to the boil, add the scampi and turn the heat down. Simmer for 1½–2 minutes. Remove with a slotted spoon

and set aside to cool.

4 Separate the orange corals from the scallops and remove and discard the black membrane. Poach the scallops for 3–5 minutes in the liquor, adding the corals for the last minute of the cooking time. Drain and leave to cool.

5 Remove the sauce from the heat and allow to cool. Remove the cooled mussels from their shells and discard the shells.

6 To arrange, pour the sauce into individual ramekins and place one on each plate. Arrange the scampi and mussels on the plates. Slice the scallops in half horizontally and arrange them with the corals placed decoratively on top. Serve accompanied by fingerbowls and large napkins.

✋✋ 45 minutes, plus cooling

Monkfish salad

Monkfish (*ange de mer* in French) tastes like lobster or scampi, but is much less expensive. Monkfish salad makes a light, refreshing lunch dish or an unusual starter and is the perfect partner for the dry white wine of Spain – choose from a Penedés or Rioja.

Serves 4
350 g /12 oz tail piece of
   monkfish
1 medium-sized fennel bulb
For the dressing
60 ml /4 tbls olive oil
30 ml /2 tbls lemon juice
1 garlic clove, crushed
2.5 ml /1/2 tsp fresh tarragon,
   chopped
2.5 ml /1/2 tsp fresh chervil,
   chopped
2.5 ml /1/2 tsp fresh basil,
   chopped
salt
freshly ground black pepper

For the court bouillon
2 carrots, peeled and finely
   chopped
1 medium-sized onion,
   finely chopped
2 celery stalks, cleaned
   and chopped
bouquet garni of fresh herbs
30 ml /2 tbls lemon juice
300 ml /10 fl oz dry white wine
6 black peppercorns, crushed
salt
To serve
2 small or 1 large lettuce heart
stuffed olives

1 Trim the base and the fronds from the fennel. Slice the bulb finely and put in a bowl. Blend the dressing ingredients together and pour over the fennel. Leave to marinate for 2 hours.
2 Meanwhile put all the court bouillon ingredients into a saucepan with 600 ml /1 pt water. Bring to the boil then simmer for 15 minutes. Cool slightly.
3 Put the monkfish in a saucepan and strain the court bouillon over the fish. Bring slowly to the boil, cover, reduce the heat and simmer for about 10 minutes or until the flesh just flakes.

4 Carefully remove the fish with a slotted spoon and leave to cool.
5 With a sharp knife, cut the cold fish into 4 × 1.2 cm /1½ × ½ in pieces and toss with the fennel and its dressing. Chill for 30 minutes.
6 Finely shred the lettuce heart and arrange around the edge of a plate. Pile the fish in the centre and decorate with olives. Serve immediately.

2½ hours including marinating

Sardines in white wine

Fresh sardines are plentiful and cheap in Portugal and they are often baked on a layer of potatoes in a white wine and tomato sauce. Red mullet are also delicious cooked this way. Serve a dry white wine, such as a Portuguese white Dão.

Serves 4

8 fresh sardines, gutted
4 medium-sized potatoes
2 medium-sized onions
105 ml /7 tbls olive oil
salt
freshly ground black pepper
freshly grated nutmeg

15 ml /1 tbls tomato purée
125 ml /5 fl oz white wine,
   such as Dão
5 ml /1 tsp dried thyme
For the garnish
black olives
lemon slices

1   Heat the oven to 180C /350F /gas 4. Slice the potatoes and onions on a mandolin or very finely with a sharp knife.
2   Put 45 ml /3 tbls of the olive oil in a casserole dish large enough to hold the fish in one layer. Swirl the oil around so the bottom of the dish is thoroughly coated. Place the potatoes in a thin layer at the bottom of the dish and cover with the onions. Season with salt, freshly ground black pepper and nutmeg. Pour over 30 ml /2 tbls of oil. Bake for 40 minutes.
3   Rinse the sardines carefully under cold water and pat dry. Place the sardines neatly in one layer on top of the baked potatoes and

onions. Set on one side.
4   Mix the tomato purée with the white wine and pour over the fish. Season with salt and freshly ground black pepper, sprinkle over the thyme and 30 ml /2 tbls oil. Bake for 15 minutes, basting occasionally if the potatoes become too dry.
5   Garnish with the black olives and lemon slices if wished. Serve immediately.

1¼ hours

486

Stir-fried beef with corn

This Chinese-style dish can be served as part of a Chinese meal or try it on its own with soft noodles. Either way it is a good accompaniment for wines from the Northern Napa Valley, such as a Chardonnay.

Serves 4-6
15 ml /1 tbls dry sherry
15 ml /1 tbls soy sauce
7.5 ml /1½ tsp cornflour
500 g /1 lb rump steak, thinly sliced across the grain
15 ml /1 tbls oil
1 small onion, quartered

125 g /4 oz mange tout
5 ml /1 tsp salt
400 g /14 oz canned miniature corn cobs, rinsed and drained
400 g /14 oz canned straw mushrooms, drained
10 ml /2 tsp sugar
plain boiled noodles, to serve

1 In a bowl, blend the sherry and soy sauce into the cornflour. Add the beef and turn it so that it is thoroughly coated.
2 Heat the oil in a wok or frying-pan. Fry the onion for 2 minutes over a high heat. Remove the beef from the cornflour mixture with a slotted spoon, reserving the liquid. Add the beef to the frying-pan and stir fry until lightly browned. Add the mange tout and the salt and stir fry for another 30 seconds.
3 Add the baby corns and the straw mushrooms and stir fry for 1

minute. Add the sugar to the frying-pan and blend.
4 Blend the remaining cornflour liquid with 10 ml /2 tsp cold water and stir into the pan. Cook for another minute until thickened. Serve as part of a Chinese meal or pile the stir-fried beef and vegetables onto plain boiled noodles.

 20 minutes

Normandy veal escalopes

Flavoured with calvados and cream, the classic ingredients of Normandy cooking, this delicious dish would be suitable for a dinner party. Serve with a full-bodied white Sancerre.

Serves 4

4 escalopes of veal, slightly beaten
2 medium-sized red dessert apples
50 g /2 oz butter
salt
freshly ground pepper

30 ml /2 tbls lemon juice
60 ml /4 tbls calvados
200 ml /7 fl oz thick cream
To garnish
sprigs of parsley
triangular croûtons

1　Peel the apples and cut into small cubes. Melt the butter in a heavy-based frying-pan over medium heat. When it starts to foam, add the apple and cook for 2 minutes. Remove with a slotted spoon and set aside.

2　Sprinkle the veal with salt and pepper and the lemon juice. Then add to the frying-pan, over medium heat. Brown the veal quickly on both sides.

3　Heat the calvados in a small pan. Set it alight, then pour it, while still flaming, over the meat, turning the heat up under the frying-pan. Rotate the pan until the flames die down. Then lower the heat and pour in the thick cream.

4　Add the apple cubes to the meat and cook gently for about 2 minutes. Stir continuously; do not allow the sauce to boil.

5　When the sauce has thickened, transfer the veal to a warmed serving dish. Arrange the apple cubes on top of the veal and pour the sauce over the apple. Garnish with parsley sprigs and croûtons and serve.

15 minutes

Watercress veal

This *nouvelle cuisine*-style dish is best served on individual plates. Serve it with a medium white wine such as Orvieto.

Serves 4
50 g /2 oz shelled, halved walnuts
1 bunch of watercress, washed
50 g /2 oz butter
1 small onion, finely chopped
150 ml /5 fl oz thick cream

salt and freshly ground pepper
lemon juice
milk (optional)
4 veal escalopes, thinly beaten out
cooked new potatoes, to serve
cooked broccoli florets, to serve

1 Put the halved walnuts in a small bowl and pour over enough boiling water to cover. Leave to stand for 10 minutes.
2 Discard the stalks from the watercress; chop the leaves.
3 Remove the walnuts from the water with a slotted spoon. Remove the thin brown skin that covers the nuts. Chop them finely.
4 In a heavy-based frying-pan, melt half the butter. When the foaming subsides, add the finely chopped onion and sauté, stirring occasionally, for about 5 minutes or until soft. Add the chopped watercress leaves, thick cream and chopped walnuts. Season with salt, freshly ground black pepper and lemon juice to taste. Cover the pan tightly and simmer gently over a very low heat for 7–10 minutes.

(Add a little milk if the sauce reduces and thickens too rapidly.)
5 Remove the sauce from the heat and purée in a blender until smooth. Return the sauce to a pan and keep warm over a low heat.
6 Meanwhile, melt the remaining butter in a frying-pan. Cut each beaten escalope into 2 evenly-shaped, smaller escalopes. Sauté over a medium heat until cooked through, 3–4 minutes.
7 To serve, arrange the veal on invidual heated plates and spoon the sauce over. Serve with tiny new potatoes and florets of broccoli.

1¼ hours

Juniper pork

Delicately flavoured with juniper berries and sweetened with pimentos, this is a light dish which would complement a wine from the Middle Moselle.

Serves 4
12 thin slices of pork fillet
10 ml /2 tsp juniper berries, crushed
salt and ground black pepper
100 g /4 oz butter

60 ml /4 tbls white wine
275 g /10 oz fresh green beans,
* topped and tailed*
350 g /12 oz canned pimentos
10 ml /2 tsp sugar

1   Put the slices of pork fillet between two sheets of greaseproof paper and beat with a meat bat or rolling pin until they are really thin. Season with the crushed juniper berries and salt and pepper.
2   Melt the butter in a large frying-pan over a low heat and add the white wine, letting it bubble for 1–2 minutes. Place 3–4 slices of pork in the pan, in one layer. Sauté for 3–4 minutes each side, remove and keep warm. Repeat until all the slices are cooked.

3   Add the beans and cook for 5 minutes over medium-low heat.
4   Stir in the pimentos and the sugar and cook for a further 4–5 minutes. Season the vegetables and arrange on a serving platter.
5   Lay the slices of pork on top of the beans and pimentos, pour over the remaining pan juices and serve immediately.

45 minutes

Pork with soured cream

This exotic-tasting dish is very simple to make. Accompanied by steamed carrot sticks sprinkled with chopped dill, and a brightly coloured mixed salad, it makes an appetizing and attractive supper dish. A dry white wine, such as Mâcon-Villages, would make an excellent partner to this meal.

Serves 4
4 loin pork chops
60 ml /4 tbls Moutarde de Meaux
   or any other coarse grain mustard
2.5 ml /½ tsp ground ginger

1.5 ml /¼ tsp freshly ground black pepper
1.5 ml /¼ tsp salt
30 ml /2 tbls olive oil
150 ml /5 fl oz soured cream

1 Place the mustard, ginger, pepper, salt and 1.5 ml /¼ tsp of the oil in a bowl and mix together.
2 Spread one third of the mustard mixture over the chops on one side only. Heat the remaining oil in a large frying-pan over moderate heat and place the chops in the pan, *uncoated* side downwards. Cook for 7–10 minutes.
3 Turn the chops over and cook for another 7–10 minutes. While cooking, spread the upturned cooked sides of the chops with another

third of the mustard mixture.
4 Once cooked, remove the chops from the pan and keep warm on a serving dish. Stir the soured cream into the juices left in the pan. Mix in the remaining mustard mixture and heat through for one minute, stirring well, then pour over the chops. Serve immediately.

 25 minutes

481

Pork paprika

The piquancy of paprika blends superbly with the full grapey flavour of a fine Rheinhessen wine.

Serves 4–6

1 kg /2 lb stewing pork
15 ml /1 tbls oil
15 g /¹⁄₂ oz butter
1 large onion, sliced
15 ml /1 tbls caraway seeds
30 ml /2 tbls mild paprika

400 g /14 oz canned peeled
* tomatoes*
salt
freshly ground black pepper
450 g /1 lb tagliatelle verdi
150 ml /5 fl oz soured cream

1 Cut the pork into 4 cm /1½ in cubes and set aside. Heat the oil and butter in a large frying-pan over moderate heat. Add the sliced onion and soften for 5 minutes.
2 Add the caraway seeds and paprika to the pan and cook for 3 minutes, stirring well with a wooden spoon. Add the pork cubes to the pan, a few pieces at a time, allowing the meat to colour lightly.
3 Pour in the tomatoes and season with salt and freshly ground black pepper. Stir well, cover and cook over a low heat for 1 hour.
4 Fifteen minutes before the pork is cooked, prepare the tagliatelle. Bring a pan of salted water to the boil, add the tagliatelle and boil for 10 minutes or until *al dente* – firm to the bite. Drain and transfer to a large platter, keep warm.
5 Stir the soured cream with a fork, then add to the cooked pork mixture. Stir the soured cream to distribute it, and allow to warm through but do not boil.
6 Spoon the pork on to the centre of the tagliatelle and serve immediately.

1½ hours

Chicken with port

Port and brandy give this casseroled chicken a luscious flavour.
Serve with a dry white Portuguese Dão.

Serves 4

1.4 kg /3 lb oven-ready chicken
salt
freshly ground black pepper
40 g /1½ oz softened butter
15 ml /1 tbls chopped mixed herbs
25 g /1 oz butter
2.5 ml /½ tsp lemon juice

500 g /1 lb button mushrooms,
* cleaned and halved*
10 ml /2 tsp cornflour
275 ml /10 fl oz thick cream
1 shallot, finely chopped
75 ml /3 fl oz port
50 ml /2 fl oz brandy

1 Heat the oven to 180C /350F /gas 4. Rub the chicken with salt and pepper. Blend together the butter and herbs and smear this over the chicken. Roast the chicken in the oven for 1¼–1½ hours, basting frequently.
2 Meanwhile, put 50 ml /2 fl oz water in a saucepan. Bring to the boil, then add 15 g /½ oz butter, lemon juice and salt to taste. Add the mushrooms and cook gently for 10 minutes.
3 Pour the cooking liquid out of the saucepan and reserve. Blend the cornflour with 15 ml /1 tbls of the cream, then stir this cornflour mixture and the rest of the cream into the mushrooms. Simmer for 2 minutes then set aside.
4 Transfer the cooked chicken to a wooden board and pour off most of the fat from the roasting tin. Divide the chicken into serving portions and set aside.

5 Add the shallot to the fat remaining in the roasting pan and cook over gentle heat for 5 minutes. Add the port and reserved mushroom juice and boil down rapidly, until reduced to about 75 ml /3 fl oz.
6 Add the mushroom mixture to the pan and simmer for 3 minutes, until the liquid is slightly thickened. Season to taste.
7 Smear the inside of a flameproof casserole with the remaining butter and arrange the chicken pieces in the casserole. Place over moderate heat and when the chicken begins to sizzle, pour the brandy over it. Ignite and shake the casserole slowly until the flames have subsided. Then pour in the mushroom mixture, cover and heat through without boiling for 5 minutes.

2½ hours